Ann Arbor High School,
June 14th 1859.

Edward A Hyde.

Dear Sir:

In compliance with the decision of the Board of Judges on Prize Essays, allow me to present you this volume as a premium for your meritorious essay on Caesar's character as a general, author and man.

Yours Very Respectfully
Dan^c B. Briggs

Prof. A. D. White
" H. S. Frieze
" A. L. Brooks
} Board of Judges.

I0754304

ADAM FERGUSON L.L.D. F.R.S.E.

PAINTED BY SIR J REYNOLDS   ENGRAVED BY W E TUCKER.

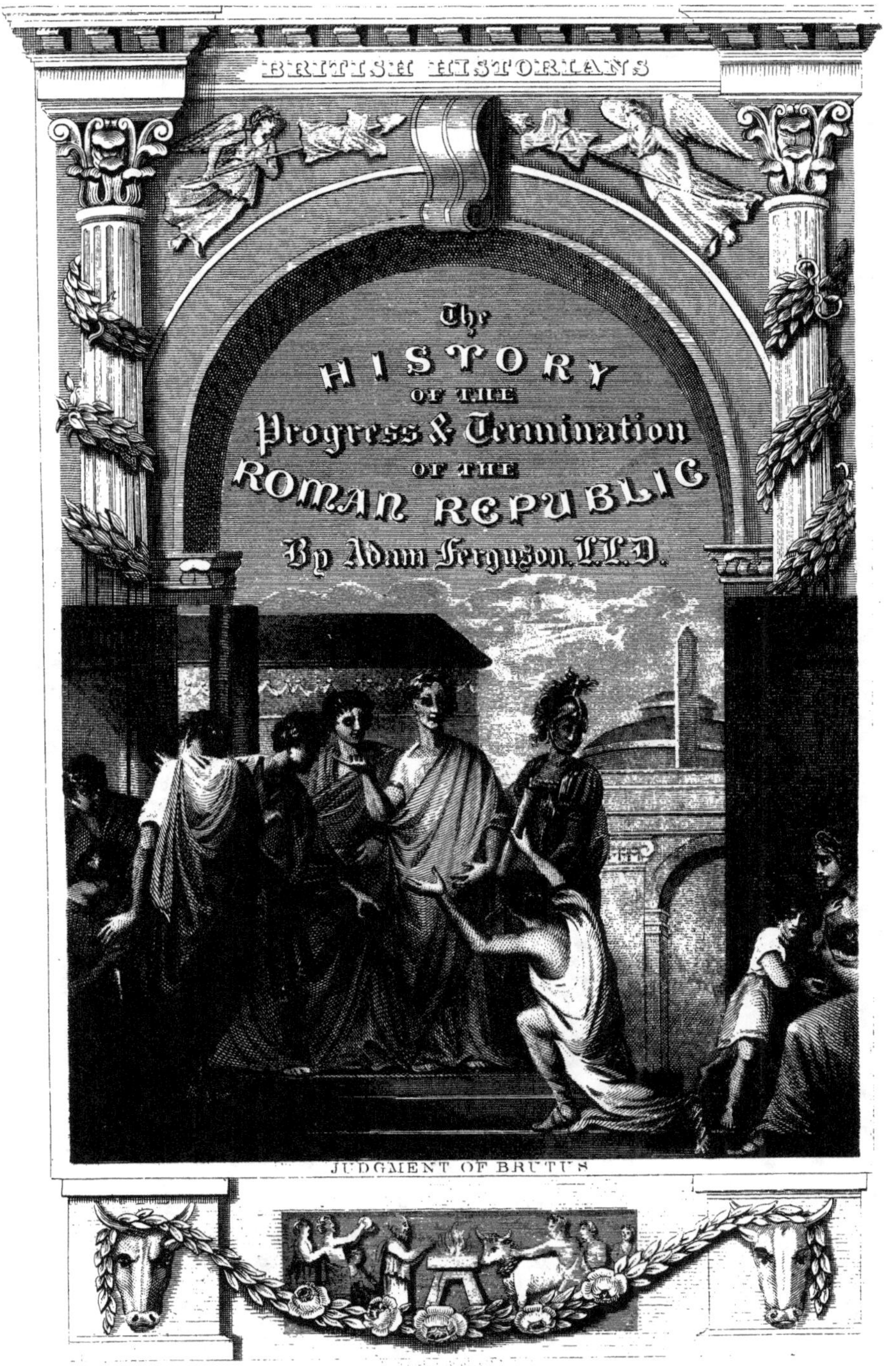

BRITISH HISTORIANS

The HISTORY OF THE Progress & Termination OF THE ROMAN REPUBLIC

By Adam Ferguson, LL.D.

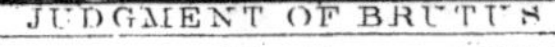

JUDGMENT OF BRUTUS

THE

HISTORY OF THE PROGRESS AND TERMINATION

OF THE

ROMAN REPUBLIC.

BY

ADAM FERGUSON, LL.D.,
PROFESSOR OF MORAL PHILOSOPHY IN THE UNIVERSITY OF EDINBURGH.

WITH

A NOTICE OF THE AUTHOR,

BY LORD JEFFREY.

NEW YORK:
J. C. DERBY, 119 NASSAU STREET.
CINCINNATI: — H. W. DERBY.
1856.

NOTICE OF THE AUTHOR.

ADAM FERGUSON was born at Logierait, in the highlands of Scotland, on the 20th of June, 1723, and was the son of a Presbyterian clergyman. In the autumn of 1738 he entered the University of St. Andrew's, where, four years after, he took the degree of Master of Arts, and he passed some time subsequently in the study of theology. In 1745, he was selected by Lord John Murray, commander of the forty-second Highland regiment, as his military chaplain, to qualify himself for which office he received ordination, although he had not studied divinity the full period of six years. He remained with the regiment until 1757, when he succeeded the celebrated David Hume as keeper of the Advocates' Library, but resigned that office in the following year. In 1759, he was elected Professor of Natural Philosophy in the University of Edinburgh; though we are told that he had not made physical science a principal object of his inquiries, nor, indeed, studied it much more than most young men do in the common course of academical instruction. Five months of preparation, however, enabled him to enter upon this office, the duties of which he performed in a manner that secured his popularity. About 1762, he founded a society known by the name of "The Poker," for procuring from the government the establishment of a militia in Scotland, and, to forward its views, wrote a satirical pamphlet, entitled "The History of Sister Peg." His first publication, however, excepting a printed sermon, was "A Defence of the Morality of Stage Plays," during the controversy respecting Home's tragedy of "Douglas." Several pamphlets were written in defence of the same views; but Mr. Ferguson's was admitted, by the opposite party, to be the only piece on that side evincing any tolerable degree of discretion.

In 1764, he was elected Professor of Moral Philosophy at Edinburgh, and entered on his duties with a degree of spirit and activity, from which the most advantageous results were anticipated. His lectures drew constantly a numerous and applauding auditory. About a year after his election to the chair of Philosophy, he published his "Essay on the History of Civil Society," which received the unanimous approval of the literary world. In a letter dated the 10th of March, 1767, Mr. Hume, congratulating him on its success, says: "I have met with nobody that had read it who did not praise it; Lord Mansfield is very loud to that purpose in his Sunday societies; I heard Lord Chesterfield and Lord Lyttleton express the same sentiments; and, what is above all, Cadell, I am told, is already projecting a second edition of the same quarto size." The style, as well as the matter, was also praised by the poet Gray; and Lord Shelburne approved of it so highly as to express a desire to patronise the author, and offered to procure him some appropriate appointment in one of the English universities, after having been informed that the government of West Florida, which he had some thoughts of conferring on him, would not be considered a suitable office. Mr. Ferguson shortly after married, and took a farm in the parish of Currie, where he gratified his taste for agricultural and horticultural pursuits.

In May, 1774, he set out for Geneva, to take charge, as tutor, of Charles, Earl of Chesterfield. The connection was dissolved in the course of the following year, and he returned to Edinburgh, where, to his astonishment and mortification, he found the chair he had held declared vacant by the town-council, though they had previously appointed, at his desire, a deputy to perform its duties. His friends, Drs. Robertson, Blair, and Black, indignantly remonstrated against this proceeding, applied to the Court of Session in his behalf, and he was, though not without much exertion, reinstated in his office. He appears to have exhibited a good deal of feeling on this occasion; and he concluded a letter to a friend, in reference to the movement of his enemies, by saying: "The fools and knaves are no more than necessary to give others something to do."

Literature and agriculture continued to occupy his time for many years. The progress of the American war called his attention to the study of politics, about 1776, in which year he published "Remarks on a Pamphlet, lately published by Dr. Price, entitled, 'Observations on the Nature of Civil Liberty,' &c." He also communicated his views, from time to time, to Sir William Pulteney, and other members of Parliament; and, on the determination of the government to send out commissioners to quell the disorders, he was appointed Secretary to the Commission. He was, in consequence, absent in the United States during the sessions of 1778 and 1779; but his duties were efficiently performed in that period by Dugald Stewart. In 1780, he had an attack of apoplexy, which, however, had no permanent effect on either his bodily or mental faculties; but he now thought it expedient to cease lecturing without notes, and therefore commenced writing a course of instruction to be read to his classes. At the same time he was busy in completing his celebrated "History of the Progress and Termination of the Roman Republic," which appeared in 1783 in three volumes quarto. This work has been translated into several modern languages, and has been justly described as one which not only delights by the clearness of its narrative and the boldness of its descriptions, but instructs and animates by profound and masterly delineations of character, as well as by the philosophical precision with which it traces the connection of events. It is written in that tone of high-minded enthusiasm which, if it can only snatch from oblivion whatever is noble and generous in the record of human actions, regards the graces of style as objects merely of secondary account, and is chiefly studious of impressing the lessons of wisdom which may be gathered from the survey of distant ages. This admirable performance will hold its place among classic English histories, notwithstanding that some points of which it treats appear in a somewhat different light from the discoveries and criticisms of more recent scholars.

In 1784, he resigned the chair of moral philosophy to Dugald Stewart, and was himself joined in the professorship of mathematics with Mr. Playfair, to entitle him to retain his salary. He now proceeded to revise the notes of his lectures on Ethics and Politics, and in 1792 published them under the title of "Principles of Moral and Political Science," in two volumes, quarto. Among modern writers, to whose suggestion he appears to have been most indebted, are Shaftesbury, Hutcheson, Montesquieu, and Adam Smith. The work has been censured for the very partial notice which it offers of the importance of religious principle; it abounds, however, in passages of great beauty on the subject of a future state, and shows an anxiety to establish the foundations of natural theology. After its publication, the author visited the continent, and was elected a member of the Academy of Berlin, and of other learned societies. He passed the winter of 1793 at Rome, and returned to Scotland in the following year, with an intention of spending the remainder of his days in rural retirement. For this purpose he fixed on Hallyards, in Manor Water, where he remained fourteen years; but at the expiration of that period, his sight and hearing having in a great measure failed, he removed to St. Andrew's, that he might more frequently enjoy the conversation of his friends. Here he gradually declined in all but his intellectual faculties, in the full vigour of which he died, on the 22d of February, 1816, in the ninety-third year of his age.

The private character of Dr. Ferguson was irreproachable; his manners were easy, elegant, and becoming both a man of the world and a philosopher. With his intimate friends, he was full of fascinating gayety and refined humour. If impatient of anything, it was of contradiction; and of assumed superiority he could rarely forbear testifying his contempt. We have his own authority for suggesting that he was indebted, for his manner, less to intercourse with polished society than to familiarity with the beautiful in nature.

The principal compositions of Dr. Ferguson, besides those we have mentioned, were "The Institutes of Moral Philosophy," and a "Memoir of Dr. Black," both of which were translated into several languages. His fame at present, however, rests upon his great work, "The History of the Progress and Termination of the Roman Republic."

CONTENTS.

BOOK I.

BOOK II.

BOOK III.

THE

HISTORY

OF

THE PROGRESS AND TERMINATION

OF THE

ROMAN REPUBLIC.

BOOK I.

CHAPTER I.

The Subject—Supposed Origin of the Roman State—Its Government—T The People—Curiæ—Centuries—Tribes—Religion—The Triumph—(Progress of the State under its Kings—Change to a Republic.

THE Roman State was originally a small principality, and one of the many little cantons, which, under the denomination of Latins, occupied the left of the Tiber, from its confluence with the Anio to the sea, and from Ostia to Circeii on the coast. Within this narrow tract, reaching in breadth inland no more than sixteen miles, and extending on the coast about fifty miles, the Latins are said to have formed no less than forty-seven independent states;[1] each of whom had a separate capital or strong hold, to which they occasionally retired for safety, with their cattle and other effects, and from which they made frequent wars on each other.[2] The country, divided into so many separate territories, we may consider as resembling some of the lately discovered islands in the Southern or Pacific Ocean,[3] where every height is represented as a fortress, and every little township, that can maintain its possessions, as a separate state. Among settlements of this description, the Romans, though they were originally no way distinguished in point of possessions or numbers, yet, in consequence of some superiority of institution or character, came to have a decided ascendant.

Beyond the Tiber on the one hand, and the Liris on the other, the contiguous parts of Italy were possessed, in the same manner with Latium, by different races of men, who, under various denominations of Etrurians, Samnites, Campanians, and others, formed a multiplicity of little nations, united by leagues for common safety, and ranged under opposite interests, with a view to some balance of power which they endeavoured to maintain. The peninsula towards one extremity,[4] was from time immemorial peopled with Grecian colonies. Towards the other, it was, in the first ages of the Roman state, overrun by nations of Gaulish extraction.[5]

The land throughout, in respect to situation, climate, and soil, was highly favoured, diversified with mountain and plain, well wooded and watered, replenished with useful materials, fit to yield pasture for numerous herds, and to produce abundance of corn, wine, and oil. And, what is still of more importance, was already become the flourishing nursery of ingenious men, ardent and vigorous in their pursuits, though, in respect to many arts and inventions, yet in a state of great simplicity or ignorance.

The Romans, who made their first step to dominion by becoming heads of the Latin confederacy, continued their progress to the sovereignty of Italy; or, after many struggles with nations possessed of resources similar to their own, united the forces of that country under their own direction, became the conquerors of many kingdoms in Asia and Africa, as well as in Europe; and formed an empire, if not the most extensive, at

1 Dionys. Halicar. lib. iv. 2 Liv. lib. i. c. 5. &c.
3 See Cook's Voyage to New Zealand.

4 Magna Græcia. 5 Gallia Cisalpina.

least the most splendid of any that is known in the history of mankind. In possession of this seeming advantage, however, they were unable to preserve their own institutions; they became, together with the conquests they had made, a prey to military government and a signal example of the vicissitudes to which prosperous nations are exposed.

This mighty state, remarkable for the smallness of its origin, as well as for the greatness to which it attained, has, by the splendour of its national exertions, by the extent of its dominion, by the wisdom of its councils, or by its internal revolutions and reverses of fortune, ever been a principal object of history to all the more enlightened nations of the western world. To know it well, is to know mankind; and to have seen our species under the fairest aspect of great ability, integrity, and courage. There is a merit in attempting to promote the study of this subject, even if the effect should not correspond with the design.

Under this impression the following narrative was undertaken, and chiefly with a view to the great revolution by which the republican form of government was exchanged for despotism; and by which the Roman people, from being joint sovereigns of a great empire, became, together with their own provinces, the subjects, and often the prey, of a tyranny which was equally cruel to both.

As in this revolution men of the greatest abilities, possessed of every art, and furnished with the most ample resources, were acting in concert together, or in opposition to each other, the scene is likely to exhibit what may be thought the utmost range or extent of the human powers; and to furnish those who are engaged in transactions any way similar, with models by which they may profit, and from which they may form sound principles of conduct, derived from experience, and confirmed by examples of the highest authority.

The event which makes the principal object of this history, has been sometimes considered as a point of separation between two periods, which have been accordingly treated apart—the period of the republic, and that of the monarchy. During a considerable part of the first period, the Romans were highly distinguished by their genius, magnanimity, and national spirit, and made suitable attainments in what are the ordinary objects of pursuit—wealth and dominion. In the second period, they continued for some time to profit by the attainments which were made in the former, and while they walked in the tract of the commonwealth, or practised the arts and retained the lessons which former ages had taught, still kept their possessions. But after the springs of political life, which were wound up in the republic, had some time ceased to act; when the state was become the concern of a single person, and the vestige of former movements were effaced, the national character declined, and the power of a great empire became unable to preserve what a small republic had acquired. The example, whether to be shunned or imitated, is certainly instructive in either period; but most so in the transition that was made from one to the other; and in the forfeiture of those public advantages, of which the Roman people, in some part of their course, availed themselves with so much distinction, and which, in the sequel, they abused with so much disorder at home, and oppression of their subjects abroad.

With this object before me, I hasten to enter on the scenes in which it begins to appear; and shall not dwell upon the history of the first ages of Rome; nor stop to collect particulars relating to the origin and progress of the commonwealth, longer than is necessary to aid the reader in recollecting the circumstances which formed the conjuncture in which this interesting change began to take place.

For this purpose, indeed, a general description of the state and its territory, such as they were in the beginning of this transaction, might have been sufficient; but as it is difficult to fix the precise point at which causes begin to operate, or at which effects are complete, I have indulged myself in looking back to the origin of this famous republic, whether real or fabulous, and shall leave the reader to determine, at what time he will suppose the period of authentic history to begin, or at what time he will suppose the causes of this revolution to operate, and to produce their effects.

As it is impossible to give, in mere description, a satisfactory account of a subject which is in its nature progressive and fluctuating, or to explain political establishments without some reference to the occasions whence they arose, I have, upon these accounts, endeavoured to give, even to the first part of my labours, the form of narration; and, together with the progress of political institutions in the state, remarked its territorial acquisitions and conquests, in the order in which they were made. In proportion as the principal object of the history presents itself, I shall wish, as far as my talents and the materials before me allow, to fill up the narration, and give to every scene of the transaction its complete detail. When this is done, and the catastrophe is passed, I shall wish again to contract my narration; and as I open with a summary account of what preceded my period, close with a similar view of its sequel.

The Romans are said to have made their settlement in the end of the sixth, or beginning of the seventh Olympiad,[1] about two hundred years before the accession of Cyrus to the throne of Persia, seven hundred years before the Christian æra, and long before the date of any authentic profane history whatever. The detail of their story is minute and circumstantial; but on this account is the more to be suspected of fiction: and in many parts, besides that of the fable, with which it is confessedly mixed, may, without any blameable scepticism, be rejected as the conjecture of ingenious men, or the embellishments of a mere tradition, which partakes in the uncertainty of all other profane history of the same times, and labours under the obscurity which hangs over the origin of all other nations.[2]

That the Roman state was originally a small one, and came by degrees to its greatness, cannot be doubted. So much we may safely admit on the faith of tradition, or in this instance infer, from the continuation and recent marks of a progress which the people were still making, after they became an object of observation to other nations,[3] and after they began to keep records of their own: that they had been an assemblage of herdsmen and warriors, ignorant of letters, of money, and of commercial arts, inured to depredation

1 Dionys. Hal. lib. i. 2 Liv. lib. vi.
3 Dionys. Hal. lib. i.

and violence, and subsisting chiefly by the produce of their herds, and the spoils of their enemies, may be safely admitted; because we find them, in the most authentic parts of their history, supplying these defects, and coming forward in the same direction, and consequently proceeding from the same origin, with other rude nations; being, in reality, a horde of ignorant barbarians, though likely to become an accomplished nation.

In the first accounts of their settlement, it is said that they mustered three thousand men on foot and three hundred on horseback.[4] Their establishment being effected by surprise or by force, and their people consisting of armed men who had every acquisition to make at the expense of their neighbours, they were naturally in a state of war with the country around them. They took post on the Palatium, a small height on the Tiber, which, according to former traditions, had been previously occupied by five different races of men, who, in a country so precariously settled, were frequently changing their places.[5] Their city was first the model of a Roman camp, fortified with a square breast-work and ditch, to serve as an occasional retreat to themselves and their cattle. Their leader, or chief, was the sole magistrate or officer, either civil or military. The members of the commonwealth were distinguished into different classes or ranks, under the names of patrician and plebeian, patron and client. "The patron," says Dionysius, "was to protect, to give counsel; and, whether present or absent, was to his clients what the father is to his family. The clients, in return, were to contribute to the support of their patron, to aid him in placing his children in marriage; and, in the case of his being taken by an enemy, were to pay his ransom; or of his being condemned in a fine, were to discharge it for him."[6]

The limits of prerogative and privilege, as in other rude societies, were yet imperfectly marked. It was the prerogative of the king to lead in war, and to rule in peace; but it is probable that he no more wished to deliberate, than to fight alone; and, though he may have done either occasionally, yet numbers of his followers were ever ready to attend him in both. The people acknowledged him as their leader, or prince; but they themselves, as in other instances of the same kind, were accustomed, on remarkable occasions, to assemble; and, without any concerted form of democracy, became the sovereign power, as often as their passions engaged them to act in a body. The superior class of the people as naturally came to have their meetings apart, and may have assembled frequently, when the occasion was not sufficient to require the attention of the whole.[7] Hence probably the establishments of the senate and of the popular assemblies, which were called the *Comitia*, and were both of so early a date as to be ascribed to the first of their kings.[8]

Even this founder of the state, we are told, was distinguished by his ushers or lictors carrying before him the axe and the rods, as the emblems of his power, and the instruments of his justice. The names of the senators were entered in a list, and they were separately called to their meetings. Assemblies of the people were intimated by the sound of a horn. The citizens were distinguished into curiæ, centuries, and tribes—divisions under which they formed their several compartments, for military array, religious ceremonies, or political deliberations. When met to decide on any public question, each division apart collected the votes of its members, from thence formed a vote for the curia or century; and, by the majority of these, determined the whole. The curiæ were fraternities, or divisions of the people, which met for the performance of religious rites: each had its separate priest, and place of assembly. When the curiæ were called on matters of state, they retained part of their religious forms; opened their meeting with observing the auspices, or signs of futurity; and if these were unfavourable, could not proceed on business. The augurs, therefore, in this mode of assembly, had a negative on the proceedings of the people.

The centuries were formed on a more artful idea, to make power accompany wealth. The people were divided into classes, according to the rate of their fortunes: each class was divided into centuries; but the number of centuries in the different classes was so unequal, that those of the first or richest class made a majority of the whole; and when the centuries of this class were unanimous, they decided the question. By this institution, the rich were masters of the legislature, though not without some compensation to the poor, as the several classes were charged with taxes and public services, in the same proportion in which they were vested with power.

The people, when thus assembled, were distinguished in their classes by their ensigns and arms, and, though called together on political affairs, were termed the army.[9]

In the first ages of this principality or commonwealth, the meetings of the people were held first by curiæ, and afterwards by centuries. The practice of voting by tribes was of a later date than either, and was the device of a popular party to exclude the auspices, to level the condition of ranks, and by these means to turn the channels of power in their own favour. The people were formed into their classes and centuries, to elect their officers, to enact laws, or to deliberate on other affairs of state; but they did not without struggle or contest always acquiesce in this mode of assembly. The poorer citizens often insisted to be called in the curiæ, and afterwards in the tribes, to decide on affairs which the rich would have referred to the centuries alone. The question on these occasions went to the foundation of the constitution, and implied a doubt whether the state was to be governed by the balance of numbers, or the balance of property.[10]

4 Liv. lib. i. c. 4. 5 Dionys. Hal. lib. i.
6 Ibid. lib. ii. c. 10.
7 De minoribus rebus Principes, de majoribus omnes consultant. Tacit. de Moribus Germ. 8 Dionys. lib. i.

9 Dionys. Hal. lib. iv. c. 16, 17, 18. Liv. lib. i. c. 43.
10 State of the classes and centuries at the establishment of the census:

VALUATION.

Class.	*Romans.*	*Sterling.*	*No. of Cent.*
1.	100,000	£.322 18*s.*	98
2.	75,000	242 3	21
3.	50,000	161 9	21
4.	25,000	80 14	21
5.	11,000	35 10	31
6.	——	——	1
Total, ...			193 From
First class, ...			98 Sub.
			95
Majority of the first class, ...			3

To these original springs of the political frame may be joined those of religion, which in all governments must have a considerable force; and in this have always been supposed a principal power to regulate its movements. Here indeed, there being no distinction of clergy and laity, the authority of the statesman, augur, and priest, was united in the same persons, or in the same orders of men: and as, in the mind of every citizen, notwithstanding the high measure of his superstition, the sword of state was preferred to the altar, the politician and warrior availed himself of the respect which was paid to the priest, and made superstition itself subservient to the purposes of state. With presages and prodigies he encouraged or restrained the people in their desires and pursuits; he bound them with vows and with oaths, to a degree that has not been equalled by mankind in any other instance; and, with reference to this circumstance in particular, it has been observed, that the seeds of Roman greatness were laid in the implicit respect with which every citizen revered the first institutions of his country.[1]

The wants by which the Romans were impelled in the first state of their settlement, made it necessary for them to vanquish some of their neighbours, or to perish in the attempt. Valour, accordingly, in their estimation, was the principal quality of human nature, and the defeat of an enemy the chief of its fruits. Every leader who obtained a victory made his entry at Rome in procession; and this gave rise to the triumph, which continued, from the first to the last age of the commonwealth, to be the highest object of ambition.

Historians, admiring the effect of this and of other practices of an early date among the Romans, have represented their founder, and his immediate successors, as philosophers, statesmen, and able tutors, who, with a perfect foresight of the consequences, suggested the maxims which gave so happy a turn to the minds of men in this infant republic. They are said to have taught, that by frugality and valour the Romans were to conquer the world: that they ought not to lay waste the lands which they conquered, but to possess them with colonies of their own people: that they ought not to slay the vanquished, but transport their captives to Rome, as an accession to the number of their own citizens: that they ought not to make war without provocation, nor to commence hostilities until they had demanded and had been refused reparation of wrongs. In whatever begree we suppose these maxims to have been expressed or understood in the councils of Rome, it is certain that the successful conduct of the state in these particulars was sufficient to have suggested the idea that they were known.

To the other fortunate customs which may be traced up to those early times of the state, we may join that of the census, by which the people, at every period of five years, took a regular account of the numbers and estates of their citizens, as the best measure they could have of their own progress or decline, and the surest test of their policy and conduct as a nation.

The Romans reckoned in the first period of their history, a succession of seven kings,[2] to each of whom they ascribed the invention of their several institutions. To Romulus, the mixed form of their government, the establishment of the senate and assemblies of the people, the ranks of patrician and plebeian, the relations of patron and client. To Numa, the religion of the people, and their regard to oaths. To Servius Tullius, the census, or periodical muster; and so on.—But whether we suppose these institutions to have been the suggestion of particular occasions, or the invention of ingenious men, directed by a deep premeditation of all their effects, there is no doubt that such institutions existed in very early times, and served as the foundation of that policy which distinguished the Roman state.

The monarchy of Rome is said to have lasted two hundred and forty-four years, a period in which the numbers of the people, and the extent of their settlement, had greatly increased. During this period, they had drawn many of their neighbours to Rome, and sent many of their own people to occupy settlements abroad. By the inrolment of aliens, they procured a certain increase of people; and by spreading their colonies around, they made acquisitions of territory, and extended the nursery of Roman citizens. We find, nevertheless, that, by the last part of this policy, they incurred a danger of losing the people whom they thus established or bred up in new settlements, however little removed from the metropolis. Men had not yet learned to consider themselves as the citizens of one place, and inhabitants of another. In departing from Rome, the colonies ceased to be inrolled in any tribe or ward of that city, or of its district; or to be ranked in any class of the people. They ceased, of course, to be called upon to vote in any of the assemblies, which they no longer attended. They formed notions of an interest separate from that of their original country, so much, that the colonies which had been planted by one prince, resisted the power of his successors; and conquests, where the Roman citizens were mixed with the natives, in order to keep them in subjection, were sometimes in danger of being lost. The colony itself took a part in the discontents of the people they were sent to restrain, and became parties with the vanquished in their quarrel with the victors.[3] But, notwithstanding frequent instances of this sort among the Roman colonies, the memory of their descent and the ties of consanguinity, the pride of their distinction as Romans, the capacity which every colonist retained of returning to Rome, and of being reinstated in the rolls of the people, for the most part preserved their attachment to Rome, and made them still a part of her strength, and a principal source of her greatness.

During this period of the kingly government, the numbers that were inrolled in the city and its territory, increased from three thousand and two hundred to eighty thousand men of an age

A property of 100,000 asses or pounds of copper entitled the owner to a place in the first class, 75,000 to a place in the second, 50,000 to a place in the third, 25,000 to a place in the fourth, 11,000 to a place in the fifth, and the remainder of the people, having no valuation, or having less than that of the fifth class, were thrown into the sixth or last class. The whole were divided into 193 centuries, of which the first class contained 80 centuries of foot, and 18 of horsemen, in all 98; being a majority of the whole. The sixth class formed no more than one century, as appears from the inspection of the preceding table.

1 See Machiavel's Discourses on Livy

2 Romulus, Numa, Tullus Hostilius, Ancus Martius. Tarquinius Priscus, Servius Tullius, Tarquinius Superbus

3 Liv. lib. iii. c. 4.

fit to carry arms.[4] The number of Roman tribes or wards of the city was augmented from three to twenty-one. The kingdom itself extended over the greater part of Latium, and had an intimate alliance with the whole of it. The city of Rome was become the principal resort of all the Latin confederates, the place of their meetings for devotion or pleasure, and the seat of their political consultations.[5]

To accommodate and secure this populous and growing community, several of the heights contiguous to their original settlement were, during the same period, successively occupied, the marshes between them were drained by excavations and works of great magnificence, of which a considerable part is still entire. The city itself, instead of an earthen rampart, was surrounded with towers and battlements of hewn stone.[6]

Change to republic.

So far it appears, that while every successive prince gratified his own ambition by subduing some neighbouring district or village, and brought an accession of riches or territory to his country, the genius of monarchy was favourable to the growth of this rising empire. But when princes became satiated with conquests abroad, or began to meditate schemes to increase their own importance at home, their ambition took a different direction, and led them to aim at making the kingdom hereditary, and the people more subservient to their pleasure. Under this direction of the monarch's ambition, the state, as Montesquieu observes, was likely to become stationary, or even to decline. A revolution became necessary, in order to preserve it in its former progressive state.

U. C. 244.

Such a revolution, we are told, took its rise from the resentments of the people, excited by abuses of power, and was hastened by a momentary indignation, roused by an insult offered by a son of the king to a Roman matron. As the political evils which this revolution was intended to remedy were, *the state of degradation and weakness to which the senate had been reduced*, the *usurpation of hereditary succession to the crown*, and the *general abuses of government*, suitable remedies were sought for to these evils, by restoring the numbers and power of the senate, by abolishing the royalty, and by substituting in its place an elective and temporary magistracy.

The principal part of the revolution consisted in substituting the consuls, two annual magistrates, in place of the king. These officers were chosen in the assembly of the centuries. The officer who was to preside at the election erected his standard, and pitched his tent in the field of Mars,[7] a meadow which lay on the banks of the Tiber, above the city. The people repaired to him in arms, and, distinguished by the ensigns and armour of their different classes, proceeded to make their election.

That the city might not be surprised while its defenders were thus abroad in the fields, a guard was posted, with its colours displayed, on the Janiculum, a hill on the right of the Tiber, which overlooked the river and contiguous plain. If an enemy appeared during the election, the guard had orders to strike their ensigns; and on this signal every century repaired to its post of alarm, and questions of state were suspended until the danger was removed. As it became an article of superstition, that the centuries could not proceed in any business without having an ensign displayed on the Janiculum, it was in the power of any person, by striking the ensign, to break up an assembly of the people: and this expedient for stopping the progress of any business was accordingly made use of at different times to the end of the republic.[8]

It was meant that the consuls should succeed to all the powers of the king; and in order to enforce their authority, a penalty of five oxen and two sheep was denounced against every person who refused to obey them.[9] Their joint and divided command, with the limited term of one year, which was to be the duration of their power, were thought sufficient securities against the abuse of it.

The government, by this revolution, devolved on the senate and nobles. The plebeians, in the first formation of it, were favoured by the admission of a certain number of their order to fill up the senate, which had been reduced in its numbers by the tyranny of the late king; and they were declared, in case of any oppression, to

---

4 Liv. lib. i. c. 44.

5 Dionys. Hal. lib. iv. p. 250.

6 The stones employed in building the walls of Rome, were said each to have been sufficient to load a cart.

The common sewers were executed at a great expense. It was proposed that they should be of sufficient dimensions to admit a wagon loaded with hay, (Plin. lib. xxxvi. c. 15.) When these common sewers came to be obstructed, or out of repair, under the republic, the censors contracted to pay a thousand talents, or about 193,000*l.* for clearing and repairing them, (Dionys. Hal. lib. iii. c. 67.) They were again in disrepair at the accession of Augustus Cæsar, and the reinstating them is mentioned among the great works of Agrippa. He is said to have turned the course of seven rivers into these subterraneous passages, to have made them navigable, and to have actually passed in barges under the streets and buildings of Rome. These works are still supposed to remain; but, as they exceed the power and resources of the present city to keep them in repair, they are quite concealed, except at one or two places. They were, in the midst of the Roman greatness, and still are, reckoned among the wonders of the world, (Liv. lib. i. c. 38;) and yet they are said to have been works of the elder Tarquin, a prince whose territory did not extend, in any direction, above sixteen miles; and, on this supposition, they must have been made to accommodate a city that was calculated chiefly for the reception of cattle, herdsmen, and banditti. Rude nations sometimes execute works of great magnificence, as fortresses and temples, for the purposes of war and superstition; but seldom palaces, and still more seldom works of mere convenience and cleanliness, in which, for the most part, they are long defective. It is not unreasonable, therefore, to question the authority of tradition in respect to this singular monument of antiquity, which so greatly exceeds what the best accommodated city of modern Europe could undertake for its own conveniency. And as those works are still entire, and may continue so for thousands of years, it may be suspected that they were even prior to the settlement of Romulus, and may have been the remains of a more ancient city, on the ruins of which the followers of Romulus settled, as the Arabs now hut or encamp on the ruins of Palmyra and Balbeck. Livy owns, that the common sewers were not accommodated to the plan of Rome, as it was laid out in his time; they were carried in directions across the streets, and passed under buildings of the greatest antiquity. This derangement indeed he imputes to the hasty rebuilding of the city after its destruction by the Gauls; but haste, it is probable, would have determined the people to build on their old foundations, or at least not to change them so much as to cross the direction of former streets.

7 Campus Martius.

8 See Book III. Chapter III.

9 Plutarch, in Vit. Poplicola.

have a right of appeal from any sentence or command of the magistrate to an assembly of the people at large. This was understood to be the great charter of every citizen. But the patricians alone could be chosen into the newly established offices of state. They alone were to furnish the ordinary succession of members to the senate, and, by their inrolment in the first and second classes, to have a decided majority in all the meetings or *comitia* of the centuries;[1] that is, in all assemblies of the people that were called to elect officers of state, to enact laws, or to judge of appeals. By these several provisions in their favour, they were in possession of a complete aristocracy, which they claimed as hereditary in their families, but which they were not likely to retain, without much discontent and animosity on the part of their subjects.

CHAPTER II.

Form of the Republic—Dissension of Parties—First Dictator—Secession of Plebeians—Tribunes of the People—Their Objects—Distribution of Corn—Division of Lands—Pretensions of the Plebeians—Commission to compile Laws—Decemvirs—Twelve Tables—Intermarriage of Ranks—Claim of the Plebeians to the Consulate—Military or Consular Tribunes—Censors—Ædiles—Præfectus Annonæ—Fortune of the Republic—Reduction of Veiæ—Destruction of Rome by the Gauls—Rebuilding of the City.

U. C. 244. THE government of Rome, as it is represented after the expulsion of the king, was become entirely aristocratical. The nobles had the exclusive possession of office, without any third party to hold the balance between themselves and the people. The consuls were the sole executive magistrates, and the only ministers of the senate; they were understood to come in place of the king; performed all the functions of royalty; and, in the manner of the kings, to whom they succeeded, united in their own persons all the dignities of the state, those of *judge*, *magistrate*, and *military leader*.

Such, at the first institution of the commonwealth, was, both in respect of government and manners, the simplicity or rudeness of this community. The people, however, in their new situation, were gradually and speedily led, by the accumulation of their affairs, by the contest of their parties, and by the wants of the public, to a variety of establishments, in which they separated the departments of state, more equally distributed its powers, filled up the lists of office, and put themselves in a posture to wield with advantage their strength as it increased, and to avail themselves of every circumstance that occurred in their favour.

While the exiled king was endeavouring, by continual invasions, to recover his power, disputes arose between the parties who had joined to expel him;[2] creditors, supported by the aristocracy, of which the nobles were now in full possession, became severe in the exaction of debts, or the patrons laid claim to more than the clients were willing to pay.[3] The state was distracted at once by its enemies from abroad, and by the dissension of parties at home. The authority of the new government not being sufficient to contend with these difficulties, the senate resolved to place themselves and the commonwealth, for a limited time, under the power of a single person, who, with the title of Dictator, or Master of the people,[4] should at his pleasure dispose of the state, and of all its resources.

U. C. 452 or 455.*

---

1 Dionys. Hal. lib. v.

2 In these original disputes between the patricians and plebeians at Rome, it is implied that they frequently or commonly stood in the relation of creditor and debtor, as well as of patron and client. And we may account for this circumstance in either of two ways: first, by supposing that the client was, in some degree, tributary to his patron, as the vassal was tributary to his lord in the original state of modern nations. Dionysius of Halicarnassus has laid some foundation for this supposition, in the passage above cited. Or we may suppose, in the second place, that the debts in question were money or effects actually borrowed by the client and lent by the patron. The first supposition is most agreeable to the manners of modern times; but the last is more likely to have been the fact in the original state of the Romans, and of ancient republics in general. Among them the great distinction of persons was that between freemen and slaves The rich freeman was supplied with every thing he wanted by the labour of his slaves. The necessitous freeman toiled with his own hands in labouring a small piece of ground, or in tending a few beasts. He had no trade by which to supply the luxuries of the rich, or by which, as in modern times, to make them his debtors. When he wanted their aid he was obliged to borrow; and there was, perhaps, but one occasion on which he had credit for this purpose; when he was going to war, and when he both had a reasonable excuse for borrowing, and a probable prospect of being able to pay, perhaps with interest, from the spoils of an enemy. But when his hopes failed, he might become insolvent, and exposed to all the severities of which we read such complaints in the early part of the Roman history.

There is, throughout this history, sufficient evidence that the popular party were on the side of the debtor. The prejudices of this party operated against the exaction of debts. Their influence was employed in reducing the interest of money; in having it abolished, and in having it detested, under the invidious appellation of usury They even strove, on occasion, to abolish debts: the result was far from being favourable to the necessitous borrower; he was obliged to pay for the risk, the penalties, and the obloquy to which the lender was exposed in transgressing the laws.

3 Dionys. Hal. lib. 5.

4 Magister Populi.

* The date of the nomination of the first dictator is uncertain. Liv. lib. ii. Some place it nine years after the expulsion of the kings; Dionys. twelve years.

This officer was invested with power to punish the disorderly without trial and without appeal; to arm the people, and to employ their forces on any service; to name his own substitute, or second in command; and to act without being, even at the expiration of his office, accountable either to the senate or to the people. The circumstances that were probably accidental in the first nomination of this extraordinary officer, were afterwards repeated as unalterable forms in every successive appointment of the same kind. It became the prerogative of the senate to resolve that a dictator should be named, and of the consul to name him. The ceremony was performed in the dead of night;[5] and as soon as the nomination was known, the lictors, or ministers of justice, armed with their axes and rods, withdrew from the ordinary magistrate, to attend this temporary lord of the commonwealth.

This was the first political expedient to which the state was directed by the exigency of its new government. The precedent came to be repeatedly followed in times of calamity or public alarm, and the whole powers of the state were occasionally entrusted to single men, on the sole security of their personal characters, or on that of the short duration of their trust, which was limited to six months. This institution was devised by the senate, to repress the disorders which broke out among the people, and to unite the forces of the commonwealth against its enemies. The next was of a different nature, and was meant to protect the plebeians against the oppression of their lords.

The inferior class of the people, almost excluded from any share in the new government, soon found that under its influence they had more oppression to fear from their patrons, than they had ever experienced from the prince they had banished. So long as the king and the senate shared in the powers of the state, the one took part with the people, when the other attempted to oppress them; and it was the ordinary interest and policy of the prince to weaken the nobles, by supporting the plebeians against them. This effect of the monarchy still, in some measure, remained, so long as the exiled king was alive, maintained his pretensions, and made the united services of the people necessary to the senate. During this period the patricians were still on their guard, and were cautious not to offend the people; but upon the death of the king, and the security which the new government derived from this event, the nobles availed themselves of their power, and enforced their claims on the people with extreme severity. In the capacity of creditors, they imprisoned, whipped, and enslaved those who were indebted to them, and held the liberties and the lives of their fellow-citizens at their mercy. The whole body of plebeians was alarmed; they saw more formidable enemies in the persons of their own nobility, than in the armies of any nation whatever. When the republic was attacked, they accordingly refused to arm in its defence. Many who had already suffered under the rod of their creditors, when called upon to enlist, showed their limbs galled with fetters, or torn with the stripes which they had received by command of their merciless patrons.

These distractions, joined to the actual presence of a foreign enemy, obliged the senate to have recourse to their former expedient, and to entrust the republic again in the hands of a dictator. Having succeeded in their first nomination, and having driven the enemy from their territories, they recurred to the same expedient again, on the return of a like occasion; but, in order to mix insinuation with the terrors of this measure, they made choice of Valerius, a person whose name was already known to the sufferers by some popular laws which they owed to his family. This officer had credit enough with the people to prevail on them to take arms, and had the good fortune to repel the enemy, by whom the state was invaded: but, upon his return, not being able to prevail on the senate to fulfil the hopes which he had given to the people, he made a speech to exculpate himself, and laid down his power. The citizens who had fought under his banner being still in the field, and, without any orders to disband, suspecting that the senate, under pretence of some war on the frontier, meant to remove them from the city, ran to their arms; and, if they had not been restrained by their military oath, and the respect they paid to the government of their country, must have entered the gates by force. But, under the impression of these motives, they fled from the walls instead of invading them, retired beyond the Anio, and took possession of a height about three miles from Rome,[6] afterwards known by the name of the Sacred Hill. Their officers followed, and endeavoured to persuade them to return to their duty; but were told, that no duty was owing to a government which had withdrawn its protection, and encouraged oppression; that free citizens own no country in which they are not permitted to enjoy their freedom.—"To what purpose," said Sicinius Bellutus, who was then at the head of this mutiny, "recall us to a city from which you have already forced us to fly by your extortion? By what new assurance can you persuade us to rely on a faith which you have repeatedly broken? By what charm can you engage us in support of a commonwealth, of which you will not allow us to be members? You mean to engross all the fruits which are to be reaped in your country, and it is well. We shall leave you to do so, and do not mean to interrupt your enjoyments."

This secession of a great body of the people having continued for several months, and in this time received a constant accession of numbers from the city and from the contiguous fields, threw the republic into the greatest disorder; exposed its lands to be neglected or pillaged by its own inhabitants, and ravaged by numerous enemies, who took this opportunity to invade it without opposition.

The patricians had sufficient force in their own body, and in that of their faithful retainers, to guard the avenues of the city, and to secure it from surprise: but being reduced to great difficulties for want of their usual supplies of provisions, and apprehending still greater from the interruption of labour and the suspension of government, they came to a resolution to negotiate with the leaders of the mutiny; and, for this purpose, raised Sp. Cassius, a person who, though

5 Liv. lib. viii. c. 20. & lib. ix. c. 28.

6 Cicero de Claris Oratoribus, c. 14.

of a patrician family, was in high favour with the people, to the office of consul. They agreed to mitigate the severities which they had hitherto practised against insolvent debtors, and to release such of them as were actually in bonds, or had been destined to slavery.

With these concessions, a deputation was sent to the camp, and a negotiation was opened, in which the plebeians obtained, not only a full acknowledgment of their privileges, but, what was of more consequence, a power of forming assemblies apart from the nobles,[1] and of electing annual magistrates, to guard and watch over their own separate rights. "Your consuls," they said, "are not so much the officers of the commonwealth as the heads of a faction; and, in all questions that relate to the people, are parties rather than judges. It is reasonable that we too have a head or representation in the commonwealth, under which we may act, at least in our own defence."

U. C. 260. In return to this well-advised and specious requisition, the tribunitian power was established, and with it the foundations of some good, and of much harm laid in the commonwealth. Great part of the last might have been prevented, if the plebeians, now in possession of a right to nominate tribunes for the care of their interests, had from thenceforward been content with the power of election merely, had discontinued their own collective assemblies for any other purpose, and increased the number of their tribunes, to a just representative of their whole body. The return, however, was more agreeable to the spirit of the times. The people were allowed to assemble; and, instead of a representation to support and preserve their rights with steadiness and with moderation, they proceeded to elect a few leaders, who from thenceforward, were to head every popular tumult, and to raise up every wind of contention into a storm.

The tribunes were authorised, at their first institution, to forbid, or to restrain, any measures which they thought hazardous, or injurious to the rights of their constituents, but not to propose any law, nor to move any positive resolution. They were not entitled to exercise their powers beyond the walls of the city, or to absent themselves from it for a whole day, except in their attendance on the festival of the Latin allies, where the presence of all the Roman magistrates was required. A single tribune might stop the proceedings of his own body, and of the people themselves, as well as the proceedings of the senate and patrician magistrates. In the exercise of this last part of their trust, though not permitted in this age of aristocracy to mix with the senators, they had places assigned them at the doors of the senate-house, from which, as from a watch-tower, they were to observe, and on occasion to stop, the proceedings of the lords.

As the tribunes were destined to withstand the exertions of power, and were supposed, on the most dangerous occasions, to expose themselves to the axe and the sword of their adversaries, it was thought necessary to guard their persons with the most sacred fences of religion and law. For this purpose an inviolable rule was prescribed in the following terms: "Let no one offer violence to the person of a tribune; neither kill him, nor procure him to be killed; neither strike him, nor procure him to be struck. Let the person who offends against this law be accursed; let his effects be made sacred to pious uses, and let every one pursue him to death."

To render this act irrevocable, a solemn oath for the perpetual observance of it was imposed, and dreadful imprecations were denounced against any person who should propose to repeal it;[2] and such was the effect of these precautions, taken for the safety of the tribunes, that, under the republic, persons obnoxious to public justice could not be punished, while they continued to bear this sacred character. And the emperors themselves, after they had abolished all the other rights of the republic, found, under this sacred title of tribune, a refuge to their crimes and oppressions, and a protection against the designs of assassins, or the resentment of those they had offended by their tyranny.

The college of tribunes, at its institution, was not limited to any precise number of members; it consisted at first of such persons as had been most active in procuring the establishment, and continued to be filled with the most zealous partizans of the people, the number being three or more, according as persons appeared to merit this honour. But in process of time both the plebeians who aspired to this distinction, and the patricians who were jealous of it, conspired to augment the numbers.—The first, in order to make way for their own preferment; and the second, to the end that they might be the better enabled, on occasion, to disunite their enemies, and to procure the negative of a part, to arrest the proceedings of the whole. The college of tribunes was accordingly augmented by degrees to ten; and a law was made to provide that the elections should not stop short of this number.[3]

Patricians could neither elect nor be elected into this office,[4] although, in the midst of irregularities incident to all unformed, especially to all popular governments, some exceptions are mentioned, even to the last part of this rule. The tribunes were at first elected in the assembly of the curiæ, where the vote of the poorest citizen was equal to that of the most wealthy. But even here the patricians, although not absolute masters, as they were in the assembly of the centuries, having great influence, and, by holding the auspices, having even a negative on all proceedings, it was thought necessary to alter the form of the assembly in which the tribunes were elected to that of the tribes; and by this means to enable the people to make their election, without any control from the nobles, either in virtue of the authority of the senate, or the interposition of the augurs.[5]

Such was the institution of the plebeian tribunes, while the state yet knew of no other magistrate besides the consuls and the quæstors, of whom the last, even under the kings, had been employed as a species of commissaries, or providers for the army. The expedient was adopted by the senate, to quiet the animosity of parties; but tended, in fact, only to render the contest between them more equal, and to multiply the subjects of dispute. The tribunes being vested with power to assemble the people, could not long be

1 Dionys. Hal. lib vii.

2 Dionys. Halicar. lib. iv. p. 410.

3 Lex Trebonia. Liv. lib. iii. c. 65.

4 Dionys. Hal. lib. vii.

5 Dionys. Hal. lib. ix. p. 65

confined to the mere negative with which they were at first entrusted; nor was it easy, on every occasion, to distinguish the measures of attack from those of defence; and the party of the plebeians, with these officers at their head, were then in a posture, not only to preserve their rights, but likewise to gain to their order continual accessions of privilege and power. Happily for the state, there was yet much ground of this sort to be gained, without transgressing the bounds of good order, or encroaching on the authority of equitable government.

The popular leaders in this career had to break through the bar of hereditary distinction, which, it was pretended, contrary to the genius of the republic, that no personal merit and no measure of ability could remove. One of the first steps they made in pursuit of this object, was to preclude every other power in the state from a negative on their own proceedings. For this purpose it was enacted, by the authority of the tribes, that no one, under pain of death, or of an arbitrary fine, should interrupt a tribune while he was speaking to the people.[6] Being thus provided against interruption, as they were by a former law against violence to their persons, they not only took up the complaints of their constituents, they suggested new claims to be made by them, and at every succession to office, endeavoured to signalize their term by some additional establishment for the benefit of the people: they even interrupted the state in its councils and military operations, and almost in every instance hung upon the wheels of government, until the grievances they complained of were redressed, or the demands they made were complied with.

In order to increase the number of plebeian officers, whose aid the tribunes alleged were necessary to themselves, they soon after their own institution, procured that of the Ædiles, who were to inspect the markets, and have charge of the public buildings and public shows. Being subordinate to the tribunes, as well as to the consuls, they acted, upon occasion, in what related to the policy of the town, as assistants to both.[7]

U. C. 260.

As Rome was a place of arms, and subsisted in some measure by public magazines; as settlements won from the enemy were often to be disposed of to citizens; as its institutions were yet new and incomplete; and as the patricians still claimed an exclusive right to all the offices of state, there was much to occupy the cares of the public—the distribution of corn from the granaries, the division of conquered lands, the defects of the laws, and the arbitrary proceedings of the magistrates. The qualifications of candidates for the office of consul furnished, during some ages, the subject of continual debates, and frequently exposed the parties concerned in them, if they escaped the swords of their enemies, to perish by their own dissensions. Their civil and military transactions were constantly blended together. The senate frequently involved the state in war, in order to suspend its intestine divisions, and the people as often took occasion, from the difficulties in which the community was involved by its enemies, to extort a compliance with their own demands.

The first subject of contention that arose after the institution of the tribunes was a sequel of the troubles which had preceded that establishment. The secession of the people took place in Autumn, the usual seed-time in Italy; and the labours of that season having been accordingly interrupted, the city was threatened with famine; and the senate exerted all its industry in guarding against this evil.[8] After the public granaries were filled for this purpose, it became a question, upon what terms, and at what price, the poorer citizens should be supplied from thence. Their insolence in the late mutiny, and the part which they themselves, by suspending the labours of the field, had taken, in bringing on the distress with which they were now threatened, were fully stated against them in this deliberation. The opportunity was thought to be fair, to recal the several concessions which had been extorted from the senate, and, in particular, to oblige the people to part with their tribunes, and to return within the former bounds of their duty.

Such was the substance of a contumelious speech, delivered in the senate by the celebrated Caius Marcius Coriolanus. The younger nobility applauded his sentiments; but the greater part of the senate, having recently escaped from a popular storm, were unwilling to engage themselves anew in the same dangerous situation. In order, therefore, to appease the people, who were greatly incensed at the proposal which had been made to subdue them, they agreed to deliver corn from the public granaries, at a price below that of the most plentiful season. And, by this proceeding, for the present pacified the tribunes, but flattered their presumption, and encouraged them to meditate still further demands. The distress with which their constituents had been threatened was prevented, but the insult they had received from Caius Marcius was not avenged; and they cited him to appear before the tribunal of the people, to answer for his conduct to the party he had offended. The senate and patricians were disposed to protect him; but, trusting that by the majority of their votes they might be able to acquit him in the *comitia* of the centuries, the only assembly before which, from the time of its first institution, any capital charge had been hitherto laid against a citizen, they suffered the trial to proceed. In this, however, they were disappointed. The tribunes insisted, that the people should assemble in their tribes; and having prevailed in this previous question, the accused, as being already condemned by this determination relating to the form of his trial, withdrew from his sentence.[9]

U. C. 262.

Coriolanus, in resentment of this prosecution, which forced him into exile, joined the enemies of his country, and by increasing the alarm of war from abroad, helped to suspend for a while the animosities of which he himself had furnished the occasion at home. The contest in which he had engaged the parties ended with his own exile, and was not attended with any other political effects; but it merits a place in these observations, as a proof of the great influence which the plebeian party, under its new leaders, had acquired, and as an evidence of the singular state of the Roman policy, by which, in the uncertain

6 Dionys. Hal. lib. vii.

7 Ibid. lib. vi.

8 Dionys. Hal. lib. vii.

9 Ibid. lib. i. 469.

choice of different modes of assembly, the very form of the government was left undetermined, until the occasion occurred on which this government was to act.

The assembly of the centuries formed an aristocracy, that of the tribes a democracy. They did not partake in the sovereignty by any determinate rule, but each of them occasionally seized upon the whole of it; and, instead of balancing each other by regular checks and interruptions, threatened to render the administration of the Republic a continual scene of contradictions and inconsistencies. Such at least is the judgment which we are tempted, in speculation, to pass on this singular constitution, although, in the sequel of its history, it will appear to possess at least one of the highest political advantages, in being the most excellent nursery of statesmen and warriors, and in forming the most conspicuous example of national ability and success.

The calm which the approach of Coriolanus, at the head of an army of Volsci, produced within the city, was of no longer duration than the alarm which produced it. As soon as the external enemy withdrew, the parties within resumed their disputes; but on a subject which was still more important than that which had recently employed them; and which, continuing to be moved at intervals, served to the last hour of the Republic as an object of popular zeal, or furnished a specious pretence, which ambitious and designing men continually employed, to captivate the ears of the populace. This was the most popular of all propositions—an equal division of land property, known by the name of the Agrarian law.

While the Romans were making their first acquisitions of territory, their conquests were understood to be made for the people, and were accordingly divided among them, or given to those who had not a sufficient provision for the subsistence of their families.[1] But of late, during a considerable period, while the Republic barely withstood the attacks of the exiled king, or recovered the losses sustained in the wars with the numerous enemies that supported him, she had either made few acquisitions of this sort, or, suitably to the growing disparity of ranks, which, though not necessary in very small republics, becomes so in proportion as nations extend, suffered the conquered lands to pass by connivance, occupancy or purchase, into the hands of powerful citizens, who made use of these opportunities to appropriate estates to themselves.

U. C. 267. The tribunes had not yet begun to make their complaints on this subject, when they were anticipated by the consul Sp. Cassius, who, being already in high favour with the popular party, continued to flatter the passions of the inferior class, and is said to have aimed at an improper and dangerous influence in the state. He affected great zeal for the rights of the people, and proportional indignation against their oppressors. He complained, in particular, of the improper use which had been recently made of the conquered lands, by suffering them to become the property of persons who were already too rich. Having himself made some conquests, he showed how the lands of the Republic ought to have been disposed of, by making an equal division of his own acquisitions among the more indigent citizens.[2] He obtained an act of the people to appoint three commissioners to inquire into the abuses which had been committed in the disposal of lands acquired from the enemy, and to consider of the proper corrections.

The senate, and the patricians in general, were greatly alarmed; most of them had possessions that seemed to fall within the object of this inquiry. The popular party alleged, that conquered lands being acquired by the joint labours, and at the common hazard, of all the people, should be equally divided among them. The patricians contended, that these levelling principles led to confusion and anarchy; that, in a state of which all the territory was actually, and within a few centuries, acquired by conquest, these maxims could not be applied without the subversion of government, as well as of property.

In this contest Cassius appeared to have the advantage of numbers on his side; and if he had confined his views to the division of lands, under which he was said to disguise a more dangerous intention, the senate and nobles must have at least devised considerable settlements for the people, in order to elude his demands. But while Cassius alarmed the rich with danger to their property, he at the same time alarmed every citizen with danger to his personal consequence, by offering the freedom of the city to every alien, who, at his summons, crowded from all the cantons of Latium to vote in the assemblies of the Roman people. His colleague opposed this measure, and the city, for the present, was saved from the intrusion of strangers. The attempt, however, gave offence to the people, as well as to the senate; and the unhappy author of it, in order to regain the favour of his party, proposed a resolution, not only to make a gratuitous distribution of corn, but even to refund what had been formerly paid by any citizen at the public granaries. This proposal too was interpreted to his prejudice, and raised a suspicion that he meant, with the aid of aliens and of indigent citizens, to usurp the government. On this supposition all parties in the state combined against him, and he was condemned to suffer the punishment of treason.

This appears to have been the first project after the state began to have its demesne lands, and after private estates began to be accumulated, that was made to divide all territorial acquisitions in equal shares to the people. And though the author of it perished in the attempt, the project itself was entailed on the commonwealth, as a subject of dissension, and became the source of repeated demands on the part of the people.

The tribunes had no sooner accomplished the ruin of Cassius, in which they concurred with the senate, than they insisted for the execution of the law he had framed, and for the nomination of three commissioners already resolved on, for the division of conquered lands. They protected the people in refusing to serve the state in its wars, until this demand should be granted. And having absolute and irresistible power to stop all proceedings in the city, they prevented all military levies within the walls, obliged the consuls, during a certain period, to erect their standard

1 Dionys. Hal. lib. ii.

2 Liv. lib. ii. c. 41.

n the country, and there to force the herdsman and labourer to enlist, by driving away the cattle, and distraining the effects of those who were unwilling to obey them.[3]

In these exertions of political strength, the parties at Rome learned by degrees to form their different plans, whether of administration or of opposition.

The senate endeavoured to furnish the people with employment abroad, to amuse them with triumphal processions, to gratify them with partial settlements and allotments of lands; and, in order to stop the violence of their leaders, by the negative of some one of their own order, continually endeavoured to divide the college of tribunes.

The tribunes, in their turn, endeavoured, by oaths and private engagements, to secure the unanimity of their own body, or to bind the minority to follow the decision of the greater number. They taught the people to despise the partial settlements, which, to pacify or to suspend their importunities, were offered to them at a distance from Rome. They taught them to aim at a higher object—the political consequence of their order, and an equal share in the government of their country. The tribunes were honoured in proportion to the part which they took in support of this popular cause; and plebeians were successively raised to this office, in reward of the animosity they had occasionally shown to the senate, and from respect to the courage with which they had, in any case, withstood the authority of the magistrate.

At every succession, accordingly, the new tribunes endeavoured to signalize their year by suggesting some advantage to the people; and, in the course of their struggles, obtained many regulations favourable to their interest as an order in the state.

One law which has been already mentioned, and which is of uncertain date, they obtained—to substitute the assembly of the tribes for that of the curiæ in the election of tribunes.[4]

U. C. 282. Another, to exclude the patricians entirely from the assembly of the tribes.[5]

The Agrarian law itself they frequently moved, in the interval of other claims and pretensions, or brought it forward along with such claims, in order to alarm the patricians, and to force them, under apprehension of this principal object of their fears, to a compromise, or to a compliance in some other demand.

To the other circumstances, which tended frequently to revive these political flames, may be joined the arbitrary proceedings of the magistrate, and the defect of judicial forms in the commonwealth. The consuls had succeeded to the kings as sole officers of state, both civil and military; they had not sufficient forms or limitations prescribed to them in the exercise of their power.[6] This defect, which is common in the administration of rude governments, is for the most part supplied by degrees. Evils are corrected in proportion as they are felt, and the rational proceedings of one age are adopted as precedents to regulate the next. But, in the present instance, at Rome, the popular party, it is said, demanded at once a system of jurisprudence and a complete body of laws. Being opposed by the patricians, they came to consider the measure as an object of party; and they pressed the acceptance of it, as much from animosity to the magistrates, as from a desire to secure public justice, or to regulate the forms of judicial procedure. The patricians considered the project as an attack on their power; and however innocent or reasonable it may have been, endeavoured to elude the execution of it with all the arts of evasion and delay, which they had employed to prevent the division of the conquered lands, or to frustrate any other the most factious purpose of their adversaries.

In this contest the powers and artifices of both parties were fully exerted. To the great authority and address of the nobles, the people opposed an ardour that was not to be cooled by delays, to be discouraged by partial defeats, or restrained by scruples in the choice of means for the attainment of their end. From this, as from many other instances, it may be inferred, that the popular party, in the contest with their superiors, are apt to think, that the rules of veracity and candour may be dispensed with, and that the means of deceit and violence may, without any scruple, be employed in their own favour. With less honour and dignity to maintain than their adversaries, they are less afraid of imputations that detract from either; and their leaders, supported by the voice of the more numerous party, are less apprehensive of evil fame. In this contest, accordingly, fictitious plots and conspiracies were fabricated by the popular side, and fictitious designs against the liberties of the people were imputed to the patricians, in order to render them odious, and to deter them from appearing in support of their real pretensions.[7]

In the issue of these contests, the senate despairing of being able to divert the people from their purpose, agreed to the nomination of three commissioners, who should be sent into Greece to make a collection of such laws as, being found salutary in that country, might be transferred to Rome. Soon after the return of the commissioners, the senate approved their report, and concurred in the nomination of the famous decemvirs to compile a body of laws for the commonwealth.

U. C. 302. The decemvirs were appointed merely to make the draft of a new code, and to propose matter for the consideration of the senate and people, from whom alone the propositions could receive the authority of laws; yet the persons named for this purpose, as the history bears, had credit enough with the people to be vested with a temporary sovereignty, in which they superseded the authority of the senate, as well as that of the consuls, and had unlimited power over the lives and fortunes of their fellow citizens.[8] Before their commission expired, they presented a number of laws, engraven on ten tables or plates, and containing a summary of the privileges to be enjoyed by the people, of the crimes to be punished by the magistrate, and of the forms to be observed in all judicial proceedings. They at the same time informed the people, that their plan was still incomplete, that many useful additions were yet to be made;

---

3 Dionys. Hal. lib. viii. Ibid. No. 273 and No. 278.
4 Dionys. Hal. lib. ix. Liv. lib. ii. c. 56.
5 Liv. lib. ii. c. 60.
Liv. lib. iii. c. 9. Dionys. Halicar. lib. x.

7 Dionys. Hal. lib. x. 8 Ibid. No. 303.

and, upon the faith of these declarations, obtained for another year the renewal of their powers, with a change of some of the persons who were named in the commission.

In this second year of the decemvirs' appointment, two more tables or plates were added to the former ten; a circumstance from which this part of the Roman law has derived its name. This supplement, as well as the former body of laws, was received with great avidity, and the twelve tables continued to be respected at Rome, as the ancient titles by which men are supposed to hold any valuable rights are revered in all nations.[1] No complete copy of them being transmitted to modern times, we cannot fully judge of their value; but, from the fragments remaining in authors that occasionally cite them,[2] this code appears, in some clauses, to have been a first draft of the regulations which are necessary in the establishment of property, and in making private parties answerable to public judicatures in all their disputes.—The property of land was established by a fair prescription of two years, and that of other effects by a prescription of one year.—Any controversy concerning the boundaries of land property was to be determined by arbiters or jurymen appointed by the magistrate.—Parties cited to a court of justice were not at liberty to decline attendance.—Judgment in capital cases was competent only to the assembly of the people in their centuries; but this supreme tribunal might delegate its powers by a special commission.

In considering this code as a record of ancient manners, the following particulars are worthy of notice:

The distinction of patrician and plebeian was so great, that persons in these different orders were not permitted to intermarry.

The father being considered as the absolute master of his child, had a right even to kill, or expose him to sale.[3]

The interest of money was limited to one per cent;[4] but bankruptcy was treated as a crime, and, without any distinction of fraud or misfortune, exposed the insolvent debtor to the mercy of his creditors, who might put him to death, dissect or quarter him, and distribute his members among them.[5]

Mixed with laws that arose from superstition, there were others containing proofs of great national wisdom. In private every family were free to worship the gods in their own way. And in public, though certain forms were required, yet there was not any penalty annexed to the omission of them, as the punishment of offences in this matter was left to the offended god.

The people were required to build their houses two feet asunder, to leave eight feet for the ordinary breadth of streets and highways, and double this breadth at the turnings.

They were forbid to dress or to polish the wood employed in funeral piles, or to express their sorrow for the dead by wounding their flesh, tearing their hair, or by uttering indecent or lamentable cries.

Such are a few of the more singular and characteristical clauses which are mentioned among the fragments of the twelve tables. The ardour of the people to obtain this code, and the unlimited powers which they entrusted to the commissioners appointed to frame it, had nearly cost them their liberty; and thus ended the progress of their commonwealth. The two additional tables, as well as the first ten, having been posted up for public inspection, and having been formally enacted by the senate and people, the object of the decemvirs' commission was obtained, and it was expected that they were to abdicate their power;

---

1 Livy calls the twelve tables *Fons omnis publici privatique juris.* Tacitus calls them *Finis equi juris.* And Crassus, in the Dialogue of Cic. de Orat. is made to say, Bibliothecas omnium philosophorum, unus mihi videtur tabularum libellus superare. De Orat. lib. i. c. 44.

2 Vid. Gravini de Origine Juris Civilis. Pighii Anal.

3 The clause in the twelve tables relating to the father's power of sale, contains a singular limitation. Vendendi filium patri potestas esto. Si pater filium ter venundavit filius a patre liber esto. The father may sell his child, but if he has sold him three times the child shall be free. (Dionys. lib. ii. c. 27. p. 97.) This law, in its first appearance carries an implication that, until this restriction was applied, fathers practised selling their children times without limit. No law, it may be said, is made against crimes altogether unknown; and, in general, what people do, may be inferred from what they are forbid to do; and yet the clause, considered in this light, is full of absurdity. The child, to be repeatedly sold, must have repeatedly disengaged himself from slavery. After being twice sold, he must have put himself a third time in the father's power; and to render such cases the object of law in any age or country whatever, the great law of parental affection must have been strangely suspended. The question therefore may be submitted to civilians and antiquaries, whether it be not easier to suppose a mistake in the tradition or in the record, or an unnecessary precaution in the compilers of this code; than such a frequency of the circumstances presumed in this clause, as would make the offence a proper object of legislation in any age or nation whatever; and whether this law may not have been, in its original intention, what it became in the subsequent applications of it, a mere precaution in favour of the parent, that he should not be deprived of his child by surprise, and that unless he had sold him three times, he was not supposed to have sold him at all. The form by which a Roman father emancipated his son, consisted of a sale three times repeated. The father sold him and received his price. The buyer once and again re-delivered the child, and had his price returned. After the third purchase, the buyer manumitted him by a singular ceremony prescribed in the laws.

4 Nam primo duodecim tabulis sancitum, ne quis unciario (1-12 per mon. or 1 per cent. per ann.) fœnore amplius exerceret, cum antea ex libidine locupletium agitaretur: dein rogatione tribunitia ad semuncias redacta; postremo vetitæ usuræ; multisque plebiscitis obviam itum fraudibus quæ toties repressæ miras per artes rursus oriebantur Tacit. Ann. lib. vi.

Montesquieu ventures to reject the authority of Tacitus in this instance, and supposes that the law which he ascribes to the decemvirs had no existence until the year U. C. 398; when according to Livy, lib. vi. it was obtained by the tribunes M. Duellius and L. Menenius, in favour of the people. Haud æque patribus læta, insequente anno C. Martio et Cn. Manlio Coss. de unciario fœnore, a M Duellio, L. Menenio, tribunis plebis, rogatio perlata. It is indeed probable that many antiquated laws were referred to this legendary code of the twelve tables on no better authority than that of their antiquity. And so great a reduction of interest was more likely to come from tribunes acting in favour of the people, who were generally the debtors, and who soon after procured the entire abolition of the interest of money, than from the decemvirs, who, being of the aristocratical faction, took part with the creditors.

5 The clause in this code respecting insolvent debtors, is equally strange with that which respects the power of the father, and shows no less upon what atrocious ideas of what they were to permit, as well as of what they were to prohibit, the compilers of this code proceeded. Their ideas in either, it is probable, were never realized. Livy says, that debtors were *nexi et traditi creditoribus.* (Liv. lib. ii. c. 23 & 27.) But it is affirmed with great probability of truth, that no creditor ever took the full benefit of this law against his insolvent debtor, (Aul. Gel. lib. 20. c. 1.) Laws that result from custom, and are suggested by real occasions, are genuine proofs of the reigning manners; but laws enacted by special lawgivers or commissioners, only indicate what occurs to the fancy of the compiler, and what are the prohibitions he is pleased to suppose may be necessary.

but the principal persons vested with this trust, having procured it with a view to usurp the government, or being debauched by two years uncontrolled dominion in the possession of it, refused to withdraw from their station, and boldly ventured to persist in the exercise of their power after the time for which it was given had elapsed. At Rome the power of the magistrate was supposed to determine by his own resignation, and the republic might suffer a peculiar inconveniency from the obstinacy of particular persons, who continued to exercise the functions of office after the period assigned them by law was expired.

The decemvirs took advantage of this defect in the constitution, continued the exercise of their power beyond the period for which it was given, took measures to prevent the restoration of the senate and the assemblies of the people, or the election of ordinary magistrates, and, even without employing much artifice, got the people to acquiesce in their usurpation, as an evil which could not be remedied; and the usurpers, in this as in other instances, seemed to meet with a submission that was proportioned to the confidence with which they assumed their power. The wrongs of the state appeared to make little impression on parties who had an equal concern to prevent them; but a barbarous insult offered to a private family rekindled or gave occasion to the breaking out of a flame, which injuries of a more public nature only seemed to have smothered.

Appius Claudius, one of the usurpers, being captivated with the beauty of Virginia, the child of an honourable family, and already betrothed to a person of her own condition, endeavoured to make himself master of her person, by depriving her at once of her parentage and of her liberty. For this purpose, under pretence that she had been born in servitude, and that she had been stolen away in her infancy, he suborned a person to claim her as his slave. The decemvir himself being judge in this iniquitous suit, gave judgment against the helpless party, and ordered her to be removed to the house of the person by whom she was claimed. In this affecting scene, the father, under pretence of bidding a last farewell to his child, came forward to embrace her; and, in the presence of the multitude, having then no other means to preserve her honour, he availed himself of the prerogative of a Roman father, and stabbed her to the heart with a knife. A general indignation instantly arose from this piteous sight, and all parties concurred, as at the expulsion of the Tarquins, to deliver the Republic from so hateful a tyranny.[6]

U. C. 304.

The senate and patrician administration being re-established by the cheerful concurrence of the plebeians, and the former government restored with the consent of all parties, a tide of mutual confidence ensued, which led to the choice of the most popular persons into the office of consul, and procured a ready assent from the nobles to every measure which tended to gratify the people.

The danger which had been recently experienced from the exercise of uncommon discretionary powers, produced a resolution to forbid, under the severest penalties of confiscation and death, any person ever to propose the granting of any such powers. The consecration of the persons of the tribunes, which, under the late usurpation, had almost lost its effect, was now renewed, and extended, though in a meaner degree, to the ediles and inferior officers, who were supposed to act under the tribunes in preserving the rights of the people.

The patricians likewise consented to have the acts of the senate formally recorded, placed in the temple of Ceres, and committed to the care of the ediles.[7] This was in fact a considerable diminution of the power of the consuls, who had been hitherto considered as the keepers and interpreters of the senate's decrees, and who had often suppressed or carried into execution the acts of this body at pleasure.

U. C. 304.

But the most striking effect, ascribed to the present unanimity of the citizens, was the ease with which the plebeian assemblies were permitted to extend the authority of their acts to all the different orders of the commonwealth.

The *comitia*, or assemblies of the Roman people, as may be collected from the past observations, were now of three denominations; that of the curiæ, the centuries, and the tribes. In assemblies of the first and second denomination, all citizens were supposed to be present; and laws were enacted relating to the policy of the state in general, as well as to particular departments, and separate bodies of men. The centuries disposed of civil offices, and the curiæ of military commands.[8] In the assembly of the tribes, composed of plebeians alone, the tribunes were elected; and acts were passed to regulate the proceedings of their own order, beyond which, in the ancient times of the Republic, their authority did not extend. But as the senate denied the right of the tribes to enact laws that should bind the community, the plebeians, in their turn, disputed the legislative authority of the senate. The centuries alone were supposed to enjoy the right of enacting laws for the commonwealth.[9]

This distribution, however, was partial, and tended to lodge the sovereignty of the state in the hands of the patricians, who, though no more than a part of the people, were enabled, by their undoubted majority in the assemblies of the centuries as well as in the senate, to give law to the whole.

Equity and sound policy required that the plebeians should have a voice in the legislature of a commonwealth of which they made so considerable a part. This privilege appeared to be necessary, in order to secure them against the partial influence of a separate order of men. They accordingly obtained it; but in a manner that tended to disjoin, rather than to unite into one body, the collateral members of the state. Instead of a deliberative voice, by which they might concur with the senate and *comitia* of the centuries, or by which they might control and amend their decrees, they obtained for themselves a separate and independent power of legislation, by which, as a counterpoise to the patrician acts, which might pass in the centuries without their concurrence, they could, on their part, and without the

6 Liv. lib. iii. c. 37. Dionys. Hal. fine.

7 Liv. lib. iii.

8 Liv. lib. v. c. 52. Lib. ix. c. 38. Cic. ad Famil. lib. i ep. 9. Lib. vi. c. 21.

9 These were termed *Leges*; the resolutions of the senate were termed *Senatus Consulta*, and those of the tribes, *Plebiscita*.

U. C. 304. presence or consent of the nobles, make plebeian acts that could equally bind the whole community.[1]

This rude and artless manner of communicating a share of the legislature to the inferior order of the people, tended greatly to increase the intricacy of this singular constitution, which now opened, in fact, three distinct sources of legislation, and produced laws of three different denominations; decrees of the senate,[2] which had a temporary authority; acts of the centuries;[3] and resolutions of the tribes;[4] and by these means undoubtedly made way for much intestine division, distraction, and tumult.

So far animosity to the late usurpation had united all orders of men in the measures that followed the expulsion of the decemvirs; but the spirit of cordiality did not long survive the sense of those injuries, and that resentment to a common enemy from which this transient unanimity arose. The plebeians had removed some part of the establishment, in which the patricians were unequally favoured; but they bore with the greater impatience the inequalities which remained, and by which they were still condemned to act a subordinate part in the commonwealth. They were still excluded from the office of consul, and from that of the priesthood. They were debarred from intermarriage with the nobles by an express law, which had been enacted, lest the sexes from passion, forgetting distinctions, should in this manner unite their different ranks; but being now, in some measure, by the late act in favour of the *comitia* of the tribes, become joint or rival sovereigns of the state, they could not long acquiesce in these unequal conditions.

U. C. 308. A few years after the restoration of the commonwealth, Canuleius, a plebeian, being one of the tribunes, moved the celebrated act which bears his name,[5] to repeal the clause of the twelve tables which prohibited the intermarriage of patricians and plebeians. The other nine tribunes joined at the same time in a claim of more importance—that the office of consul should be laid open to all the different orders of the commonwealth, and might be held by plebeians, as well as patricians.[6] The senate, and the whole order of nobles, having for some time, by delays, and by involving the state, as usual, in foreign wars, endeavoured to suspend the determination of these questions, were at length obliged to gratify the people in the less material part of their pretensions, respecting the intermarriage of different ranks, in order, if possible, to pacify them on the refusal of the more important claim, which related to their capacity of being elected into the office of consul.

To elude their demands on this material point, it was observed, that of the sacrifices and other duties belonging to the priesthood, which, by the sacred laws of religion, could be performed only by persons of noble birth, many were to be performed by the consul, and could not, without profanation, be committed to any person of plebeian extraction; and that, by this consideration alone, the plebeians must be for ever excluded from the dignity of consul. Superstition, for the most part, being founded on custom alone, no change can be made in the custom, without appearing to destroy the religion that is founded upon it. This difficulty accordingly put a stop, for a while, to the hasty pace with which the plebeians advanced to the consulate: but this obstruction was at length removed, as many difficulties are removed in human affairs, by a slight evasion, and

U. C. 309. by the mere change of a name. The title of consul being changed for that of military tribune, and no sacerdotal function being included in the duties of this office, plebeians, though not qualified to be consuls, were allowed to offer themselves as candidates, and to be elected military tribunes with consular power. In this manner the supposed profanation was avoided, and plebeians were allowed to be qualified for the highest office of the state. The mere privilege, however, did not, for a considerable time, enable any individual of that order to attain to the honour of first magistrate of the commonwealth. The plebeians in a body had prevailed against the law which excluded them; but as separate candidates for office, still yielded the preference to the patrician competitor; or, if a plebeian were likely to prevail at any particular election of military tribunes, the patricians had credit enough to have the nomination of consuls revived in that instance, in order to disappoint their antagonists.

Together with the separation of the military and sacerdotal functions, which took place on this occasion, another change, more permanent and of greater moment, was effected. Ever since the institution of the census, or muster, the enrolment of the people was become a principal object of the executive power. In the first ages it belonged to the king, together with all the other functions of state. In the sequel, it devolved on the consuls; and they accordingly, at every period of five years, by the rules of this office, could dispose of every citizen's rank, assign him his class, place him in the rolls of the senate, or on that of the knights, or strike him off from either; and, by charging him with all the burdens of a subject, while they stripped him of the privileges of a citizen, deprive him at once of his political consequence,[7] and of his state as a Roman.[8]

These regulations were accordingly enforced, not held up into public view merely to awe the people. The magistrate actually took an account of the citizen's estate, inquired into his character, and assigned him his place; promoted him to the senate or to the knighthood; degraded or disfranchised, according as he judged the party worthy or unworthy of his freedom, of the rank which he held, or of that to which he aspired in the commonwealth.[9]

So important a trust committed to the discretion of an officer elected for a different purpose, took its rise in the simplicity of a rude age; but continued for a considerable period without any flagrant examples of abuse. It was, nevertheless, that branch of the consular magistracy which the patricians were least willing to communicate or to share with the plebeians. While they admit-

1 Dionys. Hal. p. 306. Liv. lib. iii. c. 55.
2 Senatus Consulta.
3 Leges. 4 Plebiscita.
5 Lex Canuleia. Liv. lib. iv c. 1.
6 Dionys. Hal.

7 Liv. lib. iv. c. 24.
8 The citizens who came under this predicament were termed Ærarii.
9 Liv. lib. iv. c. 24.

ted them, therefore, to be elected tribunes with consular power, they stipulated, that the charge of presiding in the census, or musters, should be disjoined from it; and that, under the title of censors, this charge should remain with persons of patrician birth.[10] They contended for this separation, not with a professed intention to reserve the office of censor to their own order, but under pretence that persons invested with the consular power, being so frequently employed in the field against the enemies of the commonwealth, could not attend to the affairs of the city, or perform all the duties of censor at their regular periods.

U. C. 310.

But whatever may have been the real motive for separating the department of censor from that of consul, the change appears to have been seasonably made; and may be considered as a striking example of that singular felicity with which the Romans, for some time, advanced in their policy, as well as in their fortunes. Hitherto the Roman consul, being a warrior, was chiefly intent on the glory he was to reap in the field, and to gain at the expense of the enemies of the state. He disdained to seize the advantages which he had in his power, in the capacity of a clerk or accountant entrusted with the census, or enrolment of his fellow-citizens; nor does it appear that any peculiar attention was given to the choice of consuls on the year of the census, as being then vested with any dangerous measures of power. But considering the height at which party disputes were then arrived, and the great consequence of a citizen's rank and place on the rolls, it was no longer safe to entrust in the same hands the civil rights of the people, and the executive powers of the state. The consul, being frequently raised to his station by party intrigues, and coming into power with the ardour of private ambition and of party zeal, might have easily, in the manner of making up the rolls of the people, gratified his own resentments, or that of his faction. The office of consul, in his capacity of military leader, was naturally the province of youth, or of vigourous manhood; but that of censor, when disjoined from it, fell as naturally into the hands of persons of great authority and experienced age; to whom, in the satiety of brighter honours, the people might safely entrust the estimate of their fortunes, and the assignment of their rank. In such hands it continued, for a considerable period, to be very faithfully discharged; and by connecting the dignities of citizen, and the honours of the state, with private as well as public virtue, had the happiest effects on the manners of the people.

The number of censors, like that of the consuls, was limited to two; but that of the consular tribunes was left undetermined, and at successive elections was augmented from three to eight. This has given occasion to some historians, who are quoted by Livy, to ascribe the institution of this office, not to the importunity of the plebeian party, but to the exigencies of the state; which being assailed by numerous enemies, and not having as yet devised the method of multiplying commanders, under the titles of proconsul, were led to substitute officers of a different denomination, whose numbers might be increased at discretion. It is indeed probable, that, in the progress of this government, new institutions, and the separation of departments, were suggested no less by the multiplicity of growing affairs, than by the pretensions of party, or by the ambition of separate pretenders to power. In the first of those ways, we are led to account for the institution of the plebeian ediles, already mentioned; for that of the præfectus annonæ, or inspector of the markets, together with the additions that were, in the course of these changes, continually made to the number of quæstors.

The quæstors had been long established at Rome; they had charge of the public funds, and followed the kings and the consuls as commissaries or provisors in the field. During the busy period which we have been now considering, their number was augmented from two to four; and the places were filled, for the most part, with patricians, though not limited to persons of this rank.

U. C. 333.

The præfectus annonæ, or inspector of the markets, was an officer occasionally named, on a prospect of scarcity, to guard against famine, and to provide for the wants of the people. Rome was in fact a place of arms, or a military station, often depending as much for subsistence on the foresight and care of its officers, as on the course of its ordinary markets. Without a proper attention to this particular on the part of the state, the people were exposed to suffer from scarcity. On the approaches of famine, they became mutinous and disorderly, and were ready to barter their freedom, and the constitution of their country, for bread. During the famine which first suggested the separation of this trust from that of the ordinary officers of state, Sp. Mælius, a Roman knight, being possessed of great wealth, engrossed great quantities of corn; and having it in his power to supply the wants of the poor, endeavoured to form a dangerous party among them, and by their means to raise himself to the head of the commonwealth. The senate took the alarm, and, as in the most dangerous crisis of the state, had recourse to the nomination of a dictator. Mælius being cited to appear before him, and having refused to answer, was put to death.

U. C. 313.

The care of supplying the people with corn, which had been at this time committed to L. Minucius, was from thenceforward entrusted to citizens of the first rank, and the office itself became necessary in the political establishment of the commonwealth.

Hitherto we have considered the Roman Republic as a scene of mere political deliberations and councils, prepared for contention, and seemingly unable to exert any united strength. The state, however, presented itself to the nations around it under a very different aspect, as a horde of warriors, who had made and preserved their acquisitions by force, and who never betrayed any signs of weakness in the foreign wars they had to maintain.

In their transition from monarchy to republic, indeed, there seems to have been a temporary intermission of natural exertions. Private citizens, annually raised to the head of the republic, did not with their elevation acquire the dignity of princes; they did not command the same respect from their fellow citizens at home, nor had the same consideration from rival nations abroad. The frequent dissensions of the people seemed to render them an easy prey to their enemies.

10 Liv. lib. iv. c. 8.

During the life of Tarquin many powers united against them in behalf of the exiled king. They were stripped of their territory, confined to the walls of their city, and deserted by their allies.[1] The fortune of the state seemed to fall with its monarchy. The event, however, belied these appearances, and the power of the annual magistracy soon became more formidable abroad, though less awful at home, than that of the monarch. The republican government sought for respite from domestic trouble in the midst of foreign war, and the forces of the state, instead of being restrained, were impelled into action by intestine divisions. The ambition with which the lower ranks of the people endeavoured to watch their superiors, the solicitude with which the higher order endeavoured to preserve its distinction, the exercise of ability which, in this contest, was common to both, enabled them to act against foreign enemies with a spirit that was whetted, but not worn out, in their domestic quarrels.

The consuls annually elected, brought to the helm of affairs a fresh vigour of mind and continual supplies of renewed ambition. Every officer, on his accession to the magistracy, was in haste to distinguish his administration, and to merit his triumph; and numerous as the enemies of the Republic appeared, they were not sufficient to furnish every Roman consul, in his turn, with an opportunity to earn this envied distinction. It was given only to those who obtained actual victories, and who killed a certain number of their enemies.[2]

In this nursery of warriors, honours, tending to excite ambition or to reward military merit, were not confined to the leaders of armies alone: the victorious soldier partook in the triumph of his leader, and had subordinate rewards proportioned to the proofs he had given of his valour. "I bear the scars," said Dentatus (while he pleaded for a share in the conquered lands to himself and his fellow-soldiers,) "of five and forty wounds, of which twelve were received in one day. I have carried many prizes of valour. Fourteen civic crowns bestowed upon me by those I had saved in battle. Three times the mural crown; having been so often the first to scale the enemies' walls. Eight times the prize of distinction in battle. Many tokens of esteem and gratitude from the hands of generals. Eighty-three chains of gold, sixty bracelets, eighteen lances, and thirty-five sets of horse-furniture, from private persons, who were pleased to approve of my services."[3]

Under the influence of councils so fertile in the invention of military distinctions, and in armies of which the soldier was roused by so many incentives to military ambition, the frequent change of commanders, which is commonly impolitic, proved a perpetual renovation of the ardour and spirit with which armies were led. In public deliberations on the subject of war, the vehement ambition of individuals proved a continual incentive to vigorous resolutions, by which the state not only soon recovered the consequence which it seemed to have lost in its transition from monarchy, but was speedily enabled to improve upon all its former advantages, as head of the Latin confederacy; frequently to vanquish the Sabines, the Hernici, the Volsci and Etruscans, and, in about a hundred years after the expulsion of Tarquin, to extend its dominion greatly beyond the territories which had been in the possession of that prince. In one direction, from Falerium to Anxur, about sixty miles; and in the other, from the summits of the Appenines to the sea: and Rome, the metropolis of this little empire, was become, with a few competitors, one of the principal states of Italy.

U. C. 344.

The first and nearest object of its emulation at this period was Veiæ, an Etruscan principality, of which the capital, situated about nine miles from Rome, was built on an eminence, and secured by precipices.

The Romans, even before the change of their government from the form of a principality to that of a republic, had been in possession of the Tiber and both its banks; but on the right of this river were still circumscribed by the Veiæntes, with whom they had waged long and desperate wars; and, as may be supposed among rivals in so close a neighbourhood, with imminent danger to both. Veiæ, according to Dionysius, was equal in extent to Athens, and, like the other Etruscan cantons, was further advanced than Rome in the arts of peace, probably better provided with the resources of war, but inferior in the magnanimity of its councils and in the courage of its people. The Veiæntes being, after a variety of struggles, beat from the field, they retired within their walls, suffered themselves to be invested, and underwent a siege or blockade of ten years. The Romans, in order to reduce them, continued during those ten years in the field, without any interruption or distinction of seasons; made secure approaches, fortifying themselves in the posts which they successively occupied, and in the end entered the place by storm.

U. C. 357.

In these operations, we are told, that they learned to make war with more regularity than they had formerly practised; and having, some little time before, appointed a military pay for such of their people as served on foot, they at this time extended the same establishment to their horsemen or knights; imposed taxes on the people in order to defray this expense, and made other arrangements, which soon after enabled them to carry their enterprises to a greater distance, and to conduct them with more order and system: circumstances which, together with the accessions of territory and power, gained by the reduction of Veiæ, rendered this event a remarkable epocha in the history of Rome.

The use which they proposed to make of their conquest was partly founded in the original policy of the state. The practice of incorporating vanquished enemies, indeed, with the Roman people, had been long discontinued: for even Tarquin, it is said, had introduced the custom of enslaving captives, and this fate the citizens of Veiæ underwent;[4] but their lands, and the city itself, offered a tempting prize to the conquerors. And accordingly it was proposed to transplant into those vacant possessions and seats one half of the Roman senate and people.[5]

This proposal was extremely acceptable to persons of inferior condition, who hoped to double

1 Dionys. Hal. lib. v. 2 Five thousand in one field.
3 Dionys. Hal lib. x. c 36. vel p. 362

4 Liv. lib. v. c. 22. 5 Ibid. c. 24

their possessions, and flattered themselves that they might double the power of the state: but it was strenuously opposed by the senate and nobles, as tending to divide and weaken the commonwealth, and as more likely to restore a rival than to strengthen themselves. It was eluded by a partial division of the Veiæn territory, in which seven *jugera*, or about four English acres, were assigned as the lot of a family; and by these means the more indigent citizens were provided for, without any hazard of dismembering the state.

But while the Romans were thus availing themselves of the spoils of a fallen enemy, and probably enjoying, on the extinction of their rival, a more than common degree of imagined security, they became themselves an example of the instability of human affairs; being assailed by a new and unlooked-for enemy, who came like a stroke of lightning on their settlement, dispersed their people, and reduced their habitations to ashes.

The Gauls, who are said to have passed the Alps in three several migrations, about two hundred years before this date, being now masters of all the plains on the Po, and of all the coasts of the Adriatic to the banks of the river Sena, where they had a settlement, which, from their name was called Sena Gallia; and being still bent on extending their possessions, or shifting their habitations, had passed the Appenines, and laid siege to Clusium, the capital of a small nation in Tuscany.[6] The inhabitants of this place made application to the Romans for succour; but could obtain no more than a deputation to intercede with the Gauls in their behalf. The deputies who were sent on this business, and commissioned to act only as mediators, having appeared in arms on the side of the besieged, the Gauls complained of their conduct as a breach of faith, and as a departure from the neutrality which the Romans professed: and being denied satisfaction on this complaint, they dropped their design on Clusium, and turned their arms against these mediators, who had violated the laws of war. They advanced on the left of the Tiber, found the Romans posted to receive them on the Allia, a small river which was the limit of the Roman territory, in the country of the Sabines, about ten miles from Rome; and, with the same impetuosity which hitherto attended them, they passed the Allia on the right of the Roman army, drove them into the angle that is formed by the confluence of the two rivers, put all who withstood them to the sword, and forced the remainder into the Tiber, where numbers perished, or, being cut off from their retreat to Rome, were dispersed in the neighbouring country.

U. C. 363.

This calamity is said to have so much stunned or overwhelmed the Roman people, that they made no farther attempt to defend their city. All the youth that were fit to carry arms retired into the capitol. The weak or infirm, whether from sex or age, fled as from a place condemned to destruction, or suffered themselves to be surprised and cut off in the streets.

The Gauls, having employed three days in the pursuit and slaughter of those who fled from the field of battle, on the fourth day advanced towards the walls of Rome. But being alarmed at first by the general desertion of the battlements, which they mistook for an ambuscade or an artifice to draw them into a snare, they examined all the avenues with care before they ventured to enter the gates. The more effectually to dislodge every enemy, they set fire to the city, reduced it to ashes, and took post on the ruins, in order to besiege the capitol, which alone held out.[7] In this state of affairs, the republic, already so formidable to all its neighbours, was supposed to be extinguished for ever. The fame of its ruin reached even to Greece, where Rome began to be considered at this time as a rising and prosperous commonwealth.[8]

The Gauls remained in possession of the ruins for six months; during which time they made a fruitless attempt to scale the rock on which the capitol was built; and being repulsed by Manlius, who, for his vigilance and valour on this occasion, acquired the name of Capitolinus, they continued to invest and block up the fortress, in hopes of being able to reduce it by famine. The Romans, who were shut up in the capitol, still preserved the forms of their commonwealth, and made acts in the name of the senate and people. Sensible that Camillus, under whose auspices they had reduced the city of Veiæ, and triumphed over many other enemies, now in exile on the score of an invidious charge of embezzling the spoils he had won at that place, was the fittest person to retrieve their affairs; they absolved him of this accusation, reinstated him in the qualification to command their armies;[9] and, in order that he might assemble their allies and collect the remains of their late army, which was dispersed in the neighbouring country, vested him with the power of dictator. In this extremity of their fortunes, he overlooked his wrongs, procured numbers to resort to his standard, and hastened to arm for the preservation of his country. He came to the relief of the capitol at a critical moment, when the besieged, being greatly reduced by famine, had already capitulated, and were paying a ransom for themselves and their remaining effects. Before this transaction was completed, he surprised the besiegers, obliged them to relinquish their prize, and afterwards, in a decisive battle that was fought in the neighbourhood of Rome, revenged the disaster which his countrymen had suffered on the banks of the Allia.[10]

Whatever may have been the true account of this famous adventure, the Romans have given it a place in their history, retained a deep impression of their danger from the Gauls, and from thence dated the origin of some particulars in their policy, which seem to have arisen from such an impression. They set apart particular funds in the treasury, to be spared in all other possible exigences of the state, and reserved for a resource in case of a Gaulish invasion. They subjected the magistrate to certain general restrictions, but allowed an exception in case of an invasion from the Gauls; and it is likely that, in the age in which they took these alarming impressions, they had not yet acquired those advantages of discipline and military skill, in which they were afterwards so much superior to the Gauls and other barbarous neighbours.[11]

6 Liv. lib. v. c. 35, &c.

7 Plutarch, in vit. Camilli. 8 Ibid.

9 Liv. lib. v. c. 32. 10 Ibid. c. 43, &c.

11 The establishment of the Legion, and the improvement made in the choice of its weapons and manner of array, are mentioned as subsequent to this date: and the

Although historians have amply supplied the detail of history before this event, they nevertheless acknowledge, that all prior evidence of facts perished in the destruction of Rome; that all records and monuments of what the Romans had formerly been, were then to be gathered from the ruins of cottages, which had been for several months trodden under foot by a barbarous enemy; that the laws of the twelve tables, the People's Charters of Right, and the Forms of the Constitution, were to be collected in fragments of plates which were dug from the rubbish of their former habitations; and that nothing remaining to mark the former position of Rome, besides the capitol, raised on its rock, and surrounded with ruins, the people deliberated whether they should attempt to renew their settlement on this ground, or transfer it to Veiæ. It had been formerly proposed to remove to that place one half of the senate and people. It was then proposed, that they should choose that as the proper ground on which to restore the name and the seat of their commonwealth. "Why," said the promoters of this design, "attempt, at a great expense, and with so much labour, to clear out the wretched ruins of a fallen city, while we have another, provided with private and public buildings of every sort, yet entire for our reception?" To this specious argument might have been opposed the consideration of the many advantages of their former situation; its place on a navigable river, its command of the passage from Latium to Etruria, and of the navigation of the Tiber from the descents of the Appenines to the sea. But motives of superstition and national pride were supposed to be of greater weight. "Would you," said Camillus, "abandon the seats of your ancestors? Would you have Veiæ restored, and Rome to perish for ever? Would you relinquish the altars of the gods, who have fixed their shrines in these sacred places; to whose aid you are indebted for so many triumphs, and to whom you owe the conquest of those habitations for which you now propose to forsake their temples?"

Convinced by this argument, the Romans, determined to remain in their ancient situation, proceeded to restore their habitations, and, in the course of a year, accomplished the work of rebuilding their city. An era from which, as from a second foundation, may be dated the rise of the commonwealth, and the beginning of a period, in which its history, though still controverted in some particulars, is less doubtful than before, or less disfigured with fable.[1]

CHAPTER III.

Scene of Foreign War and Domestic Dispute opened with reviving Rome—Faction or Conspiracy of Manlius—Condemnation—Plebeians elected into the Office of Consular Tribunes—Aspire to the Consulate—The first Plebeian Consul—Establishment of the Prætor—Patrician Ediles—The Plebeians qualified to hold all the Offices of State—The Measure of Roman Magistracy complete—Review of the Constitution—Its seeming defects—But great successes—Policy of the State respecting Foreign or Vanquished Nations—Formation of the Legion—Series of Wars—With the Samnites, Campanians—The Tarentines—Pyrrhus—Sovereignty of Italy—Different Footing on which the Inhabitants stood.

U. C. 365.

THE Romans were not allowed to restore their community, nor to rebuild their habitations in peace. They were invaded by the Equi, the Volsci, the Hernici, the Etruscans, and some of their own Latin confederates;[2] who dreading the re-establishment of a commonwealth, from which they had already suffered so much, and whose power was so great an object of their jealousy, made every effort to prevent it. During a period of one hundred and seventeen years which followed, they accordingly had to encounter a succession of enemies, in subduing of whom they became the sovereigns of Italy; while they continued to undergo internal convulsions, which, as formerly, proved the birth of political institutions, and filled up the measure of their national establishment.

During this period, the plebeians, far from being satisfied with their past acquisitions, made continual efforts to extend their privileges. The tribunes, by traducing the senate, and by displaying in their harangues the severities of the patrician creditor, and the sufferings of the plebeian debtor, still inflamed the animosity of their party; the republic itself was so feebly established, that ambitious citizens were encouraged, by means of factions raised among persons of the lower class, to have thoughts of subverting the government. In this manner Manlius, the famous champion of the capitol, who, as has been observed, by his vigilance and valour preserved that fortress from the Gauls, formed a design to usurp the sovereignty. Presuming on his merit in this and other services, he thought himself above the laws; and endeavouring by his intrigues with

Romans, it is confessed, made less progress in every other art than in that of war. Their general Camillus, at his triumph for the victory obtained over the Gauls, made his entry into Rome, having his visage painted with red; a practice, says Pliny, which is yet to be found among nations of Africa, who remain in a state of barbarity, and which this natural historian was inclined to consider as a characteristic of barbarous manners.

1 Some parts even of the history that follows, are doubtful. The names of dictators and of consuls, the reality of entire campaigns, as well as of single actions, are controverted, (Liv. lib. i. c. 5. & 26. lib. v. c. 55. lib. viii. c. 38. lib. ix. c. 15.) but that which preceded this date rests almost on tradition alone, (Liv. lib. vi. c. 1.) It serves, however, to inform us, what the Romans themselves believed; and is therefore the best comment we can have on the genius and tendency, as well as the origin, of their political institutions

2 Liv lib vi. c. 2. & 16.

the populace, to form a party against the state, he incurred, what was at Rome of all imputations the most detested, that of aspiring to be king. In opposition to this conspiracy, whether real or fictitious, the Republic was committed to the care of a dictator; and Manlius being brought before him, endeavoured to turn the suspicion of malice and envy against his accusers. He produced four hundred citizens, whom he had redeemed from their creditors and released from chains. He produced the spoils of thirty enemies slain by himself in battle; forty badges of honour conferred on him by generals under whom he had served; many citizens whom he had rescued from the enemy, and in the number of those he had saved, he pointed at Caius Servilius, second in command to the dictator, who now carried the sword of the state against the life of a person who had saved his own. And in the conclusion of his defence, "Such were the treasons," he said, "by which the friends of the people were to be sacrificed to the senate."

His merits in the public service were great, and entitled him to any reward from the people, except a surrender of their liberties. His liberality to the more indigent citizens, if it proceeded from humanity, was noble; but if it proceeded from a design to alienate their affections from the public, or transfer them to himself, was a crime; and the most splendid services, considered as the artifices of a dangerous ambition, were the objects of punishment, not of reward.

The people, it is said, while they had in their view the capitol, which had been saved by the vigilance and bravery of this unfortunate criminal, hesitated in their judgment; but their meeting being adjourned to the following day, and to a different place, they condemned him to be thrown from the rock on which he had so lately signalized his valour.[3]

Such alarms to the general state of the commonwealth, had their temporary effect in suspending the animosity of parties; but could not reconcile their interests, nor prevent the periodical heats which continually arose on the return of disputes. The plebeians had been now above forty years in possession of a title to hold the office of consular tribune, but had not been able to prevail at any election.[4] The majority of the centuries were still composed of patricians; and when candidates of plebeian rank were likely, by their personal consideration, to carry a majority, the other party, in such particular instances, had influence enough, as has been observed, to revive the election of consuls, a title from which the plebeians, by law, were still excluded.

U. C. 366.

The plebeians, however, by the zeal of their party, by the assiduity and influence of individuals who aspired to office, by the increase of their numbers in the first and second classes, by their alliance with the patrician families in consequence of marriage, at last surmounted these difficulties, obtained the dignity of consular tribune for one of their own order, and from thenceforward began to divide the votes of the centuries with the patrician candidates. They were accordingly raised in their turn to what was then the first office of the state, and in which nothing was wanting but the title of consul. To this too they were soon led to aspire; and were urged to make the concluding step in the rise of their order, by the ambition of a female patrician; who, being married into a plebeian family, bore with impatience the mortifications to which she was exposed in the condition of her new relations. She excited her husband, she engaged her own kindred among the patricians, she roused the whole plebeian party to remove the indignities which yet remained affixed to their race, in being supposed unworthy to hold the consular dignity.

U. C. 353.

U. C. 377.

Licinius Stolo, the husband of this lady, and Publius Sextius, another active and ambitious plebeian, were placed in the college of tribunes, in order to urge this point. They began the exercise of their office by proposing three very important laws: the first intended for the relief of insolvent debtors; by which all payments made on the score of interests, should be deducted from the capital, and three years be allowed to pay off the remainder.

A second law to limit the extent of estates in land, by which no citizen should be allowed to engross above five hundred jugera,[5] or to have in stock above one hundred bullocks, and five hundred goats and sheep.

A third law to restore the election of consuls, in place of consular tribunes, with an express provision that, at least, one of the consuls should be of plebeian descent.

The patricians having gained some of the tribunes to their party, prevailed upon them to dissent from their colleagues, and to suspend, by their negatives, all proceedings on the subject of these laws. The tribunes, Licinius and Sextius, in their turn, suspended the usual election of magistrates, and put a stop to all the ordinary affairs of state.

An anarchy of five years ensued,[6] during which time the Republic, bereft of all its officers, had no magistracy besides the tribunes of the people, who were not legally vested with any degree of executive power.[7] Any alarm from abroad must have suspended the contest at home, and forced the parties to a treaty: but they are said to have enjoyed, in this state of domestic trouble, uninterrupted peace with their neighbours; a circumstance from which we may infer, that, in most of their wars, they were themselves the aggressors, and owed this interval of peace to the vacancy of the consulate, and to their want of the prompters, by whom they were usually excited to quarrel with their neighbours.

In the several questions, on which the parties were now at variance, the patricians contended chiefly for the exclusion of plebeians from the office or title of consul; and, as an insuperable bar to their admission, still insisted on the sacrilegious profanation that would be incurred, by suffering the rites usually performed by the consuls to pass into plebeian hands. This argument, instead of persuading the popular leaders to desist from their claim, only made them sensible that it was necessary to remove this impediment by a previous operation, before they attempted to pass through the way which it was meant to

3 Liv. lib. vi c. 27.

4 Ibid. c. 37.

5 About 300 English acres.

6 From U. C. 377 to 382.

7 Liv. lib. vi. c. 35.

obstruct. They appeared then for a little to drop their pursuit of the consulate; they affected to respect the claim of the patricians, to retain the possession of places which had always been assigned to their order. But they moved, that the number of ordinary attendants on the sacred rites should be augmented from two to ten; and that of these one half should be named of plebeian extraction.

While the patricians continued to reject this proposal, on account of the effect it was likely to have on their pretensions in general, they gave way successively; and, at the interval of some years, first to the acts that were devised in favour of insolvent debtors; next, to the Agrarian law, or limitation of property in land; and last of all, to the new establishment relating to the priesthood, and to the communication of the consulate itself to persons of plebeian rank.

The authors of the new regulations, knowing that the majority of the centuries was composed of patricians, or was still under the influence of that order, were not satisfied with the mere privilege of being qualified to stand for the consulate. They insisted, that at least one of the consuls should be a plebeian; and having prevailed in this, as in the other contested points, the plebeian party entered immediately on the possession of their new privilege, and raised Publius Sextius, the tribune who had been so active in the cause of his constituents, to the office of consul.

U. C. 387.

But while the patricians thus incurred a repeated diminution of their exclusive prerogatives, they endeavoured, by separating the judicative from the executive power of the consul, and by committing the first to a patrician officer, under the title of Prætor, to save a part from the general wreck.

It was intended that the prætor should be subordinate, but next in rank, to the consul. He was attended by two lictors, and had his commission in very general terms, to judge of all differences that should be brought before him, and to hear the suits of the people until the setting of the sun. This unlimited jurisdiction, as we shall have occasion to observe, came to be gradually circumscribed by its own precedents, and by the accumulating edicts of successive prætors. One person at first was supposed able to discharge all the duties of this office; but the number, in order to keep pace with the growing multiplicity of civil affairs, was afterwards gradually increased.

Another political change, by which the patricians procured some compensation for what they had now surrendered, was made about the same time. The care of the public shows and entertainments had hitherto belonged to the ediles of the people. The office of edile being at its first institution expensive, was likely to become gradually more so by the frequent additions which were made to the festivals, and by the growing demands of the people for shows and amusements. The plebeians complained of this charge as a burden on their order, and the opposite party offered to relieve them of it, provided that two officers for this purpose, under the title of Curile Ediles, should be annually elected from among the patricians.[1]

By these institutions the nobles, while they admitted the plebeians to partake in the dignity of consul, reserved to their own order the exclusive right to the offices of prætor and edile: by the last of which they had the direction of sports and public entertainments; a station which, in a state that was coming gradually under the government of popular assemblies, became, in process of time, a great object of ambition, and a principal access to power.

The design or the effect of this institution did not escape the notice of the plebeian party. They complained, that while the patricians affected to resign the exclusive title to one office, they had engrossed two others, inferior only in name, equal in consideration and influence. But no exclusive advantage could be long retained by one order, while the other was occasionally possessed of the legislative and supreme executive power. All the offices, whether of prætor or edile, of dictator or censor, were, in process of time, filled with persons of either rank; and the distinction of patrician or plebeian became merely nominal, or served as a monument of the aristocracy which had subsisted in former ages. The only effect which it now had was favourable to the plebeians; as it limited the choice of tribunes to their own order, while, in common with the patricians, they had access to every other dignity in the state.

U. C. 417.

Review of the constitution.

Such is the account which historians have given us of the origin and progress of the Roman constitution. This horde, in the earliest account of it, presented a distinction of ranks, under the titles of Patrician, Equestrian, and Plebeian; and the state, though governed by a prince, had occasional or ordinary assemblies, by which it approached to the form of a republic. Assemblies to which every citizen was admitted were termed the *Comitia:* those which were formed of the superior ranks, or of a select number, were termed the Senate. Among those who had attained the age of manhood, to be noble and to be of the senate were probably synonymous terms. But after the introduction of the census, separate rolls were kept for the senate, the equestrian order, and the people. These rolls were composed by different offices in successive periods in the state. A senate was composed of a hundred members by Romulus.[2] This number was augmented or diminished at pleasure by his successors. The consuls succeeded in this matter to the prerogative of the kings; and the censors were appointed to exercise it, with the other duties of the census, as a principal part of their functions. It is remarkable, that, notwithstanding the great importance of the senate in the government of their country, so little precaution was taken to ascertain who were to be its constituent members, or to fix their legal number. The body was accordingly fluctuating. Individuals were placed or displaced at the discretion of the officer entrusted with the muster, and the numbers of the whole increased or diminished indefinitely. The officers of state, though not enrolled, had access to the senate; but their con-

1 Liv. lib. vi. c. 42.

2 Liv. lib. i. c. 8. According to Livy the senate consisted of no more than a hundred members at the death of Romulus; but, according to Dionysius, their numbers had been augmented by a popular election at the admission of the Sabines; some writers say to two hundred; others to one hundred and fifty. Dionys. lib ii c 47.

tinuing members, after their year in office expired, depended on the discretion of the censors. It seemed to be sufficient for the purposes of this constitution, that the senate should be a meeting of the superior class of the citizens.

Recapitulation. As the noble and popular assemblies had their existence under the kings, the transition from monarchy to republic in so small a state, by substituting elective and temporary magistrates in place of the king, was easy. A sufficient occasion was given to it in the abuses which were felt in the last reign of the monarchy. The disorders incident to the shock of parties, who were set free from a former controul, required, on occasion, the remedy of a discretionary authority vested in some person who might be entrusted with the public safety, and soon led to the occasional institution of a dictatorial power. The high prerogatives claimed and maintained by one party, obliged the other to assume a posture of defence, and to place themselves under the conduct of leaders properly authorised to vindicate their rights. These rights were understood, by degrees, to imply equality, and, in the successive institutions that followed, put every citizen in possession of equal pretension to preferment and honours; pretensions which were to be limited only by the great distinction which Nature has made between the capacities, merits, and characters of men, and which are subject, in every community, to be warped by the effects of education and fortune.

New departments of state, or additions to the number of officers employed in them, were continually suggested by the increase of civil affairs; and while the territory of the Republic was but a small part of Italy, the measure of her political government was full, and the list of her officers complete. Functions which, in the first or simplest ages, were either unknown or had been committed to the king alone, were now thrown into separate lots or departments, and furnished their several occupations to two consuls, one prætor, two censors, four ediles, and eight quæstors, besides officers of these different ranks, who, with the titles of proconsul, proprætor and proquæstor, and without any limitation of number, were employed wherever the exigences of the state required their service.

In this account of the Roman constitution we are come nearly to that state of its maturity[3] at which Polybius began to observe and to admire the felicity of its institutions, and the order of its administration. The plebeians were now reconciled to a government to which they themselves had access, and citizens of every rank made great efforts of industry in a state in which men were allowed to arrive at eminence, not only by advantages of fortune, but likewise by personal qualities. The senate and assemblies of the people, the magistrates and select commissioners, had each their departments, which they administered with an appearance of sovereign and absolute sway, and without any interfering of interests or jealousy of power.

The consuls were destined to the command of armies; but, while at Rome, seemed to have the highest prerogatives in the administration of all civil and political affairs. They had under their command all the other officers of state, except the tribunes of the people; they introduced all foreign ambassadors; and they alone could move the senate on any subject of deliberation, and put their acts or determinations in writing. The consuls, too, presided with a similar prerogative in the assembly of the centuries, and in that of the curiæ, proposed the question, collected the votes, declared the majority, and framed the act. In all military preparations, in making their levies as well as in the command of the army, they were vested with high degrees of discretionary power[4] over all the troops of the commonwealth, composed of Roman citizens or allies. They commanded the treasury, as far as necessary to the service on which they were employed, and had one of its commissioners, or quæstors, appointed to attend their court, and to receive their orders.

The senate, however, had the ordinary administration of the revenue, took account of its receipts and disbursements, and suffered no money to be issued without their own decree, or the warrant of the consul in actual service. Even the money decreed by the censors for the repair of public buildings, and the execution of public works, could not be issued by the quæstors without an act of the senate to authorise it. All crimes and disorders that were committed among the free inhabitants of Italy, or municipal allies of the state, all disputes of a private or public nature that arose among them, came under the jurisdiction and determination of the senate. All foreign embassies were received or despatched, and all negotiations were conducted, by this body. In such matters the people did no more than affirm or reverse what the senate, after mature deliberation, had decreed, and for the most part gave their consent as a matter of form; insomuch, that while persons, who observed the high executive powers of the consul, considered the state as monarchial; foreigners, on the contrary, who resorted on public business to Rome, were apt to believe it an aristocracy vested in the senate.

The people, notwithstanding, had reserved the sovereignty to themselves, and, in their several assemblies, exercised the powers of legislation, and conferred all the offices of state.[5] They likewise, in all criminal matters, held the supreme jurisdiction. In their capacity of sovereign, they were the sole arbiters of life and death; and even in their capacity of subjects, did not submit to restraints which, in every other state, are found necessary to government.

A citizen, while accused of any crime, continued at liberty until sentence was given against him, and might withdraw from his prosecutors at any stage of the trial, even while the last century was delivering its votes. A voluntary banishment from the forum, from the meetings of the senate, and the assemblies of the people, was the highest punishment which any citizen, unless he remained to expose himself to the effects of a formal sentence, was obliged to undergo; and it was expressly stipulated, that, even at Tibur or Præneste, a few miles from Rome, a convict who had withdrawn from judgment should be safe.[6]

3 As it stood in the fifth and sixth centuries of Rome.

4 Vid. Zonar. No. 501. Frontini Stragemata, lib. iv. Val. Max. lib. ii. c. 7.

5 In the centuries they enacted laws, and elected the officers of state. In the curiæ they appointed officers to military command.

6 The laws of Publius, which gave the power of legislation to the plebeian assemblies, and that of Valerius, which

Parts so detached were not likely to act as one body, nor to proceed with any regular concert; and the state seems to have carried, in all its establishments, the seeds of dissension and tumult. It was long supported, nevertheless, by the uncommon zeal of its members in favour of a commonwealth in which they enjoyed so much freedom, and in which they were vested with so much personal consequence.

The several members of the constitution, while in appearance supreme, were in many respects dependent on each other.

The consuls, while in office, had the meetings, and determinations of the senate and people, in a great measure, in their power; but they received this power from the people, and were accountable for the discharge of it at the expiration of their office.

The senate could resolve, but they could not execute, until they had obtained from the people a confirmation of their acts, and were obliged to solicit the tribunes for leave to proceed in any matter which these officers were inclined to oppose.

The senate was constituted, or formed, at regular periods, at the discretion of the consuls or censors, officers named by the people.

The city, nevertheless, was over-awed by the senate and officers of state. On great and alarming occasions, the people themselves were no longer sovereigns than they were allowed by the senate and consuls to hold this character. The senate and consuls having it in their power to name a dictator, could at once transfer the sovereignty of the state to a single person, and subject every citizen to his authority. Every individual held his place on the rolls at the will of the censors, and his property at the disposal of courts that were composed of senators; the servants of the public in general, who aimed at lucrative commissions, depended on the senate, as administrators of the treasury, and trustees in the collection or disbursements of the public money;[1] and every Roman youth, when embodied in the legions, entrusted his honours and his life in the hands of the consul, or commander in chief.[2]

The mass, however, was far from being so well compacted, or the unity of power so well established, as speculative reasoners sometimes think necessary for the order of government. The senate and the popular assemblies, in their legislative capacities, counteracted one another. The numbers required to constitute a legal assembly of the people, the qualification of a citizen, which entitled him to be considered as a member of the commonwealth, were still undetermined. Aliens settling at Rome were admitted on the rolls of the people, and citizens removing to the colonies were omitted. Laws, therefore, might be obtained in a clandestine manner, when the people, not sufficiently aware of the consequence of such laws, did not attend; or the question might be determined by the voice of a single alien, as often as the division was nearly equal, and a designing magistrate chose to place any number of aliens on the rolls for this purpose.[3] The state took its laws, not only from the assemblies, which were held, however irregularly, within the capital, but from military detachments and armies, when

secured every citizen in the right of appeal to the people at large, after being repeatedly re-enacted, were now in full force. (Liv. lib. x. c. 8.)

1 The influence which the senate possessed as administrators of the public treasury, according to Polybius, was very great. They had a number of commissions to give, in the collection of various duties levied on the navigators of rivers, the entry to sea-ports, the produce of mines, and demesne or public lands, chiefly let out for pasturage. They had likewise considerable disbursements on the repair of highways and public buildings, and in the execution of a variety of other works. In such transactions great numbers of people were concerned, as contractors, as partners with those who contracted with the senate, or as creditors who advanced money to enable the contractors to perform their articles. In all these several capacities the parties depended on the will of the senate, and continually attended at the doors of that assembly, soliciting commissions, pleading for an abatement of some condition, for delay in the execution of some article, or relief in the case of unforeseen hardship or loss.

2 Polyb. lib. vi. c. 10, 11, 12, 13, 14.

3 In the settlement of Romulus, recruits of every quality, whether outlaws, fugitives, or captives, were received without distinction.—In the first ages of the Republic, aliens settling at Rome were admitted as citizens, and even placed on the rolls of the senate.—The Tarquins, and the first of the Claudian family, were emigrants from the neighbouring cantons.—After the establishment of the census, or periodical muster, the king, the consuls, and last of all, the censors, made up the rolls of the senate and people at pleasure. They admitted upon it very readily every inhabitant of the city who claimed to be enrolled; but when a right of voting in any of the popular assemblies at Rome came to be considered as a privilege of moment, the inhabitants of Latium crowded to Rome in order to obtain it. They were sometimes put upon the rolls by one consul, and forbid the city by his colleague; and in every such case the negative, by a maxim of the Roman policy, prevailed.—Such as actually settled at Rome, sooner or later found means to be inserted in the tribes; and the towns of Latium complained, that they were deserted by numbers of their people, who resorted to Rome for this purpose, and that they were likely to be depopulated. They obtained a law, by which Latin emigrants were excluded from the rolls of the Roman people, except they had left offspring to replace them in the country towns they had left. And this seems to have been the first law enacted at Rome to regulate or restrain the naturalization of aliens. Some authors have affirmed, that, even while aliens were so easily admitted on the rolls of the people, Roman citizens, accepting of settlements in the colonies, forfeited their political rights. In this, however, it is probable, that the effects of mere absence have been mistaken for an express and formal exclusion. Whoever ceased to give in his name at the census, or whoever left his ward or tribe in the city to live at a distance, was not enrolled in the ward, nor placed in any class. It did not follow, however, that he had forfeited his right, or might not claim it as often as he attended the census. In this case he was upon a foot of equality with every other citizen, and in the same manner received or rejected at the will of the censor, or other officer who took the muster.

In this account of the Roman colonies, writers have followed the account of Sigonius, whose opinion, in every circumstance relating to the Roman history, is of great authority. In this particular, however, it happens, that the principle passage he has quoted in support of his opinion, is by some accident strangely perverted. Livy relates, lib. xxxiv. c. 42. that the people of Ferentium, in the year of Rome five hundred and fifty-seven, started a new pretension, by which all Latins who gave their names to be inscribed in any Roman colony should be considered as Roman citizens; but that the senate rejected this claim when offered by persons who were annexed to the colonies of Puteoli, Salernum, and Buxentum. *Novum jus eo anno a Ferentinatibus tentatum, ut Latini, qui in coloniam Romanam nomina dedissent, cives Romani essent. Puteolos, Salernumque et Buxentum adscripti coloni, qui nomina dederunt quum ob id se pro civibus Romanis ferrent; senatus judicavit non esse eos cives Romanos.* There was a distinction between Roman colonies and colonies of Roman citizens. The first might be Latins, or other allies, planted under the authority of the Roman state. The second were probably citizens. And the whole amount of this passage was to prove, that Latins were not to be considered as Roman citizens, merely because they resided in some colony of Roman citizens. But the quotation of Sigonius is as follows, and gives a wonderful perversion to the passage in question: *De antiquo Jure Italiæ*, lib. ii. c. 3

abroad in the field.[5] Yet, under all these defects as we have repeated occasions to observe, they enjoyed the most envied distinction of nations, continual prosperity, and an almost uninterrupted succession of statesmen and warriors unequalled in the history of mankind.

U. C. 465. In about one hundred years after they began to restore their city from the ruins in which it was laid by the Gauls, they extended their sovereignty from the farthest limits of Tuscany on the one side, to the sea of Tarentum and the straits of Messina on the other; and as the contest of parties at home led to a succession of political establishments, their frequent wars suggested the policy which they adopted respecting foreign nations, and the arrangement of their national force.

They had for some time discontinued the practice of admitting captives into the number of their people; but continued that of extending and securing their acquisitions, by colonies of their own citizens, or of such allies as they could most securely trust. They exacted from the cantons of Italy which they vanquished, contributions of subsistence and clothing for the benefit of their armies; and they generally imposed some condition of this sort as a preliminary to every negotiation or treaty of peace.[6]

U. C. 415. Their forces consisted of native Romans, and of their allies in Italy, nearly in equal parts. The legion, says Livy, had been formerly arrayed in a continued line, or compacted column;[7] but in the course of the wars which led to the conquest of Italy, came to be formed in divisions, and had different orders of light and heavy-armed infantry, as well as cavalry. The light-armed infantry were called the Velites, and were supposed to ply in the front, on the flank, or in the rear of the army; and their service was, to keep the heavy-armed foot undisturbed by missiles till they came into close action with the enemy.

The heavy-armed foot consisted of three orders, called the Hastati, Principes, and Triarii; of whom each had its separate divisions or manipules; and those of the different orders were placed in three different rows, and at distances from each other, equal to the front of the division. By this disposition the manipules of the first and second row could either act separately, or, by mutually filling up their intervals, could complete the line, leaving the Triarii, in time of action, as a body of reserve, to support the line, or fill up the place of any manipule that might be forced by the enemy. And, in order to faciliate occasionally this change of disposition, the divisions of one row faced the intervals of the other.[8] They were armed with the pilum, which was a heavy javelin or spear to be cast at the enemy, and with a short and massy sword fitted to strike or to thrust. They bore an oblong shield, four feet high by two and a half feet broad, with a helmet, breastplate, and greaves.

In the structure of these weapons and this defensive armour, the Romans consulted at once both the principal causes of courage in a soldier, his consciousness of the means to annoy his enemy, and of a power to defend himself. And with these advantages they continued for ages to prevail in most of their conflicts, and were the model

"Quare ascripti coloni nomine quidem erant cives Romani, revero coloni. Testem postulatis? non longe abiero. Presto est Livius qui scribit, lib. xxxiv. Puteolos, Salernum et Buxentum *civium Roman.* Adscripti coloni, qui nomini dederant cum ob id se pro civibus ferrent; senatus judicasse non esse eos cives Romanos; et *alio loco* narrat Ferentinates novum jus tentâsse, ut Latini qui in coloniam Romanam nomina dedissent, cives Romani essent."

The perversion of this quotation is remarkable. Different clauses of the same sentence are quoted as separate passages in different parts of the author. The order of the clauses is so placed, that the use of the first in explaining the second is lost, and the words *civium Roman* are inserted. The passage in Livy, asserting that even Latins pleaded to be admitted as citizens, because they resided in some colony of citizens, proves the reverse of what Sigonius maintains, *viz.* that citizens removing to colonies were disfranchised.

The fact is, that, in the time of Livy and other historians, the distinction between Roman citizens, whether of the city or of the colonies, and the other inhabitants of Italy, was become a matter of antiquity and of mere curiosity; and therefore is not by them so fully and distinctly stated, as not to admit of dispute. The colonists ceasing to attend at elections, or in the assemblies of the people, and not giving in their names at the musters, subjected themselves to all the effects of positive exclusion, although it is probable no such exclusion had taken place; for even aliens were not excluded by any positive law, and might be admitted on the rolls at the discretion of the officer who presided over the muster. Antiquarians, in search of ancient constitutions, sometimes suppose that rules must have existed, in order to have the pleasure of conjecturing what they were.

5 The consul C. Marcius, U. C. 398, being encamped at Sutrium in Etruria, assembled his army in their tribes, and passed a law to raise the twentieth penny on the price of every slave that should be manumitted. The senate, being pleased with the tax, confirmed the act; but the tribunes, alarmed at the precedent, obtained a resolution, by which it was declared for the future to be capital for any person to propose any law in such detached or partial assemblies of the people. (Liv. lib. vii. c. 6.)

6 Liv. lib. viii. c. 1. et 2. Lib. ix. c 43. Lib. x. c. 5. et 37.

7 Liv. lib. viii. c. 8.

8 This account of the Roman legion is not without its difficulties. It appears irrational to break and disperse the strength of a body in this manner; and Cæsar makes no mention of any such distinction of orders, of the manipules, of the rows in which they were formed, or of the intervals at which they fought. His legion consisted of ten cohorts, formed from right to left on a continued front. Polybius, however, one of the best military historians, and himself an eye-witness of the disposition of the Roman legion in action, as well as on the parade, is very explicit in his account of it; refers to it in the description of the Roman march (Polyb. lib. vi. c. 38.) in the description of every battle (Polyb. lib. iii. c. 1, 2, 3, 4.) and (Polyb. lib. xv. c. 10.) in stating the comparative advantages of the Roman legion and Macedonian phalanx (Polyb. lib. xvii. c. 28.) The phalanx being a column of indefinite depth, close ranks, and a continued front, with lances or spears, it was impregnable to the short sword and loose order of the Romans, so long as it preserved its front entire, and the spear-man made no opening for the Roman soldier to enter within the point of his weapon.

It is observed that the Romans made their attack in separate divisions and at intervals, in order to bring on some irregularity in the front of the phalanx, and in order to make some openings by which the Roman soldier could enter with his sword, and, once within the point of his enemy's spear, could perform great slaughter with little resistance (Plutarch in vit. P. Emilii. Liv. lib. xliv. c. 41. Neque ulla evidentior causa victoriæ fuit quam quod multa passim prælia erant quæ fluctuantes; turbarant primo, deinde disjecerunt phalanges.) From this account then it is probable that the Romans did not divide their legion into orders and manipules, nor fight at intervals, until after they adopted the short stabbing sword, which is said to have been originally from Spain; and that they continued to make this disposition so long only as they had to do with enemies who used the spear and continued front; that after the social war in Italy, and their own civil wars began, they discontinued the separate manipules, and sought to strengthen themselves against an army like their own, by presenting a continued front. Livy accordingly marks the time at which the formation of manipules, at intervals, was which other nations endeavoured to imitate[1] in the form of their armies and in the choice of their weapons.

It is understood in the antiquities of this people, that when they were assembled for any purpose, whether of state or of war, they were termed the army. In their musters a plebeian was a foot soldier, the knight a horseman, and the legion a mere detachment of the whole, draughted for the year, or embodied for a particular service. The men, as well as the officers, in the first period of the history of the Republic, were annually relieved or exchanged; and even after it ceased to be the practice thus annually to relieve the private men, and after the same legions were employed during a succession of some years, yet the people, to the latest period of the commonwealth, continued to form the armies of their country; and the officer of state was still understood to command in virtue of his civil magistracy, or in virtue of a military qualification which never failed to accompany it. No citizen could aspire to any of the higher offices in the commonwealth, until he had been enrolled in the legions, either ten years if on horseback, or sixteen years if on foot; and, notwithstanding the special commissions that were occasionally given for separate objects of state or of war, civil and military rank were never disjoined. Equal care was taken to furnish the rising statesman and warrior with the technical habits of either profession; or rather to instruct him, by his occasional application to both, not to mistake the forms of office in either for the business of state or of war, nor to rest his pretensions to command on any accomplishment short of that superior knowledge of mankind, and those excellent personal qualities of penetration, sagacity, and courage, which give the person possessed of them an ascendant, as a friend or as an enemy, in any scene or department of human affairs. It may be difficult to determine, whether we are to consider the Roman establishment as civil or military; it certainly united, in a very high degree, the advantages of both, and continued longer to blend the professions of state and of war together, than we are apt to think consistent with that propriety of character which we require in each: but to this very circumstance, probably among others, we may safely ascribe, in this distinguished Republic, the great ability of her councils, and the irresistible force with which they were executed.[2]

During a period of about one hundred and twenty years after the rebuilding of Rome, the Romans were engaged in a continual series of wars; first with the Latins and with their own colonies who wished to disengage themselves from so unequal an alliance; and afterwards with the Etruscans on the one hand, and with the Samnites, Campanians, and Tarentines on the other. They quarrelled with the Samnites first in behalf of the Campanians, who, in order to obtain their protection, made a surrender of themselves and of all their possessions. This act of surrender they afterwards had occasion to enforce against the Campanians themselves, who endeavoured, when too late, to recover their liberties.

The Samnites were a fierce nation, inhabiting that tract of the Appenines which extends from the confines of Latium to those of the Apulia; and who, to the advantages of their mountainous situation, joined some singular and even romantic institutions,[3] which enabled them, during above forty years, from the time at which their wars with the Romans began, to maintain the contest,[4] and to keep the balance of power in suspense.

During the dependence of this quarrel, the Roman armies frequently penetrated into Lucania and Apulia, and before they had reduced the Samnites, were known as protectors and allies, or had forced their passage as conquerors to the southern extremities of Italy. And the state itself, under a variety of titles, was in reality the head, or held a species of sovereignty over all the nations who occupied that part of the peninsula.

The city of Tarentum, the most powerful of the Greek settlements in this quarter, having neglected her military establishments in proportion as she advanced in the arts of peace, was alarmed at the near approach of the Romans, and applied for protection to Pyrrhus the king of Epirus, at that time greatly distinguished among the military adventurers of Macedonia and Greece. They wished to employ the military skill of this prince, without being exposed to fall a prey to his ambition; and invited him to come, without any army of his own, to take the command of their people, whose numbers they magnified, in order to induce him to accept of their offer. But, like most foreign military protectors, he appears to have had, together with many schemes of ambition against those on whom he made war, some designs likewise on the state he was brought to defend. With this double intention he did not rely on the forces of Tarentum, but passed into Italy at the head of a numerous army, formed on the model of the Macedonians, and accustomed to service in the wars of that country and of Greece.

U. C. 473.

This is the first enemy whose forces can be considered as a known measure, with which to compare, or by which we can estimate, the power and military attainments of the Romans. They had been victorious in Italy, but the character and prowess of the enemies they had vanquished are unknown. This prince knew the arts of war as they were practised in Macedonia and in Greece, and was reputed one of the first captains of that or any other age.[5] He accordingly prevailed over

---

adopted. Polybius marks the continuance of it, and Cæsar evidently marks the discontinuance of it. It is extremely probable, that the last change was one of those made by Marius, and was introduced into the Roman armies in the social war.

The three orders of hastati, principes, and triarii, were extremely proper to mark the distinction of classes subsisting among Roman citizens, who were nevertheless, all of them equally bound, on occasion, to serve in the condition of private soldiers; and this may be one reason to incline us to ascribe the discontinuance of this distribution to Marius, who was a great leveller of ranks.

1 Polyb. lib. vi. c. 17—24.

2 Polyb. ib. vi. c. 17.

3 Of this sort it is mentioned, that ten of the fairest of one sex were annually selected as prizes to be won by the bravest and most deserving of the other. Strabo, lib. v. fin. The Samnites furnished Roman generals with the subject of twenty-four triumphs, but mixed with checks and disgraces more remarkable than any they had received in the course of their wars with any other nation. Florus, lib. 1. c. 16.

4 Liv. lib. x. c. 31.

5 Pyrrhus, it is said, was struck with the military aspect of the Romans and admired in particular the form of their

the Romans in some of their first encounters; but found that partial victories did not subdue this people, nor decide the contest. Having vast schemes of ambition in Sicily and Africa, as well as in Italy, he suddenly suspended his operations against the Romans, to comply with an invitation he received from Syracuse, to possess himself of that kingdom in behalf of his son, who had some pretensions to it in the right of Agathocles, from whom he was descended.

In order to pursue this object, he endeavoured to obtain a peace or cessation of arms in Italy; but was told, that, in order to treat with the Romans, he must evacuate their country and return to his own.[6] With this answer he passed into Sicily; and after some operations which were successful, though not sufficiently supported by his partizans in that country to obtain the end of his expedition, he returned again into Italy for the defence of Tarentum; but found that during his absence the Romans had made a considerable progress, and were in condition to repay the defeats they had suffered in the beginning of the war. Having brought this matter to the proof in several encounters, he committed the defence of Tarentum to one of his officers; and after this fruitless attempt to make conquests beyond the Ionian sea, in which he had employed six years, he returned to his own country.

U. C. 481. The Romans continuing the war against Tarentum, in about two years after the departure of Pyrrhus from Italy, made themselves masters of the place. Here, it is mentioned, they found, for the first time, the plunder of an opulent city, containing the models of elegant workmanship in the fine arts, and the apparatus of an exquisite luxury. "In former times," says Florus, "the victorious generals of Rome exhibited in their triumphs herds of cattle driven from the Sabines and the Volsci, the empty cars of the Gauls, and broken arms of the Samnites: but in that which was shown for the conquest of Tarentum, the procession was led by Thessalian and Macedonian captives, followed with carriages loaded with precious furniture, with pictures, statues, plate, and other ornaments of silver and gold.[7] Spoils which, we may guess, in the first exhibition of them, were valued at Rome more as the public trophies of victory, than felt as the baits of private avarice, or the objects of a mean admiration. The Roman citizen as yet lived content in his cottage, furnished in the rudest manner; and he subsisted on the simplest fare, the produce of his own labour. Curius Dentatus, the consul who obtained this triumph, having the offer of fifty *jugera* as a reward from the public for his services, would accept of no more than seven. This, he said, is the ordinary portion of a citizen, and that person must be an unworthy member of the commonwealth who can wish for more.[8]

encampments. The Greeks always endeavoured to avail themselves of natural strengths, and accommodated the disposition of their camp to the ground; but the Romans, trusting only to their artificial works, pitched on the plain, and always encamped in the same form. Plutarch in vit. Pyrrhi.

6 Liv. Epitome, lib. xiii. Plutarch in vit. Pyrrhi.

7 Florus, lib. i. c. 18.

8 A Roman citizen in this period might, by the law of Licinius, have an estate of five hundred *jugera*, or about three hundred acres; but the ordinary patrimony of a noble family was probably far below this measure; and the lot of a citizen in the new colonies seldom exceeded seven *jugera*. The people were lodged in cottages and slept on straw, (Plin. lib. xviii. c. 3. Cicer. pro Rossio, Val. Max. lib. iv. c. 3.) The Romans, till a little before the siege of Tarentum, had no coin but copper, and estimated considerable sums more commonly by the head of cattle than by money. They coined silver for the first time U. C. 485. Gold was known as a precious material, and was sometimes joined with oxen in the reward of distinguished services. Liv. lib. iv. c. 50. Ibid. Epitome, lib. xv.

U. C. 481. From the reduction of Tarentum the Romans may be considered as the sovereigns of Italy, although their dominion was extremely ill defined, either in respect to its nature or to its extent. They but in a few instances laid claim to absolute sovereignty, and least of all over those who were most submissive to their power. It was their maxim to spare the obsequious, but to crush the proud;[9] an artful profession, by which, under the pretensions of generosity and magnanimity, they stated themselves as the sovereign nation. Under this presumptuous maxim their friendship was to be obtained by submission alone; and was, no less than their enmity, fatal to those who embraced it. The title of ally was, for the most part, no more than a specious name, under which they disguised their dominion, and under which they availed themselves of the strength and resources of other nations, with the least possible alarm to their jealousy or pride.

With the Latins they had early formed an alliance offensive and defensive, in which the parties mutually stipulated the number of troops to be furnished by each; the respective shares which each was to have in the spoils of their common enemies, and the manner of adjusting any disputes that might arise between them. This was the league which the Latins were supposed to have so frequently broken, and of which the Romans so often exacted the observance by force.[10]

In the first struggles which they made to restore their settlement destroyed by the Gauls, and in the subsequent wars they had to maintain, during a hundred years, in support of their new establishment, different cantons of these original confederates, as well as many of their own colonies, had taken very different parts, and in the treaties which ensued, obtained, or were sentenced to, different conditions; some were admitted to the freedom of Rome, and partook in the prerogative of Roman citizens. A few were, by their own choice, in preference to the character of Roman citizens, permitted to retain the independency of their towns, and were treated as allies. Others, under pretence of being admitted to the freedom of Rome, though without the right of suffrage, were deprived of their corporation establishments, and with the title of citizens, treated as subjects. A few were governed in form by a military power, and by a præfect or magistrate annually sent from Rome.[11]

9 Parcere subjectis et debellare superbos.

10 Dionys. Hal. lib. vi. p. 415. Liv. lib. vi. c. 10. lib. ix. c. 43.

11 The city of Capua, together with its district of Campania, was the first example of a provincial government established by the Romans in any of their conquests. The Campanians, in order to be protected against the Samnites, had delivered themselves up to the Romans. But they soon after became sensible of their folly, in trusting their defence to any force but their own, or in resigning their power as a state, with a view to preserve any thing else. When they perceived this error, they endeavoured, in conjunction with some of their neighbours, to form a party against their new masters; and being defeated in

From this unequal treatment arose the variety of conditions by which the natives of Italy were distinguished, as colonies, municipal towns, allies, præfectures, or provincial governments, until about 181 years after this date, when, as will be mentioned in the sequel, the whole was put upon the same footing by the general admission of all the Italians upon the rolls of the Roman people.

CHAPTER IV.

Limits of Italy—Contiguous Nations—Ligurians—Gauls—Greek and Phœnician Colonies of Gaul and Spain—Nations of Illyricum—Of Greece—Achæan League—Thebans—Athenians —Asiatic Nations—Pergamus—Syria—Egypt—Carthage—The Mamertines of Messina— Occasion of the first War with Carthage—Losses of the Parties—Peace—State of the Romans —Political or Civil Institutions—Colonies—Musters—Operation on the Coin—Increase of the Slaves—Gladiators—Different Results of the War at Rome and Carthage—Mutiny and Invasion of the Mercenaries at Carthage—End of this War—Cession of Sardinia—War with the Illyrians—First Correspondence of Rome with Greece.

U. C. 481. AS the Romans, at the time to which our last observations refer, were become the sovereigns of Italy, or, by their ascendant in so powerful a country, were enabled to act a distinguished part among the nations around it; it is proper in this place to carry our observations beyond the boundaries of that Peninsula, and enumerate the powers that were then established on different sides of it, or beyond the narrow seas by which it was surrounded.

Italy was not then supposed to comprehend the whole of that tract which has in later times been known under this name. Being bounded, as at present, on the south and east by the seas of Sicily and bay of Tarentum, it extended no further to the north-west than to the Arnus on the one hand, and to the Rubicon on the other. Beyond these limits the western coasts were inhabited by a number of tribes, which, under the name of Ligurians, occupied the descents of the Appenines and the south of the Alps quite to the sea-shore. On the other side of the Appenines, from Senegallia to the Alps, the rich and extensive plains on both sides of the Po were in the possession of Gaulish nations, who were said, some centuries before, to have passed the mountains, and who were then actually spread over a fertile tract of more than twelve hundred miles in circumference. They consisted of nine different hordes, that were supposed to have passed the Alps at different times. Of these the Laulebecii, Insubres, Cenomani, and Veneti occupied the northern banks of the Po, including what are now the states of Milan, Venice, and other parts of Lombardy on that side of the river. The Anianes, Boii, Ægones, and Senones, were settled to the southward, from the Po to the descents of the Appenines, and on the coasts of the Hadriatic to Senegallia, over what are now the states of Parma, Modena, Bologna, and Urbino. In this favourable situation they appear to have abated much of their native ferocity, though without acquiring, in any considerable degree, the arts that improve the conveniences of life. They fed chiefly on the milk or the flesh of their cattle, and were occupied entirely in the care of their arms and of their herds. By these, and the ornaments of gold, of which they were extremely fond, they estimated their riches. They were divided into tribes or cantons, and lived in cottages huddled together, without any form of towns or of villages. The leader of every horde was distinguished by his retinue, and valued himself chiefly on the number of his followers. They had made frequent encroachments on the states of Etruria and Umbria, but were met at last, and stopped in their progress, by the Romans. Such of them as were settled within the Rubicon, and from thence to Senegallia, had, about three years before the arrival of Pyrrhus in Italy, been obliged to acknowledge the authority of the Roman state.[1]

The coasts of the Mediterranean, to the westward of Italy, had been known to the nations of Greece and of Asia, and had received many colonies from thence, which formed trading settlements, and remained altogether distinct from the natives. Such were the Greek colonies at Marseilles, Emporiæ, Saguntum, and the Tyrian colony at Gades on the coast of the ocean. On the other side of Italy, and round the Hadriatic, were settled a number of small nations, the Istrians, Dalmatians, and Illyrians; of which, at the time when the Romans became acquainted with the navigation of this gulf, the Illyrians, being the chief or principal power, extended eastward to the confines of Macedonia.

U. C. 421. Alexander the Great had finished the career of his victories about sixty years before this date. His hereditary dominions, as well as his personal conquests, were dismembered, and become the patrimony of officers, who had learned under him to affect the majesty and the power of kings. Macedonia was governed by Antigonus Dozon, who,

---

their attempts to recover their independence, were treated with the severity that is commonly employed against rebel subjects. Their senate and popular assembly, under pretence of suppressing seminaries of faction, were abolished, and a præfect or governor annually appointed (Liv. lib. ix. c. 20.) A similar course, under the same pretence, was soon after taken with Antium, (Liv. lib. ix. c. 21.) This had been the principal sea-port of the Volsci, and long the head of many formidable combinations against the Romans.

1 Polyb. lib. ii. c. 17. 19. 29.

together with the principality of Pella, held under his dependence Epirus, Thessaly, and Greece, to the Isthmus of Corinth. He had contended with Pyrrhus, the late invader of Italy, for part of this territory; and, by the death of this adventurer, was now in possession of the whole.

On one part of the coast of the Ionian sea, and on the Gulf of Corinth, were settled the Etolians, who, during the prosperity of Greece, had been an obscure and barbarous horde; but had now, by the confederacy of a number of cantons, laid many districts around them under contribution, and acted a distinguished part in the wars and transactions that followed.

On the other side of the Gulf of Corinth a similar confederacy was formed by the Achæan league. The name of Achæa, in the fabulous ages, was the most general denomination of Greeks. When other names, of Dorians and Ionians, of Athenians and Spartans, became more distinguished, the name of Achæans was appropriated to the tribes who occupied the sea-coast, or the Gulf of Corinth, from Elis to Sicyon. On this tract twelve little cantons, Dymæ, Phara, Tritæa, Rhipes, Thasium, Patræ, Pellene, Ægium, Bura, Carynia, Olenos, and Hellice,[2] having changed their government from principalities to republics, formed themselves into a league for their common defence. Hellice had been, from time immemorial, the seat of their assembly; but this place having been overwhelmed by an inundation of the sea, their meetings were transferred to Ægium.

In the more famous times of Sparta, Athens, and Thebes, these little cantons being situated on a poor and rocky shore, without shipping and without harbours,[3] were of no consideration in the history of Greece; they took no part in the defence of that country from the invasions of Darius, or of Xerxes, or in the divisions that followed under the hostile banners of Sparta and of Athens. They began, however, to appear in support of the liberties of Greece against Philip the father of Alexander, and partook with the other Greeks in the defeat which they received from that prince at Chæronea, and in all its consequences. Their league was accordingly dissolved by the conqueror, and some of their cantons separately annexed to the Macedonian monarchy. But about the time that Pyrrhus invaded Italy, Dymæ, Patræ, Pharæ, and Tritæa, found an opportunity to renew their ancient confederacy. They were joined in about five years afterwards by the canton of Ægium, and successively by those of Bura and Carynia. These, during a period of about twenty years, continued to be the only parties in this famous league. They had a general congress, at which they originally elected two annual officers of state, and a common secretary. They afterwards committed the executive power to one officer; and under the famous Aratus of Sicyon, united that republic, together with Corinth and Megara, to their league.[4]

About the time when the Romans became masters of Tarentum, this combination was become the most considerable power of the Peloponnesus, and affected to unite the whole of it under their banners; but Sparta, though greatly fallen from the splendour of her ancient discipline and power, was still too proud, or too much under the direction of her ambitious leaders, to suffer herself to be absorbed in this upstart confederacy; she continued for some time its rival, and was at last the cause, or furnished the occasion, of its fall.

The Thebans and Athenians, though still pretending to the dignity of independent nations, were greatly reduced, and ready to become the prey of any party that was sufficiently powerful to reach them, by breaking through the other barriers that were still opposed to the conquest of Greece.

In Asia, a considerable principality was formed round the city of Pergamus, and bore its name. Syria was become a mighty kingdom, extending from the coasts of Ionia to Armenia and Persia. This kingdom had been formed by Seleucus Nicanor, a principal officer in the army of Alexander, and it was now in the possession of his son, Antiochus Soter.

Egypt, in the same manner, had passed from the first Ptolemy to his son Philadelphus, who, upon the expulsion of Pyrrhus from Italy, had entered into a correspondence with the Romans. This kingdom included the island of Cyprus; and, having some provinces on the continent of Asia, extended from Cœlo-Syria, of which the dominion was still in contest with Antiochus, to the deserts of Lybia on the west and on the south. Beyond these deserts, and almost opposite to the island of Sicily, lay the famous republic of Carthage, which was now possessed of a considerable territory, surrounded by the petty African monarchies, out of which the great kingdom of Numidia was afterwards formed.

The city of Carthage is said to have been founded about a hundred years earlier than Rome, and was now unquestionably farther advanced in the commercial and lucrative arts, and superior in every resource to Rome, besides that which is derived from the national character, and which is the consequence of public virtue.

In respect to mere form, the constitution of both nations was nearly alike. They had a senate and popular assemblies, and annually elected two officers of state for the supreme direction of their civil and military affairs;[5] and even at Carthage the departments of state were so fortunately balanced, as to have stood for ages the shock of corrupt factions, without having suffered any fatal revolution, or without falling into either extreme of anarchy or tyrannical usurpation. The frequent prospect, indeed, which the Carthaginians had, of incurring these evils, joined to the influence of a barbarous superstition, which represented the gods as delighted with human sacrifices, probably rendered their government in so high a degree inhuman and cruel. Under the sanguinary policy of this state, officers were adjudged, for mistakes or want of capacity, as well as for crimes, to expire on the cross, or were condemned to some other horrible punishment equally odious and unjust.[6]

The Carthaginians being, like Tyre, of which they were supposed to be a colony, settled on a

2 Pausanius, lib. vii. c. 6.
3 Plutarch. in Vit. Arat. p. 321.
4 Polyb. lib. ii. c. 3. and Pausanias, lib. vii.

5 Aristob. Polit. lib. ii. c. 11.
6 Orosius, lib. iv. c. 6

peninsula, and at first without sufficient land or territory to maintain any considerable numbers of people, they applied themselves to such arts as might procure a subsistence from abroad; and became, upon the destruction of Tyre, the principal merchants and carriers to all the nations inhabiting the coasts of the Mediterranean sea. Their situation, so convenient for shipping, was extremely favourable to this pursuit; and their success in it soon put them in possession of a territory by which they became a landed as well as a naval power. They visited Spain, under pretence of giving support and assistance to the city of Gades, which, like themselves, was a colony from Tyre. They became masters of Sardinia, and had considerable possessions in Sicily, of which they were extremely desirous to seize the whole. From every part of their acquisitions they endeavoured to derive the profit of merchants, as well as the revenue of sovereigns.

In this republic, individuals had amassed great fortunes, and estimated rank by their wealth. A certain estate was requisite to qualify any citizen for the higher offices of state; and, in the canvas for elections, every preferment, whether civil or military, was venal.[7] Ambition itself, therefore, became a principle of avarice, and every Carthaginian, in order to be great, was intent to be rich. Though the interests of commerce should have inculcated the desire of peace, yet the influence of a few leading men in the state, and even the spirit of rapacity which pervaded the people, the necessity to which they were often reduced of providing settlements abroad for a populace who could not be easily governed at home, led them frequently into foreign wars, and even engaged them in projects of conquest. But notwithstanding this circumstance, the community stifled or neglected the military character of their own citizens, and had perpetual recourse to foreigners, whom they trusted with their arms, and made the guardians of their wealth. Their armies, for the most part, were composed of Numidians, Mauritanians, Spaniards, Gauls, and fugitive slaves from every country around them. They were among the few nations of the world who had the ingenuity, or rather the misfortune, to make war without becoming military, and who could be victorious abroad, while they were exposed to be a prey to the meanest invader at home.

Under this wretched policy, however, the first offices of trust and command being reserved for the natives, though the character of the people in general was mean and illiberal, yet a few, being descended of those who had enjoyed the higher honours of the state, inherited the characters of statesmen and warriors; and, instead of suffering by the contagion of mercenary characters, they derived some additional elevation of mind from the contrast of manners they were taught to despise. And thus, though the state, in general, was degenerate, a few of its members were qualified for great affairs. War, and the other objects of state, naturally devolved on such men, and occasionally rendered them necessary to a sedentary or corrupted people, who, in ordinary times, were disposed to slight their abilities, or to distrust their power. They became unfortunately a party for war in the councils of their country, as those who were jealous of them became, with still less advantage to the public, a party for peace; or, when at war, a party who endeavoured to embarrass the conduct of it; and, under the effects of misfortune, were ever ready to purchase tranquillity by the most shameful and dangerous concessions.

Carthage being mistress of the sea, was already long known on the coasts of Italy: she had treaties subsisting with the Romans above two hundred years, in which they mutually settled the limits of their navigation, and the regulations of their trade. And the Romans, as parties in these treaties, appear to have had intercourse with foreign nations by sea, earlier than is stated in the other parts of their history.

U. C. 244. In the first of those treaties, which is dated in the consulate of L. Junius Brutus and M. Horatius, the first year of the commonwealth, the Romans engaged not to advance on the coast of Africa, unless they were forced by an enemy, or by stress of weather, beyond the Fair Promontory, which lay about twenty leagues to the westward of the Bay of Carthage.

It was agreed, that, even in these circumstances, they should remain no longer than five days, and supply themselves only with what might be necessary to refit their vessels, or to furnish them with victims for the usual sacrifices performed at sea. But that in Sardinia, and even in Africa, to the west of this boundary, they should be at liberty to trade and to dispose of their merchandise without paying any duties besides the fees of the crier and clerk of sale; and that the public faith should be pledged for the payment of the price of all goods sold under the inspection of these officers.

That the ports of Sicily should be equally open to both nations.

That the Carthaginians, on their part, should not commit any hostilities on the coast of Latium, nor molest the inhabitants of Ardæa, Antium, Laurentium, Circeii, Terracina, or of any other place in alliance with the Romans; that they should not attempt to erect any fortress on that coast; and that if they should land at any time with an armed force, they should not, upon any account whatever, remain a night on shore.

By a subsequent treaty, in which the states of Utica and Tyre are comprehended as allies to both parties, the former articles are renewed with additional limitations to the navigation and trade of the Romans, and with some extension to that of the Carthaginians. The latter, for instance, are permitted to trade on the coast of Latium, and even to plunder the natives, provided they put the Romans in possession of any strong-holds they should sieze on shore; and provided they should release, without ransom, such of the allies of the Romans as became their prisoners.

U. C. 474. Upon the arrival of Pyrrhus in Italy, with an armament which equally alarmed both nations, the Romans and Carthaginians again renewed their treaties with an additional article, in which they agreed mutually to support each other against the designs of that prince, and not to enter into any separate treaty with him inconsistent with this defensive alliance: and further stipulated, that, in the wars which were expected with this enemy, the Carthaginians, whether as principals

---

7 Polyb. lib. vi. c. 54.

or auxiliaries, should furnish the whole shipping, both transports and armed gallies; but that the expense of every armament should be defrayed at the charge of that party in whose behalf it was employed.[2]

In observance probably of the last of these treaties, and by mutual concert, though with considerable jealousy and distrust of each other, the forces of these nations combined in reducing the garrison which Pyrrhus had left at Tarentum. Each had their separate designs on the place; and when its fate was determined, from thenceforward considered the other as their most dangerous rival for dominion and power. Pyrrhus, even when they were joined in alliance against himself, is said to have foreseen their quarrels, and to have pointed at the island of Sicily as the first scene of their contest.

The Carthaginians were already in possession of Lylibæum, and of other posts on this island, and had a design on the whole. The Romans were in sight of it; and, by their possession of Rhegium, commanded one side of the Straits. The other side was occupied by the Mamertines, a race of Italian extraction, who, being placed at Messina by the king of Syracuse to defend that station, barbarously murdered the citizens, and took possession of their habitations and effects.

This horrid action was afterwards imitated by a Roman legion posted at Rhegium during the late wars in Italy: these likewise murdered their hosts, and seized their possessions; but were punished by the Romans, for this act of cruelty and treachery, with the most exemplary rigour. They were conducted in chains to Rome, scourged and beheaded by fifties at a time. The crime of the Mamertines was resented by the Sicilians in general with a like indignation; and the authors of it were pursued, by Hiero king of Syracuse in particular, with a generous and heroic revenge. They were, at length, reduced to such distress, that they were resolved to surrender themselves to the first power that could afford them protection. But, being divided in their choice, one party made an offer of their submission to the Carthaginians, the other to the Romans. The latter scrupled to protect a crime of which they had so lately punished an example in their own people.[3] And, while they hesitated on the proposal, the Carthaginians, favoured by the delay of their rivals, and by the neighbourhood of their military stations, got the start of their competitors, and were received into the town of Messina.

This unexpected advantage gained by a power of which they were jealous, and the danger of suffering a rival to command the passage of the Straits, removed the scruples of the Romans; and the officer who commanded their forces in the contiguous parts of Italy, had orders to assemble all the shipping that could be found on the coast from Tarentum to Naples, to pass with his army into Sicily, and endeavour to dispossess the Carthaginians from the city of Messina.

As soon as this officer appeared in the road with a force so much superior to that of his rivals, the party in the city, that favoured the admission of the Romans, took arms, and forced the Carthaginians to evacuate the place.[4]

U. C. 490. Here commenced the first Punic war, about ten years after the departure of Pyrrhus from Italy, eight years after the surrender of Tarentum, and in the four hundred and ninetieth year of Rome. In this war, the first object of either party was no more than to secure the possession of Messina, and to command the passage of the Straits which separate Italy from Sicily; but their views were gradually extended to objects of more importance, to the sovereignty of that island, and the dominion of the seas.

The contest between them was likely to be extremely unequal. On the one side appeared the resources of a great nation, collected from extensive dominions, a great naval force, standing armies, and the experience of distant operations. On the other, the ferocity or valour of a small state, hitherto exerted only against their neighbours of Italy, who, though subdued, were averse to subjection, and in no condition to furnish the necessary supplies for a distant war; without commerce or revenue, without any army but what was annually formed by detachments from the people, and without any officers besides the ordinary magistrates of the city; in short, without any naval force or experience of naval or distant operations.

Notwithstanding these unpromising appearances on the side of the Romans, the commanding aspect of their first descent upon Sicily procured them not only the possession of Messina, but soon after determined Hiero, the king of Syracuse, hitherto in alliance with the Carthaginians, to espouse their cause, to supply their army with provisions, and afterwards to join them with his own. Being thus reinforced by the natives of Sicily, they were enabled to recal part of the force with which they began the war; continued, though at a less expense, to act on the offensive; and drove the Carthaginians from many of their important stations in the island.[5]

While the arms of the Romans and of Hiero were victorious on shore, the Carthaginians continued to be masters of the sea, kept possession of all the harbours in Sicily, overawed the coasts, obstructed the military convoys from Italy, and alarmed that country itself with frequent descents. It was evident, that, under these disadvantages, the Romans could neither make nor preserve any maritime acquisitions; and it was necessary, either to drop the contest in yielding the sea, or to endeavour, on that element likewise, to cope with their rival. Though not altogether, as historians represent them, unacquainted with shipping, they were certainly inferior to the Carthaginians in the art of navigation, and altogether unprovided with ships of force. Fortunately for them, neither the art of sailing, nor that of constructing ships, was yet arrived at such a degree of perfection as not to be easily imitated by nations who had any experience or practice of the sea. Vessels of the best construction that was then known were fit to be navigated only with oars, or in a fair wind and on a smooth sea. They might be built of green timber; and, in case of a storm, could run ashore under any cover, or upon any beach that was clear of rocks. Such ships as these the Romans, without hesitation, undertook to provide.

2 Polyb. lib. iii. c. 3. 3 Ibid. lib. i. c. 10.
4 Ibid. lib. i. c. 12.

5 Polyb. lib. i.

Having a Carthaginian galley, accidentally stranded at Messina, for a model, it is said, that, in sixty days from the time that the timber was cut down, they fitted out and manned for the sea one hundred gallies of five tier of oars, and twenty of three tier. Vessels of the first of these rates carried three hundred rowers, and two hundred fighting men.

The manner of applying their oars from so many tiers, and a much greater number which they sometimes employed, has justly appeared a great difficulty to the mechanics and antiquarians of modern times, and is confessedly not well understood.

The Romans, while their gallies were building, trained their rowers to the oar on benches that were erected on the beach, and placed in the form of those of the real galley.[1] Being sensible that the enemy must be still greatly superior in the management of their ships and in the quickness of their motions, they endeavoured to deprive them of this advantage, by preparing to grapple, and to bind their vessels together. In this condition the men might engage on equal terms, fight from their stages or decks as on solid ground, and the Roman buckler and sword have the same effect as on shore.

With an armament so constructed, still inferior to the enemy, and even unfortunate in its first attempts, they learned, by perseverance, to vanquish the masters of the sea on their own element; and not only protected the coasts of Italy, and supported their operations in Sicily, but, with a powerful fleet of three hundred and thirty sail, overcame at sea a superior number of the enemy, and carried the war to the gates of Carthage.[2]

On this occasion took place the famous adventure of Regulus; who being successful in his first operations, gave the Romans some hopes of conquest in Africa: but they were checked at once by the defeat of their army,
U. C. 498. and the captivity of their general.
This event removed the seat of the war again into Sicily; and the Romans, still endeavouring to maintain a naval force, suffered so many losses, and incurred so many disasters by storms, that they were, during a certain period of the war, disgusted with the service at sea, and seemed to drop all pretensions to power on this element. The experience of a few years, however, while they endeavoured to continue their operations by land without any support from the sea, made them sensible of the necessity they were under of restoring their shipping; and they did so with a resolution and vigour which enabled them once more to prevail over the superior skill and experience of their enemy.

In this ruinous contest both parties made the utmost efforts, and the most uninterrupted exertion of their forces. Taking the forces of both sides, in one naval engagement, five hundred gallies of five tier of oars, with two hundred and fifty thousand men, and in another, seven hundred gallies, with three hundred and fifty thousand men, were brought into action;[3] and in the course of these struggles the Romans lost, either by tempests or by the hands of the enemy, seven hundred gallies; their antagonists, about five hundred. In the result of these destructive encounters, the Carthaginians, beginning to balance the inconveniences which attended the continuance of war against the concessions
U. C. 512. that were necessary to obtain peace,
came to a resolution to accept of the following terms:

That they should evacuate Sicily, and all the islands from thence to Africa:

That they should not for the future make war on Hiero king of Syracuse, nor on any of his allies:

That they should release all Roman captives without any ransom:

And within twenty years pay to the Romans a sum of three thousand Euboic talents.[5]

Thus the Romans, in the result of a war, which was the first they undertook beyond the limits of Italy, entered on the possession of all that the Carthaginians held in the islands for which they contended; and, by a continuation of the same policy which they had so successfully pursued in Italy, by applying to their new acquisitions, instead of the alarming denomination of *subject*, the softer name of *ally*, they brought Hiero, who was sovereign of the greater part of Sicily, into a state of dependence on themselves.

Their manners, as well as their fortunes, were a perfect contrast to those of the enemy they had vanquished. Among the Romans, riches were of no account in constituting rank. Men became eminent by rendering signal services to their country, not by accumulating wealth. Persons of the first distinction subsisted in the capacity of husbandmen by their own labour; and, with the fortunes of peasants, rose to the command of armies, and the first offices of state. One consul, of the name of Regulus, was found by the officer who came to announce his election, equipped with the sheet or the basket, and sowing the seed of his corn in the field. Another, better known, of the same name, while he commanded in Africa, desired to be recalled, in order to replace the instruments of husbandry, which, to the great distress of his family, and the hazard of their wanting food, a fugitive slave had carried off from his land. The senate refused his request, but ordered the farm of their general to be tilled at the public expense.[6]

The association of pomp and equipage with rank and authority, it may be thought, is accidental, and only serves to distract the attention which mankind owe to personal qualities. It nevertheless appears to be in some measure unavoidable. Superiority is distinguished, even in the rudest nations, by some external mark. Duillius had his piper and his torch, in honour of the first naval victory obtained by his country;[7] and the Romans acknowledged the external ensigns of state, although they were still rude in the choice of them.

At this time, when the nation emerged with so much lustre beyond the boundaries of Italy the parties which divided the state, and whose animosity sharpened so much the pangs which

1 Polyb. lib. i. c. 20, 21
2 Ibid. lib. i. c. 27.
3 Ibid. lib. i. c. 26.
4 Polyb. c. 63.
5 Ibid. c. 62, &c.
6 Valer. Maxim. lib. iv. c. 4. Liv. Epitom. lib. xviii. Seneca ad Albinam. c. 12. Auctor de versibus illustribus.
7 Liv. Epitom. lib. xvii. xviii.

preceded the birth of many of its public establishments, had no longer any object of contest. The officers of state were taken promiscuously from either class of the people, and the distinction of plebeian and patrician had in a great measure lost its effect. A happier species of aristocracy began to arise from the lustre of personal qualities, and the honours of family, which devolved upon those who were descended from citizens who had borne the higher offices of state, and were distinguished in their country's service.

The different orders of men in the commonwealth having obtained the institutions for which they severally contended, the number of officers was increased, for the better administration of affairs, which were fast accumulating. Thus a second prætor was added to the original establishment of this office; and the persons who held it were destined to act either in a civil or military capacity, to hear causes in the city, or to command armies in the field. They were assisted in the first of these functions by a new institution, that of the centumvirs, or the hundred, who were draughted from the tribes, and appointed, during the year of their nomination, under the direction of the prætors, to take cognizance of civil disputes. The number of tribes being now completed to thirty-five, and three of the centumvirs being draughted from each, made the whole amount to a hundred and five.[8]

The city, during the late destructive war, sent abroad two colonies, one to Castrum Innui, a village of the Latins, the other to Firmium in the Picenum, on the opposite side of the peninsula, intended rather to guard and protect the coast, than to provide for any superabundance of the people, whose numbers at this time underwent a considerable diminution;[9] the rolls having decreased in the course of five years, from two hundred and ninety-seven thousand two hundred and twenty-seven, to two hundred and fifty-one thousand two hundred and twenty-two.[10] The revenue, to which citizens who were accustomed to pay with their personal service, had little to spare from their effects, and which was at all times probably scanty, being often exhausted by the expenses of the late war, brought the community under the necessity of acquitting itself of its debts, by diminishing the weight, or raising the current value of its coin. The ass, which was the ordinary measure of valuation, being the libra, or pound of copper stamped, and hitherto containing twelve ounces, was reduced in its weight to two ounces.[11]

The contribution now exacted from Carthage amounting to about two hundred and seventy-nine thousand pounds, together with the rents to be collected in Sicily, were likely to be great accessions of wealth to such a state.

The spoils of their enemies, for the most part, consisted of prisoners who were detained by the captor as his slaves, or sent to market to be sold. They had made a prize of twenty thousand captives in their first descent upon Africa; and the number of slaves in Italy was already become so great as to endanger the state.[12]

The favourite entertainments of the people were combats of armed slaves, known by the name of gladiators, derived from the weapons with which they most frequently fought. Such exhibitions, it is said, were first introduced in the interval between the first and second Punic war by a son of the family of Brutus, to solemnize the funeral of his father. Though calculated rather to move pity and cause horror, than to give pleasure, yet, like all other scenes which excite hopes and fears, and keep the mind in suspense, they were admired by the multitude, and became frequent on all solemn occasions or festivals.

In the circumstances or events which immediately followed the peace between Rome and Carthage, these nations showed the different tendency of their institutions and manners. The Romans, in the very struggles of a seemingly destructive contest, had acquired strength and security, not only by the reputation of great victories, but still more by the military spirit and improved discipline and skill of their people by sea and by land. Although their subjects in Italy revolted, and their allies withdrew their support, yet both were soon reduced, at the first appearance of these veteran soldiers who had been formed in the service of the preceding war.

The Carthaginians, on the contrary, had made war above twenty years without becoming more warlike; had exhausted their resources, and consumed the bread of their own people in maintaining foreign mercenaries, who, instead of being an accession of strength, were ready to prey on their weakness, and to become the most formidable enemies to the state they had served. Their army, composed, as usual, of hirelings from Gaul, Spain, and the interior parts of Africa, estimated their services in the war which was then concluded at a higher value than the state was disposed to allow, and attempted to take by force what was refused to their representations and claims. Being assembled in the neighbourhood of Carthage to receive the arrears of their pay, the senate wildly proposed, in consideration of the distressed condition of the public revenue, that they should make some abatement of the sums that were due to them. But the state, instead of obtaining the abatements which were thus proposed, only provoked men with arms in their hands to enter into altercations, and to multiply their claims and pretensions. The mercenaries took offence at the delays of payment, rose in their demands upon every concession, and marched at last to the capital, with all the appearances and threats of an open and victorious enemy. They issued a proclamation on their march, inviting all the provincial subjects of the commonwealth to assert their freedom, and, by

8 Liv. Epitom. lib. xx.

9 Livy, in different places, mentions between thirty and forty Roman colonies subsisting in Italy in the time of the second Punic war. (Liv. lib. xxvii. c. 9 et 38.) Velleius Paterculus reckons about forty planted in Italy after the recovery of Rome from its destruction by the Gauls. (Lib. i. c. xv.) And Sigonius, collecting the names of all the colonies mentioned by any Roman writer as planted in Italy, has made a list of about ninety. But this matter, which so much interests this very learned antiquarian and many others, was become, as we have mentioned, a subject of mere curiosity, even in the times of the writers from whom our accounts are collected; as all the Italians were by that time admitted on the roll of Roman citizens by the law of L. Julius Cæsar, and in consequence of the Marsic law, U. C. 663.

10 Liv. Epitom. lib. xix.

11 Plin. Hist. Nat. lib. xxxiii. c. 3.

12 Zonar. lib. ii. Orosius, lib. ii. c. 7.

the numbers that flocked to them from every quarter, became a mighty host, to which the city had nothing to oppose but its walls. To effectuate the reduction of Carthage, they invested Tunis and Utica, and submitted to all the discipline of war from the officers whom they themselves had appointed to command.

In this crisis, the republic of Carthage, cut off from all its resources and ordinary supplies, attacked with that very sword on which it relied for defence, and in a situation extremely deplorable and dangerous, having still some confidence in the ability of their senators, and in the magnanimity of officers tried and experienced in arduous and perilous situations, was not altogether reduced to despair. Although the people had committed their arms into the hands of strangers, the command of armies had been still reserved to their own citizens; and now, by the presence and abilities of a few great men, they were taught to assume a necessary courage, to put themselves in a military posture, and to maintain, during three years, and through a scene of mutual cruelties and retaliations, unheard of in the contests of nations at war, a struggle of the greatest difficulty. In this struggle they prevailed at last by the total extirpation of this vile and outrageous enemy.[1]

During the dependence of this odious revolt, in which a mercenary army endeavoured to subdue the state which employed them, the Romans preserved that character for generosity and magnanimity of which they knew so well how to avail themselves, without losing any opportunity that offered for the secure advancement of their power. They refrained from giving any countenance even against their rival to such unworthy antagonists. They affected to disdain taking any advantage of the present distresses of Carthage, and refused to enter into any correspondence with a part of the rebel mercenaries, who, being stationed in Sardinia, offered to surrender that island into their hands. They prohibited the traders of Italy to furnish the rebels with any supply of provisions or stores, and abandoned every vessel that presumed to transgress these orders, to the mercy of the Carthaginian cruisers which plied before the harbours of Tunis and Utica. Above five hundred Roman prisoners, seized by these cruisers, were detained in the jails of Carthage. At the termination, however, of this war, when the Carthaginians were far from being disposed to renew any quarrel whatever, the Romans fixed on this as a ground of dispute, complained of piracies committed against the traders of Italy, under pretence of intercepting supplies to the rebels; and, by threatening immediate war upon this account, obtained from the state itself a surrender of the island of Sardinia, which they had refused to accept from the rebels, and got an addition of two hundred talents to the sum stipulated in the late treaty of peace, to make up for their pretended losses by the supposed unwarrantable capture of their ships.[2]

Upon this surrender the Sardinians bore with some discontent the change of their sovereigns; and, on the first prohibition of their usual commerce with Carthage, to which they had been long accustomed, took arms, and endeavoured for some time to withstand the orders which they were required to obey.

Soon after the Romans had reconciled these new acquired subjects to their government, had quelled a revolt in Tuscany, and vanquished some cantons of Liguria, whom it is said they brought to submit as fast as the access to that country could be opened, they found themselves at peace with all the world;[3] and, in token of this memorable circumstance, shut the gates of the temple of Janus; a ceremony which the continual succession of wars, from the reign of Numa to the present time, had prevented, during a period of four hundred and thirty years; a ceremony, which, when performed, marked a situation as transient as it was strange and uncommon.

U. C. 519.

Fresh disturbances in some of the possessions recently seized by the republic, and a quarrel of some importance that carried her arms for the first time beyond the Hadriatic, embroiled her anew in a succession of wars and military adventures.

The Illyrians had become of late a considerable nation, and were a party in the negotiations and quarrels of the Macedonians and the Greeks. Having convenient harbours and retreats for shipping, they carried on a piratical war with most of their neighbours, and, in particular, committed depredations on the traders of Italy, which it concerned the Romans, as the sovereigns of this country, to prevent. They accordingly sent deputies to complain of these practices, to demand a reparation of past injuries, and a security from any such attempts for the future. The Illyrians at this time were under the government of Teuta, the widow of a king lately deceased, who held the reins of government as guardian to her son. This princess, in answer to the complaints and representations of the Romans, declared, that in her kingdom no public commission had ever been granted to make war on the Italians; but she observed, that the seas being open, no one could answer for what was transacted there; and that it was not the custom of kings to debar their subjects from what they could seize by their valour. To this barbarous declaration one of the Roman deputies replied, that his country was ever governed by different maxims; that they endeavoured to restrain the crimes of private persons by the authority of the state, and should, in the present case, find a way to reform the practice of kings in this particular. The queen was incensed; and resenting these words as an insult to herself, gave orders to waylay and assassinate the Roman deputy on his return to Rome.[4]

In revenge of this barbarous outrage, and of the former injuries received from that quarter, the Romans made war on the queen of Illyricum, obliged her to make reparation for the injuries she had done to the traders of Italy, to evacuate all the towns she had occupied on the coast, to restrain her subjects in the use of armed ships, and to forbid them to navigate the Ionian sea with more than two vessels in company.

1 Polyb. lib. i. c. 67—fine.

2 Polyb. lib. i. c. 88. lib. iii. c. 10. Appian de Bell. Punic. p.

3 Florus, lib. ii. c. 3 Eutrop. lib. ii.

4 Polyb. lib ii. c. 8.

The Romans, being desirous of having their conduct in this matter approved of by the nations of that continent, sent a copy of this treaty, together with an exposition of the motives which had induced them to cross the Adriatic, to be read in the assembly of the Achæan league. They soon after made a like communication at Athens and at Corinth, where, in consideration of the signal service they had performed against the Illyrians, then reputed the common enemy of civilized nations, they had an honorary place assigned them at the Isthmian games; and in this
U. C. 525. manner made their first appearance in the councils of Greece.[5]

CHAPTER V.

Progress of the Romans within the Alps—Origin of the second Punic War—March of Hannibal into Italy—Progress—Action on the Tecinus—On the Trebia—On the Lake Thrasimenus—Battle of Cannæ—Hannibal not supported from Carthage—Sequel of the War—In Italy—And Africa—Scipio's Operations—Battle of Zama—End of the War.

THE city of Rome, and most of the districts of Italy, during the dependence of the last enumerated wars which were waged at a distance and beyond the seas, began to experience that uninterrupted tranquillity in which the capital and interior divisions of every considerable nation remain, even during the wars in which the state is engaged. They had indeed one source of alarm on the side of Cisalpine Gaul, which they thought it necessary to remove, in order to obtain that entire security to which they aspired. The country of the Senones, from Sena Gallia to the Rubicon, they had already subdued, even before the arrival of Pyrrhus in Italy; but the richest and most fertile tracts on the Po were still in the possession of the Gaulish nations; and it had been proposed, about four years after the conclusion of the first Punic war, to erect a barrier against the invasion of this people, by occupying with Roman colonies the country of the Senones, from Sena Gallia to the Rubicon. Although the inhabitants to be removed to make room for these settlements had been subject to the Romans above forty years, yet their brethren on the Po considered this act of violence as an insult to the Gaulish name, resolved to avenge it, and invited their countrymen from beyond the Alps to take part in the quarrel.

In consequence of their negotiations and concerts, in about eight years after the Romans were settled on the Rubicon, a great army of Gauls appeared on the Roman frontier. These nations used to make war by impetuous assaults and invasions, and either at once subdued and occupied the countries which they over-ran, or, being repulsed, abandoned them without any farther intention to persist in the war. Their tumultuary operations, however, were subjects of the greatest alarm at Rome, and generally produced a suspension of all the ordinary forms of the commonwealth. On a prospect of the present alarm from that quarter, the senate apprehending the necessity of great and sudden exertions of all their strength, ordered a general account to be taken of all the men fit to carry arms, whether on foot or on horseback, that could be assembled for the defence of Italy; and they mustered, on this famous occasion, above seven hundred thousand foot and seventy thousand horse.[6] From this numerous return of men in arms, the state was enabled to make great detachments, which they stationed under the consuls and one of the prætors separately, for the defence of the commonwealth. The Gauls, having penetrated into Etruria, where the prætor was stationed, attacked and obliged him to retire. The consuls, however, being arrived with their several armies in different directions to support the prætor, renewed the conflict with united force, and put the greater part of the Gaulish invaders to the sword.

In the year following, the Romans
U. C. 529. carried the war into the enemy's country; and in about three years more, passed the Po, and made themselves masters of all the plains on that river quite to the foot of the Alps. To secure this valuable acquisition they projected two colonies of six thousand men each, one at Cremona and the other at Placentia, on the opposite sides of the Po; but were disturbed in the execution of this project, first, by a revolt of the natives, who justly considered these settlements as military stations, intended to repress and keep themselves in subjection; and afterwards, by the arrival of a successful invader, who, by his conduct and implacable animosity, appeared to be the most formidable enemy that had ever attempted to shake the power, or to limit the progress of the Roman state.

The Republic had now enjoyed, during a period of twenty-one years from the end of the first Punic war, the fruits not only of that ascendant she had acquired among the nations of Italy, but those likewise of the high reputation she had gained, and of the great military power she had formed in the contest with Carthage. The wars that filled up the interval of peace with this principal antagonist, were either trivial or of short duration; and the city itself, though still rude in the form of its buildings, and in the manners of its people, probably now began to pay a growing attention to the arts of peace. Laws are dated in this period which have a reference to manufacture and to trade. Clothiers are directed in the fabric of cloth, and carriers by water are directed in the

---

5 Polyb. lib. ii. c. 12. Appian in Illyr.

6 Polyb. lib. ii. c. 22—24, &c. Liv. Epitom. lib. xxi.

size of their vessels.[1] Livius Andronicus and Nevius introduced some species of dramatic entertainments, and found a favourable reception from the people to their farcical productions.[2]

U. C. 513.

But whatever progress the people were now inclined to make in the useful or pleasurable arts of peace, they were effectually interrupted, and obliged to bend the force of their genius, as in former times, to the arts of war, and to the defence of their settlements in Italy.

The Carthaginians had been for some time employed in Spain, making trial of their strength, and forming their armies. In that country Hamilcar, an officer of distinguished fame in the late war with the Romans, and in that which ensued with the rebel mercenaries, had sought refuge from that disgust and those mortifications which in the late treaty of peace, he felt from the abject councils of his country. And having found a pretence to levy new armies, he made some acquisitions of territory, to compensate the losses which Carthage had sustained by the surrender of Sardinia and of Sicily.

Spain appears to have been to the trading nations of Greece, Asia, and Africa, what America has been, though upon a larger scale, to the modern nations of Europe—an open field for new settlements, plantations, and conquests. The natives were brave, but impolitic, and ignorant of the arts of peace, occupied entirely with the care of their horses and their arms. These, says a historian, they valued more than their blood.[3] They painted or stained their bodies, affected long hair with gaudy ornaments of silver and of gold. The men were averse to labour, and subsisted chiefly by the industry of their women. Their mountains abounded in mines of copper and of the precious metals; insomuch that, on some parts of the coast, it was reported that the natives had vessels and utensils of silver employed in the most common uses.[4] A fatal report! such as that which afterwards carried the posterity of this very people, with so much destructive avidity, to visit the new world; and is ever likely to tempt the dangerous visits of strangers, who are ready to gratify their avarice and their ambition at the expense of nations to whose possessions they have no reasonable or just pretension. The Spaniards were at this time divided into many barbarous hordes or small principalities, which could neither form any effectual concert to prevent the intrusion and settlement of foreigners, nor possessed the necessary docility by which to profit by foreign examples, whether in the form of their policy or the invention of arts.

The Carthaginians had made their first visits to Spain under pretence of supporting the colony of Gades, which, like themselves, was sprung from Tyre. They made a settlement under the name of New Carthage, in a situation extremely favourable to the communication of Spain with Africa, and in the neighbourhood of the richest mines. Hamilcar, after a few successful campaigns, in extending the bounds of this settlement, being killed in battle, was succeeded by his son-in-law, Hasdrubal, who continued for some years to pursue the same designs.

The Romans, in the mean while, were occupied on the coast of Illyricum, or amused with alarms from Gaul. They were sensible of the progress made by their rivals in Spain; but imagining that any danger from that quarter was extremely remote, or while they had wars at once on both sides of the Hadriatic, being unwilling to engage at the same time with so many enemies, were content with a negotiation and a treaty in which they stipulated with the Carthaginians that they should not pass the Iberus to the eastward, nor molest the city of Saguntum. This they considered as a proper barrier on that side, and professed for the inhabitants of that place the concern of allies. Trusting to the effect of this treaty, as sufficient to limit the progress of the Carthaginians in Spain, they proceeded, in the manner that has been mentioned, to contend with the Gauls for the dominion of Italy, which hitherto, under the frequent alarms they received from this people, was still insecure.[5]

Hasdrubal, after nine years' service, being assassinated by a Spanish slave, who committed this desperate action in revenge of an injury which had been done to his master, was succeeded in the command of the Carthaginian troops in Spain by Hannibal, the son of Hamilcar. This young man, then of five and twenty years of age, had, when a child,[6] came into Spain with his father, seemed to inherit his genius, and preserved, probably with increasing animosity, his aversion to the Romans. Being reared and educated in camps, and from his earliest youth qualified to gain the confidence of soldiers, he on the death of Hasdrubal, by the choice of the troops was raised to the command of that army, and afterwards confirmed in it by the senate of Carthage.

The Carthaginians had now for some time ceased to feel the defeats and the sufferings which had induced them to accept of the late disadvantageous conditions of peace, and were sensible only of the lasting inconveniences to which that treaty exposed them. They had long felt, from the neighbourhood of the Romans, an insurmountable bar to their progress. They had felt, during above seventeen years from the date of their last treaty of peace, the loss of their maritime settlements, and the decline of their navigation. They had felt the load of a heavy contribution, which, though restricted to a particular sum, had the form of a tribute, in being exacted by annual payments; and they entertained sentiments of animosity and aversion to the Romans, which nothing but the memory of recent sufferings and the apprehension of danger could have so long suppressed.

Hamilcar, together with a considerable party of the senate, were supposed to have borne with the late humiliating peace only that they might have leisure to provide for a subsequent war. "I have four sons," this famous warrior had been heard to say, "whom I shall rear like so many lions' whelps against the Romans." In this spirit he set armies on foot to be trained and accustomed to service in Spain, and had already projected the invasion of Italy from thence.

Whatever may have been the military services which the Carthaginians devised, the execution of

1 Lex Metilia de Fullonibus. Lex Claudia lib. xvii. c. 21.
2 Cicer. in Bruto, p. 35. A Gall.
3 Justin, lib. xliv. c. 2.
4 Strabo, lib. iii.
5 Polyb. lib. ii. c. 13.
6 At nine years of age.

them was secured by the coming of Hannibal to the head of their army. He was well formed for great enterprise, and professed an hereditary aversion to the Romans. In the first and second year of his command he continued the operations which had been begun by his predecessors in Spain; but during this time, although he made conquests beyond the Iberus, he did not molest the city of Saguntum, nor give any umbrage to the Romans. But, in the third year after his appointment, his progress alarmed the Saguntines, and induced them to send a deputation to Rome to impart their fears.

At the arrival of this deputation from Saguntum, the Romans had fitted out an armament under the command of the consul L. Emilius Paulus, destined to make war on Demetrius the prince of Pharos, a small island on the coast of Illyricum. This armament, if directed to Spain, might have secured the city of Saguntum against the designs of Hannibal; but the Romans still considered any danger from that quarter as remote and continued to employ this force in its first destination. They paid so much regard, nevertheless, to the representations of the Saguntines, as to send deputies into Spain, with orders to observe the posture of affairs, and to inform the Carthaginian officer on that station, of the engagements which had been entered into by his predecessor, and of the concern which the Romans must undoubtedly take in the safety of Saguntum. The return which they had to this message gave sufficient intimation of an approaching war; and it appears that, before the Roman commissioners could have made their report, the siege of Saguntum was actually commenced by Hannibal. He had already formed his design for the invasion of Italy, and, that he might not leave to the Romans a place of arms and a powerful ally in the country from which he was about to depart, determined to occupy or destroy that place. He was impatient to reduce Saguntum before any succours could arrive from Italy, or before any force could be collected against him, so as to fix the theatre of the war in Spain. He pressed the siege, therefore, with great impetuosity, exposing his person in every assault, and exciting, by his own example, with the pickaxe and spade, the parties at work in making his approaches.[7] Though abundantly cautious not to expose himself on slight occasions, or from a mere ostentation of courage, yet in this siege, which was the foundation of his hopes, and the necessary prelude to the farther progress of his enterprise, he declined no fatigues, and shunned no danger, that led to the attainment of his end. He was nevertheless, by the valour of the besieged, which they exerted in hopes of relief from Rome, detained about eight months before this place, and deprived at last of great part of its spoils by the desperate resolution of the citizens, who chose to perish, with all their effects, rather than fall into the enemy's hands. The booty, however, which he saved from this wreck, enabled him, by his liberalities, to gain the affection of his army, and to provide for the execution of his design against Italy.

U. C. 534.

The siege of Saguntum, being an infraction of the late treaty with the Romans, was undoubtedly an act of hostility; and this people incurred a censure of remissness, uncommon in their councils, by suffering an ally, and a place of such importance, to remain so long in danger, and by suffering it at last to fall a prey to their enemy, without making any attempt to relieve it. It is probable, that the security they began to derive from a frontier, far removed from the seat of their councils, and covered on every side by the sea, or by impervious mountains, rendered them more negligent than they had formerly been of much slighter alarms. They expected to govern by the dread of their power, and proposed to punish, by exemplary vengeance, the insults which they had not taken care to prevent.

The attention of the Romans, during the dependence of this event, had been fixed on the settlements they were making at Cremona and Placentia, to keep in subjection the Gauls, and on the naval expedition which they had sent under the consul Emilius to the coast of Illyricum. This officer, about the time that Hannibal had accomplished his design on Saguntum, and was retired for the winter to his usual quarters at New Carthage, had succeeded in his attack on Demetrius prince of Pharos, had driven him from his territories, and obliged him to seek for refuge at the court of Macedonia, where his intrigues proved to be of some consequence in the sequel of these transactions.

The people of Rome being amused with these events, and with a triumphal procession, which, as usual, announced their victory, proceeded in the affairs of Spain according to the usual forms, and agreeably to the laws which they had, from time immemorial, prescribed to themselves in the case of injuries received—sent to demand satisfaction; complained at Carthage of the infraction of treaties; and required that Hannibal with his army should be delivered up to their messengers; or if this were refused, gave orders to denounce immediate war. The Roman commissioner, who spoke to this effect in the senate of Carthage, having made his demands, held up the lappet of of his gown, and, said "Here are both peace and war; choose ye."—He was answered, "We choose that which you like best."—"Then it is war," he said; and from this time both parties prepared for the contest.

U. C. 535.

Hannibal had been long devising the invasion of Italy, probably without communicating his design even to the councils of his own country. The war being now declared, he made his dispositions for the safety of Africa and Spain; gave intimation to the army under his command, that the Romans had required them to be delivered up, as a beast which commits a trespass is demanded in reparation for the damage he has done.[8] If they felt a proper resentment of this indignity, he warned them to prepare for an arduous march. He was in the eight and twentieth year of his age when he entered upon the execution of this design; an undertaking which, together with the conduct of it has raised his reputation for enterprise and ability to an equal, if not to a higher pitch, than that of any leader of armies whatever.

The Romans, a few years before, had mustered near eight hundred thousand men, to whom

7 Polyb. lib. iii. 17.

8 Velut ob noxam sibi dedirunt tularet populus Romanus. Liv. lib. xxi. c. 30.

the use of arms was familiar, to whom valour was the most admired of the virtues, and who were ready to assemble in any numbers proportioned to the service for which they might be required: the march from Spain into Italy lay across tremendous mountains, and through the territory of fierce and barbarous nations, who might not be inclined tamely to suffer a stranger to pass through their country, or lose any opportunity to enrich themselves with his spoils.

From such topics as these, historians have magnified the courage of this celebrated warrior at the expense of his judgment. It is probable, however, that both were equally exerted in this memorable service. In the contest of nations, that country which is made the seat of the war, for the most part labours under great comparative disadvantage, is obliged to subsist the army of its enemy as well as its own, is exposed to devastation, to hurry, confusion, and irresolution of councils; so much that, in nations powerful abroad, invasions often betray great incapacity and weakness, or at least fix the whole sufferings of the war upon those who are invaded. Hannibal, besides this general consideration, had with great care informed himself of the real state of Italy, and knew, that though the Roman musters were formidable, yet much of their supposed strength consisted of discordant parts; a number of separate cantons recently united, and many of them disaffected to the power by which they were cemented together. Most of the inhabitants of that country, being the descendants of different nations, and distinguished by various languages, still retained much animosity to each other, and most of all to their new masters. Those who had longest borne the appellation of Roman allies, even the colonies themselves, as well as the conquered nations, had occasionally revolted, and were likely to prefer separate establishments to their present dependance on the Roman state. The Gauls and Ligurians, even the Etruscans, had been recently at war with those supposed masters of Italy, and were ready to resume the sword in concert with any successful invader. The Gauls on the Po were already in arms, had razed the fortifications which the Romans had begun to erect at Cremona and Placentia, and forced the settlers to take refuge at Mutina. Every step, therefore, that an invader should make within this country, was likely to remove a support from the Romans, and to add a new one to himself. The Roman power, composed of parts so ill cemented, was likely to dissolve on the slightest touch. Though great when employed at a distance, and wielded by a single hand, yet broken and disjointed by the presence of an enemy, it was likely to lose its strength; or, by the revolt of one or more of its districts, might furnish a force that could be successfully employed against itself. A few striking examples of success, therefore, for which he trusted to his own conduct, and to the superiority of veterans hardened in the service of many years, were likely to let loose the discontents which subsisted in Italy, and to shake the fidelity of those allies who composed so great a part of the Roman strength. Even with a less favourable prospect of success, the risk was but small, compared to the chance of gain. A single army was to be staked against a mighty state; and a few men, that could be easily replaced, were to be sacrificed in an enterprise which, if successful, was to make Carthage the mistress of the world; or even if it should miscarry, might inflict on her enemy a deeper wound than she herself was likely to suffer from the loss.

Hannibal collected together for this expedition ninety thousand foot and twelve thousand horse. In his march to the Iberus, he met with no interruption. From thence to the Pyrenees, being opposed by the natives, he forced his way through their country; but apprehending some inconvenience from such an enemy left in his rear, he stationed his brother Hanno, with ten thousand foot and one thousand horse, to observe their motions, and to keep them in awe. After he had begun to ascend the Pyrenees, a considerable body of his Spanish allies deserted him in the night, and fell back to their own country. This example he had reason to believe, would prove contagious; and as the likeliest way to prevent its effects, he gave out, that the party which had left him being no longer wanted for the purposes they served on the march, were returned by his orders to their own country; that he meant to spare a few more of the troops of the same nation, as being unnecessary in the remaining parts of the service; and actually dismissed a considerable body to confirm this opinion. By these separations, or by the swords of the enemy, his numbers, in descending the mountains, were reduced from ninety to fifty thousand foot and nine thousand horse, with seven and thirty elephants.[1]

U. C. 534. This celebrated march took place in the year of Rome five hundred and thirty-four, and in the consulate of Publius Cornelius Scipio and Tiberius Sempronius Longus. The Romans, as usual on such occasions, raised two consular armies, and proposed, by immediate armaments directed to Spain and to Africa, to fix the scene of the war in the enemy's country.

Sempronius assembled an army and a fleet in the ports of Sicily, and had orders to pass into Africa. Scipio embarked with some legions for Spain, and, touching on the coast of Gaul, first learned, that a Carthaginian army was marching by land into Italy. This intelligence determined him to land his troops at Marseilles, and to send out a detachment of horse to observe the country, and to procure farther and more particular information of the enemy.

Hannibal had arrived on the Rhone at some distance above its separation into two channels, and about four days' march from the sea. In order to effect the passage of the river, he instantly collected all the boats that could be found on its extensive navigation. At the same time, the natives, being unacquainted with strangers in any other capacity than that of enemies, assembled in great numbers to dispute his farther progress in their country.

Finding so powerful a resistance in front, he delayed the embarkation of his army on the Rhone, and sent a detachment up the banks of the river to pass it at a different place, and to make a diversion on the flank or the rear of the enemy who opposed him.

The division employed on this service, after a march of twenty-five miles, found the Rhone separated into branches by small islands, and at a

1 Polyb. lib. iii. c. 35—42.

convenient place got over on rafts to the opposite shore; and being thus in the rear, or on the right of the Gaulish army, hastened towards them in order to give an alarm on that quarter, while Hannibal should pass the river in their front.

On the fifth day after the departure of this party, Hannibal, having intelligence that they had succeeded in passing the Rhone, made his disposition to profit by the diversion they were ordered to make in his favour. The larger vessels, which were destined to transport the cavalry, were ranged towards the stream, to break the force of the current; and many of the horses were fastened to the stern of the boats. The smaller canoes were ranged below, and were to carry over a body of foot.

The Gauls, seeing these preparations, left their camp, and advanced to meet the enemy. They were drawn up on the banks of the river, when the Carthaginian detachment arrived on their rear, and lighted fires as a signal of their approach. Hannibal observing the smoke, notwithstanding the posture which the enemy had taken to resist his landing, instantly put off from the shore: both armies shouted; but the Gauls being thrown into great consternation by the report and effects of an attack which they little expected on their rear, without resistance gave way to the Carthaginians in front, and were speedily routed. Hannibal, having thus lodged himself on the eastern banks of the Rhone, in a few days, without any farther interruption or loss, passed that river with his elephants, baggage, and the remainder of his army.

Soon after the Carthaginian general had surmounted this difficulty, intelligence came that a Roman army had arrived on the coast, and was disembarked at Marseilles. To gain further and more certain information of this enemy, he, nearly about the same time that Scipio had sent a detachment on the same design, directed a party of horse to examine the country. These parties met; and, after a smart engagement, returned to their several armies with certain accounts of an enemy being near.

Scipio advanced with the utmost despatch to fix the scene of the war in Gaul; and Hannibal hastened his departure, being equally intent on removing it, if possible, into Italy. The last, in order to keep clear of the enemy, directed his march at a distance from the sea coast, and took his route by the banks of the Rhone. After four days march from the place where he had passed this river, he came to its confluence with another river, which was probably the Isere, though by Polybius himself, who visited the tract of this march, the place seems to be mistaken for the confluence of the Rhone and Saone.[2] Here he found two brothers contending for the throne of their father, and gained a useful ally by espousing the cause of the elder. Being, in return for this service, supplied with arms, shoes, and other necessaries, and attended by the prince himself, who with a numerous body covered his rear, he continued his march during ten days, probably on the Isere; and, about a hundred miles above the place where he had passed the Rhone, began to make his way over the summit of the Alps; a labour in which he was employed with his army during fifteen days.[3]

The natives, either fearing him as an enemy, or proposing to plunder his baggage, had occupied every post at which they could obstruct his march; assailed him from the heights, endeavoured to overwhelm his army in the gorges of the mountains, or force them over precipices, which frequently sunk perpendicular under the narrow paths by which they were to pass.

Near to the summits of the ridge, at which he arrived by a continual ascent of many days, he had his way to form on the sides of frozen mountains, and through masses of perennial ice, which, at the approach of winter, were now covered with recent snow. Many of his men and horses, coming from a warm climate, perished by the cold; and his army having struggled, during so long a time, with extremes to which it was little accustomed, was reduced from fifty thousand foot and nine thousand horse, the numbers which remained to him in descending the Pyrenees, to twenty thousand foot and six thousand cavalry, a force, in all appearance, extremely disproportioned to the service for which they were destined.[4]

The Roman consul, in the mean time, had,

2 In the manuscripts of Polybius, the river which falls into the Rhone at this place was called by a name unknown in that country. The first editors, to correct the mistake, changed this unknown name for that of the Arar. But it is extremely probable, that they ought to have made it the Isara, as the confluence of the Isere and the Rhone corresponds much better with the distances and marches mentioned by Polybius. Four marches, for instance, from the place at which Hannibal had passed the Rhone, and four more from thence to the sea.

3 This famous route has been a subject of different opinions, and of some controversy. In a country tha is raised into vast mountains, round which the way must be found by narrow valleys, and the channels of rivers, it is impossible to decide any question of this sort from the map. Polybius visited the ground, in order to satisfy himself on the tract of this famous route; and, from this circumstance, as well as from his general knowledge of war, is undoubtedly the best authority to whom we can have recourse in this question. By his account, Hannibal, after four marches from the place at which he had passed the Rhone, came to the confluence of this with another river, which is evidently the Isere. From thence, having continued his route ten days on the river, and marched about a hundred miles, he began to ascend the summit, and was employed in that difficult work fifteen days. This account may incline us to believe, that Hannibal followed the course of the Isere from its confluence with the Rhone to about Conflans; that, having surmounted the summit, he descended into Italy by the channel of another river, or the Vale of Aoste. Such are the passages by which ridges of mountains, in every instance, are to be traversed. It is indeed asserted, or implied in the text of Polybius, that Hannibal marched ten days on the Rhone after its confluence with the Arar or Isara; but it is probable, that, in visiting a barbarous country, in which the Romans had yet no possessions, and with the language of which he was unacquainted, he may have mistaken the Isere for the Rhone, and consequently the Rhone for the Arar or Saone The Rhone and Isere take their rise from the same ridge, and run nearly in the same directions. In this account of the course of the supposed Rhone which he visited, he mentions nothing of the Lake of Geneva, which is scarce ly possible, if he had seen it. Polyb. lib. iii. c. 47.

According to this conjecture, Hannibal having marched by the vale of Isere, Grenoble, Chamberry, and Mountmelian and descended by the vale of Aoste, must have passed the summit at or near the lesser abbey of St. Bernard.

As mountains are penetrated by the channels of rivers, it is probable that Hannibal, if he were himself to explore his passage, would try the course of the first considerable river he found on his right descending from the Alps, which was the Isere; but if, as is extremely probable, he had well-instructed guides, it is not likely that they would lead him so long a circuit as he must have made by the course and sources of the Rhone, when, in fact, he had one equally practicable, and much nearer, by the Isere on one side of the Alps, and the Durea Baltea on the other

4 Polyb. lib. iii. c. 55. Liv. lib. xxi.

in search of his enemy, directed his march to the Rhone; and in three days after the departure of Hannibal, had arrived at the place where he had passed that river but was satisfied that any further attempts to pursue him in this direction, would only carry himself away from what was to be the scene of the war, and from the ground he must occupy for the defence of Italy; he returned therefore without loss of time to his ships; sent his brother, Cneius Scipio, with the greater part of the army, to pursue the objects of the war in Spain; and he himself with the remainder, set sail for Pisa, where he landed and put himself at the head of the legions which he found in that quarter; and which had been appointed to restore the settlements of Cremona and Placenti. With these forces he passed the Po, and was arrived on the Tecinus, when Hannibal came down into the plain country at some distance below Turin.

The Carthaginian general, at his arrival in those parts, had moved to his right; and, to gratify his new allies the Insubres, inhabiting what is now the dutchy of Milan, who were then at war with the Taurini or Piedmontese, he laid siege to the capital of that country, and in three days reduced it by force. From thence he continued his march on the left of the Po; and, as the armies advanced, both generals, as if by concert, approached with their cavalry, or light troops, mutually to observe each other. They met on the Tecinus, with some degree of surprise on both sides, and were necessarily engaged in a conflict, which served as a trial of their respective forces, and in which the Italian cavalry were defeated by the Spanish and African horse. The Roman consul was wounded, and with much difficulty rescued from the enemy by his son Publius Cornelius, afterwards so conspicuous in the history of this war, but then only a youth of seventeen years of age, entering on his military service.[1]

The Roman detachment, it seems, had an easy retreat from the place of this encounter to that of their main army, and were not pursued. Scipio, disabled by his wound, and probably from the check he had received sensible of the enemy's superiority in the quality of their horse, determined to retire from the plains; repassed the Po, marched up the Trebia, and to stop the progress of the Carthaginians, while he waited for instructions or reinforcements from Rome, took post on the banks of that river. While he lay in this position, an alarming effect of his defeat, and of the disaffection of some Gauls who professed to be his allies, appeared in the desertion of two thousand horsemen of that nation, who went over to the enemy.

The Roman senate received these accounts with surprise, and with some degree of consternation. An enemy was arrived in Italy, and had obliged the consul, with his legions, to retire. The forces which they had lately mustered were numerous, but consisted in part of doubtful friends or of declared enemies. They supposed all their late vanquished subjects on the Po to be already in rebellion, or to be mustered against them in the Carthaginian camp. And, notwithstanding the numerous levies that could have been made in the city, and in the contiguous colonies; notwithstanding the expediency of carrying the war into Africa, as the surest way of forcing the Carthaginians to withdraw their forces from Italy for the defence of their own country, they, with a degree of pusillanimity uncommon in their councils, ordered the other consul, Sempronius Longus, to desist from his design upon Africa; they recalled him with his army from Sicily, and directed him, without delay, to join his colleague on the Trebia, and if possible, to stop the progress of this daring and impetuous enemy.

The consul Sempronius, therefore, after he had met and defeated a Carthaginian fleet on the coast of Sicily, and was preparing for a descent on Africa, suddenly changed his course, and having turned the eastern promontories of Sicily and Italy, steered for Ariminum, where he landed; and, having performed this voyage and march in forty days, joined his colleague, where he lay opposed to Hannibal on the Trebia.

By the arrival of a second Roman consul, the balance of forces was again restored, and the natives still remained in suspense between the two parties at war. Instead of a deliverance from servitude, which many of them expected to obtain from the arrival of foreigners to balance the force of the Romans, they began to apprehend, as usual in such cases, a confirmation of their bonds, or a mere change of their masters. When the contest should be ended, they wished to have the favour of the victor, and not to share in the fortunes of the vanquished. They had, therefore, waited to see how the scales were likely to incline, and had not repaired to the standard of Hannibal in the manner, it is probable, he expected; and this, with every other circumstance of the war, forced him to rapid and hazardous counsels. Being too far from his resources to continue a dilatory war, he hastened to secure the necessary possessions on the Po; and by the reputation of victory, to determine the wavering inhabitants to declare on his side. For these reasons he ever pressed on the enemy, and sought for occasions to draw them into action. He had been, ever since the encounter on the Tecinus, cautiously avoided by Scipio; who, even after he was reinforced by the other consular army, endeavoured to engage his colleague likewise in the same dilatory measures; but Sempronius, imputing this caution to the impression which Scipio had taken from his late defeat, and being confident of his own strength, discovered to the Carthaginian general an inclination to meet him, and to decide the campaign by a general action. Sempronius was farther encouraged in this intention by his success in some encounters of foraging parties, which happened soon after he had arrived on this ground; and Hannibal, seeing this disposition of his enemy, took measures to bring on the engagement in circumstances the most favourable to himself.

He had a plain in his front, through which the Trebia ran, and parted the two armies. He wished to bring the Romans to his own side of the river, and to fight on the ground where his army was accustomed to form. Here, besides the other advantages which he proposed to take, he had an opportunity to place an ambuscade, from which he could attack the enemy on the flank or the rear, while they should be engaged in front. It was the middle of winter, and there

1 Polyb. lib. x. c. 3.

were frequent showers of snow. The enemy's infantry, if they should ford the river, and afterwards remain any time inactive, were likely to suffer considerably from the effects of wet and cold. Hannibal, to lay them under this disadvantage, sent his cavalry across the fords, with orders to parade on the ground before the enemy's lines; and, if attacked, to repass the river with every appearance of flight. He had, in the mean time, concealed a thousand chosen men under the shrubby banks of a brook, which fell into the Trebia beyond the intended field of battle. He had ordered his army to be in readiness, and to prepare themselves with a hearty meal for the fatigues they were likely to undergo.

When the Carthaginian cavalry, passing the river as they had been ordered, presented themselves to the Romans, it was but break of day, and before the usual hour of the first meal in the Roman camp. The legions were, nevertheless, hastily formed, and pursued the enemy to where they were seen in disorder to pass the river; and there, by the directions of their general, who supposed he had gained an advantage, and with the ardour which is usual in the pursuit of victory, they passed the fords, and made a display of their forces on the opposite bank. Hannibal, expecting this event, had already formed his troops on the plain, and made a show of only covering the retreat of his cavalry, while he knew that a general action could no longer be avoided. After it began in front, the Romans were attacked in the rear by the party which had been posted in ambush for this purpose; and this being added to the other disadvantages under which they engaged, they were defeated with great slaughter.

The legions of the centre, to the amount of ten thousand men, cut their way through the enemy's line, and escaped to Placentia. Of the remainder of the army, the greater part either fell in the field, perished in attempting to repass the river, or were taken by the enemy. In this action, although few of the Africans fell by the sword, they suffered considerably by the cold and asperity of the season, to which they were not accustomed; and of the elephants, of which Hannibal had brought a considerable number into this country, only one survived the distress of this day.[2]

In consequence of this victory, Hannibal secured his quarters on the Po; and by the treachery of a native of Brundusium, who commanded at Clastidium, got possession of that place, after the Romans had fortified and furnished it with considerable magazines for the supply of their own army. In his treatment of the prisoners taken at this place, he made a distinction between the citizens of Rome and their allies: the first he used with severity, the others he dismissed to their several countries, with assurances that he was come to make war on the Romans, and not on the injured inhabitants of Italy.

The Roman consul, Sempronius, was among those who escaped to Placentia. He meant, in his despatches to the senate, to have disguised the amount of his loss; but the difficulty with which his messenger arrived through a country over-run by the enemy, with many other consequences of his defeat, soon published at Rome the extent of that calamity. The people, however, rose in their ardour and animosity, instead of being sunk. As awakened from a dream of pusillanimity, in which they had hitherto seemed to confine their views to the defence of Italy, they not only commanded fresh levies to replace the army they had lost on the Trebia, but they ordered the consul Scipio to his first destination in Spain, and sent forces to Sardinia, Sicily, Tarentum, and every other station where they apprehended any defection of their allies, or any impression to be made by the enemy.[3]

The unfortunate Sempronius, being called to the city to hold the election of magistrates, escaped, or forced his way through the quarters of the enemy. He was succeeded by Caius Flaminius and Cn. Servilius; the first, being of obscure extraction, was chosen in opposition to the nobles, to whom the people imputed the disasters of the present war. He was ordered early in the spring to take post at Arretium, that he might guard the passes of the Appenines and cover Etruria, while the other consul was stationed at Ariminum to stop the progress of the enemy, if he attempted to pass by the eastern coast.

Hannibal, after his first winter in Italy, took the field for an early campaign; and being inclined to counsels the most likely to surprise his enemies, took his way to Etruria, by a passage in which the vales of the Appenines were marshy, and, from the effects of the season, still covered with water. In a struggle of many days with the hardships of this dangerous march, he lost many of his horses and much of his baggage; and himself, being seized with an inflammation in one of his eyes, lost the use of it. Having appeared, however, in a quarter where he was not expected, he availed himself of this degree of surprise with all his former activity and vigour.

The character of Flaminius, who was raised by the favour of the people in opposition to the senate, and who was now disposed to gratify his constituents by some action of splendour and success, encouraged Hannibal to hope that he might derive some advantage from the ignorance and presumption of his enemy. He therefore endeavoured to provoke the new consul, by destroying the country in his presence, and to brave his resentment, by seeming, on many occasions, to expose himself to his attacks. He even ventured to penetrate into the country beyond him with an appearance of contempt. In one of these movements he marched by the banks of the Lake Thrasimenus, over which the mountains rose with a sudden and steep ascent. He trusted that the Roman consul would follow him, and occupied a post from which with advantage to attack him, if he should venture to engage amidst the difficulties of this narrow way. On the day in which his design was ripe for execution, he was favoured in concealing his position on the ascent of the mountains by a fog which covered the brows of the hills; and he succeeded in drawing the Roman consul into a snare, in which he perished, with the greater part of his army.

The loss of the Romans in this action amounted to fifteen thousand men who fell by the sword, or who were forced into the lake and drowned. Of those who escaped by different ways, some continued their flight for fourscore miles, the dis-

2 Polyb. lib. iii. c. 74.

3 Polyb. lib. iii. c. 75.

tance of this field of battle from Rome, and arrived in the city with the news of this disastrous event. On the first reports great multitudes assembled at the place from which the people were accustomed to receive a communication of public despatches from the officers of state; and the prætor, who then commanded in the city, being to inform them of what had passed, began his account of the action with these words: "We are vanquished in a great battle; the consul, with great part of his army, is slain." He was about to proceed, but could not be heard for the consternation, and the cries which arose among the people: insomuch, that persons who had been present in the action confessed, they heard these words with a deeper impression, than any they had received amidst the bloodshed and horrors of the field; and that it was then only they became sensible of the whole extent of their loss.

To increase the general affliction, farther accounts were brought, at the same time, that four thousand horse, which had been sent, upon hearing that Hannibal had passed the Appenines, by the consul Servilius, to support his colleage, were intercepted by the enemy and taken. The senate continued their meetings for many days without interruption; and the people, greatly affected with the weight of their mortifications and disappointments, committed themselves with proper docility to the conduct of this respectable body. In considering the cause of their repeated defeats, it is probable that they imputed them more to the difference of personal qualities in the leaders, than to any difference in the arms, discipline, or courage of the troops. In respect to the choice of weapons, Hannibal was so much convinced of the superiority of the Romans, that he availed himself of his booty on the Trebia and the Lake Thrasimenus, to arm his African veterans in their manner.[1] In respect to discipline and courage, although mere detachments of the Roman people were likely, in their first campaigns, to have been inferior to veterans, hardened in the service of many years under Hamilcar, Hasdrubal and Hannibal himself, yet nothing is imputed by any historian to this point of disparity. They are not said to have been backward in any attack, to have failed their general in the execution of any plan, to have disobeyed his orders, to have been seized with any panic, or, in any instance, to have given way to the enemy until, being caught in some snare by the superiority of the general, they fought with disadvantage, and perished in great numbers on the field.

The result of the senate's deliberations was to name a dictator. This measure, except to dispense with some form that hampered the ordinary magistrate, had not been adopted during an interval of five and thirty years. The choice fell upon Quintus Fabius Maximus, who seemed to possess the vigilance, caution, and vigour which were wanted in this arduous state of affairs. In proceeding to name him, the usual form which, perhaps, in matters of state, as well as in matters of religion, should be supposed indispensable, could not be observed. Of the consuls, of whom one or the other, according to ancient practice, ought to name the dictator, one was dead; the other, being at a distance, was prevented by the enemy from any communication with the city. The senate, therefore, to elude the supposed necessity of his presence, resolved that not a dictator, but a pro-dictator, should be named; and that the people should themselves choose this officer, with all the powers that were usually entrusted to the dictator himself. Fabius was accordingly elected pro-dictator, and in this capacity named M. Minutius Rufus for his second in command, or general of the horse.

While the Romans were thus preparing again to collect their forces, Hannibal continued to pursue his advantage. He might, with an enemy more easily subdued or daunted than the Romans, already have expected great fruit from his victories, at least he might have expected offers of concession and overtures of peace: but it is probable that he knew the character of this people enough, not to flatter himself so early in the war with these expectations, or to hope that he could make any impression by a nearer approach to the city, or by any attempt on its walls. He had already, by his presence, enabled the nations of the northern and western parts of Italy to shake off the dominion of Rome. He had the same measures to pursue with respect to the nations of the south. The capital, he probably supposed, might be deprived of the support of its allies, cut off from its resources, and even destroyed; but while the state existed could never be brought to yield to an enemy.

Under these impressions the Carthaginian general, leaving Rome at a great distance on his right, repassed the Appenines to the coast of Picenum, and from thence directed his march to Apulia. Here he proceeded, as he had done on the side of Etruria and Gaul, to lay waste the Roman settlements, and to detach the natives from their allegiance to Rome. But while he pursued this plan in one extremity of Italy, the Romans took measures to recover the possessions they had lost on the other, or at least to prevent the disaffected Gauls from making any considerable diversion in favour of their enemy.

For this purpose, while Fabius Maximus was assembling an army to oppose Hannibal in Apulia, the prætor, Lucius Posthumius, was sent with a proper force to the Po. Fabius having united the troops that had served under the consul Servilius, with four legions newly raised by himself, followed the enemy. On his march he issued a proclamation, requiring all the inhabitants of open towns and villages in that quarter of Italy to retire into places of safety, and the inhabitants of every district to which the enemy approached, to set fire to their habitations and granaries, and to destroy whatever they could not remove in their flight.[2] Though determined not to hazard a battle, he drew near to the Carthaginian army, and continued from the heights to observe and to circumscribe their motions Time alone, he trusted, would decide the war in his favour, against an enemy who was far removed from any supply or recruit, and in a country that was daily wasting by the effect of his own depredations.

Hannibal, after endeavouring in vain to bring the Roman dictator to a battle, perceived his design to protract the war; and considering inaction as the principal evil he himself had to fear, frequently exposed his detachments, and even his whole army, in dangerous situations. The ad

1 Polyb. lib. iii. c. 115.

2 Liv. lib. xxii. c. 11

vantages he gave by these acts of temerity were sometimes effectually seized by his wary antagonist, but more frequently recovered by his own singular conduct and unfailing resources.

In this temporary stagnation of Hannibal's fortune, and in the frequent opportunities which the Romans had, though in trifling encounters, to measure their own strength with that of the enemy, their confidence began to revive. The public resumed the tranquillity of its councils, and looked round with deliberation to collect its force. The people and the army recovered from their late consternation, and took advantage of the breathing-time they had gained, to censure the very conduct to which they owed the returns of their confidence and the renewal of their hopes. They forgot their former defeats, and began to imagine that the enemy kept his footing in Italy by the permission, by the timidity, or by the excessive caution of their leader.

A slight advantage over Hannibal, who had too much exposed his foraging parties, gained by the general of the horse in the absence of the dictator, confirmed the army and the people in this opinion, and greatly sunk the reputation of Fabius. As he could not be superseded before the usual term of his office was expired, the senate and people, though precluded by law from proceeding to an actual deposition, came to a resolution equally violent and unprecedented, and which they hoped might induce him to resign his power. They raised the general of the horse to an equal command with the dictator, and left them to adjust their pretensions between them. Such affronts, under the notions of honour which in modern times are annexed to the military character, would have made it impossible for the dictator to remain in his station. But in a commonwealth, where, to put any personal consideration in competition with the public, would have appeared absurd, seeming injuries done by the state to the honour of a citizen, only furnished him with a more splendid occasion to display his virtue. The Roman dictator continued to serve under this diminution of his rank and command, and overlooked with magnanimity the insults with which the people had requited the service he was rendering to his country.

Minutius being now associated with the dictator, in order to be free from the restraints of a joint command, and from the wary counsels of his colleague, desired, as the properest way of adjusting their pretensions, to divide the army between them. In this new situation he soon after, by his rashness, exposed himself and his division to be entirely cut off by the enemy. But being rescued by Fabius, he too gave proofs of a magnanimous spirit, confessed the favour he had received, and committing himself, with the whole army, to the conduct of his colleague, he left this cautious officer, during the remaining period of their joint command, to pursue the plan he had formed for the war.[3]

At this time, however, the people, and even the senate, were not willing to wait for the effect of such seemingly languid and dilatory measures as Fabius was inclined to pursue. They resolved to augment the army in Italy to eight legions, which, with an equal number of the allies, amounted to eighty thousand foot and seven thousand two hundred horse; and they intended, in the approaching election of consuls, to choose men, not only of reputed abilities, but of decisive and resolute counsels. As such they elected C. Terentius Varro, supposed to be of a bold and dauntless spirit; and, in order to temper his ardour, joined with him in the command L. Emilius Paulus, an officer of approved experience, who had formerly obtained a triumph for his victories in Illyricum, and who was high in the confidence of the senate, as well as in that of the people.

In the autumn before the nomination of these officers to command the Roman army, Hannibal had surprised the fortress of Cannæ on the Aufidus, a place to which the Roman citizens of that quarter had retired with their effects, and at which they had collected considerable magazines and stores. This, among other circumstances, determined the senate to hazard a battle, and to furnish the new consuls with instructions to this effect.

These officers, it appears, having opened the campaign on the banks of the Aufidus, advanced by mutual consent within six miles of the Carthaginian camp, which covered the village of Cannæ. Here they differed in their opinions, and, by a strange defect in the Roman policy, which, in times of less virtue, must have been altogether ruinous, and even in these times was ill-fitted to produce a consistent and well-supported series of operations, had no rule by which to decide their precedency, and were obliged to take the command each a day in his turn.

Varro, contrary to the opinion of his colleague, proposed to give battle on the plain, and with this intention, as often as the command devolved upon him, still advanced on the enemy. In order that he might occupy the passage and both sides of the Aufidus, he encamped in two separate divisions on its opposite banks, having his larger division on the right of the river, opposed to Hannibal's camp. Still taking the opportunity of his turn to command the army, he passed with the larger division to a plain, supposed to be on the left of the Aufidus, and there, though the field was too narrow to receive the legions in their usual form, he pressed them together, and gave the enemy, if he chose it, an opportunity to engage. To accommodate his order to the extent of his ground, he contracted the head and the intervals of his manipules or columns, making their depth greatly to exceed the front which they turned to the enemy.[4]

He placed his cavalry on the flanks, the Roman knights on his right towards the river, and the horsemen of the allies on the left.

Hannibal no sooner saw this movement and disposition of the enemy, than he hastened to meet them on the plain which they had chosen for the field of action. He likewise passed the Aufidus, and, with his left to the river, and his front to the south, formed his army upon an equal line with that of the enemy.

He placed the Gaulish and Spanish cavalry on his left facing the Roman knights, and the Numidians on his right facing the allies.

The flanks of his infantry, on the right and the left, were composed of the African foot, armed in the Roman manner, with the pilum, the

3 Plutarch. in vit. Fab. Max.

4 Ποιεων το βαθος εν ταις Σπειραις Πολλαπλασιον τε μετοπου. Vide Polyb

heavy buckler, and the stabbing sword. His centre, though opposed to the choice of the Roman legions, consisted of the Gaulish and the Spanish foot, variously armed and intermixed together.

Hitherto no advantage seemed to be taken on either side. As the armies fronted south and north, even the sun, which rose soon after they were formed, shone upon the flanks, and was no disadvantage, to either. The superiority of numbers was greatly on the side of the Romans; but Hannibal rested his hopes of victory on two circumstances; first, on a motion to be made by his cavalry, if they prevailed on either side of the enemy's wings; next, on a position he was to take with his centre, in order to begin the action from thence, to bring the Roman legions into some disorder, and expose them, under that disadvantage, to the attack which he was prepared to make with his veterans on both their flanks.

The action accordingly began with a charge of the Gaulish and Spanish horse, who, being superior to the Roman knights, drove them from their ground, forced them into the river, and put the greater part of them to the sword. By this event the flank of the Roman army, which might have been joined to the Aufidus, was entirely uncovered.

Having performed this service, the victorious cavalry had orders to wheel at full gallop round the rear of their own army, and to join the Numidian horse on their right, who were still engaged with the Roman allies. By this unexpected junction, the left wing of the Roman army was likewise put to flight, and pursued by the African horse; at the same time the Spanish cavalry prepared to attack the Roman infantry, wherever they should be ordered, on the flank or the rear.

While these important events took place on the wings, Hannibal amused the Roman legions of the main body with a singular movement that was made by the Gauls and Spaniards, and with which he proposed to begin the action. These came forward, not in a straight line abreast, but swelling out to a curve in the centre, without disjoining their flanks from the African infantry, who remained firm on their ground.

By this motion they formed a kind of crescent convex to the front. The Roman manipules of the right and the left, fearing, by this singular disposition, to have no share in the action, hastened to bend their line into a corresponding curve; and, in proportion as they came to close with the enemy, charged them with a confident and impetuous courage. The Gauls and Spaniards resisted this charge no longer than was necessary to awaken the precipitant ardour with which victorious troops often blindly pursue a flying enemy. And the Roman line being bent, and fronting inwards to the centre of its concave, the legions pursued where the enemy led them. Hurrying from the flanks to share in the victory, they narrowed their space as they advanced, and the men who were accustomed to have a square of six feet clear for wielding their arms, being now pressed together, so as to prevent entirely the use of their swords, found themselves struggling against each other for space, in an inextricable and hopeless confusion.

Hannibal, who had waited for this event, ordered a general charge of his cavalry on the rear of the Roman legions, and at the same time an attack from his African infantry on both their flanks; by these dispositions and joint operations without any considerable loss to himself, he effected an almost incredible slaughter

U. C. 537.

of his enemies. With the loss of no more than four thousand, and these chiefly of the Spanish and Gaulish infantry, he put fifty thousand of the Romans to the sword.

The consul, Emilius Paulus, had been wounded in the shock of the cavalry; but when he saw the condition in which the infantry were engaged, he refused to be carried off, and was slain.[1] The consuls of the preceding year, with others of the same rank, were likewise killed. Of six thousand horse only seventy troopers escaped with Varro. Of the infantry three thousand fled from the carnage that took place on the field of battle, and ten thousand who had been posted to guard the camp were taken.

The unfortunate consul, with such of the stragglers as joined him in his retreat, took post at Venusia; and with a noble confidence in his own integrity, and in the resources of his country, put himself in a posture to resist the enemy, till he could have instructions and reinforcements from Rome.[2]

This calamity which had befallen the Romans in Apulia, was accompanied with the defeat of the prætor Posthumius, who, with his army, on the other extremity of the country, was cut off by the Gauls. A general ferment arose throughout all Italy. Many cantons of Grecian extraction, having been about sixty years subject to Rome, now declared for Carthage. Others, feeling themselves released from the dominion of the Romans, but intending to recover their liberties, not merely to change their masters, now waited for an opportunity to stipulate the conditions on which they were to join the victor. Of this number were the cities of Capua, Tarentum, Locri, Metapontus, Crotona, and other towns in the south-east of the peninsula. In other cantons, the people being divided and opposed to each other with great animosity, severally called to their assistance such of the parties at war as they judged were most likely to support them against their antagonists. Some of the Roman colonies, even within the districts that were open to the enemy's incursions, still adhered to the metropolis; but the possessions of the republic were greatly reduced, and scarcely equalled what the state had acquired before the expulsion of Pyrrhus from Italy, or even before the annexation of Campania, or the conquest of Samnium. The allegiance of her subjects and the faith of her allies in Sicily were greatly shaken. Hiero, the king of Syracuse, who had some time, under the notion of an alliance, cherished his dependance on Rome, being now greatly sunk in the decline of years, could no longer answer for the conduct of his own court, and died soon after this event, leaving his successors to change the party of the vanquished for that of the victor.

Hitherto the nations of Greece and of Asia had taken no part in the contest of those power-

---

1 He has received from the poet the following honourable grave: Animæ que magnæ prodigum Paulum superante Pœno. Hor. Car lib. i. Ode 12.

2 Liv. lib. xxiii

ful rivals. But the Romans having already interfered in the affairs of Greece, and made their ambition be felt beyond the Adriatic and the Ionian Sea, the news of their supposed approaching fall was received there with attention: it awakened the hopes of many who had suffered from the effects of their power. Among these Demetrius, the exiled king of Pharos, being still at the court of Macedonia, and much in the confidence of Philip, who had recently mounted the throne of that kingdom, urging that it was impossible to remain an indifferent spectator in the contest of such powerful nations, persuaded the king to prefer the alliance of Carthage to that of Rome, and to join with Hannibal in the reduction of the Roman power; observing, that with the merit of declaring himself while the event was yet in any degree uncertain, the king of Macedonia would be justly intitled to a proper share of the advantages to be reaped in the conquest.

Philip accordingly endeavoured to accommodate the differences which he had to adjust with the Grecian States, and sent an officer into Italy to treat with Hannibal, and with the Carthaginian deputies who attended the camp. In the negotiation which followed it was agreed, that the king of Macedonia and the republic of Carthage should consider the Romans as common enemies; that they should pursue the war in Italy with their forces united, and make no peace but on terms mutually agreeable to both. In this treaty the interest of the prince of Pharos was particularly attended to; and his restoration to the kingdom from which he had been expelled by the Romans, with the recovery of the hostages which had been exacted from him, were made principal articles.[3]

Hannibal, from the time of his arrival in Italy, after having made war for three years in that country, had received no supply from Africa, and seemed to be left to pursue the career of his fate with such resources as he could devise for himself; but this alliance with the king of Macedonia, promised amply to make up for the deficiency of his aids from Carthage; and Philip, by an easy passage into Italy, was likely to furnish him with every kind of support or encouragement that was necessary to accomplish the end of the war.

The Romans were apprised of this formidable accession to the power of their enemy, as well as of the general defection of their own allies, and of the revolt of their subjects. Though taxes were accumulated on the people, and frequent loans obtained from the commissaries and contractors employed in the public service, their expenses began to be ill supplied. There appeared not, however, in their councils, notwithstanding all these circumstances of distress, the smallest disposition to purchase safety by mean concessions of any sort. When the vanquished consul returned to the city, in order to attend the nomination of a person who, in this extremity of their fortunes might be charged with the care of the commonwealth, the senate, as conscious that he had acted at Cannæ by their own instructions, and had, upon the same motives that animated the whole Roman people, disdained, with a superior army, to stand in awe of his enemy, or to refuse him battle upon equal ground, went out in a kind of procession to meet him; and, upon a noble idea that men are not answerable for the strokes of fortune, nor for the effects of superior address in an enemy, they overlooked his temerity and his misconduct in the action; they attended only to the undaunted aspect he preserved after his defeat, returned him thanks for not having despaired of the commonwealth;[4] and from thence forward continued their preparations for war, with all the dignity and pride of the most prosperous fortune. They refused to ransom the prisoners who had been taken by the enemy at Cannæ, and treated with sullen contempt, rather than severity, those who by an early flight had escaped from the field; being petitioned to employ them again in the war, "We have no service," they said, "for men who could leave their fellow citizens engaged with an enemy." They seemed to rise in the midst of their distress, and to gain strength from misfortune. They prepared to attack or to resist at once, in all the different quarters to which the war was likely to extend, and took their measures for the support of it in Spain, in Sardinia and Sicily, as well as in Italy. They continued their fleets at sea; not only observed and obstructed the communications of Carthage with the seats of the war, but having intercepted part of the correspondence of Philip with Hannibal, they sent a powerful squadron to the coast of Epirus; and, by an alliance with the States of Etolia, whom they persuaded to renew their late war with Philip, found that prince sufficient employment on the frontiers of his own kingdom, effectually prevented his sending any supply to Hannibal, and, in the sequel, reduced him to the humiliating necessity of making a separate peace.

In the ordinary notions which are entertained of battles and their consequences, the last victory of Hannibal at Cannæ, in the sequel of so many others that preceded it, ought to have decided the war; and succeeding ages have blamed this general for not marching directly to the capital, in order to bring the contest to a speedy termination by the reduction of Rome itself. But his own judgment is of much more weight than that of the persons who censure him. He knew the character of the Romans and his own strength. Though victorious, he was greatly weakened by his victories, and at a distance from the means of a reinforcement or supply. He was unprovided with engines of attack; and, so far from being in a condition to venture on the siege of Rome, that he could not undertake even that of Naples, which, after the battle of Cannæ, refused to open its gates; and, indeed, soon after this date he received a check from Marcellus in attempting the siege of Nola.[5]

The Romans, immediately after their disaster at Cannæ, prepared again to act on the offensive, formed a fresh army of five and twenty thousand men, which they sent, under the dictator Junius Pera, to collect the remains of their late vanquished forces, and to annoy the enemy wherever they might find him exposed.

Hannibal kept in motion with his army to protect the cantons that were inclined to declare on his side; but together with the extent and multi-

3 Liv. lib. xxiii. c. 33.

4 In the famous and admired expression, Qui de republica non desperasset.

5 Liv. lib. xxiii. c. 14, 15, 16.

plication of his new possessions, which obliged him to divide his army in order to occupy and to secure them, he became sensible of his weakness; and, with the accounts sent to Carthage of his victories, he likewise sent representations of his losses, and demanded a supply of men, of stores, and of money. He was indeed in his new situation so much in want of these articles, that, having in the three first years of the war apparenty raised the reputation of Carthage to the greatest height, and procured to his country more allies and more territory in Italy than were left in the power of the Romans, together with Capua, and other cities, more wealthy than Rome itself, and surrounded with lands better cultivated, and more full of resources, yet his affairs from thenceforward began to decline.

Armies are apt to suffer no less from an opinion, that all the ends of their service are obtained, than they do from defeats, and from despair of success. The soldiers of Hannibal, now elated with victory, perhaps grown rich with the plunder of the countries they had overrun, and of the armies they had defeated; and presuming that the war was at an end, or that they themselves ought to be relieved, or sent to enjoy the rewards of so glorious and so hard a service, became remiss in their discipline, or indulged themselves in all the excesses, of which the means were to be found in their present situation. Being mere soldiers of fortune, without a country, or any civil ties to unite them together, they were governed by the sole authority of their leader, and by their confidence in his singular abilities. Although there is no instance of their openly mutinying against him in a body, there are many instances of their separately and clandestinely deserting his service. The Spanish and Numidian horse, in particular, to whom he owed great part of his victories, upon some disappointment in their hopes, or upon a disgust taken at the mere stagnation of his fortune, went over in troops and and squadrons to the enemy.[1] His hopes from the side of Macedonia were entirely disappointed, the power of that nation having full employment at home.[2] He found himself unable, without dividing his forces, to preserve his recent conquests, or to protect the Italians who had declared for him. Some of his possessions, therefore, he abandoned or destroyed; and the natives of Italy, become the victims of his policy, or left to the mercy of the Romans whom they had offended, became averse to his cause, or felt that they could not rely on his power to protect them.[3] Moved by these considerations, he made earnest applications at Carthage for reinforcements and supplies, to enable him to continue the war. But the councils of that republic, though abject in misfortune, were insolent or remiss in prosperity. Being broken into factions, the projects of one party, however wise, were frustrated by the opposition of the other. One faction received the applications of Hannibal with scorn. "Do victories," they said, "reduce armies to the want of reinforcements and of supplies, even against the very enemies they had vanquished? And do the acquisitions of Hannibal require more money and men to keep them than were required to make them? Other victorious generals are proud to display the fruits of their conquests, or bring home the spoils of their enemies to enrich their own country, instead of draining it to support a career of vain and unprofitable victories."

These invectives concluded with a motion, which, on the supposition that the advantages gained by Hannibal were real, was well-founded in wisdom and sound policy: that the occasion should be seized to treat with the Romans, when the State had reason to expect the most advantageous terms. But this counsel either was, or appeared to be, the language of faction; and no measures were adopted, either to obtain peace, or effectually to support the war.

The friends, as well as the enemies of Hannibal, contributed to the neglect with which he was treated. In proportion as his friends admired him, and gloried in his fortune, they acted as if he alone were able to surmount every difficulty; and they accordingly were remiss in supporting him. The republic, under the effects of this wretched policy, with all the advantages of her navigation and of her trade, suffered her navy to decline, and permitted the Romans to obstruct, or molest, all the passages by which she could communicate with her armies in Spain and Italy, or her allies in Sicily and Greece.[4] They voted indeed to Hannibal, on the present occasion, a reinforcement of four thousand Numidian horse, forty elephants, and a sum of money. But this resolution appears to have languished in the execution; and the armament, when ready to sail, was suffered to be diverted from its purpose, and ordered to Spain instead of Italy.[5]

Notwithstanding these mortifications and disappointments, Hannibal still kept his footing in Italy for sixteen years; and so long gave sufficient occupation to the Romans, in recovering, by slow and cautious steps, what he had ravished from them in three years, and by a few daring examples of ability and valour. When the war had taken this turn, and the Romans, by the growing skill and ability of their leaders, as well as by the unconquerable spirit of their people, began to prevail, Hannibal, receiving no support directly from Africa, endeavoured to procure it from Spain by the junction of his brother Hasdrubal, to whom he recommended a second passage over the Alps, in imitation of that which he himself had accomplished. Every attempt of this sort, however, had been defeated, during six years, by the vigour and abilities of the two Scipios, Cnæius and Publius, and afterwards by the superior genius of the young Publius Scipio, who succeeding the father and the uncle, as will be seen in the sequel, supported, with fresh lustre, the cause of his country.

The two Scipios, after some varieties of fortune, though, while they acted together, they were generally successful, having, in the seventh year of this war, separated their forces, were both, within the space of forty days, betrayed or deserted by their allies, and cut off by the superior force of the enemy.

The natives of Spain had, by their want of union and military skill, as has been mentioned, suffered many foreign establishments to be made in their country; they had permitted the Carthaginians, in particular, to possess themselves of a considerable territory; but afterwards, in order to

1 Liv. lib. xxiii. c. 46.
2 Ibid. lib. xxvi. c. 28, 29. Lib. xxviii. c. 4.
3 Ibid. lib. xxvii. c. 1 and 16.
4 Liv. lib. xxviii. c. 4.
5 Ibid. lib. xxiii. c. 13 and 32.

remove them from thence, accepted of the protection of the Romans; and, in the sequel, occasionally applied to either of these parties for aid against the other, being, during the greater part of this war, the unstable friends, or irresolute enemies of both.

A service of so much danger, so little in public view, and at a distance from the principal scenes of the war, was not sought for as an opportunity to accumulate fame. The young Scipio, fired with the memory of his father and of his uncle, who had fallen in that service, and, instead of being deterred by their fate, eager to revenge their fall, courted a command, which every other Roman is said to have declined. This young man, as has been observed, had begun his military services, in the first year of this war, on the Tecinus, where he had the good fortune to rescue his father. He was afterwards present at the battle of Cannæ, and was one of the few, who, from that disastrous field, forced their way to Canusium. Being chosen commander by those who escaped to this place, he prevented the effect of a desperate resolution they had taken to abandon Italy. Many of the severer forms of the commonwealth having been dispensed with in the present exigences of the state, Scipio had been chosen edile, though under the standing age, being only turned of twenty-four, one year younger than Hannibal was when he took the command of the army in Spain, and four years younger than he was when he marched into Italy.

Such particulars relating to men of superior genius and virtue, are in the highest degree interesting to mankind. It is even pleasing to know, that this young man was, according to Livy, tall and graceful in his person, with a beautiful countenance and engaging aspect.

The Romans had been hitherto preserved in all the extremities of their fortune by the superiority of their national character, and by means of political establishments, which, although they do not inspire men with superior genius, yet raise ordinary citizens to a degree of elevation approaching to heroism; enabling the states they compose to subsist in great dangers, and to await the appearance of superior men. They had not yet opposed to Hannibal an officer of similar talents, or of a like superiority to the ordinary race of mankind. Scipio was the first who gave indubitable proofs of his title to this character.[6] Upon his arrival in Spain, with a fleet of thirty galleys, and ten thousand men, he found the remains of the vanquished Romans retired within the Iberus, where, under the command of T. Fonteius and Lucius Marcius, they had scarcely been able to withstand the further progress of the enemy.[7] There he accordingly landed, and fixed his principal quarters for the winter at Tarragona. By his information of the posture of the enemy, it appeared, that they had placed all their magazines and stores at New Carthage; and that, thinking this place sufficiently secured by a garrison of a thousand men, they had separated their army into three divsions, and were gone in different directions to extend their possessions, or to cover the territories they had acquired. Of these divisions, none were nearer to their principal station than ten days' march.

Upon these informations, Scipio formed a project to surprise the town of New Carthage, though at a distance from Tarragona of above three hundred miles. He rested his hopes of success on the security of his enemies, and on the prospect of being able to accomplish the greater part of his march before his design should be suspected, or before any measures could be taken to prevent him. For this purpose he disclosed it to Lælius alone; and gave him orders to steer for that place with his fleet, while he himself made hasty marches by land. This city was situated, like Old Carthage, on a peninsula, or neck of land, surrounded by the sea. Scipio took post on the isthmus, fortified himself towards the continent, from which he had reason to expect some attempt would be made to relieve the place, and secured himself on that side, before he attacked the town.

In his first attempts on the ramparts he was repulsed; but observing, that at low water, the walls were accessible at a weaker place than that at which he made his assault; and having encouraged his men by informing them that the god of the sea had promised to favour them, which they thought to be verified by the seasonable ebb which ensued, he there planted his ladders, and forced his way into the town. Here he made a great booty in captives, money, and ships.[8]

In this manner Scipio conducted his first exploit in Spain; and having carried on the war with equal ability and success for five years, he obliged the Carthaginians, after repeated defeats, to abandon that country. He himself, while Hasdrubal attempted to join his brother Hannibal in Lucania, and Mago to make a diversion in his favour in Liguria, returned to Rome. He was yet under thirty years of age, and not legally qualified to bear the office of consul. But having an unquestionable title to the highest confidence of his country, the services which he had already performed procured a dispensation in his favour. He was accordingly raised to the consulate; and when the provinces came to be assigned to the officers of state, he moved that Africa should be included in the number, and be allotted to himself: "There," he said, "the Carthaginians may receive the deepest wounds, and from thence be the soonest obliged for their own safety to recall their forces from Italy."

This motion was unfavourably received by the greater part of the senate; it seemed to be matter of surprise, that, while Rome itself lay between two hostile armies, that of Hannibal in Brutium, and that of Maga in Liguria or Gaul, the consul should propose to strip the republic of so great a force as would be necessary for the invasion of Africa.[9] The fatal miscarriage of Regulus on that ground in a former war, the unhappy effects of precipitant counsels in the beginning of the present, were cited against him, and the desire of so arduous a station was even accounted presumptuous in so young a man.

Among the difficulties which Scipio met with in obtaining the consent of the senate to the execution of his plan, is mentioned the disinclination of the great Fabius, who, from a prepossession in favour of that dilatory war, by which he himself had acquired so much glory; and by which at a

6 Liv. liv. xxvi. c. 18, 19, &c.

7 Ibid. c. 19 and 20.

8 Polyb. lib. x. c. 9—15—17. Appian de Bell. Hispan

9 Appian de Bell. Punic. p. 4.

ime when procrastination was necessary, he had retrieved the fortunes of his country, obstinately opposed the adopting of this hazardous project.

It had been, for the most part, an established maxim in the counsels of Rome, to carry war, when in their power, into the enemy's country. They had been prevented in the present case only by the unexpected appearance of Hannibal in Italy, and were likely to return to the execution of their first design as soon as their affairs at home should furnish them with a sufficient respite. We may, therefore, conceive what they felt of the difficulties of the present war, from this and other circumstances; that even after fortune had so greatly inclined in their favour, they did not yet think themselves in condition to retaliate on the enemy; or safe against the designs which Hannibal might form in Italy, if they should divide their forces, or detach so great a part of them as might be necessary to execute the project of a war in Africa.

They concluded, however, at last, with some hesitation, that Scipio, while the other consul should remain opposed to Hannibal in Italy, might have for his province the island of Sicily, dispose of the forces that were still there, receive the voluntary supplies of men and of money which he himself might be able to procure; and if he found, upon mature deliberation, a proper opportunity, that he might make a descent upon Africa. Agreeably to this resolution, he set out for the province assigned him, having a considerable fleet equipped by private contribution, and a body of seven thousand volunteers, who embarked in high expectation of the service in which he proposed to employ them.[1]

While Scipio, by his exertions in Spain, was rising to this degree of eminence in the councils of his country, the war, both in Sicily and in Italy, had been attended with many signal events, and furnished many proofs of distinguished ability in the course of its operations, highly interesting to those who are qualified to receive instruction from such examples of conduct, and from the experience of great events. But in the summary account of the steps by which the Romans ascended to empire, we can only point out the tract by which they advanced; and, with a few general observations on the means, hasten to contemplate the end which they attained.

The fortunes of Hannibal, as we have already remarked, had been some time on the decline. Capua and Tarentum, notwithstanding his utmost efforts to preserve them, had been taken by the Romans. While the first of these places was besieged, he endeavoured to force the enemy's lines: and being repulsed, made a feint, by a hasty march towards Rome itself, to draw off the besiegers. By this movement he obtained a sight of that famous city; but again retired without having gained any advantage from this intended diversion. His allies, in Sicily, were entirely overwhelmed by the reduction of Syracuse; but that which chiefly affected his cause, by cutting off all hopes of future supplies or reinforcements, was the fall of his brother Hasdrubal. This officer had found means to elude the forces of Scipio in Spain; and attempted, by pursuing the tract of his brother into Italy, to join him in that country. In this design he actually surmounted all the difficulties of the Pyrenees and of the Alps, had passed the Po and the Rubicon, and advanced to the Metaurus before he met with any considerable check. There, at last, he encountered with the Roman consuls, M. Claudius Nero and M. Livius Salinator, and was defeated with the loss of his whole army, amounting to fifty thousand men, of whom not one escaped being taken or slain.[2]

On this occasion, the Romans, who had so long left their possessions in the country a prey to the enemy, began to enjoy some degree of security, returned to their ruined habitations, and resumed the labours of the field. Hannibal, as overwhelmed with despair or affliction, confessed, that he could no longer be in doubt of the fate that awaited his country.[3] From this time he contracted his quarters, withdrew his posts from Apulia, gave intimation to all his allies in Italy, who had much to fear from the resentment of the Romans, that they should retire under the covert of his army in Brutium. Here he himself remained on the defensive; and, as if sensible that his career in Italy was nearly at an end, erected those curious monuments which are cited by Polybius, and on which were recorded the particulars of his march from Spain to Italy, and the numbers of his army at different periods of the war.[4]

In the following year, Mago, as we have observed, being unable to effect any considerable service in Spain, had orders to make sail for Italy, and once more endeavour to reinforce the army of Hannibal. But, having lost some time in a fruitless attempt on New Carthage, and a report in the mean time having spread of Scipio's intention to invade Africa, he received a second order to land at Genua; and, that he might distract or employ the forces of the Romans at home, endeavour to rekindle the war in Liguria and Gaul.

Such was the state of affairs when Scipio proposed to invade Africa, passed into Sicily, and employed the whole year of his consulate in making preparations. In this interval, however, having access by sea to the coasts which were occupied by Hannibal in Italy, he forced the town of Locri, and posted a garrison there, under the command of Pleminius, an officer, whose singular abuses of power became the subjects of complaint at Rome, and drew some censure on Scipio himself, by whom he was employed, and supposed to be countenanced.

Scipio was said, on this occasion, not only to have connived at the outrages committed by Pleminius, whom he had stationed at Locri, but to have been himself, while at Syracuse, abandoned to a life of effeminacy and pleasure, unworthy of a person entrusted with so important a command. It may appear strange, that this censure should arise from his having shown a disposition at Syracuse to become acquainted with the learning of the Greeks. His enemies gave out, that he affected the manners of that people; that he passed his time among books, and in public places of conversation and exercise. Upon these surmises, a commission was granted to the prætor of Sicily, with ten senators, two tribunes of the people, and one of the ediles, who had orders to join the

1 Appian de Bell. Punic.

2 Liv. lib. xxvii. c. 49.

3 Agnoscere se fortunam Cartnaginis. Liv lib. xxvii fine.

4 Liv. lib. xxviii. fine

prætor in that island. To these instructions were given, that if they found Scipio accessary to the disorders committed at Locri, or reprehensible in his own conduct, they should send him in arrest to Rome: but that, if they found him innocent, he should continue in his command, and be suffered to carry the war wherever he thought most expedient for the good of the commonwealth.

The members of this formidable court of inquest, having landed at Locri, in their way to Sicily, ordered Pleminius, with thirty of his officers, in chains to Rome: and from Locri, proceeding to Syracuse, they reported from thence, that Scipio was no way accessary to the crimes committed by the troops in garrison at Locri: and that within the district of his own immediate command the allies were fully protected, and the troops preserved in such order and discipline,[5] as, whenever they should be employed, gave the most encouraging prospect of victory.

Such was the report in favour of this young man, who appears to have been the first Roman statesman or warrior, who showed any considerable disposition to become acquainted with the literature and ingenious arts of the Greeks. In this particular, his Carthaginian rival is said to have advanced before him, having long studied the language and learning of those nations; and having in his retinue some persons from Greece to aid him in the use of their writings.

Scipio, while he commanded the Roman army in Spain, having already conceived his design upon Africa, had with this view opened a correspondence with Syphax, king of Numidia; and had actually made a visit in person to this prince, who, being at variance with Carthage, was easily prevailed upon to promise his support to the Romans, in case they should carry the war into that country. The Roman general, now ready to embark with a considerable army, sent Lælius with the first division, probably to examine the coast, to choose a proper station at which to fix the assembling of his fleet, and to call upon the king of Numidia to perform his engagements.

This division of the fleet, at its first appearance, was supposed to bring the Roman proconsul, with all his forces, from Sicily; and the Carthaginians, whatever reason they might, for some time, have had to expect this event, were in a great measure unprepared for it. They had their levies to make at home, and troops to hire from abroad; their fortifications were out of repair, and their stores and magazines unfurnished. Even their fleet was not in a condition to meet that of the enemy. They now hastened to supply these defects; and, though undeceived with respect to the numbers and force of the first embarkation, they made no doubt that they were soon to expect another; accordingly they continued their preparation, and took every measure to secure themselves, or to avert the storm with which they were threatened.

They had recently made their peace with Syphax, king of Numidia; and, instead of an enemy in the person of this prince, had obtained for themselves a zealous ally. He had broke off his engagements with Scipio and the Romans, tempted by his passion for Sophonisba, the daughter of Hasdrubal, a principal citizen of Carthage, who refused to marry him on any other terms. But this transaction, which procured to the Carthaginians one ally, lost them another; for this high-minded woman, who, instead of a dower, contracted for armies in defence of her country, had formerly captivated Massinissa, another Numidian prince, that, being deprived of his kingdom by Syphax, had received his education, and formed his attachments, at Carthage.[6] Massinissa, while he had hopes of an alliance with the family of Hasdrubal, engaged all his partisans in Numidia in behalf of the Carthaginians; and he himself fought their battles in person. But, stung with his disappointment, and the preference which was given to his rival, he determined to court the favour of their enemies; had made advances to Scipio, before his departure from Spain; and, now, hearing of the arrival of the Roman fleet, hastened to Hippo, where Lælius had come to an anchor, and made offer of his assistance, with that of his friends in the kingdom of Numidia.

Such was the state of parties in Africa, when this country was about to become the scene of war. The Carthaginians, still in hopes of diverting the storm, sent earnest instructions to both their generals to press upon the Romans in Italy, and to make every effort to distract or to occupy their forces, and to leave them no leisure for the invasion of Africa. They sent, at the same time, an embassy to the king of Macedonia, to remind him of the engagements into which he had entered with Hannibal, and to represent the danger to which he and every other prince must be exposed from a people so ambitious as the Romans, if they were suffered to unite, by a conquest, the resources of Carthage with those of Rome.

Philip, at the earnest entreaty of many Grecian states, who were anxious that the Romans should have no pretext to embroil the affairs of Greece, had, in the preceding year, made a separate peace first with the Etolians, and afterwards with the Romans themselves;[7] and was now extremely averse to renew the quarrel. The occasion, however, appeared to be of great moment; and he listened so far to the remonstrances of the Carthaginians, as to furnish them with a body of four thousand men, and a supply of money.

By such measures as these, hastily taken on the approach of danger, the Carthaginians endeavoured to make amends for the former remissness of their counsels. Hitherto they appear to have considered the war with little concern, and to have left their exertions to the ambition of a single family, by whom the state was engaged in this quarrel.[8] They neglected their strength at home, in proportion as they believed the enemy to be at a distance; and were indifferent to national objects, while their private interests were secure.

The harbour of Hippo, about fifty miles wes from Carthage, and under the Fair Promontory being seized by Lælius, furnished a place of re ception for Scipio's fleet. This officer accord ingly sailed from Sicily with fifty armed galleys and four hundred transports. As he had reaso to expect that the country would be laid wast before him, great part of this shipping was em ployed in carrying his provisions and stores. Th

5 Liv. lib xxix. c. 20.

6 Appian de Bell. Hispan. p. 275.

7 Liv. lib. xxix. c. 13.

8 The sons of Hamilcar.

numbers of his army are not mentioned. His first object was to make himself master of Utica, situated about half way between Carthage and Hippo, the place where he landed. He accordingly, without loss of time, presented himself before it; but soon found himself unable to execute his purpose. The country, to a considerable distance, was laid waste or deserted by the natives, and could not subsist his army. The Carthaginians had a great force in field, consisting of thirty thousand men, under Hasdrubal, the son of Gisgo, together with fifty thousand foot and ten thousand horse, under Syphax, king of Numidia, who now advanced to the relief of Utica.

Scipio, on the junction and approach of these numerous armies, retired from Utica, took possession of a peninsula on the coast, fortified the isthmus which led to it, and in this station having a safe retreat, both for his fleet and his army, continued to be supplied with provisions by sea from Sardinia, Sicily, and Italy. But being thus reduced to act on the defensive in the presence of a superior enemy, and not likely, without some powerful reinforcements from Italy, to make any further impression on Africa, he had recourse to a stratagem which, though amounting nearly to a breach of faith, was supposed to be allowed in war with an African enemy.

The combined armies of Carthage and Numidia lay in two separate encampments, and, it being winter, were lodged in huts covered with brushwood and the leaves of the palm. In these circumstances the Roman general formed a design to set fire to their camp, and in the midst of the confusion which that alarm might occasion, to attack them in the night. In order to gain a sufficient knowledge of the ground, and of the ways by which his emissaries must pass in the execution of this design, he entered into a negotiation, and affected to treat of conditions for terminating the war. His deputies, under this pretence, being freely admitted into the enemy's station, brought him minute information of their position, and of the avenues which led to different parts of their camp.

Scipio being possessed of these informations, broke off the treaty, advanced with his army in the night, and in many different places at once, set fire to Hasdrubal's camp. The flames, being easily caught by the dry materials, spread with the greatest rapidity. The Carthaginians supposing that these fires were accidental, and having no apprehension of the presence of an enemy, ran without arms to extinguish them: and the Numidians, with still less concern, left their huts to gaze on the scene, or to lend their assistance. In this state of security and confusion Scipio attacked and dispersed them with great slaughter;[1] and being, in consequence of this action, again master of the field, he returned to Utica, and renewed the siege or blockade of that place.

In such a surprise and defeat as the African armies had now received, they were likely to have lost their arms and their baggage, and to have nowhere sufficient numbers together to withstand an enemy; on this supposition, it had been already proposed at Carthage to have recourse to their last resort, the recalling of Hannibal from Italy. But this motion, upon a report from Hasdrubal and Syphax, that they were again arming and assembling their forces, and that they were joined by a recruit of four thousand men, newly arrived from Spain, was for some time laid aside These hopes, however, were speedily blasted by a second defeat which the combined army received before they were fully assembled, and by a revolution which ensued in the kingdom of Numidia, where Syphax, pursued by Massinissa and Lælius, was vanquished and driven from his kingdom, which from thenceforward became the possession of his rival, and a great accession of strength to the Romans. On this calamity Hasdrubal being threatened by the populace of Carthage with vengeance for his repeated miscarriages, and being aware of the relentless and sanguinary spirit of his countrymen, durst not trust himself in their hands; and in a species of exile, with a body of eight thousand men that adhered to him, withdrew from their service.

In this extremity there was no hope but in the presence of Hannibal; and expresses were accordingly sent both to Mago and himself, to hasten their return into Africa, with all the forces they could bring for the defence of their country.

Hannibal, it is probable, had for some time been prepared for this measure, having transports in readiness to embark his army; yet he is said to have received the order with some expressions of rage. "They have now accomplished," he said (speaking of the opposite faction at Carthage,) "what, by withholding from me the necessary supports in this war, they have long endeavoured to effect. They have wished to destroy the family of Barcas; and rather than fail in their aim, are willing to bury it at last under the ruins of their country."[2]

While the Carthaginians were thus driven to their last resource, Scipio advanced towards their city, and invested at once both Tunis and Utica, which, though at the distance of above thirty miles from each other, may be considered as bastions on the right and the left, which flanked and commanded the country which led to this famous place. His approach gave the citizens a fresh alarm, and seemed to bring their danger too near to suffer them to await the arrival of relief from Italy. It appeared necessary to stay the arm of the victor by a treaty; and thirty senators were accordingly deputed to sue for peace. The deputies, in their address to the Roman proconsul, laid the blame of the war upon Hannibal, supported, as they alleged, by a desperate faction who had adopted his wild designs. They entreated that the Romans would once more be pleased to spare a republic which was again brought to the brink of ruin by the precipitant counsels of a few of its members.

In answer to this abject request, Scipio mentioned the terms upon which he supposed that the Romans would be willing to treat of a peace. A cessation of arms was agreed to, and a negotiation commenced; but it was suddenly interrupted and prevented of its final effect by the arrival of Hannibal. This general, after many changes of fortune, having taken the necessary precautions to secure his retreat, in case he should be called off for the defence of Carthage; now in the seventeenth year of the war, and after he had supported himself sixteen years in Italy, by the

1 Polyb. lib. xiv. c. 5. Liv. lib. xxx. c. 6.

2 Liv. lib. xxx. c. 20.

sole force of his personal character and abilities, against the whole weight, institutions, resources, discipline, and national character of the Romans, transported his army from thence, landed at Hadrumetum, at a distance from any of the quarters occupied by the Romans, and drew to his standard all the remains of the lately vanquished armies of Carthage, and all the forces which the republic was yet in a state to supply.

U. C. 551.

This event produced a change in the counsels of Carthage, and inspired the people with fresh presumption. They now slighted the faith which they had lately engaged to Scipio, and seized on all the Roman vessels, which, trusting to the cessation of arms, had taken refuge in their bay. They even insulted the messenger whom the Roman general sent to complain of this outrage; and thus hostilities, after a very short truce, were renewed with redoubled animosity and rancour on both sides.

The people of Carthage, under dreadful apprehensions of becoming a prey to the Romans, sent a message to Hannibal, then at Hadrumetum, to hasten his march, requesting him to attack the enemy, and at any hazard to relieve the city from the dangers and hardships of a siege. To this message he made answer, that in affairs of state the councils of Carthage must decide; but in the conduct of war, the general who commands must judge of his opportunity to fight.

The forcing of Hannibal to evacuate Italy was a victory to Scipio; as this was the first fruit which he ventured to promise from the invasion of Africa. With this enemy, however, in his rear, it was not expedient to continue the attack of Tunis or Utica. He withdrew his army from both these places, and prepared to contend for the possession of the field.

The Carthaginian leader, having collected his forces at Hadrumetum, marched to the westward, intending to occupy the banks of the Bagrada, and from thence to observe and counteract the operations of his enemy. Scipio, intending to prevent him, or to occupy the advantageous ground on the upper Bagrada, took his route to the same country; and while both directed their march to Sicca, they met on the plains of Zama.

When the armies arrived on this ground, neither party was in condition to protract the war. Hannibal, whose interest it would have been to avoid any hazardous measures, and to tire out his enemy by delays, if he were in possession of his own country, or able to protect the capital from insult, was in reality obliged to risk the whole of its fortunes, in order to rescue it from the hands of the enemy, or to prevent their renewing the blockade.

Scipio was far advanced in an enemy's country, which was soon likely to be deserted by its natives, and exhausted of every means of subsistence; he was far removed from the sea, the principal and only secure source of any lasting supply; surrounded by enemies; a great army under Hannibal in his front; the cities of Utica, Carthage, and Tunis, with all the armed force that defended them, in his rear.

In such circumstances both parties probably saw the necessity of immediate action; and the Carthaginian general, sensible of the unequal stake he was to play, the safety of his country against the fortune of a single army whose loss would not materially affect the State from whence they came, chose to try the effect of a negotiation and for this purpose desired a personal interview with Scipio.

In compliance with this request, the Roman general put his army in motion, and the Carthaginians advancing at the same time, they halted at the distance of thirty stadia, or about three miles from each other. The generals, attended by a few horse, met on an eminence between their lines. Hannibal began the conference, by expressing his regret that the Carthaginians should have aimed at any conquests beyond their own coasts in Africa, or the Romans beyond those of Italy. "We began," he said, "with a contest for Sicily; we proceeded to dispute the possession of Spain, and we have each in our turns seen our native land overrun with strangers, and our country in danger of becoming a prey to its enemies. It is time that we should distrust our fortune, and drop an animosity which has brought us both to the verge of destruction. This language indeed may have little weight with you, who have been successful in all your attempts, and who have not yet experienced any reverse of fortune; but I pray you to profit by the experience of others. You now behold in me a person who was once almost master of your country, and who am now brought, at last, to the defence of my own. I encamped within five miles of Rome, and offered the possessions round the forum to sale. Urge not the chance of war too far. I now offer to surrender, on the part of Carthage, all her pretensions to Spain, Sardinia, Sicily, and every other island that lies between this continent and yours. I wish only for peace to my country, that she may enjoy undisturbed her ancient possessions on this coast; and I think that the terms I offer you are sufficiently advantageous and honourable to procure it."

To this address Scipio replied, "That the Romans had not been aggressors in the present or preceding wars with Carthage: that they strove to maintain their own rights, and to protect their allies; and that, suitably to these righteous intentions, they had been favoured by the justice of the gods: that no one knew better than himself the instability of human affairs, nor should be more on his guard against the chances of war. The terms," he said, "which you now propose might have been accepted of, had you offered them while yet in Italy, and had proposed, as a prelude to the treaty, to remove from thence; but now, that you are driven from every post, you propose to surrender; and are forced, not only to evacuate the Roman territory, but are stripped of part of your own. These concessions are no longer sufficient; they are no more than a part of the conditions already agreed to by your countrymen, and which they, on your appearance in Africa, so basely retracted. Besides what you now offer, it was promised on their part, that all Roman captives should be restored without ransom; that all armed ships should be delivered up; that a sum of five thousand talents should be paid, and hostages given by Carthage for the performance of all these articles.

"On the credit of this agreement we granted a cessation of arms, but were shamefully betrayed by the councils of Carthage. Now to abate any part of the articles which were then stipulated, would be to reward a breach of faith, and to in struct nations hereafter how to profit by perfidy. You may therefore be assured, that I will not so much as transmit to Rome any proposal that does not contain, as preliminaries, every article formerly stipulated, together with such additional concessions as may induce the Romans to renew the treaty. On any other terms than these, Carthage must vanquish, or submit at discretion."[1]

From this interview both parties withdrew with an immediate prospect of action; and on the following day, neither having any hopes of advantage from delay or surprise, came forth into the plain in order of battle.

Hannibal formed his army in three lines with their elephants in front.

Scipio drew forth his legions in their usual divisions, but somewhat differently disposed.

Hannibal had above eighty elephants, with which he proposed to begin the action. Behind these he formed the mercenary troops, composed of Gauls, Ligurians, and Spaniards. In a second line he placed the Africans and natives of Carthage; and in a third line, about half a quarter of a mile behind the first, he placed the veterans who had shared with himself in all the dangers and honours of the Italian war. He placed his cavalry in the wings opposite to those of the enemy.

Scipio posted Lælius with the Roman cavalry on his left, and Massinissa with the Numidian horse on his right. He placed the manipules, or divisions of the legions, not as usual, mutually covering their intervals, but covering each other from front to rear. His intention in this disposition was to leave continued avenues or lanes, through which the elephants might pass without disordering the columns. At the head of each line he placed the Velites, or irregular infantry, with orders to gall the elephants, and endeavour to force them back upon their own lines; or, if this could not be effected, to fly before them into the intervals of the heavy-armed foot, and, by the ways which were left open between the manipules, to conduct them into the rear. It being the nature of these animals, even in their wild state, to be the dupes of their own resentment, and to follow the hunter by whom they are galled into any snare that is prepared for them;[2] the design thus formed by Scipio to mislead them, accordingly proved successful. As soon as the cavalry began to skirmish on the wings, Hannibal gave the signal for the elephants to charge. They were received by a shower of missile weapons from the Roman light infantry, and, as usual, carried their riders in different directions. Some broke into their own line with considerable disorder, others fled between the armies and escaped by the flanks, and many, incited with rage, as Scipio had foreseen, pursued the enemy that galled them through the intervals of the Roman divisions quite out of the action; and in a little time the front of the two armies was cleared of these animals, and of all the irregulars who had skirmished between them in the beginning of the battle.

In the mean time the first and second line of Hannibal's foot had advanced, to profit by the impression which the elephants were likely to make. The third line still remained on its ground, and seemed to stand aloof from the action.

In this posture, the first line of the Carthaginian army, composed of Gauls and Ligurians, engaged with the Roman legions; and, after a short resistance, were forced back on the second line, who, having orders not to receive them, nor allow them to pass, presented their arms. The fugitives were accordingly massacred on both sides, and fell by the swords of their own party, or by those of the enemy.

The second line, consisting of the African and native troops of Carthage, had a similar fate; they perished by the hands of the Romans, or by those of their own reserve, who had orders to receive them on their swords, and turn them back, if possible, against the enemy.

Scipio, after so much blood had been shed, finding his men out of breath, and spent with hard labour, embarrassed with heaps of the slain, scarcely able to keep their footing on ground become slippery with mud and gore, and in these circumstances likely to be instantly attacked by a fresh enemy, who had yet borne no part in the contest, he endeavoured, without loss of time, to put himself in a posture to renew the engagement.

His cavalry, by good fortune, in these hazardous circumstances, were victorious on both the wings, and were gone in pursuit of the enemy. He ordered the ground to be cleared; and his columns, in the original form of the action, having been somewhat displaced, he ordered those of the first line to close to the centre; those of the second and third to divide, and, gaining the flanks, to form in a continued line with the front. In this manner, while the ground was clearing of the dead, probably by the Velites or irregular troops, he, with the least possible loss of time, and without any interval of confusion, completed his line to receive the enemy. An action ensued, which, being to decide the event of this memorable war, was likely to remain some time in suspense; when the cavalry of the Roman army, returning from the pursuit of the horse they had routed, fell on the flank of the Carthaginian infantry, and obliged them to give way.

Hannibal had rested his hopes of victory on the disorder that might arise from the attack of his elephants, and if this should fail, on the steady valour of the veterans, whom he reserved for the last effort to be made, when he supposed that the Romans, already exhausted in their conflict with the two several lines whom he sacrificed to their ardour in the beginning of the battle, might be unable to contend with the third, yet fresh for action and inured to victory. He was disappointed in the effect of his elephants, by the precaution which Scipio had taken in opening his intervals, and in forming continued lanes for their passage from front to rear; and of the effect of his reserve, by the return of the enemy's horse, while the action was yet undecided.[3] Having taken no measures to secure a retreat, nor to save any part of his army, he obstinately fought every minute of the day to the last; and when he could delay the victory of his enemy no longer, he quitted the field with a small party of horse, of whom many, overwhelmed with hunger and fatigue, having fallen by the way, he arrived with a few, in the course of two days and two nights, at Hadrumetum. Here he embarked and proceeded by sea to Carthage. His arrival convinced his countrymen of the extent of their loss. Seeing Hannibal without an army, they believed them-

1 Polyb. lib. xv. c. 6, 7, 8. 2 Vid. Buff Hist. Nat.

3 Polyb lib xv. c. 16.

selves vanquished; and, with minds unprovided with that spirit which supported the Romans when overthrown at Thrasimenus and Cannæ, were now desirous, by any concessions, to avert the supposed necessary consequences of their fate.

The riotous populace, that had so lately pursued with vengeance, and threatened to tear asunder the supposed authors of peace,[4] were now silent, and ready to embrace any terms that might be prescribed by the enemy. Hannibal, knowing how little his countrymen were qualified to contend with misfortune, confessed in the Senate, that he was come from deciding, not the event of a single battle, but the fate of a great war, and advised them to accept of the victor's terms.[5] They accordingly determined to sue for peace.

In the mean time the Roman army, in pursuit of its victory, was returned to the coast; and having received from Italy a large supply of stores and military engines, together with a reinforcement of fifty galleys, was in a condition, not only to resume the siege of Utica and Tunis, but likewise to threaten with a storm the capital itself; and, for this purpose, began to invest the town and block up the harbour.

Scipio being himself embarked, and conducting the fleet to its station, was met by a Carthaginian vessel that hoisted wreaths of olive and other ensigns of peace. This vessel had ten commissioners on board, who were authorized to declare the submission of Carthage, and to receive the victor's commands.

The ambition of Scipio might have inclined him to urge his victory to the utmost; that he might carry, instead of a treaty, the spoils of Carthage to adorn his triumph at Rome. But the impatience with which the consuls of the present and of the preceding year endeavoured to snatch from his hands the glory of terminating the war, may, with other motives, have induced him to receive the submission of the vanquished upon the first terms that appeared sufficiently honourable, and suited to the object of the commission with which he had been entrusted.

In allusion to this circumstance, he was heard to say, that Claudius, by his impatience to supplant him in this command, had saved the republic of Carthage.[6] But men seldom act from any single consideration; and Scipio is, in all probability, justly supposed to have had other and nobler motives than this jealousy of a successor. He is even said to have spared the rival of his country, in order to maintain the emulation of courage and of national virtue. This motive Cato, who had served under him in the capacity of quæstor, and who was not inclined to flatter, did him the honour to assign in a speech to the senate.[7]

Scipio, having appointed the Carthaginian commissioners to attend him at Tunis, prescribed the following terms:

That Carthage should continue to hold in Africa all that she had possessed before the war, and be governed by her own laws and institutions:

That she should make immediate restitution of all Roman ships or other effects taken in violation of the late truce:

Should release or deliver up all captives deserters, or fugitive slaves, taken or received during any part of the war:

Surrender the whole of her fleet, saving ten gallies of three tier of oars:

Deliver up all the elephants she then had in the stalls of the republic, and refrain from taming or breaking any more of those animals:

That she should not make war on any nation whatever without consent of the Romans:

That she should indemnify Massinissa for all the losses he had sustained in the late war:

And, to reimburse the Romans, pay a sum of ten thousand talents,[8] at the rate of two hundred talents a year for fifty years:

That the state should give hostages for the performance of these several articles, such as Scipio should select from the noblest families of Carthage, not under fourteen, nor exceeding thirty years of age:

And that, until this treaty should be ratified, they should supply the Roman forces in Africa with pay and provisions.

When these conditions were reported in the senate of Carthage, one of the members arose, and, in terms of indignation, attempted to dissuade the acceptance of them: but Hannibal, with the tone of a master, interrupted and commanded him silence. This action was resented by a general cry of displeasure; and Hannibal, in excuse of his rashness, informed the senate, that he had left Carthage while yet a child of nine years old; that he was now at the age of forty-five; and, after a life spent in camps and military operations, returned for the first time to bear his part in political councils; that he hoped they would bear with his inexperience in matters of civil form, and regard more the tendency than the manner of what he had done; that he was sensible the proposed terms of peace were unfavourable, but he knew not how else his country was to be rescued from her present difficulties; he wished to reserve her for a time in which she could exert her resolution with more advantage. He hoped that the senate would, in the present extremity, accept, without hesitation, and even without consulting the people, conditions which, though hard, were, notwithstanding, less fatal to the commonwealth than any one could have hoped for in the night that followed the battle of Zama.[9]

U. C. 552. The conditions were accordingly accepted, and deputies were sent to Rome with concessions, which in some measure stripped the republic of her sovereignty. The ratification of the treaty was remitted to Scipio, and the peace concluded on the terms he had prescribed.

Four thousand Roman captives were instantly released: five hundred galleys were delivered up and burnt: the first payment of two hundred talents was exacted, and, under the execution of this article, many members of the Carthaginian senate were in tears. Hannibal was observed to smile, and being questioned on this insult to the public distress, made answer, That a smile of scorn for those who felt not the loss of their country, until it affected their own interest, was an expression of sorrow for Carthage.

4 Appian de Bell. Punic. p. 31.
5 Polyb. lib. xv. c. 4—17. Liv. lib. xxx. c. 31.
6 Appian de Bell. Punic. p. 36. 7 Ibid.
8 Near two millions sterling.
9 Polyb. lib. xv. c. 18. Liv. lib. xxx. c. 37.

CHAPTER VI.

State of Rome at the Peace with Carthage—Wars with the Gauls—With the Macedonians—Battle of Cynocæphalæ—Peace—Freedom to Greece—Preludes to the War with Antiochus—Flight of Hannibal to that Prince—Antiochus passes into Europe—Dispositions made by the Romans—Flight of Antiochus to Asia—His Defeat at the Mountains of Sipylus—Peace and Settlement of Asia—Course of Roman Affairs at Home, &c.

IN the course of the war, which terminated in so distinguished a superiority of the Roman over the Carthaginian republic, the victors had experienced much greater distress than had, even in the last stage of the conflict, fallen to the share of the vanquished. The greater part of their territory, during a series of years, lay waste; was ruined in its habitations, plundered of its slaves and its cattle, and deserted of its people. The city itself was reduced to a scanty supply of provisions that threatened immediate famine.[1] Among other modes of taxation devised at this time, the monopoly of salt was established or renewed; but every public fund that was constituted in the ordinary way being insufficient, the state had recourse to the voluntary contribution of its members, and called for their plate and other ornaments of silver and gold to defray the expenses. They debased their silver coin by a great mixture of alloy, and farther reduced the copper Ass from its late coinage at two ounces to one.[2] The numbers of the people on the rolls, either by desertion or by the sword of the enemy, uncommonly fatal in such a series of battles, were reduced from two hundred and seventy thousand to nearly the half.[3]

In the musters and levies, no less than twelve colonies at once withheld their names, and refused their support. Yet, proof against the whole of these sufferings, the Romans maintained the conflict with a resolution which seemed to imply, that they considered the smallest concession as equivalent to ruin. In the farther exertion of this unconquerable spirit, when the pressure of this war was removed, their fortunes rose to a flood of prosperity and greatness, proportioned to the low ebb to which they seemed to have fallen in the course of it.

They joined, in Sicily, to their former possessions, the city of Syracuse, and the whole kingdom of Hiero. In Spain, they succeeded to all the possessions, to all the claims and pretensions of Carthage, and became masters of all that had been the subject of dispute in the war. They brought Carthage herself under contribution, and reduced her almost to the state of a province.

On the side of Macedonia and Illyricum, in their treaty with Philip and his allies, they retained to themselves considerable pledges, not only of security, but of power; and began to be considered in the councils of Greece, as the principal arbiters of the fortunes of nations.

In Italy, where their progress was still of greater consequence, they became more absolute masters than they had been before the war.—The cantons, which, in so general a defection of their other allies, had continued faithful to them, were fond of the merit they had acquired, and were confirmed in their attachment by the habits of zeal which they had exerted in so prosperous a cause. Those, on the contrary, who had revolted, or withdrawn their allegiance, were reduced to a state of submission more entire than they had formerly acknowledged; and the sovereignty of this whole country being, till now, precarious and tottering, derived, from the very storm which had shaken it, stability and force.

But, notwithstanding the splendour of such rapid advancement, and of the high military and political talents which procured it, if by any accident the career of the Romans had been stopt at the present era, their name, it is probable, would never have appeared on the record of polished nations, nor they themselves been otherwise known than as a barbarous dynasty, that fell a prey to some more fortunate pretenders to dominion and conquest.

The Romans, being altogether men of the sword, or of the state, made no application to letters or sedentary occupations. Cato is introduced by Cicero as saying, That it had been anciently the fashion at Roman feasts to sing heroical ballads in honour of their ancestors: but that this custom had been discontinued in his own time, and it is probable, from the great change which their language underwent in a few years, that they had no popular or established compositions in writing, or even in vulgar tradition, by which the uniformity of language has, in other instances, been longer preserved.—They had hitherto no historian, poet, or philosopher; and it was only now, that any taste began to appear for the compositions of such authors. Fabius, Ennius, and Cato, became the first historians of their country, and raised the first literary monuments of genius that were to remain with posterity.[4]

The inclination which now appeared for the learning of the Greeks was, by many, considered as a mark of degeneracy, and gave rise to the never-ending dispute, which, in this as in other nations, took place between the patrons of ancient and modern manners. The admirers of ancient times, being attached to what they received from their ancestors, were disposed to reject every new improvement, and seemed willing to stop the progress of ingenuity itself. The gay, and the fashionable, on the other hand, liked what was new; were fond of every change, and would ever adopt the latest invention as the model of propriety, elegance, and beauty.

To the simplicity of the Roman manners in other respects, and to the ability of the most accomplished councils of state, was joined a very

1 Polyb. Excerptæ Legationes.
2 Plin. Nat. Hist. lib. iii. c. iii.
3 These were probably the citizens, fit to carry arms, residing in the city; for it was not yet the practice to enrol those who did not offer their names at Rome.
4 In the sixth century of Rome

gross superstition, which led to many acts of absurdity and cruelty. In this particular it appears, that the conceptions of men are altogether unconnected with their civil and political, as well as military character; and that the rites they adopt, even when innocent, and the most admissible expressions of worship, do not deserve to be recorded for any other purpose, than to show how far they are arbitrary; and how little, in many instances, they are directed, even among nations otherwise the most accomplished, by any rule of utility, humanity, or reason.

A little time before the breaking out of the late war, the Roman senate, upon the report of a prophecy that the Gauls and the Greeks were to possess the city, ordered a man and a woman of each of those nations to be buried alive in the market-place; supposing, we may imagine, that, by this act of monstrous injustice and cruelty, they were to fulfil or elude the prediction.[5] They attended to the numberless prodigies that were annually collected, and to the charms that were suggested to avert the evils which those prodigies were supposed to presage, no less than they did to the most serious affairs of the commonwealth.[6] They frequently seemed to impute their distresses more to the neglect of superstitious rites, than to the misconduct of their officers, or to the superiority of their enemies. Fabius, who, by perseverance and steadiness, had the merit of restoring their affairs, was no less celebrated for his diligence in averting the effect of prodigies and unhappy presages, than he was for the conduct and ability of a cautious and successful commander.[7] Even Scipio is said to have been influenced by his dreams, and to have pretended to special revelations.

From such examples as these, we may learn the fallacy of partial representations of national character, and carefully to guard against drawing any inference from the defects or accomplishments which a people may exhibit of one kind, to establish those of another.

The peace with Carthage was introduced with some popular acts in favour of those who had suffered remarkably in the hardships and dangers of the war. Large quantities of corn that had been seized in the magazines of the enemy, were sold in the city at a low price, and a considerable distribution of land was made to numbers of the people in reward of their long and perilous services.

These precedents, however reasonable in the circumstances from which they arose, were the sources of great abuse; private citizens, in the sequel, were taught to rely on public gratuities, and were made to hope, that, in the midst of sloth and riot, they might subsist without care, and without industry. Soldiers were taught to expect extraordinary rewards for ordinary services; and ambitious leaders were instructed how to transfer the affection and the hopes of the legions from the republic to themselves.

The treaty with Carthage, while it terminated the principal war in which the Romans were engaged, left them at leisure to pursue a variety of quarrels, which still remained on their hands, rather than bestowed entire peace. The Insubres, and other Gaulish nations on the Po, although they had not taken the full advantage which the presence of Hannibal in Italy might have given them against the Romans, were unable to remain at peace, and were unwilling to acknowledge the sovereignty of any nation over their own. Having a Carthaginian exile, of the name of Hamilcar, at their head, they attempted again to dislodge the colonies of Cremona and Placentia; and on that side, with various events for some years, furnished occupation to the arms of the republic.

Philip, notwithstanding the treaty of peace, which, about three years before, he had concluded with the Romans, had lately supplied the Carthaginians with an aid of four thousand men, and a sum of money. Of the men he had sent to the assistance of Carthage, many had been taken at the battle of Zama, and detained as captives. Trusting, however, to the authority of his crown, he sent, during the dependence of the treaty between the Romans and Carthaginians, a message to demand the enlargement of those Macedonian captives. To this message the senate replied with disdain, that the king of Macedonia appeared to desire a war and should have it.

The people, nevertheless, wearied and exhausted with the late contest, engaged in this war with uncommon reluctance. The senate, they thought, was directed by the ambition of a few members, who never ceased to seek for new subjects of triumph, and for fresh occasion of military honours. But notwithstanding their aversion to enter into a war upon these motives, they were persuaded to give their consent upon a representation of the great progress which was making by the king of Macedonia, and the supposed necessity of carrying the war into his own country, in order to check or prevent his designs upon Italy.

Philip, from being the head of a free confederacy, in which the Achæans, and many other states of Greece, were united, aspired to become the despotic sovereign of that country; and, either by insinuation or force, had made himself master of most places of consequence round the Ægean sea, whether in Europe or Asia. Upon the death of Ptolemy Philopater, and the succession of an infant son of that prince to the throne of Egypt, Philip had entered into a treaty with Antiochus, king of Syria, to divide between them the possessions of the Egyptian monarchy; and in order to be ready for his more distant operations, was busy in reducing the places which still held out against him in Greece, and in its neighbourhood.

For this purpose he sent an army with orders to take possession of Athens, and was himself employed in the siege of Abydos. The Athenians sent a message to Rome to sue for protection. "It is no longer a question," said the consul Sulpicius, in his harangue to the people, "whether you will have a war with Philip, but whether you will have that war in Macedonia or in Italy. If you stay until Philip has taken Athens, as Hannibal took Saguntum, you may then see him arrive in Italy, not after a march of five months, and after the passage of tremendous mountains, but after a voyage of five days from his embarkation at Corinth."

These considerations decided the resolution of the Roman people for war; and the officers, yet remaining in Sicily at the head of the sea and the land forces that had been employed against Carthage had orders, without touching on Italy, to make sail for the coast of Epirus.

5 Plutarch in Vit. Marcell. 6 Vide Liv. passim.
7 Plutarch. in Vit. Fab. Max.

U. C. 552. The consul Sulpicius was destined to command in that country. He found, upon his arrival, that Attalus, the king of Pergamus, and the republic of Rhodes, had taken arms to oppose the progress of Philip. In concert with these allies, and in conjunction with the Dardanians and other cantons who joined him on the frontiers of Macedonia, the Roman consul was enabled to relieve and to protect the Athenians. But the other states of Greece, though already averse to the pretensions of Philip, and impatient of his usurpations; even the Etolians, though the most determined opponents of this prince, seemed to be undecided on this occasion, and deferred entering into any engagement with the Romans. The reputation of the Macedonian armies was still very high; and it was doubtful, whether these Italian invaders, considered as an upstart and a barbarous power, might be able to protect the states that declared for them against the vengeance of so great a king.[1]

The two first years of the war elapsed without any decisive event. Philip took post on the mountains that separate Epirus from Thessaly, and effectually prevented the Romans from penetrating any farther. But, in the third year, Titus Quintius Flamininus, yet a young man under thirty years of age, being consul, and destined to this command, brought to an immediate issue a contest which, till then, had been held in suspense.

The Roman legion, except in its first encounters with Pyrrhus, had never measured its force, or compared its advantages with any troops formed on the Grecian model, and, to those who reasoned on the subject, may have appeared greatly inferior to the Macedonian phalanx. One presumption, indeed, had appeared in favour of the legion, that both Pyrrhus and Hannibal thought proper to adopt its weapons, though there is no account of their having imitated the line of battle or form of its manipules.

The phalanx was calculated to present a strong and impenetrable front, supported by a depth of column, which might be varied occasionally to suit with the ground. The men were armed with spears of twenty-one or twenty-four feet in length. The five first ranks could level and carry their points to the front of the column. The remainder rested their spears obliquely on the shoulders of those that were before them; and in this posture, formed a kind of shed to intercept the missiles of the enemy; and, with their pressure, supported, or urged, the front of their own column.

In the shock of the phalanx and legion, it is computed, that every single man in the front of the legion, requiring a square space of six feet in which to ply his weapons, and acting with his buckler and sword, had ten points of the enemy's spears opposed to him:[2] nevertheless, the strength of the phalanx being entirely collected in front, and depending on the closeness of its order; when attacked on the flank or rear, when broken or taken by surprise, and unformed, it was easily routed, and was calculated only for level ground, and the defence of a station accessible only in one direction.

1 Plutarch in Vit. Flamin. p. 407. 2 Polyb. lib. xvii. c. 23.

The Roman legion could act on its front, its flank, or its rear. Each division, or manipule, and even the men that composed it, could act apart; and, if they had space enough to ply their weapons, could scarcely be taken by surprise, or be made to suffer for want of a determinate order. It was serviceable, therefore, upon any ground, and, except on the front of the phalanx, had an undoubted advantage over that body.

In its ordinary form, the legion made its attack by separate divisions, at considerable intervals; and this mode of attack had a tendency to break and disjoin the front of the phalanx. The divisions of the second line were made to face the intervals of the first, in order to take advantage of any disorder that might arise from the impression made on the enemy, whether they repulsed and pursued, or gave way to the divisions that attacked them.

Such are reasonings which occurred to military men, at least after the events of the present war. In the mean time the Romans, in whatever degree they comprehended this argument, had sufficient confidence in their own weapons, and in their loose order, to encounter the long spear and compacted force of their enemy.

When Flamininus arrived in Epirus, Philip received him in a rugged pass, where the Aous bursts from the mountains that separate Epirus from Thessaly. This post was strong, and could be defended even by irregular troops; but the phalanx, in this place, had none of its peculiar advantages; the Romans got round it upon the heights, and obliged the king of
U. C. 555. Macedonia to retire. He fled through Thessaly, and, to incommode the enemy in their attempts to pursue him, laid waste the country as he passed.

The flight of Philip determined the Etolians to take part in the war against him; and the Roman general, after the operations of the campaign, being to winter in Phocis on the gulf of Corinth, found, that the greater part of the Achæan states were likewise disposed to join him. He took advantage of this disposition, and got possession of all the towns in the Peloponnesus, except Corinth and Argos, which hitherto had been in alliance with the enemy.

In the following spring, Philip, having with great industry collected and disciplined the forces of his kingdom, received Flamininus in Thessaly. The armies met in the neighbourhood of Pheræ; but the country, being interspersed with gardens, and cut with plantations and hedges, the king declined a battle, and withdrew. Flamininus, knowing that he had magazines at Scotusa, supposed that he was gone towards that place, and followed by a route that was separated from that of the king by a ridge of hills. In the first day's march, the Romans and Macedonians were hid from each other by the heights; on the second day they were covered by a thick fog, which hindered them from seeing distinctly even the different parts of their own armies.

The scouts and advanced parties on both sides, had, about the same time, ascended the heights, to gain some observation of their enemy. They met by surprise, and could not avoid an engagement. Each party sent for support to the main body of their respective armies. The Romans had begun to give way, when a reinforcement arrived, that enabled them in their turn, to press on the enemy, and to recover the height from which they had been forced. Philip was determined not to hazard his phalanx on that unfavourable ground, broken and interspersed with little hills; which, on account of their figure, were called the Cynocephalæ.[3] He sent, nevertheless, all his horse and irregular infantry to extricate his advanced party, and to draw them off with honour. Upon their arrival, the advantage came to be on the side of the Macedonians; and the Roman irregulars were forced from the hills in the utmost disorder. The cry of victory was carried back to the camp of the king. His courtiers exclaimed that now was the time to urge a flying enemy, and to complete his advantage. The king hesitated, but could not resist the general voice. He ordered the phalanx to move; and he himself at the head of the right wing, while his left was marching in column, had arrived and formed on the hill.—On his way to this ground, he was flattered with recent tracts of the victory which had been gained by his troops.

Flamininus, at the same time, alarmed at the defeat of his light infantry, and seeing a kind of panic likely to spread through the legions, put the whole army in motion, and advanced to receive his flying parties. In that point of time the fog cleared up, and showed the right of the Macedonian phalanx already formed upon the height.

Flamininus hastily attacked this body, and being unable to make any impression, gave up the day, on that quarter, for lost. But, observing that the enemy opposite to his right were not yet come to their ground, he instantly repaired to that wing, and, with his elephants and light infantry, supported by the legions, attacked them before the phalanx was formed, and put them to flight.

In this state of the action, a tribune of the victorious legion, being advanced in pursuit of the enemy, as they fled beyond the flank of their own phalanx on the right, took that body in the rear; and, by this fortunate attempt, in so critical a moment, completed the victory in all parts of the field.

Thus Philip, if his phalanx had any advantage over the legion of the Romans, had not, in two successive encounters, been able to avail himself of it; and it may well be supposed, that, in the movements of armies, which often require them to act on varieties of ground, the chances were greatly in favour of the more versatile body.[4]

From this field the king of Macedonia fled with a mind already disposed not to urge the fate of the war any farther. He retired to the passes of the mountains that surround the valley of Tempe, and from thence sent a message to the Roman general with overtures of peace.

It was a fortunate circumstance in the manners and policy of the Romans, that the same motives of ambition which urged the rulers of the state to war, likewise, on occasion, inclined the leaders of armies to peace, made them admit from an enemy the first offers of submission, and embrace any terms on which they could for themselves lay claim to a triumph.

The prayer of the republic, in entering on a war, included three objects, safety, victory, and enlargement of territory.[5] Every general endeavoured to obtain these ends for his country; but, in proportion as he approached to the completion of his wishes, he became jealous of his successor, and desirous to terminate the war before any other should come to snatch out of his hands the trophies he had won. This people appeared, therefore, on most occasions, willing to spare the vanquished, and went to extremities only by degrees, and urged by the ambition of successive leaders, who, each in his turn, wished to make some addition to the advantages previously gained to his country. At the same time, the state, when furnished with a fair pretence for reducing a province to subjection, made the most effectual arrangements to accomplish this purpose.

Flamininus, on the present occasion, encouraged the advances that were made to him by Philip, granted a cessation of arms, gave him an opportunity to continue his applications for peace at Rome, and forwarded the messenger whom he sent on this business. The senate, on being informed that the king of Macedonia cast himself entirely on the mercy and justice of the Romans, named ten commissioners to be joined with Flamininus, and to determine, in presence of the other parties concerned in the war, what were to be the terms on which peace should be granted.

U. C. 557.

The time was not yet come for the Romans to lay hold of any possessions beyond the sea of Ionia. They had passed into that country as the protectors of Athens, were now satisfied with the title of deliverers of Greece; and, under pretence of setting the republics of that quarter free, detached them from the Macedonian monarchy; but, in this manner, made the first step towards conquest, by weakening their enemy, and by stripping him of great part of that power with which he had been able to resist them in the late war.

They obliged the king of Macedonia to withdraw his garrisons from every fortress in Greece, and to leave every Grecian city, whether of Europe or Asia, to the full enjoyment of its own independence and separate laws.

To secure the effects of this treaty, they obliged him to surrender all his ships of war, except one galley, on which, it was said, were mounted sixteen tier of oars, requiring a height above the water, and dimensions in every part, more fitted for ostentation than wieldiness or use.

They made him reduce his ordinary military establishment to five hundred men, and forbade him entirely the use of elephants.

For themselves, they desired only to have the Roman captives restored, deserters delivered up, and a sum of one thousand talents to reimburse the expense of the war.[6]

By this treaty the Romans not only weakened their enemy, but acquired great accessions of reputation and general confidence. They announced themselves as protectors of all free nations; and in this character took an ascendant, which, even over the states they had rescued from foreign usurpations, by degrees might rise into sovereignty and a formal dominion.

To give the greater solemnity to the gift of liberty which they made to the Grecian states, they had this act of splendid munificence proclaimed at the Isthmus of Corinth, in presence of great multitudes from every part of Greece met to solemnize the ordinary games; and, in return,

3 The name implies, that these h... resembled the head of a dog.

4 Polyb. lib. xvii. c. 22.

5 Liv. lib. xxxi. c. 5.

6 Liv. lib. xxxiii. c. 51.

were extolled by the flatterers of their power, or the dupes of their policy, as the common restorers of freedom to mankind.

The Romans hastened the completion of the treaty, by which they disarmed the king of Macedonia, upon having received information that Antiochus, king of Syria, was in motion with a mighty force, and, without declaring his intentions, made sail towards Europe. This prince succeeded to the kingdom of Syria a few years before Ptolomy Philopater began to reign in Egypt, or Philip in Greece; and was nearly of the same age with those princes. In his youth he waged war with the kingdom of Egypt for the possession of Cælo-Syria, and with the Satraps or governors of his own provinces, who attempted to render themselves independent, and to dismember his kingdom. His success in reuniting all the members of his own monarchy, put him in possession of a great empire, which reached from the extremities of Armenia and Persia to Sardis and the seas of Greece. The splendour of his fortunes procured him the title of Antiochus the Great. The crown of Egypt had been, for some time, the principal object of his jealousy and of his ambition. He had made an alliance with Philip, in which the common object of the parties was to avail themselves of the minority of Ptolomy: but he was not aware, in time, how much the king of Macedonia stood in need of his support against the Romans; or how much it was his interest to preserve that kingdom as a barrier against the encroachments of an ambitious people, who now began to direct their views to the East He advanced, however, though now too late, by the coast of Asia to the Hellespont, with a fleet and an army rather destined for observation, than for any decided part in a war which was brought to a conclusion about the time of his arrival in those parts.

At Lysimachia, the Roman deputies, who were charged with the adjustment and execution of the late treaty, met with Antiochus, and remonstrated against some of his proceedings on the coast of Asia, as affecting the possessions both of Philip and of Ptolomy. They complained of his present invasion of Europe with a hostile force. "The Romans," they said, "had rescued the Greeks from Philip, not to deliver them over to Antiochus." They demanded a restitution of all the towns he had taken from Ptolomy, and enjoined him to refrain from any attempts on the freedom of Greece.

To these remonstrances and requisitions the king of Syria with scorn replied, That he knew the extent of his rights, and was not to be taught by the Romans: that they were busy in setting bounds to the ambition of other states, but set no bounds to their own; advised them to confine their views to the affairs of Italy, and to leave those of Asia to the parties concerned.

During the conferences which were held on these subjects, each of the parties, without communicating what they heard to the others, received report of the death of Ptolomy, the infant king of Egypt; and they separated from each other, intent on the evils to be apprehended, or the benefits to be reaped, from this event.

This report, in which both parties were soon after undeceived,[1] occasioned the return of Antiochus into Syria, and suspended for some time a war which he was disposed to carry into Egypt.

Under pretence of observing the motions of that prince, the Romans, although they had professed an intention to evacuate the Greek cities, still kept possession of Demetrias, a convenient seaport in Thessaly, and of Chalcis on the straits of Eubœa; and Flamininus, under pretence of restraining the violence of Nabis, the tyrant of Lacedæmon, and of restoring the tranquillity of that country,[2] still remained with an army in the Peloponnesus.

While the Romans were carrying their fortunes with so high a hand in this part of the world, and defeating armies hitherto deemed invincible, they received a considerable check in Spain.

That country had been recently divided into two provinces; and though now possessed by the Romans, without the competition of any foreign rival, it continued to be held by a very difficult and precarious tenure, that of force, opposed to the impatience and continual revolts of a fierce and numerous people.

Spain had already furnished to Italy its principal supplies of silver and gold. At every triumph obtained in that country, the precious metals were brought in considerable quantities to the treasury of Rome; but were purchased for the most part with the blood of her legions, and led her into a succession of wars, in which she experienced defeat as well as victory. About the time that Flamininus had terminated the war in Macedonia, the Proconsul Sempronius, in the nearer province of Spain, was defeated with the loss of many officers of rank. He himself was wounded in action, and soon after died.

Even the Roman possessions in Italy were not yet fully recovered from the troubles that had arisen in the time of the late war with Carthage. The Gaulish nations on the Po still continued in a state of hostility. The slaves, of which the numbers had greatly increased in Etruria, and other parts of the country, being mostly captives taken from enemies inured to arms and to violence, interrupted their servitude with frequent and dangerous insurrections. Having persons among them, who had been accustomed to command as well as to obey, they often deserted from their masters, formed into regular bodies, and encountered the armies of the republic in battle.[3]

The ridge of the Appenines beyond the confines of Etruria and the Roman frontier, still harboured fierce and numerous tribes known by the name of Ligurians and Gauls, who not only often and long defended their own mountains and woods, but likewise frequently invaded the territory of the Romans. Here, or in Spain, during the recess of other wars, there was a continual service for the consuls and prætors, and a continual exercise to the legions. The state, nevertheless, though still occupied in this manner with petty enemies and desultory wars, never lost sight of the great objects of its jealousy, from whom were to be apprehended a more regular opposition, and better concerted designs against its power. Among these, the Carthaginians were not likely to continue longer at peace than until they recovered their strength, or had the prospect of some powerful support.—Antiochus, possessed of all the resources of Asia, was ready to join with

1 Liv. lib. xxxiii. c. 41.

2 Liv. lib. xxxiii. c. 43.

3 Ibid lib. xxviii. c. 36

this or any other state that was inclined to check the advancement of the Roman power.

U. C. 558. About a year after the conclusion of the war with Philip, the Romans received intelligence, that the Carthaginians had entered into a correspondence with Antiochus; and as their supposed implacable enemy, Hannibal, was then in one of the first offices of state at Carthage, it was not doubted that the secret intrigues of those parties were hostile to Rome. It was determined, therefore, to send a proper commission into Africa, under pretence of an amicable mediation, in some differences that subsisted between Massinissa and the people of Carthage; but with injunctions to the commissioners to penetrate, if possible, the designs of the Carthaginians; and, if necessary, to demand that Hannibal, the supposed author of a dangerous conspiracy against the peace of both the republics should be delivered up.

This great man, from the termination of the late war, had acquitted himself, in the political departments, to which he had been appointed, with an integrity and ability worthy of his high reputation as a soldier; but his reformations in a corrupted state had procured him enemies at home, not less dangerous than those he had encountered abroad.[4] Upon the arrival of the Roman deputies, he suspected that the commission regarded himself, and made no doubt that a faction whose ambition he had restrained, and many particular persons whom he had recently incensed by the reformation of certain abuses in which they were interested, would gladly seize that opportunity to rid themselves of a powerful enemy, and from fear or some other motives, prevail on a corrupted people to deliver him up to the Romans. It is said, that he had been long prepared for an emergence of this sort, and, without any embarrassment, appeared, upon the arrival of these messengers, in all the functions of his public character; but at night withdrew to the coast, and set sail for Asia.[5] He was received by Antiochus at Ephesus, and treated as a person worthy to direct the councils of a great king; an office too much exposed to envy for the favourites of a court, or even for the prince himself long to endure.

From this time forward the king of Syria, supposed to be governed by the counsels of Hannibal, became the principal object of attention and of jealousy at Rome; and though he seemed to remain in tranquillity during about three years after the acquisition of this formidable counsellor, yet it was not doubted that the first violent storm was to burst from that quarter.

Flamininus had, during the greater part of this interval, remained in Greece; had been occupied in settling the affairs of that country, and in observing the Etolians, who, being dissatisfied with the late peace, endeavoured to raise a spirit of discontent against the Romans. He made war at the same time against Nabis the tyrant of Lacedæmon; and though he failed in his attempt to force this famous usurper in his own capital, he obliged him to evacuate Argos, and to cede all his possessions on the coast. By these means he removed all the dangers with which any of the states of the Achæan league had been threatened, and restored them to the full possession of their freedom.

To leave no ground of jealousy or distrust in Greece, Flamininus persuaded the Roman commissioners to evacuate Demetrias, Chalcis, and Corinth, which they were disposed to retain in the prospect of a war with Antiochus; and having thus concluded the affairs that were entrusted to him, he returned into Italy, and made his entry at Rome in a triumphal procession, which lasted three days, with a splendid display of spoils, captives, and treasure.[6]

All the troubles of Greece, at the departure of Flamininus, seemed to be composed; these appearances, however, were but of short duration. Nabis was impatient under his late concessions; and flattering himself that the Romans would not repass the sea merely to exclude him from the possession of a few places of little consequence on the coast of the Peloponnesus, began to employ insinuation, corruption, and open force, in order to recover the towns he had lost. In this design he was encouraged by the Etolians, who flattered him with the hopes of support, not only from themselves, but likewise from Antiochus, and even from Philip; all of whom had an evident interest in repressing the growing power of the Italian republic. The Etolians had expected, at the close of the war with Philip, to come into the place of that prince, as the head of all the Grecian confederacies, and to have a principal share in the spoils of his kingdom. They urged the Roman commissioners to the final suppression of that monarchy; and, being disappointed in all their hopes, complained of the Romans, as bestowing upon others the fruits of a victory which had been obtained chiefly by their means, and as having, under the pretence of setting the Greeks at liberty, reduced that country into a weak and disjointed state, which might in any future period render it an easy prey to themselves.

Flamininus accordingly had, in all his measures for the settlement of Greece, found from this people a warm and obstinate resistance. He found them endeavouring to form a powerful confederacy against the Romans, and for this purpose engaged in intrigues with Nabis, Philip, and Antiochus; applying to each of them in terms suited to the supposed injuries they had severally received in the late war, or in the negotiations that followed.

At the conclusion of the peace with Philip, Antiochus thinking himself by the effect of that treaty aggrieved, in respect to the freedom granted to some cantons in Thrace, on which he derived a claim from his ancestors, sent an embassy to Rome with remonstrances on that subject. The Romans made answer, in the capacity which they had assumed of the deliverers of Greece, that they would oppose every attempt to enslave any Grecian settlement; and as they had no designs on Asia, they expected that the king of Syria would not intermeddle in the concerns of Europe. While they gave this answer to the ambassador of Antiochus, they resolved under pretence of treating with the king, to send commissioners, in their turn, to observe his motions.

The famous Scipio Africanus is mentioned by some historians as having been of this commission, and as having had some conversations with Hannibal, which are recorded to the honour of both. Livy, however, seems to reject these particulars as fabulous, while he admits that the apparent in-

4 Liv. lib. xxxiii. c. 45—49.

5 Ibid. c. 46—49.

6 Liv. lib. xxxiv. c. 52.

timacy of Hannibal with the Roman commissioners, very much diminished the part which this formidable counsellor held in the confidence of the king.[1]

At this time it became known that Antiochus was meditating the invasion of Italy as well as of Greece; that the first of these objects was to be committed to Hannibal, who undertook to prevail on the republic of Carthage to take a principal share in the war; and that, for this purpose, he had sent a proper person to concert measures with his party at Carthage; but the intrigue being discovered, the Carthaginians, in order to exculpate themselves, sent an account of it to Rome.

Before this intelligence had been received, the Roman commissioners were set out for Asia, and, according to their instructions, passed through Pergamus to consult with Eumenes the sovereign of that kingdom, who having reason to dread the power of Antiochus employed all his credit to engage the Romans in a war with that prince. They had an audience of the king of Syria at Apamea, and a conference afterwards, on the object of their commission, with a principal officer of his court at Ephesus. This minister made no scruple to charge the Romans with the real designs of ambition, which they endeavoured to disguise under the pretence of procuring the liberties of Greece. "Your conduct," he said, "where you are in a condition to act without disguise, is a much better evidence of your intention, than any professions you may think proper to make in Greece or in Asia, where, by assuming a popular character, you have so many parties to reconcile to your interest. Are not the inhabitants of Naples and of Rhegium Greeks, as well as those of Lampsacus and Smyrna? You are extremely desirous to set the Greeks at liberty from the dominion of Antiochus and Philip, but have no remorse in subjecting them to your own."

The deputies of the cities whose interest was in question were present at these conferences, and each pleaded the cause of his country; but without any other effect than that of convincing the parties concerned, that a war could not long be avoided. The Romans, alarmed by the intelligence received from Carthage during the dependance of this conference, had already begun to prepare for hostilities; and upon the report of their commissioners from Asia, still continued to augment their forces by sea and by land. Under pretence of repressing the violences committed by Nabis, they ordered one army into Greece, and stationed a second on the coast of Calabria and Apulia, in order to support the operations of the first.

The Romans had reason to consider the Etolians as enemies, and even to distrust the intentions of many of the republics lately restored to their liberty, who began to surmise, that under the pretence of being relieved from the dominion of Philip, they were actually reduced to a state of dependance on Rome.

To obviate the difficulties which from these surmises might arise among the Grecian republics, the Roman senate sent a fresh commission into that country, requiring those who were named in it to act under the direction of Flamininus, the late deliverer of Greece. These commissioners found the principal cities of that country variously affected: a general meeting of the States being called to receive them at Demetrias, they were, by some of the parties present at this meeting, reproached with a design, under pretence of restoring the Greeks to their liberties, of separating them from every power that was fit to protect them; and they were likewise reproached with a design of establishing their own tyranny, under pretence of opposing that of every other state.

This species of blasphemy, uttered against a power which the majority of those who were present affected to revere, raised a great ferment in the council; and the persons who had thus ventured to insult the Romans being threatened with violence, were forced to withdraw from Demetrias, and to take refuge in Etolia. The remaining deputies of Greece endeavoured to pacify the Roman commissioners, or at least entreated them that they would not impute to so many different nations, what was no more than the frenzy of a few individuals.

The Etolians had already invited Antiochus to pass into Europe. The measure was accordingly under deliberation in the council of this prince. Hannibal warmly recommended the invasion of Italy as the most effectual blow that could be struck at the Romans. "At home," he said, "their force is still composed of disjointed materials, which will break into pieces when assailed by the immediate touch of an enemy; and the most effectual power that can be raised up against them, is that which may be formed from the ruins of their own empire. But if you allow them to remain in quiet possession of Italy, and to stretch out the arms of that country to a distance, their resources are endless, and their strength irresistible." He made an offer of himself for this service, demanding a hundred galleys, ten thousand foot, and a thousand horse. With this armament he proposed to present himself on the coast of Africa, and from what further reinforcements or supplies he could derive from Carthage, to effect his descent upon Italy.

These counsels, however, were given in vain. Hannibal, as a person likely to reap all the glory of every service in which he bore any part, was become an object of jealousy to the court of Antiochus, and to the king himself. His advice being received with more aversion than respect, served to determine the king against every measure he proposed. "Such a monarch," it was said by the courtiers, "could not be under any necessity to employ foreign aid or direction:—his own force was sufficient to overcome the Romans in any part of the world:—the recovery of Greece must be the first object of his arms:—the people of that country, whenever his galleys appeared, would crowd to the shores to receive him:—the Etolians were already in arms for this purpose:—Nabis was impatient to recover the possessions of which he had been stripped by the Romans:—Philip must eagerly fly to his standard, and embrace every opportunity to revenge the indignities which had been lately put upon himself and his kingdom."[2]

U. C. 562. Flattered with these expectations, Antiochus set sail for Europe with ten thousand foot, some elephants, and a body of horse. He was received at De-

1 Liv lib. xxxv. c. 14

2 Liv. lib. xxxv c 18. et 42.

metrias with acclamations of joy; but soon after, in the sequel, came to understand that his allies in that country had sent for him to bear the burden of the war, and were devising how they should reap for themselves the advantages that might be made to arise from it.

The Etolians, at whose instance Antiochus had come into Greece, were still divided. One party among them contended for peace, and alleged that the presence of the king of Syria was a fortunate circumstance, as it might give them an opportunity to negotiate with greater advantage. Another party contended for immediate war; insisting that force alone could obtain any equitable terms from such a party as that they had to do with.

Flamininus was present in the assembly of Etolia when these debates took place relating to the resolution for peace or war with the Romans. He observed to the party who contended for war, that, before they proceeded to this extremity, they ought to have made their representations at Rome, and to have waited for an answer from thence. "We shall make our representations, and demand our answer," said a principal person in the assembly, still thinking of a descent upon Italy, to be effected by Hannibal, "perhaps where we are least expected, on the banks of the Tiber."[3]

The resolution for war with the Romans was accordingly taken in this assembly, and Antiochus was declared head of the confederacy to be formed for mutual support in the conduct of it. This prince endeavoured to obtain a declaration to the same effect from the Achæans and Bœotians; but being disappointed in his application to those states, he left part of his forces at Demetrias, and he himself having negotiated his admission at Chalcis on the Straits of Eubœa, retired, as if he had come to act upon the defensive, behind the Euripus, and established his court at that place for the winter.

Mean time the Romans prepared themselves as for a struggle of great difficulty, and probably of long duration.[4] They considered the abilities of Hannibal, employed to conduct the forces of Asia, as a sufficient ground of alarm. Their first object was to guard Italy and their other possessions. An army of observation was for this purpose stationed at Tarentum. A numerous fleet was ordered to protect the coast. The prætors and other officers of state, with proper forces under their command, had charge of the different districts of Italy that were suspected of inclining to the enemy, or of being disaffected to the commonwealth. The instructions given to these officers, were, to observe what was passing in the several quarters to which they were sent, but to avoid every occasion of animosity or tumult that might open a way for the admission of an enemy, or show an invader where to direct his attack.

Having made these dispositions for their own security, they proceeded to form an army which was to act offensively, and to fix the scene of the war in their enemy's country. Bæbius, a prætor of the preceding year, under pretence of opposing Nabis, who had renewed the war in the Peloponnesus, had already passed into Epirus with a considerable force. Acilius Glabrio, one of the consuls of the present year, to whose lot this province had fallen, was understood to have in charge the farther preparations that were making for a war in that country, and hastened the assembling of an army and fleet sufficient to disconcert the measures of the parties that were supposed to be forming against the Romans.

The usual tithes of corn were ordered from Sardinia, and double tithes from Sicily, to supply the army in Epirus. Commissaries likewise were sent to Carthage and Numidia, in order to purchase supplies from thence. And with such a sense of its importance did the Romans enter on this war, that the consul Cornelius issued an edict, prohibiting all senators, and all those who were entitled to be admitted into the senate, to absent themselves from Rome above one day at a time, and requiring that no more than five senators should on the same day be absent from the city.

The equiqment of the fleet was retarded by a dispute that arose with eight of the maritime colonies or sea-ports, who pretended to a right of exemption from the present service. But their plea, upon an appeal to the tribunes, and a reference from them to the senate, was over-ruled.

Antiochus passed the winter at Chalcis in a manner too common with princes of a mean capacity, who put every matter of personal caprice on the same footing with the affairs of state. Being enamoured of a Grecian beauty, he employed the attention of his court on feasts and processions, devised for her entertainment, and to enhance his pleasures. His reputation declined, and his forces made no progress either in numbers or discipline.

In the spring he lost some time in forming confederacies with petty states, which are ever under the necessity of declaring themselves for the prevailing power, and who change their side with the reverses of fortune. Having traversed the country from Bœotia to Arcania, negotiating treaties with such allies as these, he had passed into Thessaly, and had besieged Larissa, when the Roman prætor began to advance from Epirus.

After the contending parties had thus taken the field, and the armies of Rome and of Syria were about to decide the superiority on the frontiers of Macedonia, Philip seemed to remain in suspense, having yet made no open declaration to which side he inclined. He had felt the arms of the Romans, and had reason to dread those of Antiochus.

The princes who divided the Macedonian empire were not only rivals in power, they were in some degree mutual pretenders to the thrones which they severally occupied; Philip, probably considering Antiochus, in this capacity, as the principal object of his jealousy, took his resolution to declare for the Romans; and having accordingly joined the prætor on the confines of Thessaly, their vanguard advanced to observe the position and motions of the enemy.

Antiochus, upon the junction of these forces, thought proper to raise the siege of Larissa.— From this time forward he seemed to have dropped all his sanguine expectations of conquest in Europe, was contented to act on the defensive, and when the Roman consul arrived in Epirus, and directed his march towards Thessaly, he took post at the Straits of Thermopylæ, intending to shut up this passage into Greece; but being dislodged from thence, his army was routed, the greater part of it perished in the flight, and he

3 Liv. lib. xxxv. c. 33. 4 Appian Syriacæ, p. 95.

himself, with no more than five hundred men, escaped to Chalcis, his former retreat in Eubœa, from whence he soon after set sail for Asia.

Upon the flight of Antiochus, the Etolians alone remained in the predicament of open enemies to the Romans. They were yet extremely irresolute and distracted in their councils. After having brought the king of Syria into Europe, they had not supported him with a sufficient force; and now, upon his departure, being sensible of their danger from the Romans, a powerful enemy whom they had greatly provoked, they endeavoured to persuade the king to return; representing to him how much he was concerned to furnish that arrogant people with a sufficient occupation in Greece, to prevent their passing into Asia. They at the same time made offers of pacification and of submission to the Romans, but were received in a manner which gave them no hopes of being able to palliate the offence they had given. The consul advanced into their country, laid siege to Naupactus, and having reduced that place and the whole nation to great distress, agreed to a cessation of arms, only while they sent deputies to Rome to implore forgiveness and to make their peace with the senate. Such was the posture of affairs when Lucius Cornelius Scipio, being elected one of the consuls for the ensuing year, was destined to succeed Acilius Glabrio in Etolia; and, with his brother Publius, the victor in the battle of Zama, who was to act as second in command, had orders to prosecute the war against the kingdom of Syria.

These leaders being arrived in Greece, and intent on the removal of the war into Asia, willingly accepted of the submission of all the towns that had incurred any suspicion during the stay of Antiochus in Europe; and leaving the difference which remained to be settled with the Etolians in a state of negotiation, they proceeded without delay, by the route of Macedonia and Thrace, towards the Hellespont.

In passing through these countries, they were conducted and furnished with all the necessary supplies of provisions and carriages by Philip.

The fleets of Asia and Europe, during this march of the Roman army, contended for the command of the seas. That of Europe, which was joined by the navy of Rhodes, and even by that of the Carthaginians, who, to vindicate themselves from any blame in the present war, had taken part with their rival, after various encounters, obtained the victory in a decisive battle, which made them entire masters of the sea, and opened all the ports of Asia to the shipping of the Romans.

The king of Syria had fortified Sestos and Abydos on the Hellespont, and Lysimachia on the isthmus of Chersonesus, with an apparent resolution to dispute the march and passage of the Scipios at all these different stations, but on the total defeat of his navy, he either considered those places as lost, or, fearing to have his forces separately cut off in attempting to defend them, he withdrew his garrisons from Lysimachia, Sestos, and Abydos; and while he thus opened the way for his enemies to reach him, gave other signs of despondency, or of a disposition to sink under adversity, making overtures of peace, and offering to yield every point which he had formerly disputed in the war. In reply to these offers he was told, That he must do a great deal more; that he must submit to such terms as the Romans were entitled to expect from victory.—But as he continued to assemble his forces, he chose rather to stake his fortune on the decision of a battle; and having in vain endeavoured to make himself master of Pergamus, the capital of Eumenes, he fell back on Thyatira, and from thence proceeded to take post on the mountains of Sypylus, where he meant to contend for the empire of Asia.

In the mean time the Scipios advanced to the Hellespont, and without any resistance passed the Strait. This was the first time that any Roman army set foot on Asia; and being met by the deputies of the king with the overtures of peace that have been mentioned, sent accounts to Rome of their arrival, and made a halt for some days.

This descent was considered by the Romans as an epoch of great renown; and the messenger who brought the accounts of it was received with processions and solemn rites. Supplications and prayers were offered up to the gods, that this first landing of a Roman army in Asia might be prosperous for the commonwealth.

U. C. 562.

Publius Scipio, the famous antagonist of Hannibal, soon after his arrival in Asia, was taken ill; or, what may be supposed for his honour, being desirous not to rob his brother of any share in the glory which he perceived was to be easily won against the present enemy, he affected indisposition, and remained at a distance from the camp. Lucius, thus left alone to command the Roman army, advanced upon the king, attacked him in the post he had chosen, and in a decisive victory, dispersed the splendid forces of Asia, with all their apparatus of armed chariots, horses, and elephants, harnessed with gold.

The king himself fled with a few attendants, passed through Sardis in the night, and continued his flight to Apamea in Pisidia, where he expected to be out of the reach of his pursuers.

Thyatira, Sardis, and Magnesia soon after opened their gates to the Romans; and the king himself by a messenger from Apamea, again made haste to own himself vanquished, and to sue for peace.

The Romans, to display a moderation which they frequently affected in the midst of their victories, renewed the same conditions which they had prescribed on their arrival in Asia; and a cessation of arms being granted, officers from Antiochus, and from all the other parties concerned in the approaching treaty, repaired to Rome, in order to receive the final decision of the senate and people, on the future settlement of their affairs.

Eumenes, the king of Pergamus, on this occasion, attended in person, and, together with the republic of Rhodes, who had distinguished themselves by their zeal and faithful services in the late war, became the principal gainer in the treaty.

It was agreed by the senate, that the preliminary articles already prescribed by the consul should be confirmed:

That, according to these articles, Antiochus should resign all his pretensions in Europe, and contract the boundaries of his kingdom in Asia within the mountains of Taurus:

That he should pay to the Romans, at successive terms, five thousand talents to reimburse the expense of the war:

To Eumenes four hundred talents on the score of a debt that had been due to his father.

And, for the performance of these conditions, should give twenty hostages, such as the Romans should name.

In the farther execution of this treaty, the Romans again appeared to be solicitous only for the interest of their allies, and required no more than indemnification for themselves. They appointed ten commissioners to repair into Asia, and there to determine the several questions that might arise relating to the settlement of that country. In the mean time they published to all parties the following instructions, as the basis on which the commissioners were to proceed:

That the preliminaries of the peace with Antiochus already offered should be ratified:

That all the provinces which he was to evacuate, except Caria and Lycia, were to be assigned to Eumenes:

That these provinces, bounded by the Meander on the east, should be given to the republic of Rhodes:

That all the Greek cities which had been tributary to Eumenes should continue so, and all which had been tributary to Antiochus should be set free.[1]

A settlement was accordingly soon after made in Asia in these terms; and the Romans, while they were hastening to universal dominion, appeared to have no object beyond the prosperity of their allies: they were merciful to the vanquished, and formidable only to those who presumed to resist their arms. In the midst of their conquests, they reserved nothing to themselves besides the power of giving away entire kingdoms and provinces; or, in other words, they reserved nothing but the power of seizing the whole at a proper time, and, for the present, the supreme ascendant over all the conquered provinces that were given away, and over those who received them.

The Etolians were now the only parties in Greece who pretended to hold their liberties, or their possessions, by any other tenure than that of a grant from the Romans.

During the dependance of the war in Asia, the Etolians were making continual efforts to recover their own losses, and to preserve the city of Ambracia, then besieged by the Romans; but, upon the defeat of Antiochus, the Ambraciots surrendered at discretion, and the Etolians sued for peace.

Ambracia had been the capital of Pyrrhus, and now furnished the captor with a plentiful spoil of statues, pictures, and other ornaments to adorn his triumph. The Etolians, at the intercession of the Athenians, were allowed to hope for peace on the following terms.[2]

That they should not allow to pass through their country the troops of any nation at war with the Romans:

That they should consider the allies of Rome as their allies, and the enemies of Rome as their enemies:

That they should make instant payment of two hundred talents in silver, the standard of Athens; and of three hundred more at separate instalments within six years:

That if they chose to make these payments in gold rather than silver, the proportion should be one of gold to ten of silver; and that they should give hostages for the performance of these several articles.[3]

While the Etolians were on these terms concluding a peace, or rather obtaining a pardon, the Consul Manlius, who had succeeded the Scipios in Asia, willing, if possible, to bring back into Italy, together with the victorious legions, some pretence of a triumph for himself, led his army against the Galatians. These were the descendants of a barbarous horde, which had, some ages before, migrated from the north of Europe, visited Italy and Greece in their way, and stopped on the Halys in the Lesser Asia, where they made a settlement, round which they levied contributions quite to the shores of the Euxine, the Mediterranean, and Egean Seas. Their forces had lately made a part in the army of Antiochus, and they had not yet acceded to the peace which that prince had accepted. By these means they furnished the Roman Consul with a pretence for invading their country; and being unable to resist him, submitted at discretion. In thus extinguishing the remains of every hostile combination, the Romans took care to satisfy the world that it never was safe to take part against them in any confederacy, and that, while they never abandoned any ally of their own, they were in condition to compel the powers, with whom they were at war, frequently to abandon theirs.

Thus ended the first expedition of the Romans into Asia: in the result of which, without seeming to enlarge their own dominions, they had greatly reduced the powers both of the Syrian and Macedonian monarchies; and by restoring, whether from inclination or policy, every state to its independence, they had balanced a multitude of parties against each other, in such a manner, as that no formidable combination was likely to be formed against themselves; or if any one, or a few parties, should presume to withstand their power, many others were ready to join in the cry of ingratitude, and to treat any opposition that was made to them as an unworthy return to those who had so generously espoused the cause of mankind.

The pacification of Asia and Greece left the republic at leisure to manage its ordinary quarrels with nations unsubdued on the opposite frontier. In the west, hostilities had subsisted without interruption, during the whole time that the state was intent on its wars in the East; and triumphal processions were exhibited by turns from those opposite quarters.

In Spain the commanders were, for the most part, annually relieved, and the army annually recruited from Italy. The variety of events which are mentioned, and the continuance of the war itself, are sufficient to evince that no decisive victories were obtained, or conquests finally made. On the coast of Spain there were many Greek or African settlements established for commerce. Of these the Romans, either as having supplanted the Carthaginians, formerly their masters, or as having subdued the natives, were still in possession. But the interior parts of the country were occupied by many hordes, who appear to have been collected in townships and fortified stations,

1 Polyb. Excerptæ Legationes, c. 35. 2 Ibid. c. 28.

3 Polyb. Excerptæ Legationes, c. 28.

from which they assembled to oppose the Roman armies in the field, or in which they defended themselves with obstinate valour. Though often defeated, they still renewed the contest. Tiberius Sempronius Gracchus, in the year of Rome five hundred and seventy-four, about ten years after the peace with Antiochus, is said to have received the submission of one hundred and three towns of that country.[1] The troubles of Spain were, nevertheless, renewed under his successors, and continued to occupy the Roman arms with a repetition of similar operations, and a like variety of events.

The war in Liguria was nearly of the same description with that in Spain; continued still to occupy a certain part of the Roman force; and, both before and after the late expedition to Greece and Asia, was for some years the principal employment of both the consuls. Here, however, the Romans made a more sensible progress towards an entire conquest than they made in Spain. They facilitated their access to the country by highways across the mountains; they reduced the numbers of the enemy by the sword and by the ordinary distresses of war; and, after the experience of many pretended submissions and repeated revolts of that people, who seemed to derive the ferocity of their spirit, as well as the security of their possession, from the rugged and inaccessible nature of their country, it was determined to transplant the natives to some of the more accessible parts of Italy, where the lands, being waste from the effect of former wars, were still unoccupied and at the disposal of the republic.[2]

CHAPTER VII.

State of Italy—Character of the Roman Policy—Death of Scipio and of Hannibal—Indulgence of the Romans to the King of Macedonia—Complaints against Philip—Succession of Perseus, and Origin of the War—Action on the Peneus—Overtures of Peace—Progress of the War—Defeat of Perseus at Pidna, by Paulus Emilius—His Flight and Captivity—Settlement of Macedonia and Illyricum—Manners of the Romans.

BY the methods above related the Romans proceeded to extend their dominion over all the districts around them, and either brought to their own standard, or disarmed, the several nations who had hitherto resisted their power. While they were about to accomplish this end, the Transalpine Gauls, still having their views directed to the southward of the mountains, made some attempts at migration into Italy, in one of which they settled a party of their people at Aquileia. The Romans were alarmed, and ordered these strangers to be dislodged and reconducted across the Alps.

This circumstance suggested the design of securing the frontier on that side by a colony; and for this purpose a body of Latins was accordingly sent to Aquileia, a settlement which nearly completed the Roman establishments within the Alps. The country was now, in a great measure, occupied by colonies of Roman and Latin extraction, who, depending on Rome for protection, served, wherever they were settled, to carry the deepest impressions of her authority, and to keep the natives in a state of subjection to her government.

The domestic policy of the state, during this period, appears to have been orderly and wise beyond that of any other time. The distinction between patrician and plebeian was become altogether nominal. The descendants of those who had held the higher offices of state, were, in consequence of the preferments of their ancestors, considered as noble. Instead of a title of nobility, the son named his father and grandfather, who had been vested with public honours. And as the plebeians now found no difficulty in obtaining the offices of state, they were continually opening the way of their posterity to the rank of nobles. "Thus I," said Decius Mus,[3] while he pleaded to have the priesthood, joined to the other honours which the different orders of the people enjoyed in common, "can cite my father in the rank of consul; and my son can cite both his grandfather and me."[4] The plebeians were entitled by law to claim one of the consul's seats, and frequently occupied both.

The authority of the senate, the dignity of the equestrian order, and the manners of the people, in general, were guarded, and, in a great measure, preserved, by the integrity and strict exercise of the censorial power. The wisest and the most respected of the citizens, from every condition, were raised into office; and the assemblies whether of the senate, or the people, without envy, and without jealousy, suffered themselves to be governed by the counsels of a few able and virtuous men. It is impossible otherwise to account for that splendour with which the affairs of this republic, from the time of the first Punic war to that of the last wars with Macedonia and Carthage, though committed to hands that were continually changing, were, nevertheless, uniformly and ably conducted.

The spirit of the people was in a high degree democratical; and though they suffered themselves to be governed by the silent influence of personal authority in a few of their citizens, yet could not endure any species of uncommon pre-eminence; even that which arose from the lustre and well-founded pretensions of distinguished merit.

The great Scipio, with his brother Lucius, on their return from Asia, encountered a prosecution, unworthily supported by a popular clamour; which brought them to trial on a formal charge of secreting part of the treasure received from Antiochus. It is likely, from the manner in which Publius Scipio disdained to answer this charge, that he carried his personal spirit too high for

---

1 Liv. lib. xl. c. 50. et passim. 2 Liv. lib. xl. c. 38.
3 Vid. B. i. c. 3.

4 Liv. lib. x. c. 8.

democratical government, which can allow no private merit to come in competition with the rights of the people to sovereignty, and of individuals to equal attention in the state. At his first citation on the libel which was brought against him, seeming not to hear the person who accused him, he reminded the people, that this was the anniversary of that day on which they had gained the victory at Zama; and desired that they would follow him to the temples, in which he was to return thanks to the gods for that important event. He was followed accordingly by the whole multitude, and the accuser for that time was deserted. At his second citation, he called for the paper of accounts, on which he had entered all the sums he had received in Asia; and, while the people expected that he was to satisfy them by a state of particulars, he tore the scroll in their presence; and, taking the privilege of a Roman citizen, retired, without deigning to give any answer, and went as an exile into a country village of Italy, where he soon after died.

The same year likewise terminated the life of his antagonist Hannibal. This great man, himself a sufficient object of jealousy to nations, was, by an article in the late treaty of peace with Antiochus, to have been delivered up to the Romans; and had, in order to avoid that danger, retired into Crete. From thence he took refuge with Prusias, king of Bithynia, where the enmity of Rome still pursued him, and where an embassy was sent to demand that he should be delivered up. As soon as he knew that this demand was actually made, and that the avenues to his dwelling were secured in order to seize him, he took poison, and died.

The Romans had been so well satisfied with the part which was taken by Philip in the late war with Antiochus, that they released his son Demetrius, then at Rome, a hostage for payment of the father's tribute, of which they likewise remitted a part. They even connived at his recovering some of his former possessions, and made no inquiry into the numbers of his troops, in which he greatly exceeded the establishment prescribed by the last treaty. They continued in this disposition during four years after the late peace with the king of Syria; and, in this interval, permitted the kingdom of Macedonia, by the improvement of its revenue, and the increase of its people, in a great measure to recover its former strength.

These circumstances of prosperity, however, did not fail to excite apprehension in the minds of all those who, holding independent possessions in that neighbourhood, were exposed to be the first victims of this reviving power; and representations, to awaken the attention of the Romans on this subject, were accordingly made at Rome, from Eumenes, the king of Pergamus, and from all the petty princes and small communities on the frontier of Macedonia.

On receiving these admonitions, the senate, in their usual form, sent to the country from whence they were alarmed, a select number of their members to make inquiry into the real state of affairs. Before a tribunal thus constituted, the king of Macedonia was cited to appear as a private party, first at Tempe, to answer the charge of the Thessalians, and afterwards at Thessalonica, to answer that of Eumenes. After a discussion, sufficiently humbling to a sovereign, he received sentence, by which he was required to evacuate all the places he had occupied beyond the ancient limits of his kingdom. This sentence he received with indignation and resentment, which were too unguardedly expressed, and which rendered him thenceforward an object of continual attention and of jealousy to the Romans.

A second commission was granted to see the sentence of the first put in execution; and as soon as it became publicly known, that the Romans were willing to receive complaints against Philip, and were disposed to protect every person who incurred his displeasure, ambassadors from the princes of Asia, and persons of every condition, from all the cities of Greece, and from all the districts in the neighbourhood of Macedonia, resorted to Rome with complaints against the king, some of a private, and others of a public nature. The city was crowded with strangers, and the senate was occupied, from morning to night, in hearing the representations that were made by their allies on the subject of the usurpations and oppressions they had suffered.

Philip, to divert the storm, had sent his younger son, Demetrius, to answer the several charges which were expected to be brought against him; and, in the end, obtained a resolution of the senate to accommodate matters on an amicable footing. This resolution was grounded on pretence of the favour which the Romans bore to Demetrius, who had long resided as a hostage in their city. "The king will please to know," they said, "that he has done one thing extremely agreeable to the Romans, in trusting his cause to an advocate so well established in their esteem and regard."[5]

This language of the Roman senate respecting Demetrius, together with dangerous suggestions from some of his own confidants, probably inspired the young man with thoughts, or rendered him suspected of designs, injurious to the rights of Perseus, his elder brother. This prince took the alarm, and never ceased to excite the suspicions already formed in the breast of the father, until he prevailed in securing his own succession by the death of his younger brother.[6]

Philip, having ordered the execution of one son to gratify the jealousy of the other, lived about three years after this action, suffering part of the punishment that was due to him on that account, in the most gloomy apprehensions of danger from his surviving son, and died in great solicitude for the fate of his kingdom.

Perseus, nevertheless, in ascending the throne of Macedonia, gave hopes of a better and happier reign than that of his predecessor. He was immediately acknowledged by the Romans; and, during a few years after his accession, appeared to have no cause of disquietude from this people. Although he had adopted the measures of his father, and endeavoured by attention to his revenue, his army, and magazines; and by forming alliances with some of the warlike Thracian hordes in his neighbourhood, to put his kingdom in a posture of defence, and in condition to assert its independence; yet he appears to have excited less jealousy in the minds of his neighbours. The progress which he made seems to have escaped the attention of the Romans; until, at last awakened by the report of a secret correspondence which he carried on with the republic of Carthage, they thought proper to send a deputation into Macedonia, in order to observe his motions.

---

5 Polyb. Excerpt. Legat. c. 46. Liv. lib. xxxix. 46, 47
6 Liv. lib. xl. c. 24.

By the deputies employed in this service, the Romans obtained intelligence, that Perseus had made advances to the Achæans as well as to the Carthaginians, and to other states; and was likely to form a powerful party among the Greeks.

From this time forward the leaders of the Roman councils seemed to have taken a resolution to remove this subject of jealousy, and to suppress the Macedonian monarchy. They renewed their attention to the state of parties in Greece, and endeavoured to reconcile all the differences that might incline any of those republics to oppose them in the execution of their design. They encouraged the king of Pergamus, who afterwards appears to have repented of the part which he took in that matter, to state his complaints. They brought him to Rome in person, and cited him before the senate to give a complete detail of the circumstances that were alarming in the policy of Perseus. Eumenes, having been thus brought forward as a formal accuser, and being to return through Greece, in order to offer his devotions at the temple of Delphi, was assaulted and wounded by a party who meant to assassinate him; and this design, with some other acts of violence, being imputed to Perseus, served as a pretence for the war which followed.

The Roman senate had already granted two separate commissions, the one of a deputation to visit Macedonia, and to observe the motions of Perseus; the other of an embassy into Egypt, to confirm their alliance with Ptolemy. On hearing of the attempt that had been made to assassinate Eumenes, they directed one of the prætors, Caius Sicinius, with a proper force, to pass into Epirus; and, in order to secure their access into that country, to take possession of Apollonia, and other towns on the coast. But a misunderstanding then subsisting between the consuls, and other principal men of the senate, caused some obstruction in the farther immediate prosecution of the war.

Perseus however, alarmed by the arrival of a Roman force in his neighbourhood, sent an embassy to Rome with expostulations on the subject, and with offers, by every reasonable concession that the senate or the people could require, to avert the storm which threatened him. But the Romans, affecting resentment of the injuries they pretended to have received, ordered his ambassador, without delay, to depart from Italy; and gave intimation, that, if for the future he should have any thing to offer, he might have recourse to the commander of the Roman army in Epirus.

The interview, which Perseus soon after had with the Roman commissioners, terminated with the strongest signs of hostility on both sides.[1] The king, however, having taken minutes of what passed at their conference, sent copies to all the neighbouring states, in order to exculpate himself from any guilt in the approaching war; and as the event afterwards showed how much it was the interest of every state to support him, he being the only power that could give them any protection against the Romans; so numbers, already moved by this apprehension, were inclined to favour his cause. The Rhodians, then a formidable naval power, though restrained by fear from an open breach with the Romans, yet gave sufficient evidence of this disposition. Eumenes, likewise, though a principal instrument in fomenting the present quarrel, soon became averse to its consequences. The Bœotians and Epirots, as well as the Illyrians, openly declared for the king of Macedonia.[2]

These circumstances were stated at Rome as additional grounds of complaint against the king; and his endeavours to vindicate the part he had acted, were considered as attempts to form a hostile confederacy against the republic.

Additional fleets and armies were accordingly assembled, and directed towards Epirus; and a declaration of war was issued in the form of an act of the Roman people.

The Romans had now, during about twenty-five years, borne a principal part among the nations that surrounded the Mediterranean sea. The ascendant they had gained in all their wars or treaties, had made them common objects of fear or respect to all the contiguous powers of Europe, Asia, and Africa. The Macedonians, however, as the latest conquerors of the world, still retained a very high reputation for military skill and valour. The events of the late war rather surprised mankind, than convinced them of any decided superiority on the part of the Roman arms. The novelty of a new enemy, the mistakes or misconduct of the late king, might have accounted for his ill success. The kingdom had now been above twenty years exempted from any signal calamity, had re-established its armies, and filled its magazines and its coffers. The military establishment amounted to forty thousand men; the greater part formed and disciplined upon the plan of the phalanx, and supported with numerous troops of irregulars from the warlike cantons of Thrace. The king himself, in the vigour of manhood, sensible that the storm could not be diverted, affected rather to desire than to decline the contest; and, under all these circumstances, nations seemingly least interested in the consequences, were intent on the scene that was about to be opened before them.

Eumenes, supposed to be incited by inveterate animosity to Perseus, and by recent provocations, prepared to fulfil his professions in behalf of the Romans.

Ariarathes, the king of Cappadocia, equally inclined by policy to wish for a counterpoise to the Macedonian power, but having recently formed an alliance by marriage with the family of Perseus, determined to be neutral in the war.

Ptolemy Philomater, who then filled the throne of Egypt, was a minor. Antiochus Epiphanes, who had lately succeeded his brother Seleucus, in the kingdom of Syria, having been some time a hostage at Rome, affected in his own court the manners of a Roman demagogue; but was chiefly intent on his pretensions to Cœlesyria, which he hoped to make good under favour of the approaching conjuncture formed by the minority of Ptolemy, and by the avocation of the Roman forces in Greece.

The Carthaginians, and the king of Numidia, while they severally preferred their complaints against each other before the Roman senate, vied likewise in their professions of zeal for the Roman republic, and in their offers of supply of men, horses, provisions, or ships.

Gentius, the king of Illyricum, had incurred the jealousy of the Romans; but remained undetermined what part he should take.

Cotys, a Thracian king, declared openly for

1 Liv. lib. lxii. c. 25.

2 Polyb. Exceptæ Legationes, c. 64—67.

Perseus. The people of Greece, in their several republics, were divided among themselves. The popular parties in general, being desirous to exchange the government of their own aristocracies for that of a monarchy, favoured the king of Macedonia. The leading men were either inclined to the Romans, or wished to balance the rival powers, so as to have, in the protection of the one some security against the usurpations of the other.[3]

The Romans had committed an error by sending a small force into Epirus, which the king of Macedonia might have cut off before it could be properly supported from Italy; but their commissioners, then in that country, had the address to amuse the king with a negotiation, and to divert him, during the first year of the war, from any attempt on Apollonia, or on any other station then in possession of the Roman troops.

In the following summer, about seven years after the accession of Perseus to the throne of Macedonia, the war in that kingdom being committed to the Consul Licinius, this general followlowed the army which had been transported to the coast of Epirus; and while the Roman fleet, with their allies, assembled in the straits of Eubœa, the armies on both sides began their operations. The Macedonians encamped at Sycurium on the declivity of mount Ossa. The Roman consul penetrated into Thessaly; and, having passed the river Peneus, took post at Scea, twelve miles from the camp of the enemy. Here he was joined by Attalus, brother to the king of Pergamus, with four thousand men, and by smaller bodies collected from different states of Greece.

Perseus endeavoured to lay waste the kingdom of Pheræ, from which the Romans drew the greatest part of their subsistence; and an action ensued, in which the whole cavalry and light infantry of both armies being engaged, the Romans were defeated; and the consul, no longer able to support his foraging parties on that side of the Peneus against a superior enemy, decamped in the night, and repassed the river.

Although this victory had a tendency to raise the hopes of the king, it was by him wisely considered as a fit opportunity to renew the overtures of peace; and, in order to bring on a negotiation, it was resolved, that the condition which, under the misfortune of repeated defeats, had been offered by his father, should be made the preliminaries of the present treaty.

It appeared to the king, and to those with whom he consulted, that, in the sequel of a victory, this would appear an act of moderation, not of fear; that all neutral powers, who dreaded the consequences of a decided superiority on either side, would favour the person who should propose to have peace re-established on moderate terms; and that the Romans, being induced to terminate the war under the effects of a defeat, would from thenceforward respect the Macedonian monarchy, and be cautious how they disturbed its tranquillity.

But if in this manner the opportunity was perceived, and wisely laid hold of by the councils of Perseus, it by no means escaped the Roman council of war, which was assembled to receive the proposals of the king.

The Romans, whether from national spirit or policy at all times declined entering on negotiations or treaties in consequence of defeats. They spurned the advances of a victorious enemy, while they received those of the vanquished with condescension and mildness. They accordingly, in the present case, treated the concessions of Perseus with disdain, haughtily answering, that he must submit at discretion.[4]

This reply was received at the court of Perseus with extreme surprise. But it produced still farther concessions; and instead of resentment from the king, a repetition of his message with an offer to augment the tribute which had been paid by his father.[5]

The remainder of the summer having passed in the operations of foraging parties, without any considerable action, the Romans retired for the winter into Bœotia. On this coast the fleet, having met with no enemy at sea, had made repeated descents to distress the inhabitants who had declared for the king. The consul took possession of his quarters, without any resistance, in the interior parts of the country; and in this, with the progress that was made by the army employed on the side of Illyricum in detaching that nation from Perseus, consisted the service of the first campaign.

Licinius, at the expiration of the usual term, was relieved by his successor in office, A. Hostilius Marcius. This commander, being defeated and baffled in some attempts he made to penetrate into the kingdom of Macedonia, appears to have made a campaign still less fortunate than that of his predecessor; and the senate, at the end of the summer, having ordered him home to preside at the annual elections, sent a deputation to visit the army, and to inquire into the cause of their miscarriages, and the slowness of their progress.

The Romans, although they had experienced disappointments in the beginning of other wars, particularly in their first encounters with Pyrrhus and with Hannibal; and had reason to expect a similar effect in the opening of the present war, appear to have been greatly mortified and surprised at this unpromising aspect of their enterprise. They were engaged with an enemy renowned for discipline, who had made war a trade, and the use of arms a profession; while they themselves, it appears, for a considerable period after the present war, even during the most rapid progress of their arms, had no military establishment besides that of their civil and political constitution, no soldiers besides their citizens, and no officers but the ordinary magistrates of the commonwealth.

If this establishment had its advantages,[6] it may have appeared, on particular occasions, likewise to have had its defects. The citizen may have been too much a master in his civil capacity to subject himself fully to the bondage of a soldier; and too absolute in his capacity of military officer to bear with the control of political regulations. As the obligation to serve in the legions was general and without exception, many a citizen, at least in the case of any distant or unpromising service, would endeavour to shun his duty. And the officer would not always dare to enforce disagreeable duty on those by whom he himself was elected, or on whom he in part depended for farther advancement.

At the beginning of this war, the legions were

3 Liv. lib. xlii. c. 29—30.

4 In adversis vultum secundæ fortunæ gerere, moderari animos in secundis. Liv lib. xlii. c. 62.

5 Polyb. Excerpt. Legat. c. 69.

6 Vid. B. i. c. 3.

augmented from five thousand two hundred foot and two hundred horse, to six thousand foot and three hundred horse;[1] and, probably, to raise the authority of the consul more effectually into that of a commander-in-chief, he was commissioned to name the tribunes, as well as the centurions of the army, that were to serve under his orders: but, upon a complaint that this extension of the consul's powers did not, by enforcing the discipline of the army, serve the purpose for which it was made, the people resumed their right of election in the appointment even of inferior officers. The deputies, now sent into Macedonia, by the senate, reported, that the legions employed in that country were extremely incomplete, numbers both of the lower officers and private men being, by the dangerous indulgence of their leaders, suffered to absent themselves from their colours.[2] This abuse we may apprehend to have been frequent in a service that was to be performed by citizens who had the choice of their own commanders. And from speculative ideas on the subject, if we were not bound to be governed by experience as the preferable tutor, we should be apt to reject, as an improper mode of forming armies, that establishment by which the Romans conquered the world.

It is probable, that not only the defect of subordination in the beginning of every war, but that of skill, likewise, in the use of their peculiar weapons, made, in the Roman armies, a great disparity between raw and veteran troops.

The use of the buckler and sword required great skill, agility, and muscular strength; all of them the effect of exercise and of continued practice.

The experience of the soldier who survived many actions tended to confirm his courage, because his escape was in a great measure the effect of his skill, or of his strength; and upon a return of similar dangers, gave him confidence in himself.

In battles the strong and the skilful escaped, the weak and the awkward were likely to perish; and every action not only exercised the arms of those that survived, but made a selection of the vigorous and skilful to be reserved for future occasions.

Hence, probably, in the Roman armies, much more than in those of modern Europe, the practised soldier had a great superiority over the novice; and citizens, when brought into the field by rotation, had much to learn in the course of every campaign.

In the present contest, the checks of the first and the second year of the war, though extremely mortifying to the Romans, were received without any signs of irresolution, or change of their purpose. In the third year after hostilities commenced, the command of the army in Macedonia devolved on Q. Marcius Philippus, who, being chosen one of the consuls, drew his province as usual by lot. This officer had been employed in one of the late deputations that were sent into Greece; had shown his ability in the course of negotiations which preceded the war; and now, by his conduct as a general, broke through the line by which the king had endeavoured to secure the passes of the mountains, and to cover the frontier of his kingdom. But, when he had penetrated into Macedonia, he found himself at the end of the season, and for want of proper supplies of provisions on that side of the mountains, unable to pursue the advantage he had gained. Here, therefore, he staid only to deliver his army to Emilius Paulus, who had been named to succeed him. This was the son of that Paulus, who, being one of the consuls who commanded the Roman army at Cannæ, threw away his life rather than survive that defeat. The son was now turned of sixty;[3] and by the length of his service, and the variety of his experience in Liguria and Spain, was well acquainted with the chances of war.

Emilius Paulus, upon his election, in order that he might not be liable to answer for the faults of his predecessors, moved, that deputies should be sent into Macedonia to review the army, and to make a report of its state before he entered upon the command. His speech to the people, when about to depart for his province, carries a striking allusion to the petulant freedom with which, it seems, unsuccessful commanders were censured, or traduced in the popular conversations at Rome, and carries a defiance with which he proposed to silence the blame that might afterwards be cast on himself. "Let such as think themselves qualified to advise the general," he said, "now accompany me into Macedonia. They shall have a passage on board my ship; and, in the field, be welcome to a place in my tent and at my table; but if they now decline this offer, let them not afterwards pretend to judge of what they neither see nor understand. Nor let them set up their own opinion against that of a fellow-citizen, who is serving the public to the utmost of his ability, and at the hazard of his life and of his honours."

Emilius, upon his arrival in Macedonia, found the king entrenched on the banks of the Enipeus, with his right and left covered by mountains, on which all the passes were secured.—After some delay, during which he was employed in observing the enemy's disposition, or in improving the discipline of his own army, he sent a detachment to dispossess the Macedonians of one of the stations which they occupied on the heights, with orders to the officer who commanded in this service, that, if he succeeded in it, he should fall down on the plain in the rear of the enemy; he himself, in the mean time, made a feint to attack them in front.

The post on the heights being forced, Perseus relinquished his present disposition, and fell back towards Pydna on the banks of the Aliacmon. Here it became necessary for him, either to hazard a battle, or, on account of the nature of the country behind him, to separate his forces.

He preferred the first, and made choice of a plain that was fit to receive the phalanx, and was skirted with hills, on which his light troops could act with advantage.

Here too the Roman consul continued to press upon him, and was inclined to seize the first opportunity of deciding the war. Both armies, as by appointment, presented themselves on the plain in order of battle, and Emilius Paulus seemed eager to engage; but, as he himself used to confess, having never beheld an appearance so formidable as when the Macedonians levelled their spears, he thought proper to halt.[4] Though much disconcerted, he endeavoured to preserve his countenance, and would not recede from his

1 Liv. lib. xliii. c. 12. 2 Ibid. c. 11.

3 Plutarch in Vit. Emil. p. 157.
4 Polyb. Fragment. vol. iii. p. 243.

ground; and that he might encamp his army where they now stood, ordered the first line to remain under arms, and ready to attack the enemy, while those who were behind them began to intrench; having in this manner cast up a breast-work of considerable strength, he retired behind it, and under that cover completed the fortifications of a camp in the usual form.

In this position he waited for an opportunity to draw on an engagement, when the enemy should be less prepared to receive him, or not have time to avail themselves so much of that formidable order which constituted the strength of the phalanx.

This occasion soon afterwards seemed to be offered by a skirmish which happened in the fields between the two armies. A horse, having broke loose from the camp of the Romans, fled towards that of the Macedonians, was followed by the soldiers from whom he escaped, and met by their enemy from the opposite camp. These parties engaged, and each being joined by numbers from their respective armies, brought on at last a general action. The ground was favourable to the phalanx; and the Macedonians, though hastily formed, still possessed against the Romans the advantage of their weapons, and of their formidable order. They filled up the plain in front, and could not be flanked. They had only to maintain their ground, and had no occasion to discompose their ranks, in time of the action, by any change of position. They accordingly withstood with ease the first shock of the Roman legions; but were broken and disjointed in the sequel by the seemingly irregular attacks which were made at intervals by the manipules, or the separate divisions of the Roman foot. The parts of the phalanx that were attacked, whether they were pressed in, or came forward to press on their enemy, could not keep in an exact line with the parts that were not attacked. Openings were made, at which the Roman soldier, with his buckler and short sword, could easily enter. Emilius, observing this advantage, directed his attack on those places at which the front of the phalanx was broken; and the legionary soldier, having got within the point of his antagonist's spear, pierced to the heart of the column, and in this position made a havoc which soon threw the whole into disorder and general route.[5]

Twenty thousand of the Macedonians were killed in the field, five thousand were made prisoners in their flight; and six thousand that shut themselves up in the town of Pydna were obliged to surrender at discretion.[6]

After this defeat, the king of Macedonia, with a few attendants, fled to Pella, where, having taken up his children and the remains of his treasure, amounting to ten thousand talents, or about two millions of pounds sterling,[7] he continued his flight to Amphipolis, and from thence to Samothracia, where he took refuge in the famous sanctuary of that island.

Emilius pushed on to Amphipolis, receiving the submission of all the towns and districts as he passed. The prætor, Octavius, then commanding the Roman fleet, beset the island of Samothracia with his ships; and, without violating the sanctuary, took measures that effectually prevented the king's escape.

5 Plutarch in Vit. Emil. p. 173.
6 Liv. lib. xliv. c. 40 7 Justin. lib. xxxiii. c. 1.

This unfortunate prince, with some of his children, delivered themselves up to the prætor, and were conducted to the camp of Emilius. The king threw himself on the ground, and would have embraced the victor's knees, when the Roman general, with a condescension that is extolled by ancient historians, gave him his hand, and raised him from the ground, but reproached him as the aggressor in the late contest with the Romans; and with a lesson of morality, which tore up the wounds of the unfortunate monarch, bid the young men who were present look on this object as an example of the instability of fortune, and of the vicissitude of human affairs.

While the war in Macedonia was coming to this issue, that in Illyricum had a like termination, and ended about the same time in the captivity of the king.

News of both were received at Rome about the same time, and filled the temples, as usual, with multitudes who crowded to perform the public rites of thanksgiving that were ordered by the senate. Soon after which, embassies arrived from all the kings and states of the then known world, with addresses of congratulation on so great an event. The senate proceeded to form a plan for the settlement of Macedonia.

It was resolved to extinguish the monarchy, to divide its territory into four districts, and in each to establish a republican government, administered by councils and magistrates chosen by the people. This among the Greeks, could bear the interpretation of bestowing absolute liberty. Ten commissioners were named to carry this plan into execution in Macedonia, and five were appointed for a similar purpose in Illyricum. Emilius was continued in his command, and the army ordered to remain in Macedonia until the settlement of the province should be completed.

The commissioners, agreeable to their instructions, fixed the limits of the several districts, and, probably to perpetuate the separation of them, or to prevent any dangerous communication between their inhabitants, prohibited them to intermarry, or to hold any commerce in the property of land, from one division to another.

To some other restrictions, which had more a tendency to weaken or to dismember this once powerful monarchy, than to confer freedom on the people, they joined an act of favour, in considerably diminishing their former burdens, reducing their tribute to one half of what they had usually paid to their own kings; and, to facilitate or to secure the reception of the republican form which was devised for them, they ordered all the ancient nobles, and all the retainers of the late court, as being irreconcileable with the equality of citizens under a republic, to depart from the kingdom, and to choose places of residence for themselves in Italy.

A like plan was followed with respect to Illyricum, which was divided into three districts; and the kings both of Macedonia and of this country with many other captives, were conducted to Rome to adorn the triumph of their conquerors.

Perseus is said to have lived as a prisoner at Alba, about four years after he had been exhibited in this procession. Alexander, one of his sons, had an education calculated merely to procure him subsistence, and was afterwards, as a scribe or a clerk, employed in some of the public offices at Rome.

While the event of the Macedonian war was

yet undecided, and no considerable advantage, either of conduct or fortune, appeared on the side of the Romans; they still preserved the usual arrogance of their manner, and interposed with the same imperious ascendant in the affairs of Greece, Asia, and Africa, that they could have done in consequence of the most decisive victory. It was at this time that, by the celebrated message of Popilius Lænas, they put a stop to the conquests of Antiochus Epiphanes in Egypt. This prince, trusting to the full employment with which the Roman forces were engaged, had ventured to invade this kingdom, and was in possession of every part of it, except the city of Alexandria. He was occupied in the siege of this place when Popilius arrived and delivered him an order of the senate to desist. The king made answer, That he would consider of it. "Determine before you pass this line," said the Roman, tracing a circle with the rod which he held in his hand. This people, however, had occasion, during the dependence of the Macedonian war, to observe that few of their allies were willing to support them in the extremes to which they seemed to be inclined. The Epirots had actually declared for the king of Macedonia. The Rhodians had offered their mediation to negotiate a peace, and threatened hostility against either of the parties who should refuse to accept of it. Even Eumenes was suspected of having entered into a secret concert with Perseus, although the fall of that prince prevented any open effects of their treaty.

The Romans, nevertheless, disguised their resentment of these several provocations, until their principal enemy, the king of Macedonia, was subdued; after they had accomplished this end, they proceeded against every other party, with a severity which was then supposed to be permitted in the law of nations, and no more than proportioned to their supposed offence. They gave orders to Emilius, in passing through Epirus, to lay that country under military execution. Seventy towns were accordingly destroyed, and a hundred and fifty thousand of the people sold for slaves.

The senate refused to admit the ambassadors of Rhodes, who came to congratulate the Roman people on their victory at Pydna. They stripped those islanders of the provinces which had been granted to them on the continent by the late treaty with Antiochus, and ordered them to discontinue some duties levied from ships in passing through their sound, which made a considerable part of their revenue.

While Eumenes was coming in person to pay his court to the senate, they resolved to forbid the concourse of kings to Rome. Their meaning, though expressed in general terms, was evidently levelled at this prince; and they ordered, that when he should arrive at Brundusium, their resolution should be intimated to him, to prevent his nearer approach.

They in reality, from this time forward, though in the style of allies, treated the Grecian republics as subjects.

Such was the rank which the Romans assumed among nations; while their statesmen still retained much of their primeval rusticity, and did not consider the distinctions of fortune and equipage as the appurtenances of power or of high command. Cato, though a citizen of the highest rank, and vested successively with the dignities of consul and of censor, used to partake in the labour of his own slaves, and to feed with them from the same dish at their meals.[1] When he commanded the armies of the republic, the daily allowance of his household was no more than three medimni, or about as many bushels of wheat for his family, and half a medimnus, or half a bushel of barley for his horses. In surveying his province he usually travelled on foot, attended by a single slave who carried his baggage.[2]

These particulars are mentioned perhaps as peculiar to Cato; but such singularities in the manners of a person placed so high among the people, carry some general intimation of the fashion of the times.

A spirit of equality yet reigned among the members of the commonwealth, which rejected the distinctions of fortune, and checked the admiration of private wealth. In all military donations the centurion had no more than double the allowance of a private soldier, and no military rank was indelible. The consul and commander-in-chief of one year served not only in the ranks, but even as a tribune or inferior officer in the next; and the same person who had displayed the genius and ability of the general, still valued himself on the courage and address of a legionary soldier.

No one was raised above the glory to be reaped from the exertion of mere personal courage and bodily strength. Persons of the highest condition sent or accepted a defiance to fight in single combat, in presence of the armies to which they belonged. Marcus Servilius, a person of consular rank, in order to enhance the authority with which he spoke when he pleaded for the triumph of Paulus Emilius, informed the people that he himself, full three and twenty times, had fought singly with so many champions of the enemy, and that in each of these encounters he had slain and stripped his antagonist. A combat of the same kind was afterwards fought by the younger Scipio, when serving in Spain.

The sumptuary laws of this age were suited to the idea of citizens who were determined to contribute their utmost to the grandeur of the state; but to forego the means of luxury or personal distinction. Roman ladies were restrained, except in religious processions, from the use of carriages any where within the city, or at the distance of less than a mile from its walls; and yet the space over which they were to preserve their communications extended to a circuit of fourteen miles, and began to be so much crowded with buildings or cottages, that, even before the reduction of Macedonia, it was become necessary to restrain private persons from encroaching on the streets, squares, and other spaces reserved for public conveniency. In a place of this magnitude, and so stocked with inhabitants, the female sex was also forbid the use of variegated or party-coloured clothes, or of more than half an ounce of gold in the ornament of their persons. This law being repealed, contrary to the sentiments of Cato, this citizen, when he came, in the capacity of censor, to take account of the equipages, clothes and jewels of the women, taxed each of them tenfold for whatever was found in her wardrobe exceeding the value of one thousand five hundred denarii, or about fifty pounds sterling.[3]

1 Plutach. in Vit. Catonis, p. 330.
2 Ibid. p. 335 and 338.
3 Liv. lib. xxxiv. c. 1—6.

The attention of the legislature was carried into the detail of entertainments or feasts. In one act the number of the guests, and in a subsequent one the expense of their meals, were limited. By the Lex Tribonia, enacted about twenty years after the reduction of Macedonia, a citizen was allowed, on certain high festivals, to expend three hundred ases, or about twenty shillings sterling; on other festivals of less note, one hundred ases, or about six shillings and eight pence; but during the remainder of the year, no more than ten ases, or about eight pence; and was not allowed to serve up more than one fowl, and this with a proviso that it should not be crammed or fatted.[4]

Superstition made a principal article in the character of the people. It subjected them continually to be occupied or alarmed with prodigies and ominous appearances, of which they endeavoured to avert the effects by rites and expiations, as strange and irrational as the presages on which they had grounded their fears. Great part of their time was accordingly taken up with processions and public shows, and much of their substance, even to the whole annual produce of their herds,[5] was occasionally expended in sacrifices, or in the performance of public vows. The first officers of state, in their functions of the priesthood, performed the part of the cook and the butcher; and, while the senate was deliberating on questions of great moment, examined the entrails of a victim, in order to know what the gods had determined. "You must desist," said the Consul Cornelius, entering the senate with a countenance pale and marked with astonishment; "I myself have visited the boiler, and the head of the liver is consumed."[6]

According to the opinions entertained in those times, sorcery was a principal expedient employed by those who had secret designs on the life of their neighbour. It was supposed to make a part in the statutory crime of poisoning; and the same imagination which admitted the charge of sorcery as credible, was, in particular instances, when any person was accused, easily convinced of his guilt; insomuch that some thousands were at times convicted together of this imaginary crime.[7]

The manners of the people of Italy were at times subject to strange disorders, or the magistrate gave credit to wild and improbable reports. The story of the Bacchanals, dated in the year of Rome five hundred and sixty-six, or about twenty years before the conquest of Macedonia, may be considered as an instance of one or the other.[8] A society, under the name of Bacchanals, had been instituted, on the suggestion of a Greek pretender to divination.[9] The desire of being admitted into this society prevailed throughout Italy, and the sect became extremely numerous. As they commonly met in the night, they were said at certain hours to extinguish their lights, and to indulge themselves in every practice of horror, rape, incest, and murder; crimes under which no sect or fraternity could possibly subsist, but which, in being imputed to numbers in this credulous age, gave occasion to a severe inquisition, and proved fatal to many persons at Rome, and throughout Italy.

The extreme superstition, however, of those times, in some of its effects, vied with genuine religion; and, by the regard it inspired, more especially for the obligation of oaths, became a principle of public order and of public duty, and in many instances superseded the use of penal or compulsory laws.

When the citizen swore that he would obey the call of the magistrate to enlist in the legions; when the soldier swore that he would not desert his colours, disobey his commander, or fly from his enemy; when a citizen, at the call of the censor, reported on oath the amount of his effects; the state, in all those instances, with perfect confidence relied on the good faith of her subjects, and was not deceived.

In the period to which these observations refer, that is, in the sixth century of the Roman state, the first dawning of literature began to appear. It has been mentioned that a custom prevailed among the primitive Romans, as among other rude nations, at their feasts to sing or rehearse heroic ballads which recorded their own deeds or those of their ancestors.[10] This practice had been some time discontinued, and the compositions themselves were lost. They were succeeded by pretended monuments of history equally fallacious, the orations which, having been pronounced at funerals, were, like titles of honour, preserved in the archives of every noble house, but which were rather calculated to flatter the vanity of families, than to record the truth.[11]

The Romans owed the earliest compilations of their history to Greeks; and in their own first attempts to relate their story employed the language of that people.[12] Nævius and Ennius, who were the first that wrote in the Latin tongue, composed their relations in verse. Livius Andronicus, and afterwards Plautus and Terence, translated the Greek fable, and exhibited in the streets of Rome, not the Roman, but Grecian manners. The two last are said to have been persons of mean condition; the one to have subsisted by turning a baker's mill, the other to have been a captive and a slave. Both of them had probably possessed the Greek tongue as a vulgar dialect, which was yet spoken in many parts of Italy, and from this circumstance, became acquainted with the elegant compositions of Philemon and Menander.[13] Their comedies were acted in the streets, without any seats or benches for the reception of an audience. But a nation so little studious of ordinary conveniences, and contented to borrow their literary models from neighbours, to whom, being mere imitators, they continued for ages inferior, were, however, in their political and military character, superior to all other nations whatever, and, at this date, had extended a dominion,
U. C. 586. which originally consisted of a poor village on the Tiber, to more empire and territory than is now enjoyed by any kingdom or state of Europe.

4 Plin. lib. x. c. 50.
5 The Ver Sacrum was a general sacrifice of all the young of their herds for a whole year.
6 Liv. lib. xli. c. 15.
7 Ibid. lib. xxxix. c 41. 8 Ibid. c. 8. and sequen
9 Venificium.

10 Cic. de Claris Oratoribus, c. 19.
11 Ibid. p. 394. 12 Dion. Hal. lib. i. p. 5.
13 The people of Cumæ, about this time, applied for leave to have their public acts, for the time, expressed in Latin.

THE

HISTORY

OF

THE PROGRESS AND TERMINATION

OF THE

ROMAN REPUBLIC.

BOOK II.

CHAPTER I.

State, Manners, and Policy of the Times—Repeated Complaints from Carthage—Hostile Disposition of the Romans—Resolution to remove Carthage from the Coast—Measures taken for this Purpose—Carthage besieged—Taken and destroyed—Revolt of the Macedonians—Their Kingdom reduced to the Form of a Roman Province—Fate of the Achæan League—Operations in Spain—Conduct of Viriathus—State of Numantia—Blockade of Numantia—Its Destruction—Revolt of the Slaves in Sicily—Legal Establishments and Manners of the City.

THE reduction of Macedonia was in many respects a remarkable era in the history of Rome. Before this date Roman citizens had been treated as subjects, and permitted themselves to be taxed. They were required at every census to make a return of their effects upon oath, and, besides other stated or occasional contributions to the public, paid a certain rate on the whole value of their property. But upon this event they assumed more entirely the character of sovereigns; and, having a treasury replenished with the spoils of that kingdom, exempted themselves from their former burdens.

The accession of wealth, said to have put them in this condition, is variously reported. Livy quotes Valerius Antias as stating it at *millies ducenties*, or about a million sterling; Velleius Paterculus states it at double this sum, and Pliny at somewhat more.[1] But the highest of these computations scarcely appears adequate to the effect supposed. It is more likely that the ordinary income of the treasury, consisting of the sums so frequently deposited at the triumphs of victorious leaders, the tributes received from Carthage and Syria, the rents of Campania, the tithes of Sicily and Sardinia, with the addition of the revenue recently constituted in Macedonia, put the Romans at last in condition to exempt themselves from taxation; an effect which no perishing capital placed at once in their coffers could be supposed to produce. The Roman treasury, when examined about ten years after this date, was found to contain, in bars of gold and silver, and in coin, not much more than half a million sterling:[2] a sum which, without a proper and regular supply, must have been soon exhausted.

From the conclusion of the war with Perseus, the Romans for twenty years, do not seem to have been engaged with any considerable enemy; and their numerous colonies, now dispersed over Italy, from Aquileia to Rhegium, probably made great advances, during this period, in agriculture, commerce, and the other arts of peace. Among their public works are mentioned, not only temples and fortifications, particulars in which men attain to magnificence even in rude ages, but likewise aqueducts, market-places, pavements, highways, and other conveniences, the preludes or attendants of wealth and commerce.

Cato, in pleading against the repeated election of the same person into the office of consul, exclaimed against the luxury of the times, and alleged, that so many citizens could not support their extravagance by any other means than that of draining the provinces by virtue of their repeated appointments to command. "Observe," he said, "their villas, how curiously built, how richly furnished with ivory and precious wood. Their very floors are coloured or stained in the Punic fashion."[3]

1 Velleius, lib. 1. c. 9. Plin. lib xxxiii. c. 3.

2 Plin. lib. xxxiii. c. 3. In gold 16,810 Æ. in silver 22,070 Æ. and in coin 620,854,000 H. S. Arbuthnot on Ancient Coins.

3 Vid. Pompeium Festum.

Lex Annalis. The Romans had formerly made laws to fix the age at which citizens might be chosen into the different offices of state.[4] And on the occasion on which Cato made this speech, they excluded the same person from being repeatedly chosen. They likewise made those additions to former sumptuary laws which have been already mentioned. The census, or enrolment of the people, began to be made with more care than formerly: even the Latin allies, though migrating to Rome, were excluded from the rolls;[5] and the people generally mustered from three to four hundred thousand men.

While the Romans had no war to maintain with the more regular and formidable rivals of their power, they still employed their legions on the frontier of their provinces in Spain, Dalmatia, Liguria, and on the descents of the Alps. They opened, for the first time, an intercourse with the Transalpine nations, in a treaty of alliance with the republic of Marseilles; in consequence of which, they protected that mercantile settlement from the attacks of fierce tribes, who infested them from the maritime extremities of the Alps and Appenines. They were in general the umpires in the differences of nations, gave audience in all their complaints, interposed with their forces as well as authority, and disposed of provinces and kingdoms at their pleasure. They kept a vigilant eye on the conduct and policy of all the different powers with whom they were at any time likely to be embroiled, and generally conducted their transactions with independent nations as they adjusted the first settlement of their own acquisitions, by commission and deputations sent from the senate to decide, with the least possible delay, on such matters as might arise in the place to which their deliberations referred.

The number of commissioners employed in these services, for the most part, was ten. These took informations, formed plans, and made their reports for the final decision of the senate, and, by the frequency of these appointments, it appears that the members of the senate, in rotation, had an opportunity of becoming acquainted with that world which they were destined to govern.

The senate itself, though, from its numbers and the emulation of its members, likely to embarrass affairs by debate, delay, and the rash publication of all its designs, in reality possessed all the advantages of decision, secrecy, and despatch, that could be obtained in the most select executive council. This numerous assembly of Roman statesmen appeared to have maintained, during a long period, one series of consistent and uniform design; and kept their intentions so secret, that their resolutions, for the most part, were known only by the execution. The king of Pergamus made a journey to Rome, in order to excite the Romans to a war with his rival, the king of Macedonia. He preferred his complaints in the senate, and prevailed on this body to resolve on the war; but no part of the transaction was public till after the king of Macedonia was a prisoner at Rome.[6]

4 It appears that, by this law, being questors at thirty-one, they might rise to the consulate at forty-three.

5 Plutarch, in the life of Flamininus, mentions a law by which the censors were obliged to enrol every freeman that offered. The Latins complained, that their towns were depopulated by emigrations to Rome. Liv. lib. xli. c. 8.

6 Valer. Maxim. lib. ii. c. 2.

During the present respite from any considerable war, the Romans balanced the kingdoms of Pergamus, Bithynia, and Cappadocia against each other, in such a manner as to be able, at pleasure, to oppress any of those powers that should become refractory or formidable to their interest.

They made the kingdom of Syria devolve on a minor, the son of Antiochus; and, under the pretence of this minority, sent a commission to take charge of the kingdom. But their commissioners were, with the connivance of the court, assaulted in a riot at Antioch; some of them were killed, and others forced to fly from the country.

Demetrius, the son of Seleucus, who ought to have succeeded to his father in the monarchy of Syria, being, at the death of that prince, a hostage at Rome, had been supplanted by his younger brother, the father of that minor prince who was now acknowledged by the Romans.

Upon the insult that had been thus offered to the Roman commission at Antioch, Demetrius thought it a favourable opportunity to urge his claim, and to prevail on the senate to restore him to the succession of his father's crown: but these crafty usurpers, notwithstanding the offence they had received from those who were in possession of the monarchy, preferred the advantages which they had over a minor king, to the precarious affection or gratitude of an active spirited prince, educated at Rome, and taught by their own example to know his interest; and they accordingly denied his request.

Demetrius, however, made his escape from Rome, and, by the death of the minor and his tutor, got unrivalled possession of the kingdom of Syria. To pay his court to the Romans, as one of the first acts of his reign, he sent the murderer of their late commissioner, Octavius, in chains, to be punished at their discretion. But the senate disdained to wreck their public wrongs on a private criminal; or, having cause of complaint against the nation itself, were not to be satisfied with the punishment of a single person. They suffered the prisoner, as beneath their attention, to depart.

As patrons of the kingdom of Egypt, they promoted the division of that country between the two brothers, who were then joined in the sovereignty, and rivals for the sole possession of the throne.[7]

During the dependence of these transactions, the senate had repeated complaints from Africa, which ended in a war that proved fatal at last to the ancient rivals of their power. In the conduct of this war, being now less dependent than formerly on the opinion of the world, they, contrary to their usual pretensions to national generosity and liberality, sacrificed, without reserve, entire nations to the ambition, or to the meanest jealousy, of their own republic.[8]

The province of Emporiæ, a district lying on the coast, and the richest part of the Carthaginian territory, had been violently seized by Gala king of Numidia, and father of Massinissa. It had been again restored by Syphax, when he supplanted the family of Gala on the throne of that kingdom; but now again usurped by Massinissa on recovering the crown by the power of the Romans, to whose favour he trusted; and the Carthaginians, precluded by the late treaty from making war on any ally of the Romans, had recourse to complaints and representations, which

7 Polyb. Excerptæ Legationes. 8 Ibid No. 142

they made at Rome, both before and after the reduction of Macedonia. The Roman senate had, for five and twenty years, eluded these complaints, and, during this time, was in the practice of sending commissioners into Africa, under pretence of hearing the parties in this important dispute, but with instructions or dispositions to favour Massinissa, and to observe, with a jealous eye, the condition and the movements of their ancient rival.[1]

The Carthaginians, yet possessed of ample resources, and, if wealth or magnificence could constitute strength, still a powerful nation; being weary of repeated applications, to which they could obtain no satisfying answer, took their resolution to arm, and to assert by force their claim to the territory in question.

They were met in the field by the army of Massinissa, commanded by himself, though now about ninety years of age, and were defeated.[2]

This unfortunate event disappointed their hopes, and exposed them to the resentment of the Romans, who considered the attempt they had made to do themselves justice, as a contravention of the late treaty, and a departure from the articles of peace between the two nations.

The expediency of a war with Carthage had been for some time a subject of debate in the Roman senate. Deputies had been sent into Africa, to procure the information that was necessary to determine this question. Among these, Cato, being struck with the greatness, wealth, and populousness of that republic, and with the amazing fertility of its territory, when he made his report in the senate, carried in his lap a parcel of figs which he had brought from thence. "These," he said, "are the produce of a land that is but three days' sail from Rome. Judge what Italy may have to fear from a country whose produce is so much superior to its own. That country is now in arms; the sword is drawn against Massinissa; but when thrust in his side, will penetrate to you. Your boasted victories have not subdued the Carthaginians, but given them experience, taught them caution, and instructed them how to disguise, under the semblance of peace, a war which you will find marshalled against you in their docks and in their arsenals." This, and every other speech on this subject, Cato concluded with his famous saying, "That Carthage should be destroyed."[3]

Scipio Nasica, another speaker in this debate, contended for peace. He represented the forces of Carthage as not sufficient to alarm the Romans; or, if really greater than there was any reason to suppose them, no more than were requisite to exercise the virtues of a people already, for want of proper exertion, begun to suffer some abatement in their vigilance, discipline, and valour.

In this diversity of opinions, it appeared soon after, that the senate took a middle course; resolved not to destroy, but to remove the inhabitants of Carthage to a new situation, at least ten miles from the sea.[4]

The Carthaginians, after their late unfortunate adventure with Massinissa, were willing to preserve their effects, and to purchase tranquillity by the lowest concessions. But as the measure now proposed by the Roman senate amounted to a deprivation of all that property which is vested in houses or public edifices, and an entire suppression of all those local means of subsistence which could not be easily transferred, it was not supposed that their consent could be easily obtained, and it was accordingly resolved to keep the design a secret, until effectual means were prepared for its execution.

The consuls, without any declaration of war, were instructed to arm, and to pass with their forces into Sicily. As their arrival on that island, which was then in a state of profound peace, evidently implied a design upon Africa, the people of Utica, that they might have the merit of an early declaration in favour of the Romans, sent a deputation to make them a tender of their port and town, as a harbour and place of arms for the accommodation of their forces. The Carthaginians were distracted with opposite counsels. They laid the blame of the war with Massinissa on Hasdrubal and his abettors, whom they ordered into exile; but, without coming to any other resolutions, sent a deputation, with full powers to conclude as circumstances might seem to require, and agree to whatever they should find most expedient for the commonwealth. These deputies, on their arrival at Rome, finding no disposition in the senate to treat with them upon equal terms, resolved to arrest, by the most implicit submission, the sword that was lifted up against their country. They accordingly confessed the imprudence of their late conduct, and implored forgiveness. They quoted the sentence of banishment passed upon Hasdrubal and his party, as an evidence of their contrition for the hostilities lately offered to Massinissa; and they made a formal surrender of their city and its territory to be disposed of at the pleasure of the Romans.

In return to this act of submission, they were told, that the Romans approved their behaviour, and meant to leave them in possession of their freedom, their laws, their territory, and of all their effects, whether private or public: but, as a pledge of their compliance with the measures that might be necessary to prevent the return of former disputes, they demanded three hundred hostages, the children of senators, and of the first families in Carthage. This demand being reported in the city gave a general alarm; but the authors of these counsels were too far advanced to recede. They tore from the arms of their parents the children of the first families in the commonwealth; and, amidst the cries of affliction and despair, embarked those hostages for Sicily. Upon this island they were delivered over to the Roman consuls, and were by them sent forward to Rome.

The commanders of the Roman armament, without explaining themselves any further, continued their voyage, and, by their appearance on the coast of Africa, gave a fresh alarm at Carthage. Deputies from the unfortunate inhabitants of that place went to receive them at Utica, and were told, that they must deliver up all their arms, ships, engines of war, naval and military stores. Even these alarming commands they received as the strokes of fate, which could not be avoided. "We do not mean," said one of the deputies, "to dispute your commands; but we entreat you to consider, to what a helpless state you are about to reduce an unfortunate people

1 Polyb. Excerpt. Legat. c. 118. Liv. lib. xl. c. 17.
2 Liv. Epitome, lib. xlviii. Appian. de Bell. Punic, p. 38.
3 Delenda est Carthago.
4 Appian in Punicis. Plutarch in Vit. Catonis. Zonaras, lib. ix. c. 26. Oros. lib. iv. c. 22. Velleius, lib. c 12. Polyb. Excerptæ Legationes, No. 142.

who, by this hard condition, will be rendered unable to preserve peace among their own citizens at home, or to defend themselves against the meanest invader from abroad. We have banished Hasdrubal in order to receive you. we have declared him an enemy to his country, that you might be our friends: but when we are disarmed, who can prevent this exile from returning to occupy the city of Carthage against you? With twenty thousand men that follow him, if he comes into the direction of our government, he will soon oblige us to make war on you."[5] In answer to this piteous expostulation, the Roman generals undertook the protection of Carthage, and ordered commissaries to receive the several articles that were to be delivered up, and to see the arsenals and the docks destroyed.

It is reported, that there were delivered up to these commissaries forty thousand suits of armour, twenty thousand katapultæ, or large engines of war, with a plentiful store of darts, arrows and other missiles.

So far the Romans proceeded with caution, well knowing the veneration which mankind entertain for the seats and tombs of their ancestors, with the shrines and consecrated temples of their gods; and dreading the effects of despair, as soon as the Carthaginians should perceive how much they were to be affected in their private and public property. But now, thinking their object secure, they proceeded to declare their intentions. The consul called the Carthaginian deputies into his presence, and beginning with an exhortation, that they should bear with equanimity what the necessity of their fortune imposed, intimated, the definitive resolution of the Roman senate, that the people of Carthage should relinquish their present situation, and build on any other part of their territory, not less than eighty stadia, or about ten miles, removed from the sea. The amazement and sorrow with which these orders were received, justified the precautions which the Romans had taken to secure the execution of them. The deputies threw themselves upon the ground, and endeavoured, from motives of pity, or of reason, to obtain a revocation of this cruel and arbitrary decree. They pleaded the merit of their implicit submission, their weakness, their inability any longer to alarm the jealousy of Rome, circumvented, disarmed, bound to their duty by hostages the most precious blood of their commonwealth. They pleaded the faith which was plighted by the Romans, the hopes of protection they had given, and the reputation they had justly acquired, not only for national justice, but for clemency and generosity to all who sued for mercy. They pleaded the respect which all nations owed to the shrines and the consecrated temples of their gods; the deplorable state into which numbers of their people must be reduced, expelled from their habitations and immoveable possessions, the principal articles of their property, and the hopeless condition of others, who, inured to subsist by the advantages of a maritime situation, were entirely disqualified to support themselves or their children at a distance from the sea.

The Roman consul replied by repeating the express orders of the senate, and bid the Carthaginians remember, that states were composed of men, not of ramparts and walls. That the Roman senate had promised to spare and protect the republic of Carthage; and that they had fulfilled this engagement by leaving the people in possession of their freedom and their laws. That the sacred places should remain untouched, and that the shrines of the gods would still be within the reach of their pious visits. That the distance to which it was proposed to remove Carthage from the sea was not so great as the distance at which Rome herself was situated from it; and that the Romans had taken their resolution, that the people of Carthage should no longer have under their immediate view that element which opened a way to their ambition, had tempted them first into Sicily, afterwards into Spain, and last of all into Italy, and to the gates of Rome; and which would never cease to suggest projects dangerous to themselves, and inconsistent with the peace of mankind. "We go, then," said the deputies of Carthage, "to certain death, which we have merited by having persuaded our fellow-citizens to resign themselves into the hands of the Romans. But if you mean to have your commands obeyed, you must be ready to enforce them; and by this means you may save an unfortunate people from exposing themselves, by any act of despair, to worse sufferings than they have yet endured."

The deputies accordingly, being followed at a distance by twenty galleys of the Roman fleet, set sail for Carthage. They were received on the shore by multitudes, who crowded to hear the result of their negotiations; but the silence they preserved, under pretence that it was necessary to make their report first to the senate, spread a general dismay. In the senate their message was received with cries of despair, which soon conveyed to the people in the streets a knowledge of the conditions imposed upon them. And this nation, who, about forty years before, had consented to betray their principal citizen into the hands of their enemy, and who had lately resigned all the honours and pretensions of a free state, now kindled into rage at the thoughts of being obliged to forego so great a part of their wealth, and to remove their habitations. They burst into the place where the senate was assembled, and laid violent hands on all the members who had advised or borne any part in the late degrading submissions, or who had contributed to bring the state into its present helpless condition. They took vengeance, as is common, with a corrupted populace, on others, for faults in which they themselves had freely concurred; and, as awake to new sentiments of honour, they reviled the spirit of their own commonwealth, ever ready to barter national character for profit, to purchase safety with shameful concessions, and to remove a present danger, by giving up what is the only security of nations against any danger, the reputation of their vigour, and the honour of their arms.

While the multitude indulged themselves in every species of riot, a few had the precaution to shut the gates, to stretch the chain which protected the entrance of the harbour, and to make a collection of stones on the battlements, these being the only weapons they had left to repel the first attacks of the Romans. The remains of the senate, too, without reflecting on the desperate state of their affairs, resolved on war. Despair and frenzy succeeded in every breast to dejection and meanness.

Assemblies were called to reverse the sentence

5 Polyb. Excerpt. Legat. c. 142.

of banishment lately pronounced against Hasdrubal, and against the troops under his command. These exiles were entreated to hasten their return for the defence of a city bereft of arms, ships, military and naval stores. The people, in the mean time, with an ardour which reason, and the hopes of success during the prosperity of the republic could not have inspired, endeavoured to replace the arms and the stores which they had so shamefully surrendered. They demolished their houses to supply the docks with timber. They opened the temples and other public buildings to accommodate the workmen; and, without distinction of sex, condition, or age, became labourers in the public works, collected materials, furnished provisions, or bore a part in any labour that was thought necessary to put the city in a state of defence. They supplied the founders and the armourers with the brass and iron of their domestic utensils; or, where these metals were deficient, brought what they could furnish of silver and gold. They joined, with the other materials which were used in the roperies, their hair, to be spun into cordage for the shipping, and into braces for their engines of war.

The Roman consuls, apprised of what was in agitation, willing to await the returns of reason, and to let these first ebullitions of frenzy subside, for some days made no attempts on the city. But, hearing of the approach of Hasdrubal, they thought it necessary to endeavour, before his arrival, to possess themselves of the gates. Having in vain attempted to scale the walls, they were obliged to undergo the labours of a regular siege; and, though they made a breach, were repulsed in attempting to force the city by storm.

Hasdrubal had taken post on the creek which separated the peninsula of Carthage from the continent, maintained his communication by water, and supplied the inhabitants with provisions and arms. The Romans, seeing that they could not reduce the city while Hasdrubal retained this post, endeavoured to dislodge him, but were defeated, and obliged to raise the siege. They had already spent two years in this enterprise, changed their commanders twice, but without advancing their fortunes. They began to incur the discredit of having formed against a neighbouring commonwealth an invidious design which they could not accomplish. Enemies in every quarter, in Greece, Macedonia, and Spain, were encouraged to declare against them; and even Massinissa, unwilling to see their power substituted for that of Carthage, and jealous of the avidity with which they endeavoured to become masters in Africa, and to snatch from his hands a prey in which he thought himself entitled to share, withdrew his forces, and left them singly to contend with the difficulties in which they began to be involved.

But the Romans were animated by those mortifications which are apt to discourage other nations. They imputed the miscarriage of their troops to the misconduct of their generals; and they clamoured for a better choice. Scipio, by birth the son of Emilius Paulus, and by adoption the grandson of Scipio Africanus, having distinguished himself in Spain and in Africa, and being then arrived from the army to solicit the office of edile, was thought worthy of the supreme command; but being about ten years under the legal age, the law was suspended in his favour, and his appointment to the province of Africa, in preference to his colleague, was declared without the usual method of casting lots.

The Carthaginians were now reinstated in their consideration, and in their rank among nations, and had negotiations with the neighbouring powers of Mauritania and Numidia, whose aid they solicited with alarming reflections on the boundless ambition, and invidious policy of the Romans. They even conveyed assurances of support to the Achæans, to the pretended Philip, an impostor, who, about this time, laid claim to the throne of Macedonia; and they encouraged with hopes of assistance the subjects of that kingdom, who were at this time in arms to recover the independence of their monarchy.

The mere change of the commander, and better dicipline in the Roman army, however, soon altered the state and prospects of the war. The first object of Scipio was to cut off the communications of the Carthaginians with the country, and to intercept their supply of provisions and other articles necessary to withstand a siege.

Carthage was situated at the bottom of a spacious bay, covered on the west by the promontory of Apollo, on the east by that of Hermes, or Mercury, at the distance of about fifteen leagues from each other. The city stood on a peninsula joined to the main land by an isthmus about three miles in breadth, and covering a bason or harbour, in which their docks and their shipping were secured from storms and hostile attacks The Byrsa, or citadel, commanded the isthmus, and presented at this only entrance to the town by land, a wall thirty feet thick and sixty feet high. The whole circumference of the place was about twenty miles.[1]

The besiegers, by their shipping, had access to that side of the town on which the walls were washed by the sea; but were shut out from the harbour by a chain which was stretched across the entrance. Hasdrubal had taken post on the bason over against the town, and by these means still preserved the communication of the city with the country. Scipio, to dislodge him from this post, made a feint at a distant part of the fortifications to scale the walls, actually gained the battlements, and gave an alarm which obliged the Carthaginian general to throw himself into the city. Scipio, satisfied with having obtained his end, took possession of the post which the other had abandoned; and being now master of the isthmus, and the whole continental side of the harbour, advanced to the walls of the Byrsa. In his camp he covered himself as usual with double lines; one facing the fortifications of the enemy, consisting of a curtain twelve feet high, with towers at proper intervals, of which one in the centre was high enough to overlook the ramparts, and to afford a view of the enemy's works. The other line secured his rear from surprise on the side of the country; and both effectually guarded the isthmus, and obstructed all access to the town by land.

The besieged, however, still received some supply of provisions by sea; their victuallers took the benefit of every wind that blew fresh and right into the harbour, to pass through the enemy's fleet, who durst not unmoor to pursue them; and Scipio, to cut off this resource, projected a mole

1 Orosius, lib. iv. c. 22. Liv. Epitome, lib. li.

from the main land to the point of the peninsula across the entrance of the harbour. He began to throw in his materials on a foundation of ninety feet, with an intention to contract the mound as it rose to twenty-four feet at the top. The work, when first observed from Carthage, was considered as a vain undertaking; but when it appeared to advance with a sensible progress, gave a serious alarm.

The Carthaginians, to provide against the evils which they began to foresee from this obstruction at the entrance of their harbour, undertook a work more difficult, and more vast than even that of the besiegers, to cut across the peninsula within their walls, and to open a new passage to the sea; and this they had actually accomplished by the time that the other passage was shut. Notwithstanding the late surrender of all their shipping and stores, they had at the same time, by incredible efforts, assembled or constructed a navy of sixty gallies. With this force they were ready to appear in the bay, while the Roman ships lay unmanned and unrigged, secure against any danger from an enemy whom they supposed shut up by impenetrable bars; and in these circumstances, if they had availed themselves of the surprise with which they might have attacked their enemy, must have done great execution on the Roman fleet. But having spent no less than two days in clearing their new passage after it was known to be open, and in preparing for action, they gave the enemy likewise full time to prepare. On the third they engaged, fought for the whole day without gaining any advantage; and, in their retreat at night, suffered greatly from the enemy, who pressed on their rear.

While the besiegers endeavoured to obstruct this new communication with the sea, the besieged made a desperate attempt on their works by land. A numerous body of men, devoting their lives for the defence of their country, without any arms, and provided only with matches, crossed the harbour, and, exposing themselves to certain death, set fire to the engines and towers of the besiegers; and, while they were surrounded and put to the sword, willingly perished in the execution of their purpose.

In such operations the summer elapsed; and Scipio, with the loss of his engines, and a renewal of all the difficulties which he had formerly to encounter at sea, contenting himself with a blockade for the winter, discontinued the siege.

His command being prolonged for another year, he resumed his attack in the spring; and finding the place greatly reduced by despair and famine, he forced his way by one of the docks, where he observed that the battlements were low and unguarded. His arrival in the streets did not put him in possession of the town. The inhabitants, during six days, disputed every house and every passage, and successively set fire to the buildings whenever they were obliged to abandon them. Above fifty thousand persons of different sexes, who had taken refuge in the citadel, at last accepted of quarter, and were led captive from thence in two separate divisions, one of twenty-five thousand women, and another of thirty thousand men.

Nine hundred deserters, who had left the Roman army during the siege, having been refused the quarter which was granted to the others, took post in a temple which stood on an eminence, with a resolution to die with swords in their hands, and with the greatest effusion of blood to their enemies. To these Hasdrubal, followed by his wife and his children, joined himself; but not having the courage to persist in the same purpose with these deserters, he left the temple, and accepted of quarter. His wife, in the mean time, with more ferocity or magnanimity than her husband, laid violent hands on her children, and, together with the dead bodies, threw herself into the flame of a burning ruin. The deserters, too, impatient of the dreadful expectations which they felt, in order to hasten their own fate, set fire to the temple in which they had sought a temporary cover, and perished in the flames.

The city continued to burn during seventeen days; and all this time the soldiers were allowed to seize whatever they could save from the flames, or wrest from the hands of the dying inhabitants, who were still dangerous to those who approached them. Scipio, in beholding this melancholy scene, is said to have repeated from Homer two lines containing a prophecy of the fall of Troy. "To whom do you now apply this prediction?" said Polybius, who happened to be near him; "To my own country," he said, "for her too I dread in her turn the reverses of human fate."[2]

Scipio's letter to the senate is said to have contained no more than these words: "Carthage is taken. The army waits for your further orders." The tidings were received at Rome with uncommon demonstrations of joy. The victors, recollecting all the passages of their former wars, the alarms that had been given by Hannibal, and the irreconcilable antipathy of the two nations, gave orders to raze the fortifications of Carthage, and even to destroy the materials of which they were built.

A commission was granted by the senate to ten of its members to take possession of territories which were thus deprived of their sovereign, to model the form of this new province, and to prepare it for the reception of a Roman governor. And thus Carthage, the only instance in which the human genius ever appeared greatly distinguished in Africa; the model of magnificence, the repository of wealth, and one of the principal states of the ancient world, was no more. The Romans, incited by national animosity, and an excess of jealousy, formed a design more cruel towards their rival than at first view it appeared to be, and in the execution of it became actors in the scene of horror far beyond their original intention. By the milder law and practice of modern nations, we are happily exempted from the danger of ever seeing such horrid examples repeated, at least in any part of the western world.

While the event of this mighty siege was still in dependence, the Romans had other wars to maintain on the side of Macedonia and Greece, where the natural progress of their policy, suited to the measures which they had taken with other nations, now ended in the open and avowed usurpation of a sovereignty which they had long disguised under the specious titles of alliance and protection.

Macedonia being ill fitted to retain the republican form into which it had been cast by the Romans, after some years of distraction, and an

2 For the history of the destruction of Carthage see the authors above cited, p. 80.

attempt at last in favour of a pretended son of the late king, to recover its independence and its monarchy, underwent a second conquest.

Andriscus, an African of uncertain extraction, being observed to resemble the royal family of Macedonia, had the courage, under the name of Philip, to personate a son of that unfortunate monarch, and to make pretensions to the crown. With this object in view he went into Syria to solicit the aid of Demetrius, but was, by this prince, taken into custody, and transported in chains to Rome. The Romans paid little regard to so contemptible an enemy, and even allowed him to escape. After this adventure, the same impostor appeared a second time in Macedonia, and, with better fortune than he had in the first attempt, drew to his standard many natives of that country and of Thrace. In his first encounter he even defeated Juventius the Roman prætor, and was acknowledged king; but soon after fell a prey to Metellus, and furnished the Romans with an obvious pretence for reducing the kingdom of Macedonia to the ordinary form of a province.

The states of the Achæan league, at the same time, being already on the decline, hastened, by the temerity and distraction of their own councils, the career of their fortunes to the same termination.

The Romans, even while they suffered this famous republic to retain the show of its independence, had treated its members in many particulars as subjects. At the close of the war with Perseus, they had cited to appear at Rome, or taken into custody as criminals of state, many citizens of Achaia, who had, in that contest, appeared to be disaffected to the Roman cause. Of these they had detained about a thousand in different prisons of Italy, until, after a period of seventeen years, about three hundred of them, who survived their confinement, were set at liberty, as having already suffered enough; or as being no longer in condition to give any umbrage to Rome.[1] Polybius being of this number, acquired, during his stay in Italy, that knowledge of Roman affairs which appears so conspicuous in the remains of his history. When at liberty, he attached himself to Scipio, the son of Emilius, and being well versed in the active scenes which had recently passed in his own country, and being entirely occupied with reflections on matters of state and of war, no doubt contributed by his instructions in preparing this young man for the eminent services which he afterwards performed.

The Romans, while they detained so many Greek prisoners in Italy, in a great measure assumed the administration of affairs in Greece, disposed of every distinction, whether of fortune or power, and confined these advantages to the advocates of their own cause, and to the tools of their own ambition.[2] They received appeals from the judgments of the Achæan council, and encouraged its members, contrary to the express conditions of their league, to send separate embassies to Rome. The steps which followed are but imperfectly marked in the fragments of history which relate to this period. It appears that the Spartans, having been forced into the Achæan confederacy, continued refractory in most of its councils. By some of their complaints at Rome, they obtained a deputation, as usual, from the senate to hear parties on the spot, and to adjust their differences. The Achæan council, incensed at this insult which was offered to their authority without waiting the arrival of the Roman deputies, proceeded to enforce their own decrees against the republic of Sparta, marched an army into Laconia, and defeated, with some slaughter, at the gates of Lacedemon, the inhabitants of that city who ventured to oppose them. The Roman commissioners arriving after these hostilities had commenced, summoned the parties to assemble at Corinth, and, in name of the senate, gave sentence, that Lacedemon, Corinth, Argos, Heraclea, and Orchomenos, not having been original members of the Achæan confederacy, should now be disjoined from it; and that all the cities which had been rescued from the dominion of Philip, should be left in full possession of their freedom and independency.

Multitudes from all the different states of the league being on this occasion assembled at Corinth, a great riot ensued. The Roman deputies were insulted and obliged to leave the place; and in this manner commenced a war in which the Romans, because they hoped to establish their sovereignty in Greece without any convulsion, and had full employment for their forces in Africa, Spain, and Macedonia, engaged with great reluctance. They renewed their commission, and named other deputies to terminate the disputes in Achaia; but the states of the Achæan league, imputing their conduct in this particular to fear, and to the ill state of their affairs in Africa, while Carthage was likely to repel their attack, thought that they had found an opportunity to exclude for ever from their councils the overbearing influence of this arrogant nation.[3] They were encouraged with hopes of support from Thebes, Eubœa, and other districts of Greece, where the people were averse to the dominion of the Romans; and they therefore assembled an army to assert their common rights, and to enforce their authority over the several members of their own confederacy.

Unfortunately for their cause, Metellus had then prevailed in Macedonia, and was at leisure to turn his forces against them. He accordingly moved towards the Peloponnesus, still giving the Achæans an option to avert the calamities of war, by submitting to the mandates of the Roman senate. These, he said, were no more, than that they should desist from their pretensions on Sparta, and the other cantons who applied for the protection of Rome.

But the Achæans thought it safer to resist, than to be disarmed under these stale pretences; they took the field, passed through the isthmus of Corinth, and, being joined by the Thebans, marched to Thermopylæ with a view to defend this entry into Greece. In this, however, they were disappointed, being either prevented from seizing the pass, or driven from thence by Metellus. They were afterwards intercepted in their retreat through Phocis, where they lost their leader Critolaus, with a great part of his army.[4] Diæus, who succeeded him as head of the confederacy, assembled a new force, consisting of fourteen thousand foot and six thousand horse, took post on the isthmus of Corinth, and sent four thousand men for the defence of Megara, a

1 Pausanias in Achaicis.
2 Polyb. Excerpt. Legat. c. 103.
3 Polyb. Excerpt. Legat. c. 144.
4 Orosius, lib. v. c. 3. Pausanias in Achaicis.

place which still made a part in the expiring confederacy of independent Greeks.

Metellus, who after his victory had made himself master of Thebes, advanced to Megara, dislodged the Achæans from thence, and continued his march to the isthmus. Here he was superseded by Mummius, the consul of the present year, who, with the new levies from Rome, made up an army of twenty-three thousand foot and three thousand five hundred horse. The enemy, having gained an advantage over his advanced guard, were encouraged to hazard a battle under the walls of Corinth, and were defeated. The greater part fled into the town, but afterwards in the night withdrew from that place. Their general Diæus fled from the field of battle to Migalopolis, whither he had sent his family; having killed his wife, to prevent her falling into the hands of the enemy, he himself took poison, and died.

Such are the imperfect accounts which remain of the last efforts made by the Greeks to preserve a freedom, in the exercise of which they had acted so distinguished a part. As they never were surpassed by any race of men in the vigour with which they supported their republican establishments, so they appeared to retain their ingenuity and their skill in many arts, after they had lost the military and political spirit which constitutes the strength and security of nations; and in this latter period, which preceded their extinction, as the Achæan league was dissolved on having incurred the resentment of the Romans, so the unhappy remnant of the Spartan republic perished in having accepted their protection. The enmity and the friendship of the Romans being equally fatal, these and every other state or republic of Greece, from this time forward, ceased to be numbered among nations, having fallen a prey to a power, whose force nothing could equal but the ability and the cunning with which it was exerted.

Such, at least, is the comment which we are tempted, by the conduct of the Romans, on the present occasion, to make on that policy, with which about fifty years before this date, Flamininus, to detach the Grecian cities from Philip, proclaimed, with so much ostentation at the isthmus of Corinth, general independence, and the free exercise of their own laws to all the republics of Greece. That people, when they meant to ingratiate themselves, surpassed every state in generosity to their allies, they gained entire confidence, and taught nations, who were otherwise in condition to maintain their own independence, to rely for protection on that very power from which they had most to fear for their liberties; and in the end, under some pretence of ingratitude or affront, stripped of every right those very states who had most plentifully shared in their bounty.

In this policy there were some appearances of a concerted design, which was at one time liberal and generous beyond example, at another time cruel and implacable in the opposite extreme, equally calculated to gain or to terrify, in the cases to which either species of policy was suited. It is, however, probable, that they were led by the changing state of their interests, and followed the conjuncture without any previous design. In this sort of conduct the passions are wonderfully ready to act in support of the judgment; and we may venture to admit, that the Romans sometimes felt the generosity which they professed to employ, and of which the belief was so favourable to the success of their affairs. In a different conjuncture, in which they were no longer equally obliged to manage the temper of their allies, they became more impatient of contradiction, and gave way to their resentment on any the slightest occasions, or to their ambition without control. Their maxim, to spare the submissive, and to reduce the proud,[5] whether founded in sentiment or cunning, was a principle productive of the extremes of generosity and arrogance observed in their conduct; it led them by degrees to assume a superiority in every transaction, and as their power increased, rendered this power proportionably dangerous to other nations.

On the third day after the action which happened in the isthmus of Corinth, the victorious general entered the city; and considering that the inhabitants had a principal part in the late insult offered to the Roman commissioners, determined to strike a general terror into all the members of the league by the severities to be executed against this people. Mummius, though, with the rest of his countrymen of this age, ill qualified to distinguish the elegant workmanship of the Grecian artists,[6] of which great collections had been made at Corinth, ordered all the statues and pictures to be set apart for his triumph; and, with this reserve, gave the town, abounding in all the accommodations and ornaments of a wealthy metropolis, to be pillaged by the soldiers. He razed the walls, and reduced the city to ashes.

Thus Corinth perished in the same year with Carthage. The fortifications of Thebes, and of some other towns disaffected to the Romans, were at the same time demolished; and the arrangements to be made in the country of Greece were committed to deputies from the Roman senate. By their order, the Achæan league was dissolved, and all its conventions annulled. The states which had composed it were deprived of their sovereignty, subjected to pay a tribute, and placed under the government of a person annually sent from Rome with the title of the Prætor of Achaia.[7]

The Romans now appeared openly, perhaps for the first time, in the capacity of conquerors. The acquisition of revenue in Macedonia, which, about twenty years before this date, had first taught them to exempt themselves from taxation, excited from thenceforward an insatiable thirst of dominion: and their future progress is marked by the detail of wars which they maintained on their frontier, not in defence of the empire, but for the enlargement of possessions already too great.

In Spain, where they still met with resistance, they had acted in all the different periods of their wars, either on the offensive or defensive, according as the state was, or was not, at leisure from the pressure of their enemies, or according as the generals she employed were ambitious or pacific

On the conclusion of the peace with Philip the Roman territory in Spain had been divided into two provinces, and furnished the stations of two separate commanders annually sent from

5 Parcere subjectis, et debellare superbos.

6 He delivered them to the masters of ships, with his famous threat, that if any of these curiosities were lost, they should be obliged to replace them.

7 Pausanias, lib. vii. c. 16. Polyb. Excerptæ de Virtutibus et Vitiis.

Rome. On the renewal of the war in Macedonia, and during the continuance of it, three provinces were again united under one government. But upon the defeat of Perseus, and the reduction of Macedonia, they were separated for ever.

From that time the ambition of the Romans seems to have operated in Spain with the same effect as in other parts on the boundaries of their empire. They pressed upon the natives, not merely to secure their own territory from inroad and depredation, but to gain new accessions of dominion and wealth. They advanced to the Tagus, endeavoured to penetrate the mountains beyond the sources of that river; and on that side involved themselves in a continual struggle of many years' duration, with the Lusitanians, Gallicians, and Celtiberi.

In these wars, the Roman officers were actuated by their avarice, as well as by their ambition, and were glad of occasions to quarrel with an enemy, amongst whom the produce of rich mines of silver and of gold were known to abound, and where plentiful spoils were so likely to reward their services.

The theatre of the war in Spain was not so conspicuous, nor the conduct of generals so strictly observed, as they were in Africa, Asia, or Greece; and such as were employed in that service, therefore, the more to hasten their conquests, ventured upon acts of treachery or breach of faith with the cantons around them, which the senate did not commonly avow; and they also ventured upon acts of extortion and peculation in their own governments, which gave occasion to the first complaints of this sort that were brought to Rome.

The proconsul Lucullus, having accepted of the surrender of a town, and being received into it in consequence of a capitulation, nevertheless put the inhabitants to the sword and carried off their effects. Galba, commanding in Lusitania, or the western province of Spain, soon afterwards circumvented, by a like act of perfidy and cruelty, some of the inhabitants whom he could not otherwise reduce. These examples probably retarded, instead of forwarding, the progress of the Roman arms, and confirmed that obstinate valour with which the natives of Spain disputed every post in defence of their country; and with which they maintained the contest against a succession of Roman generals, prætors, or consuls, who were employed to subdue them. This contest they continued or renewed, at short intervals, with various success, from the first expedition of the Scipios to the last of Augustus.

At the beginning of the last war with Carthage, the Lusitanians, incensed by the act of treachery which was committed by the Roman general Galba, reassembled in numerous parties under Viriathus, who had himself escaped from the massacre on that occasion, and who entertained an implacable resentment to the authors of it. This leader, according to the Roman historians, had been originally a herdsman, afterwards a chief of banditti, and last of all the commander of an army which had often defeated the legions of Rome, and threatened their expulsion from Spain. He seems to have known how to employ the impetuous valour of a rude people against troops not less valiant than his own countrymen, though more depending on discipline; and to have possessed what the Spaniards retained, even down to the days of Cæsar, the faculty of turning the want of order to account against an enemy so much accustomed to order, as, in a great measure, to rely upon it in most of their operations. With him an apparent rout and dispersion of his followers was the ordinary prelude to a violent attack; and he commonly endeavoured, by pretended flights and disorderly movements, to draw the enemy into rash pursuits or precipitant marches, and seized every advantage which they gave him with irresistible address and valour. He continued about ten years to baffle all the attempts which the Romans made to reduce Lusitania. He had projected a league and defensive confederacy with the other free nations of Spain, when he was assassinated, as he lay asleep on the ground, by two of his own followers, supposed to be in concert with the Roman general.

The Romans, upon this event, found the western and northern parts of Spain open to their inroads. In little more than a year afterwards, a Roman army under Brutus passed the Duero,[1] and penetrated quite to the coast of Gallicia, from which they reported, with more than the embellishments and exaggerations of travellers, that the sun was seen from this distant region, when he set in the evening, to sink and extinguish himself with a mighty noise in the Western Ocean.

The natives of this country, however, did not think themselves subdued by being thus overrun. They retired, with their cattle and effects, into places of strength; and, when required to pay contributions, replied, That their ancestors had left them swords to defend their possessions, but not any gold to redeem them.

Such were the occupations of the Roman arms in the western division of Spain, while they were equally engaged in the eastern province, under Cato the elder, Tiberius Gracchus, and others, who endeavoured to secure what the state had already acquired, or to extend its limits.—These generals obtained their several triumphs, and joined to the Roman possessions on the coast considerable acquisitions in the inland part of the country. Their progress, however, on this side had been greatly retarded by the obstinate valour of the Numantians, and other cantons of the Celtiberi, who had maintained the contest during fifty years, and at last had formed a general confederacy of all the interior nations of Spain, to be conducted by Viriathus, when their measures were broken by the death of that formidable leader.

Numantia was the principal strong hold, or, as we may conçeive it, the capital of a small nation. Their lodgment, or township, was contained within a circumference of about three miles, situated among the mountains of Celtiberia, or Old Castile, and at the confluence of the Durius with another river, both of which having steep banks, rendered the place, on two of its sides, of very difficult access. It was fortified on the third side with a rampart and ditch.

The people could muster no more than eight or ten thousand men; but these were greatly distinguished by their valour, reputed superior in horsemanship to every other nation of Spain, and equal to the Romans in the use of the shield and the stabbing sword. They had already gained

1 Durius.

many victories over the Roman armies which had been employed to reduce them. They had obliged Pompey, one of the Roman generals, contrary to the practice of his country, to accept of a treaty, while the advantage of fortune was against him. They obliged the consul Mancinus to save his army by a capitulation.[2] Neither of those treaties indeed were ratified by the Roman senate. To expiate the breach of the last, the consul Mancinus, who concluded it, together with Tiberius Gracchus, his questor, were ordered to be delivered up to the hands of the enemy, and to suffer in their own persons for the failure of engagements which they could not fulfil. Tiberius Gracchus appealed to the people, was saved by their favour, and from this time is supposed to have received that bias which he followed in the subsequent part of his political conduct. Mancinus acquiesced in the sentence of the senate, was presented naked and in fetters at the gates of Numantia, as a sacrifice to the resentment of that nation, for the breach of a treaty which the Romans determined not to observe. But the victim was nobly rejected, and the Numantians insisted on the conditions they had stipulated, saying, that a public breach of faith could not be expiated by the suffering of a private man.[3]

These transactions passed about ten years after the destruction of Carthage, and the Romans, mortified with the length and ill-success of the war with Numantia, had recourse again to the services of Scipio.

They had formerly dispensed, in his favour, with the law that required a certain age as a qualification for the office of consul; and now, in order to employ him a second time, they were obliged to suspend another law, which prohibited the re-election of the same person into that office.

Upon the arrival of Scipio in Spain, it is said that he found the Roman army, discouraged by repeated defeats, withdrawn into fortified stations at a distance from the enemy, detesting the hardships of a military camp, indulging themselves in all the vices of a disorderly town, and subject to panics on the slightest alarm. It is said that the cries, the aspect, the painted visage, and the long hair of the Spaniard were become objects of terror.[4]

Among the reformations which Scipio made to restore the vigour of the army, he cleared the camp of its unnecessary followers, amongst whom are mentioned women, merchants, and fortune-tellers; he restricted the quantity of baggage, reduced the furniture of the kitchen to the spit and the pan; and the tables of officers to plain food, roasted or boiled. He prohibited the use of bedsteads in camp, and set the example himself of sleeping on a straw mat; likewise restrained the infantry from the use of horses on the march, and obliged them to carry their own baggage.

Though possessed of superior numbers he declined a battle, and avoided every route on which the enemy were prepared to receive him; took advantage of a superior address in managing his resources, and damped the ardour of a fierce people by slow operations; he laid waste the country around them, and by degrees obliged them to retire within their own ramparts, and to consume what was raised or provided within the circuit of their walls.

2 Eutropius, lib. iv. c. 8.
3 Appian de Bell. Hispan. p. 302.
4 Florus.

Scipio had been joined on his march to Numantia by Jugurtha, the grandson of Massinissa, who, on their service, made his first acquaintance with the Romans, and brought a reinforcement of twelve elephants, with a considerable body of horse, of archers and slingers. At its arrival the army amounted to sixty thousand men. But Scipio did not attempt to storm the town; he took a number of posts which he successively fortified, and, by joining them together, completed a double line of circumvallation, equal in strength to the walls which were opposed to him. He had his curtains, his towers, his places of arms corresponding to those of the place; and he established an order of service and a set of signals, in case of alarm by day or by night, which resembled more the precautions of an army on its defence, than the operations of a siege. His intention was to reduce the Numantians by famine, an operation of time, during which, from so warlike a nation, he might be exposed to surprise, or to the effects of despair.

The place besieged being at the confluence of rivers navigable with small vessels, which descended with great rapidity on the stream, or which could, with the favour of proper winds, even remount in the sight of the enemy, the people, for a while, procured some supplies by water. Numbers of them swimming with great address, and diving at proper places, to avoid being seen by the besiegers, still passed through the lines, and preserved a communication with the country, until the rivers also were barred across their channels by timbers, that were armed with sword-blades and spikes of iron.

The Numantians were still in hopes of succour from their allies. Five aged warriors undertook, each with his son for a second, to pass through the lines of the enemy, and to sue for relief from the neighbouring nations. They succeeded by night in the first part of their attempt, cut down the Roman guard, threw the camp into some confusion, and escaped before the occasion of the alarm was known. But their cause was become desperate, and too likely to involve in certain ruin any friend who embraced it. Their suit, nevertheless, was attended to at Lutia, the head of a small canton, forty miles from Numantia.

The young men of this place took their resolution in favour of the injured Numantians; but Scipio had notice of their intention time enough to prevent its effect. He hastened to the place, and having accomplished this march of forty miles in eight hours, surprised the inhabitants, had four hundred young men delivered up to him, and ordered their right arms to be struck off. By this dreadful act of severity, he secured himself from any danger on that quarter, and impressed the other states of that neighbourhood with terror.

The Numantians, in the mean time, were pressed with famine, and having no hopes of relief, sent a deputation to try the clemency of their enemy. "What was once a happy state," they said, "content with its own possessions, and secure in the valour of its citizens, is now reduced to great distress, for no other crime than that of having maintained their freedom, and of having defended their wives and their children.

"For you," they continued, addressing themselves to Scipio, "who yourself are said to possess so many virtues, it would become you to espouse the cause of this injured nation, and procure to them terms which they could with honour prefer to their present distresses. Their expectations are moderate, for they have felt the reverses of fortune. It is now in your power to receive their submission under any tolerable conditions, or to see them perish in some act of despair, which may prove fatal to many of their enemies, as well as to themselves."

Scipio replied, That he could not grant them any terms; that they must surrender at discretion.

Upon the return of this answer they resumed their former obstinacy, and held out until they had consumed every article of provision within their walls; endeavoured to turn their shields and other utensils of leather into food, devoured the dead bodies, and even preyed on each other.

The end of this piteous scene is variously reported. By some it is said, that, in the last stage of despair, the Numantians sallied forth to purchase death by the slaughter of their enemies; that, in the execution of this purpose, they for some time exposed themselves with the most frantic rage, till the greater part being slain, a few returned into the town, set fire to the houses, and, with their wives and children, perished in the flames.[1]

By others it is said, that they agreed to surrender on a certain day, but that when this day came they begged for another; alleging, that many of their people, yet fond of liberty, had determined to die, and wished for one day more, that they might the more deliberately execute their purpose. Such was the aversion to surrender at discretion, which the fear of captivity, and that of its ordinary consequences among ancient nations, had inspired. The few of this high-minded people who survived the effects of despair, falling into the enemy's hands, were stripped of their arms. Fifty were reserved, as a specimen of the whole, to adorn the victor's triumph. The remainder were sold for slaves, and the walls of their strong hold were levelled with the ground. The prisoners, even after they had laid down their arms and submitted to mercy, retained the ferocity of their looks, and cast on their victors such glances of indignation and rage, as still kept the animosity of enemies awake, and prevented the returns of pity. As these particulars strongly mark the defects which still subsisted in the supposed law of war among ancient nations, the reader will probably bear with the shock that is given to his feelings of compassion, for the sake of the picture which it is necessary to give of the manners of the times.

If we judge of Numantia from the resistance it made to the Roman arms, it having been one of their most difficult conquests, we must consider it as a state of considerable power. Its reduction gave immediate respite from war in Spain. Scipio and Brutus returned nearly together from their provinces in that country, and had their separate triumphs in the same year.

These operations against Numantia, Carthage, Macedonia, and Greece, were accompanied with a revolt of the slaves in Sicily, and with a number of other wars less considerable in Illyricum, Thrace, and Gaul. Of these the revolt of the slaves merits the greater attention, on account of the view it gives of the state of the countries now under the immediate jurisdiction of Rome. The island of Sicily having been the first acquisition which the Romans made beyond the limits of Italy, had been for some time in a state of domestic tranquillity, and undisturbed by any foreign enemy. Its lands were become the property of Roman citizens, who here, as on their estates in Italy, cultivated plantations to supply with corn, wine, and oil, the markets and granaries of Rome. The labour was performed by slaves. These were led in chains to the fields, or confined in vaults and fortified workhouses at the several tasks they were employed to perform. As the proprietors of land had many reasons to prefer the labour of slaves to that of freemen, who were distracted by their political engagements, and subject to be called upon or pressed into the military service, the number of slaves continually increased. They were, for the most part, prisoners of war; and some of them being of high rank, unused to submission, and animated with fierce passions of indignation and scorn, were ready, upon every favourable opportunity, to take arms against their masters, and often to shake the state itself with a storm which was not foreseen until it actually burst.

About ten years after the destruction of Carthage, and four years before that of Numantia, this injured class of men were incited to revolt in Sicily by Eunus, a Syrian slave; who, at first under pretence of religion, and by the fame of miracles he was supposed to perform, tempted many to break from their bondage; traversed the country, broke open the vaults and prisons in which his fellow-sufferers were confined, and actually assembled an army of seventy thousand men. With this force, in four successive campaigns, he made a prosperous war on the Roman prætors, and often stormed the entrenchments of the Roman camp.

This leader, however, being ill-qualified to improve his victories, and having no concerted plan for the government or subsistence of his followers, in a country that was gradually ruined by their own devastations, was at length, by the caution and superior conduct of Perperna, or Publius Rutilius, gradually circumscribed in his depredations, defeated, and obliged to take refuge in Enna, a fortified place, where about twenty thousand of his followers were put to the sword, and the remainder, as an example, to deter slaves from the commission of a similar offence, were nailed to the cross, near the most frequented highways, and in the most conspicuous parts of the island.

While the Roman armies were thus employed in the provinces, or on the frontier of their extensive conquests, Italy itself had long enjoyed a perfect security, the lands were cultivated, and the country stocked with people, whether aliens or citizens, freemen or slaves. From about three hundred thousand,[2] which, in this period, were the ordinary return of the census, the citizens soon after augmented to above four hundred thousand;[3] and Scipio, under whose inspection as censor this return was made, hearing the crier repeat the prayer which was usual at the closing of the rolls, "That the republic might increase

1 Orosius. lib. v. c. 7. Florus, lib. ii. c. 18.

2 Three hundred and twenty thousand.

3 Four hundred and twenty-eight thousand three hundred and forty-two.

in the numbers of its people, and in the extent of its territory;" bid him pray that it might be preserved, for it was already great enough. It is probable that, in the view of this sagacious observer, the marks of corruption already began to appear in the capital; and a tree, which still continued for a century to make such vigorous shoots from its branches, already bore some marks of decay in its trunk.

The offices of state, and the government of provinces, to which those who had filled them succeeded, began to be coveted from avarice, as well as from ambition. Complaints of peculation and extortion, which were received about this time from Spain and Macedonia, pointed out the necessity of restraining such oppressions, and suggested some penal laws, which were often, and in vain, amended and revived.

An action was instituted in favour of the provinces, against governors, or their attendants, who should be accused of levying money without the authority of the state, and an ordinary jurisdiction was granted to one of the prætors, to hear complaints on this subject. The penalty at first was no more than restitution, and a pecuniary fine; it was gradually extended to degradation, and exile.

No. 604. Lex Calpurnia de Repetundis. Questiones perpetuæ.

These reformations are dated in the time of the last war with Carthage, and are ascribed to the motion of Culpurnius Piso, then one of the tribunes. Before this time all jurisdiction in criminal matters belonged to the tribunal of the people, and was exercised by themselves in their collective capacity, or occasionally delegated to a special commission. Few crimes were yet defined by statute, and ordinary courts of justice for the trial of them were not yet established. In these circumstances criminals of state had an opportunity not only to defend themselves after a prosecution was commenced, but likewise to employ intrigue, or exert their credit with the people, to prevent or evade a trial.

To supply these defects, a list of statutory crimes now began to be made, and an ordinary jurisdiction was established. Besides extortion in the provinces, which had been defined by the law of Culpurnius,[4] murder, breach of faith, robbery, assault, poisoning, incest, adultery, bribery, false judgment, fraud, perjury, &c. were successively joined to the list; and an ordinary jurisdiction for the trial of such crimes was vested in a jury of senators, over whom the prætor, with the title of quæsitor, presided.

The number of prætors, corresponding to this and other growing exigencies of the state, was now augmented to six; and these officers, though destined, as well as the consuls, to the command of armies and the government of provinces, began, during the term of their magistracy, to have full occupation in the city. On this account it was not till after the expiration of the year for which they had been elected, that they drew lots for a province. A like policy was soon after adopted in the destination of consuls, and all the other officers of state, who, being supposed to have sufficient occupation in Italy and Rome during the year of their appointment, were not destined to any foreign service till that year was expired.

With these establishments, calculated to secure the functions of office, the use of the ballot was introduced, first in elections, and afterwards in collecting opinions of judges in the courts of justice:[5] a dangerous form of proceeding in constitutions tending to popular license, and where justice is more likely to suffer from the unawed passions of the lower people, than from any improper influence of superior rank; and where the authority of the wise, and the sense of public shame, were so much required, as principal supports of government.

An occasion for the commission of new crimes is frequently taken from the precautions which are employed against the old. From the facility with which criminal accusations now began to be received, a new species of crime accordingly arose. Calumny and vexatious prosecutions commenced by disappointed competitors against persons in public trust, became so frequent as to require the interposition of laws. On this account it was enacted, upon the motion of Memmius, that all persons in office, or appointed to command in the provinces, might decline answering a criminal charge until the expiration of their term, or until their return from the service to which they were destined;[6] and persons of any denomination might have an action of calumny against the author of a false or groundless prosecution. Whoever was convicted of this offence was to be branded in the face with the initials of his crime.

By these establishments the city of Rome, long resembling a mere military station, made some progress in completing the system and application of her laws. Literary productions, in some of their forms, particularly in the form of dramatic compositions, as hath been already observed, began to be known. The representation of fables was first introduced under pretence of religion, and practised as a sacred rite to avert the plague or some public calamity. This entertainment was fondly received by the people, and therefore frequently presented to them by the ediles, who had the charge of such matters. Literature, however, in some of its less popular forms, was checked, as a source of corruption.

U. C. 592. In the year of Rome five hundred and ninety-two, that is, about eight years after the reduction of Macedonia, the Roman senate, upon a report from M. Pomponius, the prætor, that the city was frequented by philosophers and rhetoricians, resolved, that this officer, agreeably to his duty to the republic, should take care to remove all such persons in the manner his own judgment should direct;[7] and, in about six years after this date, an embassy having come from Athens, composed of scholars and rhetoricians, who drew the attention of the youth by the display of their talents, an uncommon despatch was given to their business, that they might not have any pretence for remaining too long in the city.

A proposal which was made during this period, to erect a theatre for the accommodation of the spectators at their public shows, was rejected with great indignation, as an attempt to corrupt the manners of the people. The materials which had been collected for this work were publicly sold, and an edict, at the same time, was pub-

4 Parricidium, vis publica, latrocinium, injuria, veneficium, incestus, adulterium, captæ pecuniæ corrupti, judicii fals., perjurium.

5 Lex Gabinia Tabellaria.

6 Lex Memmia de reis postulandis. Lex Cassia Tabellaria.

7 A. Gellius, lib. xv. c. 11

lished, that no one should ever resume this design, or attempt to place any bench or seat for the accommodation of the spectators at any theatrical entertainment in the city, or within a mile of its walls.[1] It was thought an act of effeminacy, it seems, for the Roman people to be seated; and it is undoubtedly wise, in matters of small moment, however innocent, to forbid what is considered as an evil, and, in remitting established severities, to let the opinion of innocence at least precede the indulgence.

The sumptuary laws already mentioned, respecting entertainments and household expenses, were, under the name of Didius, the person who proposed the renewal of them, revived;[2] and, with some alterations, extended to all the Roman citizens dispersed over Italy.

Such was the antidote which the policy of that age provided, in the capital of a great empire, against luxury and the ostentation of wealth; distempers incident to prosperity itself, and not to be cured by partial remedies. They were by the Romans (who knew better how to accomplish the celebrated problem of Themistocles, *in making a small state a great one*, than they knew how to explain the effects of its greatness) commonly imputed to some particular circumstance, or accidental event. To the spoils of Tarentum, they said, and of Asia,[3] to the destruction of our principal rivals, the Carthaginians; to the mighty show of statues, pictures, and costly furniture, which were brought by Mummius from Corinth, we owe this admiration of finery, and so prevailing a passion for private as well as for public wealth.

In this manner they explained the effects of a progress which they themselves had made in the acquisition of so many provinces; in the growing security and riches of a mighty city, from which all foreign alarms were far removed; and to which the wealth of a great empire, either in the form of private fortune or of public treasure, began to flow with a continued and increasing stream.[4]

CHAPTER II.

Extent of the Roman Empire—Political Character of its Head—Facility with which it continued to advance—Change of Character, Political as well as Moral—Character of the People or Commons—Dangerous Humours likely to break out—Appearance of Tiberius Gracchus—His project to revive the Law of Licinius—Intercession of the Tribune Octavius—The Republic divided—Disputes in the Comitia—Deposition of the Tribune Octavius—Commissioners appointed for the Division of Lands—Tiberius Gracchus sues to be re-elected Tribune—His Death—Immediate Consequences—Proceedings of Carbo—Embassy of Scipio—Foreign Affairs—Violence of the Commissioners—Domestic Affairs.

IN the manner that has been summarily stated in the preceding chapters, the Romans completed their political establishment, and made their first and their greatest advances to empire, without departing from the policy by which they had been preserved in the infancy of their power. They were become sovereigns of Macedonia, Greece, Italy, part of Africa, Lusitania, and Spain; yet, even in this pitch of greatness, made no distinction between the civil and military departments, nor gave to any citizen an exemption from the public service. They did not despise any enemy, neither in the measures they took, nor in the exertions they made to resist him: and as the fatal effects which they and all the other nations of the ancient world were long accustomed to expect from defeats, were no less than servitude or death, they did not submit to any enemy in consequence of any event, nor under the pressure of any calamity whatever.

Other nations were accustomed to rise on victories, and to sink under defeats; to become insolent or mean with the tide of their fortunes. The Romans alone were moderate in prosperity, and arrogant when their enemies expected to force their submission.

Other nations, when in distress, could weigh their sufferings against the concessions which they were required to make; and, among the evils to which they were exposed, preferred what appeared to be the least. The Romans alone spurned the advances of a victorious enemy; were not to be moved by sufferings; and, though they cautiously avoided difficulties that were likely to surpass their strength, did not allow it to be supposed that they were governed by fear in any case whatever. They willingly treated with the vanquished, and were ready to grant the most liberal terms when the concession could not be imputed to weakness or fear. By such free and unforced concession, indeed, they established a reputation for generosity, which contributed, no less than their valour, to secure the dominion they acquired.

With the same insinuating titles of allies or protectors, by which they had, in the infant state of their policy, brought all the cantons of Latium to follow their standard; they continued to take the ascendant over nations whom they could not have otherwise subdued. But as they were liberal in their friendships, so, after repeated provocations seemed to justify a different conduct, they were terrible in their resentments, and took ample compensation for the favours they had formerly bestowed.

By their famous maxim in war, already mentioned, That the submissive were to be spared, and the proud to be humbled, it became necessary for them, in every quarrel, to conquer or to perish; and, when these were the alternatives proposed by them, other nations were entitled to consider them as common enemies. No state has a right to make the submission of mankind a necessary condition to its own preservation; nor are many states qualified to support such pretensions. Some part of this political character, however, is necessary to the safety, as well as to the advancement,

---

1 Val. Maxim. lib. ii. c. 4.

2 Lex Didia.

3 Asia primum devicta luxuriam misit in Italiam. Plin. lib. xxxiii. c. 11.

4 Liv. lib. xxxix. c. 6. Plin. lib. xxxvii. c. 1.

of nations. No free state or republic is safe under any other government or defence than that of its own citizens. No nation is safe that permits any ally to suffer by having espoused its cause, or that allows itself to be driven, by defeats or misfortunes, into a surrender of any material part of its rights.

The measure of the Roman conquests, in the beginning of the seventh century of Rome, though great, was yet far from being full; and the people had not hitherto relaxed the industry, nor cooled in the ardour with which prosperous nations advance, but which they frequently remit in the height of their attainments and of their power.

The constitution of the commonwealth still afforded a plentiful nursery of men for both the civil and military departments; and this people accordingly continued for some time to advance with a quick pace in the career of their conquests. They subdued mighty kingdoms with as great, or greater facility, than that with which they had formerly conquered villages and single fields.

But the enlargement of their territory, and the success of their arms abroad, became the sources of a ruinous corruption at home. The wealth of provinces began to flow into the city, and filled the coffers of private citizens, as well as those of the commonwealth. The offices of state and the command of armies were become lucrative as well as honourable, and were coveted on the former account. In the state itself the governing and the governed felt separate interests, and were at variance, from motives of avarice, as well as ambition; and, instead of the parties who formerly strove for distinction, and for the palm of merit in the service of the commonwealth, factions arose, who contended for the greatest share of its spoils, and who sacrificed the public to their party-attachments and animosities.

Two hundred and thirty years had elapsed since the animosities of patrician and plebeian were extinguished by the equal participation of public honours. This distinction itself was in a great measure obliterated, and gave way to a new one, which, under the denomination of nobles and commons, or illustrious and obscure, without involving any legal disparity of privileges, gave rise to an aristocracy, which was partly hereditary, founded in the repeated succession to honours in the same family; and partly personal, founded in the habits of high station, and in the advantages of education, such as never fail to distinguish the conditions of men in every great and prosperous state.

These circumstances conferred a power on the nobles, which, though less invidious, was not less real than that which had been possessed by the ancient patricians. The exercise of this power was lodged with the senate, a body which, though by the emulation of its members too much disposed to war, and ambitious of conquest, was probably never surpassed in magnanimity, ability, or in steadiness, by any council of state whatever.

The people had submitted to the senate, as possessed of an authority which was founded in the prevailing opinion of their superior worth; and even the most aspiring of the commons allowed themselves to be governed by an order of men, amongst whom they themselves, by proper efforts and suitable merit, might hope to ascend. The examples of preferment, and the rise of individuals, from the lowest to the highest ranks of the commonwealth, though for the most part received with some degree of jealousy by those who were already in possession of the higher condition, were nevertheless frequent, and extinguished all appearance of an exclusive pretension to the honours of the state in any order or class of the people.

The knights, or the equestrian order, being persons possessed of estates or effects of a certain valuation,[1] formed between the senate and the people an intermediate rank, who, in consequence of their having a capital, and being less engaged than the senators in affairs of state, became traders, contractors, farmers of the revenue, and constituted a species of moneyed interest in the city, and in the provinces.

Such, during the latter part of the period of which the events have been already related, was the distribution of rank in this commonwealth. But circumstances which appear to be fixed in the political state of nations, are often no more than a passage in the shifting of scenes, or a transition from that which a people have been, to what they are about to become. The nobles began to avail themselves of the high authority and advantages of their station, and to accumulate property as well as honours. The country began to be occupied with their plantations and their slaves. The number of great landed estates, and the multiplication of slaves, kept pace together. This manner of stocking plantations was necessary or expedient in the circumstances of the Romans: for if the Roman citizen, who possessed so much consequence in his military and political capacity, had been willing to become a hireling and a servant, yet it was not the interest of masters to entrust their affairs to persons who were liable to be pressed into the legions, or who were so often called away to the comitia and assemblies of the people.

Citizens contended for offices in the state as the road to lucrative appointments abroad; and when they had obtained this end, and had reigned for a while in some province, they brought back from their governments a profusion of wealth ill acquired, and the habit of arbitrary and uncontrolled command. When disappointed in the pursuits of fortune abroad, they became the leaders of dangerous factions at home; or when suddenly possessed of great wealth, they became the agents of corruption to disseminate idleness, and the love of ruinous amusements, in the minds of the people.

The seclusion of the equestrian order from the pursuit of political emolument or honour, and the opportunities they had, by contracts and by farming the revenue, to improve their fortunes in a different way, confirmed them in the habits of trade, and the attention to lucrative considerations.

The city was gradually crowded with a populace, who, tempted with the cheap or gratuitous distribution of corn, by the frequency of public shows, by the consequence they enjoyed as members of the popular assemblies, or perhaps dislodged from the country by the engrossers of land, and the preference which was given to the labour of slaves over that of freemen, flocked from the colonies and municipal towns to reside at Rome. There they were corrupted by idleness and indigence, and the order itself was continually debased by the frequent accession of emancipated slaves.

The Romans, who were become so jealous of their prerogative as citizens, had no other way of

1 400,000 Roman money, or about 3,000*l*.

disposing of a slave, who had obtained his freedom, than by placing him on the rolls of the people; and from this quarter accordingly the numbers of the people were chiefly recruited. The emancipated slave took the name of his master, became a client, and a retainer of his family; and at funerals and other solemnities, where the pomp was distinguished by the number of attendants, made a part of the retinue. This class of men accordingly received continual additions, from the vanity or weakness of those who chose to change their slaves into dependent citizens; and numbers who had been conducted to Rome as captives, or who had been purchased in Asia or Greece, at a price proportioned to the pleasurable arts they possessed, became an accession to that turbulent populace, who, in the quality of Roman citizens, tyrannized in their turn over the masters of the world, and wrecked on the conquerors of so many nations the evils which they themselves had so freely inflicted on mankind.[1]

Citizens of this extraction could not for ages arrive at any places of trust, in which they could, by their personal defects, injure the commonwealth; but they increased, by their numbers and their vices, the weight of that dreg, which, in great and prosperous cities, ever sinks, by the tendency of vice and misconduct, to the lowest condition. They became a part of that faction who are ever actuated by envy to their superiors, by mercenary views, or by abject fear; who are ever ready to espouse the cause of any leader against the restraints of public order; disposed to vilify the more respectable ranks of men; and by their indifference on the subjects of justice or honour, to frustrate every principle that may be employed for the government of mankind, besides fear and compulsion.

Although citizens of this description were yet far from being the majority at Rome, yet it is probable that they were in numbers sufficient to contaminate the whole body of the people; and, if enrolled promiscuously in all the tribes, might have had great weight in turning the scale of political councils. This effect, however, was happily prevented by the wise precaution which the censors had taken to confine all citizens of mean or slavish extraction to four of the tribes. These were called the tribes of the city, and formed but a small proportion of the whole.[2]

Notwithstanding this precaution, we must suppose them to have been very improper parties in the participation of sovereignty, and likely enough to disturb the place of assembly with disorders and tumults.

While the state was advancing to the sovereignty of Italy, and while the territories successively acquired were cleared for the reception of Roman citizens, by the reduction and captivity of the natives, there was an outlet for the redundancy of this growing populace, and its overflowings were accordingly dispersed over Italy, from Rhegium to Aquileia, in about seventy colonies. But the country being now completely settled, and the property of its inhabitants established, it was no longer possible to provide for the indigent citizens in this manner; and the practice of settling new colonies, which had been so useful in planting, and securing the conquests which were made in Italy, had not yet been extended beyond this country, nor employed as the means of securing any of the provinces lately acquired. Mere colonization, indeed, would have been an improper and inadequate measure for this purpose; and in time of the republic never was, in any considerable degree, extended beyond sea. The provinces were placed under military government, and were to be retained in submission by bodies of regular troops. Roman citizens had little inclination to remove their habitations beyond the limits of Italy; and if they had, wou'd have been unable, in the mere capacity of civil corporations and pacific settlements, to carry into execution the exactions of a government which they themselves, now become inhabitants and proprietors of land in those provinces, would have soon been interested to oppose: for these reasons, although the Roman territory was greatly extended, the resources of the poorer citizens were diminished. The former discharge for many dangerous humours that were found to arise among them, was in some measure shut up, and these humours began to regorge on the state.

While the inferior people at Rome sunk in their characters, or were debased by the circumstances we have mentioned, the superior ranks, by their application to affairs of state, by their education, by the ideas of high birth and family-distinction, by the superiority of fortune, began to rise in their estimation, in their pretensions, and in their power; and they entertained some degree of contempt for persons, whom the laws still required them to admit as their fellow-citizens and equals.

In this disposition of parties so dangerous in a commonwealth, and amidst materials so likely to catch the flame, some sparks were thrown that soon kindled up anew all the popular animosities which seemed to have been so long extinguished. We have been carried, in the preceding narration, by the series of events, somewhat beyond the date of transactions that come now to be related. While Scipio was employed in the siege of Numantia, and while the Roman officers in Sicily were yet unable to reduce the revolted slaves, Tiberius Gracchus, born of a plebeian family, but ennobled by the honours of his father, by his descent on the side of his mother from the first Scipio Africanus, and by his alliance with the second Scipio, who had married his sister, being now tribune of the people, and possessed of all the accomplishments required in a popular leader, great ardour, resolution, and eloquence, formed a project in itself extremely alarming, and in its consequences dangerous to the peace of the republic.

Like other young men of high pretensions at Rome, Tiberius Gracchus had begun his military service at the usual age, had served with reputation under his brother-in-law, Scipio, at the siege of Carthage, afterwards as questor, under Mancinus in Spain, where the credit of his father, well known in that province, pointed him out to the natives as the only person with whom they would negotiate in the treaty that ensued. The disgrace he incurred in this transaction gave him a distaste to the military service, and to foreign affairs. When he was called to account for it, the severity he experienced from the senate, and the protection he obtained from the people, filled his

1 Velleius, lib. ii. c. 4.

2 Liv. lib. ix. c. 46. When this precaution was taken by Fabius Maximus, the tribes amounted to thirty-one. See the successive additions by which the tribes were brought up to this number, Liv. lib. vi. c. 5. lib. vii. c. 15. lib. viii. c. 17. lib. ix. c. 20.

breast with an animosity to the one, and a prepossession in favour of the other.[3]

Actuated by these dispositions, or by an idea not uncommon to enthusiastic minds, that *the unequal distribution of property, so favourable to the rich, is an injury to the poor;* he now proposed in part to remedy or to mitigate this supposed evil, by reviving the celebrated law of Licinius, by which Roman citizens had been restrained from accumulating estates in land above the value of five hundred jugera,[4] or from having more than one hundred of the larger cattle, and five hundred of the lesser.

In his travels through Italy, he said, he had observed that the property of land was beginning to be engrossed by a few of the nobles, and that the country was entirely occupied by slaves, to the exclusion of freemen: that the race of Roman citizens would soon be extinct,[5] if proper settlements were not provided to enable the poor to support their families, and to educate their children; and he alleged, that if estates in land were reduced to the measure prescribed by law, the surplus left would then be sufficient for this purpose.

Being determined, however, as much as possible, to prevent the opposition of the nobles, and to reconcile the interest of both parties to his scheme, he proposed to make some abatements in the rigour of the Licinian law, allowing every family holding five hundred jugera in right of the father, to hold half as much in the right of every unemancipated son; and proposed, that every person who should suffer any diminution of his property in consequence of the intended reform, should have compensation made to him; and that the sum necessary for this purpose should be issued from the treasury.

In this manner he set out with an appearance of moderation, acting in concert with some leading men in the state and members of the senate, such as Appius Claudius, whose daughter he had married, a senator of the family of Crassus, who was then at the head of the priesthood, and Mutius Scævola, consul.

To complete the intended reformation, and to prevent for the future the accumulation of estates in land, the sale or commerce of land was from thenceforward to be prohibited; and three commissioners were to be annually named, to ensure the execution and regular observance of this law.

This project, however plausible, it is probable, was extremely unseasonable, and ill suited to the state of the commonwealth. The law of Licinius had passed in the year of Rome three hundred and seventy-seven, no more than fourteen years after the city was restored from its destruction by the Gauls, and about two hundred and fifty years before this date; and though properly suited to a small republic, and even necessary to preserve a democracy, was, in that condition of the people, received with difficulty, and was soon trespassed upon even by the person himself on whose suggestion it had been moved and obtained: that it was become obsolete, and gone into disuse, appeared from the abuses which were now complained of, and to which its renewal was proposed as a remedy. It was become in a great measure impracticable, and even dangerous in the present state of the republic. The distinctions of poor and rich are as necessary in states of considerable extent, as labour and good government. The poor are destined to labour, and the rich, by the advantages of education, independence, and leisure, are qualified for superior stations. The empire was now greatly extended, and owed its safety and the order of its government to a respectable aristocracy, founded on the possession of fortune, as well as personal qualities and public honours. The rich were not, without some violent convulsion, to be stript of estates which they themselves had bought, or which they had inherited from their ancestors. The poor were not qualified at once to be raised to a state of equality with persons inured to a better condition. The project seemed to be as ruinous to government as it was to the security of property, and tended to place the members of the commonwealth, by one rash and precipitate step, in situations in which they were not at all qualified to act.

For these reasons, as well as from motives of private interest affecting the majority of the nobles, the project of Tiberius was strenuously opposed by the senate; and from motives of envy interest, or mistaken zeal for justice, as warmly supported by the opposite party. At the several assemblies of the people which were called to deliberate on this subject, Tiberius, exalting the characters of freemen contrasted with slaves, displayed the copious and pathetic eloquence in which he excelled. All the free inhabitants of Italy were Romans, or nearly allied to this people. He observed how much, being supplanted by the slaves of the rich, they were diminished in their numbers. He inveighed against the practice of employing slaves, a class of men that bring perpetual danger, without any addition of strength to the public, and who are ever ready to break forth in desperate insurrections, as they had then actually done in Sicily, where they still occupied the Roman arms in a tedious and ruinous war.[6]

In declaiming on the mortifications and hardships of the indigent citizen, he had recourse to the arguments commonly advanced to explode the inequalities of mankind. "Every wild beast," he said, "in this happy land has a cover or place of retreat. But many valiant and respectable citizens, who have exposed their lives, and who have shed their blood in the service of their country, have not a home to which they may retire. They wander with their wives and their children, stripped of every possession, but that of the air and the light. To such men the common military exhortation, *to fight for the tombs of their fathers, and for the altars of their household gods*, is a mockery and a lie. They have no altars; they have no monuments. They fight and they die to augment the estates, and to pamper the luxury of a few wealthy citizens, who have engrossed all the riches of the commonwealth. As citizens of Rome, they are entitled *the masters of the world*, but possess not a foot of earth on which they may rest."[7]

He asked, whether it were not reasonable to apply what was public to public uses? whether a freeman were not preferable to a slave, a brave man to a coward, and a fellow-citizen to a stranger?

3 Cicero de Claris Oratoribus, c. 27.
4 Little more than half as many acres.
5 Plutarch in Tib. Gracch.

6 Appian. de Bell. Civ.
7 Plutarch. in Vit. Tib. Gracch.

He expatiated on the fortune, and stated the future prospects of the republic. Much, he said, she had acquired, and had yet more to acquire; that the people, by their decision in the present question, were to determine, whether they were, by multiplying their numbers, to increase their strength, and be in a condition to conquer what yet remained of the world? or, by suffering the resources of the whole people to get into the hands of a few, they were to permit their numbers to decline, and to become unable, against nations envious and jealous of their power, even to maintain the ground they already had gained?

He exhorted the present proprietors of land, whom the law of division might affect, not to withhold, for the sake of a trifling interest to themselves, so great an advantage from their country. He bade them consider whether they would not, by the secure possession of five hundred jugera, and of half as much to each of their children, be sufficiently rewarded for the concessions now required in behalf of the public; put them in mind that riches were merely comparative; and that, in respect to this advantage, they were still to remain in the first rank of their fellow citizens.[1]

By these and similar arguments he endeavoured to obtain the consent of one party, and to inflame the zeal of the other. But when he came to propose, that the law should be read, he found that his opponents had availed themselves of their usual defence; had procured M. Octavius, one of his own colleagues, to interpose with his negative, and to forbid any farther proceeding in the business. Here, according to the forms of the constitution, this matter should have dropped. The tribunes were instituted to defend their own party, not to attack their opponents; and to prevent not to promote innovations. Every single tribune had a negative on the whole. But Tiberius, thus suddenly stopped in his career, became the more impetuous and confirmed in his purpose. Having adjourned the assembly to another day, he prepared a motion more violent than the former, in which he erased all the clauses by which he had endeavoured to soften the hardships likely to fall on the rich. He proposed, that, without expecting any compensation, they should absolutely cede the surplus of their possessions, as being obtained by fraud and injustice.

In this time of suspense, the controversy began to divide the colonies and free cities of Italy, and was warmly agitated wherever the citizens had extended their property. The rich and the poor took opposite sides. They collected their arguments, and they mustered their strength. The first had recourse to the topics which are commonly employed on the side of prescription, urging that, in some cases, they had possessed their estates from time immemorial; and that the lands they possessed were become valuable, only in consequence of the industry and labour which they themselves had employed to improve them: that, in other cases, they had actually bought their estates: that the public faith, under which they were suffered to purchase, was now engaged to protect and secure their possession: that, in reliance on this faith, they had erected, on these lands, the sepulchres of their fathers; they had pledged them for the dowries of their wives and the portions of their children, and mortgaged them as security for the debts they had contracted: that a law regulating or limiting the farther increase or accumulation of property might be suffered; but that a law, having a retrospect, and operating in violation of the rights, and to the ruin of so many families, was altogether unjust, and even impracticable in the execution.

The poor, on the contrary, pleaded their own indigence and their merits; urged that they were no longer in a capacity to fill the station of Roman citizens or of freemen, nor in a condition to settle families or to rear children, the future hopes of the commonwealth: that no private person could plead immemorial possession of lands which had been acquired for the public. They enumerated the wars which they themselves, or their ancestors, had maintained in the conquest of those lands. They concluded, that every citizen was entitled to his share of the public conquests; and that the arguments which were urged to support the possessions of the nobles, only tended to show how presumptuous and insolent such usurpations, if suffered to remain, were likely to become.

This mode of reasoning appears plausible; but it is dangerous to adopt by halves even reason itself. If it were reasonable that every Roman citizen should have an equal share of the conquered lands, it was still more reasonable, that the original proprietors, from whom those lands had been unjustly taken, should have them restored. If, in this, the maxims of reason and justice had been observed, Rome would have still been a small community, and might have acted with safety on the principles of equality which are suited to a small republic. But the Romans, becoming sovereigns of a great and extensive territory, must adopt the disparities, and submit to the subordinations, which mankind universally have found natural, and even necessary, to their government in such situations.

Multitudes of people from all parts of Italy, some earnestly desirous to have the law enacted, others to have it set aside, crowded to Rome to attend the decision of the question; and Gracchus, without dropping his intention, as usual, upon the negative of his colleague, only bethought himself how he might surmount, or remove this obstruction.

Having hitherto lived in personal intimacy with Octavius, he tried to gain him in private; and having failed in this attempt, he entered into expostulations with him, in presence of the public assembly; desired to know, whether he feared to have his own estate impaired by the effects of the law; for if so, he offered to indemnify him fully in whatever he might suffer by the execution of it: and being still unable to shake his colleague, who was supported by the countenance of the senate and the higher ranks of men in the state, he determined to try the force of his tribunitian powers to compel him, laid the state itself under a general interdict, sealed up the doors of the treasury, suspended the proceedings in the courts of the prætors, and put a stop to all the functions of office in the city.

All the nobility and superior class of the people went into mourning. Tiberius, in his turn, endeavoured to alarm the passions of his party; and believing, or pretending to believe, that he himself was in danger of being assassinated, had a number of persons with arms to defend his person.

1 Appian de Bell. Civ

While the city was in this state of suspense and confusion, the tribes were again assembled, and Tiberius, in defiance of the negative of his colleague, was proceeding to call the votes, when many of the people, alarmed by this intended violation of the sacred law, crowded in before the tribe that was moving to ballot, and seized the urns. A great tumult was likely to arise. The popular party, being most numerous, were crowding around their leader, when two senators, Manlius and Fulvius, both of consular dignity, fell at his feet, embraced his knees, and beseeched him not to proceed. Overcome with the respect that was due to persons of this rank, and with the sense of some impending calamity, he asked, "What they would have him to do?" "The case," they said, "is too arduous for us to decide; refer it to the senate, and await their decree."

Proceedings were accordingly suspended until the senate had met, and declared a resolution not to confirm the law. Gracchus resumed the subject with the people, being determined either to remove, or to slight the negative of his colleague. He proposed, that either the refractory tribune, or himself, should be immediately stripped of his dignity. He desired that Octavius should put the question first, Whether Tiberius Gracchus should be degraded? This being declined as irregular and vain, he declared his intention to move in the assembly, on the following day, That Octavius should be divested of the character of tribune.

Hitherto all parties had proceeded agreeably to the laws and constitution of the commonwealth; but this motion, to degrade a tribune, by whatever authority, was equally subversive of both. The person and dignity of tribunes, in order that they might be secure from violence, whether offered by any private person, public magistrate, or even by the people themselves, were guarded by the most sacred vows. Their persons, therefore, during the continuance of their office, were sacred; so long their character was indelible, and, without their own consent, they could not be removed by any power whatever.

The assembly, however, being met in consequence of this alarming adjournment, Tiberius renewed his prayer to Octavius to withdraw his negative; but not prevailing in this request, the tribes were directed to proceed. The votes of seventeen were already given to degrade. In taking those of the eighteenth, which would have made a majority, the tribunes made a pause, while Tiberius embraced his colleague, and, with a voice to be heard by the multitude of the people, beseeched him to spare himself the indignity, and others the regret, of so severe, though necessary, a measure. Octavius shook: but, observing the senators who were present, recovered his resolution, and bid Tiberius proceed as he thought proper. The votes of the majority were accordingly declared, and Octavius, reduced to a private station, was dragged from the tribunes' bench, and exposed to the rage of the populace. Attempts were made on his life, and a faithful slave, that endeavoured to save him, was dangerously wounded; but a number of the more respectable citizens interposed, and Tiberius himself was active in favouring his escape.

Lex Sempronia. This obstacle being removed, the act so long depending, for making a more equal division of lands, was passed; and three commissioners, Tiberius Gracchus, Appius Claudius, his father-in-law, and his brother Caius Gracchus, then a youth serving under Publius Scipio at the siege of Numantia, were named to carry the law into execution.

This act, as it concerned the interest of almost every inhabitant of Italy, immediately raised a great ferment in every part of the country. Persons holding considerable estates in land were alarmed for their property. The poor were elated with the hopes of becoming suddenly rich. If there was a middling class not to be greatly affected in their own situation, they still trembled for the effects of a contest between such parties. The senate endeavoured to delay the execution of the law, withheld the usual aids and appointments given to the commissioners of the people in the ordinary administration of public trusts, and waited for a fit opportunity to suppress entirely this hazardous project. Parties looked on each other with a gloomy and suspicious silence. A person, who had been active in procuring the Agrarian law, having died in this critical juncture, his death was alleged to be the effect of poison administered by the opposite party. Numbers of the people, to countenance a report to this purpose, went into mourning; even Gracchus, affecting to believe a like design to be forming against himself, appeared, with his children and their mother, as suppliants in the streets, and implored the protection of the people. Still more to interest their passions in his safety, he published a list of the acts which he then had in view, all tending to gratify the people, or to mortify the senate. Attalus, king of Pergamus, having, about this time, bequeathed his dominions and his treasure to the Romans, Gracchus procured an act to transfer the administration of this inheritance from the senate to the people; and to distribute the money found in the treasury of Pergamus to the poorer citizens, the better to enable them to cultivate and to stock the lands which were now to be given them. He obtained another act to circumscribe the power of the senate, by joining the equestrian order with the senators in the nomination to juries, or in forming the occasional tribunals of justice.

These, with the preceding attempts to abolish or to weaken the aristocratical part of the government, were justly alarming to every person who was anxious for the preservation of the state. As the policy of this tribune tended to substitute popular tumults for sober councils and a regular magistracy, it gave an immediate prospect of anarchy, which threatened to produce some violent usurpation. The sacred office which he so much abused, had served, on occasions, to check the caprice of the people, as well as to restrain the abuse of the executive power. The late violation it had suffered, was likely to render it entirely unfit for the first of these purposes, and to make the tribune an instrument to execute the momentary will of the people, or to make the continuance of his trust depend upon his willingness to serve this purpose. Tiberius heard himself arraigned in the forum, and in every public assembly, for the violation of the sacred law. "If any of your colleagues," said Titus Annius (whom he prosecuted for a speech in the senate,) "should interpose in my behalf, would you have him also degraded?"

The people in general began to be sensible of the enormity they themselves had committed, and Tiberius found himself under a necessity of pleading for the measure he had taken, after it had been carried into execution. The person of the tribune, he observed, was sacred; because it was consecrated by the people, whom the tribunes represented; but if the tribune, inconsistent with his character, should injure where he was appointed to protect, should weaken a claim he was appointed to enforce, and withhold from the people that right of decision which he was appointed to guard, the tribune, not the people, was to blame for the consequences.

"Other crimes," he said, "may be enormous, yet may not destroy the essence of the tribunitian character. An attempt to demolish the capitol, or to burn the fleets of the republic, might excite a universal and just indignation, without rendering the person of the tribune who should be accused of them less sacred. But an attempt to take away the power by which his own office subsists, and which is centred in himself only for the better exertion of that power, is a voluntary and criminal abdication of the trust. What is the tribune but the officer of the people? Strange! that this officer may, by virtue of authority derived from the people, drag even the consul himself to prison, and yet that the people themselves cannot depose their own officer, when he is about to annul the authority by which he himself is appointed.

"Was ever authority more sacred than that of king? It involved in itself the prerogatives of every magistrate, and was likewise consecrated by holding the priesthood of the immortal gods. Yet did not the people banish Tarquin? and thus, for the offence of one man, abolish the primitive government, under the auspices of which the foundations of this city were laid.

"What more sacred at Rome than the persons of the vestal virgins, who have the custody of the holy fire? Yet are they not for slight offences sometimes buried alive? Impiety to the gods being supposed to cancel a title which reverence to the gods had conferred, must not injuries to the people suppress an authority which a regard to the people has constituted?

"That person must fall, who himself removes the base on which he is supported. A majority of the tribes creates a tribune; cannot the whole depose? What more sacred than the things which are dedicated at the shrines of the immortal gods? yet these the people may employ or remove at pleasure. Why not transfer the tribunate, as a consecrated title, from one person to another? May not the whole people, by their sovereign authority, do what every person in this sacred office is permitted to do, when he resigns or abdicates his power by a simple expression of his will?"

These specious arguments tended to introduce the plea of necessity where there was no foundation for it, and to set the sovereign power, in every species of government, loose from the rules which itself had enacted. Such arguments accordingly had no effect where the interest of the parties did not concur to enforce them. Tiberius saw his credit on the decline. He was publicly menaced with impeachment, and had given sufficient provocation to make him apprehend that, upon the expiration of his office, some violence might be offered to himself.[1] His person was guarded only by the sacred character of the tribune. The first step he should make in the new character he was to assume, as commissioner for the division of lands, was likely to terminate his life. He resolved, if possible, to take shelter in the tribunate another year, and, to procure this favour from the people, gave further expectations of popular acts; of one to shorten the term of military service, and of another to grant an appeal to the people from the courts of justice lately established.

The senate, and every citizen who professed a regard to the constitution, were alarmed. This attempt, they said, to perpetuate the tribunitian power in the same person, tends directly to tyranny. The usurper, with the lawless multitude that supports him, must soon expel from the public assemblies every citizen who is inclined to moderation; and, together with the property of our lands, to which they already aspire, make themselves master of the state. Their leader, it seems, like every other tyrant, already thinks that his safety depends upon the continuance of his power.

In this feverish state of suspense and anxiety, great efforts were made to determine the elections. The time of choosing the tribunes was now fast approaching: Roman citizens, dispersed on their lands throughout Italy, were engaged in the harvest, and could not repair to the city. On the day of election the assembly was ill attended, especially by those who were likely to favour Tiberius. He being rejected by the first tribes that moved to the ballot, his friends endeavoured to amuse the assembly with forms, and to protract the debates, till observing that the field did not fill, nor the appearance change for the better, they moved to adjourn to the following day.

In this recess Tiberius put on mourning, went forth to the streets with his children, and, in behalf of hapless infants, that might already be considered as orphans, on the eve of losing their parent in the cause of freedom, implored the protection of the people; gave out that the party of the rich, to hinder his being re-elected, had determined to force their way into his house in the night, and to murder him. Numbers were affected by these dismal representations: a multitude crowded to his doors, and watched all night in the streets.

On the arrival of morning and the approach of the assembly, the declining appearance of his affairs suggested presages; and the superstition of the times has furnished history with the omens, by which himself and his friends were greatly dismayed. He, nevertheless, with a crowd of his partizans, took his way to the capitol, where the people had been appointed to assemble. His attendants multiplied, and numbers from the assembly descended the steps to meet him. Upon his entry a shout was raised, and his party appeared sufficiently strong, if not to prevail in their choice, perhaps by their violence to deter every citizen of a different mind from attending the election.

A chosen body took post round the person of Tiberius, with direction to suffer no stranger to approach him. A signal was agreed upon, in case it were necessary to employ force. Mean time the senators, on their part, were hastily assembled in the temple of faith, in anxious deliberations on the measures to be followed.

When the first tribe delivered their votes, a confusion arose among the people. Numbers from the more distant parts of the assembly began to press forward to the centre. Among others, Fulvius, Flaccus a senator, yet attached to

1 Orosius, lib. v. c. 8.

Tiberius being too far off to be heard, beckoned with his hand that he would speak with the tribunes. Having made his way through the multitude, he informed Tiberius, that a resolution was taken in the senate to resist him by force; and that a party of senators, with their clients and slaves, was arming against his life. All who were near enough to hear this information, took the alarm, snatched the staves from the officers that attended the tribunes, and tucked up their robes as for immediate violence. The alarm spread through the assembly, and many called out to know the cause, but no distinct account could be heard. Tiberius having in vain attempted to speak, made a sign, by waving his hand round his head, that his life was in danger. This sign, together with the hostile and menacing appearances that gave rise to it, being instantly reported in the senate, and interpreted as a hint given to the people, that it was necessary he should be crowned, or that he should assume the sovereignty, the senate immediately resolved, in a form that was usual on alarming occasions, that the consul should provide for the safety of the state. This resolution was supposed to confer a dictatorial power, and was generally given when immediate execution or summary proceedings were deemed to be necessary, without even sufficient time for the formalities observed in naming a dictator. The consul Mucius Scævola, who had been in concert with Tiberius, in drawing up the first frame of his law, but who probably had left him in the extremes to which he afterwards proceeded; on the preesnt occasion, however, declined to employ force against a tribune of the people, or to disturb the tribes in the midst of their legal assembly. "If they shall come," he said, "to any violent or illegal determination, I will employ the whole force of my authority to prevent its effects."

In this expression of the consul there did not appear to the audience a proper disposition for the present occasion. The laws were violated: a desperate party was prepared for any extremes: all sober citizens, and even many of the tribunes, had fled from the tumult: the priests of Jupiter had shut the gates of their temple; the laws, it was said, ought to govern; but the laws cannot be pleaded by those who have set them aside, and they are no longer of any avail, unless they are restored by some exertion of vigour, fit to counteract the violence that has been offered them. "The consul," said Scipio Nasica, "deserts the republic; let those who wish to preserve it, follow me." The senators instantly arose, and moving in a body, which increased as they went, by the concourse of their clients, then seized the shafts of the fasces, or tore up the benches in their way, and, with their robes wound up, in place of shields, on their left arm, broke into the midst of the assembly of the people.

Tiberius, surrounded by a numerous multitude, found his party unable to resist the awe with which they were struck by the presence of the senate and nobles. The few who resisted were beat to the ground. He himself, while he fled, being seized by the robe, slipped it from his shoulders and continued to fly; but he stumbled in the crowd, and while he attempted to recover himself, was slain with repeated blows. His body, as being that of a tyrant, together with the killed of his party, amounting to about three hundred, as accomplices in a treasonable design against the republic, were denied the honours of burial, and thrown into the river. Some of the most active of his partisans that escaped, were afterwards cited to appear, and were outlawed or condemned.

Thus, in the heats of this unhappy dispute, both the senate and the people had been carried to acts of violence that insulted the laws and constitution of their country. This constitution was by no means too strict and formal to contend with such evils; for, besides admitting a general latitude of conduct scarcely known under any other political establishment, it had provided expedients for great and dangerous occasions, which were sufficient to extricate the commonwealth from greater extremities than those to which it had been reduced in the course of this unfortunate contest.

The people, when restrained from their object by the negative of one of their tribunes, had only to wait for the expiration of his office, when, by a new election, they might so model the college as to be secure of its unanimous consent in the particular measures to which they were then inclined. The precipitant violation of the sacred law, a precedent which, if followed, must have rendered the tribunes mere instruments of popular violence, not bars to restrain oppression, filled the minds of the people with remorse and horror, and gave to the senate and nobles a dreadful apprehension of what they were to expect from a party capable of such a profane and violent extreme.

The policy of Tiberius Gracchus on the other hand, the laws he had obtained, his own re-election to secure the execution, and the sequel of his plan, seemed to threaten the republic with distraction and anarchy, likely to end in his own usurpation, or in that of some more artful demagogue. But even under those gloomy expectations the senate could, by naming a dictator, or by the commission which they actually gave to the consul, have recourse to a legal preventive, and might have repelled the impending evil by measures equally decisive and powerful, though more legal than those they employed. But the consul, it seems, was suspected of connivance with the opposite party, had received his own commission coldly, and could not be entrusted with the choice of a dictator.

In these extremities, the violent resolution that was taken by the senate appears to have been necessary; and probably for the present saved the republic; preserved it indeed, not in a sound, but in a sickly state, and in a fever, which, with some intermissions, at every return of similar disorders, threatened it with the dissolution and ruin of its whole constitution.

The disorders that arise in free states which are beginning to corrupt, generally furnish very difficult questions in the casuistry of politicians. Even the struggles of virtuous citizens, because they do not prevent, are sometimes supposed to hasten the ruin of their country. The violence of the senate, on this occasion, was by many considered with aversion and horror. The subversion of government, that was likely to have followed the policy of Gracchus, because it did not take place, was overlooked; and the restitution of order, effected by the senate, appeared to be a tyranny established in blood. The senators themselves were struck with some degree of remorse, and, what is dangerous in politics, took a middle course between the extremes. They were cautious not to inflame animosities, by any immoderate use of their late victory, nor by any immediate opposition to the execution of the popular law. They wished to atone for the violences lately committed against the person of its author; they permitted Fulvius Flaccus and Papirius Carbo, two of the most daring leaders of the popular faction, to be elected commissioners for the execution of the Agrarian law, in the room of Tiberius and Appius Claudius, of whom the latter also died about this time; and, in order to stifle animosities and resentments, consented that, under pretence of an embassy to Pergamus, Scipio Nasica should be removed from Rome. In consequence of this commission, this illustrious citizen, the lineal descendant of one of the Scipios who perished in Spain in the time of the second Punic war, himself an ornament to the republic, died in a species of exile, though under an honourable title.

In the midst of such agitations, foreign affairs were likely to be much overlooked. They proceeded, however, under the conduct of the officers to whom they were entrusted, with the usual success; and the senate, having the reports made nearly about the same time, of the pacification of Lusitania, the destruction of Numantia, and the reduction and punishment of the slaves in Sicily, named commissioners to act in conjunction with the generals commanding in those several services, in order to settle their provinces.

Brutus and Scipio had their several triumphs; one with the title of Galaicus, for having reduced the Gallicians; the other, still preferring the title of Africanus to that of Numantinus, which was offered to him for the sack of Numantia.

The arrival of this respectable citizen was anxiously looked for by all parties, more to know what judgment he might pass on the late operations at Rome, than on account of the triumph he obtained over enemies once formidable to his country. He was the near relation of Gracchus, and might, under pretence of revenging the death of that demagogue, have put himself at the head of a formidable party. He was himself personally respected and beloved by numbers of the citizens, who had carried arms under his command, who were recently arrived in Italy crowned with victory, and who might possibly, under pretence of vindicating the rights of the people, employ their arms against the republic. But the time of such criminal views on the commonwealth was not yet arrived. Scipio already, upon hearing the fate of Gracchus, had expressed, in some words that escaped him, his approbation of the senate's conduct "So may every person perish," he said, "who shall dare to commit such crimes."[1] Soon after his arrival from Spain, Papirius Carbo, the tribune, called upon him aloud, in the assembly of the people, to declare what he thought of the death of Gracchus. "I must think," he said, "that if Gracchus meant to overturn the government of his country, his death was fully merited." This declaration the multitude interrupted with murmurs of aversion and rage. Upon which Scipio, raising his tone, expressed the contempt under which it seems that the populace of Rome had already fallen. "I have been accustomed," he said, "to the shout of warlike enemies, and cannot be affected by your dastardly cries." Then, alluding to the number of enfranchised slaves that were enrolled with the tribes of the city, upon a second cry of displeasure, he continued, "Peace, ye aliens and step-children of Italy.[2] You are now free, but many of you I have brought to this place in fetters, and sold at the halbert for slaves." Some were abashed by the truth and all by the boldness of this contemptuous reproach, and showed that popular assemblies, though vested with supreme authority, may be sometimes insulted, as well as courted, with success.

The part which Scipio took on this occasion was the more remarkable, that he himself was to be reckoned among the poorer citizens, and might have been a gainer by the rigorous execution of the Licinian law. His whole inheritance, according to Pliny, amounted to thirty-two pounds, or three hundred and twenty ounces of silver, which might be now valued at about two hundred and eighty pounds sterling.

Lex Papiria Tabellaria Tertia.

Papirius Carbo spent the year of his tribunate in fomenting the animosity of the people against the senate, and in promoting dangerous innovations. He obtained a law, by which the votes of the people, in questions of legislation as well as election,[3] and the opinions of the judges in determining causes, were to be taken by ballot.

He was less successful in the motion he made for a law to enable the same person to be repeatedly chosen into the office of tribune. He was supported in this motion by Caius Gracchus; opposed by Scipio, Lælius, and the whole authority of the senate,[4] who dreaded the perpetuating in any one person a power, which the sacredness of the character, and the attachment of the populace, rendered almost sovereign and irresistible.

While the interests of party were exerted in these several questions at home, the state was laying the foundation of new quarrels abroad, and opening a scene of depredation and conquest in what was then the wealthiest part of the known world. Soon after the death of Attalus, king of Pergamus, who had bequeathed his kingdom to the Romans, Aristonicus, his natural brother, being the illegitimate son of Eumenes, made pretensions to the throne of Pergamus, and was supported by a powerful party among the people. The Romans did not fail to maintain their right: Crassus, one of the consuls of the preceding year, had been sent with an army into Asia for that purpose, but in his first encounter with Aristonicus, was defeated and taken. He was afterwards killed while a captive in the hands of the enemy; having intentionally provoked one of his guards to lay violent hands on him, and thus ended a life which he thought was dishonoured by his preceding defeat.

U. C. 622.

The following year, the consul Perpenna being sent on this service, and having, with better fortune than Crassus, defeated and taken Aristonicus, got possession of the treasure and kingdom of Attalus, but died in his command at Pergamus. From this time the Romans took a more

1 Plutarch in Vit. Tiberii Gracchi.

2 Velleius Paterculus, lib. ii. c. 4.

3 Cic. de Legibus lib iii. 4 Cic. de Amicitia.

particular concern than formerly in the affairs of Asia. They employed Scipio Emilianus, with Sp. Mummius, and L. Metellus, on a commission of observation to that country. We are told that the equipage of Scipio upon this occasion consisted of seven slaves; and this, as a mark or characteristic of the times, is perhaps more interesting than any thing else we could be told of the embassy. The object of the commission appears to have related to Egypt as well as to Asia,[5] though there was not any power in either that seemed to be in condition to alarm the Romans. Ptolemy Euergetes had succeeded to the throne of Egypt, but was expelled by the people of Alexandria. Antiochus, king of Syria, had been recently engaged in a very unsuccessful war with the Parthians; and it had not yet appeared how far it concerned the Romans to observe the king of Pontus, or to consider of the measures to be taken against him for the security of their possessions in Asia.

In whatever degree the Roman embassy found worthy objects of attention in the state of the Asiatic powers, matters were hastening in Italy to a state of great distraction and ferment, on account of the violence with which the Agrarian law was put in execution by Papirius Carbo, Fulvius Flaccus, and Caius Gracchus, the commissioners appointed for this purpose. As the law authorized them to call upon all persons possessed of public lands to evacuate them, and submit to a legal division; they, under this pretence, brought into question all the rights of property throughout Italy, and took from one and gave to another as suited their pleasure; some suffered the diminution of their estates with silent rage; others complained that they were violently removed from lands which they had cultivated, to barren and inhospitable situations; even they who were supposed to be favoured, complained of the lots they received. Many were aggrieved, none were satisfied.

Moved by the representations which were made of these abuses, Scipio, at his return from Asia, made an harangue in the senate, by which he drew upon himself an invective from Fulvius, one of the commissioners. He did not propose to repeal the law, but that the execution of it should be taken out of the hands of so pernicious a faction, and committed to the Consul Sempronius Tuditanus, who remained in the administration of affairs in Italy, while his colleague Aquilius had gone to Asia to finish the transaction in the conduct of which Perpenna died.

It is mentioned that Scipio, in this speech to the senate, complained of insults and threats to his own person, which induced all the members, with a great body of the more respectable citizens, to attend him in procession to his own

U. C. 624.

house. Next morning he was found dead in his bed;[6] and, notwithstanding the suspicions of violence transmitted by different authors, nothing certain appears upon record; and no inquest was ever made to discover the truth of these reports. This illustrious citizen, notwithstanding his services, had incurred so much the displeasure of the people, that he had not the honours of a public funeral. If he had not died at this critical time, the senate, it was supposed, meant to have named him dictator, for the purpose of purging the state of the evils with which it was now oppressed.

The occasion, however, was not sufficient to make the senate persist in their intention to name a dictator; nor is there any thing material recorded as having happened during a few of the following years. Quintus Cæcilius Metellus Macedonicus, and Quintus Pompeius, were censors; both of plebeian extraction; of which this is recorded as the first example. Metellus, at the census, made a memorable speech, in which he recommended marriage, the establishment of families, and the rearing of children. This speech being preserved, will recur to our notice again, being read by Augustus in the senate, as a lesson equally applicable to the age in which he lived.

The people who were fit to carry arms, as appeared at their enrolment, amounted to three hundred and seventeen thousand eight hundred and twenty-three. But what is most memorable in the transactions of this muster, was the disgrace of Caius Attinius Labeo, who, being struck off the rolls of the senate by Metellus, afterwards became tribune of the people; and, by the difficulty with which the effect of his unjust revenge came to be prevented, showed the folly of making the will of any officer sacred, in order to restrain the commission of wrongs.

Metellus, in returning from the country, about noon, while the market-place was thin of people, found himself suddenly apprehended by this vindictive tribune, and ordered to be thrown immediately from the Tarpeian rock. The people assembled in crowds, were sensible of the tribune's breach of the sacred trust reposed in him; and, accosting Metellus by the name of father, lamented his fate; but, unless another tribune could be found to interpose in his favour, there was no other power in the commonwealth that could, without supposed profanation, interrupt a tribune even in the commission of a crime. Metellus struggled to obtain a delay, was overpowered and dragged through the streets, while the violence he suffered made the blood to spring from his nostrils. A tribune was with difficulty found in time to save his life; but Attinius having, with a lighted fire and other forms of consecration, devoted his estate to sacred uses, it is alleged that he never recovered it.[7]

Such was the weak state to which the government was reduced by the late popular encroachments, that this outrageous abuse of power was never punished; and such the moderation of this great man's family, that though he himself lived fifteen years in high credit after this accident, saw his family raised to the highest dignities, and was carried to his grave by four sons, of whom one had been censor, two had triumphed, three had been consuls, and the fourth, then prætor, was candidate for the consulate, which he obtained in the following year; yet no one of this powerful family chose to increase the disturbances of the commonwealth, by attempting to revenge the outrage which their father had suffered.[8]

Lex Attinia.

Caius Attinius is mentioned as being the person who obtained the admission of the tribunes, in right of their office as members of the senate.[9]

5 Val Max. lib. iv. c. 3

6 Cic. de Amicitia.

7 Plin. lib. vii. c. 44. Cicero, in pleading to have his house restored to him, though devoted to sacred uses, states the form of consecration in the case of Metellus but denies the effect of it. Pro domo sua, c. 47.

8 Plin. lib. vii. c. 44.

9 A. Gellius, lib. xiv. c. 8.

The Consul Sempronius, though authorized by the senate to restrain the violence of the commissioners who were employed in the Agrarian law, declined that hazardous business, and chose rather to encounter the enemy in the province of Istria, where he made some conquests and obtained a triumph.

In the same turbulent times lived Pacuvius, the tragic poet, and Lucilius, inventor of the satire. The latter, if we suppose him to be the same whose name is found in the list of questors, was a person of rank, and moved in the line of political preferment.

Historians mention a dreadful eruption of Mount Etna, the effect of subterraneous fires, which, shaking the foundations of Sicily and the neighbouring islands, gave explosions of flame, not only from the crater of the mountain, but likewise from below the waters of the sea, and forced sudden and great inundations over the islands of Laparé and the neighbouring coasts.

CHAPTER III.

State of the Italian Allies, and the Views which now began to be conceived by them—Appearance of Caius Gracchus—Resolution to purge the City of Aliens—Consulate and factious Notions of Fulvius Flaccus—Conspiracy of Fregellæ suppressed—Caius Gracchus returns to Rome—Offers himself Candidate for the Tribunate—Address of Cornelia—Tribunate and Acts of Caius Gracchus—Re-election—Proposal to admit the Inhabitants of Italy on the Rolls of Roman Citizens—Popular Acts of Gracchus and Livius—The Senate begin to prevail—Death of Caius Gracchus and Fulvius.

THE eruption of Mount Etna, and the other particulars relating to the natural history of Italy, with the mention of which we concluded our last chapter, were considered as prodigies, and as the presages of evils which were yet to afflict the republic. At this time indeed the state of Italy seemed to have received the seeds of much trouble, and to contain ample materials of civil combustion. The citizens, for whom no provision had been made at their return from military service, or who thought themselves partially dealt with in the colonies, the leaders of tumult and faction in the city, were now taught to consider the land-property of Italy as their joint inheritance. They were, in imagination, distributing their lots, and selecting their shares.

U. C. 627.

In the mean time, the inhabitants of the municipia, or free towns, and their districts, who, not being citizens, served the state as allies, had reason to dread the rapacity of such needy and powerful masters. They themselves likewise began to repine under the inequality of their condition. They observed, that while they were scarcely allowed to retain the possessions of their ancestors, Rome, aided by their arms, had gained that extensive dominion, and obtained that territory, about which the poor and the rich were now likely to quarrel among themselves. "The Italian allies," they said, "must bleed in this contest, no less than they had done in the foreign or more distant wars of the commonwealth."—They had been made, by the professions of Tiberius Gracchus, to entertain hopes that every distinction in Italy would soon be removed, that every freeman in the country would be enrolled, as a citizen of Rome, and be admitted to all the powers and pretensions implied in that designation. The consideration of this subject, therefore, could not be long delayed, and the Roman senate, already struggling with attacks of their fellow-citizens, had an immediate storm to apprehend from the allies.

The revolutions of the state had been so frequent, and its progress from small beginnings to a great empire had been so rapid, that the changes to which men are exposed, and the exertions of which they are capable, no where appear so conspicuous, or are so distinctly marked.

In the first ages the political importance of a Roman citizen appears not to have been felt or understood. Conquered enemies were removed to Rome, and their captivity consisted in being forced to be Romans, to which they submitted with great reluctance. It is not to be doubted that every foreigner was welcome to take his place as a Roman citizen in the assembly of the people, that many were admitted into the senate,[1] and some even on the throne.[2] It is likely, also, that the first colonies considered themselves as detached from the city of Rome, and as forming cantons apart; for we find them, like the other states of Italy, occasionally at war with the Romans.

But when the sovereignty of Italy came to be established at Rome, and was there actually exercised by the collective body of the people, the inhabitants of the colonies, it is probable, laid claim to their votes in elections, and presented themselves to be enrolled in the tribes. They felt their consequence and their superiority over the municipia, or free towns in their neighbourhood, to whom, as a mark of distinction and an act of munificence, some remains of independence had been left. Even in this state, the rolls of the people had been very negligently compiled, or preserved. The kings, the consuls, the censors, who were the officers, in different ages of the state, entrusted with the musters, admitted on the rolls such as presented themselves, or such as they chose to receive. One consul invited all the free inhabitants of Latium to poll in the assemblies of the people; another rejected them, and in time of elections forbid them the city.—But notwithstanding this prohibition, aliens that were brought to Rome on a foot of captivity, were suffered by degrees to mix with the citizens.[3] The inhabitants of the free towns, removing to Rome upon any

1 The Claudian family were aliens.

2 Tarquinius Priscus was of Greek extraction and an alien om Tarquinii.

3 This happened particularly in the case of the Campanian

creditable footing, found easy admission on the rolls of some tribe. The towns complained they were depopulated. The Romans endeavoured to shut the gates of their city by repeated scrutinies, and the prohibition of surreptitious enrolments: but in vain. The practice still continued, and the growing privilege, distinction, and eminence of a Roman citizen, made that title become the great object of individuals, and of entire cantons. It had already been bestowed upon districts whose inhabitants were not distinguished by any singular merit with the Roman state. In this respect all the allies were nearly equal; they had regularly composed at least one-half in every Roman army, and had borne an equal share in all the dangers and troubles of the commonwealth; and, from having valued themselves of old on their separate titles and national distinctions, they began now to aspire to a share in the sovereignty of the empire, and wished to sink for ever their provincial designations under the general title of Romans.

Not only the great power that was enjoyed in the assembly of the people, and the serious privileges that were bestowed by the Porcian law, but even the title of citizen in Italy, of legionary soldier in the field, and the permission of wearing the Roman gown, were now ardently coveted as marks of dignity and honour. The city was frequented by persons who hoped separately to be admitted in the tribes, and by numbers who crowded from the neighbouring cantons, on every remarkable day of assembly, still flattering themselves, that the expectations which Gracchus had raised on this important subject might soon be fulfilled.

U. C. 627.

Consuls; M. Æmilius Lepidus, L. Aurelius Orestes.

In this state of affairs, the senate authorized Junius Pennus, one of the tribunes, to move the people for an edict to prohibit, on days of election or public assembly, this concourse of aliens, and requiring all the country towns to lay claim to their denizens, who had left their own corporations to act the part of citizens at Rome.

On this occasion, Caius Gracchus, the brother of the late unfortunate tribune, stood forth, and made one of the first appearances, in which he showed the extent of his talents, as well as the party he was like y to espouse in the commonwealth. This young man, being about twenty years of age when the troubles raised by his elder brother had so much disturbed the republic, and when they ended so fatally for himself, had retired upon that catastrophe from the public view, and made it uncertain whether the fate of Tiberius might not deter him, not only from embracing like dangerous counsels, but even from entering at all on the line of political affairs. His retirement, however, he spent in such studies as were then come into repute, on account of their importance, as a preparation for the business of courts of justice, of the senate, and of the popular assemblies; and the first appearance he made gave evidence of the talents he had acquired for these several departments. His parts seemed to be quicker, and his spirit more ardent, than that of his elder brother; and the people conceived hopes of having their pretensions revived, and more successfully conducted, than under their former leader. The cause of the country towns, in which he now engaged, was specious, and tended to form a new, a numerous, and a formidable party in Italy, likely to join in every factious attempt which might throw the public into disorder, and make way for the promiscuous admission of aliens on the rolls of the people. This cause, however, was fraught with so much confusion to the state, and tended so much to lessen the political consequence of those who were already citizens, that the argument in favour of the resolution to purge the city of aliens prevailed, and an act to that purpose accordingly was passed[4] in the assembly of the people.

It deserves to be recorded, that amidst the inquiries set on foot in consequence of this edict, or about this time, Perpenna, the father of a late consul,[5] was claimed by one of the Italian corporations, and found not to have been a citizen of Rome. His son, whom we have already mentioned, having vanquished and taken Aristonicus, the pretended heir of Attalus, died in his command at Pergamus; and he is accordingly said to have been a rare example of the caprice of fortune, in having been a Roman consul, though not a Roman citizen. This example may confirm what has been observed of the latitude which officers took in conducting the census.

The fires of sedition which had sometime preyed on the commonwealth were likely to break out with increasing force upon the promotion of Fulvius Flaccus to the dignity of first magistrate. This factious citizen had blown up the flame with Tiberius Gracchus, and having succeeded him in the commission for executing the Agrarian law, never failed to carry the torch wherever matter of inflammation or general combustion could be found. By his merit with the popular party he had attained his present eminence, and was determined to preserve it by continuing his services. He began the functions of his office by proposing a law to communicate the right of citizens to the allies or free inhabitants of Italy; a measure which tended to weaken the power of the senate, and to increase the number of citizens greatly beyond what could be assembled in one collective body. Having failed in this attempt, he substituted a proposal in appearance more moderate, but equally dangerous, that whoever claimed the right of citizen, in case of being cast by the censors, who were the proper judges, might appeal to the people.[6] This would have conferred the power of naturalization on the popular leaders; and the danger of such a measure called upon the senate to exert its authority and influence in having this motion also rejected.

U. C. 628.

M. Plautius Hipsius, M. Fulvius Flaccus.

Leges Fulviæ.

When the consul appeared to be fairly entered on his career, and, by uniting the power of the supreme magistracy with that of a commissioner for dividing the property of lands, was likely to break through all the forms which had hitherto retarded the execution of the Agrarian law, he was with difficulty persuaded to assemble the senate, and to take his place. The whole body joined in representations against these dangerous measures, and in a request that he would withdraw his motions. To these applications he made

4 Sextus Pompeius Festus in voce Republica. Cicero in Bruto in Officiis, lib. iii.
5 Valerius Maximus, lib. iii. c. 4.
6 Appian. de Bell. Civ. lib. i.

no reply,[1] but an occasion soon offered, by which the senate was enabled to divert him from his purpose. A deputation arrived from Marseilles, then in alliance with Rome, to intreat the support of the republic against the Salyii, a neighbouring nation, who had invaded their territories. The senate gladly embraced this opportunity to find a foreign employment for the consul, decreed a speedy aid to the city of Marseilles, and appointed M. Fulvius Flaccus to that service. Although this incident marred or interrupted for the present his political designs, yet he was induced, by the hopes of a triumph, to accept of the command which now offered, and, by his absence, to relieve the city for a while from the alarms which he had given. Caius Gracchus, too, was gone in the capacity of proquestor to Sardinia; and the senate, if they could by any pretences have kept those unquiet spirits at a distance, had hopes of restoring the former order of the commonwealth.

In this interval some laws are said to have passed respecting the office and conduct of the censors. The particulars are not mentioned; but the object probably was, to render the magistrate more circumspect in the admission of those who claimed to be numbered as citizens. Such was likely to be the policy of the senate, in the absence of demagogues, who, by proposing to admit the allies on the rolls of the people, had awakened dangerous pretensions in every corner of Italy. It soon appeared how seriously these pretensions were adopted by the country towns; for the inhabitants already bestirred themselves, and were beginning to devise how they might extort by force what they were not likely to obtain with consent of the original denizens of Rome. A suspicion having arisen of such treasonable concerts forming at Fregellæ, the prætor Opimius had a special commission to inquire into the matter, and to proceed as he should find the occasion required. Having summoned the chief magistrate of the place to appear before him, he received, upon a promise of doing no violence to his person, full information of the combinations that had been forming against the government of Rome. So instructed, he assembled such a force as was necessary to support him in asserting the authority of the state; and thinking it necessary to give a striking example in a matter of so dangerous and infectious a nature, he ordered the place to be razed to the ground.[2]

U. C. 629.
C. Cassius Longinus, C. Sextius Calvinus.

By this act of severity, the designs of the allies were for a while suspended, and might have been entirely suppressed, if the factions at Rome had not given them fresh encouragement, and hopes of success or impunity. This transaction was scarcely past, when Caius Gracchus appeared in the city to solicit the office of tribune; and, by his presence revived the hopes of the allies. Having observed, that the proconsul Aurelius Cotta, under whom he served as proquestor in Sardinia, instead of being recalled, was continued in his command, and furnished with reinforcements and supplies of every sort, as for a service of long duration; and suspecting that this measure was pointed at himself, and proceeded from a design to keep him at a distance from the popular assemblies, he quitted his station in Sardinia, and returned without leave. He was called to account by the censors for deserting his duty; but defended himself with such ability and force, as greatly raised the expectations which had already been entertained by his party.[3]

The law, he said, required him only to carry arms ten years, he had actually carried them twelve years; although he might legally have quitted his station of questor at the expiration of one year, yet he had remained in it three years. However willing the censors may have been to remove this pest from the commonwealth, they were too weak to attempt any censure in this state of his cause, and in the present humour of the people. They endeavoured, in vain, to load him with a share in the plot of Fregellæ; he still exculpated himself: and, if he had possessed every virtue of a citizen, in proportion to his resolution, application, eloquence, and even severity of manners, he might have been a powerful support to the state. In a speech to the people, on his return from Sardinia, he concluded with the following remarkable words: "The purse which I carried full to the province, I have brought empty back. Others empty the wine casks which they carry from Italy, and bring them from the provinces replenished with silver and gold."[4]

In declaring himself a candidate for the office of tribune, Caius Gracchus professed his intention to propose many popular laws. The senate exerted all their influence to disappoint his views; but such were the expectations of the popular party throughout all Italy, that they crowded to the election in greater numbers than could find place in the public square. They handed and reached out their ballots at the windows and over the battlements; and Gracchus, though elected, was, in consequence of the opposition given to him, only fourth in the list.[5]

Cornelia, the mother of the Gracchi, who, ever since the death of her son Tiberius, lived in retirement in Campania, upon hearing of the career which her son, Caius, was likely to run, alarmed at the renewal of a scene which had already occasioned her so much sorrow, expostulated with him on the course he was taking; and, in an unaffected and passionate address, spoke that ardent zeal for the republic, by which the citizens of Rome had been long distinguished.

This high-minded woman, on whom the entire care of her family had devolved by the death of her husband, whilst the children were yet in their infancy, or under age, took care, with unusual attention, to have them educated for the rank they were to hold in the state, and did not fail even to excite their ambition. When Tiberius, after the disgrace of Mancinus, appeared to withdraw from the road of preferments and honours, "How long," she said, "shall I be distinguished as the mother-in-law of Scipio, not as the mother of the Gracchi?" This latter distinction, however, she came to possess; and it has remained with her name, but from circumstances and events which this respectable personage by no means ap-

1 Val. Max. lib. ix. c. 5.
2 Liv. lib. lx. Velleius Obsequens. Cic. lib. ii. De Inventione; De Finibus v. Ibid. Rhetorius, lib. iv.
3 Plutarch. in C. Graccho.
4 A. Gellius, lib. xv. c. 12.
5 Plutarch, Appian, Orosius, Eutrop. Obsequens.

peared to desire. In one fragment of her letters to Caius, which is still preserved, "You will tell me," she said, "that it is glorious to be revenged of our enemies. No one thinks so more than I, if we can be revenged without hurt to the republic; but if not, often may our enemies escape. Long may they be safe, if the good of the commonwealth requires their safety." In another letter, which appears to be written after his intention of suing for the tribunate was declared, she accosts him to the following purpose: "I take the gods to witness, that, except the persons who killed my son Tiberius, no one ever gave me so much affliction as you do in this matter. You, from whom I might have expected some consolation in my age, and who, surely, of all my children, ought to be most careful not to distress me! I have not many years to live. Spare the republic so long for my sake. Shall I never see the madness of my family at an end? When I am dead, you will think to honour me with a parent's rites: but what honour can my memory receive from you, by whom I am abandoned and dishonoured while I live? But, may the gods forbid you should persist! if you do, I fear the course you are taking leads to remorse and distraction which will end only with your life." [6]

These remonstrances do not appear to have had any effect. Caius, upon his accession to the tribunate, proceeded to fulfil the expectations of his party. The Agrarian law, though still in force, had met with continued interruption and delay in the execution. It was even falling into neglect. Caius thought proper, as the first act of his magistracy, to move a renewal and confirmation of it, with express injunctions, that there should be an annual distribution of land to the poorer citizens.[7] To this he subjoined, in the first year of his office, a variety of regulations tending either to increase his popularity, or to distinguish his administration. Upon his motion, public granaries were erected, and a aw was made, that the corn should be issued from thence monthly to the people, two parts in twelve under the prime or original cost.[8]

Lex Sempronia agraria.

Lex frumentaria.

This act gave a check to industry, which is the best guardian of manners in populous cities, or wherever multitudes of men are crowded together.

Caius likewise obtained a decree, by which the estates of Attalus, king of Pergamus, lately bequeathed to the Romans, should be let in the manner of other lands under the inspection of the censors; but the rents, instead of being made part of the public revenue, should be allotted for the maintenance of the poorer citizens.[9]

Another, by which any person deposed from an office of magistracy by the people, was to be deemed for ever disqualified to serve the republic in any other capacity.[10] This act was intended to operate against Octavius, who, by the influence of Tiberius, had been degraded from the office of tribune; and the act took its title from the name of the person against whom it was framed.

An act to regulate the co[illegible]tions of the military service,[11] by which no one was obliged to enter before seventeen years of age, and by which Roman soldiers were to receive clothing as well as pay;[12] possibly the first introduction of a uniform into the Roman legions: a circumstance which, in modern times, is thought so essential to the character of troops, and the appearance of an army.

By the celebrated law of Porcius, which allowed of an appeal to the people, every citizen had a remedy against any oppressive sentence or proceeding of the executive magistrate; but this did not appear to Gracchus a sufficient restraint on the officers of state. He proposed to have it enacted, that no person, under pain of a capital punishment, should at all proceed against a citizen without a special commission or warrant from the people to that effect. And he proposed to give this law a retrospect, in order to comprehend Popilius Lænas[13] who, being consul in the year after the troubles occasioned by Tiberius Gracchus, had, under the authority of the senate alone, proceeded to try and condemn such as were accessary to that sedition. Lænas perceived the storm that was gathering against him, and chose to avoid it by a voluntary exile. This act was indeed almost an entire abolition of government, and a bar to the exercise of such ordinary powers as were necessary to the peace of the commonwealth. A popular faction could withhold every power, which, in their apprehension, might be employed against themselves; and in their most pernicious designs had no interruption to fear from the dictator named by the senate and consuls, nor from the consul armed with the authority of the senate for the suppression of disorders; a resource to which the republic had frequently owed its preservation. As we find no change in the proceedings of the state upon this new regulation, it is probable that the absurdity of the law prevented its effect.

While Gracchus thus proposed to make all the powers of the state depend for their existence on the occasional will of the people, he meant to render the assemblies of the people themselves more democratical, by stripping the higher classes of the prerogative, precedence, or influence they possessed, in leading the public decisions. The centuries being hitherto called to vote in the order of their classes, those of the first or highest class, by voting first, set an example which was often followed by the whole.[14] By the statute of Gracchus, the centuries were required, in every question, to draw lots for the prerogative, and gave their votes in the order they had drawn.

Under this active tribune, much public business, that used to pass through the senate, was engrossed by the popular assemblies. Even in the form of these assemblies, all appearance of respect to the senate was laid aside. The rostra, or platform on which the presiding magistrate stood, was placed in the middle of an area, of which one part was the market-place, surrounded with stalls and booths for merchandize, and the courts of justice; the other part, called the comitium, was open to receive the people in their public assemblies; and on one side of it, fronting the rostra, or bench of the magistrates, stood the curia, or senate-house. The people, when any one was speak-

6 Fragmenta Corn. Nepotis ab Andrea Scotto collecta, edita cum scriptis Corn. Nepotis.

7 Liv. lib. lx. Velleius, lib. ii. Hyginus de Limitibus. Appian, de Viris Illustribus.

8 Semisse et tricenti, for a half and a third, &c. Liv. Plutarch Appian. ibid.

9 Florus, lib. iii. c. 15. Cicer. in Verrem.

10 Privilegium in Octavium.

11 De militum commodis.

12 Plutarch. in C. Graccho.—Lex Sempronia de [illegible]bertate civium.

13 Cicer. in Cluentio; pro Rabino; pro domo su[illegible]

14 The first century was called the prerogative.

ing, stood partly in the market-place, and partly in the comitium. The speakers directed their voice to the comitium, so as to be heard in the senate. This disposition, Gracchus reversed; and directing his voice to the forum, or market-place, seemed to displace the senate, and deprive that body of their office as watchmen and guardians of the public order in matters that came before the popular assemblies.[1]

At the time that the tribune Caius Gracchus engaged the minds of his contemporaries, and furnished history chiefly with these effects of his factious and turbulent spirit, it is observed, that he himself executed works of general utility; bridges, highways, and other public accommodations through Italy. And that the state having carried its arms, for the first time, over the Alps, happily terminated the war with the Salyii, a nation of Gaul, whose territory became the first province of Rome in that country. And that Caius Sextius, consul of the preceding year, was authorized to place a colony in the neighbourhood of the hot springs, which, from his name, were called the Aquæ Sextiæ, and are still known by a corruption of the same appellation.[2]

From Asia, at the same time, it was reported, that Ariarathes, the king of Cappadocia, and ally of the Romans, was murdered, at the instigation of Mithridates, king of Pontus, whose sister he had married; that he had left a son for whom Mithridates affected to secure the kingdom; but that the widowed queen having fallen into the hands of Nicomedes, king of Bithynia, this prince, in her right, had taken possession of Cappadocia, while Mithridates, in name of his nephew, was hastening to remove him from thence. On this subject a resolution was declared in the assembly of the people at Rome, that both Nicomedes and Mithridates should be required immediately to evacuate Cappadocia, and to withdraw their troops. This resolution Caius Gracchus opposed with all his eloquence and his credit, charging his antagonist aloud with corruption, and a clandestine correspondence with the agents, who, on different sides, were now employed at Rome in soliciting this affair. "None of us," he said, "stand forth in this place for nothing. Even I, who desire you to put money in your own coffers, and to consult the interest of the state, mean to be paid, not with money indeed, but with your favour and a good name. They who oppose this resolution likewise covet, not honours from you, but money from Nicomedes; and they who support it, expect to be paid by Mithridates, not by you. As for those who are silent, they, I believe, understand the market best of all. They have heard the story of the poet, who being vain that he had got a great sum of money for rehearsing a tragedy, was told by another, that it was not wonderful he had got so much for talking, when I, said the other, who it seems knew more than he was wished to declare, have got ten times as much for holding my tongue. There is nothing that a king will buy at so great a price, on occasion, as silence."[3]

Such, at times, was the style in which this popular orator chose to address his audience. Individuals are won by flattery, the multitude by buffoonery and satire. From the tendency of this speech, it appears to have been the opinion of Gracchus, not that the Romans should sequester the kingdom of Cappadocia for the heirs of Ariarathes, but that they should seize it for themselves. The question, however, which now arose relating to the succession to this kingdom, laid the foundation of a tedious and bloody war, of which the operations and events will occur in their place.

U. C. 639. *C. Fannius, Cn. Domitius Ahenobarbus.*

Gracchus, on the approach of the election of consuls, employed all his credit and influence to support Caius Fannius, in opposition to Opimius, who, by his vigilance and activity in suppressing the treasonable designs of the allies at Fregellæ, had incurred the displeasure of the popular party; and Fannius being accordingly chosen, together with Cn. Domitius Ahenobarbus, Gracchus proceeded to offer himself as a candidate to be re-elected into the office of tribune. In this he followed the example of his brother Tiberius in a step, which, being reckoned illegal as well as alarming, was that which hastened his ruin. An attempt had been since made by Papirius Carbo to have the legality of such re-elections acknowledged; but this having failed, Caius Gracchus, with great address, inserted in one of his popular edicts, a clause declaring it competent for the people to re-elect a tribune, in case he should need a continuation of his power in order to fulfil his public engagements. To avail himself of this clause, he now declared, that his views in behalf of the people were far from being accomplished. Under this pretence he obtained a preference to one of the new candidates, and greatly strengthened the tribunitian power by the prospect of its repeated renewals, and duration for an indefinite time.

Upon his re-election, Caius, continuing his administration upon the same plan of animosity to the senate, obtained a law to deprive that body of the share which his brother had left them in the courts of justice; and ordaining, that the judges, for the future, should be draughted from the equestrian order alone, a class of men, who, being left out of the senate, and of course not comprehended in the laws that prohibited commerce, had betaken themselves, as has been observed,[4] to lucrative professions, were the farmers of the revenue, the contractors for the army, and, in general, the merchants who conducted the whole trade of the republic. Though they might be considered as neutral in the disputes of the senate and people, and therefore impartial where the other orders were biassed, there was no class of men more likely to prostitute the character of judges for interest or actual hire. This revolution in the courts of justice accordingly may have contributed greatly to hasten the approaching corruption of manners, and the disorders of the government.

Lex Sempronia Judiciaria.

Lex de Provinciis ordinandis.

The next ordinance prepared by Gracchus, or ascribed to him, related to the nomination of officers to govern the provinces; and, if it had been strictly observed, might have made some compensation for the former. The power of naming such officers was committed to the senate, and the arrangements were to be annually made before the election of consuls. This

1 M. Varro de Re Rustica, lib. i. c. 2. Cic. de Amicitia. Plutarch. in vit. Caii Gracchi.

2 At Aix, in Provence. 3 A. Gellius, lib. ii. c. 10.

4 Page 91

continued to be law, but was often overruled by the people.[5]

In the same year, the boldest and most dangerous project that had ever been formed by any of the popular leaders, that for admitting the Italian allies upon the rolls of the Roman people, already attempted by Fulvius Flaccus, was again renewed by Caius Gracchus; and, upon the utmost exertion of the vigilance and authority of the senate, with great difficulty prevented.

The rumour of this project having brought multitudes to Rome, the senate thought it necessary to give the consuls in charge to clear the city, on the day that this important question was expected to come on, of all strangers, and not to suffer any aliens to remain within four miles of the walls. During the dependence of this question, Gracchus flattered the poorer citizens with the prospect of advantageous settlements, in certain new colonies, of six thousand men each, which he proposed to plant in the districts of Campania and Tarentum, the most cultivated parts of Italy, and in colonies, which he likewise proposed to send abroad into some of the richest provinces. Such settlements had been formerly made to occupy and secure recent conquest; they were now calculated to serve as baits to popular favour, and as a provision made by the leaders of faction, for their own friends and adherents.

The senate, attacked by such popular arts, resolved to retort on their adversaries; and for this purpose instructed Marcus Livius, another of the tribunes, to take such measures as should, if possible, supplant Gracchus in the favour of the people. Livius, professing to act in concert with the senate, proposed a number of acts: one to conciliate the minds of the allies, by giving them, while they served in the army, the same exemption from corporeal punishment which the Roman citizens had enjoyed.

Lex Livia de Tergo Civium Latini Nominis.

Another, for the establishment of twelve different colonies, each of three thousand citizens. But what, possibly, had the greatest effect, because it appeared to exceed in munificence all the edicts of Gracchus, was an exemption of all those lands, which should be distributed in terms of the late Sempronian law, from all quit-rents and public burdens, which had hitherto, in general, been laid on all possessions that were held from the public.[6] It was proposed to name ten commissioners to distribute lands thus unincumbered to the people; and three colonies are mentioned, Syllaceum, Tarentum, and Neptunia, as having been actually sent abroad this year, and probably on these terms.

Lex Rubria.

About the same time it was decreed, that the city of Carthage might be rebuilt for the reception of a colony of six thousand Roman citizens. This decree bears the name, not of Sempronius or of Livius, but of Rubrius, another tribune of the same year.

The senate readily agreed to the settlement of these colonies, as likely to carry off a number of the more factious citizens, and to furnish an opportunity likewise of removing from the city, for some time, the popular leaders themselves, under pretence of employing them to conduct and to settle the families destined to form those establishments. Accordingly, Caius Gracchus, and Fulvius Flaccus, late consul, and now deeply engaged in all these factious measures, were destined to take charge of the new colonists, and to superintend their settlement.[7]

U. C. 632.

Con. L. Opimius, Q. Fab. Maximus.

In the mean time, the senate, in the election of Opimius to the consulship of the following year, carried an important object to the reputation and interest of their party, and conceived hopes of being able, by the authority of this magistrate, to combat the designs of Gracchus more effectually than they had hitherto done. He was accordingly retained in the administration of affairs in Italy, while his colleague, Fabius, was appointed to command in Gaul. Caius Gracchus, having the presumption to offer himself a third time candidate for the office of tribune, was rejected, and had the mortification to find, that the authority of the senate began to prevail; and, as they had credit enough to procure his exclusion from any share in the magistracy, so they might be able to frustrate or reverse many of the acts he had obtained in favour of his party.

By the repulse of Gracchus and his associates, the aristocratical party came to have a majority, even in the college of tribunes. Questions of legislation were now likely to be determined in the assembly of the centuries; and this circumstance alone, while the senate was able to retain it, was equal to an entire revolution of the government. The centuries, under the leading of an active consul, were likely to annul former resolutions with the same decision and rapidity with which they had been passed. Much violence was expected, and the different parties, recollecting what had happened in the case of Tiberius Gracchus, took measures not to be surprised by their antagonists; for the most part came to the place of assembly in bands, even under arms, and endeavoured to possess the advantage of the ground as in the presence of an enemy.

Minucius, one of the tribunes, in consequence of a resolution of the senate, pretending that he was moved by some unfavourable presages, proposed a repeal or amendment of some of the late popular acts; and particularly, to change the destination of the colony intended for Carthage, to some other place. This motion was strenuously opposed by Fulvius Flaccus, and by Caius Gracchus, who treated the report of presages from Africa as a mere fiction, and the whole design as proceeding from the inveterate hatred of the nobles to the people. Before the assembly met, in which this question was to be decided, these popular leaders attempted to seize the capitol, but found themselves prevented by the consul, who had already with an armed force secured that station.

In the morning after they had received this disappointment, the people being assembled, and the consul being employed in offering up the customary sacrifices, Gracchus, with his party, came to their place in the comitium. One of the attendants of the consul, who was carrying away the entrails of the victim, reproached Gracchus, as he passed, with sedition, and bid him desist from his machinations against the government

5 Florus, lib. iv. c. 13. Sallust. de Bell. Jugurth. No. 621. Cicero de Provinciis Consularibus.

6 Plutarch. Paulus Minutius de Legibus Romanis.

7 Plutarch. Appian. Orosius.

of the commonwealth. On this provocation, one of the party of Gracchus struck the consul's officer with his dagger, and killed him on the spot. The cry of murder ran through the multitude, and the assembly began to break up. Gracchus endeavoured to speak, but could not be heard for the tumult; and all thoughts of business were laid aside. The consul immediately summoned the senate to meet; and having reported what had happened in the comitium, and what appeared to him the first act of hostility in a war, which the popular faction had prepared against the state, he received the charge that was usual on perilous occasions, to provide, in the manner which his own prudence should direct, for the safety of the commonwealth. Thus authorized, he commanded the senators and the knights to arm, and made proper dispositions to secure the principal streets. Being master of the capitol and forum, he adjourned the assembly of the people to the usual place on the following day, and cited the persons accused of the murder to answer for the crime which was laid to their charge.

In consequence of this adjournment, and the consul's instructions, numbers in arms, repaired to the comitium at the hour of assembly, and were ready to execute such orders as they might receive for the public safety. Gracchus and Fulvius refused to answer the citation, and the capitol being secured against them, they took post, with a numerous party in arms, on the Aventine hill, which was opposite to the capitol, and from which they equally looked down on the forum and place of assembly. Being again cited to appear at the tribunal of the Roman people, they sent a young man, one of the sons of Fulvius, to capitulate with the consul, and to settle the terms on which they were to surrender themselves. Upon this message they were told, in return, that they must answer at the bar of the assembly, as criminals, not pretend to negotiate with the republic, as equals; that no party, however numerous, was entitled to parley with the people of Rome: and to this answer the messenger was forbid, at his peril, to bring any reply. The party, however, still hoped to gain time, or to divide their enemies; and they ventured to employ young Fulvius again to repeat their message. He was seized by the consul's orders. Gracchus and Fulvius, with their adherents, were declared public enemies; and a reward was offered to the person who should kill or secure them. They were instantly attacked, and after a little resistance, forced from their ground. Gracchus fled by the wooden bridge to the opposite side of the river, and was there slain, either by his own hand, or by that of a faithful servant, who had undertaken the task of saving him in his last extremity from falling into the power of his enemies. Fulvius was dragged to execution from a bath where he attempted to conceal himself. The heads of both were carried to the consul, and exchanged for the promised reward.

In this fray the party of the senate being regularly armed and prepared for slaughter, cut off the adherents of Caius Gracchus and Fulvius in greater numbers than they had done those of Tiberius; they killed about three thousand two hundred and fifty in the streets, and confined great numbers, who were afterwards strangled in the prisons. The bodies of the slain, as the law ordained, in the case of treason, being denied the forms of a funeral, were cast into the river, and their estates confiscated.[1]

The house of Fulvius was razed to the ground, the area laid open for public uses; and, from these beginnings, it appeared that the Romans, who, in the pursuit of their foreign conquests, had so liberally shed the blood of other nations, might become equally lavish of their own.

CHAPTER IV.

State of Order and Tranquillity which followed the Suppression of the late Tumults—Appearance of Caius Marius—Foreign Wars—Complaints against Jugurtha—Appearance of the Cimbri—War with Jugurtha—Campaign and Treaty of Piso—Jugurtha comes to Rome with a Safe-Conduct—Obliged to retire from thence—Campaign of Metellus—Of Marius—Jugurtha betrayed by Bocchus—His Death, after the Triumph of Marius—This General re-elected, in order to command against the Cimbri.

THE popular party had, in the late tumults, carried their violence to such extremes, as disgusted and alarmed every person who had any desire of domestic peace; and in their ill-advised recourse to arms, but too well justified the measures which had been taken against them. By this exertion of vigour, the senate and ordinary magistrates, recovered their former authority; affairs returned to their usual channel, and the most perfect order seemed to arise from the late confusions. Questions of legislation were allowed to take their rise in the senate, and were not carried to the people, without the sanction of the senate's authority. The legislative power was exercised in the assembly of the centuries, and the prohibitory or defensive function of the tribunes, or representatives of the people, was such, as to prevent the abuses of the executive power in the hands of the aristocracy, without stopping the proceedings of government, or substituting a democratical usurpation in its place. Even the judicative power, vested in the equestrian order, promised to have a salutary effect, by keeping a balance between the different ranks and distinctions of men in the republic.

The aristocratical party, notwithstanding the ascendant they had recently gained, did not attempt to rescind any of the regular institutions of Gracchus; they were contented with inflicting punishments on those who had been accessary to the late sedition, and with re-establishing such of the nobles as had suffered by the violence of the popular faction. Popilius Lænas,

1 Appian. Plutarch. Orosius, lib. v. c. 12. Florus, lib. iii. c. 15. Auctor de Viris Illustribus, c. 65.

driven into exile by one of the edicts of Gracchus, or by the persecution to which it exposed him, was now recalled upon the motion of Calpurnius Piso, one of the tribunes.[2]

As the state of parties was in some measure reversed, Papirius Carbo thought proper to withdraw from the popular side; and, by the credit of those now in possession of the government, was promoted to the station of consul, and yielded the first fruits of his conversion by defending the cause of his predecessor Opimius, who, at the expiration of his consulate, was brought to trial for having put Roman citizens to death without the forms of law. Carbo, though himself connected with those who suffered, now pleaded the justice and necessity of the late military executions; and, upon this plea, obtained the acquittal of his client.

U. C. 633.

Publius Manlius, and C. Papirius Carbo.

This merit on the part of Carbo, however, did not so far cancel his former offences as to prevent his being tried and condemned in the following year, as an accomplice in the sedition of Gracchus. He was supposed to have been accessary to the death of Scipio; and his cause not being warmly espoused by any party, he fell a sacrifice to the imputation of his heinous crime. It is said, that, upon hearing his sentence, he killed himself.[3]

Octavius, one of the tribunes of the present year, moved an amendment of the law obtained by Gracchus, respecting the distribution of corn from the public granaries, probably to ease the treasury in part of that burden; but the particulars are unknown.

Lex Octavia Frumentaria.

About this time the celebrated Caius Marius began to appear in the public assemblies of the people. He was a person of obscure birth, and rustic manners, formed amidst the occupations of a peasant,[4] and the hardships of a legionary soldier, but of a resolute spirit, and insatiable ambition. He was a native of Arpinum, and without any other apparent title than that of being a denizen of Rome, laid claim to the honours of the state. He is remarkable for having suffered more repulses in his first attempts to be elected into office, and for having succeeded more frequently afterwards, than any other Roman citizen during the existence of the commonwealth.

Marius, after being disappointed in his first canvass for the office of tribune, succeeded in the following year. The acts which were passed under his tribunate, and which bear his name, do not carry any violent expressions of party-spirit, nor give intimation of that insatiate ambition with which he afterwards distressed his country; the first related to the conduct of elections, and provided some remedy for an evil which was complained of in the manner of soliciting votes. The space between the rails, by which the citizens passed to give in their ballots, was so broad as to admit, not only those who came to vote, but the candidates likewise, with their adherents and friends, who came to importune and to overawe the peop'e in the very act of delivering their votes. Marius proposed to put an end to this practice, and to provide for the entire freedom of the people, by narrowing the entrance, so that only the voters could pass. A party of the nobles, with Aurelius Cotta the consul at their head, not knowing with what a resolute spirit they were about to contend, being averse to this reformation, prevailed on the senate to withhold its authority, without which any regular question on this subject could not be put to the people. But Marius, in the character of tribune, threatened the consul with immediate imprisonment, if he did not move to recall this vote of the senate. The matter being reconsidered, Lucius Metellus, who was first on the rolls, having given his voice for affirming the first decree, was ordered by Marius into custody; and there being no tribune to intercede for him, must have gone to prison, if the dispute had not terminated by the majority agreeing to have the matter carried to the people, as Marius proposed, with the sanction of the senate's authority.

Lex Maria de Suffragiis.

In another of the acts of Marius, the republic was still more indebted to his wisdom and courage in withstanding an attempt of one of his colleagues to flatter the indigent citizens at the expense of the public treasury, by repealing the recent regulation of Octavius, and lowering the terms on which corn was distributed from the granaries. This was an ordinary expedient of tribunitian faction. Marius opposed it as of dangerous consequence. And his conduct in this matter marked him out as one not to be awed by any party, and a person who, into whatever party he should be admitted, was destined to govern. The times indeed were likely to give more importance to his character as a soldier than a citizen; and in that he was still farther raised above the malice of those who were inclined to revile or undervalue what were called his upstart pretensions.[5]

From the time that the Romans first passed into the Transalpine Gaul, as auxiliaries to the republic of Marseilles, they had kept on foot in that neighbourhood a military force; and, by planting colonies at convenient stations, showed their intention of maintaining possessions on that side of the Alps. Betultus, or Betultich, a prince of the country, who was supposed able to raise a force of two hundred thousand men, attempted to expel these intruders, but was defeated, first by the proconsul Fabius, afterwards by Domitius Ahenobarbus, and furnished these generals with the subjects of their respective triumphs. This prince himself became a captive to Domitius, and was carried to Rome, where he was led in procession, distinguished by his painted arms and his chariot of silver, the equipage in which it was said he usually led his army to battle.[6]

U. C. 633.

It appears that the Romans had employed elephants in the first wars they made in Gaul; for the victory of Domitius is attributed to the effect that was produced by these animals.[7]

Quintus Marcus succeeded Domitius in the command of the forces which were employed in Gaul; and continued to gain ground on the natives, who appeared from different cantons successively to resist his arms. He planted a colony at Narbo, to strengthen the frontier of the newly-acquired province on one side; and as the Romans had hitherto always passed by sea into

2 Cicero in Bruto.
3 Valerius Max. lib. iii. c. 7. Cicero in Bruto.
4 Juvenal. Sat. viii. Plin. lib. xxxiii. c. 11.

5 Plutarch. in Mario.
6 Velleius Pater. Ammianus Marcell. lib. xv. Ene Padionus in Verrinam Secundam. Val. Max. lib. v. c. 9
7 Suetonius in Vita Neronis.

that country, he endeavoured to open a passage by the Alps in order to have a communication by land with Italy on the other. In the course of these operations the Stæni, an Alpine nation that opposed him, were entirely cut off.

About this time the Roman generals obtained their triumphs on different quarters, in the Baleares and in Dalmatia, as well as in Gaul; and the republic did not meet for some years with an enemy able to resist her power, except on the side of Thrace and the Danube, where the proconsul Cato was defeated; and where a resistance was for some years kept up by the natives.

But of the foreign affairs which occupied the attention of the Romans, the most memorable was the contest of pretenders to the crown of Numidia, which, by the death of Micipsa, the son and successor of Massinissa, came to be disposed of about this time. The late king had two sons, Adherbal and Hiempsal. He had likewise adopted Jugurtha, the natural son of his brother Manastabal, whom he had employed at the head of his armies, thinking it safer to gain him by good offices, than to provoke him by a total exclusion from favour. He had formed a project, frequent among barbarous and despotic sovereigns, but always ruinous, to divide his territories; and he hoped that, while he provided for his own sons, he should secure to them, from motives of gratitude, the protection and good offices of Jugurtha, whom he admitted to an equal share with them in the partition of his kingdom. The consequences of this mistaken arrangement soon appeared in the distractions that followed, and which arose from the ambition of Jugurtha, to make himself master of the whole. For this purpose he formed a secret design against the lives of both the brothers, of whom the younger, Hiempsal, fell into his snare, and was assassinated. Adherbal, being more cautious, obliged his crafty enemy to declare himself openly, took the field against him with all the forces he could raise, but was defeated, and obliged to take refuge in the Roman province, and from thence thought proper to pass into Italy, in order to lay his complaints before the senate and people of Rome.

Massinissa, the grandfather of this injured prince, had given effectual aid to the Romans in their wars with Carthage; and, upon the final reduction of that republic, was rewarded with a considerable part of its spoils. From this time forward the Romans expected, and the king of Numidia paid to them, a deference like that of a vassal or tributary prince to his sovereign lord. Upon the faith of this connection, Adherbal now carried his complaints to Rome; and Jugurtha, knowing how ready the Romans were, in the character of arbitrators, to consider themselves as the sovereigns of other nations, thought proper to send deputies on his part, to counteract the representations of his rival.

This crafty adventurer had served under Scipio at the siege of Numantia, where he had an opportunity of observing the manners and discipline of the Romans, and accommodated himself to both. He was equally distinguished by his implicit submission to command, as by his impetuous courage, and by the ability of his conduct in every service. He had even then probably directed his views to the succession of Numidia, and saw of what consequence the Romans might prove in deciding his fortunes. He had studied their character, and had already marked out the line he was to follow in conducting his affairs with that people. They appeared to be a number of sovereigns assembled together, able in council and formidable in the field; but, in comparison to the Africans in general, undesigning and simple. With the pride of monarchs they began, he imagined, to feel the indigence of courtiers, and were to be moved by considerations of interest rather than force. His commissioners were now accordingly furnished with ample presents, and with the means of gratifying the principal persons at Rome in a manner that was suited to their respective ranks and to their influence in the commonwealth.

In the choice of this plan Jugurtha, like most politicians that refine too much, had formed a system with great ingenuity, and spoke of it with a specious wit; but had not taken into his account the whole circumstances of the case in which he engaged. Rome, he supposed, was a city to be sold. He forgot that, though many Romans could be bought, no treasure was sufficient to buy the republic; that to buy a few, made it necessary for him to buy many more; that as he raised expectations, the number of expectants increased without limit; that the more he gave, the more he was still expected to give; that in a state which was broke into parties, if he gained one by his gifts, that alone was sufficient to rouse the other against him. And accordingly, after lavishing his money to influence the councils of Rome, he was obliged to have recourse to arms at last, and to contend with the forces of the republic, after he had exhausted his treasure in attempting to corrupt her virtue.

Although Jugurtha had many partizans at Rome, such was the injustice of his cause, or the suspicion of corruption in those who espoused it, that they durst not openly avow their wishes. They endeavoured to suspend the resolutions which were in agitation against him, and had the matter referred to ten commissioners who should go into Africa, and in presence of the parties settle the differences which subsisted between them. There indeed he practised his art on the Roman commissioners with better success than he had experienced with the senate and people. He prevailed upon them to divide the kingdom, and to favour him in the lot which should be assigned to himself: knowing that force must ultimately decide every controversy which should arise on the subject, he made choice, not of the richest, but of the most warlike division; and indeed had already determined that, as soon as the Romans left Africa, he should make an end of the contest by the death of Adherbal; trusting that, by continuing to use the specific which it was said he had already applied, he might prevail on the Romans to overlook what they would not, on a previous request, have permitted.

He accordingly, soon after the departure of the Roman commissioners, marched into the territories of Adherbal, shut him up in the town of Cirta; and, while the Romans sent him repeated messages to desist, still continued the blockade, until the mercenaries of Adherbal, tired of the hardships they were made to endure, advised, and, by their appearing ready to desert, forced him to commit himself to the mercy of Jugurtha, by whom he was immediately put to death.

By these events, in about seven years from the

death of Micipsa, Jugurtha had attained to the object of his highest desires; but the arts which procured him a crown, likewise rendered his state insecure. He was disappointed in his expectation to pacify the Romans. The money he dealt went into the coffers only of a few, but his crimes roused the indignation of the whole people. Practised statesmen or politicians are seldom roused by mere feelings of indignation on the subject of private wrongs. They have, or pretend to have, reasons of state to suppress the consideration of individuals. The greater part of the Roman senate accordingly, whether acting on maxims of policy, or won by the presents of Jugurtha, received the complaints which were lodged against him with indifference; but the assembly of the people, moved by the cries of perfidy and murder which were raised by the tribunes, received the representations of his conduct with indignation and rage. These passions were inflamed by opposition to the nobles, who were supposed to favour the murderer. Neither the most deliberate statesman nor the most determined partizan of Jugurtha durst appear in his cause, nor propose to decline a war with that prince, although it was likely to be attended with considerable difficulties; and was to be undertaken at a time when a cloud hung over Italy on the side of Gaul, a quarter from which the Romans always expected, and often experienced, the most terrible storms.

U C. 640.

About the time that Adherbal laid his complaints against Jugurtha before the senate of Rome, a new enemy had appeared. The north of Europe, or of Asia, had cast off a swarm, which, migrating to the south and to the west, was first descried by the Romans on the frontier of Illyricum, and presently drew their attention to that side. The horde was said to consist of three hundred thousand fighting men, conducting their families of women and children, and covering the plains with their cattle. The consul Papirius Carbo was ordered to take post in Illyricum, to observe the motions of this tremendous host. He was alarmed with their seeming to point towards the district of Aquileia; and putting himself, with too little precaution, in their way, could not withstand their numbers, and was overwhelmed as by a tempest.

This migrating nation the Romans have called by the name of Cimbri, without determining from whence they came. It is said that their cavalry amounted to no more than fifteen thousand; that it was their practice to despise horses, as well as the other spoils of their enemies, which they generally destroyed: and from this circumstance it may be argued, that they were not of Scythian extraction, nor sprung from those mighty plains in the northern parts of Asia, where military force has from time immemorial consisted of cavalry, where horses were valued above every other species of acquisition or property; and that they must have been bred amongst mountains and woods, where this animal is not equally useful. On their helmets, which were crested with plumes of feathers, they carried the gaping jaws of wild beasts. On their bodies they wore breastplates of iron, had shields painted of a conspicuous colour; and carried two missile javelins or darts, and a heavy sword. They collected their fighting men, for the most part, into a solid square, equally extending every way: in one of their battles it was reported that the sides of this square extended thirty stadia, or between three and four miles. The men of the foremost ranks were fastened together with chains locked to their girdles, which made them impenetrable to every attack, and gave them the force of a torrent, in sweeping obstructions before them. Such were the accounts with which the Romans were alarmed on the approach of this tremendous enemy.

Although, by the defeat of Carbo, Italy lay open to their devastations, yet they turned away to the north and westward, and keeping the Alps on their left, made their appearance again on the frontier of the Roman province in Narbonne Gaul, and from thence passed into Spain, where they continued to alarm Roman settlements, and kept Rome itself in suspense, by the uncertainty of the tract they might afterwards choose to pursue.

U. C. 642.

Pub. Cornelius, Scipio Nasica.
L. Calpurnius, Piso, Bestia.

Such was the state of affairs, when the popular cry and generous indignation of the Roman people forced the state into a war with Jugurtha. The consul Piso was appointed to command in Numidia. The necessary levies and supplies for this service were ordered, and Jugurtha could no longer doubt that the force of the Roman republic was to be employed against him; yet, in hopes to avert the storm, he sent his son with two proper assistants, in the quality of ambassadors to Rome, chiefly trusting to the arts of insinuation he had hitherto practised, and to the distribution of presents and of money. Their arrival being reported to the senate, a resolution of this body passed, that unless they brought an offer from Jugurtha to surrender his person and his kingdom at discretion, they should be required in ten days to depart from Italy.

This answer being delivered to the son of Jugurtha, he presently withdrew, and was followed by a Roman army, which was prepared to embark for Africa. The war was conducted at first with great vivacity and success: but Jugurtha, by offering great public concessions or private gratifications, prevailed on the consul to negotiate. It was agreed, that, upon receiving a proper hostage on the part of the Romans, the king himself should repair to their camp, in order to conclude the treaty. In the articles that were made public, the king agreed to surrender himself at discretion, and to pay a large contribution in horses, corn, elephants, and money; but in secret articles, which were drawn up at the same time, the consul engaged that the person of the king should be safe, and that the kingdom of Numidia should be secured to him.

During these transactions the time of the expiration of Piso's command drew near, and he himself was called into Italy to preside at the approaching elections. His report of the treaty with Jugurtha was received with suspicion, and the cry of corruption resumed by the popular party. "Where is this captive?" said the tribune Memmius; "if he have surrendered himself, he will obey your commands; send for him; question him in respect to what is past. If he refuse to come, we shall know what to think of a treaty which brings impunity to Jugurtha, princely fortunes to a few private persons, ruin and infamy to the Roman republic." Upon this motion the prætor Cassius Longinus, a person of approved merit and unshaken integrity, was hastened into Africa, with positive instructions to bring the king of Numidia to Rome. By the safe conduct which Cassius brought on the part of the republic, and by his own assurances of protection, Jugurtha was prevailed on to commit himself to the faith of the Romans. He laid aside his kingly state and attendants, set out for Italy, and determined to appear as a suppliant at Rome. Upon his arrival, being called into the public assembly, Memmius proposed to interrogate him on the subject of his supposed secret transaction with certain members of the senate; but here Bebius, another of the tribunes, interposed his negative; and, notwithstanding that the people exclaimed, and even menaced, this tribune persisted. And before this bar to the farther examination of Jugurtha could be removed, an incident took place, which occasioned his sudden departure from Italy.

Massiva, the son of Gulussa, being the grandson and natural representative of Massinissa, and the only person besides Jugurtha who remained of the royal line of Numidia, had been persuaded by Albinus, the consul elected for the ensuing year, to state his pretensions before the Roman senate, and to lay claim to the crown. Jugurtha, though at Rome, and in the power of those who were likely to resent his crimes, gave a specimen of the bold and sanguinary counsels to which he was inclined, employed against this competitor the ordinary arts of his court, and had him assassinated. The crime was traced to its author, but the safe conduct he had received could not be violated; and he was only commanded, without delay, to depart from Italy. On this occasion he left Rome with that memorable saying; "Here is a city to be sold, if any buyer could be found."

U. C. 643. *M. Minucius Rufus & Posthum. Albinus.*

The consul Albinus soon followed Jugurtha, to take the command of the Roman army in Africa; and being eager to perform some notable action before the expiration of his year, which was fast approaching, he urged the king of Numidia, with all the forces he could assemble in the province; but found that he had to do with an enemy who had the art to elude his impetuosity, and from whose apparent conduct no judgment could be formed of his real designs. This artful warrior often advanced with a seeming intention to hazard a battle, when he was most resolved to decline it; or he precipitantly fled, when he meant to return upon his enemy, and take advantage of any disorder he might incur in a too eager pursuit. His offers of submission, or his threats, were equally fallacious; and he used, perhaps in common with other African princes, means to mislead his enemy, which Europeans, ancient as well as modern, have in general condemned. He made solemn capitulations and treaties with a view to break them, and considered breach of faith, like a feint or an ambush, as a stratagem licensed in war. The Europeans have always termed it perfidy to break the faith of a treaty, the Africans held it stupidity to be caught in the snare.

By the artifices of Jugurtha, accordingly, or by the remissness of his antagonist, the war was protracted for another year, and the consul, as the time of the election drew near, was recalled, as usual, to preside in the choice of his successor. At his arrival the city was in great agitation. The cry of corruption, which had been raised against many of the nobles, on account of their supposed correspondence with Jugurtha, gave an advantage to the popular party, and they determined to improve it, by raising prosecutions to the ruin of persons, either odious to the people, or obnoxious to the equestrian order, who then had the power of judicature in their hands.[1] Three inquisitors were accordingly named by special commission to take cognizance of all complaints of corruption that should be brought before them; and this commission was instantly employed to harass the nobility, and to revenge the blood which had been shed in the late popular tumults. Lucius Calpurnius, Piso, Bestia, C. Cato, Spurius Albinus, and L. Opimius, all of consular dignity, fell a sacrifice on this occasion to the popular resentment. The tribune Mamilius, upon whose motion this tribunal had been erected, with his associates, apprehending that, upon the expiration of their trust, the heat of the prosecutions might abate, moved the people that they might be continued in their office; and, upon finding themselves opposed by the influence of the senate and all the ordinary powers of the state, they suspended, by virtue of their tribunitian power, the election of consuls, and for a whole year kept the republic in a state of absolute anarchy.

In this interval Aulus Albinus, left by his brother, the late consul, in the command of the army in Africa, determined to improve the occasion by some honourable action. He left his quarters in the winter, and marched far into the country, hoping that by force or surprise he might possess himself of the Numidian treasures or magazines. Jugurtha encouraged him in this design, affected fear, retired with precipitation wherever the Romans presented themselves; and, to increase the presumption of their general, sent frequent messages to implore his pity. He at the same time endeavoured to open a correspondence with the Thracians and other foreigners, then serving in the Roman camp. Some of these he corrupted; and when he had drawn the Roman army into difficult situations, and prepared his plan for execution, he suddenly advanced in the night to the Roman station; and the avenues being entrusted, as he expected, to the Thracians and Ligurians whom he had corrupted, and by whom he was suffered to pass, he surprised the Romans in their camp, and drove them from thence in great confusion to a neighbouring height, where they enjoyed, during night, some respite from the enemy; but without any resource for subsistence, or hopes of recovering their baggage.

In the morning Jugurtha desired to confer with the prætor; and representing how much the Romans, stripped of their provision and equipage, were then in his power, made a merit of offering them quarter, on condition that they would conclude a treaty of peace, and in ten days evacuate his kingdom.

These terms were accordingly accepted: but the capitulation, when known at Rome, gave occasion to much indignation and clamour. It was voted by the senate not to be binding, and the consul Albinus, in order to repair the loss of the public, and to restore the credit of his own family, made hasty levies, with which he proposed to re-

1 Cicero de Claris Oratoribus. Sallust. in Be. Jugurth

new the war in Numidia, but not having the consent of the tribunes to this measure, he was obliged to leave his forces behind him in Italy, and joined the army without being able to bring any reinforcement. He found it in no condition to face the enemy, and was contented to remain in the province till a successor should be named.

U. C. 644.

Q. Cæcilius Metellus Numidicus, M. Junius Silanus.

Resentment of the disgraces incurred in Africa, and fear of invasion from the Cimbri, who, having traversed Spain and Gaul, were still on their march, appear to have calmed for a little time the animosity of domestic factions at Rome. The consular elections were suffered to proceed, and the choice of the people fell on Quintus Cæcilius Metellus and M. Junius Silanus; the first was appointed to the command of the army in Numidia, the second to observe the motions of the Cimbri on the frontiers of Gaul, and to turn them aside, if possible, from the territory of Rome. About this time those wandering nations had sent a formal message to the Romans, desiring to have it understood on what lands they might settle,[2] or rather, over what lands they might pass in migration with their herds. This request being refused by the senate, they opened a passage by force, overcame in battle the consul Silanus, and, probably without intending to retain any conquest, continued to move wherever the aspect of the country tempted their choice.

Metellus proceeded to Africa with a considerable reinforcement; and, having spent some time in restoring the discipline of the army which had been greatly neglected, and in training his new levies to the duties and hardships of the service, he directed his march to the enemy's country, and in his way, had frequent messages from Jugurtha, with professions of submission and of a pacific disposition.

When the Roman army entered on the territory of Numidia, they accordingly found the country prepared to receive them in a friendly manner; the people in tranquillity, the gates of every city left open, and the markets ready to supply them with necessaries.

These appearances, with the known character of Jugurtha, creating distrust, only excited the vigilance of Metellus. They even provoked him to retort on the Numidian his own insidious arts. He tampered with Bomilcar, and the other messengers of Jugurtha to betray their master, and promised them great rewards if they would deliver him into the hands of the Romans, either living or dead.

Jugurtha, not considering that his known character for falsehood must have destroyed the credit of all his professions, even if he should at any time think proper to make them sincere, and trusting to the effect of his submissive messages in rendering the enemy secure, made a disposition to profit by any errors they should commit, and hoped to circumvent and destroy them on their march. For this purpose he waited for them on the descents of a high mountain, over which they were to pass in their way to the Muthul, a river which helped to form the situation of which he was to avail himself. He accordingly lay concealed by its banks, until the enemy actually fell into the snare he had laid for them. With the advantage of the ground and of numbers, he maintained, during the greater part of the day, a contest with troops who possessed, against his irregulars, a great superiority of order, discipline, and courage; but not having found the Romans, as he expected, in any degree off their guard, he was, in the event of that day's action, obliged to fly with a few horse to a remote part of his kingdom.

This victory obtained over Jugurtha appeared to be an end of the war. His army was dispersed, and he was left with a few horsemen, who attended his person, to find a place of retreat, and to choose a station at which to assemble new forces, if he meant to continue the war.

The Numidians were inured to action. The frequent wars of that continent, the wild and unsettled state of their own country, made the use of horses and of arms familiar: but so void was the nation of military policy, and its people so ignorant of order, that it was scarcely possible for the king to fight two battles with the same army. If victorious, they withdrew with their plunder; if defeated, they supposed all military obligations at an end: and in either case, after an action, every one fled where he expected to be soonest in safety.

Metellus, after the late engagement, finding no enemy in the field, was for some time uncertain to what part of the kingdom Jugurtha had directed his flight. But having intelligence that he was in a new situation assembling an army, and likely to form one still more numerous than any he had yet brought into the field, tired of pursuing an enemy on whom defeats had so little effects, he turned away to the richer and more cultivated parts of the kingdom. Here the plunder of the country might better repay his labour, and the enemy, if he ventured to defend his territory, might more sensibly feel his defeats. Jugurtha perceiving his intention, drew his forces towards the same quarter, and soon appeared in his rear.

While Metellus was endeavouring to force the city of Zama, Jugurtha pierced into his camp, and, though repulsed from thence, took a post, by which he made the situation of the Romans, between the town and his own army, so uneasy, as to oblige them to raise the siege.

This the Numidian prince thought a proper opportunity to gain some credit to his pacific professions. He made an offer accordingly to surrender at discretion, and actually delivered up great part of his arms and military stores; but this purpose, if ever sincere, he retracted, and again had recourse to arms.

U. C. 645.

Servius Sulpicius Galba, Q. Hortensius Nepes, Marcus Aurelius Scaurus.

The victory which had been obtained in Africa, flattered the vanity of the Roman people, and procured to Metellus, in the quality of proconsul, a continuation of his former command. The troops he had posted in Vacca being cut off by the inhabitants, he made hasty marches in the night, surprised the place, and, without having allowed the authors of that outrage more than two days to enjoy the fruits c their perfidy, amply revenged the wrong they had done to the Roman garrison.

But the success of Metellus did not hasten the ruin of Jugurtha so fast as his own misconduct, in the jealous and sanguinary measures which he

2 Florus, lib. iii. Liv. lib. lxv.

ook to suppress plots and conspiracies, either real or supposed to be formed against his life, by persons the most in his confidence.

Bomilcar, still carrying in his mind the offers which had been made by Metellus, and willing to have some merit with the Romans, into whose hands he and all the subjects of Jugurtha were likely soon to fall, formed a design against his master, and drew Nabdalsa, a principal officer in the Numidian armies, to take part in the plot. They were discovered in time to prevent the execution of their design, but they made Jugurtha from thenceforward consider the camp of his own army as a place of danger to himself, rendered him distrustful, timorous, and unquiet; frequently changing his company and his quarters, his guards and his bed. Under these apprehensions, by which his mind was considerably disordered and weakened, he endeavoured, by continual and rapid motions, to make it uncertain where he should be found; and he experienced at last, that private assassination and breach of faith, although they appear to abridge the toils of ambition, are not expedient even in war; that they render human life itself, for the advantages of which war is undertaken, no longer eligible or worthy of being preserved. Weary of his anxious state, he ventured once more to face Metellus in the field, and being again defeated, fled to Thala, where he had left his children and the most valuable part of his treasure. This city too, finding Metellus had followed him, he was obliged to abandon, and, with his children and his remaining effects, fled from Numidia, first to the country of the Getuli, barbarous nations, that lived among the mountains of Atlas south of Numidia, and whom he endeavoured to arm in his cause. From thence he fled to Bocchus, king of Mauritania, whose daughter he had married; and having persuaded this prince to consider his quarrel with the Romans as the common cause of all monarchies, who were likely in succession to become the prey of this arrogant and insatiable power, he prevailed on the Mauritanian to assemble his army, and to attempt the relief of Numidia.

Jugurtha, in conjunction with his new ally, directed his march to Cirta, and Metellus perceiving his intention, took post to cover that place. But while he was endeavouring, by threats or persuasions, to detach the king of Mauritania from Jugurtha, he received information from Rome that he was superseded in the command of the army; and from thenceforward protracted the war, under pretence of messages and negotiations, and possibly inclined to leave it with all its difficulties entire to his successor.

Marius, having served under Metellus, had with great difficulty, and not without some expressions of scorn on the part of his general, obtained leave to depart for Rome, where he meant to stand for the consulship. He accordingly appeared in the capacity of candidate for this honour, and by vaunting, instead of concealing, the obscurity of his ancestors; by inveighing against the whole order of nobility, their dress, their city manners, their Greek learning, their family images, the stress they laid on the virtue of their forefathers to compensate the want of it in themselves; but more especially by arraigning the dilatory conduct of Metellus, and by promising a speedy issue to the war, if it should be entrusted to himself; a promise, to which the force and ability he had shown in all the stations he had hitherto filled, procured him some credit; he so far won upon the people, that he was chosen consul, in opposition to the interest of the nobles, and to the influence of all the leading men of the senate. His promotion was in a particular manner galling to Metellus, whose reputation he had attacked, and to whose station in Africa, by an express order of the people, in contempt of the arrangement which had been made by the senate, he was now to succeed.

U. C. 626.

L. Cassius Longinus, C. Marius.

Upon the nomination of Marius, the party who had opposed his preferment did not attempt to withhold the reinforcements which he asked for the service in which he was to command. They even hoped to increase his difficulties by suffering him to increase the establishment of his province. The wealthier class of the people alone were yet admitted into the legions; and being averse to such distant services, were likely to conceive a dislike to the persons by whom they were forced to enlist. Marius in this capacity might lose some part of the popular favour which he now enjoyed, and become less formidable to his rivals in the state. But this crafty and daring politician, by slighting the laws which excluded the necessitous citizens from serving in the legions, found in this class of the people a numerous and willing supply. They crowded to his standard, and filled up his army without delay, and even without offence to those of a better condition, who were pleased with relief from this part of their public burdens.

This was a remarkable and dangerous innovation in the Roman state, and may be mentioned among the steps which hastened the ruin of the commonwealth. From this time forward the sword began to pass from the hands of those who were interested in the preservation of the republic, into the hands of others who were willing to make it a prey. The circumstances of the times were such, indeed, as to give warning of the change. The service of a legionary soldier was become too severe for the less indigent order of citizens, and now opened to the necessitous the principal road to profit as well as honour. Marius, to facilitate his levies, was willing to gratify both; and thus gave beginning to the formation of armies who were ready to fight for or against the laws of their country, and who, in the sequel, substituted battles for the bloodless contests which hitherto had arisen from the divisions of party.

The new consul, unrivalled in the favour of the people, obtained whatever he required; and, being completely provided for the service to which he was destined, embarked for Africa with a great reinforcement, and in a few days arrived at Utica. Upon his arrival, the operations of the war were resumed, and carried into the wealthiest provinces of Numidia, where he encouraged his army with the hopes of spoil. The new levies, though composed of persons hitherto excluded from the military service, were formed by the example of the legions already in the field, and who were now well apprised of their own superiority to the African armies. Bocchus and Jugurtha, upon the approach of this enemy, thought proper to separate, and took different routes into places of safety in the more difficult and inaccessible parts of the country.

This separation was made at the suggestion of

Jugurtha, who alleged that, upon their appearing to despair, and to discontinue all offensive operations, the Roman general would become more secure and more open to surprise. But Marius, without abating his vigilance, pressed where the enemy gave way, over-ran the country, and took possession of the towns they had left. To rival the glory which Metellus had gained in the reduction of Thala, he ventured on a like enterprise, in the face of similar difficulties, by attacking Thapsa, a place surrounded with deserts, and in the midst of a land destitute of water, and of every resource for an army. Having succeeded in this design, he ventured, in his return, to attack another fortress, in which, it being supposed impregnable, the royal treasures were lodged. This strong hold was situated on a rock, which was every where, except at one path that was fortified with ramparts and towers, faced with steep and inaccessible cliffs. The garrison permitted the first approaches of the Romans with perfect security, and even derision. After some fruitless attacks, Marius, with some imputation of folly in having made the attempt, was about to desist from the enterprise, when a Ligurian, who had been used to pick snails on the cliffs over which this fortress was situated, found himself, in search of his prey, and by the growing facility of the ascent, led to a height from which he began to have hopes of reaching the summit. He accordingly surmounted all the difficulties in his way; and the garrison being then intent on the opposite side of the fortress to which the attack was directed, he returned unobserved. This intelligence he carried to Marius, who without delay ordered a detachment of chosen men, with an unusual number of trumpets and instruments of alarm, to follow the direction of this guide. He himself, to divert the attention of the besieged, and to be ready, on receiving the proposed signal from within, to make a vigorous and decisive assault, advanced to the walls. The Ligurian, with much difficulty, endeavoured to effect his intentions. The soldiers who followed him were obliged to untie their sandals and their helmets, to sling their shields and their swords, and, at difficult parts of the rock, could not be persuaded to advance until their guide had repeatedly passed and repassed in their sight, or had found stumps and points of the stone at which they could fasten cords to aid their ascent. The summit was to be gained at last by the branches of a tree which, being rooted in a cleft of the rock, grew up to the edge of the precipice. By the branches of this tree the whole party passed, and, climbing near to its top, landed at last on the summit. They instantly sounded their trumpets and gave a sudden alarm. The besieged, who had been drawn to the walls to resist the enemy who attacked them in front, were astonished with this sound in their rear, and soon after, greatly terrified with the confused flight from behind them of women, children, and men unarmed, and being at the same time vigorously attacked at their gates, were no longer able to resist, suffered the Romans to force their way at this entrance, and in the end to become masters of the fort.

Whilst Marius was engaged in the siege of this place he was joined by the questor Sylla, who had been left in Italy to bring up the cavalry, which were not ready to embark at the departure of the consul. This young man was of a patrician and noble family, but which had not, for some generations, borne any of the higher offices of state. He himself partook in the learning which then spread into Italy, from a communication with the Greeks, and had passed the early part of his life in town-dissipation or in literary studies, of which the last were considered at this time at Rome as a species of corruption almost equal to the first. He was yet a novice in war, but having an enterprising genius, soon became an object of respect to the soldiers, and of jealousy to his general, with whom he now laid the foundation of a quarrel more fatal to the commonwealth than that which had subsisted between the present and preceding commander in this service.

The king of Numidia, stung by the sense of what he had already lost, and expecting no advantage from any further delays, determined, in conjunction with Bocchus, to make a vigorous effort, and to oblige Marius, who was then moving to his winter quarters, yet to hazard a battle for the preservation of what he had acquired in the preceding campaign. The king of Mauritania had been inclined to remain neutral, or to enter on a separate treaty with the Romans; but being promised a third part of the kingdom of Numidia, in case the Romans were expelled from thence, and the war should be brought to a happy conclusion, he once more brought forward his army, and joined Jugurtha.

The prosperous state of the Romans, undisturbed for some time by the opposition of any enemy in the field, inspired them with some degree of negligence or security, by which they were exposed to surprise. About an hour before the setting of the sun, their march was interrupted by the attack of numerous parties, who, without any settled order, occupied the fields through which they were to pass, and seemed to intend, by assailing them on every side, to begin the night with a scene of confusion, of which they might afterwards more effectually avail themselves in the dark. In an action begun under these disadvantages, it was supposed, that the Roman army might be entirely defeated, and in a country with which they were not acquainted, and in circumstances for which they were not at all prepared, being unable to effect a retreat, surrender at discretion.

Jugurtha, with his usual intrepidity and conduct, profited by every circumstance which presented itself in his favour. He brought the troops, of which his army was composed, whether Getulians or Numidians, horse or foot, to harass the enemy in their different ways of fighting, and where they could easiest make their attacks. Wherever a party was repulsed, he took care to replace it; and sometimes affected to remit his ardour, or to fly with every appearance of panic, in order to tempt the Romans to break from their ranks. Marius, notwithstanding, with great dexterity and presence of mind, maintained the form of his march; and, before night, got possession of some heights on which he could secure his army. He himself, with the infantry, chose that which had the steepest ascent, and ordered Sylla, with the cavalry, to take his post on a smaller eminence below. That his position might not be known to the enemy, he prohibited the lighting of fires, and the usual sounding of trumpets at the different watches of the night. The Numidians had halted on the plain where night overtook them, and were observed at the break of day, reposing in great security, and without any seeming apprehension of danger from an enemy, who was supposed to be flying, and who, on the preceding day, had, with some difficulty, escaped from their hands. Marius resolved to attack them in this situation, and gave orders, which were communicated through the army, that at a general sound of the trumpets, every man should stand to his arms, and with a great shout, and beating on his shield, make an impetuous attack on the enemy. The design, accordingly, succeeded. The Numidians, who had often affected to fly, were driven into an actual rout. Great numbers fell in the flight, and many ensigns and trophies were taken.

After this victory, Marius with his usual precautions, and without remitting his vigilance, on a supposition that the enemy was dispersed, directed his march to the towns on the coast, where he intended to fix his quarters for the winter. Jugurtha, well apprised of his route, proposed again to surprise him before he should reach the end of his journey; and, for this purpose, avoided giving him any premature or unnecessary cause of alarm. He prepared to attack the Roman army in the neighbourhood of Cirta, which was to be the end of their labours, and near to which he supposed that they would think themselves secure from any further attempts of their enemy. In the execution of this design, he, with the greatest ability, conducted his troops to the place of action, and there too made every effort of conduct and resolution. But the match being unequal, he was obliged to give up the contest; and, with his sword and armour all bathed in blood, and almost alone, is said to have left the field, in which, for the first time, he had taken no precautions for re-assembling his army, and on which his Numidians were accordingly routed, to rally no more!

U. C. 647.

C. Attilius Scrannus. Quintus Servilius Cætico.

Upon these repeated defeats, Bocchus despaired of the fortunes of Jugurtha, and sent a deputation to Marius, requesting a conference with himself, or with some of his officers. He obtained an interview with Sylla and Manlius; but, upon their arrival, had taken no fixed resolution, and was still kept in suspense, by the persuasion of those of his court who favoured the interest of Jugurtha. Marius, being continued in his command, resumed the operations of the war, and was about to attack the only place which yet remained in the hands of the enemy. When the king of Mauritania, alarmed by this circumstance, took his resolution to sue for peace, he sent a deputation of five chosen persons, first to the quarters of Marius, and, with this general's permission, ordered them to proceed from thence to Rome. These deputies, being admitted into the senate, made offers of friendship in the name of their master; and were informed, in return, that he must give proofs of his friendly disposition to the Romans, before they could believe his professions, or listen to any terms of peace. When this answer was reported to Bocchus, he was not at a loss to understand that the Romans wished him to deliver up the king of Numidia into their hands; and seems to have conceived the design of purchasing peace, even on these terms. Sylla being already personally known to him, he made choice of this officer as the person with whom he would treat, and desired he might be sent to his quarters. The Roman questor accordingly set out with a small party. On the way he was met by Volux, the son of the king of Mauritania, with a thousand horse: him he considered as of doubtful intention, whether come as a friend or an enemy; but coming with professions of friendship from the king his father, and with orders to escort the Roman questor, they proceeded together. On the second day after this junction, Volux came in haste to the quarters of Sylla, and informed him, that the advanced party had discovered Jugurtha posted on their route, with a considerable force, and earnestly pressed the Romans to endeavour to make their escape in the night.

Sylla could no longer command his suspicions, and, sensible that he had imprudently, without hostage or other security, ventured too far on the faith of an African prince, proudly refused to alter his march; desired that the Mauritanian prince, if he thought proper, should depart; but informing him at the same time, that the Roman people would know how to avenge the injury done to their officers, and would not fail to punish the perfidy of the king his father. Volux made protestations of his innocence; and as the Roman questor could not be prevailed on to save himself by flight, this prince insisted to remain, and to share in his danger. They accordingly kept on their way, passed through the troops of Jugurtha, who, though disposed to offer violence to the Romans, had yet some measures to observe with the king of Mauritania, whose son was in the company; and while, contrary to his usual character, he remained undecided, the prey escaped him, and got out of his reach.

Jugurtha sent persons of confidence immediately to counteract the negotiations of Sylla at the court of Bocchus; and each of these parties solicited the king of Mauritania to betray the other. The Numidians endeavoured to persuade him, that, with such a hostage as Sylla in his hands, he might still expect some honourable terms from the Romans; and Sylla, on the other part, represented, that, as the king of Mauritania had offended the Romans, by abetting the crimes of Jugurtha, he must now expiate his guilt by delivering him over to justice. It was the inclination of this prince to favour Jugurtha; but it was his interest, as well as his intention, to gain the Romans. While he was still in suspense, he gave equal encouragement to both parties; and, without being finally determined what he should do, appointed the Roman questor and the king of Numidia to meet him without any escort, or number of men in arms, reserving to the last moment the power of determining against the one or the other. He had placed a body of his own troops in ambush, and, soon after the parties were met, gave a signal, which his men understood to be for seizing Jugurtha. The Numidians, who attended their king, were slain; he himself was put in chains, and delivered up to the Roman questor. Sylla with the exultation of a hunter, received this lion in his toils; and, though he lived to perform much greater actions, still appears to have valued himself most on the success of this commission. He boasted so much of his prize, that he became from that moment, an object of jealousy to Marius, and was considered as a person advancing too fast in the same career of renown.[1] It was understood among the Romans, that the commander-in-chief, upon any service, in any division or province of the empire, enjoyed the triumph for victories gained, even in his absence, by his lieutenants, or by those who served under his command; and Marius probably thought that Sylla took more to himself than was due upon this occasion. The desire of being the person who put the finishing hand to any service, however accomplished, was not peculiar to these officers. It was an effect of the Roman policy in making the rewards of honour depend so much on events, without regard to the means which were employed to produce them. From this circumstance, the citizens of this republic were as desirous of having the reputation of successful adventures affixed to their names, as courtiers in modern Europe are desirous to have titles of nobility, or badges of their sovereign's favour.

The war being thus at an end, Marius appointed a thanksgiving; and, while he was offering the customary sacrifices, the news arrived from Rome that the people had dispensed with the law in his favour, and again had made choice of him for consul of the following year. This choice was determined by the great alarm which the Romans had taken on the approach of the barbarous nations, who, like a meteor, had, for some years, traversed the regions of Europe, and, with uncertain direction, were said to destroy wherever they moved. The Romans had repeatedly stood in their way, and had provoked a resentment, which these barbarians were supposed, in haste, to wreck upon Italy. They were at first heard of under the name only of Cimbri: but were now known to consist of many nations, under the appellations of Ambrones, Teutones, Tectosagi, and others; and had gained accessions of force by the junction of the Tigurini, and other Gaulish nations, who, either by choice or compulsion, were made a part in this mighty host, whose movements the Romans considered as chiefly directed against themselves.

U. C. 648.
P. Rutilius Rufus, Cn. Mallius.

Besides the armies commanded by the consuls Carbo and Silanus, who had fallen victims to this barbarous enemy, other considerable bodies, under Scaurus and Cassius, had perished by their hands; and other misfortunes, from the same quarter, were coming apace. At the time that Marius had finished the war with Jugurtha, Quintus Servius Cæpio, having the former year commanded in Gaul, where he destroyed or pillaged the city of Tolosa, and made a great booty, consisting, according to Justin, of one hundred thousand pounds weight of gold, and one million five hundred thousand pounds weight of silver, was now, in his turn, to meet with this enemy; the consul Mallius or Manilius had orders to join him; and all the troops they could assemble were thought necessary to withstand the barbarians. These generals united their forces on the Rhone, but without a proper disposition to act in concert; they were accordingly defeated in battle; eighty thousand Romans, amongst whom were the two sons of the consul Manilius, were killed in the action; forty thousand attendants of the army were massacred in cold blood. Both camps were taken.

After this victory the lords of the Cimbri, being assembled in council, called before them Aurelius Scaurus, formerly a Roman consul, lately second in command to one of the vanquished armies, and now a prisoner. They questioned him with respect to the forces in Italy, and the route to be taken across the Alps: to these questions he made answer, that it would be in vain for them to invade that country: that the Romans on their own territory, were invincible. And, in return to these words, it is said, that a barbarian struck the prisoner with his dagger to the heart. It is further said of this barbarous council, that they came to a resolution to spare no prisoners, to destroy the spoils of the slain, to cast all the treasures of gold and silver into the nearest river, to destroy all horses with their saddles and furniture, and to save no booty whatever; and it must be confessed, that in this their resolutions were guided by a policy well accommodated to the manner of life they chose to maintain. Wealthy possessions frequently disqualify even settled nations for the toils of war, but to migrating tribes, they would be certain impediments and the means of ruin.[2]

These accounts of the character of an enemy and of the fate of Roman armies which ventured to encounter them, were received at Rome with amazement and terror. The citizens changed their dress and assumed the military habit. Rutilius, the consul, who had remained in the administration of affairs in Italy, had instructions from the senate to array every person that was fit to bear arms. No one who had attained the military age was exempted. It is mentioned, that the son of the consul himself was turned into the ranks of a legion. There was little time to train such levies; and the usual way was thought insufficient. The fencing-masters, employed to train gladiators for the public shows, were brought forth, and distributed to instruct the citizens in the use of their weapons.[3] But the expedient, on which the people chiefly relied for deliverance from the dangers which threatened them, was the nomination of Marius to command against this terrible enemy.

This officer, upon hearing of his re-election, set out for Italy, and, with his legions and their captives, entered Rome in triumph; a spectacle, of which Jugurtha, in chains, with his unfortunate children, were the principal figures. When the procession was over, the captive king was led to a dungeon, under orders for his immediate execution. As he was about to be stripped of his ornaments and robes, the executioner, in haste to pluck the pendants from his ears, tore away the flesh, and thrust him naked into a dungeon below ground. He descended into this place with a smile, saying, "What a cold bath is here?" He pined about six days, and expired. A kind and an able commander, would, in such a situation, have been an object of respect and of pity, if we did not recollect, that he was the murderer of Adherbal and Hiempsal, the innocent children of his benefactor. And if we did not receive some consolation from being told, that his own children, who were likewise innocent, were exempted from the lot of their father, and honourably entertained in Italy.

Marius, in this triumph, is said to have brought into the treasury three thousand and seven

1 Plutarch. in Mario et in Sylla.

2 Orosius, lib. v. c. 16. Eutrop. lib. v.
3 Valer. Max. lib. ii. c. 3.

pounds, or thirty thousand and seventy ounces of gold, and fifty-seven thousand seven hundred and fifty ounces of silver; and in money, two hundred and eighty-seven thousand denarii.[1] He entered the senate, contrary to custom, in his triumphal robes, probably to insult the nobles, who used to despise him as a person of obscure extraction, born in a country town, and of a mean family: but finding that this was considered as an act of petulance, and generally condemned, he withdrew and changed his dress.

The kingdom of Numidia was dismembered; part was put into the possession of Bocchus as a reward for his late services; and part reserved for the surviving heirs of Massinissa.

U. C. 649.

Consuls; C. Marius 2do. C. Flavius Fimbria.

As the law respecting the consulate now stood, no one could be elected in absence, nor re-elected into this office, till after an interval of ten years. Both clauses were dispensed with in favour of Marius, under pretence of continuing him at the head of the army, but as he might still have remained at the head of the army, and have rendered the same services to the state in the quality of proconsul, his re-election may be ascribed to his own ambition, and to his jealousy of other rising men in the state. Being considered as head of the popular party, his elevation was an object of zeal to the tribunes, and was intended to mortify those who affected the distinctions of ancient family. Contrary to the usual form, and without casting lots, he was preferred to his colleague in the appointment to command in Gaul. Having his choice of all the armies at that time in Italy, he took the new levies, lately assembled and disciplined by Rutilius, in preference to the veterans, who had served in Africa under Metellus and himself. It is probable that he was determined in this choice, more by desire to gratify the veterans who wished to be discharged, than by the consideration of any supposed superiority in the discipline to which the new levies had been trained.[2]

Upon the arrival of Marius in his province it appeared, that the alarm taken for the safety of Italy was somewhat premature. The barbarians in their battles only meant to maintain the reputation of their valour, or to keep open the tract of their migrations. They had found the lands from about the higher parts of the Danube and the Rhine, through Gaul and across the Pyrennees into Spain, and to the ocean, convenient for their purpose, and sufficiently extensive. They had yet meditated no war with the Romans, or any other nation; but did not decline the encounter where they met with resistance. At present they continued their migrations to the westward, without any intention to cross the Alps, or to visit the nations who inhabited within those mountains.

We have nothing recorded in history concerning the movements of these wandering nations, during the two subsequent years, except what is related of their adventure with Fulvius, a Roman prætor, probably in Spain, who, in return for hostilities committed in his province, having made a feint to draw the attention of their warriors, surprised and sacked their camp. Under the apprehension, however, of their return towards Gaul and Italy, Marius continued to be elected consul, and was repeatedly named to the command of the army that was destined to oppose them. His party at Rome had, at this time, besides the exigency which justified their choice, many other advantages against their antagonists, and maintained the envious quarrel of the lower people against the nobility with great animosity and zeal

CHAPTER V.

Review of the Circumstances which revived the popular Party—Farther Account of Laws and Regulations under their Administration—State of the Empire—Fourth Consulate of Marius—Continued Migrations of the Barbarous Nations—Defeated by Marius at Aquæ Sextiæ—By Marius and Catulus in Italy.

THE senate had, for some time after the suppression of the troubles which were raised by Fulvius and the younger Gracchus, retained its authority, and restrained the tribunes of the people within ordinary bounds; but by the suspicions which arose against them, on the subject of their transactions with Jugurtha, and by the miscarriages of the war in Numidia, they again lost their advantage. It is difficult to ascertain the real grounds of these suspicions. Sallust seems to admit them in their utmost extent, and represents the whole order of nobility as mercenary traders, disposed to sell what the republic entrusted to their honour. That the presents of Jugurtha were sometimes accepted, and produced some effect, is not to be doubted; but that the aristocracy of Rome, during its short reign, was so much corrupted, is scarcely to be credited. Such a measure of corruption must have rendered the state a prey to every foreign power that was in a condition to mislead its councils, and is not consistent with that superiority which the Romans then generally possessed in their negotiations, as well as in their wars. The charge itself savours too much of that envy with which the lower class of the people at all times interpret the conduct of their superiors, and which was greatly countenanced by the partizans of Cæsar, at the time when Sallust wrote, in order to vilify and reduce the senate. We cannot, however, oppose mere conjecture to the positive testimony of Sallust, corroborated by some suspicious circumstances in the transactions of the times. Among these we may recollect the patronage which Jugurtha met with at Rome, contrary to the professions of the Romans, in behalf of justice, and the uncommon number of senators degraded at that time, by authority of the censors, Q. Cæcilius Metellus and

1 About 10,000*l*.

2 Frontius de Stragemat. lib. iv. c. 2.

Cn. Domitius Ahenobarbus,[3] which has been already mentioned in its place.

Whatever may have been the real occasion of the cry then subsisting against the nobles, we have seen that the popular party, availing themselves of it, and giving it all manner of countenance, found means to recover great part of their lost power. The tribunes, having obtained the establishment of a special commission for the trial of all those who had received bribes from Jugurtha, made the people consider their own act in constituting a court of inquiry, as sufficient to evince the reality of the crime. The prosecutions which continued to be carried on for two years, upon this supposition, served more than the subject of any former dispute to alienate the minds of men from each other, and from the public. Questions were more of a private than of a public nature, and occupied the worst of the human passions, envy, malice, and revenge. One party learned to cherish falsehood, subordination, and perjury; the other lived in continual fear of having such engines employed against themselves.

The people, in their zeal to attack the nobility under any pretence, made no distinction between errors and crimes; and, contrary to the noble spirit of their ancestors, treated misfortune, incapacity, or treachery, with equal rigour. One tribune had extended the use of the secret ballot to the trial of lesser crimes;[4] another, upon this occasion, took away all distinctions, and introduced it in the trial of capital crimes also:[5] so that the judge, without being accountable, indulged his secret malice or partial favour.[6]

Laws were made to promote the interest, as well as to gratify the animosity of the lower people. By the Agrarian law of Gracchus, certain limits were set to estates in land; but, in order to render the excess of lands, in the hands of any particular person, immediately useful to the people, it was permitted, by an amendment made during the low state of the aristocratical party, that persons in possession of more than the legal measure of land, might retain their estates, but subject to a rent to be collected for the benefit of the poorer citizens; and thus it was proposed, that without any trouble in taking possession of lands, or removing from the city, the favourites of the party should be accommodated, and reap the fruits of sedition and idleness unimpaired.[7]

U. C. 647.

Lex Servilia de Judiciis.

It was proposed by the consul Servilius Cæpio, that the senate, whose members were personally so much exposed to prosecutions, should have their share likewise in composing the juries, a privilege of which, by the edict of Gracchus, they had been deprived.[8] In whatever degree this proposal was adopted, it was again expressly repealed upon the motion of Servilius Glaucia. And Cæpio soon after experienced, in his own person, the animosity of the popular faction, being tried for miscarriage in his battle with the Cimbri. He was condemned by the judges, and afterwards, in virtue of a regulation obtained by Cassius, one of the tribunes, declared, in consequence of that sentence, disqualified to hold a place in the senate.[9]

Besides the transactions already mentioned, the following particulars, overlooked in the hurry of recording military operations and events, may serve still farther to characterize the times. M. Junius Silanus was tried for misconduct against the enemy; M. Emilius Scaurus, first on the roll of the senate, was brought to trial for contempt of religion; but both acquitted. The ardour for these prosecutions, and popular regulations, continued until the second consulate of Marius, when M. Marcius Philippus, one of the tribunes, moved to restore the law of Tiberius Gracchus, respecting the division of estates in land; and in his speech in support of this motion, affirmed, that there were not two thousand families in Rome possessed of any property in land whatever.[10] This motion, however, was withdrawn.

Among the crimes which the populace were now so eager to punish, fortunately that of peculation or extortion in the provinces was one. To facilitate complaints on this subject, not only persons having an immediate interest in the case, but all to whom any money or effects injuriously taken might have otherwise come by inheritance, were entitled to prosecute for this offence; and any alien, who convicted a Roman citizen of this crime, so as to have him struck off the rolls of the people, was himself to be inrolled instead of the citizen displaced.[11]

Domitius, one of the tribunes, attacked the aristocratical constitution even of the priesthood, and endeavoured to transfer the right of election from the order itself to the people; but superstition, which continues to influence the bulk of mankind after reason has failed, here stood in his way. The custom was against him; and, in such matters, religion and custom are the same. The people, therefore, it was confessed, could not interfere without profanation; but a certain part of the people might judge of the candidates, and instruct the college of priests whom they were to choose.[12] The same artifice, or verbal evasion, had been already admitted in the form of electing the Pontifex Maximus, now chosen by seventeen of the tribes who were drawn by lot.[13]

Lex Domitia de Sacerdotiis.

During this period, a just alarm was taken on the subject of private as well as public corruption. Liberty was conceived to imply a freedom from every restraint, and to justify licence and contempt of the laws. The aids which were given to the people to enable them to subsist in profusion and idleness; the wealth that was passing to Rome in the hands of traders, contractors, and farmers of the revenue, as well as provincial officers, by whom the profits of a first appointment were lavished in public shows, fights of gladiators, and baiting of wild beasts, to gain the people in their canvass for farther preferments; these several circumstances tended in the highest degree, to corrupt the people, and to render them unworthy of that sovereignty which they actually possessed in the prevalence of the popular faction.

3 It is already mentioned, that thirty-two senators were struck off the rolls by these magistrates.
4 Lex Cassia Tabellaria.
5 Lex Cælia Tabellaria.
6 Cicer. de Legibus, lib. iii.
7 Appian de Bell. Civ. lib. i
8 Valer. Max. lib. v c. 9.

9 Asconius Pædianus in Corneliana Ciceronis.
10 Cicer. de. Officiis, lib. ii.
11 Cicero in Balbiana
12 Asconius in Corneliana Ciceronis.
13 Cicero de Lege Agraria.

The severities which were practised in certain cases, the sumptuary laws which were provided to restrain luxury, were but feeble aids to stop such a source of disorder. It is mentioned, as an instance of such severity, that some vestals were questioned at this time for a breach of that sacred obligation to chastity, under which they were held up as a pattern of manners to the Roman women; that three of them were condemned, and, together with Roman knights, the supposed partners in their crimes, suffered extreme punishment. A temple was on this occasion erected to the goddess Venus under a new title, that of the Reformer;[1] and prayers were to be offered up in this temple, that it might please the goddess to guard the chastity of Romen women.[2]

The term luxury is somewhat ambiguous; it is put for sensuality or excess in what relates to the preservation of animal life; and for the effect of vanity, in what relates to the decorations of rank and fortune. The luxury of the Romans, in the present age, was probably of the former kind, and sumptuary laws were provided, not to restrain vanity, but to govern the appetites for mere debauch. About the time that Jugurtha was at Rome, the sumptuary law of Fannius received an addition, by which Roman citizens were not only restricted in their ordinary expense, but the legal quantities and species of food were prescribed to them. The whole expense of the table was restricted to thirty asses[3] a day, and the meat to be served up, to three or four pounds, dried or salted. There was no restriction in the use of herbs or vegetables of any sort.[4] According to A. Gellius, the law permitted, on certain days, an expense of a hundred asses; on wedding days, two hundred. It is remarkable, that this law continued to have its effect on the tables of Roman citizens after Cicero was a man.[5] The epicures of this time were obliged to make up, in the cookery of their vegetable diet, what was defective in that species of food.

About the time of the commencement of the Numidian war, the people, according to the census, amounted to four hundred and three thousand four hundred and thirty-six citizens, fit to carry arms. At this time it was that the censors, Quintus Cecilius Metellus, and Cn. Domitius Ahenobarbus, expelled thirty-two members from the senate.

While the Romans were intent on the war which subsisted in Africa, they were assailed by enemies in some of the other provinces. In Spain, hostilities, at intervals, were still renewed. In endeavouring to quell one of the revolts of the natives, the Roman prætor was killed; in another encounter, the forces employed against them were cut off; and a fresh army was transported from Italy to secure the Roman possessions.

Hostilities were likewise continued on the frontier of Macedonia, by the Scordisci, Triballi, and other Thracian nations; and the proconsul Rufus, by his victories in this quarter, obtained a triumph.

During this period, in the consulship of Attilius Serranus, and Q. Servilius Cæpio, the year after the first consulship of Marius, were born two illustrious citizens, M. Tullius Cicero, and Cneius Pompeius Strabo, afterwards distinguished by the appellation of Pompey the Great. And we are now to open the scene in which the persons on whom the fate of the Roman empire was to depend, made their several entries into life, or into public business, and began to pass through an infancy or a youth of danger, to an old age or extreme trouble, which closed with the subversion of that constitution to which they were born.

U. C. 650.

Caius Marius 3tio, L. Aurelius Orestes.

Marius having, without any memorable event, passed the year of his second consulship on the frontier of Narbonne Gaul, was, by the people, still under the same apprehension of the Cimbric invasion, re-elected into the same office, and destined for his former station. This year likewise the barbarians turned aside from his province, and left the republic at leisure to contend with enemies of less consideration, who appeared in a different quarter. Athenio, a slave in Sicily, having murdered his master, and broken open the prisons or yards in which slaves were commonly confined at work, assembled a number together, and being clothed in a purple robe, with a crown and a sceptre, affected a species of royalty, invited all the slaves of the island to assume their freedom under his protection. He acquired strength sufficient to cope with Servilius Casca, the Roman prætor, and actually forced him in his camp. He likewise defeated the succeeding prætor, Licinius Luculus;[6] and was in the third year of the insurrection, with great difficulty, reduced by the consul Aquilius. This revolt was at its height in this year of the third consulship of Marius, and it was quelled in the second year after it, the rebels being surrounded in their strong holds, and obliged to surrender for want of provisions.[7] The whole is mentioned now, that it may not recur hereafter to interrupt matters of more moment.

About the same time the Romans had been obliged to equip a naval armament under Marcus Antonius, known by the appellation of the orator, against the Cilician pirates, who had lately infested the seas. All that we know of this service is, in general, that it was performed with ability and success.[8]

From Macedonia, Calpurnius Piso reported, that the victory he had gained over the Thracians had enabled him to penetrate to the mountains of Rhodope and Caucasus.

Such was the state of the empire when Caius Marius returned from his province in Gaul, to preside at the election of consuls. He was again, by the voice of the people, called upon to resume his former trust; but he affected, from modesty, to decline the honour. His partizans were prepared for acting this part, and were accordingly, by their importunities, to force him into an office which he so modestly seemed to decline. Among these, Apuleius Saturninus, at this time himself candidate for the office of tribune, charged Marius with treachery to his country in proposing to desert the republic in times of so much danger, and with his reproaches prevailed so far as to render him passive to the will of his fellow-citi

1 Venus Verticordia.
2 Orosius, lib. v. c. 15. Jul. Obsequens. Ovid. Fast lib v.
3 About two shillings.
4 Macrobius Satur. lib. ii. c. 17.
Epist. ad Familiar. lib. vii. ad Gallum.
6 Florus, lib. iii. c. 19.
7 Florus, lib. iv. c. 19.
8 Ibid. lib. iii. c. 6. Cicero de Orator. lib. i.

zens, who wished to replace him[9] again in his former station.

U. C. 651.

Caius Marius 4to, L. Lutatius Catulus.

In this fourth consulate, the courage and military skill of Marius came to be actually exerted in this province. The barbarous nations, after their return from Spain, began to appear in separate bodies, each forming a numerous and formidable army. In one division the Cimbri and Tectosages had passed through the whole length of Gaul to the Rhine, and from thence proceeded by the Danube to Noricum or Austria, and were pointing towards Italy by the valley of Trent. The Consul Lutatius Catulus was stationed near the descent of the Alps to observe the motions of this body.

In another division, the Ambrones and the Teutones hung on the frontier of the Roman province in Gaul, between the Garonne and the Rhone, and gave out, that they meant, by the most ordinary route of the mountains, to join their allies in Italy.

Upon the approach of this formidable enemy, Marius took post on the Rhone at the confluence of that river with the Isere, and fortified his camp in the most effectual manner. The barbarians reproaching him with cowardice for having taken these precautions, sent, agreeably to their own notions of war, a formal challenge to meet them in battle; and having had for answer from Marius, That the Romans did not consult their enemies to know when it was proper to fight, they were confirmed in the contempt which they already entertained of his army, ventured to leave them behind, and proceeded in separate divisions towards Italy. Marius followed; and, with rapid marches, overtook them as they passed over the country without any precaution; some of them near to the Roman colony of Sextius,[10] and far removed from each other. Having found them under such disadvantage, and in such confusion as exposed them to slaughter, with scarcely any power of resistance, he put the greater part to the sword. Thus part of the hordes, who had for many years been so formidable to the Romans, were now entirely cut off. Ninety thousand prisoners, with Teutobochus, one of their kings, were taken, and two hundred thousand were said to be slain in the field.[11]

The news of this victory arriving at Rome, while it was known that another division of the same enemy, not less formidable, was still in the field, it was not to be doubted that the command and office of consul would be continued to Marius. The populace, incited by some of the factious tribunes, joined, with the other usual marks of their attachment to his person, that of disrespect and insolence to those who were supposed to be his opponents and rivals. Of these, Metellus Numidicus, whom he had supplanted in the command of the army against Jugurtha, was the chief. This respectable citizen, being now in the office of censor, one Equitius, an impostor of obscure and slavish extraction, offered himself to be enrolled as a citizen, under the popular designation and name of Caius Gracchus, the son of Tiberius. The censor, doubting his title, called upon Sempronia, the sister of Gracchus, to testify what she knew of this pretended relation; and, upon her giving evidence against him, rejected his claim. The populace, ill-disposed to Metellus, on account of his supposed difference with Marius, took this opportunity to insult him in the discharge of his office; attacked his house, and obliged him to take refuge in the capitol. Even there the tribune Saturninus would have laid violent hands on his person, if he had not been protected by a body of the Roman knights, who had assembled in arms to defend him. This tumult was suppressed, but not without bloodshed.

U. C. 653.

Caius Marius 5to. M. Aquilius.

While the popular faction were indulging in these marks of their dislike to Metellus, they proceeded to bestow the honours which they intended for Marius, and chose him for a fifth time consul, in conjunction with M. Aquilius. His late splendid success against one division of the wandering barbarians justified this choice, and pointed him out as the fittest person to combat the other, which was still expected from the side of Noricum to attempt the invasion of Italy. Catulus, the late colleague of Marius, commanding the troops that were stationed on the Athesis, to cover the access to Italy from the valley of Trent, was destined to act in subordination to the consul, who had given orders to hasten the march of his victorious army from the Rhone.

Catulus had taken post above Verona, thrown a bridge over the Athesis, and, in order to command the passage of that river, had fortified stations on both its banks. While he was in this posture, and before the junction of Marius, the enemy arrived in his neighbourhood. The amazing works which they performed fully served to confirm the report of their numbers. They obstructed with mounds of timber and earth the channel of the river, so as to force it to change its course; and thus, instead of passing the river, they threw it behind them in their march. They continued to float such quantities of wood on the stream above the bridge which Catulus had built, that the passage of the water being stopped, the bridge, with all the timber which was accumulated before it, was entirely carried off. The Roman army, on seeing such evidence of the numbers and strength of their enemy, were seized with a panic. Many deserted their colours, some fled even to Rome without halting. The proconsul thought proper to order a retreat; and thus, by seeming to authorise what he could not prevent, he endeavoured to save in part the credit of his army.

The level country on the Po was in this manner laid open to the incursions of the barbarians. The inhabitants of Italy were greatly alarmed: and the Roman people passed an act of attainder against all those who had abandoned their colours. Marius, who continued at Rome while the legions advanced on their march from Gaul, suspended the triumph which had been ordered him by the senate, went to receive his army at the foot of the Alps, and to hasten its junction with Catulus.

Upon the junction of the two armies, those who had lately fled recovered their courage, and the generals determined, without loss of time, to hazard a battle. It is said that the barbarians of this division were still ignorant of the disaster which had befallen their allies on the other side

9 Plutarch in Mario. 10 Now Aix, in Provence.
11 Plutarch in Mario. Orosius, lib. v. c. 16. Florus, lib. iii c. 3. Velleius. Eutropius.

of the Alps, and had sent a defiance or a challenge to fight; but that being informed of this calamity when they were about to engage, they made their attack with less than their usual ferocity and confidence. Catulus received them in front. Marius made a movement to assail them in flank; but as they were hid by the clouds of dust which every where rose from the plain, he missed his way, or could not engage till after the enemy had been repulsed by Catulus, and were already put to flight. The rout was extremely bloody; a hundred and fifty thousand were said to be slain; sixty thousand submitted to be taken prisoners. The remainder of this mighty host, even the women and children, perished by their own hands; and the race of barbarous nations who had migrated through Europe, perhaps for ages before they encountered with the Romans, now appear to have been entirely extirpated.[1]

On receiving the news of this victory at Rome the city resounded with joy, and the people, in every sacrifice they offered up, addressed themselves to Marius as a god. He had been constantly attended in this war by Sylla, who, though already an object of his jealousy, still chose to neglect the preferments of the city, and to serve in the camp. In the late victory Marius was no more than partner with Catulus. Upon the arrival of the armies at Rome, he did justice to Catulus in this particular, and admitted him to partake in his triumph. In this procession there were no carriages loaded with gold, silver, or any precious spoils of any sort; but, instead of them, the shattered armour and broken swords of an enemy; the surer marks of an honour justly won, and of a more important service performed. These were transported in loads, and piled up in the capitol.

CHAPTER VI.

Character and immoderate Ambition of Marius—Death of Nonius—Re-election of the Tribune Saturninus—His Sedition and seizing the Capitol—Death of Saturninus—Reverse in the State of Parties—Recall of Metellus—Violent Death of the Tribune Furius—Birth of Caius Julius Cæsar—Lex Cæcilia Didia—Blank in the Roman History—Sylla offers himself Candidate for the Office of Prætor—Edict of the Censors against the Latin Rhetoricians—Bullion in the Roman Treasury—Present of a Groupe in golden Figures from the King of Mauritania—Acts of Livius Drusus—Revolt of the Italian Allies—Policy of the Romans in yielding to the Necessity of their Affairs—The Laws of Plautius.

UPON the extinction of the wandering nations which had now for some time molested the empire, there was no foreign enemy to endanger the peace of Italy. The wars in Thrace and in Spain had no effect beyond the provinces in which they subsisted. The insurrection of the slaves in Sicily, by the good conduct of Aquilius the consul, to whom that service had been committed, was near being quelled.

Marius, being now returned to the city, might have quitted the paths of ambition with uncommon distinction and honour. An ordinary consulate, after his having been so often called upon in times of danger, as the person most likely to save his country, could make no addition to his glory. His being set aside in times of security and leisure, would even have been the most honourable and flattering comment that could have been made on his former elections.

But immoderate thirst of power, and extreme animosity to his rivals, not elevation of mind, were the characteristics of Marius. His ambition had hitherto passed for an aversion to aristocratical usurpations. But his contempt of family distinctions, the offspring of a vanity which made him feel the want of such honours, by clashing with the established subordination of ranks in his country, became a source of disaffection to the state itself. He formed views upon the consulate yet a sixth time; and instead of the moderation, or the satiety of honours with which he pretended to be actuated when he hoped to be pressed into office, he employed all his influence, even his money, to procure a re-election; and accordingly prevailed, together with Valerius Flaccus. He had warmly espoused the interest of this candidate against Metellus, more from animosity to the competitor, whose great authority, placed in opposition to himself, he dreaded, than from any regard or predilection for Flaccus. Being chosen, in order the more to strengthen himself in the exercise of his power, he entered into concert with the Tribune Apuleius Saturninus, and, it is probable, agreed to support this factious demagogue in his pretensions to remain in office for another year; a precedent which had taken place only in the most factious times of the republic, and which was in itself more dangerous than any other re-election whatever. The person of the tribune being sacred, his will was absolute, there was no check to his power besides the fear of being called to account at the expiration of his term; and if this fear were removed by the perpetuity of office, it was a power yet more formidable than that of the dictator, and to be restrained only by the divisions which might arise among those who were joined together in the exercise of it.

U. C. 653.

Caius Marius 6to, L. Val. Flaccus.

The faction that was formed by Marius and the tribune Saturninus, with their adherents, was farther strengthened by the accession of the prætor Glaucia. This person, while in office, and as he sat in judgment, had received an affront from Saturninus, in having his chair of state broken down, for presuming to occupy any part in the attention of the people, while an assembly called by the tribune was met. He nevertheless chose to overlook this insult, in order to be admitted a partner in the consideration which was now enjoyed by these popular leaders.

1 Plutarch. in Mario & Sylla. Orosius, lib. v. c. 16. Florus, lib iii. c. 3. Velleius Eutrop. Appian in Celtica.

Upon the approach of the tribunitian elections, the senate and nobles exerted themselves to prevent the re-election of Saturninus; and nine of the new candidates were, without any question, declared to be duly elected in preference to him. The tenth place too was actually filled by the election of Nonius Sufenas, whom the aristocracy had supported with all its influence. But the party of Apuleius, enraged at their disappointment, had recourse to violence, forced Nonius, though already vested with the sacred character of tribune, to take refuge in a work-shop, from whence he was dragged by some of the late soldiery attached to Marius, and slain. The assembly broke up, and sober persons, though reputed of the popular party, retired under the strongest impressions of affliction and terror.

Marius had reason to apprehend some violent resolution from the senate, and was in no haste to assemble that body. Mean time Glaucia, in the night, with a party armed with daggers, took possession of the capitol and place of assembly, and, at an early hour in the morning, having gone through the forms of election, announced Apuleius again tribune, in the place that was vacated by the murder of Nonius. This furious demagogue was accordingly reinstated in the sacred character, which, though recently violated by himself, was still revered by the bulk of the people. He was continually attended by a new set of men who infested the streets, freemen of desperate fortune, whom Marius, contrary to the established forms of the constitution, had admitted into the legions, and who were grown fierce and insolent, as partners in the victories of that general, and who were made to expect that, in case the popular party should prevail, they themselves should have estates in land and comfortable settlements.

Under the terror of so many assassins, who considered the nobles as enemies to their cause, Marius with his faction were become masters of the commonwealth. The better sort of the people were deterred from frequenting the public assemblies, and no one had courage to propose, that any inquiry should be made into the death of the tribune Nonius, in whose person the sacred law was again set at nought.[2]

Lex Agraria.

Apuleius hastened to gratify his party by proposing popular laws. One to seize in the name of the public, those lands on the Po which had lately been desolated by the migrations of the barbarous nations, and to distribute them in lots to the poorer citizens.[3]

Another, by which it was resolved, that in the province of Africa a hundred jugera a man should be distributed to the veterans:[4] that new settlements should be made in Greece, Macedonia, and Sicily: and that the money taken from the temple at Tolosa[5] should be employed in the purchase of lands for a like purpose: that wherever these colonies should be planted, Marius should have a power to inscribe at each of the settlements, three aliens into the list of citizens.[6]

Lex Frumentaria.

That the price, hitherto paid for corn by the people at the public granaries, should be remitted, and that corn should be distributed gratis.

Upon the intention to obtain the last of those laws being known, Q. Servilius Cæpio, one of the questors, represented, that if such a law should pass, there would be an end of industry good order, and government; and that the treasury of Rome would not be sufficient to defray the expense. He exhorted the senate to employ every measure to defeat the motion. And this body accordingly made a resolution, that whoever attempted to obtain the law in question should be deemed an enemy to his country. But Apuleius was not to be restrained by the terrors of this resolution. He proceeded to propose the law in the usual form, and had planted the rails and balloting urns for the people to give their votes, when Cæpio, with a body of his attendants, had the courage to attack the tribune, broke down the steps, and overset the balloting urns; an action for which he was afterwards impeached upon an accusation of treason, but by which, for the present, he disappointed the designs of the faction.[7]

Apuleius, to extend the power of the popular assemblies, and to remove every impediment from his own designs, brought forward a number of new regulations. One to confirm a former statute, by which the acts of the tribes were declared to have the force of laws. Another, declaring it to be treason for any person to interrupt a tribune in putting a question to the people. A third, obliging the senate to confirm every act of the tribes within five days after such act had passed, and requiring every senator, under pain of a fine, and of being struck off the rolls, to take an oath to abide by these regulations. While these motions were in debate, some one of the party who opposed them, in order to stop the career of this factious tribune, observed, that it thundered; a circumstance which, upon the ordinary maxims of the Roman augurs, was sufficient to suspend any business in which the people were engaged, and to break up their assembly. "If you be not silent," said Apuleius to the person who observed that it thundered, "you will also find that it hails." The assembly accordingly, without being deterred by this interposition of the auspices, passed acts to these several purposes. The power of the senate was entirely suppressed, their part of the legislature was reduced to a mere form, and even this they were not at liberty to withhold. Marius called them together, and proposed that they should consider what resolution they were to take with respect to a change of so much importance, and particularly with respect to the oath which was to be exacted from the members. The old warrior is said, on this occasion, to have practised an artifice by which he imposed on many of the members, and which afterwards furnished him with a pretence for removing his enemy Metellus from their councils. He declared himself with great warmth against taking the oath, and by his example led other senators to express their sentiments. Metellus, in particular, assured the assembly, that it was his own resolution never to come under such an engagement.

While the senators relied on the concurrence of Marius in refusing the oath, the time appointed for administering it nearly approached; and this consul, after the third day was far spent, assem-

2 Appian de Bell. Civil. lib. 1. Plutarch in Mario, lib. lxix. Valer. Max. lib. ix. c. 7. Orosius, lib. v c. 57. Florus, lib. iii c. 16 3 Appian de Bell. Civ. lib. i.
4 Auct. de Viris Illustribus in Saturnino.
5 Now Thoulouse. 6 Auct. de Vir Illus. in Sat

7 Auct. Rhetoricorum ad Herennium.

bled the senate, set forth the dangerous state of the commonwealth; at the same time expressed his own fears of the disturbances that might arise if the senate refused to gratify the people in this matter; and while multitudes were assembled in the streets to know the issue of their councils, he required that the oath should be administered. He himself took it, to the astonishment of the senate, and the joy of the populace assembled by Apuleius, who sounded applause through every part of the streets. Metellus alone, of all who were present, refused to comply, and withstood all the intreaties of his friends, who represented the danger with which he was threatened. "*If it were always safe to do right,*" he said, "*who would ever do wrong? But good men are distinguished, by choosing to do right even when it is least for their safety to do so.*"

On the following day the tribune Saturninus entered the senate, and, not being stopped by the negative of any of his own colleagues, the only power that could restrain him, dragged Metellus from his place, and proffered an act of attainder and banishment against him, for having refused the oath which was enjoined by the people. Many of the most respectable citizens offered their aid to defend this illustrious senator by force, but he himself declined being the subject of any civil commotion, and went into exile.

While the act, which afterwards passed for his banishment was preparing, he was heard to say, "If the times should mend, I shall recover my station; if not, it is a happiness to be absent from hence." He fixed his abode at Smyrna, conducted his retirement with great dignity during his exile, and probably felt as he ought that any censure inflicted by men of a vile and profligate character was an honour.

In these transactions elapsed the second year in which Apuleius filled the office of tribune; and, being favoured by a supineness of the opposite party, contracted in a seeming despair of the republic, he prevailed yet a third time in being vested with this formidable power. To court the favour of the people, he affected to credit what was alleged concerning the birth of Equitius; and under the name of Caius Gracchus, son of Tiberius, had this impostor associated with himself in the office of tribune. The name of Gracchus, in this station, awakened the memory of former hopes and of former resentments. The party had destined Glaucia for the consulate, and appear to have left Marius out of their councils. This will perhaps account for the conduct with which he concluded his administration in the present year.

At the election which followed, the interest of the nobles was exerted for Marcus Antonius and C. Memmius. The first was declared consul, and the second was likely to prevail over Glaucia; when, in the midst of the crowds that were assembled to vote, a sudden tumult arose; Memmius was beset and murdered; and the people, alarmed at so strange an outrage, were seized with a panic, and fled.

In the night, Glaucia, Saturninus, and the questor Saufeius, being known to be met in secret conference, all the citizens who yet retained any regard for the commonwealth, crowded together, in fear of what so desperate a faction might attempt. All the voices were united against Saturninus, the supposed author of so many disorders and murders. It was proposed, without delay, to seize his person, either living or dead but being put on his guard, by the appearance of a storm so likely to break on his head, he thought proper, with the other leaders of his party and their retainers in arms, to seize the capitol, and there to secure themselves, and to overawe the assembly of the people. It was no longer to be doubted that the republic was in a state of war.—Marius, who had fomented these troubles from aversion to the nobles, now remained undetermined what part he should act. But the senate being assembled, gave the usual charge to himself and his colleagues to avert the danger with which the republic was threatened; and both these officers, however much they were disposed to favour the sedition, being in this manner armed with the sword of the commonwealth, were obliged to employ it in support of the public peace. The senators, the knights, and all the citizens of rank repaired in arms to their standard. Antonius, consul elected for the following year, in order to hinder the partizans of the faction from resorting to the city, was stationed in the suburbs with an armed force.[1] The capitol was invested in form, and appears to have held out some days; at the end of which, in order to oblige the rebels to surrender, the pipes that supplied them with water were cut off. This had the intended effect. They submitted to such terms as were proposed to them and Marius, still inclined to treat them with favour had them confined to the hall of the senate till farther orders. In the mean time a great party of citizens, who were in arms for the defence of the republic, impatient of delay, and thinking it dangerous to spare such daring offenders, beset them instantly in their place of confinement, and put the whole to the sword.[2]

It was reported, though afterwards questioned upon a solemn occasion,[3] that Caius Rabirius, a senator of distinction, having cut off the head of Apuleius, carried it as a trophy, agreeable to the manners of those times, and had it presented for some days at all the entertainments which were given on this occasion, and at which he was a guest.

This was the fourth tribunitian sedition raised to a dangerous height, and quelled by the vigour and resolution of the nobles. Marius, who had been obliged to act as the instrument of the senate on this occasion, saw his projects baffled, and his credit greatly impaired. Plutarch relates, that he soon after chose to leave the city for some time, on pretence of a desire to visit the province of Asia, where his active spirit formed the project of new wars, for the conduct of which he was much better qualified than for the administration of affairs in peace.

Upon the suppression of this dangerous sedition, the commonwealth was restored to a state which, compared to the late mixture of civil contention and military execution, may have deserved the name of public order. One office of consul was still vacant; and the election proceeding without

U. C. 652.

M. Antonius, A. Posthumius Albinus.

1 Cicero pro C. Rabirio.

2 Plut. in Mario. Appian de Bell. Civil. lib. i. Oros. lib. v. c. 17. Flor lib. iii. Auct. de Viris Illust. Cicero in Sextiana, in Catal. lib. i. Philip. lib. viii. et pro Caio Rabirio.

3 At the trial of Rabirius, when, some years afterwards, he was accused of having killed Saturninus.

disturbance, Posthumius Albinus was joined to Antonius. Most of the other elections had also been favourable to the nobles; and the majority even of the tribunes of the people were inclined to respect the senate and the aristocracy, as principal supports of the government.

The first effect of this happy recovery was a motion to recall Metellus from banishment. In this motion two of the tribunes, Q. Pompeius Rufus and L. Porcius Cato concurred. But Marius having opposed it with all his influence, and Publius Furius, another of the tribunes, having interposed his negative, it could not at that time be carried into execution. Soon after, however, the same motion being renewed by the tribune Callidius, and Furius having repeated his negative, Metellus, son of the exile, in presence of the people, threw himself upon the ground, and embracing the tribune's knees, beseeched him not to withstand the recall of his father. The young man, from this action, afterwards acquired the sirname of Pius; and the tribune, insolently spurning him as he lay on the ground, served his cause by that act of indignity perhaps more effectually than he could have done by lending a favourable ear to his request. The people, ever governed by their present passions, were moved with tenderness and with indignation. They proceeded, without regard to the negative of Furius, under emotions of sympathy for the son, to recal the exiled father. The messenger of the republic charged with the intimation of this resolution to Metellus, found him at Tralles in Lydia, among the spectators at a public show. When the letters were delivered to him, he continued to the end of the entertainment without opening them; by this mark of indifference, treating the favour of a disorderly populace with as much contempt as he had shown to their censure.

The senate, now become the supreme power at Rome, by the distaste which all reasonable men had taken to the violence of the opposite party, were gratified, not merely with the test of superiority they had gained in the recall of Metellus, but likewise in the downfall of some of the tribunes who had been active in the late disorders. Publius Furius, now become an object of general detestation, fell a sacrifice to the law of Apuleius, which declared it treason to interrupt a tribune in putting a question to the people. Being accused by Canuleius, one of his colleagues, of violating this law, he was by the populace, who are ever carried by the torrent, and prompt for execution, prevented from making his defence; and, though a tribune, put to death. Decianus, another of the tribunes, in supporting the charge against Furius, happened to speak with regret of the death of Saturninus, a crime for which he incurred a prosecution, and was banished.[4] So strong was the tide of popularity now opposite to its late direction, and so fatal even to their own cause frequently are the precedents or rules by which violent men think to obtain discretionary power to themselves. The murder of Nonius was a precedent to justify the execution of Apuleius, and both were followed by that of Furius. The law which made it treason to interrupt the proceedings of Apuleius, was employed to prevent any interruption to the operations of his enemies against himself and his faction.

4 Val. Max. lib. viii. c. 1.

Amidst these triumphs of the aristocratical party, Sextus Titius, one of the tribunes, still had the courage to move a revival of the Agrarian law of Gracchus. The proposal was acceptable in the assembly of the people.[5] And the edict was accordingly passed; but it was observed, that while the people were met on this business, two ravens fought in the air above the place of assembly, and the college of augurs, on pretence of this unfavourable omen, annulled the decree.[6] Titius, the author of it, was soon after condemned for having in his house the statue of Saturninus.[7]

The consul Aquilius returned from Sicily, and having had an ovation or procession on foot for the reduction of the Sicilian slaves, was on the following year brought to trial for extortion in his province. He called no exculpatory evidence, nor deigned to court the favour of his judges. But when about to receive sentence, M. Antonius, who had pleaded his cause, tore open the vest of his client, and displayed to the court and the audience the scars which he bore in his breast, and which were the marks of wounds received in the service of his country. Upon this spectacle, a sudden emotion of pity or respect decided against the former conviction of the court, and unfixed the resolution, which a few moments before they had taken to condemn the accused.

Among the events which distinguished the consulate of M. Antonius and A. Posthumius Albinus, may be reckoned the birth of Caius Julius Cæsar, for whose ambition the seeds of tribunitian disorder now sown were preparing a plentiful harvest. This birth, it is said, was ushered in with many presages and tokens of future greatness. If indeed we were to believe, that nature in this manner gives intimation of impending events, we should not be surprised that her most ominous signs were employed to mark the birth of a personage who was destined to change the whole face of the political world, and to lay Rome herself, with all the nations she had conquered, under a perpetuated military government.

U. C. 655.

Q. Cæcilius Metellus Nepo, T. Didius.

Antonius and Albinus were succeeded in office by Q. Cæcilius Metellus and Titus Didius. The war still continued in Spain, and fell to the lot of Didius. Upon his arrival in the province, Dolabella, the proprætor, set out on his return to Rome, and, for his victories in Spain, obtained a triumph. Metellus remained in the administration of affairs in Italy.

Lex Cæcilia Didia.

The administration of the present year is distinguished by an act in which both consuls concurred, and which is therefore marked in the title with their joint names. The Roman people had frequently experienced the defect of their forms in the manner of enacting laws. Factious tribunes had it in their power to carry motions by surprise, and to pass in the same law a variety of clauses; and, by obliging the people to pass or reject the whole in one vote, frequently obtained, under the favour of some popular clauses, acts of a very dangerous tendency. To prevent this abuse, it was now enacted, upon the joint motion of the consuls Cæcilius and Didius,

5 Julius Obsequens. 6 Cicero de Legibus, lib. ii.
7 Ibid. pro C. Rabirio. Ibid. de Orator. lib. ii. c 28

that every proposed law should be made public three market days before it could receive the assent of the people: that all its different clauses should be separately voted: and that it should be lawful for the people to pass or reject the whole or any part of it.[1]

This law had a salutary tendency; and, though far from sufficient to prevent a return of the late evils, it served for a time to stop the current of tribunitian violence; but while the source was open, any mere temporary stagnation could only tend to increase the force with which it occasionally burst over every impediment of law or good order that was placed in its way. And the inefficacy of measures taken upon the suppression of any dangerous sedition to eradicate the evil, shows the extreme difficulty with which men are led, in most cases, to make any great and thorough reformation.

It is somewhat singular, that about this time, in the midst of so much animosity of the people to the senate and nobles, this superior class of the citizens were the patrons of austerity, and contended for sumptuary laws, while the popular tribunes contended for license. "What is your liberty," said the tribune Duronius to the people (while he moved for a repeal of the sumptuary law of Fannius), "if you may not consume what is your own; if you must be restrained by rule and measure; if you must be stinted in your pleasures? Let us shake off, I pray you, these musty remains of antiquity, and make free to enjoy what we and our fathers have gained."[2]

U. C. 656.

Cn. Cornelius Lentulus. P. Licinius Crassus.

For the petulance of these expressions, this tribune was, by the judgment of the censors, on the following year, expelled from the senate; and he took his revenge by prosecuting the censor Antonius for bribery in canvassing for his office.

Cn. Cornelius Lentulus and Publius Licinius Crassus being raised to the office of consul, the latter was appointed to relieve Didius in Spain, and the other to succeed Metellus in Italy. There is, during some years, a considerable blank in the materials from which we collect this history; little more is recorded than the succession of consuls with the number of years, and a few particulars that ill supply the interval in our accounts of what passed in the city, or in the series of important affairs abroad. So far as these particulars, however, can be referred to their respective dates, it will be proper, while we endeavour to mark the lapse of time, to record them in the order in which they are supposed to have happened.

U. C. 656.

In the present year are dated two remarkable acts of the senate; one to condemn the use of magic, another to prohibit human sacrifices:[3] the first proceeding, perhaps, from credulity in the authors of the law, the other implying some remains of a gross and inhuman superstition, which was still entertained by the people though rejected by the government.[4]

In the following consulate the kingdom of Cyrene was bequeathed to the Romans by Ptolemy Apion, the late king. But, as this people professed themselves to be the general patrons of liberty, where this blessing was not forfeited by some act of ingratitude or perfidy in their allies, they did not avail themselves of this legacy, leaving the subjects of Cyrene to retain for some time the independence of their nation with a species of popular government; and in this form they were allowed to remain as a separate state, until, in a general arrangement made of all the dependencies of the empire, they came to be reduced to the form of a province.

U. C. 658.

L. Licinius Crassus, Q. Mucius Scævola. Lex Licinia Mucia de Civibus regendis.

The following consuls gave its name and its date to an act of the people nearly of the same tenour with some of those formerly passed for the exclusion of aliens. The inhabitants of Italy still continued the practice of crowding to Rome, in expectation of obtaining in a body the prerogative of citizens, or at least of intruding themselves, as many of them separately did, into some of the tribes, by which persons of this description, from voting at elections, came themselves by degrees to be elected into the higher offices of state.

Times of faction were extremely favourable to this intrusion of strangers. Different leaders connived at the enrolment of those who were likely to favour their respective parties. And the factious tribunes, in whatever degree they may have favoured the general claim of the allies to be admitted as Romans, treated the subject as matter of opposition to the senate. They expected to raise the storm of popular animosity and tumult with the more ease, in proportion as the numbers of the people increased. By the act of Licinius and Mucius, nevertheless, a scrutiny was set on foot, and all who, without a just title, ventured to exercise any privilege of Roman citizens, were remitted to their several boroughs.[5]

In this consulate is likewise dated the trial of Servilius Cæpio, for his supposed misconduct about ten years before in his command of the army against the Cimbri. He had exasperated the popular faction, by opposing the act of Saturninus for the gratuitous distribution of corn, and his enemies were now encouraged to raise this prosecution against him. The people gave sentence of condemnation, and violently drove from the place of assembly two of the tribunes who ventured to interpose their negative in his favour. Authors, according to Valerius Maximus, have differed in their accounts of the sequel; some affirming that Cæpio, being put to death in prison, his body was dragged through the streets as that of a traitor, and cast into the river; others, that he was, by the favour of Antistius, one of the tribunes, rescued, or enabled to make his escape.[6]

C. Norbanus, who was said to be author of the riot which occasioned the condemnation of Cæpio, and the supposed cruel execution of that citizen, was on the following year brought to trial himself for mal-administration and sedition in office; but, by his own popularity, and the address of the orator Antonius, who pleaded his cause, was acquitted.[7]

The war in Spain still continued; and the Romans, having gained considerable victories, sent ten commissioners, to endeavour, in concert with Crassus and Didius, to make such arrange-

1 Cic. Philip. v. Pro domo sua. Epist. ad Atticum, lib. ii.

2 Val. Max. lib ii. c. 9.

3 Plin. lib. xxx. c. 1

4 Dion. Cassius, lib. xlii. p. 226.

5 Ascon. in Orat. pro Cornelio Majest. reo.

6 Val. Max. lib. iv. c. 7.

7 Cicero de Orator. lib. ii

ments as might tend to the future peace of those provinces: but in vain; hostilities were again renewed in the following year.

U C. 660.

C. Val. Flaccus, M. Herennius.

L. Cornelius Sylla, who had been questor in the year of Rome six hundred and forty-six, now, after an interval of about fourteen years, and without having been edile, stood candidate for the office of prætor. Whether his neglect of political honours, during this period, proceeded from idleness, or from want of ambition, is uncertain. His character will justify either construction, being equally susceptible of dissipation, and of the disdain of ordinary distinctions. The people, however, refused to gratify him in his desire of passing on to the office of prætor without being edile; as they were resolved to be gratified with the magnificent shows of wild beasts, which his supposed correspondence with the king of Mauritania enabled him to furnish. But to remove this objection to his preferment, he gave out, that as prætor he was to exhibit the same shows which were expected from him as edile: and having, in the following year, persisted in his suit, he was accordingly elected, and fulfilled the expectations of the people; insomuch, that he is said to have let loose in the circus a hundred maned or male lions, and to have exhibited the method of baiting or fighting them by Mauritanian huntsmen.[8] Such was the price which candidates for preferment at Rome were obliged to pay for public favour.

In this variable scene, where so many particular men excelled in genius and magnanimity, while the state itself was subject to the government of a capricious and disorderly multitude, P. Rutilius, late questor in Asia, exhibited a spectacle sufficient to counterbalance the lions of Sylla; and, if it were permitted in any case whatever to treat our country with disdain, an instance to be applauded of the just contempt with which the undeserved resentments of corrupt and malicious men ought to be received. Having reformed many abuses of the equestrian tax-gatherers in the province which he governed, he was himself brought before the tribunal of an equestrian jury, to be tried for the crime he had restrained in others. In this situation he declined the aid of any friend, told the judges he would make no defence; but stated the particulars by which he had offended his prosecutors, left the court to decide, and, being condemned, retired to Smyrna, where he ever after lived in great tranquillity, and could not be prevailed on, even by Sylla in the height of his power, to return to Rome.[9] Great as the state and republic of Rome was become, unmerited disgrace was certainly a just object of contempt or indifference.

The proconsuls, Didius and Crassus, were permitted to triumph for victories obtained in Spain, but had not been able to establish the peace of that country. The war which broke out afresh in one of the provinces was committed to Valerius Flaccus, and the care of the other to Perpenna, one of the consuls. Flaccus, near the town of Belgida, obtained a great victory, in which were slain about twenty thousand of the enemy; but he could not prevail on the canton to submit. Such of the people as were inclined to capitulate, deliberating on terms, were beset by their fellow-citizens, and the house in which they were assembled being set on fire, they perished in the flames.

U. C. 661.

C. Claudius Pulcher, M. Perpenna.

The war having been likewise renewed with the Thracians on the frontiers of Macedonia, Geminius, who commanded there in the quality of proprætor, was defeated, and the province over-run by the enemy.

The prætor Sylla, at the expiration of his office, was sent into Asia with a commission to restore Ariarathes to the kingdom of Cappadocia, which had been seized by Mithridates, and to restore Pylamenes to that of Paphlagonia, from which he had been expelled by Nicomedes king of Bithynia. The prætor having successfully executed both these commissions, continued his journey to the Euphrates, where he had a conference, and concluded a treaty with an ambassador from Ariarathes king of the Parthians.[10]

From an edict of the censors, Cn. Domitius Ahenobarbus and Cn. Licinius Crassus, condemning the schools of Latin rhetoric,[11] it appears that the Romans, during this period, still received with reluctance the refinements which were gradually taking place in the literary as well as in the other arts. "Whereas information," said the censors in their edict, "has been lodged before us that schools are kept by certain persons, under the title of Latin rhetoricians, to which the youth of this city resort, and at which they pass entire days in frivolity and sloth; and whereas our ancestors have determined what their children should learn, and what exercises they ought to frequent: these innovations on the customs and manners of our forefathers being, in our opinion, offensive and wrong, we publish these presents, that both masters and scholars, given to these illicit practices, may be duly apprised of our pleasure."[12] Cicero being now fourteen years of age, and employed in learning that eloquence for which he became so famous, was probably involved in this censure, as frequenting the schools which, by this formal edict of the magistrate, were condemned.

In the consulate of Marcus Philippus and Sext. Julius Cæsar, according to Pliny, there were in the Roman treasury sixteen hundred and twenty eight thousand eight hundred and twenty-nine pondo[13] of gold[14] or between sixty and seventy or eighty millions sterling. In the same year a present sent from the king of Mauritania had nearly produced a civil war in the commonwealth, and greatly inflamed the passions from which that calamity soon after arose. Bocchus, in order to remind the Romans of the merit he had acquired by delivering Jugurtha into their hands, had caused this scene to be represented in a groupe of images of gold, containing his own figure, that of Jugurtha, and that of Sylla, to whom the unhappy prince was delivered up. Marius, under whose auspices this transaction had passed, being provoked at having no place in the representation of it, attempted to pull down

8 Plin. lib. viii. c. 16.

9 Val. Max. lib. vi. c. 17. Liv. lib. lxx. Orosius, lib. v. c. 17. Cic. de Orator. et in Bruto. Pædianus in Divinationem. Velleius, lib. ii.

10 Plutarch, in Sylla. Appian. in Mithridatico. Justin. lib. xxxiii. Strabo, lib. xii.

11 Cicer. de Orator. lib. iii. c. 24.

12 A. Gellius, lib. xv. c. 11.

13 The Roman pondo of ten ounces

14 Plin. Harduem, lib. xxxiii. c. 3.

the images after they had been erected in the place of their destination in the capitol. Sylla was equally solicitous to have them remain; and the contest was likely to end in violence, if matters of greater moment had not arisen to occupy the ardent and vehement spirit of these rivals.

The expectations of all parties at Rome, and throughout Italy, were now raised by the projects of Livius Drusus, an active tribune, who, in order to distinguish himself, brought forward many subjects of the greatest concern to the public. He acted at first in concert with the leading men of the senate, and was supported by them in order to obtain some amendment in the law as it then stood with respect to the courts of justice. The equestrian order had acquired exclusive possession of the judicature. The senators wished to recover at least a share in that prerogative; and Drusus, in order to gratify them, moved for an act of which the tendency was, to restore the judicative power of the senate: to prevent opposition from the equestrian order, he proposed, at once, to enrol three hundred knights into the senate: and that the senators, who appear at this time to have amounted to no more than three hundred, might not withstand this increase of their numbers, he left to each the nomination of one of the new members, proposing, that from the six hundred so constituted the lists of judges should be taken.[1] Many of the knights were reconciled to this arrangement, by the hopes of becoming senators; but the order, in general, seem to have considered it as a snare laid to deprive them of their consequence in the government of their country; and individuals refused to accept of a place in the senate, at the hazard of so great and so sudden a change in the condition of their own order, and of the constitution of the state.[2]

Lex de Judiciis.

This tribune likewise proposed an act to debase the silver coin, by mixing an eighth of alloy. But the part of his project which gave the greatest alarm, was that which related to the indigent citizens of Rome, and to the inhabitants of Italy in general.

Lex Nummaria.

With a view to gratify the poorer citizens he proposed, that all the new settlements, projected by the law of Caius Gracchus, should now be carried into execution. The consul, Marcus Perpenna, having ventured to oppose this proposal, he was, by order of the tribune, taken into custody; and so roughly treated in the execution of this order, that, while he struggled to disengage himself, the blood was made to spring from his nostrils. "It is no more than the pickle of the turtle-fish;"[3] said the tribune, a species of delicacy, in which, it seems, among other luxuries of the table, this consul was supposed frequently to indulge himself.

Lex de Coloniis.

For the allies of Italy, Livius Drusus proposed to obtain the favourite object on which they had been so long intent, the privileges and powers of Roman citizens. In all his other proposals, he had the concurrence of some party in the commonwealth, and by persuasion, or force, had obtained his purpose; but in this he struck at the personal consideration of every citizen, and was opposed by the unanimous voice of the whole people.

Lex de Civitate Sociis danda.

This tribune used to boast, that he would exhaust every fund from which any order of men could be gratified, and leave to those who came after him nothing to give, but the air and the earth.[4] The citizens in general, however, were become tired of his favours, and the people of Italy were ill-disposed to requite the merit of a project which he had not been able to execute. Soon after the motion, which he made in favour of the Italians, had been rejected, Drusus was suddenly taken ill in the public assembly, and Papirius Carbo, another of the tribunes, made a short speech on the occasion, which, among a people prone to superstition, and ready to execute whatever they conceived to be awarded by the gods, probably hastened the fate of his falling colleague: "O Marcus Drusus!" he said, "the father I call, not this degenerate son; thou who usedst to say, The commonwealth is sacred, whoever violates it is sure to be punished. The temerity of the son has evinced the wisdom of the father." A great shout arose in the assembly, and Drusus,[5] being attended to his own house by a numerous multitude, received in the crowd a secret wound of which he died.[6] All his laws were soon after repealed, as having passed under unfavourable auspices. But the inhabitants of Italy were not to be appeased under their late disappointment, and discontents were breaking out in every part of the country, which greatly alarmed the republic.

In this state of public uneasiness, some prosecutions were raised by the tribunes, calculated to gratify their own private resentments, and tending to excite animosities. Q. Varius Hybrida obtained a decree of the people, directing, that inquiry should be made by whose fault the allies had been made to expect the freedom of the city. In consequence of an inquest set on foot for this purpose, L. Calphurnius Bestia, late consul, and M. Aurelius Orator, and other eminent men, were condemned.[7] Mummius Achaicus was banished to Delos. Emilius Scaurus, who had long maintained his dignity as princeps, or first on the roll of the senate, was cited on this occasion before the people as a person involved in the same guilt. Quintus Varius, the tribune, who accused him, being a native of Spain, Scaurus was acquitted upon the following short defence: "Q. Varius, from the banks of the Sucro, in Spain, says, That M. Emilius Scaurus, first in the roll of the senate, has encouraged your subjects to revolt; Varius maintains the charge; Scaurus denies it; there is no other evidence in this matter; choose whom you will believe."[8]

The year following, Varius himself was tried, and condemned agreeably to his own act; and while the prosecutions suspended all other civil affairs, and even the measures required for the safety of the public, the inhabitants of Italy were forming dangerous combinations, and were ready to break out in actual rebellion. They were

1 Appian. de Bell. Civ. lib. i. Auct. de Viris Illustribus, c. 66. Cicero pro Clientio.
2 Ibid.
3 Ex turdis maria. Auct. de Viris Illustribus, in L. Drus. Val. Max. lib. ix. c. 5. Florus.
4 Florus, lib. iii. c. 17. 5 Cicero in Bruto, p. 63.
6 Velleius, lib. ii. c. 13, 14. Appian. Florus, lib iii c. 17.
7 Appian. Val. Max. lib. viii. c. 6. Cicero in Bruto
8 Cicero pro M Scauro filio. Auct de Viris Illustribus, c. 72. Quintilian, lib. v. c. 12 Val. Max lib. iii. c.

exasperated with having their suit not only refused, but in having the abettors of it at Rome considered as criminals. They sent deputies to meet at Corfinium, and to deliberate on a plan of operations. Their deputies were to form a senate, and to choose two executive officers, under the denomination of consuls.

The Romans took their first suspicion of a design in agitation among their allies, from observing that they were exchanging hostages among themselves. The proconsul Servilius, who commanded in the Picenum, having intelligence to this purpose from Asculum, repaired thither, in order, by his presence, to prevent any commotion; but his coming, in reality, hastened the revolt. His remonstrances and his threats made the inhabitants sensible that their designs were known, and that the execution of them could no longer in safety be delayed They accordingly took arms, and put to the sword the proconsul Servilius, with his lieutenant, and all the Roman citizens who happened to be in the place. The alarm immediately spread throughout all the towns that were concerned in the plot; and, as upon a signal agreed, the Marsi, Peligni, Vestini, Marcini, Picentes, Ferentanæ, Hirpini, Pompeiani, Venusini, Apuli, Lucani, and Samnites, took arms, and sent a joint deputation to Rome to demand a participation in the privileges of Roman citizens; of which they had, by their services, contributed so largely to increase the value.

In answer to this demand they were told by the senate, that they must discontinue their assemblies, and renounce their pretensions; otherwise, that they must not presume to send any other message to Rome.

U. C. 663.

L. Julius Cæsar, P. Rutilius Lupus.

War being thus declared, both parties prepared for the contest. The allies mustered a hundred thousand men, in different bodies, and under different leaders. The Romans found themselves in an instant brought back to the condition in which they had been about three hundred years before; reduced to a few miles of territory round their walls, and beset with enemies more united, and more numerous than ever had assailed them at once on the same ground. But their city was likewise enlarged, their numbers increased, and every individual excellently formed to serve the state, as a warrior and a citizen. All of them assumed, upon this occasion, the sagum, or military dress; and being joined by such of the Latins as remained in their allegiance, and by such of their colonies, from different parts of Italy as continued to be faithful, together with some mercenaries from Gaul and Numidia, they assembled a force equal to that of the allies.

The consuls were placed at the head of the two principal armies; Lucius Julius Cæsar, in the country of the Samnites,[9] and Rutilius, in that of the Marsi.[10] They had under their command the most celebrated and experienced officers of the republic; but little more is preserved to furnish out the history of this war than the names of the Roman commanders, and those of the persons opposed to them. Rutilius was attended by Pompeius Strabo, the father of him who afterwards bore the title of Pompey the Great; Cæpio, Perpenna, Messala, and Caius Marius, of whom the last had already so often been consul. Cæsar had, in the army which he commanded, Lentulus, Didius, Crassus, and Marcellus. They were opposed by T. Afranius, P. Ventidius, Marcus Egnatius, Q. Pompedius, C. Papius, M. Lamponius, C. Judacilius, Hircus, Assinius, and Vetius Cato, at the head of the allies. The forces were similar in discipline and in arms. The Romans were likely to be inferior in numbers and in resources, but had the advantage in reputation, authority, and in the fame of their leaders, inured to command in the highest stations. But so well had the allies taken their measures, and with so much animosity did they support a quarrel, which they had been meditating for some years, that the Romans appeared at first unequal to the contest, and were surprised and overcome in many encounters.

The detail of these operations is imperfectly recorded; and does not furnish the materials of a relation either interesting or instructive. We must therefore content ourselves with a list of actions and events, and with the general result.

One of the consuls, Lucius Cæsar, in the first encounter of the war, was defeated by Vetius Cato near Esernia, and had two thousand men killed in the field. The town of Esernia was immediately invested, and some Roman officers of distinction were obliged to make their escape in the disguise of slaves. Two Roman cohorts were cut off at Venafrum, and that colony fell into the hands of the enemy. The other consul, Rutilius, was likewise defeated by the Marsi, and fell in the field, with eight thousand men of his army. His colleague was called to the city to preside at the election of a successor; but being necessarily detained with the army, the office continued vacant for the remainder of the campaign, while the army acted under the direction of the late consuls, Marius and Cæpio.

The corpse of Rutilius, and of other persons of rank, being brought to public funeral at Rome, so alarmed and sunk the minds of the people, that the senate decreed, that, for the future, the dead should be buried where they fell.

In the mean time, Lucius Cæsar, obtained a victory in the country of the Samnites; and the senate, in order to restore the confidence of the people, as if this victory had suppressed the revolt, resolved, that the sagum, or military dress, should be laid aside.[11]

The usual time of the consular elections being come, Cn. Pompeius Strabo and Porcius Cato were named.

U. C. 664.

Cn. Pomp. Strabo, L. Porcius Cato.

Pompey gained a complete victory over the Marsi; and notwithstanding an obstinate defence, reduced the city of Asculum, where hostilities at first had commenced, and where the Romans had suffered the greatest outrage. The principal inhabitants of the place were put to death, the remainder were sold for slaves. The other consul, Cato, was killed in the attack upon the entrenchments of the Marsi; and although Marius and Sylla, in different quarters, had turned the fortune of the war against the allies, yet the event still continued to be extremely doubtful.

The Umbrians, Etruscans, and inhabitants of

9 Now part of the kingdom of Naples.
10 Contiguous part of the ecclesiastical stat

11 Liv. lib. lxxiv. Appian. Orosius, lib. v. c. 18 Florus, lib. iii. c. 18. Velleius. Eutropius.

other districts of Italy, who had hitherto hesitated in the choice of their party, took courage from the perseverance and success of their neighbours, and openly joined the revolt. The more distant parts of the empire were soon likely to seize the contagion: they were already, by the obstruction they met with in carrying supplies of provisions or revenue, severed from the capital, and the allegiance they owed as conquered provinces, whenever they saw their opportunity to withdraw it, was likely to vanish like a dream or ideal existence.

Mithridates, the king of Pontus, did not neglect the occasion that was offered to him; he put all his forces in motion, expelled Nicomedes from Bithynia, and Ariobarzanes from Cappadocia, and made himself master of the greater part of the Lesser Asia.

In this extremity it appeared necessary to comply with the demands of the allies; but the senate had the address to make this concession seem to be an act of munificence and generosity, not of weakness or fear.

The Latins, who had continued in their allegiance, were, in consideration of their fidelity, admitted to all the privileges of Roman citizens. The Umbri and Tuscans, who either had not yet declared, or who had been least forward in the war, were next comprehended; and the other inhabitants of Italy, observing, that they were likely to obtain by favour what they endeavoured to extort by force, grew remiss in the war, or withdrew from the league, that they might appear to be forward in the general return to peace.

The Marsi, Samnites, and Lucanians, who had been the principal authors of the revolt, or who had acted with most animosity in the conduct of it, continued for some time to be excluded from the privilege of Romans. But the civil war, which soon after broke out among the citizens themselves, terminated either in the extirpation of those aliens, and in the settlement of Roman colonies in their stead, or gave them an opportunity, under favour of the party they espoused, of gaining admittance to the privilege to which they aspired: so that, in a few years, all the inhabitants of Italy, from the Rubicon to the straits of Messina, were become citizens of Rome; and a constitution of state, which had been already overcharged by the numbers that partook of its sovereignty, was now altogether overwhelmed; or if this change alone were not sufficient to destroy it, was not likely long to remain without some notable and fatal revolution. Assemblies of the people, already sufficiently tumultuary, being now considered as the collective body of all the Italians, were become altogether impracticable, or could be no more than partial tumults raised in the streets of Rome, or the contiguous fields, for particular purposes: insomuch that when we read of the authority of the senate being set aside by an order of the people, we may venture to conceive all government suspended at the instance of that party, who had then the populace of Rome at their call.

Licinius Crassus and L. Julius Cæsar were chosen censors, in order to make up the new rolls of the people. This, it is likely, was found to be a difficult and tedious work. It became necessary to scrutinize the rolls of every separate borough, in order to know who were entitled to be added to the list of Roman citizens; and this difficulty was farther increased in consequence of a law devised about this time by Papirius Carbo, in which it was enacted, that not only the natives and ancient denizens of Italy, but all who should, for the future, obtain the freedom of any Italian borough if they had a residence in Italy, and had given in their claim to the prætor sixty days, should, by that act, become citizens:[1] so that the prerogative of the Roman people continued to be in the gift of every separate corporation as well as in that of the state itself.

The number of the aliens admitted on the rolls, at this muster, is not recorded; but it was probably equal to that of the ancient citizens, and might have instantly formed a very powerful and dangerous faction in the state, if effectual measures had not been taken to guard against the effect of their influence. For this purpose, they were not mixed promiscuously with the mass of the people, but confined to eight particular tribes;[2] by this means they could only influence eight votes in thirty-five;[3] and the ancient citizens were still possessed of a great majority. But this artifice did not long escape the attention of those who were aggrieved by it, and became the subject of a new dispute.

While the Romans were meditating, or actually making this important change in the state of the commonwealth, they found leisure for matters of less moment, in which they endeavoured to provide for the peace of the city, and the administration of justice.

Lex Plotia de Judiciis. Plautius, one of the tribunes, obtained a new law for the selection of judges, by which it was enacted, That each tribe should annually elect fifteen citizens, without any distinction of rank; and that, from the whole so named, the judges in all trials that occurred within the year should be taken.[4] This law appeared to be equitable, as it gave, with great propriety, to all the different classes of men in the state, an equal right to be named of the juries; and to every party concerned, an equal chance of being tried by his peers.

Lex Plotia de Vi. The same tribune likewise obtained a law for the preservation of the public peace, by which it was declared capital to be seen in public with a weapon, or instrument of death; to occupy any place of strength in the city; to offer violence to the house of any person, or to disturb any company; to interrupt any meeting of the senate, assembly of the people, or court of justice. To these clauses Catulus subjoined another, in which he comprehended persons surrounding the senate with an armed force, or offering violence to any magistrate.[5]

---

1 Cicero pro Archia Poeta.
2 Velleius Paterculus, lib. ii. c. 20.
3 Historians mention this particular, as if eight new tribes were added to the former thirty-five; but the continual allusion of Roman writers to the number thirty-five, will not allow us to suppose any augmentation. Cicero de Lege Agraria, 2da, c. 8.
4 Pedianus in Cornelianam Ciceronis.
5 Cicero pro Cælio, et Aruspicum Responso

CHAPTER VII.

Triumph of Pompeius Strabo—Progress of Sylla—War with the King of Pontus—Rise of that Kingdom—Appointment of Sylla to Command—Policy of the Tribune Sulpicius—Sylla's Commission recalled in Favour of Marius—His March from Campania to Rome—Expels Marius and his Faction from the City—His Operations in Greece—Siege of Athens—Battle of Chæronea—Of Orchomenos—Transactions at Rome—Policy of Cinna—Marius recalled—Cinna flies, and is deprived—Recovers the Possession of Rome—Treaty of Sylla with Mithridates—He passes into Italy—Is opposed by numerous Armies—Various Events of the War in Italy—Sylla prevails—His Proscription, or Massacre—Named Dictator—His Policy—Resignation—and Death.

THE social war, though far from being successful, concluded with a triumphal procession; and the senate, though actually obliged to yield the point for which they contended, thought proper, under pretence of advantages gained on some particular occasions, to erect a trophy. They singled out Pompeius Strabo for the pageant in this ceremony; either because he had reduced Asculum, where the rebellion first broke out, or because a victory obtained by him had immediately preceded the peace. But the most remarkable circumstance in this procession was, its being, in show, a triumph of the old citizens over the new, but in reality a triumph of the latter. Ventidius Bassus, being a prisoner in the war, and led as such in the present triumph, came in the form of a captive to share in the prerogatives of a Roman; he was, in the sequel, promoted to all the honours of the state; and himself, in the capacity of a victorious general, led a procession of the same kind with that in which he made his first entry at Rome as a captive.[6]

Sylla, by his conduct and his successes wherever he had borne a separate command in this war, gave proof of that superior genius by which he now began to be distinguished. By his magnanimity on all occasions, by his great courage in danger, by his imperious exactions from the enemy, and by his lavish profusion to his own troops, he obtained in a very high degree, the confidence and attachment of his soldiers; and yet in this, it is probable, he acted from temper, and not from design, or with any view to what followed. With so careless and so bold a hand did this man already hold the reins of military discipline, that Albinus, an officer of high rank, and next in command to himself, being killed by the soldiers in a mutiny, he treated this outrage as a trifle, saying, when the matter was reported to him, That the troops would atone for it when they met with the enemy.[7]

U. C. 665.

L. Corn. Sylla. Q. Pomp. Rufus, Cons.

With the merits he had recently displayed in this war, he repaired to the city, laid claim to the consulate, and was accordingly chosen in conjunction with Quintus Pompeius Rufus.

It was thought necessary still to keep a proper force under arms in Italy, until the public tranquillity should be fully established. The army, which had acted under Cneius Pompeius Strabo, consul of the preceding year, was destined for this service; and Quintus Rufus was appointed to the command of it.

The war with Mithridates, king of Pontus, however, was the principal object of attention; and this province, together with the army then lying in Campania, fell to the lot of Sylla.

The monarchy of Pontus had risen upon the ruins of the Macedonian establishments in Asia; and, upon their entire suppression, was become one of the most considerable kingdoms of the East.

Mithridates had inherited from his ancestors a great extent of territory, reaching in length, according to the representation of his own ambassador in Appian twenty thousand stadia, above two thousand miles. He himself had joined to it the kingdom of Colchis, and other provinces on the coasts of the Euxine sea. His national troops amounted to three hundred thousand foot, and forty thousand horse, besides auxiliaries from Thrace, and from that part of Scythia which lies on the Meotis and the Tanais, countries over which he had acquired an ascendant approaching to a sovereignty. He had pretensions likewise on the kingdoms of Bithynia and Cappadocia, which he had hitherto relinquished from respect to the Romans; or of which he had deferred the effect until he should be prepared to cope with this formidable power. All his pretensions, indeed, like those of other monarchs, were likely to extend with his force, and to receive no limitation but from the defect of his power. And such were his resources, and his personal character, that, if he had encountered on the side of Europe with an enemy less able than the Romans were to withstand his progress, it is probable that in his hands the empire of Pontus might have vied with that of the greatest conquerors.

About the time that the social war broke out in Italy, Cassius Longinus, Marcus Aquilius, and C. Oppius were, in different characters, stationed in the province of Asia, and took under their protection every power in that country that was likely to oppose the progress of Mithridates.

Nicomedes, who had been recently restored to the crown of Bithynia, made hostile incursions under the encouragement of these Roman generals, even into the kingdom of Pontus. Mithridates, having made fruitless complaints to them on this subject; and thinking that the distracted state of Italy furnished him with a favourable opportunity to slight their resentment, he sent his son Ariarathes into Cappadocia with a force to expel Ariobarzanes, though an ally of the Romans, and to possess that kingdom. He took the field himself, and sent powerful armies, under his generals, against Nicomedes, and against the Romans, who had assembled all the force of their province and of their allies, to the amount of a hundred and twenty thousand men, in different

6 Val. lib. vi. c. 9. Gellius, lib. xv. c. 4. Plin. lib. 7. c. 43. Dio Cassius, 43. fine. 7 Plutarch in Sylla.

bodies, to defend their own frontier, or to annoy their enemy.

Mithridates fell separately upon the several divisions of his enemies' forces; and having defeated Nicomedes, and afterwards Marcus, obliged the Roman officers, with their ally, to retire; Cassius to Apamea, Marcus towards Rhodes, and Nicomedes to Pergamus. His fleet, likewise, consisting of three hundred gallies, opened the passage of the Hellespont, took all the ships which the Romans had stationed in those straits; and he himself soon after in person traversed Phrygia and the Lesser Asia, to the sea of Cilicia and Greece. In all the cities of the Lesser Asia, where the people now openly declared their detestation of the Roman dominion, he was received with open gates. He got possession of the person of Oppius, by means of the inhabitants of Laodicea, where this general had taken refuge with a body of mercenaries. The mercenaries were allowed to disband; but Oppius himself was conducted as a prisoner to the head-quarters of Mithridates, and, in mockery of his state as a Roman governor, was made to pass through the cities in his way, with his fasces or ensigns of magistracy carried before him.

Marcus Aquilius likewise fell into the hands of the enemy, and was treated with similar scorn; and with a barbarity which nothing but the most criminal abuse of the power he lately possessed could have deserved or provoked. Being carried round the cities of Asia on an ass, he was obliged at every place to declare, that his own avarice was the cause of the war; and he was at last put to death by the pouring of melted gold into his throat.

While Mithridates thus overwhelmed his enemies, and was endeavouring to complete his conquest of Asia by the reduction of Rhodes, he ordered his general Archelaus to penetrate by the way of Thrace and Macedonia into Greece.

Such was the alarming state of the war when the Romans, having scarcely appeased the troubles in Italy, appointed L. Cornelius Sylla with six legions that lay in Campania, to embark for Greece, in order, if possible, to stem a torrent which no ordinary bars were likely to withstand.

But before Sylla or his colleague could depart for their provinces, disorders arose in the city, which, without waiting the approach of foreign enemies, brought armies to battle in the streets, and covered the pavements of Rome with the slain.

Publius Sulpicius, tribune of the people, with a singular boldness and profligacy, ventured to tamper with the dangerous humours which were but ill suppressed in the event of the late troubles; and, as if the state had no experience of civil wars and domestic tumults, lighted the torch anew, and kindled the former animosity of the popular and senatorian parties. The severe measures hitherto taken by the senate and magistrates against the authors of sedition had, in some instances, been effectual to snatch the republic out of the hands of lawless men, and to suspend for a while the ruin of the commonwealth; but he examples so given, instead of deterring others from a repetition of the same crimes, appear only to have admonished the factious leaders to take proper precautions, and to make the necessary preparations before they embarked in designs against the state. They accordingly improved and refined by degrees on the measures which they successively took against the senate; and when the tribune Sulpicius began to act, he made his arrangements equal to a system of formal war. This tribune, according to Plutarch, had three thousand gladiators in his pay, and in despite of the law of Plautius, had ever at his back a numerous company of retainers, armed with daggers and other offensive weapons; these he called his *anti-senate;* and retained to support him in an attempt, which he was at no pains to disguise, against the authority of the senate itself. He moved the people to recall from exile all those who had fled from the city on occasion of the former disorders, and to admit the new citizens and enfranchised slaves to be enrolled promiscuously in all the tribes without regard to the late wise limitation of the senate's decree, by which they were restricted to four. By the change which he now proposed, the citizens of least consideration might come to have a majority, or a great sway in the public deliberations. The tribunes would become masters in every question, and fill up the rolls of the people in the manner that most suited their interest.

This presumptuous man himself undertook to procure the freedom of the city for every person that applied to him, and boldly received premiums in the streets for this prostitution of the privileges and powers of his fellow-citizens.

The more respectable citizens, and the magistrates, in vain withstood these abuses. They were overpowered by force, and frequently driven from the place of assembly. In this extremity they had recourse to superstition, and by multiplying holy-days, endeavoured to stop or to disconcert their antagonists. But Sulpicius, with his party, laid violent hands on the consuls, in order to force them to recall these appointments. Young Pompey, the son of the present consul, and son-in-law to Sylla, was killed in the fray. Sylla himself, who had withdrawn from the tumult, feeling that he was in the power of his enemies, and being impatient to get into a situation in which he could more effectually resist them chose for the present to comply with their demands.[1]

In the midst of these violences, the city being under an actual usurpation of tyranny, Sylla repaired to the army in Campania, with a resolution to pursue the object of his command in Asia, and to leave the tribunitian storms at Rome to spend their force. But soon after his departure, it appeared, that Marius was no stranger to the councils of Sulpicius; and that he hoped, by means of this tribune, to gratify an ambition which outlived the vigour of his faculties and the strength of his body. His first object was to mortify his rival Sylla, in revoking, by a decree of the people, the appointment of the senate, and to supersede him in the command of the army against Mithridates. A decree to this purpose was accordingly with ease obtained by Sulpicius, in one of those partial conventions, which took upon them to represent the people of Italy in the streets of Rome; and Marius, now appointed general of the army in Campania, sent the proper officers to intimate his appointment to Sylla, and to receive from him, in behalf of his successor, the charge of the army, and the delivery of

1 Plutarch in Mario, p. 526. edit. Londin. 4to

the stores. Sylla had the address to make the troops apprehend that this change was equally prejudicial to them as to himself; that Marius had his favourite legions, whom he would naturally employ; and that the same act of violence, by which he had supplanted the general, would bring other officers and other men to reap the fruits of this lucrative service in Asia. This persuasion, as well as the attachment which the army already bore to their general, produced its effect.[2]

The officers, who intimated the appointment of Marius, on declaring their commission, found that violence could take place in the camp as well as in the city. Their orders were received with scorn. A tumult arose among the soldiers; and citizens vested with a public character, formally commissioned to intimate an order of the Roman people, and delivering their commands to this purpose, were slain in the camp. In return to this outrage some relations and friends of Sylla were murdered in the city, and such retaliations were not likely soon to end on either side.[3]

Faction is frequently blind, and does not see the use that may be made of its own violent precedents against itself. Although Sylla is said to have hesitated, yet he was not a person likely to shrink from the contest, in which his own enemies, and those of the state, had engaged him. Stung with rage, and probably thinking that force would be justified in snatching the republic out of such violent hands, he proposed to the army that they should march to Rome. The proposal was received with joy; and the army, without any of the scruples, or any degree of that hesitation which is ascribed to their commander in adopting this measure, followed where he thought proper to lead them.

On this new and dangerous appearance of things, not only Marius and Sulpicius, with the persons most obnoxious on account of the insults offered to Sylla and other respectable citizens, were seized with consternation; but even the senate and the nobles were justly alarmed.

A faction, it is true, had assumed the authority of the Roman people, to violate the laws, and to overawe the state; but armies, it was thought, are dangerous tools in political contests; and no good intention on the part of their leaders, no magnanimity or moderation in the execution of their intentions, can compensate the ruinous tendency of a precedent which brings force to be employed as an ordinary resource in political divisions. Even the present state of the republic did not appear so desperate as to justify such a measure.

The senate accordingly sent a deputation to Sylla, with entreaties, and with commands, that he would not advance to the city. This deputation was received by him within a few miles of the gates. He heard the remonstrance that was made to him with patience, and seemed to be moved. He gave orders, in the hearing of the deputies, that the armies should halt; sent the proper officers to mark out a camp, and suffered the commissioners to return to their employers, full of the persuasion that he was to comply with their request. But as soon as he thought this intelligence had reached the city, and had lulled his antagonists into a state of security, he sent a detachment close on the heels of the deputies, with orders to seize the nearest gate; and he himself, with the whole army, speedily followed to support them.

The gate was accordingly seized. The people, in tumult, endeavoured to recover it; Marius secured the capitol, and summoned every man, whether freemen or slaves, to repair to his standard. His party, as they assembled, were drawn up in the streets. Sylla, in the mean time, at the head of his army, rushed through the gate, which his vanguard still maintained against the multitudes by whom they were pressed. He was greatly annoyed from the battlements and windows as he passed, and might have been repulsed by the forces which Marius had assembled, if he had not commanded the city to be set on fire, in order to profit by the confusion into which the people were likely to be thrown in avoiding or extinguishing the flames. By this expedient he drove Marius from all the stations he had occupied, forced him to abandon the city, and obliged his adherents to separate.

While the army was distributed in different quarters of a city, deformed with recent marks of bloodshed and fire, their general assembled the senate, and desired them to deliberate on the present state of affairs. Among the measures he suggested on this occasion, was a law by which Marius, with his son, and twelve of his faction, who had secreted themselves, were declared enemies of their country. This sentence was accompanied with a public injunction to seize or kill them wherever they could be found. The reasons upon which this act of attainder was granted were, that they had violated the laws of the republic, and seduced the slaves to desert from their masters, and to take arms against the state.[4]

While the officers of justice were dispersed in execution of this decree, and many others were busy in search of their private enemies, thus laid at their mercy, the tribune Sulpicius, having fled to the marshes on the coast near Laurentum, was dragged from thence and slain. His head, severed from the body, as that of a traitor, who had surpassed every leader of faction in the outrages done to the laws and the government of his country, was exposed on one of the rostra; an example afterwards frequently imitated, and which, though it could not make any addition to the evil of the times, became an additional expression of the animosity and rancour of parties against each other.[5]

Marius, upon his expulsion from Rome, retired to his own villa at Salonium; and, being unprovided for a longer flight, sent his son to the farm of one Mutius, a friend in the neighbourhood, to procure what might be necessary for a voyage by sea. The young man was discovered at this place, and narrowly escaped in a waggon loaded with straw, which, the better to deceive his pursuers, was ordered to take the road to Rome. The father fled to Ostia, and there embarked on board a vessel which was provided for him by Numerius, who had been one of his partizans in the

2 Appian. de Bell. Civ. lib. 1.

3 Plutarch. in Mario, edit [illegible] p. 526.

4 Appian. de Bell. Civil. lib. i. p. 387. The names mentioned in this act of attainder or outlawry, were Sulpicius, Marius, father and son, P. Cethegus, Junius Brutus, Cneius and Pub. Granii, Albinovanus, Marcus Suetonius.

5 Velleius Paterculus, lib. ii. c 19.

ate troubles. Having put to sea, he was forced by stress of weather to Circeii, there landed in want of every necessary, and made himself known to some herdsmen, of whom he implored relief. Being informed of the parties that were abroad in pursuit of him, he concealed himself for the night in a neighbouring wood. Next day as he was within a few miles of the town of Minturnæ, he was alarmed at the sight of some horsemen, ran with all the speed he could make to the shore, and, with much difficulty, got on board of a boat which was passing. The persons with whom he thus took refuge resisted the threats and importunities of the pursuers to have him delivered up to them, or thrown into the sea; but having rowed him to a supposed place of safety, at the mouth of the Liris, they put him on shore, and left him to his fate. Here he first took refuge in a cottage, afterwards under a hollow bank of the river, and, last of all, on hearing the tread of the horsemen, who still pursued him, he plunged himself to the chin in the marsh; but, though concealed by the reeds and the depth of the water, he was discovered and dragged from thence all covered with mud. He was carried to Minturnæ, and doomed by the magistrates of the place to suffer the execution of the sentence which had been denounced against himself and his partizans at Rome. He was, however, by some connivance, allowed to escape from hence, again put to sea, and, at the island Ænaria, joined some associates of his flight. Being afterwards obliged to land in Sicily for a supply of water, and being known, he narrowly escaped with the loss of some of the crew that navigated his vessel. From thence he arrived on the coast of Africa; but, being forbid the province by the Prætor Sextilius, continued to shift his abode among the islands or places of retirement on the coast.[1]

Marius was in his seventieth year when he made this attempt to overturn the Roman republic by means of popular tumults, and when he strove to obtain the command of an army in the busiest and most arduous service which the Roman empire had then to offer. Being forced, by his miscarriage in this attempt, into the state of an outlaw, he still amused the world with adventures and escapes, which historians record with the embellishments of a picturesque and even romantic description. A Gaulish or German soldier, who was employed at Minturnæ to put him to death, overawed by his aspect, recoiled from the task; and the people of the place, as if moved by the miracle, concurred in aiding his escape.[2] The presence of such an exile on the ground where Carthage had stood, was supposed to increase the majesty, and the melancholy of the scene. "Go," he said to the lictor who brought him the orders of the prætor to depart, "tell him that you have seen Marius sitting on the ruins of Carthage."[3]

The senate, thus restored to its authority, and, by the suppression of the late sedition, masters of the city, took the proper measures to prevent, for the future, such violations of order introduced for popular government. They resolved that no question of legislation should be agitated in the assembly of the tribes;[4] and Sylla, before he left the city, thought proper to despatch the election of consuls for the following year, but did not employ the power, which he now possessed, to make the choice fall on persons who were both of the senatorian party. Together with Octavius, who had the authority of the senate at heart, he suffered Cinna, though of the opposite faction, to be chosen, and only exacted a promise from him not to disturb the public peace, nor, in his absence, to attempt any thing derogatory of his own honour.[5]

Having in this manner restored the common wealth, Sylla set out with his army for their destination in Greece. Quintus Rufus, the other consul of the preceding year, at the same time repaired to his province in the country of the Marsi, where, as has been mentioned, he was to succeed Cn. Strabo in the command of some legions; but being less agreeable to these troops than his predecessor, the soldiers mutinied upon his arrival, and put him to death. Cn. Strabo, though suspected of having connived with them in this horrid transaction, was permitted to profit by it in keeping his station. So quick was the succession of crimes which distressed the republic, that one disorder escaped with impunity, under the more atrocious effects of another which followed it.

U. C. 666.

L. Corn. Cinna, Cn. Octavius, Cons.

When Sylla was about to depart from the city, Virgilius, one of the tribunes, moved an impeachment against him for the illegal steps he had lately taken. But the state of the war with Mithridates was urgent, and Sylla took the benefit of the law of Memmius, by which persons named to command had a privilege to decline answering any charge which should be brought against them, when going on the service to which they were appointed.

The king of Pontus, notwithstanding he had been disappointed in his attempt upon Rhodes, was become master of the Lesser Asia, had fixed his residence at Pergamus, and employed his officers, with numerous fleets and armies, to carry on the war in different quarters, making rapid acquisitions at once on the side of the Scythian and Thracian Bosphorus in Macedonia and in Greece. His general, Archelaus, had reduced most of the Greek islands, and was hastening to make himself master of the Grecian continent. Delos had revolted, and thrown off the yoke of Athens, at the time that it fell into the hands of this general. The king proposed to make use of it as a decoy to bring the Athenians themselves under his power. For this purpose he pretended a desire to restore the island, with the treasure he had seized there, to its former masters; and sent Aristion, a native of Athens, but now an officer in his own service, with an escort of two thousand men, to deliver this treasure into their hands. Aristion, being, under this pretence, received into the Piræus, continued to hold this place, with the city of Athens itself, for Mithridates, and, by means of the forces he assembled in Attica, soon after overran Bœotia, Achaia, and Laconia.

To these powerful encroachments on the Roman territory, and to the personal injuries done

1 Plutarch. in Mario, edit. Lond. p. 534.
2 Velleius Pater. lib. ii. c. 19.
3 Plutarch. in Mario.
4 Appian. de Bell. Civ. lib. 1.
5 L. Florus, lib. iii. c. 21. Appian. de Bell. Civ lib. 1

to such of their generals as had fallen into his hands, Mithridates had joined a barbarous outrage, that roused, in the highest degree, the resentment of the Roman people. He had sent orders to all his commanders in every town and station in Asia, on a day fixed, to begin a massacre of the Roman citizens that were any where settled in that country, and to publish a reward for the slaves of any Roman who should succeed in destroying their master. This order was executed with marks of insult, in which the instruments of cruelty are often apt to exceed their instructions. It is particularly mentioned, that at Ephesus, Pergamus, and other cities of Asia, entire families, taking refuge in the temples, and embracing the altars, infants with their parents, and without distinction of sex or age, were dragged from thence and murdered. The number of persons that perished in this massacre, if ever known, is no where mentioned.[6]

The resentment which was natural on this occasion, together with the real danger that threatened the empire, fully justified the contempt with which Sylla treated the impeachment of Virgilius, and the celerity with which he left the city of Rome. Having transported to Dyrachium an army of six legions, he took the route of Thessaly and Ætolia; and having raised in these countries contributions for the pay and subsistence of his army, he received the submission of the Bœotians, who had lately been obliged to declare for Mithridates, and advanced to Athens, where Aristion in the city, and Archelaus in the Piræus, were prepared to make a vigorous resistance. Mithridates, who was master of the sea, collected together, all the troops which he had distributed in the islands, and ordered a great reinforcement from Asia to form an army on the side of Bœotia for the relief of Athens.

Sylla, to prevent the enemy, hastened the siege of this place. He first made an attempt to force his way into the Piræus by scaling the walls; but being repulsed, had recourse to the ordinary means of attack. He erected towers, and raised them to the height of the battlements, got upon the same level with the besieged, and plied his missiles from thence. He shook the walls with battering engines, or undermined them with galleries, and made places of arms for his men, near to where he expected to open a breach. But the defence of the place was vigorous and obstinate, and so well conducted, that he was obliged, after many fruitless efforts, to turn the siege into a blockade, and to await the effects of famine, by which the city began already to be pressed.

It was in a little time brought to the last extremity. Those who were confined within the walls had consumed all the herbage, and killed all the animals that were to be found in the place; they were reduced to feed on the implements of leather, or other materials that could be turned into sustenance, and came at last to prey upon the carcases of the dead. The garrison was greatly diminished in numbers; and of those who remained, the greater part was dispirited and weak: but Aristion, expecting for himself no quarter from the Roman general, still showed no desire to capitulate; when Sylla, knowing the weak state to which the besieged were reduced, made a vigorous effort, stormed and forced the walls with great slaughter. Aristion, who had retired into the Acropolis, was soon afterwards taken and slain.

Archelaus, likewise greatly distressed in the Piræus, found means to escape by water, and hastened to join the army that was forming on the side of Thessaly; leaving the post he abandoned to fall into the hands of Sylla, who razed its fortifications to the ground.

The army of Mithridates advanced into Bœotia. Every part of it was sumptuously provided with all that was necessary for subsistence or parade. There was a numerous cavalry richly caparisoned; an infantry of every description, variously armed, some to use missile weapons, others to engage in close fight; a large train of armed chariots, which, being winged with scythes, threatened to sweep the plains. The whole army amounted to about a hundred and twenty thousand men. But their master, with all his ability, it appears, relied, in the manner of barbarous nations, more on their numbers than he did on their order, or on the conduct of their officers. Sylla was to oppose them with thirty thousand men.

On this inferior enemy Archelaus continually pressed with all his forces, and endeavoured to bring on a general action, which Sylla cautiously avoided; waiting for an opportunity that migh deprive the enemy of the advantage they had in the superiority of their numbers. The armies being both in Bœotia, Archelaus inadvertently took post near Cheronea, on the ascent of a steep hill that was formed into terraces by ledges of rocks, and which terminated at last in a peak or narrow summit. On the face of this hill he had crowded his infantry, his cavalry, and his chariots, and trusted that, although the ground was unfavourable to such an army, it was still inaccessible, and could not be reached by an enemy.

While Archelaus believed himself secure in this position, Sylla continued to observe him from the post he had fortified at a little distance; and was told by some natives of the country, that the hill which the enemy had occupied might be ascended in their rear, and that any part of his army might be safely conducted to the summit. Upon this information he made a disposition to engage, placed his main body against the enemy in front, and, that he might throw them into confusion by a double attack, sent a powerful detachment, with proper guides, to seize on the heights above their encampment.

The unexpected appearance of Sylla's detachment in the rear produced the alarm that was intended. Their impetuous descent from the hill drove in confusion all who came in their way from thence to the camp. The rear fell down on the front. A great uproar and tumult arose in every part. And in this critical moment Sylla began his attack, and broke into the midst of enemies who were altogether unprepared to receive him. They were crowded in a narrow space, and mixed without any distinction of separate bodies of officers or men; and, under the disadvantage of their ground, could neither resist nor retire. In the centre, numbers being trod under foot by those who crowded around them, perished by violence or suffocation; or, while they endeavoured to open a way to escape, were slain by each other's swords. Of a hundred and twenty thousand men, scarcely ten thousand

6 Appian. de Bell. Mithrid. p. 585, 586.

could be assembled at Chalcis in Eubœa, the place to which Archelaus directed his flight. Of the Romans, at the end of the action, only fifteen men were missing, and of these two returned on the following day.[1]

Archelaus, even after this rout of his army, being still master at sea, drew supplies from Asia and from the neighbouring islands; and, being secure in his retreat in Eubœa, made frequent descents on the neighbouring coasts. While Sylla endeavoured to cover the lands of Bœotia and Attica from these incursions, Mithridates made great efforts to replace his army in that country; and in a little time had transported thither eighty thousand fresh troops under Dorilaus, to whom Archelaus joined himself with those he had saved from the late disaster. The new army of Mithridates, consisting chiefly of cavalry, was greatly favoured by the nature of the ground in Bœotia, which was flat and abounding in forage. Sylla, though inclined to keep the heights on which he was least exposed to the enemy's cavalry, was obliged, in order to cover the country from which he drew his subsistence and forage, to descend to the plains in the neighbourhood of Orchomenos. There he took post among the marshes, and endeavoured to fortify himself with deep ditches against the enemy's horse. While his works were yet unfinished, being attacked by the Asiatic cavalry, not only the labourers, but the troops that were placed under arms to cover the workmen, were seized with a panic, and fled. Sylla, having for some time in vain endeavoured to rally them, laid hold of an ensign, and rushed in despair on the enemy. "To me," he said, "it is glorious to fall in this place: but for you, if you are asked where you deserted your leader, you may say, at Orchomenos." Numbers who heard this reproach returned to the charge with their general; and wherever they presented themselves, stopped the career of the enemy, and put them to flight. The Roman army at length recovered itself in every part of the field; and Sylla remounting his horse, took the full advantage of the change of his fortune, pursued the enemy to their camp, and forced them to abandon it with great slaughter.

After the loss of this second army, Mithridates appears to have despaired of his affairs in Greece; he suffered Sylla to enter into quiet possession of his winter quarters in Thessaly, and authorised Archelaus to treat of peace.

Both parties were equally inclined to a treaty; the king of Pontus urged by his losses, and the Roman proconsul by the state of affairs in Italy. Sylla, though commanding in Greece by authority from the Roman senate, had been degraded, and declared a public enemy by a resolution of the people at Rome. An officer had been sent from Italy to supersede him; and a Roman army, independent of his orders, was actually employed in the province. Mithridates, too, while he had sustained such losses in Greece, was pressed by the other Roman army in Asia, under the command of Fimbria, who, with intentions equally hostile to Sylla as to Mithridates, advanced with a rapid pace, reduced several towns on the coast, and had lately made himself master of Pergamus, where the king himself had narrowly escaped falling into his hands. In these circumstances a treaty was equally seasonable for both.

Sylla had been absent from Rome about two years, during which time, having no supplies from thence, he had supported the war by the contributions which he had raised in Greece, Ætolia, and Thessaly, and with the money he had coined from the plate and treasure of the Grecian temples.[2] The republic, in the mean time, had been in the possession of his enemies, and the authority of the senate was, in a great measure, suppressed. Soon after he left the city, Cinna, notwithstanding his engagements to Sylla, revived the project of keeping the more respectable citizens in subjection, under pretence of a government placed in the hands of the people.

The designation of the popular party was the same with that which had distinguished the followers of Tiberius and Caius Gracchus; but the object was changed, and the nominal popular faction itself was differently composed. Formerly this faction consisted of the populace of Rome and of the poorer citizens, opposed to the noble and the rich. The objects for which they at that time contended, were the distribution of corn, new settlements, or the division of lands. At present the parties consisted of the inhabitants of the country towns lately admitted, or still claiming to be admitted, on the rolls of the people on one side, and of the senate and ancient citizens on the other. The object to which the former aspired, was a full and equal participation in all the powers that belonged to the Roman people. They were far from being satisfied with the manner of their enrolment into a few particular tribes, and laid claim to be admitted without distinction among the ancient citizens, and to have consideration and power proportioned to their numbers. In this they were supported by Cinna, who made a motion in their favour in the assembly of the people, and at the same time proposed to recall Marius and the other exiles of that party from their banishment. The consul Octavius, with the majority of the senate and ancient citizens, opposed these propositions; but Cinna was likely to have a powerful support in the new people that flocked to him from the country towns, and in the friends of the exiles. On the day of assembly, multitudes of the new citizens took possession of the place of meeting, and were observed to be armed with daggers or short swords. Octavius was attended at his house by a numerous assembly of the ancient citizens, who were armed in the same manner, and waited to take such measures as the necessity of the case might require. Being told that the tribunes who had forbidden the question were violently attacked, and likely to be forced from the assembly, they came forth into the streets, and drove their antagonists, with some bloodshed, through the gates of the city. Cinna endeavoured to make head against his colleague, and invited the slaves, under a promise of liberty, to his standard. But finding it impossible within the city, that was occupied by his opponents, to withstand their force, he withdrew to the country towns, and solicited supplies from thence. He passed through Tibur and Præneste to Nola, and openly implored the inhabitants to aid him against their common enemies. On this occasion he was attended by Sertorius, and by

1 For this fact Plutarch quotes the Memoirs of Sylla.

2 Plutarch. in Sylla et Lucullo.

some other senators who had embarked in the same ruinous faction. Their solicitations at any other time might perhaps have been fruitless; but now, to the misfortune of the republic, a number of armies were still kept on foot in Italy, to finish the remains of the social war. Cn. Strabo commanded one army in Umbria, Metellus another on the confines of Lucania and Samnium, and Appius Claudius a third in Campania. These armies consisted chiefly of indigent citizens, become soldiers of fortune, were very much at the disposal of their leaders, in whose name they had been levied, to whom they had sworn the military oath, and on whom they depended for the settlements and rewards which they were taught to expect at the end of their services. They were inclined to take part in the cause of any faction that was likely, by the expulsion and forfeiture of one part of the city, to make way for preferments and fortunes to the other.

Cinna distrusted Pompey and Metellus; but hoping for a better reception from Appius Claudius, he repaired to the camp of this general, and had the address to gain the troops who were under his command.

Octavius and Merula. Mean time the senate, without entering into any particular discussion of the guilt which Cinna had incurred in the late tumult at Rome, found that, by having deserted his station, he had actually divested himself of his office as consul, and they obtained the election of L. Cornelius Merula in his place.

Marius, being informed that one of the armies in Italy, with a Roman consul at its head, was prepared to support him, made haste from his exile in Africa: he landed in Tuscany, was joined by numbers, and had an offer of being vested with the ensigns of proconsul. But intending to move indignation or pity, he declined every privilege of a Roman citizen, until the sentence of attainder or banishment, which had been pronounced against him, should be reversed. In the manner practised by suppliants, with a mean habit and ghastly figure, to which he was reduced by the distress of his exile, he presented himself to the people; but with a countenance, says his historian, which, being naturally stern, now rather seemed terrible than piteous.[3] He implored the protection of the country towns, in whose cause he too pretended to have suffered, and whose interests were now embarked on the same bottom with his own. He had many partizans among those who had composed the legions which formerly served under his orders. He had reputation and authority, and soon assembled a considerable force, with which, in concert with Cinna, with Sertorius and Carbo, he advanced towards Rome.

They invested the city in three separate divisions. Cinna and Carbo lay before it, Sertorius took post on the river above, and Marius below it. The last, to prevent supplies from the sea, made himself master of the port of Ostia; the first had sent a detachment to Arminium, to prevent any relief from the side of Gaul.

In this extremity the senate applied to Metellus, requesting that he would make any accommodation with the Italian allies, and hasten to the relief of the city. The delays which he made in the execution of hese orders enabled Cinna and Marius to prevent him in gaining the allies. The inhabitants of Italy at this time had it in their option to accept the privileges they claimed from either party; and, having chosen to join themselves with the popular faction, they threw their weight into that scale.

Metellus, however, advanced into Latium; and, being joined by the consul Octavius, took post on the Alban hill. Here they found that their troops, being inclined to favour their enemies, deserted apace. Metellus, being reduced to a few attendants, despaired of the cause, and withdrew into Africa. Octavius returned to his station in the city.

The army lately commanded by Pompeius Strabo, was now deprived of its general; he having been killed by lightning in his camp. And the senate was not inclined to repose any confidence in his men. He himself had some time hesitated between the parties; and the troops, at his death, were prepared to choose the side which was most likely to favour their interest. With so uncertain a prospect of support, the senate thought it safer to enter into a treaty with Cinna and Marius than to remain exposed to the necessity of being obliged to admit them by force. They offered to reinstate Cinna in the office of consul, and to restore Marius, with the other exiles, to their condition of Roman citizens; only stipulating that they would spare the blood of their opponents, or proceed against them according to the laws of the commonwealth. While this treaty was in dependance, Marius, affecting the modesty of a person whom the law, according to his late sentence of banishment, had disqualified to take any part among citizens, observed a sullen and obstinate silence. Even when the treaty was concluded, and the gates were laid open to himself and his followers, he refused to enter until the attainder under which he lay should be taken off, and until he was replaced in his condition as a Roman. The people were accordingly assembled to repeal their former decree. But Marius, proposing to take his enemies by surprise, did not wait for the completion of the ceremony. While the ballots were collecting, he entered the city with a band of armed men, whom he employed in taking vengeance on all those who had concurred in the late measures against him. The gates, by his orders, were secured, but most of the senators escaped. Sylla's house was demolished, many who were reputed his friends were slain, others assisted his wife and his children in making their escape. Among the signals by which Marius directed the execution of particular persons, it was understood that if he did not return a salute which was offered him, this was to be considered as a warrant for immediate death. In compliance with these instructions, some citizens of note were laid dead at his feet. And as the meanest retainers of his party had their resentments as well as himself, and took this opportunity to indulge their passions, the city resembled a place that was taken by storm, and every quarter resounded with the cries of robbery, murders, and rapes. This horrid scene continued without intermission five days and five nights.

The following are the names of a few of the principal senators who suffered: the consul Octavius was murdered in his robes of office, and in

3 Plutarch. in Mario.

presence of his lictors; two senators of the name of Cæsar, Caius and Lucius; two of the name of Crassus, the father and the son, who, attempting to escape, but likely to be taken, fell by their own hands; Attilius Serranus, Publius Lentulus, C. Numitorius, M. Bæbius, whose bodies, fastened on a hook, were dragged by a rope through the streets; Marcus Antonius, one of the first Roman senators, who had betaken himself entirely or chiefly to civil arts, and is known therefore by the name of the Orator; this senator being discovered in a place of concealment, was killed by assassins sent for the purpose. The heads of the others were exposed on the rostra; that of Antonius was placed on the table of Marius, who bore him, it seems, a peculiar degree of animosity and rancour. Catulus, once the colleague of Marius in the consulate, partner in his last and most decisive victory over the Cimbri, and without question one of the most respectable senators of the age, was included in the warrant for general execution. Marius being solicited in his favour, made answer, He must die. And this victim, choosing to avoid by a voluntary death the insults likely to be offered to him by his enemies, having shut himself up, with a brasier of burning coals, in a close chamber which was recently plastered, perished by suffocation.

Merula, the Flamen Dialis, whose name, without his own knowledge, had been inscribed consul in place of that of Cinna, now likewise, willing to maintain the dignity of his station, opened his arteries at the shrine of Jupiter, whose priest he was, sprinkled the statue of the god with his blood; on feeling the approach of death, he tore from his head the apex or crest of the order, which, by the maxims of religion, he always carried while alive, but with which on his head it would have been impious and ominous to die, and took those who were present to witness of the exactness with which he performed this duty.

Cinna himself became weary of the murders which were committed to gratify the avarice of mean and needy adventurers, or the rancour even of fugitive slaves against the masters they had deserted; he wished to terminate so horrid a scene, but it seems could not stop it otherwise than by the death of those who were employed in it. He caused great numbers of them accordingly to be surrounded and put to the sword. He proposed, in concert with Marius, to give some form or title to their government, by assuming the consulate: and although there is no doubt that they could have easily obtained the sanction of an ordinary election, yet they chose to usurp the ensigns and powers of consul without any such pretence.[1] Marius, while he took the title of consul, continued to act like a chief of banditti, connived at the disorders that were committed by his military retainers, and continued still to superintend the execution of the orders which he had given on his first entry into the city, to put his opponents to death.

In the midst of these crimes, however, the name of Sylla, and the fame of his victories in Greece, gave continual presage of a just retribution. Marius was agitated with nocturnal fears, and gave signs of a distracted mind. Some one, he imagined, in the words of a poet, continually sounded in his ears, "Horrid is the dying lion's den;" which being applied to himself, seemed to announce his approaching dissolution. He took to the excessive use of wine, contracted a pleurisy, and died on the seventh day of his illness, in the seventeenth day of his last or seventh consulate, and in the seventieth year of his age; leaving the tools he had employed in subverting the government of his country, to pay the forfeit of his crimes.

Livy, it appears,[2] had made it a question, whether Marius had been most useful to his country as a soldier, or pernicious as a citizen. It has happened unfortunately for his fame, that he closed the scene of life with examples of the latter kind. In what degree he retained his genius or abilities cannot be known. His insatiable thirst of power, like avarice in the case of other persons, seemed to grow with age. His hatred of the nobles, contracted in the obscurity of his early life, remained with him after he himself had laid the amplest foundations of nobility in his own family. And he died in an attempt to extinguish all just or regular government in the blood of those who only were qualified or disposed to sustain it.

Upon the death of Marius, the government still continued to be usurped by Cinna. Many of the senators, and other citizens, obnoxious to the prevailing party, took refuge with Sylla. This general himself was declared a public enemy; his effects were seized; his children, with their mother, having narrowly escaped the pursuit of his enemies, fled to the father in Greece.

Upon this occasion Sylla did not change his conduct in the war, nor make any concessions to the enemies of the state. He talked familiarly every day of his intention to punish his enemies at Rome, and to avenge the blood of his friends, but not till he had forced Mithridates to make reparation for the wrongs he had done to the Romans and to their allies in Asia.

Alarmed by these threats, Cinna took measures to strengthen his party; assumed, upon the death of Marius, Valerius Flaccus as his colleague in the office of consul; and, having assigned him the command in Asia, with two additional legions, trusted that with this force he might obtain possession of the province.

But Flaccus, upon his arrival in Thessaly, was deserted by part of the army, which went over to Sylla; and passing through Macedonia in his route to Asia with the remainder, a dispute arose between himself and his lieutenant Fimbria, which ended in the murder of the consul Flaccus, and in the succession of Fimbria to the command. So little deference or respect did citizens pay, in the disorder of those unhappy times, even to the government they professed to serve.

Fimbria, with the troops he had seduced to his standard, after he had assassinated their general, made a rapid progress in Asia, and hastened, as has been observed, the resolution to which Mithridates was come, of applying for peace. To this crafty prince, urged by the necessity of his own affairs, the conjuncture appeared to be favourable, when so much distraction took place in the councils of Rome. He had experienced the abilities of Sylla; he knew his eager desire to be gone for

1 Livy, Epitome, lib. viii.

2 Livy, Epitome, lib. viii. Appian. de Bell. Civil lib. i. Plutarch. in Mario. Florus, lib. iii. c. 21 Velleius Pater. lib. ii. c. 19. &c. Dio Cass. in Fragmentis.

Italy, and to be revenged of his enemies; and he expected to gain him by proffering assistance in the war he was about to wage with the opposite party at Rome.

Upon a message from Archelaus, Sylla readily agreed to an interview in the island of Delos; and here being told, in the name of Mithridates, that he should have money, troops, and shipping to make a descent on Italy, provided he would enter into a confederacy with the king of Pontus, and make war on the Romans, by whom he was now proscribed, Sylla, in his turn, proposed to Archelaus to desert Mithridates, to deliver up the fleet and the army which was under his command, and to rely for protection and reward on the faith of the Romans. They will speedily seat you, he said, on the throne of Pontus. Archelaus having rejected this proposal with horror, "And you," says Sylla, "the slave, or (if you prefer that title) the friend of a barbarous tyrant, will not betray your trust, and yet to me have the presumption to propose an act of perfidy. The fields of Cheronea and Orchomenos should have made you better acquainted with the character of the Romans."

Upon this reply Archelaus saw the necessity of purchasing the treaty he was instructed to make, and accordingly made the following concessions:

That the fleet of Pontus, consisting of seventy galleys, should be delivered up to the Romans.

That the garrisons should be withdrawn from all places which had been seized in the course of this war.

That the Roman province in Asia, together with Paphlagonia, Bithynia, and Cappadocia should be evacuated, and the frontier of Pontus, for the future, be the boundary of Mithridates's territory.

That the Romans should receive two thousand talents,[3] to reimburse their expense in the war.

That prisoners should be restored, and all deserters delivered up.

While these articles were sent to Mithridates for his ratification, Sylla in no degree relaxed the measures he had taken to secure and facilitate the passage of his army into Asia. He sent Lucullus[4] round the maritime powers of the East to assemble a fleet; and, after having made some incursions into Thrace, to gratify his army with the spoil of nations who had often plundered the Roman province, he continued his route to the Hellespont, and was met in his way by the messengers of Mithridates, who informed him that their master agreed to all the articles proposed, except to that which related to the cession of Paphlagonia; and at the same time made a merit of the preference he had given to Sylla in this treaty; as he might have obtained more favourable terms from Fimbria. "That is a traitor," said Sylla, "whom I shall speedily punish for his crimes. As for your master, I shall know, upon my arrival in Asia, whether he chooses to have peace or war."

Being arrived at the Hellespont, he was joined by Lucullus with a fleet which enabled him to pass that strait. Here he was met by another message from Mithridates, desiring a personal interview; which was accordingly held in the presence of both armies, and at which the king of Pontus, after some expostulations, agreed to all the conditions already mentioned. In this he probably acted from policy, as well as from the necessity he felt in the present state of his affairs. He still hoped, in consequence of this treaty, to turn the arms of Sylla against the Romans, and trusted that the peace he obtained for himself in Asia was to be the beginning of a war in Italy, more likely to distress his enemies than any efforts he himself could make against them. With this reasonable prospect he retired into his own kingdom of Pontus; and there, strengthening himself by alliances and the acquisition of territory on the northern coasts of the Euxine, he prepared to take advantage of future emergencies, and to profit by the state of confusion into which the affairs of the Romans were hastening.

Sylla, having brought the Mithridatic war to an issue so honourable for himself, and having every where gratified his army with the spoils of their enemies, being possessed of a considerable sum of money and a numerous fleet, and being secure of the attachment of the soldiers, who had experienced his liberality, and rested their hopes of fortune on the success of his future enterprizes, prepared to take vengeance on his enemies, and those of the republic in Italy. He proceeded, however, with great deliberation and caution; and, as if the state at Rome were in perfect tranquillity, staid to reduce the army of Fimbria, to resettle the Roman province, and to effect the restoration of the allies, Nicomedes and Ariobarzanes, to their several kingdoms of Cappadocia and Bithynia.

Fimbria being required by Sylla to resign a command which he had illegally usurped, retorted the charge of usurpation, and treated Sylla himself as an outlaw: but upon the approach of this general, being deserted by his army, he fled to Pergamus, and there put an end to his life by the hands of a slave, of whom he exacted this service. To punish the province of Asia for its defection to Mithridates, Sylla obliged the inhabitants to pay down a sum equal to five years' ordinary tax. He sent Curio to replace on their thrones the kings of Cappadocia and Bithynia, who had persevered in their alliance with Rome, and sent an account of these particulars to the senate, without taking any notice of the edict by which he himself had been stripped of his command, and declared an enemy.[5] Before he set sail, however, for Italy, he thought proper to transmit to Rome a memorial, setting forth his services and his wrongs, as well as the injury done to many senators who had taken refuge in his camp, and concluding with menaces of justice against his own enemies and those of the republic, but assuring the citizens in general of protection and security. This paper being read in the senate, struck many of the members with dreadful apprehensions; expedients were proposed to reconcile the parties, and to avert the evils which the republic must suffer from their repeated contentions. A message was sent to pacify Sylla, and earnest intreaties were made to Cinna, that he would suspend his levies until an answer could be obtained from the other. But Cinna, in contempt of these pacific intentions,
U. C. 669. took measures to prosecute the war; divided the fasces with Cn. Papirius

3 About 386,000*l.*

4 Vide Plutarch. in Lucullo.

5 Appian. de Bell Mithridat. Plutarch. in Syll

L. Cornelius Cinna 4to. Cn Papirius Carbo.

Carbo, whom without any form of election, he assumed for his colleague in consulate; and in the partition of provinces, retained for himself the administration in Italy, while he assigned to Carbo the command in the neighbouring Gaul. These titular magistrates, with all the adherents of their faction, applied in great haste to the raising of men, and securing the fidelity of the towns within the several divisions which they had received in charge.

Carbo exacted hostages for their good behaviour from all the towns in his district; but as he had not authority from the senate for this measure, he found himself unable to give it effect. To Castricius, the chief magistrate of Placentia, a person of great age, who refused to comply, he said, "Have not I your life in my power?" "And have not I," said the other, "already lived long enough?"[1]

Cinna, however, having mustered a considerable force, intended to make head against Sylla in Thessaly, through which he was expected to pass in his way to Italy, and determined to transport his army thither. But the troops being averse to embark, he himself, endeavouring to force them, was killed in a mutiny. A general disorder and anarchy infected the whole party. The election of a successor to Cinna was twice interrupted by supposed unfavourable presages, and Carbo remained sole consul.

At this time an answer arrived from Sylla to the proposals made by the senate towards a reconciliation of parties; in which he declared, "That he never could return into friendship with persons guilty of so many and such enormous crimes. If the Roman people, however, were pleased to grant an indemnity, he should not interpose, but would venture to affirm, that such of the citizens as chose, in the present disorders, to take refuge in his camp, would find themselves safer than in that of his enemy's." He had embarked his army at Ephesus, and in three days reached the Piræus, the port of Athens. Here he was taken ill of the gout, and was advised to use the hot baths at Adipsus; at which he accordingly passed some time with great appearance of ease, amusing himself with buffoons and ordinary company, as if he had no affair of any consequence in contemplation. His fleet, in the mean time, consisting of twelve hundred ships, coasted round the Peloponnesus, and took on board the army which had marched by Thessaly to Dyrachium. Being apprehensive that some part of the legions, upon landing in Italy, and with so near a prospect of returning to their homes, might desert, or, trusting to their consequence in a civil war, might become disorderly and distress the inhabitants, he exacted a special oath, by which every man bound himself, upon his arrival in Italy, to abide by his colours, and to observe the strictest order in his march through the country. The troops, wishing to remove all the remains of a distrust which had suggested this precaution, made a voluntary offer of a contribution towards the support of the war; and Sylla, without accepting the favour, set sail with the additional confidence which this proof of attachment in the army inspired.

He had, according to Appian, five Roman legions, with six thousand Italian horse, and considerable levies from Macedonia and Greece amounting in all to about sixty thousand men With this force he landed in Italy, in the face of many different armies, each of them equal or superior in number to his own. The opposite party were supposed to have on foot at different stations, above two hundred thousand men.

U. C. 670.

L. Corn. Scipio, C. Jun. Norbanus.

L. Cornelius Scipio and C. Junius Norbanus, who were its leaders, being in possession of the capitol and of the place of election, were named for consuls. Norbanus, in the name of the republic, commanded a great army in Apulia; Scipio, another on the confines of Campania. Sertorius, young Marius, with Carbo, in the quality of proconsul, and others (as Plutarch quotes from the memoirs of Sylla,) to the number of fifteen commanders, had each their armies, amounting in all to four hundred and fifty cohorts;[2] of these different bodies none attempted to dispute the landing of Sylla, nor for some days to interrupt his march.

He accordingly continued to advance as in a friendly country, and in the midst of profound peace. The inhabitants of Italy, considering the Roman nobility, in whose cause Sylla appeared, as averse to the claim they had made of being promiscuously enrolled in the tribes of Rome, were likely to oppose him, and to favour the faction which had for some time prevailed in the state. To allay their animosity, or to prevent their taking an active part against him, Sylla summoned the leading men of the country towns as he passed, and gave them assurances that he would confirm the grants which had been made to them, if they did not forfeit these and every other title to favour, by abetting the faction which had subverted the government.

On his march he was joined by Metellus Pius, who, as has been observed, after a fruitless attempt, in conjunction with the consul Octavius, to cover Rome from the attack of Marius and Cinna, had withdrawn to Africa; and being forced from thence by Fabius, returned into Italy. Being in Liguria, where he still retained the character of proconsul, he endeavoured to keep some forces on foot, and to sustain the hopes of his party, when so great a change was made in their favour by the arrival of the army from Greece.

Sylla was likewise, about the same time, joined by Cneius Pompeius, son to the late consul Pompeius Strabo, who, though too young for any public character, had assembled a considerable body of men to make himself of consequence in the present contest. Being now only about nineteen years of age, he was remarked for engaging manners, and a manly aspect, which procured him a general favour and an uncommon degree of respect.[3] This distinction being unsought for, was possibly considered by him as his birth-right, and gave him an early impression of that superiority to his fellow-citizens which he continued to assume through the whole of his life. He had served in those legions with which Cinna intended to have carried the war against Sylla into Asia or Greece; but, being averse to the party, he withdrew when the army was about to embark, and disappearing suddenly, was supposed to have

1 Val. Max. lib. vi. c. 2.

2 About 225,000 men.

3. Plutarch. in Mario

been murdered by the order of Cinna, a suspicion, which, among other circumstances, incited the soldiers to that mutiny in which the general was killed. Sylla appears himself to have been won by the promising aspect of this young man, and received him with distinguishing marks of regard.

Numbers of the senate and nobles, who had hitherto remained exposed at Rome to the insults of their enemies, now repaired to the camp of Sylla. The consul Norbanus, being joined by young Marius, lay at Canusium. Sylla, while he was preparing to attack them, sent an officer with overtures of peace; these they rejected with marks of contempt. This circumstance had an effect which Sylla perhaps foresaw and intended. It roused the indignation of his army, and, in the action which followed, had some effect in obtaining a victory in which six thousand[4] of the enemy were killed, with the loss of only seventy men to himself.

Norbanus, after this defeat, retreated to Capua; and, being covered by the walls of that place, waited the arrival of Scipio, who intended to join him with the army under his command. Sylla marched to Teanum to prevent their junction; and, on the approach of Scipio, proposed to negotiate. The leaders, with a few attendants, met between the two armies, and were nearly agreed upon terms of peace; but Scipio delayed his final consent until he should consult with Norbanus at Capua. Sertorius was accordingly despatched to inform Norbanus of what had passed, and hostilities were to be suspended until his return; but this messenger, probably averse to the treaty, broke the truce, by seizing a post at Suessa which had been occupied by Sylla; and the negotiation had no other effect than that of giving the troops of both armies, as well as their leaders, an opportunity of conferring together; a circumstance which, in civil wars, is always dangerous to one or other of the parties. In this case the popularity of Sylla prevailed; and the soldiers of his army, boasting of the wealth which they had acquired under their general, infected his enemies, and seduced them to desert their leader. Scipio was left almost alone in his camp; but Sylla, receiving the troops who deserted to him, made no attempt to seize their general, suffered him to escape, and, with the accession of strength he had acquired by the junction of this army, continued his march towards Rome. Norbanus at the same time evacuated Capua, and, by forced marches in a different route, endeavoured to prevent him.

About this time, Sertorius, who, before the war broke out, had, in the distribution of provinces, been appointed propraetor of Spain, despairing of affairs in Italy, in which probably he was not sufficiently consulted, repaired to his province, and determined to try what the genius of a Roman leader could effect at the head of the warlike natives of that country.

The chiefs of the Marian party, who remained in Italy, made efforts to collect all the forces they could at Rome. Carbo, upon hearing that the army of Scipio was seduced to desert their general, said, "We have to do with a lion and a fox, of which the fox is probably the more dangerous enemy of the two."

Norbanus, soon after his arrival in the city, procured an edict of the people, by which Metellus, and the others who had joined Sylla, were declared enemies to their country. About the same time a fire broke out in the capitol, and the buildings were burned to the ground. Various suspicions were entertained of the cause; but as no party had any interest in this event, it was probably accidental, and served only to agitate the minds of the people, prone to superstition, and apt to find alarming presages in every uncommon event.

The remainder of the season was spent by both parties in collecting their forces from every quarter of Italy, and the term of the consuls in office being nearly expired, Carbo procured his own nomination to succeed them, and inscribed the name of Marius, scarcely twenty years of age, as his colleague. This young man is by some said to have been the nephew, by others the adopted son, of the late celebrated C. Marius, whose name had so long been terrible to the enemies, and at length not less so to the friends, of Rome.

U. C. 671.
C. Marius,
Cn. Pap. Carbo.

At this time the senate consented to have the plate and ornaments of the temples coined for the pay of the supposed consular armies. They were, however, notwithstanding this act of obsequiousness, believed to incline to the opposite party, and not to be trusted in case the city were attacked. The members being assembled together by orders of the prætors, Damasippus and Brutus, the most suspected, were taken aside and put to death; of this number, Quintus Mucius Scævola, Pontifex Maximus, flying to the temple in which he was accustomed to discharge his sacred office, was killed in the porch.

The military operations of the following spring began with an obstinate fight between two considerable armies commanded by Metellus and Carinas. The latter being defeated with great loss, Carbo hastened to the scene of action, in order to cover the remains of the vanquished army.

In the mean time Sylla, being encamped at Setia, and having intelligence that the young Marius was advancing against him, put his army in motion to meet him, forced him back to Sacriportum, near Præneste, where an action soon after ensued, in which Marius was defeated.

The routed army having fled in disorder to Præneste, the first who arrived were received into the place; but as it was apprehended the enemy might likewise enter in the tumult, the gates were shut, and many, being excluded, were slaughtered under the ramparts. Marius himself escaped, by a rope which was let down from the battlements to hoist him over the walls.

In consequence of this victory Sylla invested Præneste; and as great numbers were thus suddenly cooped up in a town, which was not prepared to subsist them, he had an immediate prospect of seeing them reduced to the necessity of surrendering at discretion. Committing the charge of the blockade to Lucretius Ofella, he himself, with part of the army, proceeded to Rome. Metellus, in a second action, had defeated the army of Carbo, and Pompey that of Marius near Sena; and the party of Sylla being victorious in every part of Italy, the city was prepared to receive him as soon as he appeared at the gates. The partizans of the opposite faction withdrew and left him master of the capital.

4 Plutarch. in Syll. edit. Londin. p 83

Sylla having posted his army in the field of Mars, he himself entered the city, and calling an assembly of the people, delivered an harangue, in which he imputed the disorder of the times to the injustice and cruelty of a few factious men, who had overturned the government, and sacrificed the best blood of the republic to their ambition and to their personal resentments. He exhorted all well-disposed men to be of good courage, and assured them that they should soon see the republic restored. In the mean time, he gratified his army with the spoils of the opposite party, declaring the effects of all those to be forfeited who had been accessary to the crimes lately committed against the state. After this first specimen of his policy in the city, leaving a sufficient force to execute his orders, he hastened to Clusium, where Carbo, being joined by a considerable reinforcement from Spain, was preparing to recover the metropolis, or to relieve his colleague Marius, who was reduced to great distress in Præneste.

The events which followed the arrival and operations of Sylla in Tuscany were various, but for the most part unfavourable to Carbo, whose force, by desertions and the sword, was declining apace. The issue of the war seemed to depend on the fate of Præneste, and the whole force of the party was therefore directed to the relief of that place. The Lucanians and Samnites, who had espoused the cause of Marius, and who, by his favour, had obtained the freedom of Rome, apprehending immediate ruin to themselves, in the suppression of a party by whom they had been protected, determined to make one great effort for the relief of Marius.

They were joined in Latium by a large detachment sent by Carbo, under Carinas and Marcius, and made an attempt to force the lines of the besiegers at Præneste, and to open the blockade of that place. But having failed in this design, they turned, with desperation, on the city of Rome, which was but slightly guarded by a small detachment which had been left for that purpose. Sylla being informed of their intention, with hasty marches advanced to the city, and found the enemy already in possession of the suburbs, and preparing to force the gates.

It was about four in the afternoon when he arrived, after a long march. Some of his officers proposed, that the troops, being fatigued, should have a little time to repose themselves; and that, for this purpose, they should remain on the ramparts until the following day. Sylla, however, proposing, by his unexpected presence, and by coming to action at an unusual hour, to surprise the enemy, gave orders for an immediate attack. The event for some time was doubtful; the wing that was led by himself gave way, or was forced from its ground; but the other wing under Crassus had a better fortune, put the enemy to flight, and drove them to Antemnæ.

The action, though thus various in the different parts of it, became, in the event, completely decisive. Eighty thousand of the Marian party were killed in their flight, and eight thousand taken. Carbo, in despair of the cause, fled into Sicily. The troops that were blocked up in Præneste, having no longer any hopes of relief, surrendered themselves, and the whole party was dispersed or cut off. Marius attempted to escape by the galleries of a mine, and being prevented, killed himself. His head was carried to Sylla, and by his order exposed in the market-place. "That boy," he said, "should have learnt to row before he attempted to steer!"

Sylla being now master of the republic, all men were in anxious expectation of the sequel; nor was it long before they had a specimen of the measures he was likely to pursue. About six or eight thousand of those who were supposed to be the vilest instruments of the late usurpations and murders, being taken prisoners in the war, or surprised in the city, were, by his direction, shut up in the circus, and instantly put to death.

While this horrid scene was acting, he had assembled the senate, at a little distance, in the temple of Bellona; and as most of the members then present had either favoured, or at least tamely submitted to the late usurpation, he made them a speech on the state of the republic, in which he reproached many of them as accessary to the late disorders, and admonished them, for the future, to respect the legal government and constitution of their country. In the midst of these admonitions, the cries of those who were slaughtered in the circus, reaching their ears, the assembly was greatly alarmed, and many of the members started from their seats. Sylla, with a countenance stern, but undisturbed, checked them as for an instance of levity. "Be composed," he said, "and attend to the business for which you are called. What you hear are no more than the cries of a few wretches, who are suffering the punishment due to their crimes." From this interruption he resumed his subject, and continued speaking till the massacre of these unhappy victims was completed.

In an harangue which he afterwards delivered to the people, he spoke of his own services to the republic, and of the misdemeanour of others, in terms that struck all who heard him with terror. "The republic," he said, (if his opinion were followed,) "should be purged; but whether it were so or no, the injuries done to himself and his friends should be punished." He accordingly ordered military execution against every person who had been accessary to the late massacres and usurpations; and while the sword was yet reeking in his hands, passed great part of his time, as usual, in mirth and dissipation with men of humourous and singular characters. He deigned not even to inquire into the abuses that were committed in the execution of his general plan. The persons who were employed in it, frequently indulged their own private resentment and their avarice in the choice of victims. Among these, Catiline, then a young man, had joined the victorious party; and he plunged, with a singular impetuosity, into the midst of a storm which now overwhelmed a part of the city. He is said, among other persons to whom he bore an aversion, or whose effects he intended to seize, to have murdered his own brother, with strange circumstances of cruelty and horror.

While these dreadful murders, mixed with many examples of a just execution, were perpetrated, a young man, C. Metellus, had the courage to address himself to Sylla in the senate, and desired he would make known the extent of his design, and how far these executions were to be carried? "We intercede not," he said, "for the condemned; we only intreat that you would relieve out of this dreadful state of uncertainty all those whom in reality you mean to spare."

Sylla, without being offended at this freedom, published a list of those he had doomed to destruction, offering a reward of two talents for the head of each, and denouncing severe penalties against every person who should harbour or conceal them. Hence arose the practice of publishing lists of the persons to be massacred, which, under the odious name of proscription, was afterwards imitated with such fatal effects in the subsequent convulsions of the state.

The present proscription, although it promised some security to all who were not comprehended in the fatal list, opened a scene, in some respects, more dreadful than that which had been formerly acted in this massacre. The hands of servants were hired against their masters, and even those of children against their parents. The mercenary of every denomination were encouraged, by a great premium, to commit what before only the ministers of public justice thought themselves entitled to perform; and there followed a scene, in which human nature had full scope to exert all the evil of which it is susceptible, treachery, ingratitude, distrust, malice, and revenge; and would have retained no claim to our esteem or commiseration, if its character had not been redeemed by contrary instances of fidelity, generosity, and courage, displayed by those who, to preserve their friends and benefactors, or even to preserve strangers, who took refuge under their protection, hazarded all the dangers with which the proscribed themselves were threatened.

In consequence of these measures, about five thousand persons of consideration were put to death, among whom were reckoned forty senators, and sixteen hundred of the equestrian order.

From these beginnings the Romans had reason to apprehend a tyranny, more sanguinary perhaps than any that ever afflicted mankind. "If in the field you slay all who are found in arms against you," said Catulus,[1] "and in the city you slay even the unarmed; over whom do you propose to reign?"

These reproaches were by Sylla received as jests; and the freedom and ease of his manners, as well as the professions he made of regard to the commonwealth, were imputed to insensibility, and to a barbarous dissimulation, which rendered his character more odious, and the prospect of his future intentions more terrifying.

In comparing the present with the late usurpations, men recollected, that Marius, from his infancy, had been of a severe and inexorable temper; that his resentments were sanguinary, and even his frowns were deadly; but that his cruelties were the effect of real passions, and had the apology of not being perpetrated in cold blood; that every person on whom he looked with indifference was safe; and that even when he usurped the government of the state, as soon as his personal resentments were gratified, the sword in his hand became an innocent pageant, and the mere ensign or badge of his power. But that Sylla directed a massacre in the midst of composure and ease: that as a private man he had been affable and pleasant, even noted for humanity and candour;[2] that the change of his temper having commenced with his exaltation, there were no hopes that the shedding of blood could be stopped while he was suffered to etain his power. His daring spirit, his address, his cunning, and his ascendant over the minds of men, rendered the prospect of a deliverance, if not desperate, extremely remote. The republic seemed to be extinguished for ever; and if the rage of blood, after the first heat of the massacre, appeared to abate, it was stayed only for want of victims, not from any principle of moderation, or sentiment of clemency.

Such was the aspect of affairs, and the grounds of terror conceived even by those who were innocent of the late disorders; but to those who had reason to fear the resentment of the victor, the prospect was altogether desperate. Norbanus, having fled to Rhodes, received at that place an account of the proscriptions, and, to avoid being delivered up, killed himself. Carbo, being in Sicily, endeavoured to make his escape from thence, but was apprehended by Pompey, and killed. All the ordinary offices of state were vacated by the desertion or death of those who had filled or usurped them.

Sylla had hitherto acted as master, without any other title than that of the sword; and it was now thought necessary to supply the defect. He retired from the city, that the senate might assemble with the more appearance of freedom. To name an interrex was the usual expedient for restoring the constitution, and proceeding to elections in a legal form after the usual time had elapsed, or when by any accident the ordinary succession to office had failed. Valerius Flaccus was named. To him Sylla gave intimation, that, to resettle the commonwealth, a dictator, for an indefinite term, should be appointed, and made offer of his own services for this purpose. These intimations were received as commands. Flaccus, having assembled the people, moved for an act to vest Sylla with the title of dictator, which gave him a discretionary power over the persons, fortunes, and lives of all the citizens.

No example of this kind had taken place for a hundred and twenty years preceding this date. In the former part of this period, the jealousy of the aristocracy, and, in the latter part of it, the negative of the tribunes, had always prevented a measure from which they severally apprehended some danger to themselves. It was now revived in the person of Sylla with unusual solemnity, and ratified by an act of the people, in which they yielded up at once all their own claims to the sovereignty, and submitted to monarchy for an indefinite time. Sylla having named Valerius Flaccus for his lieutenant or commander of the horse, returned to the city, presenting a sight that was then unusual, a single person, preceded by four-and-twenty lictors, armed with the axe and the rods; and it was not doubted that these ensigns of magistracy were to be employed, not for parade, but for serious execution, and were speedily to be stained with the blood of many citizens, whom the sword had spared The dictator, being attended likewise by a numerous military guard, in order that the city, in all matters in which it was not necessary for himself to interpose, might still enjoy the benefit of the usual forms, he directed the people to assemble, and to fill up the ordinary lists of office.

Lucretius Offella, the officer who had commanded in the reduction of Præneste, presuming

1 Probably the son of him who perished in the tyranny of Marius.
2 Plutarch. in Sylla.

on his favour with the dictator, and on his consequence with the army, offered himself for the consulate. Being commanded by Sylla to desist, he still continued his canvass, and was, by order of the dictator, put to death, while he solicited votes in the streets. A tumult immediately arose; the centurion, who executed this order against Offella, was seized, and, attended by a great concourse of people, was carried before the dictator. Sylla heard the complaint with great composure, told the multitude who crowded around him, that Offella had been slain by his orders, and that the centurion must therefore be released. He then dismissed them, with this homely but menacing apologue. "A countryman at his plough, feeling himself troubled with vermin, once and again made a halt to pick them off his jacket; but being molested a third time, he threw the jacket, with all its contents, into the fire. Beware," he said, "of the fire; provoke me not a third time."[1] Such was the tone of a government, which, from this example, was likely to be fatal to many who had concurred in the establishment of it, as well as to those of the opposite party.

U. C. 672.

M. Tullius Decula, Cn. Corn. Dolabella.

Sylla, soon after his elevation to the station of dictator, proceeded to make his arrangements and to new-model the commonwealth. The army[2] appeared to have the first or preferable claim to his attention. He accordingly proposed to reward them by a gift of all the lands which had been forfeited by the adherents of the opposite party. Spoletum, Interamna, Præneste, Fluentia, Nola, Sulmo, Volaterra, together with the countries of Samnium and Lucania, were depopulated to make way for the legions who had served under himself in the reduction of his enemies. In these new inhabitants of Italy, whose prosperity depended on his safety, he had a guard to his person, and a sure support to his power. By changing their condition from that of soldiers to landholders and peasants, he dispelled, at the same time, that dangerous cloud of military power, which he himself or his antagonists had raised over the commonwealth, and provided for the permanency of any reformations he was to introduce into the civil establishment. The troops, from soldiers of fortune, became proprietors of land, and interested in the preservation of peace. In this manner, whatever may have been his intention in this arbitrary act of power, so cruel to the innocent sufferers, if there were any such, the measure had an immediate tendency to terminate the public confusion. Its future consequences, in pointing out to new armies, and to their ambitious leaders, a way to supplant their fellow-citizens in their property, and to practise usurpations more permanent than that of Sylla, were probably not then foreseen.

The next act of the dictator appears more entirely calculated for the security of his own person. A body of ten thousand men, lately the property of persons involved in the ruin of the vanquished party, having their freedom and the right of citizens conferred on them, were enrolled promiscuously in all the tribes; and as the enfranchised slave took the name of the person from whom he received his freedom, these new citizens became an accession to the family of the Cornelii, and in every tumult were likely to be the sure partizans of Sylla, and the abettors of his power. They had received a freedom which was connected with the permanency of his government, and foresaw, that, if the leaders of the opposite party, in whose houses they had served, should be restored, they themselves must return into the condition of slaves; and they accordingly became an additional security to the government which their patron was about to establish.

So far Sylla seemed to intend the security of his own person, and the stability of his government; but in all his subsequent institutions, he had a view to restore the aristocracy in its legislative and judicative capacity, to provide a proper supply of officers for conducting the accumulated affairs of the commonwealth, to furnish hands for every department, and to guard against the growing depravity of the times, by extending and securing the execution of the laws. He began with filling up the rolls of the senate which had been greatly reduced by the war, and by the sanguinary policy of the parties who had prevailed in their turns. He augmented the number of this body to five hundred; taking the new members from the equestrian order, but leaving the choice of them to the people.

Lex de Judiciis.

The legislative power of the senate, and the judicative power of its members were restored. The law that was provided for the last of these purposes consisted of different clauses. By the first clause it was enacted, that none but senators, or those who were entitled to give their opinion in the senate,[3] should be put upon any jury or list of the judges.[4] By the second, that, of the judges so selected, the parties should not be allowed to challenge or reject above three.

By a third clause it was provided, that judgment, in trials at law, should be given either by ballot, or openly, at the option of the defendant; and by a separate regulation, that the nomination of officers to command in the provinces, with the title of proconsul, should be committed to the senate.

During the late tribunitian usurpation, the whole legislative and executive power had, under pretence of vesting those prerogatives in the assembly of the tribes, been seized by the tribunes. But Sylla restored the ancient form of assembling the people by centuries, and reduced the tribunes to their defensive privilege of interposing by a negative against any act of oppression; and he deprived them of their pretended right to propose laws, or to harangue the people. He moreover added, that none but senators could be elected into the office of tribune; and, to the end that no person of a factious ambition might choose this station, he procured it to be enacted, that no one who had borne the office of tribune could afterwards be promoted into any other rank of the magistracy.

With respect to the offices of state, this new founder of the commonwealth revived the obsolete law which prohibited the re-election of any person into the consulate, till after an interval of

1 Appian. in Bell. Civil. lib. i. Plutarch in Sylla.

2 It appears tha, Livy reckoned forty-seven legions, Epitome, lib. lxx x.

3 All the officers of state, even before they were pu upon the rolls, were entitled to speak in the sena[illegible]

4 Tacit. Annal. lib. xi. Cic. pro Cliento

ten years; and enacted, that none could be elected consul till after he had been questor, edile, and prætor. He augmented the number of prætors from six to eight; that of questors to twenty; and, to guard against the disorders which had recently afflicted the republic, declared it to be treason for any Roman officer, without the authority of the senate and people, to go beyond the limits of his province, whether with or without an army, to make war, or to invade any foreign nation whatever.

He repealed the law of Domitius relating to the election of priests, and restored to the college the entire choice of their own members.

He made several additions to the criminal law, by statutes against subornation, forgery, wilful fire, poisoning, rape, assault, extortion, and forcibly entering the house of a citizen; and a statute making it penal to be found with deadly weapons of any sort. To all these he added a sumptuary law, of which the tenor is not precisely known; but it appears to have regulated the expense at ordinary[5] meals and at funerals, and to have likewise settled the price of provisions.

These laws were promulgated at certain intervals, and intermixed with the measures which were taken to restore the peace of the empire. In order to finish the remains of the civil war, Pompey had been sent into Sicily and Africa, and C. Annius Luscus into Spain. In this province, Sertorius had taken arms for the Marian faction; but being attacked by the forces of Sylla, and ill supported at first by the Spaniard, he fled into Africa. From thence, hearing that the Lusitanians were disposed to take arms against the reigning party at Rome, he repassed the sea, put himself at their head, and in this situation was able, for some years, to find occupation for the arms of the republic, and for its most experienced generals.

Soon after the departure of Sylla from Asia, Murena, whom he had left to command in that province, found a pretence to renew the war with Mithridates; and, having ventured to pass the Halys, was defeated by that prince, and afterwards arraigned as having infringed the late treaty of peace. Sylla listened to this accusation, disapproved the conduct of Murena, and sent first A. Gabinius, and afterwards Minucius Thermus, to supersede him in the province.

Mean time Sylla himself exhibited a splendid triumph on account of his victories in Asia and Greece. The procession lasted two days. On the first, he deposited in the treasury fifteen thousand pondo of gold,[6] and a hundred and fifteen thousand pondo of silver;[7] on the second day thirteen thousand pondo of gold,[8] and seven thousand pondo of silver.[9] There was nothing that had any reference to his victory in the civil war, except a numerous train of senators, and other citizens of distinction, who, having resorted to his camp for protection, had been restored by him to their estates, and their dignities, and now followed his chariot, calling him father, and the deliverer of his country.

Upon the return of the elections, Sylla was again chosen consul, together with Q. Cæcilius

5 Gellius, lib. ii c. 24.

6 Reckoning the pondo at ten ounces, and 4*l*. an ounce, this will make about 600,000*l*.

7 About 287,500*l* 8 About 520,000*l*.

9 About 140,000*l* Plin. lib. xxxiii. initio.

U. C. 673.

L. Corn. Sylla, Q. Cæcil. Metell. Pius.

Metellus. The latter was destined at the expiration of his office, to command against Sertorius in Spain. Sylla himself still retained the dictatorial power, and was employed in promulgating some of the acts of which the chief have been mentioned.

Pompey having, in the preceding year, by the death of Carbo, and the dispersion of his party, finished the remains of the civil war in Sicily, was now ordered by the senate to transport his army into Africa. There Domitius, a leader of the opposite faction, had erected his standard, assembled some remains of the vanquished party, and received all the fugitives who crowded for refuge to his camp. Pompey accordingly departed from Sicily, leaving the command of that island to Memmius, and embarked his army, consisting of six legions, in two divisions; one landed at Utica, the other in the bay of Carthage. Having come to an engagement with Domitius, who had been joined by Jarbas, an African prince, he obtained a complete victory over their united forces, and afterwards penetrated, without any resistance, into the kingdom of Numidia, which, though dependant on the Romans, had not yet been reduced to the form of a province.

The war being ended in this quarter, Sylla thought proper to supersede Pompey in the province, and ordered him to disband his army, reserving only one legion, with which he was to wait for his successor. The troops were greatly incensed at this order; and, thinking themselves equally entitled to settlements with the legions who were lately provided for in Italy, refused to lay down their arms. They earnestly intreated their general to embark for Rome, where they promised to make him master of the government. This young man, with a moderation which he continued to support in the height of his ambition, withstood the temptation, and declared to the army, that, if they persisted in their purpose, he must certainly die by his own hands; that he would not do violence to the government of his country, nor be the object or pretence of a civil war. If in reality, he had encouraged this mutiny, it was only that he might have the honour of reclaiming the soldiers, and of rejecting their offer. The ambition of this singular person, as will appear from many passages of his life, led him to aim at consideration more than power.

While Pompey was endeavouring to bring the troops to their duty, a report was carried to Rome, that he had actually revolted, and was preparing, with his army, to make a descent upon Italy. "It appears to be my fate," said Sylla, "in my old age, to fight with boys;" and he was about to recall the veterans to his standard, when the truth was discovered, and the part which Pompey had acted was properly represented. The merit of this young man on that occasion was the greater, that he himself was unwilling to disband the army before they should return into Italy to attend a triumph, which he hoped to obtain; and that the resolution he took to comply with his orders, proceeded from respect to the senate, and the authority of the state.

Sylla, won by the behaviour of Pompey on this occasion, was inclined to dispense with his former commands, and, accordingly, moved the assembly of the people, that the legions serving in Africa might return into Italy.

This motion was opposed by C. Herennius, tribune of the people, who ventured to employ the prerogative of his office, however impaired, against the power of the dictator. But Sylla persisted; obtained a law to authorize Pompey to enter with his army into Italy; and when he drew near the city, went forth with a numerous body of the senate to receive him. On this occasion, it is said, that, by calling him the Great Pompey, Sylla fixed a designation upon him, which, in the Roman way of distinguishing persons by nicknames, whether of contempt or respect, continued to furnish him with a title for life. The times were wretched when armies stated themselves in the commonwealth as the partizans of their leader, and when the leader, by not betraying his country, was supposed to perform a great action.

Pompey, upon this occasion, laid claim to a triumph. Sylla at first opposed it as being contrary to the rule and order of the commonwealth, which reserved this honour for persons who had attained to the rank of consul or prætor; but he afterwards complied, being struck, it is said, with a mutinous saying of this aspiring young man, bidding him recollect, that there were more persons disposed to worship the rising than the setting sun.

In the triumph which Pompey accordingly obtained, he meant to have entered the city on a carriage drawn by elephants; but these animals could not pass abreast through the gates. His donation to the troops falling short of their expectation, and they having murmured and even threatened to mutiny, he said, the fear of losing his triumph should not affect him; that he would instantly disband the legions, rather, than comply with their unreasonable demands. This check, given to the presumption of the army by an officer so young and so aspiring, gave a general satisfaction. P. Servilius, a senator of advanced age, said, upon this occasion, "That the young man had at last deserved his triumph and his title."

Pompey, by his vanity in demanding a triumph contrary to the established order of the commonwealth, had impaired the lustre of his former actions; by this last act of magnanimity, in restraining the insolence of the troops, he forfeited the affections of the army; and in both these circumstances together, gave a complete specimen and image of his whole life. With too much respect for the republic to employ violent means for its ruin, he was possessed by a vanity and a jealousy of his own personal consideration, which, in detail, perpetually led him to undermine its foundations.

U. C. 674.

P. Servilius, Appius Claudius.

Upon the return of the elections, Sylla was again destined for one of the consuls; but he declined this piece of flattery, and directed the choice to fall on P. Servilius and Appius Claudius. Soon after these magistrates entered on the discharge of their trust; the dictator appeared, as usual, in the forum, attended by twenty-four lictors; but, instead of proceeding to any exercise of his power, made a formal resignation of it, dismissed his retinue, and having declared to the people, that, if any one had any matter of charge against him, he was ready to answer it, continued to walk in the streets in the character of a private man, and afterwards retired to his villa near Cumæ, where he exercised himself in hunting.[1]

This resignation throws a new light on the character of Sylla, and leads to a favourable construction of some of the most exceptionable parts of his conduct. When, with the help of the comment it affords, we look back to the establishments he made while in power, they appear not to be the acts of a determined usurper, but to be fitted for a republican government, and for the restoration of that order which the violence and corruption of the times had suspended.

That he was actuated by a violent resentment of personal wrongs, cannot be questioned; but it is likewise evident, that he felt on proper occasions for the honour and preservation of his country, in the noblest sense of these words. In his first attack of the city, with a military force, his actions showed, that he meant to rescue the republic from the usurpations of Marius, not to usurp the government himself. When he returned into Italy from the Mithridatic war, the state of parties already engaged in hostilities, and the violence done to the republic by those who pretended to govern it, will abundantly justify his having had recourse to arms. For the massacre which followed, it may be shocking to suppose that the evils of human life can require such a remedy; but the case was singular, exposed to disorders which required violent remedies, beyond what is known in the history of mankind, a populous city, the capital of a large country, whose inhabitants still pretended to act in a collective body, of whom every member would be a master, none would be a subject, become the joint sovereigns of many provinces, ready to spurn at all the institutions which were provided for the purposes of government over themselves, and at all the principles of justice and order which were required to regulate their government of others Where the gangrene spread in such a body, it was likely to require the amputation-knife. Men rushed into crimes in numerous bodies, or were led in powerful factions to any species of evil which suited their demagogues. Whatever may have been Sylla's choice among the instruments of reformation and cure, it is likely that the sword alone was that on which he could rely; and he used it like a person anxious to effect its purpose, not to recommend his art to those on whom it was to be practised.

In his capacity of a political reformer, he had to work on the dregs of a corrupted republic; and although the effect fell short of what is ascribed to fabulous legislators and founders of states, yet to none ever were ascribed more tokens of magnanimity and greatness of mind. He was superior to the reputation even of his own splendid actions; and, from simplicity or disdain, mixed perhaps with superstition, not from affected modesty, attributed his success to the effects of his good fortune and to the favour of the gods. While he bestowed on Pompey the title of Great, he himself was content with that of Fortunate. He was a man of letters, and passed the early part of his life in a mixture of dissipation and study. He wrote his own memoirs, or a journal of his life, often quoted by Plutarch, and continued it to within a few days of his death. A work possibly of little elegance, and even tainted,

1 Appian. Bell Civ. lib. i.

as we are told, with superstition; but more curious surely than many volumes corrected by the labours of retired study.

When tired of his youthful amusements, he sued for the honours of the state; but with so little appearance of any jealous or impatient ambition, that, if he had not been impelled by provocations into the violent course he pursued, it is probable that he would have been contented with the usual career of a prosperous senator; would have disdained to encroach on the rights of his fellow-citizens, as much as he resented the encroachments that were made on his own, and never would have been heard of but on the rolls of the consuls, and in the record of his triumphs. But fortune destined him for a part still more conspicuous, and in which, it may be thought, although none ever less studied the unnecessary appearances of humanity or a scrupulous morality, none ever more essentially served the persons with whom he was connected.

With respect to such a personage, circumstances of a trivial nature become subjects of attention. His hair and eyes, it is said, were of a light colour, his complexion fair, and his countenance blotched. He was, by the most probable accounts, four years old at the time of the sedition of Tiberius Gracchus, and seventeen at the death of Caius Gracchus; so that he might have perceived at this date the effect of tribunitian seditions, and taken the impressions from which he acted against them. He served the office of questor under Marius in Africa at thirty-one; was consul for the first time at forty-nine or fifty;[2] was dictator at fifty-six; resigned when turned of fifty-eight; and died, yet under sixty, in the year which followed that of his resignation.

There remained in the city, at his death, a numerous body of new citizens who bore his name: in the country a still more numerous body of veteran officers and soldiers, who held estates by his gifts: numbers throughout the empire, who owed their safety to his protection, and who ascribed the existence of the commonwealth itself to the exertions of his great ability and courage: numbers who, although they were offended with the severe exercise of his power, yet admired the magnanimity of his resignation.

When he was no longer an object of flattery, his corpse was carried in procession through Italy at the public expense. The fasces, and every other ensign of honour, were restored to the dead. Above two thousand golden crowns were fabricated in haste, by order of the towns and provinces he had protected, or of the private persons he had preserved, to testify their veneration for his memory. Roman matrons, whom it might be expected his cruelties would have affected with horror, lost every other sentiment in that of admiration, crowded to his funeral, and heaped the pile with perfumes.[3] His obsequies were performed in the Campus Martius. The tomb was marked by his own directions with the following characteristical inscription: "Here lies Sylla, who never was outdone in good offices by his friend, nor in acts of hostility by his enemy."[4] His merit or demerit in the principal transactions of his life may be variously estimated. His having slain so many citizens in cold blood, and without any form of law, if we imagine them to have been innocent, or if we conceive the republic to have been in a state to allow them a trial, must be considered as monstrous or criminal in the highest degree: but if none of these suppositions were just, if they were guilty of the greatest crimes, and were themselves the authors of that lawless state to which their country was reduced, his having saved the republic from the hands of such ruffians, and purged it of the vilest dreg that ever threatened to poison a free state, may be considered as meritorious. To satisfy himself, who was neither solicitous of praise nor dreaded censure, the strong impulse of his own mind, guided by indignation and the sense of necessity, was probably sufficient.

2 Vel. Pater. lib. ii. c. 17.

T

3 Appian. de Bell. Civ. lib. i. Plutarch. in Sylla.
4 Plutarch. in Sylla, fine.

THE

HISTORY

OF

THE PROGRESS AND TERMINATION

OF THE

ROMAN REPUBLIC.

BOOK III.

CHAPTER I.

State of the Commonwealth and Numbers of the People—Characters of Persons who began to appear in the Times of Sylla—Faction of Lepidus—Sertorius harbours the Marian Party in Spain—Is attacked by Metellus and Pompey—His Death, and final Suppression of the Party—First Appearance of C. Julius Cæsar—Tribunes begin to trespass on the Laws of Sylla—Progress of the Empire—Preparations of Mithridates—War with the Romans—Irruption into Bithynia—Siege of Cyzicus—Raised—Flight of Mithridates—Lucullus carries the War into Pontus—Rout and Dispersion of the Army of Mithridates—His flight into Armenia—Conduct of Lucullus in the Province of Asia.

THE public was so much occupied with the contest of Sylla and his antagonists, that little else is recorded of the period in which it took place. Writers have not given us any distinct account of the condition of the city, or of the number of citizens. As the state was divided into two principal factions, the office of censor was become too important for either party to entrust it with their opponents, or even in neutral hands. The leaders of every faction, in their turn, made up the rolls of the people, and disposed, at their pleasure, of the equestrian and senatorian dignities.

At a survey of the city, which is mentioned by Livy,[1] preceding the admission of the Italians on the rolls of the people, the number of citizens was three hundred and ninety-four thousand three hundred and thirty-six. At another survey, which followed soon after that event, they amounted, according to Eusebius, to four hundred and sixty-three thousand:[2] and it seems that the whole accession of citizens from the country made no more than sixty-eight thousand six hundred and sixty-four. The great slaughter of Romans and Italians, in which it is said that three hundred thousand men were killed, preceding the last of these musters, and the difficulty of making complete and accurate lists when the citizens were so much dispersed, will account for the seemingly small increase of their numbers.

In this period were born, and began to enter on the scene of public affairs, those persons whose conduct was now to determine the fate of the republic. Pompey had already distinguished himself, and was a person of real consequence. He had been educated in the camp of his father, and, by accident, at a very early age; and before he had attained to any of the ordinary civil or political preferments, commanded an army. Cicero, being of the same age, began to be distinguished at the bar. He pleaded, in the second consulate of Sylla, the cause of Roscius Amerinus, in which he was led to censure the actions of Chrysogonus and other favourites of the dictator, and, by his freedom in that instance, gained much honour to himself.

Cæsar, now connected with the family of Cinna, whose daughter he had married, and being nearly related to the elder Marius, who had married his aunt, narrowly escaped the sword of the prevailing party. Being commanded to separate from his wife, he retained her in defiance of this order, and for his contumacy was put in the list of the proscribed. He was saved, however, by the intercession of some common friends, whose request in his favour Sylla granted, with that memorable saying, "Beware of him: there is many a Marius in the person of that young man." A circumstance which marked at once the penetration of Sylla, and the early appearances of an extraordinary character in Cæsar.

Marcus Porcius, afterwards named Cato of Utica, was about three years younger than Cæsar, and being early an orphan, was educated in the house

1 Liv. lib. lxiii. 2 Euseb. in Chronico.

of an uncle, Livius Drusus. While yet a child, listening to the conversation of the times, he learned that the claim of the Italian allies, then in agitation, was dangerous to the Roman commonwealth. Pompedius Silo, who managed the claim for the Italians, amusing himself with the young Cato, pressed him with caresses to intercede with his uncle in their behalf; and, finding that he was not to be won by flattery, likewise tried in vain to intimidate him by threatening to throw him from the window. "If this were a man," he said, "I believe we should obtain no such favour." In the height of Sylla's military executions, when his portico was crowded with persons, who brought the heads of the proscribed to be exchanged for the reward that was offered for them, Cato being carried by his tutor to pay his court, asked, if "no one hated this man enough to kill him?" "Yes, but they fear him still more than they hate him." "Then give me a sword," said the boy, "and I will kill him." Such were the early indications of characters which afterwards became so conspicuous in the commonwealth.

With the unprecedented degradation of the tribune Octavius, and the subsequent murder of Tiberius Gracchus, began among the parties at Rome, a scene of injuries and retaliations, with intervals of anarchy and violent usurpation, which must have speedily ended in the ruin of the commonwealth, if the sword had not passed at last into hands that employed it for the restoration of public order, as well as for the avenging of private wrongs.

It is indeed probable, that none of the parties in these horrid scenes had a deliberate intention to subvert the government, but all of them treated the forms of the commonwealth with too little respect: and to obtain some revenge of the wrongs which they themselves apprehended or endured, did not scruple in their turn to violate the laws of their country. But to those who wished to preserve the commonwealth, the experience of fifty years was now sufficient to show, that attempts to restore the laws by illegal methods, and to terminate animosities by retorted injuries and provocations, were extremely vain. The excess of the evil had a tendency to exhaust its source, and parties began to nauseate the draught of which they had been made so plentifully to drink. There were, nevertheless, some dregs in the bottom of the cup, and the supplies of faction which were brought by the rising generation, were of a mixture more dangerous than those of the former age. The example of Sylla, who made himself lord of the commonwealth by means of a military force, and the security with which he held his usurpation during pleasure, had a more powerful effect in exciting the thirst of dominion, than the political uses which he made of his power, or his magnanimity in resigning it, had to restrain or to correct the effects of that dangerous precedent. Adventurers accordingly arose, who, without provocation, and equally indifferent to the interests of party as they were to those of the republic, proceeded, with a cool and deliberate purpose, to gratify their own ambition and avarice, in the subversion of the government of their country.

J. C. 675. While Sylla was yet alive, Æmilius Lepidus, a man of profligate ambition, but of mean capacity, supported by the remains of the popular faction, stood for the consulate, and was chosen, together with Q. Lutatius Catulus, the son of him who, with Marius, triumphed for their joint victory over the Cimbri, and who afterwards perished by the orders of that usurper.

M. Æm. Lepidus, Q. Lut. Catulus, Cons.

Pompey had openly declared for Lepidus, and was told upon that occasion by Sylla, that he was stirring the embers of a fire which would in the end consume the republic. After the death of Sylla it appeared, from a mark of disapprobation well known to the Romans, that of not being mentioned in his will, that Pompey had lost his esteem. This prudent young man, however, in opposition to Lepidus and others, who wished to insult the memory of Sylla, was among the first in recommending and performing the honours that were paid to his remains.

Lepidus, upon his accession to the consulate, moved for a recall of the proscribed exiles, a restitution of the forfeited lands, and a repeal of all the ordinances of the late dictator. This motion was formally opposed by Catulus; and there ensued between the two consuls a debate which divided the city. But the party of the senate prevailed to have the motion rejected.

In the allotment of provinces the Transalpine Gaul had fallen to Lepidus; and, upon his motion being rejected in the assembly of the people, although it had been for some time the practice for consuls to remain at Rome during their continuance in office, he prepared to leave the city, in order to take possession of his province. This resolution, as it implied great impatience to be at the head of an army, gave some jealousy to the senate, who dreaded the designs of a consul desirous to join military power with his civil authority. They recollected the progress of sedition which began with the Gracchi and Apuleius raising popular tumults, and ended with Marius and Sylla leading consular armies in the city, and fighting their battles in the streets. And in this point the decisive spirit of Sylla, although it may have snatched the commonwealth from the flames by which it began to be consumed, yet showed the way to its ruin in the means which he employed to preserve it.[3] The senators were willing that Lepidus should depart from the city; but they had the precaution to exact from him an oath, that he should not disturb the public peace. This oath, to avoid the appearance of any particular distrust in him, they likewise exacted from his colleague.[4]

Lepidus, notwithstanding his oath, being arrived in his province, made preparations for war; and, thinking that his oath was binding only while he remained in office, determined to remain in Gaul at the head of his forces until the term was expired. The senate, in order to remove him from the army, appointed him to preside at the election of his successor. But he neglected the summons which was sent to him for this purpose, and the year of the present consuls was by this means suffered to elapse, before any election was made.

The ordinary succession being thus interrupted, the senate named Appius Claudius, as interrex, to hold the elections, and at the same time deprived Lepidus of his command in Gaul. Upon

3 Appian. de Bell. Civ. lib. i.

4 Ibid.

this information he hastened to Italy with the troops he had already assembled, and greatly alarmed the republic. The senate gave to Appius Claudius, and to Catulus, in the quality of proconsul, the usual charge to watch over the safety of the state. These officers accordingly, without delay, collected a military force, while Lepidus advanced through Etruria, and published a manifesto, in which he invited all the friends of liberty to join him, and made a formal demand of being re-invested with the consular power. In opposition to this treasonable act of Lepidus, the senate republished the law of Plautius, by which the prætors were required, in the ordinary course of justice, to take cognizance of all attempts to levy war against the state, and joined to it an additional clause or resolution of their own, obliging those magistrates to receive accusations of treason on holy-days, as well as on ordinary days of business.

Mean time Lepidus advanced to the gates of Rome, seized the Janiculum and one of the bridges that led to the city. He was met by Catulus in the Campus Martius, repulsed and routed. All his party dispersed; he himself fled to Sardinia, and soon after died. His son, a young man, with part of the army, retired to Alba, and was there soon after taken, and suffered for a treason in which he was engaged by his father.

Marcus Brutus, the father of him who, in the continuation of these troubles, afterwards fell at Philippi, having joined with Lepidus in this rash and profligate attempt against the republic, was obliged at Mantua to surrender himself to Pompey, and, by his orders, was put to death. But the most considerable part of the army of Lepidus penetrated, under the conduct of Perpenna, into Spain, and joined Sertorius, who was now become the refuge of one party in its distress, as Sylla had formerly been of the other. In this province accordingly, while peace began to be restored in Italy, a source of new troubles was opening for the state. The prevailing party in the city was willing to grant an indemnity, and to suffer all prosecution, on account of the late offences, to drop; the extreme to which Sylla had carried the severity of his executions, disposing the minds of men to the opposite course of indulgence and mercy.

Before the arrival of Lepidus with his army in Italy, Mithridates had sent to obtain from the senate a ratification of the treaty he had concluded with Sylla: but upon a complaint from Ariobarzanes, that the king of Pontus had not himself performed his part of that treaty by the complete restitution of Cappadocia, he was directed to give full satisfaction on this point before his negotiation at Rome could proceed. He accordingly complied; but by the time his ambassador brought the report, the Romans were so much occupied by the war they had to maintain against Lepidus and his adherents, that they had no leisure for foreign affairs. This intelligence encouraged Mithridates to think of renewing the war. Sensible that he could not rely on a permanent peace with the Roman republic, he had already provided an army, not so considerable in respect to numbers as that which he formerly had, but more formidable by the order and discipline he had endeavoured to introduce on the model of the legion. He flattered himself that the distraction under which the Romans now laboured at home, would render them unable to resist his forces in Asia, and give him an opportunity to remove the only obstruction that remained to his own conquests. He avoided, in the time of a negotiation, and without the pretext of a new provocation, to break out into open hostilities; but he encouraged his son-in-law Tigranes, king of Armenia, to make war on the Roman allies in his neighbourhood, and thereby laid the foundation of a quarrel which he might either adopt or decline at pleasure. This prince accordingly, being then building a city, under the name of Tigranocerta, for which he wanted inhabitants, made an incursion into the kingdom of Cappadocia, carried off from thence three hundred thousand of the people to replenish his new settlement.

Soon after this infraction of the peace, Mithridates, in order to have the co-operation of some of the parties into which the Roman state was divided, entered into a treaty with Sertorius, and wished, in concert with this general, to execute the project of a march, by a route afterwards practised by the barbarians who invaded the Roman empire. From the shores of the Euxine it appeared easy to pass over land to the Adriatic, and once more to repeat the operations of Pyrrhus and of Hannibal, by making war on the Romans in their own country.

Sertorius, who had erected the standard of the republic in Spain, gave refuge to the Roman exiles from every quarter, and was now at the head of a formidable power, composed of Italians as well as natives of that country. By his birth and abilities he had pretensions to the highest preferments of the state, and had been early distinguished as a soldier, qualified either to plan or to execute. He was attached to Marius in the time of the Cimbric war, and became a party with this leader in his quarrel with Sylla. His animosity to the latter was increased by the mutual opposition of their interests in the pursuit of civil preferments. At the beginning of the civil war, Sertorius took an active part, but showed more respect to the constitution of his country, and more mercy to those who were opposed to him, than either of his associates Marius or Cinna. When his party were in possession of the government, he was appointed to command in Spain, and after the ruin of their affairs in Italy, withdrew into that province. He was received as a Roman governor; but, soon after the other party prevailed in Italy, was attacked on their part by Caius Annius, who came with a proper force to dislodge him. He had established posts on the Pyrenees for the security of his province; but the officer to whom they were entrusted being assassinated, and the stations deserted, the enemy had free access on that side. Not in condition to maintain himself any longer in Spain, he embarked with what forces he had at Carthagena, and continued for some years, with a small squadron of Cilician galleys, to subsist by the spoils of Africa and the contiguous coasts. In this state of his fortunes he formed a project to visit the Fortunate Islands, and if a settlement could be effected there, to bid farewell for ever to the Roman world; to its factions, its divisions, and its troubles. But while he was about to set sail in search of this famous retreat in the ocean, he received an invitation from the unsubdued natives of Lusitania to become their leader. At heir head his abilities soon made him conspicuous. He affected to consider the Lusitanians as the senate and people of Rome, treating the establishment of Sylla in Italy as a mere usurpation. He himself took the ensigns of a Roman officer of state, selected three hundred of his followers, to whom he gave the title of senate, and in all his transactions with foreign nations, assumed the name and style of the Roman republic. In treating with Mithridates he refused to cede the province of Asia, or to purchase the alliance of that prince by any concessions injurious to the Roman empire, of which he affected to consider himself and his senate as the legal head.

While Sertorius was acting this farce, the report of his formidable power, the late accession he had gained by the junction of some of the Marian forces under the command of Perpenna, and his supposed preparations to make a descent upon Italy, gave an alarm at Rome. Metellus had been some time employed against him in Spain; but being scarcely able to keep the field, his opposition tended only to augment the reputation of his antagonist. The consuls lately elected were judged unequal to this war, and the thoughts of all men were turned on Pompey, who, though yet in no public character, nor arrived at the legal age of state preferments, had the address on this, as on many other occasions, to make himself be pointed at as the only person who could effectually serve the republic. He was accordingly, with the title of proconsul, joined to Metellus in the conduct of the war in Spain.[1] It no doubt facilitated the career of this young man's pretensions, that few men of distinguished abilities were now in view to sustain the fortunes of the republic. Such men, of whatever party, had always, in their turns, been the first victims of the late violent massacres; and the party of Sylla, which was now the republic, when considered as a nursery of eminent men, had some disadvantage, perhaps in the superiority of its leader, who was himself equal to all its affairs, and taught others to confide and obey, not to act for themselves. Pompey was not of an age to have suffered from this influence. He came into the party in its busiest time, and had been entrusted with separate commands. He had already obtained for himself part of that artificial consideration which, though it cannot be supported without abilities, often exceeds the degree of merit on which it is founded; and this consideration to the end of his life he continued to augment with much attention and many concerted intrigues. He had a genius for war, and was now about to improve it in the contest with Sertorius, an excellent master, whose lessons were rough but instructive.

U. C. 676.

D. Junius Brutus, Mam. Æmilianus Livianus.

Pompey, having made the levies destined for this service, passed the Alps by a new route, and was the first Roman general who made his way into Spain through Gaul and the Pyrenees. Soon after his arrival, a legion that covered the foragers of his army was intercepted and cut off by the enemy. Sertorius was engaged in the siege of Laura. Pompey advanced to relieve it. Sertorius, upon his approach, took post on an eminence. Pompey prepared to attack him, and the besieged had hopes of immediate relief. But Sertorius had made his disposition in such a manner, that Pompey could not advance without exposing his own rear to a party that was placed to attack him. "I will teach this pupil of Sylla," he said, "to look behind as well as before him;" and Pompey, seeing his danger, chose to withdraw, leaving the town of Laura to fall into the enemy's hands, while he himself continued a spectator of the siege, and of the destruction of the place. After this unsuccessful beginning of the war, he was obliged to retire into Gaul for the winter.[2]

U. C. 677.

Cn. Octavius, C. Scribonius Curio.

The following year, Cn. Octavius and C. Scribonius Curio being consuls, Pompey still remained in his command; and, having repassed the Pyrenees, directed his march to join Metellus. Sertorius lay on the Sucro,[3] and wished to engage him before the junction; and Pompey, on his part, being desirous to reap the glory of a separate victory, an action ensued, in which the wing on which Pompey fought was defeated by Sertorius; but the other wing had the victory over Perpenna. As Sertorius was about to renew the action on the following day, he was prevented by the arrival of Metellus. "If the old woman had not interposed," he said, "I should have whipt the boy, and sent him back to his schools at Rome."

This war continued about two years longer with various success, but without any memorable event, until it ended by the death of Sertorius, who, at the instigation of Perpenna, was betrayed and assassinated by a few of his own attendants. Perpenna, having removed Sertorius by this base action, put himself at the head of the army, and endeavoured to keep them united, at least until he should be able to purchase his peace at Rome. He was, however, deserted by numbers of his own people, and at last surprised by Pompey, and slain. He had made offers to disclose the secrets of the party, and to produce the correspondence which many of the principal citizens at Rome held with Sertorius, inviting him to return into Italy, and promising to join him with a formidable power. The letters were secured by Pompey, and, without being opened, were burned. So masterly an act of prudence, in a person who was yet considered as a young man, has been deservedly admired. It served to extinguish all the remains of the Marian faction, and reconciled men, otherwise disaffected, to a situation in which they were assured of impunity and concealment.

While Pompey was thus gathering laurels in the field, C. Julius Cæsar, being about seven years younger, that is, twenty-three years of age, was returned from Asia; and to make some trial of his parts, laid an accusation against Dolabella, late proconsul of Macedonia, for oppression and extortion in his province. Cotta and Hortensius, appearing for the defendant, procured his acquittal. Cicero says, that he himself was then returned from a journey he had made into Asia, and was present at this trial. The following year Cæsar left Rome, with intention to pass some time under a celebrated master of rhetoric at Rhodes.

1 Claudius, in making this motion, alluding to the insignificance of both consuls, said, that Pompey should be sent pro consulibus.

2 Plutarch. in Pompeio et Sertorio. Appian. Liv Obsequens. Frontinus Stratagem. lib. ii. c. 5.

3 The Xucar, which falls into the Bay of Valentia

In his way he was taken by pirates, and detained about forty days, until he found means to procure from Metellus a sum of fifty talents,[1] which was paid for his ransom. He had frequently told the pirates, while yet in their hands, that he would punish their insolence; and he now told them to expect the performance of his promise. Upon being set on shore, he assembled and armed some vessels on the coast, pursued and took his captors. Leaving his prisoners where he landed, he hastened to Junius Silanus, the proconsul of Bithynia, and applied for an order to have them executed; but being refused by this officer, he made his way back with still greater despatch, and, before any instructions could arrive to the contrary, had the pirates nailed to the cross. Such lawless banditti had long infested the seas of Asia and of Greece, and furnished at times no inconsiderable employment to the arms of the republic. Servilius Vatia, who afterwards bore the title of Isauricus, had lately been employed against them, and after clearing the seas, endeavoured likewise to destroy or secure their ports and strongholds on shore. They, nevertheless, recovered this blow, and continued to appear at intervals in new swarms, and to the great interruption of commerce by sea, and of all the communications in the empire.

Under the reformations of Sylla, which, by disarming the tribunitian power, in a great measure shut up the source of former disorders, the republic was now restored to some degree of tranquillity, and resumed its attention to the ordinary objects of peace. The bridge on the Tiber, which had been erected of wood, was taken down and rebuilt with stone; bearing the name of Æmilius, one of the questors under whose inspection the fabric had been reared; and as a public work of still greater consequence, it is mentioned, that a treatise on agriculture, the production of Mago a Carthaginian, and in the language of Carthage, was, by the express orders of the senate, now translated into Latin. At the reduction of Carthage, the Romans were yet governed by husbandmen, and, amidst the literary spoils of that city, this book alone, consisting of twenty-eight rolls or volumes, was supposed to merit public attention, and was secured for the state. A number of persons, skilled in the Punic language, together with Silanus, who had the principal charge of the work, were employed in translating it.[2]

The calm, however, which the republic enjoyed under the ascendant of the aristocracy, was not altogether undisturbed. In the consulate of Cn. Octavius and C. Scribonius Curio, the tribune Licinius made an attempt to recover the former powers of the office. He ventured, in presence of both the consuls, to harangue the people, and exhorted them to reassume their ancient rights. As a circumstance which serves to mark the petulant boldness of these men, it is mentioned that the consul Octavius, on this occasion, being ill, was muffled up, and covered with a dressing which brought flies in great numbers about him. His colleague Curio, having made a vehement speech, at the close of it, the tribune called out to Octavius, "You never can repay your colleague's service of this day; if he had not been near you, while he made this speech, and beat the air so much with his gesticulations, the flies must by this time have eaten you up."[3] The sequel is imperfectly known; but the dispute appears to have been carried to a great height, and to have ended in a tumult, in which the tribune Licinius was killed.

Upon a review of Sylla's acts intended to restore the authority of the senate, it may be questioned, whether that clause in the law relating to the tribunes, by which all persons having accepted of this office were excluded from any further preferment in the state, may not have had an ill effect, and required correction. It rendered the tribunate an object only to the meanest of the senators, who, upon their acceptance of it, ceasing to have any pretensions to the higher offices of state, were, by this means, deprived of any interest in the government, and exasperated against the higher dignities of the commonwealth. Aurelius Cotta, one of the consuls that succeeded Cn. Octavius and Curio, moved perhaps by this consideration, proposed to have that clause repealed, and was warmly supported by the tribune Opimius, who, contrary to the prohibition lately enacted, ventured to harangue the people; and for this offence, at the expiration of his office, was tried and condemned.[4]

U. C. 678.

L. Octavius, C. Aurelius Cotta.

By the defects which the people began to apprehend in their present institutions, or by the part which their demagogues began to take against the aristocracy, the Roman state, after a very short respite, began to relapse into its former troubles, and was again to exhibit the curious spectacle of a nation divided against itself, broken and distracted in its councils, which nevertheless prevailed in all its operations abroad, and gained continual accessions of empire, under the effect of convulsions which shook the commonwealth itself to its base; and, what is still less to be paralleled in the history of mankind, was to exhibit the spectacle of a nation, which proceeded in its affairs abroad with a success that may be imputed in a great measure to its divisions at home.

War, in the detail of its operations, if not even in the formation of its plans, is more likely to succeed under single men than under numerous councils. The Roman constitution, though far from an arrangement proper to preserve domestic peace and tranquillity, was an excellent nursery of statesmen and warriors. To persons brought up in this school, all foreign affairs were committed with little responsibility and less control. The ruling passion, even of the least virtuous citizens, during some ages, was the ambition of being considerable, and of rising to the highest dignities of the state at home. They enjoyed the condition of monarchs in the provinces; bu they valued this condition only as it furnished them with the occasion of triumphs, and contributed to their importance at Rome. They were factious and turbulent in their competition for power and honours in the capital; but, in order the better to support that very contest, were faithful and inflexible in maintaining all the pretensions of the state abroad. Thus Sylla, though deprived of his command by an act of the opposite party at Rome, and with many of his friends, who escaped from the bloody hands of their per-

1 Near to 10,000*l.*

2 Plin. lib. xviii. c. 3.

3 Cicero de Claris Oratoribus.

4 Cicero, 3tio, in Verrem, et Pædianus, ibid

secutors, condemned and outlawed, still maintained the part of a Roman officer of state, and prescribed to Mithridates, as might have been expected from him in the most undisturbed exercise of his trust. Sertorius, in the same manner, acting for the opposite faction, in some measure preserved a similar dignity of character, and refused to make concessions unworthy of the Roman republic. Contrary to the fate of other nations, where the state is weak, while the conduct of individuals is regular; here the state was in vigour, while the conduct of individuals was in the highest degree irregular and wild.

The reputation, as well as the arms of the Romans, procured them accessions of territory without labour, and without expense. Kingdoms were bequeathed to them by will; as that of Pergamus, formerly, by the will of Attalus; that of Cyrene by the will of Ptolemy Apion; and that of Bithynia, about this time, by the will of Nicomedes. To the same effect, princes and states, where they did not make any formal cession of their sovereignty, did somewhat equivalent, by submitting their rights to discussion at Rome, and by soliciting grants from the Romans of which the world now seemed to acknowledge the validity, by having recourse to them as the basis of tenures by which they held their possessions. In this manner, the sons of the last Antiochus, king of Syria, stated themselves as subjects or dependents of the Roman people, having passed two years at Rome, waiting decisions of the senate, and soliciting a grant of the kingdom of Egypt, on which they formed some pretensions.

In Asia, by these means, the Roman empire advanced on the ruin of those who had formerly opposed its progress. The Macedonian line, in the monarchy of Syria, was now broke off, or extinct. The kingdom itself, consisting of many provinces, began to be dismembered, on the defeat of Antiochus at Sipylus, by the defection of provincial governors and tributary princes, who, no longer awed by the power of their former master, entered into a correspondence with the Romans, and were by them acknowledged as sovereigns. In this manner the states of Armenia, long subject to the Persians, and afterwards to the Macedonians, now became the seat of a new monarchy under Tigranes. And, to complete this revolution, the natives of Syria, weary of the degeneracy and weakness of their own court, of the irregularity of the succession to the throne of their own kingdom; weary of the frequent competitions which involved them in blood, invited Tigranes to wield a sceptre which the descendants of Seleucus were no longer in condition to hold. This prince, accordingly, extended his kingdom to both sides of the Euphrates, and held Syria itself as one of its divisions.[5]

In these circumstances, the Romans were left undisturbed to re-establish their province in the Lesser Asia: and under the auspices of Servilius, who, from his principal acquisition in those parts, had the name Isauricus, were extending their limits on the side of Cilicia, and were hastening to the sovereignty of that coast, when their progress was suddenly checked by the re-appearance of an enemy, who had already given them much trouble in that quarter.

Mithridates, king of Pontus, who appears to have revived in his own breast the animosities of Pyrrhus and of Hannibal against the Romans, had never ceased, since the date of his last mortifying treaty with Sylla, to devise the means of renewing the war. Having attempted in vain to engage Sylla in a league with himself against the Romans, he made a similar attempt on Sertorius in Spain. Affecting to consider this fugitive, with his little senate, as heads of the republic, he pressed for a cession of the Roman province in Asia in his own favour, and in return offered to assist the followers of Sertorius with all his forces in the recovery of Italy. In this negotiation, however, he found, as has been already remarked, that whoever assumed the character of a Roman officer of state, supported it with a like inflexible dignity. Sertorius refused to dismember the empire, but accepted of the proffered aid from Mithridates, and agreed to send him Roman officers to assist in the formation and discipline of his army.

The king of Pontus, now bent on correcting the error which is common in extensive and barbarous monarchies, of relying entirely on numbers, instead of discipline and military skill, proposed to form a more regular army than that which he had assembled in the former war; and, however little successful in his endeavours, meant to rival his enemy in every particular of their discipline, in the use of their weapons, and in the form of their legion. With troops beginning to make these reformations, and amounting to one hundred and twenty thousand foot, and sixteen thousand horse, he declared war on the Romans, and, without resistance, took possession of Cappadocia, and Phrygia, beyond the bounds they had set to his kingdom. As he was to act both by sea and by land, he began with customary oblations to Neptune and to Mars. To the first he made an offering of a splendid carriage, drawn by white horses, which he precipitated and sunk in the sea; to the other he made a sacrifice, which, as described by the historian,[6] filled the imagination more than any of the rites usually practised by ancient nations. The king, with his army, ascended the highest mountain on their route, formed on its summit a great pile of wood, of which he himself laid the first materials, and ordered the fabric to be raised in a pyramidical form to a great height. The top was loaded with offerings of honey, milk, oil, wine, and perfumes. As soon as it was finished, the army around it began the solemnity with a feast, at the end of which the pile was set on fire, and in proportion as the heat increased, the army extended their circle, and came down from the mountain. The flames continued to ascend for many days, and were seen, it is said, at the distance of a thousand stadia, or above a hundred miles.[7]

After this solemnity was over, Mithridates endeavoured to animate and to unite in a common zeal for his cause the different nations that were collected from remote parts of the empire, to form his army. For this purpose he enumerated the successes by which he had raised his kingdom to its present pitch of greatness, and represented the numerous vices of the enemy with whom he was now to engage, their divisions at home and

5 Strabo. lib. xi. fine

6 Appian. 7 Ibid. de Bell. Mithridat.

their oppression abroad, their avarice, and insatiable lust of dominion.

The Romans were some time undetermined whom they should employ against this formidable enemy. Pompey, being still in Spain, saw with regret this service likely to fall to the share of another; and he had his partizans at Rome who would have gladly put off the nomination of any general to this command, until he himself could arrive with his army to receive it. He accordingly about this time wrote a letter to the senate, complaining, in petulant terms, of their neglect, and of the straits to which the troops under his command were reduced for want of pay and provisions, and threatening, if not speedily supplied, to march into Italy. The consul Lucullus, apprehending the consequence of Pompey's presence in Italy, at the head of an army, and wishing not to furnish him with any pretence for leaving his present province, had the army in Spain completely supplied, and, at the same time, took proper measures to support his own pretensions to the command in Asia. From his rank as the consul in office, he had a natural claim to this station; and from his knowledge of the country and of the war[1] with this very enemy, in which he had already borne some part under Sylla,[2] was entitled to plead his qualifications and his merits.

When the provinces came to be distributed, the difficulties which presented themselves in Asia were thought to require the presence of both the consuls. The kingdom of Bithynia, which had been lately bequeathed to the Romans, was in danger of being invaded before they could obtain a formal possession of this inheritance; at the same time that the enemy, by whom they were threatened, was not likely to limit his operations to the attack of that country. Of the consuls, Cotta was appointed to seize on the kingdom of Bithynia, and Lucullus to lead the army against Mithridates wherever else he should carry the war. Cotta set out immediately for his province. Lucullus, being detained in making the necessary levies, followed some time afterwards; but before his arrival in Asia, the king of Pontus had already invaded Bithynia, defeated the forces of Cotta, and obliged him to take refuge in Chalcedonia. The king of Pontus, being superior both by sea and by land, over-ran the country in the neighbourhood of this place; and, having broke the chain which shut up the mouth of the harbour, he entered and burnt some Roman gallies, which were stationed there. Not thinking it advisable to attack the town of Chalcedonia, he turned his forces against Cyzicus, a port on the Propontis, blocked up the place both by sea and by land; and, being well provided with battering engines, and the other necessaries of a siege, he had hopes of being soon able to reduce it by storm. The inhabitants, nevertheless, prepared for their defence, in expectation of being speedily relieved by the Romans.

Such was the state of affairs when Lucullus arrived in Asia; and having joined his new levies to the legions which had served under Fimbria, and to the other troops already in the province, he assembled an army of about thirty thousand men, with which he advanced to re-establish Cotta in his province, and to relieve the town of Cyzicus. The king of Pontus, being elated by his successes, and by the superiority of his numbers, gave no attention to the motions of Lucullus, suffered him to get possession of the heights in his rear, and to cut off his principal supplies of provisions and forage. Trusting, however, that his magazines would not be exhausted before he should have forced the town of Cyzicus to surrender, he continued the siege. But his engines not being well served, and the defence being obstinate, his army began to be distressed for want of provisions, and it became necessary to lessen his consumption. For this purpose he secretly moved away part of his cavalry. These were intercepted by the Romans on their march, and cut off or dispersed; and the king being reduced with the remainder of his army to the greatest distress, embarked on board one of his gallies, ordered the army to force their way to Lampsacus, while he himself endeavoured to escape with his fleet. The army being attacked by Lucullus, the greater part of them perished in passing the Asopus and the Grannicus. The king himself, having put into Nicomedia, and from thence continued his voyage through the Bosphorus to the Euxine, was overtaken on that sea by a storm, and lost the greatest part of his fleet. His own galley being sunk, he himself narrowly escaped in a barge.

The whole force with which the king of Pontus had invaded Bithynia, being thus dispelled like a cloud, Lucullus employed some time in reducing the towns into which any of the troops of Mithridates had been received; and having effectually destroyed the remains of the vanquished army, took his route by Bithynia and Galatia towards Pontus. At his entrance into this kingdom was situated the town of Amysus, a considerable fortress on the coast of the Euxine, into which the king had thrown a sufficient force to retard his progress. Mithridates, under favour of the time he gained by the defence of this place, assembled a new army at Cabira, near the frontier of Armenia. Here he mustered about forty thousand foot, and a considerable body of horse, and was soliciting the Scythians, Armenians, and all the nations of that continent to his aid. Lucullus, in order to prevent, if possible, any further reinforcements to the enemy, committed the siege of Amysus to Murena, and advanced with his army into the plains of Cabira. On this ground the Roman horse received repeated checks from those of the enemy, and were kept in continual alarm, until their general, having time to observe the country, avoided the plains, on which the king of Pontus, by means of his cavalry, was greatly superior. Though very much straitened for provisions, Lucullus kept his position on the heights until the enemy should be forced to a

1 Vide Ciceronis in Lucullo, c. 1 & 2.

2 Plutarch. in Lucull. initio. edit. Lond. 4to. vol. iii. p. 137.

Cicero is often quoted to prove that Lucullus, at this time, was a mere novice in war, and owed the knowledge by which he came to be distinguished, to speculation and study, not to experience. It is observed by lord Bolingbroke, that Cicero had an interest in having it believed, that great officers might be formed in this manner; and it is probable, that he affected to consider the part which was assigned to Lucullus by Sylla, as mere civil employment. He is mentioned as having charge of the coinage with which Sylla paid his army, and of the fleet with which he transported them into Asia: but it is not to be supposed, that these were the only operations confided by Sylla to a lieutenant of so much ability.

general action. The skirmishes which happened between the foraging parties drew considerable numbers from the respective armies to engage; and the troops of Mithridates, having been routed in one of these partial encounters, the king took a resolution to decamp in the night, and remove to a greater distance from the Romans. As soon as it was dark, the equipage and the attendants of the leading men in the camp, to whom he had communicated this resolution, began to withdraw; and the army, greatly alarmed with that appearance, was seized with a panic, and could not be restrained from flight. Horse and foot, and bodies of every description, crowded in disorder into the avenues of the camp, and were trod under foot, or in great numbers perished by each other's hands. Mithridates himself, endeavouring to stop and to undeceive them, was carried off by the multitude.

The noise of this tumult being heard to a great distance, and the occasion being known in the Roman camp, Lucullus advanced with his army to take advantage of the confusion, in which the enemy were fallen, and by a vigorous attack put many to the sword, and hastened their dispersion.

The king was, by one of his servants, with difficulty mounted on horseback, and must have been taken, if the pursuing party had not been amused in seizing some plunder, which he had ordered on purpose to be left in their way. A mule, loaded with some part of the royal treasure, turned the attention of the pursuers, while he himself made his escape.

In his flight he appeared to be most affected with the fate of his women. The greatest number of them were left at the palace of Pharnacea, a place that must soon fall into the hands of the enemy. He therefore despatched a faithful eunuch with orders to put them to death, leaving the choice of the manner to themselves. A few are particularly mentioned. Of two, who were his own sisters, Roxana and Statira, one died uttering execrations against her brother's cruelty, the other extolling, in that extremity of his own fortune, the generous care he took of their honour. Monimé, a Greek of Miletus, celebrated for her beauty, whom the king had long wooed in vain with proffers of great riches, and whom he won at last only by the participation of his crown, and the earnest of the nuptial rites, had ever lamented her fortune, which, instead of a royal husband and a palace, had given her a prison, and a barbarous keeper. Being now told, that she must die, and that the manner of her death was left to her own choice, she unbound the royal fillet from her hair, and, using it as a bandage, endeavoured to strangle herself. It broke in the attempt: "Bauble," she said, "it is not fit even for this!" then stretching out her neck to the eunuch, bid him fulfil his master's purpose. Berenice of Chios, another Grecian beauty, had likewise been honoured with the nuptial crown; and, having been attended in her state of melancholy elevation by her mother, who, on this occasion, likewise resolved to partake of her daughter's fate; they chose to die by poison. The mother intreated that she might have the first draught; and died before her daughter. The remainder of the dose not being sufficient for the queen, she put herself likewise into the hands of the executioner, and was strangled. By these deaths, the barbarous jealousy of the king was gratified, and the future triumph of the Roman general deprived of its principal ornaments.

Lucullus, after his late victory, having no enemy in the field to oppose him, passed through the country, and entered without molestation into many of the towns in the kingdom of Pontus. He found many palaces enriched with treasure, and adorned with barbarous magnificence; and, as might be expected under such a violent and distrustful government, every where places of confinement crowded with prisoners of state, whom the jealousy of the king had secured, and whom his supercilious neglect had suffered to remain in custody even after his jealousy was allayed.

Mithridates, from his late defeat, fled into Armenia, and claimed the protection of Tigranes, who, being married to his daughter, had already favoured him in his designs against the Romans.

This powerful prince, now become sovereign of Syria as well as Armenia, still continued his residence in the last of these kingdoms at Tigranocerta, a city he himself built, filled with inhabitants, and distinguished by his own name. On the arrival of Mithridates to sue for his protection, Tigranes declined to see him, but ordered him a princely reception in one of the palaces.

Lucullus continued his pursuit of this flying enemy only to the frontier of Armenia, and from thence, sending Publius Clodius, who was his brother-in-law, to the court of Tigranes, with instructions to require that Mithridates should be delivered up as a lawful prey, he himself fell back into the kingdom of Pontus, and soon after reduced Amysus, together with Sinope, and other places of strength, which were held by the troops of the king.

The inhabitants of these places had been originally colonies from Greece, and having been subdued by the Persians, were, on the arrival of Alexander the Great, from respect to their origin, restored to their freedom. In imitation of this example, and agreeably to the profession which the Romans ever made of protecting the liberties of Greece, Lucullus once more declared those cities to be free. Having now sufficient leisure to attend to the general state of the Roman provinces in Asia, he found, that the collectors of the revenue, under pretext of levying the tax imposed by Sylla, had been guilty of the greatest oppressions. That the inhabitants, in order to pay this tax, borrowed money of the Roman officers and merchants at exorbitant interest; and, when the debts became equal to their whole effects, were then distrained for payment, under pain of imprisonment and even tortures: that private persons were reduced to the necessity of exposing their children to sale, and corporations of selling the pictures, images, and other ornaments of their temples, in order to satisfy these inhumane creditors. Willing to restrain, or correct these abuses, the proconsul ordered, that where the interest exacted was equal to the capital, the debt should be cancelled; and in other cases, fixed it at a moderate rate. These acts of beneficence or justice to the provinces were, by the farmers of the revenue, represented as acts of oppression and cruelty to themselves, and were, among their connexions, and the sharers of their spoils at Rome, stated against Lucullus as subjects of complaint and reproach.

CHAPTER II.

Escape and Revolt of the Gladiators at Capua—Spartacus—Action and Defeat of Lentulus the Roman Consul—And of Cassius the Prætor of Gaul—Appointment of M. Crassus for this Service—Destruction of the Gladiators—Triumph of Metellus and Pompey—Consulship of Pompey and Crassus—Tribunes restored to their former Powers—Consulate of Metellus and Hortensius—War in Crete—Renewal of the War in Pontus and Armenia—Defeat of Tigranes—Negotiation with the King of Parthia—Mutiny of the Roman Army—Complaints of Piracies committed in the Roman Seas—Commission proposed to Pompey—His Conduct against the Pirates—His Commission extended to Pontus—Operations against Mithridates—Defeat and Flight of that Prince—Operations of Pompey in Syria—Siege and Reduction of Jerusalem—Death of Mithridates.

SOON after the war, of which we have thus stated the event, had commenced in Asia, Italy was thrown into great confusion by the accidental escape of a few gladiators from the place of their confinement at Capua. These were slaves trained up to furnish their masters with a spectacle, which, though cruel and barbarous, drew numerous crowds of beholders. It was at first introduced as a species of human sacrifice at funerals, and the victims were now kept by the wealthy in great numbers for the entertainment of the people, and even for private amusement. The handsomest, the most active, and the boldest of the slaves and captives were selected for this purpose. They were sworn to decline no combat, and to shun no hardship, to which they were exposed by their masters; they were of different denominations, and accustomed to fight in different ways; but those from whom the whole received their designation, employed the sword and buckler, or target; and they commonly fought naked, that the place and nature of the wounds they received might the more plainly appear.

U. C. 680.

M. Teren. Varro. C. Cass. Varus.

Even in this prostitution of valour, refinements of honour were introduced. There were certain graces of attitude which the gladiator was not permitted to quit, even to avoid a wound. There was a manner which he studied to preserve in his fall, in his bleeding posture, and even in his death. He was applauded, or hissed, according as he succeeded or failed in any of these particulars. When, after a tedious struggle he was spent with labour and with the loss of blood, he still endeavoured to preserve the dignity of his character, dropped or resumed the sword at his master's pleasure, and looked round to the spectators for marks of their satisfaction and applause.[1]

Persons of every age, condition, and sex, attended at these exhibitions; and when the pair who were engaged began to strain and to bleed, the spectators, being divided in their inclinations, endeavoured to excite, by their cries and acclamations, the party they favoured; and when the contest was ended, called to the victor to strike, or to spare, according as the vanquished was supposed to have forfeited or to have deserved his life.[2] With these exhibitions, which must create so much disgust and horror in the recital, the Romans were more intoxicated than any populace in modern Europe now are with the baiting of bulls, or the running of horses, probably because they were more deeply affected, and more violently moved.

Spartacus, a Thracian captive, who, on account of his strength and activity, had been destined for this barbarous profession, with about seventy or eighty of his companions, escaped from their place of confinement, and arming themselves with such weapons as accident presented to them, retired to some fastness on the ascent of Mount Vesuvius, and from thence harassed the country with robberies and murders. "If we are to fight," said the leader of this desperate band, "let us fight against our oppressors, and in behalf of our own liberties, not to make sport for this petulant and cruel race of men." Multitudes of slaves from every quarter flocked to his standard. The præfect of Capua armed the inhabitants of his district against them, but was defeated.

This feeble and unsuccessful attempt to quell the insurrection, furnished the rebels with arms, and raised their reputation and their courage. Their leader, by his generosity in rejecting his own share of any booty he made, by his conduct and his valour, acquired the authority of a legal commander; and, having named Crixus and Oenomaus, two other gladiators, for his subordinate officers, he formed the multitudes that resorted to him into regular bodies, employed a certain number to fabricate arms, and to procure the necessary accommodations of a camp, till at length he collected an army of seventy thousand men, with which he commanded the country to a great extent. He had already successively defeated the prætors Clodius, Varinus, and Cossinius, who had been sent against him with considerable forces, so that it became necessary to order proper levies, and to give to the consuls the charge of repressing this formidable enemy.

Spartacus had too much prudence to think himself fit to contend with the force of the Roman state, which he perceived must soon be assembled against him. He contented himself, therefore, with a more rational scheme of conducting his army by the ridge of the Appenines, till he should gain the Alps from whence his followers, whether Gauls, Germans, or Thracians, might separate, each into the country of which he was a native, or from which he had been originally brought.

U. C. 681.

L. Gell. Poplicola. Cn. Corn. Lent. Clodianus.

While he began his progress by the mountains, in order to execute this project, the consuls, Gellius and Lentulus, had already taken the field against him. They at first surprised and cut off a considerable body under Crixus, who had fallen

---

1 Cicer. Tusculanarum, lib ii. c. 17.

2 Cicero pro Sexto, c. 27. Tuscul. Quæst. Spartacus, lib. ii. c. 17

drwn from the heights in order to pillage the country. But Lentulus afterwards pressing hard upon Spartacus, who led the main body of the rebels, brought on an action, in which the consular army was defeated with considerable loss. Cassius, too, the prætor of Cisalpine Gaul, having advanced upon him with an army of ten thousand men, was repulsed with great slaughter.

In consequence of these advantages, Spartacus, might no doubt have effected his retreat to the Alps; but his army being elated with victory, and considering themselves as masters of Italy, were unwilling to abandon their conquest. He himself formed a new project of marching to Rome; and for this purpose destroyed all his useless baggage and cattle, put his captives to death, and refused to receive any more of the slaves, who were still in multitudes resorting to his standard. He probably expected to pass the Roman armies without a battle, and to force the city of Rome itself by an unexpected assault. In this he was disappointed by the consuls, with whom he was obliged to fight in the Picenum; and, though victorious in the action, he lost hopes of surprising the city. But still thinking himself in condition to keep his ground in Italy, he only altered his route, and directed his march towards Lucania.

The Romans, greatly embarrassed, and thrown into some degree of consternation, by the unexpected continuance of an insurrection which had given them much trouble, exposed their armies to much danger, with little prospect of honour; not being courted, as usual, for the command, they imposed it on Marcus Crassus, then in the rank of prætor, and supposed to be a person of consequence, more on account of his wealth than of his abilities; though in this service, after others had failed, he laid the foundation of a more favourable judgment. They at the same time sent orders to Pompey, who had finished the war in Spain, to hasten into Italy with his army; and to the proconsul of Macedonia, to embark with what forces could be spared from his province.

Crassus assembled no less than six legions, with which he joined the army which had been already so unsuccessful against the revolt. Of the troops who had misbehaved he is said to have executed, perhaps only decimated, four thousand, as an example to the new levies, and as a warning of the severities they were to expect for any failure in the remaining part of the service.

Upon his arrival in Lucania he cut off ten thousand of the rebels who were stationed at a distance from the main body of their army, and he endeavoured to shut up Spartacus in the peninsula of Brutium, or head of land which extends to the Straits of Messina. The gladiators desired to pass into Sicily, where their fellow-sufferers, the slaves of that island, were not yet entirely subdued, and where great numbers at all times were prepared to revolt; but they were prevented by the want of shipping. Crassus at the same time undertook a work of great labour, that of intrenching the land from sea to sea with a ditch fifteen feet wide, and as many deep, extending, according to Plutarch, three hundred stadia, or above thirty miles. Spartacus endeavoured to interrupt the execution of this undertaking; but being repulsed in every attack, his followers began to despond, and entertained thoughts of surrendering themselves. In order to supply by despair what they lost in courage, he put them in mind that they fought not upon equal terms with their enemies; that they must either conquer or be treated as fugitive slaves: and, to enforce his admonitions, he ordered one of his captives to be nailed to the cross in sight of both armies. "This," he said to his own people, "is an example of what you are to suffer if you fall into the enemy's hands."

Whilst Crassus was busy completing his line, Spartacus prepared to force it; and, having provided faggots and other materials for this purpose, filled up the ditch at a convenient place, and passed it in the night with the whole body of his followers. He directed his march to Apulia, but was pursued, and greatly harassed in his flight.

Accounts being received at once in the camp of Crassus and in that of Spartacus, that fresh troops were landed at Brundusium from Macedonia, and that Pompey was arrived in Italy, and on his march to join Crassus, both armies were equally disposed to hazard a battle; the gladiators, that they might not be attacked at once by so many enemies as were collecting against them; and the Romans under Crassus, that Pompey might not snatch out of their hands the glory of terminating the war. Under the influence of these different motives, both leaders drew forth their armies; and when they were ready to engage, Spartacus, with the valour rather of a gladiator than of a general, alighting from his horse, and saying aloud, in the hearing of his followers, "If I conquer to day, I shall be better mounted; if not, I shall not have occasion for a horse;" he plunged his sword into the body of the animal. With this earnest of a resolution to conquer or to die, he advanced towards the enemy; directing the division in which he himself commanded to make their attack where he understood the Roman general was posted. He intended to decide the action by forcing the Romans in that quarter; but, after much bloodshed, being mangled with wounds, and still almost alone in the midst of his enemies, he still continued to fight till he was killed; and the victory of course declared for his enemy. About a thousand of the Romans were slain; of the vanquished the greatest slaughter, as usual in ancient battles, took place after the flight began. The dead were not numbered; about six thousand were taken, and, in the manner of executing the sentence of death on slaves, they were nailed to the cross in rows, that lined the way from Capua to Rome. Such as escaped from the field of battle, being about five thousand, fell into the hands of Pompey, and furnished a pretence to his flatterers for ascribing to him the honour of terminating the war.

The mean quality of the enemy, however, in the present case, precluded even Crassus from the honour of a triumph; he could have only an ovation or military procession on foot. But instead of the myrtle wreath, usual on such occasions, he had credit enough with the senate to obtain the laurel crown.[1]

Pompey too arrived at the same time with new and uncommon pretensions, requiring a dispensation from the law and established forms of the commonwealth. The war he had conducted in Spain being of the nature of a civil war against Roman citizens or subjects, with a Roman general

1 A. Gellius, lib. v.

at their head, did not give a regular claim to a triumph: Pompey himself was yet under the legal age, and had not passed through any of the previous steps of questor, edile, and prætor; yet on the present occasion he not only insisted on a triumph, but put in his claim likewise to an immediate nomination to the office of consul.

It now became extremely evident, that the established honours of the state, conferred in the usual way, were not adequate to the pretensions of this young man: that he must have new and singular appointments, or those already known bestowed on him in some new and singular manner. His enemies observed, that he avoided every occasion of fair competition; that he took a rank of importance which he did not submit to have examined; and that he ever aspired to stand alone, or in the first place of public consideration and dignity. His partizans, on the contrary, stated the extraordinary honours which had been done to him, as the foundation of still farther distinctions.[1] In enumerating his services upon his return from Spain, they reckoned up, according to Pliny, eight hundred and seventy-one towns, from the Pyrennees to the extremities of that country, which he had reduced; observed that he had surpassed the glory of all the officers who had gone before him in that service; and, in consequence of these representations, though still in a private station, he was admitted to a triumph, or partook with Metellus in this honour.

Pompey had hitherto, in all the late disputes, taken part with the aristocracy; but not without suspicion of aiming too high for republican government of any sort. While he supported the senate, he affected a degree of pre-eminence above those who composed it, and was not content with equality, even among the first nobles of his country. He acquiesced, nevertheless, in the mere show of importance, without assuming a power which might have engaged him in contests, and exposed his pretensions to too near an inspection. Upon his approach at the head of an army from Spain, the senate was greatly alarmed; but he gave the most unfeigned assurances of his intention to disband his army as soon as they should have attended his triumph. The senate accordingly gave way to this irregular pretension, and afterwards to the pretension, still more dangerous, which without any of the previous conditions which the law required, he made to the consulate. Crassus, who had been prætor in the preceding year, now stood for the same office, entered into a concert with Pompey, and, notwithstanding their mutual jealousy of each other, they joined their interests, and were elected together.

U. C. 683.

M. Licin. Crassus Cn. Pomp. Magnus.

Under the administration of these officers some important laws are said to have passed, although most of the particulars have escaped the notice of historians. It appears that Pompey now began to pay his court to the people; and, though he professed to support the authority of the senate, wished to have it in his power, on occasion, to take the sense of what was called the assembly of the people against them, or in other words, to counteract them by means of the popular tumults which bore this name.

The tribunes Quinctius and Palicanus, had for two years successively laboured to remove the bars which had, by the constitution of Sylla, been opposed to the tribunitian power. They had been strenuously resisted by Lucullus and others, who held the office of consul, during the dependence of the questions which had arisen on that subject. By the favour of Pompey and Crassus, however, the tribunes obtained a restitution of the privileges which their predecessors, in former times of the republic, had so often abused; and, together with the security of their sacred and inviolable character, and their negative in all the proceedings of the state, they were again permitted to propose laws, and to harangue the people; a dangerous measure, by which Pompey at once rendered fruitless that reformation which was the only apology for the blood so lavishly shed, not only by Sylla, but likewise by himself. Caius Julius Cæsar, at the same time, having the rank of legionary tribune conferred upon him by the choice of the people, was extremely active in procuring those popular acts; a policy in which he was more consistent with himself than Pompey, and only pursued the course of the party with which he embarked in his youth.[2]

Under this consulate, and probably with the encouragement of Pompey, the law of Sylla, respecting the judicatures was, upon the motion of the prætor, Aurelius Cotta, likewise repealed; and it was permitted to the prætors to draught the judges in equal numbers from the senate, the knights, and a certain class of the people,[3] whose description is not clearly ascertained. This was, perhaps, a just correction of Sylla's partiality to the nobles; and if it had not been accompanied by the former act, which restored the tribunitian power, might have merited applause.

Lex Aurelia Judiciaria.

In the mean time, corruption advanced among all orders of men with a hasty pace; in the lower ranks, contempt of government; among the higher, covetousness and prodigality, with an ardour for lucrative provinces, and the opportunities of extortion and flagrant abuse. As the offices of state at Rome began to be coveted with a view to the appointments abroad, with which they were followed, Pompey, in order to display his own disinterestedness, with an oblique reproof to the nobility who aspired to magistracy with such mercenary views, took a formal oath in entering on his consulate, that he would not, at the expiration of his office, accept of any government in the provinces; and by this example of generosity in himself, and by the censure it implied of others, obtained great credit with the people, and furnished his emissaries, who were ever busy in sounding his praise, with a pretence for enhancing his merit. It may, however, from his character and policy in other instances, be suspected, that he remained at Rome with intention to watch opportunities of raising his own consideration, and of obtaining, by the strength of his party, any extraordinary trust or commission of which the occasion should arise.

Pompey, in the administration of his consulate, had procured the revival of the censors' functions. These had been intermitted about sixteen years, during great part of which time the republic had been in a state of civil war; and

1 Vid. Cic. pro. Lege Manilia.

2 Sueton. in C. Jul. Cæsar ib. i.

3 Tribuni Ærarii.

the prevailing parties, in their turns, mutually had recourse to acts of banishment, confiscations, and military executions against each other. In such times, even after the sword was sheathed, the power of censor, in the first heat of party-resentment, could not be safely intrusted with any of the citizens; and the attempts which were now made to revive it, though in appearance successful, could not give it a permanent footing in the commonwealth. The public was arrived at a state in which men complain of evils, but cannot endure their remedies.

L. Gellius Poplicola and Cn. Cornelius Lentulus, being intrusted, in the capacity of censors, to make up the rolls of the people, mustered four hundred and fifty thousand citizens. They purged the senate with great severity, having expunged sixty-four from the rolls, and among those C. Antonius, afterwards consul, assigning as their reason, that he, having the command on the coasts of Asia and Greece, had pillaged the allies, and mortgaged and squandered his own estate. But what most distinguished this censorship was an incident, for the sake of which, it is likely, the solemnity of the census had been now revived.

It was customary on those occasions for the knights to pass in review, each leading his horse before the censors. They were questioned respecting their age, their services, and the persons under whose command they had served; and if they had already served the ten years prescribed by law, they received an exemption from future services, and were vested with the privileges which were annexed to this circumstance. At this part of the ceremony the people were surprised to see their consul, Pompey the Great, descending into the market-place, leading his horse in quality of a simple knight, but dressed in his consular robes, and preceded by the lictors. Being questioned by the censors, whether he had served the stated number of years, he answered that he had, and all of them in armies commanded by himself. This farce was received with loud acclamations of the people; and the censors having granted the customary exemption, rose from their seats, and, followed by a great multitude, attended this equestrian consul to his own house.[4]

It is observed that Crassus and Pompey, although they entered on office in concert, yet differed in the course of their administration on subjects which are not particularly mentioned. As Crassus was in possession of great wealth, he endeavoured, by his liberalities, to vie with the imposing state and popular arts of his colleague. He gave an entertainment to the whole people at ten thousand tables, and distributed three months' provision of corn. To account for his being able to court the people in this manner, it is said that he inherited from his father a fortune of three hundred talents, or near sixty thousand pounds; that he increased it, by purchasing at a low price the estates of those who were proscribed in the late troubles, and by letting for hire the labour of a numerous family of slaves, instructed in various arts and callings; and was become so rich by these means, that when, some time after this date, he was about to depart for Asia, and consecrated the tenth part of his estate to Hercules, he was found to possess seven thousand one hundred talents, or about one million three hundred and seventy thousand and three hundred pounds sterling.[5]

Pompey at the expiration of his year in the consulship, in observance of the oath he had taken, remained at Rome in a private station; but, agreeably to the character he formerly bore, maintained the reserve and stateliness of a person raised above the condition of a citizen, or even above that of the first senators of consular rank. Other candidates for consideration and public honours endeavoured, by their talents and eloquence, to make themselves necessary to those who had affairs to solicit with the public, or even to make themselves feared. They laboured to distinguish themselves as able advocates or formidable accusers at the bar, and to strengthen their interest by procuring the support of those to whom their talents either were or might become of importance. Pompey, on the contrary, stating himself as an exception to common rules, avoided the courts of justice and other places of ordinary resort, did not commit his talents to the public judgment, nor present his person to the public view; took the respect that was paid to him as a right; seldom went abroad, and never without a numerous train of attendants.[6] He was formed for the state of a prince, and migh have stolen into that high station even at Rome, if men, born to equality, could have suffered an elevation which was not supported by adequate abilities; or had been willing, when troubled with faction, to forego their own importance, in order to obtain peace and the comforts of a moderate government. The pretensions of Pompey, however, were extremely disagreeable to the senate, and not otherwise acceptable to the people, than as they tended to mortify the pride of that order of men.

U. C. 684.

Q. Hortensius, Q. Cæcil. Metellus Creticus.

The consulate of Crassus and Pompey was succeeded by that of Q. Hortensius and Q. Cæcilius Metellus. In the distribution of provinces, Crete, with the command of an armament to be sent into that island, fell to the lot of Hortensius; but this citizen, having acquired his consideration by his eloquence in pleading the causes of his friends, and being accustomed to the bar, perhaps in a degree that interfered with his military character, declined to accept of this government; leaving it, together with the command of the army that was to be employed in the reduction of the island, to his colleague Metellus, who afterwards received the appellation of Creticus, from the distinction he acquired in this service.

The Cretans, and most of the other seafaring people on the confines of Asia and Europe, had in the late war taken an active part against the Romans. They had, by the influence of Mithridates, and by their own disposition to rapine and piracy, been led to prey upon the traders, and upon the carriers of the revenue that were frequently passing from the provinces to Rome. The desire of sharing in the profits that were made by this species of war, had filled the sea with pirates and freebooters, against whom the Romans sent forth a succession of officers, with

4 Plutarch. in Pompeio.

5 Plutarch. in Crasso. As the interest of money was prohibited at Rome, under the denomination of usury, but in fact was unlimited, the annual returns from such a capital must have been immense.

6 Plutarch. in Vit. Pomp.

extensive commands, on the coasts both of Asia and Europe. Among others, M. Antonius had been employed in this service, and was accused of abusing his power, by oppressing the Sicilians and the people of other maritime provinces, who were innocent of the crimes he was employed to repress. In a descent on the island of Crete he was defeated and killed,[1] and left the Romans engaged with the people of that island in a war which was thought to require the presence of one of the consuls. The lot, as has been observed, fell on Hortensius, but was transferred to his colleague Metellus.

U. C. 685.

L. Cæc. Metellus, Q. Mar. Rex.

Such was the state of affairs, and such the destination of the Roman officers, when Lucullus received from Tigranes a return to the demand which he made of having Mithridates delivered up as his prisoner. This prince, at the arrival of Clodius, who bore the message, had made a progress to the coasts of Phœnicia, and to the farther extremities of his empire. To verify the state and title which he assumed of King of Kings, he affected, when he mounted on horseback, to have four captive sovereigns to walk by his stirrup, and obliged them, on other occasions, to perform every office of menial duty and servile attendance on his person. Lucullus, instead of the style which was affected by this prince, had accosted him in his letter only with the simple title of king. His messenger, however, was admitted to an audience, and made his demand that Mithridates, a vanquished prince, whose territories were already in the possession of the Romans, should be delivered up to adorn the victor's triumph. This, if refused, said the bearer of the message, the Roman general would be entitled to extort by force, and would not fail, with a mighty army for that purpose, to pursue his fugitive wherever he was received and protected. Tigranes, unused even to a plain address, much less to insult and threats, heard this demand with real indignation; and though, with an appearance of temper, he made offer of the customary presents and honours to the person who delivered it, he took his resolution against the Romans, and, from having barely permitted Mithridates to take refuge in his kingdom, determined to espouse his cause. He gave for answer to Clodius, that he would not deliver up the unfortunate king, and that, if the Romans invaded his territories, he knew how to defend them. He soon afterwards admitted Mithridates into his presence, and determined to support him with the necessary force against his enemies.

Upon receiving this answer from Tigranes, Lucullus resolved without delay to march into Armenia. He chose for this expedition two legions and a body of horse, on whom he prevailed, though with some difficulty, to enter on a new war at a time when they flattered themselves that their labours were ended, and that the rewards they expected were within their reach. With hasty marches he arrived on the Euphrates, and passed that river before the enemy were aware of his approach. Tigranes treated the first reports of his coming with contempt, and ordered the person who presumed to bring such accounts to be punished. But being assured, beyond a possibility of doubt, that an enemy was actually on his territories, he sent Metrodorus, one of his generals, at the head of a considerable force, with orders to take alive the person of Lucullus, whom he was desirous to see, but not to spare a man of the whole army besides.

With these orders, the Armenian general set out on the road by which the Romans were supposed to advance, and hastened to meet them. Both armies, on the march, had intelligence of each other. Lucullus, upon the approach of the enemy, halted, began to intrench, and, in order to gain time, detached Sextilius, with about three thousand men, to observe the Armenians, and, if possible, without risking an action to amuse them till his works were completed. But such was the incapacity and presumption of the enemy, that Sextilius, being attacked by them, gained an entire victory with but a part of the Roman army; Metrodorus himself being killed, his army was put to the rout with great slaughter.

After this victory Lucullus, in order the more effectually to alarm and to distract the Armenians, separated his army into three divisions. With one he intercepted and dispersed a body of Arabs, who were marching to join the king; with another he surprised Tigranes himself, in a disadvantageous situation, and obliged him to fly with the loss of his attendants, equipage, and the baggage of his army. At the head of the third division he himself advanced to Tigranocerta, and invested that place.

After these disasters Tigranes made an effort to assemble the force of his kingdom; and bringing into the field all the troops of his allies, as well as his own, he mustered an army of one hundred and fifty thousand heavy-armed foot, fifty-five thousand horse, and twenty thousand archers and slingers. He was advised by Mithridates not to risk a battle, but to lay waste the country from which the Romans were supplied with provisions, oblige them to raise the siege of Tigranocerta, and repass the Euphrates, with the disadvantage of having an enemy still in force to hang on their rear. This counsel of Mithridates, founded in the experience he had so dearly bought, was ill suited to the presumption of the king. He therefore advanced toward the Romans impatient to relieve his capital, and the principal seat of his magnificence. Lucullus, trusting to the specimens he had already seen of the Armenian forces, ventured to divide his army, and, without raising the siege, marched with one division to meet this numerous enemy. In the action that followed, the Armenian horse being in the van, were defeated and driven back on the foot of their own army, threw them into confusion, and gave the Romans an easy victory, in which, with very inconsiderable loss to themselves, they made a great slaughter of the enemy, The king himself, to avoid being known in his flight, unbound the royal diadem from his head, and left it to become a part in the spoils of the day.

Mariæus, who commanded in Tigranocerta hearing of his master's defeat, and fearing a revolt of the Greeks and other foreigners, who had been forced to settle at that place, ordered them to be searched and disarmed. This order they looked on as the prelude to a massacre, and crowding together, defended themselves with the staves and other weapons they could seize. They surrounded a party that was sent to disperse

1 Pædianus in Orat. in Verrem

them, and having by that means got a supply of arms, they took possession of a tower which commanded one of the principal gates, and from thence invited the Romans to enter the place. Lucullus accordingly seized the opportunity, and became master of the city. The spoil was great; Tigranes having collected here, as at the principal seat of his vanity, the wealth and magnificence of his court.

Mithridates, who had been present in the late action, met the king of Armenia in his flight; and, having endeavoured to re-establish his equipage and his retinue by a participation of his own, exhorted him not to despair, but to assemble a new force, and to persist in the war. They agreed, at the same time, on an embassy to the king of Parthia, with offers of reconciliation on the part of Tigranes, who, at this time, was at war with that prince, and of satisfaction on the subjects in contest between them, provided the Parthians would join in the confederacy against the Romans. They endeavoured to persuade the king, that he was by no means an unconcerned spectator in the present contest; that the quarrel which the Romans now had with the kings of Armenia, and Pontus, was the same with that which they formerly had with Philip and with Antiochus; and which, if not prevented, they would soon have with Arsaces, and was no other than his being possessed of a rich territory, which tempted their ambition and avarice. Those republicans, they said, originally had not any possessions of their own, and were grown rich and great only by the spoils of their neighbours. From their strong hold in Italy, they had extended their empire on the west to the coast of the ocean; and, if not stopped by the powerful monarchies that lay in their way, were hastening to reach a similar boundary on the east. The king of Parthia, they added, might expect to be invaded by these insatiable conquerors, and must now determine whether he would engage in a war joined with such powerful allies, of whom one by his experience, the other by his resources, might enable him to keep the danger at a distance from his own kingdom,[2] or wait until these powers being overthrown, and become an accession to the Roman force, he should have the contest to maintain in his own territory singly and unsupported from abroad. To these representations Arsaces seemed to give a favourable ear, agreed to the proposed confederacy, on condition that Mesopotamia, which he had formerly claimed, was now delivered up to him. At the same time he endeavoured to amuse Lucullus with offers of alliance against the king of Armenia.

In this conjuncture it probably was, that Lucullus, in the apprehension of being superseded and deprived of the honour of terminating the war, made his report that the kingdom of Mithridates was now in his possession, and that the kingdom of Tigranes was also in his power; and therefore, that the senate should, instead of a successor, send the usual commission to settle the form of the province, and to make a proper establishment to preserve the territories which he had already subdued. But after these representations were despatched, it became apparent that the king of Parthia had deceived him with false professions, while he actually made great progress in his treaty with the kings of Armenia and Pontus, and meant to support them with all his force In resentment of this act of treachery, and to prevent the effects of it, Lucullus proposed to carry the war into Parthia; and, for this purpose, ordered the legions that were stationed in Pontus to march without delay into Armenia.

These troops, however, already tired of the service, and suspecting that they were intended for some distant and hazardous enterprise, broke out into open mutiny, and refused to obey their officers. This example was soon afterwards followed by other parts of the army; and the general was obliged to confine his operations to the kingdom of Armenia. He endeavoured, by passing the mountains near to the sources of the Euphrates and the Tigris, to penetrate as far as Artaxata, the capital of the kingdom. By this march he forced Tigranes once more to hazard a battle, and obtained a victory; but his own army, notwithstanding their success, were so much discouraged with the change of climate, which they experienced in ascending the mountains of Armenia, and with the early and severe approach of winter in those high lands, that they again mutinied, and obliged their general to change the plan of his operations. He turned his march to the southward, fell down on Mesopotamia, and, after a short siege, made himself master of Nisibis, a rich city in that territory, where, with other captives, he took Guras, brother to the king, who commanded in the place.

Here, however, the mutinous spirit still continuing to operate in the Roman army, it began to appear, that the general, who had so often overcome the kings of Pontus and Armenia, was better qualified to contend with an enemy, than to win or to preserve the good-will of his own troops. A report being spread that he was soon to be recalled, he, from that moment, lost the small remains of his authority; the legions deserted their colours, and treated, with contempt or indifference, all the attempts he made to retain them.

This mutiny began in that part of the army, which, having been transported into Asia, under the command of Valerius Flaccus, had murdered this general, to put themselves under the command of Fimbria, and afterwards deserted their new leader to join with Sylla. Such crimes, under the late unhappy divisions of the republic, either remained unpunished, or were stated as merits with the party in whose favour the crime was committed. These legions, however, were, by Sylla, who was not willing to employ such instruments, or to intrust his own, or the fate of the commonwealth in such hands, left in Asia, under pretence of securing the province; and they accordingly made a considerable part in the armies successively commanded by Murena and by Lucullus. The disposition which they now showed, and that of the whole army, to disorder and mutiny, was greatly excited by the factious spirit of Publius Clodius, the relation of Lucullus, who, having himself taken offence at the general, gave this specimen of his future conduct in the state, by endeavouring to stir up rebellion among the troops. "We who have already undergone so many hardships," he said, "are still kept on foot to escort the camels that carry the treasures of our general, and made to pursue, without end, a couple of barbarous princes, that

2 Letter of Mithridates in the Fragments of Sallust.

lead us over deserts, or uncultivated wastes, while the soldiers of Pompey, after a few campaigns in Spain, or in Italy, are enjoying the fruits of their labour in comfortable settlements, procured by the favour of their leader."

Lucullus was so much aware of the decline of his authority, that he did not choose to expose it, by attempting to effect even a mere change of position. He hoped, that while he issued no orders of any moment, the resolution of his army not to obey him might remain a secret to the enemy. This state of affairs, however, soon became known to Mithridates, and filled him with hopes of being able to recover his kingdom. That he might not suffer the opportunity to escape him, he fell back into Pontus, with what troops he had then under his command, and, by his authority and influence over his own subjects, soon augmented his force, penetrated among the scattered quarters of the Romans, who were left to occupy the country, and separately surprised or destroyed considerable bodies of their troops. Among these, he attacked and defeated Fabius, the officer who was trusted with the general command in that kingdom; and though now turned of seventy, exposed his own person in the action, and received a wound which stopped him in the pursuit, and by that means prevented the full effect of his victory.

Lucullus, being informed of what had passed in Pontus, had influence enough with the army to put them in motion towards that kingdom with some appearance of order; but before his arrival, Mithridates had shut up Fabius in Cabira, and defeated Triarius with considerable slaughter. Here again the old man was wounded; and, to satisfy the army that he was not dead, was raised up into view, and remained in sight of the army while his wound was dressed. In this last defeat the Romans lost twenty-four legionary tribunes, one hundred and fifty centurions, and seven thousand men.

It was not doubted, however, that Lucullus, on his arrival, if the army had been disposed to act under him, would have been able soon to retrieve his affairs: but he was at this time superseded; and it was known in the army, that Acilius Glabrio was set out from Rome to assume the command. The legions, therefore, under pretence that Lucullus was no longer their general, and that they themselves, by a decree of the people, had received their dismission, refused to obey him; and the men of his army, in great numbers, actually took the route of Cappadocia on their return to Italy.

This was the state of affairs when the commissioners, who, upon the report of Lucullus, had been sent by the senate to settle the kingdom of Pontus in the form of a province, actually arrived. They found the proconsul destitute of power in his own camp, and Mithridates whom they believed to be vanquished, again master of his own kingdom, and joining to the experience of old age all the ardour and enterprise of youth.[1]

The Roman army in Asia, as a prelude to their present defection, had been taught to upbraid the parsimony of their own general by a comparison with the liberality and munificence of Pompey, and in this comparison showed a disposition to change their leader, which, it is not doubted, Pompey, by his intrigues, and with the aid of his agents, greatly encouraged. He could in reality ill brook the private station to which, by his late oath, in entering on the consulate, he had bound himself. He studied to support the public opinion of his importance, and wished for an occasion to derive some advantage from it; but nothing had occurred for two years that was worthy of the high distinction to which he aspired. The command in Asia he coveted the more, that it was secured to Lucullus by the splendour of his own successes, and by the unanimous judgment of the senate and nobles, who knew his faithful attachment to their order, and his fidelity to the aristocratical part of the constitution. The difficulties in that service were over, and nothing but the glory of terminating the war remained. Pompey, either from envy to Lucullus, or from a design to open a way to this glory for himself, contributed to the nomination of Glabrio, and to the nomination of the prætors, who were sent with separate commands into the provinces of Asia and Bithynia. If, upon this change, the war should become unsuccessful, or languish, he had hopes to be called for by the general voice of the people, as the only person fit to bring it to a happy conclusion. Meantime a project was started, which was likely to place him near to this scene of action, and to facilitate his removal, if judged expedient, to the command of the army in Pontus.

The pirates still continued to infest the seas, and were daily rising in their presumption, and increasing in their strength. They received continual accessions of numbers from those, who, by the unsettled state of Asia, were forced to join them for subsistence. The impunity which they enjoyed during the distractions of the Roman commonwealth, and the profits they made by their depredations, encouraged many who frequented the seas to engage in the same way of life. They had been chased, and numbers of them taken by M. Antonius, the orator, by Servilius Isauricus, and, last of all, by C. Antonius, the father of him who, in the capacity of triumvir, is to become so conspicuous in the sequel of this history. But they had their retreats; and, upon the least remission of vigilance in the Roman officers, they again multiplied apace, put to sea in formidable squadrons, and embarked such numbers of men, as not only enabled them to scour the seas, but likewise to make descents on the coasts, to enter harbours, destroy shipping, and pillage the maritime towns. They even ventured to appear off the mouth of the Tiber, and to plunder the town of Ostia. All the coasts of the empire were open to their depredations. The Roman magistrates were made prisoners in passing to and from their provinces; and citizens of every denomination, when taken by them, were forced to pay ransom, kept in captivity, or put to death. The supply of provisions to Italy was rendered extremely difficult, and the price in proportion enhanced. Every report on these subjects was exaggerated by the intrigues of Pompey, who perceived, in this occasion of public distress, the object of a new and extraordinary commission to himself.

Frequent complaints having been made, and frequent deliberations held on this subject in the senate, Gabinius, one of the tribunes, at last pro-

1 Appian. Bell. Mithridat. Plutarch. in Lucullo. Dio sius

posed, that some officer of consular rank should be vested, during three years, with absolute powers, in order to put an effectual stop to these outrages, and to eradicate the cause of them, so as to secure for the future the inhabitants of the coast, as well as to protect the navigation of the seas. As Gabinius was known to be in concert with Pompey, the design of the proposition was manifest; and it was received in the senate with great aversion. "For this," it was said, "Pompey has declined the ordinary turn of consular duty upon the expiration of his office, that he might lie in wait for extraordinary and illegal appointments." Gabinius being threatened with violence if he should persist in his motion, thought proper to withdraw from the assembly.

A report was immediately spread in the city, that the person of the tribune Gabinius had been actually violated; multitudes assembled at the doors of the senate-house, and great disorders were likely to follow; it was judged prudent for the senate to adjourn; and the members dreading some insult from the populace, retired by separate ways to their own houses. Gabinius, without farther regard to the dissent of the senate, prepared to carry his motion to the people; but the other nine tribunes were inclined to oppose him. Trebellius and Roscius, in particular, promised, by their negative, to put a stop to any farther proceedings on that business. Pompey, in the mean time, with a dissimulation which constituted part of his character, affected to disapprove of the motion, and to decline the commission with which it was proposed to vest him. He had recourse to this affectation, not merely as the fittest means on the present occasion to disarm the envy of the nobles, and to confirm the people in their choice; but still more as a manner of proceeding which suited his own disposition, no less desirous to appear forced and courted into high situations, than solicitous to gain and to hold them. He thus provoked the citizens of his own rank, no less by the shallow arts which he practised to impose on the public, than by the state which he assumed. He could scarcely expect to find a support in the order of nobles, and least of all among those who were likely to become the personal rivals of his fortune in the commonwealth: and yet it is mentioned, that Julius Cæsar, now about two-and-thirty years of age, and old enough to distinguish his natural antagonists in the career of ambition, took part with the creatures of Pompey on this occasion. He was disposed to court the people, and to oppose the aristocracy; either of which principles may explain his conduct in this instance. He had himself already incurred the displeasure of the senate, but more as a libertine than as a disturber of the state, in which he had not hitherto taken any material part. In common with the youth of his time, he disliked the senators, on account of the remaining austerity of their manners, no less than the inferior people disliked them on account of their aristocratical claims to prerogative. But whatever we may suppose to have been his motives, Cæsar, even before he seemed to have formed any ambitious designs of his own, was ever ready to abet those of every desperate adventurer who counteracted the authority of the senate, or set the orders of government at nought; and seemed to be actuated by a species of instinct, which set him at variance with those forms of a civil nature, which checked the license of faction.[2]

On the day on which the question on the motion of Gabinius was to be put to the people, Pompey appeared in the Comitium; and, if we may judge from the speech which is ascribed to him, employed a dissimulation and artifice somewhat too gross even for a popular assembly. He took occasion to thank the people for the honours he had so often received; but complained, that, having already toiled so much in the public service, he still should be destined for new labours. "You have forgotten," he said, "the dangers I encountered, and the fatigues I underwent, while yet almost a boy, in the war with Cinna, in the wars in Sicily and in Africa, and what I suffered in Spain, before I was honoured with any magistracy, or was of age to have a place in the senate. But I mean not to accuse you of ingratitude; on the contrary, I have been fully repaid. Your nomination of me to conduct the war with Sertorius, when every one else declined the danger, I consider as a favour; and the extraordinary triumph you bestowed in consequence of it, as a very great honour. But I must entreat you to consider, that continued application and labour exhaust the powers of the mind as well as those of the body. Trust not to my age alone, nor imagine that I am still a young man, merely because my number of years is short of what others have attained. Reckon my services and the dangers to which I have been exposed; they will exceed the number of my years, and satisfy you, that I cannot longer endure the labours and cares which are now proposed for me. But if this be not granted me, I must beg of you to consider what loads of envy such appointments are likely to draw upon me from men, whose displeasure, I know you neither do, nor ought to regard, although to me their envy would be a great misfortune: and I confess, that, of all the difficulties and dangers of war, I fear nothing so much as this. To live with envious persons; to be called to account for miscarriage, if one fails in public affairs; to be envied, if one succeeds; who would choose to be employed on such conditions? For these, and many other reasons, I pray you to leave me at rest; leave me to the care of my family, and of my private affairs. As for the present service, I pray you to choose, among those who desire the employment, some proper person; among so many, you cannot surely be at a loss. I am not the only person that loves you, or that has experience in military affairs. There are many, whose names, to avoid the imputation of flattery, I will not mention."

To this speech Gabinius replied; and, affecting to believe the sincerity of Pompey's declarations, observed, that it was agreeable to the character of this great man, neither to desire command, nor rashly to accept of what was pressed upon him. "They who are best able to surmount difficulties," he said, "are likewise least inclined to engage in them. But it is your business, fellow-citizens, to consider, not what is agreeable to Pompey, but what is necessary to your own affairs; not to regard those who court you for offices, but those who are fit to discharge the duties of them. I wish we had many persons of this description, besides the man I have pro-

2 Zonoras, An. lib. x. c. 3.

posed to your choice. Did we not all wish for such persons likewise, when we searched among the young and the old for some one whom we could oppose to Sertorius, and found none but himself? But wishes cannot avail us; we must take men as they are; we cannot create them. If there be but one man formed for our purpose, with knowledge, experience, and good fortune, we must lay hold of him, and seize him, if necessary, even by force. Compulsion here is expedient and honourable for both parties; for those who employ it, because it is to find them a person who can conduct their affairs; for him who suffers it, because he is to have an opportunity of serving his country, an object for which no good citizen will refuse to expose his person, or to sacrifice his life.

"Do you think that Pompey, while yet a boy, was fit to command armies, to protect your allies, to reduce your enemies, to extend your empire; but that now, in the prime of life, ripe in wisdom and experience, he can serve you no longer? You employed the boy, you suffer the man to be idle. When a private citizen of equestrian rank, he was fit for war and affairs of state: now he is a senator, he is fit for nothing! Before you had any trial of him, you made choice of him for the most important trust; now that you have experience of his ability, of his conduct, and of his success, you hesitate. Is the present occasion less pressing than the former? Is the antagonist of Sertorius not fit to contend with pirates? But such absurdities cannot be received by the Roman people. As for you, Pompey, submit to the will of your fellow-citizens. For this you were born, for this you were educated. I call upon you as the property of your country; I call upon you as its defence and safe-guard; I call upon you to lay down your life, if necessary. This I know, if your country require it, you will not, you cannot refuse.

"But it is ridiculous to accost you in this manner; you, who have proved your courage and your love to your country in so many and such arduous trials. Be ruled by this great assembly. Despise the envy of a few, or study the more to deserve the general favour. Let the envious pine when they hear of your actions, it is what they deserve. Let us be delivered from the evils that surround us, while you proceed to end your life as you began it, with success and with glory."

When Gabinius had finished his speech, Trebellius, another of the tribunes, attempted to reply; but such a clamour was immediately raised by the multitude that he could not be heard. He then, by the authority of his office, forbad the question; and Gabinius instantly proposed to have the sense of the tribes, whether Trebellius had not forfeited the character of tribune? Seventeen tribes were of this opinion, and the eighteenth would have made the majority, when Trebellius thought proper to withdraw his negative. Roscius, another of the tribunes, intimated by signs (for he could not be heard) that a second should be joined with Pompey in this commission. But the clamour was renewed, and the meeting likely to end in riot and violence. Then all opposition to the motion was dropped. In this state of affairs, Gabinius, trusting that, in the present humour of the people, no man would dare to oppose the measure, and wishing to increase the honour of Pompey's nomination, by the seeming concurrence of some of the more respectable citizens, called upon Catullus, who was then first on the roll of the senate, to deliver his opinion, and led him up into the rostra for this purpose.

This citizen, by the equability of his conduct, and by his moderation in support of the aristocracy, had great authority even with the opposite party. He began his speech to the people with professions of public zeal, which obliged him to deliver with plainness what he thought was conducive to their good, and which entitled him to a deliberate hearing, before they should pronounce on the merits of what he was about to deliver. "If you listen," he said, "something may still be offered to inform your judgment; if you break forth again into disorders and tumults, your capacity and good understanding will avail you nothing. I must begin with declaring my opinion, that powers so great, and for so long a time, as are now proposed for Pompey, should not be committed to any single citizen.

"The precedent is contrary to law, and in itself, in the highest degree, dangerous to the state. Whence came the usurpations of Marius, but from the habit of continued command; from his being put at the head of every army, entrusted with every war, and no less than six times re-elected consul in the space of a few years. What inflamed to such a degree the arrogant spirit of Sylla, but the continual command of armies, and the continual power of dictator? Such is human nature, that, in age as well as in youth we are debauched with power; and if inured for any time to act as superiors, we cannot submit afterwards to the equal and moderate station of citizens.

"I speak not with any particular reference to Pompey; I speak what the law requires, and what I am sure is for your good. If high office and command be an honour, every one who had pretensions should enjoy them in his turn; if they be a load or a burden, every one ought to bear his part. These are the laws of justice and of republican government. By observing them, republics have an advantage over every other state. By employing many men in their turns, they educate and train many citizens for the public service, and have numbers amongst whom they may choose the fittest to serve on every particular emergence. But if we suffer one or a few to engross every office of public service or public trust, the list of those who are qualified for any such trust will decrease in proportion. If we always employ the same person in every public service, we shall soon have no other person to employ. Why were we so much at a loss for experienced commanders when Sertorius appeared to threaten Italy with an invasion? Because command, for a considerable time before that period, had been engrossed by a few, and those few alone had any experience. Although, therefore, I have the highest opinion of Pompey's abilities for this service, I must prefer to his pretensions the public utility and the express declaration of the laws.

"You annually elect consuls and prætors: to what purpose? to serve the state? or to carry for a few months the ensigns of power? If to serve the state, why name private persons with unprecedented commissions to perform what your magistrates are either fit to perform, or are not fit to have been elected?

"If there be any uncommon emergency that

requires more than the ordinary exertions of government, the constitution has provided an expedient. You may name a dictator. The power of this officer has no bounds, but in respect to the place in which it is to be exercised, and to the time during which it is to last. It is to be exercised within the limits of Italy, where alone the vitals of the state can be exposed to any great or pressing attack; it is limited to six months, a sufficient period in which to remove the cause of any sudden alarm. But this unlimited power, which is now proposed for so long a time, and over the whole empire, must end in calamities, such as this and other nations have suffered from the ambition and usurpation of arbitrary and seditious men.

"If you bestow unlimited power by sea and by land on a single man, in what manner is he to exercise his power? Not by himself in person, for he cannot be every where present; he must have lieutenants or substitutes who act under his orders. He cannot even attend to what is passing at once in Egypt and in Spain, in Africa, Syria, and in Greece. If so, then why may not those who are to act be officers named by you, and not by any intermediate person; accountable to you, and not to another; and in the dangers they run, animated with the prospect of honour to themselves, not to a person who is unnecessarily interposed between them and their country? Gabinius proposes to invest this officer with authority to name many lieutenants; I pray you consider, whether these officers should depend upon any intermediate person, or upon yourselves alone? and whether there be sufficient cause to suspend all the legal powers, and to supersede all the magistrates in the commonwealth, and all the governors of provinces in every part of your empire, in order to make war on pirates?"

So much of what Catullus is supposed to have delivered on this occasion is preserved among the fragments of Dion Cassius. It is mentioned by others, that the audience expressed their goodwill and respect for this senator in a compliment which they paid to him, probably near the close of his speech, when urging some of his former arguments, he asked, "If this man to whom alone, by thus employing him in every service, you give an opportunity of learning the profession of a statesman or soldier, should fall, to whom will you next have recourse?" The people answered, with a general acclamation, *To yourself.*[1] They revered, for a moment, the candour and ability of this eminent citizen, but could not withstand the arts of Pompey, and the tide of popularity, which then ran so much in his favour.

This day being far spent in debate, another day was appointed in which to collect the votes, when a decree passed to vest Pompey with the supreme command over all the fleets and armies of the republic, in every sea without distinction or limit, and on every coast within four hundred stadia, or fifty miles of the shore. This commission took place in Italy, and extended throughout every province, during three years from the time of passing the edict.

As Pompey owed these extraordinary powers entirely to the tribune Gabinius, he intended to have employed him next in command to himself; but the law which excluded the tribunes from succeeding to any such commands, in the first year after the expiration of their office, stood in the way of this choice; and Pompey did not persist in it.

Upon the publication of an edict investing an officer of such renown with so high powers for restoring the navigation of the seas, corn and every other article of importation at Rome, considerably fell in their price. The friends of Pompey already triumphed in the success of their measure, and he himself soon after, notwithstanding the meanness of the enemy opposed to him, gained much credit by the rapid, decisive, and effectual measures he took to obtain the end of his appointment. Although it was the middle of winter, a season too rough, even in the Mediterranean, for such shipping as was then in use, he gave orders to arm and put to sea as many vessels as could be collected on every part of the coast. In a little time he had returns of two hundred and seventy gallies fit for service, one hundred and twenty thousand foot, and four thousand horse embodied on the coasts to which his command extended. That the pirates might be every where attacked at once, and find no refuge by changing their usual places of retreat, he divided the maritime parts of the empire into separate districts, appointed lieutenants with full powers in each, assigned their stations, and allotted their quotas of shipping and troops. He himself, with a squadron of sixty ships, proposed to visit every quarter, and to give his presence where it should be most required. He began with the coasts of Spain and Gaul, and the seas of Sardinia and Corsica; and in passing from thence, while the fleet coasted round the peninsula of Italy, he himself went on shore, and travelled by land to meet them at Brundusium. In this journey, upon his approach to Rome, he enjoyed, in all respects, the state of a great monarch, was received with acclamations by the people, and was courted by multitudes of every condition who went forth to receive him. All his complaints and representations were received as commands. The consul Piso, being supposed not to forward his levies with sufficient alacrity, would have been degraded, if Pompey himself had not interposed to prevent a motion which the tribune Gabinius intended to make for this purpose.

The fleet being arrived at Brundusium, Pompey hastened to join it, and from thence passed by the stations of his several lieutenants in the seaports of Macedonia and Greece, to the coasts of Pamphylia and Cilicia, which were the principal resort of the pirates. Such of these banditti as he took in his way, were treated with mildness; and this circumstance, together with the great preparations which were reported from every quarter to be making against them, with the small hopes they had of being able to escape, induced them, in great numbers, to surrender themselves. In the bay of Cilicia he found a squadron of their ships assembled, and ready to cover the harbours at which they had been accustomed to collect their stores, and to lodge their booty. They separated, however, upon his appearance, took refuge in different creeks of that mountainous coast, and afterwards surrendered at discretion, delivering up all the forts they had erected, with all their stores of timber, cordage, and sails, of which they had made a considerable provision.

By these means the war was finished about

1 Cicero pro Lege Manilia.

the middle of summer, six months after the nomination of Pompey to this command. In that time seventy-two gallies were sunk, three hundred and six were taken, and a hundred and twenty piratical harbours or strong-holds on shore were destroyed. Ten thousand of the pirates were killed in action, and twenty thousand, who had surrendered themselves, remained prisoners at the end of the war. These Pompey having sufficiently deprived of the means of returning to their former way of life, transplanted to different parts of the continent, where the late or present troubles, by thinning the inhabitants, had made room for them. Upon this occasion he repeopled the city of Soli in Cilicia, which had been lately laid waste, and forcibly emptied of its inhabitants by Tigranes, to replenish his newly established capital of Tigranocerta in Armenia. After this re-establishment of Soli, the place, in honour of its restorer, came to be known by the name of Pompeiopolis.[1]

Whilst Pompey was thus employed in disposing of the pirates on the coast of Cilicia, he received a message from Lappa in the island of Crete, now besieged by Metellus, intimating that the people of this place, although they held out against Metellus, were willing to surrender to Pompey. This sort of preference, implying estimation and popular regard, was one of the temptations which Pompey was supposed unable to resist; he accordingly, without consulting with Metellus, sent an officer to receive the surrender of Lappa.

Metellus had now been near two years in the island of Crete, had almost entirely reduced it, and had a near prospect of that triumph, which he afterwards actually obtained, with the title of Creticus, on account of this conquest. Pompey's commission, as commander-in-chief of all the sea and land forces of Rome, within fifty miles of the coast, no doubt extended to this island; but it was justly reckoned invidious to interfere in the province of a proconsul, whose appointment preceded his own. And this step revived all the former imputations against him, that he considered himself as every one's superior, strove to suppress every growing fame, and threw his personal consideration as a bar in the way of every rising merit. Metellus, stung with resentment, and trusting to the support of the senate, ventured to contemn his orders, even after Octavius, who had been sent by Pompey to take the inhabitants of Lappa under his protection, had entered the town, and in his name commanded Metellus to desist from the attack of a place already in possession of the Romans. He nevertheless continued the siege, forced the town to surrender, and threatening to treat Octavius himself as a rebel, obliged him to leave the island. The senate, without otherwise deciding the controversy which was likely to arise on this subject, afterwards acknowledged Metellus as the conqueror of Crete, and decreed him a triumph in that capacity.[2]

The dispute, however, at this time might have led to disagreeable consequences, if Pompey, while he was preparing to pass into Crete against Metellus, had not found another object of more importance to his plan of greatness.[3] Lucullus had always appeared to him a more formidable rival in power and consideration than Metellus, and the war in Pontus and Armenia likely to furnish a more ample field of glory than the destruction of pirates.

Mithridates, though once nearly vanquished, was, by means of the distractions which, communicating from the popular factions at Rome, had infected the army of Lucullus, enabled to renew the war with fresh vigour. Knowing that the Roman general was no longer obeyed, he not only returned, as has been mentioned, into his own kingdom, but, together with Tigranes, began to act on the offensive, and made excursions even into Cilicia. Acilius Glabrio, the proconsul appointed to succeed in the command of the Roman army, hearing the bad state of affairs, stopped short in Bithynia, and even refused to furnish Lucullus with the reinforcements he had brought from Italy. In these circumstances the province of Asia, likely to become a principal source of revenue to the commonwealth, was in imminent danger of being wrested from their hands. The friends of Pompey seized the opportunity to obtain a farther enlargement of his powers. Manilius, one of the tribunes, in concert with Gabinius, moved the people to extend his commission to the provinces of Phrygia, Bithynia, Cappadocia, and Pontus; and of course to commit the war in Armenia and Pontus to his direction. This motion was strenuously opposed by Catulus, Hortensius, and all the principal members of the senate. It was supported by Marcus Tullius Cicero and by Caius Julius Cæsar, who both intended on this occasion, to court the popular party, by espousing the cause of a person so much in favour with the people.

Cicero was one of the first of the Romans who rested his consideration entirely on civil accomplishments, and who became great by the services he was qualified to render his friends in a civil capacity, without any pretensions to the merit of a soldier. The character of a pleader was become one of the most powerful recommendations to public notice, and one of the surest roads to consequence and civil preferments. Cicero, with a fine genius and great application, was supposed to excel all who had gone before him in this line of pursuit. His talents were powerful instruments in his own hands; they rendered him necessary to others, and procured him the courtship of every party in its turn. He was understood to favour the aristocracy, and was inclined to support the senate, as the great bulwark of the state, against the licence of the populace, and the violence of factious leaders. But being now prætor with a near prospect of the consulate, he sacrificed much to his ambition in the pursuit of preferments, which were new in his family, and which the ancient nobility were disposed to envy him. His speech, upon the motion of Manilius, was the first he had ever made in a political character; it is still extant, and does more honour to his talents as a pleader, than to his steadiness in support of the constitution and government of his country.[4] He turned aside, by artful evasions, the wise councils of Hortensius and Catulus; and, under pretence of setting forth the merits of Pompey, and of stating precedents in his favour, dazzled his audience, by enumerating the irregular

1 Dion Cassius, lib. xxxvi. c. 20.

2 Liv. Epit. Plutarch. in Pompeio. Dion Cass. lib. xxxv.

3 Dion Cass. lib. xxxvi. c. 28.

4 Cicer. Orat. pro Lege Manilia.

honours which they themselves had already conferred on this object of their favour.

With such able advocates, in a cause to which the people were already so well disposed, the interest of Pompey could not miscarry; and an addition was accordingly made to his former commission, by which he became in reality sovereign of the fairest part of the empire. Upon the arrival of this news in Cilicia, where he then was, he affected surprise and displeasure. "Are my enemies," he said, "never to give me any respite from war and trouble?" He had talents undoubtedly, sufficient to support him in the use of means less indirect; but a disposition to artifice, like every other ruling passion, will stifle the plainest suggestions of reason, and seems to have made him forget, on the present occasion, that his own attendants at least had common penetration. They turned away from the farce which he acted with shame and disgust;[5] and he himself made no delay in showing the avidity with which he received what he thus affected to dislike; laid aside all thoughts of other business; immediately despatched his orders to all the provinces that were now subjected to his power; and, without passing his mandates through the hands of Lucullus, summoned Mithridates, then with an army of between thirty and forty thousand men on the frontier of Pontus, to surrender himself at discretion. This prince, being then in treaty with Phraates, who had lately succeeded his father, Arsaces, in the kingdom of Parthia, and being in expectation of a powerful support from that quarter, refused to listen to this imperious message; being disappointed in his hopes of assistance from the Parthians, and finding that Phraates had joined in a league with his enemies, he at first endeavoured to pacify the Roman general; but finding that his advances for this purpose had no effect, he prepared for a vigorous resistance.

Pompey set out for Pontus, and in his way had an interview with Lucullus, who was then in Galatia. They accosted each other at first with laboured expressions of respect and of compliment on their respective services, but ended with disputes and sharp altercations. Pompey accused Lucullus of precipitation, in stating the kingdom of Pontus as a Roman province, while the king himself was alive and at liberty. Lucullus suspected that the late mutiny had been fomented by the emissaries of Pompey, to make way for his own succession to the command. He persisted in maintaining the propriety of the report which he had made to the senate, and in which he had represented the kingdom of Pontus as conquered, and in which he had desired that commissioners should be sent as usual to secure the possession; observed, that no province could be kept, if the troops stationed to preserve it refused to obey their general; that if such disorders were made the engine of politics in the competition of candidates for office, the republic had worse consequences to fear than the loss of any distant province; that although the fugitive king had taken advantage of the factions at Rome and in the army, to put himself again at the head of some forces, he had not yet recovered any considerable portion of his kingdom, nor been able to disturb the commissioners of the senate, who were employed in settling the province; that there was nothing left for a successor, but the invidious task of snatching at the glory which had been won by another.

From this conference Pompey entered on the command with many indications of animosity to Lucullus; he suspended the execution of his orders; changed the plan of his operations; remitted the punishments, and recalled the rewards he had decreed to particular persons, in a manner which seemed to justify the suspicion of his having encouraged the late disorders, suffering them to pass with impunity; and treating with the usual confidence even the legions which had refused to obey the orders of their general. His own authority, however, seemed to be secured by the animosity of the army to their late commander, and by their desire to contrast their own conduct, and the success of the war under their present leader, with that which had taken place under his predecessor. Finding himself, therefore, at the head of numerous and well-affected forces, both by sea and by land, he lined the whole coast of the Egean and Euxine sea with his galleys, and, at the head of a great army, advanced in search of the enemy.

Mithridates, upon the approach of Pompey, continued retiring before him towards the Lesser Armenia, laid waste the country through which the Roman army was to pass, and endeavoured to distress them by the want of provisions and forage.

For several days successively the armies encamped in sight of each other. Mithridates chose his stations, so that he could not be safely attacked; and as his object was to pass the Euphrates without being forced to a battle, he generally decamped in the night, and, by his superior knowledge of the country, passed through ways in which the Roman army could not hastily follow without manifest danger of surprise. Pompey, sensible that, upon this plan of operations, the king of Pontus must effect his retreat, took a resolution to pass him by a forced march, not in the night, but in the heat of the day, when the troops of Asia were most inclined to repose. If he should succeed in this design, and get between their army and the Euphrates, he hoped to force them to a battle, or oblige them to change their route. He accordingly, on the day he had chosen for this attempt, doubled his march, passed the enemy's camp at noon-day unobserved, and was actually posted on their route, when they began to decamp, as usual, on the following night. In the encounter which followed, having all the advantages of a surprize, and in the dark, against an army on its march, and little accustomed to order, he gained a decisive victory, in which he cut off or dispersed all the forces on which the king of Pontus relied for the defence of his kingdom.[6]

Mithridates escaped with a few attendants; and, in this extremity, proposed to throw himself again into the arms of Tigranes; but was refused by this prince, who was himself then attacked by a rebellion of his own son. Upon this disappointment he fled to the northward, passing by the sources of the Euphrates to the kingdom of Colchis, and from thence, by the eastern coasts of the Euxine, to the Scythian Bosphorus, now

5 Plutarch. in Pompeio.

6 Dio. Cass. lib. xxxvi. c. 32.

the Straits of Cossa, in order to take refuge in the Chersonesus, or Crim Tartary, at Panticapæa, the capital of a kingdom which he himself had acquired, and which he had bestowed on Machares, one of his sons. Upon his presenting himself at this place, he found that Machares had long since abandoned his father's fortunes; and, upon hearing of the ill state of his affairs on his first flight from Lucullus into Armenia, had sent, as an offering of peace, a golden crown to that general, and sued for the protection of the Romans. The father, highly provoked with this act of pusillanimity or treachery, assembled a force among his Scythian allies, and, deaf to all offers of submission or entreaties of this undutiful son, dragged him from the throne, and either ordered him to be put to death, or made his situation so painful, that he thought proper to put an end to his own life.

In this manner Mithridates entered anew on the possession of a kingdom, in which he had not only a safe retreat, but likewise the means of executing new projects of war against his enemies. By the maxims of the Romans, no kingdom was supposed to be conquered, till the king was either killed, taken, or forced to surrender himself; and Pompey, by this flight of the king of Pontus, found himself under a necessity either of pursuing him into his present retreat, or of doing what he had blamed in Lucullus, by making his report of a conquest before it was fully completed. While he was deliberating on the measures to be taken in these circumstances, he was invited by Tigranes, son to the king of Armenia, then in rebellion against his father, to enter with his army into that kingdom, and to give judgment on the differences subsisting between the father and the son.

In consequence of this invitation, Pompey marched into Armenia, joined the rebel prince, and, under pretence of supporting the son, was about to strip the father of his kingdom, when this monarch, with an excess of meanness, proportioned to the presumption with which he had enjoyed his prosperity, now resolved to cast himself entirely upon the victor's mercy. For this purpose he desired to be admitted into Pompey's presence, and, with a few attendants, presented himself for this purpose. Being told, at the entrance of the camp, that no stranger could pass on horseback, he dismounted, and was conducted on foot to the general's tent. Still bearing the diadem on his head, he took it from thence, and offered to lay it on the ground at Pompey's feet; but was told with great courtesy, that he might resume it; that, by submitting himself to the generosity of the Romans, he had not lost a kingdom, but gained a faithful ally.[1] At the same time, under pretence of reimbursing the expense of the war, a sum of six thousand talents, or about one million one hundred and twenty-eight thousand pounds sterling, was exacted from him; and he himself, to this great sum which was paid to the state, added a gratuity to the army of a talent[2] to each of the tribunes, ten minæ[3] to each of the centurions, and half a mina[4] to each private man.

Pompey, in disposing of the two Armenias, which were now in his power, allotted Sophene, or the Lesser Armenia, on the right of the Euphrates, to Tigranes the son, reserving Syria and Phœnicia, to which Antiochus, the last representative of the Macedonian line, had been restored by Lucullus, together with Cilicia and Galatia, to the disposal of the Romans.

Tigranes the father with great submission acquiesced in this partition; but the son, who probably expected to have been put in the possession of the whole of his father's kingdom, was greatly discontented, and, while Pompey was yet in Armenia, entered into a correspondence with the king of Parthia, and solicited his assistance to overturn this establishment. On account of these practices, whether real or supposed, the son was taken into custody, carried into Italy, and made a part in the ornaments of the victor's triumph.[5]

The Roman general, having in this manner disposed of the kingdom of Armenia, and secured the permanency of his settlement by the confinement of the rebel prince, resumed the thoughts of pursuing Mithridates into his present retreat. For this purpose he left Afranius in Armenia, with a force sufficient to secure his rear, and to prevent any disturbance on this side of the Euphrates. He himself passed the Araxes, and wintered on the Cyrus, or the Cyrnus, on the confines of Albania and Iberia. In the following summer, having defeated the natives of those countries in repeated encounters, he advanced to the mouth of the Phasis, where he was joined by his fleet, then plying in the Euxine sea, under the command of Servilius. Here he appears to have deliberated, whether he should attempt to pursue Mithridates any farther; but upon considering the difficulties of the voyage, and of the march along a coast and a country entirely unknown, unfurnished with any safe harbour for his ships, or even with any means of subsistence to his army by land, he took his resolution to return, and to avail himself, in the best manner he was able, of the possessions which had been abandoned to him by the flight of the king.[6] With this resolution he directed his march, by the coast, back into the kingdom of Pontus; and, finding no resistance, took all his measures as in a conquered province. At one place he found a considerable treasure, which Stratonice, one of the concubines of the king, by whom he had a son named Xiphares, disclosed to him, on condition that, if the chance of war should throw Xiphares into the hands of the conqueror, his life should be spared. But this unhappy son was exposed to other dangers besides those the mother apprehended. Mithridates, upon hearing of the price which was paid for his life, ordered him to be slain. "That woman," he said, "should have likewise bargained with me in favour of her son." At other places the Roman army found the vestiges of great magnificence, joined to monuments of superstition and of cruelty. They found some productions of an art, in which the king was supposed to be master, relating to the composition of poisons, and of their antidotes, and some records of dreams, together with the interpretations, which had been given by his women.

From Pontus, Pompey, having made a proper

1 Dio. Cass. lib. xxxvi. c. 35. Plutarch. in Pompeio.
2 93*l.* 15*s.* 3 32*l.* 5*s.* 10*d.*
4 1*l.* 12*s.* 3½*d.* Vid. Arbuthnot of Ancient Coins.

5 Plutarch. in Pompeio, ad p. 458.
6 Dio. Cas lib. 37. c. 3. Plutarch. in Pompeio. Appian. in Mithridat.
7 Plutarch. in Pompeio, p. 462.

disposition of the fleet in the Euxine, to cover the coast from any attempts which Mithridates might make from the Bosphorus and opposite coasts, set out for the kingdom of Syria, which he now determined to seize in behalf of the Romans. Lucullus had already, agreeably to the policy of his country, and under pretence of setting the Syrians free, separated their kingdom from the other possessions of Tigranes: but the pretence upon which he acted in this matter being sufficient to prevent his seizing upon Syria as a Roman province, he was content with restoring it to Antiochus, the last pretender of the Macedonian line, who had lived eighteen years in the greatest obscurity in Cilicia. Pompey now proposed to complete the transaction, by seizing for the Romans themselves, what the other affected only to restore to the lawful owner;[8] and this intended owner now pleaded in vain against the Romans that right of descent from the Macedonian line, which Lucullus had employed with so much force to supplant Tigranes.[9]

On the march into Syria, Pompey, either in person or by his lieutenants, received the submission of all the principalities or districts in his way, and made the following arrangements. The Lesser Armenia, once intended for Tigranes the son, he gave to Dejotarus, king of Galatia,[10] who afterwards was long continued on the frontier of the empire as a faithful dependant, and with possessions which served as a barrier against hostile invasions from that quarter. Paphlagonia was given to Attalus and Pylæmenus, who were likewise liberal tributaries to the Roman officers, and vigilant guards on the frontiers of the empire. Upon his arrival at Damascus, he had many applications from the late subjects or dependants of the Syrian monarchy; among others, from Hyrcanus and Aristobulus, two brothers contending for the sovereignty of Judea, who now repaired to him for judgment, and requested the interposition of his power in behalf of the party he should be pleased to favour.

Of these rivals, who were the sons of Alexander, late high priest of the Jews, Hyrcanus the elder had succeeded to his mother Alexandra, whom the father had left his immediate successor in the throne; but was dispossessed by his younger brother Aristobulus, who, being of a more active spirit, had formed a powerful faction among the people.

Hyrcanus took refuge among the Arabs, and prevailed upon Aretas, the chieftain of some powerful tribe of that people, to support him with an army, in recovering the sovereignty of the Jews. In conjunction with this ally, he accordingly laid siege to Jerusalem, but was disappointed of his object by Scaurus, one of Pompey's lieutenants, who being then in Syria, at the request of Aristobulus, from whom he received a present of three hundred talents, or about fifty-seven thousand and nine hundred pounds sterling, interposed, and obliged the Arabs to raise the siege. Upon the arrival of Gabinius, whom Pompey had sent before him into Syria, Aristobulus thought proper to make him likewise a present of fifty talents, and by these means remained in possession of the sovereignty at the arrival of Pompey.

It is alleged that each of the contending parties made their presents to the general himself; Hyrcanus in particular, that of a beautiful piece of plate, admired for its workmanship and weight, being the imitation of a spreading vine, with its leaves and fruit in massy gold;[11] and these circumstances merit attention, as they furnish some instances of the manner in which great riches, now in so much request at Rome, were amassed by Roman generals in the course of their services. Besides what they gained in this manner, it is likely that every conquest they effected, every revolution they brought about, and every protection they granted, were extremely profitable.

Pompey, on hearing the merits of the question between the two brothers, declared for Hyrcanus, and advanced towards the city, to execute the decree he had passed. Upon his approach he was again met by Aristobulus, who made fresh offers of submission, and of a public contribution in money; and Pompey sent forward Gabinius to take possession of the place, in terms of this submission. But upon a report that the gates were still kept shut by the party of Aristobulus, who yet remained in his camp, he ordered this prince into confinement, and advanced with his army.

The citizens being divided, those who espoused the cause of Hyrcanus were willing to receive the Romans; the others, who were attached to Aristobulus, retired into the temple, and broke down the bridge by which this edifice was joined to the streets, and made every other preparation to defend themselves to the last extremity.

The gates of the city, in the mean time, were thrown open by the party of Hyrcanus; and the Romans being admitted, took possession of all the principal stations within the walls, and prepared to attack the temple. This building had all the advantages of a citadel, built on a height, surrounded with natural precipices, or with a deep ditch, overhung with lofty battlements and towers. Pompey sent for battering engines to Tyre, and cut down all the woods in the neighbourhood to furnish materials for filling up the ditch, raising his mound of approach,[12] and erecting his towers. All his works were with great obstinacy counteracted by those who had taken refuge in the temple. He observed, however, in the course of his operations, that the people within, although they defended their persons when attacked on the Sabbath-day, yet they did not labour, either in repairing any of their own defences, or in opposing or demolishing the works of the besiegers. He accordingly took advantage of this circumstance, made no assaults on that day, but carried on his attack in filling up the ditch, and carrying on his approach. In this manner his towers, without interruption, were raised to the level of the battlements, and his engines playing from thence, made great havoc among the besieged. The Jews, however, even under the discharge of the enemy's missiles, still continued at the altar to perform their usual rites. While they were engaged in these holy exercises they took so little precaution against the dangers to which they were exposed, that numbers perished in offering up the sacrifices, and mingled their blood with that of the victims.

In the third month after the siege began, one of the towers of the temple was brought in ruin

8 Justin. lib. xl. c. 1 and 2.
9 Appian. in Mithridat. p. 244.
10 Eutrop. lib. vi.
11 Joseph. Antiq. lib. xiv. c. 2.
12 The Agger.

to the ground; and Faustus, the son of Sylla, with two centurions at the head of the divisions they commanded, entered the breach, and putting all whom they met to the sword, made way for more numerous parties to follow them, and covered the avenues and porches of the temple with the slain. The priests, who were even then employed in the sacrifices, waited for the enemy with great composure, and, without discontinuing their duties, were slain at the altars. Numbers of the people threw themselves from the precipices; and others, setting fire to the booths in which they had lodged under the walls of the temple, were consumed in the flames. About twelve or thirteen thousand perished on this occasion, without any proportional loss to the besiegers, or to those who conducted the storm.

Pompey, being master of the temple, and struck with the obstinate valour with which the people had devoted themselves to its preservation, was curious to see the interior recess. This place, into which no one was ever admitted besides the high priest, he supposed to contain the sacred emblems of that power who inspired his votaries with so ardent and so unconquerable a zeal. And he ventured, to the equal consternation and horror of his own party among the Jews, as of those who opposed him, to enter with his usual attendants into the Holy of Holies. He found it adorned with lamps, candlesticks, cups, vessels of incense, with their supports all of solid gold, with a great collection of the richest perfumes, and a sacred treasure of two thousand talents, or about three hundred and eighty-six thousand pounds sterling.

Having satisfied his curiosity, it is mentioned that he respected the religion of the place so much as to have left every part of this treasure untouched, and to have given directions that the temple itself should be purified, in order to expiate the profanation of which he himself had been guilty. He restored Hyrcanus to the priesthood or sovereignty of the kingdom, but charged him with a considerable tribute to the Romans, and at the same time stripped the nation of all those possessions or dependencies in Palestine and Cœlesyria, which had been acquired or held in subjection by their ancestors. Such were Gadara, Scythopolis, Hyppus, Pella, Samaria, Marissa, Azotus, Jamana, Arethusa, Gaza, Joppa, and Dora, with what was then called Strato's Tower, and afterwards Cesarea. Under pretence of restoring these several places to their liberties, they were detached from the principality of the Jews, but in reality annexed to the Roman province of Syria.[1]

Pompey now recollecting that he had formerly carried his arms to the shores of the Atlantic, and to the boundaries of Numidia and of Spain; that he had recently penetrated to the coasts of the Euxine, and to the neighbourhood of the Caspian Sea; to the end that he might not leave any part of the known world unexplored by his arms, now formed a project to finish this round of exploits, by visiting the shores of the Asiatic or Eastern Ocean: a circumstance which was to complete the glory of his approaching triumph, and raise him, as his flatterers were pleased to observe, to a rank above every conqueror of the present or any preceding age.[2]

1 Joseph. de Bell Jud. lib. i. & vii. & Ant. lib. xiv. c. 6.
2 Plutarch. in Pom. p. 463

But while Pompey was employed in the settlement of Syria, in the reduction of Jerusalem, and meditating these farther conquests, Mithridates was busy in making preparations to renew the war. Having heard of the extremities to which the citizens of Rome had been frequently reduced by the invasion of the Gauls and of Hannibal, and by the insurrections of their own subjects and slaves, he concluded that they were weakest at home, or might be attacked with the greatest advantage in Italy. He again, therefore, resumed the project of marching an army of Scythians by the Danube and the Alps. He visited all the princes in his neighbourhood, made alliances with them, which he confirmed by giving to some of them his daughters in marriage, and persuaded them, by the hopes of a plentiful spoil, to join with him in the project of invading Europe. He even despatched his agents into Gaul, to secure the co-operations of nations on that side of the world, and trusted that, on his appearance in Italy, many of the discontented inhabitants would join him as they had joined Hannibal; and that the slaves, so lately at open war with their masters, would likewise be a plentiful supply of recruits to his army.

These projects, however, appeared to his own nation too hazardous and vast. They were suited to the state of a king who wished to perish with splendour; but not to that of subjects and followers who had humbler hopes, and who chose to be governed by more reasonable prospects of success. The king himself, while he meditated such extensive designs, being confined by an ulcer in his face, had been for a considerable time concealed from public view, and had not admitted any person to his presence besides some favourite eunuchs. The minds of his subjects, and of his own family in particular, were much alienated from him by some late acts of barbarous severity against Machares and Xiphares, two of his children, who with some others, as we have mentioned, had incurred his resentment.

Pharnaces, another son, attended the father; and, though disposed to betray him, was still much in his confidence. The people of Phanagoria, a town on the shore of the Bosphorus, opposite to the fortress at which the king now resided, together with the inhabitants of the country, pretending a variety of provocations, revolted against him; and the army, during his confinement, losing the usual awe of his person, mutinied, and acknowledged Pharnaces for king. They assembled round the fort in which Mithridates was lodged, and which he had garrisoned with a chosen body of men. When he appeared on the battlements, and desired to know their demands: "To exchange you," they said, "for Pharnaces; an old king for a young one." Even while he received this answer, and while many of his guards deserted him, he still hoped that, if he were at liberty, he might retrieve his affairs. He desired, therefore, by repeated messages, to know whether he might have leave to depart in safety? But none of the messengers he sent with this question being suffered to return, he apprehended that there was a design to deliver him up into the hands of the Romans. Under this apprehension he had recourse to his last resort, a dose of poison, which, it is said, he always carried in the scabbard of his sword. Being to employ this sovereign remedy of all his evils, he dismissed, with expressions of kindness and gratitude, such of his attendants as still continued faithful to him; and being left with two of his daughters, who earnestly desired to die with their father, he allowed them to share in the draught, and saw them expire. But the portion which he had reserved for himself not being likely to overcome the vigour of his constitution, or, as was believed in those credulous times, being too powerfully counteracted by the effect of many antidotes he had taken against poison, he ordered a faithful slave who attended him, to perform with his sword what was in those times accounted the highest proof, as it was the last act, of fidelity in a servant to his master.

Accounts of this event was brought to Pompey, while his army was encamped at the distance of some days' march from the capital of Judea, in his way to Arabia. The messengers appeared carrying wreaths of laurel on the points of their spears; and the army, crowding around their general to learn the tidings, were informed of the death of Mithridates. This they received with acclamations, and immediately proceeded to make all the ordinary demonstrations of joy. Pompey, having now accomplished the principal object of the war, dropped his design on Arabia, and directed the march of his army towards Pontus. Here he received the submission of Pharnaces, and, with many other gifts, was presented with the embalmed corpse of the king. The whole army crowded to see it, examined the features and the scars, testifying, by these last effects of their curiosity, the respect which they entertained for this extraordinary man. He had, with short intervals, occupied the arms of the Romans during forty years; and, though he could not bring the natives of Asia to match with the Roman legions, yet he frequently, by the superiority of his own genius, stood firm in distress, or rose from misfortune with new and unexpected resources. He was tall, and of a vigorous constistution, addicted to women, and, though superior to every other sort of seduction, to this his ardent and impetuous spirit made him a frequent and an easy prey. He appears to have loved and trusted many of that sex with boundless passion. By some of them he was followed in the field; others he distributed in his different palaces; had many children, and entertained more parental affection than commonly attends the polygamy of Asiatic princes; yet even towards his own sons, as well as towards every one else, on occasions which alarmed the jealousy of his crown, he was sanguinary and inexorable.

Pompey proceeded to settle the remainder of his conquests; and, besides the arrangement already mentioned, annexed the kingdom of Pontus to the province of Bithynia, gave the Bosphorus to Pharnaces, and put the province of Syria, extending to the frontier of Egypt, under the government of Scaurus. He had now, from the time of his appointment to succeed Lucullus, for about three years, had the sole direction of the affairs of the Romans in Asia;[1] and had exchanged with the king of Parthia provoking messages, which, in a different conjuncture, might have led to immediate war. But the cirumstances were not yet ripe for such a measure, and Pompey had provided sufficient materials for a triumph, without attempting to break through those boundaries on which so many Roman generals were doomed to disappointments, and on which the progress of the empire itself was destined to stop.

Without entertaining any farther projects for the present, he set out with two legions on the route of Cilicia towards Italy, having Tigranes, son to the king of Armenia, together with Aristobulus, late usurper of the Jewish throne, with his family, two sons and two daughters, as captives to adorn his triumph.[2]

CHAPTER III.

Growing Corruption of the Roman Officers of State—The Love of Consideration changed for Avarice, Rapacity, and Prodigality—Laws against Extortion—Catiline a Candidate for the Consulship—Conspiracy with Autronius—Competition for the Consulate—Election of Cicero and Antonius—Condition of the Times—Agrarian Law of Rullus—Trial of Rabirius—Cabals of the Tribunes—Of Catiline—His Flight from the City—Discovery of his Accomplices—Their Execution.

U. C. 686.

C. Calpurnius Piso, M. Aul. Glabrio.

ABOUT the time that Pompey obtained his commission to command with so extensive a power in the suppression of the pirates, the tide began to run high against the aristocratical party. The populace, led by some of the tribunes, were ever ready to insult the authority of the senate; and the vices of particular men gave frequent advantages against the whole order of nobility. Corruption and dangerous faction prevailed at elections, and the preferments of state were generally coveted, as steps to the government of provinces, where fortunes were amassed by every species of abuse, oppression, and violence. Envy and indignation concurred in rousing the people against these abuses. Cornelius, one of the tribunes, proposed a severe law against bribery, by which persons convicted of this crime should be disqualified for any office of state. The senate wished to soften the rigour of this law, by limiting the penalty to a pecuniary fine; and the consul, Calpurnius Piso, moved for an edict to this purpose, in order to anticipate and to preclude the more violent law of Cornelius. But the tribune prevailed, and obtained an act imposing the severer penalty. He likewise, by another decree of the people, attacked the discre-

Lex Cornelia de Ambitu.

1 Dion Cass. lib. xxxvii. c. 6.
2 Joseph. de Bell. Jud. lib. i. c. 7.

tionary jurisdiction of the prætors,[1] obliged them to be more explicit in the edicts they published, and to observe them more exactly.

The crime of extortion in the provinces, however, was the great disgrace of the Romans. To have found an effectual remedy for this evil, would have done more honour to the commonwealth than they had derived from all their conquests. Severe laws were accordingly enacted, complaints were willingly received, and prosecutions encouraged. Candidates for popularity and public favour generally began with endeavouring to bring some offender under this title to public justice; but the example of this state, after all, has left only this piece of instruction to mankind: That just government over conquered provinces is scarcely to be hoped for, and least of all where republics are the conquerors.

Manilius, one of the tribunes of the people, in order to strengthen the inferior class of his constituents, had obtained by surprise an act,[2] by which the citizens of slavish extraction were to be promiscuously inrolled in all the tribes. This act, having drawn upon him the resentment of the senate, compelled him to seek for security under the protection of Gabinius and Pompey. With this view he moved his famous act, in which Cicero concurred, to vest Pompey with the command in Asia. This motion procured him a powerful support, and, on some occasions, the general voice of the people in his favour. Soon after this transaction, being prosecuted for some offence at the tribunal of Cicero, who was then prætor, and being refused the usual delays, the prætor was obliged to explain this step in a speech to the people; in which he told them, that he meant to favour Manilius, and that, his own term in office being about to expire, he could not favour him more effectually, than by hastening his trial, and by not leaving him in the power of a successor, who might not be equally disposed in his favour. Such were the loose and popular notions of justice then prevailing at Rome.[3]

Lex Manilia.

At the election of consuls for the following year, there occurred an opportunity to apply the law against bribery. Of four candidates, Publius Autronius Pætus, Publius Cornelius Sylla, L. Aurelius Cotta, and L. Manlius Torquatus, the majority had declared for the former two; but these being convicted of bribery, were set aside, and their competitors declared duly elected.

About the same time L. Sergius Catilina, who has been already mentioned as one of the most violent executioners of Sylla's proscriptions, having returned from Africa, where he had served in the capacity of prætor, and intending to stand for the consulate, was accused of extortion in his province, and stopped in his canvass by a prosecution raised on this account. In his rage for this disappointment, he was ripe for any disorder; and, being readily joined by Autronius and Piso, formed a conspiracy to assassinate their rivals,[4] to massacre the senate, to seize the ensigns of power, and, with the aid of their faction, to lay hold of the government.[5] Julius Cæsar and Crassus are mentioned by Suetonius as accomplices in this plot. Crassus was to have been named dictator, and Cæsar his general of the horse.[6] Cæsar was to have given the signal for the execution of the massacre, by uncovering his shoulders of his gown; but Crassus having relented, absented himself from the senate on the day appointed, and Cæsar, though present, omitted to give the signal, by which means the whole was disconcerted. Sylla was tried some years after as an accessory, and was defended by Cicero.

Many of those who, by their birth and distinction, were destined to run the career of political honours, found their fortunes, by the extravagant expence of public shows, and in gratuities to the people, by bribes to private persons, as well as by their own debauchery and prodigality, ruined before they attained their end. They sought to repair their ruin by any unwarrantable means,[7] and were ready to engage in any dangerous design. The state appears to have apprehended an increase of this danger from the number of foreigners, who, from every quarter, crowded to Rome, as to the general resort of persons who wished to gratify their own extravagance, or to prey upon that of others. Under this apprehension, an edict was obtained, upon the motion of C. Papius, tribune of the people, to oblige all strangers to leave the city: but it is likely, that the state was in greater danger from natives than foreigners. Catiline, having prevailed upon Clodius, by the consideration of a sum of money, to drop the prosecution, which had been intended against him, was left to offer himself a candidate for the consulate of the following year.[8]

Lex Papia de Peregrinis.

The office of censor had been revived in the persons of Catulus and Crassus; but these officers found that its authority, so powerful in former times, was now of little effect. They scarcely ventured to give it a trial within the city; and, having differed about the enrolment of citizens residing beyond the Po, and about some other particulars, they resigned their power.[9] Censors were again named in the following year, but with no greater effect; some of the tribunes, fearing to be degraded from the senate, forbade them to proceed in making up the roll.[10]

U. C. 689.

C. J. Cæsar, C. Mar. Figulus.

In the next consulate, Caius Julius Cæsar, at this time thirty-five years of age, entered on his career of popularity and ambition. Being edile, together with Marcus Bibulus, he not only concurred with his colleague in all the expensive shows that were given to the people, but gave separate entertainments on his own account. The multitudes of gladiators he had assembled on this occasion gave an alarm to the magistracy, and he was ordered not to exceed a certain number. In the administration of his office as prætor, he took some steps that were likely to revive the animosity of the late parties of Marius and Sylla; and, notwithstanding the act of indemnity which had passed, raised prosecutions on a charge of assassination, against all those who had put any citizen to death in execution of Sylla's proscription.[11] From this time, Suetonius observes, that Cicero dated the beginning of Cæsar's project to subvert

1 Dio. Cass. lib. xxxvi. c. 23.
2 Ibid lib. xxxvi.
3 Plutarch. in Vit. Cicer.
4 Cic. in Catil. i. c. 6.
5 Dion. lib. xxxvi. &c.
6 Sueton. in Cæsar.
7 Plutarch. in Vit. Ciceronis
8 Cicero de Aruspicum Responsis
9 Dion, lib. xxxvi. Plutarch. in Crasso.
10 Ibid. Plut.
11 Sueton. in Vit. C. J. Cæsaris.

the republic, and to make himself master of the state.[12]

What has most distinguished this consulate, however, is the competition of candidates for the succession to that office on the following year, and the consequences of the election which followed. The candidates were M. Tullius Cicero, C. Antonius, son of the late celebrated orator, L. Sergius Catilina, P. Sulpitius Galba, and L. Cassius Longinus, Quintus Cornificius, and Licinius Sacerdos.

Cicero was the first of his family who had ever resided, or enjoyed any honours, at Rome. He was a native of Arpinum, a country-town of Italy, and was considered as an obscure person by those who were descended of ancient families, but had great consideration on account of his eloquence and the consequences of it, to all such as had any interests at stake before the tribunals of justice. Being solicited by Catiline to undertake his defence on a trial for malversation in Sicily, he did not at once reject the request, nor always deny his aid to the factious tribunes in support of their measures. He was undoubtedly, like other ambitious men at Rome, disposed to court every party, and willing to gain individuals;[13] and had of late, in particular, considerably strengthened his interest, by having supported the pretensions of Pompey, and by having joined the popular tribunes, in what they proposed in behalf of that officer. He was, notwithstanding, probably by his aversion to appear for so bad a client as Catiline, saved from the reproach of having espoused his cause; and by his known inclination in general to support the authority of the senate, he disposed the aristocratical party to forgive the occasional part which he took with the tribunes in particular questions, not immediately supposed to affect their government.

In the course of this competition for the consulship, Antonius and Catiline joined interests together, and spared no kind or degree of corruption. Cicero complained of their practices in the senate, and moved to revive the law of Calpurnius against bribery, with an additional penalty of ten years' banishment.[14] Catiline considered this measure as levelled against himself; and incited by this provocation, as well as by the animosity of a rival, was then supposed to have formed a design against Cicero's life, and to have expressed himself to this purpose, in terms that gave a general alarm to the electors, and determined great numbers against himself. He had drawn to his interests many persons of infamous character and desperate fortune, many youths of good family, whom he debauched or encouraged in their profligacy. His language, at their meetings, was full of indignation at the unequal and supposed unjust distribution of fortune and power. "All the wealth of the state, all authority," he said, "is engrossed by a few, while others of more merit, are kept in poverty and obscurity, and oppressed with debts." He professed his intention, when in office, to remove these grievances, to cancel the debts of his friends, to enrich them by plentiful divisions of land, and to place them in the highest stations.

These declarations, being made to a numerous meeting, were ill concealed. Curius, one of the faction, boasted to Fulvia, a woman of rank, with whom he had a criminal correspondence, that a revolution must soon take place, and specified the particular hopes and designs of their party. This woman mentioned the subject to her own confidents, but concealed the author of her information. In the mean time, Catiline was considered as a person of the most dangerous designs, and was opposed in his election by all who had any regard to public order, or to the safety of the commonwealth. Cicero, at the same time, being supported by the senate, was elected, together with Caius Antonius. The latter stood candidate upon the same interest with Catiline, and was preferred to him only by a small majority.

U. C. 690.

M. Tullius Cicero, C. Antonius.

By this event the designs of Catiline were supposed to be frustrated; but the consuls were not likely to enter on a quiet administration. The tribunitian power, from the time of its restoration, was gradually recovering its force, and extending its operations. Every person that could give any public disturbance, that could annoy the senate, or mortify any of its leading members; every one that had views of ambition adverse to the laws, or who wished to take part in scenes of confusion and tumult; every person oppressed with debt, who wished to defraud his creditors; every person who, by his profligacy or crimes, was at variance with the tribunals of justice, was comprehended under the general denomination of the popular party. The Roman people had once been divided into patrician and plebeian, next into noblemen and commoners; but now they took sides with little regard to former distinctions against or for the preservation of public order. In the assembly of the centuries, as well as in that of the tribes, the disorderly and the profligate began to prevail; and as it was impossible that the collective body of the people could meet, the comitia, for the most part, was but another name for such riotous assemblies, as were made up of the persons who haunted the streets of Rome. The minds of sober men were full of fear and distrust, alarmed with surmises of plots, and various combinations of desperate persons, who united their influence, not to carry elections or attain to preferments, but to overturn the government, or to share in its spoils.[15]

Lex Servilia Agraria.

One of the tribunes of the present year, Servilius Rullus, soon after his admission into office, under pretence of providing settlements for many of the citizens, promulgated the heads of an Agrarian law, which he carried to the senate and the people. The subject of former grants was now in a great measure exhausted, and all Italy was inhabited by Roman citizens. This tribune proposed a new expedient to open settlements for the indigent, not by conquest, but by purchase. It was proposed that all estates, territories, or possessions of any sort, which belonged to the republic, should be sold; that all acquisitions of territory recently made, and the spoils taken from any enemy should be disposed of in the same manner; that

12 Sueton. Vit. C. J. Cæs c. ix. Suetonius supposes, that Cicero alluded to the conspiracy of Autronius and Syl-- in which Crassu- as well as Cæsar, was said to be engaged.

13 Ep. ad Atticum, lib. i. ep. 2.

14 Dio. lib xxxvii. c. 39.

15 Cicero de Lege Agraria.

the money arising from such sales should be employed in purchasing arable and cultivable lands, to be assigned in lots to the needy citizens; and that, to carry this law into execution, ten commissioners should be named in the same manner in which the pontiffs were named, not by the whole people, but by seventeen of the tribes selected by lot: that these commissioners should be judges, without appeal, of what was or was not public property; of what was to be sold, of what was to be bought, and at what price; that they were to receive and judge of the accounts of every consul, or other officer, except Pompey, commanding in any province, where any capture was made, or new territory acquired: and in short, that they should, during five years, which was the intended term of their commission, be the sole masters of all property within the empire, whether public or private.

On the day that the new consuls entered on their office, when they returned in procession from the capitol, and gave the first meeting to the senate, Rullus had the presumption to propose this law, and to move the conscript fathers, that they would be pleased to give it the sanction of their approbation and authority in being carried to the people. Upon this occasion, Cicero made his first speech in the character of consul. The former part of it is lost; the remainder may be reckoned among the highest specimens of his eloquence. In this and the two speeches he delivered to the people, on the same subject, he endeavoured to demonstrate (if we may venture to imitate his own expressions) that, from the first clause of this law to the last, there was nothing thought of, nothing proposed, nothing done but the erecting, in ten persons, under the pretence of an Agrarian law, an absolute sovereignty over the treasury, the revenue, the provinces, the empire, the neighbouring kingdoms and states; and, in short, over all the world as far as it was known to the Romans. He painted in such lively colours the abuses which might be committed by Rullus, and by his associates, in judging what was private and what public property, in making sales, in making purchases, in planting the colonies; and so exposed the impudence of the cheat, by which it was proposed to surprise the people into the granting of such powers, the absurdity and the ruinous tendency of the whole measure, that it was instantly rejected, and its author hissed from the assembly, and treated as an object of ridicule and scorn.

The splendour of the consul's eloquence, on this occasion, appeared with great distinction, and the spirit of the times continued to furnish him with opportunities to display it.[1] Roscius Amerinus, having been tribune of the people a few years before, had, by the authority of his office, set apart some benches in the theatre for the equestrian order. This gave offence to the people, so that Roscius was commonly hissed when he appeared at any of the public assemblies. On some one of these occasions the consul interposed; and, in a popular harangue, secured the attachment of the knights to himself, and reconciled the people to the distinction which had been made in favour of that body.

There happened under the same consulate a business of greater difficulty, being a motion to restore the sons of the proscribed to the privilege of being chosen into the offices of state, of which they had been deprived by an ordinance of Sylla. Their fate was undoubtedly calamitous and severe. Many of them who had been too young to have incurred the guilt of their party, were now come of age, and found themselves stript of their birthright, and stigmatized with this mark of dishonour. It was proposed, in their behalf, to take away this cruel exclusion. But Cicero, apprehending that this proposal tended to arm and to strengthen persons, who, from long use, had contracted an habitual disaffection to the established government, powerfully opposed the motion, and succeeded in having it rejected.[2]

Though the orations on the two subjects last mentioned have perished, great part of that which he spoke on the trial of C. Rabirius still remains. This man, of a great age, a respectable senator at the distance of six-and-thirty years, was brought to trial as an accomplice in the death of Apuleius Saturninus, the factious tribune, who, as has been related, having seized the capitol, was, by the consuls Marius and Valerius Flaccus, acting under the authority of the senate, and attended by all the most respectable citizens in arms, forced from his strong-hold, and put to death as a public enemy.

Titus Atius Labienus, one of the tribunes, was the declared prosecutor of C. Rabirius; but historians agree, that this tribune acted at the instigation, and under the direction, of C. Julius Cæsar. The intention of the popular party was, by making an example of this respectable person in so strong a case, where the authority of the senate, and the commands of the most popular consul, where even the prescription of so old a date should have repelled every danger, effectually, for the future, to deter every person from acting in support of the senate, or from opposing force to the designs of factious tribunes, however turbulent or dangerous.

The senate, and all the friends of government, were greatly alarmed, and united in defence of Rabirius. The popular party, as already described, the ambitious, the profligate, the bankrupt, who were earnest to weaken the hands of government, and in haste to bring on scenes of confusion and trouble, took the opposite side.

The prosecutor laid his charge for treason of the most heinous kind, and destined the accused to die on the cross, the ordinary manner of executing the sentence of death on the slaves. "The executioner stalks in the forum," said Cicero "and the cross is erected for a Roman citizen in the field of Mars." The accusation was first brought before the prætor who possessed the ordinary jurisdiction in such cases. This magistrate empannelled two judges, who were to determine in this mighty cause. These were Caius Julius and Lucius Cæsar. At this court the defendant was condemned; and with appearances of animosity, on the part of Caius Cæsar, that greatly increased the alarm. This rising citizen had always courted the populace, and was strongly supported by them. That he should aim at honours and power, it was said, is common; but that he wished to provide impunity for the dis-

1 It is probable that Cicero did not write in order to speak, but wrote after he had spoken, for the use of his friends. Epist. ad Atticum. lib. ii. c. 1.

2 Plin. lib. vii. c. 30

turbers of the commonwealth, was alarming. The crime of Rabirius, even if he could be convicted of it, had been committed the year before Cæsar was born. In the person of the accused every circumstance, even on the supposition of a true charge, pleaded for compassion and even for respect: the fact, at the same time, was denied, and a positive evidence was brought, that another had received a reward for killing Saturninus: but the policy of the faction required this victim; and the sentence must have been executed, if the condemned had not fled, by appeal, to the judgment of the people, where indeed his cause might be reckoned more desperate than if it had been before a select court. The parties attended this trial with great ardour. Hortensius conducted the appeal and defence. Cicero pleaded in behalf of justice and government; painted the age, the infirmities, the forlorn state of the defendant, who had survived his relations and his friends. He pointed out the danger to government and to order from this precedent, in terms that must have melted every heart, not callous from ambition, faction, or profligacy of manners: but in vain. Even in the assembly of the centuries, the majority was hastening to affirm the sentence, when Q. Cæcilius Metellus Celer, then prætor, and one of the augurs, hastened to the Janiculum, and tore down the ensign which was planted there as a sign of peace. A silly piece of superstition stopt the proceedings of those whom neither justice nor compassion, nor regard to government could restrain.

It was established, as has been formerly noticed,[3] that the assembly of the centuries could not proceed without this signal in view. In the first ages of Rome, the enemy were always at the gate. While the people were assembled in the field on one side of the city, they were in danger of being assailed on the other. When they assembled, therefore, in the field of Mars, a guard was always posted on the Janiculum, and an ensign displayed. If any enemy appeared, the ensign was taken down, the assembly dismissed, and the people took to their arms. This ceremony, like many other customs both of superstition and law, remained after the occasion had ceased; and it was held illegal or impious in the people to proceed in any affair without the ensign in view. By this means the trial was put off, and the prosecutors, despairing of being able to work up the people again into an equal degree of violence, dropt the prosecution. The cause still remained undecided, and the power of the senate to defend its own authority, continued in a state of suspense.

The tribune Labienus laid aside all thoughts of renewing the prosecution, in order to pursue the object of some other popular acts; one in particular, to repeal the almost only remaining ordinance of Sylla; that which related to the election of priests. The right of election was again taken from the college, and, according to the law of Domitius, given to seventeen of the tribes that were to be drawn by lot. This change was intended to open the way of Caius Julius Cæsar into that office; and he was accordingly promoted to it in the following year.

Others of the tribunes likewise endeavoured to distinguish themselves by acts of turbulence and sedition. Metellus Nepos endeavoured to repeal that clause of the act against bribery and corruption, which declared the party convicted to be disqualified for any of the offices of state. This tribune, though sufficiently disposed to disorderly courses, had many connections among the most respectable citizens, and was persuaded, in this instance, to drop his design.

But among the several confederacies into which the popular party was divided, none was more desperate, nor supposed more dangerous, than that of Catiline, the late disappointed candidate for the consulship. His rival Cicero had intimation, before the elections, of a design formed by this desperate faction against his own person, and still continued to observe them. He entered into a correspondence with Fulvia, who had given the first hints of a dangerous conspiracy; and, by means of this woman, procured the confidence of Curius, who gave him minute information of all the proceedings of the party.

In public, Catiline again professed himself a candidate for the office of consul, in competition with Servius Sulpicius, P. Muræna, and J. Silanus. He boasted of support from Antonius; but Cicero to divert his colleague from this dangerous connection, made him every concession. Having, in drawing lots for the provinces of Gaul and Macedonia, drawn the latter, which was thought to be preferable, he yielded it up to Antonius; and by this, and every other means in his power, persuaded him to value the secure possession of dignities and honours, lawfully obtained, in preference to expectations formed on the projects of a few desperate men.

In secret, Catiline encouraged his adherents by professing to have many resources, and to be supported by numbers who were ready to take arms at his command. In a numerous meeting of his party in October, a few days before the consular elections, he opened the whole of his design; and in the speech which he made on that occasion, is said to have used expressions to the following purpose: "The distressed can rely for relief only on those who have a common cause with themselves. Whoever, in his own fortune, is at ease, will not regard the misery of others. If you would know how I stand affected to the parties which now divide the commonwealth, *rich creditors* and *needy debtors*, recollect what every one knows, that I have no safety but in the destruction of the one, and in the relief of the other that my interest is the same with yours, and that I have courage to attempt what may be necessary, for your benefit."

From the strain of this passage, the description of a party to whom it was with propriety addressed, may be easily collected. Cicero, who had frequently taxed Catiline with dangerous designs, now determined to lay the whole of his intelligence before the senate; and for this purpose deferred the consular elections, which were to have been held on the eighteenth of October, to a future day, and assembled the senate. Catiline having with the other members attended, and hearing the charge, did not pretend to deny or to palliate his words. "There are," he said, "in this republic, two parties; one weak both in its members and head; the other, strong in its members, but wanting a head: while I have the honour of being supported by this party, it shall have a head." Upon these words, a general cry

3 See book i. c. 1.

of indignation arose in the senate; but no resolution was taken. Many, who were there present as members, were pleased to see the senate itself insulted; and Catiline, as if in condition to brave all his enemies, was, in all his expressions, equally unguarded in the streets and in the senate. To Cato, who, in the public forum, some days before this meeting, had threatened him with a prosecution: "Do," he said, "but if you light a flame in my fortunes, I will extinguish it under the ruins of the commonwealth."[1]

A prosecution was actually raised against him in the name of Lucius Paulus, a young man of distinction, for carrying arms against the public peace. On this occasion, however, he thought proper to dissemble his thoughts, and offered to commit his person to custody till his innocence should appear. "No one," he said, "who knows my rank, my pretensions, and the interest I have in the preservation of the commonwealth, will believe, that its destruction is to be apprehended from me, and that its safety is to come from a native of Arpinum."[2] He offered to commit himself to the custody of Cicero, of Metellus, or of any other magistrate, till this injurious aspersion were removed. To this offer the consul replied, That he who did not think himself safe within the same ramparts with Catiline, would not receive him into his house.[3]

By one effect of the unparalleled freedom now enjoyed by Roman citizens, persons accused of the most dangerous crimes were at liberty, during the dependence of their trial, either to proceed in perpetrating their crime, or to withdraw from justice. This effect was derived from the laws of Valerius and Porcius, which secured against violence or the power of the magistrate, the person of every citizen, until he were finally condemned by the people. In support of this privilege, which was salutary, when the abuse of power in the magistrate was to be dreaded more than the license of crimes in the subject, the Romans persisted even after vice was become too strong for the laws, and when exemption from every just restraint was fatally mistaken for liberty. The state had now been thrown, on many occasions, into the most violent convulsions, because there was no ordinary or regular method of preventing disorders, or of suppressing them on their first appearance.

Catiline, soon after the elections, at which, by he preference given to Muræna and Silanus, he received a fresh disappointment in his hopes of the consulship, sent Mallius, or Manlius, an experienced soldier, who had served with himself under Sylla, to prepare for an insurrection in the district of Etruria. This officer, in the end of October, under pretence of giving refuge to debtors from the oppression of their creditors, had actually assembled a considerable body of men.[4] Accounts at the same time were received, that Publius Sylla was making a large purchase of gladiators at Capua, and insurrections were accordingly apprehended on the side of Campania and Apulia. In this state of affairs, continual nformations being brought of Catiline's designs, ne senate gave in charge to the consuls to watch over the safety of the state; and these officers accordingly put chosen bodies of men under arms, and secured all the posts of consequence in the city. Metellus, the conqueror of Crete, who still remained without the walls in hopes of a triumph, was appointed to command on the side of Apulia. The prætor Metellus Celer was sent into Cisalpine Gaul, in order to secure the peace of that province;[5] and the consul Antonius was destined to suppress the insurrection of Mallius at Fæsulæ.[6]

Catiline meanwhile remained in the city, and had frequent consultations for the preparation and the execution of his plot. At a meeting of the party, held in the beginning of November, in the house of M. Porcius Lecca,[7] a general massacre of the principal senators was projected. The conspirators severally chose their stations, and undertook their several parts. Two in particular, who were familiar in Cicero's house, undertook next morning, under pretence of a visit, to surprise and assassinate the consul. But he being the same night apprised of his danger by Fulvia, gave the proper orders, and the intended murderers, upon their appearance at his door, were refused admittance. He immediately after assembled the senate in the temple of Jupiter. Catiline presented himself with his usual presumption; and Cicero, as appears from an oration which he then delivered, instead of laying the matter in form before the senate, accosted Catiline in a vehement invective, urging him to be gone from the city, where all his steps were minutely observed, where his meaning was understood, and precautions taken against all his designs. "I told you," said the consul, "that your emissary Mallius would be in arms by the first of November; that you intended a massacre of the senators about the same time. I now repeat the memorable words you made use of when you were told, that many of the senators had with drawn from the city. You should be satisfied, you said, with the blood of those who remained. Were you not surrounded, hemmed in, and beset on every side by the guards posted to watch you? Did your intention to surprise Præneste, on the night of the first of November, escape me? Did you not find precautions taken that argued a knowledge of your design? There is nothing, in short, that you do, that you prepare, that you meditate, which is not heard, which is not seen, which is not felt by me in every circumstance. What of last night? Were you not at the house of Porcius Lecca? Deny it! I have evidence. There are here present persons who were of your company. But where are we? What manner of government or republic is this? The enemies and destroyers of the commonwealth make a part in its highest councils! We know them, and yet they are suffered to live! But, be gone. The time of enduring you is past. The world is convinced of your guilt. Stay only till there is not a single person that can pretend to doubt of it; till your own partizans must be silent, and till the clamour, which they would willingly raise against every necessary act of government, be suppressed."

This being the general tendency of the consul speech, fraught with such alarming matter, and

1 Cicero Orat. pro Muræna.
2 The town of which Cicero was native.
3 Cicero in Catilinam, i. c. 3.
4 Ibid
5 Cicero in Catilinam, c. 12
6 Now Florence.
7 Cicero pr. Pub Sylla, c. 16

urged with so much confidence, the audience was seized with terror, and numbers, who happened to be on the same bench with Catiline, withdrew from his side. He himself arose, and attempted to vindicate his character, but was silenced with a general cry of indignation; upon which he left the senate; and, after concerting farther measures with those of his party, not thinking that a longer stay in the city could be of any use to his affairs, he withdrew in the night, leaving letters behind him to some of the senators, in which he complained, that, by a combination of his enemies, he was driven into exile; and that, rather than be the occasion of any disturbance in the commonwealth, he was willing to retire. While these letters were handed about in the city, he took his way, preceded by the ushers and ensigns of a Roman proconsul, straight for the camp of Mallius, and entered into a state of open war. The features of this man's portrait are probably exaggerated by the vehement pencils and lively colourings of Cicero and of Sallust. He is represented as able to endure hardships of any kind, and as fearless in any danger; as, from his youth, fond of discord, assassinations, and bloodshed; as having, under pretence of Sylla's proscription, murdered his own brother to possess his estate; as having murdered his own child, to remove the objection made to him by a woman who refused to marry him with the prospect of being a step-mother. He is represented as rapacious, prodigal, gloomy, impetuous, unquiet, dissembling, and perfidious; a description, of which the horrors are probably amplified; but for which it cannot be doubted there was much foundation, as he far exceeded in profligacy and desperation all those who, either in this or the former age, were, by their ambition or their vices, hastening the ruin of the commonwealth.

Cicero always professed to have particular intelligence of the progress of Catiline. This, according to Sallust, he owed to Fulvia, by whose means he obtained a correspondence with Curius; but he himself, in none of his orations, gives any intimation of the manner in which he obtained his information. It is probable that Curius insisted on being concealed, that he might not be exposed to the rage of the conspirators as an informer and a traitor. On this account the consul, although he was minutely apprised of particulars, was obliged to adopt the plan he hitherto followed, to urge the conspirators into open hostilities, and a full declaration of their purpose. He had succeeded with respect to Catiline; but his accomplices were yet very numerous in the city, and were taking their measures to co-operate with those who were in arms.

In this state of affairs, Fabius Sanga, a Roman citizen of distinction, came to the consul, and informed him, that the ambassadors of the Allobroges, a people then inhabiting what is now called the territory of Geneva, and part of Savoy, whose patron he was, had made him privy to a very momentous affair; that, upon being disappointed in a suit, on which they had been employed to the senate, they had been carried by P. Umbrenus to Publius Cornelius Lentulus, the prætor, who condoled with them on the subject of the wrong they had received, assured them of redress if they would merit the favour of a party that was soon to have the ascendant at Rome; and proposed that they should, immediately upon their return to their own country, prevail on their nation to march an army, for this purpose, into Italy. Cicero immediately laid hold of this intelligence, as affording means to bring the plot to light, and furnish a sufficient evidence to convict the conspirators. He desired Sanga to encourage the correspondence, to advise the ambassadors to insist on proper credentials to be shown to their countrymen, to procure a list of the Roman citizens who, in case they should rise in rebellion against the Romans, were to become bound to protect them; and when they should be thus provided, and about to depart, he instructed Sanga to bring him intimation of their motions, that they might be secured, with their writings, and other evidence of the facts to be ascertained. Sanga, having instructed the ambassadors accordingly, gave notice of their motions to the consul. In the evening before they were to depart, Cicero ordered the prætors, L. Flaccus and C. Pontinus, to march by different ways, and in small parties, after it was dark, a sufficient armed force to intercept the ambassadors of the Allobroges. The parties were stationed on different sides of the river, at the bridge called Milvius, without knowing of each other, and without having any suspicion of the purpose for which they were placed, farther than arose from their having been told that they were to seize any person who should attempt to pass. About three o'clock in the morning the ambassadors entered on the bridge with a numerous retinue; and being challenged, and commanded to stop by the party that was placed to intercept them, they endeavoured to force their way; and some blood was shed. But on the appearance of the prætors, with their ensigns of office, the ambassadors ceased to resist. Their despatches were secured. Volturcius, a Roman citizen, who was found in their company, was taken and searched. Letters were found upon him, in different hands, and under different seals, addressed to Catiline. These, together with the prisoners, were immediately carried back to the city.

The consul being apprised of the success which attended this part of his design, sent, before any alarm could be taken by the party, messages to Gabinius, Statilius, Cethegus, and Lentulus, desiring to see them at his own house. The three former came with the messenger; but Lentulus was newly gone to bed, and, by his delay, gave some cause to suspect that he was aware of his danger. He too, however, came; and the house of Cicero was presently crowded, not only with numbers of the equestrian order that were in arms for the defence of his person, but likewise with many senators whom he desired to be present. The ambassadors of the Allobroges, now prisoners, were likewise conducted thither, and the letters found upon them were produced unopened. Cicero declared his intention to assemble the senate without delay, in order to lay the whole matter before them. Many of the company were of opinion, that the letters should be first opened, in order to see whether they contained any matter of so much moment, as to require assembling the senate, at a time when so great an alarm was likely to be taken. Cicero, however, having no doubt of the contents of the letters, and of the importance of the matter, overruled those scruples, and the senate was accordingly called. Meantime the Allobroges dropped some expressions which implied, that arms were concealed in the house of Cethegus. This occasioned a search being then made, and a considerable quantity of daggers and swords were accordingly found.

At the meeting of the senate, Volturcius was first examined; he denied his knowledge of any treasonable designs, but appeared disconcerted; and, upon being reminded of the reward that had been offered for the discovery of any plot against the state, and of the danger to which he himself would be exposed in prevaricating, he confessed, that the letters seized in his custody were sent by the prætor Lentulus and others: that he had besides a verbal message to Catiline, informing him that the plan was now ready for execution; that the station of every person was assigned; that some were appointed to set fire to the city in different places, and some to massacre their enemies in the midst of the confusion that was likely to be occasioned by the fire; and desiring that Catiline, in order to support his friends, and to profit by the diversion they were to make in his favour within the walls, should issue a proclamation to arm the slaves, and that he himself should march directly to Rome.

The deputies of the Allobroges being next introduced, acknowledged, that they had been charged by Lentulus, Cethegus, Statilius, and Cassius, with assurances of support to the council of their nation, confirmed by oath, accompanied with directions, without delay, to march a body of horse into Italy, where they should be joined by a numerous infantry, and receive proper directions in what manner they should farther proceed; that, to encourage them, Lentulus quoted a prophecy, found in the collection of the Sybils, by which he himself was pointed out as the third of the Cornelii,[1] destined to arrive at the sovereignty of Rome: that the conspirators had differed about the time of executing their design. Lentulus was of opinion it should be deferred to the holy-days in December; that Cethegus, notwithstanding, and the others, were impatient, and desired a nearer day.

The supposed conspirators were next called in their turns; and the letters, with the seals unbroken, were exhibited before them. Cethegus, being the first examined, persisted in denying his knowledge of any conspiracy; accounted for the arms that were found in his house, by saying, He was curious of workmanship of that nature, and always bought what he liked. He maintained his countenance well, till his letter was produced, and then fell into great confusion, as the seal was immediately known to be his.

Lentulus next, with great confidence, denied the charge; affected not to know either Volturcius or the ambassadors; asked them upon what occasion they ever could pretend to have been admitted into his house? He, however, owned the seal affixed to the letter that was now produced against him. It was the head of his grandfather. But the letter being opened, was found to be unsigned, and in the following general terms: "The bearer will inform you who I am. Fear nothing. Remember where you stand; and neglect nothing. Call in every aid, even the meanest." While he persisted in his denial, some one asked him, If he had never quoted the Sybiline oracles to these Gauls? Confounded with this question, he forgot his disguise, and confessed.

Gabinius too was at last brought to own his guilt; and in this manner the conspiracy was fully laid open. L. Julius Cæsar, the consul of the former year, in the presence of Lentulus, who was married to his sister, gave his opinion, that this unhappy man should be immediately put to death. "This," he said, "is no unprecedented measure. My grandfather, Fulvius Flaccus, was slain by order of the consul Gabinius. His son was taken into custody and put to death in prison." In the mean time Lentulus was ordered to divest himself of the office of prætor, and, together with his accomplices, was committed to close imprisonment. This Cornelius Lentulus was distinguished by the name of Sura. He had been consul about eight years before, and was afterwards, for his debaucheries, struck off the rolls of the senate. He had now again condescended to accept of the office of prætor, in order to recover, in the capacity of a magistrate, his seat in the senate.

A proclamation was issued to apprehend M. Cæparius, who had been sent to raise an insurrection in Apulia, together with P. Furius, Magius Chilo, and P. Umbrenus, who had first introduced the Gaulish ambassadors to Gabinius. The senate voted thanks to the consul Cicero for his great vigilance, and for the consummate ability he had shown in the discovery and suppression of this treasonable design; to the prætors, for the faithful execution of the consul's orders; and to Antonius, his colleague, for having detached himself from men with whom he was known to have been formerly connected. A public thanksgiving to the gods was likewise decreed in honour of the consul, and in consideration of this deliverance of the city from fire, of the people from massacre, and of Italy from devastation and war.

An assembly of the people being called, Cicero gave this account of the proceedings in a speech which is still extant,[2] and early on the following day assembled the senate to deliberate on the farther resolutions to be taken with respect to the prisoners. An agent had been busy in the night to raise some disturbance in favour of Lentulus; but the design of setting fire to the city struck the people in general with so much horror, that not only such as were possessed of property, but every inhabitant trembled for his own person, and for the safety of his house. The avenues to the senate, the capitol, the forum, all the temples in the neighbourhood, by break of day, were crowded with armed men. The consul had summoned the equestrian order in arms to protect the senate, and citizens of every rank came forth to strengthen the hands of the magistrates.

When the senate met, the members differed in their judgment. Junius Silanus, one of the consuls-elect, being called up first in order, declared himself for a sentence of death. Tiberius Nero differed from him, and proposed perpetual imprisonment. The majority, however, joined Silanus, until Caius Julius Cæsar spoke. This able advocate declared against the opinion of Silanus, not as too severe, but as contrary to law; and insisted on the danger of a precedent which migh[t]

1 The former two were Cinna and Sylla.

2 In Catil. 3.

set the life of every citizen at the mercy of a vote in the senate. Death, he said, was the common destination of all men; what no one could avoid, and what the wise frequently coveted. It was not, therefore, a punishment; and he did not propose to mitigate, but to increase, the severity of the sentence in this case. He proposed, therefore, that the estates of the prisoners should be confiscated; that their persons should be committed for life to the keeping of the most secure and best affected towns in Italy; and that it should be declared treason for any one hereafter to move the senate or the people for any mitigation of their punishment.

Cæsar might be considered as uttering what the popular faction were to urge, and as laying the ground upon which the proceedings of the senate, and the conduct of each particular member, might be afterwards arraigned before the people. The terrors of the Porcian and Sempronian laws, when likely to be urged by so powerful an advocate, alarmed the greater part of the senate. Silanus is said to have retracted his opinion. The consul submitted the question to the judgment of the senate, and declared his willingness to execute any decree they should form. He treated Cæsar with great respect, and laid hold of the severe terms in which he spoke of the conspiracy, as a pledge of his future conduct, in case the proceedings of government, with respect to the matter now before them, should hereafter be questioned or brought under review. "The senate," he observed, "had no cause to dread the imputation of cruelty. It was mercy to prevent, in the most effectual manner, a crime to be perpetrated in so much blood. If this crime were not prevented, they were to see that city, the resort of nations, and the light and ornament of empire, perish at one blow. They were to see heaps of her citizens unburied, and lying in their blood; to see the fury of Cethegus let loose in murder; to see Lentulus become a king, Catiline commanding an army, and every where to hear the cries of mothers, to see the flight of children, and the rape of virgins. If the father of a family," he continued, "should spare a slave who had shed the blood of his children, who had murdered his wife, and set fire to his dwelling, how should such a father be considered—as cruel, or as void of affection?

"He desired them not to regard what was given out, of their not being in condition to attempt any thing vigorous against those men. He himself, as first magistrate, had not neglected the necessary precautions; and the general ardour with which all ranks of men concurred in the defence of their families, their properties, and the seat of empire, rendered every resolution they could take secure of the utmost effect. The forum is full, all the temples in its neighbourhood are full, all the streets and avenues to this place of assembly are full of citizens of every denomination, armed for the defence of their country. He requested that the senate would issue their orders before the sun went down, and seemed to apprehend dangerous consequences, if these matters were left undetermined, and the city exposed to the accidents of the following night. For himself, he professed to have taken his resolution. Although he felt the occasion full of personal danger, he would execute the orders of the conscript fathers," he said; "but, if he fell in the attempt, implored their protection for his wife and his children."[3]

All this appears to have passed in debate before Cato spoke. This virtuous citizen, then about thirty-three years of age, had, in the former part of his life, taken a very different course from the youths of his own time, and, both by his temper and education, was averse to the libertine principles which had crept into the politics and the manners of the age. He spoke chiefly in answer to Caius Cæsar, who, he observed, seemed to mistake the question. "We are not inquiring," he said, "what is the proper punishment of a crime already committed, but how we may defend the republic from an imminent danger with which it is threatened. It is proposed to send the prisoners to safe keeping in the country. Why into the country? Because perhaps the faction of profligate citizens is more numerous in Rome, and may rescue them. Is Rome the only place to which profligate men may resort, or are prisoners of state most secure where the force of government is least? This proposal is surely an idle one. if the author of it professes to entertain any fear of these men. But if, in this general alarm of all the city, he and such persons be not afraid, so much the more cause have we to be on our guard. We are beset with enemies, both within and without the walls. While Catiline with fire and sword is hastening to your gates, you hesitate, whether you will cut off or spare his associates, that are taken with the torch in their hands and the dagger at your breast! You must strike those who are now in your power, if you mean to intimidate those who are coming to support their designs. The remissness or the vigour which you now show will be felt in the camp of Catiline, and will be attended with suitable effects. I am therefore of opinion, that we order these men, agreeably to the practice which our ancestors followed in all cases of treason and of open war against the commonwealth, to immediate death."

Such is said to have been the speech of Cato, by which the senate was determined in the very momentous resolution which was taken on the present occasion; and however little we may be inclined to consider such compositions in many parts of ancient history as records of fact, much credit is due to this representation, as it is given by a person who himself became a partizan of Cæsar, and as the speech itself must have been offered to the perusal of many who were present at the delivery of it.[4] The execution of the prisoners was accordingly determined, and Cornelius Lentulus, in the beginning of the following night, was, by order of the consul, committed to a vaulted dungeon under ground, and strangled. His accomplices had the same fate; and the minds of men, though somewhat quieted of their fears, were nevertheless stunned with the scene, and beheld with amazement a patrician of the Cornelian family, of the first rank in the commonwealth, who himself had been consul, suffering, without any formal trial, by the hands of the common executioner of justice.[5]

While these things were in agitation at Rome

3 Cicero in Catilinam, orat. iv.

4 The more credit is due to this account of Cato's speech, that the speech which is ascribed to Cicero by the same historian, is a faithful extract from the oration which still remains.

5 Sallust. Bell. Catil. Cur ergo in sententiam Catonis? quia verbis luculentioribus et pluribus, rem

Catiline was endeavouring to augment his force in the field. He found about two thousand men under Mallius. These he formed into two legions, and as his party increased he completed their numbers. He refused for some time to enrol his fugitive slaves, of whom many took refuge in his camp; thinking it would discredit and weaken his cause to rest any part of it on this support. But the freemen that joined him being ill armed, he was obliged to keep in the neighbourhood of the mountains, and frequently to change his ground, to avoid an engagement with the consul; and he endeavoured to gain time, in hopes that the intended blow being struck at Rome, a general defection of the opposite party would ensue. But when accounts came that his design had failed in the city, and that his principal associates were no more, those who were inclined to his cause were discouraged, and numbers who had already joined him began to fall off, he determined to remove to a distance from his enemies; and for this purpose directed his march to a pass in the Apennines, by which he might escape into Gaul. This design the Prætor Metellus had foreseen, made a forced march to prevent the effect of it, and Catiline at last, finding himself beset on every quarter, determined to hazard a battle. Of the armies that were in the field against him he chose to face that of Antonius; either because it lay on his route to Rome, and, if defeated or removed, might open his way to the city, or because he hoped to meet in the commander of it some remains of inclination in his favour. In whatever degree these hopes were at first reasonably conceived, they ceased to have any foundation; as Antonius, being taken ill had left the army under the command of Petreius. With this commander Catiline engaged in battle, and, after many efforts of valour and of conduct, fell with the greater part of his followers, and thus delivered the state from a desperate enemy, whose power was happily not equal to his designs, and who has owed much of his celebrity to the orator and the historian, who have made him the subject of their eloquent compositions. Sallust appears to have been so intent on raising and finishing particular parts of his work, that he neglected the general order of his narrative. I have, therefore, in most parts of the relation, preferred the authority of Cicero to his. This great man was undoubtedly best informed, and he rested so much of his reputation on this transaction, that he loses no opportunity of returning to it, and in different parts of his writings, when collected, has furnished a pretty full narration of circumstances respecting the origin and termination of this wild and profligate attempt to subvert the government of the republic.

CHAPTER IV.

Character of the Times—Philosophy—Opposite Tenets and Votaries—Proceedings of the Senate—Tribunate of Metellus, Nepos, and of Cato—Proposal to recal Pompey at the Head of his Army frustrated—His arrival in Italy—And Triumph.

IT may appear strange, that any age or nation should have furnished the example of a project conceived in so much guilt, or of characters so atrocious as those under which the accomplices of Catiline are described by the eloquent orator and historian,[1] from whose writings the circumstances of the late conspiracy are collected. The scene, however, in this republic, was such as to have no parallel, either in the past or in the subsequent history of mankind. There was less government, and more to be governed, than has been exhibited in any other instance. The people of Italy were become masters of the known world; it was impossible they could ever meet in a fair and adequate convention. They were represented by partial meetings or occasional tumults in the city of Rome; and to take the sense of the people on any subject was to raise a riot. Individuals were vested with powers almost discretionary in the provinces, or continually aspired to such situations. The nominal assemblies of the people were often led by profligate persons, impatient of government, in haste to govern. Ruined in their fortunes by private prodigality, or by the public expense in soliciting honours; tempted to repair their ruins by oppression and extortion where they were entrusted with command, or by desperate attempts against the government of their country if disappointed in their hopes. Not only were many of the prevailing practices disorderly, but the law itself was erroneous;[2] adopted indeed at first by a virtuous people, because it secured the persons and the rights of individuals, but now anxiously preserved by their posterity, because it gave a license to their crimes.

The provinces were to be retained by the forces of Italy; the Italians themselves by the ascendant of the capital; and in this capital all was confusion and anarchy, except where the senate, by its authority and the wisdom of its counsels, prevailed. It was expedient for the people to restrain the abuses of the aristocratical power; but when the sovereignty was exercised in the name of the collective body of the Roman people, the anarchy and confusion that prevailed at Rome spread from one extremity of her dominion to the other. The provinces were oppressed, not upon a regular plan to aggrandize the state, but at the pleasure of individuals, to enrich a few of the most outrageous and profligate citizens. The people were often assembled to erect arbitrary powers, under

eandem comprehenderat. Cicer. ad Atticum, lib. xii. epist. 21.

1 Cicero in Sallust.

2 Lex Valeria et Porcia de tergo Civium lata. Liv. lib. ii. c. 8. lib. iii. c. 55. lib. x. c. 9. By these laws a Roman citizen could not be imprisoned, any more than suffer punishment, before conviction; he might stop any proceeding against him by an appeal to the people at large; and, being at liberty during trial, might withdraw whenever he perceived the sentence likely to be given against him.

the pretence of popular government. The public interests and the order of the state were in perpetual struggle with the pretensions of single and of profligate men. In such a situation there were many temptations to be wicked; and in such a situation, likewise, minds that were turned to integrity and honour had a proportionate spring to their exertions and pursuits. The range of the human character was great and extensive, and men were not likely to trifle within narrow bounds; they were destined to be good or to be wicked in the highest measure, and, by their struggles, to exhibit a scene interesting and instructive beyond any other in the history of mankind.

Among the causes that helped to carry the characters of men in this age to such distant extremes, may be reckoned the philosophy of the Greeks, which was lately come into fashion, and which was much affected by the higher ranks of men in the state.[3] Literature being, by the difficulty and expense of multiplying copies of books,[4] confined to persons having wealth and power, it was considered as a distinction of rank, and was received not only as a useful, but as a fashionable accomplishment. The lessons of the school were considered as the elements of every liberal and active profession, and they were practised at the bar, in the field, in the senate, and every where in the conduct of real affairs. Philosophy was considered as an ornament, as well as a real foundation of strength, ability, and wisdom in the practice of life. Men of the world, instead of being ashamed of their sect, affected to employ its language on every important occasion, and to be governed by its rules so much as to assume, in compliance with particular systems, distinctions of manners and even of dress. They embraced their forms in philosophy, as the sectaries in modern times have embraced theirs in religion; and probably in the one case honoured their choice by the sincerity of their faith and the regularity of their practice, much in the same degree as they have done in the other.

In these latter times of the Roman republic the sect of Epicurus appears to have prevailed; and what Fabricius wished, on hearing the tenets of this philosophy, for the enemies of Rome, had now befallen her citizens.[5] Men were glutted with national prosperity; they thought that they were born to enjoy what their fathers had won, and saw not the use of those austere and arduous virtues by which the state had increased to its present greatness. The votaries of this sect ascribed the formation of the world to chance, and denied the existence of Providence. They resolved the distinctions of right and wrong, of honour and dishonour, into mere appellations of pleasure and pain. Every man's pleasure was to himself the supreme rule of estimation and of action. All good was private. The public was a mere imposture, that might be successfully employed, perhaps to defraud the ignorant of their private enjoyments, while it furnished the conveniencies of the wise.[6] To persons so instructed, the care of families and of states, with whatever else broke in upon the enjoyments of pleasure and ease, must appear among the follies of human life. And a sect under these imputations might be considered as patrons of licentiousness, both in morality and religion, and declared enemies to mankind. Yet the Epicureans, when urged in argument by their opponents, made some concessions in religion, and many more in morality. They admitted the existence of gods, but supposed those beings of too exalted a nature to have any concern in human affairs. They owned that, although the value of virtue was to be measured by the pleasure it gave, yet true pleasure was to be found in virtue alone; and that it might be enjoyed in the highest degree even in the midst of bodily pain. Notwithstanding this decision on the side of morality, the ordinary language of this sect, representing virtue as a mere prudent choice among the pleasures to which men are variously addicted, served to suppress the specific sentiments of conscience and elevation of mind, and to change the reproaches of criminality, profligacy, or vileness, by which even bad men are restrained from iniquity, into mere imputations of mistake, or variations of taste.

Other sects, particularly that of the Stoics, maintained, almost in every particular, the reverse of these tenets. They maintained the reality of Providence, and of a common interest of goodness and of justice, for which Providence was exerted, and in which all rational creatures were deeply concerned. They allowed, that in the nature of things there are many grounds upon which we prefer or reject the objects that present themselves to us, but that the choice which we make, not the event of our efforts, decides our happiness or our misery; that right and wrong are the most important and the only grounds upon which we can at all times safely proceed in our choice, and that, in comparison to this difference, every thing else is of no account; that a just man will ever act as if there was nothing good but what is right, and nothing evil but what is wrong; that the Epicureans mistook human nature when they supposed all its principles resolvable into appetites for pleasure, or aversions to pain; that honour and dishonour, excellence and defect, were considerations which not only led to much nobler ends, but which were of much greater power in commanding the human will; the love of pleasure was grovelling and vile, was the source of dissipation and of sloth; the love of excellence and honour was aspiring and noble, and led to the greatest exertions and the highest attainments of our nature. They maintained that there is no private good separate from the public good; that the same qualities of the understanding and the heart, wisdom, benevolence, and courage, which are good for the individual, are so likewise for the public; that these blessings every man may possess, independent of fortune or the will of other men; and that whoever does possess them has nothing to hope, and nothing to fear, and can have but one sort of emotion, that of satisfaction and joy; that his affections, and the maxims of his station, as a creature of God, and as a member of society, lead him to act for the

---

3 Vid Cicero's Philosophical Works.

4 The grandees had their slaves sometimes educated to serve as secretaries to themselves, or as preceptors to their children.

5 See Plutarch. in Pyrr. The philosopher Cyneas, in the hearing of Fabricius, entertained his prince with an argument, to prove that pleasure was the chief good. Fabricius wished that the enemies of Rome might long entertain such tenets.

6 Cicero in Pisonem.

good of mankind; and that for himself he has nothing more to desire, than the happiness of acting this part. These, they said, were the tenets of reason leading to perfection, which ought to be the aim of every person who means to preserve his integrity, or to consult his happiness, and towards which every one may advance, although no one has actually reached it.

Other sects affected to find a middle way between these extremes, and attempted, in speculation, to render their doctrines more plausible; that is, more agreeable to common opinions than either; but were, in fact, of no farther moment in human life than as they approached to the one or to the other of these opposite systems.

Cæsar is said to have embraced the doctrines of Epicurus; Cato those of Zeno. The first, in compliance with fashion, or from the bias of an original temper. The other, from the force of conviction, as well as from the predilection of a warm and ingenuous mind. When such characters occur together, it is impossible not to see them in contrast. When Sallust writes of the proceedings of the senate, in the case of the Catiline conspiracy, he seems to overlook every other character, to dwell upon these alone. Cæsar, at the time when this historian flourished, had many claims to his notice;[1] but Cato could owe it to nothing but the force of truth. He was distinguished from his infancy by an ardent and affectionate disposition. This part of his character is mentioned on occasion of his attachment to his brother Cæpio, and the vehement sorrow with which he was seized at his death. It is mentioned, on occasion of his visit to the dictator Sylla, when he was with difficulty restrained by the discretion of his tutor from some act or expression of indignation against this real or apparent violator of public justice. He had from his infancy, according to Plutarch, a resolution, a steadiness, and a composure of mind not to be moved by flattery, nor to be shaken by threats. Without fawning or insinuation, he was the favourite of his companions, and had, by his unaffected generosity and courage, the principal place in their confidence. Though in appearance stern and inflexible, he was warm in his affections, and zealous in the cause of innocence and justice. Such are the marks of an original temper affixed by historians as the characters of his infancy and early youth. So fitted by nature, he imbibed with ease an opinion, that profligacy, cowardice, and malice, were the only evils to be feared; courage, integrity, and benevolence, the only good to be coveted; and that the proper care of a man on every occasion is, not what is to happen to him, but what he himself is to do. With this profession he became a striking contrast to many of his contemporaries; and to Cæsar in particular, not only a contrast, but a resolute opponent; and though he could not furnish a sufficient counterpoise, yet he afforded always much weight to be thrown into the opposite scale. They were both of undaunted courage, and of great penetration; the one to distinguish what was best; the other to distinguish the most effectual means for he attainment of any end on which he was bent. It were to mistake entirely the scene in which they were engaged, to judge of their abilities from the event of their different pursuits. Those of Cato were by their nature a series of struggles with almost insurmountable difficulties: those of Cæsar a constant endeavour to seize the advantages of which the vices and weaknesses of the age, except when he was resisted by persons bent on the same purpose with himself, gave him an easy possession. Cato endeavoured to preserve the order of civil government, however desperate, because this was the part it became him to act, and in which he chose to live and to die. Cæsar proposed to overturn it; because he wished to dispose of all the wealth and honours of the state at his own pleasure.

Cæsar, as versatile in his genius as Cato, was steady and inflexible, could personate any character, and support any cause; in debate he could derive his arguments from any topic; from topics of pity, of which he was insensible; from topics of justice and public good, for which he had no regard. His vigour in resisting personal insults and wrongs appeared in his early youth, when he withstood the imperious commands of Sylla to part with his wife, the daughter of Cinna, and when he revenged the insults offered by the pirates to himself; but while his temper might be supposed the most animated and warm, he was not involved in business by a predilection for any of the interests on which the state was divided. So long as the appetites of youth were sufficient to occupy him, he saw every object of state, or of faction, with indifference, and took no part in public affairs. But even in this period, by his application and genius, in both of which he was eminent, he made a distinguished progress in letters and eloquence. When he turned his mind to objects of ambition, the same personal vigour which appeared in his youth, became still more conspicuous; but, unfortunately, his passions were ill directed, and he seemed to consider the authority that was exercised by the senate, and the restraints of the law on himself, as an insult and a wrong.

Cæsar had attained to seven-and-thirty years of age before he took any part as a member of the commonwealth. He then courted the populace in preference to the senate or better sort of the people, and made his first appearance in support of the profligate, against the order and authority of government. With persons of desperate fortune and abandoned manners, he early bore the character of liberality and friendship. They received him as a generous patron, come to rescue them from the morose severity of those who judged of public merits by the standard of public virtue, and who declared against practices, however fashionable, which were inconsistent with public safety. Himself, a person of the greatest abilities, and the most accomplished talents, having an opportunity to live on terms of equality with the greatest men that have yet appeared in the world, he chose to start up as the chief among those who, being abandoned to every vice, saw the remains of virtue in their country with distaste and aversion. When he emerged from the avocations of pleasure, or from the sloth which accompanies the languor of dissipation, his ambition or desire to counteract the established government of his country, and to make himself master of the commonwealth, became extreme. To this passion he sacrificed every sentiment of friendship or animosity, of honour, interest, resentment,

1 Sallust attached himself to Cæsar, and was employed by him in the civil wars.

or hatred. The philosophy which taught men to look for enjoyment indiscriminately wherever it pleased them most, found a ready acceptance in such a disposition. But while he possibly availed himself of the speculations of Epicurus to justify his choice of an object, he was not inferior to the followers of Zeno, in vigorous efforts and active exertions for the attainment of his ends. Being about seven years younger than Pompey, and three years older than Cato; the first he occasionally employed as a prop to his ambition, but probably never ceased to consider him as a rival; the other, from a fixed animosity of opposite natures, and from having felt him as a continual opponent in all his designs, he sincerely hated.

Cato began his military service in the army that was formed against the gladiators, and concluded it as a legionary tribune, under the prætor Rubrius, in Macedonia, while Pompey remained in Syria. He was about three-and-thirty years of age when he made his speech relating to the accomplices of Catiline; and by the decisive and resolute spirit he had shown on this occasion, came to be considered as a principal support of the aristocracy, or of the authority of the senate.[2] To this body, as usual, every flagrant disorder repressed was a victory. The discovery of a design so odious as that of Catiline, covered under popular pretences, greatly weakened their antagonists. One of the first uses they proposed to make of their advantage, was to have Cato elected among the tribunes of the subsequent year. His services were likely to be wanted in opposition to Metellus Nepos, then arrived from the army of Pompey, with recommendations from his general to offer himself a candidate for the same office; and, as was expected, to start some new gratification to the ambition or vanity of this insatiable suitor for personal consideration.

It had not yet appeared what part Pompey was to take in the disputes that were likely to arise on the legality or expedience of the late measures; but it is not to be doubted, that he wished to hold the balance of parties, and that he would come prepared for the part that was most likely to promote his own importance. Metellus was sent on before him to be supported by his friends in the canvass for the office of tribune, and with instructions to take such measures as were likely to favour the pretensions of his general. The leading men of the senate were now, for some time, aware of the intrigues of Pompey, and bore, with indignation, the personal superiority which he affected even to the first and most respected of their order. They took occasion, in the present crisis, to mortify him by admitting Lucullus and Metellus Creticus to the triumphs to which, by their victories in Pontus and in Crete, they were long entitled. Hitherto their claims had been overruled by the popular faction, either to annoy the senatorian party, to which they were attached, or to flatter Pompey, who was supposed to be equally averse to the honours of both. They had waited in Italy about three years, and, in the manner of those who sue for a triumph, had abstained from entering the city, and still retained the fasces or ensigns of their late command.[3]

Lucullus, having obtained the honour that was due to him, seemed to be satisfied with the acknowledgment of his right; and, as if merely to show with what sort of enemy he had fought, he entered the city with a few of the Armenian horsemen cased in armour, a few of the armed chariots winged with scythes, and about sixty of the officers and courtiers of Mithridates, who were his captives. He ordered the spoils he had gained, the arms and ensigns of war, the prows of the gallies he had taken, to be displayed to public view in the great circus, and concluded the solemnity with giving a feast to the people. The senate hoped for his support against the ambition of Pompey, and the factious designs of the popular leaders; but he was disgusted, and scarcely ever after took any part in the affairs of state.

The triumph of Metellus Creticus did not take place till after the accession of the following consuls, P. Junius Silanus and Lucius Muræna, after whose election, Cicero, before he had vacated his own office of consul, had occasion to defend his own intended successor, Muræna, against a charge of corruption brought upon the statute of Calpurnius, by Servius Sulpicius, one of his late competitors, supported by Cato and others. The oration of Cicero on this occasion is still extant, and is a curious example of the topics, which, under popular governments, enter even into judicial pleadings. Great part of it consists in a ridicule of law terms; because Sulpicius, one of the prosecutors, was accustomed to give counsel to his friends who consulted him in matters of law; and in a ridicule of the stoic philosophy, because Cato, another prosecutor, was supposed to have embraced the doctrines of that sect. Cato made no other remark on this pleading, but that the republic was provided with a merry consul. The argument appeared sufficiently strong on the side of Muræna, and he was acquitted.

At the close of this trial, Cicero, about to resign his power with the usual asseveration, upon oath, that he had faithfully, and to the best of his abilities, discharged his trust; he proposed, at the same time, to harangue the people, but was ordered by Metellus, already elected, and acting in capacity of tribune, to confine himself to the terms of his oath. He accordingly refrained from speaking; but instead of swearing simply, that he had been faithful to his trust, he took an oath that he had preserved the republic.[4] It was on this occasion, probably, that Cato, now another of the tribunes, in a speech to the people, alluding to the suppression of the late conspiracy, called Cicero the father of his country;[5] and from this time entered upon an opposition to his colleague, Metellus, which was not likely to drop while they continued in office.

U. C. 691.

D. Junius Silanus, L. Muræna.

Soon after the accession of the new magistrates, a storm began to gather, which, though still aimed at the party of the senate, burst at last in a personal attack upon the late consul, who had been the author or instrument of the senate in the summary proceedings against the accomplices of Catiline. Metellus Nepos seems to have come from Asia, and to have entered on the office of tribune, with a particular design to bring about the introduction of Pompey with his army into Rome; and he was joined in this project by Caius Julius Cæsar,

2 Plutarch in Caton. edit. Londin p. 238.
3 Cicero in Lucullo.
4 Plutarch. in Cicerone.
5 Cicer. in Pisonem, c. 3.

now in the office of prætor,[1] who chose to support the tribune, as an act of hostility to the senate, if not as the means of disembarrassing himself from the present forms of the commonwealth.

In consequence of a plan concerted with Cæsar, the tribune Metellus moved in the senate, as had been usual in the times of its highest authority, for leave to propose a decree in the assembly of the people, recalling Pompey from Asia at the head of his forces, in order to restore the constitution of the commonwealth, which, in the terms he afterwards employed to the people, had been violated by the arbitrary administration of Cicero. This was the first attempt of the party to inflame the minds of the people on the subject of the late executions; and Pompey was, in this manner, offered to the popular party as their leader, to avenge the supposed wrongs they had received. Cato, when the matter was proposed in the senate, endeavoured to persuade Metellus to drop it, reminded him of the dignity of his family, which had been always a principal ornament and support to the state. This treatment served only to raise the presumption of Metellus, and brought on a violent altercation between the tribunes. The senate applauded Cato, but had not authority enough to prevent the motion which was proposed from being made to the people.

Metellus, apprehending an obstinate resistance from his colleague, endeavoured to fill the place of assembly with his own partizans; and, on the evening before the meeting, in order to intimidate his opponents, paraded in the streets with a numerous attendance of men in arms. The friends and relations of the other tribunes earnestly beseeched them not to expose themselves to the danger with which they were threatened. But, on the following day, the other party being already assembled by Metellus, at the temple of Castor, and the place having been in the night occupied by persons under his direction, armed with sticks, swords, and other offensive weapons,[2] Cato went forth attended only by Minucius Thermus, another of the tribunes, and a few friends. They were joined by numbers in the streets, who could not accompany them to their place, being prevented by the multitude of armed men that already crowded the avenues and the steps of the temple. But they themselves, from respect to their office, being suffered to pass, dragged along with them through the crowd, as an aid, in case any violence were offered, Munatius, a citizen much attached to Cato. When they came to the bench of tribunes, they found that Metellus, with the prætor Julius Cæsar, had taken their places there; and that, in order to concert their operations in the conduct of this affair, they were closely seated together. Cato, to disappoint this intention, forced himself in betwixt them, and, when the ordinary officer began to read the intended decree, interposed his negative, and forbade him to proceed. Metellus himself seized the writing, and began to read; but Cato snatched it out of his hands. Metellus endeavoured to repeat the substance of it from his memory. Thermus clapped his hand to his mouth. A general silence remained in the assembly, till Metellus, having made a signal for his party to clear the comitium of their enemies, a great tumult and confusion arose; and the tribunes who opposed Metellus were in imminent danger. The senators had met in mourning, to mark their sense of the evils which threatened the commonwealth; and now, under the apprehension of some signal calamity, gave a charge to the consuls to watch over the safety of the state, and empowered them to take such measures as might be necessary to preserve or to restore the public peace.[3]

In consequence of this charge, the consul Muræna appeared with a body of men in arms, had the good fortune to rescue Cato and Minucius Thermus; and probably by this seasonable interposition effaced any remains of misunderstanding which might have subsisted between Cato and himself, on account of the prosecution for bribery which followed the late elections.[4]

Metellus, after the tumult was composed, having again obtained silence, began to read the proposed decree; but the senatorian party, headed by the consuls, being then in the comitium, he found it impossible to proceed; and, together with the prætor Caius Julius Cæsar, retired from the assembly. From this time, these officers made no attempt to resume their motion, but complained that the government was usurped by a violent faction, under whom even the persons of the tribunes were unsafe; and Metellus, as if forced to break through the rules which obliged the tribunes to constant residence at Rome, abandoned the city, even left Italy, and fled to the camp of Pompey in Asia, from which he was lately arrived.[5] He had already threatened his opponents at Rome with the resentment and military power of his general, and now endeavoured to excite the army and their commander to follow the example which had been set to them by Sylla and his legions, when oppressed citizens, a description in which he now comprehended himself, fled to them for protection and revenge.

It may well be supposed, that Cæsar, remembering his own escape from the ruin of the Marian faction, and considering Pompey as the head of an opposite interest, and a principal obstacle to his own ambition, must look upon him with some degree of personal dislike and animosity; but his conduct on this occasion sufficiently showed how little he was the dupe of any passion or sentiment which had a tendency to check his pursuits. Meaning for the present only to weaken the senate, and to step in before them in the favour of Pompey; he undertook the cause even of a rival, and would have joined the populace, in delivering the commonwealth into his hands, rather than remain under a government which he hated. But if he really meant to overthrow the senate by force, he mistook his instrument. Pompey, no doubt, aspired to the sovereignty of the empire, and wished to reign in the city with a military power; but even this he desired to receive as the fruit of consideration and personal respect, and he ever hoped to make the people bestow it, and even force him to accept of it as their gift. For this purpose he encouraged so many agents and retainers to sound his praise; and for this purpose he had recently sent Metellus Nepos from his camp to take upon him the functions of a popular tribune; but having failed of his object, he by no means could think of extorting it by

1 Sueton in Jul. Cæs. c. 16.
2 Plutarch. in Catone, edit. Londin. p. 241, &c.
3 Plutarch. in Catone, edit. Londin. p. 241, &c.
4 Plutarch. ibid. 5 Dio. Cass. lib xxxvii. c. 43

force. No one ever courted distinction with a more incessant emulation to his rivals; but he was entirely dependent on the public opinion for any satisfaction he enjoyed in the possession of power. Trusting to this last part of his character, Cæsar, though himself of unbounded ambition, was not yet alarmed at the elevation of Pompey, and thought that he was safe even in offering him the dominion of the state. Pompey was, at this conjuncture, with his army moving towards Italy, and his coming was matter of great solicitude to the friends of the commonwealth, who feared that, in return to the affront of his not being invited to come with his army, upon the motion of Metellus, he would employ it in person to enforce his commands. Upon his arrival at Brundusium, however, as formerly upon his return from Africa, he dispelled those fears by an immediate dismission of the troops, with instructions merely that they would attend at his triumph. He himself came forward to Rome with the single equipage of his proconsular rank. Multitudes of every condition went forth to receive him, and with shouts and acclamations recompensed the moderation with which he acquiesced in the condition of a citizen.

Cæsar, from whatever motive he acted in regard to Pompey, gave every other sign of disaffection to the senate, and employed the name of this rising favourite of the people, to mortify such of the members in particular as were objects of personal animosity to himself. The repairs or rebuilding of the capitol being finished about this time, the honour of dedicating the edifice, and of being named in the inscription it was to bear, had, by a resolution of the senate, been conferred on Catulus, under whose inspection the work was executed. But Cæsar, affecting to procure this honour for Pompey, alleged that Catulus had embezzled the money allotted for this service; that much yet remained to be done; and moved, that the inscription of Catulus should be erased; that the completion of the work being left to Pompey, should carry an inscription with his name.[6] Here he probably acted as much from antipathy to one, as from an intention to flatter the other. But the design being extremely odious to the whole body of the nobles, who saw, with indignation, in that proposal an attempt to affront a most respectable citizen, in order to flatter the vanity of one person, and to gratify the profligate resentments of another, Cæsar was obliged to withdraw his motion.[7]

It was probably during this year in which Cæsar was prætor, and before the arrival of Pompey from Asia (although historians refer it to an earlier date,) that Cæsar promoted, as has been already mentioned, prosecutions upon a charge of assassination against some persons concerned in the execution of Sylla's proscriptions. The prætors were appointed by lot to carry particular laws into execution. The law respecting assassination appears to have been the lot of Cæsar; and he was entitled in virtue of his office, the jurisdiction of which was still very arbitrary, to extend, by his edict or plan of proceeding for the year, the description of the crime under his cognizance to any special case.

While he seemed to have formed so many designs against the peace of the commonwealth, and in the capacity of prætor supported them with the authority of a magistrate, the senatorian party made a powerful exertion of their influence to have him suspended, and actually obtained a decree for this purpose. He affected at first to slight their authority; but finding that a power was preparing to enforce it, perhaps at the hazard of his life, he laid aside for some time the robes and badges of magistracy, dismissed his lictors, and abstained from the functions of prætor, until, having rejected an offer of the people to restore him by force, he was, with proper marks of regard, for this instance of moderation, reinstated, by an act of the senate.[8]

The aristocratical party, at the same time, to confirm and perpetuate the evidence on which they proceeded against the accomplices of Catiline, continued their prosecutions on this subject, and obtained sentence of condemnation, in particular, against a citizen of the name of Vergunteius, and against Autronius, who, about two years before, having been elected consul, was set aside upon a charge of bribery; and who, from the disgust which he took to the senate upon that occasion, had connected himself with the more desperate party. Publius Sylla, in the same predicament with Autronius, was tried; but, being defended by Cicero, in an eloquent harangue which is still extant, was acquitted.

Cæsar likewise was accused by Vectius as accessary to the conspiracy of Catiline; but it is not likely that he was concerned farther than by the general encouragement he gave to every party at variance with the senate. Opposition to this body was called the interest of the people, and was adopted by every person who had any passions to gratify by crimes of state, or who wished to weaken the government, to which they themselves were accountable. Among the supporters of this interest, Crassus also was accused, but probably on no better grounds than Cæsar.

The whole of these proceedings, however, were suspended by the approach of Pompey. This leader had now drawn the attention of all men upon himself, was quoted in every harangue as the great support of the empire, and courted by multitudes, who, without inquiry, affected to be classed with his admirers and friends. The contagion spread like a fashion among the vulgar of every description. He himself affected indifference to this mighty tide of renown, though not without much dignity and state, which he tempered with affability, employing the greatness he possessed to give the more value to his condescensions. His manner, though acceptable to the people and the army, was disagreeable to the senate. Having previously sent Piso, one of his lieutenants, before him to stand for the consulate, he had the presumption to desire that the senate would defer the elections until he himself could be present to canvass for his friend. The senate, according to Dio, complied with his desire; but, according to Plutarch, rejected the proposal with disdain. This author imputes the resolution, which they took upon this occasion, to Cato, and subjoins, that Pompey endeavoured to gain this opponent by a proposed marriage with one of his near relations; and that Cato declined the connection, saying,

6 Sueton. in Jul. Cæsare, c. 15.
7 Dio. Cass. lib. xlvii. c. 44.
8 Sueton. in Jul. Cæsare c. 16.

that he should not be caught in a female snare. Piso, however, was elected together with Valerius Messala, and entered on his office before the triumph of Pompey.

U. C. 692.

M. Pub. Piso Calpurnius, M. Val. Messala Niger.

This solemnity followed soon after; and, though continued for two days, could not make place for all the magnificent shows that had been provided for it. The list of conquests exceeded that which had ever been produced at any other triumph. Asia, Pontus, Armenia, Cappadocia, Paphlagonia, Medea, Colchis, Iberia, Albania, Syria, Cilicia, Mesopotamia, Phœnicia, Judea, Arabia, Scythia, Crete,[1] with the sea in all its coasts. Among the people or potentates subdued, were the Basterni, Mithridates, and Tigranes. Among the captures, a thousand fortresses, nine hundred cities reduced, eight hundred galleys taken, above two millions of men in captivity. Towns repeopled, not less than three hundred and ninety-nine. To this pompous list, it was subjoined by his friends, that, this being his third triumph, he had been round the known world, and had triumphed over all the three parts of the earth, Africa, Europe, and Asia.

After rewarding the soldiers, of whom none received less than fifteen hundred denarii,[2] he carried to the treasury twenty thousand talents.[3] He led, among his principal captives, besides the chief pirates, Tigranes, son to the king of Armenia, with his wife and his daughter,—Zozimé, the queen of Tigranes,—the father of Aristobulus, king of the Jews,—a sister of Mithridates, with five sons, and some Scythian women; the hostages of the Iberii, and the Commageni; together with trophies for every battle he had fought, making in all a more splendid exhibition than any that was to be found on the records of the state.

The triumphal processions of Pompey merit more attention than those of any other person, because they contained a public evidence of his character. Others took the benefit of an established practice to publish and to ratify the honours they had acquired; but Pompey, it is likely, would have invented the triumph, even if it had not been formerly thought of; and it is not to be doubted, that he over-ran some provinces in which the enemy were subdued, or in which they were so weak, as not to be able to make any resistance, merely to place them in the list of his conquests; and that he made some part of his progress in Asia to collect curiosities and ornaments for this pompous scene.

The triumph, in its ordinary form, contained only such exhibitions as had a reference to the service in which it was obtained; the captives and spoils of the enemy, with effigies and representations where the originals, by any accident, could not be displayed. But in these solemnities, executed for the honour of Pompey, were admitted whatever could distinguish or signalize the occasion. Among these, according to the record transcribed by Pliny,[4] there were many costly ornaments of gold and of precious stones, which were fabricated on purpose to be shown. Tables or plates, used for some species of play, made of one entire crystal; a representation of the moon in gold, weighing thirty pondo; tables, utensils, statues, crowns, models of different sorts in gold and precious stones, with the representation of a mountain in gold, having lions, deer, and other animals upon it: and what serves as an evidence that these exhibitions were not limited to the spoils actually taken in war, there is mentioned an image of Pompey himself incrusted with pearls. The whole conducted with more arrangement and order, than were necessary, perhaps, in the disposition of any of the battles which the triumph was intended to celebrate.

Among the images, representations, and memorials which were carried before the victor on this occasion, there was held up to view a state of the public revenue, from which it appeared, that, before Pompey's time, it amounted to no more than fifty millions;[5] and that the addition which he alone brought to it amounted to eighty-five millions.[6]

Soon after this pomp was over, an assembly of the people was called in the circus Flaminius. to receive the address of this victorious general; but, from the extreme caution not to offend any party, the speech which he made, upon this occasion, was acceptable to none. "It gave no hopes," says Cicero,[7] "to the poor; no flattery to the rich; no satisfaction to the good; no encouragement to the profligate." Pompey was suffered to possess the highest place in the consideration of the public, merely because he assumed it; and he preserved his dignity, by never committing his reputation without being prepared, and having concerted a variety of arts by which it might be supported.

1 Plin. Nat. Hist. lib. vii. c. 26.
2 About 50*l.*
3 About 3,860,000*l.*
4 Nat. Hist. lib. xxxvii. c. 2.
5 416,666*l.*
6 708,333*l.* Plutarch in Pompeio, edit. Lond. p 479
7 Cicer. ad Atticum, lib. i. ep. 14.

CHAPTER V.

Transactions at Rome, and in the Provinces—Julius Cæsar appointed in the Quality of Propræ tor to his first Province of Lusitania—Trial of Clodius—Proposed Adoption into a Plebeian Family to qualify him for the Office of Tribune—Cæsar a Candidate for the Consulship · The Triumvirate of Cæsar, Pompey, and Crassus—Consulship of Cæsar—Motion of Vatinius, to confer on Cæsar, for Five Years, the Command in Gaul—Marriage of Pompey to Julia—Of Cæsar to Calpurnia—Plot of Vettius—Consulate of Lucius Calpurnius and A. Gabinius—Attack made upon Cicero—His Exile.

POMPEY, at his departure from Syria, left that province with two legions under the command of Æmilius Scaurus, one of his lieutenants. This officer occupied the country from the Euphrates to the frontier of Egypt, and continued the war which his predecessor had begun with the Arabs.

Caius Antonius, the late colleague of Cicero in the consulate, soon after the defeat of Catiline, proceeded to the province of Macedonia, of which, by the arrangements of the year, he had been appointed governor. He entered his province with the ensigns of victory, which had been obtained by the defeat of Catiline; but these he soon forfeited by his misconduct in a war against the Thracians, and by the disgrace which he otherwise incurred for the mal-administration of his province. Complaints were exhibited against him for extortion. On this occasion it had been reported by himself, or by some of his family, that, having agreed to divide the profits of his government with Cicero, part only was exacted on his own account. This allegation, Cicero, in a letter to Atticus, mentions with indignation; and, being asked to undertake his defence, questions whether he can decently do so under this imputation.[8] But as he soon afterwards undertook the cause of Antony, and employed his interest to have him continued in his command, it is probable that this imputation either gained no credit, or was entirely removed.[9]

The Allobroges, though deprived of the support they were made to expect from the party of Catiline, nevertheless took arms, and invaded the Roman province of Gaul. After a variety of events, they were repulsed by Pontinius, who then commanded the Roman forces in that quarter, and forced to retire into their own country.[10]

About the same time, Caius Julius Cæsar, upon the expiration of his term in the office of prætor, obtained his first military command, being appointed by lot to the government of Lusitania, where, under different pretences, he found an opportunity to quarrel with the natives, to show his capacity for war, and to lay some ground for his claim to a triumph.[11] In pushing his way to the preferments which he now held in the state, he had ruined his fortune by largesses, public shows, and entertainments to the people, by his lavish bounty in private to needy and profligate citizens, and in supporting every desperate cause, against the senate and the government; and is reported to have said of himself, that he needed one hundred and fifty millions Roman money, or one million two hundred thousand pounds sterling, to be worth nothing.[12] When about to depart from the city, he was pressed by his creditors, and had recourse to Crassus, who became his surety for great sums.[13]

A person who, in any other state, than that of Rome, could suppose such a fortune reparable, must have thought of means alarming to the state itself; but Cæsar had now quitted the paths of pleasure for those of ambition; and, in an empire which extended over so many opulent provinces, could easily proportion his wealth to the extent of his power. Although the province into which he was then sent was none of the richest, and was only a step to somewhat farther, more considerable, and more likely to supply him with the means of pursuing the objects of his ambition, he was nevertheless reported to have supplied his own wants, and to have enriched his army.[14]

In passing the Alps, on his way into Spain, at a village on the way, one of his company observed, that "*Here too there were probably parties and contests for power.*" "Ay," said Cæsar, "and I would rather be the first man in this place than the second at Rome.[15]" Upon his arrival in Lusitania, he made the necessary augmentation of the army, and soon overran all the districts that were disposed to resist his authority. With the same ability with which he conducted his military operations, he supported the dignity of a Roman governor, no less in the civil than in the military department. Historians, upon an idea which occurred to them, that the disorder in his own affairs might have rendered him partial to insolvent debtors, are at pains to acquit him of any such charge, and observe that he gave proofs of the contrary, and for the most part ordered two thirds of the debtor's effects to be sequestrated for the use of his creditors.[16]

While these things passed in the provinces, the city was occupied with ordinary affairs, and suffered an increase of the political distempers with which the public had been for some time infected. The expense and dissipation attending the public shows, in particular, were augmented to a great degree. Lucius Domitius Ahenobarbus exhibited the baiting of a hundred bears by African huntsmen;[17] and whereas such entertainments had formerly ended at one meeting, they were now continued through many acts,[18] and were intermitted only while the people retired to their meals.

The office of censor, as appears from the transactions which are mentioned relating to the farms

8 Vid. Cicero ad Atticum, lib. i. ep. 12.
9 Ad Familiar. lib. v. ep. 5.
10 Dio. lib. xxvii. 11 Dio. c. 52, &c.

12 Appian. de Bell. Civ. lib. ii. p. 715.
13 Ibid. About 160,000*l*. Plutarch in Cæsare.
14 Plutarch. in Cæsare, edit. Lond. p. 111.
15 Ibid. 16 Ibid. p. 112.
17 Plin. Nat. Hist lib viii. c. 36.
18 Dio. Cass. lib. xxxvii. c. 47.

of the revenue and the rolls of the senate, was in being at this time, although the names of the persons by whom it was exercised are not recorded. The censors are said to have let the revenues of Asia at a rate, of which the farmers afterwards complained, alleging, that their own avidity in grasping at the profits to be made in this new province had misled them.[1] They likewise put upon the rolls of the senate all who had ever held any office of magistracy, and by this addition increased the number of members beyond the former and ordinary rate.[2]

About the same time happened the memorable trial of Publius Clodius, for the scandal he had given by profaning the sacred rites in Cæsar's house. This debauchee was supposed, for some time, to have sought for an opportunity of a criminal correspondence with Pompeia, Cæsar's wife; but to have been prevented, if not by her own discretion, at least by the attention and vigilance of her family.[3] In these circumstances, in the preceding year, it fell to the lot of Pompeia, as being wife to one of the prætors in office, to celebrate, at her house, the festival of a certain female deity,[4] worshipped by the Romans; and at whose rites women alone were admitted. Every male domestic, even the husband was obliged to absent himself from home while the rites were administered. Clodius took this opportunity to carry on his intrigue; he put himself in a female dress, and, being young and of an effeminate aspect, expected to pass for a woman.[5] Pompeia was supposed to be apprised of the design, and to have stationed a female slave to receive and conduct her paramour through the apartments. Being met, however, by another slave who was not in the secret, his voice betrayed him. A cry of amazement and horror was immediately raised, communicated through all the apartments, and the occasion of it discovered to the matrons, who were met to celebrate the rites. Clodius escaped, but not without being known. The college of pontiffs made a report, that the sacred rites had been profaned. The senate resolved, that inquiry should be made into the grounds of the scandal; and that the people should be moved to authorise the prætor to select, without drawing lots, proper judges for the trial of the accused.

Clodius, by the suspicion of an incestuous commerce with his own sister, the wife of Lucullus; by his perfidy in seducing the troops of that general to mutiny, and by his profligacy on every occasion, had incurred a general detestation; and many of the senators combined, as the likeliest way of removing him from the commonwealth, in urging the prosecution against him.

He himself, foreseeing this storm, had taken refuge in the popular party, and endeavoured to silence the voice of infamy, by professing extraordinary zeal for the people, and vehement opposition to the senate. These parties accordingly became interested in the issue of his cause. The popular leaders endeavoured to preserve him as a useful instrument, and the senate to remove him as a vile and dangerous tool from the hands of their enemies. Even Cæsar, though personally insulted, and so far moved by the scandal which had been given in his own house as to part with his wife, still affected to consider as groundless the charge that was brought against the accused and being asked, why he had parted with a woman who, upon this supposition, must appear to be innocent, said, that his wife must not only be innocent, but above imputation. Pompey, to avoid giving offence, declined to favour either party; but being called upon in the assembly of the people to declare his opinion, whether this trial should proceed according to the decree of the senate; made a long speech, full of respect to the nobles, and of submission to the senate, whose authority, in all questions of this sort, he said, should ever with him have the greatest weight. He afterwards, in the senate itself, being called upon by Messala the consul, delivered himself to the same purpose; and when he had done, whispered Cicero, who sat by him, that he thought he had now sufficiently explained himself; intimating probably, that he meant to comprehend, in this declaration, his judgment with respect to all the acts of the senate which had passed relating to the accomplices of Catiline.[6]

The consul Piso was instructed to carry to the people, for their assent, an act for the better conduct of the trial of Clodius, dispensing with the usual mode of draughting judges by lot, and authorising the prætor to select them, that he might name the more respectable persons. On the day on which this motion was to be made, a numerous party of young nobility appeared for the defendant. His hirelings and retainers crowded the comitium. Even Piso, who moved the question, dissuaded the people from passing the law, and allowed the friends of Clodius to put a ridiculous trick on the assembly, by distributing to the people, as they came forward to vote, two ballots, which, instead of being, as usual one negative and the other affirmative, were both negative. This trick being observed, Cato suspended the ballot, and strongly remonstrated against the proceeding of the consul.[7] He was supported by Hortensius and Favonius. The assembly broke up, and the affair again returned to the senate. The members were importuned by Clodius, who cast himself at their feet as they entered; they, nevertheless, confirmed their former resolution by a majority of four hundred to fifteen.[8]

Hortensius, however, having proposed that, instead of the motion which the consuls had been instructed to make for the selection of the judges, the tribune Fusius should move the people to grant commission for the trial, leaving the judges, as usual, to be drawn by lot; an edict was framed and passed to this effect. Hortensius, who conducted the trial, was confident that no jury could acquit the accused. The court accordingly, in all their proceedings, seemed at first inclined to severity. They even applied for a guard to protect their persons against the partizans of the criminal; but the majority, nevertheless, suffered themselves to be corrupted, and took money in the course of the trial. Of fifty-six judges that were inclosed, twenty-five gave their voice to condemn, and thirty-one to acquit. Catulus, on this occasion, asked the majority to what purpose they had desired a guard? "Was it," he said, "to secure the money you expected to receive for your votes?"[9]

1 Cicer. ad Atticum, lib. i. ep. 17.
2 Dio. lib. xxxvii. c. 46.
3 Plutarch. in Cæsare, edit. Lond. p. 109.
4 Called the Bona Dea.
5 Cicero ad Atticum. lib. i. 12, 13.

6 Cicero ad Atticum, lib. i. epist. 13, 14. 16.
7 Ibid. 8 Ibid. ep. 14.
9 Dio. Cas. lib. xxxvii. c. 46. Cic. ad Att. lib. i. ep. 16

Soon after this judgment the senate resolved that inquiry should be made concerning those judges who had been corrupted in the trial. And by this resolution gave a general offence to the equestrian order, who considered it as an imputation on their whole body.[10]

Pompey, in the course of this transaction, had been obliged to declare himself for the senate; but his object was to be on good terms with all parties, and to manage his interest, by having some of his creatures always chosen into the highest offices of state. He offered, as candidate for the consulate of the following year, Afranius, one of his dependants, who is represented by Cicero as a person of mean character, and who, having no personal dignity, nor any credit with the people, was to be supported in his canvass by money alone. Pompey himself, and the consul Piso, openly employed bribery in obtaining votes in his favour.[11]

A variety of resolutions were obtained in the senate to restrain these practices. Two of them were proposed by Cato and Domitius. The first was levelled against the consul Piso, and gave permission, on the suspicion of illicit practices respecting elections, to visit the house even of a magistrate. By the other it was declared, that all those who were found distributing money to the people should be considered as enemies to their country.[12]

The senate, at the same time, encouraged Lurco, one of the tribunes, to propose a new clause to corroborate the laws against bribery. By this clause promises of money made to the people, if not performed, did not infer guilt; but, if performed, subjected the guilty person from thenceforward to pay to each of the tribes an annual tax of three thousand Roman money, or about twenty-four pounds sterling; and there being thirty-five tribes, this tax amounted in all to about eight hundred and forty pounds of our money. That the tribune might not be interrupted in carrying this law, the senate farther resolved, that the formalities or restrictions of the Lex Ælia and Fufia[13] should not be opposed to him.[14] It appears, however, that the liberality of Pompey prevailed against these precautions, as Afranius was elected, together with Q. Cæcilius Metellus Celer.

Soon after the election of these officers, the farmers of the revenue of Asia, supported by the whole equestrian order, complained, as has been mentioned, of the terms of their contract, in which they alleged that they had greatly exceeded what the funds of that province could afford, and made application to the senate for relief. Their plea was contested for some months with great animosity on both sides.[15]

Upon the accession of the new consuls, several other matters, tending to innovation and public disturbance, were introduced. Metellus Nepos, late tribune, being now in the office of prætor, procured a law to abolish the customs payable at any of the ports of Italy. The Romans, as has been observed, upon the accession of wealth derived from Macedonia, had exempted themselves from all the ancient assessments, and they now completed the exemption of all the Italians from every tax besides that of quit-rents for public lands, and the twentieth penny on the value of slaves when sold or emancipated. They were become the sovereigns of a great empire, and as such, thought themselves entitled to receive, not obliged to pay, contributions.[16]

The tribune Herennius, at the same time, made a motion for an act to enable Publius Clodius to be adopted into a plebeian family, which, though an act of a more private nature than any of the former, tended still more to embroil the parties of the senate and the people. This factious and profligate person had entertained great resentments against many of the senators on account of the prosecution he had lately incurred, and against Cicero in particular, who, having been called as an evidence on his trial, gave a very unfavourable account of his character. The summary proceedings against the accomplices of Catiline, in which Cicero presided as consul, exposed him to the resentment of the popular faction; and Clodius now proposed to qualify himself to be elected tribune of the people, in order to wreak his vengeance on that magistrate in particular, as well as on the other abettors of the senatorian party. The motion, however, for the present was rejected, though not finally dropt, by Clodius himself, nor by the popular faction, whose cause he professed to espouse.[17]

Two other motions were made in which Pompey was deeply interested: one, to ratify and confirm all his acts in the province of Asia: another, to procure settlements for the veterans who had served under his command. The first, as it implied a reflection on Lucullus, many of whose judgments Pompey had reversed, roused this statesman from the care of his household and his table, to that of the republic.[18] He opposed this motion with vigour, and insisted that the acts of Pompey should be separately examined, and not confirmed in a single vote. In this he was supported by Catulus, by Cato, by the consul Metellus, and by the senate in general. Afranius, though vested with the consulate, and acting almost as the agent of Pompey, had neither dignity nor force to support such a measure; and Pompey, finding it rejected by the senate, declined carrying it to the people.[19]

The other proposal, relating to the provision to be made for the soldiers of Pompey, was, by L. Flavius, one of the tribunes, moved in the assembly of the people, under the title of an Agrarian law. In this act, to prevent the imputation of partiality to any particular description of men, certain gratuities were projected for the indigent citizens in general;[20] and, to enable the commonwealth to extend its bounty, it was proposed first of all to revoke the conveyance of certain lands, which, having belonged to the public in the consulate of P. Mucius and L. Calpurnius, were sold by the senate; and that the price should be restored to the purchasers. It was proposed likewise to seize certain lands which had been confiscated by Sylla, but not appropriated; and to

10 Cicero ad Att. lib. i. ep. 17. 11 Ibid. ep. 16.
12 Cicero ad Att. lib i. ep. 16.
13 These were formalities and restrictions provided to check the precipitate passing of laws.
14 Cicer. ad Atticum, lib. i. ep. 16.
15 Ibid. lib. i. ep. 17, 18. lib. xxvii. c. 51.

16 Ibid. lib. ii. ep. 16. Dio. Cass.
17 Dio. Cass. liv. xxxvii. c. 51.
18 Plutarch. in Lucullo, edit. Lond. p. 197.
19 Dio. lib. xxxvii. c. 49. 20 Ibid. lib. 50.

allot, during five years, the revenues of the late conquests in Asia to purchase lands, which should be distributed in terms of this act.[1]

The consul Metellus Celer, supported by the senate, strenuously opposed the passing of this law. The tribune persisted with great obstinacy, and, to remove the obstruction he met with, committed the consul to prison. The whole senate would have attended him thither, and numbers accordingly crowded to the place, when the tribune, vested with the sacred defences of his person, to bar their way, planted his stool or chair of office in the door of the prison; and, having seated himself upon it, "This way," he said, "you cannot pass; if you mean to enter, you must pierce through the walls."[2] He declared his resolution to remain all night where he sat. The parties were collecting their strength, and matters were likely to end in greater extremities than suited the indirect and cautious conduct of Pompey. This politician, although he engaged all his friends to support the motion of Flavius, affected to have no part in the measure, and now probably instructed the tribune to remove from the doors of the prison. Flavius accordingly withdrew of a sudden, saying, he had done so at the request of the prisoner, who begged for his liberty.[3]

It is supposed that Pompey, on this occasion, severely felt the checks which his ambition received from the senate; that he regretted for a moment the dismission of his army, and wished himself in condition to enforce what his craft or his artifice had not been able to obtain. The error he had committed in resigning the sword, if he conceived it as such, might have still been corrected by recovering the possession of some considerable province, which would have given him the command of an army and of proper resources to support his power. He, nevertheless, appears to have preferred the scene of intrigue in the city and the capital of the empire; a choice in which he was probably confirmed by Cæsar, who professed great attachment to him, and who was about this time returned from the government which he held as proprætor in Lusitania.

This officer, according to Dio, had found some pretence for a war with the nations on the frontier of the Roman province; had obliged them to take refuge in some of the islands on the coast, and afterwards reduced them in that retreat. His object was to return to Rome with the reputation of victory, to obtain a triumph, and to offer himself as a candidate for the consulship of the following year. For this purpose he quitted his province without waiting for a successor, and, upon his arrival at Rome, halted as usual with the ensigns of his military command at the gates of the city, applied for a triumph, and, at the same time made interest for votes at the approaching election.[4] The senate, and the friends of the republic in general, were become extremely jealous of his designs, and of his credit with the people. From a libertine he was become an ardent politician, seemed to have no passion but ambition or animosity to the senate; without committing himself he had abetted every factious leader against them, and seemed to be indifferent to consideration or honours, except so far as they led to power. Cicero and Cato were at this time the principal, or most conspicuous, members of the senate. The first was possessed of consular rank, great ingenuity, wit, and accomplished talents: the other, possessed of great abilities and an inflexible resolution, embraced the cause of the republic with the same ardour that others engaged in pursuing the object of their own ambition, their pleasures, or personal interests. He had penetration enough to perceive in Cæsar, long before the senate in general was alarmed, a disposition to vilify the aristocracy, and, in conjunction with needy and profligate citizens, to make a prey of the republic. Under this apprehension he opposed him with a degree of keenness which Cæsar endeavoured to represent as a personal animosity.

The senators in general, now aware of their danger from Cæsar, were disposed to resist his applications, whether made for honours or for public trust. They, on the present occasion, disputed his pretensions to a triumph: and, while he remained without the city in expectation of this honour, refused to admit him on the list of candidates for the office of consul. But the day of election being fixed, Cæsar, without hesitation, preferred the consulate to the triumph, laid down the ensigns of his late military command, assumed the gown, and entered the city as a candidate for the consulship.[5]

The people were at this time divided into a variety of factions. Pompey and Crassus distrusted each other, and both were jealous of Cæsar. Their divisions strengthened the party of the senate, and furnished that body with the means of thwarting separately many of their ambitious designs. This Cæsar had long perceived, and had paid his court both to Pompey and Crassus, in order to hinder their joining the senate against him. The expedience of this precaution now appeared more clearly than ever, and he is supposed to have separately represented to these rivals the advantage which their enemies derived from their misunderstanding, and the ease with which, if united, they might concert among themselves all the affairs of the republic, gratify every friend, and disappoint every enemy. Upon this representation Pompey and Crassus were reconciled, and agreed to act in concert with Cæsar, and to support him in his pretensions, at the approaching elections.[6]

This private combination, which remained some time a secret, was afterwards, by a kind of mockery, alluding to the ordinary names of public office, taken from the number of those who were joined in them,[7] called the triumvirate. In the mean time, these supposed leaders of opposite factions, in abating their violence against each other, took a favourable appearance of moderation and candour. They paid their court separately to persons whom they wished to gain, and flattered them with hopes of being able to heal the divisions of their country. This sort of court they paid in particular to Cicero; and by their flatteries, and real or pretended admiration of his talents, seemed to have got entire possession of his mind. Pompey affected to place the merits

1 Cicero ad Att. lib. i. ep. 19.
2 Dio. lib. xxxvii. p. 50.
3 Dio. Cas. lib. xxxvii p. 50.
4 Ibid. c. 50, &c.
5 Sueton. in Cæsare, c. 18. Dio. lib. xxxvii. c. 54.
6 Dio. Cass. lib xxxvii. c. 54, 55. Plutarch. in Pompeio, Cæsare, et Crasso.
7 As the Decemvirs, Septemvirs, &c

of Cicero greatly above his own. "I, indeed," he said, "have served my country, but this man has preserved it."[8] The senators, with whom Cicero had hitherto acted, were alarmed; and it appears that Atticus, about this time, had taxed him with leaving his party, to commit himself into the hands of their enemies. In his answer to this imputation, he seems to have flattered himself that he had made acquisition of Pompey, not surrendered himself into his power; at least, that he had reclaimed or diverted him from the dangerous projects in which he had been lately engaged, and that he thought himself likely to succeed in the same manner with Cæsar: so much, that he triumphed in the superiority of his own conduct to that of Cato, who, by his austerity and vehemence, had alienated the minds of men otherwise well disposed to the republic,[9] "while I," he said, "by a little discretion, reclaim, or even disarm its enemies."[10]

Few persons were naturally possessed of more penetration than Cicero, although it will afterwards appear how egregiously he was mistaken on this occasion; but he chose not to see what checked his vanity, or prevented his enjoying the court which was paid to him by Pompey and Cæsar. His own glory intercepted every other object from his view, and made him the dupe of every person who professed to admire him, and secretly displeased with every one who did not pay him, on every occasion, the expected tribute of praise; a description under which Cato, though his most sincere well-wisher and friend, appears at this time to have fallen.

Cæsar, to the other arts which he employed to secure his election, added the use of money, which he obtained by joining his interest, in opposition to Bibulus with that of Lucceius, another of the candidates possessed of great wealth. He himself having squandered his fortune, as has been observed, was still greatly in debt, and Lucceius willingly furnished the money that was given to the people in the name of both. This illegal proceeding, together with the menacing concerts of which he began to be suspected with Pompey and Crassus, greatly alarmed the friends of the republic. They determined to support Bibulus against Lucceius; and, in order to give Cæsar a colleague who might occasionally oppose his dangerous intentions, they even went so far as to contribute sums of money, and to bid for votes as high as their opponents. In this crisis, even Cato owned it was meritorious to bribe.[11]

During the dependence of this contest, the senate, by the death of Lutatius Catulus, was deprived of an able member, and the people of a fellow-citizen of great integrity, moderation, fortitude, and ability; a model of what the Romans in this age should have been, in order to have preserved their republic. He partook with Cato in the aversion which Cæsar bore to the most respectable members and best supporters of the senate, and would probably have taken part with him likewise in the continual efforts he made to preserve its authority. The aristocratical party, notwithstanding this loss, prevailed in carrying the election of Bibulus against Lucceius; and though they could not exclude Cæsar from the office of consul, they hoped, by means of his colleague, to oppose and to frustrate his designs.[12]

Cæsar, well aware of their purpose, opened his administration with a speech praising unanimity, and recommending good agreement between those who are joined in any public trust. While he meant to vilify the senate, and to foster every disorderly party against them, he guarded his own behaviour, at least in the first period of his consulship, with every appearance of moderation and candour, paid his court not only to leaders of faction, but to persons of every description, and while he took care to espouse the popular side in every question, was active likewise in devising regulations for the better government of the empire: so that the senate, however inclined to counteract his designs, as calculated to raise himself on the ruins of the commonwealth, could scarcely, with a good grace, oppose him in any particular measure. He set out with a project for the relief of indigent citizens having numerous families, including the veterans and disbanded soldiers of Pompey; proposing to settle them on some of the public lands in Italy. He gave out that he expected the concurrence of Cicero in this measure, sent him a message by Balbus,[13] with assurances *that he meant to consult with Pompey and himself in all matters of importance*, and *that he had hopes of bringing Crassus into the same mind:* words, from which it is manifest that the coalition of these persons was not yet publicly known. "What a fine prospect I have before me," says Cicero to Atticus; "a perfect union with Pompey, even with Cæsar if I please; peace with my enemies, and tranquillity in my old age." But his heart misgave him; the honours of his former life recurred to his mind. With his great talents, he was destined to transmit a more honest fame to posterity, and to become the lamented victim of his country's betrayers, not the detested associate of their crimes.[14]

This consulate is distinguished by the passing of many laws, particularly this, which was devised for the settlement of citizens on certain public lands; and therefore known by the title of the Agrarian law. On this act Cæsar was to rest his popularity, and his triumph over the senate. He gave out that he was to make a provision for twenty thousand citizens, without any burden to the revenue. But he well knew that his antagonists would perceive the tendency of the law, and not suffer it to pass without opposition; and he affected great moderation in the general purpose, and in framing every part of his plan; affecting solicitude to obtain the consent of the senate; but, in reality, to make their opposition appear the more unreasonable and the more odious to the people. He declared, that he did not mean to strip the revenue of any branch that was known to carry profit to the public, nor to make any partial distribution in favour of his friends; that he only meant to plant with inhabitants certain un-

8 Cicero ad Atticum, lib. ii. epist. 1.

9 Alluding to the opposition which Cato gave to the farmers of the revenue, in their petition for an abatement of their rent. But Cato followed his judgment in this matter; and there is no reason to prefer the judgment of Cicero to his.

10 Cicero ad Atticum, lib. ii. epist. 1.

11 Sueton. in Caio Cæsare, c. xix. Appian. de Bell. Civil. lib. ii.

12 Plutarch. Appian. Dio. Sueton. &c.

13 Dio. Cass. lib. viii. initio. Plutarch. in Cæsare In Pompeia, Pompeio, Lucullo, Catone, &c. &c. Sueton. in Cæsare. Appian. de Bell. Civil. lib. ii.

14 Cicero ad Atticum, lib. ii. ep. 3.

profitable wastes, and to provide for a number of citizens, who, being indigent and uneasy in their circumstances, filled the city itself with frequent disorders and tumults; and that he would not proceed a step without consulting the senate, and persons of credit and authority in the state.

In a way to save these appearances, and with these professions, Cæsar formed the first draught of an act which he brought to the senate for their approbation, and the support of their authority in proposing it to the people. It was difficult to find topics on which to oppose a measure so plausible, and conducted with so much appearance of moderation and candour. But the tendency of the act itself was evidently not to promote the peace of the commonwealth, but to constitute a merit in the party that procured it, and to give power to those who were to be entrusted with its execution.

In great and populous cities indigent citizens are ever likely to be numerous, and would be more so, if the idle and profligate were taught to hope for bounties and gratuitous provisions, to quiet their clamours, and to suppress their disorders. If men were to have estates in the country because they are factious and turbulent in the city, it is evident that public lands, and all the resources of the most prosperous state, would not be sufficient to satisfy their claims.

The commissioners appointed for the distribution of such public favours, would be raised above the ordinary magistrates, and above the laws of their country. They might reward their own creatures, and keep the citizens in general in a state of dependence on their will. The authors of such proposals, while they were urging the state and the people to ruin, would be considered as their only patrons and friends "It is not this law I dread," said Cato; "it is the reward expected for obtaining it."

Odious as the task of opposition on such difficult ground might appear to the people, this senator did not decline it. Being asked his opinion in his turn, he answered, That he saw no occasion for the change that was now proposed in the state of the public lands; and entered on an argument with which he meant to exhaust the whole time of the sitting of the senate, and to prevent their coming to a question. He was entitled, by his privilege as a member in that assembly, to speak without interruption, and might, if he chose to continue speaking, persist until all the members had left the house. Cæsar suspecting his design, and finding it impossible otherwise to silence him, ordered him into custody. The whole senate instantly rose in a tumult. "Whither go you before the meeting is adjourned?" said Cæsar to Petreius, who was moving from his side. "I go," said the other, "into confinement with Cato. With him a prison is preferable to a place in the senate with you." The greater part of the members were actually moving away with Cato, and Cæsar felt himself at once stripped of the disguise of moderation he had assumed, and dreaded the spirit which he saw rising in so numerous a body of men, who, on former occasions, had maintained their authority with becoming vigour. He had relied on their want of decision, and on their ignorance of their own strength. But his rashness broke the charm. He wished that the prisoner would procure some friend among the tribunes to interpose; but Cato, seeing him embarrassed, and the senate engaged in the cause, went off in the custody of the lictor without any signs of reluctance. Cæsar immediately recollecting himself, and never hurried too far by any passion, despatched a tribune of his own party, with secret directions to rescue the prisoner; and this being done, the senators again returned to their places. "I meant," said Cæsar, "to have submitted this law to your judgment and correction; but if you throw it aside, the people shall take it up."[1]

Cæsar, upon this occasion, increased his own popularity, and diminished that of his enemies in the senate, who were supposed in this, as in some other instances, to withstand with keenness, every measure that was devised for the comfort of the people. The imputations cast out against him by Cato and others, were supposed to proceed from malice or cynical prejudices. He found himself strong enough to extend his bounty to the people, so as to comprehend the lands of Campania, which were hitherto considered as unalienable, and the richest demesne of the public, together with a valuable district near the confluence of the Vulturnus and the Sabbatus, formerly consecrated to pious uses. In these valuable tracts of land there was sufficient subject for an ample provision for the soldiers of Pompey, and for the retainers of those who, together with Crassus and Cæsar himself, were proposed to be commissioners for carrying this act into execution.

At the first assembly of the people, Cæsar proposed his scheme to impropriate the lands of Campania, with the above additions; and first of all called on his colleague Bibulus to declare his mind on the subject. Bibulus spoke his dissent; and in vehement terms declared, that no such alienation of the public demesne should be made in his consulate. Cæsar next called upon Pompey, though in a private station; and the audience, ignorant of the concert into which these leaders had entered, were impatient to hear him on the subject of a measure which was likely to elevate a supposed rival so high in the favour of the people. To the surprise of all who were present, Pompey applauded the general design, and, in a speech of considerable length, discussed all the clauses of the act, and with great approbation of each. When he had done speaking, Cæsar, alluding to what had dropped from his colleague, and affecting to fear the interposition of force; "Will you support us," he said to Pompey, "in case we are attacked?"—"If any one," said the other, "shall lift up a sword against you, I shall lift up both sword and shield."[2] Crassus being called upon, spoke to the same purpose. The concurrence of these leaders portended the unanimous consent of all parties; and a day being fixed for putting the question, the assembly for the present adjourned.

To oppose a measure so popular, and from which such numbers had great expectations, no means remained so likely to succeed as superstition. To this aid Bibulus accordingly had recourse, and by virtue of the authority with which he was vested, proclaimed a general fast, and a suspension for the present year of all the affairs

1 Dio. lib. xxxviii. c. 1, 2, 3. Plutarch. Sueton. Appian, &c.

2 Cicero ad Att. lib. ii. Plutarch. in Pompeio. Dio. Cass. lib. xxxviii. c. 5.

of state. The design of this suspension, and the extravagant length of time to which it was extended, probably enabled his colleague to treat it with contempt, and to proceed in the design of putting his question, as if no such proclamation had been issued. The assembly was accordingly summoned in the temple of concord. Cæsar, early in the morning, secured all the avenues and the steps of the portico with an armed force; had Vatinius, one of the tribunes of the people, who was entirely devoted to his interest and even in his pay,[3] stationed with this party, in order to take the odium of all violent measures on himself. Bibulus, however, attended by numbers of the senate, and three of the tribunes, who were prepared, by their negative, to put a stop to every proceeding, came into the place of assembly with a firm countenance; he protested against the legality of any meeting to be formed in a time of general fast; but the opposite party being in possession of the temple, forced him from the steps, broke the ensigns of the lictors, wounded the tribunes that interposed in his defence, and effectually removed all farther obstruction to their own designs. The question then being put, the law passed without opposition, including a clause to oblige every senator, under pain of exile or death, to swear to the observance of it.

This oath was probably a snare laid by Cæsar for the most resolute of his opponents, like that which was formerly laid by Marius, on a like occasion, for Metellus Numidicus, and by which that virtuous citizen was actually for some time removed from the commonwealth.[4]

Metellus Celer, the late consul, together with Cato and Favonius, were likely to have fallen into this snare. They at first declared their resolution not to swear to the observance of any such ruinous law; but on maturer consideration, they became sensible that in this they were serving the cause of their enemies. "You may have no need of Rome," said Cicero to Cato, "and may go into exile with pleasure; but Rome has need of you. Give not such a victory to her enemies and your own." Upon these considerations it was determined to comply.[5]

Bibulus, on the day following that of his violent expulsion from the assembly of the people, assembled the senate, complained of the outrage he had received, and submitted the state of the republic to their consideration. But even this assembly, though consisting of above six hundred of the most powerful citizens of Rome, not destitute even of courage, were declined in their spirit, and became averse to exertions of vigour. They were occupied with their villas, their equipages, and the other appurtenances of wealth and of high rank. "They appear," says Cicero upon this occasion, "to think that even if the republic should perish, they will be able to preserve their fish-ponds."

The consul Bibulus, even Cato, though far removed from any ambiguity of conduct, saw no possibility of resisting the torrent. The first retired to his own house, and from thence forward, during the remainder of the year, did not appear in any public place. Cato absented himself from the senate.[6]

While Cæsar engrossed the full exercise of the consular power, Bibulus was content with issuing his edicts or manifestos in writing, containing protests, by which he endeavoured to stop all proceedings in public affairs on account of the religious fast, or continuation of holidays, which he had instituted to restrain his colleague. In these writings he published violent invectives against Cæsar, in which, among other articles, he charged him with having had a part in the conspiracy of Catiline.[7] The tribune Vatinius, in return, issued a warrant to commit the consul Bibulus to prison; and, in order to seize him, attempted to break into his house; but in this he was foiled, and the parties continued, during the remainder of this consulate, in the same situation with respect to each other.

In dating the year, instead of the consulate of Cæsar and Bibulus, it was called by some wag the consulate of Julius and Cæsar.[8] This able adventurer, though suspected of the deepest designs, went still deeper in laying his measures for the execution of them than his keenest opponents supposed. He found means to tie up every hand that was likely to be lifted up against himself; as those of Pompey and Crassus, by their secret agreement, of which the articles were gradually disclosed in the effect. He confirmed to Pompey all the acts of his administration in Asia, and, by putting him on the commission for dividing the lands of Campania, and for settling a colony at Capua, gave him an opportunity, which the other earnestly desired, of providing for many necessitous citizens of his party. He flattered Crassus sufficiently, by placing him on the same commission, and by admitting him to a supposed equal participation of that political consequence which the triumvirs proposed to secure by their union. He gained the equestrian order, by granting a suit which they had long in dependence, for a diminution of the rents payable by the revenue farmers in Asia.[9] These he reduced a third; and with that order of men acquired the character of great liberality and candour. He himself was the only person who in appearance was not to profit by these arrangements. He was occupied, as his retainers pretended, in serving the republic and in promoting his friends; was the general patron of the distressed and the indigent, and had nothing to propose for himself.

With his consent and under his authority, Fufius, one of the prætors, and Vatinius, one of the tribunes, obtained two laws, both of them equitable and salutary: the first relating to the use of the ballot in the comitia, or assembly of the people: the other, relating to the challenge of parties in the nomination of judges or juries. The introduction of the ballot in political questions had greatly weakened the influence of the aristocracy over the determinations of the people; and resolutions were frequently carried in this manner, which no party, nor any particular order of men, were willing to acknowledge as their

---

3 Cicero in Vatinium. Cæsar was reported to have said at Acquileia, some time after this date, when Vatinius was disappointed of the edileship, that he had no business with honours, being intent on money only; and that he was paid for all his services in the tribunate.

4 See book ii. c. 6.

5 Plutarch in Catone. Appian. de Bell. Civil lib. ii.

6 Cicero pro Sextio. Plutarch. in Catone.

7 Sueton. in C. Cæsare.

8 Ibid. c. 20. Dio. Cass. lib. xxxvii. c. 6. 8.

9 Cicero ad Att. lib. ii. ep. 1. Appian. de Bell. Civil lib. ii. p. 433.

measure. The nobles imputed the absurd determinations to the majority that was formed by the people, and these sometimes retorted the imputation. To leave no doubt in such matters for the future, Fufius proposed that the orders of Patrician, Equestrian, and Plebeian, should ballot apart.[1] This regulation had some tendency to restore the influence of the superior classes.

Vatinius proposed that in criminal actions, when the judges were drawn by lot, the defendant and prosecutors might, in their turns, challenge, or strike off from the list, persons to whom they took a particular exception.[2]

Cæsar himself was busy in devising new regulations to reform the mode of elections, and to improve the forms of business in some of the public departments. By one of his acts the priests were to be elected agreeably to the former laws of Atius and Domitius, with this difference, that candidates might be admitted even in absence. By another of his acts, regular journals were to be kept in the senate and in the assemblies of the people, and all their proceedings recorded for the inspection of the public. By a third, persons convicted of treason were subjected to new penalties, and governors of provinces to additional restraints in the exercise of their power. Such officers were not allowed to receive any honorary gift from their provinces, until their services being considered at Rome, were found to have entitled them to a triumph.[3] They were restrained from encroaching on the right of any state or principality beyond the limits of their province. They were obliged to leave copies of their books and of their acts at two of the principal towns in their government,[4] and immediately upon their arrival at Rome, to give in a copy of the same accounts to the treasury. They were doomed to make restitution of all subjects received in extortion, not only by themselves, but by any of their attendants.[5]

With these acts Cæsar adorned his consulate, and in some measure discountenanced the party which was disposed to traduce him. He is, nevertheless, accused of having stolen from the treasury, to which he had access in the capacity of consul, bars of gold weighing three thousand pondo, and of having concealed the theft by substituting brass gilt, and of the same form, in its place.[6]

Whatever foundation there may have been for this report, it soon appeared that Cæsar had objects of a more serious nature, could copy, on occasion, the example of Pompey, and, in his manner, cause what was personal to himself to be proposed by others, whom he might be free to support or disavow according to the reception which his proposal met from the public. It cannot be doubted that he now conceived the design of bringing a military force to support his pretensions in the city. Hitherto kingly power being odious at Rome, whoever had aspired to it had always perished in the attempt, and the mere imputation, however supported, was fatal. The most profligate party among the populace were unable or unwilling to support their demagogues to this extent; and the people in general became jealous of their most respectable citizens, when it appeared that merit itself approached to monarchical elevation. Marius, by the continued possession of the highest offices, and by the supreme command of armies, had acquired a species of sovereignty which he knew not how to resign. Cinna came into partnership with Marius, and wished to govern after his decease. Sylla, to avenge his own wrongs and those of his friends, to cut off a profligate faction, and restore the republic, took possession of the government. He led his army against usurpers, and had the power to become himself the most successful usurper, as he was put in possession of a sovereignty which he no doubt might have retained. So far he was a model to every ambitious adventurer, and pointed out the only means which could insure to a single person the sovereignty of Rome. Catiline, with his accomplices, Lentulus and Cethegus, had vainly attempted to overturn the state, or to usurp its government, by means of a profligate party among the populace or citizens of desperate fortune.[7] Cæsar was become head of the same party; but an army like that of Sylla, a convenient station, and the resources of a great province, were necessary to support the contest, and to carry it against his rivals, as well as against the republic itself, to a favourable issue.

The republic had taken many precautions to prevent the introduction of military power at Rome. Although the functions of state and of war were entrusted to the same persons, yet the civil and military characters, except in the case of a dictator, were never united at once in the same person. The officer of state resigned his civil power before he became a soldier, and the soldier was obliged to lay aside his military ensigns and character before he could enter the city; and if he sued for a triumph in his military capacity, must remain without the walls till that suit was discussed. The command of armies and of provinces in the person of any officer was limited to a single year at a time, at the end of which, if it were not expressly prolonged, it was understood to expire, and to devolve on a successor named by the senate.

That no leader of a party might have an army at hand to overawe the republic, no military station was supposed to exist within the limits of Italy. The purpose, however, of this precaution was in some measure frustrated by the near situation of a province in which an army was kept within the Alps. Italy was understood to extend only from the sea of Tarentum to the Arnus and the Rubicon: beyond these boundaries, on the northwest, all those extensive and rich tracts on both sides of the Apennines, and within the Alps, which now make the dutchies of Ferrara, Bologna, Modena, Milan, the states of Piedmont and Venice, with the dutchy of Carniola, and the whole of Lombardy, were considered, not as a part of Italy, but as a province termed the Cisalpine Gaul, and, like the other Roman pro-

1 Dio. lib. xxxviii. c. 8. 2 Ibid. Appian.

3 Cicero ad Att. lib. v. ep. 16. et lib. vi. ep 7.

4 Cicero ad Famil. lib. ii. ep. 17. et lib. v. ep. 20.

5 Ibid. in Vatinium pro Sext.

6 Sueton. in Jul. c. 54. Cæsar is said to have sold the gold bullion he brought from Spain at 3000 H. S. or about 25*l.* of our money. This will make his supposed theft about 75 000*l.*

7 Speaking of the imaginary danger to a state of being overturned by the rabble; we might as much fear, said a witty writer of the present age, that a city would be drowned by the overflowing of its own kennels.

vinces, was to be held by a military officer, supported by an army.

This then was the most commodious station at which a political adventurer might unite the greatest advantages, that of having an army at his command, and that of being so near the capital as to be able, by surprise, to occupy the seats of government whenever his designs were ripe for such an attempt.

Sylla had an army devoted to his pleasure; but, having the seas of Asia and Ionia to pass in his way to Italy, could not, without giving an alarm from a great distance, and without putting his enemies on their guard, approach to the city. He therefore, when he had this object in his view, made no secret of his purpose.

Cæsar had formed a design on the commonwealth, and acted from his original disposition, and a deliberate intention to make himself master of it; not urged, like Sylla, by great provocations, and the suggestion of singular circumstances. He arranged his measures like the plan of a campaign, which he had the ability to digest, and the patience to execute with the greatest deliberation. He proposed to make himself master of an army at the gates of Rome, and to have the resources of a province contiguous to the capital. He secured the possession of these advantages by an unprecedented prolongation of the usual appointments for five years; so that the people themselves could not, without a breach of faith, recal their grant upon any sudden alarm of the improper use he might propose to make of their favours.

The Cisalpine Gaul, or that part of Italy which lay from the Rubicon to the Alps, was peculiarly suited to the purpose of Cæsar. But the distribution of the provinces was still within the prerogative of the senate; and the provincial governments were filled by their appointment, in pursuance of an express regulation ascribed to Caius Gracchus, and known, from his name, by the title of the Sempronian law.[8] Cæsar had ever been at variance with the greater part of the senate. In the office of prætor he had been suspended by their authority. In his present office of consul he had set them at open defiance. He had no prospect of being able to obtain from them the choice he had made of a province; and the proposal to put him in possession of the Cisalpine Gaul for a term of years, joined to the preceding parts of his conduct, would have given a general alarm, and opened at once the whole extent of his design.

It was necessary, therefore, in order to obtain this object, to set aside the authority of the senate, and to procure his nomination by some degree of surprise. The tribune Vatinius accordingly, upon a rumour that the Helvetii, or the nations inhabiting from mount Jura to the Alps, were likely to cause some commotion on the frontier of Gaul, moved the people to set aside the law of Sempronius, and, by virtue of their own supreme power, to name Cæsar as proconsul of the Cisalpine Gaul and Illyricum for five years with an army of three legions. The senatorian party, as might have been expected, were greatly alarmed at this proposal. They vainly, however, hoped to evade it by substituting another appointment for Cæsar in place of this province. It was proposed to make him superintendant of the public forests throughout the empire; a charge which, though not, in our acceptation of the word, a province, however, like every other public department in that empire, known by this name. This substitute for the government of the Cisalpine Gaul was thought to be the better chosen, that it neither implied nor required the command of an army, and was to withhold the engine of military power from a person so likely to abuse it. This weak attempt, however, against so able an adversary, only tended to expose the meaning of those by whom it was made, and by showing to the senate their own weakness, hurried them into concessions which perhaps might have been otherwise avoided. In order that Cæsar might not owe every thing to the people and nothing to them, they extended his command at once to both sides of the Alps. On the one side of these mountains he had a station from which to overawe the city: on the other, he had a great extent of territory, and a theatre of war on which he might form an army and inure them to service. The senate, seeing he had already, by a vote of the people, obtained the first with an army of three legions for five years; and imagining that it was no longer of any use to oppose him; or hoping to occupy his attention, or to wear out the five years of his command in wars that might arise beyond the Alps, they joined to his province on the Po that of the Transalpine Gaul, with an additional legion. In this manner, whether from these or any similar reasons, it is affirmed by some of the historians,[9] that the senate even outran the people in concessions to Cæsar; and to this occasion is referred the memorable saying of Cato: "Now you have taken to yourselves a king, and have placed him with his guards in your citadel."[10]

Cæsar at the same time, on the motion of the tribune Vatinius, was empowered to settle a Roman colony on the lake Larius at Novum Comum, with full authority to confer the privilege of Roman citizens on those who should settle in this place. Having obtained the great object of his consulate, in his appointment for a term of years to the command of an army within the Alps, he no longer kept any measures with the senate, nor allowed them any merit in the advantages he had gained. He was aware of their malice, he said, and had prevailed in every suit, not by their concession, but in direct opposition to their will. Though capable of great command of temper, and of the deepest dissimulation when in pursuit of his object, he appears, on this and other occasions, to have had a vanity which he indulged, in braving the world when his end was obtained.[11] As he insulted the senate when no longer depending on their concurrence for any of his objects, so he no longer disguised his connexion with Pompey and Crassus, or the means by which in his late measures, the concurrence of these rivals had been obtained.

As such combinations and cabals generally have an invidious aspect to those who are excluded from them, the triumvirate, for so it began to be called in detestation and irony, not-

8 Lex Sempronia, vid. b. ii. c. 3.

9 Sueton. in Jul. Cæsare, c. 22.

10 Plutarch. in Catone. Dio. Cass. lib. xxxviii. Appian. de Bell. Civil. lib. ii.

11 Sueton. in Cæsare, lib. ii. c. 22.

withstanding the popularity or influence enjoyed by those who had formed it,[1] became an object of aversion and general abuse.[2] They were received at all public places with groans and expressions of hatred. An actor, performing on the public theatre, applied to Pompey a sentence of reproach, which occurred in the part he was acting. The application was received with peals of applause, and called for again and again.[3]

The edicts that were published by Bibulus in opposition to Cæsar were extolled, and received with avidity. The places of the streets at which they were posted up were so crowded with multitudes assembled to read them, that the ways were obstructed. Cæsar and Pompey endeavoured to lessen the effect of these edicts in speeches to the people, but were ill heard. Pompey lost his temper and his spirit, and sunk in his consideration as much as Cæsar advanced in power. It became manifest even to the people, that Cæsar had procured their conjunction for his own conveniency;[4] but Pompey himself probably felt that he was too far advanced to recede.

The senate, and all the most respectable citizens of Rome, though unanimous in their detestation of the design that was formed by Cæsar, Pompey, and Crassus, to dispose of the republic at their pleasure, yet either were, or believed themselves, unable to cope with the power of so many factions united. Cæsar, in order to hold by force what he gained by artifice, and by some degree of surprise, filled the streets with his retainers in arms, and showed, that, in case of any attempt to recal what had been so weakly given up to him, he was in condition to resist, and to lay the city in blood. If he were driven from Rome, he had provided within the Alps an army of two or three complete legions, with which he could maintain his province, or even recover his possession of the city. Every one censured, complained, and lamented; but there was little concert, and less vigour, even among the members of the senate.

Cato, with his declared disapprobation of the late measures, was reduced to the single expedient of assisting Bibulus in drawing up the edicts or manifestos against the proceedings of Cæsar, which were, at this time received with so much avidity by the people.

Cicero now declined taking part in any affair of state; but being known for an advocate, was courted in this capacity by many citizens, who had affairs in dependence before the courts of justice, and apprehending an attack which was likely to be made upon himself, on account of the transactions of his consulate, he avoided, as much as possible, giving offence to any of the parties which divided the commonwealth. The storm was to be directed against him by Publius Clodius, under whose animosity to the governmen of the nobles, and to Cicero in particular, it was perceived for some time to be gathering.[5]

This bustling profligate having, in the former year, in order that he might be qualified for tribune of the people, got himself adopted into a plebeian family, could not obtain the necessary ratification of the deed of adoption in the assembly of the curiæ, until his cause was espoused by Cæsar, who seems to have taken his part, in resentment of some insinuations thrown out against himself by Cicero, in pleading for M. Antonius, his late colleague in the consulate. Antonius being, as has been mentioned, on account of his administration in Macedonia, accused of extortion, was defended by Cicero, who took that occasion to lament the state of the republic, brought under subjection as it was by a cabal which ruled by violence, and in contempt of the law. Cæsar was greatly provoked: "This person," he said, "takes the same liberty to vilify the reputation of others, that he takes to extol his own;" and upon those expressions, considered as a warning of the part which Cicero was likely to take in his absence, he determined not to leave him at the head of the senatorian party to operate against him. His destruction might be effected merely by expediting the formality of Clodius's adoption into a plebeian family, to qualify him for tribune of the people;[6] and Cæsar, on the very day in which he received this provocation from Cicero, permitted the act of adoption to pass in the assembly of the curia.

Pompey likewise concurred in executing this deed of adoption for Clodius, and assisted in the quality of augur to carry it through the religious forms. Clodius, in the mean time, gave out, that he had no design on the tribunate, but was soliciting an embassy to Tigranes king of Armenia. Cicero was so much blinded by this pretence, that he was merry in his letter to Atticus on the absurdity of Clodius, in having himself degraded into a plebeian, merely to qualify him to appear at the court of Tigranes. He was merry likewise with his not being put on the commission of twenty for the execution of Cæsar's Agrarian law. "Strange!" he said, "that he who was once the only male creature in Cæsar's house, cannot now find one place among twenty in this list of his friends."[7]

The more effectually to impose upon Cicero and his friends, Cæsar affected to believe, that the intention of Clodius was against himself, and taken up with the animosity of a person who had already attempted to dishonour his house;[8] and he pretended to dispute the validity of his adoption, and of consequence, his qualification to be elected a tribune. Pompey joined in the same vile artifice. "Nay," says Cicero, upon hearing of their pretended opposition to Clodius, "this is perfect tyranny. Only send the proper officers to me, and I will give my affidavit, that Pompey told me himself he had assisted as augur in passing that decree."[9]

With these transactions the year of Cæsar's

1 The titles of duumvirs, triumvirs, and so on, were the designations of legal commissions at Rome acting under public authority; such title was given to the private coalition of these adventurers in mere irony.

2 Cicer. ad. Att. lib. ii. ep. 16.

3 "To our misfortune thou art great." He was called upon to repeat these words again and again innumerable times. "The time will come when thou shalt rue this state;" likewise repeated with peals of applause, &c. Cicero ad Att. lib. ii. epist. 19. Val. Max. lib. vi. c 2.

4 One of the sentences, so much applauded in its application to him at the theatre, was, "Eandem virtutem tempus veniet cum graviter gemes."

5 Cicero ad Att. lib. ii. epist. 19, 20, 21, 22, 23.

6 Dio. Cass. lib. xxxviii c. 10. &c. Plutarch. in Cicerone. Cicero pro domo sua, de Provinciis Consularibus, &c.

7 Cicer ad Att. lib. ii. epist. 7.

8 In the intrigue with Cæsar's wife.

9 Cic. ad Att. epist. 10. Vol. 12.

consulate drew to a close. He ratified his treaty with Pompey, by giving him his daughter Julia in marriage. During the former part of the year, this lady had been promised to Servilius Cæpio, and had been of great use to her father, by securing the services of Cæpio against Bibulus. Servilius, on his disappointment, was pacified by the promise of Pompey's daughter. Cæsar himself married the daughter of Calpurnius Piso, who, together with Gabinius, the creature of Pompey, was destined to succeed in the consulate, and who was, by this alliance, secured in the interest of Cæsar. "Provinces, armies, and kingdoms," said Cato on this occasion, "are made the dowries of women,[10] and the empire itself an appendage of female prostitution."

In this situation of affairs, and among parties who dealt in impositions and artifices, as well as in open and daring measures, some particulars are recorded, which, to gain our belief, require some acquaintance with the manners of the times. Vettius, a citizen of some note, who had been employed by Cicero in the time of his consulship to gain intelligence of the Catiline conspiracy, now himself appeared as the author of a plot, of which the origin and the issue were matter of various conjecture. Knowing that Curio, a young man of high rank, and a declared enemy of Cæsar, was on bad terms likewise with Pompey, he told him in confidence, that he himself had determined to assassinate Pompey, and proposed to Curio to join with him in that design. The young man communicated the matter to his father, and the father to Pompey, who laid it before the senate. Vettius being examined in the senate, at first denied any intercourse with Curio, but afterwards confessed, that he had been drawn into a conspiracy with this young man, with Lucullus, Brutus, Bibulus, and some others, who had formed a design on Pompey's life.

It was strongly suspected, that Cæsar had employed Vettius to frame this imposture, in order that he might engage some of those persons in a criminal correspondence; and that it was intended, as soon as he had laid some foundation for an imputation of guilt against them, that he should, with a party of slaves, armed with daggers, put himself in the way of being taken; that he should at first deny the plot, but afterwards suffer himself to be forced, by degrees, to confess, and to declare his pretended accomplices; that this plan was disconcerted by the early intimation which Curio gave to his father, before all the circumstances intended to give it an air of probability were in readiness.

It was scarcely possible, however, that Cæsar should have committed his reputation to the hazard of detection in so infamous a project. He laid hold of it indeed with some avidity, and endeavoured to turn it against his opponents. After Vettius had been examined before the senate, and was committed to prison for farther examination, Cæsar presented him to the people, and brought him into the rostra, to declare what he knew of this pretended bloody design. The prisoner repeated his confession but varied in the account of his accomplices, particularly in leaving Brutus out of the list; a circumstance likewise, in the scandal of the times, imputed to the partiality of Cæsar, and considered as proof of his clandestine relation to this young man. Vettius was remanded to prison, and a process commenced against him on the statute of intended assassination. A trial must have probably disclosed the whole scene, and for this reason was said to have been prevented, by the sudden death of Vettius, who was supposed to have been strangled by order of Cæsar in prison.[11]

U. C. 695.
L. Calpurnius Piso Cesonianus,
A. Gabinius Nepos.

By the influence of Pompey and Cæsar, Gabinius and Piso were elected consuls; and, by their connivance, Clodius became tribune of the people. The ascendant they had gained, however, was extremely disagreeable to many of the other officers of state, and even to some of the tribunes. L. Domitius Ahenobarbus and C. Memius Gemellus joined in an accusation against Cæsar, late consul, for proceedings in office contrary to law and religion. Cæsar, for some time, affected to join issue with him on these questions, and to submit his cause to judgment; but apprehending delay and trouble, without any advantage from such an enquiry, he pleaded his privilege as a person destined for public service; and accordingly, without staying to answer this charge, withdrew from the city, and continued to make his levies, and to assemble his army in the suburbs of Rome.

In this posture of affairs, one of the quæstors, who had served under Cæsar in his consulship, was convicted of some misdemeanor;[12] and the opposite party, as if they had of a sudden broke the chains in which they were held, commenced suits against all the tools that had been employed by him in his late violent measures. Gabinius had been charged with bribery by Caius Cato, then a young man. But the prætor, whose lot it was to exercise the jurisdiction in such cases, being under the influence of Pompey, evaded the question. Caius Cato complained to the people, and, having said that Pompey usurped a dictatorial power, narrowly escaped with his life.[13]

Vatinius was accused before the prætor Memmius, who willingly received the accusation; but all proceedings were suddenly stopped by the interposition of Clodius in the capacity of tribune; and the attention of the people and of the senate soon came to be more entirely occupied with the designs of this factious adventurer.

The ruin of Cicero appears to have been the principal object which Clodius proposed to himself in entering on the office of tribune; and this, though affecting to be of the popular party, he pursued chiefly from motives of personal animosity and resentment. Cicero had given evidence against him on his trial, and afterwards in the senate made him the object of his wit and invective.[14] He is generally represented by Cicero as effeminate and profligate, void of discretion or prudence. On the present occasion, however, he seems to have managed with considerable steadiness and address. He acted evidently in concert with Cæsar, Pompey, and Crassus; but probably had not from them any particular direction in what manner he was to proceed.

Ever since the summary proceedings which

10 Plutarch. in Catone.

11 Cicero ad Att. lib. ii. epist. 24. Sueton. in Cæsare, c. 20.

12 Sueton. in Nerone, c. ii. et in Cæsare, c. 23.

13 Cicero ad Quint. Frat lib. i. epist. 2.

14 Cicer. ad Att. lib. i.

were employed against the accomplices of Catiline, the danger of this precedent was a favourite topic with the popular faction. Clodius professed that the object of his tribunate was to provide a guard against this danger. He began with paying his court to different parties and different orders of men in the republic, by proposing acts favourable to each; and he stated his motion for the better securing of the people against arbitrary executions, which he meant in the end to apply to Cicero, as but one of many regulations intended by him for the benefit of the public, and which he joined with some acts of gratification to private persons. He gained the present consuls by procuring them lucrative appointments, at the expiration of their year in office; to Piso, Macedonia including Achaia; to Gabinius, Syria with a considerable addition beyond the usual bounds of the province.[1] He gained the indigent part of the people by an act to remit all the debts which were due for corn at the public granaries; and by ordering, for the future, the distributions from thence to be made gratuitously.[2] He, at the same time, procured another act extremely agreeable to many of the citizens, for restoring and increasing the number of corporations which had been abolished about nine years before, on account of the troubles to which they gave rise.

The meeting of corporate bodies, in a city so much addicted to faction and tumult, had been the cause of frequent disorders. As persons, affecting to govern the state, endeavoured to gain the people, by indulging their passions for idleness and pleasure, with games, theatrical entertainments, combats of gladiators, and the baiting of wild beasts; so the head of every corporate body, though upon a smaller scale, had his feasts, his entertainments, and shows, forming his party of retainers, on occasion, to maintain his pretensions by force. The renewal, therefore, of such establishments, a measure which carried to every tradesman in his stall the feeling and consequence of a Crassus, a Pompey, and a Cæsar, affecting to govern the world in their respective ways, was greedily adopted by the lower people. And Clodius took the opportunity of the first popular meetings to awaken and to direct their zeal to his own purpose.[3] He even gained a considerable party in the senate by affecting to circumscribe the discretionary power of the censors over this body. Many of the members had reason to dread the censorial animadversions, and were pleased with an act which he obtained to provide, that for the future, no one could be struck off the rolls of the senate without a formal trial, and the concurrence of both the censors.[4]

Joined to so many arts practised to reconcile different parties to the measures he affected to take for the security of the people's liberties, Clodius promulgated his law of provision against arbitrary executions, and gave it a retrospect which was undoubtedly meant to comprehend the summary proceedings which had been held against Cethegus and Lentulus in the consulate of Cicero. While the subject was in dependence, he thought of two circumstances that might operate against him, and which he was therefore determined to prevent. One was, the practice of recurring to the celestial auspices by which the proceedings of the people were sometimes suspended; and the other was, the opposition which he might expect from Cato, who was likely to consider the cause of the senate and the republic as involved in that of the magistrate, who had preserved the state by executing their decrees. To secure himself against the first, he procured an edict to prohibit all persons from observing the heavens while the people were deliberating on any affair of state; and to obviate the second, he thought of a pretence for a temporary removal of Cato from Rome.

In the preceding consulate, Cato, though armed as he was solely with the reputation of integrity, unable to prevent the progress of a ruinous faction affecting popular measures, yet by his unremitted opposition, he forced them, on occasion, to show what Pompey in particular was extremely desirous to conceal, that they prevailed by corruption and force, not by what they pretended, the free choice of their fellow-citizens. Clodius foreseeing a like opposition, and possibly a disappointment in his design against Cicero, if Cato continued at Rome, devised a commission to employ him in foreign service. Ptolomy, king of Cyprus, had put a personal affront on Clodius, by refusing to pay his ransom when taken by pirates on the coast of Asia near to that island. He now took an opportunity to be revenged on him, by procuring an act to forfeit his kingdom and his treasure; and by making Cato the instrument of his revenge, he proposed to free himself at the same time from the interruption which this citizen was likely to give to his projects at Rome.[5]

At an interview with Cato, Clodius had the impudence to pretend great admiration of his virtue; told him, that the commission to reduce Cyprus into the form of a province was solicited by many; but that he knew of none who, by his faithfulness and integrity, was so well qualified for the trust as Cato, and that he meant to propose him to the people. "That," said Cato, "I know is a mere artifice; not an honour, but an indignity intended to me." "Nay," said Clodius, "if you do not go willingly, you shall go by force;" and on that very day moved and obtained his nomination from the people. Lest the affair of Cyprus should not detain him a sufficient time, he was farther charged in his commission to repair to Byzantium to restore some exiles, and to quiet some troubles which had arisen at that place.

Cæsar and Pompey likewise concurred in procuring this commission to Cato, in order to remove a powerful support from the prætors Memmius and Domitius, whose proposal to repeal all the acts of Cæsar was yet in dependence.

The storm was now prepared to fall upon the magistrate who had presided in the suppression of Catiline's party, and no man had any doubt of its direction. Cato, before he left Rome, seeing Cæsar in possession of the gates with an army, and ready, in the event of any tumult, *under pretence of quieting disorders*, to enter the city by force, and to seize on the government; and apprehending, that the cause in dependence, however just, was altogether desperate, earnestly

1 Plutarch. in Cicerone.
2 Pædianus in Pisoniana. Dio. lib. xxxviii. Cicero pro Domo sua.
3 Dio. lib. xxxviii. c. 13. Cicero in Pisonem, c. 4. et Ascanius, ibid.
4 Ibid. See a summary of these acts. Cicero pro Sextio, from c. 15 to c. 28.
5 Cicero pro Sextio.

exhorted Cicero, rather to yield and to withdraw from the city, than to bring matters to extremities in the present state of the republic.[6]

Cicero, however, was for some time undecided. Having secured the support of L. Ninius Quadratus, one of the tribunes, he proposed to obstruct the proceedings of his enemy, and to give a negative to all his motions. Afterwards, upon assurances from Clodius, that the purpose of the act was altogether general, and had no special relation to himself, he was prevailed on not to divide the college of tribunes, or to engage his friends in the invidious task of giving a negative to a law, that was intended merely to guard the people against arbitrary proceedings.[7]

Clodius, having obtained this advantage, no longer made any secret of his design against Cicero, and boasted of the concurrence of Cæsar and Pompey. In this neither of these professed friends of Cicero denied the imputation;[8] but excused themselves in private by pleading, that while their own acts of the preceding year were still questioned by the prætor, it was necessary for them to keep terms with so violent a tribune;[9] but Pompey, together with this apology for his present conduct, gave Cicero the strongest assurances of future protection. "This tribune," he said, "shall kill me before he injure you." It is not credible that Pompey then meant to betray him; it was sufficiently base that, in the sequel, he did not keep his word. On the contrary, when his aid came to be most wanted by his injured friend, he retired to the country, under pretence of business; and being at his villa near Alba, where Lentulus, Lucullus, and many of the most respectable senators repaired to him with the warmest entreaties in behalf of a person to whose eloquence and panegyric he owed so many of his honours, he coldly referred them to the ordinary officers of state for protection, saying, that as a private citizen he could not contend with a furious tribune at the head of an armed people.[10]

In the mean time, the consul Gabinius, though under the absolute direction of Pompey, promoted the attack against Cicero, and checked every attempt that was made in his favour. When the equestrian order, together with numbers of the most respectable citizens from every quarter of Italy, crowded in mourning to Rome, and presented a memorial to the senate in his behalf; and when the members proposed to take mourning, and to intercede with the people, Gabinius suddenly left the chair, broke up the meeting, went directly from thence to the assembly of the people, where he threw out injurious insinuations against the senate, and mentioned the meetings which had been held by the equestrian order, as riotous and seditious tumults; said, that the knights ought to be cautious how they revived the memory of that part which they themselves had acted in the violent measures which were now coming under review, and which were so likely to meet with a just retribution from the people.

In this extremity Cicero attempted to see Pompey in person at his country-house; but while the suppliant was entering at one door, this treacherous friend withdrew at another.[11] No longer doubting that he was betrayed by a person on whom he had so fully relied, he began to be agitated by a variety of counsels and projects. He was invited by Cæsar to place himself in the station of lieutenant in his province of Gaul; and, in that public character abroad, to take refuge from the storm that was gathering against him in Italy. But this, from a person who had so much contributed to raise the storm, was supposed to proceed from a design to insult or betray him; or at best to reduce him to a state of dependence on himself. Being attended by a numerous body of citizens, chiefly of the equestrian order, who had taken arms in his cause, he sometimes had thoughts of defending himself by force at other times, he despaired of his fortunes, and as appears from his letters, proposed to kill himself; and was diverted from this intention only by the entreaties and anxious care of his friends.

Such was the state of affairs, when Clodius assembled the people to pass the act he had framed against arbitrary executions. He had summoned them to meet in the suburbs, that Cæsar, who on account of his military command was then excluded from the city, might be present. This artful politician being called upon among the first to deliver his opinion; with an appearance of moderation and unwillingness to bear hard on any person to whom the law might apply, referred the people to his former declarations; said, that every one knew his mind on the subject of arbitrary executions; that he approved the act which was now proposed, as far as it provided against such offences for the future; but could not approve of its having a retrospect to any transaction already passed.

While Cæsar thus, in delivering his own opinion, affected to go no farther than consistency and a regard to his former conduct seemed to require, he permitted or directed his party to go every length with Clodius, and meant either to ruin Cicero, or force him to accept of protection on the terms that should be prescribed to him.

When the general law had passed, there was yet no mention of Cicero; and his enemies might have still found it a difficult matter to carry the application to him; but he himself, in the anguish of his mind, anticipated the accusation, went forth in mourning to the streets, and implored mercy of every citizen with an aspect of dejection, which probably did not encourage any party to espouse his cause. He was frequently met in this condition, and insulted by Clodius, who walked in the streets, attended by an armed rabble; and he determined at last to abandon the city. Being escorted by a company of his friends, he passed through the gates in the middle of the night on the first of April, took the road of Lucania, and intended to have made his retreat into Sicily, where the memory of his administration in the capacity of quæstor, and the continued effects of his patronage at Rome, were likely to procure him a favourable reception.[12] But Clodius, immediately upon his departure, having carried a special attainder, by which, in the language of such acts, he was interdicted the use of fire and water; and by which every person within five hundred miles of Italy was forbid, under severe

6 Plutarch. in Catone. 7 Dio. lib. xxxviii. c. 14.
8 Cicero post Reditum in Senatum.
9 Ibid. pro Sextio, c. 17 et 18.
10 Cicero in Pisonem.

11 Plutarch. in Cicerone.
12 Vid. Actionem in Verrem.

penalties to harbour him; Virgilius, the prætor of Sicily, though his friend, declined to receive him. He turned from thence to Brundusium, passed into Macedonia, and would have fixed his residence at Athens; but apprehending that this place was within the distance prescribed to him by the act of banishment, he went to Thessalonica in his way to Cyzicum. Here he had letters that gave him intimation of some change in his favour, and entertaining some prospect of being speedily recalled, he accordingly determined to wait the issue of this hope.

We have better means of knowing the frailties of Cicero, than perhaps is safe for the reputation of any one labouring under the ordinary defects of human nature. He was open and undisguised to his friends, and has left an extensive correspondence behind him. Expressions of vanity in some passages of his life, of pusillanimity in others, escape him with uncommon facility. Being at least of a querulous and impatient temper, he gives it full scope in his exile, perhaps not more from weakness, than from design to excite his friends to redouble their efforts to have him restored. He knew the value of fortitude as a topic of praise, and might have aspired to it; but would it not, he may have questioned, encouraged his party to sleep over his wrongs? In any other view, his complaints resemble more the wailings of an infant, or the strains of a tragedy composed to draw tears, than the language of a man supporting the cause of integrity in the midst of undeserved trouble.—"I wish I may see the day," he writes to Atticus, "in which I shall be disposed to thank you for having prevailed upon me not to lay violent hands on myself; for it is certainly now matter of bitter regret to me that I yielded to you in that matter."[1]

In answer to the same friend, who had chid him for want of fortitude, "What species of evil," he says, "do I not endure? Did ever any person fall from so high a state? in so good a cause with such abilities and knowledge? with so much public esteem? with the support of such a respectable order of citizens? Can I remember what I was, and not feel what I am? Stript of so many honours, cut off in the career of so much glory, deprived of such a fortune, tore from the arms of such children, debarred the view of such a brother, dearer to me than I was to myself, yet now debarred from my presence, that I may spare him what he must suffer from such a sight, and myself what I must feel in being the cause of so much misery to him. I could say more of a load of evils which is too heavy for me to bear; but I am stopped by my tears."[2]

From the whole of this correspondence of Cicero in his exile, we may collect to what degree the unjust reproaches which he had suffered, the desertion of those on whom he relied for support, the dangers to which he left his family exposed, affected his mind. The consciousness of his integrity, even his vanity forsook him; and his fine genius, no longer employed in the forum or in the senate, or busied in the literary studies which amused him afterwards[3] in a more calamitous time of the republic, now, by exaggerating the distress of his fortunes, preyed upon himself. It appeared from this, and many other scenes of his life, that although he loved virtuous actions, yet his virtue was accompanied with so insatiable a thirst of the praise, to which it entitled him, that his mind was unable to sustain itself without this foreign assistance; and when the praise which was due to his consulate was changed into obloquy and scorn, he seems to have lost the sense of good or of evil in his own conduct or character; and at Thessalonica, where he fixed the scene of his exile, sunk or rose in his own esteem, as he seemed to be valued or neglected at Rome.[4]

CHAPTER VI.

Cæsar takes Possession of his Province—Migration of the Helvetii—Their Defeat—War with Ariovistus—Return of Cæsar for the Winter into Italy—Great Concourse of Citizens to his Quarters—Motion to recal Cicero—Disorders that followed upon it—Consultations of Pompey and Cæsar—Augmentation of the Army in Gaul—Second Campaign of Cæsar—Operations on the Aisne—On the Meuse and Sambre—Battle with the Nervii—Successful Attempt for the Restoration of Cicero—Controversy Relating to his House—Repeated Riots of Claudius—Trial of Milo.

WHILE the transaction which terminated in the exile of Cicero was still in dependence, Cæsar, although, by assuming the military character, he had disqualified himself to take any part in civil affairs, had actually gone from the city and embodied his legions, yet he still remained in the suburbs of Rome to observe the issue of that business, and to direct the conduct of his party. He thought himself too much interested in the event to leave it entirely under the direction of Pompey, with whom his own connexion was precarious, and might be of short duration. He was inclined to ruin, if he could not gain, a person whose talents and character made him of so much consequence to the parties who contended for power in the state. Having failed in his attempt to gain him as a dependent, and to carry him as part of his own retinue into Gaul, he secretly promoted the designs of Clodius, and employed his own retainers and friends against him, until he saw the purpose accomplished.

The provinces of which Cæsar had obtained the command, comprehended, as has been observed, under the denomination of the two Gauls, considerable territories on both sides of the Alps. Cisalpine Gaul, which was joined to Italy, extended to Lucca, not far from Pisa on one side

1 Cicero ad Att. lib. iii. epist. 3.

2 Ibid. epist. 10.

3 See the Book of Tuscular Questions.

4 Vid. Cicero ad Att. lib. iii.

of the Apennines, and to the Rubicon, not far from Ariminum on the other. Beyond the Alps, the whole territory from the Mediterranean to the Rhine and the Meuse, was known by the name of Gaul. A part of this tract, which was bounded by the Rhone, the mountains of Auvergne, the Garonne, and the Pyrenees, was already a Roman province, including, together with Languedoc and Dauphiné, what, from its early subjection to the Romans, is still named Provence.

The remainder of the country was divided into three principal parts, occupied by the Aquitani, the Celtes, and the Belgæ, nations differing in language, establishments, and customs. The first division extended from the Pyrenees to the Garonne; the second from the Garonne to the Seine; and the third from thence to the Meuse and the Scheld.

In each of these tracts there was a multiplicity of separate cantons and independent communities, of which Cæsar had occasion to enumerate no less than four hundred. Even the smallest of these communities, by his account, was broken into parties and factions, who had separate objects, and were engaged in opposition to each other. The people, in general, were held in a state of dependence by two separate orders of men, whose condition and character may account for the manifold divisions and animosities that took place in their country. One order was ecclesiastical, composed of the Druids, who, by their profession, had the keeping of such mysteries, and the performance of such rites as were then in use; and, having over their fellow-citizens the claim to a hierarchy, had, among themselves, in the various pretensions to preferment and rank in their own order, continual objects of competition, jealousy, and quarrels.

The other order was entirely military, and consisted of persons whose principal distinction arose from the number of their armed adherents; and who, therefore, vied with each other in the multitude of their retainers, or in the force of their parties.[5]

The country, we learn, in general, was interspersed with what are called towns, and what were, in reality, safe retreats, or places of strength. It abounded in corn and cattle, the resources of a numerous people; armies were collected, and political assemblies were statedly, or occasionally called: but how the people were accommodated, or in what degree they were supplied with the ordinary productions of mechanic or commercial arts, is no where described.

In these particulars, however, as they were probably less skilful than the Italians, so they surpassed the Germans, to whom they yielded in the reputation of valour; and they were now in reality on the eve of becoming a prey to the rapacity and ferocity of the one, or to the ambition, refined policy, and superior arts of the other.

Among parties, who were already so numerous, and likely to be divided indefinitely by family or personal jealousies, Cæsar was about to find the occasions, which he undoubtedly sought for, of raising his reputation in war, of enriching himself and his dependents, and of forming an army inured to service, and attached to himself. While he was yet in Italy, he had intimation of a wonderful project formed by the Helvetii, natives of the tract which extends from the Jura to the Alps, and of the valleys which divide those mountains, to quit their own country in order to exchange it for a better settlement, in a less inclement region, on the lower and more fertile plains of Gaul.

They had taken, for this purpose, an exact account of their own numbers in every canton, and mustered no less than three hundred and fifty-eight thousand souls, of whom ninety-two thousand were warriors, or men fit to bear arms. To put this multitude in motion, a great apparatus of provisions, of horses, and of carriages was necessary; and they allotted two years for the necessary preparations. This time was now elapsed, and the swarm began to dislodge on the twenty-fifth of March of the year in which Cæsar was to take possession of his province. On receiving the alarm, he set out from Italy, and with hasty journeys arrived at Geneva, where to prevent surprise, he broke down the bridge of the Rhone, and took other measures to preclude the access of strangers to his province.

In the mean time the Helvetians sent a pacific message, desiring, that they might be allowed to pass the Rhone, and giving assurances that they would abstain from every sort of hostility on their march through the Roman province. Cæsar, in order to gain time, affected to take their request into consideration, promised to give them an answer by the middle of April; and in this manner amused them, while he assembled the legion, that was dispersed in different parts of the province, and ordered new levies to be made with the greatest despatch. At the same time, he fortified the banks of the river, from the Lake of Geneva, to the narrow pass[6] at which the Rhone enters between the Jura and the Vuache, and from thence running under cliffs, and steep mountains, renders the access from Helvetia to Gaul either impracticable or easily obstructed.

Being thus prepared for his defence, he, on the return of the Helvetian deputies, gave them for answer, That the Romans never allowed strangers to pass through their country; and that if any attempt were made on his province, he should repel it by force. Upon receiving this answer, the Helvetians, though too late, endeavoured to effect the passage of the Rhone, and made repeated attacks, either where the river was fordable, or where it admitted the use of rafts or of boats, but were repulsed in every attempt, and were at last obliged to turn to the right, where, by the consent of the Sequani, their neighbours in that part of the country, they passed over the Jura into Gaul.

Cæsar, probably not more alarmed for the safety of his province, than desirous to render it a scene of action, determined to observe the migrations of this enemy, and to seize the occasion they furnished him of forming his troops to service. For this purpose he himself, in person, repassed the Alps, and without any regard to the limitations of his commission, which restricted his military establishment to three legions, ordered additional levies, and with the forces assembled near Aquileia, returned to his northern province. In this march he met with opposition from the inhabitants of the mountains, who endeavoured to ob-

5 Cæsar de Bell. Gall. lib. vi. c. 10—20.

6 Fort l'Ecluse.

struct his way: but he had traversed the country of the Allobroges, and passed the Rhone above its confluence with the Soane,[1] when he had intelligence, that the Helvetii, having cleared the passes of Jura, and marched through the country of the Sequani, were arrived on the Soane; and although they had hitherto, agreeably to their stipulations with the natives, abstained from hostilities, that they threatened the nations inhabiting beyond this river with fire and sword.

Upon application made to him for protection from the natives inhabiting between the Soane and the Loire, this willing auxiliary continued his march; and being informed, that of the Helvetii, who had moved in four divisions (this being the number of their cantons,) the three first had already passed the Soane; and that the fourth division being to follow, yet remained on the nearer bank of the river, he marched in the night with three legions, surprised this rear-division; and, having put many of them to the sword, forced the remainder to take refuge in the neighbouring woods.

As soon as the main body of Cæsar's army arrived on the Soane, he constructed a bridge, and passed that river in his way to the enemy. The Helvetians, sensible of their loss in the late action, and alarmed at the rapidity of his motions, he having executed in one day the passage of a river which had detained them above ninety days, sent a deputation to treat with the Roman proconsul, and to obtain, if possible, his permission to execute their project of a new settlement on amicable terms. They offered, in case they were allowed to sit down in quiet, to leave the choice of the place to himself; bidding him remember, at the same time, that "the arms of the Helvetii had, on former occasions, been felt by the Romans. That the recent fate of a single canton taken by surprise ought not to flatter him too much; that the Helvetians had learned from their fathers to rely more on valour than on artifice or on negotiation; but that they did not wish to have their present migration signalized with any massacres, nor their new settlement stained with Roman blood."

To this message, Cæsar replied, "That he could recollect to have heard of insults which had been offered to the Romans by their nation, and to which they now probably alluded: that he likewise had more recent provocations which he knew how to resent; nevertheless, if they meant to comply with his demand, to repair the injuries they had done to the Allobroges[2] and to the Edui[3], and to give hostages for their future behaviour, that he was willing to grant them peace."

Upon this reply the Helvetian deputies withdrew, saying, That it was the practice of their countrymen to receive, not to give hostages; and both armies moved on the following day: the Helvetians, in search of some quarter where they might settle without interruption; and Cæsar, to observe their motions, and to restrain them from plundering the country of his allies. Both continued on the same route during fifteen days, with no more than an interval of five or six miles between the front of one army and the rear of the other.

On this march Cæsar's cavalry, having rashly engaged themselves on unfavourable ground, received a check; and he himself, being obliged to follow the course of the Soane, by which he received his provisions, was likely to lose sight of the enemy, when he had intelligence, that they had taken post at the foot of a hill, about eight miles in his front, and seemed to have formed a resolution to receive him, in that position, if he chose to attack them. Having examined the ground on which they were posted, and observing, that the height in their rear was not by nature inaccessible, nor sufficiently secured against him, he despatched Labienus in the night at the head of two legions, with orders to possess himself of the eminence, and to fall down from thence on the enemy's rear whenever he saw them attacked by himself in front. Labienus accordingly got possession of the hill, and Cæsar advanced towards the foot of it to occupy the attention of the enemy, and to attack them in front. But the purpose of this disposition was frustrated by the misinformation of an officer of horse, who, being advanced before the army, reported, that the enemy still appeared on the height, and that Labienus probably had failed in his attempt to seize it. Cæsar, disconcerted by this information, made a halt, in which he lost so much time as to give the enemy an opportunity to decamp, and to retire in safety. He nevertheless continued his pursuit for one day longer, and at night encamped about three miles in their rear. But being obliged, on the following day, to alter his route in order to receive a supply of provisions, the enemy believed that he was retreating, and began to pursue in their turn. He halted on a rising ground to perceive them, placed his new levies with the baggage on the higher ground, and the choice of his army on the declivity towards the plain. Here the enemy advancing to attack him, after an obstinate engagement which lasted from one in the afternoon till night, were defeated with the slaughter of about two hundred thousand of their people; and the remainder, amounting to no more than one hundred and thirty thousand souls, reduced to despair by the sense of their losses, and the want of subsistence, surrendered at discretion. Cæsar ordered them back into their own country, charging the Allobroges to find them subsistence, until they should be able to provide for themselves. The Boii, however, a part of this unfortunate migration, were received by the Edui, who, to gain this accession of people, allotted part of their own lands to accommodate these strangers.[4]

At the end of this first operation of Cæsar, while great part of the summer yet remained, another service on which to employ his army soon presented itself The nations who inhabited the banks of the Soane and the Loire, being sensible of the deliverance they had received from a storm, which, by the uncertainty of its direction, alarmed every quarter of Gaul, sent deputies to congratulate the Roman general on his late victory, and to propose that they might hold, under his protection, a general convention of all their states. The object of their meeting, as it soon appeared, was to obtain some relief from the common oppression they underwent from the tyranny of

1 Then the Arar.

2 Inhabitants of what is now the territory of Geneva, and part of Savoy.

3 Occupying the country between the Soane and the Loire

4 Cæs. de Bell. Gal. lib. i. c. 28, 29.

Ariovistus, a German chief, who, when the Gauls were at war among themselves, had been invited as an auxiliary to one of the parties, and had obtained the victory for his allies: but took for the reward of his services possession of one third of their territory, which he bestowed on his own people, and assumed for himself the sovereignty of the whole. His force was daily augmented by the continual arrival of more emigrants from Germany; so that, from fifteen thousand men, with whom the chief had arrived, his followers had multiplied to a hundred and twenty thousand. To accommodate this numerous people, he had recently made a demand of another third of the territory of the Sequani, and was extending his possessions from the neighbourhood of the Rhine to the Soane. Most of the nations on this tract had been obliged to submit to a contribution levied by these strangers, and to give hostages for the regular payment of it.

The unfortunate nations who, by trusting to the protection of a barbarous prince, had exposed themselves to this calamity, now applied for relief to another power, whose pretensions in the end were likely to be equally dangerous to their freedom. Sensible of the hazard to which they exposed their hostages by entering into any open concert against the Germans, they made their application to Cæsar in secret, and found him sufficiently willing to embrace every opportunity of rendering his province a theatre of action to his army, and of renown to himself. He sent without delay a message to Ariovistus, desiring to have a conference with him on affairs that concerned the general interests of Gaul. This haughty chieftain replied with disdain, "That if the Roman general meant to have an interview with him, his place of residence was known; that he neither could trust himself in the quarters of Cæsar, without an army, nor would be at the expense of assembing one, merely for the satisfaction of a conference with him."

Cæsar renewed the message with an express requisition that the hostages of the Edui should be restored; that Ariovistus should abstain from hostilities against this people, or against any other ally of the Romans; and that he should not suffer any more of his countrymen to pass the Rhine.

To this message Ariovistus replied, That he had conquered the possessions which he held in Gaul, and that he knew of no power who had a right to direct him in the use of his conquests; that whoever attacked him should do so at his peril; and that Cæsar, if he thought proper, might try the spirit of his people; they were ready to receive him, and had not for fourteen years slept under any cover.

Cæsar, not to seem backward in accepting this challenge, and in compliance with a maxim which he often observed with success, *That his blows should anticipate his threats, and outrun the expectations of his enemy*, advanced upon the Germans before they could think him in condition to act against them. For this purpose, without communicating his design to any person of his own army, he repassed the Soane, and ascended by the course of the Douse to Vesontio, now Besançon, a place of strength, which he understood Ariovistus meant to seize, as the principal resort of his forces.

Here, for the first time, his intention of making war on the Germans began to be suspected in his own army; and the legions, taking their account of the strength and ferocity of that enemy from the report of the Gaulish auxiliaries, were greatly alarmed. Many citizens of distinction who had crowded to the standard of Cæsar, as to a place of victory and honour, now, under various pretences, applied for leave to retire. Their example spread a kind of panic in the army, and both men and officers muttered their resolution not to obey, if they should be ordered upon what they were pleased to consider as a service so unreasonable and wild.

Cæsar being thus called upon to exert that undaunted courage and masterly eloquence by which he was distinguished on many occasions, assembled all the officers of his army, and reprimanded them for attempting to penetrate the designs of their general, or for pretending to question the propriety of his motions. The matter in dispute with Ariovistus, he said, might be terminated in an amicable manner. This chieftain had very lately made advances of friendship to the Romans, had been favourably received, and there was no reason to believe that he would now wantonly provoke their resentment. "But if he should, of whom are you afraid. Of a wretched remnant of the Cimbri or Teutones, already vanquished by Marius? Of a people confessedly inferior to the Helvetians, whom you have subdued? But some of you, I am told, in order to disguise your own fears under the affectation of wisdom, talk of difficulties in the ways by which you are to pass, and of the want of provisions which you are likely to suffer. I am not now to learn from such persons as you what I owe to my trust, nor to be told that an army must be supplied with provisions. But our allies are ready to supply us in greater quantities than we can consume, and the very country we are to pass is covered with ripe corn. As for the roads you shall speedily see and judge of them. I am little affected with what I hear of a design to abandon me in case I persist in this expedition. Such insults, I know, have been offered to commanders, who, by their avarice or by their miscarriages, had forfeited the regard or the confidence of their troops; what will happen to me a little time will discover. I meant to have made a longer halt at this place, but shall not defer giving you an opportunity to show, whether regard to your duty, or the fear of a supposed enemy, is to have the greatest effect on your minds. I mean to-morrow, at two in the morning, to decamp, and shall proceed, if no other part of the army follows me, with the tenth legion alone."

This speech had a very sudden effect. The tenth legion, having been formerly distinguished by their general, felt this expression of confidence as an additional motive to deserve it, and sent a deputation of their officers to return their thanks. The whole army soon vied in excuses for their late misbehaviour, and in assurances of their resolution to support their general in any service on which he might be pleased to employ them. He accordingly decamped at the hour appointed; and making a circuit of forty miles, to avoid some difficulties which lay on the direct road, after a continual march of seven days, in which he was conducted by Divitiacus, a native of Gaul, he arrived within twenty-four miles of the German quarters.

Upon this unexpected arrival, Ariovistus, in his turn, thought proper to desire a conference with Cæsar. He proposed that they should meet on horseback, and be attended only by cavalry. In this part of his army, which was composed chiefly of Gaulish horse, Cæsar was weak. But, not to decline the proposal that was made to him, he mounted his supposed favourite legion on the horses of the Gauls, and with this escort came to the place appointed for the conference.

It was an eminence in the midst of a spacious plain, about half-way between the two armies. The leaders, each attended by ten of his officers, met at the top of the hill. Their escorts drew up at the distance of two hundred yards on each side.

Cæsar began the conference, by reminding Ariovistus of the honours recently bestowed upon him by the Roman senate, who ordered him the usual presents, and gave him the title of king. "The Edui," he said, "were the allies of the Roman people; they had formed this connexion in the height of their prosperity, and when they were supposed to be at the head of the Gaulish nations; that it was not the custom of the Romans to let nations suffer by their alliance, but to render it in every instance, to the party who embraced it, a source of prosperity and honour. He therefore renewed his former requisition, that Ariovistus should not make war on the Edui, or on any nation in alliance with Rome; that he should remit their tribute, and release their hostages; and, if he could not send back into their own country such of the Germans as were already on this side of the Rhine, that he should at least prevent the arrival of any more from that quarter."

In answer to these propositions, Ariovistus replied, That he had been invited into Gaul by the natives of this country; that he had done them services, and had exacted no more than a just reward; that, in the late quarrel betwixt them and himself, the Gauls had been the aggressors, and had suffered no more than the usual consequences of a defeat; that to indemnify him for his losses, they had subjected themselves to a tribute, and had given hostages for the regular payment of it. "Am not I too," he said, "by your own account, in alliance with the Romans? Why should that alliance, which is a safeguard and an honour to every one else, be a loss and a misfortune to me? Must I alone, to preserve this alliance, resign the advantage of treaties, and remit the payments that are due to me? No; let me rather be considered as an enemy than as an ally upon these conditions. My countrymen have passed the Rhine, not to oppress the Gauls, but to defend their leader. If strangers are to be admitted here, the Germans, as the first occupiers, have a right prior to that of the Romans. But we have each of us our province. What do Roman armies on my territory? I disturb no possession of yours. Must I account to you likewise for the use which I make of my own?"

To this pointed reply Ariovistus subjoined a reflection, which showed that he was not unacquainted with the state of parties at Rome. "I know," he said, "that the Romans are not interested in this quarrel, and that, by cutting you off, I should perform an acceptable service to many of your countrymen. But I shall take no part in your internal divisions. Leave me; make war where you please; I shall not interpose in any matter which does not concern myself."

Cæsar continued to plead the engagements which the Romans had contracted with many of the nations who now claimed their protection. "If conquest could give any right to possession," he said, "we are the first conquerors. We have long since subdued the Arverni; but it is not our practice to enslave every nation we vanquish, much less to forsake those we have once patronised." While he yet spoke the German horse had advanced, and even began to throw darts, which made it expedient for Cæsar to break up the conference. He accordingly withdrew, giving strict orders to his people not to return the insults of the enemy.

In a few days after this conference, the German chieftain proposed another personal interview, or, if that were declined, desired that some person of confidence should be sent with whom he might treat. Being gratified in the second part of this alternative, but intending no more by this request than a mere feint to lull the enemy into some degree of security, he pretended to take offence at the quality of the persons who were sent to him, ordered them into custody, and on the same day put his army in motion upon a real design, which showed that, barbarian as he was he understood the plan, as well as the execution, of military operations. Observing that the Romans derived their subsistence from the country behind them, he made a movement, by which he passed their camp, took a strong post about eleven miles in their rear, and by this means intercepted their ordinary supply of provisions.

Cæsar for many days successively endeavoured, by forming on the plain between the two armies, to provoke the enemy to a battle; but having failed in this purpose, he was obliged to divide his army, and to place it in separate posts, which he fortified, in order to recover a communication with the country behind him. He learned that the Germans had borne with great impatience the defiances he had given them; but that they were restrained from fighting by the predictions of their women, who foretold that their own people would be defeated, if they should hazard a battle before the change of the moon.

The Germans, notwithstanding the awe in which they stood of this prediction, endeavoured to dislodge one of the divisions of Cæsar's army, and, having failed in that attempt, were afterwards attacked by the Romans in their camp, and defeated with great slaughter. Ariovistus himself, with the remains of his followers, fled to the Rhine, about fifty miles from the field of battle, passed that river in a small canoe; numbers of his people perished in attempting to follow him, and the greater part of those who remained were overtaken, and put to the sword by Cæsar's cavalry.

In this manner Cæsar concluded his first campaign in Gaul; and laid the foundation of his future conquests in that country, by stating himself as the protector of its native inhabitants against the Helvetii and the Germans, two powerful invaders who were likely to subdue it. He placed his army for the winter among the nations whom he had thus taken under his protection, and set out for Italy, under pretence of attending to the affairs of his province on that side of the Alps; but more probably to be near to Rome, where he had many political interests at stake, friends to support, and enemies to oppose, in their canvass for the offices of state. His head quarters were fixed at Lucca, the nearest part of his province to Rome; and that place began to be frequented by numbers who were already of his party, or who desired to be admitted into it, and with whom he had previously made his own terms in stipulating the returns they were to make for the several preferments in which he undertook to assist them.

At the election of consuls for this year, P. Cornelius Lentulus Spinther was joined with Q. Cæcilius Metellus Nepos, of whom the latter had, in the capacity of tribune, distinguished himself as an instrument of the most dangerous factions. Lentulus had lately attached himself entirely to Pompey, and, by the influence of this patron, probably now prevailed in his election. He had been edile in the consulate of Cicero, and had taken a vigorous part in those very measures for which Cicero was now suffering in exile.[1] He was likely to favour the restoration of that injured citizen, and upon this account was now the more acceptable to Pompey, who, having an open rupture with Clodius, was disposed to mortify him by espousing the cause of his enemies.

Clodius, soon after his late victory over Cicero, greatly rose in his presumption, and, forgetting that he prevailed more by the connivance of Pompey and Cæsar, and by the support of their friends, than by any influence of his own, ventured to set Pompey himself at defiance, to question the validity of his acts in the late settlement of Asia, to set the young Tigranes, still the prisoner of Pompey, at liberty,[2] and proposed to restore him again to his kingdom. In the debates which arose on these measures in the assembly of the people, Pompey had the mortification to find that the sarcasms of Clodius were received by the audience in general with applause, as well as by the partizans of the senate, in particular, with marks of satisfaction. Chiefly governed by vanity, and impatient of obloquy, he absented himself from the public assemblies during the remainder of Clodius's term in office, and was ready to embrace every measure by which he might be revenged of that factious tribune, or regain his own credit with the more respectable class of the citizens.[3]

Encouraged by this division among their enemies, the majority of the senate, who justly considered the cause of Cicero as their own, had ventured, on the twenty-ninth of October, while Clodius was yet in office, to move for his recall. Eight of the tribunes concurred in urging this motion, and it was rejected only in consequence of the negative of Ælius Ligur, one of the college whom Clodius had prepared to act this part, and whom he was ready to support by force, if the opposite party should persist in their motion.[4]

Upon the election of the new consuls and tribunes for the following year, better hopes of success were entertained by the friends of Cicero. Lentulus declared that the restoration of this exile should be the first object of his administration; and that he would not fail to move it on the day that he entered on office. Metellus too, the brother-in-law of Clodius, though always inclined to favour the popular faction, could not in this matter set himself in opposition to Pompey and declared his intention to concur with the consul.[5] Milo, Sextius, and six more of the tribunes, with all the prætors except Appius Claudius, the brother of Publius, declared their intention to take an active part in forwarding this measure.

Encouraged by these appearances, Cicero left his retreat at Thessalonica, and arrived at Dirrachium, before the twenty-fifth of November, to be at hand to consult with his friends on the steps that were to be previously taken. Meantime the consuls-elect had their provinces assigned. Lentulus was destined to command in Cilicia and Cypress, and Metellus in the farther province of Spain. Both were amply gratified in every article of their appointments, in order to confirm them in the interest of the senate; but Cicero expressed great anxiety lest these concessions should be found premature; and, being made before the new tribunes entered on office, or could have their voice in these destinations, was afraid lest it might alienate their affections from his party, and render them less zealous to move for his recall. The consul, Lentulus, notwithstanding, kept his word; and, on the first of January, the day of his entering on office, moved the senate to resolve that Cicero should be immediately recalled from banishment; that all persons opposing his return should be declared enemies to their country; and that if the people should be disturbed by violence in passing this decree, it should, nevertheless, be lawful for the exile to avail himself of it.[6]

U. C. 696.

P. Cor. Lentulus Spinther, Q. Cæcil. Metell. Nepos.

This motion was received in the senate with general applause. Eight of the tribunes were zealous in support of it. On the contrary, two members of the college, Numerius and Serranus, were gained by Clodius to oppose it. Serranus, however, could venture no farther at this meeting than to plead for a delay. But he was prevailed upon, during the intervening night, to interpose his negative, and the motion accordingly could proceed no farther in the senate.

It was resolved, notwithstanding, to propose a law to the people for Cicero's restoration; and a day was fixed for this purpose. Early in the morning of that day Fabricius, one of the tribunes in the interest of the exile, endeavoured to occupy the place of assembly with an armed force, but found that Clodius, with a numerous troop of gladiators, was there before him. A conflict ensued, in which Fabricius, together with Cispius, another of the tribunes who came to his assistance, with all the party of the senate, were driven from the forum.

Clodius, at the head of his gladiators, with swords already stained in blood, pursued his victory through the streets. The temple of the nymphs, in which were kept some public records which he wished to destroy, was set on fire;[7] the houses of Milo and Cæcilius the prætor were attacked. "The streets, the common sewers, the

1 Cicero ad Att. iii. lib. ep. 22.
2 Vid. Ascon. Padian. in Orat. pro Milone.
3 Plutarch. in Vit. Cicer. p. 475 et 476
4 Cicero ad Att. lib. iii. ep. 23.

5 Cicero ad Att. lib. iii. ep. 24.
6 Cicero ad Att. lib. iii. ep 26. et in Orat. post reditum.
7 Cicero pro Milone, 27 Parad 4 d. Haruspicum Responsio 27.

river," says Cicero, "were filled with dead bodies, and all the pavements were stained with blood." No such scene had been acted since the times of Octavius and Cinna, when armies fought in the city for the dominion of the empire.[1]

Quintus Cicero escaped by hiding himself under the dead bodies of his own servants, who were slain in defending his house. The tribune Publius Sextius actually fell into the hands of his enemies, received many wounds, and was left for dead among the slain. This circumstance, however, alarmed the party of Clodius not less than it alarmed his opponents. The odium of having murdered, or even violated the person of a tribune, was likely to ruin their interest with the people; and they proposed to balance this outrage by putting to death Numerius, another tribune, who, being of their own side, should appear to be killed by the opposite party; but the intended victim of this ridiculous and sanguinary artifice, receiving information of their design, avoided being made the tool of a party at the expense of his life, and made his escape.[2]

After so strange a disorder, parties for some months, mutually afraid of each other, abstained from violence. The tribune Milo commenced a prosecution against Clodius for his crimes; but it was for some time eluded by the authority of Appius Claudius, brother of the accused, who was now in the office of prætor; and the courts, when actually called, were repeatedly dispersed by the armed party of gladiators, with which Publius Clodius himself infested every public place. It was vain to oppose him without being prepared to employ a similar force, and Milo accordingly had recourse to this method. He purchased a troop of gladiators, and of bestiarii, or baiters of wild beasts, and the remainder of those who had been employed by the ediles Pomponius and Cosconius, and who were now in the market for sale. He ordered the bargain to be secretly struck, concealing the name of the buyer, lest the opposite party, suspecting the design, should interpose to prevent him.

So provided, Milo ventured to encounter with Clodius. Their parties frequently engaged in the streets, and the populace, fond of such shows, enjoyed the spectacle which was presented to them in every corner of the city.[3]

While the disorders which thus arose from the disputes relating to Cicero's restoration were daily augmenting, he himself fell from the height of his hopes to his former pitch of dejection and sorrow. The attempt which had been made in his favour might have succeeded, if Pompey had been fully prepared to concur in it. But all the measures of the triumvirate, being concerted at the quarters of Cæsar, Pompey was obliged, after declaring his own inclinations on the subject, to consult his associate, and found him by no means inclined to restore a citizen who was likely to be of so much consequence, and who was to owe the favour of his restoration to any other than himself. The tribune Sextius, before the late dissolution, had made a journey into Gaul, to obtain the consent of Cæsar to this measure, but could not prevail; and it is probable that this artful politician was unwilling to restore an exile who was likely to ascribe the principal merit of that service to Pompey, and, by his own inclinations in favour of the senate, to become an accession to a party which Cæsar wished to degrade and to weaken by every means in his power. It was to strengthen himself against the senate that Cæsar made his coalition with Pompey and Crassus; and from animosity to this body, he wished to crush every person of consequence to their party, and to favour the pretensions of every ambitious citizen who ventured to act in open defiance of their government.

Pompey, in the mean time, though committing himself as a tool into the hands of Cæsar, was flattered with the appearance of sovereignty which he enjoyed in the city, and willingly supported Cæsar in every measure that seemed to fix his attention abroad, consented to the repeated augmentations of the army in Gaul, and approved of every enterprise in which their leader was pleased to employ them.

In this year, which was the second of Cæsar's command, two more additional legions were by his orders levied in Italy; and under pretence of an approaching war with the Belgæ, a nation consisting of many cantons in the northern extremities of Gaul, this reinforcement was made to pass the Alps to the northward in the spring. As soon as the forage was up, he himself followed in person, took the field, and, in the usual spirit of his conduct, endeavoured by the rapidity of his motions, to frustrate or to prevent the designs of his enemies.

His force now consisted of eight Roman legions, besides numerous bodies of horse and foot from different cantons in Gaul, archers from Crete and Numidia, and slingers from the Balearian islands; so that it is likely the whole may have amounted to about sixty thousand men. The greater part of his army had wintered on the Soane[4] and the Douse,[5] as protectors, not as masters of the country, being received only in the character of allies. Cæsar having now taken numbers of their people into his army as auxiliaries or as hostages, and having spent twelve days in preparing for his march, took his route to the northward, under pretence of carrying the war into the enemy's country, or of preventing them from gaining, to their supposed confederacy against the Romans, any of the nations in the southern parts of Gaul.

His way lay through the high, though level, countries, now termed Burgundy and Champagne, in which the Soane, the Moselle, the Meuse, and the Seine, with so many other considerable rivers, that run in different directions, have their source. After a march of fifteen days, he arrived in the canton of the Remi,[6] where he found a people, though of the Belgic extraction, disposed to receive him as a friend, and to place themselves under his protection.

From this people he had a confirmation of his former intelligence relating to the designs of the Belgic nations, and an account of the forces which they had already assembled. From the track of country that is watered by the rivers, which are now called the Oise, the Scheld and the Meuse, he understood that no less than three

1 Orat. pro Sext. c. 35, 36. 38.
2 Cicero pro Sextio.
3 Cicero ad Att. lib IV. ep. 2.

4 Anciently named the Arar.
5 The Dubis.
6 Now the district of Rheims.

hundred and fifty thousand men could be mustered, and were actually assembled, or preparing to assemble, against him. To prevent the junction of this formidable power, or to distract part of its force, he detached part of his Gaulish auxiliaries to make a diversion on the Oise, while he himself advanced to the Aisne,[7] passed this river and fortified a station on its northern bank. Having a bridge in his rear, he left six cohorts properly intrenched before it, to secure his communication with the country behind him.

While he remained in this post, the Belgæ advanced with a great army, attacked Bibrax, a place of strength about eight miles in his front; and having spent many hours in endeavouring to reduce it, were about to renew their assault on the following day. But Cæsar having in the night thrown into the garrison a considerable reinforcement of archers and slingers, the appearance of this additional strength on the battlements induced the enemy to desist.

They nevertheless continued to advance, laid waste the country, and came within two miles of his camp. They had a front, as appeared from their fires, extending about eight miles.

Cæsar, considering the numbers and reputation of this enemy, thought proper to proceed with caution. He observed them for some days from his entrenchments, and made several trials of their skill in partial encounters before he ventured to offer them battle. But being encouraged by the event of these trials, he chose a piece of sloping ground that lay before his camp, and was fit to receive his army. As the enemy's front was likely to extend farther than his, he threw up entrenchments on the right and left to cover his flanks; and with this security, to prevent his being surrounded, drew forth his army. The Belgæ too were formed on their part; but the ground between the two armies being marshy, neither thought proper to pass that impediment in presence of the other; and after a few skirmishes of the horse and irregular troops, the Romans re-entered their camp. The enemy, upon this event, disappointed in their expectations of a battle, took their way to the fords of the Aisne,[8] in order to pass the river, and get possession of the bridge in the rear of the Romans. Cæsar had intelligence of this movement from the officer who was stationed to guard that post; and marching instantly with all the cavalry, archers, and slingers of the army, he arrived in time to overtake them, while yet entangled in the fords, and obliged them to retire.

The Belgæ, having made these successive attempts with much impetuosity, but without proper foresight, soon appeared to be ill qualified to maintain a permanent war with such an enemy. They were disheartened by their disappointments, and alarmed by the rumour of a diversion which Cæsar had caused to be made in a part of their own country. They had exhausted their provisions, and found themselves under the necessity to break up their camp. It was therefore resolved in their general council, that their forces, for the present, should separate; and if any of their cantons should be afterwards attacked by Cæsar, that the whole should assemble again for their common defence.

With this resolution they decamped in the night, but with so much noise and disorder that Cæsar suspected a feint, or an intention to draw him into a snare. He therefore remained in his lines till the morning, when it appeared that they were actually gone, and were seen at a distance on the plain moving in the greatest disorder, and as in a total rout, striving who should soonest get beyond the reach of their enemies. He pursued them with his cavalry so long as it was day, and, though with great bravery resisted in his attacks on their rear, made considerable havoc. At the approach of night he discontinued the pursuit, and withdrew again to the camp he left in the morning. On the following day he moved with his whole army, and, that the enemy might not have time to re-assemble their forces, determined to penetrate into the heart of their country. In the beginning of his march he followed the course of the Aisne, and in his way reduced the Suessones and Bellovaci, two cantons that lay on the right and the left, near the confluence of this river with the Oyse. From thence, being himself to march to the northward, to visit the banks of the Sambre and the Meuse, he detached the young Crassus, with a considerable force, towards the sea coasts, to occupy those cantons which now form the provinces of Normandy and Bretanny.

Part of the country through which the Meuse and the Sambre passed, now forming the dutchy of Hainault, was then occupied by the Nervii, one of the fiercest of the Belgic nations, who, having heard with indignation of the surrender of the Bellovaci and Suessones, their neighbours, prepared for resistance, sent such of their people as, by their sex or age, were unfit to carry arms into a place of security, assembled all their warriors, and summoned their allies to a place of general resort. They took post on the Sambre, where the heights on both sides of the river being covered with woods, enabled them to conceal their numbers and their dispositions. They had intelligence that Cæsar, except in presence of an enemy, usually moved his legions with intervals between them, which were occupied by their baggage; and they made a disposition to surprise him on the march, and under this disadvantage. For this purpose they chose their ground on the Sambre, and agreed that the van of the Roman army should be suffered to pass unmolested, but that the appearance of the first column of baggage should be the signal for a general attack to be made at once from all the different stations in which their parties were posted.

Cæsar, in the mean time, about three days after he had marched from Samarobriva, now supposed to be Amiens, being apprised that he was come within ten miles of the river, on the banks of which the enemy was posted, altered the form of his march, placed six legions, clear of incumbrance, in the van of his army, next to these the whole of his baggage, and in the rear the two legions that were last levied in Italy. When he entered the open grounds on the Sambre, a few parties of horse appeared, but were soon driven into the woods by his cavalry. The legions that came first to their ground began, as usual, to intrench, and received no disturbance till the column of baggage came in sight. At this signal multitudes of the enemy presented themselves on every side, drove in the cavalry

7 Jasara and Axona.
8 Axona.

that were posted to cover the working parties, and in many places were close in with the main body of the army before the infantry had time to uncover their shields, or to put on their helmets. The Roman soldier, nevertheless, ran to his colours, and, without waiting for the orders of his general, from whose abilities, on this occasion, he could derive no advantage, endeavoured to join his companions in the order to which they were accustomed.

The event of this tumultuary action was various in different places. The Nervii, in one part of the action, forced the imperfect works of the Roman camp: but in another part of it were themselves forced from their ground, and driven in great numbers into the river. Some of the Roman legions were broken, lost the greater part of their officers, and when Cæsar arrived to rally them, were huddled together in confusion. He was reduced to act the part of a mere legionary soldier, and, with a shield which he took from one of his men, joined in the battle, and in this manner, by his presence and by his example, kept the enemy at bay, until he was relieved by the arrival of two legions of the rear-guard, and of two others, that were sent by Labienus to support him.

This seasonable relief, where the Romans were most distressed, changed the fortune of the day; and the confusion, which in the beginning of the action had been turned to so good account by the Nervii, now became fatal to themselves. The greater part of them fell in heaps on the ground where they first began the attack. The few who attempted to fly were met at every opening of the woods by parties of the enemy, by whom they were forced into the thickets or put to the sword; and as they fell in the end with little resistance, many became a prey to the followers of the legions, who put themselves in arms and bore a part in the massacre. Of four hundred chiefs only three escaped; and of an army of sixty thousand men, no more than five hundred left the field of battle. The piteous remains of this nation, consisting of superannuated men, of women, and of children, sent, from the marshes in which they had been concealed, a message to implore the victor's mercy; but it does not appear in what manner he disposed of them.

Another enemy yet remained in the field. The Attuatici, descendants of the Cimbri and Teutones, the late terrors of Gaul, of Spain, and of Italy, being settled below the confluence of the Sambre and the Meuse, had been on their march to join the Nervii, when they heard of this unfortunate action; and then withdrew to their own country. Being pursued by Cæsar, they shut themselves up in their principal fortress. Here they made a voluntary submission; and being commanded to lay down their arms, threw such a quantity of weapons from the battlements, as almost filled up the ditch to the height of the ramparts. But Cæsar, having delayed taking possession of the place till the following day, the besieged, whether they only meant to deceive him, or repented of their surrender, took arms again in the night, and in a sally endeavoured to surprise the Roman army. But four thousand of them being killed in this desperate attempt, and the remainder being forced into the town, were, in consequence of their former breach of faith, to the amount of fifty thousand persons, sold for slaves.

Thus Cæsar having, in the second year of his command, penetrated to the Meuse and the Scheld, and being master of the eastern frontier of Gaul as far as the Rhine, and even from beyond that river having received some offers of submission; being master too of several cantons in Normandy and Bretanny, which had submitted to the young Crassus, placed his army for the winter in the midst of these conquests, and himself, as at the end of the former campaign, set out for Italy and the neighbourhood of Rome.

Here the principal point which he left in contest between the parties, relating to the restoration of Cicero, had been for some time determined. Clodius had found a proper antagonist in Milo, and, as often as he himself, or any of his party, appeared in the assemblies of the people, or in the streets, was every where attacked with his own weapons.

Every one agreed, that if the laws could not give protection to the citizens who were most willing to be governed by them, they should not by their formalities screen the disorderly and profligate in the practice of every species of crime.

Clodius had now for some months lain under an impeachment from Milo, and had declared himself candidate for the office of edile, endeavouring by violence, and by the artifices of his brother, to put off the trial till after the elections, when, if he should be vested with any public character, he might be able to screen himself under the privilege of his office. His own credit, however, and the fear which citizens entertained of his armed banditti, who were now in a great measure restrained by Milo, had abated so much, that the party of the senate determined to make another vigorous effort for the restoration of their exiled member.

This business was accordingly again moved in the senate; and about the beginning of June a decree was passed in the fullest terms for the restoration of Cicero. The consul was charged with the farther conduct of this measure as of the utmost consequence to the commonwealth. This officer accordingly issued a proclamation, in terms employed only on the greatest occasions, requiring all who had the safety of the republic at heart to support him in the execution of this decree. There was, in consequence of this proclamation, a great concourse of citizens from all parts of Italy. The enemies of the measure shrunk and withdrew their opposition. The act passed in the assembly of the people on the fourth of August. Cicero had been so confident of this event, that he on the same day sailed from Dyrrachium, and on the following arrived at Brundusium. On the eighth day, being still at this place, he had intimation of the act being passed, set out for Rome, and continued his journey through multitudes of people, who were assembled on the roads to testify their joy upon his return: he entered the city on the fourth of September.

Next day he addressed the senate in a harangue, which is still extant, composed of lavish panegyric or vehement invective, corresponding to the demerit or merit of parties in his late disgrace and restoration. The multitudes that were assembled on this occasion, their impatience to see him, their acclamations and wonderful unanimity, raised him once more to his former pitch of glory, and appeared to repay all the services he had rendered to the public, and to compensate all the sorrows of his late disgrace. The whole matter was, to persons of reflection, an evidence of that weakness with which this ingenious man suffered himself to be affected by popular opinion, and of the levity with which multitudes run into different extremes.

During these transactions Cæsar was at a great distance, in the northern extremities of Gaul, engaged with fierce and numerous enemies, and involved in difficulties, concerning which there were various reports, and of which the issue, with respect to himself and his army, was supposed to be uncertain. In these circumstances, however willing Pompey may have been to persevere in the measures concerted with Cæsar, it is probable that he found himself unable to resist the force of the senate, which was now exerted to obtain the restoration of a person who had taken so distinguished a part in their measures.

It is possible likewise, that in these circumstances Pompey may have taken upon him to act independently of Cæsar, though he afterwards, in trying to gain Cicero to the party of the triumvirate, affected to give Cæsar equal merit with himself in procuring his recall, and he appealed to Quintus, the brother of Marcus Cicero, for the truth of this assertion.[1] Cicero himself, however, was not disposed to give Cæsar any credit upon this account; and, though both Cæsar and Crassus, after the matter was decided, affected to concur in it, yet he does not seem to have believed them sincere. He imputes to Cæsar an active part in the injury he had received, but none in the reparation that was done to him.[2]

Pompey, not the less jealous of Cæsar for their pretended union, and sensible of the advantage he had gained in a military command of so long a duration at the gates of Rome, now wished to propose for himself some appointment of equal importance. The moment of cordiality in the senate on their recovering a favourite member, and the first emotions of gratitude in the breast of Cicero, whom he had obliged, appeared to form a conjuncture favourable for such a proposition; and he laid, with his usual address and appearance of unconcern, the plan of a motion to be made for this purpose.

The importation of corn into Italy had lately miscarried, and a great scarcity and dearth had followed. The populace being riotous upon this complaint, had in the theatre attacked with menaces and violence numbers of the wealthy citizens who were present, and even insulted the senate itself in the capitol. A report industriously raised by the enemies of Cicero was propagated, to make it be believed that the distress arose from his engrossing for some time the attention of the state; and it was represented, in opposition to this clamour, that the late corn act of Clodius, and the misconduct of one of his relations, intrusted by him with the care of the public granaries, was the cause of this distress. It was insinuated by the adherents of Pompey, that no man was fit to relieve the people besides himself; that the business should be committed to him alone; and Cicero was called upon, as he entered the senate, to make a motion to this purpose, as bound to procure some relief to the people, in return to their late cordiality in his cause.

Cicero had probably owed his recall to the declarations of Pompey in his favour; and, however little reason he had to rely on his friendship, it was convenient to appear on good terms with him. He suffered himself, therefore, to be carried by the stream that seemed to run in favour of this fashionable leader. As if the necessity of the case had suggested the measure, he moved the senate that a commission, with proconsular power over all the provinces, should be granted to Pompey to superintend the supplies of corn for the city. The senate, either of themselves disposed to grant this request, or won by the eloquence of their newly recovered member, instructed the consuls to frame a resolution to this purpose, and carry it to the assembly of the people for their assent.

Here C. Messius, one of the tribunes, proposed to enlarge the commission, and to comprehend the superintendency of the revenue, with an allotment of fleets and armies suited to the extent of this unprecedented trust. Pompey, observing that this additional clause was ill received, denied his having any share in proposing it, and affected to prefer the appointment intended for him in terms of the act which had been proposed to be drawn up by the consuls. His partizans, however, still pleaded for the extension of the commission as proposed by Messius, but in vain. The extravagance of the proposal gave a general alarm, not only to the senate, but even to the party of Cæsar, who wished to employ Pompey against the senate; but not to arm him with a military force, or to give him in reality that sovereignty of which he so much affected the appearances.

The extraordinary commission, now actually granted to Pompey, although it was exorbitant in respect to the influence it gave him over all the producers, venders, buyers, and consumers of corn throughout the whole empire; yet, as it did not bestow the command of an army, fell short of the consequences which Cæsar principally dreaded in his rival; and though probably the cause of some jealousy, did not produce any immediate breach between them.

Pompey, being entitled by this commission to appoint fifteen lieutenants, put Cicero at the head of the list; and this place was accepted of by him, on this express condition, that it should not prevent his standing for the office of censor, in case an election took place on the following year.[3] He was now in the way of recovering his consideration and his dignity, but was likely to meet with more difficulty in respect to his property, which Clodius had taken care to have forfeited, having even demolished his house, and consecrated the ground to pious uses. This last circumstance had placed a bar in his way, which could not be removed without a formal decree of the pontiffs.

The college met on the last of September to hear parties in this cause. A violent invective having been pronounced by Clodius against his antagonist, Cicero replied in that oration, which is still extant among his works on the subject of his house.[4] The question was, Whether the

1 Cicero ad Familiar. lib. i. ep. 9.
2 Orat. in Senat. post Reditum, c. 15.
3 Cicero Orat. in Senat. post Redit. c. 13. ad Att.
4 Pro Domo sua

ground on which Cicero's house had formerly stood, being formally consecrated, could be again restored to a profane or common use? The pontiffs appear to have been unwilling to give any explicit decision. They gave a conditional judgment, declaring, that the consecration of Cicero's ground was void, unless it should be found that this act had been properly authorized by the people. Both parties interpreted this judgment in their own favour; and the senate was to determine, whether, in the act of consecration, the consent of the people had been properly obtained.

The senate being met on the first of October, and all the parties who were members of it being present, Lucullus, in the name of the pontiffs, his collagues, reported, That they had been unanimous in their judgment to revoke the act of consecration, unless it should be found, that the magistrate, who had performed that ceremony, had been properly authorized by the people; but that this was a question of law now before the senate. A debate ensued, in which Lentulus Marcellinus, consul-elect for the following year, gave his opinion against the legality of the consecration: he was followed by numbers, and the judgment of the senate was likely to be on that side. Clodius, to put off the question, spoke for three hours, and would have prevented the senate's coming to any resolution, if the members, becoming impatient, had not silenced him by their interruptions and clamours.

A resolution being moved for in the terms that had been proposed by Marcellinus: the tribune Serranus, who had formerly suspended the decree for the recall of Cicero, now again interposed with his negative. The senate, nevertheless, proceeded to engross the decree, in which it was resolved, that the ground on which Cicero's house had formerly stood, should be again restored to him in property; that no magistrate should presume to contest the authority of the senate in this matter; and if any interruption were given in the execution of this decree, that the tribune, who now interposed with his negative, should be accountable for the consequences. Serranus was alarmed. His relation, Cornicinus, to give him the appearance of greater importance, and an opportunity to recede with dignity, laid himself on the ground at his feet, and besought him, by his intreaties, to say, that he would not insist for the present on the negative he had given; but he begged the delay of a night to consider of the matter. The senate, recollecting the use which he formerly made of such a delay on the first of January, was disposed to refuse it, when, upon the interposition of Cicero himself, it was granted; and he having thought proper to withdraw his negative entirely, the act accordingly passed on the second of October. Cicero was allowed two millions Roman money[1] to rebuild his house in town; five hundred thousand[2] to rebuild his villa at Tusculum, and two hundred and fifty thousand[3] to rebuild that at Formiæ. The first sum he seems to have considered as adequate to his loss, but complains of the other two.[4] He proceeded, without delay, to take possession of his ground, and to employ workmen in rebuilding his house. He had made some progress, when Clodius, on the third of November, came with an armed force, dispersed the workmen, and attacked the house of Quintus Cicero that was adjoining, set it on fire, and kept a guard of his retainers in the streets till it was burnt to the ground. By this act of violence, Clodius had rendered his cause, in the criminal prosecution which still hung over him, in a great measure desperate. His safety required the actual destruction of his enemies, and he had no scruple to restrain him from the most violent extremes. He accordingly attacked Cicero as he passed in the streets on the eleventh of November, attended by a company of his friends, forced them into a walled court, where they with difficulty defended themselves. Clodius, in this attack, had frequently exposed his own person, and might have been killed; but Cicero was now become too cautious for so bold a measure. "I have put my affairs," he writes to Atticus, "under a gentle regimen; and, in all the cures I am to apply for the future, have renounced the use of the surgeon's knife."

Clodius, upon this occasion, being disappointed of his design upon Cicero's life, came into the streets on the following day, which was the twelfth of November, with a number of slaves provided with lighted torches, and escorted by a party armed in form with shields and swords. They made directly for a house belonging to Milo, with intention to set it on fire, took possession of that of P. Sylla, in its neighbourhood, as a fortress in which to defend themselves, and to keep off all assistance, till the house they were to set on fire should be burnt to the ground.

While they were about to execute this purpose, a number of Milo's servants, led by one Flaccus, sallied forth against the incendiaries, killed several of the most forward, put the rest to flight, and would not have spared Clodius himself, if he had not availed himself of the retreat, which, in entering on this design, he had prepared for his party.

On the following day, Sylla made his appearance in the senate, in order to exculpate himself; but Clodius still remained shut up in his own house. It appears scarcely credible, that a state could subsist under such extreme disorders; yet the author of them had been long under prosecution for crimes of the same nature; and it was still a question, whether the charge against him should be heard, or whether he should not be allowed to take refuge in one of the offices of state, to which he was sure of being named by the people, provided the elections were allowed to precede his trial.

Marcellinus, the intended consul of next year, moved the senate to hasten the prosecution, and to join the late disorders committed by the criminal to the former articles of the charge which lay against him. But Metellus Nepos, one of the present consuls, and the relation of Clodius, having formerly found means to put off the trial, was now determined to prevent it altogether, by hastening the election of ædiles, in which Clodius was candidate. He endeavoured to prevent any immediate determination of the senate by prolonging the debate. But the majority of the members were greatly exasperated, and resolved, that the trial of Clodius for these repeated acts of violence and outrage should precede the elections. The consul Metellus, notwithstanding, was determined to give him a chance to have refuge from this

1 About 16,145*l.* 16*s.* 8*d.* 2 About 4,036*l.* 5*s.*
3 About 2,018*l.* 4*s.* 6*d.*
4 Ad Atticum, lib. iv. epist. 2.

prosecution in the public office to which he aspired, and would have brought on the elections on the nineteenth of November, if he had not been prevented by Milo, who in the middle of the preceding night, had, with an armed force, occupied the place of assembly, and was prepared to observe the heavens, and to announce some of the celestial presages of unfavourable events, in case other methods to suspend the elections should not have prevailed.

Metellus, and the two brothers, Appius the prætor, and Publius Clodius, being apprised of this intention, and of the power with which it was supported, did not make their appearance in the field, and Milo kept his station till noon, when he withdrew with the general applause of the senate, and of the more orderly citizens.

The meeting, or assembly of the people, being adjourned to next day, Metellus, in order to lull the vigilance of Milo, assured him, that there was no occasion to occupy posts in the dead of the night; that he meant to do nothing before it was day; that if any one meant to suspend the election, he should, in the morning, be found in the market-place, and there submit to the forms which any one was legally entitled to plead against his proceeding. Milo, accordingly, at break of day, repaired to the market-place, where he expected to be joined by the consul; but soon afterwards was told, that Metellus had deceived him, was hastening to the field of Mars, where the elections were commonly held, and would instantly begin to call the votes, when it would be too late to interpose even under the pretence of religion. Upon this information, he immediately pursued and overtook him before the election began; and, by declaring his intention to observe the heavens, once more frustrated the designs of the faction.

On the twenty-first, the people could not assemble by reason of the public market; and their meeting being called for the twenty-third, Milo again took possession of the field with an armed force; and Cicero, who concludes a letter to Atticus with describing this state of affairs, made no doubt of Milo's success.[5] What passed on this day is uncertain; but it is known, that Clodius at last prevailed; that, being elected ædile, he was, by the privilege of his office, screened from the prosecution that was intended against him and being himself safe, did not fail upon the expiration of Milo's tribunate, to retort the charge upon his prosecutor; and accordingly brought him to trial on the second of February, for acts of violence and breach of the peace.

U. C. 697.
Cn. Corn. Lentulus Marcellinus, L. Marc. Philippus.

Pompey, as well as Cicero, appeared in defence of Milo; and they succeeded in having him acquitted, while they incurred a torrent of reproach and invective on the part of the prosecutor. The market-place was crowded with the partizans and retainers of Clodius: he had instructed them to reply to his interrogations, and to direct all their abuse on Pompey. "Who starves the people for want of corn? Pompey. Who wants to be sent to Alexandria? Pompey." This farce greatly disturbed the concerted dignity of this politician. His principal object was consideration, and he could not endure contempt. He was on bad terms with the senate; and they listened to the invective of his personal enemies with apparent satisfaction. He complained to Cicero that the people were alienated from him; that the nobility were his enemies; that the senate was adverse, and the youth in general ill disposed to him.[6] He had indeed submitted to become the agent of Cæsar at Rome; and, with the friends of the republic, incurred the odium of their joint measures, while the other was rising every day in military reputation, and was forming an army almost at the gates of Rome, with which he held every party in the republic in awe. Pompey, on this occasion, really did, or affected to believe, that a design was formed against his own life; he assembled a numerous party of his retainers from the country, and absented himself, during some time from the senate and from the assemblies of the people.

CHAPTER VII.

Return of Cato from Cyprus—His Repulse at the Election of Prætors—Arrival of Ptolemy Auletes at Rome—Visit of Pompey and Crassus to Cæsar's Quarters at Lucca—Renewal of their Association—Military Operations in Cæsar's Province—Violent Election of Crassus and Pompey—Provinces—Of Crassus in Syria—Of Pompey in Spain for five years—Crassus departs for Syria.

THE particulars we have related in the last chapter have led us on to the middle of February, in the consulate of Lentulus Marcellinus and L. Marcius Philippus. The first was attached to the forms of the republic, and was a strenuous partizan of the senate. His election was probably a continuation of the victory which this party had obtained in the restoration of Cicero. Philippus was now nearly related to Cæsar, having married his niece, the widow of Octavius; and possibly owed his preferment in part to that connexion. He was, by this alliance, become the step-father of young Octavius, now a boy of ten years of age, brought up by his mother in the house of her second husband. This appears to have been a man of great moderation, no way qualified to be a party in the designs or usurpations of the family with which he was now connected.

Some time before these consuls entered on office, in the end of the preceding year, Marcus Cato arrived from having executed his commission to Byzantium and Cyprus. The business upon which he had been sent to the first of these places, was to restore some exiles who had been driven from their country in the violence of faction. At the second he was to seize the treasure

5 Cicero ad Att. lib. iv. epist. 3.
6 Cicer. ad Quint. frat. lib ii. epist. 3.

and the other effects of Ptolemy, and to reduce his kingdom to the form of a Roman province. This measure, by all accounts, was unjust, and the office highly disagreeable to Cato; but he was determined to perform it with the punctuality and respect due to all the orders of the state. While he himself went to Byzantium, he sent forward Canidius to Cyprus, to intimate the commands of the Roman people, and to exhort the king to submission. Upon his return to Rhodes, in his way to Cyprus, he had intelligence, that this prince, unable to bear the ruin of his fortunes, had in despair, killed himself. His treasure was seized, and his effects sold: the whole yielded to the treasury about seven thousand talents of silver. Upon the approach of Cato to Rome, the magistrates, the senate, and multitudes of the people went forth to receive him. The senate thought proper in this manner to distinguish their friends, and to favour them with some marks of consideration, in order to balance, if possible, the public honours that were frequently lavished on their enemies. For the same purpose likewise they resolved to insert the name of Cato among the prætors of this year; but this honour he himself rejected as unprecedented and illegal. The year following, however, when he stood candidate for this office in the ordinary form, he was rejected; and Vatinius, the well-known tool of Cæsar, who had been employed by him in all measures that were too mean for himself to acknowledge, was chosen.[1]

Cæsar, as has been observed on different occasions, had a serious antipathy to Cato, considered him as a determined and resolute opponent; and accordingly employed all his influence to exclude him from the offices of state, and probably had a particular pleasure in procuring him a repulse, by the preference of so mean an antagonist as Vatinius, who had the present majority of votes against him. But, in mentioning this event, Valerius Maximus is pleased to reverse the form of expression, usual in speaking of disappointed candidates, saying, "That the list of prætors for this year had not the honour of Cato's name."[2]

Cato, in the execution of his late commission, had taken exact inventories of all the effects sold at Cyprus; but his books being lost, or burnt in a vessel that took fire on the voyage, Clodius frequently threatened him with a prosecution to account for the sums he had received; and in this he was seriously instigated by Cæsar, who from his winter quarters at Lucca, watched all the proceedings at Rome.

From this station, the proconsul of Gaul, although he could not attend in person, sent his agents to the city, took part in every transaction of moment that related to his adherents or to his enemies. It appeared to be his maxim, that no man should be his friend or his enemy without feeling the suitable effects. Memmius, who had been prætor with Domitius Ahenobarbus, and who had joined his colleague in the prosecution that was commenced against Cæsar at the expiration of his consulate, having since been prætor of Bithynia, and accused of misconduct in his province, was attacked by him in a memorial which he drew up to be employed in support of the charge. Memmius, in defending himself, recriminated, and spared no kind of invective; and in the issue of this matter had the good fortune to escape from the resentment of his enemy.

The power of Cæsar, aided by his influence in so important a station, was daily increasing; and as he spared no pains to crush those whom he despaired of gaining, so he declined no artifice to gain every one else. All the spoils of his province were distributed in gratuities at Rome. He knew the state of every man's family, and where he could not reach the master, paid his court to the mistress, or to the favourite slave. While in his winter quarters at Lucca, many senators resorted from Rome to pay their court; of these no less than two hundred were said to have been present at one time; and so many of them in public characters, that the lictors, who paraded at the entrance of his quarters with the badges of office, amounted to one hundred and twenty.[3]

During this winter, a question relating to the restoration of Ptolemy Auletes to the throne of Egypt, gave rise to warm debates in the senate. This prince had been dethroned by his subjects; and, conceiving that he had sufficient credit with many persons at Rome, who had experienced his bounty, he repaired thither to solicit his own restoration. In his way he had an interview with Marcus Cato at Cyprus, and was advised by him to return to Egypt, and to accept of any terms from his own people, rather than to enter on such a scene of anxiety and mortification, as he should find every suitor for public favour engaged in at Rome. The giddiness of the multitude, the violence of the parties of which one was sure to oppose what the other embraced, the avarice of those who might pretend to be his friends, and whose rapacity the treasures of his kingdom could not assuage, were sufficient to deter the king from proceeding on his voyage. But the importunity of his attendants, who wished to have him restored without any concessions to his subjects, confirmed him in his former resolution. He accordingly proceeded to Rome; and, to the great encouragement of his hopes, was favourably received by Pompey, who was then possessed of the reigning influence in the city, and who considered this as a proper opportunity to have a military commission joined to the civil one of which he was already possessed.

In the mean while the people of Alexandria, not knowing to what place their king had withdrawn, imagined that he was dead, and put his daughter Berenice in possession of the kingdom. Being afterwards informed, that he had steered for Italy, and was likely to engage the Romans against them, they sent a deputation to counteract his solicitations in the Roman senate. But these deputies being intercepted, and murdered by his order, he proceeded, without opposition, in his application at Rome, and obtained a decree for his restoration to the crown.

The king of Egypt, by having procured an act in his own favour, yet made but a small progress in the business on which he was come. New difficulties arose in the choice of a person to carry the decree of the senate into execution, which greatly retarded its effect.

Soon after this decree had passed, Lentulus Spinther, consul of the present year, being destined at the expiration of his magistracy in the

1 Plutarch. in Vit. Catonis, et Cicero in Vatinium.
2 Val. Max. lib. vii. c. 5.

3 Plutarch. in Cæsare.

city to command in Cilicia and Cyprus, had inserted the business of restoring the king of Egypt as a part of his own commission. But after Lentulus was gone for his province, this part of the commission, probably by the influence of Pompey, who had views on that expedition, as the object of a military command for himself, was recalled. A strong party of the nobles, however, being jealous of the state which Pompey affected, and of his continual aim at extraordinary powers, conceived an expedient to disappoint him on this occasion, or to render the commission unworthy of his acceptance. In visiting the books of Sybils, verses were said to be found, containing an injunction to the Romans, not indeed to withhold their friendship from a king of Egypt soliciting their protection, but "to beware how they attempted to restore him with a military force." The authenticity of this oracle was acknowledged, or declared by the augurs; and the tribune Caius Cato, who was averse to the cause of Ptolemy, availed himself of it, to suspend the effect of the resolution which had been already taken in favour of that prince. The senate and people were divided in their opinions. One party urged that Pompey should be appointed to restore the king of Egypt to his throne; others agreed that he might be appointed, provided that he undertook the commission, as proconsul, attended by two lictors, and, in the terms of the oracle, without any military force.[4] Pompey himself affected to think, that the business should have been left as it was in the department of Lentulus the proconsul of Cilicia and Cyprus; but his retainers, so long as they had any hopes of rendering this a military commission, or of making it a pretence for placing their patron again at the head of an army, never ceased to urge that he should be employed in it.

Ptolemy himself likewise wished to have this business devolve upon Pompey, as the most likely person to command the force of the commonwealth, and to employ it effectually in his favour. But both despairing at last of success, Ptolemy retired to Ephesus; and, fearing the resentments he had provoked in the contest with his own people, and in the late murder of their deputies, he took refuge in the temple of Diana; a retreat from which he was conducted, about two years afterwards, by Gabinius, and replaced on his throne.[5]

Pompey was disgusted with his disappointment in not being named to this service, and probably more by the little respect that was paid to him by all parties while he lay under the lash of continual invectives from Clodius, and from Caius Cato. Having obtained, on the fifth of April, a grant of some money towards executing his office of general surveyor of corn for the people; and having heard his own and Cæsar's embezzlement of the public treasure, especially in the alienation of the revenues of Campania, severely censured in the senate,[6] he left Rome on pretence of applying the sums with which he was now entrusted for the purchase of corn in Sardinia and Sicily. In his way he passed by Lucca, and, together with Crassus, augmented the number of attendants who paid their court at the quarters of Cæsar.

At an interview of these three leaders they renewed their former confederacy; and it being known that Domitius Ahenobarbus was to stand for the next election of consuls, Cæsar, considering how much a citizen so determined in opposition to himself, instigated by Cato, and supported by the party of the senate, might attempt or execute against him in his absence, proposed, that the opposition to this candidate should not be committed to any person of inferior consideration in their party; but that Pompey and Crassus should themselves enter the lists, in order to exclude Domitius from the consulate.[7]

It was agreed likewise, at this conference, that, upon the expiration of the term for which they were to hold this office, Pompey should have the province of Spain, Crassus that of Syria, each with a great army: that Cæsar should be continued in his present command, and have such additions to the establishment of his province as might enable him to support an army of eight Roman legions, with the usual accompaniments of auxiliaries and irregular troops. Such was already the state of his forces,[8] including a legion of native Gauls; he having, contrary to the express limitation of his commission, by which he was restricted to three legions, made this enormous augmentation. This convention, like the former, was for some time kept a secret, and only began to be surmised about the usual time of the elections.

Soon after these matters were settled, Crassus being to remain in Italy, Pompey proceeded on his voyage to Sardinia, and Cæsar repaired to his army in Gaul, where the war in different places had been renewed in his absence. Among the dispositions he had made for the winter, the young Crassus was left to command on the coasts of the British channel; and Galba, another of his lieutenants, was posted among the Alps to protect the traders of Italy at a principal pass of these mountains. This officer had dislodged the natives from many of their strong holds, whence they were accustomed to infest the highways, and to lay such as passed into Italy under contributions; and he took hostages for their good behaviour for the future. He fixed his quarters, during the winter, at Octodorus, now supposed to be the village of Martinach in the Vallé, situated at the foot of the mountains over which travellers pass in the route of the greater abbey of St. Bernard. Here he remained for some time in quiet possession of his post; but the natives observing, that the legions under his command had been greatly reduced by the services of the preceding campaign, and by the detachments which he had recently made from his quarters, formed a design to surprise and to cut him off. For this purpose, the inhabitants of the village in which he was quartered suddenly withdrew from him, and soon after appeared with multitudes of their countrymen on the neighbouring mountains. From thence they made a furious attack on the Roman entrenchment, continually sending fresh numbers to relieve those who became fatigued, or who had exhausted their weapons.

The Romans, on the first prospect of this at-

4 Dio. lib. xxxix. c. 12—16. Cicero ad Lentulum. Epist. ad Familiares, lib. vii.
5 Liv. Epitom. Decad. xi. lib. 5.
6 Cicero ad Quint. frat. lib. ii. ep. 5 et 6.

7 Suet. in Cæsare, c. 24.
8 Ibid.

tack, had deliberated, whether they should not abandon their post; but had resolved to maintain it, and were now become sensible that they must perish, if they could not, by some impetuous sally, disperse the numbers that were assembled against them. For this purpose, they determined to break from their lines, and to mix with the enemy sword in hand; a manner of fighting, in which by the superiority of the Roman shield and sword, they always had a great advantage. They accordingly sallied from their entrenchment, and, with the slaughter of ten thousand of the enemy, who began the attack with thirty thousand, obliged them to retire. Galba, nevertheless, not thinking it prudent to remain in a situation in which he had been exposed to so much danger, retired, for the remainder of the winter, to the neighbourhood of Geneva.

The war had broke out at the same time in the quarters of Crassus, at the other extremity of the province Some nations, who had made their submission, and given hostages at the end of the preceding campaign, repented of this step, and entered into a concert to recover their liberties. They began with seizing the Roman officers who had been stationed among them as commissaries to provide for the subsistence of the army, and they detained them as pledges for the recovery of their own hostages.

The principal authors of this revolt were the inhabitants of what is now termed the coast of Britanny, between the rivers Vilaine and Blavet. They trusted to the strength of their situation on small islands, or peninsulas, that were joined to the continent only by some narrow beach or isthmus, which the sea, at high water, overflowed. They depended likewise on the strength of their shipping, in the use of which, by the practice of navigation on that stormy sea, and by their frequent voyages even to Britain, they were extremely expert. They supplied the want of canvass and hempen cordage with hides and thongs of leather, and the want of cables with iron chains, to which they fastened their anchors.

Cæsar, having received intelligence of this enemy, while he remained in his quarters at Lucca, sent orders to build as many ships as possible upon the Loire, and to assemble mariners from the neighbouring coasts. Apprehending, at the same time, a general defection of the province, and perhaps a descent from the Germans, that were ever ready to profit by the distress or divisions of their neighbours, he sent Labienus with a large body of horse to the Moselle, at once to awe the Belgic nations, and to guard the passage of the Rhine. He sent also Titurius Sabinus with a proper force into Normandy, where the natives were already in arms; and the young Crassus to the Garonne, to give the natives of Gascony sufficient occupation in their own country, and to prevent their junction with the authors of this revolt.

He himself made haste to join the troops that were stationed in Britanny, and ordered Decimus Brutus to assemble his fleet, and to make sail without loss of time for the bay of Vannes. After his arrival on the coast, he met with all the difficulties which he had reason to expect from the nature of the country, and from the disposition and skill of its inhabitants. The enemy had retired from the continent to their strong holds on the promontories or head-lands, in which they were periodically surrounded by the sea. Being attacked at one station, they withdrew in their boats to another; and by their situation seemed to be secure from any enemy, who was not in a condition to make his attack, at once, both by sea and by land. They eluded a land attack by embarking on board of their vessels and an attack from the sea, by landing from their boats, which they drew up on the beach.

Cæsar, to decide the event of this singular contest, was obliged to wait the arrival of his shipping. As soon as it appeared, the natives, sensible that their fate depended on the event of a sea-fight, embarked the most expert of their warriors, got under sail with all their force, amounting to two hundred and twenty vessels, and steered directly for their enemy. While the fleets drew near to each other, the shores were crowded with spectators; and the army with Cæsar himself came forth on the heights, from which they could behold the scene.

The Romans being inferior to their enemy in the use of their sails, as well as in the strength of their vessels, endeavoured to supply their defect, as usual, by an effort of address and unexpected contrivance. They had provided themselves with scythes, fastened to shafts of a proper length, in order to cut the enemy's rigging, and let loose or discompose their sails; and having thus, in the first encounter, disabled many of their ships, they grappled with them, and boarded them sword in hand.

The Gauls, seeing a great part of their fleet thus irrecoverably lost, would have escaped with the remainder; but were suddenly becalmed, and being, from ten in the morning till night, continually exposed to the attack of the Romans, were all either taken or destroyed; and the nation thus bereft of its principal strength and the flower of its people, surrendered again at discretion.

Under pretence that they had violated the law of nations, in seizing the persons of officers who were stationed among them in a public character, their leaders were put to death, and their people sold for slaves.

The inhabitants of the lower banks of the Seine, at the same time having been defeated by Titurius, returned, agreeably to what was said to be the character of Gaulish nations, to their former submission, with the same levity with which they had thrown it aside.

The nations inhabiting the banks of the Garonne were still inclined to resist the approaches of Crassus to their country. To the advantage of numbers, they joined a lively courage, of which the Romans themselves had frequently felt the effects. Every chief was attended by a number of followers, whom he called his soldurii, and who had devoted themselves to his service. While the chieftain lived, the soldurii fared in every thing alike with himself; but if he perished by violence, they too must die, and there was no instance of their failing in this part of their engagement.

Crassus being arrived on the Garonne, and warned by the example of other Roman officers, who had fallen or miscarried in this service, deferred passing the river till he had augmented his force by the junction of some troops from Toulouse, and other parts of the Roman province. Being thus reinforced, he proceeded against the natives who were divided into many little hordes, of which Cæsar has, on this occasion, enumerated twelve, jealous of each other, and unwilling to join even in their common defence. They accordingly, notwithstanding their valour, fell separately into the hands of the Romans, and in the end were vanquished, or made their submission.

By these conquests, the former acquisitions of Cæsar on the Seine and the Marne, had a direct communication with the districts of Toulouse and Narbonne, or what was already called the Roman province of Gaul. Cæsar himself, having re-established peace in those tracts which are now termed Britanny and Normandy, closed the campaign with a march northward, where he penetrated through the marshes and woods into Brabant; but being stopped by heavy rains, and the approach of winter, he returned on his route, without making any settlement; and having put his army into winter quarters among the nations who had lately revolted, he set out as usual for Italy. There his presence was greatly wanted by Pompey and Crassus, who, on the approach of the elections, were likely to meet with unexpected difficulties in executing the plan lately concerted between them.

At Rome, the spring and part of the summer had passed in disputes between persons connected with the opposite parties. Clodius had attacked Cicero in his own person, in his effects, and in the persons of his friends. P. Sextius, who, in the character of tribune, had been so active in the recall of this injured exile, and who had exposed his life in the riots to which that question gave rise, was now accused, and brought to trial for supposed acts of violence committed by him in the course of those contests. He was defended with great zeal by Hortensius, and with a proper gratitude by Cicero; and by their joint endeavours was, on the twelfth of March, acquitted by the unanimous verdict of his judges.[1]

After this trial was over, a piece of superstition, curious as it forms a picture of the age, gave occasion to a fresh dispute between Cicero and his enemy Clodius. Upon a report, that horrid noises and clashing of arms had been heard under ground in one of the suburbs, the senate thought proper to take the subject under consideration, and they referred it for interpretation to the college of Aruspices. This body delivered in judgment, that the gods were offended, among other things, by the neglect and profanation of the holy rites, and by the prostitution of sacred places to profane uses. This response Clodius endeavoured to apply to the case of Cicero's house, once consecrated and set apart for religion, and now again profaned by being restored to his former owner. Cicero endeavoured to remove the charge of profanation from himself to Clodius, by reviving the memory of his famous adventure in Cæsar's house. "If I quote any more recent act of impiety," says he, "this citizen will recall me to the former instance, in which he intended no more than adultery." He proceeded, however, to apply the response of the Augurs to a late intrusion of Clodius in rushing into the theatre with an armed rabble, while the games were celebrating in honour of the great goddess.

The senate for two days together listened to the mutual invectives of both parties, and were entertained with their endeavours to surpass each other in declarations of zeal for religion. Cicero, however, by the goodness of his cause, the force of his admirable talents, and perhaps still more by the aid of the triumvirate, whose favour he earnestly cultivated, prevailed in the contest.

This martyr in the cause of the senate, ever since his return from banishment, courted the formidable parties, whose power, at least to hurt, he had experienced. He committed, or affected to commit, himself entirely into the hands of Pompey; and, with a declaration of much attachment also to Cæsar, composed a flattering panegyric, which this leader received with great pleasure,[2] probably more on account of the breach it was likely to make among his opponents in the senate, than on account of the satisfaction he received from it, or of any real accession of strength it gave him in the pursuit of his designs. By this conduct Cicero disgusted his former friends, and felt his situation in the city so painful, that he absented himself, during great part of the summer, from Rome; a circumstance which interrupted the course, or changed the subject, of those letters to which we are indebted for the best record of the times.

We have indeed great reason to regret any interruption of materials from which the history of this consulate might be collected. The republic seems in part to have recovered its dignity by the able and resolute conduct of Marcellinus, and by the tacit concurrence of his colleague Philippus, who, though connected with Cæsar, did not cooperate in the execution of his designs.[3] By the influence of these consuls, the applications made to the senate by Gabinius, now commanding in Syria, for certain customary honours were rejected.[4] This refusal was intended to mortify Pompey, who protected Gabinius, and who himself was commonly treated by Marcellinus with great freedom and severity. The aristocratical party recovered their courage, and Domitius Ahenobarbus, by their influence, was in a fair way to succeed in his election for consul of the following year.

The tribunes, excited chiefly by Caius Cato, espoused the opposite interest, and proposed many resolutions to the people, in order to favour their designs. The consul Marcellinus endeavoured to interrupt them by the appointment of fasts and holidays, in which it was not lawful to transact affairs in the assembly of the people. The tribunes, in their turn, suspended the election of consuls, and in this were encouraged by Pompey and Crassus, who feared the effect of a choice to be made under the direction of Marcellinus, and had not even openly declared their own intentions to offer themselves. Their late interview with Cæsar, and the part they since took, had created suspicion of their views. Marcellinus put the question to Pompey in the senate, whether he desired the consulate for himself? And this politician, long unaccustomed to make plain declarations, answered indirectly, That if there were no ill-disposed citizens in the commonwealth, he should have no such desire. Crassus, to the same question, made a like evasive reply, That he should be governed by what he judged

1 Cicero ad Quin. Frat. lib. ii. epist. 4. Orat. pro Sext.

2 Cicero ad Att. lib. iv. ep. 5.

3 Cic. ad Quint. Frat. lib. ii. ep. 6.

4 Ibid. ep. 7

best for the state. Both appear to have perceived that they were to rely for success chiefly on popular tumults; and as these would come to be employed with great disadvantage against such an able and resolute magistrate as Marcellinus, they took measures to defer the elections until the term of the present consuls in office should expire.[1]

They found the tribune Caius Cato, a proper instrument for their purpose, secured his negative, and employed it repeatedly to suspend the elections. The republic, upon the approach of the new year, being to lose its former magistrates, without any succession of new ones, was likely to fall into a state of great confusion. The senate went into mourning, and discharged every member from assisting at any of the public diversions. In this state of suspense and public alarm, Publius Clodius, who had for some time been at variance with Pompey, as if gained by the sympathy of measures on this occasion, was reconciled to him, and attacked Marcellinus with continual invectives.

In this manner the year was suffered to elapse without any election of consuls. The fasces dropped from the hands of Marcellinus and Philippus, and an interregnum ensued. Pompey and Crassus then openly appeared as candidates for the vacant offices of state. Young Crassus came from the army in Gaul, attended by a numerous body of citizens then serving under Cæsar: they brought a considerable accession of votes to the party of their general, and were themselves not likely to be outstripped by their opponents in acts of sedition and the use of force. Domitius Ahenobarbus alone, supported by the councils of his kinsman Marcus Cato, had the courage to persist in a contest with these powerful and dangerous antagonists. The time of election being fixed, he went before break of day to occupy his place in the field of Mars, but found his way already obstructed by a disorderly populace, and even by men in arms. The slave who carried a light before him was killed. Some of his friends, particularly Marcus Cato, was wounded;[2] and his adherents not being in condition to dispute the ground with the force that was assembled against them, retired to their own houses, leaving Pompey and Crassus to be named without opposition.

In the same manner the faction of the triumvirate overruled every other election, procured the preference, which has already been mentioned, of Vatinius to Cato, and filled every office with their own creatures. They carried the appointment of ediles by actual force, and at the expense of the lives of some of those who opposed them. Pompey himself having been entangled in one of these tumults, retired to change his clothes, which were stained with blood. They were disappointed in the nomination only of two of the tribunes, Publius Acquilius Gallus and Ateius Capito, who were of the opposite party.

U. C. 698.

Cn. Pompeius Magnus. 2do; M. Licinius Crassus.

These events, however, were, by the contest which arose on every question, deferred for all the months of winter and spring. The offices of prætor were not filled up by the middle of May.[3] The elections had begun for this purpose some time before; but it being observed that Marcus Cato had the first centuries, Pompey, under a pretence, allowed by the Roman superstition, that he was to observe the heavens, interposed to suspend the ballot. The faction employed the time which they obtained by this delay in procuring votes, and were so unguarded in giving money, that they laid themselves open to a criminal prosecution, and had reason to apprehend that whatever election they made would be disputed at law. To prevent this consequence, Afranius, a person entirely under the direction of Pompey, moved in the assembly of the people for a dispensation from the statute of bribery in the case of elections then depending for the office of prætor; and having obtained this extraordinary indulgence, secured to the party the fruits of their influence and of their money.[4]

Among the acts of Pompey and Crassus, in their second consulate, are mentioned some regulations respecting the courts of justice by which the juries, though taken in equal numbers from the senate, the equestrian order, and the mass of the people, were nevertheless limited to persons of considerable property. There are likewise mentioned some resolutions then passed to enforce the laws against murder, and to amend those against bribery by additional penalties, together with a sumptuary law to check the extravagance and prodigality of the age. "So willing were these magistrates," said Hortensius, "to compensate by their acts for the defects of their practice, that they made laws even to limit the expense of the table." Such professions to reform the age were probably intended to retrieve the character which the popular leaders had lost by the violence and bare-faced corruption of their recent canvass, and to mark their administration with some measures that might seem to disprove the imputations commonly laid to their charge.

Pompey, at the same time, had an opportunity to signalize his consulate, by opening, during the present year, the magnificent theatre which he himself, or his freedman Demetrius, had erected for the accommodation of the people at their public shows. At this solemnity were exhibited many dramatic performances and entertainments of every sort. Among these, in the course of five days, no less than five hundred lions were let loose and killed by African huntsmen; and the whole concluded with the baiting of eighteen elephants, animals that seemed to have sagacity enough to be conscious of the indignity and the wrong which they suffered. By their piteous cries they moved compassion in the breasts even of that barbarous rabble, for whose entertainment they were slain.[5]

The allotment of provinces, which was the principal object of this consulate, was for some time kept from the view of the people. Pompey continued to profess that he did not intend to accept of any province whatever. But the public gave no credit to such declarations on his part; and his own partizans were accustomed to press upon him what he affected to decline.[6] Every one, therefore, in all conversations, endeavoured to accommodate him in a province, some with

1 Dio lib. xxxix. c. 37.
2 Plutarch in Crass. Pompeio, &c.
3 Cicer. ad Quint. Frat. lib. ii. ep. 9.

4 Cicer. ad Quint. Frat. lib. ii. ep. 9.
5 Dio. lib. xxxix. Cicero ad Familiar. lib. vii. Plin. lib. viii. c. 7.
6 Cicero ad Att. lib. iv. ep. 9.

Syria, others with Spain and Africa; to all which suggestions, or officious projects, he affected indifference, or even aversion. Trebonius, however, at this time tribune of the people, made a motion, which was soon understood to be the real mind of Pompey, and the actual result of his counsels: that the province of Syria should be assigned to Crassus; that of Spain, together with Africa, to himself; each in imitation of Cæsar's appointment in Gaul, to continue for five years, with such establishments of men and of money as the necessity of the service during that period might require. This motion was made in execution of the original plan concerted with Cæsar, and it served to bring to light the object of their late conference at Lucca, which had so much alarmed the friends of the republic.

On the day that this motion was made in the assembly, Marcus Cato, by means of the tribunes Atteius Capito and Acquilius Gallus, obtained leave to address the people. He endeavoured to disappoint the purpose of the meeting, by occupying so much of their time as to prevent their coming to any decision. Being commanded silence, and persisting to speak, he was ordered by Trebonius into custody. In this manner, however, the first day was spent, and the assembly adjourned to the next morning.

The tribunes Atteius and Gallus, suspecting that means might be used to exclude them from the assembly which was then to be held, took measures to secure their admission. For this purpose Gallus remained all night in the senate-house, which fronted the Comitia or place of assembly. But this device was turned against himself; the opposite party having placed a guard to confine him in that place during the greater part of the following day. His colleague Atteius, with Cato, Favonius, and some others, eluded the parties that were placed to intercept them, and found their way to the place of assembly. When the question was put, Cato, being lifted up into view by those of his friends who were about him, gave an alarm that it thundered; an intimation ever held by the religious customs of the Romans to be ominous, and sufficient to suspend their procedure in any business of state. He was, however, on this occasion forced from the comitium with the slaughter of some of his friends, who resisted the force that was employed against them. About the same time the tribune Acquilius was wounded in forcing his way from the senate-house, and a great concourse of people was forming round him as he stood bleeding in the streets. Violence to the person of a tribune was still considered with religious horror, and the consuls, in whose behalf this tumult had been raised, fearing the consequence of suffering such a spectacle to remain in the view of the people, ordered the multitude to withdraw, and removed the tribune, still bleeding of his wounds, from the public view.

In the sequel of these operations, Pompey and Crassus obtained the provinces in question, and in the terms proposed; they proceeded to fulfil their part of the late engagement to Cæsar, by moving that his command should be continued during an additional term of five years more. "Now, indeed," said Cato, addressing himself to Pompey, "the burden is preparing for your own shoulders. It will one day fall on the republic, but not till after it has crushed you to the ground."

These arrangements being made, the officers thus appointed proceeded to take charge of their trust. Pompey, the newly named proconsul of Spain, under pretence of a war subsisting with the Vaccei, raised the establishment of his province to four legions, two of which Cæsar soon after, under pretence of more urgent service in Gaul, had the address to borrow from him.

Pompey either had not yet begun to perceive what Cato suggested to him, that the greatest difficulty he had to fear, in preserving the eminence to which he aspired, was the emulation of Cæsar; and that the sword must determine the contest between them; or he flattered himself that, like the person who stays at the helm, he was to command the vessel; and by remaining at the seat of government, while his associates and rivals accepted of appointments at a distance, that he continued to preside as sovereign, and supreme dictator of the whole. Under the influence of these conceptions, although his proper station was Spain, he either procured, or at least availed himself of, a motion that was made by some of the tribunes to detain him in Italy; and fancied, while he sent his own lieutenants, Afranius and Petreius, as private agents for himself into that province, that even Cæsar and Crassus, though in a more public character, were however to act in a subordinate station to himself.

Crassus ever considered riches as the chief constituents of power, and he expected, with the spoils of Asia, to equal the military or political advantages that were likely to be acquired by his rivals in Europe. From the levies and other preparations which he made for his province, it soon appeared that he intended a war with the Parthians, the only antagonists which the Romans had left on the frontier of Syria. Observing that he was likely to meet with an opposition to this design from the senate and from the tribunes, who exerted their powers to interrupt his preparations, and took measures to detain him at home, he became the more impatient to set out for his province, and left Rome before the expiration of the year for which he was elected into the office of consul. The tribune Atteius endeavoured to stop him, first by his tribunitian negative, next by actual force, and last of all by solemn imprecations, devoting the consul himself, and all who should follow him on that service, to destruction.

While Crassus passed through the gates of Rome, on his intended departure for Asia, this tribune, with a lighted fire, the usual form of devoting a victim to the infernal gods, denounced a curse, which greatly alarmed many of the followers of Crassus. This piece of superstition he might, in his own mind, have justly contemned: but it was imprudent to slight the effects of it on the minds of the people, and on the minds of his own army. In the apprehension of both he was by this form doomed to destruction, and proceeded in the war at the head of troops ill prepared to ward off calamities, which they were thus made to believe hung over them, in consequence of imprecations of which they did not question the efficacy.

THE

HISTORY

OF

THE PROGRESS AND TERMINATION

OF THE

ROMAN REPUBLIC.

BOOK IV.

CHAPTER I.

State of the Commonwealth—Administration of the Provinces—Operations of Cæsar in Gaul, Germany, and Britain—State of Pompey at Rome—Progress of Crassus into Syria—Kingdom of Parthia—Invasion of Crassus beyond the Euphrates—Second Invasion of Cæsar in Britain.

THE provincial appointments of Pompey and Crassus, with that which was at the same time prolonged to Cæsar, seemed to dismember the empire, if not to expose the republic itself to great danger.

Of these three adventurers, Pompey and Cæsar, apart from the evil particularly apprehended in any of their measures, were in themselves subjects of a very dangerous character: neither possessed that dignity of mind which fits the citizen for the equality of persons in a republican state; neither could acquiesce in the same measures of consideration or power which other senators had enjoyed before him; neither could be at ease where he did not command as master, or appear at least as the principal object in every scene in which he was employed.

This paltry ambition, some ages before, might have been held in contempt by the meanest of the people, or must have shrunk before that noble elevation of mind by which the statesman conceived no eminence besides that of high personal qualities employed in public services, or before the austere virtue which confined the public esteem to acts of public utility, supported by unblemished reputation in private life. But in the present age, there was a fashion which set such antiquated notions at defiance, controlled the authority of the state itself, and bestowed on private adventurers the attachment which belonged to the commonwealth, and the deference which was due to its legal head.

In the progress of this republic the character of parties has already repeatedly changed, and the danger to be apprehended from them accordingly varied.

In the first periods of its history, citizens were divided on the supposed distinctions of birth; and, in the capacities of patrician or plebeian, strove for prerogative or privilege with much emulation, as separate orders of men in the commonwealth, but with little jealousy of personal interests.

In a subsequent period, when the invidious part of the former distinction was removed, citizens having no longer the same subject of animosity, as being born to different pretensions, they entered more fully on the competition of individuals, and the formation of separate factions. They strove for the ascendant of aristocratical or democratical government, according to the interest they had formed to themselves in the prevalence of either. They were ready to sacrifice the peace and honour of the public to their own passions, and entered into disputes accordingly, which were in the highest degree dangerous to the commonwealth. They thought personal provocations were sufficient to justify public disorders; or, actuated by vehement animosities, they signalized their victories with the blood of their antagonists. But, though sanguinary and cruel in their immediate executions, they formed no deliberate plans of usurpation to enslave their country, nor formed a system of evils to continue beyond the outrage into which they themselves were led by their supposed personal wrongs or factious resentments.

We are now again once more to change the scene, and to have under our consideration the conduct of men who were in reality as indifferent to any interest of party as they were to that of the republic, or to any object of state; who had no resentments to gratify, or who easily sacrificed those which they felt to the purposes of a cool and deliberate design on the sovereignty of their country. Though rivals, they could occasionally enter into combinations for mutual support, frequently changed their partizans, and had no permanent quarrel but with those who uniformly wished to preserve the republic. They were surrounded by persons who admired the advantages of wealth or of power which were gained at the expense of their country, and who indeed were ready to extol the virtues of any adventurer who led a numerous list of retainers to share in the spoils of the commonwealth.

Peace had now, for some years, except in that part where Cæsar commanded, been established throughout the empire. Instead of military operations, the state was occupied in directing the farms of the revenue, in hearing complaints of oppression from the provinces, and in appointing the succession of military governors. Besides the disputes which have been mentioned relating to the provincial appointments of Crassus and Cæsar, there arose a question on the subject of provinces to be assigned to their immediate predecessors in the consulate, Marcellinus and Philippus. It was strongly urged that Piso, Gabinius, and even Cæsar should be recalled to make way for officers who were entitled to similar command in their turns. This measure was supported in part by Cicero, who vehemently contended, that Piso and Gabinius should be superceded; but urged the continuance of Cæsar in his station, a circumstance for which this able adventurer had taken sufficient precaution not to leave it in hazard from the issue of this debate.

Piso, the nearer relation of Cæsar, in the event of these deliberations, was actually recalled, and, upon his return to the city, complained to the senate, in terms of great asperity, of the injury done to his character. Cicero had ever treated Piso and Gabinius, though in reality but the instruments of Pompey and Cæsar, as the principal authors of his late calamities; and, upon the present occasion, had pronounced against Piso that violent invective which still remains among his works, and which the subsequent conduct of the person against whom it was directed in a great measure disproved.

Gabinius had for some years enjoyed the government of Syria, and during this time had ventured to employ the force of his province in a manner, which, together with some other offences, drew upon him, at his return to Rome, the animadversion of the senate.

It has been mentioned that Ptolemy Auletes, king of Egypt, in exile from his kingdom, had applied to the Romans for aid in recovering his crown; that his suit had been granted, but rendered ineffectual by the regard which was paid to a supposed oracle, which forbade his being reinstated with a military force; that he had withdrawn to Ephesus, and taken sanctuary in the temple, where he waited for some change of fortune in his favour. Lentulus, the governor of Cilicia, to whom the business of restoring him, though without military force, had been committed by the senate, deliberated whether he should not venture to disregard the restriction imposed upon him; march with an army to restore the king of Egypt; possess himself of the wealth which was to be found in effecting such a revolution, and trust to the influence of his friends at Rome in procuring his pardon from the senate, and even their approbation of what he should have done.

Upon this question, Cicero advised Lentulus, if he had a force sufficient to undertake the enterprise, not to lose an opportunity of performing a service which, though not authorised, could be afterwards vindicated. But the business still remained in suspense, when Gabinius arrived in Syria, and probably, by an advice from Pompey to the same purpose with that of Cicero to Lentulus, undertook, in opposition to a decree of the senate and of the augurs, the restoration of this exile to his throne. Having received or bargained for a great sum of money in return for this service, he advanced with a fleet and an army towards Egypt, passed through Palestine, and on his way raised a contribution in that country.

Berenicé, the daughter of Ptolemy, now in possession of the crown, had married Archelaus; and, in order to strengthen her hands against her father, had assumed her husband as a partner in the throne. But the forces of these associated sovereigns were defeated by Gabinius, and Ptolemy was restored to his kingdom. Gabinius, with the treasure amassed on this occasion, hoped to be secure against the attacks which, at his return to Rome, were likely to be made upon him, for his contempt of the senate, and of the oracle, and for the extortion of which he was accused at the same time in Palestine, a part of his own province

In this busy time of Cæsar's faction at Rome, he himself upon an alarm of an invasion from Germany, had been called to defend the northern extremity of Gaul. Two separate hordes, the *Tenchteri* and *Usupetes*, pretending to be driven by superior force from the usual tract of their migrations, had united together, and presented themselves on the banks of the Rhine. The native inhabitants of the right of that river instantly abandoned their habitations, and collecting all the boats that could be found on it to the opposite side, made a disposition to stop the passage of these invaders.

The Germans, observing the precautions which were taking against them, affected to lay aside the design of passing the Rhine; and, by changing their course, made a feint to divert the attention of their antagonists. In execution of this purpose, they continued for three days to retire from the river. At the end of this time, supposing that their opponents would be off their guard, and returned to their ordinary way of life, they suddenly turned their whole cavalry, and in one night repassed the ground over which they had marched on the three preceding days, surprised a sufficient number of boats with which to accomplish their passage, dislodged the natives of the country on the left of the river before them, and from thence continued their migrations betwixt the Rhine and the Meuse, over what is now called the dutchies of Juliers, of Limburg and Luxemburgh.

These invaders amounted, by Cæsar's account, to upwards of four hundred thousand souls;[1] a number which exceeds that of the inhabitants of any city in Europe, besides London and Paris, and which may perhaps raise some suspicion of

1 Cæsar de Bell. Gall. lib. iv. c. 15.

error in copying the text, or of exaggeration in the commentary, which was itself intended to raise the character of Cæsar at Rome. On the question relating to the probability of so great a number, it may be observed, that those migrating nations, certainly unacquainted with many of the arts which are practised to supply and accommodate populous cities, were likewise exempt from the want of such supplies, and acquiesced in what was necessary to mere subsistence. Such nations have less skill and industry than the manufacturer and the trader in a settled and well regulated city; but they have less waste and less misapplication of labour to superfluous and unprofitable purposes than take place in great cities.

The German nations of this age, although they had opportunities to observe among their neighbours the advantages of land property, and of agriculture supported by skill and industry, yet frequently preferred the state of migration, and from policy declined making any permanent settlement, lest the care of property, and the study of unnecessary accommodation, should corrupt or enervate their people. Their favourite occupation was hunting, which they considered as a preparation for war. They traversed the woods and pasture lands, with numerous herds, and subsisted chiefly by milk, flesh, and game. They likewise knew the use of corn, of which they sometimes took a crop from favourable lands; but without remaining any longer than one season to cultivate any particular portion of ground.

They moved in great and numerous bodies, that must to a great extent have covered the face of the country over which they passed; but the body thus moving together were distinguished into separate clans and fraternities, led by their headmen or chiefs, who kept order in their several divisions. They allowed private parties to make war beyond the limits of their own country, and to choose their leaders for this purpose. In peace, the separate clans had no band of connexion. If they had at any time a general government which comprehended the whole of their tribes, it was but a temporary expedient, to which they had recourse in war, and on other pressing occasions.

Under such equality of condition, every individual, who was of a proper age, was obliged to labour for himself, and to subsist by what he procured; and he employed his labour only in procuring what was necessary. In these circumstances, it was not likely that commodities should accumulate; but the numbers of the people, if we may rely on the testimony of Cæsar in this place, or on the evidence of ancient history in general, was certainly great.[1]

The Suevi, before whom the present invaders of Gaul had retired, were said to consist of a hundred cantons, each furnishing annually a thousand men for war, and a like number for the care of their herds and domestic concerns. Such clouds gathering on the frontiers of Cæsar's province, required his presence. He accordingly assembled his army, and advanced between the Rhine and the Meuse.

The Germans, in general, were accustomed to despise the Gauls, and the present invaders expected no formidable opposition on this side of the Rhine; they had ventured to divide their forces, and had sent the great body of their horse upon an excursion beyond the Meuse to scour the lower parts of the country, and upon Cæsar's approach, they offered to treat with him. "They neither sought (they said) nor would they decline a war with the Romans. It was their way to repel injuries with the sword, not to elude them by negotiation. But in the present case, they should nevertheless condescend so far as to assure the Roman general, that they had passed the Rhine from necessity, and not with any intention to invade his province. That if he were pleased to receive them as friends, they were in condition to merit this title, should be content with the ground they had gained, or accept of any other which he might choose to assign them." Cæsar replied, "That while they remained in Gaul, he could not consider them as friends. That if they repassed the Rhine, he had allies in Germany, with whom he should endeavour to join them in a league of defence against the common enemy, by whom they had been thus forced to relinquish their usual bounds."

Having received this answer, the German deputies, to make their report, and to receive the command of their nations, desired a cessation of arms for three days. But Cæsar suspecting that they only meant to amuse him, and to gain time for the junction of all their forces, refused to comply with this request, and continued his march. Being arrived within twelve miles of their camp, he was again met by their deputies, with fresh intreaties that he would advance no farther, at least, that he would give to the cavalry, who made the vanguard of his army, orders to abstain from hostilities for three days: that in this time, they might have an answer from the German nations mentioned in their last conference, and know whether such a league could be formed, as was then proposed, to give them some prospect of safety in returning to their usual haunts.

Cæsar, upon this occasion, seems to have granted a cessation of arms; though on account of what afterwards happened, he is willing to diminish the extent of his own engagement, and to impute the breach of faith which followed to his enemies. He agreed to advance no farther than four miles for the convenience of water, and sent an order to his vanguard to abstain from hostilities. This order, however, had no effect. His advanced guard, consisting of five thousand horse, had an encounter with eight hundred of the enemy.

When this encounter happened, the Germans were not yet joined by the great body of their horse. They had earnestly sued for a cessation of hostilities; it was not likely that they would have begun the attack. Yet Cæsar accused them of a design, with this small party, to surprise the whole of his cavalry.

On the day which followed this skirmish of the cavalry, the leaders and principal men of the Germans leaving their own camp unfurnished with officers, in perfect security, came in great numbers to that of Cæsar to exculpate themselves, to convince him of their pacific dispositions, and to prevent the farther progress of his army. This he thought a favourable opportunity to cut off, by a complete surprise, this enemy entirely, and to finish the war. Having accordingly secured the persons of their leaders, who had thus

1 Cæsar de Bell. Gall. lib. iv. vi.

put themselves in his hands, he advanced with his whole army directly to their camp, easily overcame the few that took arms to oppose him, and without distinction of sex or age, put the whole to the sword. The country, over all the ways by which they endeavoured to escape from the camp, at which the slaughter began, to the confluence of the Rhine and the Meuse, was strewed with the slain.[2]

The Roman people, though seldom sparing of the blood of their enemies, were shocked at the recital of this extraordinary massacre; and when Cæsar, on account of this victory, applied for a thanksgiving, and for the usual honorary decrees of the senate, he was charged with having wantonly invaded the nations of Gaul, and of having dishonoured, by an act of treachery, the arms of the Republic. It was proposed to deliver up his person to those injured nations, that he might expiate, by his own sufferings, so many acts of injustice and impiety, which the gods might otherwise avenge on his country.

The German horse, that by their absence had escaped this calamity which befel their countrymen, appear soon after to have repassed the Rhine, and to have taken refuge with some of the hordes who lived near the sources of the Roer and the Lippe. Thither Cæsar, to spread the terror of his arms, soon afterwards pursued them; and passed the river, not in boats and by surprise, as the Germans were accustomed to do, but in a manner which he seems to have chosen, as better suited to the dignity of the Roman state; he projected a bridge, which was executed in ten days, with much ingenuity, and some ostentation of his power and skill. This work being finished, he placed proper guards at both its extremities, and advanced with the main body of his army into the contiguous parts of Germany, where, on account of the reception given in that quarter to the cavalry who had escaped the late massacre on the Meuse, he laid the country under military execution.

Cæsar, from the place at which he had passed the Rhine, appears to have gone up the eastern side of the river, where he visited the Ubii, a nation inhabiting over against what are now the cities of Bonne and Cologn. Here he had intelligence, that the Suevi, a nation consisting, as has been observed, of a hundred cantons, and mustering two hundred thousand warriors, who were divided into two squadrons that took the field, and conducted the domestic affairs of the nation by turns, were preparing to oppose him; that they had actually sent their wives, children, and superannuated men into places of safety, and had assembled their warriors to meet him. This nation, having an ascendant over all the cantons of Germany, considered it as a proof of their valour, that no nation could pretend to settle on the tract of their migrations, or within reach of their excursions; and that the country, to a great distance around them, was accordingly waste. In their own movements, they never halted above a year to raise a single crop from fields, which, to keep up the martial spirit of their nation, and to preclude the desire of property, with the other passions that accompany settlement, they successively abandoned.

Cæsar, not being prepared to enter on a war with such an enemy, and being sensible that a defeat might expose his army to ruin, while even a victory could procure him no adequate advantage, having remained eighteen days on that side of the Rhine, and employed no more than twenty-eight days in the whole service, chose, while he still had the reputation of victory unimpaired, to repass that river, and to break down his bridge.

This singular man, whose abilities were equal to any task, and who had no occasion to court the public admiration by measures concerted on purpose to obtain it, was, nevertheless, not above ostentation, and gave way to it not only where it might contribute to impose on an enemy, but even where it would do no more than gratify his own vanity, or increase the fame of his actions at Rome. To this motive we may venture to impute the design, which, at an advanced season of the year, and at the end of the same summer in which he had, between the Meuse and the Rhine, vanquished the numerous army of the Tenchteri and Usepetes, in which he had passed the Rhine, and insulted the warlike nations of Germany, even on their own ground, he now projected the invasion of Britain, though surrounded by the ocean, and untouched by the arms of any foreign invader. To carry this design into immediate execution, as soon as he had repassed the Rhine, he continued his march through the low countries, and collected his forces in the neighbourhood of the Portus Itius and Gesoriacum.[3] While we perceive the features of vanity in the leader, we must admire the hardiness and vigour of the troops who could accomplish these services.

The extent of this island, the numbers and character of its people, were then unknown on the continent. Cæsar having in vain endeavoured to procure information in these particulars, sent a galley with orders to explore the coast, and to observe the countenance of the natives. He ordered all his shipping, and even those vessels which he had employed the preceding year against the Veneti,[4] to sail round the Cape of Britanny into the British channel, and repair to the straits which separate this island from the continent.

On the report of these preparations, which evidently pointed at Britain, some of the natives, willing to avert by negotiation the storm which threatened them, sent to the Roman proconsul a submissive message, and offered to come under his protection.

Cæsar, founding a claim to the possession of the island on these advances which were made to him, proceeded with more boldness to the execution of his enterprise. That the natives of the country he was leaving might not create any trouble in his absence, he obliged them to give hostages, and made a proper disposition of his army to keep them in awe. He had assembled at the most convenient haven on the Gaulish side, now supposed to be the Wissan, between Calais and Boulogne,[5] eighty transports or ships of burden, with a number of galleys to accommodate the officers of rank, and their equipage. The remainder of his shipping was yet detained,

2 That branch of the Rhine which falls into the Meuse, changes its name for that of Wall.

3 Calais and Boulogne.

4 In the Bay of Biscay, about Vannes.

5 See Danville's Geography of ancient Gaul.

by contrary winds, in a creek at some miles distance, supposed to be Boulogne; thither he sent his cavalry, with orders to embark on board the ships where they lay. He himself went on board, with the infantry of two legions, at the former haven, and having found a favourable wind and moderate weather, weighed about ten at night, and reached the coast of Britain, on the following day, at ten in the morning. The cliffs, where he first came near to the shore, were high and steep, and the hills were covered with numerous bodies of foot, of men on horseback, and even in wheel carriages, from which the natives of this country were accustomed to make war. It being impossible to land under such difficulties, and in the face of this opposition, he bore away, as it is probable, to the northward about eight miles, with a favourable wind, to some part of the flat shore[1] which surrounds the Downs; and here, in the manner of ancient debarkations, for which the shipping of those times was built, ran his transports aground, and prepared to land.

In the mean time the Britons, who in their march on the hills had kept pace with the Roman galleys, came down to the strand, and advanced even some way into the water to oppose the descent. As the surf on that shore usually runs high, and the Romans, from where their vessels struck, had some way to wade in water that was too deep to allow them the free use of their weapons, they remained on board, and durst not meet the enemy under such disadvantages. Cæsar seeing his men unusually backward, did not think proper in these circumstances to urge them farther; but ordered some of the lightest vessels, which were mounted with missile engines, or manned with archers and slingers, to row as near to the shore as they could on the right and the left of the landing-place, and from thence to gall the enemy. This disposition succeeded so well, that the beach close to the water was presently cleared, and the Romans were left to descend from their ships, and to wade undisturbed to the land.

The Britons, seeing their enemy in possession of the shore, offered to surrender, and were about to deliver their hostages, when an accident happened, which encouraged them again to take arms. On the fourth day after the Roman infantry had landed, a second division of ships, with the cavalry, appeared in sight; but before they could reach the land, were dispersed by a violent storm; part was driven back on the coast of Gaul, part carried down the British channel, and cast in distress on the contiguous shores. Even the shipping, from which the legions had disembarked, lying aground in the surf, or at anchor in a high sea and spring-tide, with which the Italians were unacquainted, were set adrift, or filled with water, many of them beat to pieces or greatly shattered, and rendered unserviceable.

By these misfortunes, Cæsar, although he had made no provision to subsist for the winter in Britain, was in danger of being obliged to remain in it for want of shipping. The natives retracted their late submission, began to drive away the cattle, and to lay waste the country within reach of the Roman camp. They flattered themselves that the enemy would be obliged to depart, or must perish for want of provisions; and that they would, by the example of so vain and calamitous an attempt, deter every stranger for the future from invading their island.

Cæsar, in the mean time, while he employed all his workmen with the greatest diligence in repairing his ships, endeavoured to collect some provisions, and to form a magazine. The natives assembled in great bodies to intercept his foragers, and obliged him to cover them with the whole force of his army. The legions were at first greatly disconcerted by the unusual effect of the British chariots, and by the want of their own cavalry; but as they prevailed in every close fight, the Britons were soon obliged to renew their former submission, and became bound to deliver double the number of hostages they had formerly stipulated. But Cæsar not thinking it proper, with shattered vessels, at the mercy of autumnal winds and stormy seas, to await the performance of this article, ordered the hostages to be sent after him into Gaul, re-embarked with his army, and with the first favourable wind repassed to the continent. At his arrival, he found that the Gauls, upon the report of his late misfortunes, had revolted; that one of his transports, with three hundred men on board, having parted with the fleet, and landing at a separate place, were attacked; and that it was necessary to send the remains of his cavalry to their relief. The Morini, inhabiting what are now the districts of Calais and Dunkirk, with other nations of the low countries, had taken arms against the officers he had stationed to keep them in awe. The campaign therefore concluded with the operations which were necessary to quell this revolt. Labienus subdued the Morini. Quintus, Titurius, Sabinus, and Lucius Cotta having laid waste great part of the low countries, fell back to the coast.

The Roman army was soon after put into winter quarters: and Cæsar, as if sensible that he had made his attempt on Britain with too small a force, and whatever representation he might give of particulars, had incurred the imputation of a miscarriage, gave orders to refit his fleet, and to add, during the winter, as many more ships as possible, built upon a construction more fit for that service, broader, and more capacious in the hull, for the reception of men and horses, and lower in the gunwale, for the convenience of landing. The timber was probably taken from the neighbouring forests; but the materials of his rigging, it is said, were brought from Spain. Having taken these measures to enable him at a more convenient season to renew his expedition into Britain, he set out as usual for Italy, and for the neighbourhood of Rome.

Here he found Pompey and Crassus employed, as has been already related, in obtaining for themselves, and for him, the objects which they had severally in view. Crassus had fixed his thoughts on the treasures of the east, and projected the sale of kingdoms, of which he hoped to have the disposal in that part of the world. Pompey too was gratified in his wishes, had got the command of an army and the patronage of a great province, while he continued at Rome to enjoy his consideration, and was vested with a species of monarchy, in wielding the united powers of the party. Cæsar had provided, what he knew in the end was to decide every controversy, a great

1 Planum et apertum littus. See Cæsar's Commentaries.

army, inured to service, and in a station which gave an easy access to Italy, and the command of Rome. As if secure of their interests, they permitted the election of consuls to

U. C. 699.

L. Dom. Ahenobarbus, App. Claud. Pulcher.

proceed without disturbance; and suffered Lucius Domitius Ahenobarbus, a professed partizan of the senate, together with Appius Claudius, to be elected consuls; Marcus, Cato, and Milo, to be placed in the list of prætors; and several citizens, well affected to the senate, to be admitted into the college of tribunes.

The winter and spring, however, were inactive on the part of the aristocracy. Cato, probably, did not see any public object in which to engage with advantage beyond the duties of his office, in which he endeavoured to restrain by his authority, and by his example, the extravagance and luxury of the age. The dangerous powers which had been recently granted to persons, from whose ambition the republic had much to fear, no doubt greatly alarmed the senate; but this body, though led by Domitius, one of the consuls, by Cato and Milo, two of the prætors, and supported by many of the tribunes, did not think themselves entitled to dispute the validity of those grants, nor to attempt the revocation of what had been so recently confirmed by the people.

Pompey, now master of Spain and part of Africa, with an adequate army, still under the pretence, as has been mentioned, of his commission to furnish the public granaries with corn, remained in Italy, and passed the greater part of his time among his country villas, executing the duties of general purveyor with the assistance of his lieutenants, and managing his intrigues in the city by means of his agents and friends. He was attended by numbers of every rank and condition, who resorted to him with the assiduity of real courtiers, and with a servility, which, in a republic, implied the utmost corruption of manners. He even maintained the appearances of royalty in the state which he assumed, as well as in the influence he acquired. While he himself affected reserve and moderation, in order to appear worthy of his rank, his retainers ever treated him as a great prince, and with his connivance fomented disorders tending to shake the government of the senate; to the end that the republic might be forced to rely on him for support, while he himself affected to decline the burden.

In the management of these intrigues, and in the full hopes of their success, Pompey was now left by Crassus, as well as by Cæsar. The first, in his impatience to take possession of his government, had broken through all the impediments that were placed to hinder his departure from Rome, made haste to Brundusium with his army, embarked, notwithstanding the unfavourableness of the season, and with considerable loss, both of men and of shipping in a storm, made his passage into Macedonia. The prohibition of the prætor still sounded in his ears. He dreaded a vote of the senate or people to recall his commission. It appears, that soon after his departure, a motion had been actually made for this purpose; and that Cicero, though formerly on ill terms with Crassus, being taught by his late sufferings to court the favour of those who could either hurt or protect him, appeared on this question in his favour, and claimed a share in the merit of obtaining the decision that was given to confirm his commission.[2]

But without attending to the state of these deliberations at Rome, Crassus continued his march by Macedonia and the Hellespont into Asia. In passing through Galatia, finding Dejotarus, sovereign of that principality, then of an advanced age, occupied in a work that is becoming at every age, building a new city, and making a settlement for more people; he is said to have observed to the prince, that it was somewhat too late, at his age, to form projects of new settlements; "nor are you very early," replied the other, "in your undertaking the conquest in Parthia."

Crassus was turned of sixty, and having ever considered riches as the surest means of arriving at eminence and power, now joined, to the rapacity of a youthful ambition, the avarice of age. Upon his arrival in Syria, he pillaged the temple of the Jews, and laid hold of treasure wherever else he could find it. He made a pretence of the military levies to be made in the provinces for extorting money; and afterwards, reserving the money he had raised for his own use, neglected the levies. He required of the different districts of his province, and of the neighbouring allies, large quotas of men, and military stores, merely that they might buy exemptions with proportional sums of money.[3] In the same spirit of avarice and rapacity, he invaded the Parthians without any authority from the state, and even without the pretence of a quarrel.

The Parthians, like other dynasties which before or since have arisen in that part of the world, or in the neighbourhood of the Euphrates and the Tigris, were of Scythian extraction. On the decline of the Macedonian power, about two hundred years before the present date, a swarm from the north had migrated to the lower banks of the Tigris, overran the country round Ctesiphon, continued to harass the neighbourhood by their depredations; and, at last, being commanded by Arsaces, the founder of this new kingdom, took possession of an extensive country, and though under a new name, in fact restored the monarchy of Persia.[4]

The Parthian, or new Persian monarchy, being yet in its vigour, was the most formidable power that now any where appeared within reach of the Roman arms. Its forces consisted almost entirely of horse. Part intended for regular charges, cased in heavy armour, and using the lance; part mounted in a lighter manner for expedition and swiftness, and using the bow. While in the field they were attended by herds of spare horses, which they pastured, or drove in the rear of their armies. With this supply, upon any occasional loss, they new-mounted their cavalry, or, having reliefs of fresh horses, performed amazing marches, and frequently presented themselves to their enemies, where it was not expected they could appear. They had different notions of victory and defeat from other nations; they always counted it a victory, when, by their flights, they drew an enemy into straits by hasty and

2 Cicero ad Famil. lib. v ep. 8. ad Crassum.
3 Plut. in Crasso, 11. Dio. Cass. lib. iv. c. 13.
4 Justin. lib. lxi. Dio. Cass. lib. xl, xli.

unguarded pursuits,[1] and often enjoyed the greatest advantage when they seemed to be routed and to fly.

When Crassus advanced to the Euphrates, Orodes king of Parthia, then engaged in a war with Artabazes, on the side of Armenia, sent a deputation to expostulate with the Roman general on the cause of his hostile approach; Crassus made answer, that he would give the reasons of his coming when he arrived at Seleucia, "here," said one of the Parthian messengers (showing the palm of his hand,) "hair will grow before you shall arrive at Seleucia." Crassus proceeded in his march, passed the Euphrates, and ravaged Mesopotamia without any resistance. Having continued his operations until the end of the season, he returned for the winter into Syria.[2] Upon his arrival in this province, he was joined by his son Publius, who had served some years in a considerable rank in the army in Gaul, and was now detached by Cæsar with a thousand horse, and many marks of honour, to act under his father in Syria.

This invasion of Mesopotamia, after the season had become far spent, served only to alarm and provoke the enemy, without procuring any advantage to the arms of the Romans; and hostilities were likely to proceed in the spring with great animosity, when Crassus was to prosecute the war which he had thus commenced on such dangerous ground.

Cæsar, in the mean time, found continual occupation for his troops in Gaul, or in the neighbourhood of that province. He himself, with his usual activity, having been in Italy in the beginning of winter, and having conferred with the persons with whom he entrusted the management of his affairs at Rome, proceeded to Illyricum, upon a report, that this part of his province was infested by the incursions of the Pyrustæ, a warlike tribe on the frontier. Upon his arrival, the invaders withdrew, and were disowned by their nation. The state denied, that they had ever given a commission to make war on the Roman province, became bound for the future to restrain the depredations of private adventurers, and gave hostages for the observance of this article.

Early in spring, Cæsar returned from this expedition to the quarters of his army in the low countries, and found, that in consequence of the orders he had given at the end of the preceding campaign, no less than six hundred transport vessels, and twenty-eight galleys, were actually built in different harbours from Ostend to Boulonge, and in a few days might be ready for sea. He accordingly ordered them to be launched, and directed the whole to assemble at the same port from which he sailed on the preceding year, in order to receive the army on their intended invasion of Britain. But, before his departure, being informed that certain nations on the Moselle were meditating a revolt, and were soliciting the Germans to come over the Rhine to their assistance, to the end that he might not leave any enemy on foot in his rear, and that he might secure the peace of Gaul in his absence, he marched to the Moselle with four legions and eight hundred horse. Upon his arrival he had the good fortune to find the people divided between two leaders, who, being jealous of each other, made their submission separately, and gave the necessary hostages as a pledge for their future behaviour.

With these securities, Cæsar returned to the coast, found all his armed galleys and five hundred and sixty of his transports actually assembled; the other forty transports had been put back by contrary winds, and were still retained at the port at which they had been built. The force intended for this expedition to Britain consisted of five legions, amounting possibly, on the probable supposition that they were not complete, to about twenty thousand men,[3] together with a body of Gauls, including many of their chiefs, whom Cæsar chose to retain with his army, rather as hostages for the fidelity of their countrymen, than as auxiliaries in the war. The fleet consisted of five hundred and sixty transport vessels, twenty-eight armed galleys, with many tenders and small craft, provided by officers for their own conveniency, and for the reception of their equipages; in all eight hundred sail.

The wind being northerly for five-and-twenty days[4] after the fleet was assembled, the troops still remained on shore. At the expiration of this time the wind changed, and the troops began to embark, but were suddenly interrupted by the desertion of a Gaulish chief, who, being averse to the service, thought this a favourable opportunity to disengage himself with his followers. Cæsar considered this desertion as a declaration of war, and being sensible of the danger he might incur in case of any disaster, by having such enemies in his rear, suspended the embarkation, and sent a party of horse in pursuit of the fugitive, who, being overtaken, was killed in attempting to defend himself. His followers were brought back and obliged to embark for Britain.

On the return of the party employed in this service the embarkation proceeded, and being completed at sunset of the same day, the wind being still fair, the fleet weighed, and got into the channel; but the wind soon after having failed, or shifted more to the west, and the tide being set to the northward, they were carried a considerable way in that direction past the port for which they had steered. At day-break, they saw the land of Britain on their left, and seemed to leave some conspicuous part of the island, probably the south foreland, astern: but with the turn of the tide, and the help of their oars, they arrived at noon at a convenient part of the coast not far distant from the landing-place of the former year, but less exposed to the sea. This place we may suppose to have been *Pigwell Bay*, beyond the mouth of the Stour, or the entry to Sandwich Haven.[5]

1 Dio. Cass. lib. xl. c. 15.

2 Dio. lib. xl. Plut. in Crasso.

3 The legions, at the end of this campaign, were reduced to 3,500.

4 See Cæsar's Commentaries.

5 Mr. d'Anville, on a supposition that Cæsar must have passed into Britain by the shortest possible line, fixes upon Hith, about eight miles west of Dover, as the place of his landing in his first invasion of Britain, and, consequently, on some other contiguous part as the place of his landing in the second invasion; but this does not agree, either with the description of the coast, being *planum et apertum littus*, or with the sequel of the story, which places some such river as the Stour to be passed in his march, about twelve miles from the shore. The coast at Hith, though not altogether inaccessible, is steep and hilly, and would have exposed Cæsar to difficulties in his first opera-

The Britons had assembled as formerly to oppose the descent of the Romans; but, on the appearance of so great a fleet, were intimidated, and withdrew from the coast.

Cæsar, flattering himself that he had found a safer road for his ships than that at which he had stationed them in the preceding year, left his fleet at anchor, and guarded against any attempts of the natives by a body of ten cohorts and three hundred horse, that were properly entrenched on the shore. Being informed that the Britons had their forces assembled on a small river (probably the *Stour*), at the distance of ten or twelve miles from his landing-place, he put his army in motion in the night, and at break of day came up with them, dislodged them from their post, and obliged them to withdraw to a place of retreat in that neighbourhood, which, on occasion of their own wars, had been fortified in their manner with a moat, and ramparts of wood. To reduce them in this strong hold, he erected some works, and made regular approaches; but as he had not invested the place, the only effect of his attack was, to force the enemy to abandon it, and to continue their retreat. He had taken his resolution to pursue them on the following day, and had begun his march in three divisions, when it appeared, that the element which is the safeguard of Britain, though not always sufficient to keep its enemies at a distance, yet is subject to accidents which render the attempt of invaders very difficult, and their condition, even when on shore, sufficiently hazardous. To this purpose a messenger overtook Cæsar on his march with tidings, that all his ships, in a storm which arose in the preceding night, had been driven from their anchors, had run foul of each other, that many of them were stranded and wrecked, and all of them greatly damaged.

Cæsar, on this report, suspended his march, and, having fixed the main body of his army in a well-fortified camp; he himself, with a proper escort, returned to the coast. At his arrival, he found that forty of his ships were irrecoverably lost; but that the remainder, though greatly damaged, might be refitted. For this purpose he gave orders in his army, that all who had been instructed in the trade of a carpenter should repair to the sea-port to be employed in refitting the fleet; he called many workmen likewise from Gaul, and gave directions for building a number of new vessels on different parts of that coast; and to guard, for the future, against such accidents as had lately befallen his ships, he ordered that they should be drawn on shore. In this work the army was incessantly employed for ten days, and without intermission even in the night. The fleet, at length, being in this manner secured from the dangers of the sea, and covered by an entrenchment on the side of the land, he returned to his camp, and resumed the operations of his army.

It appears that the natives of Britain, being divided into many small cantons, or separate principalities, and, as usual in such cases, frequently at war among themselves, had been actually at variance when Cæsar arrived; but, during the short respite which the disaster that had befallen his fleet had given them, that they had agreed to suspend their own quarrels, and were assembled in greater numbers than formerly, under Cassivelaunus, a chieftain of Middlesex, or, as Cæsar describes him, a prince residing on the northern banks of the Thames, and at about seventy or eighty miles from the sea.

This chieftain brought into the field a numerous army of infantry, of horsemen, and armed chariots. His knowledge of the woods enabled him to harass the Romans on their march, and, following the tracts that were clear of underwood, not only to gall them with missiles from the thickets, but to charge them likewise with his horsemen and chariots, even in places where the ground seemed least fitted for the movement of such bodies. Encouraged with his success in this species of warfare, he ventured to attack the whole cavalry of the Roman army, which, being on a foraging party, were supported by an entire legion. But the Britons being, in this attempt, defeated with great slaughter, their chief lost courage, or was deserted by his followers, and never more attempted to face the Romans.

Cæsar, finding this enemy remit his ardour, advanced with a quicker pace. From his silence on the subject of any difficulty in passing the Medway, we must suppose him to have followed the vale of the Stour to Ashford, and from thence to have kept on the plains to Maidstone, near to which place the river Medway is everywhere naturally fordable; and from the length of his march, being about eighty miles from the sea, when he came upon the banks of the Thames, we may suppose him to have arrived on that river at the reach which runs from south to north, somewhere between Kingstone and Brentford. There he observes, that the only ford in the river was fenced and guarded; that a row of sharp stakes was driven under water; that the opposite bank was lined with a palisade, and manned by a numerous body of the natives. He nevertheless proceeded to force his way, and by the impetuosity of his attack, drove the enemy from their post, and, without any loss, effected his passage, although his men were obliged to wade up to the chin.

Cassivelaunus had, for some time, made no attempt to resist the Roman army; he had contented himself with observing their motions, and with endeavouring to strip the country before them of every particular by which they could profit on their march. Cæsar, on his part, advanced with the precautions necessary against such an enemy, and, as they had destroyed what could be of immediate use to his army, he destroyed what was left, in order to force the natives to submission. In this state of the war, having leisure and opportunity to observe the condition of the country and the manners of the people, he gives the following account of both: "That on the coast there were colonies from the neighbouring continent, still distinguished by the names of the countries from whence they had come; that these colonies being possessed of agriculture, and well stocked with cattle, were extremely populous; that they had money made of iron or brass; the first of which metals, with great quantities of tin, were found in their own island; the other metal was imported from abroad; that the winter was milder here than in Gaul; that the woods of Britain furnished the same timber with those of Gaul, except the fir and the beech;

---

tions on shore, which he could not possibly have omitted to mention.

and that the houses were built in the same manner in both countries." From this account of the coast he proceeds to observe, "That the inland parts were occupied by the original natives, who, with little corn, subsisted chiefly by milk and the other produce of their herds; that, by a particular superstition, although possessed of hares, of geese, and other fowls, they were forbid to eat of these animals; that they were curious in the ornaments of the person; affected to have bushy whiskers, and long hair; that they stained or painted their bodies of a blue colour, and had no clothes besides the skins of beasts; that they associated in small clubs or fraternities of ten or a dozen in number." And adds a circumstance in which, if he were not deceived, as is common enough to foreigners, by some appearances which were not sufficiently explained to him, he gives a striking example of the diversity which takes place among mankind in settling the canon of external actions. The brothers, the father, and the son, though separately married, and reputed the parents of children, brought forth by their respective wives, yet, without jealousy or imputation of evil, lived with those wives in common.[1]

Cæsar, being on the left of the Thames, made an alliance with the Trinobantes, supposed to have been the inhabitants of Essex and Suffolk. The sovereign of this canton having, in some quarrel with his own people, been expelled from his dominion, had taken refuge with Cæsar in Gaul, and was now, by force of the Roman arms, restored to his kingdom. Five other principalities made their submission at the same time. Cassivelaunus retired to his principal fortress, which, consisting of a palisade and a ditch situated in the least accessible part of the woods, was by the natives, as Cæsar is pleased to express himself, called a town, and was in reality, in case of alarm, a place of retreat for themselves and their cattle. On the approach and attack of Cæsar on one side, Cassivelaunus retired by an outlet on the other, leaving some herds of cattle, and many of his men, to fall into the enemy's hand.

After this defeat, the British prince endeavoured, as a last resource, to give Cæsar some trouble in his rear; and for this purpose sent an order to the four princes of Kent, to assemble their people, and endeavour to force the Roman station, and destroy the Roman shipping, where they lay on the coast. They accordingly attacked the intrenchment, but were repulsed; and Cassivelaunus himself, reduced to despair by the defection of so many of his countrymen, and by his repeated defeats, determined to make his submission. The season of the year being far advanced, and Cæsar, desirous to retire with honour from a country in which he was not prepared to make any settlements, accepted this on easy terms.

A certain tribute was imposed on the nations inhabiting the banks of the Thames, hostages taken for the payment of it, and the invaders, with a numerous assemblage of prisoners, then the only or principal spoils of this island, retired to their ships, which, not being sufficient to receive them at one embarkation, were obliged to return for a second; and in this way successively, without any material accident, transported the whole of the Roman army into Gaul.

CHAPTER II.

Death of Julia the daughter of Cæsar and the wife of Pompey—Trial of Gabinius—Detection of an infamous Transaction of Memmius and Ahenobarbus—Revolt of the Low Countries—Military Execution against the Inhabitants of the Country between the Rhine and the Meuse—Operations of Crassus in Mesopotamia—His Death—Competition for the Consulate—Death of Clodius—Riot in the City—Pompey sole Consul—Trial of Milo.

WHILE the Roman army was in Britain, there happened, by the death of Julia, the daughter of Cæsar and the wife of Pompey, a great change in the discontinuance of the relation which subsisted between them, and in the separation of their supposed political interests. The connection which then came to be dissolved, had been devised as a bond of confederacy between parties whose interfering objects of ambition must have otherwise, on many occasions, excited their mutual jealousy. Neither the father-in-law, nor the son, was likely to sacrifice his ambition to mere affection, but each may have expected, that the other should be, in some degree, the dupe of his relation, and should abate a little of the jealousy to which he was, by his situation and his objects, so naturally inclined. This passion, however, we may believe was far from having been extinguished in the mind of either. The choice which Pompey made of Spain for his province, with a military command for a term of five years, probably proceeded from a desire to retain his superiority over Cæsar, and to have in his power, in case of a breach between them, a province, though less contiguous to Italy than that which was held by Cæsar, not less fitted to furnish formidable armies and the resources of war.

Notwithstanding these effects of jealousy, while the familiar relation of father-in-law and son subsisted between Cæsar and Pompey, and while Crassus continued to hold a species of balance in their councils, they seemed to acquiesce in a participation of consequence and power. But the death of Julia, and that likewise of the child of which she had been delivered only a few days before her death, put an end, not only to any real cordiality in this connection, but even to any semblance of friendship, and rendered them, from this time forward, mutually jealous of the advantages they severally gained, whether in respect to force in the provinces, or to state and popularity at Rome.

It is observed, that, from this date, Cæsar became more than formerly attentive to reports from the city, and more careful of his intelligence

1 See Cæsar's Commentaries on his last expedition to Britain.

from thence;[2] and that he endeavoured to gain every person who might be of consequence in deciding the contest which he perceived must arise. Among these he paid his court in particular to Cicero, who was likely, about this time, to devote himself to Pompey, and whom he wished, at least, to keep in suspense between them: for this purpose, as appears from their correspondence, he applied, as usual, to his vanity, and, while he was piercing the woods of Britain in pursuit of Cassivelaunus and his painted followers,[3] affected to read and to admire verses which were sent to him by a person much more esteemed for his prose than his poetry.

The Roman army had been tempted into Britain by the hopes of finding mines of silver, but were disappointed; for, besides slaves, they found no booty in that island. Such probably likewise were the principal spoils of Gaul; yet we find their general, in consequence of his conquests in that country, enabled to expend great sums in supporting his influence at Rome. While Pompey procured his own appointment to the command of an army, in order to keep pace with Cæsar in the provinces, Cæsar, in his turn, projected public works at Rome to vie with the magnificence of Pompey, and with that of other citizens, who made such works a part of their policy, to gain the people. For this purpose Cæsar proposed to build a Basilica,[4] and to enlarge the forum, at an expense of six millions Roman money, or about fifty thousand pounds; to rail in the field of Mars with marble ballisters, and to surround the whole with a colonade or portico extending a thousand paces, or about a mile.

In these several works Cæsar affected to consult or to employ Cicero in a manner which flattered his vanity, and renewed his hopes of being able also to direct his councils,[5] in what related to matters of state.

In the mean time, parties in the city, though engaged on the side of different competitors for office at the approaching elections, were likewise intent on the cause of Gabinius. This officer, while yet in his province, had been impeached for disobeying the orders of the senate, and for contempt of religion in his expedition to Egypt. But having, by the influence of Pompey, and of Cæsar, eluded his first attack, he set out for Rome in great confidence, and, on his journey, gave out, that he was to demand a triumph. But, upon his approach to the city, hearing in what manner the senate and people were affected towards him, he thought proper to make his entry in the night; and being arrived, on the eighteenth of September, did not even venture to appear in the senate for ten days. No less than three prosecutions were preparing against him; for treason, for extortion in his province, and for other crimes. The first day on which he presented himself in the senate, the consuls, when he would have withdrawn, commanded him to stay. And, having called the farmers of the revenue from Syria, who attended with a complaint from the province, bid them state their charge.

An altercation ensued, in which Cicero, mindful of the injuries he had received from Gabinius, took a principal part against him, and pronounced an invective, which the other returned with the abusive appellation of fugitive, in allusion to his late exile.[6] Yet, soon after, when this criminal was brought to trial for extortion in his province, Cicero, as will afterwards be mentioned, undertook, at the solicitation of Pompey, to appear in his defence.

Before this trial for extortion took place, C. Memmius, one of the tribunes, on the ninth of October delivered to the people, with great force, a charge of treason against Gabinius.[7] The judgment of the tribes being called, and sentence of condemnation likely to pass, while the lictors were preparing to seize their prisoner, his son, a young man, with much filial piety, a virtue highly esteemed by the Romans, threw himself at the feet of the tribune, and being rudely spurned on the ground, happened to drop his ring, the badge of Roman nobility; the spectators were moved; Lelius Balbus, another of the tribunes, interposed, and, with the general approbation of the people, commanded the process to stop.[8]

The other prosecutions nevertheless were continued against Gabinius. One before the prætor Alfius, in which, though the majority of the judges voted to acquit, there were twenty-two, out of seventy, who voted guilty.[9] Another before Cato, on a charge of depredation in his province, to the amount of quater millies, four hundred millions Roman money, or about three millions sterling; in this last was condemned, and forced into exile. At this trial, Pompey and Cæsar continued to employ their influence in his favour. And Cicero, although he had hitherto treated Gabinius as the author of his own exile, being reconciled to Pompey and Cæsar, no longer continued at variance with a person, who had been no more than their tool or instrument in procuring his misfortunes, and condescended, on this occasion, though ineffectually, to plead his cause.[10]

The approaching elections gave rise to competitions and intrigues more connected with the state of the republic, and more an indication of the manners which then prevailed. The poorer citizens came to depend for their subsistence on the distributions of corn and other gratuities, which were made or procured by those who courted popularity, or who aspired to the offices of state. Corruption became every day more flagrant and less disguised; and the laws against bribery were losing their force for want of persons to prosecute a crime, of which so many either wished to reap the benefit, or which many were so strongly tempted to commit. To supply this defect, Cato moved in the senate, that every one elected into office should be subjected to an inquest, even if no one should prosecute;[11] and actually obtained an edict, requiring the ordinary judges, that were named for trials within the year, to take cognizance of the means by which candidates succeeded to office; and to set those aside who were found to have incurred the penal-

2 Cicero ad Quint. frat. lib ii. ep. 15. et lib. iii. ep. 1.
3 Ibid. lib. ii. ep. ult. Ad Atticum, lib. iv. ep. 16.
4 What the Romans called a Basilica or palace, was a kind of exchange, containing porticoes for merchants, and other public accommodations.
5 Cicero ad Att. lib. iv. ep. 16.

6 Cicero ad Quint. frat. lib. iii. 7 Ibid.
8 Val. Max. lib. viii. c. 1.
9 Cicero ad Att. lib. iv. ep. 16
10 Dio. lib. xxxix. c. 63. Cicero ad Quint. frat lib. iii. ep. 1 et 3.
11 Plutarch. Cicero ad Att. lib. iv. ep. 16.

ties of corruption.[1] The tribunes interposed their negative, or suspended the effect of this resolution, until an act of the people should be obtained to confirm it. The proposal gave great offence to the parties concerned; and Cato, being attacked by the populace, narrowly escaped with his life. He afterwards, in a full assembly of the more respectable citizens, was favourably heard on this subject. But Terentius, one of the tribunes, still persisting in his negative, this attempt to restrain the corrupt practices of those who canvassed for office had no effect.

The candidates themselves, in the mean time, if each could have trusted the laws for restraining others, as well as himself, from the practice of giving money; or if any number of them could have relied upon an agreement to be entered into among themselves to refrain from it, would, it is probable, have been glad to be relieved from an abuse which rendered their pretensions so expensive and so precarious. Moved by these considerations, candidates for the office of the tribune entered into an agreement not to bribe, and deposited each a sum of money[2] in the hands of Cato, to be forfeited by any person who should be found acting in contravention to their treaty.[3] One of them, however, was detected in giving money, and accordingly forfeited his pledge.

In the competition for the consulate, corruption was carried to the greatest excess. An office was opened, at which the candidates dealt out money to the people, who came in the order of their tribes to receive it.[4] A gratuity of ten millions of sesterces,[5] was offered to any person who should secure the vote of the first century, or, as it was called, the *Prerogativa*. The demand for money to be employed in this species of traffic became so great, that by the first of July, interest rose from four to eight per cent.[6] All the four candidates, Memmius, M. Scaurus, Cn. Domitius, and M. Messala, mutually raised prosecutions for bribery against each other; and in the course of these transactions, it appeared that Caius Memmius, once a vehement partizan of the senate, had made his peace with Cæsar, and was now supported by his party at Rome.

Memmius, it may be remembered, having been prætor at the expiration of Cæsar's consulate, brought a charge of high misdemeanour in office against him. And Cæsar appeared for some time to resent this attack; but was in reality as little to be diverted from his purpose by resentment, as he was by affection, and knew how to choose his friends from among those who had the resolution to provoke, as well as from among those who inclined to serve him. Cæsar accordingly made use of this opportunity to separate Memmius from the rest of his enemies, and by his means brought to light a scene of corruption, in which Memmius himself, with other professed supporters of the senate, had been concerned, and which furnished Cæsar, and the supposed popular party, with a great triumph against these pretenders to purity and public virtue.

It appeared that, among other irregularities at Rome in the administration of government, even laws, and supposed acts of the senate or people, could be forged or surreptitiously obtained. The present consuls, Cn. Domitius Ahenobarbus, and Ap. Claud. Pulcher, entered into a compact with those two who were candidates to succeed them, Caius Memmius and C. Domitius Calvinus: the two first, to secure their own nomination to lucrative provinces at the expiration of their consulship: the two others now standing for this office, to secure their elections. The parties agreed to forge an edict of the senate and of the people, fixing the consular provinces. And a sum of money was deposited by the candidates in the hands of the consuls, to be forfeited, if they did not support this forgery, with the evidence of three augurs, who should vouch for the passing of the law in the assembly of the people, and two senators of consular dignity, who should swear they were present when this allotment of provinces was confirmed by the senate, although it was notorious that no meeting of the senate had been held for this purpose.

Memmius being gained by the parties of Cæsar and Pompey, was persuaded to sacrifice his own reputation in order to ruin that of Domitius Ahenobarbus. He laid this strange agreement, which had been drawn up in writing, together with the bonds which had been granted upon it, before the senate. Appius Claudius braved the detection; but Ahenobarbus, professing himself to be of a party which contended for purity and reformation of manners, incurred much disgrace and reproach.

From this transaction it should appear, not only that the assemblies of the people were extremely irregular and tumultuary, and might be made up of such persons as were by any party purposely brought to the comitium; but that even the meetings of the senate might be packed; that their proceedings were carelessly recorded, and might be easily forged. The numbers required to form a comitium or assembly of the people not being fixed, any convention of persons brought from any part of Italy, occupying the usual place of assembly, might take upon them the designation and powers of the Roman people; and as the fluctuating sovereignty of the people by this means passed from one party to another, its orders were often surreptitious and contradictory, and every law might be considered as the mandate of a party or faction, not as the will of the community.[7] Great as these disorders were, there were at all times numerous parties who had an interest in the continuance of them; and the age, though suffering under the most grievous abuses, was still more averse to the necessary reformations.

The infamy of this recent transaction produced a delay of the elections, until the term of the present consuls in office was expired. An interregnum accordingly ensued. The partizans of Pompey hinted the necessity of naming a dictator. He himself affected great reserve, in expectation that when the present troubles came to their height, the powers necessary to suppress them would, by general consent, be pressed into his hands.

In the mean time, Cæsar, whose councils had so great a share in determining these events, was detained in the northern parts of Gaul, and was

1 Cicero ad Att. lib. iv. ep. 16.

2 Quingena, 500,000 Roman money, about 4000*l*.

3 Plutarch. Cicero ad Att. lib. iv. ep. 15 ad Quint. frat. lib. ii. c. 12.

4 Ad Att. lib. iv. ep. 17.

5 About 80,000*l*.

6 Ad Quint. frat. lib ii. ep 15. Idibus quintilibus fœnus fuit bessibus ex triente

7 Dion. Cassius, lib. xxxix. c. 65.

obliged, contrary to his usual practice, to pass the whole winter on this side of the Alps. On his return from Britain, finding that the harvest in Gaul had been unfavourable, he was tempted, in order to facilitate the subsistence of his army, to extend his quarters much farther than had been his ordinary practice. Labienus, with one division, was sent to the Moselle; Titurius Sabinus, with another, to the neighbourhood of the Meuse, near to what are now the districts of Liege and Maestricht. Quintus Cicero was posted on some of the branches of the Scheld or the Sambre, in the county of Hainault. And the whole army, by this disposition, extended from the Seine to the Meuse, about Maestricht, and from the sea to the neighbourhood of Treves. The distance at which the posts were placed from each other being observed by the natives, who still bore with impatience the intrusion and usurpation of these strangers, tempted them to form a design against each of these quarters apart, and by cutting them off, to rid their country for ever of these imperious and insatiable guests, who acted as proprietors in every territory on which they were received, and branded every act of resistance to their unjust usurpation with the name of defection and rebellion.

In execution of this design, Ambiorix, leader of the nations which were situated in the angle, above the confluence of the Meuse and the Rhine, and round the quarters of Sabinus, which are supposed to have been at a place which is now called Tongres, suddenly presented himself with a numerous body before the Roman station, and endeavoured to force the intrenchment; but being repulsed, had recourse to an artifice in which he succeeded. Affecting a great regard for the Romans, he desired that he might have an opportunity to communicate to their general a matter of the most serious importance. An officer being sent to him upon this request, he pretended to disclose, with the utmost regret, a secret design formed by the Gauls to cut off the Roman army; gave notice that a great body of Germans had already passed the Rhine to join in the execution of this design; that he himself had been very much averse to the project; but had been obliged to give way to the popular impetuosity of his countrymen, which he could not resist; that all he could do was to warn the Romans of their danger, to the end that they might, in the most effectual manner, consult their own safety. If they chose, while it was in their power, to withdraw, and to gain the nearest station of their own people, he had influence enough to hinder their being molested on the march: but if they should hesitate for any time, or wait till the Germans arrived, it would no longer be in his power to avert the storm with which they were threatened.

This admonition, even from an enemy, after a long debate in the council of war, determined Sabinus to quit his present situation. He accordingly began a march of fifty miles towards the quarters of Quintus Cicero. And falling into a snare, which the treacherous chieftain had laid for him, perished, with an entire legion and five cohorts, of whom the greater part were put to the sword. Some got back to the station they had left, but finding no security in that place, killed themselves in despair. A very few escaped, by the woods, to Labienus on the Moselle.

The natives, thus encouraged by the success of their first operation, pushed on to the quarters of Quintus Cicero, armed and assembled the country as they passed and arrived with such expedition, that they intercepted all the parties which were abroad in search of wood, provisions, or forage, and made so unexpected an attack on the Roman station, as left Cicero scarcely time sufficient to man his entrenchments. They renewed the artifice which they had practised with so much success against Sabinus. But Cicero, though unacquainted with the manner in which that officer had been betrayed, determined to remain in his camp, and as soon as possible to give intimation of his danger to Cæsar. For this purpose he strengthened his post with additional works, and published a reward to the first person who should succeed in carrying intelligence to the nearest quarter of the Roman army.

The enemy being about sixty thousand men, formed a circle, facing to the centre, quite round the Roman intrenchment; and, the more effectually to cut off all communication of supplies or intelligence from without, effected a line of circumvallation, consisting of a ditch fifteen feet wide, and a breastwork eleven feet high, extending over a circumference of fifteen miles.[8] In this work, being unprovided with intrenching tools, they were obliged to cut the turf with their swords. But having begun it by a sufficient number of hands in all its parts at once, they, according to Cæsar's account, completed the whole in three hours.

From this line, which they formed by the direction of some Italian deserters, they made regular approaches to the Roman intrenchment; and having pushed their turrets quite up to the ditch, threw, by means of their slings, red hot bullets and burning darts into the thatch with which the huts of the camp were covered; set them on fire; and, in the midst of the confusion which arose from this circumstance, endeavoured to scale the palisade and the parapet.

While Cicero continued, with great ability and courage, to withstand these attacks, the persons who endeavoured to carry the tidings of his situation to Cæsar were repeatedly intercepted, and cruelly tortured, to deter others from renewing the same attempt. The intelligence, however, by means of a native Gaul, who, availing himself of the dress, manners, and language of his country passed unobserved through the lines of the enemy, was at last carried to the head quarters of the Roman army.

Cæsar, as usual, trusting more to despatch and rapid execution than to the numbers of his men, left a legion at Samarobriva[9] to guard his stores, magazines, and baggage, and with two other legions, not exceeding seven thousand men, being all that, without hazarding an improper delay, he could assemble, hastened his march to the quarters of Cicero. He despatched two messengers, one to Labienus, with orders, if possible, to put the troops under his command in motion towards the Meuse, and another to Quintus Cicero himself, with hopes of assurances of immediate relief. The first messenger found Labienus beset with a numerous army of Gauls, and therefore unable to move; the other, having come to the foot of

8 Cæsar de Bell. Gallico, lib. v. c. 42.
9 Amiens

Cicero's intrenchment, cast the billet which contained the intelligence, wound up on the shaft of a dart, against one of the towers, where it stuck, and hung for some days unobserved; but being found at last, it was carried to Cicero, and gave notice of Cæsar's approach. At the same time the fire and the smoke of his camp began to appear on the plain, and gave both parties equal intimation of his coming.

The Gauls, without delay, got in motion with all their force, and having abandoned their lines of circumvallation, advanced to meet Cæsar. Cicero sent him intelligence of this movement of the enemy. The armies arrived nearly at the same time on the opposite sides of a brook running in a hollow track between steep banks, which neither party in the presence of the other could venture to pass.

Cæsar, supposing that the great inequality of his numbers might inspire the Gauls with contempt, endeavoured, by exceeding his usual caution, to feed their presumption. He affected to choose a ground that was fit to secure his camp; and contracting its limits, crowded both his legions within the dimensions which were usually occupied by one. In this posture he meant to await the effects of the enemy's temerity, or, if they declined passing the brook, to avail himself of the security they were likely to feel, and to attack them in their own camp by surprise.

The event justified Cæsar in his expectation. The Gauls, trusting to the superiority of their numbers, thought they had nothing to dread but the escape of their enemy; and they accordingly passed the rivulet, with intention to force his lines. Instead of defending his camp, he poured forth his army at once from all its avenues, and, with the advantage of a surprise upon those who came to attack him, and by the great superiority of the Romans, when mixed sword in hand with an enemy, routed, dispersed, or forced to lay down their arms, the greater part of this multitude which came to attack him with so much ferocity and confidence.

By this victory Cæsar not only relieved Quintus Cicero, whom he joined the same evening, but likewise dispelled the cloud which hung over the other quarters of his army, of which many had been at the same time invested by the natives. These insurrections, however, which kept all the inhabitants of the low countries in motion, even in the most unfavourable season, gave him the prospect of an early and a busy campaign, and so much disconcerted the plan which he had formed for the winter, that he was hindered from making his usual journey across the Alps.

During this necessary stay in Gaul, it does not appear that the interests which Cæsar commonly studied were suffering in any considerable degree at Rome. The civil government in the city was hastening fast to its ruin, and the longest sword was soon likely to decide the sovereignty of the empire. The office of consul was unoccupied, and continued to be so from the beginning of January to the middle of July. In all this time there was no administration of justice,[1] nor any exercise of magistracy, besides that of the interrex, who, during the five days of his appointment, was supposed to have no other object besides the elections of consuls. This object was vainly attempted by every successive interrex The popular tumults were fomented by the tribunes who were in the interest of Pompey; and some prodigy or unfortunate presage, was continually alleged, to prevent the elections. The senate striving to put an end to these disorders, even ventured to commit to prison Q. Pompeius Rufus, a tribune, who seemed to be most active in disturbing the public peace. The occasion seemed ripe for the execution of Pompey's design; and accordingly another tribune, Lucceius Hirrus, known to be in the secret of Pompey's intrigues, moved that he should be named dictator.[2] He himself, as usual on such occasions, absented himself from the assembly, and still kept it in his power to avow or disown the measures of his creatures.

This motion was strongly opposed by Cato, and appeared to be extremely disagreeable to all the principal members of the senate.[3] Pompey therefore thought proper to disclaim it, denied his having encouraged the tribune to make it, and even refused to accept of the dictatorship; adding, That he had been called to the exercise of great powers earlier than he himself had expected; and that he had always resigned his powers earlier than had been expected by any one else.[4] In this was expressed the great object of Pompey's ambition; he preferred this point of estimation to the possession of power. The odium of the proposed measure fell upon Lucceius Hirrus, the tribune who moved it, and had nearly brought upon him a deposition or degradation from his office. Cato, willing to gain Pompey, or to confirm him in the virtue he assumed, pronounced an encomium on this act of moderation, recommended the republic to his care, and encouraged him in the resolution he had taken, to prefer the esteem of his fellow-citizens even to the power of disposing of their lives and fortunes at his pleasure. Pompey from thenceforward joined with the senate in bringing on the elections; and accordingly, after seven months interval of confusion and anxiety, Cn. Domitius Calvinus and M. Valerius Messala were chosen and entered on office in the month of July

U. C. 700.

Cn Dom. Calvinus M. Val Messala, Coss.

While Pompey was endeavouring, by his intrigues in the city, to make a species of monarchy in his own person appear to be necessary, Cæsar was in fact providing himself with the only means which, in so distracted a state, can either acquire or preserve such a power. He was joining three additional legions to the establishment of his province; and, under pretence of his late loss on the Meuse, or of his fears of a general defection in Gaul, he had the address to bring into his own service a legion which had been recently formed in Italy under the commission of Pompey. These he now borrowed, and either actually debauched, or rendered of doubtful fidelity if ever it should be proposed to recall or employ them against himself.

While he took these measures for the augmentation of his forces, and before the end of winter, having intelligence that the Nervii, or the inhabitants of the county of Hainault, held frequent consultations together, and were about to take

1 Plutarch. in Pompeio, p. 4?3.

2 Plutarch. in Pompeio. D. Con. Cicero epist. ad Quint. frat. lib. iii. ep. 9.

3 Ibid. 4 Plutarch. in Vit. Pompeii.

arms, he determined to prevent them; and for this purpose, with four legions drawn from the nearest quarters, he marched into their country, and, without meeting with any opposition, destroyed their habitations, moved away their cattle, and made many prisoners. He continued these severities until the natives, reduced to great distress, implored his mercy, and gave hostages for their future submission.

Having, in the course of this winter, called the nations of Gaul to a general convention at an island in the Seine,[5] he began the operations of the following summer by punishing some of the cantons,[6] who had absented themselves from that assembly, and who, by this act of disrespect, had incurred his resentment, or given him suspicion of hostile intentions. The principal object of the campaign, however, was the punishment of Ambiorix and his countrymen, by whom, as has been related, Sabinus, with a legion and five cohorts, had been circumvented and cut off in the beginning of the preceding winter.

As the Romans scarcely appear to have conceived that any people had a right to withstand their invasions, and treated as rebellion every attempt a nation once vanquished made to recover its liberties, Cæsar states it as necessary for the credit of the Roman army, for the security of their quarters, and for preventing such acts of supposed perfidy for the future, that the subjects of Ambiorix should suffer an exemplary punishment. To secure this effect, he projected two expeditions; one to the right and the other to the left of this enemy's country, with intention to preclude them from any retreat or assistance on either side. He penetrated into the woods and marshes of Brabant, or on the left of the Meuse, and obliged the inhabitants to come under engagements not to assist or harbour his enemies.

From thence, still avoiding to give any alarm to the nation which was the principal object of these operations, and having formerly sent his baggage under an escort of two legions to the Moselle, he now followed in the same direction with the whole army; and finding that Labienus had, by a recent victory, vanquished all his enemies in that quarter, he continued his march to the Rhine, constructed a bridge on that river a little way higher up than the place at which he had formerly passed it, and once more set foot upon German ground.

The Suevi, and other great migrating nations of that continent, having moved to the eastward, leaving nothing behind them but deserts, on which no army could subsist, he contented himself with exacting hostages from the Ubii and other contiguous nations, to secure their neutrality, or rather to make sure of their concurrence in the future operations of the war. And with these pledges here passed the Rhine, broke down part of his bridge, and left a guard of twelve cohorts properly intrenched to secure the remainder.

From thence he sent forward his cavalry, with orders to make quick and silent marches into the countries between the Rhine and the Meuse, and himself followed with the infantry. Hitherto Ambiorix and his countrymen, who were the principal objects of all these operations, had taken no alarm, and had enjoyed such perfect security, that the leader himself, upon the arrival of Cæsar's horse, narrowly escaped, and had no more than time, by a general intimation, to warn his people to consult their own safety. They accordingly separated, part hid themselves in the contiguous marshes, others endeavoured to find refuge with some neighbouring nations, or fled to the islands that were formed at the confluence of the Meuse and the Rhine.

Cæsar, as if he had been forming a party of hunters, separated his army into three divisions; sent Labienus with one division to pursue those who had fled to the confluence of the two rivers; Tribonius with the second up the course of the Meuse; and he himself, in pursuit of Ambiorix, directed his march to the Scheld. His orders were, that each division should put all they met to the sword, and calculate their time so as to return to the place of general rendezvous in seven days.

To render this execution the more complete, all the neighbouring nations were invited to partake in the spoils of a country that was doomed to destruction. Among the parties who were allured by this invitation, two thousand German horse had passed the Rhine, and continued to ravage all before them in a body. Cæsar, in making a disposition for his present march, had lodged the whole baggage of his army at the station, (supposed to be Tongres) which in the preceding winter had been fortified for the quarters of Sabinus. Here the works being still entire, he left a guard with his baggage under the command of Quintus Tullius Cicero.

The Germans, in the present instance, knowing no distinction of friend or enemy, ceased to plunder the natives of the country, and turned all their thoughts on seizing the baggage of the Roman army. Their coming was so little expected, that the traders and suttlers who had erected their stalls and displayed their merchandise, as usual, without the intrenchment, had no time to save their effects. Numbers of Cicero's baggage-guard were abroad in search of forage. The remainder with difficulty manned the avenues of their post, and must have been forced, if the foragers, upon hearing the noise with which the Germans began the attack, had not returned to their relief, and forced their way through the enemy, who, mistaking them for the vanguard of Cæsar's army, thought proper to consult their own safety by an immediate flight.

Cæsar, upon his return to the post at which he had left his baggage, censured the officer commanding the guard for having divided his party, and for having omitted, on the supposition of any degree of security whatever, any part of the precautions usual upon such a duty. He proceeded to complete the revenge he had projected against the unhappy followers of Ambiorix, with sending parties in every direction to burn every house, and lay waste every field that had been formerly spared or overlooked; and this being done on the approach of winter, made the destruction complete, as the few who escaped the sword were certain to perish by famine, or by the asperity of the season.

Cæsar having in this manner made an example, which he supposed was to overawe all the nations of that neighbourhood, he withdrew with his army from a country in which he had made it impossible for any numbers of men to subsist

5 Now Paris. 6 The Senones and Carnutes.

and having stationed two of his legions on the Moselle and the remainder on the Marne, on the Seine, and the Loire, he himself hastened into Italy, where all his views and preparations ultimately centred. The scene of political intrigue, in which Crassus had hitherto bore a part with Pompey and himself, was now, in consequence of recent events on the other extremity of the empire, about to undergo a great change, that was likely to affect the conduct of all the parties concerned.

In the spring, Crassus had taken the field on the frontier of Syria, with seven legions, four thousand horse, and an equal number of light or irregular troops. With this force he passed the Euphrates, was joined by an Arabian chieftain, who is mentioned by historians under different names, of Acbarus[1] or Ariamnes, in whom, on account of his supposed knowledge of the country, the Roman general had placed great confidence. Here he expected likewise to have been joined by Artabazes, king of Armenia; but Orodes, now on the throne of the Parthians, prevented this junction, by invading the kingdom of Armenia in person, while he left Surena, a young warrior of great reputation, in Mesopotamia, to oppose the Romans.

Crassus intended to have followed the course of the Euphrates to where it approaches nearest to Seleucia and Ctesiphon, the capital of the Parthian kingdom; but was dissuaded by Ariamnes, who prevailed on him to direct his march eastward on the plains to meet Surena, as not in a condition to oppose him. Some parties too, that were advanced to examine the country, reported that they had been on the tract of departing cavalry, but that no enemy was any where to be seen. Thus Crassus was induced to quit the Euphrates, and agreeably to the directions of his guide, took the rout of Carræ eastward. This place he fortified in his way, and occupied with a garrison. From thence, in a few marches, he arrived in sandy and barren plains, without trees, herbage, or water. While the army, though discouraged by these appearances, still continued its march, a few horsemen belonging to the advanced guard returned to the main body with signs of terror, and brought an account that their division had been surrounded by numerous bodies of horse, and to a few cut off; that the enemy were advancing apace, and must soon appear. Crassus at first fearing to be outlined by the enemy, extended his front as far as he possibly could; but recollecting that the Parthians were all on horseback, and by the rapidity of their motions might easily gain either or both his flanks, so that it was proper to present a front in every direction, he changed his disposition from a line to a square, having his cavalry on the angles.

The Roman army being thus compacted, the Parthians appeared on every side, came within reach of an arrow-shot, and galled them without intermission. The weapons of the Romans in this situation availed them nothing; even the shield could not cover them from arrows, that showered from every quarter, and in many different directions. They stood, however, in their place with some degree of courage, in hopes that the quivers of the Parthians must soon be exhausted, and that this enemy would be obliged either to join them in close fight, or to retire. But they found themselves deceived in this expectation, observing that the enemy had a herd of camels in their rear, loaded with arrows, and that the quivers of those in the front were continually replenished from thence. At the same time Ariamnes, the Arabian, deserted, and was perceived to go over to the enemy. The desertion of this traitor, by discovering that his pretended attachment, and his counsel, which had been unhappily followed, was only a piece of barbarous treachery to draw the army into its present situation, completed the general discouragement which the Romans had already begun to feel. They crowded together in despair, and oppressed with heat and thirst, or stifled with dust, they continued for a while, like beasts caught in a snare, to present an easy prey to their enemies.

In this extremity, Crassus determined to make an effort with his cavalry to drive the enemy so far off, as not to be able to reach his infantry with their arrows. His son Publius accordingly formed the Roman horse into one body, and made a general charge. The Parthians gave way in seeming disorder. The young man advanced with great impetuosity as against a flying enemy, and in hopes of completing his victory: but the Parthians, under cover of the dust which every where arose, instead of flying before him, as he supposed, were actually turning on his flanks, and even falling behind him to encompass his rear. The legions at the same time, happy to be relieved from the attack of the enemy, quitted their ground, and for a little resumed their march, which enabled the Parthians the more effectually to surround the horse; but the father, recollecting the danger to which he exposed his son, again prevailed on them to halt. In this situation, a few of the horse arrived, with accounts that they had been surrounded, that Crassus, the son, was slain, and the whole cavalry cut off, except a few who escaped to the father with these melancholy tidings.

Night, however, was fast approaching, and the Parthians, on a sudden, withdrew, sensible that their way of fighting would expose them to many disadvantages in the dark. It was always their practice to retire at night to a considerable distance from the enemy whom they had harassed by day, and upon these occasions they generally fled like an army defeated, until they had removed so far as to make it safe for them to pasture their horses, and to store up their arms. Crassus, apprised of this practice, took the benefit of the night to continue his retreat, and abandoning the sick and wounded of his army, made a considerable march before it was day. But the advance he had gained, was not sufficient to hinder his being overtaken by the same enemy, and again involved in the same distress. Having his defeats and his flights renewed on every succeeding day, he arrived at last at the post which he had fortified at Carræ, and there found some respite from the attacks of the enemy. At this place, however, it was not possible to make any considerable stay, as the whole provisions of the army were lost or consumed, and such supplies as the country around might have furnished, were entirely in the power of the enemy. Nor was it convenient to depart immediately. The moon was then at the full, and night was almost as favourable to the Parthians as day. In these circumstances, it was determined to wait for the

1 Plutarch. et Dion. Cass.

wane of the moon, and then, if possible, to elude the enemy again by marches in the night.

In this interval, the army mutinied against Crassus, and offered the command to Caius Cassius; but he, although desired even by Crassus himself, declined to accept of it.[2] The troops of consequence no longer obeyed any command, and separated into two bodies. The first went off by the plains on the nearest way into Syria: the other took the route of the mountains; and if they could reach them before the enemy, hoped to escape into Cappadocia or Armenia. The first division was accompanied or commanded by Cassius, who, though with considerable loss, led them back to Syria. The other, with Crassus, himself, was pursued by Surena, and harassed on every ground where the Parthian horse could ply on their flank or their rear. Being exposed to frequent losses, they suffered a continual diminution of their numbers, and were not likely to be long in condition to avoid the enemy, or make any resistance.

Surena, apprehending that these remains of the Roman army might gain the mountains before he could force them to surrender, sent a deputation to Crassus, proposing at some intermediate place, between the two armies, a conference, to which each should bring a stipulated number of attendants. While this message was delivering, Surena himself appeared at a little distance on an eminence, waved with his hand, and in token of peace, unbent his bow. Crassus distrusting the faith of this barbarous enemy, who was supposed to hold perfidy lawful, as a stratagem of war, declined the conference; but his troops, weary of continual fatigue and danger, and flattering themselves that by an accommodation an end might be speedily put to their sufferings, expressed such a desire of the conference, as their general, in this situation, could not safely withstand. He put himself, therefore, with a few friends, under the direction of Surena's messengers, and submitted to be led to their general; but on the way, finding himself treated as a prisoner, he refused to proceed, and having made some resistance, was slain. The army separated into sundry divisions, a few escaped into Armenia or Syria, the greater part fell into the enemy's hands.[3]

Thus died Crassus, commonly reputed a rare instance of ambition, joined with avarice, and a mean capacity. It is not to be doubted, that in point of ambition he even rivalled Pompey and Cæsar; and it is probable, therefore, that his avarice was merely subservient to this passion. It is quoted, as a saying of his, that no man who aspired to a principal place in the republic should be reputed rich, unless he could maintain an army at his own expense.[4] Such was the use of wealth, which, in place of equipages, horses, and dogs, occurred to a rich man of that age at Rome. Of his capacity we cannot form a high opinion, either from the judgment of his contemporaries, or from his own conduct.[5] It appears, indeed, that he owed his consequence more to his wealth, than to his genius or personal qualities of any kind. On account of his wealth, probably, he was considered by Cæsar and Pompey as a person, who, if neglected by them, might throw a weight into the scale of their enemies; and he was admitted into their councils, as a person fit to witness their transactions, and on occasion to hold the balance in suspense between them These circumstances placed him among the competitors for the principal influence at Rome, and makes his death an era in the history of those factions which were hastening to overwhelm the republic. By this event, his associates Cæsar and Pompey, already disjoined by the dissolution of their family connection, were left to contend for the superiority, without any third person to hold this species of balance between them.

The calm which had succeeded the late election of consuls was but of short duration. The time of electing their successors was fast approaching, and the candidates Scipio, Milo, and Hypsæus, were already declared. Clodius, at the same time, stood for the office of prætor. Scipio was by birth the son of Metellus Pius, adopted into the Cornelian family by Scipio Nasica. His daughter, in consequence of this adoption, bearing the name of Cornelia, the widow of young Crassus, was recently married to Pompey, who, upon this connection, supported Scipio, his father-in-law, in his pretensions to the consulate. Milo had a powerful support from the senate, in whose cause he had retorted the arts and violence of the seditious demagogues against themselves. Clodius had great interest with the populace, and from inveterate animosity to Milo and to his party, joined all his interest with Scipio and Hypsæus against him.

It is in the nature of human things to advance, in accumulating the good or evil to which they tend. These competitors, in contending for the streets and the usual places of canvassing the people, joined to the former arts of distributing money, and of exciting popular tumults, the use of an armed force, and a species of military operations in the city. Three parties in arms every day paraded in different quarters of the town, and wherever they encountered, violence and bloodshed generally followed. The opposite parties of Hypsæus and Milo had fought a battle in the *Via Sacra;* many of both sides were killed, and the consul Calvinus was wounded in attempting to queil the riot.

These disorders so long obstructed the elections, that the term of the present consuls in office expired, before the nomination of any successors; and every legal power in the commonwealth being suspended, the former state of anarchy, with accumulated distractions, again ensued. The senate and the other friends of Milo, would gladly have hastened the elections, but were hindered by the partizans of the other candidates. The populace too, enjoying this season of gratuities, of entertainments, and of public shows, in which the competitors continued to waste their fortunes, were glad to have the canvass prolonged.[6]

U. C. 701.

When the senate proposed to have recourse to the remedy usual in such disorders of the state, by naming an interrex, the only title under which any person could preside in restoring the magistracy by an election of consuls, they were forbid

2 Dio. lib. iv. c. 28.
3 Dio Cass. lib. xl. Plutarch. in Crass.
4 Cicero de officiis, lib. i. c. 8.
5 Is igitur mediocriter, a doctrina instructus; augustius etiam a natura, &c. Cicero de claris oratoribus, c. 66. Ad Atticum, lib. iv. ep. 13.

6 Pædianus in Argument. Orat. pro Milone.

by the tribune Munatius Plancus, who was supposed to co-operate with Pompey in some design, to be favoured by deferring every measure that was proposed for the restoration of order.

In the midst of this scene, which kept the minds of men in fear of some general calamity, an accident happened which brought the disorder to a height, and forced every party to accept of a remedy. On the 13th of the kalends of February, or the 20th of January, Milo going to Lanuvium, a town about fifteen miles from Rome, of which he was chief magistrate, about three o'clock in the afternoon, met with Clodius returning from his country seat at Aricia. Milo was in a carriage with his wife Fausta, the daughter of Sylla, and a friend Fusius. He had a numerous escort, amounting to some hundreds of servants in arms, and, in particular, was attended by two noted gladiators, Eudamus and Birria. Clodius was on horseback, with a retinue of thirty servants likewise in arms. It is likely that this encounter was altogether accidental; for the companies continued on their way without any disturbance, till Birria, the gladiator, unwilling to pass without giving some specimen of his calling, as he straggled a little behind his party, quarrelled with some of the followers of Clodius. A fray ensued: Clodius himself returned to quell it, or to punish the authors of it; but meeting with little respect among the gladiators, received a wound in the shoulder, and was carried to be dressed in the inn at Bovillæ, near to which place the disturbance began. Milo being told of what had passed, likewise returned to the place; and thinking it safer to end their quarrels there, than await the revenge of an enemy thus provoked, who would not fail, at the head of his faction in the city, to rouse the fury of the populace against him, encouraged his people to pursue their advantage; they accordingly forced their way into the inn, dragged Clodius from thence, and having killed him, and dispersed all his followers, left him dead of many wounds in the highway.

Sextus Tedius, a senator, happening to pass, put the body into his own carriage, and sent his servants with it to Rome. They arrived before six at night, and proceeding directly to the house of the deceased, which stood on the palatine hill over the forum, laid the corpse in the vestibule.

The servants of the family, and multitudes from the streets, immediately crowded to see this spectacle. Fulvia, the wife of Clodius, stood over the body, and with loud lamentations uncovered and pointed out the wounds of her deceased husband. The crowd continued to increase all night, and until break of day, when Q. Munatius Plancus, and Q. Pompeius Rufus, tribunes of the people, likewise repaired to the same place, and gave orders to carry the dead body naked to the market-place, and there to leave it exposed to public view on the rostra; and at the same time accompanied this spectacle with inflammatory harangues to the people.

Sextus Claudius, kinsman of the deceased, soon after removed the body from the market-place to the senate-house, meaning to reproach the order of senators as accessory to the murder. The populace, who still followed in great numbers, burst into the place, tore up the benches, and brought into a heap the materials, with the tables and desks of the clerks, the journals and records of the senate, and having set the whole on fire, consumed the corpse on this extraordinary pile. The fire soon reached the roof, and spread to the contiguous buildings. The tribunes, Plancus and Rufus, who were all this while exhorting the people to vengeance, were driven from the rostra by the flames which burst from the buildings around them. The senate-house, the porcia basilica, and other edifices were reduced to ashes.

The same persons, by whom this fire had been kindled, repaired to the house of M. Lepidus, who, upon the first alarm of an insurrection, had been named interrex, forced into the hall, broke down the images of the family ancestors, tore from the looms the webs, in weaving of which the industry of Roman matrons was still employed, and destroyed what else they could reach. From thence, they proceeded to attack the house of Milo, but there met with a more proper reception. This house, during the riots, in which the master of it had borne so great a part, was become a kind of fortress, and among the other provisions made for its defence, was manned with archers, who plied those who attacked it with arrows from the windows and terrace, in such manner as soon obliged them to withdraw.

The rioters being repulsed from the house of Milo, crowded to the temple, in which the consular fasces, during the interregnum, were kept, seized them by force, and carried them to the houses of Scipio and Hypsæus, the present popular candidates for the consulate; these, without any other form of election, they pressed to assume the ensigns of consular power. But not having prevailed in this proposal, they proceeded to the house of Pompey, saluting him with mixed shouts of consul or dictator, according as they wished him to assume the one or the other of these titles or dignities.

From this time, for some days, an armed populace, mixed with slaves, continued, under pretence of searching for Milo and his adherents, to pillage every place they could enter.[1] And the partizans of the candidates, Hypsæus and Scipio, thinking they had Milo at a disadvantage, beset the house of the interrex; and, though it was not customary for the first in this nomination to proceed to the elections, they clamoured for an immediate assembly of the people for this purpose. The party of Milo, though professing likewise to join the same clamour for an immediate election, came to blows with their opponents, and protected the house and the person of the interrex from farther violence.

Milo, himself, who was at first supposed to have fled or gone into exile, hearing of the excesses committed by the opposite party, and of the general inclination of the more sober part of the citizens to check and disappoint their violence, ventured again to appear in the city, and at the head of his friends renewed his canvass. A succession of officers, with the title of interrex, continued to be named at the expiration of every usual term of five days; but such was the confusion and distraction of the scene, that no election could be made. The senate, under the greatest alarm, gave to the interrex, and to the tribunes of the people, to whom they joined

1 Appian de Bell. Civ. lib. ii.

Pompey, who, by virtue of his proconsular commission as purveyor of corn for the people, held a public character in the state, the usual charge given to the consuls, to watch over the safety of the republic. They even recommended to Pompey to make the necessary levies throughout Italy, and to provide a military force to act for the commonwealth, in repressing the disorders which were committed by the candidates for office.

Under the protection of such temporary expedients, to restrain the violence with which all parties endeavoured to do themselves justice, some applied for redress, in the way of prosecution and civil suit. The two Claudii, nephews of the deceased Publius Clodius, demanded that the slaves of Milo, or those of his wife Fausta, should be put to the torture, in order to force a discovery of the manner in which their uncle was killed. The two Valerii, Nepos and Leo, with Lucius Herennius Balbus, joined in the same demand. On the opposite party, a like demand against the slaves of the deceased Publius Clodius was made by Cælius, one of the tribunes; and a prosecution for violence and corruption was entered by Manlius Cenianus against Hypsæus and Scipio, the competitors of Milo, for the office of consul.

Milo, in answer to the demand that was made to have his slaves put to the torture, pleaded that the persons, now demanded as slaves, were actually freemen, he having manumitted them as a reward for their faithful services in defending his person against a late attempt made by Clodius on his life. It was alleged, on the other hand, that they were manumitted to evade the law, to preserve them from the torture, and to screen himself from the evidence which they might in that manner be obliged to give. M. Cælius and Manlius Cenianus being tribunes, and disposed to favour Milo, had ventured to vindicate him to the people, and to load Clodius as the aggressor, and the intended assassin in the fray which cost him his life. Cicero too, with great zeal and courage, while the friends of Milo were yet unsafe in the streets, maintained the same argument in the senate, and before the people.[2] Milo, however, would have been glad to make a composition; and as Pompey had all along, in the competition for the consulate, favoured not only Scipio but likewise Hypsæus against him, he offered to drop his pretension in favour of those candidates, if Pompey would agree to suppress the prosecutions that were commencing against him. To these proposals Pompey refused to listen. He probably thought the election secure for his friends, and by affecting a zeal for justice, hoped to increase his authority with the people.

The partizans of Pompey, in the midst of this wild and disorderly state of affairs, were busy in renewing the cry which they had raised in the former interregnum, that he should be named dictator, for the re-establishment of order, and the restoration of the public peace. Such an extraordinary power had never been at any time more wanted in the republic; but the times, in which it might be safely applied, were no more. The name of dictator recalled the memory of Sylla's executions, and it appeared to be uncertain against whom they might now be directed

2 Ascon. Pædian. in Argument. Orat. pro Milone.

To avoid the title more than the power of dictator, Bibulus moved in the senate, that all the present candidates for the consulate should be set aside, and that the interrex should assemble the people for the election of Pompey sole consul. Cato, to the surprise of every body, seconded this motion. He observed, that any magistracy was preferable to none, and that if the republic must be governed by a single person, none was so fit for the charge as the person now proposed. Pompey being present, thanked Cato for this declaration of his esteem, and said he would accept of the charge, in hopes of being aided by his counsel. Cato made answer, in terms, meant to be literally interpreted, but which in other instances of the same kind, under an aspect of sullenness, have been intended to flatter, that he meant no favour to Pompey, and deserved no thanks from him: that his intention was to serve the republic.

It was resolved, in terms of this motion, that Pompey should be presented to the people as sole candidate for the office of consul, and that after two months were elapsed, he might propose any other candidate to be joined in this office[3] with himself. The election was accordingly brought on by the interrex Servius Sulpitius, on the twenty-fourth of February, and Pompey declared sole consul,[4] with a commission from the senate to arm, if necessary, the inhabitants of Italy, for the better establishment of order in the city.

Pompey sole Consul.

The first object of Pompey, in the high and unprecedented dignity which was now conferred upon him, appears to have been the framing of some laws to restrain for the future such disorders as had lately prevailed, and to bring criminals to justice. For this purpose, he obtained an act to enforce the laws which already subsisted against violence and corruption; and to regulate the form of proceeding in trials on such criminal accusations.

By the regulations now suggested by Pompey, every trial was to end in four days. The examination of evidence might occupy the three first; the hearing of parties, and the judgment, the fourth. The prosecutor was allowed two hours to support his charge, and the defendant three hours to make his defence. The number of advocates was restricted, and the use of commendatory characters prohibited.[5] The quæsitor, or judge criminal, was to be chosen from among those who had held the office of consul, and eighty judges or jurors were to be impannelled, and obliged to attend the trial. After the evidence and pleadings were heard, the parties were then allowed each to challenge or reject fifteen of the jury or judges, or five from each of the orders of which they were composed: and the court being thus reduced to fifty-one, they were to be inclosed and to give judgment.[6]

Corruption was become so frequent, and so much a necessary art in conducting elections, that it was difficult to find any one willing to prosecute this crime. To remedy this defect, a clause was enacted in the law of Pompey, by which any person formerly convicted of bribery, might obtain a remission of the penalties he had

3 Plutarch. in Vit. Pomp. et Catonis, Dio. lib. xl.
4 Ascon. Pædian. in Argument. Orat. pro Milone.
5 Dio. Cass. lib. xl. c. 53. 6 Ascon. Pæd. ibid.

incurred by convicting any one other person of a crime equal, or by convicting two persons, though of a crime less heinous than his own. By these means, it was proposed that one conviction should produce still more in succession. That conviction, in every instance, should be attended with infamy; but that the pains of law should ultimately rest on such a person as could not find another on whom to shift the burden from himself.[1]

These regulations were made with a particular view to the trial of Milo, now arraigned on the statutes both of corruption, and of violence or assassination. The passing of these laws was opposed on this account by the friends of the accused, who alleged, that they were not acts of legislation, but acts of attainder, having a retrospect to the case of a party concerned in a past transaction. Cælius the tribune, and Cicero, maintained this argument. Pompey replied with impatience, that if he were hindered to proceed in a legal way, he should employ force.[2] He appeared to entertain some animosity against Milo, such at least as they who love to govern, have to others who appear not to be easily governed. He either had, or affected to have, apprehensions of danger to his own person, confessed or affected this apprehension in the senate, and retired, as for safety, to his own house in the suburbs: there he retained, for the guard of his person, a party of armed men; and there too, under the same affectation of withdrawing from violence, he caused the assemblies of the senate to be held.

The aristocratical or senatorian party was much interested in the preservation of Milo: they had been frequently assailed by the popular rioters, who set the laws at defiance; and as the laws had not always been of sufficient force to protect their persons, it was their interest to protect those who, on occasion, had set aside the laws in their defence. The argument, in equity, indeed was strong on the side of Milo. During the late suspension of government, the factions were rather separate parties at war, than subjects enjoying the protection, and amenable to the jurisdiction of any civil power whatever. They who procured or prolonged this state of anarchy, were alone chargeable with the consequences. In this contest, which could not be maintained without force or violent measures, the friends of the republic and of the senate were badly circumstanced. They contended for laws, and a constitution which might be turned against the very irregularities which had been necessary to their own preservation, while the opposite faction, if defeated, might claim the protection of forms, which they had endeavoured to subvert.

It would have been just, perhaps, to have closed the late scene of confusion with a general indemnity, and to have taken precautions for the regular uninterrupted exercise of government in future. This, however, would not have calmed the resentments of those who were aggrieved, and Pompey determined to signalize his government by a more specious appearance of justice. Domitius Ahenobarbus was chosen commissioner for the trial of Milo, on the charge of murder; and the other judges, taken from among the most respectable of each order in the commonwealth, were impannelled in terms of the late statute. The criminal was cited to answer this charge on the fourth of April; and on the same day, to answer a charge of corruption brought against him in the ordinary court of the prætor Manlius. Marcellus appeared for him at the bar of the prætor, and procured a delay until the other trial should be ended.

The court, it appears, was assembled in the forum or open market-place. There was a tribunal or bench railed in for the judges. The whole space was crowded with multitudes of people. The prosecutors began with examining Cassinius Schola, who had been in company with Clodius when he was killed. This witness gave direct evidence to the fact, and exaggerated the atrocity of the crime. Marcellus would have cross-questioned him; but the populace, and many others who assembled in the crowd, who favoured the prosecution, raised a menacing cry, which alarmed the accused and his counsel so much, that they claimed the protection of the court. They were accordingly received within the rails, and the judge applied to the consul, who had taken his station near to the place of assembly, in order to restrain, by his presence, any disorders that might arise at the trial. Pompey, who was then attended only by his lictors, was himself likewise alarmed by that disorderly shout, and said, that for the future, a proper force should be provided to keep the peace. He accordingly, on the following day, filled every avenue, which led to the forum, with men under arms; and, upon some tumult among the populace, gave an order that the place should be cleared. In the execution of this order numbers were killed.

Under the impression made by this vigorous exertion of power, the witnesses continued to be examined for two days without any disturbance. Among these the inhabitants of Bovillæ, the family and relations of Clodius, and his wife Fulvia, were examined on the several circumstances that fell within their knowledge, and left no doubt remaining with respect to the fact. The minds of men every day became more intent on the issue: so that, on the fourth day, when the parties were to plead, all other business was suspended in the city; the shops and offices were shut.

There appeared for the prosecutors Appius Claudius, M. Antonius, and Valerius Nepos. They began at eight, and spoke till ten. For the defender appeared Q. Hortensius, M. Marcellus, M. Calidius, Faustus Sylla, M. Cato, and M. T. Cicero, of whom the last only attempted to speak. Some were of opinion, that, as the fact was undeniable, it ought to be justified on the plea of necessity and public expedience. Cicero himself thought this too bold a plea, and therefore chose that of self-defence, alleging that Clodius was the aggressor, and intended to assassinate Milo. It is remarked of this celebrated orator, that he began all his orations under considerable solicitude and awe of his audience. On this occasion, when he stood up to speak, the partizans of Clodius, who were likewise inveterate enemies to himself, endeavoured to disconcert him with clamours and menacing cries. The unusual sight of military guards, commanded by an officer, who was supposed to be prejudiced against his client, it is said, so far overcame and sunk his spirit, that he spoke feebly, and con

1 Dio. Cass lib. xl. c. 52.

2. Ascon. Pædian. in Argument. Orat. pro Milone.

cluded abruptly; and that what he actually delivered was far short of that masterly oration which he composed, and afterwards published under the title of Milo's defence.

The accused, however, even in this alarming scene, stood at the bar with an undaunted countenance; and while every one else, in imitation of the senators, appeared in mourning, he alone appeared in an ordinary dress. When judgment was given, and the ballots inspected, it appeared that, of the senators, twelve condemned, and six, or perhaps rather five, acquitted; of the knights, thirteen condemned, and four acquitted; of the Tribuni Ærarii, or representatives of the plebeian order, thirteen condemned, and three or four acquitted. And Milo, upon the whole, was condemned by thirty-eight against thirteen.

Before sentence was pronounced, being still at liberty to withdraw, he retired into exile, and fixed his residence at Marseilles. Thither Cicero sent him a copy of an oration in his defence, composed at leisure, as an effort of his eloquence, and a specimen of what could be urged in the cause. The packet containing this writing, it seems, was delivered to read to Milo while he sat at dinner. "How lucky it was," he said, "that this oration was not actually spoken, I should not now have been eating these excellent fish at Marseilles."[3] These marks of indifference make a striking contrast to the figure which Cicero himself had exhibited in his exile. If he could have thus trifled with apparent or unmerited disgrace, that single addition of constancy and force to his character would have undoubtedly placed him as high in the order of statesmen, as, by the other parts of his character, he stands in the list of ingenious men and virtuous citizens.

Milo was likewise soon after condemned, in absence, by the prætor, upon a charge of bribery and corruption. Some of his competitors, particularly Hypsæus and Scipio, were brought to trial for the same offence. The tribune Munatius Plancus and Pompeius Rufus were, at the expiration of their office, tried and condemned for the share they had in the fire which consumed the senate-house, and in the assault which was committed on the house of M. Lepidus the interrex.

3 Asconius Pædianus et Argument et Notis in Orat pro Mil. Dio. Cass. lib. xl Plut. in Pompeio, Catone. &c.

CHAPTER III.

Character of Pompey in Capacity of sole Consul—Privilege of Cæsar to be admitted as Candidate for the Office of Consul, without resigning his Province—General Revolt of the Gauls—Operations in that Country—Blockade and Reduction of Alesia—Distribution of Cæsar's Army in Gaul.

POMPEY in his dignity of sole consul, having joined a legal authority to the personal elevation which he always affected, possessed much of the influence and consideration of a real monarch; and it would have been happy, perhaps, for the state, if he could have made such a dignity hereditary, and a permanent part of the constitution, or given to the commonwealth that reasonable mixture of kingly government, of which it appears to have stood so greatly in need. In his present elevation he rose for a while above the partialities of a factious leader, and appeared to adopt that interest which the sovereign ever has in the support of justice. He even seems to have personated the character of a prince, or to have considered himself as above the rank of a citizen. Among other instances to this purpose, is mentioned his haughty saying to Hypsæus, late candidate for the consulate, now under prosecution for bribery, who, as Pompey passed from the bath to supper, put himself in his way to implore his protection, "Detain me not," he said, "you only make supper too cool for no purpose."[4] In the midst of the solicitations of his courtiers and flatterers, he even ventured to dispense with his own regulations. Contrary to the rule he himself had laid down for the direction of criminal trials, he furnished Munatius Plancus, when brought to the bar, with a commendatory testimony, "I cannot prefer this writing of Pompey," said Cato, "to the law of which he himself is the author." On account of this saying, Plancus, when the judges came to be inclosed, thought proper to reject Cato: the accused was nevertheless condemned.[5]

Besides the measures taken to punish past offences, it was thought necessary to devise some laws to prevent for the future, or to lessen the temptation to the commission of such dangerous crimes. The principal source of the late disorders appeared to be the avidity of candidates for those offices of state, which led immediately to the government of lucrative provinces. To remove this temptation, it was ordained, at the suggestion of Pompey, that no man could be appointed to a province till five years after the expiration of that office, whether of consul, prætor, or quæstor, in virtue of which he claimed a proportionate station in the provinces.

Before the enacting of this law, however, Pompey had the address to procure for himself a prolongation of his government in Spain for five years. This circumstance, which continued to give him the command of an army abroad, while he likewise bore the highest civil office in the state at home, set a very dangerous precedent for the commonwealth.

Cæsar's command in Gaul was soon to expire; and, according to the laws then in force, he must even resign it before he could aspire to the consulate, or pretend to cope with his rival in civil preferments. It had been wisely ordained by the laws, that the persons offering themselves as candidates for the office of consul, should appear in person to sue for it; and that no man, without resigning his command and dismissing his army,

4 Val. Max. lib. ix. c. 5.

5 Plutarch. in Pompeio, p. 484.

could enter the city, or even go beyond the limits of the province in which he had governed. By this regulation it was intended to prevent the conjunction of civil power in the state with the command of an army. Pompey, however, though vested with such a command in Spain, had contrived to be exempted from the observance of this law; and, under pretence that his office of general purveyor of corn for the Roman people did not confine him to any station, and in reality extended to the whole empire, or had a particular reference to Italy, still continued to reside in the city of Rome.

Cæsar, to keep pace with his rival, openly aspired to the same privilege with Pompey, and claimed, as a mere instance of equal treatment, what the other had obtained; but what, if bestowed on himself, with his other advantages, must have given him a great and immediate superiority. The army he commanded was already in the most advantageous situation. The addition of consular power at Rome, to that of general in both the Gauls, was joining Italy itself to his provinces, and putting him at once in possession of the empire. Any opposition made to his authority as consul would be construed as rebellion against the state itself. Pompey would be driven at once from the helm of affairs to the command of a distant province, in which he, at most, could only defend himself; but not entertain any designs on the sovereignty of Italy, which would be covered from his attempts by the Pyrenees and the Alps, and the great armies of Gaul.

With these objects in his view, Cæsar instructed his partizans among the tribunes to move, that, being continually engaged in a hazardous war, which required his presence, and being necessarily detained abroad in the service of his country, he might be exempted from the law, which required the candidates for office to attend their canvass in person, and might therefore be elected into the consulate without presenting himself to the people for that purpose.

This proposition was sufficiently understood by the leading men of the senate, and by the few who joined with them in support of the commonwealth. It was known to be intended that Cæsar should have a privilege of being elected consul, without resigning his province, or dismissing his army; and they withstood the motion as of the most dangerous consequence. But Pompey, who ought likewise, for his own sake, to have been alarmed at the progress of Cæsar, and at the uncommon advantage at which he now aimed, was either lulled into security by the artifices of his rival, or thought himself sufficiently raised above any danger from this or any other quarter. He had accepted, in his own person, many unprecedented honours, and was possibly unwilling to contend for forms which, at some future period, might limit his own pretensions. Cato loudly renewed his suspicion of Cæsar's designs. Cicero could not be neutral in any dispute that should arise between Cæsar and Pompey. He had been banished by the one, and restored by the other. Besides the personal consideration he owed to Pompey on this occasion, his natural bias was on the side of the senate, and for the support of the forms which were provided for the safety of the commonwealth. He nevertheless suffered himself to be dazzled with the court which Cæsar had paid to him for some time, with a view to this very question; he condemned the indiscreet zeal of Cato, who, in his opinion, was ruining the cause of the republic by setting both Cæsar and Pompey at defiance, while he himself, by temporising, and by managing the inclinations of these parties, had secured them both in its interests. He stated the danger of a quarrel with Cæsar at this time, supported as he was by a powerful army, and in the bowels of Italy; but did not consider that he was then giving up, without a quarrel, all that any quarrel could extort.

The army of Cæsar was not then so well prepared to follow him against his country, nor he himself furnished with the same colours of justice, under which he afterwards made war on the commonwealth. If a civil war were to be dreaded, to temporise, in this instance, was to give a delay which proved favourable to the enemy, or rather, in effect, to deliver up the republic, without a contest, to that fate which the prudent counsels in question were intended to remove. Under colour of this prudence, nevertheless, Cicero, as well as Pompey, supported the tribunes in their motion, and obtained for the proconsul of Gaul the dispensation he desired, to retain his army, while he offered himself a candidate for the highest office of the state at Rome.

Cæsar, immediately upon his arrival on that side of the Alps in the beginning of winter, observing the distractions which took place in the city upon the murder of Clodius, affected much zeal for the laws which had been so grossly violated in that instance; and, under pretence of furnishing himself with the means of supporting the state against those who were inclined to disturb it, ordered new levies in every part of his provinces, and made a considerable addition to his army; but, contented for the present with the privilege he had obtained of suing for the consulate, without quitting his province, or resigning his military power, he left the state, as before, apparently in the hands of Pompey; and, in the middle of winter, on the report of a general defection of all the Gaulish nations, repassed the Alps.

Most of the nations that lay beyond the mountains of Auvergne, the original limits of the Roman province, roused by the sense of their present condition, or by the cruel massacre lately executed in a part of their country, were actually in arms. They had submitted to Cæsar, or were separately gained by him, under the specious pretence of alliance or protection against their enemies; and with the title of ally, suffered him to become their master. But the violence with which he had threatened the canton of the Carnutes,[1] for absenting themselves from the convention which he had assembled on the Seine, and the merciless severities executed by him against the unfortunate natives of the tract between the Rhine and the Meuse,[2] convinced all the nations of Gaul that they were reduced to the condition of slaves; and that every exertion they made for liberty was to be punished as a crime. They saw the folly of their former dissentions, and suspended all their animosities to enter into a general concert for their common safety. The occasion, they said, was favourable for the recovery of their country. The Romans were dis

1 Now Chartres.
2 Now chiefly Liege and Guelderland.

tracted at home, and Cæsar had sufficient occupation in Italy. His army could not act in his absence. The present time, they concluded, was the favourable opportunity to shut out the Romans for ever beyond the Cevennes, or even to force them to retire within the Alps.

All the nations on the Seine, the Loire, and the Garonne, quite round to the sea-coast, received these representations with joy. They held private meetings, and instead of exchanging hostages, which would have been too public a measure, and have led to a discovery of their designs, they plighted their faith by a more secret form, commonly practised among them on great occasions, that of pressing their banners together.

The people of the Carnutes[3] undertook to begin hostilities; and accordingly, on a day fixed, surprised the town of Genabum,[4] where they put many Roman traders, together with the commissary-general of the army, to death.

It was the custom of the Gauls to convey intimation of such events by means of a cry which they raised at the place of action, and repeated wherever the voice was heard, till, passing almost with the velocity of sound itself, it gave the speediest information of what was done. In this manner, intelligence of what had been transacted at Genabum at the rising of the sun, was, before night, propagated in every direction to the distance of a hundred and sixty miles, and put all the nations within this compass in a ferment. Its first and principal effects, however, were produced in the country of the Arverni.[5] Here Vercingetorix, a youth of heroic spirit and great capacity, assembled his retainers, took possession of Gergovia, now Clermont, the capital of his country, and from thence sent messengers in every direction to urge the execution of the measure lately concerted for the general freedom of Gaul. He himself, in return for his zeal, being chosen the common head of the confederacy, in this capacity, fixed the quota of men and of arms to be furnished by each separate canton, and took hostages for the regular observance of the conditions to which the several parties had agreed.

Vercingetorix having assembled a considerable army, sent a part of his force to act on the Garonne, and to harass the frontiers of the Roman province, while he himself moved to the Loire, in order to rouse the nations of that quarter, who appeared to be too secure; and he accordingly brought to his standard all the warriors of those cantons that lay on the left of that river. His party on the Garonne, at the same time, were joined by all the nations of Aquitania, and, in formidable numbers, threatened with immediate destruction the cities of Thoulouse and Narbonne, or such part of their districts at least as were open to invasion.

Thither Cæsar, with all the forces he could assemble upon his arrival from Italy, immediately repaired; and, having put the province of Narbonne in a condition not to be insulted, proceeded to give the enemy an alarm in their own country. His object was, if possible, to put himself at the head of the legions which he had left on the northern frontiers of his new acquisitions. He did not choose that those legions should move in his absence so far as to expose themselves to be cut off by the natives. Nor was it easy for himself, with the force under his command, to penetrate through so many enemies as lay in his way to join them. It was yet winter, and the mountains were deeply covered with snow. This circumstance, which increased his difficulties, as it was likely to render the enemy secure, still encouraged him to make his attempt. He accordingly passed the mountains[6] which lay in his way, at a time when the snow, in many places, being six feet deep, must be removed with shovels, and when that passage was supposed to be entirely impracticable. After he had surmounted this difficulty, his object being to draw the attention of the prince of the Arverni to his own country, he sent his cavalry abroad in numerous parties to destroy with fire and sword the people with their habitations and possessions. When he thought the alarm was sufficiently spread, and must have reached the Gaulish army on the Loire, he pretended, that his presence was required in the province behind him, gave the command of the troops in Auvergne to Decimus Brutus, then a young man; giving him orders at the same time to keep his parties abroad, and to continue to harass the country as he himself had done.

Having taken these measures to fix the attention of the enemy in one quarter, Cæsar, with a few attendants, made haste to pass in a different direction to Vienna on the Rhone, where he was received by a party of horse, which he had appointed at that place to wait his orders; and, under this escort, without halting by day or by night, he passed by Bibracte[7] and the country of the Lingones,[8] to the nearest quarter of his army on the Seine, and while he was yet supposed to be in Auvergne, had actually assembled his legions which had been distributed on the course of that river.

Vercingetorix having notice that Cæsar, in this manner, had passed him, and that the Roman army on the Seine was in motion, perceived that the invasion of his own country had been no more than a feint, and that the chief force of the enemy was to be expected from a different quarter, he resumed the operations which he had intermitted on the Loire, and endeavoured to possess himself of a post in the territory of Bibracte, where the people still professed themselves to be in the alliance of the Romans.

Cæsar, notwithstanding the difficulty of procuring provisions and forage so early in the season, thought himself under a necessity of opposing the progress of the enemy. For this purpose he left his baggage, under the guard of two legions, at Agendicum;[9] and from thence, with the remainder of the army, proceeded to Genabum,[10] leaving Trebonius by the way to take possession of a town which the natives, after a little show of resistance, had surrendered.

Upon his arrival before Genabum, the Gauls, who were in arms at that place, resolved to abandon the town; and shutting the gates against the Romans on one side, endeavoured to escape by the bridge of the Loire on the other. But Cæsar, having notice of their design, forced open their gates, and overtook them, while crowded together in the entrance of the bridge, and in the

3 Chartres 4 Orleans. 5 Auvergne.

6 The Cevennes.
7 Afterwards Augustudonum, now Autun.
8 Langres. 9 Sens. 10 Orleans.

narrow streets which led to it, put the greater part to the sword, and, under the pretence of revenging the massacre of the Roman traders, who had been cut off at this place, ordered that the town should be destroyed. From thence he penetrated into the country of the Bituriges,[1] on the left of the Loire; and, on his way towards Avaricum,[2] the capital of that district, forced every place that opposed his passage.

Vercingetorix, observing the rapid progress of the Romans, and knowing that the Gauls, being without order or discipline, could not withstand them in battle, declined an engagement, but endeavoured to distress the enemy by delays and want of provisions. He had authority enough with his own people to persuade them to lay their country waste every where within many miles of Cæsar's route. Twenty towns of the Bituriges were burnt in one day. Avaricum alone, contrary to the opinion of Vercingetorix, and at the earnest request of its inhabitants, who undertook to defend it to the last extremity, was spared.

Thither, accordingly, Cæsar advanced as to the only prize that was left. He attacked the place, under great disadvantages, in the midst of a country that was entirely laid waste, and trusting for the daily subsistence of his army to the Ædui beyond the Loire, who, notwithstanding their professions, were far from being hearty in his cause, or diligent in sending their supplies of provisions to his camp. Such as they sent were intercepted by Vercingetorix, who had occupied a strong post with his army, and infested the highways with his parties. In these circumstances, Cæsar's army was sometimes reduced to great distress, he himself, to pique the resolution of his soldiers, affected a willingness to raise the siege, whenever they were pleased to intimate, that they could endure it no longer; "We are got into a difficult situation," he used to observe; "if the troops are discouraged, I shall withdraw." To this affected tenderness for the sufferings of his men, he was every where answered, with intreaties that he would not dishonour them, by supposing that any hardships could oblige them to forfeit the character they had acquired by the labour of so many successful campaigns. He accordingly continued the attack of Avaricum under all his discouragements.

The place was covered on two sides by a river and a morass, and was accessible only on the third. The walls of the town were ingeniously constructed with double frames of wood, having compartments or pannels filled up with masonry and large blocks of stone. The masonry secured the timber from fire, and the frames preserved the masonry against the effects of the battering ram, which could act only on the stones contained within a single pannel or division of the frame, without ruining at once any considerable part of the wall, or effecting a breach. The Roman army approached to this wall by the most laborious and difficult methods which were practised. They began, in the ancient form of attack, at a proper distance, and on a breadth of eighty-three feet, to lay a sloping mound,[3] which rising by degrees on the plain, formed, as it advanced, an easy ascent to the level of the battlements. The earth on the sides of this mound was supported by timbers, hurdles, and faggots, and the workmen in front were covered with mantlets and moveable penthouses. The besieged, that they might still overtop the besiegers, raised their walls by additional frames of wood, which they covered with raw hides, as a security against the burning arrows and shafts which were darted against them.

In this contest the works on both sides were raised about eighty feet, and the besieged endeavoured to keep the advantage of superior height, not only by raising their own walls, but likewise by undermining and sinking the mound of the besiegers. They made galleries under the foundation of their own wall to the bottom of the enemy's mound, by which they endeavoured to remove the earth and other materials from below, as fast as they were accumulated above. They came from their sally-ports on different sides of the mound, and endeavoured to set fire to the wood by which the earth was supported. In all these particulars showing that they possessed the arts of defence in common with ancient nations.[4] Vercingetorix, in the mean time, continued to harass the Roman army from without, intercepted their supply of provisions, and, by means of the river and the morass, maintained his communication with the town, and sent in frequent relief.

Notwithstanding all these difficulties, Cæsar by degrees brought forward and raised his mound of approach to the height of the battlements; so that by a single assault he might determine the fate of the town. And while both parties were preparing for a last effort, he took the opportunity, as he frequently did, of a heavy rain to make his attack. The besieged, as he supposed, had taken shelter from the weather, and were in that instant put off their guard. He got possession of the battlements with little resistance, and drove the parties who manned them before him from the walls. The inhabitants formed in the streets, and the Romans who had entered, extending their line to right and left along the ramparts, were about to occupy the battlements over the whole circumference of the place, when the garrison, observing their danger, began to escape by the gates. In the confusion that followed, the town was sacked, and could make no resistance. Of forty thousand persons who had taken shelter in it, no more than eight hundred escaped. This massacre was joined to that lately performed at Genabum, under the pretence of completing the vengeance which was due for the murder of the Roman traders who were put to death at the breaking out of the present revolt.

The Gauls, as usual on every calamitous event, were greatly disheartened, and were about to despair of their cause, when their leader reminded them, that, contrary to his judgment, they had reserved this place from the general devastation, and had themselves undertaken to defend it; that what they suffered was the consequence of a mistake, and might be retrieved by abler conduct. His authority as usual rose on the ill-success of counsels which he had not approved, and brought an accession of numbers to his standard.

Cæsar, finding a considerable supply of stores and provisions at Avaricum, remained some days to relieve and to refresh his army. The country around him, however, being entirely laid waste, or occupied by parties of the enemy, it became

1 Now Berri. 2 Bourges. 3 The Agger.

4 Cæsar de Bell. Gall. lib. vii. c. 22, &c. Vid. Thucidid. lib. ii. in the siege of Platæa.

necessary for him to repass the Loire, and to open his communication with a country of which the inhabitants still professed to be in alliance with the Romans, and having had their possessions covered by the river from the incursions of the enemy in their late devastations, were still in condition to supply his camp. As in this movement he seemed to retire and to give up the ground he had disputed with the prince of the Arverni, he pretended that he was called to settle a dispute which had arisen among the Ædui, relating to the succession of the chief magistrate, or head of their canton. Having repassed to the right of the Loire without any loss, he made a demand on his allies of that side for ten thousand men on foot, and all the horses they could furnish.

He now had enemies on every quarter, and it was good policy to keep them divided, and to occupy them separately. For this purpose he sent four legions towards the Seine; while he himself took the route of Noviodunum,[5] at the confluence of the Loire and Allier; and there leaving his money, spare horses, and unnecessary baggage, he continued his march on the banks of the Allier, with intention to pass that river, and to invade the Arverni, from whom this revolt had originated, and whose chief was now at the head of it. This prince, knowing that the river Allier is never fordable till autumn, and till the melting of snows on the Cevennes begin to abate, ordered all the bridges upon it to be demolished, and hoped to prevent the Romans from passing it during the greater part of summer. As soon as Cæsar marched from Noviodunum, he presented himself on the opposite bank of the river, and regulated his motions by that of the enemy. The two armies commonly decamped, marched and encamped again in sight of each other; and Cæsar never affected to elude the vigilance of the Gauls, till he saw an opportunity to do so with advantage.

It happened that one of the bridges of the Allier had been but imperfectly destroyed; most of the piles were yet fast in the ground, and appeared above water; so that a passage might be effected in a few hours. The country around was woody, and furnished cover, or a place of ambush, to any number of men. From these circumstances Cæsar conceived the design to over-reach the enemy. He put his army in motion as usual, but himself remained with a sufficient detachment in the neighbourhood of the ruined bridge, which he meant to repair. In order that the Gauls might not be led to suspect that any part of his army was left behind, he ordered that those who were to move should divide, and present the same number of separate bodies, the same distinction of colours and standards, which they were accustomed to show on a march of the whole army; at the same time, as he knew that the Gauls would endeavour to keep pace with his people, in order to hasten and increase their distance, he ordered them to make a quicker and a longer march than usual. When he supposed that this feint or stratagem had taken its full effect, he began to work on the piles which were left in the river, and in a few hours repaired the bridge so effectually, that he passed with a division of the army he had reserved for this purpose, and instantly fortified a post to cover them on the opposite bank. From thence he sent orders to recall the main body; and before the enemy were apprised of his design, had re-united all his forces on the left of the river.

Vercingetorix, as soon as he had intelligence that the Romans had passed the Allier fell back to Gergovia,[6] the capital of his own principality, in order to take measures for the safety of that place. It being situated on a height having an ascent of above a mile from the plain, and surrounded by other hills, which made part of the same ridge, he ordered a stone wall to be built six feet high about half way up the ascent to the town, and encamped as many as the space could contain within the circuit of this wall. He occupied the other hills at the same time with separate bodies, having communications with each other and with the town. By this disposition Cæsar found all the approaches of the place commanded, and no possibility of investing the whole by lines of circumvallation, or by any chain of posts. He pitched his camp at some distance from the foot of the hill, and from thence in a few days got possession of a height in his way to the town, on which he posted two legions, with a line of communication, fortified on both its flanks, leading from this advanced station to his main encampment.

In this posture Cæsar foresaw, that all the heights in his neighbourhood being in possession of the enemy, while he pressed upon the town, he himself might be hemmed in, and cut off from all the supplies necessary for the support of his army. To preserve his communication, therefore, with the Allier and the Loire, he ordered his allies from the opposite side of these rivers to advance with the forces he had formerly required of them, to occupy the country in his rear, and to cover his convoys. They accordingly took the field; but their leaders having been for some time inclined to favour the general cause of the Gauls, they thought this a favourable opportunity to declare their intentions. Being arrived within thirty miles of Cæsar's army, they halted; and, upon a report which was industriously spread amongst them, that he had murdered some of their countrymen who were already in his camp, they put all the Romans in their company to death, and took measures to join their countrymen who were assembled for the defence of Gergovia. They had not yet moved to execute this resolution, when Cæsar had notice of what was intended, and with his usual diligence arrived, after a march of thirty miles, with four legions and all his cavalry, in time to prevent its effects. He presented himself as a friend; and thinking it safest for the present to disguise his resentment, he produced into public view all the persons who were said to have been killed by his orders, convinced such as had been deceived of their error, and brought them, with the seeming cordiality of allies, to his camp.

Cæsar made a merit with the Ædui of this act of clemency towards their people; but found that the spirit of defection was not confined to these detachments; that it had pervaded the nation; that the violence committed in the camp was an effect of the resolutions adopted by the whole people; that, in pursuance of the same measures, his purveyors and commissaries had been assault-

5 N[illegible]ers.

6 Now supposed to be the neighbourhood of Clermont

ed and pillaged even where they thought themselves secure, as in a friend's country; and that he could no longer rely on the affections of any nation in Gaul.

The leaders of the Ædui, however, on hearing of the lenity that was shown to such of their people as were in the power of Cæsar, pretended to return to their duty; and Cæsar, not to break at once with the only supposed ally which remained to him beyond the Cevennes, affected to consider the late disorders as the effect of a mere popular tumult, and declared himself willing to rely on the wisdom of the state itself for the reparation of wrongs which a few ill-advised persons of their country had committed.

This able commander appears, on many occasions, to have trusted greatly to the superiority of the Roman soldiers, as well as to that of his own reputation and conduct as a general. His confidence in both was required in the highest degree to support him in continuing, or even in attempting, a siege under his present difficulties, beset by numerous enemies, who were in appearance ably conducted; while he himself was deserted by those who were reputed his friends.

In his last march to repress the defection of his allies, he had left his camp exposed to the attacks of the enemy, and defended only by two legions against the whole force of so many nations as were assembled for the defence of Gergovia. These seized their opportunity in his absence, made a vigorous attack, and must have prevailed, if he had not returned with the utmost celerity to relieve his camp.

With the same confidence in the superiority of his men, Cæsar soon afterwards made an attempt to force the wall, which, as has been mentioned, the Gauls had built on the ascent of the hill which led to the town; and having made a feint on the opposite side with part of his horse, joined by the followers of the army mounted on horseback, who showed themselves at a distance to appear like cavalry, he drew the enemy from the place he meant to attack, actually passed the wall, and made himself master of part of their camp. A few of his men penetrated even into the town; but not being supported were surrounded and slain; even those who had succeeded at first under favour of the feint by which he had drawn off the enemy, were, upon the return of the Gauls to the defence of their camp, repulsed with considerable loss. In consequence of this defeat, it was no longer doubtful that Cæsar would be under the necessity of raising the siege.

In order to begin his retreat without any appearance of fear, he formed his army two days successively on the plain before his entrenchment, and offered the enemy battle. On the third day he decamped; and, with the credit he derived from this species of defiance or challenge, in three days he arrived at the Allier, repaired his bridge, and repassed undisturbed by the enemy. His passage, of the same river, a short time before, was esteemed as a victory, and his return, without having gained any advantage, and merely for the safety of his army, was undoubtedly considered as a defeat. The low state of his fortunes, checked and baffled by a Gaulish leader, yet a youth, and unexperienced, encouraged the nations on the right of the Loire, even while he was advancing towards them, to declare for the liberties of Gaul; and as a commencement of hostility, they carried off or rifled the treasure he kept for the pay of his army, and seized all the spare horses and baggage which he had left at Noviodunum,[1] as at a place of security at the confluence of the Allier and the Loire.

He himself was yet inclosed between these two rivers, having enemies on every side, and no magazines or stores for the supply of his army He deliberated whether he should not fall back on the province of Narbonne; but the danger to which he must expose Labienus, commanding a division of the Roman army on the Seine, the difficulty of passing the mountains of Auvergne, then occupied by his enemies, and the discredit which his arms must incur from such a retreat, prevented him. He determined, therefore, to advance; passed the Loire by a ford above its confluence with the Allier; found a considerable supply of provisions and forage in the country of the Ædui, and continued his march from thence to the Seine.

Labienus, with the troops he commanded in that quarter, had besieged Lutetia, the original germ from which the city of Paris has grown, then confined to a small island in the Seine, and had made some progress in the siege, when he heard of Cæsar's retreat from Gergovia, of the defection of the Ædui, and of preparations which were making by the nations on his right against himself. In these circumstances, he laid aside his design on Lutetia, and ascended by the left of the Seine to the country of the Senones, through which Cæsar was now advancing to meet him. In passing the river at Melodunum,[2] he was attacked by the enemy, but obtained a considerable victory; and, with the credit of this event in his favour, continued his march to a place which is now called Sens, near to which he was soon afterwards joined by Cæsar.

While the Romans were thus re-uniting their forces on the Seine, Vercingetorix had passed the Loire, and held a general convention of the Gaulish nations at Bibracte. He was attended by deputies of all the cantons from the Moselle to the Loire, except the Treviri, Remi, and Lingones.[3] The first stood in awe of the Germans, who kept them in continual alarm. The two last professed an attachment to the Romans, who were still masters of the field in their neighbourhood.

The leader of the Gaulish confederacy being at this meeting confirmed in his command, made a requisition for an augmentation of force, chiefly of cavalry, and accordingly increased this part of his army to fifteen thousand. To the end that he might give the Romans sufficient occupation in their own defence, he projected two separate invasions of the province of Narbonne: one to be executed by the nations which lay between the Rhone and Garonne, towards Thoulouse the other, from the Soane and the upper parts of the Loire, towards Geneva and the left of the Rhone. He himself, though still determined to avoid any general action, was to harass the enemy in their movements, and to cut off their supplies of provisions.

Cæsar, on his part, wished to open his communication with the Roman province, that he might have access to cover it against the designs

1 Nevers. 2 Now Melun.
3 Now Treves, Rheims, and Langre.

of the enemy, and to avail himself of its resources for the subsistence of his army. For this purpose, it was necessary for him to return, by the Soane and the Rhone, through a level country which was in possession of the enemy, to whom he was greatly inferior in cavalry. He sent into Germany for a reinforcement of horse; and the natives of that part of the continent being already sensible, that wherever they were admitted to act as soldiers of fortune, they were qualifying themselves to act as masters, without scruple bestowed their services for or against any cause; two thousand of them joined Cæsar, but so ill mounted that he was obliged to supply them with horses, by borrowing such as belonged to his officers of infantry, and as many as could be spared from his cavalry. To compensate their defect in horse, the men were brave, and, in many of the operations which followed, turned the event of battles, and determined the fate of the war.

The Roman army being thus reinforced, Cæsar began his march to the southward; and having passed the heights at the sources of the Seine, found the Gauls already posted in three separate divisions, contiguous to the different routes he might take, with numerous flying bodies of horse, ready to harass him in any movement he should make in their presence. By continuing his march, he soon gave their leader an opportunity to try his fortune in a sharp encounter, in which the whole cavalry of both armies came to be engaged. The Gauls were routed chiefly by the valour and address of the Germans, to whom Cæsar imputed his victory. This event was decisive in respect to the cavalry, that part of both armies on which it was supposed that the fate of the war must turn. And Vercingetorix, not to expose his infantry to the necessity of a general action, instantly retired to the heights from which the Seine, and a number of other rivers which mix with it before its confluence with the Marne, have their source. Cæsar, no longer apprehensive of the enemy's horse, resumed the confidence with which he always pursued his advantages, and followed his flying enemy into this retreat.

Vercingetorix, with his very numerous army, took post at Alesia, a place raised on a hill at the confluence of two rivers; the point on which it stood being the termination of a ridge which separated the channels by which these rivers descended to the plain. The fields on one side were level, on the other mountainous. The Gauls were crowded together on the declivity of the hill of Alesia, under the walls of the town, and in that position thought themselves secure from any attack. But not aware of the resources, enterprise, and genius of their enemy, while they endeavoured to render themselves inaccessible, they had got into a place in which they might be cooped up; and Cæsar immediately began to surround them, making a proper distribution of his army, and employing working parties at once on a chain of twenty-three posts and redoubts.

Vercingetorix, though too late, perceiving the enemy's design, sent his cavalry to collect what provisions could be found in the neighbouring country; but these troops, in consequence of their late defeat, not being able to keep the field against the Roman and German horse, he proposed to diminish the consumption within his lines by dismissing them altogether, giving them instructions to make the best of their way to their several cantons, and there to represent the situation in which they had left the army, and the necessity of making a great and speedy effort from every quarter to relieve it. He had eighty thousand men under his command, and might be able to subsist them for thirty days, and no longer.

Cæsar, from the enemy's having sent away their cavalry, concluded that they meant to act on the defensive, and to remain in their present situation until they should be relieved. With little apprehension of disturbance, therefore, from within his lines, he proceeded to execute amazing works; at once to secure his prey and to cover himself against any attempts which might be made to rescue them. This great commander owed many of his distinguished successes to the surprising works which he executed; so far exceeding the fears or apprehensions of his enemy, that they found themselves unexpectedly forced into difficulties with which they were not prepared to contend.

The Roman armies in general, and those which served under Cæsar in particular, had learned to make war with the pick-ax and the shovel, no less than with the javelin and the sword, and were inured to prodigies of labour as well as of valour. In the present case they were made to execute lines of circumvallation and countervallation over an extent of twelve or fourteen miles. They began with digging, quite round the foot of the hill, a ditch twenty feet wide, with perpendicular sides, in order to prevent any surprise from the town. At the distance of four hundred feet from this ditch, and beyond the reach of the enemy's missiles, was drawn the line of countervallation, consisting of a ditch fifteen wide, and a rampart twelve feet high, furnished, as usual, with a palisade. At a proper distance from this first line which fronted the town, so as to leave a proper interval for the lodgement and forming of his army, he drew another line, consisting of the same parts and dimensions, fronting the field. From the nature of the ground, part of these works were upon the hills, and part in the hollows or valleys; and the ditches, wherever the level permitted, or could not carry off the water, were allowed to be filled.

As he had reason, at least after the distress of a blockade began to be felt, to expect from a garrison, which exceeded his own army in numbers, the most vigorous sallies from within; and, by the united exertions of all the Gaulish nations in behalf of their friends, every effort that could be made from without; and as his own army, consisting of no more than sixty thousand men, could not equally man, in every place, works of such extent, he thought it necessary to cover his lines with every species of outwork then practised in the art of attack or defence, the *cippi*, *liliæ*, and the *stimuli*.

The first were forked stakes, or large branches of trees planted in rows in the bottom of a ditch five feet wide, bound together to prevent their being pulled up separately, and cut short and pointed to wound the enemy who should attempt to pass them.

The second, or liliæ, consisted of single stakes sharpened and made hard in the fire, planted in the bottom, of tapering or conical holes, of which there were many rows placed in quincunx; so that a person who had passed in the interval of any two must necessarily fall into a third. This device was commonly masked or concealed with slender brushwood covered with earth.

The last, or the stimuli, were wooden shafts set in the ground and stuck thick with barbed hooks, to fasten or tear the flesh of those who attempted to pass them in the night, or without the necessary precautions.

All these several works, it appears, the Roman army completed, considerably within the thirty days for which Vercingetorix had computed that his provisions might last. Both parties concerned in this blockade, without any attempt to hasten the event, seemed to wait for the several circumstances on which they relied for the issue. Cæsar trusted to the effects of famine, and the Gauls to the assistance of their friends, who were in reality assembling in great numbers from every quarter to effect their relief. They are said to have mustered at Bibracte[1] no less than two hundred and forty thousand foot, with eight thousand horse. But if these numbers are not exaggerated, they may be considered as a proof how far those nations were ignorant of the circumstances on which the fortunes of armies really turn. The supreme command of this multitude was given to Comius, a chieftain of one of the northern cantons, who having some time made war in conjunction with the Romans, owed the rank which he held in his own country to the favour of Cæsar, but could not resist the contagion of that general ardour with which his countrymen now rose to recover their freedom.

While this great host was assembling, the unhappy garrison of Alesia received no tidings of relief. Their provisions being near exhausted, they began to despair of succour. A council was held to deliberate on their conduct, and to form some plan of escape. Some were of opinion that they ought to surrender themselves, and to implore the victor's mercy. Others, that they should make a general sally, endeavour to cut their way through the enemy, and escape or perish with swords in their hands. Critognatus, a warrior of rank from the canton of the Arverni,[2] treated the opinion of those who proposed to surrender as mean and dastardly; that of the second, as brave rather in appearance than in reality. "Bravery," he said, "does not consist in sudden efforts of impatience and despair, but in firmly enduring for any length of time what the circumstances of war may require. Shall we think merely, because we have no communication with our friends, that they have deserted us, and do not intend to make any effort to save us? Against whom do you think Cæsar hath constructed so many works in his rear? Against whom does he man them in your sight with so much care? He has intelligence, although you have not, that a powerful army is preparing to relieve you. Take courage, and wait the coming of your friends. Even if your provisions should fail, the example of former times will point out a resource. Your ancestors, being surrounded by the armies of the Cimbri and the Teutones, rather than surrender themselves, fed on the bodies of those who were unserviceable in the war; and by this expedient held out till the enemy was obliged to retire. And yet, on that occasion, our ancestors had less cause than we have to make every effort of constancy and fortitude. Their enemies were passing, and meant only to plunder a country which they were soon to abandon; our enemies come to bind us in perpetual chains, and to establish a dominion at which human nature revolts."

The Gauls kept their resolution to hold out, but rejected the means that were proposed to supply their necessities, or reserved them for a time of greater extremity. The proposition of Critognatus is, by Cæsar, who was himself the unprovoked author of so much distress, and who continued, without remorse, to gratify his ambition at the expense of so much blood, mentioned with horror as an act of nefarious cruelty.[3] So much are men affected with appearances which shock the imagination more than with the real measure of what is hurtful to mankind. What followed, however, was probably no less cruel on the part of the Gaulish army than it was on the part of Cæsar; the first, to lessen the consumption of food, turned out the women, children, and unarmed inhabitants of the town to the mercy of the enemy; and Cæsar, in order to accumulate the sufferings of the besieged, would neither relieve nor suffer them to pass. From these circumstances we may presume, although it is not mentioned, that they must have perished a spectacle of extreme anguish and suffering in the presence of both armies.

In the midst of these extremities, Comius, with the united force of the Gaulish nations, at last appeared for the relief of Alesia, and with their multitudes covered the neighbouring hills. Being favoured by the nature of the ground, they were enabled to advance within five hundred paces, or less than half a mile, of Cæsar's lines. On the following day the cavalry on both sides began to act. The Gaulish horse, trusting to their superiority in number, or to the defensive plan which the Romans were likely to follow on the present occasion, drew forth on the plain below the town, and proposed to encourage their friends by braving the enemy. Cæsar thought it necessary to repel this species of insult, and sent his cavalry to accept the challenge. An action began about noon, and lasted till the setting of the sun, when the Gaulish horse, who till then had maintained the fight with great obstinacy and valour, being taken in flank by the Germans in Cæsar's service, were obliged to give way. Both sides, on this occasion, had mixed parties of infantry with their horse; and the Gaulish foot, who were engaged in this action, being now abandoned to the swords of the enemy, fled in the utmost confusion to the rear of their own army.

After this action nothing passed for a day and a night; but it appeared that, during this time, the Gaulish army in the field were collecting faggots and hurdles to fill up the trenches of Cæsar, and preparing graplings to tear down the palisade and the parapet; and that they only waited till these preparations should be finished to make a vigorous attempt to raise the siege. They accordingly came down in the middle of the night, and, with a great shout, the only signal they supposed could be understood by their friends in

1 Autun. 2 Auvergne.

3 Nec prætereunda videtur oratio Critognati propter ejus singularem ac nefariam crudelitatem. De Bell Gall. lib. vii. c. 76.

town, gave a general assault on Cæsar's line of circumvallation, as far as their numbers could embrace it, and without any choice of place.

Cæsar had assigned to every legion and separate body of men their station, and had repeatedly, to render them familiar with his disposition, given the alarm, and taught them to repair to their posts; he had placed Mark Antony and Trebonius, with a body of reserve, to succour any part of the lines that might be in danger of being forced. So prepared, he now received, without any surprise, the general assault of the Gauls. His men suffered considerably from the first shower of missiles that came from so numerous an enemy; but as soon as the assailants advanced to the outworks, and felt themselves entangled in the snares which had been laid for them, and against which they had taken no precaution, they were sensible that they fought at a great disadvantage, and desisted at once from this rash and inconsiderate attempt.

The besieged, in anxious expectation of what was to pass in the field, hearing the shout that was raised by their friends, returned it to make known their intention to co-operate in every attack, and instantly begun to employ the preparations which they likewise had made to fill up the trenches, or force the lines. They continued, during the greater part of the night, to cast such materials as they could throw into the broad ditch at the foot of the hill; but, when day appeared, seeing that their friends had retired, without making any impression on the exterior line, they too, not to expose themselves in an attempt in which they were not to be seconded, withdrew to their station on the hill.

From this disappointment the Gauls, both within and without the blockade, were sensible of their error in having made an attack before they had examined the enemy's works. To correct this mistake, they visited the whole circumference of Cæsar's lines. They observed, in a particular place, that the exterior line was interrupted by a hill which it could not embrace without making a great circuit. That Cæsar, to avoid so great an addition to his labour, and so much outline to defend, had encamped two legions in that place with their usual entrenchment, which formed a kind of fortress on the summit of the hill, trusting to this camp as a redoubt that would connect his defences on that side.

This place was chosen by the Gauls for a second and better concerted attempt than the first; and they determined, instead of the night to make their attack at noon-day, when the enemy were most likely to be off their guard. Five-and-fifty thousand men were selected for this service; and they began their march early in the night, arrived at their ground before break of day, and lay concealed under a ridge of hills till noon. At this time they came forward, furnished not only with grappling irons to tear down the palisade, which was formed on the parapet, but with hurdles and faggots to fill up the ditch, and to smother the stimuli from which they had suffered so much in their former attacks.

Cæsar, though not thrown off his guard, either by the time of the day, or by his former success, was sensible, that he was now attacked in his weakest place. He ordered Labienus instantly, with six cohorts, to support the legions that were posted in that station; and as he had reason to expect, at the same time, a general assault, both from within and from without his lines, to favour this principal attack, he ordered every separate body to its post of alarm; and he himself, with a considerable reserve, took a station from which he could best observe the whole, and be ready to sustain any part that was pressed. He had given Labienus instructions, in case he found that the lines could not be defended, to sally forth, and to bring the action to an issue, in which the Romans were generally found to have an advantage by mixing with the enemy sword in hand.

The Gauls, who were shut up on the heights of Alesia, only waiting to second the attempts of their friends in the field, began the action on their part nearly about the same time; and the Romans, being alarmed with hostile cries and shouts, at once both in their front and in their rear, were in danger of being seized with a panic, from which the best troops, on occasion, are not exempted.

Labienus was so much pressed where the Gauls made their principal effort, that Cæsar detached two several parties from his reserve to sustain him. First, a body of six cohorts under Decimus Brutus, and afterwards a body of seven cohorts under Fabius. At length, upon receiving information that Labienus had not been able to prevent the enemy from passing the intrenchment, but that he meant, with all the troops who had joined him from different stations, amounting to nine-and-thirty cohorts, to make a general sally according to his instructions, and to mix with the enemy sword in hand; he himself instantly moved to support him.

Cæsar had, by this time, observed, that the enemy, by a gross misconduct, had made no feint or no attempt on any other part of the lines to favour their principal attack; and he therefore, with those he still retained as a body of reserve, not only left the post of observation he had taken in the beginning of the action, but ventured even to unfurnish some other parts of the line as he passed, and advanced with great rapidity to join in the sally which Labienus was about to attempt. In his coming he was known from afar by the conspicuous dress which he generally wore in time of battle; and his arrival, on this occasion, with the reinforcement which he brought, greatly animated that part of his army, which had begun to despair of the event. He had, in this critical moment, with his usual genius and presence of mind, ordered his cavalry to get out of the lines; and, while the foot were engaged in front, to take the enemy in flank or in the rear. If the event had been otherwise doubtful, this movement alone, it is probable, must have secured it in his favour. The Gauls, although in the attack they had acted with ardour; yet lost courage when pushed to defend themselves; and, upon the appearance of Cæsar's cavalry in their rear, took to flight, and were pursued with great slaughter.

This flight at once decided the fate of both attacks; of the Gauls, who were shut up in Alesia, and of their countrymen, who had come to their relief. During the night, those in the field, discomfited by their repulse, were separating, leaving their chieftains, and dispersing in different directions. Many fell a prey to the parties who were sent in pursuit of them. Those from within the lines, who had suffered so long a blockade, now seeing all their hopes of relief at an end, were no longer disposed to contend with their fate. Vercingetorix having assembled the leaders together, told them, That, as he had undertaken this war, not from motives of private ambition, but from an earnest desire to recover, if he could, the freedom of his country, so he was now ready to become a sacrifice to the safety of his countrymen, and in any manner they thought proper to dispose of him, whether dead or alive, was willing to be made the means of appeasing the victor's revenge.

At this consultation it was determined to surrender; and Vercingetorix suffered himself to be delivered up. With respect to the treatment he received, Cæsar is silent; but it is probable, that, like other captive chiefs, on such occasions, he was destined to grace the future triumph of his conqueror; though, upon a fair review of the parts they had severally acted, likely to furnish a comparison not altogether to his advantage, and in some respects fit to obscure his glory.

The other prisoners also, except those who belonged to the cantons of the Ædui and Arverni, underwent the ordinary fate of captives; and, in this capacity, were exposed to sale, or divided as plunder among the troops. Cæsar reserved the prisoners of the Ædui and Arverni, on this occasion, to serve him as hostages in securing the submission of their respective cantons, and in obtaining from thence an immediate supply of provisions.

CHAPTER IV.

Cæsar remains in Gaul—Pompey assumes Piso into the office of Consul—Succession of Servius Sulpicius and M. Claudius Marcellus—Arrangement for the Provinces—Motion to recall Cæsar—Continued Debates in the Senate—Operations of Cæsar in Gaul—Intrigues in the City—Affairs in the other Provinces—Campaign of Cicero—Succession of Consuls—State of Parties in the City and in the Senate—Arrival of Cæsar in Italy in the Spring—Return to Gaul—Parts with two Legions to Pompey and the Senate—Alarm of Cæsar's March—The Consul Marcellus commits his Sword to Pompey.

THE seventh and the most difficult campaign of the war in Gaul being now at an end, Cæsar sent Labienus, with two legions beyond the Soane;[1] Caius Fabius, with two more, to the heads of the Marne and the Meuse; other officers with separate bodies, amounting in all to three legions, into different stations beyond the Loire and towards the Garonne; Quintus Tullius Cicero, with some other officers, to a station allotted them on the Soane, to superintend the formation of magazines and the supply of provisions, which were chiefly transported by the navigation of that river.

Cæsar himself having now no other object of equal importance with that of securing the possession of a country so populous and of so great extent, from which he might draw such resources of men and of revenue, as must put him on the foot of a great monarch, determined to pass the winter on this side of the Alps. He had obtained a dispensation from the law which excluded him from the consulate, so long as he retained his army; but as it was not yet time to avail himself of his privilege, he resolved, by remaining at a distance, as much as possible to shun the notice of such parties at Rome as were known to observe his proceedings, and to state them as matter of general alarm. He nevertheless did not suffer any thing of moment to pass in the city without taking some part by means of his agents and partizans, and was continually employed in gaining to his interests all those who were likely to come into office, or who, by their personal consideration, were of any importance in the state, and ever strove to exclude from office such as were disinclined to himself, or who could not be gained.

Pompey had now, for some months, exercised the office of sole consul. In that time he had, in some measure, restored the authority of government, and had exercised it with moderation. He had shown himself qualified to act the part of an excellent prince, though ill qualified to endure the equality which is claimed by the citizens of a commonwealth. His continual desire of unprecedented honours was one of the evils that distressed the republic. This evil, however, was partly mitigated by the facility with which he parted with power. Having enjoyed his present dignity from the first of March to the beginning of August, he took for colleague his father-in-law Metellus Scipio, suspending the prosecution under which he then lay, for bribery, in soliciting votes at a preceding election.

The newly elected colleague of Pompey, desirous to signalize his administration by some act of reformation, moved and obtained the repeal of the act in which Clodius had so greatly circumscribed the power of the censors; and he attempted to revive the authority of this magistracy, but in vain. Few citizens, now in public view, could bear the rigorous inspection of this once awful tribunal, as few had the courage to undertake or to exercise its trust. The institution accordingly had fallen into disuse, because it was not fitted to the times. And there being few of the people that were fit either to censure, or that could bear to be censured, it was not in the power of laws to revive what the general sense and manners of the age had abolished.

Disorders arising from the weakness of government had come to that extreme at which states must either correct themselves, or undergo some fatal change. The example of punishments inflicted, and of prosecutions still carried on against persons lately in office, for the illegal methods employed at elections, deterred many from offering themselves for any of the offices of state; and the late law, excluding consuls, prætors, and other magistrates from any provincial appoint-

1 The Arar.

ments for five years after the expiration of their term, removed one powerful motive by which citizens were induced to seek for such honours.

At the elections for the ensuing year only three candidates appeared; M. Marcellus, Servius Sulpicius, and M. Cato: all of them supposed to be of the senatorian party; but very differently considered by those who now endeavoured to rule the state. Marcellus had, in fact, recommended himself to Pompey; and Sulpicius, as afterwards appeared, had been gained by Cæsar; and both were warmly espoused by those powerful patrons in the present contest in opposition to Cato, whose success might have proved a considerable obstruction to Cæsar's designs.

It is observed of this competition, that it was carried on without bribery or tumult. As the competitors were supposed to be all of the senatorian party, the senators thought their interest secure whichever of the candidates should prevail. And as the senatorian party divided upon the occasion, the influence of Cæsar and Pompey easily cast the balance on the side of Sulpicius and Marcellus. Cato, during the competition, continued in the same habits of friendship as usual with both; and when the choice was decided in their favour, instead of withdrawing from public view, as was common under such disappointments, he went to the field of Mars as usual from the assemblies of the people, stript and went to exercise, and continued from thence forward to frequent the forum in his common undress. To those who condoled with him, or pressed him to continue his suit for another year, as he had done when first disappointed of the prætorship, he made answer, That he thought it was the part of a good man to undertake the public service, whenever he was intrusted with it, and to make his willingness known, but not to court the public for employments as a favour to himself. "The people," he said, "at the time that they refused me the prætorship, were under actual violence: in this case, they have made a free choice, and it appears that I must either violate my own mind, or renounce their good-will. My own mind is of more consequence to me than their favour; but, if I retain my character, I shall not be so unreasonable as to expect consideration from persons to whom it is not agreeable."[2]

U. C. 702. *Serv. Sulpicius, M. Claud. Marcellus, Coss.*

When the new consuls were received into office, their immediate predecessors being by the late act precluded for five years from holding any provincial government, it became necessary to fill stations of this sort with those who had formerly been in office, and who hitherto had not been appointed to any command in the provinces. Accordingly Bibulus, who had been the colleague of Cæsar in his consulate, was appointed to the government of Syria, vacant by the death of Crassus. Cicero was named to succeed Appius Claudius in Cilicia and Cyprus, Accius Varus was appointed prætor in Africa, and P. Cornelius Spinther in Achaia. Pompey, who had hitherto enjoyed a dispensation from the law, in continuing to hold by his lieutenants the government and command of the army in Spain, while he filled the office of consul in the city, now professed an intention to take possession of his province in person, and he actually set out from Rome for this purpose; but was induced to suspend his journey by a motion, which was made in the senate by Marcellus, soon after his accession to the office of consul.

Cæsar was now in possession of a very important privilege, which entitled him to sue for the consulate, without resigning the command of his army. His view in coveting this privilege; his continual augmentation of the troops in his province; his address in attaching the army to himself; his insinuation; his liberality; his assiduity to gain every person that could be won, and to preclude from power every one likely to oppose himself: the whole tendency of his conduct, and the enormous power he had acquired, began to be observed, and gave a general alarm. What Cato had so often represented to no purpose, began to be generally perceived; and persons, formerly the least attentive to the warnings they received, would now have been glad to remove Cæsar from the post of advantage they had given him.

The greater part of the senate had become remiss in their attendance, and regardless even of their own political interests. The few who exerted themselves, were distracted with personal jealousies and distrust of each other. Cicero in particular, who before his banishment had been strenuous on the side of the aristocracy, now grown timorous from the sufferings he had incurred, was chiefly attentive to his own safety, which he studied by paying his court to the prevailing powers. There was no bar in Cæsar's way, beside the great consideration and the jealousy of Pompey, who had assisted him in procuring his privilege to stand for the consulate in absence; but now saw its tendency, and wished to recall it. It was probably, therefore, with the approbation of Pompey, though after his departure from Rome, that the consul Marcellus, while the senate was deliberating on the other removes and appointments in the provincial governments, proposed that, the war in Gaul being finished, Cæsar should be recalled; or, if his friends insisted on his being continued in his command, that he should not be admitted on the list of candidates for the consulate, until he presented himself personally for this purpose.

This motion gave rise in the senate to warm debates, which were frequently adjourned, and as often resumed. The consul Sulpicius, supported by numbers of the tribunes who were in the interest of Cæsar, opposed the proceeding. Pompey himself, under pretence that he waited the issue of these debates, stopped short in his journey to Spain, passed some time at Ariminum in reviewing the new levies which were destined to reinforce the troops of his province; and at last, being summoned to attend the senate on the fifteenth of August, to consider of the provincial arrangements,[3] he returned to Rome.

On this day, Pompey affected to censure the violence with which it had been proposed to recall, before the expiration of his term, an officer legally appointed. He acknowledged his opinion, that Cæsar ought not to unite the government of a province, and the command of an army, with the dignity of consul; but dissuaded the senate from taking an immediate resolution on that

2 Plutarch. in Canton, p. 268.

3 Cicer. Epist. ad Familiar, lib. viii. ep. 4. Dio Cass. lib. iv. c. 58, 59.

head. The debate was adjourned to the first of September.[1] Then no meeting of the senate could be formed; but as soon as the subject was again resumed, the late consul Cornelius Scipio, the father-in-law to Pompey, proposed, that on the first of March, when the persons destined to succeed the present consuls must have entered on office, a day should be fixed to consider of the province of Gaul, and moved that this question should be resumed in preference to every other business.[2] Marcellus accordingly prepared, and laid before the senate, a decree for this purpose on the last of September. By the first clause of this decree, the consuls elected for the following year were required, on the first of March, to move in the senate the consideration of the consular provinces, to admit no other business to precede or to be joined with this, and to suffer no interruption in the meetings of the senate, even on account of the assemblies of the people. By the same clause, it was resolved, That the three hundred senators, appointed judges for the year, might be called off from their sittings in the courts to attend the senate on this business; and if it should be necessary to make any motion on this subject in the assemblies of the people at large, or of the Plebeians[3] separately, that the consuls Sulpicius and Marcellus, the prætors, the tribunes, or such of them as shall be agreed upon, should move the people accordingly.

To this clause were prefixed, in the usual form, the names of twelve senators, as the authors or movers of it.

By a second clause, bearing the same names, a caution was entered against any obstruction to be given in this business by persons empowered to control the senate's proceedings; and it was resolved, that whoever should put a negative on this decree, should be declared an enemy to his country; and that the senate, notwithstanding any such negative, should persist in recording its own decree, and in carrying its purpose into execution. In the face of this resolution, the tribunes C. Cælius, L. Venicius, P. Cornelius, C. Vibius Pansa, interposed their negatives.

By another clause, the senate resolved, that on the same day, the case of the armies of the republic should be taken into consideration, and all who claimed their dismission, either on account of the length of service, or any other consideration, should be heard; and that this likewise should be entered as a decree of the senate, notwithstanding any negative interposed to the contrary. Here the tribunes C. Cælius and C. Pansa, again forbad the decree. The last clause related to the mode of carrying into execution the purpose of the Pompeian law, with respect to the nomination of proprætors to the province of Cilicia, and the other eight prætorian provinces; and on this clause likewise, the two last mentioned tribunes entered their negative.[4]

Thus the resolutions of the senate, though preserved in their own records, were, by the continual interposition of the tribunes, prevented from having any real effect. And Cæsar, from the disputes which had arisen on his account, had sufficient warning, if this had been necessary, to prepare himself for an approaching conflict. It is indeed, likely, that though in action the principal characters of his mind were decision and rapidity, yet no man ever laid his designs more deep, looked forward to consequences more remote, or waited with more patience the proper time for the execution of his purpose. He had now, by the unremitted application of eight years, acquired the advantage, for the sake of which he had coveted the command in Gaul; he was at the head of a numerous army, which he had gradually augmented from two or three legions, the establishment of his province, to twelve, well inured to service, and attached to his person. He was in possession of a privilege to stand for the consulate, without disbanding his army; and when he should unite the first civil and political authority in the state, with an army at the gates of the capital, there is no doubt that he might be considered as sovereign of the empire. His apparent right to the advantages he had gained was such, that the resolutions of the senate against him, however necessary to the preservation of the commonwealth, might have the semblance of injustice, and were likely to engage both his own army and the populace of Rome in his quarrel. He himself prepared for the issue, by removing every cause of embarrassment in his province, and by paying fresh court to the legions under his command with gratifications and bounties.

He had dispersed or destroyed all the great armies, which the utmost efforts of the Gaulish nations, in the preceding campaign, had been able to assemble against him; but he had not reconciled the spirits of that people, nor inured them to his government. He had a plausible ground, therefore, from which to refute the allegations of the senate, who proceeded in their resolutions against him, on a supposition, that the war in his province was ended; and at the same time, had a fair pretence to gratify his army with the spoils of the country. For these purposes, soon after he had placed his army in winter quarters, he had intelligence, or affected to believe, that the war was likely to break out afresh in different cantons; and under this pretence, took occasion to carry his legions successively into action. Leaving M. Antony to command at Bibracte[5] on the right of the Loire, he himself, with the eleventh and twelfth legions, passed that river, took the canton of the Bituriges by surprise, plundered their habitations, carried many of the people into captivity, and continued to lay waste the country, until they and all the neighbouring cantons on the left of the Loire, to avert these calamities, surrendered themselves at discretion.

From this expedition, in which he spent forty days, he returned to his quarters, and ordered the two legions, which had been thus employed, a gratuity of two hundred sestertii, or about thirty shillings a man to the private soldiers; and of about two thousand sestertii, or sixteen pounds, to the centurions. This money, it is observed by the historian,[6] was not immediately paid; but was retained by Cæsar as a pledge in his own hands, or remained as a debt due to the army, giving to every individual a special interest in the safety and success of his general.

About eighteen days after this first division of the army was brought back to its quarters, other

1 Cicero ad Familiar, lib. viii. ep. 9.
2 Ibid. 3 Ad Populum Plebemve ferrent. Ibid.
4 Cicero ad Familiar. lib. viii. ep. 8.
5 Afterwards Augustodunum, now Autun.
6 Hist. de Bell. Gallico.

two legions were employed on a like expedition between the Loire and the Seine.[7] The inhabitants of this tract were to suffer military execution, upon a complaint that they infested the newly acquired subjects of Cæsar beyond the Loire. He accordingly marched to protect his new allies; and being arrived in the country, from whence they were said to be invaded, found the supposed enemy, by the devastations of the preceding campaign which had ruined their towns and villages, reduced to live in temporary huts, in which they withstood with difficulty the inclemency of the season, and were rather objects of pity than of hostile resentment. On the approach of the Romans, they fled to the woods, where they perished in great numbers, from the effects of famine and cold. To force them to an immediate surrender, or to cut off all hopes of advantage from delay, Cæsar made a disposition to prevent their having any respite from their present sufferings. He ordered the ruins of Genabum[8] to be repaired as a place of arms, quartered his legions there, and kept the horse and light infantry in the field to pursue the natives, to seize their persons, and to multiply the evils to which they were exposed. In this service too, it was likely that the army was rewarded by the distribution of captives, the only spoils of such an enemy, and came to have a demand on Cæsar for gratuities equal to those which had been granted to the eleventh and twelfth legions.

These operations led on to the spring, when a more real service took place on the frontiers of the low countries. From that quarter, the people of the Remi[9] had given information, that the Bellovaci, or inhabitants of what is now called the Beauvais, with other cantons on the right of the Oise, were actually arming, and meant to make war on the Romans and their allies.

On this intimation, Cæsar thought proper again to call forth the eleventh legion into service; and it is remarkable that this legion, though now in its eighth campaign, is expressly said to have been thus employed out of its turn, in order to improve a discipline, in which, when compared to the other legions, they were deemed to be still defective. The eighth and ninth legions, the one from the station of Fabius, and the other from that of Labienus, were ordered to join them in the country of the Suesones,[10] near the confluence of the Oise and the Aisne. With this force Cæsar passed the Oise; but arrived too late to surprise his enemy. The Bellovaci,[11] with some of their neighbours, apprehending, from the fate of the nations on the Loire, that they could not rely for safety on their innocence, nor on the care which they had taken to avoid giving offence to the Romans, had taken arms for their own security, and had retired with all their effects to a strong post. They had a hill in their front, beyond which there lay a morass, and in that situation they thought themselves sufficiently secure without any artificial work.

Cæsar posted himself in their neighbourhood; and supposing that the superiority of their numbers would inspire them with confidence, took measures to augment their presumption, and to derive some advantage from the errors they were likely to commit, under the effects of this disposition. He affected unusual caution, fortified his camp with uncommon care, scarcely ventured abroad to cover his foragers, and seemed to be entirely occupied in securing himself.

The enemy, however, continued to avoid any general action, and were satisfied with the successful war they were suffered to make on the foraging parties which were sent from the Roman camp. Being joined by five hundred German horse, they attacked and destroyed the cavalry, which had come to the assistance of Cæsar from the cantons of the Remi and Lingones,[12] and on which he chiefly relied for covering the avenues to his camp. By this loss he might have been in a little time reduced to great distress, or even forced to retire, if he had not procured a speedy reinforcement, by ordering Trebonius, with the two legions lately stationed at Genabum,[13] and a third from Avaricum,[14] to join him without delay.

The Gauls, on hearing of this great accession of strength to their enemy, and recollecting the fatal blockade and ruin of their countrymen at Alesia, determined to change their ground. They began to execute this resolution in the night, by removing their sick, wounded, and baggage; but had made so little progress at break of day, that their intention was discovered, and Cæsar, before they began their march, had time to pass the morass, and to take possession of the rising ground in their front. This he did with the greatest despatch; and though he did not think it expedient to attack them in their present position, he had it in his power to take advantage of any movement they should make, and continued to awe them and to keep them in suspense.

The Gauls, therefore, instead of being able to depart, as they expected before day-light, were obliged to continue to front the enemy, in order to cover the retreat of their baggage. They still flattered themselves, that Cæsar before night would be obliged to retire to his camp; but observing, that while the greater part of his army continued in readiness for action, he began to entrench himself where he stood, they bethought themselves of a stratagem to elude his design. They brought forward the wood and straw, which remained, as usual, on the ground of their late encampment, laid them in a continual train along the front, and having set them on fire, produced such a line of smoke, as darkened the whole fields between the two armies. Under this cover, they began their retreat, and before Cæsar could venture to penetrate the cloud of smoke in pursuit of them, had gained a considerable distance. On the first sight of this uncommon appearance, he suspected their design, and began to advance; but the precautions, which he was obliged to take, in order to guard against an ambuscade or surprise, gave the Gauls the time they wanted to effect the first part of their retreat undisturbed.

Before night they halted again, about ten miles from their former station, and recurred to the same means they had hitherto employed to distress the Roman army. They succeeded in most of their attempts on the parties that were sent abroad by Cæsar to procure him provisions; and having reduced him to the necessity of depending entirely for the subsistence of his army on what

7 To the country of the Carnutes.
8 Now Orleans.
9 Rheims. 10 The Soissons. 11 The Beauvais.
12 Rheims and Langres. 13 Orleans. 14 Bourges

a particular district could supply, they formed a design, with the choice of their army, to surround and cut off the parties, which they expected he must employ on that service. Cæsar had intelligence of their design, and prepared, in his turn, to counteract them. He placed his army in a proper position to surprise the great detachment they had made; and having thus taken or destroyed the flower of their army, obliged the remainder, who were thrown into despair by so great a loss, to surrender themselves at discretion; in consequence of this surrender, he got possession of all the cantons in that neighbourhood.

The Belgic nations being thus finally subdued, and Cæsar having no longer any enemy to oppose him in the field, except a few desperate bands from different parts of the country, who, either from fear of his severity, or aversion to his government, had deserted their settlements, he determined to act against them in different quarters at once, and to cut off the retreats, which, in case of distress, this remnant of the nations who lately opposed him mutually gave to each other. He sent C. Fabius, with twenty-five cohorts, to act on the left of the Loire; the twelfth legion towards the sources of the Garonne, with orders to cover the approaches to Narbonne from the incursions of any stragglers, whom his intended severities might force upon desperate attempts on that side. He himself, with Labienus and Mark Antony, proceeded to the Meuse, where the territories of the late unfortunate Ambiorix,[1] beginning to be re-peopled, and the nation reinstated under its former leader, were become again the object of his vengeance. To convince this unhappy people, that they were not to enjoy peace under the government of a prince who had presumed to circumvent and to destroy a part of the Roman army, he renewed his military execution against them, issuing his orders, as in the former instance, to spare neither sex nor age.

While Cæsar himself was employed in this manner, C. Fabius being arrived at the place of his destination, between the lower parts of the Loire and the Garonne, found a considerable force in arms against Caninius Rebilus, the Roman officer, who was stationed in that quarter. The natives had laid siege to a fortress that was in possession of the Romans; but alarmed by the approach of Fabius, they withdrew, and endeavoured to pass the Loire to the northward. In this attempt, being intercepted in their march, and obliged to fight the Roman detachment, they were defeated with great slaughter. After this calamity, about five hundred, who escaped from the field under Drapes, a prince of that country, formerly distinguished in the war against the Romans, took their flight in the opposite direction, and proposed to attack the Roman province of Narbonne, in order to compensate their losses with its spoils.

Fabius in consequence of his victory, received the submission of all the nations from the Loire to the Seine, and quite down to the sea coast; and having taken measures to secure his conquest, followed Drapes to the southward, overtook him beyond the Garonne, and obliged him, being no longer in condition to make any attempt on the Roman province, to take refuge at Uxellodunum,[2] a place of strength, situated on a steep rock, at the confluence of some of those streams, which, falling from the Cevennes, form the Garonne by their junction.

Here Caninius and Fabius having joined their forces together, made dispositions to invest their enemy; but before their works were completed, Drapes, while he had yet access to the fields, willing to spare the magazines which he had made up in the town, ventured abroad with a detachment, at the head of which he was surprised and taken. The natives, however, who remained in the place, being supplied for a considerable time with provisions, resolved on a vigorous defence; and, by keeping the Roman army for some time at bay, began to raise up anew the hopes and expectations of the nations around them. Cæsar thought the reduction of this place an object that required his own presence. Having therefore sent Labienus to the Moselle, and having left M. Antony to command in the low countries, he himself, with his usual despatch, crossed great part of Gaul, and appeared on the Garonne, equally unexpected by his own people, and by the enemy who were besieged in the town of Uxellodunum.

The place being strong by nature, and in no want of provisions, could be forced only by cutting off its access to water. For this purpose Cæsar lined the banks of the river with archers and slingers, and effectually prevented the besieged from supplying themselves from thence. He proceeded next to exclude them from the use of a spring which burst from the rock in the approach to their town; for having got the command of the ground, he pushed a mine to the source from which the water came, diverted it from its former direction, and, by depriving the besiegers of this last resource, obliged them to lay down their arms and trust to his mercy. In this, however, they experienced what the author,[3] from whom these accounts are taken, considered as more than the usual severity of ancient war. Cæsar, according to this historian, having given proof of his clemency, bethought himself now of an example of justice; and for this purpose ordered such as had carried arms in defence of Uxellodunum to have their hands struck off.[4] And this refined act of cruelty being joined to the many barbarous executions with which the conquest of that country had been achieved, thus ended the war in Gaul.

The usual time of putting the troops into winter quarters not being arrived, Cæsar thought proper to visit the nations upon the Adour, or what is now called Gascony;[5] the only part of his new conquests in the acquisition of which he had not acted in person. He marched through this country at the head of two legions, and was every where received with the most perfect submission. From thence he repaired to Narbonne, the capital of his original province, held the usual meetings for the despatch of civil affairs, and made a disposition for the quarters of his army during the winter. By this disposition two le-

1 Now Liege, Juliers, and Guelderland.

2 Supposed to be Cadenau.

3 Hist. de Bell. Gall. lib viii. c. 44.

4 Cæsar quum suam lenitatem cognitam omnibus sciret.—Omnibus qui arma tulerant manus precidit. Vitam concessit quo testator esset pœna improborum De Bell Gall. lib. viii. c. 44.

5 Aquitania

gions were stationed in the high country, from which spring the Garonne and the Loire, or in the territories of the Limovaci and Arverni;[6] two at Bibracté between the Soane and the Loire; two between the Loire and the Seine;[7] and the remaining four under the command of Trebonius, Vatinius, and Quintus Tullius Cicero, in different parts of the low countries. To this extremity of his new conquests he himself repaired, and fixed his quarters at Nemetocenna,[8] in the centre of his northern stations.

By this distribution of his army, Cæsar formed a kind of chain from the frontier of his original province, quite through the heart of his new acquisitions to the Meuse and the Scheld. And by his seeming anxiety for the safety of the northern extremities of his province, and still more by his own distance from Italy, he probably lulled for a while the vigilance or jealousy of his principal opponents at Rome. His own attention, however, to the state of politics was never less remitted.

Mark Antony, a person profligate and dissipated, but when the occasion required exertion, daring and eloquent, destined to be frequently mentioned in the sequel of this history, now began to be employed by Cæsar in the affairs of the city; and, under pretence of standing for the priesthood, was sent from Gaul, where he had recently served in the army, to bear a principal part among the agents and emissaries of his general. These agents were continually busied in magnifying his services, and in gaining to his interest every person of consideration who could in any degree advance or obstruct his designs. In the conquest of Gaul, they alleged that he added to the patrimony of the Roman people a territory of no less than three thousand miles in circumference, and a revenue of forty millions Roman money.[9] They took care at the same time, in his name and by his directions, under the pious pretence of celebrating the memory of his daughter, the late wife of Pompey, to cajole the people with public entertainments and feasts; and proceeded to execute, at a great expense, the splendid works which Cæsar had formerly ordered.

He himself, at the same time, was careful to secure the affections of the army; doubled their pay, and was lavish in all the other articles which were derived from his bounty. Besides his occasional liberality to the legions in time of the war, he gave, or engaged himself to pay, to each particular soldier, what to persons of that condition was a considerable object. In the city he even entered into the secrets of every family, and, as has been mentioned, gained the master by courting the mistress or favourite slave. His purse was ever open to gratify the covetous with presents, to relieve the necessitous, and to silence the creditors of those who were oppressed with debt. He encouraged the prodigal to squander their patrimonies, and freely lent them the aids which their extravagance rendered necessary to them. He kept a correspondence at the same time with dependant and foreign princes; and took upon him the protection of provincial towns, in order to secure their affection and their confidence.[10]

While Cæsar was thus extending his influence in the empire, he had amused Pompey by assigning to him, in all their arrangements, what was apparently the place of honour and of importance at the head of affairs at Rome; as he had gratified Crassus likewise by leaving him to choose the most lucrative government, while he himself submitted to be employed as a mere provincial officer, to explore a barbarous country, and to make war with its natives. But by thus yielding the supposed preference of station to his rivals, he actually employed them as the willing tools and ministers of his own ambition. The former, with all his disposition to emulation and jealousy, and perhaps for some time the dupe of these artifices, imagined that Cæsar advanced by his permission, and that the present state of parties was the fruit of his own address. As he himself, for the most part, endeavoured to obtain his ends by means indirect and artificial, he was the more easily duped by those who affected to be deceived by him, and who were able to overreach him. Although it was impossible for him now to remain any longer insensible to the superiority which Cæsar had acquired, or to those still more important objects at which he was aiming, yet he had not hitherto taken his part openly nor directly against him, but contented himself with employing others in ill-concerted and ineffectual attacks, which he sometimes disowned, and always feebly supported. At last, and in the prosecution of the measures of which we have observed the beginning in the senate, he hazarded the whole authority of that body against Cæsar, without having provided any military power to enforce their commands.

Pompey himself, while most under the influence of ambition, and when he had it most in his power to trample on the civil constitution of his country, had shown a respect for the commonwealth, which kept him within bounds that were consistent with this species of government; and he imagined that no man could presume to surpass himself in pretensions to rise above the ordinary level. In the course of debates relating to the present state of affairs, he generally spoke ambiguously, or affected to disbelieve the designs that were imputed to Cæsar; but finding, on the last motion which was made to recall him from Gaul, that the eyes of the whole senate were turned upon himself, he was forced to break silence; and, with some degree of embarrassment, said, that although it was his opinion, that the proconsul of Gaul could not, in consistence with justice, be instantly recalled, yet that after the first of March he should have no difficulties on the subject. "But," says one of the senators, "what if this motion should then have a negative put upon it?" "I shall make no distinction," replied Pompey, "between Cæsar's refusing to obey the order of the senate, and his procuring some one here to forbid that order." "But what if he persist in demanding the consulate while he retains his province and his army?" "What," replied Pompey, "if my own child should offer me violence?"[11]

After the attempt which had been made to fix

6 Limoges and Auvergne. 7 At Tours and Chartres. 8 Supposed to be Arras.

9 Plutarch. in Vit. Catonis, p. 268. Sueton. in Jul. Cæs. c. 25. Between about three and four hundred thousand pounds.

10 Sueton. in Jul. Cæs. c. 26, 27, 28.

11 Cicer. Epist. ad Familiares, lib. viii. ep. 8.

the question of Cæsar's recall for the first of March, Pompey being at Naples, was taken ill, and supposed to be in danger. His recovery gave a general satisfaction, of which he had afterwards very flattering proofs in his progress through Italy. He was every where met by processions, found the ways strowed before him with flowers, and was received by multitudes, who appeared to be frantic with joy for the return of his health.

Whatever part Pompey himself or his emissaries may have had in procuring these demonstrations of respect and affection, it is probable he was highly flattered with them, and either mistook them himself, or hoped that others should mistake them, as the proofs of a consideration and power which no attempt of his rival could overset or impair.

The principal attention of all parties, during this summer and autumn, as has been mentioned, had been turned to the affairs of Cæsar, and the dangerous tendency of the course he pursued: and they were but for a little while diverted from this object by an alarm on the side of Syria. The Parthians, encouraged by their late success against Crassus, passed the Euphrates with a great army, commanded by Pacorus, son to Orodes, under the direction of Osaces, a veteran and experienced leader. They had, during the preceding winter, made an alliance with the king of Armenia, and were to be joined by his forces in this invasion. The disaster of Crassus had rendered the Parthian name terrible at Rome; and this inte ligence struck a momentary panic in the city, as if an enemy were already at the gates. Some proposed to give Pompey the command in Syria; some to send Cæsar thither; and others, to send both the present consuls to the army with a proper reinforcement.[1]

But before these measures could be determined, or before any reinforcement could be ready to join the army in Syria, the people were relieved of their fears by Caius Cassius, the general then commanding in that province, who had obliged the Parthians to withdraw from Antioch; in their retreat attacked them, and made great slaughter. Osaces in that action received some wounds, of which, in a few days afterwards, he died, and the Parthian army continued in their retreat during the following year beyond the Euphrates; sensible, in their turn, that a war carried over the wastes of that desolated frontier might be ruinous to any power by which it was attempted.

Bibulus, the present proconsul of Syria, soon after the retreat of the Parthians, arrived in his province, and, according to the established practice of the Romans, laid his pretensions to a triumph for the victory which, under his auspices, though before his arrival, had been obtained by his lieutenant.

This invasion of Syria, as well as some disturbances in his own province, furnished Cicero, at the same time, with the occasion of some military operations, of which we have a particular account, in his letters, and which, though not material to the military history of the times, are not unworthy of notice, as they relate to this eminent personage. He had taken possession of his command in Cilicia, and however better fitted by his habits for the forum and the political assemblies at Rome than for the field, possessed abilities to qualify him for any station, put himself at the head of an army, and prepared for the defence of his province. He had set out from Rome in May; and having had a conference with Pompey at Tarentum, arrived at Brundusium on the twenty-first of that month.[2]

The military establishment of Cilicia being no more than twelve thousand foot and two thousand horse, Cicero applied for an augmentation of it, and on the fourth of June was still a Brundusium, waiting for an answer to this application. But finding that his request, having been opposed by the consul Sulpicius,[3] was unsuccessful, he set sail from that place, arrived at Actium on the fifteenth of that month, and, passing through Athens, reached his province on the last of July. Here he found the troops, in consequence of a mutiny which had recently broke out among them, separated from their officers, dispersed in places of their own choosing, the men of entire cohorts absent from their colours, and considering themselves as exempt from any authority or government whatever. Trusting to the respect that was due to the name and commission of proconsul, he ordered M. Annius, one of his lieutenants, to assemble as many as he could of the mutinous troops, and to encamp at Iconium in Licaonia. There he joined them on the twenty-fourth of August; and having intelligence of the Parthian invasion, took measures for the security of his province; marched, without loss of time, to Cybistra, on the frontier of Cappadocia; took under his protection the king Ariobarzanes, who was then threatened by a powerful faction in his own kingdom, and by receiving him as a prince in alliance with the Romans, dispelled the storm that had been gathered against him. He accepted, at the same time, of the offer that was made by Dejotarus, to join him with all his forces; and being in this situation when he received accounts that the Parthians had presented themselves before Antioch, he supposed that his presence might be wanted to cover his own frontier on the side of Syria. He accordingly moved to that quarter, in order to secure the passes of the mountains. Here, however, he learnt, that the storm had blown over; that the enemy had retired, and had sustained a considerable loss in their retreat; and that Bibulus was then at Antioch. This intelligence he communicated to Dejotarus, intimating, at the same time, that his assistance was no longer necessary.

The province of Cilicia had been for some years subject to the Romans; but the inhabitants of the mountainous parts had never acknowledged their authority, nor even that of their own national sovereigns. Cicero, on his arrival in the neighbourhood of their country, finding that the people had retired to their strong holds, and were still determined to oppose his authority, formed a design to surprise them; and, for the better execution of his project, made a feint to withdraw to Epiphania, where he halted for a day, as if to refresh his troops. On the day following, which was the eleventh of October, in the evening, he put his army again in motion towards the mountains, and before morning arrived in the midst of his enemies, who by this time had returned to

1 Cicer. Epist. ad Familiares. lib. viii. ep. 10.

2 Cicero ad Familiar. lib. iii. ep. 3.

3 Ibid.

their usual habitations; cut them off separately, pursued such as fled, forced their strong holds, and in about sixty days reduced some towns and a considerable tract of country, which had never before acknowledged the Roman government.

The troops, on this occasion, saluted Cicero with the title of imperator; which, being usually given to victorious leaders,[4] was commonly understood as the suffrage of the army for obtaining a triumph. He himself, accordingly, on this circumstance, together with the service which gave occasion to it, afterwards grounded his claim of that honour. This claim he scarcely seems to have seriously entertained; he even treats it as a jest in some of his letters; yet the triumph being in these latter times considered rather as the means of acquiring a certain rank in the commonwealth, than as the just reward of military merit, he submitted his claim to the senate, and urged his friends to support it. His conduct as governor of a province, at a time when this station was supposed to give a license to every species of rapine and oppression, did honour to his own disposition, and to those literary studies, in which he was taught to choose the objects of his ambition and his habits of life. In this character he declined, both for himself and for his attendants, all those presents, contributions, and even supplies of provisions, of which custom or law had authorised the Roman governors, in passing through the provinces, to avail themselves. In his command he distinguished himself by his humanity, condescension, and disinterestedness; was easy of access and hospitable; open, in particular to all persons of literary merit and ingenuity, whom he entertained without ostentation. In such situations other Roman generals, though of great merit, indulged themselves in what was the custom of their times; they drained the provinces to accumulate their own fortunes, or placed their money there at extravagant interest. He was governed by different maxims, and wished to rise above his contemporaries by the fame of his disinterestedness, as well as of his ingenuity and civil accomplishments. Other citizens might possess greater steadiness, and force or elevation of mind; but his fine genius, his talents, and fair disposition, of which his weakness indeed often prevented the full effect, still rendered him an important acquisition to either of the parties in the commonwealth. And as they endeavoured to gain, so they even seemed to acquire, his support in their turns.

Whilst the affairs of the respective provinces were thus administered by the commanders to whom they were intrusted, the usual time of elections at Rome being arrived, L. Æmilius Paulus, and C. Claudius Marcellus were elected to succeed to the consulate for the following year. Soon after these elections attempts were made, though without effect, to carry into execution some of the regulations devised by Pompey, in his late administrations, to check the corruption of the times. Calidius had been engaged in the last competition, and immediately upon his disappointment was brought to trial for illegal means employed in his canvass. He was acquitted; and, in resentment, retorted the charge on Marcellus, in order, if possible, to annul his election; but failed in the attempt.

4 Cicero ad Familiar. lib. xv. ep. 4.

Of those who were now elected consuls, Caius Marcellus, as well as his relation and immediate predecessor Marcus Marcellus, was understood to be in the interest of Pompey. Æmilius Paulus, a senator of rank, and of course interested in the preservation of the republic, the honours of which he was so well entitled to share, was expected to support the measures of the senate, and adhere to the established forms. Together with internal tranquillity, the government seemed to recover its ancient severity. Appius Claudius, late proconsul of Cilicia, and Calpurnius Piso were chosen censors, and appeared to have authority enough to carry into execution the powers lately restored to this office by the ordinance of Scipio. It was expected that these censors would hold an even balance between the factions. Appius favoured Pompey, and Piso, from his relation of father-in-law to Cæsar, was necessarily disposed to check the partiality of his colleague. The hopes of the senate were likewise considerably raised by the unexpected nomination of Caius Scribonius Curio to be one of the tribunes. Servius Pola, after being elected into this office, had been convicted of bribery, the election was set aside, and Curio substituted in his place. This young man was of an honourable family; and possessing talents which qualified him for the highest preferments, naturally set out on a foot of independence, and joined those who were for maintaining the freedom of the commonwealth, and their own equal pretensions to honour and power. Being active and bold, as well as eloquent, the senators were fond of a partizan who was likely to take upon himself much of that fatigue and danger which many of them were willing, even where their own estates and dignities were concerned, to devolve upon others.

U. C. 703.

L. Æmilius Paulus, and C. Claudius Marcellus.

The new magistrates accordingly entered on office with high expectations that the dangerous pretensions of ambitious citizens, particularly those of Cæsar, would be effectually checked. The consuls were possessed of a resolution of the senate, requiring them to proceed to the business of Cæsar's province by the first of March. This resolution wanted only the consent of the tribunes to render it a formal act of the executive power, of which this branch was by the constitution lodged in the senate. But one of the tribunes having forbid the decree, M. Marcellus, late consul, moved that application might be made to this officer to withdraw the negative, which prevented the effect of what the senate had resolved. But the motion was rejected by a majority[5] of the senate itself; and many other symptoms of Cæsar's great influence, even over this order of men, soon after appeared.

This able politician, probably that he might not seem to have any views upon Italy, had fixed his quarters, and that of his army, in the low countries, and at the extremity of his recent conquests. But instead of seizing every pretence, as formerly, for making war on the natives of Gaul, he endeavoured to quiet their fears, and to conciliate their affections;[6] and while he kept the whole province in a state of profound tranquillity, collected money, provided arms, and completed

5 Cicero ad Familiar. lib. viii. ep. 13.
6 Hist. de Bell. Gall. lib. viii. c. 49.

his legions, as if preparing for a dangerous and important war. His distance from Italy lulled the jealousy of his opponents, and enabled him to carry on his operations unobserved. He spared no expense in gaining accessions to his interest; and when promises were accepted, seemed to make them with unbounded confidence in the means on which he relied for the performance of them. In this he acted as on the eve of a great revolution, the event of which was to raise him above the want of resources, or above the necessity of a scrupulous faith with private persons. He actually remitted at this time great sums of money to Rome; and no less than fifteen hundred talents, or about 289,500*l*, to the management of the consul Æmilius alone, who was supposed to expend this money in erecting public buildings for the use of the city. But not being superior to corruption, at least not to that which was addressed to his vanity, in being made agent and trustee for so popular a leader as Cæsar, he disappointed the hopes of his friends, and in all the contests which arose during his consulate,[1] became an active partizan for the person who had honoured him with so flattering a trust.

It was likewise very early observed in these debates, that the zeal of Curio, who set out with violent invectives against Cæsar, began to abate; that he for a while endeavoured to divert the attention of the public to other objects;[2] and at last fairly withdrew himself from the support of the senate, and espoused the interest of Cæsar in every question.

This interest was now likewise strengthened by the accessions brought to it in consequence of the disputes of the censors. These magistrates concurred in expurging from the rolls of the senate such as were of servile extraction, and many even of noble family, on account of some infamy or blemish in their character. But Appius, having carried his affectation of zeal beyond what the age could bear, and being suspected of partiality to Pompey's friends, gave offence to Piso, who, by protecting many citizens who were stigmatized by his colleague, gained them to the interest of Cæsar. From these several causes this party became very numerous even in the senate, and continued to suspend any decrees that were proposed to deprive Cæsar of his command, or to recall the extraordinary privilege which had formerly been granted to him.

It was afterwards discovered, in the sequel of these transactions, that Curio, some time before he openly declared himself for Cæsar, had been actually gained by him. This young man, like the youth of that age in general, had dissipated his fortune, and contracted immense debts. His popularity was the effect of his profusion; and the load of his debts made him a very uncertain friend to government, and to laws which supported the just claims of his creditors against him. He readily listened to Cæsar, who offered to relieve him of this burden, and actually paid his debts to a great amount;[3] according to some reports, to the amount of ten millions Roman money;[4] according to others, of six times that sum.[5]

Curio, after he took his resolution to join Cæsar, continued to speak the language of his former party, and to act in concert with them, until he should find a plausible excuse for breaking with them. Such a pretence[6] he sought by starting many subjects of debate without consulting them, and by making proposals in which he knew that the leading men of the senate would not concur. To this effect he devised a project for the reparation of the highways, offering himself to have the inspection of the work for five years. And when much time had been spent in fruitless debates on this subject, he insisted, that a considerable intercalation should be made to lengthen the year, to give him sufficient time to ripen his projects. Being opposed in this by the college of Augurs,[7] he employed his tribunitian power to obstruct all other business, and separated himself entirely from his friends in the senate.

Curio, having in this manner withdrawn himself from his former party, did not at once openly join their opponents; but, with professions of independence, affected to oppose the errors of both; and, by this artful conduct, seemed to have received the instructions, or to have imitated the policy of his leader. When the great question of Cæsar's recall was revived, he inveighed, as formerly, against the exorbitant powers which had been committed to this general, and urged the necessity of having them revoked; but subjoined, that the powers granted to Pompey were equally dangerous, and proposed, that both should be ordered to disband their armies, and return to a private station. The partizans of Pompey insisted, that the term of his commission was not yet expired; nor that of Cæsar's, replied Curio. If either is to be disarmed, it is proper that both should be so; if only one army be disbanded, we are certainly the slaves of that which remains.

There were probably now three parties in the state; one devoted to Cæsar, another to Pompey, and a third that meant to support the republic against the intrigues or violence of either. The latter must have been few, and could not hope to be of much consequence, except by joining such of the other two, as appeared by the character of its leader least dangerous to the commonwealth. Cæsar had shown himself in his political course, a dangerous subject, and an arbitrary magistrate. In the capacity of a subject, he had supported every party that was inclined to commit disorder in the state, or to weaken the hands of government. In that of a magistrate he spurned every legal restraint, acted the part of a demagogue, supporting himself by popular tumults, and the credit of a faction, against the laws of his country; and it was the general opinion of considerate persons, that his thirst of power and emolument was not be satiated without a total subversion of government: that if, in the contest which seemed to impend, his sword should prevail, a scene of bloodshed and rapine would ensue, far exceeding what had yet been exhibited in any calamity that had ever befallen the republic. The description of his adherents,[8] and the character of persons that crowded to his standard, justified the general fear and distrust which was entertained of his designs. All who had fallen under the sentence of the law, all who

1 Appian. Plutarch.
2 Cicero ad Familiar lib. viii. ep. 6.
3 Plutarch. Dio. Sueton. Appias.
4 Velleius, lib. ii. c. 48.—80,729*l*. See Arbuthnot's Tables.
5 Valerius Maximus, lib. ix.
6 Dio. Cass. lib. xl. c. 61. Appian de Bello Civile.
7 Cicero ad Familiar. lib. viii. ep. 6.
8 Cicero ad Atticum, lib. v : 7.

dreaded this fate, all who had suffered any disgrace, or were conscious they deserved it; young men who were impatient of government; the populace who had an aversion to order; the bankrupt, to whom law and property itself were enemies; all these looked for his approach with impatience, and joined in every cry that was raised in his favour.

Pompey, the leader of the opposite party, had never ceased to embroil the state with his intrigues, and even invaded the laws by his impatience for extraordinary and unprecedented honours; yet, when possessed of power, he had employed it with moderation, and seemed to delight in receiving these singular trusts by the free choice of his country; not in extorting them, not in making any illegal use of them, nor in retaining them beyond the terms prescribed by his commission. It appeared, that in nothing he had ever injured the commonwealth so deeply, as in caballing with Cæsar while he rose to his present elevation, from which he was not likely to descend, without some signal convulsion in the state.[9]

This comparison of the parties which were now to contend for power at the hazard of the republic, made it easy for good citizens to choose their side. But they nevertheless naturally wished to prevent the contest from coming to extremities; as in the event of the war, which they dreaded, it was scarcely possible to avoid a military government. They considered the proposal of Curio as a mere pretence to justify Cæsar in keeping possession of his army; but they saw that there was no force in the republic sufficient to resist him. They wished to arm Pompey for this purpose; but were prevented, either by the confidence which he still gave them of his own superiority, or by their fear of precipitating the state into a civil war, by seeming to take any precautions against it.

Cæsar would have considered every attempt to arm the republic as a declaration against himself; and was ready to commence hostilities before any such measure could be carried into execution. The proposal for disarming at once both Cæsar and Pompey, in the mean time, was extremely acceptable to the popular party, who perpetually sounded the cry of liberty against the senate, and lately too against Pompey himself, who, on account of the spirit of his administration when last in office, and the severity of his prosecutions against bribery and other offences, which are not odious to the vulgar, was become in a considerable degree unpopular, and supposed to aim at a tyranny. With such powers as Pompey already possessed, it was reckoned an effort of courage to oppose him. And Curio, in coming from the senate, with the lustre of having acted so bold a part, was received by the populace with shouts and acclamations, was conducted to his house over ways strewed with flowers, and, like a victor in the circus, presented with chaplets and garlands, in reward of his courageous, patriotic and impartial conduct. This happened about the time that Pompey, as has been observed, was making a show of his great popularity in the country towns, where he was received with feasts, processions, and acclamations, on occasion of his recovery from a supposed dangerous illness. Cæsar too had a like reception in the towns of the Cisalpine Gaul; but it is likely, that of these three pretenders to popularity, Pompey was most elated with his share of the public favour, and the most likely to mistake these appearances of consideration for the stable foundations of power. Under this mistake probably it was, that when one of his friends asked him, with what force he was to oppose Cæsar if he should march into Italy with his army? "In Italy," he answered, "I can raise forces with a stamp of my foot." He was, however, greatly alarmed by the motion which had been made by Curio, and by the reception it met, both in the approbation of the senators, and in the acclamations of the people. He wrote a letter, on this occasion, to the senate, in which he acknowledged the services of Cæsar, and mentioned his own. "His late consulate," he said, "was not of his seeking; it was pressed upon him to save the republic in the midst of great dangers; the command he then bore had devolved upon him in consequence of his having been consul, and was given for a term of years, yet far from being expired; but he was ready, nevertheless, without waiting for the expiration of his term, to resign with alacrity what he had accepted with reluctance." He continued, on every occasion, to repeat the same professions, adding, "That he made no doubt his relation and his friend Cæsar would cheerfully make a like sacrifice to the fears and apprehensions of his fellow-citizens; and that, after many years of hard struggle with warlike enemies, he would now hasten to retire in peace, and to solace himself in the midst of domestic repose."

Pompey, for the most part, chose to dissemble his sentiments, and advanced to his purpose by indirect means; he was, therefore, like most artful men, easily over-reached by persons who perceived his designs; and probably, on the present occasion, was the only dupe of his own artifices, or of those that were employed against him. Curio, in the senate, openly attacked this part of his character, insisting that actions, and not professions, were now to be regarded: that the army of Cæsar was, to the republic, a necessary defence against that of Pompey; that nevertheless, both should be ordered to disband, under pain of being declared, in case of disobedience, enemies to their country; and that an army should be instantly levied to enforce these orders. "Now," said he, "is the time to reduce this assuming and arrogant man, while you have a person who can dispute his pretensions, and who can wrest those arms out of his hands, which he never would have willingly dropped."

The friends of Cæsar, in the senate, offered to compromise the dispute; and provided Pompey retired to his province, and Cæsar were allowed to retain the Cisalpine Gaul with two legions, they proposed, in his name, to disband the remainder of his army, and to resign the other part of his provinces. "Observe the dutiful citizen and good subject," said Cato, "how ready he is to quit the northern parts of Gaul, if you only put him in possession of Italy and of the city; and how ready to accept of your voluntary submission, rather than employ your own army against you to enforce it."[10]

In the result of these debates, the senate, upon

9 Cicero ad Atticum, lib. vii. ep. 3.

10 Plutarch. in Catone.

the motion of the consul Marcellus, came to a vote on the following questions, which were separately stated, relating to the appointments both of Cæsar and of Pompey. On the first question, Whether Cæsar should disband his army? the *Ayes* were general throughout the house. On the second, relating to Pompey, the *Noes* greatly prevailed. Curio and M. Antony insisted, that the questions were not fairly put; and that they did not collect the sense of the senate; that the majority might be of opinion, that both should disband; and that both, therefore, should be included in the same question. To this purpose, accordingly, a third question was put; and the senate having divided, a majority of three hundred and seventy *Ayes* appeared against twenty-two *Noes*.[1] Whether these proceedings of the senate were annulled by any informality, or were deprived of effect by any other circumstance, does not appear. The only immediate consequence they seem to have produced, was an order to Pompey and Cæsar, requiring each of them to march a legion to reinforce the army in Syria, where the Parthians, though repulsed from Antioch in the preceding year, had wintered in the Cyrrhestica, a district of that province, and threatened to repeat their invasion in the present spring and summer; and this appears to have been no more than a feeble attempt to strip Cæsar of two legions, of which, when it came to be executed, he well knew how to disappoint the effect.

While the subject of Cæsar's appointments occupied all parties at Rome, he himself, with his army, passed a quiet winter in Gaul; and at the end of it, or early in the spring, set out for Italy. He employed, as a pretence for this journey, the election to a vacant place in the college of augurs, which was fast approaching; and for which his friend Mark Antony was a candidate. Many votes were to be procured in the colonies and free cities bordering on that part of his province which was beyond the Alps; and he made his journey with uncommon speed to secure them: but being informed, on the road, that the election of augurs was past, and that his friend Antony had prevailed, he nevertheless continued his journey, and with the same diligence as before he had received this information, saying, It was proper he should thank his friends for their good offices, and request the continuance of their favour in his own competition for the consulate, which he proposed to declare on the following year. He alleged, as a reason for his early application, that his enemies, in order to oppress him, or to withstand his just pretensions, had placed C. Marcellus and P. Lentulus in the magistracy of the present year, and had rejected the pretensions of Galba, though much better founded.

He was met in all the provincial towns and colonies of Cisalpine Gaul with more than a kingly reception, with sacrifices and processions every where made by innumerable crowds, which were assembled to see and admire him. Having made the circuit of this province, and sounded the dispositions of the people, he returned with great despatch to his quarters at Nemetocenna,[2] in the low countries, where he likewise wished to know the disposition as well as the state of his army; and, for this purpose, ordered the whole to assemble on the Moselle. He foresaw, that the senate might possibly pass a decree to supersede him; and that he must then depend upon the attachment of his legions, and make war, or submit, as he found them inclined; in this, however, it is probable he was in a great measure resolved, or had no doubt of their willingness to become his partners in a military adventure for the sovereignty of the empire.

In this state of affairs he assigned to Labienus his station within the Alps; and seeming to have conceived a suspicion of this officer, or rather knowing that he was not disposed to follow him, in case his commission should be withdrawn by the senate, nor to co-operate in any act of hostility against the republic, he wished to prevent the disputes which might arise on such an occasion, and to avoid the difficult task of determining how he should deal with a citizen, who being an offender against himself, was nevertheless in his duty to the state, and who either, by his impunity or by his sufferings, might start dangerous questions, and divide the opinions and affections of the soldiers. He dismissed him, therefore, from the army in the northern Gaul, to command on the Po, a station from which he could easily quit the province, and join the forces of the republic; and by this means rid him at once of a person on whom he could not rely, and whom he would scarcely dare to punish for defection. But in whatever manner we understand this separation, it is noticed, that while Cæsar himself remained with the army upon the Moselle, and made frequent movements merely to exercise the troops and to preserve their health, a rumour prevailed, that his enemies were soliciting Labienus to desert him, and to carry off the troops that were under his command. At the same time it was reported, that the senate was preparing a decree to divest Cæsar of his government, and to disband his army. These insinuations he affected to treat as groundless, observing, that he could not believe such an officer as Labienus would betray his trust; and that for himself, he was at all times ready to submit his cause to a free senate. The proposals of Curio, and his other friends, he said, had been so reasonable, that the senate would have long ago accepted of them, if that body had not been under the improper influence of his enemies.

About the same time, Cæsar received the famous order of the senate to detach a legion from his army to be transported into Syria, and employed in the Parthian war; and likewise to restore that legion which he had borrowed from Pompey. It is probable, that he had desired the last might be sent to him merely to take off a part of his rival's force; and though he now, with seeming cheerfulness, complied with the requisition to restore them, yet he afterwards complained of this measure respecting the two legions in question, as a mere artifice to turn his own forces against him. In compliance with the senate's order, he sent the fifteenth legion, then upon the Po, and relieved it by one from his present camp. In dismissing the soldiers of Pompey, he was, under pretence of gratitude for past services, most lavish of his caresses and thanks; and as an earnest of future favour, ordered each private man a gratuity of two hundred and fifty denarii.[3] By this artful conduct, while he parted with the men, he took care to retain their affec-

1 Appian de Bello Civ. lib. ii. Plutarch. in Cæsar. p. 134. 2 Arras.

3 About 5*l*.

tions, and sent them, together with his own legion, as at best but an uncertain and dubious accession of strength to his enemies.[4]

The officers who were sent to make these demands, and to conduct the troops into Italy, brought to their employers a very flattering report of the state and dispositions of Cæsar's army: that they longed to change their commander; had a high opinion of Pompey; and, if marched into Italy, would surely desert to him; that Cæsar was become odious on account of the hard service in which he had so long employed them, without any adequate reward, and on account of the suspicion that he aimed at the monarchy.[5] It is in the highest degree probable, that their crafty leader employed proper persons to hold this language to the commissioners of the senate, and to the officers of Pompey; and to utter complaints of their commander, and of the service, on purpose that they might be repeated in Italy. His own preparations were not of more importance to him than the supine security into which he endeavoured, by this and every other measure, to lull his enemies.

On the approach of winter he conducted his army back to their quarters in the low countries, and the interior parts of Gaul. Trebonius was stationed with four legions on the Scheld and the Meuse, and Fabius, with other four, between the Soane and the Loire, in the canton of Bibracte, now Autun. This disposition, like that of the former winter, was calculated to avoid giving any alarm to his opponents in Italy. He himself intended to winter within the Alps, but had no troops on that side of the mountains that could occasion any suspicion; only one veteran legion is mentioned, the thirteenth, which he had sent to replace the fifteenth; that, upon pretence of the Parthian war, had been called away from his province. Upon his arrival in Italy he affected surprise upon hearing that the two legions lately demanded from him had not been sent into Asia, but were kept in Italy, and put under the command of Pompey. He complained, that he was betrayed; that his enemies meant to disarm and circumvent him. "But while the republic is safe, and matters can be made up on amicable terms, I will bear," he said, "with any indignities, rather than involve the state in a civil war."[6]

While the factions that were likely to divide the empire were in this situation, C. Marcellus, now third of this name in the succession of consuls, together with Publius Lentulus, were chosen for the following year. Before they entered on office a rumour arose, that Cæsar, with his whole army, was actually in motion to pass the Alps. Marcellus, consul of the present year, assembled the senate; laid before them this report, and moved, that the troops then in Italy should be prepared to act, and new levies should be ordered. A debate ensued, in which Curio contradicted the report, and, by his Tribunitian authority, forbade the senate to proceed in any resolution upon this subject.

On this interposition of the tribune, the consul dismissed the assembly, using, together with other expressions of impatience, the words following: That if he were not supported by the senate, in the measures which were necessary for the preservation of the commonwealth, he should put the exercise of his power into hands more likely to make the state be respected: then, together with Lentulus, one of the consuls elected for the ensuing year, he repaired to the gardens where Pompey resided; this officer being obliged, on account of his military command, to remain without the city; and presenting his sword, bid him employ it for the defence of his country, and with it to assume the command of the forces then in Italy. To this address, Pompey, with an air of modesty, made answer, "If nothing better can be devised for the commonwealth."

4 Appian. de Bello Civile, lib. ii. Plutarch. in Vita Pompeii, p. 435.

5 Plutarch. in Vita Cæsaris, p. 133, et in Vita Pompeii. p. 486.

6 Hirtus de Bello Gallico, lib. viii. c. 46.

CHAPTER V.

Return of different Officers from their Provinces—Decree of the Senate to supersede Cæsar—Forbidden by the Tribunes—Commission to the Consuls and to Pompey—Their Resolutions—Flight of the Tribunes Antony and Quintus Cassius—Speech of Cæsar to the Legion at Ravenna—Surprise of Ariminum—March of Cæsar—Flight of Pompey and the Senate, &c.—Approach of Cæsar—Embarkation and Departure of Pompey from Brundusium—Return of Cæsar to Rome—Passes by Marseilles into Spain—Campaign on the Segra—Legions of Pompey in Spain conducted to the Var.

IN this posture of affairs, the officers, who had been sent in the preceding year to the command of provinces, were returned to Rome, and some of them remained with their ensigns of magistracy in the suburbs, to solicit the military honours to which they thought themselves entitled by their services. Bibulus, though not present in the action in which Cassius defeated the Parthians, yet being then governor of the province, and the advantage gained, with the number of the enemy slain, coming up to the legal description of those services for which the triumph was obtained, he entered his claim: and was accordingly, upon the motion of Cato, who probably wished him this consolation for the mortifications he had received in his consulate, found to be entitled to this honour. It had been long appropriated as the specific reward of victories, obtained by the slaughter of a certain number of enemies, and would have been preposterous in the case of any other merit: Cicero, nevertheless, now likewise applied for a triumph, partly in emulation to Bibulus, of whom he expresses some jealousy; and partly, that he might have a pretence for his stay in the suburbs, and for absenting himself from the senate, and from the assemblies of the people, being very much perplexed how to steer between the parties of Cæsar and Pompey, who had both applied to him by letters to join them in the present dispute.[1] He had, some time before his departure from Cilicia on his return to Rome, sent an account of his military operations to Cato, and to some others of his friends, with an earnest request, that a thanksgiving might be appointed for the victory he had obtained. Such an appointment was reckoned one of the greatest honours which a Roman officer could receive in absence, and might lead to a triumph. Cato replied in terms that were polite; but carrying some degree of indirect reproof for the improper ambition which Cicero betrayed in this request, intimating that his merit was not so much that of a general, as that of a humane, upright, and able magistrate; that he had moved the senate to pass a decree to this purpose in his favour, as thinking it more honourable than a thanksgiving, which always had a reference to some event, depending on chance or the valour of an army; but that, since Cicero had chosen to put his services on the last footing, he had a double satisfaction, that of having done what he thought incumbent on himself, and that of finding that the desire of his friend was gratified.[2]

Cicero at first received this declaration of Cato as a proper expression of friendship, and in the highest degree honourable to himself;[3] but on hearing of the military honours which were decreed to Bibulus upon Cato's motion, he was greatly provoked, and considered this conduct as partial to his rival, and invidious to himself.[4] He was instigated or confirmed in these sentiments by Cæsar, who gladly seized the opportunity to incite him against Cato. "Observe," he said, in one of his letters, which is quoted by Cicero on this subject, "the malice of the man, he affects to give you the commendations of clemency and integrity, which you did not desire, and withholds a piece of common respect, which you had asked. This conduct," continues Cicero to Atticus, "bespeaks the envy from which it proceeds. It is not sufferable, nor will I endure it. Cæsar, in his letter to me, has not missed the proper remarks." Such were the concerns that distracted the mind of this ingenious but weak man, even while he himself foresaw a conflict, in which the republic itself, and all the honours it could bestow, were probably soon to perish.

In the present situation of affairs, every resolution which the friends of the republic could take was fraught with danger, and every day increased their perplexity. To leave Cæsar in possession of his army, and to admit him with such a force to the head of the commonwealth, was to submit, without a struggle, to the dominion he meant to assume. To persist in confining him to one or other of these advantages, was to furnish him with a pretence to make war on the republic. The powers which were necessary to enable Pompey to resist Cæsar, might be equally dangerous to the republic in the possession of the one, as they were in that of the other. This person, on whom the state was now to rely, even while his own consideration, with that of every other senator, was at stake, did not seem disposed to act, until all the powers that were wanting to gratify his ambition should be put into his hands. With an appearance of ease and negligence, he went upon parties of pleasure through Italy, while every one else apprehended that Rome itself, as well as Italy, must soon become a scene of blood. At an interview with Cicero, whom, on his way to the city, he met near Naples, he himself spoke of a civil war as unavoidable.[5] Upon his return to Rome, on the twenty-sixth of December, he even seemed averse to any accommodation. He declared his mind openly that if Cæsar should obtain the consulate, even upon laying down his arms, the state must be undone; that in his opinion, whenever a vigorous opposition appeared, Cæsar would choose to retain his army, and drop his pretensions to the consulate: but, continued he, if Cæsar should proceed headlong, and bring matters to the decision of the sword, how contemptible must he appear, a mere private adventurer against the authority of the state, supported by a regular army under my command.

To justify this security, or presumption on the part of Pompey, it must be remembered that while Cæsar was forming an army in Gaul, Pompey, by means of his lieutenants, likewise formed a great army of six complete legions, and many auxiliaries, in Spain; and that if Cæsar should make any attempt upon Italy, it is probable he intended that his army should pass the Pyrennees as fast as that of Cæsar passed the Alps, occupy his province, cut off his resources, and while Pompey himself received him with the forces of Italy, that the Spanish army should press upon his rear, and place him at once between two attacks. It ought likewise to be considered, that although few troops were then actually formed in Italy, yet this was the great nursery of soldiers for the whole empire, and multitudes could, on any sudden emergency, be embodied in every part of that country.[6]

Pompey, with these securities in his hands for the final success of his views against Cæsar, suffered this rival to run his career, leaving the senate exposed to the dangers which threatened them; and under the influence of apprehensions, which he expected would render them more tractable, and more ready in every thing to comply with his own desires, than he had generally found them in times of greater security.

In the same strain of policy, Pompey had frequently ventured to foment or to connive at the growing troubles of the republic, in order to render himself the more necessary, and to draw from the senate and the people offers of extraordinary trust and power. By the address of Cato, and of other active men in the senate, he had been obliged on a late occasion, when he aimed at the powers of dictator, to be content with those of sole consul. It is probable, that he had entertained the same views on the present occasion, and permitted the evils to accumulate, until the remedy he wished for should appear to be necessary. He continued accordingly with votes and resolutions of the senate to combat Cæsar, who was at the head of a numerous army, ready on the first plausible pretence to fall upon Italy, to seize the

1 Cicero ad Att. lib. vii. ep. 1.
2 Cicero ad Familiar. lib. xv. ep. 5. 3 Ibid. ep. 6.
4 Cicero ad Att. lib. vii. ep. 2
5 Cicero ad Atticum, lib. vii. ep. 8.
6 Cic. ad Familiar. lib. xvi. ep. 12.

seats of government, and avail himself of that name and authority of the republic, on which Pompey himself so greatly relied.

U C. 704. *C. Claudius Marcellus et L. Cornelius Lentulus.* Mean time, the new year commenced, and C. Claudius Marcellus with L. Cornelius Lentulus, entered on their office as consuls. Both parties were prepared for a decisive resolution on the subject of Cæsar's claims. He himself for some years had wintered near to the northern extremity of his provinces. He was now at Ravenna, the nearest station of his army to Rome; but without any troops, besides what appear to have been the usual establishment of the Cisalpine province; that is, the thirteenth legion, which had been sent thither to supply the place of a legion, with which he had been required to reinforce the army of Syria, and three hundred horse, making in all between five and six thousand men.[7] Soon after his arrival at Ravenna, he had been visited by Curio, who, at the expiration of his tribunate, made this journey to receive his directions in respect to the future operations of the party; and after their conference, returned to Rome with a letter from Cæsar, addressed to the senate, which was presented on the first of January, at the admission of the new consuls into office.[8]

The consul Lentulus moved, that prior to any other business, the state of the republic, and that of the provinces, should be taken under consideration; and alluding to the resolutions which were already on record, relating to Cæsar's province, said, that if the senate stood firm on this occasion to their former decrees, his services should not be wanting to the commonwealth. He was seconded by Scipio, and was applauded by the general voice of the senate; but Cæsar had procured the admission of Mark Antony and of Quintus Cassius, two of his most noted and determined partizans, into the college of tribunes. These could make riots, or furnish the pretence of violence in the city, whenever the military designs of their patron were ripe for execution: they were to be the executors of what had been concerted with Curio, or whatever else should be thought proper to promote Cæsar's designs. They began with threatening to stop all proceedings of the senate, until Cæsar's letter was read; and prevailed on this meeting to begin with that paper. It was expressed, according to Cicero, in terms menacing and harsh,[9] and contained in substance a repetition of the proposals, which Cæsar had been all along making through Curio, and his other adherents at Rome, "That he should be allowed to retain the honours, which the Roman people had bestowed upon him; that he should be left upon a foot of equality with other officers, who were allowed to join civil office at Rome with military establishments in the provinces; and that he should not be singled out as the sole object of their distrust and severity."[10]

This letter was considered as an attempt to prescribe to the senate, and unbecoming the respect due to their authority. It was by many treated as an actual declaration of war. The debates were renewed on this subject for some days successively, from the first to the seventh of January. On the last of these days, a resolution was framed, ordering Cæsar to dismiss his army, and by a certain day to retire from his provinces, or in case of disobedience, declaring him an enemy to his country. The tribunes, Mark Antony and Quintus Cassius, interposed with their negative.

The hands of the senate being thus tied up by the prohibition or interdict of the tribunes, it was moved that the members should put on mourning, in order to impress the people with a deeper sense of the calamity which was likely to ensue from the contumacy of these factious officers. This likewise the tribunes forbad; but the senate being adjourned, all the members, as of their own accord, returned to their next meeting in habits of mourning, and proceeded to consider in what manner they might remove the difficulty which arose from this factious interposition of the tribunes. In the conclusion of this deliberation, it was determined to give to the consuls and other magistrates, together with Pompey, in the character of proconsul, the charge usual in the most dangerous conjunctures; *to preserve the commonwealth by such means as to their discretion should appear to be necessary.*

This charge suggested to the minds of the people, what had passed in the times of the Gracchi of Saturninus and of Catiline. The tribunes, who had occasioned the measure, either apprehended, or affected to apprehend, immediate danger to their own persons: they disguised themselves in the habit of slaves, and, together with Curio, in the night fled from Rome in hired carriages.[11] The consuls repaired to Pompey in the suburbs; and, agreeably to the order of the senate, claimed his assistance in discharging the important duties with which they were jointly intrusted. It was agreed, in concert with him, that they should support the authority of the senate with a proper military force, that they should proceed to make new levies with the greatest despatch; and in order to give effect to these preparations, that Pompey should have the supreme command over the treasury, and all the forces of the republic, in every quarter of the world.

Winter was now set in, or fast approaching. The season, although nominally in the month of January, being only about fifty days past the autumnal equinox, or about the twelfth of November, Cæsar had few troops on the side of Italy; the force of his army was yet beyond the Alps, and the officers now entrusted with the safety of the commonwealth, flattered themselves that much time might be found to put the republic in a state of defence, before his army at this season could pass those mountains, even if he should be so desperate as to make war on the commonwealth; which Pompey did not even, in this state of affairs, appear to have believed.

When Cæsar received accounts of the senate's resolution, he drew forth the troops then at Ravenna, and in a harangue enumerated the wrongs which for some years he alleged had been done to himself; complained that his enemies had now found means to excite against him even Pompey,

---

7 Appian. de Bello Civil. lib. ii. p. 447. Plut. in Cæsare.
8 Dio. Cassus, lib. xli. c. 1.
9 Cicero ad Familiar. lib. xvi. ep. 12.
10 Suetonius in Cæsare, c. 29.

11 Appian. de Bello Civili, lib. ii. Dio. Cass. lib. xli. c. 3. Cicero ad Familiar. lib. xvi. ep. 12.

a person whose honour he had always promoted with the warmest affection; that the interposition of the tribunes, in behalf of the army and of himself, had been defeated by means of threats and of actual force; that their sacred persons had been violated, in order to oppress him; that resolutions, which had never been taken but in the most dangerous and threatening conjunctures, to prevent ruinous laws from being carried by insurrection and violence, were now formed against peaceable magistrates, and in times of profound tranquillity; he therefore exhorted the army to maintain the honour of an officer, under whom they had now, for nine years, faithfully served the republic; under whom they had gained many victories in Gaul and in Germany, and reduced a most warlike province into a state of absolute submission. He was answered with a shout of applause, and a general acclamation from the ranks, that they were ready to avenge the injuries done to their general, and to the tribunes of the people.

On receiving these assurances from the troops then present, Cæsar immediately despatched an express to the quarters of the twelfth legion, which, from the time at which it afterwards joined him, appears to have been already within the Alps with orders to march. The remainder of his army being supposed in the low countries, or in the heart of Gaul, it would not have appeared to an ordinary capacity, that even in case of hostilities any decisive operation could take place before the spring. At that season, indeed, the measures now taken by both parties seemed to threaten a dangerous convulsion; but it is not to be doubted that Cæsar had foreseen, or prepared, many of the most important circumstances of the present conjuncture; that he had brought his affairs into that posture, at which he intended hostilities should commence; and that the seeming neglect with which he suffered himself to be taken with so small a force on the side of Italy, was probably the best concerted preparation he could have made for the war. While he brought no alarming force towards Rome, his antagonists continued secure, and made no effectual provision to resist him. He apprehended more danger from the legions which Pompey had formed in Spain, than from any force then subsisting in Italy, and he made his disposition against those legions, by placing the strength of his army between the Pyrennees and the Alps. There the army formed in Gaul, served him sufficiently in his design against Italy, by securing him from any interruption on that quarter. When the war broke out, being well aware that the effects of surprise are often greater than those of force, even if he had wished for more troops in Italy, it is probable that he would not have awaited their coming.

On the very day that he delivered the harangue just mentioned to the legion that was quartered at Ravenna, he ordered a chosen body of men, in the manner of stragglers roving for pleasure through the country, and armed only with swords, to take the road separately, and without any appearance of concert, to Ariminum, the first fortified place of Italy beyond the Rubicon, which was the limit of his province, there to remain, and at a certain time of the night to seize upon one of the gates. He likewise ordered a party of horse to parade at some distance from Ravenna, and there to wait for an officer who was to deliver them orders. He himself passed the day, as usual, in forming combats of gladiators, and in attending the exercises of the legion; at night he went to supper at the usual hour, and after he had taken his place, pretending business, or some slight indisposition, which called him away from the company, he mounted a carriage that waited for him, drove through a gate opposite to that of Ariminum, and having travelled for a little time in that direction, turned into the road on which he had posted the party of horse, and having joined them, marched about thirty miles before break of day, entered Ariminum by a gate which the party he had sent before him kept open; and thus without any resistance took possession of the place.

It was of importance, that the first report of hostilities at Rome should carry an account of his success; not merely of his having made an attempt. This circumstance may justify the measures which he took to surprise a place which, without so many precautions, might have been easily reduced, though at the hazard perhaps of delay for a few days. He himself, indeed, in his Commentaries, makes no mention of any such measures, nor of the doubts and hesitations under which he is said to have halted on the banks of the Rubicon, by the passing of which he entered into a state of war with the common wealth.

At Ariminum his little army, on the following day, arrived from Ravenna, and the tribunes, Mark Antony and Quintus Cassius, joined him from Rome. He presented them to the army in the disguise in which they affected to have escaped from the violence of a tyranny then established in the city. "Observe," he said, "to what extremities persons of noble birth, vested with the sacred character of tribunes are reduced, for having supported their friends, and for having pleaded the cause of an injured army."[1] The occasion was suited to popular eloquence; and this eminent master of every art did not neglect the opportunity. He is said to have acted his part with great vehemence; to have torn open his vest from his breast, and to have shed tears; frequently held up to view the hand on which he wore his ring, the common ensign of noble birth among the Romans, and declared, that he would sacrifice all the honours of his rank to reward those who were willing to support the public cause, and who adhered to himself on the present occasion. From these signs, where he was not distinctly heard, it was supposed that he promised the honours of nobility, and a large sum of money to every soldier in his army.[2]

Lucius Cæsar and the prætor Roscius, who, while the decree against Caius Cæsar was depending in the senate, made offer of their good offices to treat with him, and bring matters to an amicable accommodation, were now come without any public commission, probably to hinder their friend from taking any desperate resolution. They brought at the same time, a private message from Pompey, with some expressions of civility, and an apology, taken from the necessity of the public service, for the hardship which he supposed himself to have put upon Cæsar. Pompey, in this message, protested, "That he had

1 Appian. de Bell. Civile, lib. ii.
2 Sueton. in Cæs. c. 33.

always preferred the public to private considerations;" and subjoined, "that he hoped Cæsar would not suffer any passion to carry him into measures hurtful to the state, nor, avenging himself of his private enemies, stretch forth his hand against the republic."

Such professions had little credit with Cæsar; but if they were to be of any weight with the public, he was not likely, in his turn, to fail in the use of them. He desired those persons, by whom Pompey had favoured him with this message, to carry for answer, "That the republic had always been to him dearer than his fortune or his life; but that he could not suffer the honours which the Roman people had bestowed upon him in public, to be contemptuously torn away by his private enemies. His commission, he said, would have expired in six months; his enemies, in their eagerness to degrade him, could not bear even with this delay, but must recall him immediately. The Roman people had dispensed with his attendance at the elections, yet he must be dragged to town at that time to gratify private malice. These personal insults he had patiently borne for the sake of the public; and being resolved to disarm, requested the senate only that others should disarm as well as himself; that even this was refused, and new levies were ordered throughout Italy; that two legions which had been called off from his own army, under pretence of the Parthian war, were now retained against him; that the whole state was in arms; for what purpose but for his destruction; that, nevertheless, he would suffer any thing for the good of the commonwealth. Let Pompey repair to his province; let all parties disband, and no army whatever be assembled in Italy; let no one pretend to overawe the city; let the assemblies of the people and of the senate be free; and in order the more speedily to terminate these disputes, let the parties meet and confer together; let Pompey say where he will be waited on, or let him name a proper place of meeting; at a friendly conference every difficulty will be soon removed."[3]

From this time forward, Cæsar affected, on every occasion, to have no object in view but to prevail on his enemies, by some reasonable accommodation, to save the republic from a ruinous war, and to stop the effusion of innocent blood.[4] He continually repeated his proposals of peace, while he urged his military operations with uncommon rapidity. He ordered new levies at Ariminum, and sent Antony to occupy Arretium,[5] a pass in one of the branches of the Flaminian Way through the Apennines; and as fast as the troops could march he seized Pisaurum,[6] Faunum, Auximum, with the town of Ancona, and all the places necessary to give him the command of that district, or to open his way to Rome.

A general consternation spread over all the country before him; the people fled from their habitations, and communicated the alarm, with every sort of exaggeration, to the city. Pompey had relied much on the name and authority of the commonwealth, and no less on his own. Others thought themselves secure while this renowned and experienced commander gave them assurances of safety. Now, like a person awake from a dream, he seemed to perceive the whole was illusion. Cæsar paid no regard to the authority of the senate, nor stood in awe of the state. He was at hand, with the reputation of a general equal to Pompey, at the head of troops fresh from service, and inured to blood. The republic was but a name; and they who composed it, though respectable at a distance, were, on the approach of an enemy, irresolute, disunited, and incapable of the exertions which such an occasion required. Orders had gone forth to raise troops in every part of Italy; but no great progress in so short a time could yet have been made in that service. Besides the two legions which had served so long under Cæsar himself, there were not any forces embodied in the country. These were justly suspected of inclining to their former general; and, instead of enabling Pompey to meet the danger which threatened the commonwealth, furnished him, at the head of such troops, with particular reasons for his keeping at a distance from the enemy. In a letter to Domitius Ahenobarbus, "I sent you word," he writes, "that with these two legions I did not choose to be near Cæsar.[7] If I should retreat, therefore, at his approach, be not surprised."[8]

Domitius had been appointed to succeed Cæsar in the government of Gaul; and, with some other officers in the Picenum,[9] had made some progress in raising troops. Their numbers, perhaps, surpassed those of Cæsar. If Pompey, therefore, had thought it possible to defend the city, he must have hastened to that quarter, and have put himself at the head of those troops. But he was timorous in hazarding his own reputation, a weakness from which Cæsar was altogether exempt, and which was unworthy of the great military talents of either. Pompey seldom committed his fame where the prospect was unfavourable, or events extremely uncertain. Cæsar, on such occasions, never chose to trust his affairs in any other hands than his own.

Pompey, acting under these motives, assembled the senate, and informed them that it was necessary to abandon Rome; that he would meet them again at Capua, where he proposed to assemble his forces; that he should consider all those who remained in the capital to countenance or to witness the violences of Cæsar as equally guilty with those who should be found in his camp.

It being unlawful for the officers of the republic to absent themselves from the city, the senate passed an act to dispense with their attendance at Rome, and to enable them to exercise the powers of magistracy wherever the necessities of the state might require their presence. These preparations for dislodging the government, together with the actual flight of Pompey, damped all the courage that remained in any order or class of the people. It made Cæsar appear at once more odious and more terrible.[10] It was generally expected[11] that he would exceed either Cinna or Sylla in rapacity and cruelty;[12] and that the city, if he should surprise his opponents there, would become a scene of blood. The consuls, and most

3 Cæsar. de Bell. Civil. lib. i.
4 Cæsar. Appian. in lib viii. Ad Attium, post ep. 13.
5 Arrego. 6 Pisaro, Feno, and Osimo.

7 Meaning probably that he did not choose to give them an opportunity to desert.
8 Cicero ad Atticum, lib. viii. ep. 2. Ad Domitium.
9 March of Anconia.
10 Cicero ad Att lib. vi. ep. 11.
11 Ibid. ep. 12. 22.
12 Ibid. lib. vii. ep. 7.

of the other officers of state, set out with their ensigns of power. All night the gates were crowded with senators and other persons of rank who fled on this occasion; some with their families and most valuable effects, others alone, and distracted by the general panic, without knowing whither they were to retire, or to what fate they were leaving their families.

Cæsar, in the mean time, making a rapid march through Umbria, or what is now the dutchy of Urbino,[1] and the Picenum, or March of Ancona,[2] not only took possession of every place as he passed, but gained daily accession of strength by the junction of the new levies that had been raised to oppose him. Soldiers are averse to the losing side; and Pompey's flight put an end to his military power in Italy. The prætor Thermus had, with five cohorts, amounting, if complete, to twenty-five hundred men, taken post at Iguvium,[3] among the Apennines, on the Flaminian Way. Observing that Pompey's party in general was retreating, and that Curio was advancing towards him with a part of Cæsar's forces, he resolved to abandon his post; but as soon as he began to execute this purpose, and was on the road to Rome, the troops deserted him on the march, returned to the post from which he had removed them, and declared for Cæsar.

The dispositions of the towns of which Cæsar had got possession, made it unnecessary for him to leave any garrison behind him, and permitted him to advance with all his forces. Auxinum[4] declared for him before his arrival, and obliged Accius Varus, who held that post for the republic, to abandon it. This officer was overtaken by Cæsar's advanced parties, and, like Thermus, was deserted by his people.

At Cingulum in the Picenum, Cæsar was joined by the twelfth legion, to which, on his first motion from Ravenna, he had sent orders to march. With this accession of force, he advanced to Asculum[5] on the Fronto; and having dislodged from thence Lentulus Spinther, who commanded ten cohorts, the greater part of these troops deserted to him. The remainder put themselves under the command of Vibullius, who was just arrived from Pompey to support the hopes of the cause in that quarter.

As Cæsar made his principal push on the Adriatic side of the Apennines, the troops that were suddenly raised for the republic were, without any well-concerted plan, drawn together upon that coast. And Pompey himself had not yet openly laid aside the design of making head against Cæsar in those parts. Vibullius having assembled in all about fourteen cohorts, fell back to the Aternus, now called the Piscara, and joined L. Domitius Ahenobarbus at Corfinium, a pass in the Apennines that commanded the Valerian way to Rome. This officer having assembled twenty-five cohorts, meant to have joined Pompey wherever he should be found, and had ordered Thermus to follow with five cohorts more;[6] but imagining probably that Pompey still intended to cover Rome from the incursions of Cæsar, and that Corfinium was an important post for this purpose, he determined to observe the motions of the enemy from that place.

1 Umbria, 2 Picenum. 3 Gubio.
4 Osimo. 5 Oscule.
6 Pomp. ad Cicer. in lib. ad Att. post ep. 11.

Pompey by this time had moved from Capua to Luceria, and seemed to have taken the resolution not only of abandoning the posts that covered the access to Rome, but even all Italy, to Cæsar. The consuls, the greater part of the magistracy, and the senate, had followed him to Capua. Here was received the message which Cæsar had given to Roscius and to L. Cæsar. It contained several reflections and insinuations in the highest degree provoking to Pompey; and to this circumstance Cæsar probably trusted, that he should not be bound by any of the offers he had made, and that the odium of rejecting the peace would fall upon his enemies. But the friends of the commonwealth, deeply impressed with the necessity of their own affairs, gladly listened to any terms of accommodation. They objected indeed to the proposed interview between Pompey and Cæsar, remembering the dangerous concerts which at their meetings had been formerly entered into against the commonwealth.

Pompey himself was so sensible of the disadvantage at which he was taken, that he dissembled his resentment of the personal reflections cast on himself, and consented to conditions which he had hitherto rejected with disdain. It was agreed accordingly that he should repair to Spain, and that, his province being in profound peace, he should reduce his military establishment. Cæsar, on his part, besides the conditions he himself had offered, was required to evacuate all the towns which he had lately seized in Italy; and it was proposed that the consuls, magistrates, and senators, should return to the city, and from the usual seat of government give all the sanction of public authority to these arrangements. From such appearances it was not doubted that an accommodation must follow. And in this belief Cato, though appointed to command in Sicily, chose to abide by the senate while the treaty remained in dependence. And Cicero thought the agreement almost concluded. "The one," he wrote to his friend Atticus, "begins to repent of his precipitation, and the other is sensible he has not a force sufficient to support such a war."[7]

Cæsar therefore was likely to be caught in the snare he laid for his enemies, or obliged to lay aside the disguise which he had assumed in affecting such earnest desires for peace. To avoid either of these inconveniences, he objected to some of the conditions which the opposite party had subjoined to his proposals, and complained of the silence which they kept on others, as proceeding from a deliberate purpose to circumvent and betray him. "Pompey will repair to Spain," he said, "but when? I am required to evacuate all the towns of Italy, while Pompey and the whole senate continue in arms against me, and while my enemies not only make new levies, but employ for my destruction legions which they have actually taken away from my own army. If Pompey be sincere in desiring a peace, why does he decline the personal interview which has been proposed for that purpose?"

Cæsar had by this time, advanced with hasty marches to Corfinium, drove in a detachment from the garrison, which he found breaking down a bridge about three miles from the town, sat down under the walls, and employed three days in fortifying his camp, and in filling the maga-

7 Ad. Att. lib. vii. ep. 14

zines with corn from the neighbouring country. Being joined by the eighth legion and twenty-two cohorts of the new levies from Gaul, with three hundred auxiliary horse, he ordered proper posts to be seized on every side of the town, and effectually shut up those who were within from any relief, or from any communication with their friends. When his works began to appear against the place, Domitius published a reward to any who should carry letters to Pompey. Different messengers were despatched for this purpose, and brought for answer, that Pompey disapproved of his having allowed himself to be invested by Cæsar, had foretold him the bad consequences of this measure, and now earnestly exhorted him, if possible, to extricate himself; for that it was not in his power with these doubtful legions, which had been so lately drawn from Cæsar's army, or with new levies, to force the hardy and veteran troops of the enemy.[8]

This answer Domitius endeavoured to conceal from his army; encouraged them with hopes of a speedy relief from Pompey, and seemed intent on the defence of the place, while he was actually taking measures to get off in person, without any hopes of preserving the forces he had assembled for the commonwealth. This design being suspected, the troops surrounded his quarters in the night, took him prisoner, and to pay their court, while they delivered up their general and surrendered the town, made offer of their own services to Cæsar.

Upon this surrender, Cæsar took possession of the gates, manned the walls, and gave orders that no person whatever from his army should enter the place before it was day. He knew, that besides Domitius and Vibullius, there were many senators and Roman knights now shut up in the town. These he ordered in the morning to be brought before him, expostulated with them on the subject of their enmity to himself, and their precipitation in hurrying the state into this unnatural war. He then dismissed them with the respect that was due to Roman citizens of their rank; and being told that a considerable sum of money, amassed at Corfinium for the support of the troops, had been seized by his people, to complete this scene of unexpected moderation, by an exhibition of disinterestedness, as well as of clemency, he ordered this money to be restored to Domitius. The fame of this wonderful mildness and generosity, as he expected, was every where diffused; and though, by over-acting his part in abstaining from the public money, he furnished every thinking person with a sufficient comment on the other parts of his conduct; yet many were happy to understand, that, in this alarming contest, their lives and properties were, from any motives whatever to be spared.

Rome was now open to Cæsar; but he thought the possession of it of no moment, until he had suppressed the military arrangements that were making in the country, and had decided who was to have the possession of Italy. He therefore, on the very day on which he became master of Corfinium, detached to Sicily, under the command of Curio, the troops that deserted to him in making this conquest.[9] He himself set out for Apulia, and, before sunset, accomplished a considerable march; but while he thus urged the war with the greatest rapidity, sent messengers before him to the leaders of the opposite party, with professions of friendship and overtures of peace.

Immediately after the reduction of Corfinium, Balbus, an officer in Cæsar's army, was despatched with a message to the consul Lentulus, containing earnest entreaties, that this magistrate would return to Rome, and prevent the disorders that were likely to arise from the suspension of government. To induce him to comply with this request, Balbus had secret instructions to assure the consul of a proper appointment in the provinces at the expiration of his year in office. The bearer of this message declared, that Cæsar desired nothing so much as to join Pompey, and to make peace with him on any equitable terms. And the father of this young man, one of Cæsar's retinue, wrote, at the same time, to Cicero, that Cæsar had no object but to enjoy peace and security under Pompey.[10] But while the fame of his clemency at Corfinium, and of this wonderful disposition to peace was spread throughout Italy, and reconciled the minds of many to whom he had been till then an object of terror;[11] while he hoped to amuse his enemies, and to relax the diligence of their military preparations, he advanced with so much rapidity, that, in order to avoid him, they had no more than the time that was necessary to cross the mountains from Capua to Luceria, to fall back from thence to Canusium, and from this last place, without a halt, to Brundusium.

Pompey, while he moved in this direction, having sent Metullus Scipio, and his own son Cnæus into Syria, to provide and assemble the necessary shipping to embark his army;[12] his intention to abandon Italy began to be suspected, and shook the great authority which he still derived from his military reputation. His officers were every where deserted on the march by the new levies, who returned to offer their services to Cæsar. His own presence kept the other parts of the army together, and brought them safe to the port from which it was suspected they were to take their departure from Italy. Soon after his arrival at this port he effectually verified these suspicions, embarking a great part of his army with the consuls, while he himself, not having sufficient shipping to transport the whole, remained with a second division to wait for the return of his ships.

Such was the posture of Pompey, when Cæsar, with six legions, four of veteran troops, and two newly raised or completed from those who came over to him on the march, arrived at the gates of Brundusium. Even here, he never dropt the project of amusing his enemy with proposals of peace. Cn. Magius, an officer in the service of the commonwealth, having been taken on the march, was dismissed with great courtesy, and a message to Pompey containing a request, that he would admit Cæsar to an interview; and observing, that differences are soon made up at a

8 Pompeius ad Domitium, lib. viii. **Et** ad Atticum, post ep. 12. Cæs. de Bell. Civ

9 Cæsar. de Bello Civ. lib. i. c. 25.

10 Cicer. ad Att. lib. viii. ep. 9.

11 Ibid. ep 13. **Si mehercule neminem occidet, nec cuiquam quicquam ademerit, ab his qui eum maxime timerant, maxime diligetur.**

12 Plutarch. in Pompeio.

conference, which otherwise might occasion many journeys and messages to no purpose.

This pacific message, as in other instances, only constituted a part in the military plan of Cæsar, and was accompanied with effectual preparations for a blockade and a siege. It did not as yet appear, whether Pompey meant to transport all his troops, and to abandon Brundusium, or to keep possession of this post, in order to retain a passage into Italy, and to command both sides of the gulf. Cæsar, to try his intentions, and either to shut him up, or to hasten his departure, observing, that the entrance of the harbour was narrow, and might be shut up, began an alarming work for this purpose. He employed numerous parties to throw stones, earth, and other heavy materials into the passage between the two moles, and expected, in a little time, to be able to join them, and thus effectually to exclude all communication with the sea.

In this work the besiegers advanced, for some time, with great rapidity; but being come into deeper water, where the materials they threw in were absorbed or unsettled, and displaced by the motion of the sea, they found it necessary to change their plan, and endeavoured to shut up the harbour by means of floating rafts and hulks firmly anchored in the passage. In executing this project they were disturbed by a continual discharge of arrows, stones, and other missile weapons from vessels in the mouth of the harbour, on which proper engines were mounted for this purpose.

While the parties were thus, without intermission, engaged at the entrance of the port, Cæsar again made a show of proposing a treaty. As he had received no answer to his former message by Magius, he affected to despair of making any progress by direct applications to Pompey, and sent into the town Caninius Rebilus, one of his lieutenants, who, being in great intimacy with Scribonius Libo, had directions to make application to him, and, in Cæsar's name, to intreat his good offices in bringing on a negotiation; particularly, if possible, in procuring an interview between Pompey and himself. Representing to Libo, that if an interview were obtained, some way might be discovered to stop the issues of blood, a blessing which, in that case, would for ever be mentioned as the effect of so essential a service performed by Scribonius Libo to his country.

Pompey, upon receiving these proposals, which, though addressed to Libo, were carried directly to himself, made answer, that, in the absence of the consuls, he could not treat. In this instance, he perceived, no doubt, the insincerity of Cæsar's pacific declarations, and was not tempted to remit the vigilance of his defence, or the ardour with which he now at last prepared for the contest: yet he could not altogether prevent one advantage which Cæsar meant to reap from these repeated professions of moderation and desire of peace, that of appearing in the eyes of the people, not the author of the war, but a person forced to these extremities by the violence and obstinacy of his enemies.

After the works at the mouth of the harbour of Brundusium had been continued three days, and had made considerable progress, the transports which had carried the first division of Pompey's army returned from Dyrrachium, and as the passage at the mouth of the harbour was still open, he prepared to embark with the remainder of his forces. The inhabitants of the town, being disaffected to him, were likely to give intelligence to Cæsar of all his motions; and he made no doubt that as soon as he should withdraw his guards, they would throw open their gates; and expose him to be attacked in his rear, and possibly to lose such part of his army as might be overtaken on shore. To provide against this event, and to retard Cæsar's entry into the town, he built up the gates with solid mortar and stone, and traversed the streets with walls and large ditches, replenished with sharp stakes, which were masked, or hid with a slight covering of brushwood and earth.

When the legions began to move towards the harbour, the rear guard still endeavoured to present the usual appearances on the ramparts, by occupying every post with archers, slingers, and other light troops. These being to remain in their post while the main body was embarking, had orders, at a signal given, to abandon the walls, and to repair on board the transports which were ready to receive them.

The troops in Brundusium thus began to embark in the night, and Cæsar, having immediate intelligence of it from the town, brought forward his scaling ladders, and, as soon as the ramparts appeared to be deserted, began to ascend them in several places at once, and effected one part of his purpose, by gaining the battlements without opposition; but when he was about to descend from thence into the streets, having notice of the snares and obstructions which were placed in his way, he was obliged to halt, or to advance with so much precaution, that the enemy had time to put off from the mole, and get under sail. Only two transports, that struck, and were aground on the banks which had been formed or begun at the mouth of the harbour, fell into his hands. The remainder, with the greater part of the senate, attended by the officers of state and the ensigns of magistracy, proceeded in their passage to Epirus; thus leaving Cæsar in possession of Italy and of the seats of government, from which the world could scarcely disjoin, in their idea, the right to command.

Cæsar having, in this manner, surprised the republic, and in sixty days obliged all his opponents to evacuate Italy, and to leave him sole master of the forces which began to be mustered against him, it is probable, notwithstanding the question he states relating to the expedience of following his enemy into Epirus, that he had already taken his resolution to consider the reduction of Spain as the next object of consequence to that of Italy. In that province, which was full of resources, a regular army of seven or eight legions had been for some time formed, with an evident purpose to keep him in awe. He was threatened, therefore, with the most immediate danger from thence. Some arrangements too were yet wanting for the security of Italy. The professions which he had made of pacific dispositions, and of zeal for the republic, were to be confirmed by showing a proper respect to the forms of the constitution, and by endeavouring to restore a government which he had actually overthrown.

For these reasons, Cæsar contented himself, for the present, with having ordered shipping to be provided at the port of Brundusium, that he might amuse the enemy with appearances of his intending to continue the war on that side, or that he might be actually ready to do so, when he had elsewhere accomplished the purpose on which he was bent. Notwithstanding his pacific declarations, and his ostentation of clemency on every occasion, the people still trembled when they saw almost every citizen of reputation and honour obliged to fly from the seats of government, and, in their place, collected from different quarters of Italy, every bankrupt, every outlaw, and every person of infamous character.[1] These being at variance with the laws of their country, had flocked to Cæsar, and were received by him under the denomination of the injured and the oppressed citizens, whose wrongs he was come to redress.

With this company, still multiplying around him, having given orders to secure Brundusium from the sea, and posted there, and at Sipontum and Tarentum, each a legion; and having ordered ships from every part of the coasts of Italy and Gaul, he set out for Spain, intending, while the troops, with whom he had overrun Italy, took some repose in quarters, and while those who were destined for the service in Spain were on the march, that he himself should visit Rome, and observe the aspect of his party. His father-in-law, Calpurnius Piso, although, by his relation to Cæsar, hindered from following Pompey, yet would not countenance his son-in-law so far as to remain in the city to receive him. Marcus Lepidus, then prætor, was the officer of highest rank who continued in his place; and beside the tribunes who had been the instruments in kindling this war, was the only magistrate who resigned himself entirely to the victor's disposal. Among the tribunes, Cæcilius Metellus, though disposed to have followed the senate, being detained in the city by the sacred duties of his functions, had taken his resolution to employ the negative with which he was intrusted, in restraining the violations of law and government, which were to be expected in such a scene as was now to be opened at Rome.

Cicero, upon the commencement of hostilities, having still the ensigns of proconsul, was appointed to inspect the levies and other affairs of the republic on the coasts of Campania and Latium. Upon Pompey's retreat, he remained in this station with a mind overwhelmed with perplexity and irresolution. He affected respect and gratitude to Pompey, though he surely owed him no obligation, bore him no real affection, and blamed him highly for his flight from Italy; but in the last perhaps he only meant to justify himself for not having immediately joined him in his retreat, and for not having embarked with more decision in the cause. He sincerely lamented the state of the republic, of which he now certainly despaired, and only wished to steer a course, the safest he could for his own reputation and his person.

Cæsar, in the beginning of this contest, had contributed much to perplex the resolution of Cicero, who generally saw so many objects in every question of state, that it was difficult for him to decide between them. He had been kept undetermined by means of a flattering correspondence, in which Cæsar made repeated applications for his good offices towards preventing the present troubles. Being now in the way of Cæsar from Brundusium to Rome, he was honoured with a personal interview; at which, says Cicero to his friend Atticus, I shall study rather to appear an object of his respect than of his liking. He accordingly, on that occasion, resisted his flattery, and withstood his entreaties to attend a meeting of the senate, which Cæsar had ordered to be assembled by a messenger despatched from Formiæ. Cæsar appeared to be piqued at this refusal: "It will be supposed you condemn me," he said, "and others will be led by your example." Cicero replied, "that his case was different from that of others who had less connection with Pompey." "Come, then," continued Cæsar, "and treat of an accommodation with Pompey." "Shall I be at liberty to do so in my own way?" "Who will restrain you?" "Shall I move the senate then, that the war shall not be carried into Spain, nor into Greece? Shall I lament the treatment which Pompey has received?" "That, indeed," said Cæsar, "I shall not like to have said." "I thought so," replied the other, "and choose to absent myself." At parting, Cæsar desired him to consider of the matter. "If you desert me," he said, "I must have recourse to other counsels, and know not what I may be forced to do."[2]

Upon the arrival of Cæsar in the suburbs of Rome, such of the senators as were in the city or in the neighbourhood, assembled at his summons. He opened the meeting by enumerating the wrongs he had received, and by loading his opponents with the guilt of the present war. "He never had aspired," he said, "to unprecedented honours. The office of consul was now again open to him by the laws of the commonwealth; and the Roman people had dispensed with his personal attendance in suing for it. An act to this purpose," he said, "had been obtained in the fairest and most constitutional manner Ten tribunes had concurred in proposing it. His enemies, particularly Cato himself, had been heard at full length against it, and had practised his usual artifice for disappointing the senate or the people, by prolonging the debates. Pompey himself was consul when this act was passed. If he disapproved of the act, why did he not oppose it then? If he approved of it, why rob him now of the privilege it bestowed? He reminded this meeting of the moderation with which he himself had offered to resign his command, while others were so tenacious of theirs; or while they imposed conditions on him, to which they themselves would not submit, and chose to throw the state into confusion, rather than abate the least of their own pretensions. He observed, that his enemies had made use of a false pretence to call off two legions from his army; that they had violated the sacred character of the tribunes, who were guilty of no offence, but that of protecting him against the oppression of his enemies; that they had rejected all offers of an accommodation, or even of a conference.

"He now exhorted the senate not to desert the

1 Cicer. ad Att. lib. ix. ep. 19. Cave autem putis quemquam hominem in Italiam turpem esse, qui hinc absit. Vidi ipse Formiis universos, &c.; et Cicer. ad Att. lib. ix. ep. 1. qui hic potest se gerere non perditi vita mores ante facta ratio suscepti negotii, socii, &c.

2 Cicer. ad Atticum, lib. ix. ep. 18.

commonwealth, nor to oppose such as, in concert with him, might endeavour to restore the government; but if they should shrink in this arduous task, he should not press it upon them. He knew how to act for himself. If his opinion were followed, deputies should be now sent from the senate to Pompey, with entreaties, that he would spare the republic. He knew, that Pompey had formerly objected to his having any such deputation sent to himself, considering such advances as a concession of right in him to whom they were made, or of fear in those who made them. These," he said, "were the reflections of a narrow mind; for his own part, as he wished to overcome his enemies in the field, so he wished to excel them in acts of generosity and candour."

Such were the colours in which this artful man endeavoured to disguise his cause; and while he took effectual measures to maintain it by force, employed likewise an insinuation, and an eloquence not less dangerous than his sword. The proposals of a treaty were received in this meeting with joy; but no man was willing, after having assisted at such a meeting of the senate, to hazard his person in Pompey's camp.

While Cæsar, to reconcile all men to his cause, affected clemency even to those who were taken in arms against him, Pompey, supposing himself entrusted with the powers and severities of the law, had threatened to employ those powers and severities to the utmost extent against every person who staid behind him at Rome. Proscription and massacre of those who abandoned the commonwealth were the ordinary language at his quarters.[1] He proposed to operate in this case by fear alone, and had forgotten, that legal government itself, on certain occasions, with all its authorities and powers, stands in need of insinuation and of popular arts.

Cæsar, in taking the opposite tone, and in affecting to commit his affairs to the issue of a fair negotiation and treaty, relied on the difficulties that were likely to occur in the conduct of any negotiation; or he presumed upon these difficulties in making offers which he did not wish his enemies to accept. His intention was to load his antagonist with the blame of a war which, it is probable, he had a long time been devising. If he had really meant to renew his former concerts with Pompey, he would have employed again the same concealed methods by which those concerts had been formerly obtained, and would not have intrusted the mediation to the senate, a body which, however composed, had a natural claim to authority, and might have carried their negotiations farther than he proposed. He had ever entertained a serious aversion to the name and pretensions of the senate. Being altogether indifferent to public interests of every sort, the mediocrity of parts, that must ever appear in the majority of such a body, was to him an object of contempt. He had espoused the cause of every faction, of every tumult, of every criminal against them; and, at one time, rather than be subject to their authority, had proposed, that Pompey himself should transport his army from Asia to usurp the government. Even the few senators, who, upon the former occasion, from indifference to public questions, or from a disposition to favour his cause, had remained in the city, became the objects of his disgust. Many of them, though willing to be his instruments, were not yet formed for his purpose. When he affected to treat them with respect, they received his addresses as matter of right; when he proposed any measure, they took the matter into serious consideration, and affected to deliberate of what was to be done. "He detests the senate," said Curio to Cicero, "now more than ever; he will leave them no authority. I meant to have held my commission by a fictitious decree of that body: but he said, I should hold it of himself; and that every honour, and every power should be derived from him."[2]

Cæsar, however, meant to make this remnant of a legal assembly the tools of every ungracious or improper measure he had occasion to execute, and, in particular, to avail himself of their authority in seizing the public money. Pompey, before he left Rome, had been authorised to draw from the measures of the commonwealth whatever money he wanted for the service. At his departure, he ordered the whole to be removed; and the consul Lentulus was about to execute this order, when a sudden alarm of Cæsar's approach obliged him to desist, and left him time only to carry away the keys of the public repositories. Cæsar now moved the senate, that the doors should be opened: and that the public money should be issued from thence to defray the expense of the war.[3] To this motion the tribune Metellus Celer opposed his negative; and Cæsar, disdaining any longer to wear a mask which subjected him to the observance of insignificant forms, proceeded to the treasury, and ordered the doors to be forced. The tribune had the boldness to place himself in the way, and was about to reduce Cæsar to the disagreeable alternative of being disappointed of his purpose, or of rendering himself the object of popular detestation, by violating the sacred person of a tribune, from a veneration to which, he himself professed to have undertaken the war. On this occasion, contrary to his usual character, he appeared to have lost his temper, and threatened Metellus with immediate death. "This," he said, "is easier for me to execute than to utter." It was thought, that if the tribune had persisted, not only this officer, but numbers of the senators, and many of the more respectable citizens, whom he considered as enemies and promoters to the tribune's contumacy, would have been involved in a general massacre. "Think not," said Curio, in relating these particulars to Cicero, "that his clemency proceeds from temper, or is secured to you by any real disposition of his mind. It is a mere effect of his policy; he is naturally indifferent to blood, and, if he is provoked, will make it to run in the kennels."[4]

The tribune Metellus, however, when matters were coming to this extremity, suffered himself to be removed. The doors were forced open, all the money was taken from thence, even the sacred deposit, supposed to have remained from the time of the rebuilding of Rome after its destruction by the Gauls, and still kept as a resource for the utmost exigency of public affairs, was now carried off. I have subdued the Gauls, said

1 Cicer. ad Atticum, lib. viii. ep. 1[illegible].

2 Cicero ad Att. lib. x. ep 4.
3 Dio. Cassius, lib. xli. c. 17 et 18.
4 Cicero ad Atticum, lib. x. ep. 4.

Cæsar, and there is no longer any need of such provision against them. He is said, on this occasion, to have carried off in bars, 25,000*lb.*[5] of gold, 35,000*lb.*[6] of silver, and in coin, 40,000,000 Roman money.[7]

After this act of violence, it appears that Cæsar distrusted the affections of the people. He had proposed to harangue them in a public audience, which had been appointed for that purpose; but apprehending that he might be exposed to insult from some one in the crowd, he declined that solemnity, even avoided the public view altogether, and having passed but a few days at Rome, set out for Spain sullen and displeased. It was no longer a doubt, that his victories led to the subversion of the republic, and of every species of civil government whatever.[8]

Marcus Emilius Lepidus, who, as has been observed, was at this time prætor, and the officer of highest rank then at Rome, was left to govern the city. Mark Antony had the command of Cæsar's forces in Italy; and by the use which he made of his power, treating persons of the most respectable condition with great insolence, and indulging himself in all the extravagance of debauch, for which his genius appears to have been peculiarly fitted, increased the dismal apprehensions of the public. He is said to have travelled through Italy himself in an open litter, with Citheride, a celebrated actress, followed by seven other carriages replenished with courtezans, and even attended by his wife Fulvia, the widow of the late famous Clodius, who, to enjoy her husband's state, and partake with him in the license of his military power, connived at his infidelities, and made a part in this scandalous train.[9] The whole, a lively specimen of the purpose for which the accomplices of Catiline, and many of the followers of Cæsar wished to be masters of the republic, and a foretaste of the wanton caprice with which this overgrown republic, so long a prey to outrageous faction, was now likely to be made the subject and the sport of a military usurpation.

Soon after hostilities had commenced, Cotta had been sent to command for the republic in Sardinia, and Cato to command in Sicily. Cæsar, when about to carry the war into Spain, thought it necessary, if possible, to get the possession of these islands, as well as to reduce Pompey's forces in every other part of the empire. Having stationed Dolabella, with C. Antonius, on the coast of Illyricum, he ordered Valerius, with a proper force, into Sardinia, and Curio, with three legions, to attack Cato in Sicily. The Sardinians, hearing that one of Cæsar's officers was appointed, in his name, to take possession of their island, declared for his interest, took arms against Cotta, and obliged him to fly into Africa, where he joined Accius Varus, who had occupied that province in the name of the republic.

Cato, some time after his nomination to command in Sicily, and while there were any hopes of a negotiation, remained at Capua, then the quarters of Pompey, in order to give his assistance in forming an accommodation, the least ruinous that could be obtained for the commonwealth. On Pompey's retreat into Apulia, he went into Sicily, and the province being unprovided with every means of defence, he gave orders to repair, and to build ships in all the ports of the island, and in those of the neighbouring coast of Italy. He had likewise ordered all the towns to furnish their quota of troops; but had not been able to assemble any force, when Curio landed at Messina, with the two legions destined by Cæsar to take possession of the island. Sensible that any attempts to resist this force would only expose the lives of a few well-affected citizens or subjects, who might on this occasion be disposed to support him as an officer of the republic, he discontinued his military preparations, and withdrew from the island.

This officer had often disapproved of Pompey's conduct; and on this occasion, complained particularly of the defenceless state in which he had suffered the republic to be surprised in all its possessions. Cæsar, who no doubt wished to have the suffrage of such a citizen, and of his own enemy against Pompey, represents Cato as complaining that he was betrayed, that the senate had been deceived, and that the war itself was unnecessary.[10] The conduct of Pompey, not only as a citizen, but as an officer of state and as a soldier, has been censured in many parts of this memorable contest; and it is indeed easy to spy faults after the event, and when experience has exposed them to view. Cæsar himself is said to have censured him for abandoning Italy; and it is probable would have respected him more, if in executing this resolution, instead of passing into Macedonia, he had gone to the head of his army in Spain. His celebrated saying, in leaving Brundusium, when he was about to carry the war into that country, implied an opinion to this purpose, "We go," he said, "from this general who has no army, to an army that has no general."

Cæsar's own disposition of his forces, as has been already mentioned, in assigning what appeared to have been the reason of his conduct, had been made with the greatest ability; and the more, that they gave him the appearance of a person acting without design, and suddenly forced to the measures which he embraced. In talking of ordinary men, we may err in imputing too much to design and concert; but with respect to Cæsar, the mistake to be feared, is not perceiving the whole extent of his foresight and plan. He at once armed himself with a military force, and artfully guarded the appearances under which he was to use it. When the senate passed their resolution against him, he seemed to be caught unprepared to resist; but the senate was still less prepared to attack. He had artfully avoided giving them any cause of suspicion, by any unnecessary assemblage of forces on the side of Italy, while he had sufficient strength to take the full benefit of the consternation into which they were thrown by his first alarm. Though long meditating the invasion of Rome with an army, he contrived an incident, in the flight of the tribunes, to make it appear the effect of a sudden provocation, and of his zeal in a popular cause. When we consider that Mark Antony was the tribune who furnished this pretence

According to Arbuthnot, ch. 18.

5	£678,125	0	0	
6	94,937	10	0	
7	322,916	13	4	Vid. Plin. lib. xxxiii. c. 3.
	£1,095,982	3	4	

8 Cic. ad Att. lib. x. ep. 4. Ibid. lib. x. et xiii.

10 Cæs. de Bell. Civ. lib. xxx.

there is no doubt that Cæsar had his choice of the time at which it should be presented to him.

At this conjuncture, the greater part of his army still remained beyond the Alps, and in the precise situation in which they were most likely to be wanted to encounter the first considerable difficulty that would probably arise in the war, from the veteran legions which had been levied for Pompey, and which were stationed under Afranius and Petreius in Spain.[1] If these legions had attempted to pass the Pyrennees, the army of Cæsar was stationed in Gaul to intercept them, and he was accordingly secure of being able to finish the war in Italy, without any interruption from thence. When this service was effected, his army in Gaul remained in the most advantageous position, from which to enter upon what was likely to become the second object of his enterprise, the reduction of Spain.

The antagonists of Cæsar, without any apprehension of these dispositions, and perfectly secure before hostilities commenced, were completely surprised, overwhelmed, and routed in every quarter on which they attempted to make any defence. Armies indeed had been formed in Italy, according to the saying of Pompey, *at the stamp of his foot;* but they were armies that served the purpose of his enemies, not that of the republic, or his own; and though raised to secure Italy against Cæsar, became in the reduction of Italy itself an accession to his force, and were ready to be sent in separate divisions to occupy different provinces of the empire in his name; insomuch, that while Cæsar himself, with the strength of the veteran legions with which he had conquered Gaul, hastened into Spain to reduce what was the most formidable part of his rival's power, his officers were detached with separate bodies of these newly acquired troops, into Sardinia, Sicily, and Africa.

Pompey, although he had never visited his government in person, nor sought for occasions of war, as Cæsar, in order to form his army and inure them to service, had done in Gaul, had nevertheless formed a great military establishment, consisting of seven Roman legions, with five thousand horse, and eighty cohorts of provincial infantry, equal in number to eight legions more; and Cæsar had reason to believe, that this great force, if the war could have been protracted in Italy, would have come upon his rear, cut off his resources in Gaul, or obliged him to defend himself on the north of the Alps. He accordingly, instead of bringing into Italy the legions that lay in the low countries, or the interior parts of his province, had moved them only to the neighbourhood of Narbonne, to be near the confines of Spain, from which this storm was to be dreaded; and meant, if the success of his affairs in Italy should admit of it, that these legions should cross the Pyrennees, and fix the scene of the war amidst his rival's possessions.

Spain had been formerly divided into two provinces, under two separate Roman governors; but the whole being united under Pompey, was committed by him to three lieutenants, Varro, Petreius, and Afranius. The first commanded, from the river Guadiana westward to the extremities of Lusitania[2] and Gallicia; the second, from the Guadiana eastward to the mountains of Murcia; and the third, from thence to the Pyrennees.

Soon after the war broke out in Italy, Pompey sent Vibullius into Spain, with orders to these officers to assemble their forces, and to prepare for the defence of their province. Varro affected indifference in the quarrel, or an equal regard to the opposite parties concerned in it. An accident, he said, had placed him under the command of Pompey; but he had an equal attachment to Cæsar. The other two, from regard to the commonwealth, or from fidelity to their commander-in chief, engaged with more zeal in the cause. They determined, in concert with Vibullius, to leave Varro in the western province, while they themselves drew the principal part of their force towards the eastern frontier; and by occupying the passes of the mountains, or some strong post on the Ebro, endeavoured to defend the country intrusted to their care, until Pompey should either arrive in person to take the command on himself, or until, having rallied his forces in Macedonia, he should bring the scene of the war again into Italy. For this purpose, they took post at Ilerda,[3] a place of strength on the Segro, and about twenty miles above the confluence of this river with the Cinea; Afranius with three legions, Petreius with two more, together with five thousand horse, and eighty cohorts of provincial infantry.

Such were the dispositions that were making in Spain, when Cæsar, having expelled his rival from Italy, took possession of Rome, and having passed a few days in that city, in the manner above related, set out for his army in the province of Narbonne.

Being to pass by Marseilles, he intended to take possession of that city; but the inhabitants were already disposed to favour his antagonists, and shut their gates against him. This ancient Greek colony, after having long defended their settlement against the rude tribes in their neighbourhood, had placed themselves at last under the protection of the Romans; but with a reserve of all their immunities, and an exemption from all the burdens of a Roman province. Cæsar proposed to have entered their city as a neutral place, and to prevail on the citizens to receive him, cited the examples of Rome itself, and of all the other cities of Italy, who had opened their gates, and given a passage to his army, without taking any part in the present disputes. To this proposal, the people of Marseilles made answer, That in every case where the Romans were divided among themselves, every ally in their situation must so far preserve their neutrality, as not to receive the forces of either party within their walls, and that in the present case particularly, they lay under such high obligations to the leaders of both parties, that they must carefully avoid giving offence to either.

It soon after appeared, however, that this plausible answer was intended merely to gain time. Vibullius had passed by Marseilles in his way to Spain, and had delivered to the people of that place a message from Pompey, with assurances of support; on which they fully relied. The receipt of this message, was followed by a reso-

1 See pages 256, 257, the preceding parts of this chapter.

2 Portugal.

3 Now called Lerida

lution to admit the officers and men of Pompey's party into their town, and to exclude his antagonists.

Domitius Ahenobarbus, after he had been dismissed from Corfinium, no ways affected by the ostentatious clemency of Cæsar, had, in pursuance of the senate's appointment to the government of Gaul, repaired to that province, raised some troops, with which he was expected to take possession of Marseilles, and actually, in a few days after this answer was given to Cæsar, entered the harbour of that place with seven ships, and some land forces on board. Upon his arrival, the people of this republic called in to their assistance the force of some neighbouring cantons from the mountains; repaired their fortifications; replenished their magazines; employed many hands in fabricating arms; and took every other precaution that was necessary, in case they should be attacked, to enable them to make a vigorous defence.

Cæsar being greatly provoked, invested the town with an army of three legions; and having ordered some ships to be built on the Rhone, prepared to assail it at once by sea and by land. He committed the attack by land to Trebonius; and that from the sea to Decimus Brutus. While he was making these preparations, a report prevailed that Pompey was passing the seas into Africa, and intended, with the troops which were in that province, and a body of Numidian cavalry, to reinforce, and to take the command of his army in Spain. It is probable that Cæsar, in like circumstances, would have even taken a shorter road to the head of his army. He appears at least to have believed this report of his enemy, or to have thought it extremely probable, and to have been somewhat alarmed. As if the prospect of meeting with Pompey, having under his direction a well-appointed and regular force, had rendered him doubtful of the affections of his own men, he mentions an artifice practised by himself on this occasion, which may be considered as a specimen of his address, and of the influence which he employed with his army. He borrowed money from the officers, and gave it in gratuities to the soldiers; thus taking a pledge for the fidelity of the one, and purchasing that of the others by his bounty.

While Cæsar was yet employed in opening the siege of Marseilles, he ordered Fabius, who commanded his forces at Narbonne, to advance into the Pyrennees; and if the passes were open or slightly guarded, to penetrate into Spain, and occupy some advantageous station on the frontier of that country. This officer accordingly, having forced the passes of the Pyrennees, penetrated to the Segra, or, as it was then called, the Sicoris; and took post on the right of this river, in the front of the united armies of Afranius and Petreius, who were encamped near the town of Ilerda.

Fabius, not to be interrupted by occasional floods in his communication with the country through which he had passed, and to keep open the ordinary route from Gaul, laid two bridges upon it, at the distance of four miles from each other. By these communications, he was chiefly supplied with provisions; and as the Spanish army had an easy access by the bridge of Ilerda to intercept his supplies, it was necessary to cover every convoy and foraging party with numerous and powerful escorts. Two entire legions, under the command of Plancus, had marched on this service, and were to be followed by a body of cavalry. After the infantry had passed the river, and the cavalry was entered on the bridge, it broke down, and deprived those who were already over, of any communication with the camp. The timber and wreck of the bridge floating by the town of Ilerda, gave the enemy intimation of what had happened, and suggested the design to scour the country on the left of the Segra, with a powerful detachment, in order to intercept any parties who might by this accident be cut off from the main body of the army. For this purpose, Afranius marched with four legions, and might have taken or destroyed those who remained under Plancus on the left of the river, if this officer had not retired to a height, on which he was able for some time to resist the superior numbers of his enemy. In the mean while, Fabius suspecting the danger to which his detachment was exposed, despatched two legions more by the other bridge to support the former. On the appearance of this reinforcement, Afranius, whose plan in the present campaign was altogether defensive, thought proper to retire, without hazarding an action, in which he might be exposed to a too hasty decision of the cause.

Two days after this adventure, Cæsar, with an escort of nine hundred horse, arrived in the camp of Fabius. Having examined the situation of both armies, and ordered the bridge on the Segra to be rebuilt, he proceeded as usual to act on the offensive, and to occupy the enemy's attention with successive operations against them, by which he left them no leisure to form any designs of their own. It was his fortune, indeed, in this and other periods of the present war, to need a speedy decision, which made him take measures that forced his enemies to remain on the defensive, and inspired his men with a notion of their own superiority; an opinion which, after it has been some time received, seldom fails to verify itself.

In a few days after his arrival, he advanced with his army in three divisions to the foot of the hill on which the Spanish army was encamped, and while they continued to observe, and endeavoured to penetrate his intentions, he began to break ground, and to make a lodgement for himself in that place. That his purpose might not be known, until the work was considerably advanced, he kept the first and second lines under arms, and ordered the third, without raising a parapet, or planting their palisades, to sink a ditch fifteen feet wide, and of a sufficient length to cover his front. This being done, he retired with his whole army behind it, and ordered them to lie upon their arms all night. Under cover of this temporary entrenchment, he on the following day completed the usual fortifications of his camp, and brought forward the tents and baggage of his army, which till then had remained under a proper guard on his former ground.

Being now in possession of a post within four hundred paces, or less than half a mile of the enemy's lines; and having a view of the ground which lay between their camp and the town of Ilerda, extending about three hundred paces, and mostly plain, with a small height in the middle of it, he formed a project to seize the height; and knowing that the enemy lodged their magazines and stores in Ilerda, proposed to cut off their communication with the town. In this view, he drew up a body of three legions in a proper position, from which to execute his purpose; and ordered the front rank[1] from one of those legions to start from their colours, and with the utmost speed to gain the height which he intended to occupy. The sudden movement of this body explained his design to the enemy, and they instantly put all the piquets and extraordinary guards of their camp in motion to prevent its effects. Having a nearer way, and the advantage of the ground, they prevented Cæsar's party; and being in possession of the height before they came up, repulsed and beat them back to their main body. Here too, they pursued their advantage; and as they rushed with little regard to order, but with an appearance of undaunted courage, on the flanks as well as the front of the legions which Cæsar had advanced, they put the whole in some degree of confusion, and forced them back to the heights in their rear.

While the leaders of the Spanish army probably committed an error in not redoubling their blow, or remained in suspense. Cæsar issued from his camp with a fresh legion to support the flying division of his army, obliged the enemy to retire in their turn, and having overtaken them before they could reach their camp, obliged them to take refuge under the walls of the town.

The ground at the foot of these walls was steep, and the access to it was by lanes and narrow ways. Thither the troops, with whom Cæsar had renewed the action, flushed with victory, had followed the enemy, and got into a situation in which they could not gain any advantage, nor retire without loss. The parties, however, continued to skirmish during five hours, and being continually reinforced from their respective armies, a general engagement was likely to ensue on ground extremely unfavourable to Cæsar.

In order to extricate himself with the least possible appearance of disgrace, he ordered a general charge, and having drove his antagonists before him to the foot of the wall, he sounded a retreat from thence, and brought off his men, before the enemy could rally or return to the pursuit.

In this manner, Cæsar retired to his camp with considerable loss, and foiled in his design; but on account of the last impression he made on the enemy, with some pretensions to a victory, of which to support the courage of his troops, he did not neglect to avail himself.

In a few days after this miscarriage, the army of Cæsar suffered a worse and more alarming calamity. The summer being far advanced, and the snow on the Pyrennees melting, all the rivers which are supplied from thence, rose on a sudden to their greatest height. The Segra carried off both the bridges erected by Fabius, and baffled all the endeavours that were used to restore them. As often as any attempt was made for this purpose, the work was interrupted by the enemy from the opposite bank, or the materials were swept away by the flood. Neither the Segra nor the Cinca were passable, and the country between them, though extending in breadth about thirty miles, being exhausted, could no longer furnish any supply of provisions to Cæsar's camp.

About the time that the army began to feel their distress, a convoy which arrived from Gaul, consisting of many carriages, escorted by a large body of Gaulish horse, and accompanied with many officers and persons of distinction, who came to witness the glories of this campaign, the whole, together with their attendants and equipage, amounting to about six thousand men, were attacked by Afranius, and with great loss obliged to take refuge in the neighbouring mountains.

In consequence of this disaster, and under the sense of the present, and apprehension of the future distress, the modius[2] of corn sold in Cæsar's camp for fifty denarii, or at the rate of thirty shillings a peck. All their attempts to procure a supply were frustrated by the difficulties of their situation, or by the vigilance of the enemy. As the height of the floods was a permanent effect of the season, in swelling every river which descends from mountains that retain their snow in the summer, and as the enemy were plentifully supplied from their magazines in the town of Ilerda, or had, by the bridge of that place, an open communication with the fertile country which is now named Catalonia on their right, Cæsar could have no immediate prospect of relief. The Spanish army accordingly triumphed in their good fortune, and sent exaggerated accounts of their advantage to all parts of Spain, to Italy, and to Macedonia. Many persons, who had hitherto hesitated in the choice of their party, were now determined. Varro began to exert himself in his province, and levied two entire new legions in the name of Pompey. Many hastened from Italy into Macedonia, to be the carriers of such agreeable tidings, or to have the merit of declaring themselves of the party of the republic, while the issue of the war yet remained in any degree of suspense.

The triumphs, however, which anticipate events are often deceitful; and, by the overweening security and confidence which they inspire, give an able enemy great advantage, even in his distress, or facilitate the changes of fortune in his favour. Afranius and Petreius, while they trusted to the ordinary course of the seasons, were not sufficiently upon their guard against the superior resources of so able an adversary. They suffered him to build, unobserved, a number of boats, upon a construction which his workmen had learned in Britain; having a keel in the ordinary form, and some timbers of strength on the sides; but, instead of plank, finished between these timbers with basket-work, and covered with hides. These vessels being of easy carriage, were transported by land about twenty miles above Cæsar's camp; and in a first embarkation ferried over a party sufficient to make a lodgement on the opposite bank. Cæsar continued to reinforce this party, until, having an entire legion intrenched on that side, he ventured to employ his carpenters openly in constructing a bridge, which they began at once from both sides of the river. This work was completed in two days, and again gave him access to the left of the Segra, where he surprised some of the enemy's

1 Unius Legionis Antesignanos. Cæsar. de Bell. Civil. lib. i. c. 43.

2 Little more than a peck.

parties, and procured immediate relief by a supply of provisions to his own camp.

About the time that Cæsar had effected this change in the state of his army, he had news of a naval fight on the coast of Gaul, in which his fleet, under Decimus Brutus, had defeated that of the enemy, and given a speedy prospect of the reduction of Marseilles. This report, together with the disappointment he had recently given to the hopes of his enemies, had at once all the effects of victory, and made him appear more formidable than he was supposed to be, even before the distresses which he had lately experienced. His antagonists, from a state of sanguine expectation, sunk into a proportional degree of despondency, and became so much in awe of his superior conduct, that they abandoned the country on the left of the Segra to his foragers, and never ventured, except in the night, to go abroad for the necessary supplies of their own camp. These events affected the natives of the country in a still higher degree, and brought them from every quarter to make a tender of their services in supplying Cæsar with provisions, or in seconding him in his military operations.

In conjunction with the natives, who were now become his allies, Cæsar again found himself in condition to act on the offensive, and to devise new alarms for the enemy. His first object was to render the passage of the river at all times practicable; and as he had failed in his purpose of separating the Spanish army from the town of Ilerda, he now proposed to extend his command of the country, and to form a chain of posts, by which he might circumscribe the town itself, together with the enemy's camp, which depended upon it.

The bridge which he had lately built was at too great a distance, and he experienced the insecurity of such communications over torrents, which came with such force and so much inequality from the mountains. Instead, therefore, of attempting to erect any more bridges, he proposed to render the river fordable, by separating its course into many different channels; and for this purpose made a number of cuts, of about thirty feet deep, through the plain, to receive as much of the waters of the Segra as might sufficiently drain the principal stream.

The enemy, as soon as they understood the purpose of these operations, were greatly alarmed. They foresaw that Cæsar, having the passage of the river secured, might command its opposite banks below, as well as above the town of Ilerda, block up the bridge of that place, and, with the aid of the country around him, which, since the late defection of its inhabitants, was ready to support him in all his designs, might have it in his power to prevent their supplies, and distress them, in their turn, for want of provisions.

To remove from a situation in which they were exposed to so many evils, they resolved instantly to abandon their present station, and to retire beyond the Ebro, where the people, either from fear or affection, were still in their interest. They proceeded to the execution of this purpose with much seeming precaution and foresight. Having fixed upon a proper place at which to lay a bridge over the Ebro, they ordered all the boats, within a certain distance on that river and on the Segra, to be collected together for that purpose. They placed a proper garrison in Ilerda, to check the motions of the enemy in their rear, or if he attempted to reduce that place, to employ his forces until they themselves should have effected their retreat, and made their arrangements in the new position they intended to take.

As their first movement in filing off from their present encampment, and in passing through the town of Ilerda, encumbered with all their baggage, was likely to detain them some time in presence of the enemy, and exposed them to the attacks of his cavalry and light troops, they intended no more on the first day, than to file off by the bridge; and they fixed on a post at which they might halt on the left of the Segra, and make the proper dispositions to continue their march. This post they sent two legions before them to occupy and to secure.

Having taken these preparatory steps, they decamped, defiled without molestation through the town of Ilerda, and came to the ground on which they had taken care to secure their reception; here they halted until the middle of the night, when they again were in motion. They had a plain of some miles before them, bounded by a ridge of hills, which they were to pass in their way to the Ebro. They might be exposed to Cæsar's light troops in crossing this plain; but as soon as they reached the mountains, they could, by securing the passes in their rear, effectually prevent any farther attack from the enemy. Thither they accordingly directed their march; but Cæsar, who had observed their intentions, and who had so far succeeded in his operations on the river as to be able to ford it with his horse, sent the greater part of his cavalry, in the beginning of the night, with orders to hang upon the rear of the enemy, and by all possible means to retard their progress.

This service the cavalry performed with so much success, that at break of day the Spanish army, in consequence of the frequent interruptions they had received, were still to be seen from Cæsar's camp. The cavalry, as often as the enemy got in motion, were observed to attack them, but when the enemy halted, appeared to stop or retire, and were pursued in their turn. The army of Cæsar being spectators of this scene became extremely impatient, and with the greatest ardour pressed to be led against the enemy. Even officers crowded to their general, and begged they might be allowed to try the ford; they observed of what consequence it was, that an enemy who had been driven with so much labour from one post, should not be suffered to retire in safety to another situation, from which they might renew the war.

Cæsar, affecting to be moved by these representations, and to be prevailed upon to do what it is probable he earnestly desired, instantly made his dispositions to pass the river. He selected the least firm and vigorous men of every cohort for the guard of the camp; placed lines of horse in the river above and below the ford, to break the force of the stream, and to save those who might be overpowered by the strength of the current; in this manner he passed his infantry between the double lines of cavalry without the loss of a man. They had a circuit of six miles to make, in order to avoid the town of Ilerda; but notwithstanding this delay, and the advantage which Afranius and Petreius had gained by beginning their march at midnight, and by their not being discovered until it was day, such were the interruptions given by the cavalry, and the speed with which the legions of Cæsar advanced, that they overtook the enemy's rear about three in the afternoon, and occasioned at once a general halt in every part of their column.

Petreius and Afranius, stunned by the unexpected arrival of Cæsar at the head of his whole army, formed on a rising ground to receive him; and both armies seemed to prepare for immediate action. But Cæsar, knowing the necessity which the enemy were under of pursuing their retreat, and the prospect he had of increasing his advantage on the march, did not think it necessary to attack them when in order of battle; he took his ground, however, so near them,[1] that he could profit by every advantage they gave him, and in every attempt they should make to change their situation, could push them into all the disorders of a general rout.

In this position of the two armies, the Spaniards having some time remained in order of battle, again attempted to resume their march; but having soon experienced the difficulties of that attempt with an enemy so near them, and being faint with hunger and the fatigue of so many tedious and fruitless operations, they determined to halt and wait for the return of night. They had now no more than five miles to pass on the plain, and hoped, by a rapid motion in the night, to traverse this space before Cæsar could overtake them, or before he could oblige them to halt any where short of the mountains, where they looked for a perfect security.

Both parties appeared to be fixed on their ground for the night, when some prisoners that were brought to Cæsar gave information that the enemy were in motion, and must in a little time be so far advanced as to reach the hills before he could give them any effectual trouble. On this sudden emergence, although his army was by no means ready to march, he ordered every trumpet to sound, as if he were actually in motion. This feint, however slight, had its effect, the enemy believed that they were to be instantly attacked, or closely pursued on the march, when disordered and encumbered with baggage; they desisted from their intention, and gave the signal to halt.

Afranius and Petreius, thus baffled in the execution of the first part of their plan, which had been so reasonably formed, began to lose courage, and remained on this ground all night, and the following day perplexed with irresolution and various counsels. So far, however, they determined, that before so vigilant an enemy it was safer to march by day than by night; and in this mind they remained yet a second night in the present position.

In this interval Cæsar, having leisure to visit the country over which they were to pass, found it practicable to turn their flank and get to the hills before them. He accordingly moved in the night, and at break of day, before the enemy judged it safe to decamp, he appeared on their right; but seeming to retire, and to leave them at liberty to continue their retreat. So long as his march had this appearance, they were pleased to think that he had moved for want of provisions, and applauded themselves for having patiently waited so joyful an event. But as soon as he had got a sufficient way to his left, he changed his direction, and marched with all possible speed to reach the mountains. They were no longer at a loss to perceive his design, or the danger with which they themselves were threatened. And they instantly, without striking their tents or packing their baggage, moved in the greatest haste to prevent him.

In this operation, Cæsar was now become certain of one or other of two great advantages; either that he should reach the pass of the mountains before the enemy, and so cut off their retreat; or, if they got there before him, that he should be left in possession of their camp and their baggage. He prevailed, however, in the trial of speed, got the first of these advantages by being before them at the ascent of the mountains, where he found a ledge or terras that was sufficiently capacious to receive his army, and which gave him entire command of the pass.

Afranius, on seeing Cæsar in possession of this ground, sent a considerable party to try the ascent of the mountains at a different place, and to gain the summits behind him; in hopes that, if this way was practicable, he might follow with his whole army, and descend from thence to the Ebro. But the party he employed on this service was, in presence of both armies, surrounded by Cæsar's horse, and put to the sword. The rest of the army, without making any attempt to rescue their friends, beheld this scene with a kind of torpid dejection. They dropped their arms, and staggered in their ranks. The troops of Cæsar, who well understood these signs of extreme terror, became to a degree of mutiny impatient for action; and he himself was sensible that the enemy might in that moment be attacked with the greatest advantage; but as he now thought himself sure of being able to reduce them without a blow, he was unwilling to give them an opportunity, however unlikely to avail them, of making their escape by the chance of a battle. While he endeavoured accordingly to restrain the unseasonable ardour of his own men, the leaders of the Spanish army had time to retire with theirs, and led them back to the camp which they had left in the morning, and to the melancholy possession of tents and of baggage, which they had been willing to abandon, in order to effect their escape.

Cæsar having left proper guards to secure the passes of the mountains, followed the enemy, and took post, as before, so near them, that they could not move without being exposed to his insults.

In this position of the two armies, the sentinels and advanced guards had an opportunity to talk together; they mutually regretted the unhappy quarrel in which they were engaged, and both officers and men becoming by degrees more familiar, met between the lines, and even exchanged visits in their opposite camps. Officers of the Spanish army proceeded so far as to talk of an accommodation, and got over their scruples in treating without proper authority from their generals, by proposing to stipulate some honourable terms for them in the peace which they proposed to conclude.

Cæsar was apprised of this correspondence, and, however irregular, connived at a circumstance which he hoped his superior popularity

1 The want of cannon or fire-arms enabled a superior army to remain almost in contact with that it intended to harass.

and the splendour of his fortune, would turn to his own account. He flattered himself, that as he had been able to seduce the troops of Pompey in Italy, so he might now deprive his antagonists of the army they had formed in the field to oppose him.

The Spanish generals, being intent on a work they were executing to secure their access to water, remained for some time unapprized of the disorderly correspondence subsisting between the two armies; and Afranius, when he came to the knowledge of what was passing, seemed to observe it with great indifference; but Petreius was greatly alarmed, ran with the officers and the guard who usually attended his person to the space between the lines, dispersed all those who were found in conference together, and put all the soldiers of Cæsar's army who fell in his way to the sword. From thence he went through the camp, and with tears exacted from every legion apart fresh oaths of fidelity to Pompey. He afterwards assembled the whole at the usual place of audience, before the general's tent; and in a speech composed of insinuation and reproach, endeavoured to confirm them in their duty; and, to the end that he might effectually cut off all hopes of conciliation, ordered all the soldiers of Cæsar's army that could be found within his intrenchments to be brought before him and slain.

Cæsar, at the same time, having many officers and men of the Spanish army in his camp, might have retaliated these acts of severity; but he chose rather to contrast the character of clemency he himself had assumed, with the austere and merciless policy of his enemies; and for this purpose gave their freedom to such officers or men as chose to return to their own party, and rewarded with preferments and honours such of them as were inclined to remain in his service.

Afranius and Petreius, by the timely discovery of these irregular practices, having escaped the disgrace of being delivered up to the enemy, to be treated at his discretion, or to be spared only as objects of pity at the intercession of their own army, continued their plan of operations; but by persevering in their resistance, they only enabled their adversary to give still more evident proofs of his superior skill and address. They were sensible that their present post could not be long maintained; it had been taken, in their haste to reach the mountains, from necessity, as an immediate respite from the attacks of an enemy who annoyed their march; and, besides other inconveniences, had a difficult access to water, the brook or river from which they were to be supplied being exposed to the discharge of arrows, darts, and other missiles from the enemy. Their bread, which they had calculated to serve them on the whole route to the Ebro was near exhausted, and they had no immediate prospect of supply. They entered therefore into anxious deliberation on the choice of a retreat, by which they might soonest get beyond reach of an enemy who pressed them with such unremitted alarms. They hesitated whether they should return to Ilerda, where they still had some magazines, or should attempt to reach Tarraco[2] on their left, at the distance of about fifty miles. The length and difficulty of the way, in which they would be exposed to Cæsar's attacks, determined them against the last; and they chose the first, as promising the nearest and most immediate relief from their present distresses. They accordingly, without any precaution, decamped, and directed their march to Ilerda.

The Spanish infantry were now more exposed than they had been on any of their former marches; for their cavalry had been so often discomfited, and had lost courage so much, that they could not be kept to their place in the column, and were now actually received for safety into the centre of the infantry; the rear was therefore cruelly annoyed by Cæsar's horse, supported by the whole force of his legions. In ascending the heights, which were frequent in their way, they had the better of the enemy, by throwing their javelins and darts on those who attempted to pursue them from below; and with this superiority they made a stand on every ascent, to force their pursuers back to some distance; but in descending the hills, the same advantage being taken against themselves, they generally ran in great disorder to the plains. And in this manner, the ground being uneven, their march consisted of alternate steps and precipitate flights, extremely fatiguing, and likely to end in a general rout.

The leaders of the retiring army, to prevent this fatal consequence, thought proper again to form upon a rising ground, and attempted a stratagem to amuse the enemy, and to gain some advance on the march before him. For this purpose, affecting to make some permanent lodgment in the place where they halted, they threw up a breast-work, but neither pitched their tents nor unloaded their baggage, and were ready to depart the moment their pursuer gave them an opportunity, by quitting the order of march. Cæsar, trusting to the effects of his late attacks, and to the appearances which the enemy presented, had no suspicion of their purpose, gave orders to pitch, and even suffered his cavalry to separate in parties to forage. This was no sooner observed from the Spanish army, than they instantly resumed their march. It was then about noon, and they made some way undisturbed.

Cæsar seeing himself over-reached, instantly put his legions in motion, without striking their tents or packing their baggage, and leaving orders for the cavalry to follow him as soon as they could be assembled, endeavoured to keep close to the enemy's rear. He was in this situation when the cavalry rejoined him, and, by renewing with double ardour their former operations, obliged the Spanish army again to suspend their march, and, in despair, to take some respite from the continual attacks with which they were harassed, by halting again in a field, which they had no time to examine, and in which they were accordingly very much exposed.

On this ground Cæsar had again a fair opportunity to attack them, and, with little doubt of the event, to terminate the war by a battle; but he persisted in his purpose of forcing this unfortunate army to surrender without any loss or hazard to himself. In this mind he continued to observe them with a degree of insulting indifference. They soon became sensible of the great disadvantage of the position in which they had halted, and endeavoured to change it, without exposing themselves to the enemy, who was so near as to be able to disturb them in every mo-

2 Tarragona.

tion they attempted to make; for this purpose they broke ground for a new intrenchment in their rear, and retiring as besiegers advance in the attack of a fortress, changed their situation under the cover of works which they successively raised.[1]

In these slow and toilsome operations they persisted all the night and the following day, and got a new position, in which they were less exposed to the enemy; but subject to a fresh inconveniency, till then unobserved, in the great distance to which they were removed from water.

As soon as this defect was perceived, which was probably not till after the soldier had consumed what he commonly carried in his flask, they discontinued their fatiguing operations; but no man ventured abroad for water, and they remained all night under dreadful apprehensions of what they might suffer from this distress.

On the following day the Spanish army advanced in array to the watering-place, and, at the hazard of a general action, proceeded to supply themselves with this necessary article. They were suffered to avail themselves of this temporary relief; but none attempted to procure any food, and they soon after, in order to supply their own immediate wants, and to lessen their consumption of water and forage, killed all the beasts of burden in their camp. While they endeavoured, by means of these temporary expedients, to await the event of any change that might offer in their favour, Cæsar formed a design to cut off all their hopes at once by a line of circumvallation. In conducting or covering this work, his legions were commonly under arms. And the enemy, sensible of the extremity to which they were soon likely to be reduced, advanced in front of their camp to interrupt him; and there might have decided their fate by an action upon equal terms. But they had no courage left; the habit of acting upon the defensive had impressed them with a sense of inferiority, and their frequent miscarriages had made them distrust the conduct of their officers. Though now in a state of suffering, from which nothing but victory could extricate them, or which nothing but the blood of their enemies could avenge, they, without making any effort for either purpose, retired again within their intrenchment.

In that situation, however, their distresses in a little time became entirely insufferable. After four days had passed in their camp without water or sustenance of any sort, their leaders desired an interview with Cæsar; and, not to expose themselves in so humbling a state to the troops of either army, begged that their meeting might be held apart from both. The conference was accepted; but Cæsar would not allow it to be held in any private place: he insisted that Afranius and Petreius should meet him in the space between the two armies; and having previously demanded, as an acknowledgment of his victory, that the son of Afranius should be delivered up as an hostage, he came to the place of meeting, surrounded by multitudes who crowded from both armies to witness the scene.

Afranius pleaded in behalf of the troops he commanded, that they had done no more than their duty to Pompey, and no more than the service of the province in which they had been stationed required; but acknowledged the distresses to which they were reduced, and implored the victor's clemency.

Cæsar, in return, upbraided the leaders of that army with their obstinate animosity to himself, and with their late cruelty to innocent men, who had committed no other offence than that of having embraced their fellow-citizens as friends, and that of being desirous to terminate this unnatural quarrel in an amicable manner. "That army," he said, "had been raised and kept on foot for the sole purpose of making war upon him. For this purpose numerous fleets had been equipped in times of profound peace, and seven entire legions, under able and experienced officers, had been kept in this peaceable province, where there was not the least pretence of a war; that every measure was concerted for his destruction; that in order to raise one citizen to uncommon honours and powers, a new species of arrangement had taken place, by which a person remaining at the gates of Rome, governing in the city and in every district of Italy, might likewise have the command in two warlike provinces, and be allowed a great military establishment in time of profound peace; that, on the contrary, in order to distress himself, the ordinary rules of the service had been set aside; and that to him alone had been denied, what had always been granted to every citizen who faithfully served the republic, the privilege of retiring, if not distinguished with honours, at least without being loaded with injuries and affronts; that he had borne these indignities, however, with patience, and mentioned them now, not as a prelude to any severities which he meant to inflict, nor as an excuse for any singular advantage he meant to take of their present distresses; that he demanded no more than peace; his antagonists should go unhurt, provided they left the province, and became bound not to serve his enemies for the future against him; that no one should be forced to take any active part on his side; that all who committed no injury against him should be considered as his friends; and that every man now in his power should be at liberty, without any other conditions than these."

It is difficult to determine whether the sword or the tongue of this singular man were most dangerous to the state he attacked. It is probable that many of his present audience were as much convinced by his eloquence, as they had been subdued by his military skill, and thought him a person no less forced to his present extremities by the wrongs he had suffered, than able to do himself justice by the force of his arms. His speech was received by the late partizans of his rival with evident signs of pleasure. To be discharged after a certain period of the most faithful services was all that a Roman soldier, in the ordinary times of the republic, could claim. To receive this favour at the hands of a victorious enemy, by whom they expected to be treated as captives, gave sudden and unexpected joy.

After the material articles were adjusted in this manner, some questions arose with respect to the time and place in which the vanquished army should be dismissed from their colours. Numbers of them, though Roman citizens, had been enlisted in Spain, and were natives or settlers in that province; others had been transported from Italy, and wished to return to their

1 Cæsar. de Bell. Civil. lib. i. c. 81.

country. It was determined, therefore, that the first should be disbanded immediately; the others march to the Var, and there be set free, and not be subject to be pressed into any service whatever. Cæsar undertook to supply them with provisions on their march. He ordered their effects, if any were found in his camp, to be restored to them. He paid his own soldiers a high price for what they were in this manner desired to restore. By this measure he gained several advantages; he lightened his baggage; he made a gratification to his own men, without the imputation of bribery; and he gained his late enemies by an act of generosity. The vanquished army accordingly came to Cæsar with all their complaints, and appealed to him even from their own officers. It was impossible for mankind to resist so much ability, insinuation, and courage.

About a third of the captive army were dismissed from their colours in Spain; the remainder passed the Pyrennees, preceded by one part of Cæsar's army, and followed by the other; who, being thus separated to the van and the rear, and always encamping close to their prisoners, led them, in terms of the capitulation, to the frontiers of Cisalpine Gaul.[2]

While the main body of Cæsar's army thus conducted the remains of the Spanish legions to the place of their destination, Varro yet remained in the western province of Spain; and Cæsar, in order either to effect a conjunction which had been concerted between them, or to force him to surrender, sent Quintus Cassius with two legions to that quarter, and himself followed with an escort of six hundred horse. Upon the report of his approach, the natives, as usual, having taken their resolution in favour of the successful party, declared for the victor. One of the legions of Varro that lay at Gades[3] advancing in form with their colours, came forward to Hispalis to receive him, and made offer of their services. Varro himself agreed to surrender the forces he commanded, both by sea and by land, and was received at Corduba. Here Cæsar held a general convention of the province; and having thanked the people for the favours they had shown to his cause, he remitted the contributions, and withdrew all the burdens which Varro, acting under the authority of Pompey, had imposed upon them. In this, as in other examples, he endeavoured to dispel the fears which his enterprise at first had occasioned, and secured the attachment of the provinces by a sense of the ease and the freedom which his success had procured them. The fleets and armies which joined him upon every conquest he made, enabled him to station troops for the security of every new acquisition, without dividing the forces on which he was to rely for the future operations of the war. He accordingly, in the present instance, left under the command of Quintus Cassius, five legions, consisting chiefly of the troops which had been levied by Varro; and he himself embarking on board a fleet which had been fitted out for his enemies, went by sea to Tarraco, now Tarragona, and from that place by land to Narbonne and Marseilles.

CHAPTER VI.

The Siege of Marseilles continued—Its Surrender—Cæsar named Dictator—Return to Rome—Mutiny at Placentia—Cæsar with Servilius Isauricus Consuls—Forces and Disposition of Pompey—Departure of Cæsar to Brundusium—Transports the first division of his Army to Acroceraunus—Message to Pompey, and their several Operations—The Lines of Dyrrachium—Cæsar baffled in his attempt to invest Pompey—Action and Defeat of Cæsar—His Retreat—March of both Armies into Thessaly—Battle of Pharsalia.

THE city of Marseilles had not surrendered to the forces which Cæsar had left under the command of Trebonius and Decimus Brutus to besiege it. Brutus, according to the dispositions which had been made to block up the place by sea, as well as by land, was stationed under the island at the mouth of the bay. His squadron consisted of twelve ships, but so hastily built, that no more than thirty days had elapsed from the felling of the timber to the launching of the vessels. They were manned, however, with the choice of Cæsar's legions; and, in order to frustrate any advantage which their antagonists might have in the construction or management of their ships, they were furnished with contrivances to grapple and make fast their gunwales to those of the enemy, in order to decide the contest with their swords.

The Marseillians had equipped ten galleys, of which the greater number, though not all, were decked. These they joined under the command of Domitius, who had been named by the senate to succeed Cæsar in Gaul, with the seven ships which this officer had brought into their harbour; and having manned them with mariners from the neighbouring coasts, they came abroad into the bay, in order to force Brutus from his station, and to open their communication with the sea. In the beginning of the action, the Marseillians being superior to Cæsar's fleet in the number of their ships, and in the skill of their mariners, had a considerable advantage. But as soon as they suffered themselves to be entangled by the grapple, the Gaulish sailors, though of a very hardy race, could not withstand the arms and discipline of the legionary soldiers, and were defeated with the loss of nine of their ships.

This was the victory already mentioned, and which contributed so much to the reputation of Cæsar's arms, while he lay before Ilerda; and which, joined to the other circumstances of his good fortune, procured him the alliance of so many nations in Spain.

While Brutus thus kept his station in the bay of Marseilles, Trebonius practised all the usual methods of attack to reduce the city. This place

2 Cæs. de Bell. Civ. lib. i. 3 Now Cadiz.

being covered on three sides by water, and on the fourth only accessible by an isthmus or neck of land, which was defended by walls and towers of a great height; he opened two separate attacks, probably on the right and the left of the isthmus, and at each of these attacks, appears to have employed the sloping mound or terrace,[1] which, in the sieges of the ancients, where the defence depended on the height of the battlements, corresponded to the sap of the moderns, and was calculated to conduct the besiegers, by a gradual ascent, to the top, as the other conducts them to the foot of the walls. This work was supported on the sides chiefly with timber, and built up with fascines, hurdles, and earth, rising in the present case to an elevation of eighty feet, and in breadth, as was formerly observed in that employed against the Bituriges,[2] probably no less than three hundred and fifty feet, so as to receive a proper column of infantry in front, and to embrace a proper extent in the walls. The workmen employed in the front of this laborious approach were covered with screens, mantlets, and penthouses of great length; and such was the consumption of timber in the construction of the whole, that the neighbouring country is said to have been cleared of its woods.

A mere trading city, long disused to war, or accustomed to rely on foreign protection, we may suppose to have been ill provided, either in the state of its arsenals, or in the spirit of its citizens for such an attack. But this little republic, still bearing the character of an independent state, being in the neighbourhood of mountains inhabited by fierce nations, who looked upon its wealth as a tempting prize, and owing its safety to the strength of its walls, and the state of its arsenals, was still suitably provided for its own defence; and the people, although long inured to peace, still kept in mind the duties which the necessities of war might oblige them to render to their country. They were now supported by the presence of the Roman proconsul, and had hopes of a speedy relief from Pompey, whom, in opposition to Cæsar, who was in rebellion against the legal government of his country, they considered as head of the commonwealth. They accordingly exerted great perseverance and valour in defence of their wall; and by a continual discharge from the battlements, and by frequent sallies, in which they set fire to the works of the besiegers, greatly retarded the progress of the siege. They had engines of a peculiar force, from which they darted arrows of a monstrous size and weight, being beams twelve feet long, and proportionally thick, and pointed with iron, which none of the screens or coverings, usually employed in making approaches, could resist; and Trebonius was accordingly obliged to proportion the strength of his timbers and penthouses, and the thickness of his parapets, fascines, and earth, on his terrace, to the weight of these enormous weapons.

While such efforts were made on both sides at this memorable siege, Pompey had detached Nasidius with sixteen galleys from the coast of Macedonia to endeavour the relief of Marseilles. This squadron had entered the straits of Messina by surprise, and, having cut out of the harbour a ship which belonged to Curio's fleet, proceeded on their destination to the coast of Gaul. Being arrived in the bay of Tauroentum, now La Ciotat, in the neighbourhood of Toulon, they sent intimation of their coming, in order to concert operations with those in the harbour of Marseilles.

The besieged were greatly animated with these hopes of relief; and having already drawn from their docks as many ships as supplied the place of those they had lost in the late engagement, they now manned them with the choice of their citizens, and determined once more to try their fortune at sea. When this fleet was about to depart, numbers of women, and many citizens, who, on account of their age, could not take part in the service, crowded to the shore, and with tears exhorted the soldiers and mariners to be mindful of their own and their country's honour, on the eve of becoming a prey to their enemies. Multitudes of people, at the same time, drew forth in procession, and crowded to the temples with prayers and supplications for the success of this last effort they were to make in defence of their commonwealth.

This bustle in the streets of Marseilles, with the motion of the shipping in the harbour, being observed from the camp of Trebonius, which was situated upon a height, and which had a view into the town, gave sufficient intimation of what was intended; and Brutus was warned to be on his guard: but the Marseillians, having found a favourable wind, had the good fortune to clear the bay, and, without any interruption from his squadron, joined Nasidius at Tauroentum. Here an action soon after ensued, in which the Marseillians made great efforts of valour; but were ill supported by Nasidius, who, unworthy of the command with which he had been entrusted, withdrew at the beginning of the action, and fled to the coast of Spain. The Marseillians, being left to sustain the contest alone, lost nine of their ships, of which five were sunk, and four were taken.

These tidings were received at Marseilles with inexpressible sorrow; but did not alter the resolution of the inhabitants to persevere in their defence, and in the use of every possible method that could be employed to protract the siege, and to give Pompey time to devise more effectual means for their safety. They accordingly, with great vigour and success, counteracted the ordinary operations of the siege, burning and demolishing a considerable part of the works which were raised up against them, and obliging the besiegers frequently to renew their labours.

The first attack, against which the besieged were not able to find an adequate defence, came from a work which had not been a part in the original plan of the siege, but had been devised by the soldiers who had succeeded each other on the guard of the agger, or mound of approach, as a lodgment or cover to secure themselves from surprise. It was at first no more than a square of ten yards, enclosed with a brick wall five feet thick; but so situated, that if it were raised to a proper height, it might cope with the battlements, and greatly annoy the besieged. To give it this consequence, masons were employed to raise it, and great efforts of ingenuity were made to protect them in their work. A moveable penthouse, of great thickness in the roof, and screened in the front and sides with net-work made of cables, or the strongest ropes, was raised on beams or

1 Agger. 2 Bourges.

rafters of a proportional strength, and contrived to be hoisted up by machinery, to keep pace with the building, and to cover the workmen as they rose on the successive courses of masonry which they laid. With these precautions, a tower was gradually raised on the foundation of the original brick wall, to the height of six stories; and being furnished with ports or embrasures on every floor, gave the besiegers, by means of their missiles, the command of all the space from thence to the ramparts. They accordingly, under the cover of engines, that made a continual discharge from this tower, filled up the ditch, and pushed up a gallery to the foot of the wall. In this position, notwithstanding all the efforts of the besieged, by a continual discharge of heavy stones from the battlements, to destroy or overwhelm the supports of their gallery, they undermined the foundation of the rampart, and brought some part of it in ruin to the ground.

The inhabitants, greatly alarmed at the sight of a breach, which might soon be enlarged to admit of being stormed, made some signals of truce, and sent to beseech Trebonius that he would suspend his operations, and wait for the arrival of Cæsar, in whose clemency they hoped to find some protection against the fury of troops, who had already threatened the inhabitants with a massacre.

Trebonius, accordingly, moved by these intreaties, and by the instructions he had received from Cæsar, not to deliver up the town, in case it fell into his hands, to the rage of the soldiers, suspended his operations, and supposing the petition of the inhabitants equal to an offer of surrender on their part, entrusted his works to slender guards, who, in their turn relying on the submissive professions of the people, were proportionally remiss in their duty. The citizens, tempted by the opportunity which was thus offered them to strike an important blow, and to throw back to a great distance, all the posts of the enemy, made a vigorous sally from the town, and being favoured by a high wind, which blew directly on the works of the besiegers, set the whole on fire, and reduced to ashes, in a few hours, what had been the labour of many months to erect.

As Trebonius had already exhausted the greater part of the materials which the country around him could furnish, it appeared difficult for him to resume the attack. But he himself, as well as the troops under his command, being greatly exasperated by the late breach of faith in the town, made every effort of ingenuity and courage to repair their losses. They substituted brick work for timber in supporting the sides and galleries of their terrace; and advanced with so rapid a progress in their new approach, that the besieged, now greatly spent with toil, and disappointed in their hopes of relief, were struck with fresh and more alarming apprehensions of what they might expect from the resentment of troops whom they had incensed with a recent and just provocation; and they returned to their suit for mercy, with more humble and more sincere intentions of submission.

While messages were passing to this effect, Domitius Ahenobarbus, sensible that he could no longer serve the cause of his party at this place, embarked with his attendants and friends on board of three galleys which still waited his orders in the harbour. Having the opportunity of a high and favourable wind, which made it unsafe for the squadron of Brutus to weigh, or to quit their anchors in pursuit of him, he endeavoured to escape from the bay. In this attempt two of his vessels were taken, the third, with himself on board, got off, and reserved him to take that share which yet remained for him in the growing misfortunes of his party throughout this disastrous war.

Such was the state of affairs when Cæsar arrived from Spain, and expecting, in the present contest for empire, to profit as much by the reputation of his clemency, as by the terror of his arms, listened to the supplications of the people of Marseilles, and took possession of the town without any act of resentment or severity whatever. While he was yet at this place, he had accounts from Rome, that his party in the city had procured an act of the people to vest him with the power of dictator. The ceremony of his nomination had, in the absence of both consuls, been performed by Marcus Æmilius Lepidus, then prætor in office, who, though a person of mean capacity, was, by the chance of his situation, involved in many of the greatest affairs that followed; and, though but a single accomplice in the crimes of this guilty age, escaped its violences, to become almost the only example of an ignominy and disgrace, which so many others had merited no less than himself.

Cæsar, being thus raised, though by an irregular step, to a legal place in the commonwealth, hastened to Rome, in order to be invested, for the first time, with the character of dictator. In his way he was stopped at Placentia by some disorders which threatened a mutiny among the troops who were assembled at that place. The legions, elated by victory, and filled with a sense of their own importance, in a contest for the sovereignty of the empire, were become impatient of discipline, and in haste to avail themselves of that military government they were employed to establish. In entering Italy they treated Roman citizens as their subjects, and the country as their property. Being restrained, they resented the severities which were practised against them, entered into cabals, and even talked of abandoning Cæsar, and of declaring for Pompey. Here, however, the usual courage and ability of this singular man supported him. He brought the mutinous troops, under arms, before him, and put them in mind how much he had ever coveted, and been anxious to obtain the affections of the soldiers; but assured them, that it was no part of his intention to earn those affections by making himself an accomplice in their crimes. "Shall we," he said, "who profess to be the deliverers of our country from oppression, become ourselves the greatest oppressors? Shall I, who am intrusted with the command of a Roman army, become the patron of licentiousness, and in order to indulge for a moment the passions of my soldiers, suffer them to ruin their own fortunes for ever? What should induce me?—The fear of violence to my person, or the danger to which my life may be exposed?—If my life were attacked, there are enow to defend it. But what is life compared to the honour of a Roman officer, which I am concerned to maintain? There are persons who have said, that they will desert my cause, and go over to Pompey. Let them.

They shall soon have an opportunity to do so. If Pompey be my enemy, what is there I should more earnestly wish than to find his cause entrusted with such men? men who make war on their friends, and disobey their officers. He had been slow," he said, "in proceeding to the fatal extremes which were now become necessary. The guilty," he continued, "had been long known to him; but he had endeavoured to conceal their offences, in hopes that remorse and shame, or the fear of justice, would have made the actual application of punishment unnecessary; but that he must now, though with the greatest reluctance, proceed to the last of remedies."

In order that he might not involve the whole of those who were present in the same desperate cause, he affected, in this harangue, to treat the offence he was to punish as the crime of a few. They were now to be set apart, he said, and their punishment should purge the army, and retrieve its honour. In pursuance of this plan, he affected to believe, that the ninth legion were the principal authors of this mutiny. He ordered a few of them for immediate execution, and boldly dismissed the whole of the legion from his service. The remainder of the army, having thus obtained an implied exculpation, in token of their own innocence, vied with each other in applauding the justice of their general. Even the legion, which was dismissed from the service, detesting as a punishment on themselves, what they had threatened to execute as an act of resentment against their commander, beset him with humble and earnest intreaties, that he might be pleased to receive them again into his service. He affected great difficulty in granting this request; but, after much solicitation, suffered himself to be gained by their professions of penitence.[1]

With a considerable accession of authority, acquired by his success in quelling this mutiny, Cæsar proceeded to Rome, where he assumed the title and ensigns of dictator; being the first example of any person, since the abdication of Sylla, entrusted with this alarming power. It was said to be conferred upon him, however, merely in compliance with form; and that there might be a proper officer, in the absence of both the consuls, to preside at the elections. His own object, at the same time, being to gain to his party the authority of legal government, and, in his conduct, to give proofs of clemency and moderation, without any intention, for the present, to perpetuate or even to exercise any of the high powers of dictator, he proceeded to hold the elections, and was himself, together with Servilius Isauricus, chosen consul for the following year. In the interval that followed, before their installation, he continued to assemble the people in the character of dictator, and obtained some laws respecting the times, and the distracted state of public affairs. Credit and trade were at an alarming stand; he procured an act to facilitate the recovery of debts, by delivering the effects of the debtor to be divided among his creditors, upon an estimate of what the different subjects might have been sold for at the time that the war broke out.

Many being supposed to hoard great sums of money, as the only means of preserving it from the violence of the times, or being unwilling to lend on such securities as were then to be had, Cæsar procured another act, by which any person was forbid to have in his possession, at once, above sixty thousand Roman money.[2]

He obtained a general act of indemnity, from which Milo alone was excepted, restoring persons of every denomination, who, at the breaking out of the war, lay under the censure of the law, and were in exile for corrupt practices in the state; and, in pursuance of this measure, procured a pardon for all the disorders which had been committed in opposition to the late government; but for none of the irregular efforts that had been made in support of it. He opened the city at once to all the inhabitants of the Cisalpine Gaul, and by a single vote gave them a title to be enrolled with the people of Rome as members of the republic.[3] In these, and in other affairs of less moment, while his troops were in motion through Italy, he employed a few days in the city, and being ready to depart, resigned the power of dictator. This resignation, made by a person possessed of a military force, and hitherto victorious, was considered as an evidence of his moderation, and served to dispel the fears of those who expected to see the immediate establishment of a military government. He was now about to assume the office of legal magistrate, and to appear in the character of Roman consul against those who, lately trusting to the name and authority of the republic with which they were vested, had treated himself and his adherents as rebels; but who now, in their turn, might appear to incur all the disadvantages of that imputation which he was about to retort upon them; and with the additional charge of an attempt to dismember the empire, and to arm so many of the provinces against the sovereignty of the state.

The competitors in this famous contest were in, or but a little past the prime of life: Pompey was fifty-seven, and Cæsar fifty. The first had been early distinguished as an officer, and for many years had enjoyed a degree of consideration, with which that of any other Roman citizen was not allowed to compare. His reputation, however, in some measure, had sunk, and that of Cæsar rose on the first shocks of the present war; but the balance was not yet absolutely settled, and the minds of many were held in anxious suspense. Cæsar, wherever he had acted in person, had always prevailed; but where he was not present, his affairs wore a less promising aspect.

His forces under Curio had acquired an easy possession of Sicily; and this officer, encouraged by his first success, transported two legions into Africa, found Varus encamped near Utica, obliged him to retire into the town, and was preparing to besiege it, when he received intelligence that Juba, king of Numidia, was advancing to its relief with all the powers of his kingdom. This prince had been induced to take part in the war by his attachment to Pompey, and by his personal animosity to Curio, who, in his tribunate, had moved for an act to deprive him of his kingdom.

1 Dio. Cass. lib. xli. c. 27—35. Appian. de Bello Civ. lib. ii. p. 547. Sueton. in Cæs. c. 69. Lucan. lib. v. p. 244.

2 About 500*l*.

3 Dio. Cass. lib. xli. c. 36, 37, 38. Cæs. de Bell. Civ lib iii

Curio, upon this intelligence, wisely withdrew from Utica to a strong post in the neighbourhood, and sent orders into Sicily to hasten the junction of the troops he had left behind him in that island. While he waited their coming, some Numidian deserters arrived at his camp, and brought accounts that Juba, with the main body of his army, had been recalled to defend his own dominions; and that only Sabura, one of his generals, with a small division, was come to give what support he could to the party of Pompey in Africa.

Upon this information, Curio formed a design to intercept the Numidian general before he could be joined by Varus; and for this purpose, leaving a guard in his camp, he marched in the night to attack the enemy, where he was informed that they lay on the banks of the Bagrada. His cavalry being advanced, fell in with the Numidian horse, and put them to flight. Encouraged by this advantage, he hastened his march to complete the victory; and Sabura, by whose art the last intelligence had been conveyed to him, likewise, after a little resistance, fled before him. By this means, Curio was gradually ensnared into the midst of Juba's forces, was surrounded, and attacked on every side. He attempted, in vain, to take refuge on a height which he had in view, and, with the greater part of his army, was put to the sword. The few who escaped, with those who had been left in the camp, endeavoured to find a passage into Sicily, and, being disappointed, surrendered themselves to Varus, by whom they were treated with clemency; but being observed, and distinguished by Juba, who arrived at Utica on the following day, were claimed as his captives, and put to death.

About the same time, Dolabella, to whom Cæsar had given the command both of his sea and land forces on the coast of Illyricum, was, by Marcus Octavius and Scribonius Libo, expelled from thence; and Caius Antonius, attempting to support Dolabella, was shut up in a small island, and, with his party, made prisoners.[4]

The principal storm, however, with which the new government was threatened, appeared on the side of Macedonia. In this country, Pompey himself was now at the head of a great force. He had transported five legions from Italy; and, since the middle of March, when his last division sailed from Brundusium, he had been in the quiet possession of Greece, Macedonia, and all the eastern part of the empire. He had sent his father-in-law, Cornelius Scipio Metellus, into the provinces of Asia and Syria, to collect the forces and the revenues of those opulent countries; and despatched his own son Cneius with instructions to assemble all the shipping that could be found on that coast. He likewise sent general orders to all the Roman officers in different parts of the empire, and to the allies or dependants of the Roman people, to join him with every power they could raise. Seven thousand citizens of rank had followed him from Italy.[5] Numbers of veterans, who had been settled in Thessaly, repaired to his standard. He was joined by one legion from Sicily, another from Crete, and two from Asia. He had two legions under Scipio in Syria, had assembled three thousand archers, and as many slingers; had hired, in the neighbourhood of Macedonia, two thousand foot and seven thousand cavalry. Dejotarus sent him six hundred horse; Ariobarzanes five hundred; Cotus, a Thracian prince, five hundred; the Macedonians furnished two hundred; five hundred being the remains of Gabinius's army, had joined him; his son brought eight hundred from his own estates; Tarcundarius three hundred; Antiochus Commagenes two hundred: amounting to fifty-five thousand legionary troops, eight thousand irregular infantry, and ten thousand six hundred horse. In all seventy-three thousand six hundred.[6]

He had likewise assembled a numerous fleet; one squadron from Egypt, of which he gave the command to his son Cneius; another from Asia, under Lelius and Triarius; one from Syria, under Caius Cassius; that of Rhodes, under Caius Marcellus and Coponius; that of Achaia and Liburnia, under Scribonius Libo and M. Octavius: the whole amounting to above eight hundred galleys, of which Bibulus had the chief command, with orders to guard the passage from Italy to Greece, and to obstruct the communications of the enemy by the Ionian sea.

Pompey had likewise formed large magazines of corn from Thessaly, Asia, Egypt, Crete, and Cyrene. The principal resort of his land forces was at Berrhœa, on the fertile plains between the Axius and Haliacmon, that run into the Bay of Thermæ. The Roman senate was represented at Thessalonica by two hundred of that body, who, together with the two consuls, held their assemblies, and assumed all the functions of the Roman state. The Roman people were likewise represented by the concourse of respectable citizens, who repaired to the army or to this place.[7] But though so many members of the government, thus violently expelled from Rome, considered themselves as the real constituents of the commonwealth, they suffered the usual time of elections to elapse, and did not attempt to preserve in their retreat the succession of officers, in opposition to the elections that were made at Rome. Claudius Marcellus and L. Cornelius Lentulus, at the expiration of their year in office, took the several commands allotted to them, as usual, under the title of proconsul.

The general had been extremely active in forming, as well as in assembling this powerful armament. He intended, early in the spring, to take possession of Dyrrachium, Apollonia, and the other towns on the coast, probably with a view to fall upon Italy, with a weight which now appeared sufficient to ensure the high reputation as a commander, which his successes, on other occasions, had procured him.

Cæsar, on his part, had drawn all his army to the coast in the neighbourhood of Brundusium; but it was not likely that he would attempt to pass a sea which was commanded by the enemy's fleet, or venture upon a coast where he had not a single port, and in the face of a superior army, now completely formed and appointed, under the command of an officer, whom no man was ever supposed to excel. The formality of entering on the office of consul, to which he had been elected, it was supposed, might detain him at Rome till after the first of January; and Pompey accordingly made no haste in taking his intended stations

4 Dio. Cass. lib. xli. c. 41 and 42.
5 Plutarch in Pompeio.
6 Cæsar. de Bello Civile, lib. iii.
7 Dio. Cass. lib. xli. 43.

on the coast of Epirus, from which he might either act on the defensive, or invade Italy as the occasion might require.[1]

It was difficult, however, to foresee what such an enemy as Cæsar might attempt. Having staid no more than eleven days at Rome, while he acted in the character of dictator, and obtained his election as consul, without waiting for his admission into office, he set out in December for Brundusium. At this place twelve legions and all his cavalry were already, by his order, assembled. He found the numbers of his army considerably impaired by disease, being come from the more healthy climates of Spain and Gaul to pass the sickly season of autumn in Apulia. In any other hands than his own, an army so reduced would have scarcely been fit for the defence of Italy against such forces as were assembled to invade it; and his march to Brundusium would have appeared altogether a defensive measure, and intended to counteract the operations of his enemy from beyond the seas. The season too appeared extremely unfavourable to any hostile attempts on Greece. Cæsar, however, had determined to prevent the designs of his enemy, and to keep him involved in all the disadvantages of a defensive war.

No more transports were collected in the harbour of Brundusium than were sufficient to receive about twenty thousand foot and six hundred horse. Cæsar, nevertheless, immediately on his arrival, informed the troops of his intentions to embark, and of his resolution to fix the scene of the war in Greece. He cautioned them not to occupy transports with unnecessary baggage and horses, and exhorted them to rely on the consequences of victory, and on his own generosity, for a full reparation of any loss they might sustain by leaving their effects behind them. He embarked seven legions in the first division, and with these he himself sailed on the fourth of February. He turned from the usual course, and steering unobserved to the right, arrived next day where the enemy, if they had really been apprised of his embarkation, were least likely to expect him, on what was reputed a very dangerous part of the coast, under a high and rocky promontory, that was called the Acroceraunus.

U. C. 705. *C. Julius Cæsar, P. Servilius Isauricus.*

As soon as the fleet had come to an anchor, Cæsar having Vibullius Rufus, one of Pompey's officers who was taken in Spain, till now detained as a prisoner, he dismissed him with a message to his general in the following terms: "That both parties had already carried their obstinacy too far, and might learn, from experience, to distrust their fortunes; that the one had been expelled from Italy, had lost Sicily, Sardinia, and Spain, with one hundred and thirty cohorts (or thirteen legions);[2] that the other had sustained the loss of an army in Africa, cut off with its general,[3] and had suffered no less by the disasters of his party in Illyricum; that their mutual disappointments might instruct them how little they could rely on the events of war; that it was time to consult their own safety, and to spare the republic; that it was prudent to treat of peace while the fortunes and the hopes of both were nearly equal; if that time were allowed to elapse, and either should obtain a distinguished advantage, who could answer that the victor would be equally tractable as both were at present?

"But since all former endeavours to procure a conference, or to bring on a treaty between the leaders themselves, had failed, he proposed, that all their differences should now be referred to the senate and people; that, in the mean time, each of them should solemnly swear, at the head of their respective armies, That, in three days, they should disband all their forces, in order that, being disarmed, they might severally be under a necessity to submit to the legal government of their country; that he himself, to remove all difficulties on the part of Pompey, should begin with dismissing all the troops that were under his command, whether in garrison or in the field." [4]

It appears that Cæsar, if these declarations had been accepted, might have been somewhat embarrassed for evasions; but equally bold in all his measures, he risked this event, or rather foresaw it could not happen, as he was sure that this offer of peace, like the former, would be rejected; and the rather, that it would be considered as an effect of his weakness, and of the danger into which he had fallen by his rash debarkation with so small a force. At any rate, there is no doubt that his message was intended, in the usual strain of his policy, to amuse his enemy, or to remove the blame of the war from himself. As he usually accompanied such overtures of peace with the most rapid movements and the boldest resolutions, the moment Vibullius set out, he disembarked his troops, and in the night despatched the transports on their return to Brundusium to bring the remainder of his army.

His landing on the coast was the first intimation received by the enemy of his intention to pass a sea, which they supposed sufficiently guarded by their fleets, and of his purpose to carry the war into a country, in which they thought themselves secure by the superiority of their numbers, and of their other resources. Bibulus, upon this alarm, put to sea, and came in time to intercept about thirty of the empty transports on their return to Italy. These he burned; and, sensible of his own remissness in suffering so great a body of the enemy to pass, he distributed his ships along the coast, and determined, for the future, to keep the sea in the face of every difficulty, and under every distress.

In the mean time, Cæsar marched directly to Oricum, where Lucius Torquatus, on the part of Pompey, was posted, with orders to defend himself to the last extremity. But Cæsar, as soon as he appeared in the character of Roman consul, preceded by the ensigns of office, prevailed on the garrison to desert their commander, and to surrender the place. Without stopping here, he proceeded to Apollonia, was received in the same manner by the inhabitants, in opposition to the officer who commanded for Pompey. In consequence of these examples he was acknowledged by all the towns of Epirus, and continued his march with the greatest despatch towards Dyrrachium, where Pompey had collected his stores, and formed his principal magazines. By his unexpected arrival he had hopes

1 Appian. de Bello Civile, lib. ii.
2 The armies of Afranius, Petreius, and Varro, &c.
3 The army of Curio and C. Antonius.
4 Cæs. de Bell. Civ. lib. iii.

of being able to surprise that important place, and to make himself master of it, before a sufficient force could be assembled to cover it.

Pompey, in execution of the plan he had formed, was on his march from Macedonia towards the coast of Epirus, when he was met by Vibullius, and received from him the first intelligence of Cæsar's landing. He was not amused with the message which this officer brought him, nor did he attempt to retort the artifice, by affecting o be deceived. He even expressed himself in terms harsh and impolitic, "That he neither chose to return to his country, nor to hold his life by the concession of Cæsar; and, without returning any answer, detached some parties towards the coast where the enemy was landed, with orders to lay waste the country, break down bridges, destroy the woods, and block up the highways with the timber they felled.[5] He sent expresses to Scipio, with an account of Cæsar's arrival in Epirus, and with orders to hasten his passage into Europe, with all the forces he had been able to assemble in Asia. He himself advanced with great diligence; and being informed on the march, that Oricum and Apollonia had already fallen into the enemy's hands, he hastened to save his magazines and stores at Dyrrachium, and without stopping, night or day, marched in such disorder, that many deserted as from a cause already ruined or desperate. He arrived, however, in time to prevent the designs of Cæsar on Dyrrachium; encamped under the walls, sent a squadron of ships immediately to retake or block up the harbour at Oricum, and ordered such a disposition of the fleet as was most likely to prevent the passage of a second embarkation from Italy.

Cæsar, finding himself prevented at Dyrrachium, halted on the Apsus; and, in order to cover Epirus and wait for the second division of his troops from Italy, prepared to intrench himself on the banks of that river. Having accordingly secured the main body of his army in this post, he himself returned with a single legion to receive the submission of the towns in his rear, and to provide for the supply of his camp.

In the mean time Bibulus, on the part of Pompey, blocked up the harbour at Oricum, and commanded the passage from Italy with his fleet.

Calenus, on the part of Cæsar, who had orders to lose no opportunity of transporting his army from Brundusium, actually embarked and put to sea; but being met by a packet from Cæsar, with intelligence of the dispositions which had been made by the enemy to intercept him, he returned, suffering one of the vessels that had accompanied his fleet to keep on her way, in order to carry an account of his motions; but she was taken by the enemy and destroyed.

Bibulus, who commanded the fleet which lay before Oricum, being precluded from the land by the parties which Cæsar had posted along the shore, forced to bring his daily supplies of wood, water, and other necessaries at a great disadvantage from Corcyra, and reduced to great distress, endeavoured, under pretence of a negotiation, to obtain a cessation of arms. But Cæsar, who came in person to Oricum, on hearing of this proposition, supposing that the design of Bibulus was to find an opportunity, under cover of the truce, to procure some supply of provisions and water, rejected the offer, and returned to his camp on the Apsus.

Pompey had advanced from Dyrrachium, and took post on the opposite bank of that river. Dion Cassius and Appian agree that he made some attempt to pass the Apsus, and to force Cæsar in this post; but that he was prevented by the breaking of a bridge, or by the difficulties of a ford. According to Cæsar's own account, the armies continued to observe each other, and the troops, separated only by a narrow river, had frequent conferences from the opposite banks. It was understood that in these interviews no hostilities should be offered. Of the two parties, that of Cæsar was the more engaging to soldiers; notwithstanding his own affectation of regard to the civil constitution of the republic, his military retainers still hoped to remain in possession of the government. He therefore encouraged the communication of his men with those of the opposite party. On this occasion Vatinius, by his direction, went forward to the bank of the river, and raising his voice, complained of the harsh treatment lately offered to Cæsar, in the contempt shown to all his overtures and advances to peace. May not one citizen, he said, send a message to another when he means only to prevent the shedding of innocent blood? He proceeded to lament the fate of so many brave men as were likely to perish in this quarrel; and was listened to with profound silence by many of both armies, who crowded to the place.

These remonstrances on the part of Cæsar, delivered by an officer of high rank, and appearing to make so deep an impression, on both armies, when reported at Pompey's quarters, seemed to be too serious to be slighted. An answer, therefore, was given by the direction of Pompey, that on the following day A. Varo should be sent to any place that should be agreed upon as safe between the two armies, and there receive the propositions that should be made to him. The parties accordingly met at a place appointed, and multitudes from both armies crowded around them. Pompey, considering the whole as an artifice to gain time, or to find an opportunity to debauch his men, probably gave instructions to break up the conference, in a way that for the future should keep the troops at a greater distance from each other. Soon after the officers met, some darts, probably by his directions, were thrown from the crowd. Both sides being alarmed by this circumstance, they instantly parted, and withdrew under a shower of missiles, in which numbers were wounded.

The fate of the war seemed to depend on the vigilance of the fleet, and on the difficulties with which Cæsar had to contend in bringing any reinforcements or supplies from Italy. Bibulus, from the effect of fatigue, was taken dangerously ill; but could not, upon any account, be persuaded to leave his station, and died on shipboard. There being nobody appointed to succeed him in the command at sea, the leader of each of the separate squadrons acted for himself without any concert. Scribonius Libo, with fifty galleys, set sail from the coast of Epirus, steered towards Brundusium, where he surprised and burnt some trading vessels, one in particular laden with corn for Cæsar's camp. Encouraged by these successes, he anchored under the island which co

5 Appian. lib. ii.

vered the mouth of the harbour: from thence he kept the town in continual alarm, landed in the night parties of archers and slingers, with which he dispersed or carried off the patroles which the enemy employed on the shore; and thus, master of the port of Brundusium, expected fully to obstruct that outlet from Italy, and to awe the neighbouring coast. To this purpose he wrote to Pompey, that the other divisions of the fleet might go into harbour; that his squadron alone, in the post he had taken, was sufficient to cut off from Cæsar all reinforcements and farther supplies. But in this he presumed too much on the first effects of his own operations. Antony, who commanded the troops of Cæsar in the town of Brundusium, by placing numerous guards at every landing-place on the contiguous shore, effectually excluded the squadron of Libo from any supply of wood or water, of which his ships, for want of stowage, could not have at any one time a considerable stock; and he reduced them to such distress for want of these articles, that they were obliged to abandon their station, and to leave the harbour again open to the sea.

In the mean time, pressing orders arrived from Cæsar to hasten the embarkation of the troops. Dion Cassius and Appian relate, that he himself being impatient of delay, embarked alone in disguise on board of a barge, with intention to pass to Brundusium; that, after he had been some time at sea, the weather became so bad, as to determine the master of the vessel to put back; but that being prevailed upon by the intreaties of Cæsar, he continued to struggle with the storm for many hours. They farther relate, that the mariners being likely to faint, the passenger at last discovered himself, and encouraged them to persist, by telling them that they carried Cæsar and his fortunes; that, nevertheless, he was forced to give way, and afterwards entrusted his orders to a messenger; but that he returned to camp before it was known that he had been absent. He himself says, that some months being past, and the winter far advanced, he suspected that some opportunities of effecting the passage of his second division had been lost; that he was become highly impatient, and wrote to hasten the embarkation; informing his officers, that they might run ashore any where between Oricum and Apollonia; as the enemy's fleet, having no harbour in those parts, were frequently obliged, by stress of weather, to depart from the coast.

Upon these orders, the troops with great ardour began to embark. They consisted of four legions and eight hundred horse, under the command of Mark Antony and Calenus. The wind being at south, and no enemy appearing in the channel, they set sail, and steered for the coast of Epirus, but were drove to the northward; and on the second day passed Apollonia, and were discovered by the enemy from Dyrrachium. As they were far to the leeward of that part of the coast on which Cæsar had instructed them to land; and as it was vain for them with this wind to attempt getting to the southward, they chose to give way at once, and steer for some convenient harbour, northward of all Pompey's stations. But in following this course, as they passed by Dyrrachium they were instantly chased by Quintus Coponius, who commanded Pompey's squadron at that place, chiefly consisting of Rhodian galleys. The wind at first was moderate, and Coponius expected easily to weather the headlands that were to leeward of his post; and, though it rose considerably after he set sail, he still continued to struggle against it. As soon as Antony observed this enemy, he crowded sail and made for the nearest harbour; being in the bay of Nympheus, about three miles beyond Lissus,[1] on the coast of Dalmatia. This bay opened to the south, and was very accessible, though not secure with the present wind. He chose, however, to risk the loss of some ships, rather than fall into the enemy's hands; and made directly for this place. Soon after he entered the harbour the wind shifted to the south-west, from which his ships were now sufficiently covered, and he debarked without any loss. At the same time the wind, in consequence of this change, blowing more directly on the land, and more violently, bore hard on Coponius, forced him upon the shore, where the greater part of his galleys, being sixteen in number, were stranded and wrecked.

Such of Antony's transports as got safe into the bay of Nympheus landed three veteran legions, with one of the new levies, and eight hundred horse. Two of his transports, one with two hundred and thirty of the new raised troops; the other, with somewhat less than two hundred veterans, being heavy sailers, fell astern; and it being night before they arrived, mistook their way, and, instead of the bay of Nympheus, came to an anchor before Lissus. Ottacilius Crassus, who was stationed with a body of horse in that place to observe the coast, manned some small boats, surrounded these transports, and offered the troops who were on board favourable terms if they would agree to surrender. Upon this summons the new levies accordingly struck; but the veterans ran their vessels ashore, and having landed, fought their way, with the loss of a few men, to Nympheus, where they joined the main body of their army that was landed with Antony.

The colony of Lissus had been settled by Cæsar, as a part of the province of Illyricum, and now appeared to favour his cause; Ottacilius therefore thought proper to withdraw with his garrison; and Antony having stationed some of the transports at this place to enable Cæsar to embark his army for Italy, if, as was reported, Pompey should attempt to remove the scene of the war into that country; and having sent the remainder back for the troops which were still left at Brundusium, he despatched messengers to Cæsar with the particulars of his voyage, and an account of the place at which he had landed.

The fleet, with this division of the army under Antony, had been seen on the coast, from the stations both of Pompey and of Cæsar, steering to the northward; but it was not known for some days what was become of them. Upon the arrival of the intelligence, that they had effected a landing to the northward, both parties determined to move to that quarter. Pompey decamped in the night, and knowing the route which Antony was likely to take, placed himself in his way, giving orders that the army, without lighting fires or sounding their trumpets, should remain in profound silence. Antony, however, having intelligence of this disposition of the enemy, did not advance. Cæsar, in the mean time, to favour

1 Cæs. de Bell. Civ. lib. iii. c. 26.

his junction, was obliged to make a considerable circuit, ascended on the banks of the river Apsus to a ford at which he passed; from thence continued his march to the northward, and seemed to advance on Pompey's right, while Antony remained in his front. In this situation, Pompey, apprehending that he might be attacked on different sides at once by Cæsar and by Antony, thought proper to quit his station; and leaving their armies to join, fell back to Asparagium, a strong post about a day's march from Dyrrachium.

Cæsar having obtained this great reinforcement, was no longer so anxious as he had hitherto been for the preservation of his possessions upon the coast. His enemies, by the superiority of their fleets, could prevent his receiving any regular supply of provisions from the sea. It was necessary for him, therefore, in order that he might have some other resource, and be in condition to act on the offensive, to extend his quarters by land, and to cover some tract of country from which he could subsist his army. For this purpose he removed from Oricum the legion that was stationed at that place; taking such precautions as were necessary to secure his shipping in the port from any surprise by sea. He drew the greater part of the vessels on shore, sunk one in the mouth of the harbour, and placed another at anchor near it, mounted with a considerable tower, and manned with a proper force. Being thus secured on the coast, he sent numerous detachments in different directions: L. Cassius Longinus, with a legion of new levies, into Thessaly; C. Calvisius Sabinus, with five cohorts and a party of horse, into Ætolia; Cn. Domitius Calvisius, with two legions, the eleventh and twelfth, into Macedonia; giving strict charge to each of these officers, that they should collect all the forage and provisions which those or the neighbouring countries could furnish.

As Pompey had relied much on the authority of government, with which he was vested at the beginning of the war, and which he believed gave his party a dispensation from the exercise of those popular arts, with which Cæsar thought proper to recommend his cause, he threatened to punish the refractory more than he encouraged or rewarded the dutiful; and he often therefore extorted services from the provinces, neglecting the necessary attention to conciliate their affections; and such were the effects of this conduct, that the detachments which now appeared on the part of Cæsar were every where favourably received. Sabinus made himself master of Ætolia. Longinus found the people of Thessaly divided, and was joined by one of the parties. Calvisius, upon his arrival in Macedonia, had deputations from many towns and districts of the province, with assurances of favour and submission; and by these means the possessions of Cæsar, even in those countries on which his antagonists had chiefly depended, began to be equal to theirs.

It was thought an unpardonable error in Pompey, thus to suffer his quarters to be overrun by an enemy who had but recently acquired a footing on the coast, and whose army was, in number of cavalry and light infantry, as well as of regular foot, greatly inferior to his own. Pompey, however, knowing the interest which Cæsar had in bringing the contest to a speedy decision, did not choose to divide his forces, and he relied for the security of the southern and inland provinces, on the legions which were soon expected to land from Asia on the eastern shores of Macedonia or Thessaly.

Scipio, being the father-in-law of Pompey, had been employed in assembling the forces of Asia, and had, by severe exactions, availed himself of the resources of that opulent province. He was still occupied in this service at Ephesus, when he received from Pompey an account of Cæsar's arrival in Epirus, and an order without delay to transport his army into Europe. He accordingly, soon after the arrival of Cæsar's detachments at their several places of destination, debarked in the bay of Therme, or of Thessalonica, and penetrated into Macedonia, directing his march towards the quarters of the two legions which Cæsar had sent thither under the command of Domitius Calvisius, and gave a general alarm on his route; but being arrived within about twenty miles of Domitius, he turned on a sudden into Thessaly, as thinking Longinus, who was stationed in that country with one legion of raw troops, might be made an easier prey.

To lighten his march, he left his baggage under a guard of eight cohorts, commanded by Favonius on the Haliacmon, a river which separates Macedonia from Thessaly, and proceeded with great despatch towards the quarters of Longinus. This officer, greatly alarmed at his sudden approach, and mistaking, at the same time, for an enemy a body of Thracian horse which were coming to his own assistance, hastily withdrew by the mountains, and continued his retreat to Ambracia. Scipio was about to pursue Longinus on the route he had taken, when he was recalled by earnest representations from Favonius, the officer he had left to guard his baggage; informing him, that his post was in the utmost danger of being forced by Calvisius, who was on his march through Macedonia for that purpose. Scipio accordingly returned with all possible despatch to the Haliacmon, and arrived at the post of Favonius, after the dust which arose from the march of the enemy had appeared on the plain; and thus came barely in time to sustain his party, and to rescue his baggage.

The armies continued to occupy the opposite banks of the Haliacmon; and as Scipio, by the flight of Longinus, was become master of all Thessaly, Calvisius continued in possession of Macedonia, and from thence secured a considerable source of supply to Cæsar's army.

It would have been of great moment to Pompey's affairs, and not inconsistent with the dilatory plan he had formed for the conduct of the war, to have risked an action between these separate bodies on the Haliacmon, rather than to have suffered his enemy to retain the command of so many posts of consequence; and Scipio accordingly passed the river with a view to bring on an engagement; but after some stay on the plain, finding no opportunity to attack the enemy with any hopes of success, he repassed the river, and having occupied his former station, there passed some partial encounters between such as were advanced on the different sides, but without any considerable event.

While so many large bodies, detached from the principal armies, were thus contending in Thessaly for the possession of the country, Pompey remained to cover the ground, which was of greater importance to him, in the neighbourhood of the sea, and the port of Dyrrachium. Having, at the distance of about a day's march in his rear, this town and harbour as a place of arms, at which he had deposited his magazines and stores, and from which he received his ordinary supply of provisions, he had taken his measures to protract the war; and trusting to his own superior resources, both by sea and by land, did not doubt that by waiting until the countries which Cæsar had occupied should be exhausted, he might force him to retire from the contest without the risk of a battle. To hasten this event, he endeavoured every where to straiten his quarters in the country, and to block up or destroy all the harbours he had on the coast.

Cneus, the eldest of Pompey's sons, commanding the Egyptian fleet, in execution of this plan which had been laid to harass the enemy, without exposing their cause to a general hazard, attacked Cæsar's principal naval station at Oricum, raised the vessel that had been sunk at the mouth of the harbour, forced the armed galley that was stationed before it, and carried off or destroyed all the ships that were laid up in the port. From thence he proceeded to Lissus, burnt thirty transports which Antony had left in the harbour; but having made an attempt on the town, was repulsed with loss.

Cæsar, on the opposite part, sensible of the interest which he had in bringing the war to a speedy decision, advanced upon Pompey, forced a place of some strength that covered his front, and encamped in his presence. The day after he arrived in this position, either to bring on a general action, or to gain the reputation of braving his antagonist, he formed his army on the plain between the two camps; but as Pompey continued firm or unmoved by this insult, and as the recent losses which Cæsar had sustained in his shipping, and on the coast, rendered his prospect of future supplies or reinforcements every day less secure, he projected a movement, by which he proposed either to force an engagement, or to preclude the enemy from all his resources in the town and harbour of Dyrrachium.

For this purpose, and that Pompey might the less suspect any important design, he decamped in the day, and having a large circuit to make, directed his march at first from Dyrrachium, and was thought to retire for want of provisions; but in the night he changed his direction, and with great diligence advanced to the town. Pompey having intelligence of the change which Cæsar had made in his route during the night, perceived his design; and having a nearer way to Dyrrachium, still expected by a rapid march to arrive before him. But Cæsar having prevailed on his men, notwithstanding the great fatigues of the preceding day, to continue their march with little interruption all night, was in possession of the only avenue to the town, when the van of Pompey's army appeared on the hills.

Pompey thus shut out from Dyrrachium, where he had placed his magazines and stores, and from the only harbour he had on the coast, was obliged to take possession of the Petra, a small promontory which covered a little creek or bay not far from the town, and there endeavoured to supply the loss of the harbour, by bringing ships of burden to unload, and by procuring supplies in boats from his magazines and stores in the town; and in this manner was still in condition to avoid any immediate risk of his fortunes in a single action.

Cæsar, on the other hand, being disappointed in the design he had formed to exclude the enemy from their magazines in the town of Dyrrachium, and seeing no likelihood of being able to bring the war to a speedy decision, his own communication with Italy being entirely cut off, and the fleets he had ordered from thence, from Sicily, and from Gaul, having met with unexpected delays, sent an officer, named L. Canuleius, into Epirus, with a commission to draw into magazines all the corn that could be found in that or the neighbouring districts, and to secure them at proper places for the use of his army. This, however, in a country that was mountainous and barren, itself commonly supplied with corn from abroad, and lately on purpose laid waste by the enemy, was not likely to furnish him with any considerable supply, or to enable him for any time to support a dilatory war. His genius was therefore at work by some speedier course to harass his enemy, and to hasten the end of the contest.

In these circumstances, however, he did not neglect his usual artifices to amuse and distract his antagonists with great professions of moderation, and with overtures of peace. On hearing of Scipio's arrival in Europe, affecting to have despaired of obtaining peace by any farther direct applications to Pompey himself, and willing to appeal to the reason of the father-in-law against the obstinacy of the son, he sent Clodius, their common friend, with letters and instructions, to inform Scipio of the great pains he had taken to obtain an equitable accommodation, "all which, he presumed, had hitherto failed, through the unhappy timidity of those he entrusted with his messages, and from their not having courage to deliver them properly to their general. But subjoined that, through the mediation of Scipio who could deliver himself with so much freedom, who could advise with so much authority; and who, being at the head of a great army attached to his person, could even enforce what was just, he might expect a different issue to propositions so fair and so reasonable. And that in this event Scipio would have the honour of being the restorer of tranquillity and good order to Italy, of peace to the provinces, and of prosperity to the whole empire." Clodius was received with respect; but on delivering his message, it appears that all farther communication was refused him as a person who came to insult or amuse with false pretensions. Cæsar, indeed, was himself, as usual, so far from trusting to the effect of these propositions, or so far from remitting his own operations in order to confirm his pacific professions, that he even redoubled his efforts in that very quarter which was entrusted to Scipio; and as he had already possessed himself of Epirus, Acarnania, and Ætolia, he carried his views still farther on that side, and sent Fusius Calenus to be joined by Longinus and Sabinus, and to endeavour, by the isthmus of Corinth, to penetrate into Achaia.

He himself at the same time engaged in a project, which to those who do not recollect the amazing works which were frequently executed by Roman armies, particularly by that of Cæsar himself, will appear so vast, and even romantic, as to exceed belief: this project was no less than to invest Pompey in his camp, though at the head of an army superior to his own, and oblige him to recede from the coast, or submit to be invested with lines, and completely shut out from the country. For this purpose he occupied several hi ls in the neighbourhood of Pompey's camp, strengthened them with forts, joined those forts by lines of communication across the valleys, and soon appeared to have projected a complete chain of redoubts, and a line of circumvallation.

Pompey, to counteract this daring project, took possession of some heights in his turn, fortified and joined them in the same manner, and while the one endeavoured to contract, the other endeavoured to enlarge, the compass of their works. The archers and slingers on both sides, as in the operations of a siege, were employed to annoy the workmen. The armies lay under arms, and fought in detail for the possession of advantageous grounds. When forced from one height which they attempted to occupy, they seized upon another that was contiguous, and still continued their line, though obliged to change its direction.

In these operations, a campaign that began in January with the landing of Cæsar on the coast of Epirus, already drew on to the middle of summer, and both parties had undergone great labour, and were exposed to peculiar distress. Cæsar's army, already inured at the blockade of Alesia, and the sieges of Marseilles and of Avaricum, to toils like those in which they were now engaged, flattered themselves with a like glorious issue to their present labours. They were in want of bread, and obliged to substitute in its place a kind of root boiled up with milk; but were comforted under this hardship with the prospect of fields which were replenished with ripening corn, and which gave the hopes of a plentiful harvest. They not only continued their countervallations with incredible toil, but turned or interrupted all the rivulets or springs that formerly watered the grounds on which the enemy were now encamped.

Pompey's army, on their part, were less inured to such toilsome operations. They had plenty of bread, which came to them with every wind, from the different coasts that were still in their possession, but were in great distress for want of water and forage: many of their horses had died; the men, too long confined to the same ground, and to the same air, which was infected with filth, and the exhalation of putrid carcases, being reduced to the use of bad water, were become extremely sickly.

Pompey, nevertheless, held his enemy at some disadvantage by the superiority of his numbers, and by the extent of line which he obliged him to form and to defend; and it appears that he availed himself of these advantages with all those abilities of a great officer, which he was justly supposed to possess. He not only forced Cæsar, without hazarding a general action, to recede from many of the heights which he attempted to occupy, and obliged him, with great labour, to widen the compass of his lines; but likewise alarmed him by various attacks on the works which he had already completed, and in some places forced open the bars which the enemy had placed in his way, and recovered his own communication anew with the country before him. But as Cæsar could present his whole army in many places to cover the works he was executing, it was impossible, without risking a general action, which Pompey avoided, entirely to stop his progress.

In the course of these operations, it appears, from the text of Cæsar's Commentaries, though incomplete, that the armies changed the ground of their principal encampments as well as the disposition of some separate posts, and mutually harassed each other with frequent surprises and alarms. And Cæsar mentions no less than six capital actions which happened in one day at the lines of circumvallation, or under the walls of Dyrrachium; and in most of them it is probable that Pompey had the advantage, as he acted on the string, or smaller circumference, while his antagonists moved on the bow, or the wider circle.

Pompey completed his own line of circumvallation to a circuit of fifteen miles, having a chain of four-and-twenty redoubts on the different hills over which it was carried. By this work he obliged Cæsar to recede half a mile beyond him, and to extend his compass to about seventeen miles in circumference.

The extremities of both their works terminated on the shore; and Cæsar having no boats or ships to oppose to the numerous craft of his enemy, ought, perhaps, by the consideration of this very circumstance, to have been diverted at first from his project. But as he sought merely for occasions of action, he was contented with the hopes of finding them even under such disadvantages. While he was obliged to remain with the strength of his army at that end of his line which was nearest the town of Dyrrachium, in order to prevent the access of Pompey to his magazines, he proposed to fortify the other extremity of it with double works, and had already thrown up, at the distance of two hundred yards from each other, two entrenchments, consisting of a parapet ten feet high, and of a ditch fifteen feet wide; one facing the lines of Pompey, the other turned to the field, in order to guard against any surprise from parties which, coming by water, might land in his rear. He was likewise about to join these entrenchments by a traverse or flank, to cover him from the sea.

Before this work was completed, Pompey made a disposition to force him at this extremity of his lines, and of consequence to open a way to his rear over the whole extent of his works. For this purpose he brought in the night six entire legions, or sixty cohorts, to that part of his own works which faced this place. He embarked a numerous body of archers, slingers, and other light troops, having their helmets and shields fortified, as it seems was the custom, with basket work, to break the force of the stones which were likely to shower from the enemy's parapets, and furnished with great quantities of fascines and other materials proper to fill up the ditch. This embarkation was effected in the night; and the officer who commanded it had orders to land part of the troops in the rear of both Cæsar's entrenchments, and another part between them where the work was still incomplete. These separate divisions were to be supported by the whole force of the legions in front, who were to take advantage of any effect which the missiles from their boats might produce on the flank or the rear of the enemy.

These attacks were accordingly made at day break, in three different places at once, and had all the consequences of a complete surprise. They fell with the greatest effect upon the station of the ninth legion, of which the piquets and other guards being instantly routed, the whole legion was put under arms to support them; but soon infected with the panic, was carried off in the flight. Antony, who occupied the nearest station on the heights, appearing in that instant with twelve cohorts, and a better countenance, stopped for a while the pursuit of the enemy, and furnished a retreat to the troops that were routed.

The alarm was conveyed to Cæsar himself, by fires lighted on all the hills, and he hastened to the ground with as many cohorts as could be spared from the posts in his way; but he came too late, Pompey had already forced the entrenchments, had burst from his confinement, and was beginning to encamp in a new position, where, without losing his communication with the sea, he rendered abortive for a long time Cæsar's purpose of excluding him from the supplies of necessaries or conveniences which were to be derived from the land, and was now in a posture to command a free access to water and forage, from the want of which he had been chiefly distressed in his late situation.

Thus Cæsar, far from reaping the fruits which he expected from the labour of so many months, began to incur the censure of a visionary projector, who presumed to practise on the ablest captain of the age the arts with which he had succeeded against ignorant barbarians, or, at most, against generals of mean capacity.

These circumstances, however, probably made no impression on Cæsar himself, nor greatly altered the confidence of his army: he presented himself again before the enemy in their new position, and pitched his camp in their presence, still determined to act on the offensive, even in the sequel of attempts in which he had failed. An action accordingly followed, of which the result is evident, although it is difficult, from the imperfect text of his Commentaries, to ascertain the detail. It appears that both armies had changed the ground which they had taken immediately after the last action; that in this remove Pompey had taken possession of the camp which Cæsar had left; and as his army, being more numerous, occupied more ground than that of Cæsar had done, he made a second entrenchment, quite round that which had been formerly occupied by Cæsar. This camp was covered by a wood on one side, and by a river, at the distance of four hundred paces, on the other.

While Pompey lay in this position, he had thrown up a line of communication from the flank of his camp to the river, in order to cover his access to water. But after he had taken this precaution, he thought proper to change his ground, and had moved about the distance of half a mile on his march to occupy a new situation, when, for some purpose that is not explained, he thought proper to send back a legion, or large detachment of his army, to resume the possession of the camp he had so recently left.

Cæsar, on his part, being occupied in fortifying a camp in the last situation he had taken, and observing this detachment sent off from the enemy, thought it gave him a favourable opportunity, by cutting it off, to recover part of the credit he had lost in the late action. While, to amuse the enemy, he ordered his men to continue the work in which they were engaged, he himself marched with twenty-three cohorts, in two divisions, under cover of the wood, came to the ground unobserved, and with the division which was led by himself, mixed with the enemy, who had already taken possession of the exterior lines, and drove them from thence to the interior intrenchment, with great slaughter. The other division being in the mean time to attack the same works at a different place, mistook the line of communication which covered the access from the camp to the river for the entrenchment of the camp itself, and before they perceived their mistake, had run along this line to a great distance in search of an entrance; when observing, at last, that the line along which they ran was not defended, the infantry went over it first, and were followed by all the cavalry; but the time which they had lost by their former mistake gave Pompey an opportunity to come to the relief of his detachment. As soon as he appeared, Cæsar's cavalry, finding themselves entangled between the line of communication, the entrenchment of the camp, and the river, began to retire with great precipitation, and were followed by the foot, who fell into great confusion. That part of Pompey's detachment, which, in the beginning of the action, had been defeated by Cæsar, seeing themselves likely to be supported, rallied in the rear-gate of the camp; and the party which Cæsar himself commanded against them, observing the precipitant retreat of the other division, saw dangers and difficulties accumulating on every side. Imagining that they were about to be surrounded, or shut up within the enemy's works, they betook them to flight, crowded back to the ditch, and, in attempting to repass it, were killed in such heaps, or were trodden under foot in such numbers, that the slain filled up the ditch, and made a passage for those that followed.

In this state of general confusion and terror, the presence and authority of Cæsar, which, on other occasions, used to be of so great effect, were entirely disregarded. The bearer of a standard, upon Cæsar's catching it, and endeavouring to stop him, quitted his hold, and continued to run without it; a rider, whose horse he had seized by the bridle, dismounted, and ran off on foot. The rout was complete; but the ditches and works, amongst which the action began, as they embarrassed the flight of the one party, so they retarded the pursuit of the other; and Pompey, who did not expect such a victory, remained in suspense. He mistook the flight of Cæsar's army for a feint, to draw him into some ambuscade. In this he was governed, probably by the high estimation for discipline and valour to which Cæsar's army was so justly entitled; but which no troops can uniformly support at all times: and if it be true, as is probable, that the flight of an army in actual rout may be always distinguished from a concerted retreat, he on this day committed an unpardonable error; and Cæsar, who may be inclined to exaggerate the oversights, though not the advantages, of his enemy, owns that he himself lost about a thousand men, with above thirty standards or colours, and owed the preservation of his army to the excessive caution or incapacity of Pompey. He himself acted indeed like a person defeated, instantly abandoned all his famous lines of Dyrrachium, and all his outposts; and to make head against the victor, brought all the scattered parts of his army together.

Pompey, in the mean time, lost the decisive moment, or was not sensible of his advantage till after the time for improving it was past. But this victory, although it had not been perceived in the precise moment in which a signal advantage could have been made of it, was presently afterwards greatly exaggerated. Pompey had from his own army the usual salutations of triumph, or received the title of Imperator, which he continued to assume, and sent his accounts of the action, by expresses, to every part of the empire; but had the moderation to abstain from the practice that was usual in the case of victories obtained over foreign enemies, that of binding his fasces and his despatches with laurel.

Cæsar, by carrying the war into Macedonia, had put himself in a very arduous situation. He had passed over a sea on which the enemy were masters, and had invaded a country of which they were in possession, with forces greatly superior to his own: but this daring adventure, which, even in its first successes, excited astonishment, now exposed him to censure, and his attempt to invest so great an officer as Pompey, at the head of an army superior to his own, appeared altogether wild and extravagant. The merit of all his former campaigns, as is common, began to be questioned by those who, after the event, can instruct and correct every general; and the glory he had gained in the former part of the war was entirely obscured. He was even said to have gained the Spanish army by corruption, and to have purchased with money the surrender which he pretended to have forced by his address and his sword. People returned to their first apprehensions, that Pompey was the greatest general which any age or nation had ever produced; that he had effectually put an end to the present contest, and had left nothing for his party to do but to reap the advantages of the victory he had obtained for them.

Some time before this event, and while the minds of men were yet in suspense, Cato, in one of the councils which had been summoned by Pompey, observed that Cæsar had acquired much popular favour by his ostentation of mercy, and by the hopes of protection which he held out to every man who did not actually take arms against him; while Pompey and his followers, by publishing threats against all who did not actually espouse their cause, had rendered the army of the republic an object of terror; he therefore moved that a proclamation should be issued, containing assurances, that every town not actually in arms should be protected, and that no blood should be shed but in the field of battle. A resolution to this purpose had been accordingly published;[1] but in the present exultation of victory was forgotten. The times were said to require exemplary justice, and to justify executions and forfeitures, not only of those who were actually in arms against their country, but of those likewise who had betrayed its cause by a mean and profligate neutrality. The favourites of Pompey already, in imagination, sated their revenge, and gratified their avarice, at the expense of the opposite party and of its abettors.[2] Every one considered the use which he himself was to make of the victory, not how it might be secured or rendered complete.

The shock which Cæsar had received in so critical a time and situation, was, not without reason, supposed to be decisive; he had abandoned his lines, and called in all his out-posts. His army appeared to sink under the weight of their misfortunes. Inferior to the enemy in numbers, greatly reduced by their losses, and fallen in their own estimation, they were not soon likely to recover courage enough to contend for the field again with so renowned and so superior an adversary.

Cæsar, however, was not overwhelmed by these appearances; he knew what was the force of an army which had been taught, by the experience of many years, to repose the utmost confidence in themselves and in their general, and which was not likely to sink, without hopes of recovery, under any single event. He considered their apparent dejection as a symptom of indignation, and of rage more than of fear or debasement; and, instead of blame or reproach, soothed them with consolation, and with the apologies which he industriously framed for their late miscarriage. He bid them recollect their former actions, and not be dismayed by a single accident which befel them in the midst of a career sustained with a spirit so much superior to that of every enemy they encountered: "If fortune has crossed us for once," he said, "we must retrieve our losses by diligence and resolution. Difficulties only excite the brave, and awaken their ardour; you have formerly experienced difficulties, and every soldier who was at Gergovia will remember the effects of perseverance and courage."

He was sensible, however, that some particular officers had set a shameful example; and he supposed that by singling out these for punishment, he might seem to exculpate the soldiers, and reinstate them in their own esteem. For this reason he dismissed, with infamy, some bearers of standards, who, he alleged, had misled the troops, whose object it is never to part from their colours. By these means the sullen dejection of the legions was changed into rage, and an ardent impatience to retrieve their honour. They did not presume to importune their general to be entrusted so soon again with his fortunes; but they imposed voluntary tasks, by way of penance, on themselves, saying, that they had deserved to be loaded with hardships. Many of the superior officers gave it as their opinion to Cæsar, that whatever resolution he might have taken for the future plan of the war, so favourable a disposition in the army, and so fair an opportunity of yet ending the contest with honour on the very ground on which they had incurred their late disgrace, should not be neglected, nor suffered to escape. Cæsar, however, did not choose to stake his fortunes on the chance of a feverish ardour, which still had some mixture of consternation, nor to rely on a fury which had more of despair than of rational confidence, against the impetuosity of a superior army recently flushed with victory. Nor was he safe to remain in his present situation, without any posts

1 Plutarch. in Vita Pompeii, p. 494.

2 Cæs. de Bell. Civ. lib. iii. c. 88.

3 Ibid.

in his rear to secure his communication with the country, and without any immediate prospect of supply for the subsistence of his army.

For these reasons, Cæsar determined, without loss of time, to decamp and to remove to some distance from the enemy.[1] In the first night after this resolution was taken, and as soon as it was dark, the sick and wounded, with all the baggage, under the escort of a legion, were sent off, with orders that they should not halt till they reached Apollonia, being a march of about thirty miles. At three in the morning the main body of the army, observing a profound silence, turned out of the camp by different gates, and took the same route. Two legions yet remained for the rear-guard. These, after a proper interval, being ready to depart, sounded the usual march to make the enemy believe the van of the army was then only beginning to move, and the whole being thus already on their way, and without any incumbrance, they soon gained a considerable distance from the enemy, who was likely to pursue them.

Pompey, as soon as he was apprised of this retreat, drew forth his army, and followed with great expedition. After marching a few miles he overtook, with his cavalry, the rear of Cæsar's army at the passage of the river Genusus; but being received by the enemy's horse, interlined with infantry, could make no impression, and saw them effect the passage of the river without any considerable loss.

Cæsar, having completed an ordinary march, took possession of the lines which he had formerly occupied at Asparagium; but not intending to remain on this ground, gave orders to the legions to rest on their arms. He sent forth his cavalry by the front gate in sight of the enemy, as if with intention to forage; but with orders to turn round the camp, and enter it again by the rear. Pompey supposing, from these appearances, that Cæsar had concluded his march, and that the business of the day was over, followed his example, pitched in the same lines, which he likewise had formerly occupied at this place, and suffered his men to stray in search of forage and wood; many also who, in the hurry with which they decamped in the morning, had left their baggage behind them, were now allowed to lay down their arms, and returned to Dyrrachium in search of it.

Cæsar, who waited only until the halt he had made should produce this effect in the camp of the enemy, again put his army in motion about noon, and without interruption on the same day completed a second march of eight miles; while Pompey's army, having already laid aside their arms and encamped, were not in condition to follow. Cæsar continued his retreat during some of the subsequent days in the same order, having his baggage advanced some hours before him: and Pompey, having lost some ground by the delay of the first day, and having harassed his army in attempting to regain it, on the fourth day entirely discontinued the pursuit.

This respite gave both parties leisure to consider the plan of their future operations. Cæsar repaired to Apollonia to lodge his sick and wounded, to pay off the arrears of his army, and to make a proper disposition for the security of the places he held on the coast. And having already one cohort at Lissus, placing three at Oricum, and four at Apollonia, he continued his route from thence to the southward. He proposed, without delay, to penetrate into Thessaly, and to occupy, for the subsistence of his army, as much as he could of that fertile country. He flattered himself, that if Pompey should follow him thither, to a distance from his magazines and his supplies by sea, the war might be continued between them upon equal terms. If he attempted to retake Oricum and the towns on the coast, he must expose Scipio and the body under his command, in the eastern parts of Macedonia, to be separately attacked; or, if he wished to preserve Scipio and his army, he would be obliged to quit his design upon Oricum in order to support them. If he should pass into Italy, it was proposed to follow him by the coasts of Dalmatia. And this last alternative of carrying the war into Italy, from the difficulties, the delays, and the discredit to which it might have exposed Cæsar's cause, appears to have been the preferable choice for Pompey. It was accordingly debated in council, whether, being master of the sea, and having abundance of shipping, he should not transport his army, recover the possession of the seat of government, and strip his antagonist of that authority which he derived from this circumstance? or, whether he should not stay to finish the remains of the war in Macedonia? The advantages likely to result from his return to Rome in the capacity of victor, after he had left it with some degree of disgrace, were obvious. But the war appeared to be so near its conclusion, that it was reckoned improper to leave any part of it unfinished. It was argued, that, by quitting the present seat of the war, Cæsar would be left to recover his forces in a country yet full of resources, and would only exchange the western part of the empire for the east, from whence Sylla had been able, and from whence Pompey himself was now about to recover the city and the possession of Italy.

But what weighed most of all in these deliberations, the safety of Scipio required the presence of Pompey in Macedonia. If he should remove his army from thence, this officer, with the forces recently arrived from Asia, would fall a sacrifice to the enemy.

Upon these motives both armies, having their several detachments in Thessaly, and separate bodies to support or to rescue from the dangers which threatened them; the generals determined to march into that country, and calculated their respective movements, so as to cut off the enemy's parties, or to sustain their own. Cæsar, by his march to Apollonia, had been turned from his way; and having the discredit of a defeat, and being supposed on his flight, was harassed or ill received by the country as he passed. The messengers, whom he had despatched to Domitius, were intercepted; and this officer, while both armies were advancing, having made some movements in Macedonia in search of provisions, and having, with the two legions he commanded, fallen into Pompey's route, narrowly escaped, and only by a few hours, being surprised and taken.

Cæsar, having arrived in time to rescue Domitius, and being joined by him as he passed the mountains into Thessaly, continued his march to

1 Cæs. de Bell. Civ. lib. iii.

Gomphi. The people of this place having refused to admit him, he scaled the walls, gave the town to be pillaged; and, intending, by this example, to deter others from retarding his march by fruitless resistance, he put all the inhabitants to the sword. When he arrived at Metropolis, the people, terrified by the fate of Gomphi, threw open their gates; and Cæsar, to contrast this with the former example, gave them protection. From thence to Larissa, where Scipio, having fallen back from the Haliacmon, then lay with a considerable army, the country was open, and Cæsar, or his parties, were every where received without opposition. Having passed all the lesser rivers which fall into the Penius, he took post on the Enipeus, which runs through the district of Pharsalia. Here he commanded extensive plains, covered with forage and with ripening corn; had a very fertile country to a great distance in his rear; and being joined not only by Domitius, but probably likewise by the legion which Longinus commanded in Ætolia, in all amounting to ten legions, he was in a condition to renew his offensive operations.

Pompey directed his motions likewise towards the same quarter; but although he had the more direct route, and was every where received as victor in the late action, was still on his march. Scipio advanced from Larissa to receive him; and being joined, they took post together on a height near Pharsalus, and in sight of Cæsar's station, at the distance of thirty stadia, or about three miles.[2] The armies being some time fixed in this position, Cæsar drew forth, in the front of his intrenchment, to provoke his antagonist. It was evidently not Pompey's interest to give an enemy, whom he had brought into considerable straits, an opportunity of relief by the chance of a battle. But as this was a defiance, and had some effect on the minds of the soldiers, it was proper to return it; and both sides, during many days, continued to turn out in the front of their respective lines. Cæsar advanced, on each successive day, still nearer to Pompey's ground; but there were some difficulties in the way of his farther approach, in which he did not choose to engage himself in the presence of an enemy, nor did Pompey choose to quit the eminence on which he had hitherto formed his line of battle.

The summer being far spent, and all the forage and corn of the neighbouring plains being consumed, Cæsar began again to suffer for want of provisions, and having no hopes of bringing the enemy to a battle on this ground, he determined to change it, for some situation in which he could more easily subsist his own army, or by moving about, harass the enemy with continual marches, and oblige them perhaps to give him an opportunity to fight them on equal terms. Having resolved on this plan, and having appointed a day on which the armies should move, the tents being already struck, and the signal to march given, while the van was passing through the rear-gate of the camp, it was observed that Pompey's army, being formed according to their daily practice, had advanced farther than usual before their lines. Cæsar immediately gave orders to halt, saying to those who were near him, "The time we have so earnestly wished for is come; let us see how we are to acquit ourselves." He immediately ordered, as a signal of battle, a purple ensign to be hoisted on a lance in the centre of the camp.[3] Appian says, that he likewise ordered the pales to be drawn, and the breast-work to be levelled in the front towards the enemy, that his army might not hope for a retreat, not even behind their intrenchments.[4]

It was evidently Pompey's interest to avoid a battle, and to wait for the effect of the distresses to which Cæsar's army must have been exposed on the approach of winter. But this is the most difficult part in war, requiring great ability in the general, together with tried courage and discipline in the troops. A general may be qualified to fight a battle, but not dexterously to avoid an enemy who presses him; an army may have that species of courage which impels them in action, but not that degree of constancy which is required to support them long unemployed in the presence of an enemy. In whatever degree Pompey himself was qualified for the part which the service required of him, he was attended by numbers of senators and persons of high rank, who, thinking themselves in a civil or political capacity, equal with their general, bore the continuance of their military subordination with pain. They said, he was like Agamemnon among the kings, and protracted a war that might have been ended in a day, merely to enjoy his command. Nursed in luxury, and averse to business, petulant in safety, useless in danger, impatient to be at their villas in the country, and their amusements in the town; and anticipating the honours and successions to office which they imagined due to their high merits in the present service, they railed at the conduct of their general, affected courage by urging him to fight, whilst in reality they only wished to terminate the suspense and anxiety of a campaign, which they had not the resolution to endure. Many of the allies, then also present in the army, who were princes of high state in their own dominions, were impatient of longer delay; and the troops of every description, in imitation of so many respectable examples, were loud in their censures of so much caution in their general.

Pompey, urged by the clamours of his army, thought himself under a necessity to come to a speedy decision, and had prepared for battle on the morning of that very day on which Cæsar was about to decamp. Although he was sensible, that in this conjuncture, it was not his interest to hazard a battle, it is probable, that he did not think the risk was great. He too, as well as others of his party, became elated and confident upon his late success.[5] His numbers greatly surpassed those of Cæsar, especially in horse, archers, and slingers; and he trusted, that, by this part of his army, he should prevail on the wings, and carry his attack to the flank, and even to the rear of the enemy. Having the Enipeus, a small river with steep banks, on his right, which sufficiently covered that flank,[6] he drew all the cavalry, amounting to seven thousand, with the archers and slingers, to his left, expecting that the event of the battle would be determined on this wing. He himself, therefore, took post to

2 Appian. de Bello Civ. lib. ii.

3 Plutarch. in Vita Pompei.
4 Appian. de Bell. Civ. lib. ii.
5 Cicer. ad Familiar. lib. vii. ep.
6 Appian. de Bello Civile, lib. ii

second the operations of the cavalry, at the head of the two famous legions which he had called off from Cæsar at the beginning of the war. Scipio was posted in the centre, with the legions from Syria, having the great body of the infantry divided on his right and his left. The right of the whole was covered by a Cilician legion, and the remains of the Spanish army which had joined Pompey under Afranius. The whole amounted to one hundred cohorts, or about forty-five thousand foot, drawn up in a line of ten men deep.[1]

Cæsar, observing this disposition, formed his army in three divisions; the left was commanded by Antony, the right by Sylla, and the centre by Cn. Domitius. The tenth legion was posted on the right, and the ninth on the left of the whole. He had eighty cohorts in the field; but these so incomplete, as not to exceed above twenty-two thousand men. He saw the disparity of his horse and irregulars on the right, having no more than a thousand horse to oppose to seven thousand of the enemy. In order to reinforce and sustain them, he draughted a cohort from each of the legions in the right to form a reserve, which he placed in the rear of his cavalry with orders to sustain them, or to repel the enemy's horse, when they should attempt as he expected, to turn his flank. This body formed a fourth division of his army, not placed in the same line with the other divisions; but facing obliquely to the right, in order to receive the cavalry that was expected to turn the flank, and to fall obliquely on the rear. He himself passed along the front of the right wing, and earnestly entreated them not to engage till they got the signal from himself. He reminded them of his continual attention to the welfare of the army, desiring them to recollect with what solicitude he had endeavoured to bring on a treaty, in order to save both armies to the republic; and how far he had always been from any disposition wantonly to shed the soldiers' blood. He was answered with shouts that expressed an impatience to begin the action. Pompey had directed the cavalry and archers assembled on his left to begin the attack; and instructed them, as soon as they had driven Cæsar's horse from the plain, to fall upon the flank and the rear of his infantry.

These dispositions being completed, a solemn pause and an interval of silence ensued. The same arms, and the same appearances presented themselves on the opposite sides. When the trumpets gave the signal to advance, the sounds were the same; many are said to have shed tears.[2] Being so near, that they had only space enough in which to acquire that rapid motion with which they commonly shocked, Cæsar's army began to rush forward, while Pompey's agreeable to the orders he had given them, remained in their places, expecting that the enemy, if they were made to run a double space in coming to the shock, would be disordered, or out of breath. But the veterans, in Cæsar's line, suspecting the intention of this unusual method of receiving an enemy, made a full stop; and, having drawn breath, came forward again with the usual rapidity. They were received with perfect order, but not with that resistance and equal force which motion alone could give. The action became general near about the same time over the whole front. Pompey's horse, as was expected, in the first charge, put Cæsar's cavalry to rout, and, together with the archers and slingers, were hastening to turn the flank of the enemy. But as soon as they opened their view to the rear, being surprised at the sight of a body of infantry which was drawn up to oppose them, and being, probably, from their confidence of victory, negligent of order; in their attempts to recover it they were thrown into the utmost confusion, and, although there was not any enemy in condition to pursue them, fled to the heights. The archers and slingers, being thus deserted by the horse, were put to the sword. And Pompey's left, on which he expected the enemy could not resist him, being flanked by the cohorts who had defeated his cavalry, began to give way Cæsar, in order to increase the impression he had made, brought forward fresh troops to the front of his own line; and while his reserve turned upon the flank, made a general charge, which the enemy no longer endeavoured to withstand.

Pompey, on seeing the flight of his cavalry, an event he so little expected, either thought himself betrayed, or despairing of the day, put spurs to his horse, and returned into camp. As he entered the prætorian gate, he called to the guards to stand to their arms, and to provide for the worst. "I go the rounds," he said, "and visit the posts." It is likely that surprise and mortification had unsettled his mind. He retired to his tent in the greatest dejection, and yet he awaited the issue.[3] His army, in the mean time, being routed, fled in confusion through the lanes of their own encampment. It was noon, and the victors, as well as the vanquished, were greatly fatigued; but Cæsar seldom left any refuge to a flying enemy, not even behind their intrenchments. He ordered Pompey's lines to be stormed, met with some little resistance from the guards that were placed on the parapet, but soon prevailed. The rout and the carnage continued through the streets and the alleys of the camp, to the rear-gate and passages through which the vanquished crowded to recover the fields, and from which, without any attempt to rally, they continued their flight to the neighbouring hills.

When Pompey's army drew forth to battle, their tents were left standing, as in full confidence of victory; and the plate, furniture, and equipage of the officers were still displayed, as if intended for show. Notwithstanding this circumstance, Cæsar had authority enough to restrain his troops[4] from plunder, and continued the pursuit. Seeing crowds of the vanquished had occupied a hill in the rear of their camp, he made haste to surround them, and to cut off their farther retreat. But they themselves having observed, that the place was destitute of water, abandoned it before they could be surrounded, and took the road to Larissa. Cæsar having ordered part of the army to keep possession of the enemy's camp, another part to return to their own, he himself, with four legions, endeavoured to intercept the fugitives in their way to Larissa.

1 Frontinus de Stratagematis.
2 Dio. Cassius, lib xli. c. 58.

3 Cass. de Bello Civ. lib. iii. c. 94.
4 The spoils of an enemy were commonly secured by the Romans in a regular manner, to be equally divided.

He had the advantage of the ground; so that after a hasty march of six miles, he got before them; and, having thrown himself in their way, obliged them to halt. They took possession of a height over a stream of water, from which they hoped to be supplied. Night was fast approaching, and the pursuers were spent with fatigue; but Cæsar yet prevailed on his men to throw up some works to prevent the access of the enemy to the brook. When overwhelmed with fatigue and distress, these remains of the vanquished army offered to capitulate; and while the treaty was in dependence many among them, who were senators and persons of rank, withdrew in the night, and made their escape; the rest surrendered at discretion. Persons of distinction, who had been formerly prisoners, and who had been set at liberty, were now put to death. Some were spared at the intercession of their friends, to whom Cæsar permitted that each should save one of the prisoners.[5] The private men took oaths of fidelity to the victor, and were enlisted in his army. Cæsar, having ordered such of his men, as had been on service all night, to be relieved from the camp, he himself marched with a fresh body the same day to Larissa.

CHAPTER VII.

Comparative Loss on the different Sides in the late Action—Pompey's Flight—His Death—Arrival of Cæsar at Alexandria—Cato, with the Fleet and Remains of the Army from Pharsalia, steers for Africa—State of Italy and of the Republican Party—Adventures of Cæsar in Egypt—Victory over Pharnaces—Arrival in Italy—Mutiny of the Legions—Cæsar passed into Africa—His Operations and Action with the Horse and Irregulars of the Enemy—Post at Ruspina—Siege of Uzita—Battle of Thapsus—Death of Cato.

IN the famous battle of Pharsalia, Cæsar, by his own account, lost no more than two hundred men, among whom were thirty centurions, officers of distinguished merit. He killed of the enemy fifteen thousand, took twenty-four thousand prisoners, with a hundred and eighty stand of colours, and nineteen Roman eagles and legionary standards; and on this occasion he cut off many senators and many of the equestrian order,[6] the flower of the Roman nobility, who were the most likely to bear up the sinking fortunes of the commonwealth.

Pompey, when he was told that Cæsar's troops had already forced his intrenchments, changed his dress, mounted on horseback, and having passed through the rear gate of the camp, made his escape to Larissa. On the road he fell in with about thirty horsemen who joined him. At the gates of Larissa he received what he wanted for his journey, but declined entering the town, saying, That he would do nothing to make a breach betwixt the inhabitants of that place and the victor.[7] From thence he passed by the valley of Tempe to the coast, and rested only one night in a fisherman's cottage. Next morning he put off from the shore in a small boat, with a few of his attendants, and coming in sight of a trading vessel, made signals, and was taken on board. In this ship he steered to Amphipolis, came to an anchor before that place, and, probably to conceal his farther intentions, issued a proclamation addressed to all the districts of Macedonia, and requiring new levies to be made, and all the youth of the province to assemble forthwith at this place. But having received some supplies of money, he remained only one night at Amphipolis. His wife Cornelia, and Sextus the youngest of his sons, were at Mitylene, in the island of Lesbos; thither he proposed to sail, and, without having settled his plan any farther, was anxious to save this part of his family from falling[8] into the hands of his enemies. Having taken them on board, and being joined by some galleys of the fleet, after a delay of some days, occasioned by contrary winds, he set sail, continued his voyage to the coast of Cilicia, and from thence to Cyprus. He meant to have landed in Syria; but being informed that the people of Antioch, upon the news of his defeat, had published a resolution to admit none of his party, he dropt that intention, and contented himself with what aids and reinforcements he obtained on the coasts of Cilicia and Cyprus. He seized the money which was found in the coffers of the farmers of the revenue; and having borrowed, or otherwise procured, considerable sums, he armed two thousand men, and having shipping sufficient to transport them, continued his voyage to Egypt.

The late king, Ptolemy Auletes, had been indebted to the Romans and the patronage of Pompey; and the kingdom being now on a respectable footing, having a considerable military force in the field; this Roman leader, though of a vanquished party, flattered himself, that in the gratitude of the Egyptian court he might find some means to reinstate his affairs.

On the death of Ptolemy, who had been restored to his throne by Gabinius, two factions had arisen in Egypt. The king leaving four children, Ptolemy the elder, Cleopatra, Arsinoe, and Ptolemy the younger, had by his will bequeathed his crown to Ptolemy the eldest of his sons, together with Cleopatra the eldest daughter. This brother and sister being by the laws permitted to marry, were in the capacity of husband and wife associated on the throne. But the council of the young king proposed to set aside the will by excluding Cleopatra. In execution of this design, having obliged her to leave the kingdom, and to fly for protection into Syria, they had taken post with a great army at Pelusium to prevent her return, she being said to have assembled a numerous

---

5 Dio. Cass. lib. xli. c. 62.
6 Appian. de Bell. Civ. lib. ii.
7 Dio. Cass. lib. xlii. c. 2.
8 Cæsar, Appian, Plutarch.

force in Asia for that purpose.[1] Pompey observing this army upon the shore, concluded that the king was present, came to anchor, and sent a message with intimation of his arrival, and of his desire to join his forces with those of Egypt.

The council of Ptolemy consisted of three persons, Achillas, who commanded the army; Photinus, a eunuch, who had the care of the finances; and Theodotus of Samos, who was the preceptor or literary tutor of the young king. These counsellors, knowing that the Romans had been named executors of the late king's will,[2] and in this capacity might restore Cleopatra to her share in the throne, and that Pompey, in name of the republic, might assume the supreme direction in Egypt, were greatly alarmed upon receiving his message, and came to a resolution to put him to death. By this atrocious action they expected to rid themselves of one dangerous intruder, and to merit the favour of his rival, who by this decisive stroke was to become the sovereign of the empire, and fully able to reward those who took a seasonable part in his quarrel.

With this intention Achillas, with a few of his attendants, came on board in a small boat, delivered a message from Ptolemy, inviting Pompey to land. In the mean time some Egyptian galleys, with an intention to secure him, drew near to his ship; and the whole army, with the king at their head, were drawn out on the shore to receive him. The size of the boat, and the appearance of the equipage which came on this errand, seemed disproportioned to the rank of Pompey; and Achillas made an apology, alleging, that deeper vessels could not go near enough to land him on that shallow part of the coast. Pompey's friends endeavoured to dissuade him from accepting of an invitation so improperly delivered; but he answered by quoting two lines from Sophocles, which implies, that *whoever visits a king, though he arrive a free man, must become his slave.* Two of his servants went before him into the boat to receive their master; and with this attendance he put off from the ship. His wife Cornelia, and Sextus the youngest of his sons, with some other friends, remained upon deck, sufficiently humbled by the preceding strokes of fortune, anxious for the future, and trembling under the expectations of a scene which was acting before them. Soon after the barge had left the ship, Pompey looking behind him, observed among the Egyptian soldiers a person whose countenance he recollected, and said to him, Surely, fellow soldier, you and I have somewhere served together. While he turned to speak these words, Achillas beckoned to the other soldiers, who understanding the signal to put the Roman general to death, struck him with their swords. Pompey was so much prepared for this event, that he perceived the whole of his situation at once, and sunk without making any struggle, or uttering one word.[3] This was done in the presence of the king of Egypt, and of his army, who were ranged on a kind of amphitheatre formed by the shore. The vessel in which the unhappy Cornelia with her family was left, and the little squadron which attended it, as if they had received a signal to depart, cut their cables and fled.

Thus died Pompey, who for above thirty years enjoyed the reputation of the first captain of his age. The title of *Great*, originally no more than a casual expression of regard from Sylla, continued, in the manner of the Romans, to be given him as a mark of esteem, and a name of distinction. He attained to more consideration, and enjoyed it longer than any other Roman citizen; and was supplanted at last, because, for many years of his life, he thought himself too high to be rivalled, and too secure to be shaken in his place. His last defeat, and the total ruin which ensued upon it, was the consequence of an overweening confidence, which left him altogether unprepared for the first untoward event. The impression of his character, even after that event, was still so strong in the minds of his enemies, that Cæsar overlooked all the other remains of the vanquished party to pursue their leader.

The accounts which Cæsar received at Larissa made him believe that Pompey must have passed into Asia; and he accordingly, on the third day after the battle of Pharsalia, set out in pursuit of him with a body of horse, ordering a legion to follow. In passing the Hellespont, he was saluted by some galleys which guarded the Straits, under Lucius Cassius. These surrendered themselves, and, with their leader, made offer of their service to the victor. From thence he continued his march by the coast of Ionia, receiving the submission of the towns in his way. And being come into Asia, he had intelligence of Pompey's operations in Cyprus, of his departure from thence, and of his continuing to steer for the coasts of Egypt. In order to be in condition to follow him hither, he put into the island at Rhodes, where he provided transports sufficient to embark the legion which he ordered to follow him from Thessaly, and another from Achaia, with eight hundred horse. To these he joined a convoy of ten armed galleys of this island, and some Asiatic ships.[4]

With this force Cæsar set sail for Alexandria, and arrived, after a passage of three days.[5] Here he learned the catastrophe of Pompey's life; and had presented to him by the courtiers of Ptolemy, who were impatient to recommend their services, the head of the deceased severed from the body, with his seal, which was known throughout the empire, being that with which his signature was put to all letters, acts, and public writings: but Cæsar either really was, or affected to be, seized with a momentary compunction; is said to have turned away from the sight, and to have wept.[6] This able actor probably had tears, as well as words, at command; and could sanctify, under the most specious appearances, the evils which his ambition had produced. From this event, however, which he thus affected to regret, and no sooner, he became secure, and seems to have dated the termination of the war. He accordingly landed without precaution, and being detained at first by the usual periodical winds of the season, became entangled in difficulties, or engaged in pleasures, which occasioned a very unaccountable stay, suspended the expectations

1 Cæsare, de Bell. Civ. lib. iii. 2 Cæsare, ibid.
3 App. de Bell. Civ. lib. ii. Plut. in Pomp. Livii epitome, lib. cxii.

4 Cæs. de Bell. Civ. lib. iii.
5 App. de Bell. Civ. lib. ii. The two legions which he led in this service amounted only to three thousand two hundred men; so much had the army in general suffered in their late campaigns.
6 App. ibid.

of the whole empire, and gave to those of the opposite party leisure to consult their safety in different ways.

Cato, upon the march of Pompey into Thessaly, had been left to command on the coast of Epirus; and his quarters, after the battle of Pharsalia, became a place of retreat to many who escaped from the field, or who, at the time of the action, had been detached on different services. He assembled great part of the fleet at Corcyra; and, with his sea and land forces united, still preserved the aspect of a vigorous party. Cicero, Cnæus the eldest son of Pompey, Afranius, Labienus, and other persons of distinction had joined him. Among these Cicero, as being the first in rank, was offered the command; and having declined it, narrowly escaped with his life from the fury of young Pompey, who considered his refusal as a desertion of the cause, and as an act of perfidy to his father, whose fate was yet unknown.[7] Cicero, being protected by Cato and others, who were present, escaped into Italy; and declining the command of an army, reserved, for scenes in which he was better qualified to act, talents which had been, on former occasions, of so much use to his fellow citizens. It appeared that Cato had even disapproved of his having joined either party in this war, and wished him to have devoted his life and his abilities entirely to those services which he was better qualified to render to his country, in the senate, and in the popular assemblies, than in the field.

It is probable that Cato had already taken his own resolution not to submit to Cæsar, nor to survive the fall of the commonwealth; but he treated with great candour such as chose to make their peace, and to retire from the storm. Having staid a sufficient time at Corcyra, to receive on board such of the vanquished army as those to take refuge in the fleet; and having afterwards put into Patræ, near the mouth of the Gulph of Corinth, for the same purpose, he still gave every one his option to continue in arms, or to retire. He seems to have supposed that Pompey was gone into Egypt, and he determined to follow him; hoping, that after the junction of this great reinforcement, he might, either there or in the province of Africa, renew the war with advantage. Being, in pursuance of this design, arrived in the African seas, but west of the frontier of Egypt, he met the unhappy Cornelia, with the young Sextus Pompeius, who had recently beheld the death of the husband and the father near the shore at Pelusium. The account which he received of this event determined him not to continue his voyage any farther to the eastward; but to return towards the Roman province of Africa, where the friends of the republic under Varus, in consequence of the defeat of Curio, and the alliance of Juba, still kept the ascendant, and lately received an accession of strength by the junction of Scipio and of Labienus, who had escaped from Pharsalia. But the periodical winds which about the same time began to detain Cæsar at Alexandria, made it impossible, or at least dangerous, for him to continue his voyage along a coast that was covered to a great extent by the famous shoals and sand-banks of the Syrtes. For these, perhaps, and other reasons which are not mentioned, Cato landed at Berenicé: and from thence conducting his army, then consisting of ten thousand men, in small divisions, through the deserts of Barca, and round the bay of the Syrtes; and having, during thirty days, encountered with many difficulties from the depth of the sands and the scarcity of water, he effected his march to the frontier of the Roman province.[8]

Cæsar, when he passed into Macedonia, had left Italy and the western provinces in a state not likely, in his absence, to create any trouble. But the uncertain, and even unfavourable aspect of his affairs, for some time after his landing in Epirus, had encouraged those who were discontented to question the validity of his acts, and to disregard his arrangements. The army in Spain having mutinied, deserted from Q. Cassius, and put themselves under the command of M. Marcellus Æserninus, who, however, did not openly declare himself for either party, till after the event was decided in favour of Cæsar.

At Rome, it is probable that few had remained besides those who were inclined to Cæsar's party, or at least such as were indifferent to both; and that some persons, even of the last description, thought they had an interest in his success, as being their only safety against the menacing declarations of his adversary, who, in all his proclamations, treated neutrality between the parties as treason to the commonwealth. But the uncertain state of his fortunes, while the event of the war remained in suspense, and still more after his defeat at Dyrrachium, encouraged or tempted numbers, even in the city of Rome, to declare for Pompey. Marcus Cælius, who, in the preceding year, had, upon disgust, or hopes of promoting his own fortune, gone with Antony and Curio to join Cæsar, and who was now, by the influence of the prevailing party, elected one of the prætors; being moved by a fresh disgust from the party he had joined, or by its apparent decline in the field, openly declared himself against Cæsar's measures, offered protection to debtors against the execution of his laws relating to bankrupts, drove his own colleague Trebonius by force from the prætor's tribunal, and gave such an alarm, that the senate thought themselves under the necessity of giving the consul Isauricus the usual charge to guard the commonwealth as in times of extreme danger. Upon this decree the consul took arms to preserve the peace, and Cælius was obliged to leave the city. About the same time Milo, who still lay under sentence of banishment, ventured, at the head of an armed force, to land on the coast, and attempted to make himself master of Capua. While he was engaged in this enterprise he was joined by Cælius; but both were soon after surrounded and cut off by the forces which Cæsar had left for the protection of Italy.[9]

These disturbances, and every appearance of opposition to the party of Cæsar, were again easily suppressed upon the news of his victory at Pharsalia. The populace, who generally range themselves on the victorious side, and who are equally outrageous in every cause they espouse, celebrated the occasion, by pulling down the statues of Pompey and of Sylla. There was

7 Plutarch. in Vit. Ciceronis. Dio. Cass. lib. xlii. c. 10—12.

8 Strabo, lib. xvii. p. 836.

9 Liv. Epitome, lib. cxi. Dio. Cassius, lib. xlii. c. 22. 26.

either no senate, and no assembly of the people to resist the torrent with which fortune now ran on the side of military government, or the names of senate and people were, without debate or difference of opinion, put to decrees, by which the supreme power of life and death over the supposed adherents of the vanquished party was committed to the victor. By these decrees, the power of making war or peace, and of naming commanders and governors in all the provinces, was committed to Cæsar. He was, by a new and unheard-of resolution, made consul for five years, dictator for twelve months, and vested with the sacred character of tribune for life. He alone was appointed to preside in all public assemblies, except those of the tribes, in which the other tribunes bore an equal part with himself.

When these decrees were presented to Cæsar, then in Egypt, he assumed the ensigns and power of dictator, and appointed Antony, who commanded in Italy, general of the horse, or second to himself in the empire. The reputation of Cæsar's clemency had encouraged many, who had recently opposed him, to lay down their arms, and to return to their habitations, trusting to this character of the victor, or to other considerations more particularly applicable to themselves. Cicero returned to Italy, and waited for Cæsar in the neighbourhood of Brundusium. Caius Cassius, who had commanded the fleet which had been assembled for Pompey from the coasts of Syria and Cilicia, having sailed to Sicily, while the army yet lay in Pharsalia, surprised and burnt the shipping, amounting to thirty-five vessels, of which twenty were decked, which Cæsar had assembled at Messina, and was about to have forced the town to surrender, when he was informed of the defeat of Pompey in Thessaly, and set sail for the coast of Asia. Here he waited for Cæsar at the mouth of the Cydnus, without being determined, whether he should attempt to destroy or submit to the victor. From the correspondence of Cassius with Cicero, it appears, that, like this distinguished senator, he was about to withdraw from the ruins of a party which he could no longer support. Cicero, nevertheless, afterwards ascribes to him a design of killing Cæsar at this place, if the prey had not escaped him by going to a different side of the river from where he was expected to land. Upon this disappointment Cassius made his submission, and delivered up his fleet.[1] Quintus Cicero went to Asia, to make his peace with Cæsar; and many, expecting him in Italy, resorted thither on the same errand. In this number, it was reported that Cato and L. Metellus meant to present themselves as persons who had done no wrong, and who came openly to resume their station in the commonwealth. Cæsar foresaw the difficulties that might arise to himself from the presence of such men; that they would greatly embarrass his government by opposing it, or, in order to rid himself of such troublesome guests, reduced him to the necessity of pulling off the mask of moderation and clemency, which he had hitherto assumed. For these reasons, he chose rather to prevent their coming, than to contend with them after they were come; and sent positive orders to Antony, to forbid Cato, Metellus, and every other person, to whom he had not given express permission, to set their foot in Italy.[2]

1 Cæsar. de Bello Civil. lib. iii.

U. C. 706.

C. Julius Cæsar Dict. Iterum M. Antonius Mag. Eq.

Such was the state of affairs at the end of the year of Rome 705, and beginning of the following year which is dated in the dictatorship of Caius Cæsar. While he himself still remained in Egypt, the government of Italy continued in the hands of Antony. All orders of men vied, in demonstrations of joy, for the success of the victor, and for the ascendant which his party had gained. They still probably hoped to have the form of the republic preserved, while no more than the administration of it should pass from the ruined party to those who were now in power: but in the first steps of the present government they found themselves disappointed. The usual election of magistrates, which, even in the height of the war had never been omitted, now at the end of it, and when no enemy any where appeared to alarm the party, were all of them, except that of the tribunes, entirely suspended or laid aside. All government centred in the person of Antony, and the administration was altogether military. He himself, immersed in debauch, past the greatest part of his time in the company of buffoons and prostitutes; frequently shifted the scene of his frolics from the town to the country, and travelled through Italy with a field equipage, and a numerous train of carriages. filled with courtezans and their retinue. In these processions he himself is said to have sometimes appeared in a carriage that was drawn by lions.[3] In this tide of success, as he was ungracious and arrogant to citizens of the highest rank, so he was indulgent to the troops, and deaf to all the complaints that were made of their violence and rapine. Being equally apt to set the example of disorder and license in his own practice, as he was to indulge them in others, his retainers frequently alarmed the city with rapes, robberies, and murders, and made the pacific inhabitants of Italy expect, with the arrival of Cæsar, a continual increase of such disorderly masters to sport on the ruins of the commonwealth.

The worst men, as usual, were the most forward in paying their court to the party in power. The nearest relations became spies or informers against each other. Fears or complaints uttered were reported as crimes. A general silence and distrust ensued, and all parties wished or dreaded the arrival of Cæsar, according as they expected to lose or to gain by the fall of the commonwealth. In this interval of expectation, men discovered their gloomy apprehensions, by propagating strange fictions of ominous appearances, or by magnifying things natural into alarming presages and prodigies.[4]

The daily expectation of Cæsar's arrival for some time, suspended all the usual factions in the city, and suppressed the hopes and designs of his opponents in all parts of the empire: but his unexpected stay at Alexandria, and the unfavourable reports of his situation, which were sometimes brought from thence, began to turn the tide of popularity at Rome, and encouraged the remains of the late republican party, now

2 Cæsar. de Bello Civil. lib. iii. ep. 8 et 7.
3 Plut. in Vita Antonii, p. 74, 75.
4 Dio. Cass. lib. xlii. c. 26

forced to take refuge in Africa, again to lift up its head.[5]

Dolabella, a young man of patrician extraction, observing the roads which others had taken, by becoming tribunes of the people, to arrive at power in the commonwealth, procured himself, in imitation of Clodius, to be adopted into a plebeian family, to the end that he might be legally qualified to hold this office; and having accordingly succeeded in this design, revived the wild projects by which the worst of his predecessors had endeavoured to debauch the lower ranks of the people. He proposed an abolition of debts, and a reduction of house-rents. Being opposed by Trebonius, one of his colleagues, their several retainers frequently, as usual, proceeded to violence in the streets; and although the senate passed a decree to suspend every question or subject of debate until the arrival of Cæsar, these tribunes continued to assemble the people, kept them in a ferment by opposite motions, and filled the public places with tumult and bloodshed.[6] Mark Antony, second in command to Cæsar, under pretence that such disorders could not be restrained without a military force, took possession of the city with an army; and while he sometimes favoured one party, and sometimes the other, continued to govern the whole at discretion.[7]

The troops about the same time became mutinous in their quarters; and these disorders rose or fell according to the reports that were propagated from Asia or Egypt relating to the state of Cæsar's affairs. The spirits and hopes of the late republican party, which yet had some footing in Africa and Spain, likewise fluctuated in the same manner. It is highly probable, that if Cæsar had pursued the other remains of this party with the same ardour with which he pursued Pompey in person, or if he could have returned to the capital immediately on the death of his rival, they never would have attempted, or would have been able to renew the contest; but the leisure which he left them, and the ill aspect of his own affairs, for some time encouraged and enabled them to recover a strength, with which they were yet in condition to dispute the dominion to which he aspired.

Cato, who, with the remains of the republican party from Epirus, had arrived on the coast of Africa, being informed that Varus still held the Roman province on this continent in the name of the republic, that Scipio was there, and that the king of Numidia persisted in his alliance against Cæsar, determined to join them. At his arrival, Scipio and Varus being on bad terms, he received an offer of the command from the general voice of the army; but his acceptance being likely to increase, rather than to appease animosities, and the preference being constitutionally due to Scipio as of consular rank, Cato had no doubts in declining it. Neither Pompey nor Scipio ever considered him as their personal friend; his services they knew were intended to the republic, and would turn against them whenever they came to make that use of their advantages to which it is likely they were both inclined. Pompey was accordingly ever jealous of Cato, and in the last part of the campaign in Thessaly chose to leave him behind on the coast. Scipio adopted the same conduct with respect to this partizan of the commonwealth, and joined to the motives of jealousy, which actuated Pompey, a distrust of the inclination recently shown by the army to prefer him in the command. In order that he might not interfere in his counsels, he assigned or suffered him to take a separate station at Utica, where he continued to be the principal support of the cause. The inhabitants of this place were obnoxious to Pompey's party; and having formerly received Curio with the forces of Cæsar, and ever favoured his interest, were now doomed to destruction, but saved at the intercession of Cato, who, in this extremity of political evils, wished not to increase the sufferings of mankind by unnecessary acts of revenge and cruelty.

The spirit of the republic thus reviving in Africa, and the party being in condition to receive all who fled to them for protection, and having the alliance of Juba, the most powerful prince of that continent, soon became formidable both by sea and by land; and if they had chosen to invade Italy in the absence of Cæsar, were in condition to have regained the capital of the empire. Young Pompey having, at the same time, passed into Spain, was favourably received by his father's adherents and clients in that province, and profiting by the misconduct of Quintus Cassius in those parts, was likely to assemble a considerable force.

Gabinius, who commanded for Cæsar on the coast of Illyricum, attempting to penetrate by land into Macedonia, was cut off by Octavius, who had assembled a remnant of Pompey's army on the confines of that kingdom. Domitius Calvisius, whom Cæsar had appointed to command in Bithynia, had received a defeat from Pharnaces the son of Mithridates; and in general, the state of his affairs in other parts of the empire was such, while he himself continued unheard of in Egypt, as to raise a suspicion of some misfortune, supposed to be the only way of accounting for his long stay in that country, and for the seeming neglect of all the advantages he had gained by a conduct hitherto in every instance decisive and rapid. Pompey had fallen by treachery in Egypt, and so might Cæsar. It was now the middle of June, and there was no intimation received in Italy of the time at which he might be expected to return. He had written no letters since the middle of December, nor had any one come from him at Alexandria since the middle of March.[8]

The imperfect accounts which remain of what passed in Egypt during this interval, are as follows: Cæsar, at his arrival, had found the young king under the direction of Pothinus; and Arsinoë, the sister of the king, in the keeping of Ganimedes, two eunuchs who had the care of their education. From his manner of receiving the present of Pompey's head, these officers conjectured that they had gained nothing by the murder of one of the rivals, who were engaged in this contest for the Roman empire; and that this action, although it freed Cæsar of an enemy whom he respected and feared, was not to be publicly avowed or rewarded by him. They

5 Cicero ad Attic. lib. xi. ep. 16.
6 Eight hundred citizens were killed in these frays.
7 Dio. Cass. lib. xlii. c. 29.

8 Cicer. ad Att. lib. xi ep. 16 et 17.

dreaded the interposition of this dangerous man in their affairs, more than they had dreaded even that of Pompey.

The troops now in Egypt, were the remains of that army with which Gabinius had restored the late king, and which he left to secure his establishment. They were recruited by deserters from the Roman provinces, and by banditti from Syria and Cilicia. They retained the form of the Roman legion; but had precluded themselves from any prospect of return to the Roman service by a mutiny, in which they had murdered the two sons of Bibulus, then proconsul of Syria. Numbers of the men were married, and had families in Egypt; they were in the practice of disposing of the lives and properties of the people, of the offices at court, and of the crown itself at their pleasure. A party of this insolent rabble, then in garrison at Alexandria, and in the character of guards to the person of the king, took offence at the parade with which Cæsar landed, and were offended with the number and show of his lictors, by which he seemed to encroach on the majesty of their sovereign. Frequent tumults arose on this account, and numbers of Cæsar's attendants were murdered in the streets. The westerly winds were then set in, and he finding himself detained in a place where he was exposed to so much insult, ordered a reinforcement of troops from Asia, and employed Mithridates of Pergamus to bring all the forces he could assemble there to his relief. The party of Cleopatra applied to him for his protection; she herself, being still in Syria, ventured to pass into Egypt, came to Alexandria by sea, and is said to have been carried, wrapped up in a package of carpet, to the presence of Cæsar.

In this manner, it is pretended that Cæsar became acquainted with the person of this celebrated woman, then in the bloom of youth, and possessed of those allurements by which she made different conquerors of the world, in their turns, for a while renounce the pursuits of ambition for those of pleasure. She is supposed at this time to have become the mistress of Cæsar, and to have made him, though turned of fifty years, to forget the empire, the republic, the factions at Rome, and the armies which in Africa and Spain were assembling against him. Under the dominion of his passion for Cleopatra, he took a resolution to carry into execution the destination made by the late king, and in the quality of Roman consul and representative of the Roman people, to whom this office had been entrusted by the will, he commanded both parties to lay down their arms, and to submit their claims to his own arbitration.

Pothinus, fearing the total exclusion of the young king, his pupil, in favour of Cleopatra, called Achillas with the army to Alexandria, in order to defeat Cæsar's purpose, and obliged him to leave the kingdom. This army consisted of twenty thousand men inured to bloodshed and violence, though long divested of the order and discipline of Roman troops. Cæsar hearing of their approach, and not being in condition to meet them in the field, seized and fortified a quarter of the town, in which he proposed to defend himself. The young Ptolemy being in his power, was prevailed on to despatch two persons of distinction with a message to Achillas, signifying the king's pleasure that he should not advance; but the bearers of this message, as being supposed to betray the interest of their master, in whose name they appeared, were by the orders of Achillas seized and slain. Cæsar, however, being still in possession of Ptolemy's person, represented Achillas as a rebel and an outlaw, and still, in the name of the king, issued repeated orders and proclamations against him.

Achillas being arrived at Alexandria, entered the city, and endeavoured to force Cæsar's quarters; but being repulsed, took possession of that part of the town which was open to him, and blocked up the remainder both by sea and land. The city being thus divided, the Egyptians and Romans fought in the streets, and from the houses which they severally occupied. Cæsar, as he despaired of being able to receive any succours by land, endeavoured to keep open his communication by sea, and sent pressing orders to Syria, Cilicia, Rhodes, and Crete, for reinforcements of men and of ships. Having early discovered that Pothinus, who was still in his power, corresponded with the enemy, he ordered him to be put to death, continued to strengthen his division of the town by additional barriers; and in order to prevent surprise, demolished and cleared away many of the buildings adjoining to his works. Achillas, finding so much unexpected resistance, sent for reinforcements, and a supply of stores and warlike engines, from every part of the kingdom. He traversed, with breast works, the streets leading to Cæsar's quarters, and demolishing the houses in his way, effected a chain of works parallel to those of Cæsar, consisting of a parapet and frequent towers. He exhorted the Egyptians to exert themselves for the independency of their kingdom; represented to them, "That the Romans were gradually assuming the sovereignty of Egypt; that Gabinius had come as an auxiliary, but acted as a master; that Pompey on being defeated in Thessaly, came into Egypt,[1] as to a property which he had a right to employ in repairing his ruined fortunes; that Pompey had fallen in vain, if Cæsar were tamely suffered to succeed him; that if this intruder were allowed to keep possession of the city, until his succours should arrive from Asia, all Egypt for the future must expect to be the slaves of the Romans."

The danger to which Cæsar was exposed, arose no less from the remains of the republican party now assembling against him in Africa than it did from the force with which he was actually assailed in Egypt. If Scipio had been apprised of his condition in that country, he might in a few days have sailed to Alexandria, and in conjunction with the Egyptians, who would now have accepted of any assistance against Cæsar, have recovered the fall of their party at Pharsalia; but the best opportunities are sometimes lost, because it is not supposed that an enemy could be so rash as to furnish them.

The scene in Egypt was frequently changing by the intrigues and the treachery of different parties in the court. Ganimedes who had the charge of the young princess, Arsinoë, being hitherto lodged in the quarters of Cæsar, found means to make his escape, together with his ward; and finding the troops disposed to lay hold of Arsinoë, as a branch of the royal family, em-

---

1 Hirtius de Bello Alexandrino.

ployed assassins to put Achillas to death; and, in name of the princess, took on himself the command of the army. His abilities as an officer, which were very considerable, and his bounty, secured to him the affection of the soldiers. He continued the attack on Cæsar's quarters, in all the ways which were already begun by his predecessor. The town being furnished with water by subterraneous passages from the neighbouring heights, he uncovered the conduits which led to Cæsar's division of the town; and, to render these conduits unserviceable, forced into them great quantities of brine from the sea. The loss however was soon supplied from wells, in which, at a moderate depth, the besiegers found plenty of fresh water.

While Cæsar thus counteracted the arts which were employed to distress him, the eighteenth legion, with a considerable supply of provisions, military stores, and engines of war, being arrived on the coast, but unable to reach Alexandria on account of the winds, he thought proper to embark and put to sea, in order to cover this reinforcement, while they made for the port. On this occasion he was attacked by the Egyptian fleet; but gained a victory, destroyed a great part of the enemy's ships, and brought his own reinforcement safe into harbour. The Egyptians, with great ardour, set to work in all the docks on the Nile, to repair the loss they had now sustained, and were soon masters of a fleet, consisting of twenty-two vessels of four tire of oars, five of five tire, and many of smaller dimensions. Cæsar had to oppose them, nine galleys from Rhodes, eight from Pontus, five from Lycia, and twelve from the coast of Asia. Five were of five tire of oars, and ten of four tire. The remainder were smaller dimensions, and most of them open. With these forces, having once more engaged off the mouth of the harbour, the Egyptians were again defeated, with the loss of one galley of five tire of oars, another of two tire taken, and three sunk. The remainder retired under cover of the mole, and of the towers of Pharos.

Soon after this action at sea, Cæsar attacked the Pharos, forced the enemy to fly from thence, most of them swimming across the harbour, killed many, and took six hundred prisoners. He forced them at the same time to abandon the tower, which commanded the entrance of the mole on that side. As he pursued them in their flight, and as the mole itself became crowded with his soldiers, who advanced to push the attack, or who came unarmed from the ships, and all the stations around, to witness this scene; the Egyptians seeing these crowds, laid hold of the opportunity, mounted the mole, threw those who were upon it into confusion, forced them over the quay into the water, or into their boats. Cæsar himself endeavoured to escape in this manner, and finding that the boat into which he went, being aground and overloaded, could not be got off, he threw himself into the water, and swam to a ship. In this tumult, he lost four hundred men of the legions, and an equal number of the fleet. The Egyptians recovered all the ground they had lost, got possession again of the tower at the head of the mole, and of the island which secured their ships.

In such operations, with various events, the parties in Egypt passed the winter and spring. Cæsar still retained the person of Ptolemy in his possession, and made use of his name to countenance his own cause, or to discredit that of his enemies; but the king being extremely averse to this use being made of his authority, and desirous to recover his liberty, entered into a concert with some officers of his army, to find a pretence for his release. In pursuit of their design, they conveyed secret intimation to Cæsar's quarters, that the troops were greatly disgusted with Ganimedes, and that if Ptolemy should make his appearance in person, they would certainly submit to his orders, and commit the whole settlement of the kingdom to the arbitration of Cæsar. The king was instructed to affect a great dislike to this proposal, and with tears intreated that he might be allowed to remain in the palace. Cæsar, either being deceived by these professions, or believing the name of the king to be of little consequence, consented to let him depart; but this artful boy, as soon as he was at liberty, laid aside his disguise, laughed at the supposed credulity of those he had deceived, and urged the attack on the Roman quarters with great animosity.

While affairs at Alexandria were in this situation, accounts were brought that Mithridates of Pergamus, whom Cæsar had sent to procure succours from Asia, was actually arrived at Pelusium with a considerable force; that he had reduced that place, and only waited for instructions from Cæsar how to proceed. These accounts were brought to both parties about the same time, and both determined to put their forces in motion. Ptolemy leaving a proper guard on his works, embarked his army on the Nile, having a considerable navigation to make by the different branches of that river. Cæsar, at the same time, put his army on board in the harbour, and having an open course by the coast, arrived at Pelusium before the king; and being joined by Mithridates, was in condition to take the field against the Egyptian army. Ptolemy, to prevent the return of Cæsar by land to Alexandria, had taken a strong post on one of the branches of the Nile; but here, after a few skirmishes, he was attacked, defeated, and driven from his station. Endeavouring to make his escape by water, the barge[2] which carried him being overloaded sunk, and himself, with all his attendants, perished.

Immediately after this action, in which the Egyptian army was routed and dispersed, Cæsar, escorted by a small party of horse, returned to Alexandria, and having received the submission of the inhabitants, made such arrangements as he thought proper in the succession to the kingdom. He placed Cleopatra on the throne, in conjunction with her younger brother, and to remove any farther occasion of disturbance to this settlement, he ordered her sister Arsinoë to be transported to Rome. He left great part of the army to support this new establishment in Egypt, and he himself, after this singular interlude, in the midst of the conquest of the Roman empire, marched with the sixth legion by land into Syria. At Antioch, he received such reports of the state of affairs, as required his presence in different quarters. Nine months were elapsed, since any orders or directions had been received from him. During this time, the factions of the city, the relaxation of discipline in the army, and the threats of invasion from Africa, had placed his affairs in

2 Hirt. de Bello Alex.

such a state of hazard, as to urge his immediate appearance in Italy and at Rome; but he thought it of consequence to his authority to leave no enemy behind him in the field,[1] nor to suffer the remains of disorder in any of the provinces through which he was to pass. Pharnaces, the son of Mithridates, to whom Pompey had assigned the kingdom of the Bosphorus, imagining that the civil wars, in which the Romans were engaged, made a favourable opportunity for the recovery of his father's dominions, had passed with an army into Pontus, and from thence invaded the lesser Armenia and Cappadocia, which had been separately allotted by the Romans to Dejotarus and to Ariobarzanes. At the instances of these princes, Domitius Calvisius, who had been despatched by Cæsar after the battle of Pharsalia with three legions to receive the submission of the Asiatic provinces, hitherto in the interest of Pompey, despatched to Pharnaces a messenger, requiring him instantly to withdraw his troops from Armenia and Cappadocia; and, in order to give the more weight to this message, he himself at the same time took the field with one Roman legion, together with two legions that had been formed by Dejotarus in the Roman manner, and two hundred Asiatic horse. He at the same time ordered Publius Sextius and C. Prætorius to bring up a legion which had been lately raised in Pontus, and Q. Patisius to join him with some light troops from Cilicia.

These forces being assembled at Camana in Cappadocia, the messenger, who had been sent to Pharnaces, returned with an answer, that the king was willing to evacuate Cappadocia; but that, having a just claim to Armenia, in right of his father, he would keep possession of that province until the arrival of Cæsar, to whose decision he was willing to submit his pretensions. Domitius, not being satisfied with this answer, put his army in motion towards Armenia. While he advanced, Pharnaces endeavoured to amuse him with negotiations, and to put him off his guard, by permitting the country to receive him with all the appearances of peace and security. Being arrived at Nicopolis, the capital of Armenia, he there received orders from Cæsar to march into Egypt; but being unwilling to quit his supposed prey, risked a battle with the forces of Pharnaces, was defeated, and obliged to fly with the remains of his army, by the route of the mountains which separated Armenia from the Roman province.

Elated with this victory, Pharnaces, at the time of Cæsar's departure from Egypt, had returned into Pontus, had taken possession of the principal towns, and with great severity exercised the sovereignty of the kingdom. About the middle of July, Cæsar, having despatched Trebonius from Antioch with an account of his own operations, and with instructions to those who commanded in Italy,[2] went himself by sea to Tarsus, where he received, as has been mentioned, the submission of Caius Cassius, who waited for his coming; and who, according to the account of Cicero, till then was undetermined, whether he should make his peace with the victor, or attempt to assassinate him.

At Tarsus, Cæsar held a convention of the principal inhabitants of Cilicia, and from thence marched into Cappadocia, stopped at Comana to make the necessary arrangements in that province, and continued his route to the frontiers of Galatia and Pontus. Hither Dejotarus, who had espoused the cause of Pompey, who had fought under his banners in Pharsalia, and who, by the gift of that unfortunate officer, still retained the sovereignty of Galatia, came to make his submission. He laid down his diadem, and the ensigns of royalty; and, presenting himself in the habit of a suppliant, pleaded, that, in the late war, the eastern part of the empire, being subject to Pompey, the princes of that quarter had not been free to choose their party; that he was himself not qualified to decide in a question on which the Roman people was divided; that he thought it his duty to follow the Roman standard wherever it was erected, without considering by whom it was carried. Cæsar, rejecting the plea of ignorance or incapacity, insisted, that any prince in alliance with the Romans could not be ignorant who were consuls in the year that succeeded the consulate of Lentulus and Marcellus, and who were actually in the administration of the state at Rome; that they could not be ignorant who was at the head of the republic, and in possession of the capital, and of the seat of empire; and who of consequence was vested with the authority of the commonwealth. But that he himself, in the capacity of a private man, was willing, in consideration of this prince's age, his character, and the intercession of his friends, to forgive the part which he had taken against him. He desired him, therefore, to resume the crown and other ensigns of royalty, and to keep possession of his kingdom, reserving the discussion of the title, by which he held any particular territory, to a future day.

Being joined by a legion which Dejotarus had lately formed in the Roman manner, Cæsar's force now consisted of this, together with the remains of the two legions that escaped with Domitius from Nicopolis, and of the sixth, which had accompanied himself from Egypt, now reduced by the sword, and by the fatigues of service, to no more than a thousand men. With this army he advanced towards Pontus. Upon his approach, Pharnaces sent forward a messenger to present him, in honour of his late victories, with a crown of gold, and made offers of submission, expecting to appease him, or to fill up the time until Cæsar should be obliged, by the necessity of his affairs, to give his presence elsewhere. "Come not against me," he said, "as an enemy: I never took part with Pompey, nor declared war against Cæsar. Let me not be treated with more severity than Dejotarus, who did both." Cæsar replied, that he would listen to Pharnaces when he had acted up to his professions; that he had forgiven Dejotarus, and many others, with pleasure, the injury done to himself; but that he could not so easily overlook insults which were offered to the Roman state; and that he did not pardon wrongs done in the provinces of the Roman empire, even by those of his own party. "Your not having joined with Pompey," he said, "has saved you from being a partner in his defeat, but was not the cause of my victory." With this reply to the messages of Pharnaces, Cæsar demanded the instant surrender of the kingdom of Pontus, and full reparation of all the

1 Hirt de Bello Alex.
2 Cicer. ad Attic. lib. xi. ep. 23

damages sustained by any Roman citizen settled in that province. Pharnaces professed an intention to comply with these demands; but under various pretences delayed the performance of his promise. He had fixed on a hill in the neighbourhood of Ziela, a place that became famous by the victory which his father Mithridates had there obtained over a Roman army, under the command of Triarius: and in order to secure himself, repaired his father's lines, and seemed to be determined to maintain this post.

Cæsar, having lain for some days within five miles of the enemy, advanced to an eminence separated from the camp of Pharnaces only by a narrow valley sunk between steep banks. He came upon this ground in the night, and began to intrench himself as usual, having a party under arms to cover the workmen. As at break of day the greater part of his army appeared to be at work, this seemed to be a favourable opportunity to attack them; and Pharnaces began to form for this purpose. Cæsar, imagining that he only meant to give an alarm, and to interrupt his workmen; even after he was in motion, did not order the legions to desist from their work, nor to arm: but seeing him descend into the valley, and attempt to pass it in the face of his advanced guard, he sounded to arms, and was scarcely formed when the enemy had passed both banks of the vale to attack him.

The troops of Pharnaces began the action with an ardour that was suited to the boldness with which they had advanced; and Cæsar's contempt of their designs had nearly exposed him to a defeat. But the action, which was doubtful every where else, was decided by the veterans of the sixth legion, before whom the enemy began to give way, hurried with precipitation down the declivity, and fell into a general rout. Pharnaces fled with a few attendants, and narrowly escaped being taken.[3] This victory gave Cæsar an opportunity to compare his own glories with those of Sylla, of Lucullus, and of Pompey; and was on this account, probably, regarded by him with singular pleasure. "How cheap is fame," he said, "when obtained by fighting against such an enemy?"[4] And in the triumphs which he afterwards led in the sequel of these wars, the trophies of this particular victory were distinguished by labels, containing these words, "I came, I saw, I vanquished."[5]

From the peculiar ostentation of the ease with which this victory was obtained, appearing to Cæsar as a measure of his own superiority to Sylla and Pompey, we may suspect that vanity, not less than ambition, was the spring of that emulation from which he had raised such a flame in the empire.[6] Having, by this defeat, extinguished all the hopes and pretensions of Pharnaces, he restored Domitius Calvisius to his command in that quarter, and to a general inspection of affairs in Asia. This province, which had furnished a principal supply to the public revenue of the state, as well as to the private fortune of Roman adventurers, was now made to pay large contributions in name of arrears of what had been promised to Pompey, or of forfeiture for offences committed against the victorious party.

Cæsar, having issued his orders for the contributions to be levied in Asia, set out by Galatia and Bithynia towards Greece, in his way to Italy; he landed at Tarentum, having been near two years absent from Rome. Many citizens had waited near twelve months at Brundusium, in anxious expectation of his coming, and under great uncertainty of the reception they were to meet with. Cicero, being of this number, set out for Tarentum as soon as he heard of Cæsar's arrival, and met him on the road. When he presented himself, Cæsar alighted from his carriage, received him with marks of respect, and continued to walk and to discourse with him aside for some time. There is no particular account of what passed between them in this conversation. On the part of Cicero, probably, were stated the reasons which he assigns, in a letter to Atticus, for his conduct before the battle of Pharsalia, bearing, that he had been averse to the war, that he thought the republic had nothing to gain by the victory of either party, and that he joined Pompey, more influenced by the opinion of others, than decided in his own.[7] Under these impressions, though courted by Cæsar, who wished to have the credit of his name in support of the measures now to be taken at Rome, he chose to withdraw to a life of retirement, and devoted his time to literary amusements and studies. At this time he probably composed most of his writings on the subject of eloquence, as he did some time afterwards those which are termed his philosophical works.[8]

U. C. 706.
C. Jul. Cæsar, M. Æmilius Lepidus.

Cæsar arrived at Rome in the end of the year seven hundred and six of the Roman era, in which he had been named a second time dictator. This year, as has been related, he had passed chiefly in Egypt. Being elected, together with M. Æmilius, consul for the following year, he applied himself, for a little time, in the capacity of civil magistrate, to the affairs of state; endeavoured to restore the tranquillity of the city, which had been disturbed in his absence, and to wipe away the reproach which the levities of Antony had brought on his party. He stifled the unreasonable hopes of a general abolition of debts, with which Dolabella had flattered the more profligate part of the community. He told the people, on this occasion, that he himself was a debtor; that he had expended his fortune in the public service, and was still obliged to borrow money for the same purpose. With respect to the general policy of the city, and the case of insolvent debtors, he revived the laws which he himself had procured, about two years before, in his way from Spain to Epirus. But while he appeared to be intent on these particulars, his thoughts were chiefly occupied in preparing to meet the war which the remains of the ancient senate and of the republican party were resuming against him in Africa.

This province, in which Varus, supported by the king of Numidia, had been hitherto able to keep his station as an officer of the commonwealth, was now become the sole or the principal

3 Hirtius de Bello Alex. Velleius. Florus. Liv. Epitome, &c.
4 Appian. de Bell. Civ. lib ii p. 185.
5 The famous words, *Veni, vidi, vici.*
6 Sueton. in Vit. Cæsaris, c. 47.

7 Cicer. ad Att. lib. xi. ep. 11.
8 Ibid. lib. xv. ep. 13.

refuge of the republican party. Three hundred citizens, many of them senators and exiles from Italy, as well as settlers in that province, had assembled at Utica, and considering every other part of the empire as under the influence of a violent usurpation, stated themselves as the only free remains of the Roman republic; held their meetings in the capacity of senate and people; authorized, under these titles, the levies that were made in the province, and contributed largely to supply the expense of the war. Many officers of name and of rank, Labienus, Afranius, Petreius, as well as Scipio and Cato, with all the remains they had saved from the wreck at Pharsalia, were now ready to renew the war on this ground. The name of Scipio was reckoned ominous of success in Africa, and that of Cato, even if the origin or occasion of the present contest were unknown, was held a sufficient mark to distinguish the side of justice, and the cause of the republic.

These leaders of the republican party having a considerable force at sea, and having access to all the ports, not only of Africa, but likewise of Sicily, Sardinia, and Spain, had furnished themselves plentifully with all the necessaries for war.[1] They had mustered ten legions, which, according to the establishment of that time, may have amounted to fifty thousand Roman foot. They had twenty thousand African horse, a great body of archers and slingers, with a hundred and twenty elephants. They expected to be joined by the king of Numidia, who, to the established character of his countrymen for stratagem and valour, joined the glory of his late victory over Curio; and was supposed to muster, at this time, besides numerous bodies of horse, of archers, of slingers, and a great troop of elephants, thirty thousand foot, armed and marshalled, for the most part, in the manner of the Roman legion.[2]

The army already in Africa, as well as the remains of the sea and land forces of Pompey, who were lately arrived from Macedonia, were willing, as has been mentioned, to have placed Cato at their head. But the established order of the commonwealth, for which all the party contended, requiring that Scipio, who was of consular rank, should have the preference, Cato, who had no more than the rank of prætor, and who could not be accessary to the infringement of any established or constitutional form, declined the command. By this circumstance we are deprived of an opportunity to judge how far the military abilities of this great man kept pace with his integrity, judgment, and courage, in civil and political affairs.

Scipio being the officer of highest rank in the republican party, and having the supreme command of their forces, notwithstanding that the coasts of Italy were exposed to his attempts, and notwithstanding that the condition of Cæsar himself, if his situation at Alexandria had been known, gave sufficient opportunities for enterprise, took all his measures for a defensive war.

Such was the state of affairs in Africa when Cæsar, who, with all his military character and authority, frequently experienced the difficulty of commanding mere soldiers of fortune, taught to divest themselves of civil principle, or regard to public duty, was likely to perish in a mutiny of his own army, and to end his career by the swords which he himself had whetted against the republic.

The legions, which after the defeat of Pompey had been ordered into Italy, becoming insolent in the possession of a military power which they saw was to be formed on the ruins of the commonwealth, and feeling their own importance, especially in the absence of their leader, would not be commanded by subordinate officers; nor did they, on the return of Cæsar himself, discontinue habits of disorder and license which they had some time indulged. Being stationed in the neighbourhood of Capua, from whence it was expected they should embark for Africa, they decamped without orders, and marched towards Rome; paid no regard to the authority of Sallust, who, in the capacity of prætor, with which he had been vested by Cæsar, endeavoured to stop them, killed many officers and persons of rank who ventured to oppose them, and threw the city into great consternation. On the approach of this formidable body, Cæsar himself is said to have wavered in his resolution. He had some troops attending his person, and there was a legion which Antony had stationed in the city on occasion of the late commotions. With these he at first proposed to meet and resist the mutiny; but he recollected, that even these troops might be infected with the same spirit of disobedience, and that if he were not able to command by his authority, and were forced to draw the sword against his own army, the whole foundations of the power he had erected must fail. While he was agitated by these reflections, he sent an officer with orders to inquire for what purpose the mutinous legions advanced? This officer was told, "That they would explain themselves to Cæsar." Having this answer, and expecting their arrival at the gates, he chose that they should appear to do by his permission, what they were likely to do without it; he therefore sent them another message, informing them that they had his leave to enter the city with their arms. They accordingly came in a body, and took possession of the field of Mars. There, contrary to the advice of his friends, they were received by Cæsar himself in person. Being raised on a conspicuous place, they crowded around him; and, from many different quarters at once, complained of the scanty rewards which they had received,[3] enumerated their services and the hardships they had suffered, and with one voice demanded their instant discharge. Cæsar knowing that they only meant to extort some concessions, which they hoped the consideration of the war, which was still impending in Africa, would oblige him to make; that they were far from wishing to be dismissed, or to resign those arms to which they owed their own consequence, and on which they grounded their present presumption, affected to comply with their request, owned that their demand was highly reasonable; adding, that the service for which they had been hitherto retained was now at an end, and that he was sensible they were worn out, and unfit to contend with new fatigues.

1 Dio. Cass. lib. lxii. c. 5.

2 Appian. de Bello Civile, lib. ii. Hirt. de Bello African.

3 Dio. Cass. c. 51—55.

Cæsar, in concluding a speech which he made to this purpose, employed the appellation of *Quirites*, or fellow citizens; and observed how proper it was, that all who had served out the legal time should receive the accustomed dismission. In speaking these words, he was interrupted by a general cry, that they were no Quirites, but soldiers, willing to serve. It is alleged, that the name of Roman citizens,[4] though the most respectable form of address in the political assemblies of the people, carried contempt to these military adventurers, and insinuated a state of degradation from that in which they affected to stand. An officer who was prepared for the occasion, or who wished to improve this sentiment in favour of Cæsar, desired to be heard; made an apology for what was past, and offered to pledge himself for the duty and future obedience of the troops. He was answered by Cæsar, That the services of this army were now of little moment to him; that as they desired their dismission, while by their own confession they were yet in condition to serve, he had taken his resolution, and should instantly dismiss them with the usual rewards. "No man," he said, "shall complain that in time of need I employed him, and now at my ease forget the reward that is due to him. Such as continue in the service until the public tranquillity is fully restored shall have settlements in land; such as have received promises of money at any time during the war, shall be paid now, or in a little time hereafter with interest." He concluded, however, with saying, "That as he asked no man to remain in the service, so he should not reject the duty of those who were willing to abide by their colours; that he owed this indulgence to their present requests, and to their merit on former occasions." The whole with one voice desired to be comprehended in this act of indulgence, and went headlong into all the extremes of submission, as they had lately gone into every excess of disorder and insolence. Cæsar was thus again in full possession of his power; but he did not venture to punish the authors of the mutiny. It was safer to reward such as were conspicuous in any particular merit; he therefore selected a few to be distinguished by immediate effects of his bounty, and put the remainder in motion towards Africa, where they might have an opportunity of earning future rewards and the pardon of past offences; and where they might spend against enemies that fury which, at every interval of leisure to recollect their pretensions and their consequence, they were so likely to turn against their leader.[5]

The year was now, according to the vulgar computation at Rome, and in consequence of the usual intercalations being neglected, nominally advanced to the middle of December, but was in reality little past the autumnal equinox,[6] or was in the end of September, when Cæsar, having made the proper arrangements in the city, and in the manner related, appeased the mutiny which threatened to deprive him of his army, was again in motion to carry the war into Africa. The season which was thought unfit for operations at sea, and which had actually forced his antagonist's ships into port, gave him the opportunity he wished for to effect his passage into that province. He knew that the enemy's fleet could not continue to cruize for any time to observe his motions; and that he might escape them with the advantage of a favourable wind, he had chosen the same opportunity, and in the same season, two years before, to transport his army into Macedonia against Pompey, who trusting to the numbers and vigilance of his fleet, suffered himself to be surprised, and to be dispossessed of a country which he occupied with so superior a force. Cæsar having gained so much on that occasion, by the rapidity of his motions, now made war with many accumulated advantages of reputation and power, which increased his boldness, and facilitated his success.

Having ordered troops and shipping from different quarters of Italy to assemble at Lillybæum, from whence he had the shortest passage to Africa, he himself arrived there on what was nominally the seventeenth of December, but in reality no more than the thirtieth of September; and although he found no more of his army arrived than one legion, or five thousand men, of the new levies, and six hundred horse, he ordered these, notwithstanding, to embark on board such ships as were then in the harbour; and if the wind had served, would have instantly sailed, even with this small force, trusting that he might be able to surprise some port on the opposite shore, and prepare a safe landing-place for the troops that were to follow. But while he continued wind-bound at Lillybæum, he was joined successively by a number of legions, which he ordered to embark as fast as they arrived; and, that they might be ready to put to sea with the first fair wind that served, sent the transports to lie under an island near the mouth of the harbour.

Being in this state of readiness with six legions, or about thirty thousand foot, together with two thousand horse; and the wind coming fair on the twenty-eighth of December, or, as it is computed, on the twelfth of October, he himself went on board, and leaving orders for the troops that were still in motion towards Lillybæum to follow him without delay, he set sail for the nearest land in Africa. Not knowing of any port to which he might securely repair, he could not, as usual, assign a place of general resort in case of separation, and only gave orders to the fleet to keep close together; and deferred the choice of a landing-place till after he should have observed the coast, and seen in what part of it the enemy were least guarded against a descent. Soon after he got to sea a storm arose, which dispersed the fleet; he himself, with the ships that still kept him company, after being tossed four days in a passage of no more than twenty leagues, got under the land of the promontory of Mercury, and from thence, to avoid the forces of the enemy, which were stationed near Utica and round the bay of Carthage, steered to the southward.

The coast of Africa, from this cape or promontory to the bottom of the great Syrtes, over three degrees of latitude, or about two hundred miles, extends directly to the south. It abounds with considerable towns, which, on account of their commerce, were anciently called the Emporiæ; and by their wealth, tempting the rapacity both of the Numidians and of the Carthaginians, were long a subject of contention between these

4 Quirites, Roman citizens
5 Dio. Cass. lib. xlii. c 51—55.
6 Plut. in Vita Cæsaris, p. 154.

powers. Adrumetum lay on one side of a spacious bay, bounded by the head of Clupea on the north, and that of Vada on the south. The southern coast of this bay contained, besides Adrumetum, the following seaports: Ruspina, Leptis, and Thapsus; the bay itself extending from the first of these places to the last about thirty-six miles. Scipio had secured Adrumetum and Thapsus, being the extremity of this line, with considerable forces. In order to render the province unfit for the reception of an enemy, he had laid waste the country, and had collected all the provisions and forage into these and other places of strength for the use of his own army.

Considius being stationed at Adrumetum with two legions, and Virgilius with a proper force at Thapsus, the ports of Ruspina and Leptis, as well as many of the inland towns, were entrusted to the keeping of their own inhabitants. But these, on account of the general devastations lately committed by order of Scipio, were extremely disaffected to his party, and inclined to favour any enemy against him.

Cato was stationed at Utica as the last retreat of the Roman senate, the centre of all their resources, and the seat of their councils.

Scipio had collected the main body of his army near to the same place, supposed to be the principal object of any attempt that might be made from Italy.

Labienus and Petreius had separate bodies, at proper stations, to guard the inlets of the coast round the bay of Carthage; and were so disposed of, that they could easily join and cross over land to the bay of Adrumetum upon any alarm of an enemy, from that side.

Varus had the direction of the fleet. He had kept the sea during summer and on the approach of autumn, but had then withdrawn to Utica, and laid up his ships for the stormy season.

Cæsar, however, according to his custom of taking opportunities when his enemies were likely to be off their guard, venturing to sea, even in this season, seems to have had no information to direct him on his approach to the coast, besides the general report that the enemy were strongest and most to be avoided in the bay of Carthage. In this belief he passed the headlands of Clupea and Neapolis, and stood in to the bay of Adrumetum. Being seen from the shore, he was followed by Cn. Piso from Clupea, with three thousand Numidian horse, and was received at Adrumetum by Considius, with a force greatly superior to that which he himself had brought to the coast. But so little had he attended to the strength of the enemy, or so much was he determined to brave it, that he landed near Adrumetum on the nominal first of January, or about the middle of October, with three thousand foot and a hundred and fifty horse. This hazardous step his high reputation seemed to require or to justify. The enemy might not be apprised of his present weakness, it being occasioned by the accidental separation of his fleet. They were likely to be awed by his name, and to remain at a distance long enough to let him be joined by the remainder of his army. In the mean time he supported the courage of his own people, by proceeding against the enemy with his usual confidence.

N. C. 6. *Jul. Cæsar Dictat. 3tio M. Æmil. Lepidus, M. Eq.*

The garrison of Adrumetum, upon this sudden appearance of a force which came to attack them, were thrown into some confusion, and Considius, instead of taking measures to crush so inferior an enemy before he should receive any reinforcement, thought of nothing but how to secure himself from surprise; shut his gates, manned his walls, and placed all the troops under his command at their posts of alarm. Cæsar, to confirm him in this disposition, sent him a summons to surrender at discretion; and afterwards, at the suggestion of Plancus, who had been in habits of intimacy with Considius, endeavoured to corrupt or to gain him by an insinuating message; but this officer, being more a man of integrity than he had shown himself to be an able general, ordered the bearer of the message to be put to death, and sent the letter unopened to Scipio.

Cæsar having received no return to his message, and suspecting that his attempt to corrupt the commander of the forces at Adrumetum might betray his weakness, after only one night's stay in this dangerous situation, determined, on the day after he landed, to remove to some place of greater security. With this view he marched to the southward, and though harassed in his rear by the enemy's horse, continued his march without any considerable interruption or loss. As he advanced to Ruspina, a deputation from the inhabitants of that place came forward to meet him, with offers of every accommodation it was in their power to supply, and of an immediate reception into their town. He encamped one night under their walls; but being inclined to see more of the coast, and not being in condition to divide his little force, he proceeded with the whole to Leptis. Here he was received with equal favour; and having entered the town, took measures to protect the inhabitants from the licentiousness of his own people.

This was a convenient post for the reception of his transports; and a few of them accordingly, having some cohorts of foot and troops of horse on board, it being now the third day after he himself had debarked, or about the twentieth of October, put in to the harbour of Leptis. By the report of persons who came in these ships he learnt, that numbers of the fleet, after they had parted company, appeared to be steering for Utica; a course by which they must either run into the hands of the enemy, or lose much time before they could correct their mistake, or recover their way to the southward.

In a state of anxious suspense, occasioned by these circumstances, Cæsar seems to have deliberated, whether it were not proper for him again to embark; and in consequence of his doubts, probably, though under pretence of the want of forage, he still kept his cavalry on board, and with great difficulty continued to supply them with fresh water from the land. But as soon as he determined to keep his footing in Africa, he landed his cavalry, and took the necessary measures to procure supplies of provisions by sea. He sent back the empty transports to receive any troops that might be arrived at Lillybæum, and ordered ten galleys from the harbour at Leptis to cruise for the missing ships of his last embarkation. He despatched expresses to Sardinia and other maritime provinces, with orders to hasten the reinforcements of troops and the supplies of provisions which were expected from thence;

and having intelligence that the enemy had some magazines in the island of Cercina, near the coast of Africa, he sent thither Crispus Sallustius, the celebrated historian, now serving in his army, to endeavour to secure those magazines for his use.

Being determined to keep both the ports of Ruspina and Leptis, which the enemy seemed to have abandoned to him, he was now, by the arrival of the cohorts which joined him at Leptis, in condition to garrison the town with three thousand men, while he himself returned with the remainder of those who were landed, to keep his possession, at the same time, of Ruspina. This place being unprovided of every necessary for the support of a garrison, he determined to try what provisions could be found in the neighbourhood to subsist his troops till they could be otherwise supplied, or enabled to penetrate farther into the country. For this purpose he advanced with the whole of his little army to forage, followed by all the carriages that could be assembled, and had them loaded with corn, wood, and other necessaries, to form some species of magazine for the troops he intended to place in the town. As soon as he had effected this service, it appeared that he had taken the resolution to go in person in search of the transports, on board of which the greater part of his army was dispersed. And with this view having posted ten cohorts at Ruspina, he himself, with the seven others, that made the whole of his strength now on shore, went down to the harbour, which was about two miles from the town, and embarked in the night.

The troops that were to be left at Ruspina, without the leader, in whom their confidence was chiefly reposed, were aware of their danger; so few, surrounded with numerous armies who were likely to assemble against them. They had now been three days on shore, and the enemy had full time to be apprised of their situation and of their weakness. The presence of their general had hitherto supported their courage; they relied on his abilities to repair the effects whether of mistake or temerity; but in his absence they lost all hopes, and expected to become an easy prey to their enemies.

Cæsar, however, fully determined to put to sea, having past the night on board, still continued at anchor; when at break of day being about to weigh, some vessels came in sight, and were known to be a part of the fleet which he so anxiously looked for. These were soon followed by other ships which appeared successively, and brought him the greater part of the six legions with which he had originally sailed from Lillybæum. Being thus prevented in his intended excursion, he returned to Ruspina, and took post between the town and the shore.

In the mean time it appears, that Labienus and Petreius, commanding the horse and light troops of Scipio's army, in the angle that is formed by the promontory of Clupea, between the bays of Carthage and Adrumetum, having intelligence that Cæsar was landed, with the utmost diligence assembled their forces, and marched towards the coast from which they had received the alarm.

Cæsar had taken a defensive station behind the town of Ruspina, the place which he chose for the resort and safe reception of his convoys and reinforcements by sea; but he was far from limiting his plan of operations to the defence of this place. On the fourth or fifth day after his landing, although by his own account he had yet no intelligence of the enemy's motions, he thought proper to continue the alarm he had given, and marched from Ruspina with a body of thirty cohorts, or about fifteen thousand foot, and four hundred horse, to penetrate into the country to observe its situation, or to extend the source of his supplies. After he had begun his march for this purpose, and was about three miles from his camp, the parties that were advanced before him fell back on the main body, and informed him that they had been in sight of an enemy. Soon after this report clouds of dust began to rise from the plain, and about noon an army appeared in order of battle. To observe them more nearly, Cæsar, after he had made the signal for the cohorts to form, and to be covered with their helmets, went forward with a small party to view the enemy. He saw bodies of cavalry in every part of the field; and from the imperfect view which could be had of them, as the air was clouded with dust, he supposed their line to consist entirely of horse. He thought himself secure against such an enemy, provided he could sufficiently extend his front and cover his flanks; and for this purpose he divided his small body of horse to the right and the left; and that he might not be outlined, diminished the depth to increase the length of his ordinary column. In making this disposition, however, he had mistaken the enemy's force; it did not consist, as he supposed, entirely of cavalry, but of troops of horse interspersed at intervals with bodies of foot, and he had not observed that considerable detachments were sent under cover of the hills to turn his flanks, and fall upon his rear.

Under these disadvantages on the part of Cæsar, the action began in front by a scattered charge of the Numidian horse, who came in squadrons from the intervals at which they were placed among the infantry, and advancing at full gallop, threw their javelins and darts, and presently retired to their former situation. In this retreat, under cover of the infantry whose intervals they occupied, they instantly rallied, and prepared to repeat the charge.

While Cæsar's infantry was occupied in front with this unexpected mode of attack, his horse were defeated on the wings; and the enemy, in consequence of the disposition they had made, were already on his right and left, even began to close on his rear, and, by the superiority of their numbers, were enabled to continue the impression they made on every side; his men giving way, to shun the arrows and darts of the enemy, were pressed from the flanks to the centre, so that they were forced into a circle, without any distinction of front or rear, and were galled with a continual discharge of missiles, which did great execution.[1]

Cæsar, who so far had suffered himself to be surprised and overreached, in this difficult situation, took the benefit of that confidence which his known ability and presence of mind ever procured him from his troops. Recollecting that the enemy must have weakened their line in

1 Cæsaris copiis in orbem compulsis, intra cancellos omnes conjecti pugnare cogebantur.

every part, by attempting to stretch it over so great a circumference, he prevailed on his legions again to extend their ranks, ordered the cohorts to face alternately to the right and the left, and making a front in both directions, charged the enemy on the opposite sides, and drove them in both ways to a distance from the ground. Without attempting, however, to improve his advantage, or to urge the pursuit, he took the opportunity of the enemy's flight to effect his own retreat, and fell back to the camp behind Ruspina, from which he had moved in the morning.

The speedy march of Labienus and Petreius, from a distance which could not be less than eighty or a hundred miles, accomplished by the fourth or fifth day after the arrival of Cæsar, and their disposition on the day of battle, to avail themselves of their numbers and manner of fighting, was able and spirited. But the event is sufficient to show that the use of mere missile weapons in the open plain, against troops who are armed and disciplined for close fight, although it may harass and distress an enemy, cannot have any decisive effect.

In about three days after this encounter, Cæsar had intelligence that Scipio himself was advancing with the whole force of his infantry, consisting of eight legions, or about forty thousand men, and four thousand regular horse: an army which he was not in condition to oppose in the field, and which obliged him, contrary to his usual practice, to adopt a plan of defence. Ruspina lay along the coast, and at the distance of two miles from the shore. As his army lay behind the town; covering part of the space between it and the sea with the fortifications of his camp, he threw up an intrenchment from his camp on one side, and from the end of the town on the other, quite to the shore: so that, by means of the town in front, the fortifications of his camp and these lines in flank, the whole space between Ruspina and the sea was covered with works. And the harbour was thus secured from any attempts of the enemy. In order to man and defend these fortifications, he landed his engines from the galleys, and brought the mariners to serve them on shore.

The choice of this situation, cooped up in a narrow place, exposed to be deprived of any communication with the country, might, in case the enemy had seized their advantage, or in case the reinforcements which Cæsar had expected from the sea, had by any accident been long delayed, have exposed him to the greatest calamities. He himself would not have neglected to hem in an enemy so posted with a line of circumvallation; but the undertaking was too vast for those who were opposed to him, and he was suffered in safety to wait the arrival of his reinforcements, and to collect some immediate supply of provisions from the neighbouring country, as well as to receive convoys which he had ordered from every maritime province.

While Cæsar remained in this post, Scipio arrived at Adrumetum, and having halted there a few days, joined Labienus and Petreius in the station they had chosen, about three miles from the town of Ruspina. Their cavalry immediately overran the country, and interrupted the supplies which Cæsar derived from thence. The space he had inclosed within his entrenchments being about six square miles, was soon exhausted even of forage or pasture, and his horses reduced to feed on sea weed, which was steeped in fresh water, in order to purge it as much as possible of its salt.

To encourage the hopes which Scipio entertained from all these circumstances, the king of Numidia, with a powerful army, was on the march, and likely to join him before Cæsar could receive any considerable addition to his present force; but whatever might have been the consequence of this junction, if it had really taken place, it was delayed for some time by one of those strokes of fortune to which human foresight cannot extend. Publius Sitius, a Roman citizen, who had been an accomplice with Catiline in his designs against the republic, and who, on this account, had fled beyond the reach of the Roman power, had assembled a band of warriors or lawless banditti, at the head of which he made himself of consequence on the coasts of Africa, and was admitted successively to join the forces of different princes in that quarter. Being now in the service of Bogud, king of Mauritania, and being disposed to court the favour of Cæsar, or hoping to make his peace at Rome by means of a person so likely to be at the head of the Roman state, he persuaded the king of Mauritania to take advantage of Juba's absence, and with such troops as he had then on foot, to invade the kingdom of Numidia. . Juba being about to join Scipio near Ruspina, when the news of this invasion of his own country overtook him, found himself obliged not only to return on his march, but to call off from his allies great part of the Numidian light troops, who were already in their camp.

Scipio, though thus disappointed of the great accession of force which he expected to receive by the junction of Juba, and though even somewhat reduced in his former numbers, still continued to act on the offensive; and in order to brave his enemy, and to receive some species of triumph from supposed offers of battle, repeatedly formed his army on the plain between the two camps. In repeating these operations, he advanced still nearer and nearer to Cæsar's entrenchments, and seemed to threaten his camp with an attack. In return to this insult, or to take off its effects, Cæsar, knowing the strength of his works, affected to hear of the enemy's approach with indifference, and without moving from his tent, gave orders for the ordinary guards, which lay without the intrenchments, not to be discomposed, but as soon as the enemy approached them, to retire behind the parapet with the utmost deliberation; and Scipio, upon this reception, when seemingly most bent on assaulting the lines, being satisfied as usual with this display of his superiority, returned to his camp.

During these operations, and while Juba was still detained in Numidia by the diversion which Sitius had occasioned in his kingdom, Cæsar had frequent deserters from the African army, and received deputations from different parts of the country, with professions of attachment to himself as the relation of Marius, whose memory was still recent and popular in that province. Among these advances, which were made to him by the natives of the country, he had a message from the inhabitants of Acilla, a place situated about ten miles from the coast, and equally distant from Adrumetum and from Ruspina, offer ing to come under his protection, and inviting him to take possession of their town. The people of this place, like most other towns of the province, were extremely disaffected to Scipio on account of the severities which he exercised, by laying waste their possessions on the approach of Cæsar; and as they dreaded a repetition of the same measure, they were desirous to put themselves in a posture of defence against him. Cæsar accepted of their offer, and sent a detachment of his army, who turning round the enemy's flank, after a long night's march entered the town without opposition. Considius having intelligence of what was in agitation at Acilla, sent a detachment at the same time from Adrumetum to secure the place; but coming too late, and finding that the enemy had already entered the town, brought forward some more forces on the following day, and endeavoured, but in vain, to dislodge them.

While Cæsar was thus endeavouring to extend his quarters in Africa, and to enlarge the source of his subsistence, Crispus Sallustius succeeded in the design upon which he had been sent to the island of Cercina, and was able to furnish a considerable supply of provisions from thence. There arrived at the same time from Allienus, at Lillybæum, a large convoy and fleet of transports, having on board two entire legions, the thirteenth and fourteenth, together with eight hundred Gaulish cavalry, a thousand archers and slingers, and a large supply of provisions. As soon as these troops were landed, the transports were sent back to Lillybæum, in order to receive the remainder of the army which was still expected from thence. These supplies and reinforcements at once relieved Cæsar's army from the distress which they suffered; and by so great an accession of strength, amounting to twelve thousand men, put him in condition to break from the confinement in which he had some time remained, and to act on the offensive.

The first object upon this change in his affairs, was to seize upon some rising grounds in the neighbourhood of Ruspina, which Scipio had neglected to occupy, and from thence to pursue such advantage as he might find against the enemy. For this purpose, he decamped after it was dark, on the supposed twenty-sixth of January, or tenth of November, and turning by the shore round the town of Ruspina, arrived in the night on the ground which he intended to occupy. This was part of a ridge, which runs parallel to the coast, at a few miles distance from the shore, and which, on the north of Ruspina, turns in the form of an amphitheatre round a plain of about fifteen miles extent. Near the middle of this plain stood the town of Uzita, on the brink of a deep marshy tract, which is formed by the water of some rivulets that fall from the mountains, and spread upon the plain in that place. Scipio had posted a garrison in the town, and had occupied the ridge on one side of the amphitheatre beyond the marsh, but had neglected the heights, of which Cæsar now took possession. It seems, that on these heights there remained a number of towers, or a species of castles constructed by the natives in the course of their own wars. In these Cæsar was furnished with a number of separate lodgments, which he joined by lines, in order to continue his communication with the camp he had left, and with the port of Ruspina.

He had, in one night, made a considerable progress in these works, and being observed at day-break, Scipio, in order to interrupt him, advanced into the plain, and formed in order of battle, about a mile in the front of his own encampment. Cæsar, notwithstanding this movement of the enemy, did not at first think it necessary to interrupt his works; but Scipio seeming to come forward with intention to attack him, while so great a part of his army was at work, he ordered the whole under arms, still keeping the advantage of his ground on the heights. Some parties of cavalry and light troops came near enough to skirmish between the two armies, and Labienus being advanced on the right beyond the main body of Scipio's forces, Cæsar sent a detachment round a village to attack him, and obliged him to fly in great disorder, after having narrowly escaped being entirely cut off. This flight of Labienus spread so great an alarm over Scipio's army, that the whole, with precipitation, retired to their camp. Cæsar returned to his post, and without any farther interruption, continued to execute the works he had already begun. As soon as these were finished on the following day, he again formed in order of battle, to return the defiance which the enemy had so often given him, while he lay in the lines of Ruspina; and observing that Scipio remained in his camp, he marched on to the town of Uzita, which lay between the two armies. Scipio being alarmed for the safety of this place, at which he had deposited some part of his magazines, advanced to sustain the troops he had posted in the town; and Cæsar, believing that an action was likely to follow, made a halt, with the town of Uzita before his centre, having both his wings extended beyond it to the right and the left. Scipio, not to extend his front beyond the walls of the town, drew up his army in four lines, consisting of many separate bodies interspersed with elephants; but as Cæsar did not choose to attack the town, supported as it was by Scipio's army, neither did Scipio choose to expose any part of his line by advancing beyond it. Both armies having remained in this posture till sun-set, returned at night to their respective camps.

Cæsar still persisting in his design to oblige the enemy to hazard a battle in defence of Uzita, projected double lines of approach from his present camp to the town. As the place was accessible to the enemy, and when their army should be drawn up in order of battle, might be made a part of their line, it was impossible for Cæsar to invest the town, or even to approach the walls without hazard of being attacked on his flanks from the field, as well as in the centre from the town itself. In order to cover the approach which he intended to make to the walls, he carried on from his camp on the hills two intrenchments on the right and the left, forming a lane of sufficient breadth to embrace the town. Between these parallel lines his troops advanced to the walls with perfect security, and under cover from any attacks that might be made on their flanks. As soon as this lane was effected to within the necessary distance of the walls, he threw up in front a breast work opposite to the ramparts of the town, and from thence began to construct the works that were usually employed in the reduction of fortified places.

During the dependance of this siege, both par

ties received great reinforcements. Scipio was joined by the king of Numidia, who having repelled the enemy who attempted to invade his own kingdom, now came with three bodies of regular infantry, formed in the manner of the Roman legion, eight hundred heavy armed or bridled cavalry, with a great multitude of light or irregular troops. Cæsar's army, on the appearance of this new enemy, were much discouraged; but on seeing that Scipio, even after he was joined by the king of Numidia, still remained on the defensive, they resumed their former confidence, and were themselves soon after reinforced by the arrival of two more legions, the ninth and the tenth, who on their first approach to the coast, mistook for an enemy some galleys which Cæsar had stationed off the harbour of Thapsus, and under this mistake stood off again to sea, where they suffered many days from sickness, want of provisions, and of water.

These legions having been the principal authors of the late mutiny in Italy, are said to have now come without orders, intending to evince their zeal, and to court their general's favour at a time when their service might be not only acceptable, but necessary to his safety. The principal historian of this war,[1] however, relates only, that Cæsar having observed tribunes and centurions of these legions to have occupied entire transports with their own equipage, to the exclusion of the troops which were then so much wanted for the service, he took this opportunity to execute a piece of justice, which he had thought proper to remit, or to defer on a former occasion. That he dismissed several officers of these legions from the service, with the following terms of reproach: "For you, who have incited the troops of the Roman people to mutiny against the republic, who have plundered the allies, and been useless to the state; who, in place of soldiers, have filled transports with your servants and horses; who, without courage in the field, or modesty in your quarters, have been more formidable to your country than to her enemies, I judge you unworthy of any trust in the service of the republic, and therefore order you forthwith to be gone from the province, and to keep at a distance from all the stations of the Roman army."

The other incidents, which are dated by historians during the dependence of the siege of Uzita, do not serve to make us acquainted with its progress, or with the detail of its operations. The season we are told was stormy, and Cæsar's army, in order to crowd the more easily on board of the transports, had left great part of their equipage behind them in Sicily, and were now without any covering besides their shields, exposed to heavy rains and hail, accompanied with thunder and appearances of fire, which, to their great amazement, instead of the ordinary flashes of lightning, became stationary, and for a sensible time continued to flame on the points of their spears. While this storm continued, the ground upon which they lay was overflowed with water, or washed with continual torrents from the hills. Cæsar, nevertheless, persisted in the attack of Uzita, and seemed still to flatter himself that the defence of this place would lay the enemy under some disadvantage, which might furnish him with an opportunity to decide the war. The armies were accordingly often drawn out in order of battle, and were present at partial engagements of their cavalry or irregular troops, but without any general action.

In the midst of the great expectations which must have attended the operations of this siege, Cæsar had one of the many occasions, on which he was ever so ready to commit his genius, his reputation, and his life, in acts of seeming temerity, which persons of inferior ability may admire, but never can safely imitate. Varus, with a fleet of fifty galleys, had surprised and burnt the greater part of his shipping at Leptis, and was in chase of Acquila, who, with an inferior squadron, was flying before him to the southward. Cæsar apprehended that the enemy, in consequence of this advantage, if not speedily checked, must soon be masters of the sea, so as to cut off all his supplies and reinforcements from the coasts. He knew that reputation gained or lost on small occasions, often decides the greatest affairs; and that adverse circumstances, which if suffered to accumulate, may obscure the brightest fortune, can, if seasonably encountered, by daring efforts of resolution and courage, be actually turned to advantage. He instantly, therefore, went in person to Leptis, from whence he put off in a barge, and having overtaken his own squadron, which was flying before the enemy, he ordered them to put about, and steer directly against their pursuers. Varus was struck with this unaccountable change in the conduct of his enemy, and supposing them to have come in sight of some powerful support, he fled in his turn, and crowding sail, steered for the port he had left. Cæsar gave chase, overtook some of the heaviest sailers that fell astern, and forced the remainder to take refuge in the harbour of Adrumetum. Here he presented himself with an air of defiance; and having given this turn to the state of his affairs at sea, and left peremptory orders to his fleet not to resign the advantage which they had gained by the enemy's flight, he returned to the attack of Uzita. In such actions the fortunate often succeed, because the attempt appears to be impossible; and men of great ability may no doubt venture into the midst of difficulties, with which persons of inferior capacity are by no means fit to contend.

Cæsar, notwithstanding that by this stroke of fortune he preserved his communication with the sea, and received considerable supplies from thence, as well as from the country around him, in which he was favoured by the natives; yet being greatly circumscribed by the superiority of the enemy's light troops, he suffered considerably in his camp from scarcity of provisions; and being in his present operations against Uzita, to fight with a numerous army, in detail, behind the walls of a fortified town, without being able to engage them upon equal terms in any decisive action, he took his resolution to discontinue the siege, and to remove to a more advantageous station; or to undertake some enterprise, in which he was more likely to succeed. He accordingly decamped in the night, set fire to the wood and straw that was amassed upon the ground, left the lanes he had fortified with so much labour, and marching by the shore, placed his baggage between the column of the army and the sea, and thus covered it from the enemy, who he expected were to fol-

1 Hirtius.

low him by the ridge of hills which overlooked the line of his march.

The retreat of Cæsar was sufficient to confirm the leaders of the republican party, in the hopes they had formed of being able to wear him out by a dilatory war. They followed him accordingly by the heights, and having observed that he stopped at Agar, a town which he held by the affections of the natives, they took post on three several heights, at the distance of about six miles from his camp. In this position, they were not able to hinder him from making in the contiguous villages and fields a considerable acquisition of provisions and forage, which greatly relieved his army; but, to prevent his farther excursions into the country, and to secure its produce to their own use, they sent two legions, under the command of Caius Mutius Reginus, with orders to take possession of the town of Zeta, which lay about twenty miles from Agar, and on the right at some distance beyond their present camp. Cæsar had intelligence from the natives, that these troops were frequently employed abroad in collecting provisions and forage, and that they might easily be cut off, and the town be surprised. He accordingly formed a design for this purpose; and with a view to the execution of it, removed from the plain of Agar, and fortified a strong camp on a height nearer to the enemy. Here leaving a sufficient guard for his lines, he put the remainder of the army in motion in the night, passed by the enemy's stations, and surprised the town of Zeta, which he entered by break of day, while the greater part of the garrison had left the place in perfect security, and were scattered in foraging parties over the neighbouring country. Having placed a sufficient detachment to secure this new acquisition, he set out upon his return, making a disposition, not to pass the enemy unobserved, which was no longer practicable, but to force his way through any impediment they might oppose to his march. The night could no longer be of any advantage to him; he set out, therefore, by day, leading the governor of Zeta, with P. Atrius, who belonged to the association of Utica, his prisoners, together with some part of Juba's equipage, and a train of camels, loaded with plunder which he had taken in the place.

The enemy were by this time apprised of his motions. Scipio was come out of his lines; and, not far from Cæsar's route, had posted himself in order of battle. Labienus and Afranius, with a great power of cavalry and light infantry, had taken possession of some heights under which he was to pass, and were preparing to attack him on his flanks, and on his rear. Cæsar was aware of these difficulties; it was nevertheless necessary to encounter them. He trusted, that the head of his column must force its way; and he placed his whole cavalry to cover the rear of his march. When he came abreast of the enemy, being assailed, as usual, by the African cavalry with peculiar efforts of agility and cunning, he made a halt; and in order, by some great exertion, if possible, to clear his way, and procure to his people some respite in pursuing the remainder of their march undisturbed, he ordered the legions to lay down the loads which they usually carried, and to charge the enemy. They accordingly put all the Africans to flight; but no sooner resumed their march, than they were again attacked, and repeatedly forced to renew the same operations. They had already been detained four hours in passing over a hundred paces, or less than half a quarter of a mile, from the place at which they were first attacked. The sun was setting, and the enemy were in hopes of being able to oblige them to halt for the night on a field, which was destitute of water. Scipio, for this purpose, still kept the position which he had taken in the morning, and from thence observed, and occasionally supported, the operations of the light troops.

Cæsar perceived the danger to which he must be exposed, if he should halt on this ground, and saw the necessity of continuing his march; but observing, that as often as the cavalry in his rear was engaged, whether they repulsed or gave way to the enemy, he was obliged to stop in order to support them, or to wait till they had recovered their station, he thought proper to change his disposition, brought forward the horse to the head of his column, and substituted a chosen body of foot in the rear, who although under an incessant discharge from the enemy, continued to move, and enabled him, though slowly, to effect his retreat with a regular and uninterrupted pace. In this manner, notwithstanding the great danger to which he had been exposed, he regained his camp, near Agar, with a very inconsiderable loss.

Having thus got possession of Zeta, a post on the flank or rear of the enemy, Cæsar formed successive designs on Vacca, Sarsura, and Tysdra, places similarly situated round the scene of the war. His design on the first of these places was prevented by the Numidians, who, having intelligence of his coming, entered before him, and reduced the town to ashes. Both armies being in motion for some days, he forced Sarsura; but advancing to Tysdra, with the same intention, he thought proper, upon observing the strength of the place, not to make any attempt against it; and, on the fourth day, having returned to his station near Agar, the enemy likewise resumed their former position.

While Cæsar remained at this post, he received a reinforcement of four thousand men, consisting chiefly of the sick, who had been lef behind the army in Italy, and who now joined their legions, together with a body of four hundred horse, and a thousand archers and slingers. With this accession of strength, he formed a design on Tegea, which was occupied by a detachment of the enemy, supported by the whole of their army, encamped at the distance of a few miles behind the town; and having advanced, in hopes to force or surprise it, about eight miles on the plain, he was observed by Labienus and Scipio, who came forward at the same time, about four miles beyond their own station, in order to sustain their detachment. These consisting of four hundred horse, divided themselves on the right and the left of the town; and the main armies being formed in order of battle, with this post between them, Cæsar gave orders, that the party of horse, which ventured to show themselves without the walls of Tegea, should be attacked. The events which followed this first encounter, brought into action several detached bodies, both of horse and of foot, that were sent from the different sides to sustain the parties engaged, but did not lead to any general or decisive action; and both armies retired at night to their respective lines.

In many of these partial engagements which happened in this campaign, Cæsar's cavalry gave way to that of the Africans. In one of their flights Cæsar met an officer, who was running away with his party, and affecting to believe him under a mistake, took hold of his bridle, "You are wrong," he said, "for it is this way you must go to the enemy." Even the legions stood greatly in awe of the Numidian irregulars, by whom they were, on many occasions, surprised with some new feat of agility or cunning; and they were considerably intimidated by the number and formidable appearance of the elephants, which they knew not how to withstand. To fortify the minds of his men, and to prepare them to meet such antagonists, Cæsar had a number of elephants brought to his camp, armed and harnessed like those of the enemy. He exercised his horses in presence of these animals, taught his men in what places to strike, where the beast was vulnerable, and how to elude their fury. He likewise made some change in the usual exercise of the legion, such as might the better qualify his men to baffle or repel the artful and desultory attacks of the Numidians; and as he frequently employed his regular troops in foraging parties, he inured them by degrees to depart from their usual forms, without losing their courage, and to recover from any casual disorder into which they might be thrown. To show his own confidence in the superiority of his men, he frequently made an offer of battle on equal ground; and, in the manner that was, in their turns, common to both parties, drew a species of triumph from his enemy's declining to fight.

In these operations the campaign drew on to the middle of February, and had lasted about five months; during this time Cæsar had surmounted very great difficulties, arising from the dispersion of his fleet, the uncertainty of his communication with Italy, and the scarcity of provisions in a country laid waste or possessed by his enemies. He was now become master of many towns on the coast, and of a considerable extent of territory; but from the many objects which required his attention in different parts of the empire, he remained under great disadvantage in supporting a dilatory war, in which it appeared that Scipio and Labienus were resolved to persist. In order, if possible, to break their measures, he formed a design upon Thapsus, their principal garrison and sea-port on the southern boundaries of the province. With this view he decamped in the night from his station near Agar, and directing his march to the southward, arrived before Thapsus on the following day. As he had formerly, in order to secure his convoys against any attempts from thence, blocked up the harbour with his ships, he now seized all the avenues which led to the town, and invested it completely from the land.

Scipio and Juba, greatly interested to preserve a place of so much consequence, put their armies in motion, and, to counteract that of Cæsar, followed him by the route of the hills. Seeing him invest Thapsus, they took their first posts on two separate heights, about eight miles from the town. Cæsar, with his usual industry and despatch, executed lines both of circumvallation and of countervallation. By these lines, which were in the form of a crescent, terminating at both ends in the sea, he embraced the town, and proposed to encamp his army between them. Scipio was sufficiently acquainted with the ground, to know, that there was near the harbour a narrow channel, or salt-pit, separated from the sea, by a second beach or sand-bank, which it was possible the enemy might not have observed, and by which he might still have an entry to the town, or be able to throw in his succours. He therefore advanced with his whole army; and while he made a feint to interrupt Cæsar in the works he was carrying on, sent a party to occupy the sand-bank, or to throw themselves into the town of Thapsus by that communication. Cæsar, however, had already taken possession of this passage, and shut it up with three several intrenchments or redoubts, so placed as to secure it at once against any sallies from the garrison, as well as attacks from the field.

The combined army, on being thus disappointed of any communication with the town of Thapsus, remained all the day under arms, and gave the enemy an opportunity, which he often affected to desire, of terminating the war by a battle. But Cæsar, either because he had not sufficiently fortified his intrenchments to secure his rear from the town, or because he would not choose that moment to fight, when the enemy was prepared to receive him, made no advances to engage on that day.

Scipio, remaining on the same ground all night, took his resolution to encamp, and at break of day appeared to be forming the usual intrenchments. Cæsar had then probably completed his own works; and thinking the opportunity fair, or being determined not to suffer the enemy to effect a lodgment in his presence, he made the usual signal to prepare for action; and leaving a proper force to man his intrenchments against the town, drew out the remainder of his army to the field, ordered part of his fleet to get under sail, to turn a head-land in the rear of the enemy; and as soon as the action began in front, to alarm them with shouts, or a feint to land and to attack their rear. Having made these dispositions, he put his army in motion, and being come near enough to distinguish the posture of the enemy, observed, that their main body was already in order of battle, with the elephants disposed on the wings; and that numerous parties were still at work on the lines, within which they meant to encamp. He halted and made a disposition suitable to that of the enemy. His centre consisted of five legions, his wings each of four; the tenth and second legions composed the right wing, the eighth and ninth composed the left. Five cohorts, together with the cavalry, were selected to support the archers and slingers that were to begin the attack on the enemy's elephants. Cæsar himself went round every division on foot, exhorted the veterans to be mindful of the high reputation which they had to support, and recommended to the new levies to take example from those who were already possessed of so much glory, and who were instructed by long experience in the arts to be practised in the day of battle against an enemy.

While Cæsar was thus employed, the legions of Scipio appeared to reel; they at one time retired behind their imperfect works, again changed their purpose, and came back to their ground

Many of Cæsar's officers, and many of the veteran soldiers, well acquainted with this sign of distraction and irresolution, called aloud for the signal of battle. But he himself, possibly to whet their ardour, as well as to keep them in breath, again and again halted the whole line.

In this situation of the two armies, Cæsar is said to have been seized with a fit of the epilepsy, to which he was subject; a disease, which, although it attacks the seats of understanding and of sense, and suspends, for a time, all the exercises of them in the most alarming manner, does not appear from this example to impair the faculties, nor to be inconsistent with their highest measures, and their ablest exertions. The report, however, is not consistent with the narration of Hirtius. This historian, although he allows that the troops, in the last part of their motion to engage, acted without any orders; and while Cæsar wished them to advance more deliberately, that they forced a trumpet on the right to sound the usual charge, and that the whole line, without any other signal, overwhelming by force all the officers who ventured to oppose them, continued to rush on the enemy: yet he observes that Cæsar, instead of being out of condition to act, took his resolution to excite an ardour which he could not restrain; and, in order that he might bring his whole army at once with united force into action, commanded all his trumpets to sound, and himself, mounting on horseback, rode up with the foremost ranks. The battle began on the right, where the enemy's elephants being galled with a shower of arrows and stones, reeled back on the troops that were posted to sustain them, trod part of the infantry under foot, and broke over the unfinished intrenchments in their rear.

The left of Scipio's army being thus routed, the main body soon after gave way; and the whole fled to the camp which they had formerly occupied; but in their flight, being thrown into the utmost confusion, and separated from their officers, they arrived at the place to which they fled, without any person of rank to rally or command them. In this state of consternation they threw down their arms, and attempted to take refuge in the camp of their Numidian ally. But this being already in possession of the enemy, they continued their flight to the nearest heights; and being without arms, awaited their fate in a state of helpless despair. When they saw the troops that pursued them advance, they made signs of submission, and saluted the victors with a shout; but in vain. They were instantly attacked by the victorious army of Cæsar, who, though affecting clemency on former occasions, now seemed to be actuated with a paroxysm of rage and thirst of blood; contrary to the orders and entreaties of their general, they put the whole of this unarmed and defenceless multitude to the sword. They are said, on this occasion, to have seized the opportunity of satiating their revenge on some of their own officers who had offended them. One was actually murdered, another, being wounded, fled to Cæsar for protection; and many persons of distinction, senators and Roman knights, observing their danger, thought proper to withdraw to some place of concealment, till the present fury of the troops should abate.

In the beginning of this memorable action, the garrison of Thapsus had sallied, but were repulsed with loss. When the contest was over, Cæsar, to induce the town to surrender, displayed the trophies of victory; but had no answer. On the following day, he drew up his army under the walls of the town; and in that place pronounced his thanks to the legions for their behaviour, and, without any reproach for the disorder and cruelty of the preceding day, declared what were to be the rewards which he intended, at a proper time, for the veterans; and, by some immediate mark of his favour, distinguished a few who had signalized themselves. He appointed Caius Rubellius, with three legions, to continue the siege of Thapsus, and Cn. Domitius with two others to reduce Tysdra; and having sent forward M. Messala, with a body of horse on the road to Utica, he himself followed with the remainder of the army.[1]

At Utica were assembled from every part of the empire, all who were obnoxious to Cæsar, or who, from a zeal for the republic, had refused to submit to his power. On the third day after the battle, towards night, a person who had escaped from the field of battle coming to Utica, this unhappy convention of citizens was struck with the greatest alarm. Under the effects of their consternation, they met in the streets, ran to the gates, and again returned to their habitations. They crowded together in the public places, and separated by turns, and passed the night in extreme confusion. Cato represented to them, that the accounts they received might be exaggerated, and endeavoured to compose their fears. As soon as it was day he called them together, and laid before them a state of the place, or the works, military stores, provisions, arms, and numbers of men; and having commended the zeal, which they had hitherto shown in defence of the republic, exhorted them now to make the proper use of the means they had still of defending themselves, or at least of making their peace in a body: declared, that if they were inclined to submit to the victor, he should impute their conduct to necessity; but if they were determined to resist, he should reserve his sword for the last stake of the republic, and share with them in the consequences of a resolution, which he should love and admire. He contended, that they were now to consider themselves as assembled, not in Utica, but in Rome; "that the force of the republic was yet great, and might still, as on former occasions, rise again from its ruins; that the forces of Cæsar must still be distracted or separate, to make head against enemies who were appearing in different parts of the empire; that in Spain his own army had deserted from him, and the whole province had declared for the sons of Pompey; that Rome, the head of the commonwealth, was yet erect, and would not bend under the yoke of a tyrant; that his enemies were multiplying while he seemed to destroy them; that his own example should instruct them; or rather, that the courage which he exerted in the paths of guilt and of infamy, should animate those who were about, either to die with honour, or to secure for their country blessings in which they themselves were to share." At this assembly, a resolution was accordingly taken to defend the city of Utica, and numbers of slaves, who were set free by their masters for this purpose, were armed and inrolled. But it soon

1 Hirt. de Bello Af.

appeared, that the assembly consisted of persons unable to persist in this resolution, and who were preparing separately to merit the favour of the conqueror by an entire and early submission. They soon made a general profession of this design, expressed their veneration of Cato; but confessed, that they were not qualified to act with him in so arduous a scene; assured him, that if they were permitted to send a message to Cæsar, the first object of it should be to intercede for his safety; that, if they could not obtain it, they should accept of no quarter for themselves. Cato no longer opposed their intentions; but said, that he himself must not be included in their treaty; that he knew not of any right Cæsar had to dispose of his person; that what had hitherto happened in the war only served to convict Cæsar of designs which were often imputed to him, and which he always denied. He will now, at least, own, he said, that his opponents had reason for all the suspicions they suggested against him.

While matters were in this state, a party of Scipio's horse, which had escaped from the field of battle, appeared at the gates of the town, and were with difficulty, by Cato's intreaties, hindered from putting every Roman, who offered to submit to Cæsar, as well as the inhabitants of the place, to the sword. Being diverted from this act of violence, and furnished with some money for their immediate subsistence, they continued their retreat. Most of the senators, who were present, took shipping and escaped. Lucius Cæsar undertook to carry to his kinsman a petition from such of the Roman citizens as remained; and said to Cato, at parting, that he would gladly fall at the victor's feet to make *his* peace. To which Cato answered, "If I were disposed to make my peace with Cæsar, I should repair to him in person; but I have done him no wrong, I am not an object of his pardon, and shall not request what it were insolence in him to offer me as a favour." He, however, on this occasion, observed to his own son, that it would not become him to leave his father. "At a fit time," he said, "you will put yourself on the victor's mercy, but do not take part in public affairs: the times do not afford a station in which it would be proper for you to act." "And why," said the young man, "will you not take the benefit of the victor's clemency for yourself, as well as for me?" "I was born to freedom," he said, "and cannot, in my old age, be reconciled to servitude. For you these times were destined; and t may become you to submit to your fate." Having passed the day in aiding his friends to procure the means of their escape, he went to the bath, and supped as usual, without any marks of dejection or affectation of ease; and being retired to his chamber, after some time which he employed in reading, he killed himself. His attendants, upon hearing a noise which alarmed them, burst open the door, and would have dressed the wound, but he tore it up with his hand, and expired in making this effort.[1] Every one, through the day, had been anxious to know what was the design which Cato covered under the appearance of so much concern for others, and of so little care for himself. On the first report of his death, multitudes crowded to the door of his quarters, and gave the most unfeigned demonstrations of dejection and sorrow. The colony of Utica, though originally hostile to his cause, and still in the interest of Cæsar, ordered a public funeral, and erected his statue in the place of interment.

Cato died in the vigour of life, under fifty; he was naturally warm and affectionate in his temper; comprehensive, impartial, and strongly possessed with the love of mankind. But in his conduct, probably became independent of passion of any sort, and chose what was just on its own account. He professed to believe, with the sect whose tenets he embraced, that it might or might not, in particular circumstances, be expedient for a man to preserve or lay down his life; but that, while he kept it, the only good or evil competent to him consisted in the part which he took, as a friend or an enemy to mankind. He had long foreseen the dangers to which the republic was exposed, and determined to live only while he could counteract the designs that were formed against it.[2] The leader of the successful party thought proper to apologize for himself, by decrying the virtues of Cato; but the bulk of mankind, in his own and the subsequent ages, were equally pleased to extol them; and he is a rare example of merit, which received its praise even amidst the adulation that was paid to his enemies;[3] and was thought, by the impartial, equally above the reach of commendation or censure.[4]

---

1 Dio. Cass. Appian. Plutarch. Hirtius de Bello Africano.

2 Sed verè laudari ille vir non potest, nisi hac ornata sunt; quod ille ea, quæ nunc sunt, et futura viderit, et ne fierent contenderit, et facta ne videret, vitam reliquerit. Cicer. ad Att. lib. xii. ep. 4.

3 See the writings of Virgil and Horace.

4 Cujus gloriæ neque profuit quisquam laudando, nec vituperando quisquam nocuit, quum utrumque summis præditi fecerint ingeniis. Frag. Livii ex Hieronym. Prolog. lib. xi. in Oscam.

THE

HISTORY

OF

THE PROGRESS AND TERMINATION

OF THE

ROMAN REPUBLIC.

BOOK V.

CHAPTER I.

Arrival of Cæsar at Utica—Wreck of the Republican Party—Servility of the Roman People—Magnificence and Administration of Cæsar—His last Campaign in Spain—Death of the elder of Pompey's Sons—Cæsar's Return, Triumphs, Honours, and Policy in the State—Spirit of the times—Source of the Conspiracy against Cæsar—Its Progress—Death of Cæsar.

WHEN Cæsar was informed, on his march from Thapsus, that of all the principal men of the opposite party, Cato alone remained at Utica to receive him, he was at a loss to interpret his conduct, and possibly might have found it difficult to determine how he should deal with an antagonist, whom he neither could reconcile to his usurpation, nor treat as a criminal. The character of generosity towards his enemies, which Cæsar had assumed, laid him under some obligation, in point of consistency, to treat the person of Cato with respect; and the opportunity he would have had, in that instance, of exercising his clemency with so much lustre, could not have escaped him. In the busiest scene of his life he had not any party object, or any party quarrel to maintain; he had repeatedly sacrificed personal animosity to ambition; and when he took the field against the republic, he had few private resentments to gratify: he knew that an affectation of reluctance in shedding the blood of Roman citizens, the reverse of what remained so much an object of horror in the memory of Sylla, was the likeliest means to cover the effects of this destructive war, and to reconcile the people to his government.. In the bulk of his fellow citizens he had found either rubbish to be removed from the way of ambition, or tools with which he might work in removing it; they were the dupes of his policy, or open to the imputations of sinister designs or unreasonable obstinacy which he cast on his opponents. In Cato, perhaps, alone, he found a measure of estimation, which, with all his abilities and prosperous fortune, he could not neglect, and a penetration which, without management for his person, treated his politics as a system of villany devised for the ruin of the commonwealth. Cato therefore alone, of all his antagonists, he possibly hated beyond the possibility of a reconciliation.[5]

Cæsar was in reality, according to the representation of his friend Curio, neither sanguinary nor scrupulous of blood, but in the highest degree indifferent to both, and ready to do whatever was most likely to promote his designs. As he had already sufficiently provided for the reputation of clemency, he now made a freer use of his sword, and in proportion as he approached to the end of the war, or saw the means of extirpating those who were most likely to disturb his government, he dipped his hands with less scruple in the blood of his enemies. As he pursued Pompey into Egypt, under a certain impression that the death of this rival was material to the establishment of his power in Italy, so it is likely that he now hastened to Utica as a place at which he might crush the remains of the republic. On hearing of the death of Cato, however, he made use of an expression which served to discover the resolution he had taken with respect to him. "I must be allowed," he said, "to envy this man the splendour of his death, as he has refused me the honour of preserving his life." Having passed through Uzita and Adrumetum, which surrendered to him on his march, and being met by numbers who came to make their submission, he arrived at Utica in the evening, and continued all night without the gates.

Marcus Messala had already taken possession

5 Et cuncta terrarum subacta præter atrocem animum Catonis.

of the town. Cæsar entered on the following day; and having ordered the people to attend him, made a speech, in which he thanked the colony of Utica for their faithful attachment to his cause; but spoke of three hundred Roman citizens, who had contributed to support the war against him, in terms which sufficiently showed that he was no longer to court the reputation of mercy. Appian says, that as many of them as fell into his hands were by his order put to death. Hirtius relates, that he only confiscated their effects, and that this sentence was afterwards changed into a limited fine, amounting in all to two hundred thousand sestertia, or about a million and a half sterling, to be paid in three years, at six separate payments.

From this general wreck of the republican party in Africa, the leaders continued their flight in different directions. Many who surrendered themselves were spared; but most of those, who, in their attempts to escape, fell into the enemy's hands, either killed themselves, or by Cæsar's order were put to death.[1] Afranius and Faustus Sylla having joined a party of cavalry that fled by Utica from the field of battle, were intercepted by Sitius, and defending themselves, with the loss of many of their party, were taken. In a few days after this event, these prisoners, under pretence of a riot in the camp, were put to death.

Scipio, with Damasippus, Torquatus, and Plætorius Rustianus, endeavoured to escape by sea into Spain. After being tossed some days with contrary winds, they ventured to put into Hippo, on the coast of Numidia, where they met with a squadron of Cæsar's fleet, commanded by Sitius. Their vessel being boarded, they were asked with impatience, where is the general? Scipio himself made answer, the general is well; and in uttering these words stabbed himself, and went headlong into the sea.

Juba, with Petreius, having escaped from the field of battle at Thapsus, lay concealed by day, and continued their flight in the night towards Zama, a place which, at the breaking out of the war, the king of Numidia had fortified, and made the residence of his women, and the repository of his treasure and most valuable effects He knew that if he should be taken captive by a Roman general, the consequence was being led in triumph, and possibly afterwards put to death. He had therefore provided this retreat in case of an unfortunate issue to the war; intending it merely as a place at which he might die in state. With this intention he had raised, near to the royal palace, a pile of wool on which he meant to consume whatever could mark or adorn the victor's triumph; and it was his purpose, while he set these materials, and with them the whole city, on fire, to commit himself and his women to the flames.

The inhabitants of Zama had some intimation of this design, and, upon the approach of the king, not choosing to celebrate by such an offering the exit of a vanquished prince, shut their gates and refused him admittance. They likewise had the humanity to refuse sending the women to him, on a supposition that he meant they should be a sacrifice to his jealousy, or be involved in his ruin.

Juba finding himself thus disobeyed, even by his own subjects, retired to one of his country seats; and having ordered a splendid entertainment at the close of it he and Petreius fell together by their own swords. The kingdom of Numidia was converted into a Roman province, and the government of it was committed to Sallust the historian. The son of the king, yet an infant, was reserved to make a part in the procession of the victor's triumph.[2] The furniture and ornaments of his palaces were sold, and produced a considerable sum of money. Great contributions were raised at the same time in those parts of Africa which had been already subjected to the condition of a Roman province. The inhabitants of Thapsus were made to pay fifty thousand Roman sestertia;[3] those of Adrumetum, eighty thousand; those of Leptis and Tysdra paid the quotas exacted from them in corn and oil.

Cæsar having, in this manner, closed a scene in which he had destroyed fifty thousand of his opponents, who might be supposed to be the most obstinate adherents of the republican party, and having joined to the empire a territory which, by the report afterwards made in the assembly of the people, was fitted to yield an annual tribute of three hundred thousand medimni of grain, and three hundred thousand weight of oil,[4] he embarked at Utica, on the fifteenth of June, and in three days after he sailed from thence, arrived in the island of Sardinia: a part of his dominions, said Cicero, which he had not hitherto seen. Before his departure from Africa he had made necessary arrangements respecting the army; and, although he had recently availed himself of the services of the legions who had mutinied in Italy, and seemed to have forgotten their offence, yet he took the benefit of the present prosperous state of his affairs to indulge his resentment; and that they might not communicate with factious spirits in Italy, have leisure to over-rate their services, or to set an example to the rest of the army of exorbitant demands, he ordered them to be broke and disbanded in Africa. The remainder of the troops who had given him the victory in that country, he ordered, after receiving the necessary refreshments, to proceed in the voyage to Spain, where he had still some resistance to apprehend from the sons of Pompey.

Leaving the army therefore to pursue this course, Cæsar himself took shipping again in the island of Sardinia on the twenty-ninth of June; and, being some time detained by contrary winds, arrived at Rome on the twenty-sixth of the following month;[5] having since the time of his departure from Italy, on the expedition to Africa, in which he had so many difficulties to surmount, spent no more than six months.

The news of Cæsar's victory had been some time received. The principal supports of the republic had fallen at Thapsus and at Pharsalia; and as the sons of Pompey, though favourably received by their late father's adherents in Spain, were not yet supposed to be in condition to resist the victor, the revolution in his favour seemed to be complete, and every part of the Roman empire subjected to his power. Nothing now remained, but that he should take possession of

1 Dio. Cass. lib. xliii. c. 12. Appian. de Bello Civili, lib. ii. Florus, Eutropius, Hirtius.

2 Plut. in Cæs.

3 About 400,000*l*.

4 Plut. in Cæs.

5 Hirtius de Bell. Afr. c. 86.

that sovereignty to which he aspired, and in which, it soon after appeared, that to him there was a charm, even in the court that was paid to him, as well as in the possession of power.

Whatever distress the surviving members of the commonwealth may have suffered on the loss of their relations and friends, who had fallen in the late bloody transactions of this war, or whatever mortification they may have felt on the loss of their own political consequence, as partners in the empire of the world, no symptoms of aversion, or unwilling submission, appeared on the part of the people; all orders of men hastened to pay their court to the victor, and, by their servile adulations, to anticipate the state of degradation into which they were soon to be reduced.

In the name of the senate and people, a continual thanksgiving of forty days was decreed for the late victory at Thapsus. The power of dictator was conferred on Cæsar for ten years, and that of censor, which gave the supreme disposal of honours and rank in the commonwealth, and which, on account of the abuse to which it was subject, had been some time abolished, was now under a new title, that of *Præfectus Morum*, restored in his person. At the same time the nomination of some of the officers of state, formerly elected by the people, was committed to him. He was, in the exercise of these powers, to be preceded by seventy-two lictors, triple the number of those who used to attend the dictators, and he was to enjoy, for life, many of the inferior prerogatives, which, under the republic, served to distinguish the first officers of state; such as that of giving signals for the horses to start, or for the other sports to begin at the games of the circus; and that of delivering his opinion before any one else in the senate. It was likewise ordered, that he should have in the senate a gilded chair of state, placed next to that of the consul; and, as if it were intended to join ridicule with these extraordinary honours, it was decreed that as the conqueror of Gaul, in his triumphs he should be drawn by white horses, to put him on a foot of equality with Camillus, to whom this distinction had been given, as the restorer of his country from its destruction by the ancestors of that nation; that his name should be inserted, instead of that of Catullus, as the person who had rebuilt the capitol; that a car, like that of Jupiter, should be placed for him in the same temple, and near to the statue of the god himself; and that his own statue, with the title of a demi-god, should be erected on a globe representing the earth.

It is said that Cæsar refused many of the honours which were decreed to him; but in these, which he no doubt encouraged, or favourably received, he sufficiently betrayed a vanity which but rarely accompanies such a distinguished superiority of understanding and courage. Though in respect to the ability with which he rendered men subservient to his purpose; in respect to the choice of means for the attainment of his end; in respect to the plan and execution of his designs, he was far above those who were eminent in the history of mankind; yet in respect to the end which he pursued, in respect to the passions he had to gratify, he was one merely of the vulgar, and condescended to be vain of titles and honours, which he has shared with persons of the meanest capacity. Insensible to the honour of being deemed the equal in rank to Cato and Catullus, to Hortensius and Cicero, and the equal in reputation to Sylla, to Fabius, and to the Scipios, he preferred being a superior among profligate men, the leader among soldiers of fortune, and to extort by force from his fellow citizens a deference which his wonderful abilities must have made unavoidable, even if he had possessed the magnanimity to despise it.

Cæsar, soon after the distinctions now mentioned were bestowed upon him, addressed himself to the Roman senate and people, in a speech which, being supposed to proceed from a master, was full of condescension and lenity, but from a fellow citizen was fraught with insult and contumely. A speech delivered on so remarkable an occasion was likely to be in substance preserved; and under the government of his successors, by whom he was numbered with the gods, it was not likely to get abroad but with a view to do him honour. "Let no man," he said, "imagine that, under the favour of my exalted situation, I am now to indulge myself in acts, or even in expressions, of severity; or that I am to follow the example of Marius, of Cinna, of Sylla, or of most others, who, having subdued their enemies, dropt, in the height of their fortune, that character of moderation, under which they had formerly enticed men to their party. I have appeared all along in my true character, and now, in the height of my power, have no change to make in my conduct.[6] The more my fortunes advance, the more I will endeavour to use them properly. My sole object, while I endeavoured to rise above my enemies, was to secure for myself a situation in which I might exercise virtue with dignity and safety; and I shall not now imitate the examples which I myself often have condemned, nor sully the splendour of my victories by an improper use of my power.

"As the favours of fortune are won by vigour, so they are preserved by moderation, and should be most carefully preserved by those who enjoy the greatest share of them. I covet sincere affection and genuine praise; not the adulation that springs from fear and hatred. These are my serious thoughts, confirmed on reflection; and you shall find me governed by them in all the actions of my life. I do not mean to be your lord or your tyrant, but your chief and your leader. When the state has occasion for my authority, you shall find in me a dictator and a consul; but on ordinary occasions, no more than a private man.

"I have spared many who were repeatedly in arms against me. I have shut my ears to the informations of the hidden designs of others, and have destroyed all letters and papers which could lead to a detection of my secret enemies. To most of you I can have no resentment; and I do not incline to raise prosecutions against those who may think they have incurred my displeasure. Live, therefore, with me from this time forward in confidence, as children with their father. I reserve to myself the power of punishing the guilty, as far as justice requires; but will protect the innocent, and reward the deserving.

"Let not these appearances of military force alarm you. The troops which are quartered in

---

6 Dio. Cass. lib. xliii. c. 15.

the city, and which attend my person, are destined to defend, not to oppress the citizens; and they will know, upon every occasion, the limits of their duty.

"Uncommon taxes have lately been levied in the provinces and in Italy, but not for my private use. I have in reality expended my fortune, and contracted immoderate debts in the public service; and, while I myself have borne so great a part of the burden, am likewise made to bear the blame of what others have exacted." He concluded with assurances, that the arrears which were due to the troops, and the other debts of the public,[1] should be paid with the least possible inconvenience to the people.

In this speech was conveyed, not the indignant and menacing spirit of Sylla, who despised the very power of which he was possessed; but the conscious state and reflecting condescension of a prince who admired and wished to recommend his greatness. The Roman people, in former instances of usurpation, had experienced sanguinary and violent treatment, and they now seemed to bear with indifference the entire suppression of their political rights, when executed by hands, that refrained from proscriptions and murders. But as Cæsar seemed to think his present elevation the highest object of human wishes, there were some who thought their present subjection the lowest state of degradation and misery. "What should I do in such times?" says Cicero to his correspondent, "books cannot always amuse me. I go into any company, affect to be noisy, and laugh, to conceal my sorrow."[2]

The populace were gratified with shows, processions, and feasts, and with the gratuities that were given them in money. Cæsar had four separate triumphs in one month. The first for his conquest of Gaul, at which Vercingetorix, the prince of the Arverni, by a custom cruel and odious in all its parts, was led in chains, and afterwards put to death. The second for his victory in Egypt, at which Arsinoë, the sister of the queen, was exhibited in fetters, and by her youth and beauty excited a general compassion, which preserved her life. A third for the defeat of Pharnaces, where the trophies, as has already been mentioned, were marked with the words, *I came, I saw, I vanquished.* The last for the overthrow of the king of Numidia, in which the infant son of that prince was carried in procession. This captive having received a literary education at Rome, became afterwards, according to Plutarch, an historian of eminence.[3]

Although triumphs were not obtained for the defeat of fellow citizens, and nothing in these processions had reference to Pompey, yet the effigies of many considerable senators, who had fallen in the civil war, were carried before the victor's chariot.

In these processions, Cæsar is said to have carried to the treasury, in all, sixty thousand talents in money;[4] two thousand eight hundred and twenty two chaplets or crowns of gold, weighing twenty thousand four hundred and fourteen pounds.[5] He at the same time distributed to each private man of the army, five thousand denarii or drachmas, about one hundred and sixty one pounds sterling: to each centurion, double: to the tribune, quadruple: to the people, an attic mina of a hundred drachmas, or about three pounds four shillings and seven pence a man.[6]

The soldiers, who walked in these processions, in chaunting their ballads and lampoons, took the usual petulant liberties with their leader, alluded to the disorders of his youth and to the crimes of his age; and showed that they were not deceived by the professions which he made of a zeal for the rights of the people. "If you observe the laws," they said, "you shall be punished; but if you boldly transgress them all, a crown is your reward." These appearances of freedom in the troops, perhaps, flattered the people with some image of the ancient familiarity of ranks which subsisted in times of the republic; but the license of mere soldiers of fortune brings too often the reverse of freedom to the people; and in whatever manner those of Rome were qualified to judge of their own situation, it is likely that the pageants, which now entertained them, were part of the means which Cæsar employed to reconcile them to his usurpation, and to divert their thoughts from the prospect of a military government with which they were threatened. Farther to secure these effects, he continued to multiply shows and public diversions. He himself, at the close of his triumphs, walked in procession at the opening of magnificent edifices he had built, and in his return at night from this ceremony, attended by multitudes of the people, was lighted by torches borne on elephants.[7] At the same time he erected theatres, and exhibited dramatic performances in different parts of the city, and amply indulged the taste of the populace for entertainments of every sort. He introduced not only gladiators to fight in single combat, but parties on foot and on horseback to engage in considerable numbers on opposite sides, and to exhibit a species of battles. Among these he showed the manner of fighting from elephants, having forty of these animals properly mounted, and the manner likewise of fighting at sea, having vessels on a piece of water which was formed for the purpose. In most of these shows, the parties who were engaged, being captives or malefactors condemned to die, gave a serious exhibition of the utmost efforts they could make in real fight.

Among the other articles of show and expense which composed the magnificence of these entertainments, are mentioned the blinds or awnings of silk, a material then of the highest price, which were spread over the public theatres to shade the spectators from the sun, and to enable them undisturbed, from under these delicate coverings, to enjoy the sights of bloodshed and horror which were presented before them. Two human sacrifices, we are told, were at the same time offered up in the field of Mars, by priests specially named for this service. Of this shocking exhibition, the historian does not explain the occasion.[8] The whole was attended by a feast, to which the

1 Dio. Cass. lib. xliii. c. 15. &c.

2 Cic. ad Familiar. lib. ix. ep. 26. Miraris tam exhiliratam esse servitutem nostram. Quid ergo faciam?—ibi loquor quod in solum ut dicitur, et gemitum in risus maximos transfero.

3 Plut. in Cæs. Dio. Cass.

4 About 10,000,000*l.*

5 The Roman pondo consisted of ten ounces, about 800,000*l.*

6 Appian. Sueton.

7 Dio. Cass. Suetonius

8 Dio. Cass. lib. xliii. c. 24.

people were invited, and at which twenty thousand benches or couches were placed for these numerous guests.[9] So great was the concourse from the country to this entertainment, that multitudes lay in the streets, or lodged in booths erected for the occasion. Many were trampled under foot, and killed in the crowds. Among those who perished in this manner, two Roman senators are mentioned.

This method of gaining the people, by flattering their disposition to dissipation and idleness, was already familiar at Rome. It had been employed under the republic in procuring favour, and in purchasing votes by those who aspired to the offices of state. It was now intended by Cæsar to effect the revolution he had in view, and to reconcile the populace of Rome, who had for some time governed the empire, to the loss of their political consequence, in being deprived of a power which they were no longer worthy to hold. It is probable, that the arms of Cæsar were not more successful in subduing those who opposed him in the field, than these popular arts were in gaining the consent of his subjects to the dominion he was about to assume.

From this time forward, Cæsar took upon himself all the functions of government, and while he suffered the forms of a senate and popular assemblies to remain, availed himself of their name and authority without consulting with either, affixing without scruple the superscription of particular senators to the decrees or edicts, which he sent abroad into the provinces.[10] "My name," says Cicero, "is often prefixed to public deeds which are sent abroad, as having been moved or drawn up by me, and which come back from Armenia or Syria as mine, before I have ever heard of them at Rome. Do not imagine I am in jest; for I have letters from persons, whose names I never heard of before, thanking me for the honour I have done them in bestowing the title of king."[11]

Equally absolute in the city as in the provinces, Cæsar placed whoever he thought proper on the rolls of the senate; and, without regard to birth, declared some to be of Patrician rank. He recalled some who had been driven into exile for illegal practices, and reinstated in their ranks many whom the censors had degraded.[12] In all the elections, he named half the magistrates, or in a mandate, addressed to the tribes, took upon him to direct the people whom they were to choose.[13] In the exercise of so much power, he became reserved and difficult to access, familiar only with persons whom he himself had raised, and who had talents amusing or serviceable, and without any pretensions to alarm his jealousy.[14] Nevertheless, if the Romans could have overlooked what was offensive in his manner, or illegal in the powers which he had thus usurped, many of his acts were in themselves, as might have been expected from so able a personage, worthy of a great prince, and tending to reform abuses, as well as to facilitate the summary proceedings of the despotical power he had assumed.

Among the first acts of Cæsar's reign, the law of Sylla, by which the children of the proscribed had been excluded from holding any office in the state, was repealed. The judiciary law, which had undergone so many alterations, and which in its latest form, admitted some of the inferior class of the people[15] on the roll of the judges or jurymen, was now reformed, so as to limit the exercise of the judicature to the senators and knights. A scrutiny was made into the titles of those who had been in the practice to receive corn at the public granaries, and their numbers were greatly reduced.[16] Of the corporations which had been multiplied for factious purposes, many were abolished, and the original companies of the city alone were permitted to remain. Many punishments, for the better restraining of crimes, were increased. To the ordinary punishment of murder, was joined the confiscation of the whole estate; to that of some other crimes, the confiscation of one half. The kalendar was reformed upon the principles established by the Egyptian astronomers. The reckoning by lunar months, and the use of irregular intercalations, which had been frequently made for party and political purposes, had so deranged the terms, that the festivals to be observed by reapers did not happen in harvest, or those of the vintage in autumn. To restore them therefore to their proper dates in the kalendar, no less than an intercalation of sixty-seven days, or above two months, was required. This intercalation was made in the present year, between the months of November and December, so that the name of December was transferred from the time of the autumnal equinox, to that, where it still remains, of the winter solstice.

Under the government of Cæsar, sumptuary laws were framed to restrain the expense of the table; and he himself expressed a great zeal to correct the abuse which prevailed in this article. Being sensible that Italy was greatly depopulated by the distractions of the commonwealth, and by the devastations of the late civil war, he took measures to restore the numbers of the people, both by detaining the natives of Italy at home, and by inviting foreigners to settle. He gave

9 Plut. in Cæsar.

10 It is well known, that the senatûs consulta bore the names of the senators by whom they were proposed.

11 Ante audio senatûs consultum in Armeniam et Syriam esse perlatum, quod in meam sententiam factum esse dicatur, quam omnino mentionem ullam de ea re esse factam. Atque hoc nolim me jocare putes, nam mihi scito jam, a regibus ultimis allatas esse literas, quibus mihi gratias agant, quod se mea sententia reges appellaverim; quos ego non modo reges appellatos, sed omnino nato nesciebam. Cicero ad Familiares, lib. ix. ep. 15.

12 At this time, he with much difficulty was persuaded, at the intercession of the senate, to permit the return of Caius Marcellus, who at Athens, on his way into Italy, was, upon motives which have not been explained, assassinated by one of his own attendants. This Marcellus was consul, U. C. 703.

13 The words of Cæsar's mandate were, "Cæsar dictator tribui, &c. &c. commendo vobis illum, &c. &c. ut vestro suffragio suam dignitatem teneat. Sueton. in Cæsar.

14 Cicer. ad Familiar. lib. iv. ep. 9. Ib. lib. vi. ep. 14.

15 The tribuni Ærarii.

16 The leaders of faction under the republic, and no one probably more than Cæsar himself, in order to increase the numbers of their partizans, had augmented this list, and it was undoubtedly become a great abuse. Dion. Cassius says, it was at this time reduced by Cæsar to one half. Suetonius specifies the number from three hundred and twenty thousand to one hundred and fifty thousand. Plutarch and Appian state the reduction, so as to be understood of the numbers of the whole people, in comparing the muster taken before the civil war with the one now made.

premiums to those who had families: he ordered, that no citizen above twenty nor under ten, except belonging to the army, should remain out of Italy above three years at a time; and that the sons of senators, except in the family or retinue of the public officers, should not go abroad; that all landholders in Italy should employ no less than one third freemen on their lands; that all practitioners of liberal arts, particularly foreign physicians settling at Rome, should be admitted on the rolls of the people; and at the same time he extended the privilege of Romans to whole cities and provinces in different parts of the empire,[1] by these means increasing the number of Roman citizens, or at least increasing the number of those who were to bear this title. Sensible that he himself had become dangerous to the republic, by having his power as a provincial officer improperly prolonged, he took measures to prevent a similar danger to the government, of which he himself had now acquired the possession, limiting the duration of command in the provinces, if with the title of proprætor to one year, or with that of proconsul to two years; a regulation in which he showed how well he understood the nature of the ladder by which he himself had mounted to his present elevation, and how much he desired to withhold the use of it from any one else who might be disposed to tread in his steps, or to dispute his continuance in the height he had gained.

While Cæsar, on a supposition that he himself was to hold the reigns of government, was providing for the security of the power he had established in the capital, and on a supposition that he had no enemy left in the field, or that the remains of the adverse party in the provinces might be extinguished by his officers, was betaking himself to civil affairs and to popular arts, he had reports from Spain which convinced him, that his own presence might still be necessary to repress a party, which began to resume its vigour under the sons of Pompey. He had sent Didius, with the fleet and army, from Sardinia, to secure the possession of Spain; but this service was found to be more difficult than was at first apprehended. He had himself, in appearance, reduced this province; but many humours had broke out in it, while he was afterwards so much occupied in other parts of the empire. Even the troops which had joined his standard, mutinied during the uncertain state of his fortunes in Thessaly and Egypt; and though, upon the death of Cassius Longinus, and the succession of Trebonius, their discipline was in appearance restored; yet consciousness of the heinous offence they had committed against Cæsar made them doubt of his forgiveness; and, joined with the inclination and respect which they yet entertained for the family of Pompey, determined them to take part against him. They had opened a secret correspondence with Scipio, while he was yet at the head of a powerful army in Africa, and encouraged him to send a proper officer into Spain to take the command of such forces as could be raised in the province.

Young Pompey was sent for this purpose. In his way, he put into the island of Majorca, and was there some time detained by sickness, or remained in expectation that he might prevail on the natives to espouse his cause. The troops on the continent, in the mean time, even before Pompey arrived to take the command of them, declared themselves openly against Cæsar, and erased his name from their bucklers. They obliged his lieutenant Trebonius to fly from their quarters, and owned T. Quintus Scapula and Q. Apronius for their generals.

In this posture of affairs, young Pompey arrived in Spain, took the command of this army, and either received or forced the submission of the principal towns. He was likewise strengthened by the accession of all the Roman settlers in the province who retained any zeal for the republic, and by the remains of former armies who had been levied by his father, especially such of that army which had served under Afranius on the Segra, as were left in Spain; and by many officers of rank, who, having escaped from Thessaly or Africa upon the late calamities of their party, had taken refuge in this country. Among these, Labienus and Varus, with as many as could be saved from the massacre at Thapsus, were assembling anew under the standard of Pompey. The two brothers, Cnæus and Sextus, were joined together, and supported by the name of their father, which was still in high veneration; they had assembled thirteen legions. Among these, were two legions of native Spaniards, who had deserted from Trebonius;[2] one that was raised from the Roman colonists; and a fourth which had arrived from Africa, with the elder of the two brothers.

Q. Fabius Maximus and Q. Pedius or Didius,[3] the officers of Cæsar, being unable to make head against this force, remained on the defensive, and by the reports which they made to their commander, represented the necessity of his own presence in the province.

The continuance of the dictatorial power in Cæsar's person, had superseded the usual succession in the offices of state. Lepidus still remained in his station of general of horse; and, with a council of six or nine præfects being left to command at Rome, Cæsar set out in the autumn for Spain. He ordered troops from Italy to reinforce those already employed in this service, and, in twenty-seven days after his departure from Rome, arrived at Saguntum.[4]

Upon the news of Cæsar's approach, Cnæus Pompeius had assembled all his force on the Bœtis, posted his brother Sextus with a proper garrison at Corduba, and himself endeavoured to reduce Ulia, a town which still held out against him in that neighbourhood. Cæsar's first object, upon his arrival in Spain, was to preserve this place from falling into the enemy's hands. For this purpose, he detached eleven cohorts under the command of L. Julius Paciæcus, with orders, if possible, to throw themselves into the town. The night in which they marched for this purpose, being stormy and dark, they passed the first posts of the besiegers unnoticed. When near the gates, they were challenged; but the officer who led the van, having answered in a low voice, that they were a detachment ordered to the foot of the wall in search of some entry, by which, under the cover of the night, they might surprise

1 Dio. Cass. Sueton Appian.

2 Hirtius de Bell. Hisp. 3 Dio. Cass. ibid. c. 31.

4 App. de Bell Civil. lib. .i. or as Strabo writes, at Obulio, lib. iii. p. 160.

the garrison, they were suffered to pass, and presenting themselves at one of the gates, upon a signal that had been agreed upon, they were admitted into the town.

While Cæsar thus reinforced the garrison of Ulia, he himself, to make a diversion in their favour, marched up to Corduba, cut off a party that had been sent from thence to observe his motions, and threatened the town with a siege. Sextus, who was in the place, being alarmed, sent pressing representations to his brother, who accordingly abandoned his lines before Ulia, and marched to his relief. Both armies encamped on the Guadalquivir.[5] The parties that were sent forward by them to scour the country, or to cover their quarters, were engaged in daily skirmishes. But the two brothers, being in possession of the principal stations, and in condition to protract the war, continued to act on the defensive. Cæsar, on his part, made some movements in order to disconcert them, and to find, if possible, an opportunity of coming to action; but the country being hilly, and the towns generally built upon heights, every where furnished strong posts for the enemy, and prevented his making any progress. The winter at the same time approached, and exposed his army to considerable hardships from the severity of the season, and from the scarcity of provisions. Under these disadvantages, he undertook the siege of Allegua, and on the twentieth of February, after an obstinate resistance, obliged that town to surrender.[6]

C. J. Cæsar, Dict. 3tio. M. E. Lepidus, M. E. Coss.

U. C. 708.

Our accounts of these operations, which are ascribed to Hirtius, and which, with his other performances are annexed to Cæsar's Commentaries, being less perfect than other parts of the collection, all we can distinctly learn from them is, that after a variety of different movements, which gave rise to frequent skirmishes, the armies in the month of March came to encamp in the plain of Munda, about five miles from each other; that Cæsar was about to leave his station, when in the morning of his intended departure, he had intelligence, that the enemy had been under arms from the middle of the preceding night, and were meditating some attempt on his camp. This intelligence was followed by the sudden appearance of their army on some elevated grounds near the town of Munda; but as they showed no disposition to come into the plain, Cæsar, after some hesitation, advanced to attack them.

In the army of Pompey, together with the flower of a warlike people, the natives of Spain, were assembled many veterans of the Roman legions, inured to blood; many Roman citizens of rank, now pushed to despair, or warned, by the fate of their party at Thapsus, not to expect safety from the mercy of a victorious enemy, and not to have any hopes, but in their swords. Under these impressions, they waited for Cæsar's approach with a proper countenance, and on the first onset repulsed and put to flight the troops by whom they were attacked. In this extremity, Cæsar ran into the ranks of his own men; said, *they were delivering him over to boys;* laid hold of a sword and a shield, and calling out that *this then should be the last day of his life, and of their services,* took a place in the ranks as a mere legionary soldier. In this manner he renewed the action, and being reduced to the necessity of animating his men with the example of his own personal valour, committed his fortune and his life to the decision of a contest, in which his ability as an officer could no longer have any share; but while the event was still in suspense, Bogud, an African, commanding a body of horse in his service, having made an attempt to pierce into Pompey's camp, drew Labienus from his post in the field to cover it. This accident turned the fortune of the day. The troops, who till then valiantly sustained Cæsar's attack, believing that Labienus deserted them, instantly fled in disorder. The slaughter from thence forward turned as usual entirely against those who fled. Thirty thousand fell upon the field, and among them three thousand Roman citizens of high condition, with Labienus and Accius Varus at their head. Seventeen officers of rank were taken, with thirteen Roman eagles or legionary standards.

Cæsar acknowledged, that having on other occasions fought for victory, he had now been obliged to fight for his life. He had a thousand men killed, and five hundred wounded, before the enemy gave way. Part of the vanquished army retired into the town of Munda, part into the camp, and in their respective posts prepared to defend themselves to the last extremity. Cæsar, on the approach of night, took possession of all the avenues by which either might escape; and it is said, that the troops he employed in this service, instead of traverses of earth or stone to obstruct the highways, raised up mounds of the dead bodies.

Early in the morning of the following day, Cæsar having left the town of Munda in this manner blocked up or invested, set out for Corduba, which Sextus, the younger of the two brothers, upon the news of the battle, had already abandoned.

Cnæus, on seeing the rout of his own army, fled with a small party of horse on the road to Carteia.[7] Here he had collected most of his shipping and naval stores; but the news of his defeat having arrived before him, the people were divided in their inclinations. Part had already sent a deputation with an offer of their services to Cæsar; part still adhered to the family of Pompey, and from these opposite dispositions had proceeded to actual violence and bloodshed in the streets. Pompey himself was wounded in one of their scuffles, and expecting no safety in a place, in which so many of the inhabitants had declared against him, he took ship, and put to sea with thirty galleys. He was pursued by Didius, who commanded Cæsar's squadron at Gades; and being obliged in a few days to stop for a supply of water, of which he had been ill provided at his sudden departure from Carteia, he was overtaken, most of his ships destroyed, and he himself obliged to seek for safety on shore. Soon after he landed, he dismissed his attendants, or was deserted by them; and falling into the hands of the enemy, though greatly weakened by his wounds and loss of blood, he continued to

5 The Bœtis.

6 Hirtius de Bell Hisp.

7 Now Gibraltar.

defend himself, until he was overpowered and slain. His head, according to the barbarous custom of the times, was sent to the conqueror, and exposed at Hispalis.

In the preceding transactions of the war, every circumstance contributed to the fall of the republic, and to the success of Cæsar. In the very outset of the contest, half the nobility, ruined by prodigality and extravagance, had been desirous of anarchy and confusion. Citizens high in civil rank, and with fortunes entire, were generally glad to forego their political consequence in exchange for ease and safety. Even the arms which should have protected the commonwealth, were in the hands of mere soldiers of fortune, who were inclined to favour that side from which they looked for the establishment of military government; they fought to procure great power and estates for themselves, not to preserve laws which gave property and the security of wealth to others. Many of the senators indeed perceived the impending ruin, and were prevailed upon to make some efforts for the preservation of the state, but on most occasions too hastily despaired of their cause. It was not thought honourable or safe for a citizen to survive his freedom. Upon this principle, the friends of the republic, while they escaped from the enemy, perished by their own hands.

Soon after the action at Munda, Scapula, one of the officers lately at the head of the republican party in Spain, turned the practice of suicide into a kind of farce. Having retired to Corduba from the field of battle, he ordered a magnificent pile of wood to be raised and covered with carpets; and having given an elegant entertainment, and distributed his money among his attendants and servants, he mounted to the top of this fabric, and while one servant pierced the master with his sword, another set fire to the pile. Thus the victories of Cæsar were completed by his enemies; and while he gained a fresh step at every encounter, they who opposed him went headlong, and abandoned their country to its ruin.

The province of Spain, under a proper conduct of its force and resources, if it had not been able to stop at once the career of Cæsar's victories, was surely sufficient to have given him more trouble than any other part of the empire. Its natives brave, and addicted to war, were inferior to the Romans only in policy and discipline. They had been averse to the party of Cæsar, and would not, even in its highest prosperity, prefer it to the cause they had originally espoused. Being mixed with the remains of Roman armies which had been broken and dispersed in the field, they still maintained every place of defence against the conqueror; and, within the walls of cities to which they retired, defended themselves to the last extremity.

Cæsar, having been employed part of the spring and the following summer in subduing this scattered enemy, prepared to leave the province. He assembled the principal inhabitants at Hispalis; and having upbraided them with their animosity to himself and to the Roman people, he put them in mind of his early connexion with their country, as quæstor and as prætor, and of his repeated good offices in the capacity of senator and magistrate; having made a proper establishment for the government of the province, he set out for Italy,[1] and arrived at Rome in October.[2] Although it was contrary to the practice of former ages to admit of triumphs where the vanquished were fellow-citizens, he took a triumph for his late victory at Munda; and the more to amuse the people who, whatever be the occasion, are captivated with such exhibitions, he appointed separate triumphs, on the same account, to Q. Fabius Maximus, and to Didius, who had acted under him in that service.

These triumphs, over the supposed last defenders of the public liberty, and over the perishing remains of the family of Pompey, so long respected at Rome, instead of the festivity which they were intended to inspire, were attended with many signs of dejection. But none took upon him to censure, or was qualified to stem, the torrent of servility by which all orders of men were carried. The same succession of games and entertainments were ordered as in the former year. The senate and people indeed had no longer any concessions to be added to those already made to the conqueror, and it was difficult to refine on the language of adulation, which they had so amply employed in former decrees; but something to distinguish the present situation of affairs, to show the ardour of some to pay their court, and to disguise the discontent and the sorrow of others, was thought necessary on the present occasion. A thanksgiving was appointed, and ordered to continue for fifty days. The anniversary of the twentieth of April, the day on which the news of the victory at Munda was received at Rome, was ordered to be for ever celebrated with games of the circus.[3] Even they who felt a secret indignation at the elevation of a single person to act as lord of the commonwealth, concurred, in appearance, with these resolutions in honour of Cæsar.[4] They thought that the full cup was most likely to nauseate, and that extreme provocation was most likely to rouse the spirits of free men, if any yet remained.

In the concessions which were made to Cæsar, whether suggested by his friends or by his enemies, there was no attempt to preserve any appearance of the republic, or to veil the present usurpation. The senate, in presenting their several decrees, waited upon him in a body as subjects to acknowledge their sovereign; were received by him on his chair of state, and in all the form of a royal ceremony, stretching forth his hand to each as they approached. While he carried the external show of his elevation to this height, Pontius Acquilla, one of the tribunes, being seated in the exercise of his office, had suffered him, in one of his processions, to pass, without rising from his place. This he greatly resented. "Must I," he said to those who attended him, "refer the government to this tribune!" And for some days, in granting requests or petitions, he affected to guard his answers ironically, by saying, "Provided that Pontius Acquilla will permit."[5] The consulate was

---

1 Antony had set out from Rome to meet Cæsar but to the great surprise and alarm of every body, returned unexpectedly to Rome. Cicero ad Att. xii. 18. It was known afterwards, that Antony returned under the surprise of an order given by Cæsar to oblige him to pay for houses, &c. bought at Pompey's sale. Cicer. Phil. ii. 29. Ibid. xxxi. 29.

2 Velleius Paterculus.

3 Dio. Cassius.

4 Plutarch. in Cæs.

5 Sueton. in Cæs. c. 78

offered to him for ten years, but he declined it, as he destined this and the other offices of state for the gratification of his friends. He himself had assumed the title of consul in his late triumph, and immediately after resigned it to Q. Fabius Maximus.

Such, from henceforward, was to be the manner of conferring honours under the monarchy of Rome. Families had become noble in consequence of being admitted into the senate, or in consequence of having borne any of the higher offices of state, such as that of consul or prætor. Instead of titles, they recited the names of ancestors who had been in these offices, and instead of ensigns armorial, erected the effigies or images of such ancestors. Cæsar, that he might have more frequent opportunities to gratify his retainers, paid no regard to the customary establishment of the senate, and increased its numbers at pleasure, by inserting in the rolls persons of every description, to the amount of nine hundred. He augmented the number of prætors to fourteen, and that of quæstors to forty; and even, without requiring that his friends should pass through these offices, rewarded them at pleasure with the titular honours of consular, prætorian, patrician, &c.;[6] and extended his munificence likewise to the provinces, by admitting aliens separately, or in collective bodies, to the privilege or appellation of Roman citizens.

In the midst of appearances, which seemed to throw a ridicule on the ancient forms of the republic, as well as to substitute a military government in their stead, Cæsar named himself, together with Mark Antony, as consuls for the following year. This compliment paid to the civil establishment, by condescending to bear the name of legal office, though very illegally assumed, flattered the citizens with hope that he meant to govern under some form of a republic.[7] Nothing, however, followed from these appearances; the state which he affected, his dress, his laurel wreath, the colour and height of his buskins, the very seal which he chose to make use of, being the impression of a Venus armed, in ostentation of his supposed celestial extraction; the numerous guards and retinue, exceeding two thousand men, with which he was constantly attended;[8] the satisfaction with which he seemed to receive the forced servility of those whom his sword had subdued, betrayed a mind which, though possessed of real superiority, had not sufficient elevation to disdain the false appearances of it.

On the last day of the year, Q. Fabius Maximus, who had been a few months consul, died before he had vacated the office; and about noon of the same day, Cæsar, who had assembled the tribes, ordered them to take the form of the centuries, and to elect Caninius consul for the remainder of the day. Plutarch says, that Cicero exhorted the people to be speedy in paying their court to this new consul: "for this magistrate may be out of office before we can reach him." Cicero himself, referring to this farcical election, writes in a letter to one of his friends, "we have had a consulate, during which no one either ate or drank, and yet nothing extraordinary happened; for so great was the vigilance of this officer, that he never slept all the time he was in office. You may laugh at these things," he says; "but if you were here, you would cry."[9]

U. C. 709.

C. J. Cæsar, Dict. 4to. M. E. Lepidus, M. E. C. Octavius, Mag. Eq. Cn. Domitius Calvisius in sequentem annum designatus non iniit.

On the following day, Cæsar, with all the powers and ensigns of dictator, took possession of the consulate in conjunction with Antony. He intended, after having held this office for a few days in his own person, to resign it in favour of Dolabella, though a young man, still far short of the legal age. The execution of this intention, however, was some time delayed at the request of Mark Antony, who, being jealous of Dolabella, endeavoured to obstruct his preferment.

Cæsar himself passed the winter in assiduous application to civil affairs, and in forming projects to embellish the capital, and to aggrandize the empire. He made some regulations for the better government of the city. Under this title may be reckoned his prohibiting the use of letters, of purple, and of pearls, except to persons of a certain rank, and to them only at great festivals, and on remarkable occasions; together with his reviving the ancient sumptuary laws respecting the expense of the table. For the better execution of these laws, he appointed inspectors of the markets, with orders to seize all illicit articles of provision; and if any thing of this sort were known to escape the inspectors, he sent officers to seize them from the tables on which they were served. To check the luxury of the times in other articles, he imposed duties on the importation of foreign commodities.

Under the ordinary pretence, that the laws were become too voluminous, he ordered them to be digested into a code, with a view to simplify and to reduce them into a narrower compass; in this measure attempting a reformation which mankind, in certain situations, generally wish for, but which no man can accomplish without the possession of absolute power.

In the same spirit of despotical government, with which Cæsar abridged the laws, he acted at once as legislator and as a judge. As instances of his severity in the latter capacity, it is mentioned, that he annulled a marriage, because it had been contracted no more than two days after the woman had parted from a former husband; and to this he joined his punishing senators for extortion in the provinces, by expulsion from the senate.

His mind, at the same time, entertained projects of great variety and extent. To drain the great marshes which rendered the air so unhealthy, and so much land unserviceable in the neighbourhood of Rome; to cut across the isthmus of Corinth, to erect moles, and form harbours on the coast of Italy; to make highways across the Apennines; to build a new theatre that should exceed that of Pompey; to erect public libraries, and make a navigable canal from the Anio and the Tiber to the sea at Teracina; to

6 Dio. Cass. lib. xliii. c. 47.

7 Appian.

8 Cicer. ad Att. lib. xiii. ep. 52.

9 Cicero ad Familiar. lib. vii. ep. 10. Ita Caninio consule scito, nemine prandisse. Nihil tamen eo consule mali factum est. Fuit enim mirifica vigilantia qui toto suo consulatu somnum non viderit. Hæc tibi ridicula videntur: non enim ædis. Quæ si videris lachrymas non teneres.

build a magnificent temple to Mars. These projects are justly mentioned as meritorious in the sovereign of a great empire; and it must be confessed, that power would be but a wretched possession, if there were not something of this sort to be done after the toils of ambition were over.

The measure which of all others contributed most to the honour of Cæsar, did we suppose him entitled to the powers he assumed, was the general indemnity which he granted to all who had opposed him. Some he even employed in the administration of government, and promoted in the state. He placed Caius Cassius and Marcus Brutus, for this year, on the list of prætors, and entrusted them with the higher jurisdiction of the city. To the widows of many who died in opposition to himself, he restored their portions, and gave their children part of their patrimony.[1] He replaced the statues of Sylla and of Pompey, which the populace, in flattery to himself, had thrown down; "and by this means," says Cicero, "he firmly established his own.

It appeared, on many occasions, that Cæsar meant to contrast his own conduct with that of Sylla;[2] his own clemency with the bloody executions performed by the other. The comparison, no doubt, is curious, and must occur to every person who reads their story. Sylla had been excited, by extreme provocations, to turn his arms against a party in possession of the capital, and he drew his sword to punish injuries done no less to the republic than to himself. While he was master of the state, he acted indeed like a person who did not care how odious he rendered despotical power, for he did not mean to retain it. But he mixed with the resentment of a personal enemy, the high views of a noble citizen, who proposed to reform the state by clearing it of many corrupted and dangerous members. When he had accomplished this purpose, he disdained the pageantry of high station, was above receiving the adulation which proceeds from servility, or wishing to enjoy a continual precedence in the management of affairs, which requires no extraordinary capacity. Embarked by fortune on a tempestuous sea, when he had conducted the vessel safe into port, he quitted the helm; and after having been master, was not afraid to place himself among his countrymen as a fellow-citizen; and in this state of equality his greatness of mind secured to him a distinction, which no degree of precedency, and no measure of prerogative, could have bestowed.

To this character that of Cæsar, in many particulars, may be fairly considered as a contrast. He himself had stirred up the disorders which produced the civil war in which he engaged. He had no injuries either public or private to resent; his affected clemency, in sparing a few captives, in the beginning or in the course of his operations, was belied by the wantonness with which he entered on a war, in which the blood of many thousands of his fellow-citizens was to be unnecessarily shed.[3] If he had been reluctant in the shedding of blood, his mercy would have appeared, in avoiding so destructive a contest, not in ostentatiously sparing a few of the many whose lives his wanton ambition brought into h... ard. His clemency should have appeared at the Rubicon, not at Corfinium; in leaving his country to enjoy its liberties, not merely in sparing those whom no man in his senses would destroy, a people who were willing to submit, and whom he desired to govern.

Cæsar used to ridicule the resignation of Sylla as an act of imbecility,[4] and was himself fond of precedence as well as of power. The degree of vanity which he is said to had indulged, in accepting the frivolous honours which were now conferred upon him by acts of the senate, is indeed scarcely credible. Among these is mentioned a decree that he should have precedency of all magistrates, and the privilege of being always dressed in the triumphal robes; of having a gilded chair of state, and a place of distinction at all the public games; that he should be allowed to deposit a suit of armour in the temple of Jupiter Feretrius, an honour appropriated to those who, like Romulus, had killed, with their own hands, a leader of the enemy; that his lictors should have their fasces always bound with laurel; that himself, in coming from the Latin festivals, should enter the city on horseback; that he should have the title of Father of his Country, and be so designed on the coins; that the anniversary of his birth-day should be kept as a festival; that statues should be erected to him in all the towns of Italy, and in the temples of the city; that the statues, without any consideration of his titles to these honours, should be adorned with the civic and obsidionary crowns; the first a badge worn by those who had saved a fellow-citizen in battle, the second by those who had delivered the city itself from a siege.[5]

The senate and people, observing that these distinctions were agreeable to Cæsar, subjoined, that his robes should be cut in imitation of that of the ancient kings of Rome; that he should have an escort of knights and senators; that it should be permitted to swear to his destiny; that all his decrees, without exception, should be ratified; that, at the end of five years, a festival should be held in honour of him, as of a person of divine extraction; that an additional college of priests should be established to perform the rites which were instituted for that occasion; that in all gladiatorian sports, whether at Rome or in the provincial towns, one day should be dedicated to him; that a crown of gold set with gems, like those of the gods, should be carried before him into the circus, attended with a thensus or car like that on which the idols of the gods were carried; that he should have the title of Julian Jove—have a temple erected for himself, in conjunction with the goddess of Clemency—and, to complete the ridicule of these institutions, that Mark Antony should be appointed the priest of this sacred fane.[6]

From these particulars, which, to characterise

1 Sueton. Dio. lib. xliii.

2 Quonium reliqui crudelitate odium effugere non potuerunt neque victoriam diutius tenere, præter unum L. Syllam quem imitaturus non sum. Hæc nova sit ratio vincendi, ut misericordia et liberalitate nos muniamus. Cicer. ad Att. lib. ix. ep. 7.

3 It is said that 400,000 Romans perished in this contest.

4 Syllam nescisse literas qui dictaturam deposuerit. Sueton. in Jul. Cæs. lib. lxxvii.

5 Dio. Cass. lib. xliv. c. 4.

6 Ibid. c. 6.

the ambition of the person to whom they refer, and the manners of the age, are selected from those mentioned by the original historian,[7] it was no longer to be doubted, that Cæsar wished to establish a monarchy on the ruins of the republic. He himself was extremely arrogant in his behaviour, and so unguarded in his expressions as to say, That the republic was but a name, that his words should be carefully observed, for that he meant every word should have the force of a law.

To so much arrogance and affectation of kingly state, joined to absolute power, nothing was wanting but the title of King. This Cæsar himself evidently appeared to have the vanity to desire. His retainers and flatterers, on different occasions, endeavoured to surprise the people into a concession of it; but notwithstanding the powers of sovereignty, which he exercised without control, and the honours of divinity, which were decreed to him by general consent, his influence was not sufficient to reconcile the Roman people to the name of King. One of his emissaries, willing to suggest the propriety of bestowing this title, or to insinuate Cæsar's purpose of assuming it, had bound the head of one of his statues with a royal fillet. The tribunes Marullus and Cæsetius, affecting great zeal for the honour of Cæsar, as well as for the majesty of the Roman state, made inquiry after the author of an insinuation so derogatory to both; and receiving information of the guilty person, in order to check such insinuations for the future, sent him to prison. This officious interposition of the tribunes, though pretending to vindicate Cæsar himself from so odious an imputation, he received with marks of displeasure; and hearing these officers extolled as the restorers of the public liberty with the appellation of the *Bruti*, "Brutes indeed," he said they were; but took no farther notice of the matter.

Soon after this incident, some one, or a few in the assembly of the people, saluted him with the title of king. But on hearing, instead of acclamations, a general murmur of dislike, he silenced this unreasonable piece of flattery, saying, That his name was *Cæsar*, and not *king*. Here too the tribunes again interposed, and raised prosecutions against the authors of such treasonable expressions. But in this instance Cæsar lost his patience, and complained in the senate that factious men, under the pretence of discharging the public office of magistracy, propagated insinuations injurious to his character, and tending to alarm the people with false apprehensions. Such offences, he said, merit capital punishment; but he should be satisfied with degradation from office. This sentence was accordingly inflicted; and from thenceforward it was not doubted, that Cæsar aspired to the title, as well as the power of a monarch.

This opinion was still farther confirmed, when on the sixteenth of February,[8] at the *Lupercalia* (a festival, which being continued down from barbarous ages, served as a monument of primæval simplicity and rudeness), the same piece of flattery, in making tender of a crown, was renewed by Antony, then in the office of consul, and the chief confidant of Cæsar.

It was the custom in this festival of the Lupercalia, for the first officers of state, and the first of the nobles to present themselves naked in the streets, carrying thongs of undressed hide, with which they ran through the crowd, and struck at those who happened to be placed within their reach. The stroke was thought a remedy, in particular, for barrenness in women; and numbers of this sex crowded in the way to receive it.

In the ceremony now to be performed, Mark Antony bore his part as consul; and Cæsar sat on his gilded chair of state in his triumphal robes to behold the spectacle. Antony stopped before him, and presented him with a royal crown, saying, "This crown the Roman people confer upon Cæsar by my hands." A few of the spectators seemed to applaud; but Cæsar, perceiving that the people in general, by their silence, gave signs of displeasure, pushed away the crown with his hand; and upon this action, received from the people, by an universal shout of applause, an unquestionable explanation of their former silence.

To try the effect of a moderation which was so much applauded, Antony threw himself upon the ground at Cæsar's feet, repeated his offer of the crown, and hoped that the people might join him in pressing the acceptance of what was so modestly refused; but with no better success than in the former attempt.

That the merit of this refusal, however, might not be forgotten, or that the offer might be held equal to the actual investiture of the crown, an entry was made in the Fasti or public records, by the directions of Antony, "That the consul having, by the order of the Roman people, presented a crown, and offered to confer the majesty of king on Caius Julius Cæsar, perpetual dictator, he had declined to receive it."[9]

The Roman republic had, for some time, subsisted in a very disorderly state; the people having dominion over many other nations, scarcely admitted any species of government among themselves. The inhabitants of Rome, assuming the prerogatives of the collective body of Roman citizens, who now not only extended over all Italy, but were dispersed throughout the empire, generally assembled in tumults, whose proceedings nothing but force could regulate, and at every convulsion gave an immediate prospect of military government. All who wished to preserve the republic, endeavoured to extend the prerogatives of the senate, and to prevent, as much as possible, these ill-formed assemblies of the people from deliberating on matters of state; and it might, no doubt, have been still better for the empire, if the spirit of legal monarchy could at once have been infused into every part of the commonwealth; or if, without farther pangs or convulsions, the authority of a prince, tempered with that of a senate, had been firmly established. But men do not at once change their habits and opinions, nor yield their own pretensions upon speculative notions of what is suited to the state of their country. Cæsar aspired to dominion in order to gratify his personal vanity, not to correct the political errors of the times; and his contemporaries born to the rights of citizens, still contended for personal independence and equality, however impossible it might be longer to preserve

7 Dio. Cass. lib. xliv. c. 6.
8 Cicer. Philip. ii. c. 34.

9 Cicer. Philip. ii. c. 34.

any species of republic at the head of such an empire.

Ever since the expulsion of Tarquin, the name of king had been odious at Rome. The most popular citizens, as soon as they became suspected of aspiring to kingly power, became objects of aversion, and were marked out as a prey to the detestation of their country. Thus fell Manlius Capitolinus, the Gracchi, Apuleius, and others who were loaded with this imputation.

The Romans, accustomed to see vanquished kings the sport of popular insolence, led in triumph, put to death; or if suffered to live, made to languish in poverty and neglect—accustomed to see kings, who were their own allies, submitting their cause to the judgment of the Roman people, or suing for favour, considered monarchy itself as an appurtenance of servility and barbarism; and the project to give a king to the Romans as an attempt to degrade them into barbarians and slaves.

The maxim, which forbids assassination in every case whatever, is the result of prudent reflection, and has a tendency to allay the jealousy, and to mitigate the cruelty of persons who, by violent usurpations, which laws cannot restrain, have incurred the resentment of mankind. Even tyrants, it is supposed, are cruel from fear, and become merciful in proportion as they believe themselves secure; it were unwise, therefore, to entertain maxims which keep the powerful in a continual state of distrust and alarm. This prudential morality, however, was entirely unknown in the ancient republics, or could not be observed, without surrendering the freedom for which the citizens contended. Amongst them the people were obliged to consider, not what was safe, but what was necessary; and could not always defend themselves against usurpations, neither by legal forms, nor by open war. It was thought allowable, therefore, to employ artifice, surprise, and secret conspiracy against an usurper; and this was so much the case at Rome, that no names were held in greater veneration, than those of citizens who had assassinated persons suspected of views dangerous to the commonwealth; or who, by any means whatever, rendered abortive the projects of adventurers who attempted to arm any party against the legal constitution of their country.

Cæsar, having attempted to join the title of king with the powers of perpetual dictator, had reason to distrust a people who were actuated by such conceptions. He was an object of private as well as of public resentment, having usurped the government over those whom he had cruelly injured; over the fathers, the brothers, and sons of those who had fallen by his sword. He accordingly, for some time, had the precaution to keep a military guard attending his person; but, grown familiar with those he had offended, and secure in his personal courage, he dropt this precaution, and began to reign with the confidence of a lawful monarch. Although he had incurred so much resentment, he disdained to stand in awe of it, and ventured to join the confidence of innocence with the highest measures of guilt. This conduct indeed was uncommon, and the effect of a daring courage, but unworthy of the penetration and skill with which he had hitherto conducted his affairs. It may serve to confirm, what has been already observed, that, amongst the many accomplishments which he possessed, and together with the abilities which rendered him superior to every direct opposition, he was actuated by a vanity which bordered on weakness. Misled, perhaps, by this passion, he persisted in his emulation to the glory of Sylla, and would show to the world, that he who had not resigned his power could walk the streets of Rome, unattended, with as much safety as the other, who had the magnanimity to restore the constitution of his country; joined to this weakness, he had too mean an opinion of those who composed the commonwealth, greatly sunk indeed in their political characters, but not fallen into that state of personal weakness, which his security and contempt of them seemed to imply.

Above sixty citizens of noble extraction were found, who thought their late condition as members of the republic could still be recovered. Some had been stunned with their fall, but not quite overwhelmed; others, who, on specious pretences, had assisted in obtaining the victories of Cæsar, detested the monarchy which he was pleased to assume. In the first period of the civil war many imagined, that the contest was to end in substituting one party for another, not in the entire subversion of the republican government; and they were inclined, as soon as fortune should declare in favour of either party, to be reconciled with those that prevailed.[1] But when it evidently appeared, that Cæsar, by suppressing the last remains of opposition to himself in every part of the empire, meant to establish a monarchy in his own person, a secret indignation filled the breasts of those who, upon a foot of family consequence, or personal ability, had any pretensions to political importance. To such persons the dominion of an equal appeared insufferable. Many of them affected servility, in conferring the extravagant honours which had been decreed to Cæsar, as the mask of a sullen displeasure, which, conscious of a tendency to betray itself, took the disguise of the opposite extreme.

The question respecting the expedience of monarchical government did not enter into the deliberations of any one. If it had been urged that a king was necessary; it would have been asked, Who gave the right to Cæsar? If the people in general were corrupt, were the bankrupts, and outlaws, and soldiers of fortune that formed the court of Cæsar unblemished? If the great, the able, and experienced citizens, who were qualified to support the republic, were now no more, by whose sword had they perished? or who was to blame for the ruin that had befallen the commonwealth? If the corrupt arts, the treasons, the murders, encouraged or executed by Cæsar, had made a change of government necessary, the first act of that new government, for the instruction of mankind, ought to have been to punish the author of so many disorders and crimes, not to reward him with a crown.

Many of Cæsar's officers, and the nearest to his person, were as much in this mind as any other citizens; and on this supposition, so familiar was the thought of proceeding to the last extremities against him, that, when Antony came to meet Cæsar, on his return from Spain, Trebo-

1 Cicero ad Familiar.
2 Cicer. Philip. lib. II. c. 14.

nius ventured to sound his inclinations respecting a design on Cæsar's life.[3] Although Antony did not adopt the measure, he did not betray Trebonius, nor did he appear to be surprised at the proposal. It was afterwards suggested, that Antony should be invited to a share in the conspiracy; and the proposal was dropt only on account of the refusal which he had already given to Trebonius; so readily was it believed, that every noble Roman would rather share in the government of his country, as an independent citizen, than as a retainer to the most successful usurper.

It is well known, that a conspiracy accordingly was, at this time, formed against the life of Cæsar, although the first steps and the consultations of the parties are no where minutely recorded. The principal authors of it were Caius Cassius and Marcus Brutus, then prætors in the city; Decimus Brutus and Trebonius, who had both served in high rank under Cæsar himself, and of whom the first was destined by him to the command in Cisalpine Gaul, and to the consulate in the following year.

Caius Cassius was early noted for a high and impetuous spirit. It is observed, that being a boy when Sylla was at the height of his power, he struck the son of the dictator for having said, That his father was the master of the Roman people. The tutor of young Sylla having carried a complaint to Pompey, the boys were called, and questioned on the subject of the quarrel, "Do but repeat your words again," said Cassius; "and in this presence I will strike you." He had distinguished himself in Syria, by collecting the remains of the unfortunate army of Crassus, with which he repelled the attempt of the Parthians on that province. He followed Pompey in the civil war, and commanded a squadron of the fleet on the coast of Sicily at the time of the battle of Pharsalia. From thence he went into Asia, with a professed intention to wait for the arrival of the victor from Alexandria, and to drop all farther opposition against him; but even then, according to Cicero, would have put Cæsar to death, if he had not debarked on a different side of the Cydnus, from that on which he was at first expected to land.[4]

Marcus Brutus was the nephew of Cato by his sister Servilia; and so much the favourite of Cæsar, who was said to have had an intrigue with his mother, that he was by some supposed to be his son. The father of Brutus, in the civil wars of Sylla, had been on the side of Marius, and having fallen into Pompey's hands, was by him put to death. The son retained so much resentment on this account, that he never accosted or saluted Pompey till after the civil war broke out; when, thinking it necessary to sacrifice all private considerations to the public cause, he joined him in Macedonia, and was received with great marks of distinction. This young man, either on account of his uncle Cato, or on account of the expectation generally entertained of himself, was held in the highest estimation. Being taken prisoner at the battle of Pharsalia, he was not only protected by the victor, but sent into the province of Cisalpine Gaul with the title of governor; where, during the war in Africa against Scipio and the king of Numidia, he remained, perhaps, rather under safe custody than in high confidence with Cæsar. He was this year, together with Caius Cassius, who married his sister, promoted to the dignity of prætor; and though of less standing than Cassius, had the precedence by the partiality of Cæsar. This circumstance was supposed, at the time that Brutus and Cassius were actually framing their conspiracy, to have occasioned a breach between them.

Cassius is reputed to have been the prime mover in the design against Cæsar's life; and to have been the author of anonymous calls to vindicate the freedom of Rome, which were posted up or dropped in public places; and which, from the prevailing spirit of discontent, found a ready acceptance. Labels were hung upon the statues of the ancient Brutus, and billets were dropped, in the night, upon the judgment-seat of the prætor of this name, exciting him to imitate his ancestors, by restoring the republic; "You sleep, you are not Brutus;" and on the statues of his supposed ancestor, the elder Brutus, was written, "Would you were alive!" These expressions of a secret disaffection, and prognostics of some violent design, either escaped the attention of Cæsar, or were despised by him; but were easily understood by persons who looked for a deliverance from the indignities to which they felt themselves exposed. While Cassius and Marcus Brutus entered into a formal concert on this subject, numbers pined under the want of that consideration to which they thought themselves born; many were provoked by particular instances of vanity or arrogance in the present dictator;[5] and upon the least hint of a design against him, were ready to join. "I am sorry you should be ill at so critical a time," said Brutus to Legarius. "I am not ill," said the other, "if you have any intentions worthy of yourself."[6]

Great numbers daily acceded to the plot, of whom the following, besides Brutus and Cassius, are the principal names upon record: Cæcilius, and Bucolianus, two brothers; Rubrius Rex, Q. Ligarius, M. Spurius, Servilius Galba, Sextius Naso, Pontius Acquila. These had ever been on the side of the senate, or adherents of Pompey. The following had acted in the war under Cæsar; Decimus Brutus, C. Casca, Trebonius, Tullius Cimber, Minucius, and Basilus;[7] they are said in all to have amounted to sixty.[8] Cicero was known to detest the usurpation of Cæsar; to mourn over the fall of the commonwealth, over the humiliation of the senate, and the diminution of his

3 Cicer. Philip. lib. ii. c. 14.

4 Ibid. c. 11.

5 Cæsar had about this time, a visit from the queen of Egypt, who lived with him at his gardens on the Tiber. (Cicer. ad Attic. lib. xiv.) Many who overlooked his usurpation, and the violence he did to the constitution of his country, were scandalized at the intimacy in which he lived with this woman. Being accustomed to the distinctions of a court, and considering Cæsar as the monarch, she treated the citizens, who were still admitted to him on a foot of equality, as dependants and subjects. He himself, with all his state, was polite. As an apology for having made Cicero wait too long in his anti-chamber, he accosted him with saying, "How can I hope to be tolerated, when even Marcus Tullius Cicero is made to wait? If any one could forgive it, he would; but the world must detest me." Cleopatra, it is probable, made no such apology when she gave cause to complain of her arrogance.

6 Sueton. in Cæsare.

7 Appian. de Bell. Civ. lib. ii.

8 Sueton. in Cæsar

own political consequence; but he was not consulted in this design. The authors of it relied on his support, in case they should be successful; but they knew too well his ingenuity in suggesting scruples and difficulties, to bring him into their previous deliberations on so arduous an enterprize.

The conspirators, in forming their project, generally sounded the minds of persons before they made any formal or direct proposal. Brutus being in company with Statilius, Favonius, and Labio, proposed, among other problematical questions, some doubts concerning the expediency of assassinating tyrants. Favonius observed, that such actions led to civil war, and that this was worse than usurpation. Statilius said, that no wise man would engage in so hazardous an enterprise to serve a parcel of knaves and fools. Labio contended warmly with both; and Brutus changing the subject, thought no more of Statilius or Favonius, but communicated the design to Labio, who immediately embraced it.

As so many were concerned, and as they remained some time in suspense as to the proper time and place for the execution of their purpose, it is singular that the conspiracy should have come to such a height undiscovered. But Cæsar did not encourage informers; his great courage preserved him from the jealousies by which others in less dangerous situations are guided. He trusted to his popularity, to his munificence, to the professions of submission which were made to him, and to the interest which he supposed many to have in the preservation of his life. He had not only dismissed the guards, which at his return to Rome had attended him; and was commonly preceded only by his lictors and the usual retinue of his civil rank; but had suffered the veterans to disperse on the lands which had been assigned to them, unfurnished Italy of troops, and had transported the greater part of the army into Macedonia, reserving only a small body under Lepidus in the suburbs of Rome. His own mind, though fond of appearance of superiority, it is probable, was easily satiated with the pageantry of state. His thoughts became vacant and languid in the possession of a station to which he had struggled through so much blood; and his active mind still urged him to extensive projects of war and conquest.[1] He accordingly planned a series of wars which were not likely to end but with his life. He was to begin with revenging the death of Crassus, and reducing the Parthians. He was next to pass by Hyrcania and the coasts of the Caspian Sea into Scythia; from thence, by the shores of the Euxine Sea, into Sarmacia, Dacia, and Germany; and from thence, by his own late conquests in Gaul, to return into Italy;[2] for this purpose he had already sent forward into Macedonia seventeen legions and ten thousand horse.[3]

As Cæsar was likely, whatever may have been the extent of his projects, to be employed some time in the execution of them, he thought proper to anticipate the election of magistrates at Rome, and to arrange, before his departure, the whole succession to office for some years. Dion Cassius says, that his arrangement was made for three years; Appian, for five years. It is certain, that he fixed the succession to office for two subsequent years. Hirtius and Pansa were destined to the consulate in the first; Decimus Brutus and Plancus, in the second.[4] He continued to increase the number of magistrates, that he might have more opportunities to gratify his retainers and friends. The quæstors, as has been mentioned, he augmented to forty, the ædiles to six, the prætors to sixteen. Among the latter he named Ventidius, a native of Picenum, who had been taken and led in triumph, while the people of that district, with the other Italians, on account of their claim of being enrolled as citizens, were at war with Rome. Ventidius had subsisted by letting mules and carriages. In the pursuit of this business he had followed the army of Cæsar into Gaul; and becoming known to that general, was gradually trusted and advanced by him. His career of preferment continued up to the dignity of consul, and he himself, as has been formerly observed, came at last to lead, in the capacity of a victorious general, a procession of the same kind with that in which he had made his first entry at Rome as a captive.

This arrangement, in which Cæsar, by anticipating the nomination of magistrates, precluded the citizens from the usual exercise of their rights of election, made the subversion of the republic more felt than any of the former acts of his power, and gave the leaders of the conspiracy a great advantage against him. The prospect of his approaching departure from Rome, which was fixed for the month of March, urged the speedy execution of their purpose. The report of a response or prediction, which some of the flatterers of Cæsar had procured from the college of Augurs, bearing that the Parthians were not to be subdued but by a king,[5] appeared to be the prelude of a motion to vest him, in his intended expedition against the Parthians, with the title, and with the ensigns of royalty, to be borne, if not in the city, at least in the provinces.[6]

A meeting of the senate being already summoned, for the Ides, or fifteenth, of March, the proposal to bestow on Cæsar the title of king, as a qualification enjoined by the Sybils to make war on the Parthians, was expected to be the principal business of the assembly. This circumstance determined the conspirators in the choice of a place for the execution of their design. They had formerly deliberated, whether to pitch upon the Campus Martius, and to strike their blow in the presence of the Roman people assembled, or in the entry to the theatre, or in a street through which Cæsar often passed in the way to his own house.[7] But this meeting of the senate seemed now to present the most convenient place, and the most favourable opportunity. The presence of the senate, it was supposed, would render the action of the conspirators sufficiently awful and solemn; the common cause would be instantly acknowledged by all the members of that body; and the execution done would be justified under their authority. If any were disposed to resist, they were not likely to be armed; and the affair might be ended by the death of Cæsar alone, or without any effusion of blood beyond that which was originally intended.

1 Dio. Cass. Appian. Plutarch.
2 Plutarch in Cæsare.
3 Appian. de Bell. Civil. lib. ii.
4 Cicero ad Attic. lib. xiv. ep. 6.
5 Dio. Cass. lib. xliv c. 15.
6 Zonaras, lib. x. c. 14.
7 Sueton. in Cæsare.

It was at first proposed that Antony, being likely to carry on the same military usurpations which Cæsar had begun, should be taken off at the same time; but this was overruled. It was supposed that Antony, and every other senator and citizen, would readily embrace the state of independence and personal consideration which was to be offered to them; or if they should not embrace it, they would not be of sufficient numbers or credit to distress the republic, or to overset that balance of parties in which the freedom of the whole consisted. It was supposed that the moment Cæsar fell, there would not be any one left to covet or to support a usurpation which had been so unfortunate in his person. "If we do any thing more than is necessary to set the Romans at liberty," said Marcus Brutus, "we shall be thought to act from private resentment, and to intend restoring the party of Pompey, not the republic."[8]

The intended assembly of the senate was to be held in one of the recesses of Pompey's theatre. It was determined by the conspirators, that they should repair to this meeting as usual, either separately, or in the retinue of the consuls and prætors; and that, being armed with concealed weapons, they should proceed to the execution of their purpose as soon as Cæsar had taken his seat. To guard against any disturbance or tumult that might arise to frustrate their intentions, Decimus Brutus, who was master of a troop of gladiators, undertook to have this troop, under pretence of exhibiting some combats on that day to the people, posted in the theatre, and ready at his command for any service.[9]

During the interval of suspense which preceded the meeting of the senate, although in public Brutus seemed to perform all the duties of his station with an unaltered countenance; at home he was less guarded, and frequently appeared to have something uncommon on his mind. His wife Porcia suspected that some arduous design respecting the state was in agitation; and when she questioned him, was confirmed in this apprehension, by his eluding her inquiries. Thinking herself, by her extraction and by her alliance, entitled to confidence, she bore this appearance of distrust with regret; and, under the idea that the secret which was withheld from her, must be such as, upon any suspicion, might occasion the torture to be employed to force a confession; and supposing that she herself was distrusted more on account of the weakness than of the indiscretion of her sex, she determined to make a trial of her own strength, before she desired that the secret should be communicated to her. For this purpose she gave herself a wound in the thigh, and while it festered, and produced acute pain and fever, she endeavoured to preserve her usual countenance, without any sign of suffering or distress. Being satisfied with this trial of her own strength, she told her husband the particulars, and with some degree of triumph added, "*Now you may trust me; I am the wife of Brutus and the daughter of Cato; keep me no longer in doubt or suspense upon any subject in which I too must be so deeply concerned.*" The circumstance of her wound, the pretensions which she otherwise had to confidence, drew the secret from her husband, and undoubtedly from thence forward, by the passions which were likely to agitate the mind of a tender and affectionate woman, exposed the design to additional hazard of a discovery and of a failure.

But the morning of the Ides of March, the day on which this conspiracy was to be executed, arrived, and there was yet no suspicion. The conspirators had been already together at the house of one of the prætors. Cassius was to present his son that morning to the people, with the ceremony usual in assuming the habit of manhood; and he was, upon this account, to be attended by his friends into the place of assembly. He was afterwards, together with Brutus, in their capacity of magistrates, employed as usual, in giving judgment on the causes that were brought before them. As they sat in the prætor's chair they received intimation that Cæsar, having been indisposed over night, was not to be abroad; and that he had commissioned Antony, in his name, to adjourn the senate to another day. Upon this report, they suspected a discovery; and while they were deliberating what should be done, Popilius Lænas, a senator whom they had not entrusted with their design, whispered them as he passed, "I pray that God may prosper what you have in view. Above all things despatch." Their suspicions of a discovery being thus still farther confirmed, the intention soon after appeared to be public. An acquaintance told Casca, "You have concealed this business from me, but Brutus told me of it." They were struck with surprise; but Brutus presently recollected that he had mentioned to this person no more than Casca's intention of standing for ædile, and that the words which he spoke probably referred only to that business; they accordingly determined to wait the issue of these alarms.[10]

In the mean time Cæsar, at the persuasion of Decimus Brutus, though once determined to remain at home, had changed his mind, and was already in the streets, being carried to the senate in his litter. Soon after he had left his own house, a slave came thither in haste, desired protection, and said he had a secret of the greatest moment to impart. He had probably overheard the conspirators, or had observed that they were armed; but not being aware how pressing the time was, he suffered himself to be detained till Cæsar's return. Others, probably, had observed circumstances which led to a discovery of the plot, and Cæsar had a billet to this effect given to him as he passed in the streets; he was intreated by the person who gave it instantly to read it; and he endeavoured to do so, but was prevented by the multitudes who crowded around him with numberless applications; and he still carried this paper in his hand when he entered the senate.

Brutus and most of the conspirators had taken their places a little while before the arrival of Cæsar, and continued to be alarmed by many circumstances which tended to shake their resolution. Porcia, in the same moments, being in great agitation, exposed herself to public notice. She listened with anxiety to every noise in the streets; she despatched, without any pretence of

8 Dio Cass. lib. xliv. c. 15.

9 Ibid.

10 Appian. de Bell. Civil. lib. ii.

business, continual messages towards the place where the senate was assembled; she asked every person who came from that quarter if they observed what her husband was doing. Her spirit at last sunk under the effect of such violent emotions; she fainted away, and was carried for dead into her apartment. A message came to Brutus in the senate with this account. He was much affected, but kept his place.[1] Popilius Lænas, who a little before seemed, from the expression he had dropped, to have got notice of their design, appeared to be in earnest conversation with Cæsar, as he lighted from his carriage. This left the conspirators no longer in doubt that they were discovered; and they made signs to each other, that it would be better to die by their own hands than to fall into the power of their enemy. But they saw of a sudden the countenance of Lænas change into a smile, and perceived that his conversation with Cæsar could not relate to such a business as theirs.

Cæsar's chair of state had been placed near to the pedestal of Pompey's statue. Numbers of the conspirators had seated themselves around it. Trebonius, under pretence of business, had taken Antony aside at the entrance of the theatre. Cimber, who, with others of the conspirators, met Cæsar in the portico, presented him with a petition in favour of his brother who had been excepted from the late indemnity; and in urging the prayer of this petition, attended the dictator to his place. Having there received a denial from Cæsar, uttered with some expressions of impatience at being so much importuned, he took hold of his robe, as if to press the intreaty. *Nay*, said Cæsar, *this is violence.* While he spoke these words, Cimber flung back the gown from his shoulders; and this being the signal agreed upon, called out to strike. Casca aimed the first blow. Cæsar started from his place, and in the first moment of surprise, pushed Cimber with one arm, and laid hold of Casca with the other. But he soon perceived that resistance was vain; and while the swords of the conspirators clashed with each other, in their way to his body, he wrapped himself up in his gown, and fell without any farther struggle. It was observed, in the superstition of the times, that in falling, the blood which sprung from his wounds sprinkled the pedestal of Pompey's statue. And thus having employed the greatest abilities to subdue his fellow-citizens, with whom it would have been a much greater honour to have been able to live on terms of equality, he fell in the height of his security, a sacrifice to their just indignation; a striking example of what the arrogant have to fear in trifling with the feelings of a free people, and at the same time a lesson of jealousy and of cruelty to tyrants, or an admonition not to spare, in the exercise of their power, those whom they may have insulted by usurping it.

When the body lay breathless on the ground, Cassius called out, that there lay the worst of men.[2] Brutus called upon the senate to judge of the transaction which had passed before them, and was proceeding to state the motives of those who were concerned in it, when the members, who had for a moment stood in silent amazement, rose on a sudden, and began to separate in great consternation. All those who had come to the senate in the train of Cæsar, his lictors, the ordinary officers of state, citizens, and foreigners, with many servants and dependants of every sort, had been instantly seized with a panic; and as if the swords of the conspirators were drawn against themselves, had already rushed into the streets, and carried terror and confusion wherever they went. The senators themselves now followed. No man had presence of mind to give any account of what had happened, but repeated the cry that was usual on great alarms for all persons to withdraw, and to shut up their habitations and shops. This cry was communicated from one to another in the streets. The people, imagining that a general massacre was somewhere begun, shut up, and barred all their doors as in the dead of night, and every one prepared to defend his own habitation.

Antony, upon the first alarm had changed his dress, and retired to a place of safety. He believed that the conspirators must have intended to take his life, together with that of Cæsar; and he fled in the apprehension of being instantly pursued. Lepidus repaired to the suburbs, where the legion he commanded was quartered; and uncertain whether Cæsar's death was the act of the whole senate, or of a private party, waited for an explanation, or an order from the surviving consul, to determine in what manner he should act.[3] In these circumstances a general pause, and an interval of suspense and silence, took place over the whole city.

CHAPTER II.

General Consternation on the Death of Cæsar—Tumultuary Assembly of the People—Declarations of Cinna and Dolabella—Appearance of Brutus and Cassius in the Forum—Their return to the Capitol—Meeting and Debate in the Senate—Act of Oblivion—Speech of Brutus to the People—Funeral of Cæsar—Insurrection of the People—Policy of Antony—Appearance of Octavius—His Difference with Antony—Both have recourse to Arms—Aspect of Things—Antony proceeds to expel Decimus Brutus from the Cisalpine Gaul.

IN the general consternation, occasioned by the death of Cæsar, the authors of this important event appeared to be no less at a loss what to do, than the other members of the senate, on whom it was brought by surprise. The danger of executing the first part of their design had appeared so great, that they looked no farther, or they imagined that with Cæsar's life every difficulty would be ended; and that the senate and people, restored to their authority and privileges, would naturally recur to their usual forms. Finding

1 Plut. in Bruto.
2 Cicer. ad Famil. lib. xii. ep. 1. Nequissimum occisum esse.
3 Appian. de Bell. Civ. lib. ii.

themselves deserted in the senate, and not knowing to what dangers they might still be exposed, they wrapped up the left arm in their gowns; a preparation which the Romans, in the habit of using a shield, generally made when alarmed with any prospect of violence.

The conspirators thus in a body, with their swords yet stained with blood, went forth to the streets proclaiming security and liberty, and inviting every one to concur with them in restoring the commonwealth. They were joined by many who, though not accessary to the conspiracy, chose to embark with them in the present state of their fortunes. Of these are particularly mentioned Lentulus Spinther, Favonius, Acquinas, Dolabella, Murcus, Peticus, and Cinna. But observing that the people in general did not show any hearty approbation of their cause; and knowing that, besides the legion which Lepidus commanded in the suburbs, there were in the city multitudes of veterans, who having received grants of land from Cæsar, either had not yet gone to take possession of them, or having been at their settlements, had returned to pay court to their patron before his departure from Rome; and suspecting that Antony, now the sole consul and supreme officer of state, was likely to exert the powers of a magistrate against them; and being on every side beset with dangers of which they knew not the extent, they determined to take refuge in the capitol, and with the gladiators of Decimus Brutus, who had already taken possession of that fortress, to wait the issue of this general scene of suspense.

Multitudes of the people, observing that the persons who had occasioned this general alarm were themselves on the defensive, and no way inclined to extend the effusion of blood, ventured forth into the streets, and many crowded together in the forum or ordinary place of resort.[4] The first person that took any public part upon this occasion was Cinna, the son of him who had been a leader of the Marian party, brother-in-law of Cæsar, and now, by his nomination, advanced to the dignity of prætor. This relation of the deceased, to the surprise of every one, tore the prætor's gown from his own shoulders; declared that in this act he then abdicated his office, as having been unwarrantably obtained by the nomination of an usurper; and he proceeded to make a harangue to the people, in which he represented Cæsar as a tyrant, extolled the conspirators as the restorers of liberty to their country, and proposed that they should have the proper safeguards to their persons, and be invited to assist in the assembly of the people.

Dolabella, who had been nominated by Cæsar to succeed in the office of consul, which he himself was about to vacate, thinking that the intended succession was now open to him upon Cæsar's death, reversed the first part of Cinna's conduct, by assuming the robes and ensigns of consul, to which he had no title; but joined with the abdicated prætor in applauding the authors of Cæsar's death, expressed his wish that he himself had been a partner in the glory of their action, joined with Cinna, in proposing that these restorers of liberty should be invited to the assembly of the people, and that the anniversary of the present day should be observed for ever, as a festival sacred to the restoration of the commonwealth.

The partizans of Cæsar, yet unacquainted with the extent of their own danger, had absented themselves, and the assembly consisted chiefly of persons to whom these proposals were agreeable. The motions that were now made by the late prætor and the supposed consul accordingly prevailed, and the leaders of the conspiracy were invited to descend from the capitol. But of this invitation only Marcus Brutus and Cassius took the benefit. Having joined the assembly, they severally addressed themselves to the multitude with an air of dignity and consciousness of merit, as being the procurers of that liberty which the people were now to enjoy, and by which they were enabled to judge for themselves. They contrasted the late usurpation of Cæsar[5] with the free constitution of the republic; observed, that with respect to themselves, unsupported as they were by any military force, they could have no intention to supplant the usurper in the possession of his power, and could have no object besides the restoration of the laws and the freedom of their country. And they exhorted the audience, in terms rather popular, than really applicable to the present state of affairs, to make the same use of their deliverance from an usurped and violent domination which their ancestors, at the expulsion of Tarquin, had made of a similar event. They specified the merit which many persons had in this enterprise, particularly that of Decimus Brutus, who had furnished the company of gladiators, which, in entering on this business, made the principal part of their strength; and observed, that, notwithstanding the splendid fortune to which Decimus Brutus might have aspired under Cæsar's influence, he had preferred the rights of his fellow-citizens and the restoration of the commonwealth. They turned the attention of the audience on the case of Sexteius Pompeius, the only surviving son of the great Pompey, now unjustly deemed an outlaw and a rebel.[6] "In the person of this young man," they said, "you have the last of a noble family, who, in the contest for freedom, have sacrificed themselves for the republic, even he is still beset by the emissaries of the late usurper, who, pretending public authority, are armed for his destruction with swords, yet red with the blood of his father and of his brother." They moved the people, that so unjust a war should be instantly suspended, and that this young man should be restored to the rights of his ancestors; that the tribunes Cæsetius and Marullus, being unjustly degraded by Cæsar, in violation of that sacred law, which he himself, upon much less grounds, had made his pretence for a civil war, should now be restored to all their dignities.

4 Appian says, that the friends of the conspirators, by distributing money, endeavoured to form a party among the populace. The necessity of this expedient, if real, is sufficient to show how desperate the attempt was of restoring democratical government to the inhabitants of Rome, composed of the refuse of Italy, and of the provinces collected to enjoy the rewards of idleness and faction.

5 Appian. de Bello Civili, lib. ii. Dio. Cass. lib. xliv. c. 21.

6 This young man having absconded for some time after the defeat and death of his brother at Munda, had again appeared in Spain at the head of a considerable force, and defeated Asinius Pollio, who had been employed by Cæsar against him.

In these fond anticipations of freedom, the authors of this attempt to restore the republic, enjoyed for once the fruits of their labour, and spoke to a numerous assembly of the Roman people, seemingly unrestrained and unawed by military force. The city, however, had not yet recovered from the consternation with which the people was seized; the present assembly was not sufficiently attended by persons, on whom the conspirators could rely for their safety. It was thought most prudent, therefore, that Brutus and Cassius should return to their friends in the capitol, and that from this place they should treat of an accommodation with Antony, and with the other leaders of the opposite party.

On the following day, Antony, seeing that the restorers of the commonwealth remained in the capitol, and abstained from violence against any of the supposed friends or adherents of Cæsar, ventured abroad from his lurking place, and resumed the dress and ensigns of consul. In this capacity he received a message from the conspirators, desiring a conference with himself and with Lepidus. Antony, though, in times of relaxation and security, extravagant, dissipated, and in appearance incapable of serious affairs;[1] yet in arduous situations he generally belied these appearances, was strenuous, cautious, and able. He did not yet perceive how far the party of Cæsar was or was not extinguished with its leader. The only military force in Italy was at the disposal of Lepidus, of whom he was jealous. In his answer, therefore, he assumed an appearance of moderation and regard for the commonwealth, and referred every question to the senate, which he had already summoned to assemble.

In expectation of this meeting of the senate, all parties were busy in consultations, and in soliciting support to their interest. The friends of the conspirators were in motion all night visiting the senators, and preparing measures for the following day. The veterans of Cæsar, both officers and legionary soldiers, apprehending that the grants of land lately made to themselves might be recalled, went to and fro in the streets, and made application wherever they had access, with representations and threats. They even provided themselves with arms, and prepared to overawe the senate by their numbers.

In the course of the same night, Lepidus had marched into the city with the legion he commanded, and took possession of the forum. To the people who assembled around him he lamented the death of Cæsar, and inveighed against the authors of this unexpected event. By this declaration, he encouraged the partizans and retainers of the late dictator to come abroad, and rendered the streets and passages exceedingly dangerous for those who were supposed to be of the opposite party. Cinna, who, to evince his zeal for the reviving republic, had resigned the office of prætor conferred upon him by Cæsar, was attacked on his way to the senate, and narrowly escaped with his life.

Antony, in that busy night, had, by his credit with Calpurnia the widow of Cæsar, got possession of all his memorials and of all his writings, and had secured an immense sum of money which had been deposited by him in the temple of Ops.[2]

On the following day, being the eighteenth day of March, the senate assembled, as soon as it was light, in the temple of the Earth. The veterans beset the doors.[3] Dolabella presented himself, ushered in by the lictors, and took possession of one of the consuls' chairs. Antony being seated in the other, moved the assembly to take into consideration the present state of the commonwealth. He himself professed great zeal for the republic, and a disposition to peace.[4] The greater part of those who spoke after Antony justified or extolled the act of the conspirators, and moved that they should have public thanks and rewards for their services. This they supported by a charge of usurpation and tyranny against Cæsar. Upon this point, however, Antony thought proper to interpose; reminded the senators how nearly many of them were concerned in this question. "They who are to vote in it," he said, "will please to observe, that if Cæsar shall be found to have acted with legal powers, his acts will remain in force; if otherwise, all the proceedings that took place during his administration must be erased from your records; and his body, as that of a traitor and a tyrant, made fast on a hook, must be dragged through the streets, and cast into the Tiber. This sentence would affect the remotest parts of the empire, or would extend, in its application, farther perhaps than we should be able to enforce it by our arms. Part indeed is in our power. Many of us hold offices, or are destined by Cæsar's nomination to offices, either at home or abroad. Let us begin with divesting ourselves of what we now hold; and with renouncing our expectations for the future. After we have given this proof of our disinterestedness, our allies abroad will listen to us, when we speak of recalling the favours granted to them by the late dictator."

By this artful turn, which was given by Antony to the subject now under deliberation, many, who in the late arrangements made by Cæsar, held places in the senate or magistracy, or, who were by his appointment destined to succeed to high offices at home or abroad, were greatly disconcerted. Some of those who were actually in office, as retainers of the late usurpation, resigned their powers, and laid down the ensigns of magistracy on the steps where they sat; but Dolabella, who, in consequence of a destination made, though not fulfilled by Cæsar, had recently assumed the consular robes, and who, being under the legal age, had no hopes of being re-elected by the free voice of the people, notwithstanding his declaration in favour of the authors of Cæsar's death, pleaded for the necessity of sustaining all the acts and decrees of that usurper.

While the senators were engaged in debate on the terms of their first resolution, relating to the act of the conspirators and the death of Cæsar, the people, who had assembled in great multi-

1 If I am not mistaken, says Cicero upon this occasion, he minds eating and drinking even more than mischief. (Cicero ad Attic lib. xiv. ep. 3. quem quidem ego epularum magis arbitror rationem habere, quam quidquam mali cogitare.)

2 Cicero says, septies Millies H. S. about six millions sterling. Philip ii. c. 37. 4000 talents. Plut. in Anton.

3 Cicer. ad Att. lib xiv. ep. 14. Nonne omni ratione veterani qui, armati aderant, cum presidii nos nihil haberemus, defendendi fuerunt?

4 Ibid. Philip. i. c. 1.

tudes in the market-place, became impatient to know what was passing, and pressed on the doors of the temple where the senate was met, with some attempts to force or break them open.[5] On this occasion, Antony and Lepidus thought proper to go forth, under pretence of appeasing the tumult; but with a real intention to observe what, in this critical state of affairs, was the prevailing disposition of the people, with a full resolution to be governed in their own measures, by what seemed to be the will of the multitude. Finding the humour of the majority, and the disposition of the troops such as they desired, menacing and sanguinary against the conspirators, they endeavoured to inflame their passions, employing signs and gestures of indignation, rather than words, which could not be heard. Among other expressions of this nature, Antony laid open his bosom, to show the armour with which he had thought necessary, in the senate, and amidst so many concealed enemies, to guard his life. By this, and other signs which he made, he insinuated that Cæsar had fallen in consequence of his excessive confidence, and of the clemency with which he had spared those who became his murderers.

From this scene, which passed in the streets, Antony returned to the senate;[6] and the debate being resumed, Dolabella alleging the confusion which must arise from a general suspension of magistracy, and the disorders attending general elections at so critical a time, insisted, that all magistrates now in office should continue. Cicero pleaded for a general amnesty and oblivion for the past; enumerated the evils which had been brought on the republic, by the contentions and by the vindictive spirit of party; proposed that none should be questioned for Cæsar's death, nor any one be called to account for violence committed under his authority; that the arrangements made by Cæsar should remain; that every one destined to office, should in his turn succeed according to that destination; and that all the provisions made for the army should be fully secured to them.[7]

After some opposite opinions on the question had been delivered, Antony concluded the debate with a tone of more authority than he had hitherto assumed. "While you deliberated," he said, "on the conduct which you were to hold with respect to the conspirators, I chose to be silent; but when you changed the question, and proposed to condemn the dead, I ventured only to make one objection, which being removable by yourselves, ought to have been the least of all your difficulties. And yet I find it is sufficient to stop all your proceedings! What are we to think of the remaining objections? The whole fabric of the empire rests at this moment on establishments made by Cæsar; at home on the arrangements he has made in the succession to office; abroad on the grants of possessions or immunities made by him to princes, cities, corporations, and provinces, and on the several conditions he has, in return, stipulated with them on behalf of the Roman people. Imagine then, upon the subversion of what he has established, what scenes of confusion must follow. It is true, confusion at a distance may not affect you; but the scene in Italy will be sufficient to occupy your utmost attention. Will the veterans, do you think, who have not yet laid down their arms, or not lost the use of them, of whom many thousands are now in this city, will they allow themselves to be stripped of the grants which were made to them in reward of long, dangerous, and faithful services? You have heard their voice last night in the streets. You have heard their menaces against the authors of our present distresses. Will they behold with patience the body of their favourite leader dragged with ignominy in the streets? Will they bear with an indignity, which, though done to his memory, must involve a forfeiture of all that they themselves have received, or a disappointment of all they expect in reward of their services? Will the Roman people in general submit to have the principal author of their present greatness stigmatised by your decrees as a criminal, and to have his assassins rewarded with honours?—The proposal to me, in all its parts, appears wild and impracticable. Let the conspirators, if you will, escape with impunity, provided they are sensible of the favour that is shown to them; but talk not of rewards to them; nor, under pretence of censuring the conduct of your late dictator, wildly open a scene of confusion, by subverting all your present establishments. My opinion is, that the acts of Cæsar, without exception, should be ratified, and that all affairs should be suffered to move on in the channels in which he has left them. On these preliminary conditions I will submit to an accommodation, and agree that we think no more of the past."

In delivering this speech, Antony having perceived so powerful a support in the legion which now had possession of the forum, in the veterans, and in the promiscuous multitudes of people who were assembled round the doors of the senate, expressed himself with assurance and great vehemence. A decree was accordingly passed, by which all prosecutions, on account of Cæsar's death, were prohibited; all his acts, for the sake of peace, were confirmed; all his plans ordered to be carried into execution; and all the grants of land, which had been made by him to the veterans, specially ratified.[8]

This decree being to be carried to the people for their assent on the following day, and the accommodation of parties being so far advanced, the conspirators intimated an inclination to address themselves to the people; and were instantly attended by great numbers, who assembled to hear them on the ascent of the capital.[9] Brutus spoke from the steps. He explained the motives upon which his friends and himself had thought proper to betake them to their present retreat; and, in speaking on this subject, complained of the outrage which had been offered to Cinna, who, though not concerned in the death of Cæsar, was attacked, for having been supposed to approve of what they had done. He enumerated the distresses which had afflicted the commonwealth, from the time at which Cæsar commenced hostilities to the present hour; "A period, during which the best blood of the republic," he said, "was continually shedding, in Spain, in Macedonia, and in Africa, to gratify the ambition or vanity of a single man. These things

5 Appian. de Bello Civ. lib. ii.
6 Ibid.
7 Dio. Cass. lib. xliv. c. 34.
8 Appian. de Bell. Civil. lib. ii.
9 Cicer. ad Attic. lib. xv. ep. 1.

however," continued he, "we consented to overlook, and in suffering Cæsar to hold the higher offices of state, became bound, by our oath of fidelity, not to call any of his past actions in question. If we had likewise sworn to submit ourselves to perpetual servitude, our enemies might have some colour for the accusation of perjury, which we are told is now laid to our charge; but the proposal of any such engagement we should have rejected with indignation, and we trust that every Roman citizen would have done so also. Sylla, after having gratified his revenge against many who were no doubt his own enemies, at the same time that they were enemies of the public, at last restored the commonwealth; but Cæsar, without any pretence, besides the gratification of his own ambition, continued, in the city and in the provinces, to usurp all the powers of the empire. The treasury he treated as his property, and the magistrates of Rome as his creatures, to be placed or displaced at his pleasure. One of the last acts of his life, in preparing for his departure from Rome, was to fix the succession of magistrates for several years; in order that in his absence you might not, by choosing your own officers, recover the habit of exercising that freedom, and of enjoying those rights, of which he meant to deprive you for ever."

From this account of Cæsar's usurpation, Brutus proceeded to speak of the grants which had been made to the veterans. "He acknowledged the long and faithful services which those men had performed against the enemies of the commonwealth in Gaul, in Germany, and in Britain; approved of the provision which had been made for them, and assured them of his concurrence in carrying this provision into full execution. At the same time he lamented the sufferings of those who had been stripped of their ancient possessions, to make way for those new grants; proposed that they should have a compensation from the treasury, and hoped that the justice of the commonwealth would be employed in equally protecting the rights of every citizen."

This speech was received with applause; and on the following day the act of oblivion being confirmed by the people, and the children of Antony having been sent[1] as hostages to the capitol, the conspirators came down from thence, and were received with loud acclamations. After parties had saluted each other with mutual congratulations and expressions of friendship, Cassius retired to sup with Antony, and Brutus with Lepidus. The republic appeared to be thoroughly re-established. The nobles in general expressed their satisfaction in the present situation of affairs, and extolled the authors of Cæsar's death as the restorers of freedom to their country. Many, however, who had shared in the late usurpation, having tasted of military power, and being unable to acquiesce in the condition of mere citizens, however dignified, or to accommodate themselves to the restraints and formalities of legal government, were likely to prove bad members of the reviving republic. Antony in particular considered himself as the successor of Cæsar, and could not for a moment cease to think how he might grasp the sovereignty, and dispose of all the dignities and emoluments of the state.

The senate had weakly, under the show of moderation, resolved to confirm Cæsar's will and to ratify all his acts, both public and private: they had decreed that the remains of Cæsar should be honoured with a public funeral, which was to be conducted in the manner which his friends should think proper.

Antony was prepared to take advantage of these circumstances, towards preserving the party of Cæsar both in the army and in the city, not doubting that, while this party remained, he himself should remain at its head. For this purpose, he published Cæsar's will, in which he knew that there were many clauses likely to gratify the people, and to inflame their minds against his assassins. Among these, were a legacy of money to be distributed to the inferior citizens, at the rate of twenty-five attic drachmas, about two pounds ten shillings a man;[2] or, according to Octavius, quoted by Dion Cassius, 300 H. S. about the same sum; together with an assignment of his gardens on the river, as public walks for the service and pleasure of the people. Many legacies were likewise bequeathed to private persons. The inheritance with the name of Cæsar, was devised to Octavius, grandson to his sister Julia. The succession, in case of the failure of this young man, was devised to Decimus Brutus, who, at the same time, together with Mark Antony, was made guardian to the young Cæsar, and executor of the will.

Upon the publication of this will, the partizans of Antony took occasion to extol the munificence and generosity of Cæsar towards the Roman people, to blacken the conduct of the conspirators, representing that of Decimus Brutus, in particular, as equal to parricide; and Antony, in this manner having secured the public attention and favour, proceeded to celebrate the funeral with all the honours that were due to a public benefactor, and to a common parent of the people.

Cæsar's body, in the general consternation, had been left for some hours on the spot where it fell. It was at last borne on a litter by a few slaves to his own house. In this confusion, one of the arms, all over blood, was left hanging over the side of the litter; and this circumstance, though at the time in appearance unnoticed, yet remained with a deep impression on the minds of those who beheld it. On examining the body, there were found twenty-three wounds sufficiently ghastly, although no more than one or two were mortal. Antony determined to exhibit this spectacle to the people, accompanied with that of the robes, which were pierced and torn in the struggle with which Cæsar fell, and all over stained with his blood. He likewise ordered a solemn dirge to be performed, with interludes of music, agreeable to the practice at Roman funerals, and suited to that particular occasion. He himself prepared to speak the oration; and a day being fixed for the solemnity, a pile was raised in the Campus Martius, near to the tomb of Julia, the daughter of the deceased, and the wife of Pompey. Although it was intended that the body should be consumed on this pile in the Campus Martius, the funeral oration was to be spoken from the rostra in the forum, and a couch was placed there adorned with ivory and gold, on which was laid the corpse with an effigy of the deceased, covered with purple, and over it a tro-

1 Cicer Philip. i. c. 1.

2 Appian. de Bell. Civili. lib. ii.

phy, on which was to be hung the robes in which he was killed. The whole of this pageant was covered up, and adorned with a gilded canopy of state. In bearing it to the forum, the pall was carried by magistrates then in office, or by persons who had passed through the highest stations of the commonwealth. But in the procession, the streets were so crowded, that no order could be kept, and multitudes who ought to have passed in regular procession, hurried by the shortest ways to the place at which the obsequies were to be performed.[3]

Antony began the funeral oration, with an apology for intruding on the patience of many, who possibly took no particular concern in the catastrophe of Cæsar's life. "Had Cæsar been a private man," he said, "I should have proceeded to his funeral in silence; but one who has died in the first station of the republic, is entitled to public notice. And my own station as consul, were I qualified for the task, would have imposed on me a special duty on this occasion; but in this instance, the eulogium of the dead must proceed from a higher authority than mine. The senate and the people of Rome have spoken, and they have left to me only the task of repeating what they have said." After these words, he read over the decrees of the senate and people, enumerating the titles, dignities, honours, and powers which had been conferred on Cæsar. He spoke of the lustre of his family, the graces and accomplishments of his person, and of his singular abilities; gave a general account of the wars in which he had been engaged; his splendid successes and the accession of glory and of empire he had procured to the Roman state: and when he had gained so far on the attention of his audience, he addressed himself to the popular part in particular. "When you were oppressed," he said, "by a faction that engrossed all the powers and dignities of the commonwealth, Cæsar generously interposed in your behalf. When this faction had withdrawn themselves from the allegiance that was due to the government of their country; and when they had actually armed first the provinces of Spain, afterwards Macedonia, Greece, Asia, Africa, and all the eastern parts of the empire against you, he braved the storms of winter and the superior force of the enemy; he dispersed the cloud which had gathered over your heads; he carried the glory of your arms into Asia, Africa, Egypt, and yet a third time into Spain. His enemies every where experienced his valour in battle, and his clemency in victory. He pardoned many who were repeatedly in arms against him; and when he dreaded the effects of an excessive lenity towards those who appeared to be incorrigible, he sought for pretences to pardon his enemies under the show of gratifying his friends.

"On the subject of his administration in the state, I need not make any observation to you. You were witnesses of his conduct. Descended of your ancient kings, he had more glory in refusing a crown that was offered to him, than they had in wearing it with all its honours.—You loved him—you set him at the head of your priesthood—at the head of your army—at the head of the republic;—you declared his person sacred as that of your tribunes—you declared him the father of his country—you showed him to the world, adorned with the ensigns of sovereign power—your dictator, your guardian, and the terror of your enemies. But he is no more!—This sacred person is now breathless before you. The father of his country is dead: not, alas! of disease—not of the decline of years—not by the hands of foreign enemies—not far from his own country—but here within your walls, and in the Roman senate, in the vigour of health, in the midst of all his designs for your prosperity and glory. He who often repelled the swords of his enemies, has fallen by the hands of treacherous friends, or by the hands of those whom his clemency had spared.—But what availed his clemency? what availed the laws with which he so anxiously guarded the lives of his fellow-citizens? His own he could not guard from traitors. His mangled body, and his gray hairs clotted with blood, are now exposed in that forum which he so often adorned with his triumphs; and near to that place of public debate, from which he so often captivated the people of Rome with his eloquence."[4]

At this passage, it is said that Antony began to change the tone of lamentation into that of rage; that he raised his voice to indignation and threats, but that he was checked by a general murmur of the senators; and that he thought proper again to soften his expressions. "The gods," he said, "are masters of the fortunes of men. It is our part to forget the past, to look forward to the future, to cultivate peace among ourselves, and to accompany this hero with songs of praise to the mansions of the blest."—Having spoke these words, he tucked up his robe, and disengaged his arms as for some vehement action; and standing over the bier in which the effigy was laid, uncovered it; but, as starting from the sight, or struck into silence, he held up the torn and bloody garment to view, sunk again into a sorrowful tone, and prayed that it were possible for him to redeem that precious life with his own. Being interrupted with a general cry of lamentation from the people, he made a pause to hear the interlude. At a passage of the song, in which Cæsar was personated in the following words, "For this I spared, that they might murder me;" a general cry of indignation burst from the multitude; and, at the same time, the effigy of the dead, with all its wounds and stains of blood, being raised to view, the people could no longer be restrained. Part ran to avenge his blood on the persons of the conspirators, and part tore up the benches and tribunals of the magistrates, dismantled the senate-house, brought into heaps the spoils of the supposed enemies of Cæsar, and forgetting the preparations which had been made for a funeral pile in the field of Mars, brought the most precious combustible materials they could find to light a fire in the forum, on which to consume the body of the dead.

From this beginning, the people continued during the whole night to bring fresh materials. The officers who had attended the procession, stripped off the robes in which they were dressed, and cast them in the flames. Women crowded to the pile, and threw upon it, as a sacrifice to

---

3 Sueton. in Cæsar.

4 Dio. Cass. lib. xliv. c. 49.

the manes of the dead, the ornaments of their own persons, the gorgets and the prætextas of their children. The people, in general, appeared to be seized with an epidemical phrensy, of which, neither the degree of their attachment to Cæsar in his life-time, nor the manner in which they had received the first accounts of his death, had given any adequate expectations: they ran through the streets denouncing vengeance on his enemies, and proceeded to violence against every person who was represented as such. Helvius Cinna being mistaken for Cornelius of the same name, who, on the preceding day had declared his approbation of the conspiracy, was put to death by the populace, his body torn in pieces, and his head carried in procession on the point of a spear.[1] The perpetrators of this murder being led by the retainers and dependants of Cæsar's family, snatched lighted brands from the funeral pile, and attacked the houses of Brutus, Cassius, and the other conspirators. They even attempted to demolish Pompey's theatre, in which Cæsar had been killed, and lighting many fires at once in different parts of the city, threatened the whole with immediate destruction.

In these riots, though projected by Antony, the public disorder was carried to a greater height than he had wished or foreseen. His intention was to incite a popular cry against the authors of Cæsar's death, and to check the senate in any opposition they were likely to give in the execution of his own designs. But when the crimes which were committed began to reflect dishonour on the party of Cæsar, and when all persons of property were alarmed, and the city itself was threatened with ruin, he found himself obliged, with the authority of magistrate, to interpose and put an end to tumults of so dangerous a nature. For this purpose, in concert with Dolabella, he issued an edict, prohibiting the populace to assemble in arms on any pretence whatever, and posted guards in different parts of the town to secure the observance of it.

Antony having by these means restored the peace of the city, and dispersed all the crowds which had assembled, except that which still remained at the place of Cæsar's funeral, where the populace continued for some time to feed the pile, he made a journey to the country, and remained in Campania great part of April and May. During this time he was assiduous in his visits to the quarters and new settlements of the veterans, on whom he was for the future to rely for support in the pretensions, which it is probable he had already conceived, and which were much too high for the safety of the commonwealth. In his absence, one Ematius, who had formerly assumed the name of Marius, and under this popular designation had been busy in disturbing the public peace, and who, upon this account, had by the late dictator himself been driven from the city, now again appeared, affected to lead in the riotous honours which were paid to the memory of Cæsar, and, attended by the populace, erected an altar or monument on the spot where the corpse had been burnt, and drew multitudes thither as to a place of devotion. On this occasion, Dolabella, who had offended many of the more respectable citizens, by assuming, without any regular authority, the dignity of consul, now recovered their favour by a vigorous exercise of his power against this impostor, gave orders that Ematius should be put to death, many of his accomplices thrown from the Tarpeian rock, and the monument or altar they had erected should be razed to the ground.[2]

By these executions, the peace of the city seemed to be established, and even the commonwealth itself in some measure restored. Both the consuls affected the character of ordinary magistrates, showed a proper deference to the senate, and in all things endeavoured to give satisfaction to the friends of the republic. Antony upon his return to the city, consulted the principal senators upon every motion which he proposed to make, and referred the determination of every question to the free discussion of that body. He affected to have no secrets; and though empowered by the late act of the senate to carry into execution the different articles of Cæsar's will, and to complete all his intended arrangements, he did not, under this description, propose any measure but what was generally known and approved.[3]

In pursuance of this system of moderation, it was proposed by Antony, that Sextus, the remaining son of Pompey, who under the authority of the late dictator had been declared an out-law, should be restored to his country, and have a compensation in money for the losses which had been sustained by his family: and, to provide likewise for the future safety of the commonwealth, as well as for that of private persons, it was proposed that a law should be enacted to abolish for ever the name and power of dictator. At the same time, all the honorary votes which had passed in favour of Brutus and Cassius, and every act which had a tendency to mitigate the animosity of Cæsar's party, to pacify the veterans, and to incline them, without any farther disturbance, to settle on the lands which had been allotted to them, had his concurrence.

The senate, in order to terminate as soon as possible every occasion of public uneasiness or alarm, although they greatly disapproved of the reward that was given to the army, for having, in a manner, subdued the republic, and had reason to dread the precedent, yet hastened to the performance of all Cæsar's engagements, in order to deprive the veterans of any pretence for multiplying their demands, or remaining together in arms.

These circumstances had a very favourable aspect, and the storm which threatened the city and the commonwealth appeared to be laid. Many had foretold that the permission of a public funeral to Cæsar would have dangerous consequences; and during the late tumults and riots thought themselves sufficiently justified in these predictions. But their apprehensions now appeared to have been groundless, and the authors of the late moderate counsels, in which the senate was induced to temporise, and to make concessions in such matters as were of less moment, in order to appease the animosity of parties, and to obtain their consent in matters of more consequence, were now highly applauded.

All the conspirators, in the height of the late

[1] Sueton. in Cæs. Plut. Ibid. Appian. Dio. Cass. &c.

[2] Dio. Cass. lib. xliv. c. 50 et 51. App. de Bell. Civ lib. ii.

[3] Cicero Philip. lib. i. c. 1.

disorders which arose on account of Cæsar's funeral, had withdrawn from the city, and, under different honourable pretences which were furnished them by the senate, continued to absent themselves from Rome. Many of them had been formerly named to the government of provinces, and now proceeded to take possession of their lots. Decimus Brutus, in this capacity, repaired to the Cisalpine Gaul, Trebonius to Asia, and Tullius Cimber to Bythinia.

Marcus Brutus had been appointed to the government of Macedonia, and Cassius to that of Syria; but the two last being actually in office as prætors, could not take possession of provinces until the expiration of their year, nor could they regularly absent themselves from the city, without some decree from the senate to dispense with their attendance as officers of state. Under the present favourable aspect of public affairs, and after the consuls had given such evident proofs of their respect for the commonwealth, it was supposed that the authors of the late revolution might now return in safety to the capital; and Cicero himself, on this occasion, was so confident of the perfect restoration of peace to the republic, that in writing to Atticus, he assures him, that "Brutus may now walk the streets of Rome with a crown of gold on his head." In this, however, with all his penetration, he had overrated the professions, and mistaken the designs of Antony. This profligate adventurer, the more dangerous that he was supposed by his debaucheries disqualified for any deep or arduous design, had assumed the disguise of moderation and deference to the senate, merely to conceal his intentions, until he had formed a party on which he could rely. He had so far imposed on the public, by affecting to be alarmed with danger to his own person from the riots which he was employed to suppress after the funeral of Cæsar, that the senate permitted him to arm his friends; and suffered him, under their own authority, to assemble a powerful body of men, amounting to some thousands, chiefly composed of officers who had served under the late dictator, and who now submitted to act as the guards of Antony's person.[4] Being thus strengthened, when the return of Brutus and Cassius was mentioned to him, he betrayed the falsehood of his former professions. "They cannot be safe," he said, "in the midst of so many of Cæsar's retainers and friends."[5]

Antony was greatly awed by the abilities of Brutus and Cassius, by the respect which was paid them by the public, by their credit with the senate, and by their determined resolution to maintain its authority. In order, therefore, to fortify himself against them, he maintained a continual correspondence with the veterans of the late Cæsar's army, courted their attachment, and stated himself as their protector and leader. In this capacity, he made his visit to their settlements in Campania, where, it has been observed, he passed the greater part of the months of April and May. At his return, he endeavoured to strengthen himself still more, by entering into a concert with Lepidus, who, in the quality of second in command to Cæsar, or general of the horse to the dictator, remained at the head of all the military forces in Italy. He engaged himself to obtain for Lepidus the dignity of chief pontiff; and, in order to cement the union of their families, proposed a marriage of his own daughter with the son of this officer. He had been averse to the promotion of Dolabella; and, at the death of Cæsar, would have opposed his assuming the dignity of consul, if he had not been prevented at first, by the uncertainty of his own situation, and afterwards by the countenance which this intruder into public office began to receive from the senate. In these circumstances, to dispute the accession of Dolabella, would be to throw him entirely into the hands of the republican party; he thought proper, therefore, to disguise his inclinations, and took measure to gain him, or at least to set him at variance with the authors of the late conspiracy. For this purpose, he made a tender of his services to procure him an appointment to command in any of the more advantageous provincial situations.

Notwithstanding that Cassius was already appointed to the government of Syria, Antony, according to agreement, undertook to support the pretensions of Dolabella, and to aid him in supplanting Cassius at the meeting of the senate, which was to be held on the first of June. Having in this manner, with great industry and application, strengthened himself by his coalition with Lepidus and Dolabella, the one at the head of the army, the other his own colleague in the principal office of the state; and having secured the attachment and support of the veteran soldiers recently settled in Italy, he no longer kept any terms with the senatorian party, or with the friends of the republic. Having formerly obtained a resolution of the senate to confirm all the acts, and to maintain the arrangements which had been devised by Cæsar, and being master of the papers and memorials in which these were contained, he brought extracts and quotations from them in support of his several proposals, without producing the originals; and in this form commenced, in the name of the dead, a reign more arbitrary than that of the living Cæsar had been. As he had never communicated to any one the papers or memorials from which these authorities were drawn, he expunged or he inserted whatever he thought proper, or even, without taking this trouble, framed his quotations on every subject to the purpose which he meant to serve. He made Cæsar's memorials to teem with intended laws and acts of the senate, and of the people; with grants and forfeitures of lands; with the pardon of crimes and recalls from banishment; with orders for levying contributions from princes, states, and private persons; with compositions to be exacted from towns and corporations; for the ransom of their possessions, liberties, and franchises; and even with distinct resolutions and decisions relating to matters which took their rise after Cæsar's death.[6] His wife Fulvia, the widow of Clodius, likewise availed herself of this valuable mine, and sold offices and commissions, together with entire provinces and kingdoms,[7] to those who were willing to pay her price.

Among the acts of Antony, during this consulate, is mentioned, a change which he made in the judiciary law, by which he obtained, that a

4 Appian. de Bell Civ. lib. i.
5 Cicer. ad Familiar. lib. xi. ep. 1
6 Cicer. Philip. ii. c. 38.
7 Ibidem ad Atticum, lib. xiv. ep. 12.

certain number of centurions should be entered on the rolls of the judges, in place of the revenue officers[1] whom Cæsar had excluded. Relying on this and other artifices, which procured him the support of the army, he rose every day in his presumption; and while he incited Dolabella to persist in supplanting Cassius in the province of Syria, he himself proposed to supplant Brutus in his nomination to the government of Macedonia. By this appointment, he meant to place himself at the head of the army, which Cæsar, to be in readiness for his Asiatic or Parthian expedition, had transported into Macedonia; and it appeared afterwards to be his design, as soon as he had obtained the command of this army, to procure an appointment to supersede Decimus Brutus in the province of Cisalpine Gaul, and, under pre tence of expelling him from thence, to transpon this army again into Italy.

In order to obtain acts for so much of these purposes as he was then about to execute, he summoned all the members of the senate[2] to assemble on the first of June. He had brought into the city, to overawe this assembly, great numbers of the veterans, on whom he himself, besides confirming the settlements which had been assigned to them by Cæsar, had bestowed considerable favours. At this meeting of the senate, few of the members, who were inclined to oppose the consul, thought that they themselves could with safety attend. Even Hirtius and Pansa, though named for the consulate of the following year, and protected by the dignity which belonged to that destination, thought proper to absent themselves.[3]

At a call of the senate, so ill attended, Antony obtained for himself, without opposition, the government of Macedonia, with the command of the army which had been destined for Asia, but which, from Cæsar's death, had remained in that province. He at the same time obtained for Dolabella the province of Syria to the exclusion of Cassius; and by these several acts stated himself and his colleague as in open enmity with the leaders of the republican party, whom they had lately affected to court, but whom they now proceeded to strip of the preferments and honours which had been assigned to them by the commonwealth.

Under pretence of making compensation to Cassius and Brutus for the loss of the provinces of Macedonia and Syria, of which they were now deprived, Antony procured them appointments which they considered as an additional insult; that of Brutus to inspect the supplies of corn from Asia; and that of Cassius, to superintend the supplies of the same kind which were brought from Sicily.

While the senate complied with Antony in his demands on these several subjects, they endeavoured to restrain his abuse of the supposed will and memorials of Cæsar. For this purpose they appointed a committee of their own number to inspect the contents of those papers, and to attest the reality of such notes and instructions as were to be carried into execution under the authority of the senate. Antony, however, paid no regard to this appointment, nor even suffered the committee to meet in discharge of the duty for which they were named.

About this time[4], and alarmed by these violences, Cicero, who had hitherto maintained some degree of neutrality or moderation between the parties, departed from Rome. He had, before the death of Cæsar, intended to withdraw into Greece, under pretence of superintending the education of his son at Athens, and had obtained Cæsar's consent, and the leave of the senate for that purpose. On Cæsar's death, having hopes that the republic was about to revive, he took his resolution to remain in the city; but being now satisfied that these hopes were vain; or, in his own terms, observing, "that, although the tree had been cut down on the ides of March, its roots were yet entire, and made vigorous shoots," he resumed his former design of absenting himself; and instead of applying to the senate for leave, accepted from Dolabella, the newly appointed governor of Syria, a commission of lieutenancy, which he was to employ as a pretence for crossing the Ionian sea. In execution of this design he arrived on the twenty-sixth of June at Antium, where he found Brutus, with his wife Porcia, and mother Servilia, with other persons of distinction. He gave it as his opinion, that Brutus and Cassius should accept of the commissions assigned to them as inspectors of the supplies of corn from Sicily and Asia, and should repair to their several provinces for that purpose. While the company were yet deliberating on this subject, they were joined by Cassius, who, upon Cicero's repeating what he had said, answered, with a stern countenance, that he would not go into Sicily, nor accept as a favour, what was intended as an affront. He complained, that opportunities had been lost of rendering effectual the first and principal step which had been taken to deliver the commonwealth, and was inclined to blame Decimus Brutus for some part of this neglect. Cicero censured the conduct of the whole party, for not having secured the completion of a business that was so successfully begun. "You ought," he said, "immediately, upon the death of Cæsar, to have assumed the government, to have called the senate by your own authority, and to have taken advantage of the spirit that was generally raised among the people for the recovery of their legal constitution."

In the result of this conference, Brutus and Cassius, as well as Cicero, took their resolution to depart from Italy; and the two former, with so much resentment of the indignity which they had suffered in their appointment to inspect the importation of corn, that they engaged Servilia[5] to employ her influence in having this appointment expunged from the public acts or records of the senate. Before their departure, they wrote a joint letter to Antony, conveyed in expressions that were guarded and polite; but demanding an explanation of the terms in which they stood with him, and of the purposes for which he had assembled the veterans of Cæsar in such numbers at Rome. Some time after this letter was sent they drew up a joint edict or manifesto, setting forth the cause of their absence from the capital, and protesting against the violence which was daily offered to the constitution of the republic.

In answer to this letter, and to the paper with which it was followed, Antony issued a manifesto

1 Tribuni Ærarii. 2 Cicero ad Attic. lib xv ep. 6. 3 Ibid. Phil. i. c. 2.

4 The middle of June.
5 The mother of Brutus

full of invective and contumely, and which he transmitted, under a formal address, to the prætors Brutus and Cassius, accompanied with a letter in the same style. The originals of these several papers are lost; but in reply to the last, we find addressed to Antony, and signed by Brutus and Cassius, the following original preserved among the letters of Cicero:

"Brutus and Cassius, prætors, to Antony, consul, &c.

"We have received your letter, which, like your manifesto, is full of reproach and of threats, and very improper from you to us. We have done you no injury; and if we were inclined to hostilities, your letter should not restrain us. But you know our resolutions, and you presume to threaten us, to the end that our pacific conduct may be imputed to fear. We wish you all the preferments and honours which are consistent with the freedom of the commonwealth. We have no desire to quarrel with you; but we value our liberties more than we value your friendship. Consider well what you undertake, and what you can support. Do not be encouraged so much by the length of Cæsar's life, as warned by the short duration of the power he usurped. We pray to God, that your designs may be innocent; or, if they be not innocent, that they may be as little hurtful to yourself as the safety of the commonwealth can permit."[6]

These altercations led to an open breach. The prætors wrote to Decimus Brutus, Trebonius, and Cimber, to put their several provinces in a state of defence, and to make what farther provision they could of men and money as for a certain war.[7] Cicero, in continuing his voyage to Greece, had arrived on the sixth of August at Leucopetræ, beyond Rhegium; and had set out from thence; but being put back, was met by some citizens at Rhegium, just arrived from Rome, who brought him copies of the edicts or manifestos issued by Cassius and Brutus, with a report, that a full meeting of the senate was expected on the first of September; that Brutus and Cassius had sent circular letters requesting the attendance of all their friends; that Antony was likely to drop his designs; that the cause of the republic, having so favourable an aspect, his own departure was censured, and his presence was earnestly wished for.

Upon these representations, Cicero took his resolution to return to Rome, and arrived again at Pompeii, on the nineteenth of August.[8] Here, among the accounts of what had passed in the senate on the first of that month, he was informed that Piso, the father of Calpurnia, and father-in-law of the late Cæsar, had, notwithstanding this connection and his interest in the remains of the late usurpation, vigorously opposed the measures of Antony; and, on that occasion, had acquired great distinction as a man of ability, and as an upright citizen; but that not being properly supported in the senate, he had declined any farther struggle, and had absented himself on the following day.

Cicero, though not greatly encouraged by these reports, continued his journey to Rome; and having arrived, on the last of August, found that the expectations which he had been made to entertain of Antony's intentions were void of foundation; and that the outrages he was likely to commit were such, as to make it extremely unsafe for any distinguished friend of the republic to come in his power. For this reason, Cicero, on the first of September, sent an excuse to the senate, pleading the ill state of his health, which obliged him to remain shut up in his own house. Antony considered his absence from the senate as an affront to himself, or as giving too much countenance to the suspicions which were entertained of his violent intentions. Under this impression he burst into rage, and sent an officer to require the attendance of Cicero, threatening, if he persisted in his supposed contumacy, to pull down his house about his ears: the ordinary method of forcing those to submission, who shut themselves up, or took refuge in their dwellings from the sentence of the law. He was dissuaded, however, from any attempt to execute his threat; and being himself absent from the senate on the following day, Cicero ventured to take his seat, and, in the absence of the consul, delivered that oration which is entitled the first Philippic. In this speech he accounted for his late retirement from the capital, and for his present return, in terms strongly reflecting on the conduct and administration of the present consul.

Antony, in his turn, greatly exasperated by the accounts he received of Cicero's speech, prepared to reply at a subsequent meeting of the senate; and delivered himself accordingly with great acrimony against his antagonist. These mutual attacks, thus made in the absence of the parties, produced from Cicero that famous oration which is entitled the second Philippic; a model of eloquence in the style of ancient invective; but which, though put in the form of an immediate reply to imputations supposed to be made in his presence, never was at all delivered, and is to be considered as a mere rhetorical pleading in a fictitious case. The offence, however, which was given by the publication of this invective, made a principal part in the quarrel, which the parties never ceased to pursue, till it ended with Cicero's life.

While the consul Antony in this manner threw off the mask of a legal magistrate, and acted in some measure as a person who succeeded to the military usurpation erected by Cæsar, a new actor appeared on the stage of public affairs, from whose youth nothing important, it was thought, could, for some time, be expected. This was Caius Octavius, the grand nephew of Julius Cæsar, by his niece Attia, and the son of Octavius, who, in the course of state preferments, had arrived at the dignity of prætor; and in this rank, having governed the province of Macedonia, died suddenly on his return from thence. His widow the mother of this young man, married Philippus, a citizen of moderate parts, but upright intentions. In the house of Philippus the young Octavius was brought up, and passed his early years, while his grand-uncle was engaged in the most active parts of his life, and while he was insinuating himself by intrigues, or forcing his way at the head of armies to the sovereignty of the Roman empire. Elevated by his connection with this relation to a high situation and to higher views, he had followed him in the late campaign

6 Cicer. ad Fam. lib. ii. ep. 3 Dated 4th of August.
Cicer. ad Att. lib. xvi. ep. 7. 8 Ibid.

against the sons of Pompey in Spain, and was intended, though a minor, to succeed Lepidus, under the dictator, as general of the horse.

Upon the return of Cæsar into Italy, and after the army destined for the war in Asia had been transported into Macedonia, the young Octavius was sent to Apollonia, as a place at which he might continue his studies, and his military exercises, and be in the way to join the army, and to attend his uncle in the projected expedition to the East.

After Octavius had been about six months at Apollonia, a messenger arrived in the beginning of the night with accounts of Cæsar's death, bearing, that he had fallen in the senate; but without determining whether he fell by the hands of a few, or in the execution of a general resolution of the whole body. The young man was greatly dejected and perplexed in his thoughts. The military men then about him advised him to repair to the quarters of the army in Macedonia, and to put himself at their head. But his step-father Philippus, and his mother Attia, in their letters, had cautioned him against this or any other ambitious resolution; they advised him to return into Italy in the most private manner, and warned him to avoid giving any umbrage to the partizans of the republic, who had now got the ascendant at Rome, and would not allow any person whatever to tread in the dangerous steps of his late uncle.

Octavius accordingly embarked for Italy; and as he knew not what might be the disposition of the troops who were then stationed at Brundusium, he chose to land at Lupia, a place at some little distance, and on the same coast. Here he received farther accounts from Rome, with particulars of the conspiracy; the proceedings of the senate; accommodation of the parties; the tumults that arose at Cæsar's funeral; the will, and his own share in it: but his friends still persisted in recommending a private station, and advised him even to drop his pretensions to the name and inheritance of Cæsar. But this young man, though only turned of eighteen, took upon him to decide for himself in this matter. He sent an officer to sound the disposition of the garrison at Brundusium; and finding that they were inclined to revenge the death of their late favourite leader, and that they resented the other proceedings of the republican party, he proceeded in person to Brundusium in the most public manner, and was met at the gates by the troops, who received him with all the honours thought due to the son of Cæsar.

From this time forward, Octavius assumed the name and designation of his late uncle. He was soon after attended by persons of all ranks from the neighbourhood of Brundusium, and sent forward to Rome with a retinue, to which, as he passed on the way, he received continual accession of numbers. The veterans, in general, who had grants of land, flocked to him; complained of the remissness of Antony in suffering the assassins of his own friend and benefactor to go unpunished, and declared their resolution to be revenged as soon as any person appeared to lead them. Octavius thanked them for their grateful respect to his father's memory, but exhorted them to moderation and submission. He wished to know the state of parties more exactly before he should declare himself and on his [illegible]rney to Rome, young as he was, employed all the caution and wariness of age for the security of his person, lest any disguised enemies should have insinuated themselves among a multitude of professed friends, who were yet generally unknown to him. At Terracina, about fifty miles from Rome, he received a report, that the consuls had superseded Brutus and Cassius in the provinces of Macedonia and Syria, and had assigned them inferior stations, by this account, at Cyrene and Crete; that many exiles were recalled, particularly Sextus Pompeius; and that, under pretence of executing the intentions of Cæsar, many new members were admitted into the senate.[1]

Octavius, upon his arrival at Rome, found his step-father and his mother under great apprehensions from the power of the senate, and from the general dispositions which appeared in the late act of indemnity that was passed in favour of those who had borne an active part in Cæsar's death. And these apprehensions were strongly confirmed by the neglect of Antony, who took no notice of his arrival, and did not pay that attention which might be thought due to the name of Cæsar; but he neither desponded nor exposed himself by any hasty act of presumption. He said, "That, being so young a man, and in a private station, he could not expect that the first advances should be made to him from the Roman consul; that he would soon convince the senate of his dutiful intentions towards them; that all the world must applaud in him the endeavours he should make to bring the authors of his father's death to justice; that the act of indemnity, in favour of the assassins, had passed when there was no one to oppose it; but that a charge of murder, when directly brought,[2] could not be slighted by the senate, by the Roman people, nor even by Antony himself: that to decline the inheritance which was left him, would be disrespectful to the memory of Cæsar, and injurious to the Roman people, in whose behalf he was made executor of his father's will. Cæsar," he said, "has distinguished me, and honoured me; and I had rather die, than appear unworthy of such a father." His friends were silenced by the appearance of so much discretion and resolution. They broke off the conference with an advice which already appeared to be unnecessary, That he should do nothing rashly, nor embrace violent measures, where prudence might equally gain his purpose.

Next morning this young man, attended by a numerous company of his friends, repaired to the forum, and presented himself before the prætor C. Antonius, in order to declare in form his acceptance of the inheritance of his late uncle, and in order to be invested with the name of Cæsar. From thence he went to Pompey's gardens, where Antony then resided; and after being made to wait, for some time, in a manner that sufficiently expressed, on the part of Antony, a dislike to his visit, he was admitted to a conference.

The young Octavius, having been educated as the nearest relation to Cæsar, and destined to inherit his fortunes, had conceived the extent of his own importance from the height of Cæsar's power; he considered the sovereignty of the empire, in some measure, as his birthright and his own interest as the central point to which all public transactions should tend. In this confer-

1 Appian. de Bello Civile, lib. ii.

2 Ibid

ence with Antony, he is said to have betrayed more of this character than suited his present condition, or than could be reconciled with the discretion with which he had acted on other occasions. He entered with the consul on a review of his conduct as an officer of state, from the death of Cæsar to the present moment; thanked him for the regard he had in some things shown to his father's memory, and with equal confidence censured and arraigned him in others. "You did well," he said, "in opposing the thanks which the senate was about to decree to the murderers of my father and of your own benefactor and friend; and you did well in depriving Brutus and Cassius of the important provinces of Macedonia and Syria; but why preclude my just resentments by an act of indemnity? Why assign any provinces at all to those assassins? Why suffer Decimus Brutus, in particular, with so great a force to keep possession of Gaul? This is not only to spare but to arm them against me." He concluded by demanding restitution of the money which Antony had seized in the temple of Ops,[3] to the end that he might, without delay, pay off to the Roman people the legacies bequeathed to them by Cæsar.

Octavius, in this first specimen of his boldness and address, although he ventured to insult the Roman consul, paid court to the army and to the people; and perhaps wished for the reputation of having quarrelled with Antony on the subject of his remissness in avenging the death of Cæsar, and of his own impatience to pay off the contents of his will. Antony, being surprised and piqued at the arrogance of his speech, and of his pretensions, endeavoured to check his ambition, by putting him in mind, that although he was named the heir of Cæsar's estate, he must not pretend to inherit his dignities; that the Roman constitution acknowledged no hereditary powers; that he ought to remember in whose presence he stood; that the Roman consul must be equally indifferent to his approbation, or to his censure. "To me," he said, "it was owing that your uncle was not declared a usurper and a tyrant; consequently, to me it is owing that you have any other inheritance by him besides the disgrace of being related to a traitor, whose body had been dragged through the streets, and cast into the Tiber. As to any money which may have been lodged in the treasury, of that," he said, "Cæsar had already diverted too much to his own private uses; that when his receipts came to be examined and the sums not accounted for to be claimed, much public money might be found among his effects; that Cæsar himself, if living, could not refuse to make up his accounts; and that a proposal was actually in agitation to have them stated and examined."

From these altercations, Octavius and Antony parted on very ill terms, and were publicly known to have quarrelled. Octavius, from an affected zeal to put the people in possession of the legacy bequeathed to them by his father, brought his own effects to sale. Antony, on his part, promoted the inquiry into the applications of public money, and gave out, that the heirs of the late dictator would have great sums to refund, and little reversion. These heirs, in return, pleaded the late decree of the senate and people, ratifying all Cæsar's acts, and consequently precluding all inquiries into this, or any other part of his administration; but as Antony could fabricate acts of Cæsar, when wanting, to his purpose, so he could set aside or evade real acts when they stood in his way.

In the mean time the friends of the republic rejoiced at a breach which seemed to weaken their enemies, and gave them hopes, that a competition for the succession to Cæsar's power would divide the army, and shake the foundation on which that power was supported. In this contest Antony, by his age, his authority, and by his great influence in the commonwealth, having so much the advantage, they thought it safest to promote the interest of his antagonist, who was in a private station, a minor, under the direction of relations inclined to moderation, and strongly possessed with deference to the senate. Antony, by his arrogance, and the public contempt with which he treated the heir of Cæsar, gave offence to the party from which he hoped for support. Having already obtained all the ends which he proposed to himself in courting the senate, he pulled off the mask, and set them at defiance. Octavius, on the contrary, while he endeavoured to supplant his antagonist in the favour of the people, affected great deference to the senate and regard to the commonwealth. He even changed his language in public respecting the conspirators, and to their friends affected a desire to be reconciled with them. Being at the country-house of Philippus, near to that of Cicero, he took this opportunity to pay his court to a person of so much consideration in the republican party; accosted him with the title of father, and mentioning his friends of the conspiracy with respect, affected to put himself entirely under his protection.[4] Cicero being either the dupe of these artifices, or willing to encourage Octavius against Antony, seemed to listen to his professions; notwithstanding that Philippus, who was interested to save the republic, at the same time informed him that he did not believe this artful boy was sincere.[5]

While the young Cæsar thus strove to ingratiate himself with the party of the senate, his chief reliance was on the people. He opened an office for the payment of the late dictator's legacy to every one who claimed a share of it; and as these liberalities were ascribed to the deceased, and could not be made a charge of corruption against himself, he did not scruple to extend them beyond the letter of the will. He endeavoured at the same time to make it be believed, that by the oppressions of Antony he was straitened for means to perform his duty in this respect to the people; recommended to his agents to hasten the sale of his own effects at any price, and continually brought new articles to the market in order to raise money.[6] Being introduced by one of the tribunes, he delivered a harangue to the people, in which he declared his intention to exhibit shows and theatrical entertainments in honour of his late father's memory.[7] He proposed to have seated himself at the theatre in his chair of state;

3 Plut. in Antonio. Appian. de Bell. Civ. lib. ii.

4 Cic. ad Attic. lib. xiv. ep. 11. Modo venit Octavius in proximam villam Philippi, mihi totus deditus.

5 Ibid. lib. xii. ep. 15.

6 Appian. de Bell. Civ. lib. ii.

7 Cicer. ad Attic. lib xv. ep. 1.

but in this particular had the mortification of being forbid by the tribunes.[1]

Although the senators in general promoted the claims of Octavius, and considered him as a zealous confederate against Antony, who was the principal object of their fears, the conspirators saw in him the representative of their late enemy and the leader of Cæsar's army. They endeavoured to put their friends on their guard against him, and by all means in their power to counteract his popular arts. For this purpose the public entertainments, which were this year to have been given by Brutus in the quality of prætor, were provided and exhibited in his absence with great splendour. These entertainments, from animosity to the family of Cæsar, rather than from a regard to Brutus, were conducted by C. Antonius, the brother of the present consul, who presided in the place of his colleague the absent prætor, and who was desirous on this occasion to divide with Octavius the popular favour even in behalf of Brutus, with whom he was not on good terms.[2]

As such entertainments were intended by the Roman officers to ingratiate themselves with the people, so the reception they met with was considered as an indication of their success or disappointment in any object they had in view. On the present occasion the Tereus of Accius being brought on the stage, and every sentiment of liberty applicable to the times being greatly applauded, this was considered as an intimation of popular favour to the deliverers of their country, and to Brutus in particular, the giver of the feast. His friends thought this a favourable opportunity to make trial of their strength; and as the Roman people, still supposed to be the sovereigns of the world, were accustomed, like other despotical masters, to decide on the greatest affairs as matters of private passion, and in the midst of their pleasures, the aristocratical party raised a cry, that the restorers of public liberty should be recalled to their country.[3] This cry was not returned by the audience, and the performance itself was stopped by the clamours of the opposite party, until the proposal now made in favour of the conspirators should be withdrawn.

Brutus and Cassius finding their party among the people so little able to support them, saw no security but in the possession of provinces which, in case of an open attack from their enemies, might supply them with money and arms for their defence. They determined, therefore, notwithstanding the late arrangements, by which they were superseded, to repair to the provinces of which the command had been originally intended for them; Cassius to Syria, and Brutus to Macedonia and Greece. They were encouraged in the pursuance of this resolution by the divisions and quarrels which arose in the opposite party; observing that the adherents of the late Cæsar were ranged on different sides with Octavius or with Antony, and that the army itself, though extremely averse to disputes which tended to disturb their possession of the government, were likely to balance or hesitate in the choice of their leader, they left Italy with some hopes, that the republic might revive in the dissension of its enemies.

1 Cicer. ad Attic. lib. xv. ep. 2.
2 Appian. de Bell. Civ. lib. ii.
3 Cicer. ad Attic. lib. xvi. ep. 2.

The officers whom Antony had assembled as a guard to his person, ventured to expostulate with him on a breach which was so likely to reduce their force, and they exhorted him to act in concert with Octavius, at least until they had obtained a just revenge against the assassins of Cæsar. On this occasion Antony entered into the reasons of his past conduct, and accounted for the concessions which he had made to the senate, as necessary, to obtain the conditions on which the present flourishing state of the party depended. He reminded his friends that it was by his means that Cæsar's acts had been ratified; that it was by his means that, notwithstanding the late act of indemnity, the conspirators had been expelled from the city, and stripped of their provinces.

For the future, he assured them, that being possessed of a proper force, he would appear undisguised, and give sufficient proof of his regard to Cæsar's memory, and to the interest of his surviving friends.

Antony, in compliance with the intreaties which were now made to him at this conference, had an interview with Octavius; at which they were, in appearance, reconciled to each other: but their pretensions were far from being sufficiently adjusted to render the agreement of long continuance. Octavius aspired to a degree of consequence which Antony by no means thought necessary to admit in so young a person. His undoubted title to the inheritance of Cæsar, and the attachment of Cæsar's personal friends, made Antony consider his advancement as altogether incompatible with the success of his own designs. Effects of their jealousies and animosities accordingly soon after appeared, such as rendered an open breach again unavoidable.

A vacancy having happened in the college of tribunes,[4] Octavius, though far short of the legal age, was presented by his friends as a candidate for this station. Antony, without declaring himself openly against them, published an edict, threatening with prosecution any person who should make a proposition to the people contrary to law; and by these means prevented their farther proceeding in this design.

Soon after this act of authority, on the part of Antony, to check the ambition of the young Cæsar, men armed as for an assassination were discovered in the consul's house. They were not brought to any public examination; but it was given out that they had been suborned by Octavius. Whether this plot was fabricated, in order to load him with the odium of it, and to justify the measures which Antony himself meditated to take against a person supposed to have aimed at his life, or whether it was by Antony actually believed to be real, is uncertain. It occasioned a considerable ferment in the city, and the parties reasoned upon it as they were severally inclined. The friends of Antony persisted in accusing Octavius, and others recriminated, urging as a proof of Antony's design on the life of Cæsar, his having recourse in this manner to a forgery, which was evidently intended to exasperate the army and the people against his antagonist, and to justify the violence which he himself, with the first opportunity, meant to employ.[5] Cicero,

4 Appian. de Bello Civil. lib. ii. 5 Ibid.

however, says, that people of judgment believed the plot on the part of Octavius to have been real, and that they approved of it.[6]

In the late interval of military usurpation, the senators in general, though willing to resume the government, were actually unable to bear the load which it was likely to lay on their shoulders. They rejoiced at the breach between Octavius and Antony; but if these adventurers should continue to quarrel about the spoils of the commonwealth, the greater part of those who had any interest in defending it were no more than a prey to the conqueror. Clouds hung over their councils on every side. The officers who had served under Cæsar in the late civil war, were posted at the head of armies in the most advantageous situations. Asinius Pollio had the command in the farther province of Spain, Lepidus in the nearer; Plancus commanded in Gaul, and Antony in Macedonia. The veterans remained in the neighbourhood of Rome with swords in their hands, anxious for the settlements which had been lately assigned to them by Cæsar. These they did not believe to be secure, without the destruction of every law and of every form which could be cited to favour the claims of the former proprietors.

Antony made rapid advances to the military usurpation he had some time projected. Having availed himself so far of his nomination to the government of Macedonia, as to get possession of the numerous and respectable army which Cæsar, on their way to the Parthian war, had transported thither, he proceeded to exchange that province for the Cisalpine Gaul; and, under pretence of expelling Decimus Brutus from thence, had ordered the army of Cæsar to be transported back into Italy. Soon after the detection of the supposed plot of Octavius he departed from Rome, and set out for Brundusium. The troops which he had ordered from Macedonia were already arrived at that place; and as he had intelligence that Octavius had his emissaries employed to seduce them, he hastened to prevent the effect of this design, and to secure his own authority. He professed to employ this army merely in gaining possession of the province which had lately been decreed to him by the people. But in the desire of occupying, with an army, that very station from which Cæsar had so successfully invaded the republic; and which, according to the expression of Cato on the nomination of Cæsar to that province, was in reality the citadel or commanding station which gave possession of Rome, he sufficiently evinced the designs which he had formed against the republic, and no less alarmed the heir of Cæsar, who expected to be the first victim of his power, than it threatened the senate with a new and dangerous usurpation.

Under these impressions, while Antony took the road to Brundusium, Octavius repaired to Campania, and, by large donations[7] in money, engaged the veterans who were settled at Calatia, Casilinum, and Capua, to declare for himself. With this powerful support, he published his intention to withstand the consul, and took measures to procure the authority of the senate against their common enemy. He professed great zeal for the cause of the republic, and affected to put himself entirely under the direction of Cicero, now the most respectable member of the senate that was left. He intreated this experienced counsellor to favour him with an interview at Capua. "Once more," he said, in his letter upon this occasion, "save the republic." At their conference it was deliberated whether Octavius should throw himself into Capua with three hundred veterans who had joined him, and there stop Antony's march to Rome; or should cross the Apennines, to give the legions, who were marching from Brundusium, an opportunity to execute the project of defection, which he believed they were meditating in his favour. In this question he affected to be determined entirely by Cicero, who advised him to move with all the force he could assemble towards Rome.[8]

In compliance with this advice, Octavius having assembled ten thousand men, without waiting to array, or even to have them completely armed, advanced by hasty marches to prevent Antony, who about the same time had marched from Brundusium, and was hastening to advance in the same direction.[9]

The city was thrown into a great alarm by this unexpected approach of two hostile armies. Some expressed their fears of Antony, others of Octavius, and some of both. It was uncertain whether they advanced in concert to oppress the republic, or in competition to contend for its spoils. Many appearances favoured the latter supposition; and the late reconciliation gave some credit to the former.

Octavius, having the advantage of a shorter march, arrived before his antagonist; and being within two miles of the city, was received by Canutius, one of the tribunes, whom he soon after sent back into the city, with assurances, that he had assembled his party not to second, but to oppose the designs of Antony; and that his purpose was to employ all the force he could raise for the defence of the commonwealth. The tribune Canutius, in reporting what passed with Octavius, exhorted all who wished to preserve the republic to lend their assistance in execution of this design.

Upon these assurances, delivered by a tribune of the people, the gates were thrown open to Octavius, and he entered the city, though not in a military form, yet followed by a numerous band of attendants, who concealed their weapons. With this company he took possession of the temple of Castor and Pollux, and prepared to explain himself to a numerous concourse of people, who were hastening into the area or court before the temple. Being introduced by the tribune into this assembly, as a person who had matters of great moment to communicate respecting the state of the republic and the designs of Antony, he began his speech by commemorating the merits of his late adoptive father, and the ingratitude and injustice of Antony; declared, that although he had assembled his friends merely in his own defence, he was ready to employ them in the service of his country, and submitted himself entirely to such directions as he should receive from the powers established by law in the commonwealth; observed, that they could not possi

6 Cicero ad Famil lib. xii. ep. 23.

7 Five hundred Denarii, i. e. about 16*l.*

8 Appian. de Bell. Civ. lib. ii.

9 Cicero ad Att. lib. xvi. ep. 8

tly doubt of his inclination to be employed at least against his personal enemies.

It was probably in this speech, that Octavius, being to make a solemn asseveration, pointed to the statue of Julius Cæsar, with these words, "So may I arrive at my father's honours!"[1] He had two opposite and irreconcilable parties to please on this occasion, and had not learned that the only safe course in such cases is silence. He offended the partizans of the republic by the veneration he expressed for Cæsar, and by his wish to tread in his steps; and in this, perhaps, committed the only public indiscretion with which he is chargeable in any part of his conduct. But what was in reality a more dangerous effect of this error, he offended the military part of his audience by the regard he affected to entertain for the civil government of the state, and by his open declaration of war against Antony. By this declaration, military men found themselves not invited to enter, as they expected, on the secure possession of the rewards and honours which had been promised to them; but called upon to fight for empire against their late fellow-soldiers, commanded by an officer from whom they had high expectations as a friend, and much to fear as an enemy.

Soldiers of fortune being thus disappointed of the spoils which they expected to seize, and of the rewards which were now become due for former services, some of them absolutely renounced the party of Octavius; others, under pretence of providing arms and necessaries for the field, or pleading various excuses, desired leave to return to their own habitations. The greater part of the veterans actually withdrew: but Octavius, young as he was, did not sink under this untoward state of his affairs. He had ordered levies in Etruria, and in the district of Ravenna. These levies, upon the reputation of the ascendant he had gained in the city, succeeded apace, and induced military adventurers from every quarter to espouse his cause.

Many who had served under Julius Cæsar, being accustomed to the life of a soldier, though settled as landholders in Italy, were not yet rooted in the condition of citizens, or in that of husbandmen. They had yet fresh in their memories the license and the spoils of war. They saw them offered anew under the auspices of a leader who bore the name of Cæsar, and whose munificence was known. Many, therefore, who had recently left Octavius, being unwilling that others should reap the harvest in which they themselves had been invited to partake, again repaired to his standard; and, as fast as they arrived, were sent to Etruria, into different quarters, to be armed, arrayed, and furnished with all necessaries for the field.[2]

Octavius from thenceforward conducted himself between the parties with great address: to the veterans he talked of avenging Cæsar's death: to the friends of the republic he set forth the dangerous designs of Antony, affected to sacrifice all private resentment to his zeal for the commonwealth,[3] even promoted the election of Casca into the colleague of tribunes,[4] and affected in all things to be governed by the senate.

What hopes, in the mean time, could be formed for the state? Could senators entrust the age or the intention of this crafty boy, nursed, as they observed, in the midst of usurpation; and who, by arming himself without any legal authority, had given evidence of an assuming and audacious spirit? They stood in awe of Antony, and were afraid to provoke him by an open declaration. Octavius did not yet appear to be in condition to cope with the Roman consul; and if he were in condition to do so, would be likely to form designs equally dangerous to the commonwealth. Antony, with a numerous army, had all the authority of government in his hands. The dispositions of Pansa and Hirtius, the consuls named by Cæsar for the ensuing year, were yet unknown.— Although many things were transacted in name of the senate, this order of men scarcely ventured to resume their ordinary functions, and shook under the rod which Cæsar had lifted over them, even while it hung in suspense between different divisions of his remaining party.[5] Piso, the father-in-law of Cæsar, had ventured to oppose Antony. Cicero and Publius Servilius afterwards followed this example. "But all that we have gained," said Cicero, "is no more than this, that the Roman people may perceive, that whoever contends for liberty is not safe at Rome." These senators, therefore, together with L. Cotta, L. Cæsar, and L. Sulpicius, had in despair, upon seeing Antony put himself at the head of an army, absented themselves from the public assemblies.

It was evident from every circumstance, that the fate of the empire was to be determined by the sword. The troops feeling their consequence, affected indifference to every interest but their own, and presumed to treat with equal contempt, in their turns, the different persons who assumed the command of them. Of the five legions which had been quartered in Macedonia, four were landed at Brundusium when Antony arrived at that place. They turned out on his coming, but did not receive him with the usual acclamations and shouts. They closed in profound silence round the platform from which he was to speak, as having suspended their judgment, until they should know what gratuities they were to receive in reward of their services. When he mentioned four hundred sestertii, or between three and four pounds a man.[6] This being far short of the rewards that were expected for giving a new master to the commonwealth, he was answered with signs of derision. In return to this insolence, Antony assumed a tone which tended rather to exasperate than to overawe his audience. He reproached these legions with ingratitude for the favour he had recently done them, in changing their destination from Parthia to the Cisalpine Gaul; and with treachery, in having suffered to remain among them the emissaries, whom he knew that a presumptuous boy had employed to debauch them from their duty. "These," he said, "shall not escape me; in the mean time prepare yourselves to march into the province which is allotted for your station."

Antony, while he yet continued to speak, had the mortification to see entire cohorts, with their

1 Cicer. ad Att. lib. xvi. c. 15.
2 Dio. Cass. lib. xlv. c. 12. Appian. Bell. Civ. lib. ii.
3 Cicer. ad Att. lib. xv. ep. 12.
4 Ibid. lib. xvi. ep. 15.
5 Cicer. ad Att. lib. xiv. ep. 5 et 6. Ibid. ad Dolabellam, post 17.
6 Dio. Cass. lib. xlv. c. 13. or according to Appian 100=16s.

officers, withdraw from his presence, uttering words of contempt and of scorn. Seeing the desertion likely to become general,[7] and being greatly provoked, he dismissed the audience, sentenced three hundred officers and private men to immediate death, and stood by while they perished under the hands of the executioners. Fulvia, who had attended him in his journey to Brundusium, is said to have been present likewise at this scene, and to have satiated her revenge of the insults offered to her husband, with so near a view of the executions, as to have her clothes stained with blood.[8]

The offence that was taken at these cruelties gave ample encouragement to the agents of Octavius, who, notwithstanding the threats of Antony, still continued to negotiate in the quarters of his army. Papers were dropt and handed about, containing a contrast of Antony's parsimony with the liberality of Octavius. A search was made for the authors of these libels; but the bad success with which it was attended, served only to show the general disaffection of the army. The accounts, at the same time, which were brought of the progress which Octavius made in the settlements of the veterans, and of his reception at Rome, gave Antony a just sense of his danger, and made him change his tone. In a second address to the army, he made an apology for his late severities. They knew, he said, his character, that it was neither sordid nor severe; that the sums he had mentioned were no more than a present to signalize their meeting, and an earnest of his future munificence. He did not, however, at this time, make any addition to his former bounty, lest it should appear to be extorted from him by fear.

The soldiers, in appearance, satisfied with these declarations, accepted with respect the sum which had been offered to them; submitted to the changes which had been made among their officers, and marched off in divisions by the coast of the Adriatic towards Ariminum. Antony himself, with an escort of cavalry and infantry, composed of men the bravest and most attached to his person, whom he had selected from the whole army, set out for Rome. At his arrival, the horse were quartered in the suburbs; he himself, attended by a body of foot, entered the city, had a regular guard mounted in the court of his own house, ordered centinels to be posted, gave the parole, and made every disposition to prevent surprise, as in a military station. Being still vested with the office of consul, he summoned the senate to meet on the twenty-fourth of September; and, in the proclamation or summons, declared, that if any senator absented himself on that day, he should be deemed an accessary to the plot against the consul's life, which had been lately discovered, and an accomplice in the other wicked designs known to be in agitation against he republic.

Notwithstanding this pompous threat, Antony himself did not attend at the time appointed; but, by another proclamation, he again summoned the senate to meet on the twenty-eighth of the same month. He intended, on this day, to obtain a decree against Octavius; whom, in all his manifestos, he qualified with the name of Spartacus; as having, without any legal authority, presumed to levy war against the state;[9] but, as he entered the porch of the senate-house, a messenger arrived with accounts that the Legio Martia had deserted with its colours to Octavius. Before he had recovered this shock, another messenger came with a like account of the fourth legion. He entered the senate, but very much disconcerted, and unprepared to act in circumstances so different from those with which he laid his account. He avoided the mention of Octavius; and pretending to have called the assembly, without any particular business, he made a short speech and adjourned. From this meeting, hearing that one of the revolted legions had taken post at Alba, he instantly repaired to that place, in hopes of reclaiming them; but was received with a discharge of arrows and stones from the battlements, and obliged to retire. Fearing that the remainder of the army would follow this example, he ordered them an additional gratuity of five hundred sestertii, or about four pounds a man. And, to give them an immediate prospect of action, which is often the most effectual means of stifling dangerous humours in any army, he declared his intention to make war on Decimus Brutus, in order to dislodge him from the province of Gaul. In pursuance of this intention, he ordered his equipage for the field, and set up his standard at Tibur, to which place he expected that all his friends and adherents would repair.

Antony, being joined by the last of the troops from Macedonia, had still three legions belonging to that army; and these, together with the veterans settled in the neighbourhood of Tibur, who came with their ensigns and colours to offer their services, amounted in all to four legions, besides the ordinary attendance of irregular troops, and the crowds of people that flocked to his standard. With this formidable power, having for a a few days overawed the city, and drawn around him the greatest part of the senate, and of the equestrian order, with many of the people who had so lately declared for his rival, and who, in the contests of such parties, ever yield to the present power, and are the property of him who can best work on their fears; he set out on his march to Ariminum, the last place of Italy on the frontier of Gaul.

Octavius, at the same time, had assembled his forces at Alba, consisting of the two legions who had lately come over to him from Antony, one legion of new levies, together with two of the veterans lately embodied, which, not being full, were completed with the choice of his new-raised men. He made a report to the senate of the number and description of the troops he had thus assembled, and received their thanks and congratulations. It is nevertheless probable, that his services were received by this body with great distrust of their own situation, and of his designs.

Had the senate been free to choose on whose swords they were to rely for the defence of their cause, those of Cassius and Brutus, with the other conspirators, originally drawn in behalf of the republic, must have appeared the preferable choice. Uncertain, however, of the effect of any direct or public resolution in favour of those who were the authors of Cæsar's death, they left the correspondence to be maintained with them to private persons; and senators accordingly wrote

7 Cicer ad Att. lib. xvi. ep. 8.
8 Ibid. Philip. iii. c. 2 et 4.

9 Cicer. Philip. iii. c. 8.

in their private capacity, to recommend perseverance and the utmost exertion of their zeal. "Such is the state of the republic," says Cicero to Cassius; "even in the calmest times, scarcely able to support itself. What must it be in the present storm? All our hopes are in you. But if you have withdrawn yourselves merely for your own safety, we cannot have hopes, not even in you. If you intend any thing worthy of your own character, I wish I may live to see the effect. The republic, at any rate, must revive under your efforts."[1] He adjured Decimus Brutus, by the example of Octavius, who, though in a private station, raised armies for the state; he adjured him by the example of the faithful legions who deserted from Antony, to stand by the commonwealth; and in the present crisis to exert himself to the utmost, without waiting for the orders of the senate.[2]

Cicero had already proclaimed his animosity to Antony, and besides his zeal for the republic, had a particular interest in abetting any party that was formed against this dangerous enemy. Hearing that he was gone from the city, and that all the forces in its neighbourhood had declared for Octavius or for the senate, he himself ventured, on the ninth of December, to return to Rome,[3] and proposed in the senate that they should decide on the plan they were to follow in this arduous state of their affairs.

CHAPTER III.

Situation and Address of Octavius—Meeting of the Senate—Progress of Antony—His march into Gaul—Message of Octavius to Decimus Brutus—New Consuls Hertius and Pansa—Meeting of the Senate—Deputation to Antony—His Answer—Declared an enemy—Advance of Hirtius and Octavius to raise the siege of Mutina—Brutus and Cassius confirmed in the command of all the Eastern Provinces—Progress of the War in Gaul—Siege of Mutina raised—Junction of Antony and Lepidus—Consulate of Octavius.

WHEN Antony left Rome to take possession of the Cisalpine Gaul, Octavius was in arms at the gates of the city, and, though a mere youth under age, was furnished with every art which age itself could bestow, to qualify him for the part he was to act. He had gained upon the army by donations and promises; upon the senate by public professions of duty and of zeal for the republic; and, on particular members, by attentions and flattery. The legions, which had lately come over to him from Antony, having exhibited a mock fight, he ordered them, on that occasion, a special gratuity of five hundred sextertii, or four pounds a man; saying, that as this was but the representation of a battle, the reward was proportional; but if he should ever have occasion to employ them in real fights, they should have as many thousands.[4] In this situation, it became necessary for the senate, either to authorise and to avail themselves of this ultraneous support; or, by refusing it, to drive the veterans, and all the military party which still revered the name of Cæsar, into measures immediately fatal to the republic.

Upon the march of Antony towards Gaul, Octavius had already sent a message to Decimus Brutus[5] with assurances of his aid in defending that province, and of his co-operation every where else in supporting the authority of the senate. Hitherto men stood in awe of Antony, as being vested with the authority of consul, and threatening to treat his opponents as rebels to the commonwealth. Even Hirtius and Pansa, destined to succeed him in the consulship, it was supposed, would scarcely venture to take possession of the office without his consent, and the usual form of his abdication; but the prospect of a vigorous support from Octavius, relieved many from their fears of Antony, and determined them on the part they were to act.

The senate, under pretence of taking measures that the succeeding consuls might enter on their office in safety, being assembled by one of the tribunes on the nineteenth of December, a manifesto was produced from Decimus Brutus, of which no copy remains, but probably stating his right to the province of Gaul, and representing the injustice of Antony in attempting to dislodge him by force. Octavius was at the same time introduced by the tribune, and pronounced a panegyric on Brutus.[6] Cicero, in a speech which is still extant, extolled the conduct of the young Cæsar in arming the veterans, as a generous effort made at the hazard of his own life, and of his private fortune, to defend the republic. He applauded the two legions who had lately deserted from Antony; and warmly urged the senate to support Decimus Brutus in his province. He moved, that thanks should be given to these officers, and to the troops who adhered to them; and that the consuls, on the first of January, should move the senate farther to consider of the rewards that were due to the army, for the faithful services which they had rendered to the commonwealth. These public propositions he blended with a continual and vehement invective against Antony.[7] He obtained decrees of the senate to the several effects he had proposed; and having carried those decrees to the comitia or assembly of the people for their approbation, there likewise he supported them with a repetition of the same topics, and with the usual force of his eloquence.[8]

In the mean time, Antony, being arrived on the frontier of Gaul, despatched an officer to Decimus Brutus, with a copy of his own commission from the Roman people, and with an order to evacuate the province. To this message he had

1 Cicer. ad Familiar. lib. xii. ep. 2.
2 Ibid. lib. xi. ep 7. 3 Ibid. ep 5.
4 Appian. de Bell. Civ. lib. ii.
5 Dio. Cass. lib. xlv. c. 15.
6 Cicer. ad Famil. lib. xi. ep. 6. Ibid. Philip. iii. c. 5
7 Cicer. Philip. ii. 8 Ibid. Philip. iv.

for answer, that Decimus Brutus held his command by authority of the Roman senate, who alone, by the laws, were entitled to dispose of the provinces; and that he would not surrender what the laws of his country had enjoined him to defend. Antony, after having to no purpose exchanged repeated messages on this subject, continued his march into the province, and forced Brutus, with two legions and some new levies, that were under his command, to throw himself into Mutina, where he had formed some magazines from the stores and provisions he was able to collect in the neighbourhood, and where he proposed to wait for the succours which he was made to expect from Rome. Antony advanced to Bononia and Claterna, took possession of these places, and having invested Mutina, began to besiege it in form.

U. C. 710.

C. Vibius Pansa, C. Hirtius, both killed. Octavius succeeded Pansa. Upon his resignation, C. Carinus succeeded Octavius. Q. Pedius succeeded Hirtius. Ventidius succeeded Pedius, who died in office.

Such was the posture of affairs in the end of December, about ten months after the death of Cæsar.[9] On the first of January, the consuls Pansa and Hirtius, being to enter on the exercise of their office, proceeded to the senate from the temple, where they had offered the usual sacrifices; and agreeably to the order of the nineteenth of December, moved this assembly to take under consideration the present state of the republic.[10] Pansa having stated the subject, called upon his father-in-law, Q. Fusius Calenus to deliver his opinion. This senator being disposed to favour Antony advised, that they should not rashly, take any violent resolution; that they should send a deputation to the late consul, with instructions from the senate to lay down his arms, and to return to his duty. This motion was vehemently opposed by Cicero, who, in a speech still extant,[11] insisted that Antony was already in effect declared an enemy, and ought to be reduced by force, not gained by negotiation and treaty. He recounted the violences committed by him in his late consulate, particularly the acts which he promulgated under the pretence of Cæsar's memorials and will. "From the foundation of Rome to this present hour," he said, "Antony alone has had the impudence to present himself in this assembly, escorted by a military force. The kings never attempted it. The boldest adventurers, and they who were most forward to revive the kingly power, never ventured so far. I remember Cinna; I have seen Sylla; and last of all, Cæsar. These were the persons, who since the expulsion of Tarquin, made the greatest advances to kingly power. I do not say that they were unattended in the senate; or that their retinue were always unarmed; they were followed only by a few, and with concealed weapons. But this daring assassin paraded in the streets with a military power, moving in cohorts under arms, with all the forms of a regular march. He posted a body of archers with their quivers full, and even chests of spare arrows for immediate and continued action, on the very steps by which senators were to ascend into the temple of Concord; you have ordered public thanks to the troops that have drawn their swords against him; you have extolled the generous magnanimity of a young man, who, without waiting for your commission, brought a hasty power to cover the city from his violence; and are you now deliberating whether you are to soothe his fury with negotiation, or to meet it with force?[12] If you send deputies to his camp, no matter with what message, you will appear to surrender; you will appear to distrust your own cause; you will damp the ardour of your own troops; and you will shake the faith of the provinces."

Such was the purport of Cicero's speech respecting the conduct of Antony, the merits of Decimus Brutus, of Lepidus, of Octavius, of the legions, and of the veterans; and of L. Egnatuleius the tribune, who led the Legio Martia in the late choice of their party. In the close of the speech, he moved, That suitable honours should be decreed to each; that the senate should ratify all the proceedings of Brutus in defending the province of Gaul; that Lepidus should have a statue erected to him; that Octavius should have the rank of proprætor, be confirmed in his present command, and be entitled to sue for the offices of state before the legal age; that three years of the age appointed by law, should be dispensed with in behalf of Egnatuleius; that the veterans, who had taken arms under Octavius, and the legions, who had deserted from Antony to join the standard of the commonwealth, should have the gratuities that were promised to them by Octavius; and at the end of the present war should have grants of land, and a perpetual exemption to themselves and their children from every military service. In his encomium on Brutus, he insinuated the praise that was due to him, as a partner in the conspiracy against Cæsar; but, not to offend the partizans of Octavius, declined entering fully on that subject. He pledged himself for the future behaviour of Octavius. "This admirable young man," he said, "having once tasted of true glory, having found himself held forth by the senate, by the people, and by all orders of men as a citizen dear to his country, and as the guardian of the commonwealth, never can place any other species of distinction or honour in competition with this. If Julius Cæsar had found himself, at so early a period of life, in such an illustrious point of view, he never would have sought for preferment by courting the populace, nor have betaken himself to measures incompatible with the safety of his country. The mind of this young man is perfectly known to me. Love of the republic, respect to the senate, deference to good men, the desire of real glory are his ruling passions. I will therefore venture to pledge my honour in the most positive assurances to you, to the Roman people, and to the commonwealth. I promise, I undertake, I engage that C. Cæsar will continue towards the republic this conduct which he now holds, and that he will always be what you wish, and what you would choose that he should be."

Octavius, we may suppose, had, in some measure, blinded Cicero with his flattery; yet in this panegyric there was probably more of what the orator wished to recommend to Octavius, than of what he believed to be his original intention; but this designing young man was not to be caught

9 Appian. de Bell. Civ. lib. ii. 10 Ibid. lib. iii. 11 Cicer. Philip. v.

12 Cicer. Philip. v.

in such snares. He knew too well how to retort these artifices, even at an age, when others scarcely knew that such arts are practised; and the experienced Cicero, with all the penetration and wit for which he was eminent, was the dupe of a youth who possessed the deepest of all artifices, that of suffering himself in appearance to be deceived, while in reality he employed the cunning of others to his own purpose.[1]

L. Piso, with a considerable party in the senate, inclined to moderate the resolutions that were proposed against Antony. He contended that no Roman citizen could be condemned unheard; that the senate could do no more than appoint him a day of trial, and cite him to answer for himself. The time of the first meeting being already spent in this debate, the senate adjourned; and the subject being resumed on the following day, it is said[2] that Fusius Calenus, with a torrent of abuse and reproach, retorted on Cicero the invective which, on the preceding day, he had pronounced against Antony. He reproached him with the obscurity of his birth, and accused him of a presumption, which was supported only by a talent for declamation, often employed by him against the best citizens, never in bringing real criminals of state to punishment "What have you done," he said, accosting Cicero, "either at home or abroad, to merit the high degree of consideration to which you lay claim? In what war have we ever prevailed under your auspices? What accession of territory have you ever gained to the Roman state? Even in respect to your boasted talent for speaking, you do but impose upon the world the labours of retirement for the prompt effusions of eloquence; and you publish harangues, which you had neither the invention to conceive, nor the courage to deliver in the face of any public assembly, or in the midst of any real affairs." He accused Cicero of having forced Catiline into rebellion, and of having put to death, without any trial, Cornelius Lentulus, and other Roman citizens of rank; of having lighted the fire of dissension among the leaders of the present unhappy divisions that continued to tear the republic, and of having blown up the flames which still continued to consume the state; of having meanly abandoned the cause of Pompey upon his defeat at Pharsalia, and of having instigated assassins to take away the life of Cæsar, even after he himself had implored his mercy, and accepted of his protection. He reproached him with a fresh instance of ingratitude, in this attempt to turn the arms of the republic against the late consul, to whose clemency he himself was indebted for his life. Having mixed this invective with the defence, and even with the praises of Antony, he concluded with calling upon the senate to consider how absurd it would be to declare war upon a magistrate, who acted by commission from the Roman people, at the head of an army, of which they had given him the command, and in the very province which they had committed to his government; and this merely in support of a young man who had presumed, without any public authority, to levy war against a Roman officer of the highest rank, and in favour of a rebel who had presumed forcibly to retain a province, which the Roman people had ordered him to surrender. "Such men," he said, "were indeed the enemies of the republic; but he did not move for any formal declaration against them. The times," he observed, "will not suffer us to do all that ought to be done." He moved only that messengers should be instantly despatched to all the parties at war in this unfortunate contest; that all of them should be required to lay down their arms, and to submit to the decisions of the senate; that if any one of them should disobey, it would then be full time to declare him a public enemy, and to give to the consuls the usual and regular powers to guard the safety of the commonwealth and to reduce disorderly subjects to their duty.[3]

Such are the abuses of an admired art, as vile and odious in its falsehoods, as in the genuine effusions of truth it is noble and respectable; and this speech, compared with some of the former, which were delivered relating to the same persons, may serve to exhibit the variety of colours with which the same subjects and characters may be covered in debate, and by which public assemblies may be perplexed in their councils. The majority of the senate were aware however of Antony's designs, and knew the danger of suffering him to get a military establishment, and the possession of a formidable army within the Alps; and they would probably have come to a severe resolution, if one of the tribunes had not interposed for that day, and forbid their proceeding any farther on the subject.

The senate was again adjourned until the next morning, and in the mean time the relations and family of Antony, his mother, his wife, his children, and intimate friends went into mourning, passed the night in visiting the principal members, or in waiting for the people, as they passed in the streets, to implore their protection. When the senate was about to assemble, this company of suppliants took their station on the steps of the temple, and embraced the knees of the members as they passed.

This solemn council, when met, on coming to the question, took, as is common on such occasions, a middle course between the extremes which were pointed out to them. They so far treated Antony as a friend, as to order a deputation of their own members to attend him in his camp; but the message which they sent by this deputation, sounded more like a declaration of war, than an overture of reconciliation or of a peace.[4] They commanded him[5] not to disturb in his government Decimus Brutus, whom they qualified with the appellation of consul-elect; not to lay siege to Mutina; not to lay waste the province; not to make any levies of forces, or to presume to continue in arms against the authority of the senate.

L. Piso, Philippus, and Servius Sulpicius, being deputed to carry these orders, had farther in charge to signify to Decimus Brutus, and to the troops under his command, the entire approbation of the senate, and the high esteem and honour[6] in which they were held on account of their conduct. The senate at the same time entered, on their own records, the honorary decrees which had been passed in favour of Decimus Brutus, Octavius, Egnatuleius, and the army, in terms that had been proposed by Cicero; and resolved, that

1 Cicer. Philip. v.

2 Appian. de Bell. Civ. lib. iii.

3 Dio. Cass. lib. xlv. c. 18. lib. xlvi. c. 28.

4 Cicer. ad Familiar. lib. xii. ep. 24.

5 Decimus Brutus was already destined to succeed in the consulate of the following year

6 Cicer. Philip. vi.

the gratuities already paid by Octavius to the veterans, and to the legions who had lately come over from Antony, should be refunded from the treasury; that lands should be allotted, and a continual exemption be given to them from all military service after the present war.

When the deputies were gone with the message which they had received from the senate, the party of Antony at Rome endeavoured to alarm the people, and to load his enemies with all the consequences that were likely to follow from the late resolutions. They extolled the happy effects of moderation and peace, observed that Antony was a person of a daring and impetuous spirit, and ought not to have been incensed; that his party was strong; and in case of a rupture, would be joined by numbers of profligate men, for whom no attempt was too arduous, and against whom the friends of the republic could not be too much on their guard.[7]

While men were amused with such discourses at Rome, Servius Sulpicius, one of the three deputies on whom the senate chiefly relied for the effect of their commission, died on the journey. The other two were kindly received by Antony, and admitted without any jealousy or distrust to visit the approaches he had made, and the works he had erected, against the town of Mutina.

While the siege was continued without interruption, the commissioners were received with affected submission to the orders of the senate; were told that Antony would evacuate the province, disband his army, and return to a private station; that he would forget the past, and agree to a sincere reconciliation, provided that the legions then under his command, that his cavalry and his guards were properly rewarded and accommodated with grants of land, and put upon the same footing in all these respects with the troops of Octavius; provided that the arrangement of the provinces, which had been made in conjunction with Dolabella, should be confirmed; that the acts taken from the will and memoirs of his late colleague should be ratified; that no account should be required of the money which he had taken from the temple of Ops; that the septemviri, or commissioners of the treasury, should not suffer for what they had done in delivering it into his hands: that a general indemnity should pass in favour of all his adherents; that his act relating to judicatures should not be repealed; that upon these conditions he would evacuate the Gallia Togata,[8] but retain the Comata,[9] with six legions, to be completed with draughts from the troops now under Decimus Brutus; that he should have this force as long as Marcus Brutus and Caius Cassius should remain under arms; and that, at any rate, he should retain his division of the province for five years.

In this plan of accommodation, Antony endeavoured to frustrate the principal articles, by means of the conditions which he took care to subjoin; and, in order entirely to defeat the purpose of his antagonists, he sent to Rome, in the company of the deputies of the senate, his quæstor, of the name of Cotyla, with orders to solicit his interest, and to intrigue with the senators and principal citizens.[10] Complaining of the ascendant his enemies had gained in the senate, "With what countenance," he said, "can they arraign the administration of Cæsar, while they submit to that of Cicero? If they allege that Cæsar was an usurper, what is this Cicero, who pretends to dictate to the Roman senate, and to suspend the orders of the Roman people? Let him know that I claim the province of Gaul, in consequence of an appointment from the highest authority in the state, and he may be assured that I shall treat Decimus Brutus as a rebel, if he persist in withholding it from me. The life of this traitor shall atone for that noble blood which he shed in the senate-house, and shall expiate that guilt in which Cicero is fast involving the senate itself."[11]

Antony, in this commission to his quæstor, and in his public declarations, joined with the insolence of the matter, affected expressions of submission to the senate; and made a variety of proposals, either to gain time, or to curry favour with the army, whose interest he pretended tc have greatly at heart. The deputies, who had been employed on this unsuccessful business, incurred much public censure. It was unworthy of L. Piso and of L. Philippus, it was said, to hold any intercourse with a rebel, who refused to comply with the orders that were sent to him.[12] Under this sense of the matter, at a meeting of the senate, it was moved, that war should be declared against Antony, and that every senator should assume the military habit. This motion was agreed to even by Lucius Cæsar, uncle to Antony; a decree was framed upon it, and passed without opposition, by which the army under his command were required, by a certain day, to lay down their arms.[13]

Upon this resolution, obtained by those who strove for the preservation of the commonwealth, great rejoicings were made over all Italy, and it did not then appear from whence any real danger could arise to the authority of laws, which were so properly supported. The consuls, it was observed, acted with great vigour; the senate, the middling class, and the citizens in general, expressed great zeal.[14] The people crowded to have their names enrolled in the levies that were ordered.[15] The reputation which Cicero gained in bringing public affairs into this situation, set him at the head of the commonwealth; but while it placed the whole administration of the state in his hands, it made him an object of great animosity to the opposite party, and of some envy to many persons of principal consideration in his own. It was under the impression of these circumstances, he complained that senators of the first rank were lukewarm, were timid, or ill affected to the cause of the republic.[16]

The conduct of the war was committed to the consuls, and, jointly with them, to Octavius, in the capacity of proprætor. Orders were likewise despatched to Lepidus and to Plancus, to cooperate with these officers. The first was yet on his march into Spain, through the province of Narbonne; the other was posted on the Rhone.[17] The treasury being so much exhausted by the late embezzlements, that there was not money sufficient for the immediate service, it was agreed

7 Cicer. Philip. vii.
8 Within the Alps.
9 Beyond the Alps.
10 Cicero. Philip. viii.
11 Appian. de Bell. Civ. lib. iii.
12 Cicer. ad Famil. lib. xii. ep. 4.
13 Dio. Cass. lib. xlvi. c 29, 30. Cicer. Philip. viii.
14 Cicer. ad Famil. lib. xii. ep. 4.
15 Ibid. lib. xi. ep. 8.
16 Ibid.
17 Dio. Cass. lib. xlvi. c. 39.

that all citizens should pay the five and twentieth part of all their effects; that the senators should pay, over and above, a certain rate for all the houses or tenements they either possessed or let to tenants, and that in aid of these supplies, requisitions of money and of arms should be made through all the towns of Italy.

In the mean time, Octavius, without waiting for the authority with which the senate had lately invested him, had followed Antony across the Apennines, and took post with his army at the Forum Cornelii,[1] on the road from Ariminum[2] to Mutina.[3] The messages which passed between the senate and Antony, as well as the delays which the consuls, under the pretence of winter, made in advancing with their forces, gave him some degree of uneasiness. Pansa was employed at Rome in conducting the new levies. Hirtius, though destined to take the field, and to join Octavius, was still detained by indisposition.[4] Antony continued the siege of Mutina without interruption.

Octavius, after having sent many pressing messages to hasten the march of the consul, was at last joined by him at the Forum Cornelii, and they advanced together; forced the posts which Antony had established at Claterna and Bononia, and encamped at the latter of these places.[5] Here they were still separated by the Rhenus and Lavinius from the army of Antony, which covered the siege of Mutina, and were precluded from any communication with the town. They endeavoured, however, to give notice of their approach to the besieged; and for this purpose, the country being flat, they hoisted lights on the highest trees; but not relying entirely on these signals, they employed a dexterous swimmer, who undertook to pass into the town by the channel of the river, and to carry the intelligence of their arrival engraved on a plate of metal.

Upon this information, Brutus was confirmed in his resolution of defending the place to the last extremity, and prevailed on the garrison, under the hopes of a speedy relief, to persevere in the toils and dangers of their present service.[6]

The senate, notwithstanding that they considered the preservation of the republic as the common cause of all those who could hope to partake in its honours, and believed that the present consuls, Hirtius and Pansa, were sincerely embarked in its cause; and notwithstanding the confidence they placed in Octavius as opposed to Antony, they still relied chiefly on those who had taken an active part against the late usurpation of Cæsar, and looked to Brutus and Cassius for a principal support against the remains of that military faction. On this account, they had annulled the proceedings of Antony relating to the distribution of the eastern provinces, reinstated Marcus Brutus in the government of Macedonia, and Cassius in that of Syria; and, by these appointments, placed the whole resources of the commonwealth, from the Adriatic to the utmost boundary of the empire, under their authority.[7]

Marcus Brutus and Cassius had left Italy in the preceding Autumn. Brutus had passed through Lucania. Thither Porcia accompanied him, with the melancholy prospect of parting, perhaps for ever. While she endeavoured to conceal her grief, she was betrayed into tears by the sight of a picture, which represented the parting of Hector and Andromaché. One of the company, without observing the distress which Porcia seemed to feel, repeated from Homer the lines from which this picture was taken. *My father, my brother, and my husband are, Hector, all in thee.*[8] "But I cannot reply," said Brutus, "in the words of Hector, *go to thy maids, and mind thy loom;* for although Porcia is deficient in strength of body, in her mind she is formed to great affairs."[9]

Brutus, having embarked at Elea, sailed into Greece, where he was received with every mark of respect. Here he seemed to devote himself entirely to study; but had his agents employed to provide what was necessary against the storm, which he had reason to expect. He sent Herostratus into Macedonia to sound the disposition of the troops in that province, and drew about himself all the young Romans who were then at Athens, attending the different schools which still supported the reputation of that place.

While Brutus remained in Greece, a body of troops, under the command of an officer, named Apuleius,[10] with a sum of money amounting to sixteen thousand talents, collected from the revenue of Asia, were delivered up to him. The troops who had served lately under Vatinius in Illyricum, being then at Dyrrachium, deserted from their commander to join him.[11] Those under Caius Antonius, at Apollonia, followed this example. Part of Dolabella's forces, who were marching under Cinna into Asia, likewise left their party to join that of the republic.[12] As Brutus was considered in Macedonia and Thessaly as reviving the party of Pompey, many who had served under that leader, and were yet dispersed in those parts, flocked to his standard, so that the new levies he had ordered, were soon completed to the amount of four legions and five hundred horse. A great convoy, with spare arms, which Cæsar had provided for the Parthian war, and which, by the order of Antony, were then to be again returned into Italy, were intercepted by him at Demetrias. Upon the order of the senate to put him in possession of Macedonia, the greater part of the province, then under the command of Hortensius, acknowledged his authority. At his departure from Athens, many of the young Roman nobility made a part of his retinue, and among these, the son of Marcus Tullius Cicero, who, though with a genius for letters inferior to that of his father, became nevertheless distinguished as a soldier in the course of the war.[13]

Cassius, at the same time, had gone with the utmost despatch into Syria, to prevent Dolabella, who was sent by the opposite party to take possession of that province. He had received some supplies of men and of money from Trebonius, then commanding at Smyrna, and prevailed with

1 Imola. 2 Rimini. 3 Now Modena.
4 Dio. Cass. lib. xlvi. c. 35, 36.
5 Cicer. ad Familiar. lib. xii. ep. 5.
6 Dio. Cass. lib. xlvi. c. 35, 36.
7 Appian. de Bell. Civ. lib. iii.

8 Εκτοϱ, αταϱ συ μιο εσσι πατηϱ και ποτνια μητηϱ,
Ἠδε κασιγνητος,—— Iliad. lib. vi. v. 439.
9 For these particulars, Plutarch quotes young Bibulus, the son of Porcia by a former husband, who was present. Plutarch. in Bruto.
10 Cicer. Philip. xiii. 11 Dio. Cass. lib. xlvii. c. 27
12 Plutarch. in Bruto. 13 Ibid.

part of the cavalry of Dolabella, on their march through the province of Asia, to abandon their leader. With these forces, he advanced into Cilicia, reduced the city of Tarsus, and continued his march, with a respectable appearance, into his intended province.

At the arrival of Cassius, the forces of Syria were divided, and the opposite parties had actually committed hostilities against each other. The troops which had been stationed there by Julius Cæsar, had even, before his death, mutinied, and had put Sextus Julius, a young man who commanded them, to death. They submitted themselves to the command of Cæcilius Bassus, one of Pompey's officers, who, having escaped from Pharsalia, then lay at Tyre, and in this change of their leader, declared for the party of the republic. They defeated Statius Murcus, whom Cæsar had ordered, with three legions, to reduce them, and made it necessary to bring against them a reinforcement of three legions more from Bythinia, under Marcus Crispus. This officer had accordingly brought these forces, and was actually engaged in the siege of Apamea, to which Bassus had retired when Cassius arrived in Syria.

There were now in this province, engaged on opposite sides, no less than eight legions. Upon the arrival of Cassius, the two legions under Bassus declared for him; and soon after the other six, moved by the authority of his commission from the senate, or gained by his personal character and address, followed this example. Four more legions, who, intending to join Dolabella, were marching from Egypt through Palestine,[14] were intercepted, and forced to receive his orders as governor of Syria. His army, by these different accessions, amounted to twelve legions.

Upon the first suspicion that Brutus and Cassius intended to possess themselves of these important provinces, Dolabella, to whom, by the influence of Antony, the command in Syria had been assigned, set out from Rome, and with all possible diligence joined some troops that were placed to receive him on the side of Macedonia, passed the Hellespont, and continued his route to the east. In passing through the province of Asia, he had an interview at Smyrna with Trebonius, professed a friendship for him, affected great respect for his associates in the conspiracy against Cæsar, and a zeal for the restoration of the commonwealth. After this conference with the governor of the province, he put his army in motion with the most pacific appearances on the route to Ephesus; and having by these means put Trebonius off his guard, he returned in the night, surprised the city of Smyrna, seized on the person of the governor, and, with many insults, put him to the torture,[15] continuing him under it for some days, in order to extort a discovery of the treasure which he supposed to be hid in some repository of the province; but on the third day, Dolabella having satiated his mind with these cruelties, gave orders that Trebonius should be strangled, his head severed from the body, and exposed on the point of a spear, while the limbs were dragged through the streets.

This murder, being committed on the person of a Roman officer, within the very province in which he was appointed to command, raised a general indignation. Dolabella was declared a public enemy by the senate. The conduct of the war against him was committed to Caius Cassius, who was now at the head of the armies in Syria, and who, together with Marcus Brutus, was authorised by formal decrees to retain all the forces they had assembled, and all the resources of which they were possessed, and to employ them according to their own judgment, where the service of the republic seemed most to require their exertions.[16]

Thus the flames of war, which were already lighted in Italy, began to extend, and were soon communicated to every part of the empire. The opposite armies before Mutina continued during the winter to observe each other, and in their attempts to give or to withhold relief from the besieged, had frequent skirmishes and partial engagements. The chief direction of affairs at Rome, in the mean time, had devolved on Cicero, who incited the senate and the people, with all the powers of his eloquence against Antony. The soldiers in general, with their officers, were notwithstanding inclined to favour this declared enemy of the commonwealth. Ventidius in particular, who professed to range himself under Octavius, was in reality warmly attached to his rival; and, in order to serve him, formed a design to surprise Cicero, and the other heads of the republican party. For this purpose, he assembled a body of veterans in the neighbourhood of Rome, and advanced towards the city; but his design being suspected, and the persons against whom it was directed having taken the alarm, and withdrawn to places of safety, he turned away to Picenum, and there waited the issue of the campaign.[17]

The senate, during the dependance of these operations, as in full possession of the republic, devised laws, to prevent for the future those abuses which had given rise to the present disorders. They resolved, that no extraordinary commission of any kind should be given to any single person, or any provincial appointment prolonged beyond a year.[18] While they were thus employed, separate addresses were presented to them from Lepidus and from Plancus, warmly recommending an accommodation with Antony.[19] Cicero made his observations on this conduct, in a letter to Plancus of the thirteenth of the kalends of April, or twentieth of March; but he delivers himself to Lepidus on the same subject with more warmth, alluding to some recent honours which had been received by this officer, and for which he neglected to make the proper acknowledgments. "I am glad," he said, "that you wish to reconcile your fellow-citizens to each other. If you could procure them peace without slavery, you would perform a most acceptable service to your country, and acquire much honour to yourself; but if, under the title of peace, we are again to become the slaves of a profligate villain, be assured that every man in his senses will prefer death. In my opinion, therefore, it will be wise in you to desist from a proposal, which neither the senate, the people, nor any good man can approve."[20]

14 Dio. Cass. lib. xlvii. c. 26, 27 28. 15 Ibid. c. 29.

16 Cicer. Philip. xi.

17 Ibid. xii. Cicer. ad Familiar. lib. x. ep. 16.

18 Dio. Cass. lib. xlvi. c 39.

19 Cicer. Philip. xii.

20 Cicer. ad Familiar. lib. x ep. 6 -27

Notwithstanding these sentiments, publicly declared by a person, then supposed to be at the head of the republic, numbers in the city and in the senate espoused the cause of Antony. Piso, at whose house the wife and children of this supposed public enemy were entertained, openly corresponded with him. The consul Pansa proposed a fresh deputation to him with overtures of peace, and his party in the senate insidiously offered to devolve the honour of this deputation upon Cicero himself, who rejected the offer, with proper animadversion on the danger to which his life must be exposed in the camp of his enemy, and discussed with his usual eloquence the weakness of the council itself, as well as the great impropriety of his being employed in it.

While this measure was in agitation, Hirtius and Octavius appear to have sent a joint message to Antony, informing him of what had been proposed in the senate, and desiring a cessation of arms, with liberty to convey some supply to the garrison of Mutina, until the event of the senate's deliberations should be known. Antony replied in terms calculated to insinuate himself into the favour of the late Cæsar's party, and to gain the affection of the army; but full of reproach and contumely against those who pretended to espouse the cause of the commonwealth, and against the authors of the present councils at Rome. These had recently procured a decree of the senate, full of indignation against the murderers of Trebonius, and had furnished Marcus Brutus and Caius Cassius with a commission and warrant to execute public justice against Dolabella on this account. In reference to these circumstances, "I know not (said Antony, in his answer to Hirtius and Octavius) whether I should receive more satisfaction from the death of that villain Trebonius, than I feel indignation at the unjust sentence passed against Dolabella. That the Roman senate should value the life of that vile fellow Trebonius, more than they did that of Cæsar himself, the father of his country, is surely provoking enough; but what must I feel, when I see you Hirtius, whom Cæsar has raised and adorned so much, that I am persuaded you scarcely know yourself; and when I see you, young man, who have no pretence to consideration besides the name of Cæsar, which you have boldly assumed, contributing all in your power to blast the memory of Cæsar, and when I see you both endeavouring to oppress his friends, committing yourselves, with all the powers of the commonwealth, into the hands of Marcus Brutus and of Caius Cassius, who were his murderers; and when I see you joined against me to rescue from justice this assassin, Decimus Brutus, who had so aggravated a part in the same crime? But, the camp and the head quarters of Pompey it seems are to be formed anew, and to bear the name and the authority of a Roman senate, and the exile Cicero is to be set up at the head of this reviving party.

"You are employed in avenging the death of Trebonius, I am employed in avenging that of Cæsar; we, who were once the friends of Cæsar, are like a troop of gladiators to part, and from opposite sides to fight and to cut one another's throats under the direction of Cicero, who is become master of the show! But for me, I have taken my resolution, and will neither suffer the veterans to be stripped of their just rewards, nor the wrongs which are intended to myself and to my friends, to be carried into execution. If in this I am supported, and succeed, life will be sweet; if I fall, the thought of what you are to suffer, from the very party you are now endeavouring to raise up against me, will even then be some consolation. If the faction of Pompey be so insolent in its ruin, I choose that you rather than I, should experience the effect of its recovery, and of its return to power."

Antony, in all his discourses, affected to be in good understanding with Lepidus and with Plancus, who, he insinuated, were in concert with himself, and embarked in the same cause.[1] But whatever secret correspondence these officers may have held together, they and Pollio likewise professed the highest duty to the senate, and affection to the commonwealth. Plancus having, for some time after the commencement of the war, declined any open declaration, now informed the senate in a public address, That he had hitherto been taking measures to render the declaration he should make of real moment to the republic; that he had remained silent so long, not from any hesitation in the choice of his party, but from a desire more effectually to serve that party which he had long since embraced; that before he declared himself, he had secured the co-operation of his officers, the affections of his army, and of the whole province in which he was stationed; that he was now at the head of five complete legions well affected to the republic, and, in consequence of his liberalities, attached to himself; that the whole province was unanimous in the same cause; that the people, with a zeal which a concern for their own freedom or safety could not surpass, had taken arms in support of the Roman republic; that he was ready to obey the orders of the senate, either to retain his command, or to resign it to any person they should appoint to receive it from him; that he would remain in his post, or advance upon the enemy; and by the last of these measures, if it should be thought expedient, draw upon himself the whole weight of the war; that provided he could, by any means, re-establish the commonwealth, or defer its ruin, the manner of doing it was indifferent to him. Others, he said, had declared themselves for the senate, while that body, being greatly alarmed, was lavish of its commendations and of its rewards; but that if he had missed the time in which his services were likely to have been most highly valued, he had chosen the occasion which promised from them the greatest benefit to the commonwealth, a consideration which should be to him a sufficient reward for the highest service he could perform.[2]

Pollio, at the same time, wrote to Cicero, expressing a violent detestation of Antony's party, and of the designs of their leader. To be connected with such a person in any cause, he said, would be grievous; even to have acted under Cæsar, being contrary to his disposition and to his principles, was, notwithstanding the circumstances which obliged him to it, now become sufficient matter of regret. The experience of his condition under that usurper had made him more sensible of the value of freedom, and of the misery of dependence and servitude. "If any one for

1 Cicer. Philip. xiii. 2 Cicer. ad Famil. lib. x. c.8

the future," he continued, "shall pretend to usurp such powers, he shall find in me an open and declared enemy There is no danger to which I will not expose myself in the cause of freedom."[3]

While the party of the senate appeared to gain such accessions of strength by the declaration of so many military officers in the different provinces, Decimus Brutus was reduced to great straits at Mutina; and waited, under many circumstances of distress, for the opening of a campaign, in which he expected that his own fate, and that of the republic, might soon be determined. On the approach of the proper season, the consul Pansa, with the levies he had made, amounting to four legions, marched towards Gaul, and being arrived at Bononia on the fourteenth of April, was next day to have joined his colleague, who had taken post with Octavius, to observe and to impede the progress of the siege. To facilitate their junction, Hirtius had detached the legion which was called the Martia, with two prætorian bands, to occupy the passes, and to strengthen the van of Pansa's army, in case they should be disturbed on their march. Antony, at the same time, having intelligence of their route, marched in the night with two chosen legions, the second and third, two prætorian cohorts, being veteran and experienced troops, with a numerous body of irregulars and horse. He took post at a village, which was called the Forum Gallorum, and posting the horse and irregulars in open view in the field, at some distance from the village, he placed the legions and irregular infantry in ambuscade under the cover of the houses.

When Pansa's army, led by the detachment which Hirtius had sent to receive them, came in sight of Antony's horse and irregulars, they could not be restrained until the posture and strength of the enemy were examined. They broke from their ranks, and without waiting till the village shou'd be visited, they rushed through a defile in a wood or morass to intercept the enemy, who, appearing to consist of horse and light infantry alone, could, as they apprehended, have no hopes of safety but by endeavouring to escape, which it was necessary by an immediate attack to prevent. As the foremost of Pansa's army were passing in the most disorderly manner from this defile, in pursuit of their supposed prey, Antony, with the legions, placed himself in their way, and forced them to fly with great slaughter. Pansa himself was dangerously wounded, and his army obliged to take refuge in the camp from which they had marched in the morning. Here too Antony attempted to force them, but was repulsed; and fearing that his own retreat might be cut off, took his resolution to retire, and endeavoured, without loss of time, to rejoin the main body of his army which lay before Mutina.

Antony was soon justified in his apprehensions of the danger to which the farther pursuit of his victory over Pansa might have exposed him; for Hirtius, having intelligence of the movement he had made in the night, though too late to prevent its effects, had left his camp with twenty cohorts of veterans, arrived at the Forum Gallorum, and was in possession of the very ground on which Pansa had been defeated, when Antony, returning from the pursuit of his victory, fell, in his turn, into the same snare which he himself, a few hours before, had so successfully laid for his enemy, was accordingly surprised and defeated with great slaughter, and with the loss of the eagles or standards of both the legions, and of sixty ensigns of the cohorts. After this disaster, he himself, having fled with the cavalry, arrived about ten at night in his camp about Mutina,[4] from thence sent detachments abroad to collect the remains of his scattered party, or to facilitate their retreat.[5]

Pansa having been carried to Bononia on account of the wounds he had received, Hirtius took the command of his division of the army, and effected its junction with his own, and with that of Octavius.

In this state of affairs, Antony being considerably weakened by his loss in the late action, and the enemy greatly reinforced by their junction, he determined to keep within his lines, to continue the blockade of Mutina, and to await the effect of the distress into which he had already reduced the besieged. The danger to which Decimus Brutus, with the garrison, were exposed, at the same time hastened the endeavours of Hirtius and Octavius to force the besiegers to battle For this purpose, or in order to relieve the town, they made a feint to throw in succours on a side which the besiegers had deemed inaccessible, and which, on this account, they had but slightly guarded. Antony, alarmed by this attempt to render abortive all the labours he had sustained in the preceding blockade, drew forth his army to oppose them, and by this movement exposed himself to the hazard of a general engagement. While he was making his disposition to receive the enemy in the field, his lines were attacked by a sally from the town, and it became necessary to divide his forces. He himself, with that part of his army which remained with him to make head against Hirtius and Octavius, was defeated, fled to his camp, and, being pursued thither, continued to give way, until the action ended by the death of the consul Hirtius, who, after he had forced the intrenchments of the enemy, was killed, and fell near to the prætorium or head-quarters of their general.

Upon this event, Octavius, not having the qualities of a soldier which were necessary to replace the consul, suffered the victorious army, thus checked by the loss of their commander, to be driven back from the ground they had gained, and left Antony again in possession of his works.

The vanquished party, however, feeling all the effects of a defeat, and not being in condition to continue the siege, resolved to decamp in the night; and they executed this resolution unobserved and unmolested by their enemies, either from the town of Mutina or the camp. Octavius had a courage and ability more fit for the council than for the field; and Decimus Brutus, though at break of day he observed that the lines of the besiegers seemed to be evacuated, yet, as he had no intelligence from the camp, remained all that day in suspense. Even after he had received information of what had passed, of the various events of the action, and of the consul's death, and found, that he was from thenceforward to depend on Octavius for support and co-operation

3 Cicer. ad Famil. lib. x. c. 31.

4 Cicer. ad Familiar. lib. x. ep. 30
5 Appian. de Bell. Civ. lib. iii.

in the war, being greatly alarmed by the neglect which this young man had shown in not joining him the moment the communication between them was open; and not being in condition to act alone, having neither cavalry nor baggage-horses, and the troops being greatly reduced by the hardships they had suffered, he was obliged to remain inactive while the enemy continued their retreat undisturbed.[1]

On the second day after the battle, Decimus Brutus, being sent for by Pansa to Bononia to concert the future operations of the war, he learned, on his way, that this consul was dead of his wounds.

By these delays, Antony had got two days march a-head, and, without halting, reached the fens of Sabatta on the coast of Liguria. Here the country being of difficult access he thought himself secure, and made a halt, to consider of his future operations. At the same time Ventidius, who, upon the news of the defeat of his friend at Mutina, had passed the Apennines by hasty marches, followed and joined him at this place.[2]

In the first accounts of Antony's defeat that were carried to Rome, it was reported, that his army had been entirely routed; that he himself had escaped from the field of battle with only a few broken remains of his infantry unarmed; and that to recruit his numbers, he had broken open the work-houses, and set loose and enlisted the slaves.[3]

Upon these representations the senate were greatly elated; and, amidst the acclamations of the people, ordered a feast of thanksgiving, which was to last for sixty days, and renewed the proclamation in which Antony, and all who had served under his command, were declared to have forfeited all the rights of citizens, and to be enemies of their country.[4]

The commonwealth being deprived of its legal head by the death of both the consuls, Decimus Brutus, as next in succession, according to the arrangement which had been made for the ensuing year, became the principal object of consideration with the senate; and being supposed most deeply interested in the preservation of the republic, was the person on whom they chiefly relied for the support of their cause. The senators, accordingly, seemed to drop at once the high regard which they had hitherto paid to Octavius, and overlooking his pretensions and his influence over the army, gave to Brutus the command of all their forces, whether in Italy or in Gaul.

Thus ended the connexion of the young Cæsar with the friends of the republic,—an alliance which had, on both sides, probably been equally insincere. The young man, pretending to have his eyes opened by this conduct of the senate, and supposing that the party of Antony was less hostile to himself than that which had now gained the ascendant in the commonwealth, he slighted the instructions which were sent to him to take his orders from Brutus, retained the command not only of the troops which had followed his own standard, but the command likewise of a legion which had been raised for the republic by Pansa.[5] He refused to co-operate with Decimus Brutus in pursuing the late victory against Antony, and had influence enough with different bodies of the army, particularly with the fourth legion and the Martia, to hinder their obeying the orders they had received from Rome.[6]

In this manner, as the respect which was paid to Octavius by the senate vanished with the occasion which they had for his services; so all the professions he made of concern for the republic, and of zeal for its restoration, disappeared, with the interest which led him to make those professions. And Decimus Brutus, the person now acknowledged by the senate as consul-elect, and head of the republic, for whose relief Octavius affected to have assembled his forces, was left by him to finish the remains of the war against Antony, at the head of such troops as had any degree of attachment to the cause of the republic.

Decimus Brutus, when the war broke out, had a military chest of forty thousand sestertia, about three hundred and twenty thousand pounds; but the whole was now expended, and his own credit likewise exhausted. He was, from this time forward, ill supported at Rome, all motions made in his favour being opposed by the party of Octavius, as well as by that of Antony. The troops that adhered to him amounted to seven legions; these he subsisted by such resources as he himself could command. He advanced to Dertona on the fourth of May;[7] and from thence continuing his march till within thirty miles of the enemy, he received intelligence, that Antony, in a speech to his army, had declared his intention to pass the Alps, and to cast himself entirely on the friendship of Lepidus, in whose disposition he professed to have great confidence; that this proposal being disagreeable to the army, they had declared their resolution to remain in Italy, and exclaimed, That there they would conquer or perish; that Antony had been disconcerted by this declaration, and had continued a whole day undetermined as to his future operations; but in order to conform himself to the inclination of the army, and, if possible, to keep his footing in Italy, he was about to surprise Pollentia, a fortified place on the Tenarus, and had detached Trebellius with a body of cavalry for this purpose.

Decimus Brutus, upon this intelligence, sent forward three cohorts to prevent the design on Pollentia; and these having effected their march in time to secure the place, the enemy, by this disappointment, notwithstanding their late resolution to remain in Italy, were under a necessity of passing the Alps.[8] They undertook this difficult march so ill provided with every necessary, that, according to Plutarch, they had no subsistence but what was found on the route, consisting chiefly of wild herbs, fruits, and animals not commonly used for human food; but Antony himself discovered a patience and a force of mind which no man, judging by his usual way of life, could have expected from him; and, by his own example, supported the spirits of his men through the greatest distresses.[9]

1 Cicer. ad Familiar. lib. xi. ep. 13. 2 Ibid.
3 Ibid. ep. 10 4 Dio. Cass. lib. xlvi. c. 39.
5 Cicer. ad Familiar lib. xi. ep. 20.
6 Ibid ep. 10. 19. 7 Ibid. ep. 10.
8 Ibid. ep. 13 9 Plut. in Antonio.

Lepidus, in consequence of the senate's instructions, or of his own desire to be at hand to take such measures as the state of the war in Italy might require, had discontinued the march of his army into Spain, and returning through the province of Narbonne, had passed the Rhone at its confluence with the Soane; and now, hearing of Antony's march, descended on the left of these rivers, and took a situation to intercept him, not far from the coast at the Forum Vocontium, on a small river called the Argenteum, which empties itself into the sea at Forum Julii.[10]

In the mean time Antony had passed the Alps, and on the fifteenth of May arrived with the first division of his army at Forum Julii, four-and-twenty miles from the station of Lepidus. Ventidius having followed about two days' march in the rear of Antony, and having again joined him at this place, their forces consisted[11] of the second legion entire, with a considerable number of men, but without arms; the broken remains of many legions, together with a body of cavalry, of which, this part of the army having suffered least in the late action, Antony had still a considerable force. But in this position many deserted from him, and his numbers were daily diminishing; Silanus and Culeo, two officers of rank, were among the deserters.

Such was the posture of affairs, on the twenty-first of May, when Lepidus gave to Cicero the strongest assurances[12] of zeal for the commonwealth. Plancus, at the same time, had taken post on the Isere,[13] had thrown a bridge over that river, and waited for the arrival of Decimus Brutus, whom he expected to join him by the most ordinary passage of the Alps:[14] but while he lay in this position he received a message from Lepidus, informing him of Antony's approach, and expressing great distrust of many in his own army, whom he suspected of a disposition to join the enemy. Upon these representations, Plancus marched on the twentieth of May, as appears from his despatches to Rome of this date, expected to join Lepidus in eight days, and hoped, by his presence, to secure the fidelity of the army, which began to be questioned. He wrote, with great confidence, of the zeal and affection of his own troops, and was pleased to say, that he himself, unsupported by any other force, should be able to overwhelm, as he expresses himself, the broken forces of Antony, though joined by the followers of that muleteer Ventidius.[15]

In the mean time, the armies of Antony and Lepidus remaining in sight of each other, frequent messages passed between the leaders; and as no hostilities were committed, the soldiers conversed freely together, though without any apparent effect.[16] Lepidus still professed to govern himself by the orders of the senate, and to employ his army in support of the commonwealth. But while he preserved these appearances, he sent an order to countermand the junction of Plancus; and having convened his own army, as usual, around the platform,[17] from which it was the custom to harangue the troops, he addressed them in a speech, in which he repeated his professions of duty to the republic, and urged a vigorous exertion in the war. It had not yet appeared to what point these professions were tending, when he was answered with exclamations, which he probably expected, from some leading persons among the soldiers, in which they declared the wishes of the army for peace. Two Roman consuls, they said, had been already killed in this unnatural quarrel. The best blood of the republic had been spilt, and the most respectable citizens declared enemies of their country; that it was time to sheath the sword; "for our parts," they said, "we are determined that our arms, from henceforward, shall not be employed on either side."[18] From this audience the army of Lepidus proceeded to invite Antony into their camp, and presenting him to their general as a friend, terminated the war between them by a coalition, in appearance forced upon Lepidus, but probably previously concerted with himself.

Antony was now joined with Lepidus in the command of the army which had come to oppose him, and by his popularity, or superior ability, soon got the ascendant of his colleague. He found himself again at the head of a great force, composed of the remains of his late defeat, three legions that had joined him under Ventidius, and seven of which the army of Lepidus consisted.[19]

Plancus, being still upon his march, persisted in his intention to join Lepidus notwithstanding he had received an order or instruction from himself to the contrary; but having, at last, received positive information of his defection, and considering the danger to which he himself must be exposed with an inferior force against two armies united, he returned to his post on the Isere, and sent pressing instances to hasten the march of Decimus Brutus, and of other succours from Italy.[20]

Lepidus, even after the reception of Antony into his camp, addressed the senate in a solemn declaration, still asserting his affection to the commonwealth, and representing the late change of his measures as the effect of necessity imposed upon him by the troops, who, in a mutinous manner, refused to make war on their fellow-citizens. While he made these professions, he recommended to the senate the example of the army, exhorted them to drop all private animosities, to make the public good the rule of their conduct, and not to treat as a crime, the humane and merciful disposition which fellow-citizens had exercised towards each other.[21]

At the same time despatches arrived from Plancus and Decimus Brutus, both treating the pretended mutiny of the army in Gaul as a mere artifice of their general to conceal his own defection.[22] The city was greatly alarmed, even the populace, affecting a zeal for the authority of the senate, demolished the statues which had been lately erected to Lepidus. The senators, incensed not only at his treachery, but at the false professions with which he presumed to address them on the subject, proceeded to declare him a public enemy, and resolved, that all his adherents, who did not return to their duty before the first o

10 Frejus. 11 Cicer. ad Familiar. lib. x. ep. 17.
12 Ibid. 13 Isura.
14 Probably by Mount Cenis, or the channels of the Dorea Baltea and the Isere.
15 Cicer. ad Familiar. lib. x. ep. 13.
16 Appian. de Bell. Civ. lib. iii.
17 The suggestum, most commonly raised of turf.

18 Cicer. ad Familiar. lib. x. ep. 21.
19 Appian. de Bell. Civ. lib. iii.
20 Cic. ad Famil. lib. x. ep. 21.
21 Ibid. ep. 35. 22 Ibid.

September, should be involved in the same sentence. Private instructions were sent, at the same time, to Marcus Brutus, and to Caius Cassius, urging them to hasten the march of their forces for the defence of the capital.[1]

During these transactions, Octavius remained inactive on the frontiers of Italy. The demise of the two consuls opened a new scene to his ambition. This event came so opportunely for his purpose, and his own character for intrigue was so much established, that he was suspected of having had an active part in procuring the death of those officers. It was said, that he employed some emissaries to despatch Hirtius in the heat of battle; and that Pansa's wound, not being mortal, he suborned the person who dressed it, to render it so by an injection of poison. A surgeon named Glyco was actually taken into custody on this account; the suspicion remained against Octavius till the last moment of his life, and even made a part in the grievous reproaches with which his memory continued to be loaded after his death.[2] It was rejected, however, at the time, even by Marcus Brutus, who warmly interceded with Cicero in behalf of Glyco, as a person who was himself a great sufferer by Pansa's death, and who bore such a reputation for probity as ought to have secured him against this imputation.[3] The testimony of Marcus Brutus, when given in favour of Octavius, must, no doubt, be admitted as of the greatest authority, and may be allowed, in a great measure, to remove the whole suspicion.

Octavius himself gave out, that Pansa, when dying of his wounds, desired to see him in private, gave him a view of the state of parties, and advised him no longer to remain the tool of those who meant only to demolish the party of Cæsar, in order that they themselves might rise on its ruins. But from the detail of what passed in the interval between the battle of Mutina and the death of Pansa, of which Decimus Brutus sent an account to Cicero, it does not appear that Octavius could have seen Pansa. And it is probable, that this pretended advice of the dying consul was fabricated afterwards, to justify the part which Octavius took against the senate.[4] The supposed admonition of Pansa, at any rate, was probably not necessary to dissuade Octavius from continuing to support the republic longer than his own interest required. This was the great rule of his conduct, and if, until that hour, he continued to believe, that the senate intended to raise him on the ruin of Antony's party, in order that he might become their own master and sovereign of the commonwealth, he fancied surely what was not probable, and what they never professed to be their intention. The restoration of the republican government, and of the senate's authority, implied, that individuals were to be satisfied with receiving the honours of the republic in their turn; and with this prospect, Octavius himself affected to be satisfied, so long as it suited with the state of his fortunes, to act the part of a republican.

The commonwealth undoubtedly sustained a great loss in the death of the two consuls. Though trained up under Cæsar, and not possessed of any remarkable share of political virtue, they were men probably of moderate ambition, tenacious of the dignities to which they themselves and every free citizen might aspire, but not covetous of more. They were likely, therefore, to acquiesce in the civil establishment of their country, and by the dignity of their characters, to overawe the more desperate adventurers, whose views and successes were inconsistent with the safety of the commonwealth.

If the consuls, Hirtius and Pansa, had lived even with such abilities as they possessed, they might have kept Lepidus within the bounds of his duty, they might have prevented Antony from recovering the defeat which he had lately received at Mutina, and obliged Octavius, if not to drop his ambitious designs, at least to defer the execution of them to a more distant period. But, immediately after the death of these magistrates, it became evident, that this young man was dissatisfied with his situation and with his party, he not only kept at a distance from Decimus Brutus, but seemed determined not to take any part in the farther operations of the campaign. The prisoners that were in his hands he treated as friends, and by suffering them, without any exchange or ransom, to join their own army, gave hopes that he was ready to treat on reasonable terms of a reconciliation with their general. He at the same time took steps with the senate that seemed to prognosticate a rupture, made application for a triumph, in which neither his age, his rank, nor his share in the late action, or in the victory obtained over Antony, in any degree supported him; and having failed in this attempt, he declared his intention to sue for the office of consul.

Octavius, when he offered himself as a candidate for the consulate, according to Dion Cassius, affected to insist that Cicero[5] should be associated with him in the office,[6] and should take the whole administration on himself. For his own part, he said, that, in this association, he aspired only to the title of Magistrate; that all the world must know, the whole authority of government, and all the glory to be reaped in the public service would redound to his colleague; that, in this request, and in that he had made for a triumph, he had no object but to gain a situation in which he might lay down his arms with honour, as having such a public attestation in behalf of his services.[7]

Cicero, according to the testimony of the same historian, fell into the snare that was laid for him by this artful boy, supported his pretensions, and was willing to become the colleague and the tutor of this reviving Cæsar.

Octavius afterwards boasted of the artifice he had employed in this piece of flattery to Cicero, as the only means he had left, at that time, to secure the continuance of his military command.[8] But the senators, and the partizans of the conspirators, in particular, were greatly exasperated. The proposition appeared so strange, that no tribune, no person in any office, not even any private citizen, could be found to move it.[9] The ani-

1 Appian. de Bell. Civ. lib. iii.
2 Tacit. Annal. lib. i. c. 10.
3 Cicer. ad Brutum, ep. 3 edit. Olivet. tom. 9.
4 Cicer. ad Familiar. lib. xi. ep. 13.
5 Dio. Cass. lib. xlvi. c. 42.
6 Appian. de Bell. Civ. lib. iii.
7 Cicer. ad Brutum. ep. 10.
8 Plut. in Cicer.
9 Cicer. ad Brutum, ep. 18.

mosity of Cicero to Antony had already, they thought, carried him too far in supporting the pretensions of this aspiring young man. If he should prevail on the present occasion, all that the senate had hitherto done to restore the constitution would be fruitless. A person, who presumed to claim the office of consul at an age so improper, and so far short of that which the law prescribed, was likely, when possessed of this power, to set no bounds to his usurpations. In order, therefore, to elude his requisition, they were obliged to defer the elections, and, in the mean time, appointed ten commissioners under pretence of inquiring into the abuses committed in Antony's administration, and of distributing to the army the gratuities, and of executing the settlements devised for their late services, but probably with a real intention to vest these commissioners with the chief direction of affairs, until it could be determined who should succeed in the office of consul, and who should be intrusted with the safety of the republic. The partizans of the commonwealth were now, in appearance, superior to their enemies, but far from being secure in possession of the superiority they had gained.[10]

The senate, in order to exclude Octavius from this commission, without giving him any particular reason to complain of their partiality, at the same time left out Decimus Brutus; and by this equal exclusion of persons at the head of armies from the management of affairs, in which the armies were so much concerned, they enabled Octavius to fill the minds of the soldiers with distrust of the civil power, and to state the interests of the civil and military factions as in opposition to each other.[11] He no longer, therefore, disguised his aversion to the senate; complained, that they treated him disrespectfully, called him a boy, who must be amused,[12] decked out with honours, and afterwards destroyed.[13] "I am excluded," he said, "from the present commission, not from any distrust in me, but from the same motive from which Decimus Brutus is also excluded, a general distrust of every person who is likely to espouse the interests of the army; and, from these exclusions, it is evident what they intend with respect to the claims of the veterans, and with respect to their expectations of a just reward for their services."[14]

Upon the junction of Antony with Lepidus, the senate felt the necessity of paying a little more attention than they had lately done to the interest of Octavius. Instead of appointing him to act under Decimus Brutus, as they at first intended, they joined him in the command of the army; and in this new situation required him to co-operate in defending Italy against the united forces of Antony and Lepidus.

Octavius instantly communicated to the army these orders of the senate, with insinuations of the hardships which they were now to undergo on being sent on a fresh service, before they had received the rewards which were promised and due to them for the former; and he proposed, that they should send deputies to the senate with proper representations on this subject.

A number of centurions were accordingly selected to carry the mandate of the army to Rome. As they delivered their message in the name of the legions, without any mention of Octavius, this was thought a favourable opportunity to negotiate directly with the troops, without consulting their leader; and the senate accordingly sent a commission for this purpose, with the hopes that they might be able to detach the whole army from their general, or that at least they might be able to engage, in their own cause, those legions in particular, who had deserted from Antony, with professions of zeal for the commonwealth.

Octavius, to counteract this design before the commissioners employed in the execution of it arrived, drew forth his army, and in a speech complained of this and of the former injuries he had received from the senate: "Their intention," he said, "is to cut off separately all the leaders of Cæsar's party. When they have accomplished this purpose, the army too must fall at their feet.[15] They will recall the grants of land which have been made to you, and will deprive you of the just reward of all your faithful services. They charge me with ambition; but what evidence is there of my ambition? Have I not declined the dignity of prætor, when you offered to procure it for me?—My motive is not ambition, but the love of my country; and for this I am willing to run any hazard to which I myself may be exposed; but cannot endure, upon any account, that you should be stripped of what you have so dearly bought by your services in the public cause. It is now become evident, that in order to prevent the most dangerous powers from coming into the hands of your enemies, and in order to ensure the rewards to which you are so justly entitled, it is necessary that your friends should be raised to the head of the commonwealth. In the capacity of consul I shall be able to do justice to your merits; to punish the murderers of my father, to be revenged of your enemies, and at last to bring these unhappy domestic dissensions to an end."[16]

This harangue was returned with acclamations of joy, and a second deputation, to be escorted by four hundred men, was instantly appointed from the army, demanding the consulate for their general. The officers employed in this service were repeatedly admitted to audiences in the senate.[17] In answer to the objections which were drawn from the defects of their general's age and title, they urged former precedents; that of Scipio, of Dolabella, and the special act relating to Octavius himself, in whose favour ten years of the legal age were already dispensed with. One of the officers, in this singular deputation, while the senate proposed a delay in order to deliberate on the matter, is said to have shown the hilt of his dagger; and some one of the party who escorted the deputies, in resuming his arms at the door of the senate-house, was heard to say, in girding the belt of his sword, *If you will not confer the consulate on Octavius, this shall.* To these menacing insinuations, Cicero, who had jokes imputed to him, on occasions that were

10 Appian. de Bell. Civ. lib. iii.
11 Cicer. ad Familiar. lib. xi. ep. 20.
12 Ibid. ep. 21.
13 Laudandum adolescentem, ornandum, tollendum. —This last word is ambiguous. This saying was imputed to Cicero, but is peremptorily denied.
14 Sueton. in Octavio, c. 12.

15 Appian. de Bell Civ. lib. iii. 16 Ibid.
17 Dio. Cass. lib. xlvi. c. 42.

equally serious to himself and to the republic, is said to have replied, *Nay, if you pray in that language, you will surely be heard.*

While the senate delayed giving any direct answer to this military demand, they again sent a deputation of their own members with money to be distributed to the legions, hoping, by this means, to divert them from the project which they had formed in favour of their general. But Octavius being secretly apprised that a sum of money was sent to corrupt his army, and observing that the soldiers were impatient at having no immediate return to their own message, chose not to await the trial of this dangerous experiment, separated the legions into two columns, marched directly to Rome; and on his way being met by the deputies of the senate, he commanded them, at their peril, not to approach the army, or to interrupt its march.

Upon the news of his approach, the city was thrown into great consternation. The senate, believing they had erred in offering too little money to the troops, ordered the former bounty to be doubled.[1] They resolved that Octavius should be admitted to the consulate; or, according to Dion Cassius, that he should have the title and ensigns of consul, but without the actual power; that he should have a place in the senate among those who had been consuls; that he should be prætor at the first elections, and consul at the following.[2] And thus having done enough to show their fears, but not to disarm, or to lull the ambition of this presumptuous young man, they sent new deputies, with every symptom of trepidation and alarm, to intimate these resolutions.

Soon after this deputation from the senate was despatched, two legions, lately transported from Africa, and ordered for the defence of the city, having arrived at the gates, the senators, with their party among the people, resumed their courage: they were even disposed to recall their late concessions, and began to exclaim, that it were better to perish in defending their liberties, than, without any struggle, to fall a prey to their enemies. Persons of every description assumed the military dress, and ran to their arms.

There were now at Rome three legions, with a thousand horse; one legion having been left there by Pansa when he marched towards Gaul. These troops were posted on the side from which the enemy was expected, on the Janiculum and the bridge which led from thence to the city. Galleys were ordered to be in readiness at Ostia, to convey the public treasure beyond the sea, in case it should become necessary to take this measure to save it: and it was determined to seize the mother and sister of Octavius,[3] who were then supposed to be at Rome, and to detain them as hostages. But this intention was frustrated by the timely escape of these women, who, apprehending some danger, had already withdrawn from the city. Their flight, or the early precaution which they themselves, or their friends, had taken in this matter, was considered as the evidence of a long premeditated design on the part of Octavius.

Under this impression, and that of the superior force with which it was known Octavius was prepared to assail them, the senators again lost hopes of being able to resist; but they flattered themselves, that the resolution they had taken to defend the city, would not be known in time to prevent their first message to the army from being delivered. Their concessions were accordingly published among the troops; but appearing to be forced, were received with contempt, and served only to encourage the presumption of the soldiers, and to hasten their march. As the army drew near to the city, all the approaches were deserted by those who had been placed to defend them, and the advanced guard of Octavius passed to the Mons Quirinalis, without being met by any person in the quality either of friend or of enemy. But, after a little pause, numbers of his own party among the people having gone forth to receive him, the streets were instantly crowded with persons of all ranks, who hastened to pay their court.[4]

Octavius having halted his army during the night in the first streets which they entered; on the following day, with a proper escort, and amidst the shouts and acclamations of the multitude, took possession of the forum. The troops who had been assembled to oppose him, at the same time left their stations, and made an offer of their services. Cornutus, one of the officers who commanded those troops, having in vain endeavoured to prevent this defection, killed himself Cicero is said to have desired a conference with his young friend; but when he seemed to presume on his former connection, was coldly answered, that he had been slow in his present advances.

In the following night a rumour was spread, that the Martia and the fourth legion, which made a part in the army of Octavius, but supposed to be particularly attached to the senate on account of the late honorary decrees which had passed in their favour, had declared against the violent measures of their leader; that they offered to protect the senate and people in their legal assemblies, and in any resolutions they should form on the present state of the republic. Numbers of senators believed this report, and were about to resume their meetings. Crassus, one of the prætors, set out for the Picenum, where he had considerable influence, in order to assemble what forces he could raise to secure the success of this design; but before morning this report was known to be groundless, and all orders of men returned to their former dejection and submission.

At break of day Octavius removed the army from the streets of Rome into the Campus Martius. He did not suffer any acts of cruelty to be committed, or make any inquiry after those who had been forward in opposing his claims. He affected the clemency of his late uncle; but like him too, without any scruple, laid his hands on the public treasure, made a distribution to the army of the sums which had been first decreed to them; and engaged for himself, soon after, to add from his own estate what had been successively promised. Having ordered that the election of consuls should immediately proceed, he withdrew with the army, affecting to leave the people

1 Appian. de Bell. Civ. lib. iii.
2 Dio. Cass. lib. xlvi. c. 41.
3 Appian. de Bell. Civ. lib iii.

4 Appian. de Bello Civ. lib. iii.

to a free choice. And being himself elected, together with Q. Pedius, whom, without any mention of Cicero, he had recommended for this purpose, he returned in solemn procession to offer the sacrifices usual on such occasions, and entered on his office on the twenty-first of September, the day before he completed his twentieth year.[5]

On this occasion the young Cæsar, in the capacity of consul, made a speech to the troops, acknowledging their services; but avoided imputing to their interposition the honours which he had recently obtained in the city. For these honours he returned his thanks to the senate, and to the assemblies of the people. These he accosted as the sovereigns of the empire; and was answered by an affected belief of his sincerity.

In the same spirit of servility with which so many honours had been decreed to Julius Cæsar, it was enacted, that Octavius should for ever take rank of every consul, and the command of every general, at the head of his own army; that he should have an unlimited commission to levy troops, and to employ them where the necessities of the state might require;[6] that his adoption into the family of Cæsar should now be ratified in the most solemn manner by the assembly of the Curiæ; a form which the laws of the republic required in every such case, and in which he had been formerly prevented by the intrigues of Antony; that the act declaring Dolabella an enemy of his country should be repealed, and an inquest set on foot for the trial of those who had been concerned in the death of Julius Cæsar.

In consequence of this establishment, numbers were cited, and upon their non-appearance were condemned. Among these were Marcus Brutus and Caius Cassius. In giving sentence against them, the judges affected to show their ballots; and a citizen, of the name of Silicius Coronas, being of the number, likewise held up his ballot into public view; but, in the midst of this tide of servility and adulation, had the courage to acquit the accused. His courage for the present passed without animadversion, but he was reserved, with silent resentment, as an object of future punishment.[7]

CHAPTER IV.

Proceedings of the new Consul—State of the Eastern Provinces—Interview of Octavius, Antony, and Lepidus, with their Coalition—The Proscription or Massacre—Death of Cicero—Sequel of the Massacre—Succession of Consuls—Severe Exaction of Taxes—State of Sextius Pompeius—Movements of Antony and Octavius respectively—Both bend their course to the East—Posture and Operations of Brutus and Cassius—Their arrival and progress in Europe—Campaign at Philippi—First Action and Death of Cassius—Second Action and Death of Brutus.

THE republic, of which Octavius was now, in appearance, the legal magistrate, had declared open war against Antony and Lepidus; and, in consequence of this declaration, the forces of Decimus Brutus and of Plancus, as has been mentioned, had advanced to the Rhone and the Isere, but had been obliged again to retreat, in order to avoid coming to action with a superior enemy. It was considered, therefore, as the first object of the consul to reinforce that army of the republic, and to carry the decrees of the senate into execution against those who presumed to dispute their authority. He accordingly marched from the city as upon this design; but it soon after appeared, that he had been some time in correspondence with these supposed enemies of their country; that he intended to join them against the senate, and, with their forces united, to resist the storm which was gathering against them in the east, under the governors of Macedonia and Syria.

While the siege of Mutina was still in dependance, Marcus Brutus had drawn his forces towards the coast of Epirus, with intention to pass into Italy; but having received a report that Dolabella, then in the province of Asia, had transported a body of men from thence to the Chersonesus,[8] and that he seemed to intend the invasion of Macedonia, he was obliged to return for the defence of his own province; and from thenceforward, by the state of the war in Syria was hindered, during some time, from taking any part in the affairs of the west.

Dolabella, in consequence of his appointment to the government of Syria, after the murder of Trebonius, had assembled a fleet on the coast, to accompany the march of his army by land, and to dispute the possession of that province with Cassius.[9] His operations, however, began in that quarter with his receiving a great check to his hopes in the defeat of his fleet; his galleys having been dispersed, and all his transports taken by Lentulus, who had served under Trebonius, and who now commanded the fleets of Brutus and Cassius in those seas.[10] Notwithstanding the defeat of his forces at sea, he advanced by land into Cilicia; and while his antagonist lay in Palestine, to intercept the legions that were coming to join him from Egypt, he made considerable levies, took possession of Tarsus, reduced the party which Cassius had left at Ægа, and proceeded to Antioch; but finding the gates of this town were shut against him, he continued his march to Laodicæa, where he was admitted; being determined to make a stand at this place, he again assembled the remains of his fleet, in order to bring his supply of stores and provisions by sea.[11] Having encamped and intrenched his army close to the walls of Laodicæa, he threw

5 Vell. Paterculus, lib. ii. c. 65.
6 Dio. Cass. lib. xlvi. c. 39.
7 Appian. de Bell. Civ. lib. iii.
8 Cicer. ad Brutum, ep. 2.

9 Cicer. ad Famil. lib. xii. ep. 12. 10 Ibid. ep 15
11 Dio. Cass. lib. xlvii. c. 30.

down part of the ramparts, to open a communication between his camp and the town.[1]

Cassius, having intelligence of this progress made by Dolabella in Syria, and of his dispositions to secure Laodicæa, prepared to dislodge him from thence. For this purpose he advanced to Pallos, at the distance of twenty miles from the enemy's station, and took measures, by cutting off his supplies both by sea and by land, to reduce him by famine. In execution of this design, he endeavoured to procure shipping from every part of the coast, extending from Rhodes to Alexandria; but found that most of the maritime states of Asia were already drained by his enemy, or were unwilling to declare themselves for either party. The port of Sidon was the first that furnished him any supply of vessels; but the officer who commanded them having ventured to appear before Laodicæa, was unable to cope with the navy which Dolabella had collected from his late defeat; and, though he defended himself with great obstinacy, and with great slaughter of the enemy, after many ships were sunk on both sides, suffered a capture of five galleys with all their crews. Notwithstanding this check, Cassius was soon after joined by squadrons from Tyre, Aradus, and even from Cyprus. The governor of this island, contrary to the orders of Cleopatra, his sovereign, who had assembled her fleet to support Dolabella, ventured to change their destination, and to take part with Cassius.[2]

With this accession of force, Cassius being again in condition to block up the harbour of Laodicæa, presented himself for this purpose, and two engagements followed; in the first of which the advantage was doubtful; in the second, the victory declared for Cassius, and rendered him master of the coast. Holding his enemy, therefore, blocked up by sea, he continued to press upon the town from the land, and, by the fifth of June, had reduced the besieged to great distress; but while he seemed to rely entirely on the effects of this circumstance,[3] he carried on a correspondence with the garrison, and, on a day concerted with the officer on duty, was admitted into the place.

Dolabella, finding that the town was delivered up, chose to fall by the sword of one of his own men, of whom he requested the favour to save him, by this last act of duty, from falling into the hands of his enemies. The troops who had served under him acknowledged the authority of his rival, and took the oath of fidelity usual in ranging themselves under a new general. Cassius seized what money he found in the public treasury, or in the temples at Laodicæa, laid the citizens under a heavy contribution, and put some of those who had been most forward in saving his enemy to death.[4]

Such was known, some time before the battle of Mutina, to be the event of affairs in Asia; and the fortunes of Marcus Brutus and Cassius, they being supposed to have twenty legions under their command, with all the resources of the Eastern empire, were still in a thriving condition, when Octavius, soon after his nomination to the office of consul, under pretence of urging the war against Antony and Lepidus, had taken his departure from Rome, leaving his colleague, Pedius, in the administration of the city. To him he had given instructions to obtain, as of his own accord, the revocation of the acts by which Antony and Lepidus had been declared public enemies. He incited the army, at the same time, to demand a reconciliation of parties, and administered an oath to them, in which they swore not to draw their swords against any of the troops who had ever served under Cæsar. As Pedius made no mention of his colleague in making his motion in favour of Antony and Lepidus, the senate, not knowing how far it might be agreeable to Octavius, referred the whole matter to himself; and, upon his having signified his approbation, proceeded to revoke their former decree of attainder.[5] By these means Octavius, without appearing himself as the author of this change, transferred the imputation of treason from Antony and Lepidus to Brutus and Cassius, with their adherents in the late conspiracy against the life of Cæsar.

As soon as the state of parties was thus transformed, Octavius congratulated the senate on the wisdom of their measures, and from thenceforward treated with Antony and Lepidus as friends, corresponded with them on the subject of the commonwealth, and invited them, without loss of time, to return into Italy.

Under pretence of this revolution in the government, Plancus withdrew his forces from the army of Decimus Brutus, and espoused the cause, which the republic itself, under the authority of the consuls, appeared to avow. Pollio likewise followed this example.

In consequence of these separations, Decimus Brutus was left singly to withstand the force of so many enemies who were united, and now supported against him with the authority of the state itself. He still had ten legions, of which the four with which he had defended the city of Mutina during the preceding winter, were not yet recovered from the sufferings of that service. With the other six, being raw and undisciplined troops, he did not think himself in condition to continue the war against so many enemies; and he determined, therefore, to withdraw by Illyricum into Macedonia, and to join himself with the forces which were raised for the republic in that province. But in the execution of this design he found, that in civil wars armies are not easily retained on the losing side, and had occasion to observe, that they are never hearty in behalf of civil institutions against a professed intention to establish military government. On pretence of the hardships of the proposed march, he was deserted first by the new levies, and afterwards by the veterans, with all the irregulars, who, except a few Gaulish horse, went over with their colours to the enemy. Of those who remained, he, under the deepest impressions of despair, allowed as many as chose it to depart; and with only three hundred horsemen who adhered to him, set out for the Rhine, intending to make his intended retreat through Germany. But, in proportion as difficulties multiplied on his way, the little troop which attended him greatly diminished; and being reduced to ten, he imagined that, with so few in his company, he might even pass through Italy undiscovered. He ac-

1 Cicer. ad Famil. lib. xii. ep. 13.
2 Appian. de Bell. Civ. lib. iii.
3 Cicer. ad Famil. lib. xii. ep. 13.
4 Appian. de Bell. Civ. lib. iii.

5 Dio. Cass. lib. xlvi. c. 44.

cordingly disguised himself, and returned to Aquileia; but being there seized, though unknown, as a suspicious person, and being conducted to an officer of the district who knew him, he was, by the orders of Antony, put to death.[6]

Thus, while all the military powers of the east were assembled under Marcus Brutus and Cassius, with a professed design to restore the republic, those of the west were equally united for a contrary purpose. Antony and Lepidus having passed the Alps, descended the Po, and advanced towards Mutina. Octavius being already in that neighbourhood with his army, they met, with five legions of each side, on the opposite banks of the Lavinus, not far from the scene of their late hostile operations against each other. The leaders agreed to hold a conference in a small island formed by the separation and re-union of two branches of the river. To the end that they might have equal access to this island, bridges were laid on the divisions of the Lavinus by which the island was formed. The armies drew up on the opposite banks; and as the recent animosities of Antony and Octavius still left some remains of distrust between them, Lepidus first entered alone into the place that was intended for their conference; and having seen that no snares were laid by either party, he made the signal agreed on, and was joined by the other two without any attendants.

Octavius now met with Antony in a character more respectable than that in which he had formerly appeared to him, and, with the dignity of the Roman consul in office, had the place of honour assigned to him. They continued their conference during this and the two following days;[7] and at the expiration of this time made known to their armies, that they had agreed on the following articles: That Octavius, in order to divest himself of every legal advantage over his associates, should resign the consulate; that the three military leaders, then upon an equal footing, should hold or share among them, during five years, the supreme administration of affairs in the empire; that they should name all the officers of state, magistrates, and governors of provinces; that Octavius should have the exclusive command in Africa, Sardinia, and Sicily, Lepidus in Spain, and Antony in Gaul; that Lepidus should be substituted for Decimus Brutus in the succession to the consulate for the following year, and should have the administration at Rome, while Octavius and Antony pursued the war against Brutus and Cassius in the east; that the army, at the end of the war, should have settlements assigned to them in the richest districts and best situations of Italy. Among the last were specified Capua, Rhegium, Venusia, Beneventum, Nuceria, Ariminum, and Vibona.

To ratify this agreement, the daughter of Fulvia, the wife of Antony, by Clodius her former husband, was betrothed to Octavius. He was said to have already made a different choice, and consequently to have had no intention to fulfil this part of the treaty;[8] but the passions, as well as the professions, of this young man, were already sufficiently subservient to his interest.[9]

While the army was amused by the publication of these several articles, the circumstances which chiefly distinguished this famous coalition was the secret resolution, then taken, to extinguish at once all future opposition to the Cæsarian party, by massacring all their private and public enemies. They drew up a list, of which the numbers are variously reported, comprehending all those who had given them private or public offence, and in which they mutually sacrificed their respective friends to each other's resentment. Antony sacrificed his uncle Lucius Cæsar to the resentment of Octavius; who, in his turn, sacrificed to that of Antony, Cicero, with Thoranius, his own guardian, and his father's colleague in the office of prætor.[10] Lepidus gave up his own brother L. Paulus; and all of them agreed to join with these private enemies every person supposed to be attached to the republican government, amounting in all to three hundred senators and two thousand of the equestrian order, besides many persons of inferior note, whose names they deferred entering in the list until their arrival at Rome. They meant, as soon as they should be in possession of the capital, to publish the whole list for the direction of those who were to be employed in the execution of the massacre. But as there were a few whose escape they were particularly anxious to prevent, they agreed that the murders should begin, without any warning, by the death of twelve or seventeen of their most considerable enemies, and among these by the death of Marcus Tullius Cicero.[11] They ratified the whole by mutual oaths; and having published all the articles, except that which related to the massacre, the plan of reconciliation between the leaders was received by the armies with shouts of applause, and was supposed to be the beginning of a period in which military men were to rest from their labours, and to enjoy undisturbed the most ample reward of their services.

This celebrated cabal, known by the name of the Second Triumvirate, having thus planned the division or joint administration of an empire which each of them hoped in time to engross for himself, they proceeded to Rome with an aspect which, to those who composed the civil establishment of the commonwealth, was more terrible than that of any faction which had been hitherto formed for its destruction.

In former times, individuals rose to the head of parties or factions, and brought armies to their standard by the natural ascendant of superior abilities; and either disdained the advantages of usurped dominion, or knew how to employ their powers in exertions not unworthy of human reason. But in this instance, persons obscure, or only known by their profligacy, were followed by armies who conceived the design of enslaving their country. The spirit of adventure pervaded the meanest rank of the legions, and every soldier grasped at the fruits that were to be reaped in subduing the commonwealth. If no person had offered to put himself at their head, they themselves would have raised up a leader whom they might follow in seizing the spoils of their fellow-citizens.

Lepidus, noted for his want of capacity, being in the rank of prætor when Cæsar took possession of Rome, and being the only Roman officer

6 Appian. de Bell. Civ. lib. iii.
7 Ibid. lib. iv.
8 Dio. Cass. lib. xlvi. c. 54, 55, 56.
9 Ibid.
10 Sueton. in Octav. c. 27.
11 Appian. de Bell. Civil. lib. iv.

of state who was willing to prostitute the dignity of his station, by abetting the violence which was now done to the constitution, was entrusted with power, and the command of an army, merely because he brought the name and authority of a magistrate to the side of the usurpation. The use of his name had been likewise convenient to Antony in the late junction or coalition of their armies; and was now necessary or convenient to both the other parties in this famous association, as he held a kind of balance between them, and was to witness transactions in which neither was willing to trust the other.

Antony, possessed of parts which were known chiefly by the profligate use which he made of them, seeking to repair by rapine a patrimony which he had wasted in debauch; and sometimes strenuous when pressed by necessity, yet ever relapsing in every moment of ease or relaxation into the vilest debauchery or dissipation.

Octavius, yet a boy, only known by acts of perfidy and cunning above his years; equally indifferent to friendship or enmity, apparently defective in personal courage, but followed by the remains of Cæsar's army, as having a common cause with themselves in securing the advantages which they severally claimed by virtue of his authority. He was now about the twentieth year of his age, had been already two years at the head of a faction, veering in his professions and in his conduct with every turn of fortune; at one time reconciled with the authors of Cæsar's death, and courting the senate, by affecting the zeal of a citizen for the preservation of the commonwealth: at another time, courting the remnant of his late uncle's army, by affecting concern for their interests, and a solicitude for the security of the grants they had obtained from Cæsar: at variance with Antony on the score of personal insults and incompatible pretensions, even charged with designs on his life; but reconciled to him, in appearance, from considerations of interest or present conveniency. He had already, in the transactions of so short a life, given indications of all the vilest qualities incident to human nature, perfidy, cowardice, and cruelty; but with an ability or cunning which, if suffered to continue its operations, was likely to prevail in the contest for superiority with his present rivals in the empire.

Such was the received description of persons who had now parcelled among themselves the government of the world, and whose vices were exaggerated by the fears of those who were likely to suffer by the effects of their power. Under the dominion of such a junto, if any one were left to regret the loss of public liberty, or to feel the state of degradation into which citizens were fallen; if any one could look forward from the terrors of a present tyranny to the prospect of future evils; to them surely a scene of expectation was opening the most gloomy that ever had presented itself to mankind; persons, apparently incapable of any noble or generous purpose, coveting power as a license to crimes, supported by bands of unprincipled villains, were now ready to seize and to distribute, in lots among themselves, all the dignities of the state, and all the patrimony of its members.

In human affairs, however, the prospect, whether good or bad in extreme is seldom verified by the end; and human nature, when seemingly driving to the wildest excess, after a series of events and struggles, settles at last in some sort of mediocrity, beyond which it never is pushed but by occasional starts and sallies. The first entry of this triumvirate on the scene of their government, indeed, was such as could scarcely be supported in the sequel of any tyranny or usurpation whatever.

The triumvirs being on their way to Rome, their orders for the immediate execution of seventeen of the principal senators had been received before their arrival, and several were accordingly surprised and murdered in their houses, or in the streets. The first alarm appearing the more terrible, as the occasion of these murders was unknown, struck all orders of men with a general amazement and terror. The streets were presently deserted, and hushed in silence, except where armed parties skulked in search of their prey, or by the cries which they raised, gave mutual intimation of the discoveries they made. Persons who found themselves pursued, attempted to set the city on fire, in order to facilitate their own escape. Pedius, the consul, continued all night in the streets, endeavouring to prevent the calamity of a general fire. In order to quiet the minds of those who were not aimed at in this execution, he published the names of the seventeen, with assurances that the executions were not to proceed any farther.[1] It has been supposed, that the design was no farther communicated to this magistrate, and that he would have opposed the extremes to which it was carried; but, on the following night, he died of the fatigue he had incurred on this occasion, and the public assurances he had given were attended with no effect.

The triumvirs marched separately towards the city, and made their entry on three several days. As they arrived in succession, they occupied every quarter with guards and attendants, and filled every public place with armed men, and with military standards and ensigns. In order to ratify the powers they had devised for themselves, they put the articles of their agreement into the hands of the tribune Publius Titius, with instructions, that they should be proposed and enacted in the public assembly of the Roman people; and put in the form of a legal commission, or warrant, for the government they had usurped. By the act which passed on this occasion, the supreme power or sovereignty of the republic, during five years, without any reserve or limitation, was conferred on Octavius, Antony, and Lepidus; and a solemn thanksgiving being ordered for the events already passed, which led to this termination, the citizens in general, under the deepest impressions of terror and sorrow, were obliged to assume appearances of satisfaction and joy.

As the first act of this government, two lists or proscriptions were delivered to the proper officers of the army, and posted in different parts of the city; one a list of senators, the other a list of persons of inferior rank, on whom the troops were directed to perform immediate execution. In consequence of these orders, all the streets, temples, and private houses, instantly became

1 Appian. de Bell. Civ. lib. iv.
2 Dio. Cass. lib. xlvi. Appian. lib. iv.

scenes of blood.[3] At the same time, there appeared on the part of the triumvirs a manifesto, in which, having stated the ingratitude of many whom Cæsar had spared, of many whom he had promoted to high office, and whom he had even destined to inherit his fortunes, and who, nevertheless, conspired against his life, they alleged the necessity they were under of preventing the designs of their enemies, and of extirpating a dangerous faction, whom no benefits could bind, and whom no considerations, sacred or profane, could restrain. "Under the influence of this faction," they said, "the perpetrators of a horrid murder, instead of being called to an account, are entrusted with the command of provinces, and furnished with resources of men and money to support them against the efforts of public justice, and against the indignation of the Roman people. Some of these murderers," they continued, "we have already chastised; others, being at the head of powerful armies, threaten to frustrate the effects of our just resentment. Having such a conflict to maintain in the provinces, it would be absurd to leave an enemy in possession of the city, and ready to take advantage of any unfavourable accident that may befall us in defence of the commonwealth. For this reason, we have determined to cut off every person who is likely to abet their designs at Rome, and to make this desperate faction feel the effects of that war which they were so ready to declare against us and our friends.

"We mean no harm to the innocent, and shall molest no citizen, in order to seize his property. We shall not insist on destroying even all those whom we know to be our enemies; but the most guilty, it is the interest of the Roman people, as well as ours, to have removed, that the republic may no longer be torn and agitated by the quarrels of parties who cannot be reconciled.

"Some atonement is likewise due to the army insulted by the late decrees, in which they were declared enemies to the commonwealth.

"We might," they continued, "have surprised and taken all our enemies without any warning, or explanation of our conduct; but we chose to make an open declaration of our purpose, that the innocent may not, by mistake, be involved with the guilty, nor even be unnecessarily alarmed." They concluded this fatal proclamation, with a prohibition to conceal, rescue, or protect any person whose name was proscribed; and they declared, that whoever acted in opposition to this order, should be considered as one of the number, and involved in the same ruin. They declared, that whoever produced the head of a person proscribed, if a free man, he should receive twenty-five thousand Attic drachms or denarii, and if a slave, should have his liberty, with ten thousand of the same money; and that every slave killing his master, in execution of this proscription, should have his freedom, and be put on the rolls of the people in the place of the person he had slain.

At the time that this proclamation and the preceding lists were published, armed parties had already seized on the gates of the city, and were prepared to intercept all who attempted to escape. Others began to ransack the houses, and took their way to the villas and gardens in the suburbs, where it was likely that any of the proscribed had retired. By the disposition they made, the execution began in many places at once, and those who knew or suspected their own destination, like the inhabitants of a city taken by storm, were on every side surrounded by enemies, from whom they were to receive no quarter. To many, it is observed by historians, that their own nearest relations were objects of terror, no less than the mercenary hands that were armed against them. The husband and the father did not think himself secure in his concealment, when he supposed it to be known to his wife or to his children. The slaves and freedmen of a family were become its most terrible enemies. The debtor had an interest in circumventing his creditor, and neighbours in the country mutually dreaded each other as informers and spies. The money which the master of a family was supposed to have in his house, was considered as an additional reward to the treachery of his domestics. The first citizens of Rome were prostrate at the feet of their own slaves, imploring protection and mercy, or perished in the wells or common sewers, where they attempted to conceal themselves.

Persons having any private grudge or secret malice, took this opportunity to accomplish their ends. Even they who were inclined to protect or conceal the unhappy, were terrified with the prospect of being involved in their ruin. Many, who themselves, contrary to expectation, were not in the list of the proscribed, enjoyed their own safety, in perfect indifference to the distress of their neighbours; or, that they might distinguish themselves by their zeal for the prevailing cause, joined the executioners, assisted in the slaughter, or plundered the houses of the slain.

There were killed, in the beginning of this massacre, Salvius, one of the tribunes of the people, together with Minucius and Annalis, both in the office of prætors. Silicius Coronas, a person already mentioned, who being one of the judges at the citation of Marcus Brutus and Caius Cassius for the murder of Julius Cæsar, had ventured, in the presence of Octavius, to hold up into view the ballot by which he acquitted them, and who, although at that time in appearance overlooked, now perished among the proscribed.

Many tragic particulars, in these narrations, seem to be copied from former examples of what happened under Marius Cinna and Sylla, of persons betrayed by their servants, their confidants, and nearest relations, and with a treachery and cruelty, which seemed to increase with the corruptions of the age; but yet not without instances of heroic fidelity and generous courage, of which human nature itself ever appears to be capable, even in the most degenerate times.

The slave of one of the proscribed, seeing soldiers come towards the place where his master lay concealed, took the disguise of his clothes, and presented himself to be killed in his stead. Another slave agreed to personate his master, and being carried in his litter, was killed, while the master himself, acting as one of the bearers of the litter, escaped. Another having been formerly branded by his master for some offence, was easily suspected of a desire to seize this opportunity of being revenged; but he chose the opposite part. While his master fled, he put himself in the way to stop his pursuers, produced

3 Dio. Cass. lib. xlvi. Appian. lib. iv.

a head, which he had severed from a dead body in the streets, and passing it for that of his master, procured him the means of escape.

The son of Hosidius Geta saved his father by giving out that he was already killed, and by actually performing a funeral in his name. The son of Quintus Cicero, though, in the former part of his life, often on bad terms with his father and with his uncle, and often undutiful to both, ended his days in an act of magnanimity and filial affection; persevering in the concealment of his father, notwithstanding that the torture was applied to force a discovery, until the father, who was within hearing of what was in agitation, burst from his concealment, and was slain, together with his son.[1]

Quintus Cicero, who perished in this manner, was for some time in concealment with his brother Marcus, having been in the country, or having escaped from the city on the first alarm of these murders. The brothers are mentioned as being at Tusculum together, and as setting out from thence for Astura, another of Cicero's villas on the coast, intending to embark for Greece; but as Quintus was entirely unprovided for the voyage, and his brother unable to supply him, they parted on the road in agonies of grief. In a few days after this parting, Quintus having put himself under the protection of his own son, received, though in vain, that striking proof of his filial affection and fidelity, which has just been mentioned.

Marcus Cicero having got safe to Astura, embarked, and with a fair wind arrived at Circeii. When the vessel was again about to set sail, his mind wavered, he flattered himself that matters might yet take a more favourable turn; he landed, and travelled about twelve miles on his way to Rome:[2] but his resolution again failed him, and he once more returned towards the sea. Being arrived on the coast, he still hesitated, remained on shore, and passed the night in agonies of sorrow, which were interrupted only by momentary starts of indignation and rage. Under these emotions, he sometimes solaced himself with a prospect of returning to Rome in disguise, of killing himself in the presence of Octavius, and of staining the person of that young traitor with the blood of a man, whom he had so ungratefully and so vilely betrayed. Even this appeared to his frantic imagination some degree of revenge; but the fear of being discovered before he could execute his purpose, the prospect of the tortures and indignities he was likely to suffer, deterred him from this design; and, being unable to take any resolution whatever, he committed himself to his attendants, was carried on board of a vessel, and steered for Capua.[3] Near to this place, having another villa on the shore, he was again landed, and being fatigued with the motion of the sea, went to rest; but his servants, according to the superstition of the times, being disturbed with prodigies and unfavourable presages, or rather being sensible of their master's danger, after a little repose awaked him from his sleep, forced him into his litter, and hastened again to embark. Soon after they were gone, Popilius Lænas, a tribune of the legions, and Herennius, a centurion, with a party who had been for some days in search of this prey, arrived at the villa. Popilius had received particular obligations from Cicero, having been defended by him when tried upon a criminal accusation; but these were times, in which bad men could make a merit of ingratitude to their former benefactors, when it served to ingratiate them with those in power. This officer, with his party, finding the gates of the court and the passages of the villa shut, burst them open; but missing the person they sought for, and suspecting that he must have taken his flight again to the sea, they pursued through an avenue that led to the shore, and came in sight of Cicero's litter, before he had left the walks of his own garden.

On the appearance of a military party, Cicero perceived the end of his labours, ordered the bearers of his litter to halt; and having been hitherto, while there were any hopes of escape, distressed chiefly by the perplexity and indecision of his own mind, he became, as soon as his fate appeared to be certain, determined and calm. In this situation, he was observed to stroke his chin with his left hand, a gesture for which he was remarkable in his moments of thoughtfulness, and when least disturbed. Upon the approach of the party, he put forth his head from the litter, and fixed his eyes upon the tribune with great composure. The countenance of a man so well known to every Roman, now worn out with fatigue and dejection, and disfigured by neglect of the usual attention to his person, made a moving spectacle even to those who came to assist in his murder. They turned away, while the assassin performed his office, and severed the head from his body.

Thus perished Marcus Tullius Cicero, in the sixty-fourth year of his age. Although his character may be known from the part which he bore in several transactions, of which the accounts are scattered in different parts of this history, yet it is difficult to close the scene of his life, without some recollection of the circumstances which were peculiar to so distinguished a personage. He appears to have been the last of the Romans, who rose to the highest offices of state by the force of his personal character, and by the fair arts of a republican candidate for public honours. None of his ancestors having enjoyed any considerable preferments, he was upon this account considered as a new man, and with reluctance admitted by the nobility to a participation of honours. It was however impossible to prevent his advancement, so long as preferments were distributed according to the civil and political forms of the republic, which gave so large a scope to the industry, abilities, and genius of such men. Under those forms, all the virtues of a citizen were allowed to have some effect, and all the variety of useful qualifications were supposed to be united in forming a title to the confidence of the public; the qualifications of a warrior were united with those of a statesman, and even the talents of a lawyer and barrister, with those of a senator and counsellor of state. The law required,[4] that the same person should be a warrior and statesman, and it was at least expedient or customary, that he should be also a barrister, in order to secure the

1 Dio. Cass. lib. xlvii. Appian. de Bell. Civ. lib. iv.
2 Plut. in Cicerone. 3 Ibid.

4 Ten or fifteen years military service was required as a qualification for the higher offices of state. Vid Polyb. ubi supra.

public favour, and to support his consideration with the people.

Cicero was by no means the first person at Rome, who with peculiar attention cultivated the talents of a pleader, and applied himself with ardour to literary studies. He is nevertheless universally acknowledged, by his proficiency in these studies, to have greatly excelled all those who went before him, so much as to have attained the highest preferments in the commonwealth, without having quitted the gown, and to have made his first campaign in the capacity of Roman proconsul, and above ten years after he had already exercised the supreme executive power in the state.

To the novelty of this circumstance, as well as to the novelty of his family-name in the list of officers of state, was owing some part of that obloquy which his enemies employed against him; and it may be admitted, that for a Roman he was too much a mere man of the robe, and that he possibly may have been less a statesman and a warrior, for having been so much a man of letters, and so accomplished a pleader.

Cicero, whether we suppose him to have been governed by original vanity, or by a habit of considering the world as a theatre for the display of his talents, and the acquisition of fame, more than as a scene of real affairs, in which objects of serious consequence to mankind were to be treated, was certainly too fond of applause, courted it as a principal object even in the fairest transactions of his life, and was too much dependant on the opinion of other men to possess himself sufficiently amidst the difficulties which occur in the very arduous situation which fell to his lot. Though disposed, in the midst of a very corrupt age, to merit commendation by honest means, and by the support of good government, he could not endure reproach or censure, even from those whose disapprobation was a presumption of innocence and of merit; and he felt the unpopularity of his actions, even where he thought his conduct the most meritorious, with a degree of mortification which greatly distracted his mind, and shook his resolution. Being, towards the end of his life, by the almost total extirpation of the more respectable citizens and members of the senate, who had laboured with him for the preservation of the commonwealth, left in a situation which required the abilities of a great warrior, as well as those of the ablest statesmen, and in which, even such abilities could not have stemmed the torrent which burst forth to overwhelm the republic, it is not surprising that he failed in the attempt.

Antony, at the same time that he gave orders for the death of Cicero, gave directions that not only his head, but his right hand likewise, with which he had written so many severe invectives against himself, should be cut off,[5] and brought to him as an evidence of the execution.

In the course of these murders, the heads of the slain were usually presented to the triumvirs, and by their orders set up in conspicuous places, while the bodies were cast into the river, or suffered to be exposed in the streets. Antony having more resentments to gratify than either of his colleagues, had the heads of his enemies brought to him in great numbers, even as he lay on his couch at his meals. That of Cicero was received by him with the joy of victory; he gazed upon it with singular pleasure, and ordered it, together with the hand, to be exposed on the rostrum from which this respectable citizen had so often declaimed, and where these mangled parts of his body were now exposed to the view of a multitude, that used to crowd to his audience.[6] Fulvia too had her enemies on this occasion, and received the bloody tokens of their execution with a savage avidity and pleasure, which to those who judge of propriety from modern customs, or who form their opinions of the sex from the manners of modern times, will scarcely appear to be credible. When the head of Cicero, in particular, was brought to her toilet, with a peculiar and spiteful allusion to the eloquence, by which she herself, as well as her present and former husbands, had been galled, she is said to have forced open the jaw, and to have pricked and tore the tongue with the point of a bodkin, which she took from her hair.

In this horrid scene of revenge and cruelty, rapacity too had its share, many persons were proscribed, merely that their estates might be brought into the coffers of the triumvirs; and many persons were threatened, to induce them to ransom[7] their lives with money. The list received frequent additions, and underwent many alterations, some names being scratched out, and others inserted, a circumstance, by which persons of any considerable property, as well as those who were obnoxious to any of the persons in power, were kept in the most anxious state of suspense and uncertainty. Many who were spared by the public usurpers of government, fell a sacrifice to the resentment of their private enemies, or to the avarice of those who wished to possess themselves of their property;[8] and the names of many persons who had been thus slain, without any public authority, were afterwards inserted in the list of the proscribed, in order to justify the murder.

The troops were sensible of their own importance on this occasion, and set no bounds to their pretensions. They solicited grants of the houses of persons reputed to be of the opposite party; or, being the only buyers at the frequent sales which were made of forfeited estates, obtained the possession of them by a kind of fictitious purchase. Not satisfied with the price which was paid them for the blood of the proscribed, or with the extravagant gratuities which they frequently received, they were, under various pretences, hastening to seize every subject that tempted their avarice. They intruded themselves into every family, and laid claim to every inheritance; they plundered at discretion the houses of the rich, or murdered indiscriminately those who offended them, or who stood in their way to the possession of wealth; they encouraged, by their example, fugitive slaves, and disorderly persons of every description, who, forming themselves into bands in the disguise of soldiers, engaged in the same practices, and perpetrated the same crimes.

The triumvirs, whose principal object it was to secure the government, though noways interested in these extreme disorders, which far ex-

5 Plut. in Cicerone.

6 Appian. de Bell. Civ. lib. iv.
7 Dio. Cass. lib. xlvii.
8 Ibid. c. 12. Appian. de Bell. Civ. lib. iv.

ceeded what they originally projected, not daring to restrain the military violence, lest it should recoil on themselves, left for some time the lives, as well as the properties of the people, entirely at the mercy of the troops; and citizens, who were reputed to have any effects in reserve, were fain to adopt some soldier as a son, in order to obtain his protection.

Such are the particulars which are recorded of this famous transaction, which, however monstrous in those who gave rise to it, far exceeded the bounds of their original design. When the evil had in some measure spent its force, its authors were willing to divert the attention of the public, or to efface the melancholy impressions which remained. For this purpose, Lepidus and Plancus being about to enter on the office of consul for the following year, on some slight pretence of a victory gained by the army in Gaul, entered the city in procession; but suspecting that the people were more inclinable to dejection than triumph, they directed the public, by a proclamation, to give on that day the demonstrations of joy which generally made part in the reception that was given to victorious generals.[1]

The soldiers indeed were not wanting, as usual, in the petulant sarcasms and familiar abuse, in which they availed themselves of their present consequence: they sung, in their procession, scurrilous ballads, alluding to examples of parricide as well as murder committed by their chiefs in the late proscription; by Lepidus and Plancus, that of their own brothers; by Antony and Octavius, that of their nearest relations and friends.[2] But at the disposal of such masters as these, every citizen who was likely to frown on their crimes, every person whose countenance gave signs of dejection, or sorrow, every possessor of land, and every father of a family, had reason to tremble for their persons, their possessions, and the safety of their children.

Such was the aspect of affairs in Italy; but there were still some rays of hope, which shone from a distance. Not only Brutus and Cassius, in their provinces of Macedonia and Syria; but Cornificius in Africa, and Sextus Pompeius in Sicily, still held up the standard of the republic, and offered places of refuge to its friends. Sextus Pompeius stationed ships on the coast to receive them, and published rewards for the rescue or protection of his father's party, and of those unfortunate remains of the commonwealth.[3] Paulus, the brother of Lepidus, though abandoned to destruction, was suffered to escape by the soldiers of the army, from a respect to himself or to their general. Lucius Cæsar was protected by his sister, the mother of Antony. Messala escaped to Brutus. Many others, whose names only are known, took refuge with one or other of the leaders, who were in condition to contend for the republic, or for the sovereignty of the empire.

U. C. 711.
L. M. Plancus, M. Æ. Lepidus.

Lepidus and Plancus being entered on the office of consul, had in charge from the triumvirs, as the first object of their magistracy, the raising of money to supply the farther exigencies of the war. Great sums had been expected to arise from the sale of the estates of the proscribed; but the purchase of such estates was justly reckoned invidious among a certain class of the people, who declined being partakers in the spoils of innocent and respectable citizens; and it was dangerous for an ordinary citizen to appear to be rich, or in condition to buy: insomuch, that they who murdered the owner, were almost the only buyers of estates that were exposed to public sale; and the money which arose from these sales, fell greatly short of the expectations which had been entertained from them.

It was computed, that two hundred millions, Roman money, were yet wanting to supply the expense of the war.[4] In order to make up the deficiency, the male sex chiefly having hitherto suffered by the public exactions, a contribution was levied from such women related to the opposite party as were supposed to be rich. At the same time persons of every description whose estates exceeded one hundred thousand[5] Roman money, were commanded to give an account of their effects, that they might pay a tax equal to a fiftieth of their stock, and one year's income of their ordinary revenue.[6]

To enforce these exactions, hitherto unusual in Italy, much violence was necessary. The rents of houses in the city, and the produce of lands in the country were sequestrated, leaving only one half for the subsistence of the owners. In this manner, great sums of money were levied from the peaceable part of the commonwealth; but as the triumvirs had incurred a very heavy debt in their military operations, and in bounties to secure the troops in their interest, and had in prospect an arduous and expensive war against Brutus and Cassius, armed with the forces, and supported by the treasures of the east, the first sums which came in were far from being sufficient for their purpose. Additional exactions were made, under the denomination of fines or forfeitures, from those who were alleged to have given in a false state of their effects.

In imitation of the late sanguinary proscriptions, the consuls published lists of all who had incurred this penalty, and ordered their effects accordingly to be seized. The inhabitants of the towns were obliged to find subsistence for the troops that were quartered on them, and the country was pillaged, under pretence of a search that was made for the effects of rebels. The pay of the soldiers accumulating in the hands of their leaders, was considered, together with the advantages which they expected at the end of the war, as a pledge of their attachment and perseverance in the cause.[7]

Although few men were now left in Italy, who could forget their own fears so far as to think of the commonwealth, or who could be suspected of any design to restore the ancient government, yet this was made the ordinary ground of suspicion against those whom the triumvirs wished to oppress; and the desire to remove it, led all orders of men to affect a veneration for the memory of Cæsar, and to vie in their zeal to avenge his death. The anniversary of this event was made a day of mourning. A shrine was erected on the

1 Appian. de Bell. Civ. lib. iv.
2 De Germanis non de Gallis triumphant Consules.
3 Appian. ut supra. Dio. Cass. lib. xlvii. c. 12.
4 Appian. de Bell. Civ. lib. iv.
5 About eight thousand pounds.
6 Appian. ut supra.
7 Dio. Cass. lib. xlvii. c. 14, 15

place of his funeral, and was declared to be a public sanctuary, and place of refuge even to criminals. The divine or monarchical honours which were thus paid to the memory of the dead, preserved in the minds of the people that disposition to endure a master which was thought favourable to the living usurpers, and which the division of power between them might have otherwise diminished.[8]

Agreeably to the model of Julius Cæsar's arrangements, preparatory to his intended expedition into Asia, the triumvirs, before the departure of Octavius and Antony on the service to which they were destined, fixed the succession to all the offices of state for some years. They had under their command an army of forty legions, which they now separated into two divisions.[9] The one, under the direction of Antony, was assembled on the eastern coast to be in readiness to cover Italy on that side, or to pass into Macedonia, and to carry the war against Brutus and Cassius into that province. The other was destined to remain in Italy, in order to secure the head of the empire, and oppose any attempts of the opposite party by sea from Sicily or Africa, which were still in their possession.

Sextus Pompeius, the last of the family of the great Pompey, in consequence of the resolutions passed in his favour soon after Cæsar's death, had set out from Spain as admiral of the Roman navy, and fixing his station in Sicily, had a numerous fleet, and mustered considerable land forces.[10] With these, in the war which immediately followed, he wished to co-operate with the combined armies of the two consuls, Hirtius and Pansa; but was prevented by a doubt which arose, whether the veterans of Cæsar, who composed great part of that army, would act in concert with a son of Pompey?[11] Upon the coalition of Octavius with Lepidus and Antony, he again became an exile, but continued in possession of Sicily, a province, which, by the present division of the empire, was comprehended in the lot of Octavius.

Cornificius, by commission from the Roman senate, still held the province of Africa, and refused to surrender it to Sextus, an officer who had been sent by Octavius, in consequence of the same distribution, to take possession of it in his name. The dispute being likely to end in a war, the opposite parties applied to the neighbouring princes for aid; but the lieutenant of Octavius having his commission from the supreme authority then established at Rome, or being known to represent the triumphant party, was acknowledged by most of the African powers in alliance with the Romans. Being joined by their forces, he came to an action with his antagonist near Utica, and obtained a victory, in which Cornificius was killed. Lælius and Roscius, two officers of rank in the vanquished army, perished by their own hands.[12] As many as could find shipping, escaped to Pompey in the island of Sicily.

Soon after this event, Octavius, being desirous to dislodge the remains of the republican party from an island of so much consequence, sent Salvidienus with a fleet towards the straits of Messina, while he himself marched by land to Rhegium. A sea fight soon after ensued, from which the fleets retired with equal loss. Salvidienus put into the harbour of Balanus to refit; and Octavius, being arrived at Rhegium, was meditating a descent upon Sicily, when he received pressing instances from Antony to join him at Brundusium, that they might endeavour to repel the storm which was gathering from the east, and which seemed to threaten their establishments in Italy with the greatest hazard.[13]

Marcus Brutus, after fortune seemed to have declared for the republican party at Mutina, thinking himself at liberty to attend to the affairs of the east, and to support Cassius in his struggle for the possession of Syria, had passed with his army into Asia, in order to cut off all supplies from Dolabella, and to avail himself of the resources, for the pay and subsistence of the army, which were still to be found in that opulent province. While he was employed in the execution of this design, the important events already mentioned took place in that quarter. Cassius had prevailed in Syria, got entire possession of the province, was acknowledged as general by all the armies which had been assembled by either party beyond the boundaries of Cilicia; and he was meditating an expedition into Egypt, to punish Cleopatra for the part she had taken against him in his contest with Dolabella, and to raise a contribution in her country for the farther support of the war.

The victory obtained at Mutina, though by an army which till then was reputed on the side of the commonwealth, made a great change to its prejudice, giving an opportunity to its enemies to declare themselves, and to unite their forces; insomuch, that by the coalition of Octavius and Lepidus with Antony, all the remaining armies of the west were joined, not only to subdue the capital, but to carry the war into Macedonia and Asia, the last retreat of the republican interest.

Brutus being informed of these circumstances, and of the late proscriptions, sent a message to Cassius, with pressing instances to divert him from his project against Egypt, and to turn his forces to the rescue of the commonwealth from the hands of tyrants, and to avenge the innocent blood which had been so copiously shed in Italy.

Upon these representations, Cassius, having left a legion to secure the possession of Syria, marched to the westward, and in his way raised large contributions for the support of the war. Among the other measures which he took for this purpose, he surprised Ariobarzanes in his palace, and obliged him to deliver up the money then in his treasury. He pillaged the city of Tarsus; and, upon account of the support which the inhabitants of that place had given to Dolabella, subjected them for the future to a heavy tribute.[14]

About the middle of winter, Brutus and Cassius, with their armies, joined at Smyrna. These restorers of the republic had parted some months before at Pireus, one bound for Syria, the other for Macedonia; but more like exiles than Roman officers of state, without any men, shipping, or money, and under great uncertainty of their success, in obtaining possession of the provinces on

8 Dio. Cass lib. xliv. c. 18 et 19.
9 Appian. ut infra. 10 Dio. Cass. lib. xlviii. c. 17.
11 Cicer Philip. xiii.
12 Appian. de Bell. Civ. lib. iv. c. 22, &c. Dio. Cass. lib. xlviii. c. 21.

13 Appian. ut supra. 14 Ibid.

which they had their several pretensions. Their affairs now bore a different aspect; they had a numerous fleet, and a mighty land force, large sums of money already amassed, with the resources of a territory the most wealthy of any part in the Roman empire.[1] Brutus proposed that they should, without delay, transport their forces into Europe, and prevent the triumvirs from getting any footing in Macedonia or Greece; but Cassius contended, that they had yet enemies or allies of doubtful fidelity in Asia, and that it would be imprudent to leave any such behind them, or to forego the treasure which they might yet command in that country, and which would enable them to reward and to encourage their armies.

Brutus determined by these considerations, accordingly marched into Lycia, while Cassius proceeded to execute a project he had formed for the reduction of Rhodes. His fleet being on their way to turn the Capes of Asia, in order to support him in this design, the Rhodians, trusting to their superior skill and reputation as mariners, assembled all the ships they could muster, and, near to the harbour of Lindus, ventured to engage those of Cassius; but being inferior in number and weight of ships, they were defeated with considerable loss. Cassius beheld the engagement from a high land on the continent, and as soon as the ships could be again refitted,[2] ordered the fleet to Loryma, a fortified harbour in the continent, over against the island of Rhodes; from thence he embarked his army. He himself, with eighty galleys, escorted the transports in their passage, landed on the island, and besieged the capital both by sea and by land.

The Rhodians having trusted entirely to the defence of their shipping, were unprovided of all things necessary to withstand a siege. Cassius, by surprise, or by the treachery of a party within the walls, soon became master of the place, laid it under a severe contribution; and having left an officer of the name of Varus to command in the island, he returned to the continent with a great accession of reputation and wealth.

Brutus at the same time had forced the passes of the mountains, leading into Lycia, and advancing to Xanthus, summoned the town to surrender. This place had acquired much fame by the obstinate resistance of its inhabitants, or by the desperation they had shown, when forced, on former occasions, by Harpalus, the general of Cyrus, and by Alexander in his way to the conquest of Persia.[3] Upon the approach of Brutus, they razed their suburbs, and removed every building which might cover the advances of an enemy. The walls were surrounded by a ditch fifty feet deep; and this being the first impediment which Brutus had to encounter, he began the attack with a continual labour to fill it up, and to effect a passage for his engines to the foot of the rampart. Having accomplished this object, he proceeded to cover his workmen with galleries, and to erect the engines usually employed in making a breach. He was opposed by the besieged in repeated sallies, in the last of which his works were set on fire, and reduced to ashes.

In the mean time, two thousand men of the Roman army, pursuing the party who had made this sally, entered the city along with them, and not being properly supported, suffered the gates to be shut, and themselves to be cut off from all relief. Being instantly surrounded by the inhabitants, numbers of them were killed, and the remainder forced into a temple, where they endeavoured to defend themselves.

This circumstance produced the most vigorous efforts on the part of the besiegers, to force the walls, that they might rescue their friends, or make a diversion in their favour. They applied scaling-ladders to the battlements, and forcing engines to the gates; and having at last made their way into the town, that they might at once terrify the inhabitants, and give notice of approaching relief to their own party, they raised a mighty shout as they entered the streets, and continued to urge their fury, in every direction, with fire and sword. The inhabitants, unable to resist this storm, retired to their houses, and there, determined to maintain their ancient fame, chose rather to perish by their own hands, than submit to the enemy. The father of every family, beginning with the slaughter of his wife and children, proceeded to kill himself.

While the people of Xanthus were employed in the execution of this purpose, Brutus hearing the cries of desperation and of murder, supposed that his troops had refused to give quarter, and were killing the wretched inhabitants of the place, without distinction of sex or age. In order to put the speediest stop to so horrid a scene, his first thought was to bring off the troops, by sounding a general retreat; but being informed that the people were perishing, not by the cruelty of his army, but by their own desperation, he ordered to be proclaimed a general freedom and protection to all the inhabitants; but so long as any considerable number of the citizens remained, the officers who came near them, even with an offer of quarter, were answered with threats, or with showers of darts and of arrows, obliged to keep at a distance. The temples and public buildings were, with great difficulty, saved from fire; but none of the inhabitants could be rescued, besides a few women and slaves.

Brutus, greatly afflicted with this piteous catastrophe, marched with reluctance towards Patara, where the inhabitants were supposed to be infected with the same desperate spirit; and, to prevent the necessity of such fatal extremities, sent a message to prevail on the people to surrender, and to accept of his protection. The example of Xanthus appeared much too atrocious to be followed; and they submitted to pay the contributions which were exacted from them.

Lentulus, at the same time, who commanded the fleet which had been employed in transporting the army of Cassius into the island of Rhodes, forced his way into the harbour of Andriaca, the port of Myra, by breaking the chain which was stretched across the entrance; and this place being reduced, the inhabitants of Lycia sent offers of submission and of their services in the war, agreed to pay a certain tribute, and to join the fleet with their galleys. Lentulus, being accordingly reinforced with a great accession of ships, set sail for Abydus, the shortest passage into Europe, where he was ordered to wait the arrival of the land forces.

At the same time, Murcus, commanding an

1 Plut. in Bru o. 2 Appian. ut supra.
3 Ibid. lib. iv.

other squadron belonging to Brutus and Cassius, upon a report that Cleopatra, with a numerous fleet, was at sea, to effect a junction with Octavius and Antony, had been stationed at the Cape of Tenarus to intercept her; but being informed that the Egyptian fleet was dispersed, or had suffered much in a storm, he weighed from Tenarus, and steered for Brundusium, took possession of an island at the mouth of the harbour, and from thence intended to prevent the transportation of any troops from Italy to Macedonia or Greece. He had however arrived too late to effect the whole of this purpose. Great part of Antony's army was already transported, and he himself, with the remainder, waited for favourable winds to run or pass unnoticed in the night.

In this state of the war, Brutus and Cassius, having accomplished the services in which they had been severally engaged, again assembled their forces on the right of the Meander. It is said, that they began their conference on bad terms, the effect of a jealousy which had been industriously raised between them; but there did not appear any consequences of a misunderstanding; and their joint forces, without delay, began to move towards Europe, in order to check the advances which the enemy were already making in Macedonia. Having passed the Hellespont, they marched, by the isthmus of Cardia, to the coast of the bay of Melanus; here they made a halt for some days, to muster and to review their forces. The army of Cassius consisted of nine legions, that of Brutus of eight, amounting to about eighty thousand men, formed in the manner of the Roman infantry. Brutus had four thousand Gaulish and Lusitanian horse; two thousand cavalry, made up of Thracians, Illyrians, Parthians, and Thessalians. Cassius had two thousand Gauls and Spaniards, and four thousand Parthian archers mounted on horseback. They were followed likewise by some princes of Galatia, at the head of their respective forces. The whole, by this account, amounted to near a hundred thousand men. Many of the legions had been formed under Cæsar, and could not be retained in their present service, without frequent liberalities, and without a prospect, at the end of the war, of settlements. not inferior to those which were enjoyed or expected by the troops of the opposite side. The wealth of Asia, however, having put their leaders in condition to perform what was at present expected from them; all former engagements were now fulfilled, as the best earnest that could be given of future gratuities.

At the close of this muster, Cassius and Brutus, with all the officers of senatorian rank, who were then present, being assembled on a platform, raised as usual to some height from the ground, were surrounded by the army, who crowded to hear the speech of their leaders; and it was supposed, that what they were to deliver should have the effect of a manifesto or proclamation, respecting the cause in which they were engaged. Cassius spoke for himself, for his colleague, and the body of senators who attended them; addressing this motley assemblage of native Romans and aliens, of citizens and soldiers of fortune, collected from different parties, as an assembly of the Roman people deliberating on their public rights. He mentioned the mutual confidence that was natural between officers and men engaged, as they were, in a common cause; enumerated their resources with the other advantages they possessed, and took notice of the punctual discharge of all former engagements, as the best security which could be given of a fixed intention to make a suitable provision for every soldier who should contribute to bring the war to a favourable issue. "The unjust reproaches of our enemies," he said, "we could easily disprove, if we were not, by our numbers, and by the swords which we hold in our hands, in condition to despise them. While Cæsar led the armies of the republic against the enemies of Rome, we took part in the same service with him, we obeyed him, we were happy to serve under his command. But when he declared war on the commonwealth, we became his enemies; and when he became an usurper and a tyrant, we resented, as an injury, even the favours which he presumed to bestow upon ourselves. Had he been to fall a sacrifice to private resentment, we should not have been the proper actors in the execution of the sentence against him. He was willing to have indulged us with preferments and honours; but we were not willing to accept, as the gift of a master, what we were entitled to claim as free citizens. We conceived, that, in presuming to confer the honours of the Roman republic, he encroached on the prerogatives of the Roman people, and insulted the authority of the Roman senate.

"Cæsar cancelled the laws, and overturned the constitution of his country; he usurped all the powers of the commonwealth, set up a monarchy, and himself affected to be a king. This our ancestors, at the expulsion of Tarquin, bound themselves and their posterity, by the most solemn oaths, and by the most direful imprecations, never to endure. The same obligation has been entailed upon us as a debt by our fathers; and we, having faithfully paid and discharged it, have performed the oath, and averted the consequences of failure from ourselves, and from our posterity.

"In the station of soldiers, we might have committed ourselves without reflection to the command of an officer, whose abilities and whose valour we admired; but, in the character of Roman citizens, we have a far different part to sustain. I must suppose, that I now speak to the Roman people, and to citizens of a free republic; to men who have never learned to depend upon others for gratifications and favours, who are not accustomed to own a superior, but who are themselves the masters, the dispensers of fortune and of honour, and the givers of all those dignities and powers by which Cæsar himself was exalted, and of which he assumed the entire disposal. Recollect from whom the Scipios, the Pompeys, even Cæsar himself derived his honours: from your ancestors, whom you now represent, and from yourselves, to whom, according to the laws of the republic, we, who are now your leaders in the field, address ourselves as your fellow-citizens in the commonwealth, and as persons depending on your pleasure for the just reward and retribution of our services. Happy in being able to restore to you what Cæsar had the presumption to appropriate to himself, the power and the dignity of your fathers, with the supreme disposal of all the offices of trust that were established for your safety, and for the preservation of your freedom; happy in being able to restore to the tribunes of the Roman people the power of protecting you, and of procuring to every Roman citizen that justice which, under the late usurpation of Cæsar, was withheld, even from the sacred persons of those magistrates themselves.

"An usurper is the common enemy of all good citizens; but the task of removing him could be the business only of a few. The senate and the Roman people, as soon as it was proper for them to declare their judgment, pronounced their approbation of those who were concerned in the death of Cæsar, by the rewards and the honours which they bestowed upon them; and they are now become a prey to assassins and murderers; they bleed in the streets, in the temples, in the most secret retreats, and in the arms of their families; or they are dispersed, and fly wherever they hope to escape the fury of their enemies.—Many are now present before you, happy in your protection—happy in witnessing the zeal which you entertain for the commonwealth, for the rights of your fellow-citizens, and for your own. These respectable citizens, we trust, will soon, by your means, be restored to a condition in which they can enjoy, together with you, all the honours of a free people, concur with you in bestowing, and partake with you in receiving, the rewards which are due to such eminent services, as you are now engaged to perform."[1]

Such is the substance of what we receive as the speech of Cassius on this memorable occasion, and, although we may not consider these compositions as the genuine record of what was spoken, yet as they contain the ideas and reasonings of times so much nearer than ours to the date of the transactions to which they refer, it is undoubtedly fit, and often instructive, to retain the argument on which they are founded. At the close of this speech, it is said that Cassius resumed the comparison of the forces and resources of the opposite parties, stated to his army their own equality by land, and their superiority by sea; the facility with which they were to be supplied with all necessaries; and that he concluded, with a promise to pay an additional gratuity of fifteen hundred sesterces to each man.[2]

After this solemnity, the army again began to advance; and while they marched in small divisions by the route of Ænos and Doriscus, Cimber, with a squadron of galleys, having a legion and a considerable detachment of archers on board, sailed towards the coast of Macedonia, with orders to search for a proper station within the mountains of Pangeus, a ridge which, stretching from Thrace southward, terminated in the bay of Strymon, opposite to the island of Thasus. The generals, upon their arrival on the river Nessus, found that the usual passage of the mountains at Symbolus was already seized by Saxa and Norbanus, who, with the first division of Antony's forces from Italy, had traversed Macedonia, and hastened to possess themselves of this pass, in order to stop the farther progress of their enemies in Europe.

Here the eastern armies were accordingly stopped, and were likely to end their career in Thrace, while their antagonists continued in possession of Macedonia, and preserved the most convenient retreat for their shipping in the bay of Strymon. They were relieved, however, from this apprehension by Ruscopolis, a Thracian prince, who attended them, and who pointed out a different route from that which the enemy had occupied. Under this guide they marched three days among the mountains, and having crossed the summit, descended in the track of a river towards Philippi, situated on the eastern boundary of the plains of Amphipolis. This march carried them into the rear of the enemy's station, and would have enabled them to cut off their retreat, if intelligence had not been carried to Saxa and Norbanus time enough to enable them to withdraw These officers accordingly abandoned their post, fell back forty or fifty miles[3] to Amphipolis; and having put this place in the best posture they could for defence, determined to await the arrival of Octavius and Antony.

Brutus and Cassius took post at Philippi, on the declivity of the mountains, near to the pass which Saxa and Norbanus had lately abandoned. They encamped about two miles[4] from the town on two separate eminences, about a mile[5] asunder. On their right was Philippi, covered by the mountains; on the left an impassable marsh, which reached about nine miles from their camp to the sea.[6] In their front the country from Philippi, westward to Amphipolis, extending about forty or fifty miles, was flat and subject to floods and inundations of the rivers. The fleet was in harbour at Neapolis, near where the marsh, which covered the left of Cassius's camp, terminated in the sea; and Cimber had fixed on that place as the port to which all their convoys should repair, and by which they expected to be plentifully supplied with necessaries from Asia, and the coasts of the Egean sea. They formed, at the same time, a magazine in the island of Thasus, out of the reach of the enemy, at which to lodge in safety the surplus of their provisions and stores.

Antony and Octavius had been employed, during the winter, in transporting their forces into Macedonia; and having effected their passage, notwithstanding the vigilance of the enemy's fleet, their army advanced by rapid marches to the river Strymon, in order to preserve Amphipolis, and to carry the scene of the war as far as they could from Italy. Octavius had been taken ill, and remained behind at Dyrrachium. Antony, upon his arrival at Amphipolis, having found the town in a posture of defence, fixed upon it as a place of arms, for the security of his heavy baggage and stores. From thence he advanced upon the flat country, through a march of some days, and pitched in sight of Philippi, within a mile of the enemy's stations.

It was the object of the triumvirs to bring the war to a speedy issue, as they foresaw the difficulty of being long able, without any supply of provisions from the sea, to maintain so numerous an army by the sole resources of the neighbouring country. Brutus and Cassius, on the contrary, perceived their own advantage, and were determined to protract the war. They fortified their camps with great care, and joined them to each other; and to the town of Philippi on the one side, and to the morass on the other, with such works as formed a continued chain to cover their communication, for about twelve miles from the town of Philippi, to the port of Neapolis.

Antony's camp being on the plain, and in a low situation, was overlooked by the enemy, and

1 Appian. de Bell. Civ. lib. iv. 2 About 12*l*.

3 350 stadia. 4 Eighteen stadia.
5 Eight stadia. 6 Seventy. stadia.

subject to be overflowed by the torrents which fell from the hills. He made every possible effort to bring his antagonists to action, and by his forwardness in pressing them to a battle, raised the courage of his own troops, and assumed, as is common with those who act offensively, the appearance of superiority. While he yet continued in this posture, Octavius, though not entirely recovered from his illness, joined him from Dyrrachium. They took two separate stations opposite to those of the enemy; Octavius opposite to Brutus, and Antony to Cassius. The number of legions, on both sides, were equal; but those of Antony and Octavius were not complete. In cavalry they were unequal; that of Brutus and Cassius amounting to twenty thousand, while that of Octavius and Antony was no more than thirteen thousand.

Antony and Octavius, in order to force their antagonists to a battle, or to cut off their communication with the sea, formed a design to pierce the morass, and to seize upon the heights beyond it on the left of Cassius's camp. In the work which they carried on for this purpose, they were covered by the reeds, which grew to a great height in the marsh; and in ten days, without being observed, by means of timbers, hurdles, and earth, which they sunk as they advanced, accomplished a passage, and sent in the night a party of their army to occupy the opposite heights, to make lodgments, and to intercept the communication of their antagonists with Neapolis, from which they received their daily supplies.

As soon as Brutus and Cassius perceived this advantage gained by the enemy, they took measures to recover it, and to open their own access again to the sea. For this purpose they, in their turn, traversed the morass in a line which crossed the passage which the enemy had made, and pierced their highway with a deep and impassable ditch. Having in this manner cut off the enemy's parties that had passed the morass from any succours or supplies from their main body, they were about to force them, when Octavius and Antony endeavoured to recover their passage; and to divert the attention of the enemy from what they were doing in the marsh, drew forth their armies on the plain.

While Octavius was still confined by sickness, his lieutenant, or next in command, took his place in this movement, and advanced toward the intrenchment of Brutus. The light troops began to skirmish on the ascent of the hill. And, notwithstanding it was the resolution of both leaders in the republican army not to hazard a battle, except in defence of their own intrenchments, the legions of Brutus observing, from their parapet, what passed between the advanced parties in front, were so animated or incensed, as not to be restrained. They accordingly quitted their lines, attacked the wing on which Octavius was supposed to command, drove them back to their ground, and continuing their pursuit, even forced them in their camp. Octavius himself, having been carried from his bed to a litter, narrowly escaped falling into the enemy's hands.

On the other wing Antony likewise had advanced towards the camp of Cassius; but as he was observed, at the same time, beginning to work in the morass, this movement of his army was considered as no more than a feint to favour the other design. Cassius, to divert him from his operation in the marsh, drew forth his army likewise; and having greatly the advantage of the ground, did not suppose that the enemy, in such circumstances, would venture upon a general action. In this however he was disappointed. Antony, seeing Cassius expose his front, discontinued his work in the morass, mounted the height in his presence, forced him to retire, even took and pillaged his camp; and thus showed, in his turn, what are the effects of an impetuous attack upon an enemy who are disposed to think themselves secure.

These separate actions, or the preparations which were made for them, had filled up the greater part of the day. It was already dusk, and the field, for the most part, was covered with clouds of dust; so that no one could see to a distance. Those who commanded on the right in both armies, having put those who were opposed to them to flight, thought that the event was decisive in their own favour. But Brutus and Antony being informed of what had passed on the other wings of their respective armies, neither attempted to keep the advantage he had gained. Disqualified by fatigue or surprise from renewing the contest, they passed each other on the plain, and hastened back to their former stations.

Cassius, after the rout of his division, with a few who adhered to him, had halted on an eminence, and sent Titinius to the right, with orders to learn the particulars of the day on that side. This officer, while yet in sight, was met by a party of horse emerging from the clouds of dust on the plain. This party had been sent by Brutus to learn the situation of his friends on the left; but Cassius, supposing them to be enemies, and believing that Titinius, whom he saw surrounded by them, was taken, he instantly, with the precipitant despair, which, on other occasions, had proved so fatal to the cause of the republic, presented his breast to a slave to whom he had allotted, in case of any urgent extremity, the office of putting an end to his life. Titinius, upon his return, imputing this fatal calamity to his own neglect in not trying sooner to undeceive his general by proper signals, killed himself, and fell upon the body of his friend.[7] Brutus soon after arrived at the same place, and seeing the dead body of Cassius, shed tears of vexation and sorrow over the effects of an action so rash and precipitant, and which deprived the republic and himself, in this extremity, of so necessary and so able a support. This, he said, is the last of the Romans.

The surviving leader of the republican party, in order to prevent the impression which the sight of a funeral so interesting was likely to make on the army, ordered the body of Cassius to be carried to the island of Thasus, and there privately interred. He himself spent the night in re-assembling the troops who had been dispersed, formed both armies into one body, and drew the whole into one camp. He still kept his ground at Philippi, and endeavoured to support the courage of the troops, and to replace the activity and military skill of his unfortunate colleague. In his addresses to the army, he set forth the advantages they had gained as more than sufficient to compensate their losses. He represented the distressed condition of the enemy, who, hav-

7 Dio. Cass. lib. xlvii. c. 34. Appian. lib. iv.

ing already exhausted the province of Macedonia in their rear, were obliged to bring their provisions from Thessaly, which was at a greater distance, and not likely to supply them so long. "The sea-ports," he observed, "being every where blocked up, and their convoys intercepted by a fleet of above two hundred and sixty sail, the prospect of what they must speedily suffer will make them impatient for action. They will provoke," he said, "they will attempt to insult you; but this appearance of courage is a mere effect of despair. Only wait the result of these circumstances, and perseverance will render your victory easy." He supported these exhortations with giving the army full satisfaction in all their claims and pretensions, and with an additional gratuity of a thousand sesterces to each man.[1]

The leaders of the other side, at the same time, were equally employed in what was necessary to palliate the sufferings, or to raise the hopes of their own army. Though not equally in condition to make present donations, they amply supplied this defect with expectations and promises. They declared their intention of giving an additional gratuity of five thousand sesterces to each private man,[2] five times as much to the centurion, and the double of this sum to the tribune. "Judge ye," said Antony, in his address to the army, "who has suffered most by the mutual pillage of yesterday? You, who have left all your effects behind you in Italy, or the enemy, who came to their ground loaded with the spoils of Asia? Their own general, by killing himself, has proclaimed your victory. We declare you victorious, by bestowing upon you the rewards of valour to which you are entitled. If the enemy choose to dispute your claim to these rewards, let them meet us again in the field. They shall have an opportunity to-morrow, and for some days to come; if they shrink and remain behind their entrenchments, I shall leave you to determine who is vanquished in the trial of force which we have had."

Antony and Octavius accordingly drew forth their army for many days successively, and were greatly embarrassed with the resolution which appeared to be taken by the enemy, not to hazard a battle. They began to suffer greatly for want of provisions, and felt the approach of winter, which, in a marshy situation, threatened them with growing inconveniences. Brutus, to hasten the effects of the season, had turned the course of a river from the hills, and laid under water part of the plain on which they encamped.[3] At the same time a recent calamity, which befel them at sea, increased these distresses, and diminished their hopes of relief.

On the same day on which the late battle was fought at Philippi, Domitius Calvisius had sailed from Brundusium, having on board of transports two legions, of which the Martia was one, with two thousand men of the prætorian bands, and a body of horse, convoyed by some galleys, or ships of force. Being met at sea by the fleet of Brutus, consisting of a hundred and thirty sail, under Murcus and Ahenobarbus, a few of the headmost and best sailing ships escaped; but the remainder being surrounded had no resource but in the valour of the troops, who endeavoured to defend themselves with their swords, grappling and lashing their transports to the ships of the enemy; but in this attempt, being galled with missiles from the armed galleys, particularly with burning darts, by which some of the transports were set on fire, the others, to avoid the flames, were obliged to keep at a distance; and the greater part of them suffering extremely without being able to annoy the enemy, were sunk or destroyed. Calvisius himself, having been five days at sea, with difficulty escaped to Brundusium.

These tidings had their effect in both armies. In that of Brutus they inspired an unseasonable ardour, and a disposition to commit the cause of the party to the hazard of a battle; in that of Antony and Octavius, they impressed the necessity of a speedy decision. These leaders, to amuse their own troops, and to provoke the enemy, had seized, in the night, a post on the declivity below the ground which was lately occupied by Cassius. They were suffered to make a lodgment upon it by Brutus, who had not any apprehension that he could be annoyed from a situation that was so much lower than his own. On the following day it appeared, that their intention in seizing this post was to cover a movement, which they proposed to make to the right on the edge of the morass; which they accordingly executed, and pitched again in two separate encampments. In this new position they were observed to sound the morass, and either intended a feint, or had a real design, by effecting a communication with the opposite side, again to cut off every intercourse of Brutus with his ships. But finding that all the heights on the opposite side were now secured against them by intrenchments, they dropped that intention, and endeavoured, by frequent alarms, and by exposing their own parties on the plain, to engage their antagonist in a general action.

Brutus, in the mean time, having secured his own communication with Neapolis, by a proper disposition of posts from his present encampment to the sea; and trusting that his enemies must, upon the approach of winter, be obliged to evacuate Macedonia, or to separate their army for the convenience of finding subsistence, persisted in his resolution to protract the war. In this conjuncture he wrote to his friend Pomponius Atticus in the following terms: "My object is secure; for either I shall, by my victory, rescue the Romans from the servitude into which they are fallen, or perish in the attempt, and by dying myself escape from slavery. I have done my part, and wait for the issue in which public freedom or death is to follow. As for Antony, who has chosen to become the retainer of Octavius, rather than a sharer with us in the equal rights of a citizen, he has a different alternative, either now to perish with this young man, or, being the dupe of his artifices, to become hereafter the subject of his government."[4]

The troops of Brutus, however, could not be reconciled to this dilatory plan; they began to complain that a victorious army should be cooped up behind intrenchments, and should be insulted like women; even the officers, pretending to reason on the state of the war, censured their general for losing the opportunity, which so great an

1 About 8*l*. 2 About 40*l*.
3 Zonarus, l. 19. p. 38[illegible]
4 Plutarch. in Bruto.

ardour in the army gave him of deciding the contest at a blow. They alleged, that even if the attempt should prove unsuccessful, he might still return to the execution of his defensive and dilatory operations.

Brutus was aware that the army, now under his command, having been trained up as mere soldiers of fortune, had no principle of attachment to either side; that it was necessary to consult their inclinations, as well as to flatter their hopes. He remembered that Cassius had been obliged, in many things, to abate the usual rigour of his discipline; and being himself of a mild and indulgent nature, he yielded to those who were under his command; or not being able to stem the torrent which daily increased, he suffered the impatience of his own men to hurry him into a risk of all his fortunes. In about twenty days after the former action,[5] overcome by mere importunities, he drew forth his army on the declivity before his camp; the enemy, at the same time, according to their usual practice, were forming upon the plain; and both sides foresaw the approach of a general engagement.

Historians introduce their accounts of the last action at Philippi, with a detail of forms and solemnities, which, on other occasions, they have either omitted to mention, or which were not equally observed. As soon as the parole or word for the day was given over the different divisions of the respective armies, a single trumpet sounded the signal of battle; and was followed by a numerous band, which played an air, while the legions were dressing their ranks, and while the men were trying and handling their arms.

Brutus, being on horseback, passed along the lines of his own army, and exhorted his men not to quit the advantage of the ground on which they stood, by advancing too far to meet the enemy. "You have promised me a victory," he said, "you have forced me to snatch it now, rather than to wait for a more secure possession of it hereafter. It is your business to fulfil your own expectations and mine."

On the other side, Antony and Octavius were happy in having their fortunes, hitherto desperate, brought to the chance of a battle. They put their army in mind, that this was what all of them wished: "You are poor and distressed," they said, "but in the enemy's camp you will find an end to your sufferings, and the beginning of riches and plenty. From us, who are your leaders, you may expect the rewards which are due to valour, and every effect of a disposition in us which is sufficiently liberal, but which victory alone will give us the power to indulge in the manner that we wish."

In these preparations the day being far spent, and noon about three hours already past, the trumpets on both sides having sounded a general charge, made a sudden pause, and sounded again, while both armies being in motion, struck upon their bucklers, advanced with a mighty shout, and, under a shower of missile weapons of every sort, closed with their swords. They continued long with all the fury that kindles in the use of short weapons, to struggle on the same spot. The places of those that fell in the first rank were continually supplied from the ranks behind them; and the place of action began to be choked up with heaps of the slain. No stratagem is said to have been practised, or any accident to have happened, to determine the fate of the day on either side; but, after a severe contest, the army of Brutus began to give way, at first slowly, and almost insensibly; but being pressed with growing violence, they were thrown into some confusion, and gave up the day without hopes of recovery. In the disorder that followed, numbers, who fled to the camp, finding the entrances obstructed by the crowds that struggled for admission, despaired of safety there, and passed on to the heights in its rear. Octavius advanced to the enemy's camp to secure, or to keep in awe those who had taken refuge within it. Antony pursued those who were dispersed on the heights, and, at the approach of night, made the necessary dispositions to hinder those who were within the intrenchment, or those who were in the field, from rallying or assembling again; and employed parties of horse all night to scour all the avenues in search of prisoners.

Brutus himself being cut off from the camp and closely followed, Lucilius, one of his company, to give him time to escape, affecting to personate his general, and falling behind, was taken. This captive, supposed to be Brutus, the leader of the republican army, being conducted to Antony, to whom he was known, met with a reception not unworthy of his generous artifice. "You intended," said Antony, to those who brought the prisoner, with a politeness which seemed to refute some of the imputations on his character, "to bring me an enemy, but you have brought me a friend."[6]

Brutus, in the mean time, having in the dark passed a brook that ran between steep and rocky banks covered with wood, made a halt, with a few friends, on the opposite side, as in a place of safety. Being yet uncertain of the extent of his loss, he sent an officer to observe the field, and with orders, if any considerable body of the army were yet together, to light a blaze as a signal or token of its safety. This officer accordingly made his way to the camp, and finding it still in the possession of his friends, made the signal; but lest it should not be observed, he attempted to return to his general, fell into the enemy's hands, and was slain.

As, from the signal now made, it appeared to Brutus and the small company who attended him, that the camp was still in possession of their own people, they thought of making their way thither; but recollecting that the greater part of the army were dispersed, they doubted whether the lines could be defended until they could reach them, or even if they should be maintained so long, whether they could furnish any safe retreat. While they reasoned in this manner, one of their number, who went to the brook for water returned with an alarm that the enemy were upon the opposite bank; and saying, with some agitation, "We must fly." "Yes," replied Brutus, "but with our hands, not with our feet." He was then said to have repeated, from some poet, a tragic exclamation in the character of Hercules: "O Virtue! I thought thee a substance, but find thee no more than an empty name, or the slave of Fortune." The vulgar, in their traditions, willingly lend their own thoughts

5 Plutarch. in Bruto.

6 Plutarch. in Bruto.

to eminent men in distress; those of Brutus are expressed in his letter to Atticus already quoted: "I have done my part, and wait for the issue, in which death or freedom is to follow." If he had ever thought that a mere honourable intention was to ensure him success, it is surprising he was not sooner undeceived. Being now to end his life, and taking his leave of the company then present, one by one, he said aloud, "That he was happy in never having been betrayed by any one he had trusted as a friend." Some of them, to whom he afterwards whispered apart, were observed to burst into tears; and it appeared that he requested their assistance in killing himself; for he soon afterwards executed this purpose, in company with one Strato and some others, whom he had taken aside.

This catastrophe, as usual, set the imaginations of men to work; and many prodigies and presages were believed to have preceded it. A spectre, it was said, had presented itself in the night to Brutus, when he was about to pass the Hellespont, told him it was his evil genius, and was to meet him again at Philippi; that here it accordingly again appeared on the eve of the late action.

Brutus was then about thirty-seven or forty years of age.[1] Next to Cato, he, of all the Romans, was supposed to have acted from the purest motives of public virtue. Cassius had too much elevation of mind to endure a master; but Brutus was likewise too just to have usurped on the rights of his fellow-citizens, even if they had been in his power. His character, however, in some respects, is questionable; and we may not, through the disguise of manners so different from our own, be able to ascertain the truth. Cicero, who is at once the principal author of his fame and of the exceptions which are taken against it, charges him with an uncommon degree of arrogance, and complains of the tone which, while yet a young man, he took even with himself.[2] He likewise relates some particulars of a loan which one Scaptius had transacted for Brutus in the island of Cyprus, and of which the payment was exacted under the proconsulate of Cicero, with circumstances of uncommon avarice and cruelty; and that in this he even presumed to demand that the Roman proconsul should support him with all his authority. The loan was usurious, and, in exacting the payment of it, the senate of Salamis, in the island of Cyprus, had been surrounded by a party of cavalry, and shut up from the use of food. Cicero writes of this proceeding to Atticus, with every expression of blame and indignation; and yet Brutus, then a young man, continued to be held in the highest veneration and esteem by persons who were acquainted with these particulars. "If you should have no other advantage," says Atticus, in writing to Cicero, "from your present government, but the opportunity of gaining the friendship of Brutus, this alone will be enough." And Cicero himself frequently mentions Brutus, after this transaction, with peculiar expressions of admiration and love.[3] So that we must either suppose Brutus to have been innocent of this extortion and cruelty committed by his agent in Cyprus, or that such proceedings, though contrary to law, were so much authorized by the practice of the times, as to stain the manners of the age much more than the characters of individuals. Of these conjectures, perhaps, both are in part to be admitted: the law of the republic forbidding the interest of money under the denomination of usury, inflamed, rather than prevented, the evil. Under this prohibition, the necessitous borrower was made to pay for the risk and obloquy which the lender incurred by transgressing the law, as well as for the use of his money. It was impossible to prevent what is necessary in the common course of things; persons having occasion for money must borrow; and persons having money will lend, in order to reap the benefit of it. It appears to have been customary with towns in the provinces, with corporations, and with dependent princes, to borrow money at exorbitant interest from the rich at Rome; and probably to employ that money in making presents to gain the powerful.[4] Pompey had great sums owing to him in Asia, and likewise received great presents from thence. These we must admit to have been great abuses; but individuals are not always accountable for the abuses of their age, even where they have not corrected them in their own practice.

Brutus and Cassius, the last unsuccessful leaders of the republican party, even after it became a crime to mention their names with respect, were revered in secret by every person who had any memory or conception of the ancient republic, and will, in every age, be held, in estimation by those who conceive merit as independent of fortune. Even Antony, it is said, when the death of Brutus was reported to him, expressed the highest respect for his memory, covered his remains with the imperial robe which he himself wore in the field, and ordered his obsequies to be performed with the highest marks of distinction and honour;[5] in this instance, probably acting from policy, or, under all the vices of dissipation and profligacy with which he was charged, knowing how to seize the occasion of gaining the public esteem, by splendid pretensions to generosity and candour.

Octavius, who far excelled his colleague in the ordinary arts of discretion and policy, is represented as greatly inferior to him in his behaviour on the present occasion. It is said that he ordered the head of Brutus to be carried into Italy, and exposed on Cæsar's tomb; and, among other proofs of insolence and cruelty which he gave in the present prosperous tide of his fortunes, that having among his prisoners a father and son of the name of Florus, he ordered that one of them should be put to death, and that they should cast lots, or fight, to determine which should be spared. Under this cruel sentence, the father intreated that he himself might die. Octavius attended to see the execution; and, after the death of the father, likewise witnessed that of the son, who killed himself.[6]

That part of the vanquished army which fled

1 Liv. Epitome, lib. cxliv. Vel. Paterculus, c. 72.

2 Ad Attic lib. v. ep. 21, et lib. vi. ep 1. Ad me autem etiam cum rogat aliquid, contumaciter, arroganter, ἀκοινωνήτως, solet scribere.

3 Vid. lib. de Claris Oratoribus, cap. 3. &c. &c. This book is expressly dated after the return of Cicero from Cilicia

4 Cicer. ad Attic. lib v. ep. 21.

5 Plut. in Antonio et Bruto.

6 Sueton. in Octav. c. 14. Dio. Cass. dates this particular after the battle of Actium.

to the heights, being about fourteen thousand men, hearing of the death of the last of their leaders, surrendered themselves, and were equally divided between Octavius and Antony. Those who remained in the camp, or at any of the outposts of the army, likewise laid down their arms. Of the persons of rank who partook in the wreck of their party at Philippi, some escaped by sea, and joined Sextus Pompeius in Sicily, now the sole refuge of those who adhered to the commonwealth. Others killed themselves, or in the late action had refused quarter, and fought till they were slain. Among the first were Livius Drusus, the father of Livia, afterwards the wife of Octavius. Among the second were two young men of distinguished names; Cato, the son of him who died at Utica, and Lucius Cassius, nephew of the late general. Labeo, with great deliberation, prepared a grave for himself in his tent, wrote to his family at Rome, gave directions about his affairs, and then submitted himself to a person whom he had retained to put an end to his life.

It appears to have been a point of honour among the Romans of this age, to perish by their own hands rather than by that of their antagonists, otherwise they could have easily, when fortune appeared to have declared against them, forced the enemy to bestow that death which they afterwards obtained with great reluctance from their friends; and perhaps, in forcing matters to this extremity, they might have turned the fortune of battle. Cæsar seems to have owed his victory, on some occasions, to efforts of this sort, and his party in general prevailed by their perseverance under checks and difficulties, as much as by the advantage they took of their victories.[7]

CHAPTER V.

Immediate Consequences of the Event at Philippi—New Partition of the Empire made by Octavius and Antony—Their Separation—Progress of Octavius at Rome—His Friends Mæcenas and Agrippa—Alarm and Distress in Italy on the Dispossession of the Inhabitants to make way for the Troops—Jealousy of Fulvia and Lucius Antonius—Blockade and reduction of Perusia—Progress of Antony in Asia—His Stay at Alexandria—Return to Italy—Accommodation with Sextus Pompeius—Return of Octavius and Antony to Rome—Their Policy.

AMONG the immediate consequences of the late event at Philippi, is mentioned the death of Porcia, the wife of Brutus, and the daughter of Cato. Being suspected of an intention to kill herself, watched by her servants, and anxiously precluded from the ordinary means of effecting that purpose, she swallowed burning coals, and expired. This was said to have happened on hearing of her husband's death; but Plutarch cites a letter of Brutus, extant in his own time, from which it appeared that this catastrophe preceded the death of Brutus, and was imputed to the negligence of her servants, who attended her in the delirium of a fever.[8]

By the battles which had been fought in different parts of the empire, by the late massacre in Italy, and by the event of the war at Philippi, the last pillars of the commonwealth seemed to be removed, or but a few of its members were left who had any zeal for its preservation. Octavius and Antony, upon the total and decisive victory they had gained, without paying any regard to the pretensions of Lepidus, made a new partition of the empire. Octavius, to his former lot, had an addition of Spain and Numidia; Antony that of the farther Gaul and the province of Africa.[9] It was agreed between them, that Antony should prosecute the remains of the war in the east, and raise the necessary contributions to enable them to fulfil their engagements to the army: that Octavius should return into Italy, conduct the war against Sextus Pompeius, repress the designs of Lepidus, in case he should be dissatisfied with the present arrangement, and in proper time settle the veterans on the lands which had been allotted to them.—These articles were committed to writing, and the ratifications exchanged. Antony having received from Octavius a reinforcement of two legions, departed for Asia, and Octavius set out on his return to Rome.

When accounts of the final action at Philippi were received in the city, a thanksgiving was ordered; and, instead of being limited to fifty or sixty days, as in the late decrees which had passed in honour of Julius Cæsar, this festival was now to be continued for an entire year. In proportion to the approaches which the republican party made to its entire extinction, the few who remained of it carried an affectation of joy that kept pace with their real sorrow. Their fears broke forth in profuse expressions of pretended attachment and zeal for the honour of those whom they dreaded.

Under such an aspect of gladness, covering extreme anxiety or terror, the pacific inhabitants of Italy looked for the arrival of an army which was to be gratified with their richest possessions. They remembered what had passed at former military entries into Rome, and they anticipated the sufferings which were to be expected from a young man who had, during some time, and from mere policy, assumed an air of moderation, and employed every artifice to forward his purpose; but in proportion as he became secure of his end, he threw off his original mask, and concurred in *usurpations the most bloody* of any that had been known in the history of mankind.—Octavius being detained by sickness on his way to the city, these gloomy apprehensions gained force from delay. It was supposed that he deferred his arrival only while he adjusted his plan or took measures to render its effects more certain. Every one exaggerated the evil, but no one thought of a remedy. Such was the present state of a [illegible]

7 See the History of the Campaigns on the Segra at Dyrrachium, and in Africa.

8 Plut. in Bruto.

9 Dio Cass. lib. xlviii. c. 1.

less nobility and people, the remains of a commonwealth, long accustomed to dominion, retaining their haughtiness while they lost their vigour, long desirous of power, but unable to sustain the weight of a free constitution.

Octavius gave notice to the senate, that his coming was delayed by sickness, accepted the decree of a continued thanksgiving for the late victory obtained at Philippi, but desired it might be understood, that this honour was conferred on account of the exemplary justice he had done on the assassins of his father. The cunning with which he occasionally dropt this pretence, or with which he resumed it, as the motive of all his pursuits, forms a striking part in his character. He at one time co-operated with the conspirators, and declared it to be his intention, in conjunction with them, to restore the republic. He accordingly promoted the resolutions which were taken at Rome in favour of Decimus, as well as Marcus Brutus and Cassius, he promoted the election of Casca into the office of tribune; he raised an army to support them against Antony, and took into his councils the most vehement partizans of the senate. "*Even Servius Galba, holding the very dagger with which he murdered Cæsar*," said Antony to him, in his letter during the siege of Mutina, "*is now employed in your camp.*"[1] As he often, however, on former occasions, courted the army, by affecting a pious intention to avenge his father's death, so he now recurred to the same pretence, as the most likely to counterbalance the favour that was paid to the memory of Brutus and Cassius, and the general regret which attended the catastrophe of the last scene that was acted in behalf of the commonwealth.

U. C. 712. *L. Antonius, P. Servilius, Vatica Isauricus.*

About this time, Octavius was known to have in his service two officers of distinguished merit, Marcus Vipsanius Agrippa, and Caius Cilnius Mæcenas; both well qualified in their respective parts to support him in the pretensions he had formed on the empire. The first, by his courage and military abilities, was qualified to supply or to conceal his defects as a soldier; the second, by his industry, his temper, his choice of friends, and his fitness to soften the manners of the times, by diverting the minds of men from objects of public distress to the elegant and amusing occupations of literary genius, well qualified to smooth all the difficulties in the way of his civil administration. Although it had not yet appeared in what degree Octavius was to commit his affairs to such able hands, his discernment in choosing them might be considered as the presage of a fortune not depending on accidents, but founded on a real ascendant of understanding and judgment.

Upon the arrival of the young Cæsar at Rome, he gave assurance to the senate of his intention to avoid all unnecessary acts of severity.[2] But the first object of his administration being to settle the veterans on the possessions which they had been made to expect at the end of the war, he was very soon led into a scene of extreme violence, and involved in great difficulties.

At the formation of the triumvirate the army had been flattered with the hopes of being settled on the most fertile lands, or in the wealthiest cities of Italy. In order to fulfil these expectations, it was necessary to dispossess the ancient inhabitants; and as this was to be done without any pretence of forfeiture, or delinquency of any sort, the unhappy sufferers pleaded, that the lands intended for the army should be taken by lot, or in equal proportions, and in every part of the empire. But the soldiers were absolute, and not to be satisfied but by immediate possession of the lots which had been actually assigned as the reward of their services. A general order was accordingly signed for the present occupiers of those lands to remove. The victims of this severity repaired to Rome in entire families; persons of every sex, age, and condition crowded the streets, took shelter in the temples and other places of public resort, and filled the city with complaints and lamentations.[3] "The ancient inhabitants of Italy, citizens of Rome," they said, "were stripped of their possessions, and turned out to perish with their children, to make way for adventurers who had subverted the laws of their country, and who were to perpetuate the military usurpation they had established. The same violent hands which had stripped the Roman people of their sovereignty, were now to be let loose on their property. The innocent, who had taken no part in the late troubles, were to be sacrificed, merely because their possessions suited the conveniency of those who had already brought so many evils on the commonwealth. They had been promised protection from this party; but were now to suffer, from their pretended protectors and friends, greater evils than any conquered province had ever endured from the worst of its enemies."

To these complaints both the army and its leaders were equally insensible, and proceeded, in particular instances, to acts of violence, which the execution of their general purpose did not require. They kept the minds of the people in suspense by their indecision in choosing their lots; by quitting those which were at first assigned, in order to exchange them for others; and, by leaving particular persons without any regular grant or assignment, to make free with such lands as suited their conveniency. The leaders were obliged to connive at what they could not restrain, and gave way to a violence to which they owed the possession of their power.[4]

The army now considering the lands of Italy as their property, looked upon every person inclined to protect the ancient inhabitants as their enemy, resented every delay that was made in gratifying their desires, and were equally insolent to their own officers as they were to the people. A party being assembled in the Campus Martius to receive their dismission and their assignments of land; and having some time waited for Octavius, from whom they expected satisfaction in

1 Cicer. Philip. Antony t[o] [O]ctavius and Hirtius.
2 Dio Cass. lib. xlviii. c. [illegible]

3 Publius Virgilius Maro is said to have been of this injured train. Having had a small property in land near Mantua, he was stripped of it to make way for an officer of the legions; a wrong to which he so tenderly alludes in his eclogue (Nos patriæ fines et dulcia linquimus arva, nos patriam fugimus.) But being recommended to Mæcenas by Asinius Pollio, who commanded in that part of Italy, he obtained, from the respect that was due to his fine genius, a protection which humanity and justice owe equally to every other person that was involved in this calamity.—Appian. de Bell. Civ. lib. v.
4 Appian. lib v.

these particulars, became impatient and clamorous, laid violent hands on Nonius, a centurion, who endeavoured to pacify them, and even threw him into the river, where he perished. They afterwards dragged the dead body on shore, and placed it on the way by which their general was to pass, as a warning, that he himself should not slight their displeasure. Octavius being informed, before he came abroad, of this menacing insult which had been offered to his authority, saw the necessity of not appearing to be moved. He passed the dead body without seeming to observe it, made the intended distribution of land to the troops; and affecting to consider the murder of Nonius as the effect of a private quarrel, in which he was to take no part, left this dangerous meeting with an exhortation, that they should *not weaken their own cause by quarrelling among themselves.*

The cohorts which Octavius retained for the ordinary guard of his own person, treated him, on occasion, with equal disrespect. As an instance of this sort, it is mentioned, that one of their body having, at the public theatre, seated himself on the Equestrian bench, and the audience being scandalized at this act of presumption, the soldier was removed by order of his general; but his companions being made to believe that he was carried away to be put to death, placed themselves in the way of Octavius, as he passed from the theatre, and, with clamours and threats of instant revenge, demanded their fellow-soldier to be restored. Having prevailed in this particular, they called upon him to declare what usage he had received; and when they were told by himself that no violence had been offered to him, they alleged that he was hired to conceal the truth, and to betray the honour of the army, and were scarcely to be appeased by his repeated asseverations to the contrary.

In these dangerous times, enormities which were committed by disorderly persons of any description being imputed to the soldiers, were suffered to pass with impunity. Robbery and murders became frequent, and the city of Rome itself, as well as the provincial towns, was infested by persons who, either from necessity, or from the license of the times, subsisted by rapine. No property was safe, and the condition of persons of all parties equally insecure. At Rome the rent of houses fell to a fourth, and whole streets appeared to be deserted.[5]

In this distracted scene, nevertheless, there were persons who envied Octavius the hateful pre-eminence which he seemed to enjoy. Among these Manius, the person entrusted with the affairs of Mark Antony, Lucius his brother, now in the office of consul, and Fulvia his wife, aspiring to a share of the government, became impatient of an administration from which they thought themselves unfairly excluded. Not only L. Antonius, in the capacity of consul, but the others also, in right of the absent triumvir, thought themselves entitled to more consideration than they now enjoyed.

The power of distributing the lands and other rewards to the army, it was observed, gave Octavius a signal advantage over his colleague, and fixed the expectations of all men upon him alone. By these means he filled Italy with his own retainers and friends; and Fulvia complained that Mark Antony should be thus deprived of the fruits of a victory, which had been obtained chiefly by his conduct and valour. She appealed to the legions, presented herself at their quarters, and, with her children in her arms, implored, what she was pleased to call, a matter of right in behalf of her husband.

In this manner, persons representing the absent triumvir endeavoured to divide the party, and to add to the scene of political confusion already subsisting, a breach and opposition of interest among those who commanded the army. The country, at the same time, suffered from the interruption that was given by the fleets of Domitius Ahenobarbus and Sextus Pompeius, from the opposite ports of Illyricum and Sicily, to the importation of corn and other necessaries; and this circumstance, joined to the uncertainty of property, and the other causes which interrupted industry, completed the distresses of Italy.

The people, although they were willing to submit to any government, were not likely to be long able to endure their present sufferings. The friends of Antony endeavoured to load Octavius with the blame of these evils, and thought this a favourable opportunity to wrest the government out of his hands. They found fault with the provision he had made for the army as too scanty; and they joined in the complaints that were made by the sufferers, who were dispossessed of their property to make way for the soldiers. They affected a design to restore the republic; and Lucius Antonius, in the character of Roman consul, called upon the remaining friends of the commonwealth to appear in support of their legal magistrate. He professed his intention to make war even on his own brother, as well as on Octavius, if he should persist in his present usurpations, or should attempt to obstruct the restoration of the laws. But, notwithstanding his professions to this purpose, he himself, affecting to believe that his person was in danger, put his attendants under arms, and paraded the streets at the head of a military force; a measure that was ever considered at Rome as the intimation of a design to usurp the government.

Octavius, greatly provoked by these attacks which were made upon him by the representatives of Antony, repudiated the daughter of Fulvia, whom, at the formation of the triumvirate, he had betrothed merely to serve a political purpose, and whom he now returned to her family, with express declarations of his never having had any commerce with her as his wife. Fulvia, affecting to consider this insult as a prelude to greater injuries, appealed to Lepidus in behalf of his absent colleague, and withdrew to Præneste, whither great numbers of all ranks and conditions, both civil and military, flocked to her standard. Here she put herself at the head of an army, held regular councils, and, with a sword by her side, gave the parole, and frequently harangued the troops.

In these hasty advances to a rupture, representations to Antony, and preparations for war, were equally made on both sides. It was yet uncertain how the army might divide between the parties. Octavius was likely, by his presence, to command the superior number; but great part of the forces now in Italy had been levied in

[5] Dio. Cass. lib. xlviii. c. 9

the name of Antony, and still, according to the custom of those armies, bore his name on their shields. The two legions which were to have been transferred to Octavius, to replace those which he had given to Antony in Macedonia, were still retained by Lucius Antonius for his brother. The provinces of Gaul, with considerable armies, ready to march into Italy, were under the government of Ventidius, of Plancus, and of Asinius Pollio, who were the adherents of Antony, and likely to espouse his cause. Antony himself, by the superiority of his military character, had, in the course of his joint operations with Octavius, greatly surpassed him, and had acquired a high degree of reputation with the troops. It was, therefore, necessary for his rival to proceed with great caution, and not rashly to draw upon himself, in this quarrel, the weight of his colleague's authority, nor to disgust the army, by appearing to be the aggressor in a war between their leaders.

Such disputes were certainly in general disagreeable to the army, who, having subdued the republic, hoped, now at their ease, to divide its spoils. It was necessary, therefore, for Octavius, if a war should ensue, to make it appear to be the work of his enemies. For this purpose he formed at Rome a council of the principal officers; proposed that they should make inquiry into the grounds of the present dissension, and oblige those who were in fault to submit to their decrees.

Fulvia and her partizans called this military convention by a ludicrous name, which we may translate *the ammunition senate*,[1] and refused to submit their cause to so new a tribunal.

The army in general was alarmed at the prospect of seeing the civil war renewed. Two legions that had first served under Cæsar, and afterwards under Antony, being now quartered at Ancona, sent a deputation to Rome, with intreaties that the parties would avoid a rupture. They were referred by Octavius to L. Antonius, who, he said, was the aggressor; and proceeding, attended by a great concourse of people to Prænesté, where the heads of the opposite party were assembled, beseeched them to spare the republic, already too much afflicted with civil dissensions. They were told for answer, that "Octavius was the aggressor; that while his colleague was raising money for the benefit of the army, he was artfully changing the inhabitants of Italy, and occupying all the important stations of the empire with his own retainers and creatures; that the money, which, under pretence of supporting the war against Sextus Pompeius, had been taken from the treasury, was by Octavius diverted from its use, and employed in corrupting the troops of his friend; that the estates of the proscribed, under the pretence of sales, at which, besides the creatures of Octavius, there was no man to purchase, had been actually employed by him for the same purpose; that, if he really meant to avoid a rupture, he ought to do nothing without consulting the friends of his colleague, who were equally entitled with himself to share in the fruits of their common victory obtained at Philippi. But I know," said Lucius Antonius, "the falsehood of Octavius; while he amuses you with the hopes of a negotiation and treaty, and with professions of having nothing at heart besides your interest, he is arming himself with the utmost diligence, and has reinforced the garrison of Brundusium, with an evident purpose to obstruct the return of his colleague, and your principal friend, into Italy."

Octavius being in possession of the capital, in order that he might appear to have, not only the authority of government, but the countenance likewise of all the more respectable citizens of Rome on his side, called an assembly of the senate, at which he invited the Equestrian order to attend. He represented to this assembly the calamities that were now impending over Italy from the jealousy and restless ambition of a few persons, who called themselves the friends of Mark Antony, and he exhorted them with one accord to join him in averting these evils. He accordingly obtained a deputation to be sent to Prænesté, where the heads of the opposite party were still assembled, to remonstrate against their procedure. This measure however had no other effect besides that which Octavius proposed by it, that of transferring to his enemies the blame of all the evils which were expected to follow.

An expedient was proposed, more likely to prevent these evils, by a conference to be held by the military officers of the opposite sides, who, perceiving themselves about to be involved in a quarrel, were extremely averse to risk all the advantages they had already obtained, without any prospect of gain. This expedient of a military congress was suggested by the officers themselves, and was readily embraced by their leaders. Gabii being half way from Prænesté to Rome, was fixed upon as the place at which they should meet; but on the day on which they were to open their conference, parties of horse having been, from some remains of distrust, without any concert, sent forward on both sides to escort their deputies, and mutually to observe each other, they met unexpectedly on the highway, and coming to blows, numbers were killed or wounded, and the intended convention was dropped.

Each of the parties, in consequence of this accident, published a manifesto, and began to assemble in a hostile manner. Lucius Antonius had ordered new levies, and with these, joined to the troops already on foot, under the authority of his brother, and who were now stationed in the nearer province of Gaul, under Calenus, he proposed to assemble an army of eleven legions.

Octavius ordered six legions under Salvidienus, from Spain; and having already four in Italy, with a considerable body of troops, which, under the designation of Prætorian bands, made the ordinary guard of his person, he took the field to prevent the designs of his enemies.

The nobility and citizens of rank were divided; but the greater part, who had yet any hopes of seeing the civil government restored, thought themselves safer in the party of the consul Lucius Antonius, than in that of Cæsar; and accordingly repaired to his camp.

Sextus Pompeius, on the eve of a contest thus likely to divide his enemies, might have made himself of considerable consequence, or might have obtained advantageous terms from either party. His forces had been seen greatly augmented by the accession of two legions, the remains of the wreck at Philippi, that had escaped with Murcus. He might have got a footing in

1 Senatus Caligatus.

Italy, and, by the favourable disposition of many who felt the oppression of the present government, or dreaded the future effects of its tyranny, might have held the balance between the contending parties. He, nevertheless, either under the notion of leaving his enemies to waste their strength against each other, or not having a sufficient genius for such arduous enterprises, suffered the opportunity to escape, and contented himself with endeavouring to secure his possession of Sicily and Sardinia, which he hoped to retain as a patrimony independent of Rome.

Ahenobarbus, the other remaining leader or representative of the republican party, who was still hovering on the opposite coast of Italy with the remains of the fleet, which he had commanded under Brutus and Cassius, made frequent descents, and plundered the recent settlements of the veterans. He even forced his way into the harbour of Brundusium, took some galleys belonging to Octavius, and laid waste the adjacent country; but, while he was acting in a manner equally hostile to both parties, the forces of the triumvirs, indifferent to every external enemy, began to assemble against each other. Lepidus declared for Octavius, and these two having left the city together, Lucius Antonius presented himself at the gates, and was admitted. Having assembled the people, he declared that his intention was to restore the republic. His brother, he said, for the future desired no illegal powers, and was ready to join in calling Octavius and Lepidus to account for the tyranny they had lately exercised against the ancient inhabitants of Italy.

In the mean time, the event of this contest appeared to depend on the movements that were making on the side of Spain and Gaul. Salvidienus being on his march to join Octavius, Asinius and Ventidius hung on his rear. Agrippa, on the part of Cæsar, passed the Po in order to join Salvidienus; and having succeeded in this design, they obliged Asinius and Ventidius to remain on the defensive, expecting the arrival of Lucius Antonius, who was on his march to support them.

When Antonius came to a pass of the Apennines, on the Flaminian way, he found the gorges of these mountains already occupied by Agrippa and Salvidienus; not attempting to force them, he fell back to Perusia, and sent orders to Ventidius to join him by some other route; but Octavius having got possession of Sentinum and Nursia, two posts on the opposite sides of the mountains, effectually prevented the junction of his enemies, assembled all his forces in the neighbourhood of Perusia, and invested Antonius in that place. He drew a line of circumvallation, extending about fifty stadia, or six miles, and placed his army between two parallels, equally strong, against any attempts that were likely to be made from the garrison, or from the field.

Lucius Antonius being thus shut up in Perusia during the autumn, and part of winter, and all the efforts of Fulvia, Asinius, Ventidius, and Plancus, to succour him being ineffectual, he was reduced, from want of provisions, to the greatest extremities, and offered to capitulate.

Octavius, in accepting this offer, with his usual address, took measures to divide his enemies, or to sow the seeds of future jealousy among them. He affected to distinguish the regular troops, which had been formed to serve under his colleague Mark Antony, from the Roman citizens, or rather supposed disorderly persons, who had taken a part in this insurrection. The first, from pretended respect to their leader, he allowed to withdraw with honour; the others he required to surrender at discretion. In complying with this requisition, L. Antonius himself set the example, went forth in person to receive the victor's commands, and being courteously treated, alleged his duty as a civil magistrate, and his desire to restore the commonwealth, as an apology for his conduct, and implored mercy for those who had embarked with him in the same design. Octavius replied, "That as his enemies had surrendered themselves at discretion, he should make no remarks on the truth of their plea, nor talk of conditions, where he was not to be bound by a treaty; that he must now consider not only what his enemies had merited, but what was due to himself." Having found among his prisoners some of the veterans who had served under Cæsar, he was disposed to have ordered them all to be executed; but observing that this measure was extremely offensive to his own army, he confined his severities to the Roman citizens, who, he pretended, had on this occasion acted with equal animosity to the army, and to himself. To avenge the supposed injury that was done to the army, all persons of the civil description, found under arms, were put to death. Of these, Cannutius, C. Flavius, Clodius, Bythinicus, and others, are mentioned by Appian.[2] This Cannutius is said by Dion Cassius to have been the tribune, who presenting Octavius to his first audience from the people, contributed so much to the rise of his fortunes.

The greater part of the executions were performed in the presence of Octavius, and in the manner of sacrifices to the manes, or to the divinity, of Julius Cæsar. In this form, however detestable, they were supposed, in that age, to carry an aspect of piety, which sanctified the cruelty with which they were ordered, and with which Octavius himself witnessed the scene. Four hundred of the senatorian and equestrian order are said, by Dion Cassius and Suetonius, to have perished in this manner.[3] The magistrates and council of Perusia, being separately ordered to execution, implored for mercy, but had one general answer, *You must die.*[4] The place itself, whether by the desperation of its inhabitants, or by the outrage of those who were now become masters of it, was set on fire, and burnt to the ground. The country around being deserted, or laid waste with fire and sword, and cleared of its former possessors, became a prey to such followers of the army as chose to occupy it.[5]

At the date of this odious transaction, Octavius was no more than twenty-three years of age; and though, in former examples of cruelty, his youth may have been overruled or misled by the party-rage of his colleagues, yet, in this instance, he himself betrayed a merciless nature, in the effects of which he had no man to share, or to divide the blame;[6] and the world began to dread more from the separate power which he was about to establish, than they did from the joint

2 Appian. de Bell. Civ. lib. v.
3 Dio. Cass. lib. xlviii. c. 14.
4 Sueton. in Octav. c. 15.
5 Dio. Cass. lib. xlviii. c. 14 et 15.
6 Livii Epitome, lib. cxxvi.

usurpation, in which he bore a part, with persons, of whom the one was contemned for want of capacity, and the other detested for his profligate manners.

U. C. 713.

L. Dom. Calvinus, Asinius Pollio.

Before the breaking out of this war in Italy, Domitius Calvinus and Asinius Pollio had been destined consuls; and the year following that, in which these transactions passed, is accordingly dated or inscribed with their names. They were prevented, however, by this breach between the adherents of Antony and of Cæsar, from taking the formal possession of their office.

Pollio, holding his commission from Mark Antony, although he had no opportunity to act, was understood to join with the brother in the late division of their parties. While the war continued, being stationed in his province in the district of Venetia, he carried on a correspondence with Ahenobarbus, and representing Lucius Antonius, with his title of Roman consul, as legal head of the republic, endeavoured to engage that officer on his side; but, in the event of the war, this correspondence was broke off, and the military adherents of Antony being dispersed or cut off, his relations and retainers fled in different directions.

Fulvia, escorted by three thousand horse, took the road to Brundusium, and from thence, with Plancus and some other attendants, under the convoy of five galleys, sailed to Greece.[1] Julia, the aged mother of Antony, took refuge with Sextus Pompeius in Sicily. Thither likewise fled Tiberius Claudius Nero, with his wife Livia Drusilla, and her infant son, persons often to be mentioned in the sequel of this history, as principal sharers in that power which now seemed to be raised on the ruin of their fortunes. Others had recourse to the protection of Ahenobarbus on the coast of Apulia.

While the relations of Antony in Italy were engaged in this unfortunate contest, he himself had passed from Greece through Asia into Egypt, where, believing all his difficulties were at an end, he indulged his natural disposition to pleasure and dissipation. At Ephesus he had assembled the principal inhabitants of the province of Asia, proposed a contribution, and represented the occasion which obliged his colleagues and himself to make a demand for money. "They were about to disband the army," he said, "consisting of no less than twenty-eight legions, to whom were due great arrears of pay, together with deserved rewards and gratuities for past services. One of my colleagues," he continued, "is gone into Italy to provide settlements for this numerous army, or rather to remove all the inhabitants of that country, in order to make way for them. The task of finding supplies of money lies upon me, and I am persuaded you will own we are very moderate, when we demand no more than you gave to our enemies. Necessity, however, obliges us to exact, in one year, what Brutus and Cassius levied in two." "You will please then to order," said one of the audience, "two summers and two harvests in this wonderful year; for you, who can command us to pay the tax of two years in one, can likewise order the fruits of both years to be gathered in one."[2]

Antony, who paid more regard to wit than to the considerations either of humanity or justice, was pleased with this answer, and agreed that the proposed subsidy should be levied in two years, instead of one.[3] From Ephesus, he travelled by the coast towards Syria, laid heavy contributions, disposed of lands and country seats, of which he made gifts to his retainers and followers. He received frequent applications for such favours from those who attended him, under pretence that the estates, which they coveted, were either deserted or occupied by an enemy. To his cook, in particular, he is said to have given the grant of a large possession, for having pleased him in the dressing of a supper. In his own behaviour, he exhibited that dissipation and extravagance, to which he ever returned in the moments of triumph and relaxation, and showed, in the gayety and festivity of his court, a perfect contrast to the melancholy with which the inhabitants of every province were seized on his approach.[4] He had probably seen Cleopatra in Italy, during her intimacy with Julius Cæsar; and now, supposing himself come in place of that successful adventurer, as head of the empire, he thought of this prize as the reward of his labours, and possibly considered her as the principal object of his journey to the east. In order to heighten the scene of their meeting, with a farce to consist of a supposed quarrel and reconciliation, he affected to believe a report of her having ordered her fleet from Cyprus to join that of Cassius in the late war, and he sent her a formal summons to meet him in Cilicia, and to give in her answers to this heavy charge.

Cleopatra accordingly appeared on the Cydnus on board a galley, with a splendid retinue, and dazzled the Roman triumvir with the profusion of her ornaments, the elegance of her equipage, and the charms of her person. She was now about nine and twenty years of age, and being acquainted with the languages and manners of different nations, particularly instructed in the literature of the Greeks, and being in the maturity of wit and beauty, she joined the arts of a coquet, with all the accomplishments which became the birth and the high condition of a queen. Being invited to sup with Antony, she pleaded that he should begin with accepting her invitation. At their first entertainment, observing that his raillery savoured of the camp, she humoured him in this manner, and even surpassed him in the freedom of her conversation.

From thenceforward Antony laid aside all business, followed the queen of Egypt to her kingdom, leaving his own provinces exposed to an enemy, by whom they were soon after assailed and overrun; and while this storm was raging in the east, and his brother, with his other adherents in Italy, were struggling for his share in the government of the empire, and obliged to fly or submit to his rival, he passed the winter at Alexandria in frolic and dissipation.[5] To gratify the jealousy of Cleopatra, he ordered Arsinoë, her sister and competitor for the throne, who had hitherto been confined at Miletus, to be put to death. In every other particular, he suffered himself to be governed by her caprice, and with the ensigns and attendance of a Roman consul, and first officer of the state in the empire,

1 Appian. de Bell. Civ. lib. v. 2 Ibid.

3 Plut. in Antonio. 4 Ibid. 5 Ibid.

lived like a boy under the influence of his first amour. The course of his pleasures, however, was in a little time effectually interrupted, by a report of the state of his affairs in Syria and the Lesser Asia.

Pacorus, the son of the king of Parthia, had passed the Euphrates with a great army, had overrun Syria, and was making hasty advances in Cilicia. He was conducted in this expedition by Labienus, a Roman officer,[6] who, on the part of Brutus and Cassius, had resided at the court of Parthia while the fate of the empire yet remained in suspense at Philippi, and who now persuaded the Parthians to attempt the conquest of opulent provinces in their neighbourhood, which, together with the Roman republic itself, were become the possession of mere adventurers, unacknowledged and unsupported by the laws of the commonwealth.

Upon this alarm, Antony had assembled the naval forces of Asia and of Egypt, and had set sail with two hundred galleys for the coast of Phœnicia; when the misconduct and distress of his relations in Italy were reported to him, and showed him the necessity of directing thither the armament which he had fitted out against the Parthians, in order to re-establish his interest, and to save the remains of his power.[7] Having committed the command of his forces in Asia therefore to Ventidius, he steered for Greece. Upon his arrival at Athens, he was received by Fulvia, whose salutations were probably less flattering than those to which he had been lately accustomed in Egypt. The husband and the wife, on this occasion, were mutually disposed to blame and to recriminate. He complained of the flame which had been so unseasonably raised in his affairs in Italy, and she of his notorious infidelities to her bed, and of his remissness in the care of his interest. She was supposed, in fomenting the late quarrel with Octavius, to have acted so much from jealousy of Cleopatra, as to have industriously created troubles in Italy, in order to hasten the return of her husband from Egypt.

At Athens, Antony was likewise met by Scribonius Libo, the father-in-law of Sextus Pompeius, who, under pretence of conducting his mother Julia in safety to her son, brought overtures of an alliance, and proposals to form some concert for the conduct of their operations on the opposite coasts of Italy against Octavius. To this proposal, however, Antony made no decisive reply. In the late partition of the empire, Italy was not made a part in the separate lot of any of the triumvirs; but being equally open to all of them, Antony professed being on his way thither, not as an enemy of Octavius, but as his colleague in the government, equally interested with himself to preserve the capital of the empire undisturbed. In answer to Libo, therefore, he acknowledged his obligation to Sextus Pompeius, for the honourable manner in which he had treated his relation, assured him, that if an opportunity offered, he should be happy to return the favour; and that if he were obliged to make war on Octavius, he should be glad of Pompey's assistance; or, in case matters were accommodated otherwise, should not neglect his interest in adjusting the treaty.

Octavius being informed of this interview, seized the opportunity which it gave him of raising suspicions against Antony in the minds of the veterans. He published the intelligence he had received of his correspondence with the head of the Pompeian faction, and represented it as a prelude to some scheme for restoring the enemies of the late Cæsar, for re-establishing the ancient possessors of land in Italy, and, consequently, for dispossessing the veterans of the settlements recently made in their favour. By spreading these reports in the army, he took measures to strengthen himself, in case he should find it necessary to refuse his colleague a free admission into any of the ports of Italy.

Soon after the reduction of Perusia, Calenus, who commanded a considerable body of Antony's forces at the foot of the Alps, dying, Octavius repaired to the quarters of those troops, gained them over to his own interest, and, in order to secure their fidelity, made the necessary change of their officers. By these means, after he had supplanted the party of his rival in all the towns which they held in Italy, he now dispossessed them of the Cisalpine Gaul, for which their leader had so long contended against the senate.

At the arrival of Antony in Greece, Octavius could muster a land force greatly superior to any that could be formed against him, even by the junction of his rival with Ahenobarbus and Sextus Pompeius; but he was so much inferior in shipping, that if their fleets should unite, they must be masters of the coast, and prevent all the importations by which Italy was supplied from abroad. To sow the seeds of some jealousy between them, or to counteract the intrigues of Antony with Scribonius Libo and with Sextus Pompeius, he made offers of marriage to Scribonia, the sister of Libo, and aunt of Pompey's wife; and this proposal being favourably received by the brother, he sent Mucia, the mother of Sextus Pompeius, with an honourable retinue, to engage her son likewise to promote the intended alliance. By these means, he hoped to amuse, or to soften, the animosity of that family against himself; or at least, by these appearances of a friendly correspondence with Sextus Pompeius, in his turn, to alarm Antony, and thus to disconcert any plan which his rival, in the prospect of a breach with himself, might have formed for a coalition with the remains of the republican party. This marriage with Scribonia, was the second project of the same kind which Octavius had formed before the age of twenty-four, merely to lull the vigilance, or to blunt the animosity of his antagonists, while he himself continued to pursue his principal object with unremitting attention and ardour.

Antony, in every comparison with Octavius, not only had the advantage of years, but was reckoned the better soldier; and having had the principal share, if not the whole honour of the victory at Philippi, had great authority in the army, and was likely, wherever he appeared, to be favourably received by all the troops who had any where served under his command. These, however, upon his approach to Italy, under various pretences, were sent by his crafty rival into the distant provinces. Lepidus too, although he

6 Supposed to be the son of him who served under Julius Cæsar, in the reduction of Gaul, and afterwards against him in the civil war.

7 Appian. de Bell. Civ. lib. v. Plut. in Antonio.

had hitherto acquiesced in the late partition of the empire, by which he had been stripped of his equal share in the power of a triumvir; yet, as he was suffered to retain the title, and might throw his weight into the scale of either of the other parties, or furnish a pretence for some part of the army to follow him, it was thought proper, on the present occasion, to remove him to a distance. For this purpose, the government of Africa was assigned to him, and he himself, with six legions of doubtful inclinations, was dismissed to take possession of that province.

While Octavius was thus strengthening himself in Italy, or removing every object of distrust from that country, Antony, with a less pacific appearance than he had hitherto preserved, set out from Athens, and leaving Fulvia ill at Sicyon, joined at Corcyra his fleet, which had come round the Peloponnesus, and from thence sailed with two hundred galleys for the coast of Italy. He was joined by Ahenobarbus in his passage, and steered directly for Brundusium. As there was no declared quarrel betwixt himself and Octavius, he expected to be admitted into this port; but being disappointed in this expectation, he landed at some distance from the harbour, and invested or blocked up the town by sea and by land. Having thus committed hostilities, he no longer hesitated in accepting the alliance of Sextus Pompeius against Octavius, and proposed to him to make a descent some where on the opposite coast of Italy, to distract the forces of their common enemy, while he himself continued the siege of Brundusium.

Sextus Pompeius accordingly, notwithstanding that the marriage of his relation Scribonia with Octavius had taken place, not suffering himself to be imposed upon by this artifice, landed at Thurio, in the bay of Tarentum, made himself master of that place, and of the country from thence to Consentia. He, at the same time, sent Mænas, one of his admirals, into Sardinia, who got possession of that island, and gained to his party two legions that were stationed there.

Octavius sent Agrippa to oppose Pompey, while he himself advanced for the relief of Brundusium, but in a manner which confirmed the former suspicions of his personal courage. Being taken ill on the march, he stopped short at Canusium, and suffered Brundusium to fall into the hands of his rival. Agrippa acted with more vigour; pressed upon the enemy who had landed near Tarentum, obliged them to abandon their conquests, and to take refuge in their ships.

After Antony had got possession of Brundusium, it soon appeared that this unprofitable quarrel was equally disagreeable to the armies on both sides, and each of the leaders, in order to exculpate himself to the troops, endeavoured to load his antagonist with the blame. Antony complained that, without any offence on his part, the ports of Italy had been shut up against him. Octavius recriminated, by alleging the correspondence of Antony with the Pompeian party, and excused his own conduct, in the order he had given to shut the port of Brundusium, alleging, that this precaution was taken, not against Antony or the troops in his service, but against Ahenobarbus, one of the assassins of Cæsar, whom Antony had engaged to make war upon Italy.

In whatever manner these representations were received, as the troops had frequent intercourse, their mutual inclinations to peace became known to each other; and officers, who had access to both their leaders, made formal proposals to effect a reconciliation between them. Antony, to evince his willingness to spare the blood of the legions, dismissed Ahenobarbus, under pretence of employing him to execute a commission in Bithynia, and at the same time sent instructions to Sextus Pompeius to withdraw from the coast.

In this disposition of the parties, accounts were received of the death of Fulvia, an event which greatly facilitated the negotiation for peace, as it gave hopes of cementing the alliance of parties by a family connexion. It was accordingly proposed, that the sister of Octavius, and the widow of Marcellus, should be married to Antony: and, upon this basis, a treaty was framed, including a new partition of the empire, by which all the east, from the Euphrates to Codropolis on the coast of Illyricum, was assigned to Antony. The west, from thence to the ocean and the British channel, was assigned to Octavius. Italy, as the seat of government, and the principal nursery of soldiers for the support of their armies, was to be equally open to both. Lepidus was suffered to remain in the possession of Africa. Ahenobarbus was included in this treaty, and declared at peace with the heads of the empire; but Sextus Pompeius, notwithstanding his late confederacy with Antony, and his newly contracted relation with Octavius,[1] was still to be treated as an enemy. He was to be opposed by Octavius, while the war with the Parthians was supposed sufficient to occupy the forces of Antony.

Upon the conclusion of this treaty, the leaders gave mutual entertainments, and the troops, released from the unprofitable task of making war on each other, returned to the more agreeable occupation of receiving the rewards of their services. They understood, that Antony had gone into Asia to raise the money, which was wanted to pay off their arrears, and to satisfy their claims: they had manifold scores, in which they stated the rewards and gratuities which they had been made to expect on different occasions, and they now became clamorous, in particular, for the sums which had been so liberally promised them before the battle of Philippi. The same violence which they had been taught to employ against the civil government of their country, they were ready at times to turn against their own leaders. They addressed their demands, on the present occasion, chiefly to Antony. From him they required an account of the money he had collected in Asia; and surrounding him in a mutinous manner, would not have abstained from violence to his person, if they had not been pacified by Octavius, who, having been the instrument of former liberalities, had credit enough with the army to make them acquiesce in the apology which was made for the delay of their payment, and in the fresh assurances, which were now given, that all the promises which had been formerly made to them should be faithfully performed.

All discontents for the present being suspend

1 Dio. Cass. lib. xlviii. c. 28. Appian. de Bell. Civ lib. v.

ed, the legions submitted to be sent into different quarters, and the leaders, with every appearance of a perfect reconciliation, set out for Rome. They made their entry into the city together, on horseback, and dressed in triumphal robes; they were received by the people, of every rank and condition, with demonstrations of joy, which, under the sense of a deliverance from the prospect of a civil war, that had so recently threatened the inhabitants of Italy, was very general and very sincere.

The pacific appearances, with which the joint sovereigns of the empire made their entry at Rome, were confirmed by the actual marriage of Antony with Octavia; and it was expected, that the late rivals, now become brothers, by this marriage, were to govern for the future with much cordiality and mutual confidence. Antony, to evince the sincerity of this intention on his own part, put Manius, the confident of his brother and of Fulvia, to death, as being the supposed author of the late tumults in Italy; and probably, the more fully to show how far he was willing to sacrifice every consideration to his present connexion, he betrayed a secret correspondence, which Salvidienus, an officer serving under Octavius, had maintained with himself during the siege of Brundusium. This officer, in consequence of the detection, being condemned for treachery, killed himself.[2]

Upon the faith of these public renunciations of all partial attachments, Octavius and Antony, in the character of collegiate sovereigns, passed the remainder of the present year, and the whole of the following, at Rome, with great appearance of concord. This circumstance was in some measure ascribed to the discretion of Octavia, who, during the same period, was delivered of a child to Antony, and by the birth of this new relation, gave an additional pledge for the continuance of their union; but, notwithstanding these flattering appearances, Italy still suffered under the distresses of a war, subsisting with those who were in possession of Sicily and Sardinia.

Sextus Pompeius, exasperated by the treatment he had received from both parties in the late quarrel and reconciliation, and now possessed of a considerable naval force, blocked up the ports of Italy, and prevented the usual importation of corn. The inhabitants of the towns were reduced to great distress. Those of the metropolis, in particular, became outrageous, and, in contempt of the military force by which they were governed, rose in tumults, pulled down the houses of persons to whom they imputed their sufferings, and even attacked the triumvirs with reproaches and violence. Having furnished themselves with arms, they resisted the troops that were employed to quell them, and, in their frequent conflicts, covered the streets with the slain.

The triumvirs were inclined to end these troubles, by urging with vigour the war against Pompey, in order to oblige him to open the seas; but for this purpose, a great reinforcement of shipping was necessary, and a tax was imposed, in order to defray the expense of a fleet. A public burden coming so unseasonably, greatly increased the general discontent. The inhabitants of Rome, although they had suffered themselves to be stript of their political consequence as Roman citizens, still felt the wants of nature, and were provoked by exactions that affected their property: they took courage from the disorders of the times, and ventured to censure a usurpation, which they had not dared to resist. "Italy, the head of the empire," they said, "long used to exemption from all taxation, was not only torn by domestic wars, but impoverished by an extortion that was practised to support quarrels, not with foreign enemies, but with Romans, and to gratify the vanity or emulation of fellow-citizens, who exhausted all the strength of the commonwealth, merely to appropriate the government of it to themselves; for this, so many respectable citizens had been proscribed; for this, sword and famine were still permitted to rage, and the children of the first families in Rome, in order to revenge their personal wrongs, and even to procure their subsistence, were forced to act the part of banditti and of pirates."

The populace of Rome, instigated by these representations, tore down the proclamation, in which the new tax was imposed; and seeming to recover their former consequence, though now under the government of military force, they became more riotous and dangerous than they had been in the utmost abuse of their civil liberty, and in the height of their democratical power.

It became necessary, on account of the riots, and the growing scarcity of bread, to open a negotiation with Sextus Pompeius, as the speediest means of relief from the present distress. Octavius once more availed himself of the relation he had acquired to the family of Pompey, by his marriage with Scribonia, invited Libo to a visit in Italy, and by his means proposed an interview between the parties, to be held at Puteoli in the bay of Baiæ.

Sextus Pompeius having agreed to this proposal, came with his fleet upon the coast. Antony and Octavius went to Puteoli by land, attended by many of the principal citizens, and a numerous military escort. In order that the parties might meet in safety, it was proposed, that each should have a separate platform, erected on piles to be driven in the sea, reaching, on the one side, from the shore, on the other, from Pompey's ship, so as to bring the parties sufficiently near to hold their conference, though still with such a space or interval between them, as might mutually secure them from any insult or violence.

These preparations being made, the fleet of Sextus Pompeius ranged itself on the one side, and the land army of the triumvirs on the other. As the interests of all men were involved in the issue, their expectations were greatly raised. The shores, the cliffs, the high lands were covered with spectators, who gazed on the scene, and anxiously waited for the event. At the first conference, the triumvirs offered Pompey a safe return to Rome, with an equivalent for his father's estate. He demanded admission into the triumvirate, instead of Lepidus, who appeared in effect to be already excluded. As they parted without any agreement, a general dissatisfaction appeared among their adherents and followers on both sides. Pompey feared the defection of many who had hitherto followed him; and as he had lately put Murcus, a principal officer of his party, to death, from a jealousy of this sort, he was inclined to

2 Livii Epitome, lib. cxxvii

believe that many of his party were disposed to accept of any terms, and to treat for themselves.

The distresses of Italy, on the other hand, strongly urged the triumvirs to make the necessary concessions; and both parties came to a second interview, with better inclinations to adjust their differences. It was accordingly agreed, that Pompey should remain in possession of Sicily, Sardinia, and Corsica; that the Peloponnesus should likewise be ceded to him, and a sum of money be paid in compensation for the losses of his family;[1] that all the exiles now under his protection, except such as were concerned in the death of Cæsar, should be restored to their country, and to a fourth part of their former estates; that the navigation of the seas of Italy should be free, and vessels immediately suffered to pass from Sicily, and all the neighbouring countries, which were accustomed to supply the Italians with corn.

This treaty being ratified, was transmitted to Rome, and committed to the keeping of vestal virgins. Every cause of hostility or distrust between the parties being thus done away, their platforms were joined by a bridge of planks, and they embraced each other. Those, who were near enough to see this signal of peace, raised a shout, which was returned from the multitudes which crowded the ships and the neighbouring shores. Every one took a part in the joy that was occasioned by the present event, as having suffered under the distresses and hardships which were now brought to an end.

Historians, seeming to feel for those who were concerned in this transaction, have exerted their genius in describing it; and among other particulars, have recorded, that friends and relations, who had been long separated, being to meet in peace, crowded with great ardour to the strand; that persons who had no such particular motive, being seized with the general contagion, pressed to have a nearer view of the scene; that numbers were suffocated in the crowd; that many from the boats and ships leapt into the sea, and waded or swam to land, and were met from the shore by others who expected to recover their relations and friends; that shouts of joy, or cries of despair, were raised, according as they were severally successful or disappointed in this expectation: that parents and children, disappointed in the hopes of meeting each other, tore their hair, and fell into agonies of grief; the whole exhibiting, though in a supposed termination of public calamities, a lively expression of the distress which the late troubles had occasioned, and striking marks of the wounds which were recently open, and bleeding in the vitals of the commonwealth, and in the bosom of every private house.[2]

At the close of this scene, the leaders mutually invited each other to a feast. Pompey, by lot, gave the first entertainment on board his ship; he made an apology for the want of accommodation, and playing on the word *carinæ*, which signified a ship, and likewise was the name of his late father's villa and garden in the suburbs of Rome, which were occupied by Antony, "This," he said, "is now my *carinæ*." While the company were yet on board, Menas, once the slave of the great Pompey, but now emancipated, and the first sea officer in the fleet of his son, whispered him, that then was the time to revenge the death of his father and of his brother, and to recover the rank of his family, by despatching these authors of all their calamities. "Let me cut the cable," he said, "and put to sea; I promise you that none of them shall escape." "This might have been done by Menas, without consulting me," said Sextus; "but my faith is sacred, and must not be broken."

The guests accordingly were suffered to depart, without having, in any way, been made sensible of the danger they ran, and they gave entertainments in their turns. At these feasts additional articles were thought of to confirm the treaty, and to regulate the measures of the future administration. To strengthen the coalition of parties, the daughter of Sextus Pompeius was betrothed to Marcellus, the nephew of Octavius, and now the step-son of Antony. The succession to the consulate was fixed for four years. Antony and Libo were named consuls for the first year, Cæsar and Pompey were to follow, next Ahenobarbus and Sosius, and last of all Antony and Cæsar. Under the administration of these last, it was supposed that the public order and public tranquillity might be so well restored, for this was the language which the triumvirs still affected to hold, that the republic would no longer need the interposition of extraordinary powers, and might be left to run its usual course.

Sextus Pompeius set sail for Sicily; the collegiate sovereigns of the empire set out on their return to Rome; and, in their entry to the city, passed through multitudes, who, on the present occasion, gave very sincere demonstrations of joy. The people flattered themselves, that they were now to experience no more of their late distresses—no more civil dissensions—no more tearing of the father from his family, to serve in the wars—no more oppression and cruelty from the licentiousness of armies—no more desertion of slaves—no more devastation of their lands—no more interruption of agriculture—no more famine. In the return of exiles, who lately fled from the swords of their fellow-citizens, but who were now restored to the enjoyment of peace and security they might perceive, it was said, the surest evidence of a general act of oblivion for all offences, and a termination of all party animosities and disputes.

Octavius and Antony, during the remainder of their continuance together at Rome, passed their time in literary amusements, and in the fashionable pastimes of the age, cock-fighting and quail-fighting.[3] They conducted affairs of state with so much concord and silence, that no public transaction is mentioned, besides the completing of the aqueducts projected by Julius Cæsar, and the celebration of the festivals, which had been vowed for the destruction of those who had conspired against his life.[4]

---

1 15,500,000 drach. or denarii, about 500,000*l.* Zonoras, lib. x. p. 283. c. 21.

2 Dio. Cass. lib. xlviii. c. 37. Appian. de Bell. Civ. lib. v.

3 Plutarch. in Antonio.

4 Dio. Cass. lib. xlviii c. 32, 33.

CHAPTER VI.

Alarm of the Parthian Invasion of Syria—Arrangements of Octavius and Antony—Departure of the latter, and Residence at Athens—State of the Commonwealth—Marriage of Octavius with Livia—War with Sextus Pompeius—Actions near the Straits of Messina—Agrippa succeeds to the Command of Octavius' Fleet—His Victory at Sea—Flight of Sextus Pompeius—Breach between Octavius and Lepidus.

SUCH was the state of affairs at Rome, when the accounts which had been successively received from Syria, made the presence of Antony appear to be necessary in that part of the empire which had been specially committed to his care. His lieutenant Desidius Saxa, in opposing the Parthians under Pacorus and Labienus, had received a defeat, and being unable to brook his misfortune, had killed himself. In consequence of this catastrophe, the province of Syria was over-run by the enemy. Tyre, and all the principal towns on the coast were already in their hands, and the province of Cilicia lay open to their inroads.

Upon this report, Antony sent forward Ventidius, to collect such forces as yet remained in the province of Asia, and to give some present check to the immediate progress of the Parthians, while he himself proposed to follow, and to conduct the war in person. Before his departure, he obtained from the senate and people the form of an act to confirm all the arrangements which the triumvirs had made respecting the revenue, or any other department of the state. In concert with his colleague he made up the roll of the senate, and marked out the succession of consuls and other titular magistrates for eight years. In their choice of persons for these several honours, each was careful to balance the nomination of his rival with an equal number of his own dependants, clients, and persons over whom he had entire influence; and in this competition for power, they named for the offices of state mere aliens, soldiers of fortune, persons who had recently obtained their freedom, or confidential slaves manumitted for this purpose.[5]

These arrangements being made, Antony, attended by his wife Octavia, set out for Athens. Here he learned that the war in Syria was in a great measure at an end; that Pacorus, the son of the king of Parthia, with Labienus, having attacked Ventidius in his camp, were repulsed; that their forces had been afterwards routed in different encounters, and dispersed; that Pacorus himself was killed;[6] that Labienus had fled, in disguise, into Cyprus, was discovered, taken, and put to death; that the Parthians had abandoned all their conquests in Syria and in Palestine, and were hastening to repass the Euphrates.

Antony, upon the termination of a war, which so much alarmed his division of the empire, probably would have been inclined to return into Egypt; but as the presence of Octavia rendered a visit to Cleopatra improper, he determined to take his residence at Athens. From thence he distributed to his officers their several stations and provinces, and disposed of kingdoms on the frontier to princes who solicited his protection: that of Pontus he bestowed on Darius the son of Pharnaces, and grandson of Mithridates; that of the Jews and Samaritans, on Herod; that of Pysidia, on Amyntas; and that of Cilicia, on Polemon. During the winter he had dropped all the retinue of a Roman officer of state, resigned himself to ease, domestic pleasures, and the conversation of the learned.[7]

In the intervals of relaxation, some species of extravagance and dissipation ever make a part in the history of Antony's life. The reports, however, which remain of his behaviour at Athens, may, in a great measure, be considered as a part of the reproach, which his enemies, to justify their own cause, have thrown upon his memory; and which they have been able, by becoming the victorious party, to fix upon his name for ever. He is said, at some of his entertainments, to have personated Bacchus the young and irresistible conqueror of the world, and to have carried this extravagance so far, that the Athenians were encouraged to pay their court, by proposing a marriage between himself and their goddess Minerva. But to show that he carried some reason in his madness, he accepted the match, under condition that the bride should be accompanied with a suitable portion; and in this jest turned the servility of his flatterers to profit, by exacting ten millions of drachmas.[8]

But in whatever manner Antony passed his supposed leisure at Athens, Octavius, whose conduct, on most occasions, is a manifest contrast to that of his colleague, did not fail to avail himself of the advantages of his situation in Italy, the supposed head of the empire, and of the bent of the times to monarchy, by uniting, as much as possible, all the channels of influence in his own person.

The concerts of the first Cæsar with Pompey and Crassus, though named a triumvirate, were the mere effects of a private combination to overrule the public councils, and to dispose of every preferment, or place of emolument or trust. But the powers now exercised by Octavius, Antony, and Lepidus, though extorted by force, had at least the nominal sanction of a legal appointment, and were of the nature of those extraordinary commissions which had been frequently given in every age of the republic, and which were not improperly calculated for any uncommon emergence, or arduous state of affairs. A commission of triumvirate, in so great an exigency of the state, professedly given to restore its tranquillity, and re-establish public order, if it had been freely granted, was well enough suited to former precedents, and preserved the analogy of Roman

5 One Maximus being in the nomination for the office of quæstor, was claimed and adjudged to be a slave; another person of the same condition was discovered in a high station, and, as a punishment due for his presumption, was thrown from the Tarpeian rock. Dio. Cass. lib. xlviii. c. 34.

6 Plut. in Antonio.

7 Appian. de Bell. Civ. p. 714.

8 About 300,000*l*. Dio. Cass. lib. xlviii. c. 39.

forms, insomuch, that if the people had been less corrupted, the government of the republic might have been easily restored.

The titles of senate and people, of consul, prætor, and other magistrates or officers of state, were still retained, and preserved the appearance of ancient formalities, whether in the legislature, or in the exercise of executive power. The same members which formed the ancient political body were supposed to exist, though much debilitated, and sunk in disease. The senate consisted of persons willing to submit to, or known to favour, the present usurpation; such persons only were now to be found. Those of a different description had fallen in the civil wars, or perished in the late executions and massacres; and if they had still remained, would not have been suffered to take a part in the government of the state by those who, under the title of triumvirs, had engrossed all its functions. Even the pretended comitia were no longer those overbearing conventions, in which multitudes assembled in a tumultuary manner, assumed the prerogatives of the Roman people, disposed of elections, or carried their own mandates into execution with irresistible force. This part of the republican constitution was become a mere name, employed to ratify the acts of the triumvirs, and to confirm their nomination of persons to office. The forms of their meeting, however, as well as those of the senate, were retained to give a sanction to deeds which might not be supposed of permanent authority, without the well-known initials of the senate and people of Rome.[1]

As the supreme power, and the exercise of every public function, both at Rome and in the provinces, were now vested in this pretended commission, the ordinary offices of state were filled up merely for the sake of form, or rather that there might be an opportunity to oblige particular persons in their advancement to public honours. The titles of prætorian and consular rank, retained by those who had filled those offices in the commonwealth, were come to resemble the titles of honour by which the nobles are distinguished in monarchies; and men had, for some time, begun to covet the office, not on account of the power it conferred, but for the sake of the title it was to leave behind, with the persons by whom it had once been possessed.

For this reason the ancient denominations of office were not likely to be discontinued at Rome, even upon the establishment of monarchy. The regular term of a year indeed was already no longer annexed to the idea of magistracy. The honour of having been consul or prætor for a few months, for a few days, or even for a few hours, gave the precedency that was wished for; and many, as soon as they had taken possession of the office, were removed to make way for others to whom the same favour was intended.

In this manner, during the joint-residence of Octavius and Antony at Rome, Asinius Pollio, and Domitius, holding the consulate, were made to resign it, in order that two others might be admitted for a few days, of whom one was L. Cornelius Balbus, a native of Gades in Spain, and the first of his family that ever had a place on the rolls of the people as a citizen of Rome. But this new citizen had followed Julius Cæsar, and amassed a considerable fortune in his service. To others, the dignity of prætor and of edile, vacated on purpose, was transferred for a few hours. These preferments gave no claim, as in the former times of the republic, to the government of provinces; they gave no influence, and scarcely prescribed any function in the city.

In this general abuse of the civil institutions, now reduced to mere titles and forms, the tribunes of the people, by means of the superstitious regard that was paid to their persons, still retained a part of their consequence; and Octavius, instead of attempting to reduce it, affected to revere this sacred repository of the people's rights, in defence of which Julius Cæsar made war on the senate; and instead of attempting to remove the defences with which these officers were provided against violence, he procured his own name to be inscribed in their list, and took part in a sacred character which he could not destroy; in this, as in many other particulars, discovering an admirable discernment of the means that were necessary to palliate a recent usurpation; and seeming to profit by the experience of his late uncle, who, after he had overcome every serious resistance, fell a sacrifice to trifles, and to the security and ostentation with which he assumed the state of a monarch.

About this time is dated a considerable alteration made in the Roman law, by the addition of a rule respecting the effect of last wills. This rule is ascribed to Falcidius,[2] one of the colleagues of Octavius in the college of tribunes. Hitherto Roman citizens were free to bequeath their fortunes at pleasure, and to divide them in any proportion among their friends or acquaintance, whether relations or strangers; and property held a course in its passage, by succession, from one generation to another, which excluded no person whatever from the hopes of inheritance, provided he could obtain the regard of his fellow-citizens. As it was the practice of every testator, even when he had no motive for disinheriting his nearest relations, to give some testimony in his will to the merit of every friend who survived him, it was reckoned an honour to be mentioned in many wills, and persons who had not the ordinary opportunities to amass fortunes, either in the government of provinces, or in the farm of the revenues, might nevertheless become rich by an extensive and well-supported course of good offices in the city. This practice is possibly less suited to monarchy, than it is to republics, and least of all to despotical governments, where the master wishes to leave no will independent of his own. He can awe the living, but the dying escape from his influence. This feeling perhaps already began to take place in the minds of the rulers at Rome, and in the minds of those who courted their favour; and it may have suggested the law of Falcidius, by which testators were suffered to dispose, by will, of no more than three fourths of their effects; the other fourth was assigned to the heir at law.

While Antony yet resided at Athens, Octavius passed into Gaul on a progress to review his armies, and to make the proper disposition of his force in the provinces; and it began to appear, that the late treaty, which had been concluded with Sextus Pompeius, was no more than a

1 S. P. Q. R.

2 Lex Falcidia.

temporary expedient to procure relief to the inhabitants of Italy from the distresses with which they had been lately afflicted. The articles were never fully performed by either party. The family alliance, which Octavius contracted with Sextus Pompeius in his marriage with Scribonia, by whom he had issue, a daughter afterwards so famous by the name of Julia, was likewise, about this time, broke off to make way for his marriage with Livia, a name already mentioned, and to be often repeated in the subsequent parts of this history.

U. C. 715.

Ap. Claudius Pulcher, and C. Norbanus Flaccus.

Marriage had hitherto appeared to Octavius merely as the means of obtaining some political end; and he had already, in difficult transactions, twice availed himself of this expedient, although it is remarked by historians, as an evidence of his youth, that, until his marriage with Livia, his beard was not sufficiently grown to need the use of the razor. In this alliance, however, he seems to have had a different object; and was so far from being led by utility alone, that he not only overlooked the want of it, but likewise got over many other difficulties which stood in his way.

Livia Drusilla was the daughter of Livius Drusus, a citizen who had been in open enmity with Octavius and his party; and who, in despair, after the battle of Philippi, with other adherents of the republic, had fallen by his own hands. The daughter had been married to Tiberius Claudius Nero, who also was a declared enemy of the Cæsarean faction; and who, in the late contest of parties in Italy, put himself at the head of the ejected land-holders of Campania. joined Lucius Antonius, and, as has been mentioned on the reduction of Perusia, fled with his family into Sicily, where he took refuge with Sextus Pompeius. Being included in the treaty of reconciliation which was framed at Baiæ, he returned to Rome. His wife had already born him a son, afterwards well known by the name of Tiberius, and was again with child, and six months gone in her pregnancy, when it was proposed, that she should part from her present husband, and bring forth the child, of whom she was then pregnant, in the embraces of Cæsar. The priests being consulted on the legality of this marriage, desired to know, whether the pregnancy of Livia was well ascertained; and being informed that it was certain, made answer, That as there could arise no doubt concerning the parentage of her offspring, her separation from Tiberius Claudius, and her marriage with Octavius, were lawful.

The change which now took place in the family of Octavius, by his repudiating Scribonia, was considered as the prelude to a war with Sextus Pompeius. Many articles of the late treaty had never been carried into execution. The Peloponnesus, under pretence of the time which was necessary to recover some arrears that were said to be due to Antony in that province, had not, according to agreement, been delivered to Pompey. In justification of other infractions of the treaty, it was urged against him, that, contrary to the faith he had given, he continued to augment his fleet, and suffered his cruizers to commit depredations on the traders of Italy. Some pirates being taken, and threatened with the torture, alleged, in their own vindication, that they acted under his orders. The confessions of these men being published, with complaints and remonstrances, an altercation ensued that was likely to end in hostilities and open war.

After these complaints had become mutual between Octavius and Sextus Pompeius, the rupture was hastened by the defection of Menas, one of Pompey's officers, the same person who proposed to carry off Antony and Octavius, by cutting the cable while they were at dinner on board his master's ship. This officer, being intrusted with the command of a fleet in the ports of Sardinia, upon some disgust to his master, entered into a correspondence with Octavius, made offer of his service, and proposed to surrender the island. This act of perfidy became known only by the acceptance and execution of the offer. Octavius obtained the possession of Sardinia, and received Menas with sixty galleys into his service, rewarded his treachery by employing him in the same rank which he possessed under Sextus Pompeius, and by conferring upon him the gold ring, the well known badge of nobility at Rome.[3]

As this transaction took place while the treaty was yet supposed to be in force, Pompey demanded that the traitor should be delivered up to him, and the island of Sardinia restored; but was answered that he himself had been the aggressor, in giving refuge to deserters and fugitive slaves.

Pompey, on receiving this answer, proceeded to immediate hostilities.[4] He sent Menecrates, who succeeded Menas in the chief command of his fleet, to the coast of Campania, with orders to make reprisals, and to plunder Vulturnus, and some other places of that neighbourhood.

Octavius, on his part, had been some time endeavouring to supply his want of shipping, had built some vessels in the ports of Italy, which, with the addition of those he received by the desertion of Menas, put him in condition to enter on the war with advantage. He had ordered his equipments at two separate stations; the one at Tarentum, the other on the coast of Etruria; and being now to make war on Sicily, he proposed to bring his naval forces together at Rhegium, in the straits of Messina. Thither he likewise directed a powerful land army to march, in order to invade the island, and to begin the war, by expelling Pompey from the principal seat of his power. He himself came round to Rhegium with that division of his fleet which had been fitted out at Tarentum. Calvisius commanded the other division, and made sail from the coast of Etruria to the same place.

Sextius Pompeius, having notice of this disposition that was made to attack him, likewise divided his forces. He himself took post at Messina to observe Octavius, and sent Menecrates to intercept Calvisius, and to prevent the junction of their fleets.

Menecrates accordingly came in sight of his enemy in the evening of the same day, lay that night under the island Ænaria, while Calvisius came to anchor near Cumæ. Next morning, at break of day, both fleets got under sail; but Calvisius, having orders to bring his division safe to the general rendezvous at Rhegium, was desirous

3 Dio. Cass. lib. xlviii. c. 45. Orosius. Appian, &c.
4 Zonaras, lib. x. c. 23.

to avoid an engagement, and kept under the land. Menecrates, steering the same course, kept abreast of the enemy, till perceiving their design to avoid him, by lying close to the shore, he too stood in with the land to attack them.

Calvisius, finding an action unavoidable, and thinking himself inferior in the skill of his mariners, determined to bring his ships to anchor under the land, where they could not be surrounded, and where his men, if attacked, having smooth water, might use their swords as on solid ground; and he accordingly formed a line close to the shore, turning the prow and the beak of his ships to the sea.

In this position the squadron of Octavius received the shock of the enemy, and on the right, where Calvisius himself commanded, made a good defence, but in the centre, many of the ships were forced from their anchors, and stranded or burnt. Menecrates, in coming to engage, distinguished the galley of Menas, his ancient rival, and the traitor to their common master, bore down upon him, and, in the shock broke away the beak of his galley; but, in passing along his side, as the vessel brushed, lost all the oars of his own ship. They afterwards grappled, and fought till both the commanders were wounded; and Menecrates, finding himself disabled, and in danger of being taken, went headlong into the sea. His galley instantly struck, and was towed off by the enemy. This event, although the advantage was otherwise greatly on the side of Pompey, dispirited the whole squadron; and Demochares, who succeeded Menecrates in the command of Pompey's fleet, neglecting the advantage he might have reaped from the situation and loss of the enemy, withdrew to the island Ænaria, and from thence, on the following day, set sail for Sicily. Calvisius, having endeavoured to repair his damage, continued his voyage, under the land, towards Rhegium.

Octavius, at the same time, not knowing of this action, but being impatient to effect the junction of his fleets, made sail from Rhegium, and stood to the northward through the straits. When the greater part of the fleet had passed the port of Messina, he was observed by Sextus Pompeius, who put to sea, and attacked his rear. He nevertheless continued on his way through the gut, and would have declined an action, if it could have been avoided; but finding himself in danger of suffering an absolute defeat from the enemy, who, taking advantage of his course, pressed on his rear as in actual flight, he made a signal to halt; and from the same motives which determined Calvisius to form under the land, making a like disposition, he hoped, that, by being at anchor, his men might engage on equal terms with an enemy who were greatly superior in the management of their ships. In the event, however, he was much more unfortunate than Calvisius, and had great part of his fleet either stranded or burnt. He himself, while his ships were still engaged, left Cornificius to continue the fight, got on shore, and with a number of men, who had escaped from the wrecks, took refuge on the neighbouring hills.

At the approach of night, the lieutenant of Octavius, while the enemy still pressed upon him, seeing the danger of having all his ships forced on shore before morning, made a signal for the remains of the squadron to cut their cables, and stand out to sea. In making this movement, his own galley grappled with that of Demochares, and having disabled her, obliged the commander to move into another ship. At this instant the other division of Octavius's fleet, commanded by Calvisius, appeared to the northward; being seen first from the enemy's fleet, occasioned a sudden pause in the action.

Pompey, believing this to be a fresh enemy, whom, after so much loss and fatigue, he was not in condition to engage, took his resolution, to the great surprise of the squadron he had vanquished, to relinquish his prey, and retire to Messina.

Cornificius again came to anchor in the place of action, and being joined by Calvisius, passed the night in taking an account of his damage, in saving such ships as could be got off, or in removing the baggage and stores from such as were ashore. Octavius, at the same time, made fires on the hills to assemble the stragglers who had escaped from the wrecks, of whom many were found without arms or necessaries of any sort.

Towards morning, a gale of wind arose from the south, and rolled a great sea through the straits. It continued to blow all day and the following night; during which time, Menas, being an experienced mariner, had not only originally come to an anchor with his division, as far as he could from land, but continued all night to ease his anchors, by plying against the wind with his oars. Of the rest of the fleet, such ships as were near the land having drove in the night, many perished on the rocks. At break of day the wind abated; but, from the effects of the storm which had blown in the night, the strand was covered with dead bodies, and with the fragments of ships. The vessels that were still afloat, being about one half of the fleet, having stopped for a little time to save as many as they could from the wrecks, set sail in a very shattered condition for Vibo. Here they arrived without any molestation from the enemy, who were contented to have remained in safety at Messina. Octavius himself having beheld the wreck of so many of his ships, took the route of Campania by land, and made the necessary dispositions to frustrate any attempts which Pompey might make on the coast.

This summer having been spent in these undecisive operations, both parties prepared for a vigorous renewal of the contest in the following spring. Pompey himself continued to alarm the coast of Italy during the winter, and sent Apollophanes, one of his officers, to make a descent upon Africa. Octavius gave orders

U. C. 716.

M. Agrippa, L. Caminius Gallus, T. Statilius.

to repair the loss of his ships, and to recruit his land-forces. He had recourse to the assistance of Antony, who had hitherto expressed a dislike to the war, and was probably jealous of the accessions of power which Octavius was likely to gain by the destruction of Sextus Pompeius.

Antony, however, upon this requisition from his colleague, set sail from Greece, and appeared at Tarentum with a fleet of three hundred ships, though still undetermined, it is supposed, which side he should take in the present contest. But Octavia, who had accompanied her husband to Tarentum, had the address to turn the scale in favour of her brother. She undertook to be the mediator of their differences, went on shore, and procured an amicable interview between them

At this meeting they made an exchange of sea and land forces. Antony gave to Octavius a hundred and twenty ships, and had in return twenty thousand legionary soldiers. To confirm the removal of all their suspicions, Julia, the infant daughter of Octavius by Scribonia, was, on this occasion, betrothed to Antyllis, one of the sons of Antony by Fulvia; and the daughter of Antony was betrothed to Domitius. These schemes of alliance, projected in the infancy of the parties, never took effect, but were among the artifices with which the parents endeavoured to amuse each other.

Octavius and Antony now agreed, with very little hesitation, that Pompey had forfeited the consulate, the priesthood, and all the other advantages which had been yielded in his favour by the late treaty; and they made new arrangements respecting the succession to office, in behalf of themselves and their friends. The principal object in these arrangements was the gratifying their adherents with titles of rank. In the preceding year, no less than sixty-seven persons had passed through the office of prætor. This dignity, as well as that of consul, was frequently, for the sake of the title, taken up and resigned in the same day. The office of Ædile, which used to be of so much consequence under the republic, as it gave an opportunity to court the favour of the people with entertainments and shows, being now of no value on this account, and being the lowest in rank, though still expensive, was generally declined.[1]

The period for which the pretended commission of the triumvirs had been granted by the Roman senate and people being now about to expire, Octavius and Antony, without having recourse to the same form, resumed the exercise of their power for five years longer. And having, in appearance, amicably settled the several points in dispute between themselves, they separated in pursuit of their respective objects; Octavius being intent on the war with Sextus Pompeius, and Antony on that with the Parthians. But, to the great danger of their future agreement, the last was no longer attended by Octavia, who had hitherto served as a bond of union between them, and had checked the jealousies and extravagances of her husband. She had borne him a child, and was again pregnant, and being unable to attend him in the dangers to which he was likely to be exposed in the Parthian war, chose to remain in Italy, and to fix her residence at Rome.[2]

In the respect of the approaching campaign, Agrippa was recalled from Gaul, where he had been employed by Octavius in the preceding summer, and during the miscarriages on the coast of Italy. This officer, although of mean extraction, rose to the highest honours which could, in this state of his country, be attained by a citizen. As he was not born to the dignity and pretensions of a Roman senator, he cannot be accused, with others, of having betrayed that character; but coming forward amidst the ruins of the republic, and after the extinction of those virtues which were necessary to its preservation, he was the first person who understood and possessed the habits and accomplishments which are required in support of a monarchy; submission without servility or baseness, application, fidelity, and courage; estimating honours by his nearness to his prince, and merit by the degree in which he could promote his service.[3] He had in the preceding summer obtained some victories on the Rhine, and was the first Roman, after Julius Cæsar, who had passed that barrier of the German nations. Upon his arrival at Rome he might have had a triumph on account of these services; but preferring the respect that was due to his master, to the sense of his own personal consequence, he said, that it did not become him to triumph while the affairs of Cæsar were not in prosperity.

Agrippa was by his genius qualified for the execution of magnificent works, as well as for the steady and able conduct of military operations. Observing, that the disasters of the preceding year were to be imputed, in some measure, to the want of harbours and proper retreats for shipping on the western coast of Italy, he made it his first object to supply this defect, by opening a communication from the sea to the lakes of Cumæ, which were spacious basins, and when thus rendered accessible by navigable entries, might furnish every conveniency for the reception and construction of fleets. In describing the masonry which was necessary in the formation of these communications, mention is made of the peculiar advantage derived from the use of burnt earth taken from the neighbouring mountains; and which being used for sand in the composition of mortar, made an excellent cement for buildings that were to remain under water.[4]

While the summer passed in the execution of these works, and in the equipment of a proper fleet to encounter that of Pompey, Menas, repenting of his late desertion, entered into a correspondence with his former master; and being assured of pardon, withdrew with seven ships from the fleet of Octavius, then under the command of Calvisius, and returned to his former service. Octavius took this occasion to supersede Calvisius, upon an imputation of neglect, and appointed Agrippa to succeed him in the conduct of the war.

U. C. 717. *L. Gellius Poplicola, L. Munatius Plancus, M. Cocceius Nerva, P. Sulpicius Querinus.*

About a year was spent in the equipment of ships, and in training the mariners, which, for the convenience of harbours and docks, was executed as before, at two separate stations; one at Tarentum, under Statilius Taurus, where the ships which had been furnished by Antony still remained; the other in the new harbour at Puteoli, under Agrippa.

Lepidus, to second the operations of Octavius, had assembled his forces on the coast of Africa, and it was concerted that Sicily should be invaded in three places at once; at Lilybæum, the nearest part to Africa, by Lepidus; at Mylæ, on the northern side of the island, by Agrippa; and at Taurominium, on the eastern coast, by Statilius Taurus. It was projected, that the armaments equipped for these different services, should be at their places of destination as nearly as possible about the first of July.

1 Dio Cass. lib. xlviii. c. 43—53.

2 Appian de Bell. Civ. lib. v. Dio. Cass. lib. xlviii. c. 46, &c.

3 Vell. Pater. lib. ii. c. 79.

4 Dio Cass. lib. xlviii. c. 48—52.

While these preparations were making, Octavius, residing chiefly at Tarentum or at Cumæ, left the administration of civil affairs at Rome in the hands of Mæcenas, who, though not vested with any office of magistracy, or any other public character besides that of a person in the confidence of his master, possessed a supreme authority. Octavius himself, when the plan of the war was ripe for execution, joined that division of his forces which was led by Agrippa, and sailed from Puteoli at the appointed time; but after he had crossed the bay of Baiæ, to the promontory of Minerva, he met with a storm, by which many of his ships were damaged, and forced to put back into the port he had left.

This accident was likely to disconcert the operations of the campaign, or to delay the invasion of Sicily for another season. But the complaints of the people of Italy, suffering under the obstruction that was given by Pompey to the importation of corn, required an immediate relief. Some of the projected operations of the campaign were already begun, and required to be supported. Lepidus had sailed with the first division of his army, and had landed in the neighbourhood of Lilybæum, and Statilius Taurus had advanced from Tarentum to Leucopetræ, opposite to Taurominium, the place at which he was ordered to make his descent. Urged by these considerations, Octavius, with such repairs as he could accomplish, in about thirty days after he had been put back into port, again put out to sea. At Strougylé he learnt that Pompey, with the greater part of his fleet, lay off Mylæ to guard that access to the island. Thinking this, therefore, a favourable opportunity to push his other attack from Leucopetræ to Taurominium, he himself returned to the coast of Italy, landed at Vibo, went from thence by land to Leucopetræ, and put the squadron from that place in motion for their intended descent on Sicily.

While Octavius was thus employed at the other extremity of the Straits, Agrippa had come to an action with Pompey's fleet off the harbour of Mylæ, and obliged them to put back into port with the loss of thirty ships.[1] This circumstance still farther confirmed Octavius in his intention to pass with his army into Sicily; and he accordingly, without meeting with any obstruction, arrived at Taurominium, and landed his forces.

Sextus Pompeius, in the mean time, having had intimation of this design, soon after the action at Mylæ, had withdrawn in the night to Messina; and having put fresh men on board his ships, steered for Taurominium, and came in sight of the harbour soon after the enemy had disembarked. By the unexpected appearance of a fleet much superior to his own, Octavius was greatly alarmed; and leaving the command of the forces he had just landed, to Cornificius, he ordered his ships to slip their cables, and make what sail they could to recover the harbour of Leucopetræ. He himself went on board a small pinnace, in order the better to escape the pursuit of the enemy, and with a very few attendants landed in a creek on the coast of Italy. His ships were dispersed, part taken, and many stranded on the opposite shores; but he himself made his way in the night to Leucopetræ, where a division of the army, under Messala, waited for the return of the ships in which they were to follow the former embarkation.

Octavius, without being disconcerted by this disaster, or by a consciousness of the part which he himself had acted, and which served to confirm all the former imputations of cowardice, without loss of time sent immediate despatches to all the stations of his troops, to intimate his safe arrival in the camp of Messala. Before he shifted his wet clothes, or took any food, he made all the necessary arrangements; sent a pinnace to Cornificius, whom he had left in the command of the army in Sicily, with orders to defend himself to the last extremity; and another to Agrippa, with instructions to move as soon as he could, by sea or by land, to his relief. And he ordered Carinas, who with three legions lay embarked at Vibo, to sail without loss of time, and to join Agrippa at Liparé.

While Pompey passed with his fleet along the coast from Messina to Taurominium, he had ordered a great body of horse on the shore to keep pace, as nearly as possible, with the motion of his ships; and as they approached to Taurominium, while he himself should block up the harbour, to lay waste the country, or to restrain the foraging parties of the enemy.

Cornificius, whom Octavius had left in the command of his forces at this place, finding himself in danger of being surrounded, took his resolution to depart from the coast, and, if possible, to join Agrippa, who, he had reason to believe, might by this time have effected his landing at Mylæ, on the opposite side of the island. He accordingly endeavoured to convey intelligence of his design, and requested Agrippa to come forward to meet him with a proper force, and with the necessary supplies, to give relief to his army, and to favour his junction.

The route by which Cornificius was most likely to avoid Pompey's stations, led by the skirts of Mount Ætna, and over barren tracts that were still covered, instead of soil, with pumice and lava, which had been discharged from the mountain, and which were not any where supplied with vegetation or water. His way over this species of soil lay through difficult passes, occupied by the natives, who either harassed his rear, or disputed his passage in front. But after having undergone great labour and distress, and having lost a considerable part of his army by fatigue and famine, he was met by Laronius, with a reinforcement of troops and supply of provisions from Agrippa; and, upon the appearance of this relief, was suffered by the enemy to continue the remainder of his march undisturbed.

Thus the two separate divisions of the army of Octavius, with which he intended at once to have attacked the opposite sides of the island, were assembled together on the northern coast. Hither he himself soon after repaired, and began his operations by land at the head of twenty-one legions, twenty thousand horse, and above five thousand light or irregular infantry.

Pompey was yet strong in the neighbourhood of Messina, or in that angle of the island which pointed towards Italy. The ground being rugged and mountainous in the interior parts, forming a ridge from Mount Ætna to the head of Pelorus, his quarters were accessible only, or chiefly, by the roads on the coast, leading from Mylæ on the one hand, and from Taurominium

1 Orosius, lib vi. p. 266.

on the other, to Messina. Of these communications he was still master, by means of the fortresses which he possessed at Mylæ, and at Tauromininm. As he supposed that Lepidus, from the side of Africa, would attempt to co-operate with the forces of Octavius from Italy, he had stationed at Lilybæum a part of his fleet, and a considerable body of troops, commanded by Plennius, to oppose the descent and advances of the enemy on that quarter. The officer who had charge of his fleet on this station, had suffered the first embarkation of Lepidus to escape and to effect their landing; but being so fortunate as to intercept the second, he in a great measure disconcerted the intended operation on that side.

Lepidus, with that part of the army he had landed in Sicily, remained inactive in the neighbourhood of Lilybæum, until having accounts that Octavius was arrived in the island, had united the different divisions of his army at Mylæ, and had obliged Sextus Pompeius to collect all his force in the neighbourhood of Messina, he supposed that the country from thence might be open to him; and he accordingly, notwithstanding that Plennius, with a considerable body of Pompey's forces, remained behind him at Lillybæum, marched from one end of the island to the other; and having effected his junction with Octavius, they determined to press upon Pompey at once with their united forces both by sea and by land.

In execution of this plan, Agrippa made a feint to land at the head of Pelorus; and having drawn the attention of the enemy to that quarter, favoured the design of Octavius, who, in the mean time, surprised and took the fortress of Mylæ. The combined army having gained this important advantage, continued to press upon Pompey, made movements which threatened to invest Messina, and to cut off the communications of his fleet and army with the country in the neighbourhood of that city. In order to avoid these inconveniences, Pompey found himself under a necessity to hazard a battle either by sea or by land, or wherever his antagonists presented an opportunity the most likely to procure him relief. He himself relied chiefly on his naval force; and accordingly, without seeking for any advantage of situation or surprise, presented himself to the enemy near to Naulochus, between the promontories of Mylæ and Pelorus, and was there met by Agrippa.

The fleets which were now to engage, consisted of about three hundred ships on each side. When formed in order of battle, their lines were nearly of equal extent. The construction of ships was the same, and they advanced deliberately on smooth water, without any circumstance that appeared to prognosticate the victory on either side. The armies, at the same time, were drawn upon the shore, and in sight of the scene which was to be acted before them. After an obstinate fight, in which the fleet of Pompey already suffered considerably, seventeen of his ships at once withdrew from the action, and stood away for the straits of Messina. Those that were nearest the land ran upon the shore, and were wrecked or taken; the remainder being farther at sea, and cut off from their own harbours, struck, and delivered themselves up to the enemy.

The progress of the action at sea was accompanied from the land with shouts and acclamations on the one side, and with silent affliction, or with cries of despair, on the other. Twenty-eight ships of Pompey's fleet were sunk; above two hundred and fifty, being the whole that remained besides the seventeen that fled to Messina, were stranded, taken, or burnt.[2] Octavius lost only three ships.

Pompey perceiving the extent of his calamity, was seized with despair; and, without having given any orders in camp, made haste to Messina. The army he had left in the field, seeing themselves deserted by their leader, went over to the enemy. He himself, at Messina, made a feint of mustering his forces as for an obstinate defence. He called in all the ships that any where remained on the coast, and all the forces that could be found on the island.[3] But, in the midst of these pretended arrangements for a vigorous resistance, he had taken a resolution to depart from Sicily; and having a vessel prepared for his reception, accordingly embarked, with his daughter, and a few persons whom he had chosen to attend him in his flight.

As soon as the vessel, on board of which it was known Pompey had embarked, appeared under sail, all the ships which were then in the harbour put to sea, with intention to follow the same course; but without any orders or intimation of a place at which to re-assemble, in case of separation. The unfortunate leader observing, among the ships that followed him, some that were commanded by officers in whom, in the present state of his fortunes, he could not confide, wished to separate from them, and gave out that he meant to avoid the coasts; and, in order to deceive them in the night, extinguishing his lights, rowed close to the shore of Italy, and turning round the head-lands till he was opposite to Corcyra, he stood over for that island, from thence to Cephalonia, and last of all to Lesbos, where he landed at Mytilené, a place at which he had resided with his mother Cornelia, during the campaign between his father and the first Cæsar in Thessaly, and from whence he had been carried about twelve years before this date, to witness the catastrophe of his father's fortunes on the coast of Egypt. At Mytilené, notwithstanding the memory of these discouraging circumstances, and the low state of his own affairs, he met with a hospitable reception, and passed the winter in humble expectation of protection from Antony, to whose generosity he intended to commit himself.

Octavius, in the mean time, suspecting that Pompey must have taken refuge in some part of the provinces which were in the jurisdiction of his colleague, was cautious not to awaken his jealousy by presuming to violate his sanctuary, or by pretending to anticipate the resolutions he might be inclined to take on the subject of this suppliant.[4]

After the head of the Pompeian party had made so wretched an exit from Sicily, Plennius, who, soon after the departure of Lepidus from the neighbourhood of Lilybæum, had set out with six legions to join his commander, and who had come too late to be comprehended in the surrender of the army at Naulochus, threw

2 Orosius, lib. vi. c. 18.
3 Appian. de Bell Civ. lib. v.
4 Dio. Cass. lib. xlix. c. 18.

himself into Messina, more with an intention to obtain favourable terms for the troops under his command, than with any hopes to retrieve the affairs of his master.

At this time Lepidus being near to Messina, while Octavius still remained at Naulochus, invested the place, and, without consulting his colleague, granted the terms which were asked by Plennius, took possession of the town, and incorporated the troops that had served under that officer with his own army. In concluding this treaty, and in taking the advantage of it to strengthen himself, without the concurrence or participation of Cæsar, he had earnest remonstrances made to him by Agrippa, who had come with his victorious fleet to Messina; but it soon after appeared that Lepidus not only thought himself entitled to decide in that instance, but, upon the accession of strength which he now gained, began to form much higher pretensions. He now reckoned under his own standard twenty-two legions, with a numerous body of horse, and proposed not only to keep possession of Messina, but to claim the whole island of Sicily, as an appendage of his province in Africa. He accordingly sent detachments to secure the principal towns.

Octavius, already provoked at the precipitation with which Lepidus had granted a capitulation to the troops at Messina, without his concurrence, loudly complained of the measures which he took to appropriate the island of Sicily to himself, without the consent of his associates in the empire; alleged that he had been called thither as a mere auxiliary, and had borne no part of the expense incurred in the war. Lepidus, on his part, complained of the injustice which had already been done to him in withholding Spain, his original lot in the partition of the provinces; and said, if it were supposed that Africa and Sicily were more than equivalent for Spain, he was willing to surrender them both in exchange for that province.

This dispute being likely to end in a serious quarrel, the ordinary intercourse between the two camps was discontinued, and precautions were taken by their respective officers, as in the presence of an enemy. Both armies saw with dislike the symptoms of an open rupture and of a fresh war, in which soldiers, without any prospect of advantage, even to the victors, were mutually to imbrue their hands in blood, to decide a question of mere jealousy or emulation between their leaders.

In comparing the character and prospects of the chiefs to be engaged in this quarrel, the preference, in the esteem of both armies, was certainly due to Octavius. To his possession of Spain and the two Gauls, he joined that of Italy, with the metropolis, or seat of the empire. He bore the name of Cæsar, and was at the head of that formidable military power, which had broken the force of the republic, and extinguished the authority of the senate. By his means the retainers of Cæsar had obtained the preferable lots in the late distribution of settlements and military rewards.

Lepidus, on the contrary, without any party attached to his person, and without any high reputation, had been placed in the command of armies by the appointment or sufferance of others. The origin of his merit with Ju ius Cæsar, which consisted in prostituting the dignity of prætor to his first usurpations in the city, was an act of baseness. His place from thenceforward, in the military arrangements which ensued, was matter of course, or due merely to his rank, without any regard to his abilities or merit. His being admitted as a third in the present division of the sovereignty, proceeded solely from the mutual jealousies of the other two, who wished for a person to witness their transactions, and to hold some species of balance between them. In the choice which they made of Lepidus, his want of any pretensions, that could interfere with either in the design which they severally entertained of possessing the empire, was a principal recommendation.

In this comparison, Octavius was conscious of a superiority, in the opinion even of the troops who were enlisted to serve under the command of his rival. He accordingly thought this a favourable opportunity, while Antony was at a distance, and no enemy existing, either in Sicily or Italy, to avail himself of the weakness and incapacity of Lepidus, to strip him of his share in the empire, and to seize upon the province of Africa, and the army now in Sicily, as an accession to his own strength. For this purpose he employed proper agents in the camp of Lepidus, gained many of his principal officers by presents, and by the expectation of greater rewards. Having much contempt for the character of their leader, and thinking the way sufficiently prepared for an open declaration, he presented himself with a party of horse in the front of the camp, entered with a few attendants, as into the midst of his own army; and mounting an eminence, from which he might be heard by the crowds that assembled around him, he complained of the steps which had been taken by their general toward a rupture between the two armies, and expressed his sincere desire that all differences might be removed, without engaging in new scenes of blood so many valiant men who had deserved so well of their leaders.

It appears that numbers of officers and soldiers in the camp of Lepidus were prepared for the part they were to act on this occasion; they applauded the concern which Octavius expressed for the armies, and declared themselves willing to obey his commands. Others, though not in the concert, followed this example, ran to their arms, and hastened to present Octavius with their colours, in token that they received him as their general.

Lepidus, to whom this visit and its consequences were altogether unexpected, being roused by such an alarm, ran forth to the streets of the camp, sounded to arms; and, as many of the troops from mere habit obeyed his command, without considering who was their enemy, attacked Octavius, obliged him to repass through the gate at which he had entered, and to place himself under cover of the cavalry, who were waiting to receive him, and whose protection was now necessary to conduct him in safety to his own camp.

In this manner the design of Octavius, on the point of being executed, appeared to be defeated. But his declaration had made too deep an impression to be so slightly removed. The doubts which it raised, and the choice now to be made of a leader, was generally decided in favour of

Cæsar. The effect of this decision accordingly appeared in a great desertion from the camp of Lepidus, either then, or during the subsequent night. The legions, lately come over from the service of Sextus Pompeius, beginning to leave him in a body, he threw himself, with the usual guards of his person, in the way to stop them. But finding that the very body with which he expected to prevent this desertion joined those who were going over to the enemy, he mixed entreaties and threats, laid hold of an ensign-staff, and attempted by force to stop the officer that was carrying it to his rival. "*Dead or alive,*" said the bearer, "*you shall quit your hold.*" The cavalry at the same time mounted their horses, and without leaving their ground, sent a message to Octavius, desiring to know, whether he chose that Lepidus should be secured or put to death? Having for answer, that Octavius had no design upon the life of their general, they moved away without any farther notice of him.

Lepidus, seeing the desertion of his army complete, and having no longer any friends or retinue to attend his person, laid aside his imperial robes, and, in the ordinary dress of a citizen, walked towards the camp and the tent of his rival. Multitudes followed him, to gratify their curiosity, in seeing what was to pass in so new a scene. A person who, the moment before, had been at the head of a great army, and reputed a third in the sovereignty of the empire, was now, by the sudden desertion of his own troops, reduced to the condition of a private man, and was to appear as a suppliant before an antagonist whom he had recently set at defiance. To complete the scene of his humiliation, in entering the presence of Octavius, he would have thrown himself on the ground, but was prevented by the courtesy of his rival, who, content to strip him of his command, and of his personal consequence, would not accept this mark of abasement, and gave him leave to return into Italy, where he lived afterwards equally unobserved by those against whom he had been made the instrument of injustice, and by those who had made him their tool.

CHAPTER VII.

Forces of Octavius after the Acquisition of Sicily, and the Junction of the Armies of Sextus Pompeius and Lepidus—Mutiny and Separation of these Forces—Arrival of Octavius at Rome—His Reform of the Army—Expedition of Antony against the Parthians—His Retreat—The Death of Sextus Pompeius—Open Breach between Octavius and Antony—Progress of Antony and Cleopatra towards Greece—Operations of Antony and Octavius on the Gulph of Ambracia—Battle of Actium—Flight of Antony—Immediate Arrangements of Octavius after his Victory—Death of Antony—And of Cleopatra.

IN consequence of the events which had taken place in Sicily, Octavius found himself at once at the conclusion of a hazardous war, and master of all the forces which had been employed in it, whether as friends or as enemies. His fleet now consisted of near six hundred galleys with store-ships and transports; his land army of forty-five legions, which, though supposed to be incomplete, may have amounted to above two hundred thousand men. To these he joined above fifteen thousand horse and twenty thousand irregular infantry. They had been levied for different masters and in different parts of the empire, were persons of different descriptions; originally slaves, as well as freemen; natives of Spain, Sardinia, Sicily, and Africa, mixed with Italians and Roman citizens; adherents of Cæsar and of Pompey, of Antony, of Octavius, or Lepidus. It was very difficult to dispose of an assemblage consisting of such various and discordant parts. The troops that came over from Sextus Pompeius or Lepidus were to be retained by indulgence and favours, and those who had been the original support of Cæsar's fortunes had peculiar merits; all were sensible of their own consequence, and even of a power to dispose of the empire.

Octavius saw the necessity of separating such an army into different quarters before any cabals should be formed, and before any mutinous spirits had leisure to work on their minds, or to fill them with dangerous hopes or pretensions. That they might part in good humour, he made a distribution of some money, in token of his gratitude for recent services; and promised a great deal more. But what he now gave appeared to be contemptible, when compared with the reward which had been formerly given at Mutina and at Philippi, and still more, when compared with the settlements lately made for the veterans of Cæsar in Italy. These were minutely recorded, as the standard by which every legion had formed its expectations; and a general dissatisfaction was apparent in every rank and description of men. Octavius for some time affected to be ignorant of their discontent, and would have proceeded to make the arrangements he had planned for separating them, and for placing the legions in quarters remote from each other; but he had reason to doubt that his orders would not be obeyed, and still remained in suspense. When his knowledge of the mutinous spirit that prevailed in the army could no longer be dissembled, he endeavoured to soothe the most clamorous by additional marks of his favour, consisting chiefly of public honours, badges of military service to the men, and the title of senators bestowed on many of the officers. In distributing these favours, he assembled the army, and made a speech, setting forth the nature of the honours which he now conferred, and his farther intentions respecting the rewards which he meant to bestow. "These are baubles," said a tribune named Offilius, interrupting him; "children only are amused in this manner;[1] but men

---

1 Appian. de Bell. Civ. lib. v. Dio. Cass. lib. xlix. c. 13, 14.

who have exposed themselves in the services of their general, expect to be rewarded with lands and settlements." This tribune was seconded by the clamours of the whole army. Octavius retired from the audience in some disorder; and, sensible of the danger to which he had exposed himself from this time forward never ventured to meet these troops in a body, but employed secret arts in removing the heads of the mutiny.

The tribune Offilius, who had dared to interrupt his general in such mutinous terms, whether won by favour, or taken off by violence, was secretly disposed of. The legions who had served at Mutina and Philippi, amounting to twenty thousand men,[1] were separately appeased by donations and promises; were prevailed upon to accept of their discharge from the service, and, without any farther disturbance, to depart from the island.

When this party of the army was removed, Octavius affected to consider those who were gone as the sole cause of the late discontents, and the guilty, he said, being thus separated from the innocent and from the deserving, he made an additional present in money to those who remained, and held out the hopes of convenient settlements, and of plentiful fortunes, at the final expiration of their time in the service. By these artifices, and prudent measures, he effected the proposed separation, and extricated himself from a danger which frequently arises in the sequel of civil wars, and threatens the victor with an overthrow, from that very engine which he had employed to raise his fortunes.

Octavius, before his departure from Sicily, ordered a contribution to be levied of sixteen hundred talents;[2] and being no way disposed to follow out the plan of Lepidus, in the annexation of Sicily to the province of Africa, he appointed separate governors to each. Having dismissed the ships which Antony had furnished in the war, with instructions to wait at Tarentum for the orders of their own superior, he himself passed into Italy.

The messengers who had been sent with accounts of the victories obtained by Octavius in Sicily being arrived before him at Rome, all ranks of men vied with each other in the applause which they bestowed on his conduct, and in celebrating the occasion with demonstrations of joy. In the name of the senate and people, who had no longer any real political concessions to make, a variety of flattering proclamations were issued, ordering, in honour of the victor, statues, triumphal arches, processions, wreaths of laurel, anniversary rejoicings, and immediate thanksgivings to be prolonged beyond any former time assigned to such festivals. When he approached to the city, multitudes of every rank, adorned with chaplets, went forth to receive him, and conducted him in solemn procession to the temple, in which he was to perform the sacrifice of thanksgiving for his safe return.

Octavius, on the day after his arrival, proclaimed the peace which was obtained by the reduction of Sicily; and in two separate harangues, of which he gave copies in writing, one addressed to the senate, the other to the people, he gave an account of his whole conduct, from the time that he first assumed the administration of the government, to the present time. And, agreeably to the dictates of that masterly judgment with which he now, at least, began to conduct the interests of his ambition, he chose this time of victory and prosperity in which to exhibit the effects of his clemency, of his moderation, and of his disposition to spare those who, being supposed disaffected to him, were now in his power. He remitted all the arrears of taxes that were any where due within his jurisdiction, either by farmers of the revenue or by private persons. Of the honours that were decreed to himself he made choice of a few, and declined such as were in any degree invidious and burdensome to the people.

The inhabitants of Italy, and Roman citizens in general, having, among other evils, suffered greatly during the civil war, by the desertion of their slaves, who were readily received, and taken into the levies that were continually forming by different parties; Octavius took this opportunity, as far as it was in his power, at once to repair the loss which had been sustained by the master in the desertion of his slave, and to purge the army of a dangerous class of men, by whom it was overcharged and contaminated. In order to remove them in a manner that should prevent any disturbance on their part, he sent to every legion a sealed order, to be opened on a certain day, bearing, that all who had been in the condition of slaves should be secured; that as many as were claimed should be restored to their masters; and that the remainder should be put to death. According to this order, it was reported that thirty thousand were remitted to servitude, and six thousand killed.[3]

The author of this severe, but well concerted reform, now in the twenty-eighth year of his age, had, by accommodating himself, on every occasion, to his circumstances, and by successively availing himself of the support of different parties, more especially by courting the military retainers of his late uncle, set himself above the civil constitution of his country; and now, by affecting a regard to property, to civil rank, and to the peace of his fellow-citizens, he was about to make the army itself dependent on his will. From the real impression which he made by this policy, as well as from adulation and fear, the people were still farther incited to load him with public honours, and had his effigy carried at Rome, and in every country-town of Italy, among the idols of the tutelar gods.

The advantage now gained by Octavius, in the acquisition of armies and provinces lately belonging to Lepidus, were sufficient to have alarmed the jealousy of his remaining colleague and rival in the empire, if he had not been engaged, at this time, in a very hazardous enterprise beyond the frontier of his own province.

Antony during his stay in Italy or Greece, while he was chiefly attentive to the event of affairs in the western provinces, had entrusted the Parthian war to his lieutenant Ventidius. This officer acquitted himself with great honour in the discharge of his trust, recovered the province of Syria, which had been overrun by the Parthians, and drove them back beyond the Euphrates. Upon this account, he was judged worthy of a triumph, and came into Italy to receive this honour

1 Orosius, lib. vi.

2 About 175,000*l*.

3 Orosius, lib. vi. c. 18.

In the mean time, Antony was eager to gather the laurels which yet remained in this field, or was supposed to be jealous of the victories gained by his lieutenant over an enemy, who, till then, scarcely had yielded any advantage to the Roman arms. After his last visit to Italy, he had in the winter passed to Corcyra, and so far was attended by Octavia, but parted with her there, in the prospect of this arduous service; early in the spring he continued his voyage. Upon his arrival in Asia, notwithstanding the respect that was due to his alliance with Octavia and her brother, it soon appeared that he was still under the dominion of former passions. He already had two children by the queen of Egypt, who were named Alexander and Cleopatra, but whom the mother likewise distinguished, by the pompous appellations of the Sun and the Moon. Being prevented by the urgency of the service, at this season, from making a visit at Alexandria, he sent an officer of rank, Fonteius Capito, thither, to conduct Cleopatra from her own kingdom into Syria; and having received her in that province, in his way to the Euphrates, among other marks of his liberality, and of his passion, instead of trinkets and tokens of love, he made her a present of Phœnicia, Cœlesyria, Cyprus, and some part of Cilicia to be annexed to her kingdom. It was concerted between them, that at the end of the campaign he should pass the winter in Egypt; and they parted with mutual expressions of impatience for the return of this happy season.

The army, now mustered by Antony, consisted of sixty thousand Roman infantry, ten thousand Spanish and Gaulish cavalry, thirty thousand irregulars, being an assemblage of horse and foot, and of different nations. While he advanced with this force towards the Euphrates, he made his demand, that the Parthians should restore the captives and military ensigns taken with Crassus.[4] This was become a point of national honour among the Romans, and, joined to the late provocation, was made the ground of the present quarrel.

The Roman general had undertaken this invasion of the Parthians, in concert with the king of Armenia; and finding, at his arrival on the Euphrates, all the passages of the river, contrary to his expectation, strongly guarded, he continued his march, having the Euphrates on his right. When he arrived in the Lesser Armenia, the season was too far advanced to effect the service he had planned against the Parthians; but having intelligence that the Medes, or people of the Greater Armenia, had joined the enemy against him in the preceding part of the war, he formed a design on Praaspa or Phraata,[5] the capital of their country; in expectation of taking this place by surprise, he passed the Euphrates, leaving his heavy baggage and engines, with a guard of two legions, under the command of Statianus. With the remainder of the army he penetrated into the kingdom of the Greater Armenia, and presented himself at the gates of the capital.

This was a place of great strength, and every necessary precaution had been taken for its safety. Antony found that it could not be taken by assault, and the Parthians, although they hastened to its relief, knowing that the Roman army had come altogether unprepared for a siege, suffered them at first to remain before it undisturbed. They directed their whole force against Statianus, whom, with the two legions he commanded, they surprised and cut off, and by this means made themselves masters of all the equipage and baggage of the Roman army.

Antony, upon the first alarm of the enemy's intention to attack Statianus, having left the greater part of his forces before Praaspa, marched with a strong detachment to support him; but coming too late, found the field covered with the slain of the Roman legions, without either friend or enemy in sight. He understood that Artavasdes, the king of Armenia, to whose alliance he trusted in the present war, had remained an unconcerned spectator of this disaster, and he made no doubt that he was betrayed by this prince; but thought proper for the present to disguise his resentment. The loss he had sustained made it necessary for him to think of extricating his army from its present situation. Being alarmed for the safety of that part of it which he had left before Praaspa, he, with hasty marches, returned to its relief; but, at his arrival, finding no enemy near, and still flattering himself that the town might be obliged to surrender, and that it might, by its spoils, make up for the loss of his baggage, he lay before it, until he had exhausted all the provisions and forage that was to be found in the neighbouring country; and, in proportion as the other difficulties of his situation increased, began to feel himself harassed with the sallies of a powerful garrison, and the frequent attacks of numerous parties of Parthians in the field, who began to act against him from every quarter and made it equally difficult for him to decamp, or to subsist on his present ground.

Under these difficulties, the Roman general was frequently obliged to divide his forces; and leaving part to awe the town, marched with the remainder to cover his foragers, and the providers of his camp. As the enemy pressed upon him, in order to diminish the range from which he received his provisions, he saw the necessity of hazarding a battle; and for this purpose, marched from his camp with ten legions, three prætorian cohorts, and all his cavalry. The Parthians affected to abide his attack, but gave way at the first onset, and fled with every appearance of rout and confusion; they were pursued by the Roman infantry for fifty stadia, or about six miles, and by the cavalry over a hundred and fifty stadia, or about eighteen miles.

In this action, Antony flattered himself that he had put an end to his troubles from the Parthians; but, on numbering the prisoners and the slain, he found that only eighty of the enemy were killed, and thirty taken; and, on returning to his camp before the town of Praaspa, he found, that without being at all disconcerted by what had happened to them, they were returned to their former stations, and took measures, as before, to harass his camp, and to circumscribe his foraging parties. From this specimen of a victory over the Parthians, he learned to despair of being able to gain any advantage over an enemy, whose defeats were more pernicious to their antagonists than they were to themselves.[6] To

4 Plut. in Antonio.

5 Ibid. Dio. Cass. lib. xlix. c. 26, 27, 28.

6 Among the Romans who were seized with the passion of making offensive war on the Parthians,

complete his mortifications, he found that the garrison of Praaspa had made a powerful sally in his absence, driven his guards from their approaches, and destroyed all the works he had constructed against the town.[1] Judging it vain to renew his attack, or to remain any longer in his present situation, he sent a deputation to Phraates, probably rather to conceal his intended purpose of flight, than with hopes to obtain any reasonable terms of peace.

The king of Parthia received the message of Antony, seated on a golden throne, and holding in his hand a bended bow, the emblem of war. In order to sound the intentions of the Roman general, he proposed, as a preliminary to peace, that he should raise the siege of Praaspa. Antony was prepared to decamp, as soon as his messengers should be out of the hands of the enemy, but affected reluctance in agreeing to this condition, hoping that by these means he might conceal his intention, gain a few marches a-head, and reach the frontier of the Lesser Armenia, before the Parthians could take any advantage of his flight; but the king being equally refined in his artifices, perceived, in the affected reluctance of Antony to agree to what he knew to be necessary, an intention to fly, without waiting the result of a treaty, and, in this apprehension, he had his cavalry already prepared to pursue him, disputed every pass, hung upon his rear and upon his flanks, occupied the springs of water, and laid waste the country before him.

Many of the Roman army, overcome by famine and fatigue, expired on the march; others had laid down their arms, and submitted to the enemy. But those who had surrendered themselves, being cruelly treated, served, by their example, to check the inclination of others to sue for quarter, and taught the soldier to look for safety only in perseverance, and in the use of his arms. Antony himself, in every encounter, was prepared for the last extremity, and had a person retained, with orders, in case of his being likely to fall into the enemy's hands, to end his life; or, in case he were killed in battle, to disfigure his body, that it might not be known. But he passed through all these difficulties, as usual, with uncommon constancy and valour, making, in twenty-one days, a march of three hundred miles,[2] under a continual attack of the enemy, in which it is reckoned that his army was eighteen times engaged in battle.[3] At the end of this march, in reviewing the legions, with which he began to retreat, it was found, he had lost about a fourth of their number;[4] or, as Plutarch states his loss, twenty thousand foot, and four thousand horse.

It appears that Antony, upon his arrival in the Lesser Armenia, left a considerable body behind him in that country, to check the farther pursuit of the enemy,[5] and with the remainder of the army, proceeding from thence with great precipitation, and under great hardships from the season, by which he added eight thousand men more to his former losses, he arrived at Coni, a small sea-port, between Berytus and Sidon, on the coast of Syria. At this place, he was received by Cleopatra on board her fleet, and with her effected his passage by sea to Alexandria, where he endeavoured to conceal his losses, and to efface the memory of his sufferings in the midst of dissipation and pleasure.

U. C. 718.

L. Cornificius, Sextus Pompeius.

During the dependence of these events, the state of the war in Asia had been variously reported in the western parts of the empire. It was believed for some time, that the Roman army in Armenia, with its leader, had perished. On this supposition, Sextus Pompeius, who still remained in the island of Lesbos, began to resume his pretensions. He was not without hopes, that on the demise of Antony, the armies of Asia might declare for himself, and during some time, affected to receive every person who repaired to him, as the head of a party that was still of some consideration in the empire. He even proceeded to solicit the alliance of all the princes of the east, from Thrace to Pontus, and the banks of the Euphrates.[6] But upon the report of Antony's return into Syria, he laid aside his ambitious thoughts, and sent a message to sue for protection. Among other particulars, he set forth, that he had committed himself to the justice and clemency of Antony, not from despair, or from any sudden impulse whatever, but from previous thought and mature deliberation. He might have had a safe retreat, and a powerful support, he said, in Spain, where the friends of his father were yet numerous, and full of zeal; but from a thorough conviction, that the interests of Antony were the same with his own, he had preferred his alliance to any other. "Octavius," he continued, "will soon have the same quarrel with you, that he has lately had with me, and afterwards with Lepidus. He considers the empire as his property, and cannot endure a partner. His open force is not so dangerous, as the insidious professions, and the artful disguises with which he hides his designs. I make you an offer of a friendship that is sincere, and of a faith that is yet unbroken. I made you the same offer while I was master of Sicily and Sardinia, and in the height of my fortune. By accepting of it, you

Julius Cæsar is mentioned. And it is a problem, which never can be solved, in what manner this able statesman and warrior would have acquitted himself in so arduous a task. The Parthians had their haunts beyond the Tigris; and besides leaving no means on the frontier, by which an enemy could subsist in approaching them, probably presented no hold by which they could be seized, even in their own country. As they had no ground which it was absolutely necessary for them to defend, so there was no ground on which an invader could be secure from their attacks. They gave way while an enemy advanced, and reckoned it an advantage to draw him far from his resources and supports. They waited with patience, till time, hardships, disease, or want of provisions had rendered him an easy prey, or ripe for destruction; and they then pressed upon him with a ferocity and ardour, which abundantly corrected any belief of their cowardice that might have been taken from their manner of receiving his first attacks.

If Cæsar had not already conceived some new or uncommon means of reducing them, it is probable, that his first observations would have satisfied him, that he could not conquer such a people, although he might, in time, have settled a new nation on the Tigris to supplant them; and it is probable that he would have availed himself of some of their ordinary flights, to lay claim to a victory, and thus, with more ability than others of his countrymen, finish the war with a triumph at Rome.

1 Plut. in Antonio.

2 Liv. Epitome, lib. cxxix, &c.

3 Plut. in Antonio. 4 Vell. Pater. lib. ii. c. 82.

5 Dio. Cass. lib. xlix. c. 30.

6 Appian. de Bell. Civ. l.b. v.

will save the remains of a family, yet respected by the Roman people, and, by joining with me, you will gain the accession of a party, whom even adversity has not made to abandon their leader."

While Sextus Pompeius addressed himself to Antony in these terms, he endeavoured to preserve the appearance of an armed force, and hovered about with some ships on the coast of Ionia. Being pursued by Titius, who had orders from Antony to observe his motions, he sailed up the Propontis, and put into the harbour of Nicomedia. Here he again offered to negotiate;[7] but being told that he must surrender at discretion, he set fire to his ships, and attempted to escape by land. Having got into Phrygia, he was taken in his flight, and soon after, by order of Antony, was put to death.

This event being known at Rome, Octavius ordered public rejoicings. Among these was a solemn procession, led by two carriages or chariots of state; in one of them Octavius himself appeared; by the other, he marked the place that was due to Antony. Still farther, to soothe the jealousy of his colleague in the empire, he gave orders that a statue should be erected to him in the temple of Concord, and that he should have a share in the honours which had been recently decreed to himself. This indecent triumph over the last of a family, which had been so long in high estimation at Rome, was far from being acceptable to the people. The misfortunes of the young man himself, who from his earliest years had been an exile, and stript of his inheritance, he memory of his father and of the republic, filled the minds of men with secret indignation, and with a tender melancholy which they could not disguise; and though Octavius himself escaped on this occasion without any public insult, yet Titius some time afterwards exhibiting public shows in the theatre of the great Pompey, was, on account of the part which he had taken in the murder of the son, driven from thence by the execrations of the people.[8]

The forces of the empire were now parcelled in two separate lots, under the direction of masters, who were soon to entertain the views and the jealousies of separate monarchs. Octavius was become the sovereign of Rome, and occupied chiefly in removing obstructions to his government, and in consolidating the arrangements he had made in the state. He had taken measures to repress many disorders, the dregs of the civil wars, which still afflicted the city and the contiguous provinces. He had brought his armies under tolerable discipline, and even in a great measure reconciled the people to the loss of their political consequence, and of their liberties. He took care to destroy, with much ostentation, all papers and records from which those, who had acted against himself, might fear being drawn into trouble. He retained the usual names, and the forms of office; and wherever he himself was to exercise any uncommon power, he talked of it as a mere temporary expedient to obviate the disorders of the times, and spoke of his intention, in concert with Antony, to discontinue every irregular mode of administration, as soon as the war with the Parthians should be brought to a period. He even sent Bibulus into the east, with open and public instructions to concert with his colleague, the manner and time of their resignation.[9]

But Antony, acting as sovereign of the eastern empire, appeared on his part to be altogether intent on the entertainments of the court at Alexandria, on the renewal of the war which he affected to meditate against the Parthians, or on his project against Artavasdes, the king of the Lesser Armenia, who he thought had betrayed him in his late expedition. He was encouraged in his designs on that quarter, by the offers of a league, which were made to him from the king of Medea, who thinking his services, during the late invasion, ill requited by the Parthians, was now disposed to take arms against them.

Antony having accepted of this alliance, formed the project of a new invasion of Armenia, chiefly intent on his design to get the person of Artavasdes into his power; but he was, for one season, diverted from the execution of his purpose, by an incident, which brought into the scale of public councils the weight of passions and of motives at all times powerful; and at a time when the world was to be governed by the humours of a few persons, scarcely to be balanced by any other consideration whatever.

Octavia was become impatient of the neglect with which she was treated by her husband, and jealous of the preference which he gave to Cleopatra. Hearing that he was to leave Alexandria on a new Parthian expedition, she determined to place herself in his way as he passed through Syria. To enhance the pleasure of their meeting, she was furnished with a variety of presents, and, among the rest, attended by a body of two thousand chosen men, clothed and accoutred in the manner of the prætorian bands, which had been formed by her brother for the guard of his own person, and which he now sent as a token of friendship to Antony. She was arrived in Greece with this attendance when her intention became known in Egypt.[10]

On hearing of this journey of Octavia, Cleopatra being greatly alarmed, had the address to appear sunk under a weight of affliction, which she affected to bear with fortitude; but was sometimes surprised in tears, which she endeavoured to dry up, and either increased the anguish of real passion, or gave more appearance of sincerity to her dissimulation, by her affectation of a desire to conceal what she felt. Her health, in appearance, declined, and it was whispered, that her life was in danger. She herself continued obstinate in her silence; but her confidents insinuated that the fear of losing Antony was the cause of her distress, and that the day he left Alexandria, would probably be the last of her life. Thus, with a mixture probably of artifice and real passion, not uncommon in cases of this sort, the Queen of Egypt had the address to retain Antony at Alexandria, and prevailed on him to send a peremptory order to Octavia, not to advance in her intended progress to the east. He excused himself at the same time, from even excepting the presents which she brought from her brother.[11]

7 Dio. Cass. lib. xlviii. c. 18.
8 Vell. Pater. lib ii. c. 79.

9 Appian. de Bell. Civ. lib. v.
10 Dio. Cass. lib. xxxiii. Plut. in Antonio.
11 Ibid.

Upon the return of Octavia to Rome, under all the circumstances of this affront, her brother proposed that she should renounce her connection with Antony, and remove from his house; but if in this he wished her to act from resentment, her own conduct, though proceeding from a different motive, was better calculated to unite the people in avenging her quarrel. Being willing to await the return of her husband's inclinations, she remained at the head of his family, continued to manage his affairs, and acted in every particular as the mother of his children, even of those by a former marriage, and undertook the protection of such adherents and friends as came to solicit their affairs in the capitol.[1]

The unworthy treatment which Octavia received in return for so much duty, as it interested the public in her favour, so it gave an immediate prospect of a breach between the leaders, who now divided the empire. Antony and Octavius had been rivals for the succession of Cæsar's power, had frequent quarrels, which were suspended from time to time by apparent and ambiguous reconciliations. Even the marriage of Octavia was no more than a mere expedient to put off to a more convenient time a final breach, which, between parties of such opposite pretensions, must in the end be deemed unavoidable.

It is probable that Octavius, in all the vicissitudes of his connection with Antony, or with any other party, had never lost sight of the expectations he had formed from his earliest youth, not only as the heir of Julius Cæsar, but as the successor likewise to his power in the commonwealth. He united or broke with different parties, according to the state of his affairs, and procured these breaches or coalitions in the precise conjunctures that were most favourable to himself. He at one time joined with the senate, and the assassins of his uncle, to pull down the power of Antony; he afterwards joined with Antony to reduce the senate, and to destroy the republic. He courted Antony occasionally, to prevent his forming any dangerous combination with Sextus Pompeius or with Lepidus, and, in general, kept terms with him, while either of these leaders continued to be formidable, or could cast the balance by uniting against him.

This refined politician, upon becoming sole master of Italy, and of the western provinces, was now better enabled, than formerly, to brave the power of his remaining competitor in the empire; and he prepared for the contest, which could not be long avoided. He had greatly reduced his military establishment, by purging his armies of improper subjects, not only the armies which had come over to him from his antagonists, Sextus Pompeius and Lepidus, but those likewise which had been levied in common between Antony and himself. But even, after he had thus dismissed such as were of doubtful faith, and reduced his establishment to that measure which he wished to maintain, he had still remaining a greater number than his present occasions seemed to require, and he sought for pretences, under which, in the present state of tranquillity to which his division of the empire was reduced, he might avoid giving any alarm to his rival, and justify his maintaining so great a military force. For this purpose probably it was, that he formed the project of a war first in Africa, in the execution of which, he actually passed into Sicily; and being there some time detained by contrary winds, he changed his object, and sent the army destined for Africa to the opposite side of Italy, beyond the Hadriatic, to make war on the Japydes, Savi, Pannonii, and other nations on the side of Illyricum, who were more likely than the Africans to furnish his troops with the experience of real service, as well as himself with a plausible pretence for keeping them on foot. They accordingly penetrated, by his orders, beyond the frontier of the empire on that side, and were employed to gather laurels at the expense of the barbarians, by whom, he alleged, that his provinces had been often infested.

U. C. 719.

L. Scribonius Libo. M. Antonius absens. L. Sempronius Atratinus. Ex Kal. Julii. Paul. Æmilius, C. Memmius. Ex Kal. Novem. M. Herennius.

In the mean while, according to the arrangements that were made relating to the succession of consuls, Antony was elected into this office, and though not present in person on the first of January, had his name entered on the record. In accepting of this nomination, he meant no more than to ascertain his right to dispose of the consulate, and had given a commission, by which, on the very day of his admission, he vacated the office in favour of another, and brought forward a number of his friends in the course of the year. He wished by these means to make known, that although Octavius was pleased to occupy the seats of government; yet he was not to engross for his friends and retainers the ordinary honours that were enjoyed in the state.

Octavius, probably, treading as nearly as he could in the steps of his late uncle, still sought for occasions to keep his armies in service; and although he was not inclined to make war abroad, or make new acquisitions of territory to the empire, yet he affected to have many designs which required the possession of a military force. Among these, he projected an enterprise for the reduction of Britain, made the necessary preparations, and proceeded himself to the northern parts of Gaul. Here, however, his attention was again diverted to a different quarter. Having an army employed on the side of Illyricum, in separate divisions, under Agrippa and other officers, Messala and Geminus, whose names only are known: it was reported, that the division, under Geminus, acting in Pannonia, had received a check, and been obliged to retire from some parts of the country they had formerly occupied. Upon this alarm, Octavius himself thought proper to lay aside his design upon Britain; but finding, upon his arrival in Illyricum, that the supposed loss was already repaired, the enemy in different encounters defeated, and the former ground of his army recovered, he himself joined Agrippa, who was employed against the Dalmatians, and continued for some months to take a part in the campaign with this favourite officer.[2]

Antony, at the same time, as if equally disposed to have an army inured to service, sought likewise for occasions of war; and having quieted the jealousies of Cleopatra, by a seemingly irreconcilable breach with her rival, was permitted

1 Plut. in Antonio.

2 Dio. Cass. lib. xlix. c. 39.

to form projects of enterprise beyond the limits of Egypt. He renewed his designs against the kings of Armenia and Parthia. In the spring, he advanced to Nicopolis, a place so named, from the victory of Pompey over Mithridates; and supposing that the treachery of Artavasdes, in betraying Statianus, would justify any measures he could take against him, he sent repeated messages, under pretence of friendship, desiring a conference; but with a real intention of seizing his person. The more effectually to remove all suspicions of any such design, he proposed a marriage between Alexander, one of his own sons by Cleopatra, and the daughter of that prince; but not succeeding in this artifice, he advanced into the heart of Armenia, and threatened to lay the kingdom waste with fire and sword. The king being unprepared for defence, took his resolution at last to try the sincerity of Antony's professions, and was actually taken.

The first advantage which the Roman general proposed to make of this capture, was exacting a ransom; and for this purpose, the king, being carried round the fortresses of his kingdom in which the royal treasure had been deposited, was made to demand great sums of money under this pretence; but the officers, to whom this demand was addressed, knowing that their sovereign was a prisoner, shut their gates against him, and refused to comply. The army of Armenia at the same time assembled, and considering the throne as vacant, placed upon it Artaxes, the eldest son of their captive king. Being led by this young prince into immediate action with the Romans, they were defeated, and he himself was obliged to take refuge with the Parthians.

Antony contented with this victory, which gave him possession of the country, put his army into winter quarters in the Lesser Armenia, and entered into a defensive treaty with the king of Media, whose daughter, upon that occasion, was betrothed to the same son of Cleopatra, whose proposed marriage with the daughter of Artavasdes had been employed as a snare to betray that prince.

At the conclusion of these transactions, Antony set out on his return to Egypt, and meditating a triumphal procession into the city of Alexandria, destined his captive for a part in the scene, gave orders that he should be conducted thither in chains; and accordingly, upon the arrival of the troops and the equipage which were to form his retinue, he made his entry with all the parade of a Roman triumph, repeated all the forms which were usual on such occasions at Rome, made a speech to the people, and ordered a public feast. In these several particulars, seeming to place the inhabitants of Alexandria upon a foot of equality with the Roman people, and prostituting a solemn institution of the Romans to the vanity of a barbarous court, he gave much scandal and offence at Rome. Every circumstance being exaggerated by his enemies, his own extravagance gained a ready belief to every report that was circulated against him.

It has been observed, on different occasions, that Antony, although he stemmed the current of adversity with vigour and ability, was generally carried by prosperity into every excess of sensuality, extravagance, and dissipation. In this time of festivity, he assumed, in the midst of his debauch, not only the eastern dress, and all the badges of royalty, but likewise[3] the attire and designation of a god; wore the buskins, the golden crown, and the chaplet of ivy belonging to Bacchus, held the Thyrsus in his hand, and was drawn through the streets of Alexandria on a car like those which were employed in the processions of the gods.[4] It was said, that Cleopatra at the same time assumed the dress of Isis; that being seated together on thrones of gold, elevated on a lofty platform, Antony presented Cleopatra to the people, as queen not only of Egypt and Cyprus, but likewise of Africa and Cælesyria, and that he associated with her in these titles Cæsarion, her supposed son by Julius Cæsar. To his own son Alexander, in these drunken assignations of empire, it was reported that he allotted Armenia, Media, and Parthia, which, though not in his possession, he considered as a certain conquest: to Ptolomy, another of his sons, Phœnicia, Syria, and Cilicia,[5] and presented each of them to the people in the dress, and with the ensigns and the retinue suited to the several destinations; Alexander, with the Persian tiara; and Ptolomy, with the dress and diadem worn by the princes of Macedonia.

This mock distribution of the eastern kingdoms was executed in formal deeds or writings, of which copies were ordered to Rome to be deposited in the records of the temple of Vesta, and in the keeping of the virgins. And as Octavius looked forward to an immediate quarrel with Antony, the whole circumstances with which these acts had been solemnized at Alexandria, were industriously published at Rome to his prejudice. The writings, however, not being actually brought to the city before the subsequent year, in which Domitius and Sosius were consuls, part of the scandal was for some time secreted by the influence of these magistrates, who were inclined to favour Antony against Octavius in the impending contest for empire.

U. C. 720.
Imper. Cæsar iterum.
L. Volcatius Tullus.

P. Autronius Pætus.
ex Kal. Maii.
L. Flavius.

Ex Kal. Jul.
C. Fontius.

While Antony indulged himself in these extravagancies at Alexandria, Octavius, with L. Volcatius Tullus, assumed the title of consuls at Rome; but the first, at his admission, thought proper to follow the example that was lately set to him by Antony; on the first of January, vacated the office, and substituted another in his place. By like successive substitutions, he communicated this dignity in the course of the year to six different persons.

M. Acilius.
Ariola
Ex. Kal. Sept.
L. Vinucius.

Ex. Kal. Oct.
L. Lavonius.

The office of ædile, which had been generally declined on account of the expenses which attended the discharge of it, and which had been for some time discontinued, was now revived in the person of Agrippa, who, though he had been already of a higher rank, and in the station of consul, voluntarily undertook the duties of ædile; and, at his own expense, applied himself to the more serious objects of the trust, by constructing highways, erecting public works, and cleansing the common sewers, works of great antiquity, that seemed to exceed the

3 Florus, lib iv. c. 11. Dio. Cass. lib. l. c. 5.
4 Vel. Pat. lib. ii. c. 83. 5 Dio. Cass. lib. xlix. c. 41.

force of the times to which they were referred.[1] He at the same time repaired the circus, made new regulations for conducting the entertainments of that place, and himself exhibited magnificent shows.

Under this magistracy of Agrippa, the people were gratified with presents, as well as with pastimes. Articles of finery, trinkets, and even sums of money were distributed by a species of lottery. Counters or billets, entitling the bearer to certain prizes, which were marked upon each, were thrown out by handfuls to be scrambled for in the crowd. Public baths, furnished with all the usual apparatus, were provided, and attended with keepers and dressers at the public expense;[2] acts of munificence and popularity, in which it was thought proper to cultivate the public favour.

Octavius at the same time, on so near a prospect of a quarrel with Antony, who was to employ half the forces of the empire against him, had the good fortune to disengage himself from foreign wars. Those which he carried on in Dalmatia, terminated in the submission of that people, in their giving hostages for their good behaviour, and in their restoring the colours which had been taken from a Roman army they had defeated under the conduct of Vatinius. These he hung up in a portico, which bore his own name; but a triumph being decreed to him, he declined or deferred accepting of it; on this, as on many other occasions, discovering a mind, though fond of dominion, indifferent to pomp, and the exterior appearances of power.

Antony passed the summer at the head of his army in Syria, without having made any attempt against the Parthians. He renewed his defensive alliance with the king of Media; and the parties in this treaty, being to name the powers against whom they respectively wished, in the event of a war, to secure an alliance, the king of Media made particular mention of the Parthians, and Antony named Octavius. At the end of this negotiation, they mutually made an exchange of some troops.[3]

Thus Antony made no secret of the distrust which he conceived of his colleague in the empire, or of a breach, which, from their mutual jealousies and provocations, was gradually widening. He affected to treat Cæsarion, the reputed son of Julius Cæsar by Cleopatra, as the legitimate heir of the Julian family. He likewise retorted on Octavius, the artifice which had been practised against himself, by professing an intention to resign the power of triumvir. He complained of the violence which had been done to Lepidus; but asked, if Lepidus were justly deposed, why he himself was not admitted to his share in the provinces? He complained of his being excluded from a share in the spoils of Sextus Pompeius, as well as of Lepidus; and of his being excluded from Italy, which was the common seat of government to the whole empire, and which Octavius had not any right to appropriate to himself.

To these complaints Octavius replied, That Antony, without making any compensation to his colleagues in the western provinces, had seized on the kingdom of Egypt; that he had unwarrantably put Sextus Pompeius to death; that he had dishonoured the Roman name by his breach of faith with the king of Armenia, and had given no account at Rome of the spoils of that kingdom that he had presumed to dismember the Roman empire in behalf of Cleopatra, and of her children and that he supported her in an attempt to intrude into the family of Cæsar one of her spurious progeny.[4]

These mutual complaints were publicly made, and supported at Rome. Neither of the parties professed any intention of going to war; but, under various pretences, collected money, and augmented their forces. They held a continual correspondence by agents and messengers, merely to have an opportunity of observing each other's motions; and soon involved in their disputes and jealousies, not only their own immediate retainers and friends, but such as now composed the senate and assemblies of the people, who could not remain unconcerned spectators in a difference between persons who were likely again to involve the empire itself in a civil war.

U. C. 721.
Cn. Domitius Ahenobarbus,
Caius Sosius.
Ex. Kal. Jul.
L. Cornelius.
Ex. Kal. Nov.
U. Valerius.

Cneius Domitius Ahenobarbus, and Caius Sosius, having in consequence of preceding engagements succeeded to the consulate, and being attached to Antony, openly espoused his cause. Sosius, on the first of January, in entering upon his office, ventured to arraign the conduct of Octavius, enumerated the injuries which he had offered to Antony, and moved the senate for redress.

Octavius, having previous intimation of what was to be moved by the consul, and wishing to know the full extent of the charge before he should be obliged to reply, on that day, absented himself from the senate; but took care to have Nonius, one of the tribunes of the people, prepared to watch over his interest, and to put a negative on any proceeding that might be attempted to his prejudice. At the next assembly of the senate, he appeared with a numerous body of armed men, seated himself between the consuls, and from that place made his answer to the accusations, which in the former meeting had been stated against him, and retorted much blame on his enemies. He called upon Antony, in particular, to return into Italy, and to resign the triumvirate, the period for which that temporary power was created being now expired.[5]

To this defiance, on the part of Octavius, no reply being made by the friends of Antony, the assembly was adjourned for some days, during which time both the consuls thought proper to withdraw from the city; and not supposing themselves safe within the jurisdiction of a person against whom they had taken so hostile a part, continued their retreat into Asia, where Antony, whose cause they had espoused, had the means to protect them.

Octavius, pleased to find himself, by the flight of the ordinary magistrates, left master of the city, and freed from the necessity of employing immediate force against the forms of common wealth, gave them no interruption, nor attempted to prevent their escape. He even gave out, that these officers had withdrawn by his permis-

1 Plinius, lib. xxxvi. c 15.
2 Dio Cass lib. xlix. c 43.
3 Ibid. c. 44.
4 Dio. Cass. lib. l. c. 1.
5 Liv. Epitome, lib. cxxxii.

sion, and that every one else who was disposed to join his antagonist, might follow their example.[6]

Antony, when he received an account of what was thus passing at Rome, being arrived in the Lesser Armenia, on his last expedition into that country, assembled all the senators of his party who were then with his army, laid before them his grounds of complaint against Octavius, renounced in form his marriage with Octavia, and declared war on her brother.[7] At the same time, he took a solemn oath, in which he bound himself, at the end of six months, after he should have relieved Italy from the tyranny of Octavius, to restore the government entire to the senate and people, agreeably to the ancient constitution. Having taken this method to gain all those who wished for the restoration of the commonwealth, and having remitted great sums of money into Italy, to be dealt out in presents and gratuities to the army of his rival,[8] instead of pursuing the pretended object of the war in Armenia, he put his army in motion westward. Having Canidius advanced with sixteen legions, he himself conducting the queen of Egypt, who was to have her share in the enterprise, took the route of Ephesus, where all his ships were ordered to assemble. Of these he had eight hundred sail, of which Cleopatra furnished two hundred completely equipped, together with twenty thousand talents in money.[9]

The consuls Domitius and Sosius having joined Antony at Ephesus, and finding all his councils governed by the caprice of Cleopatra, and all his measures made subservient to her vanity or interest, warmly recommended that the queen of Egypt should return into her own kingdom, and there remain until the war should be at an end; but she, dreading the loss of her influence, the restoration of Octavia, and a reconciliation of parties, to which her pretensions, interests, and passions must be the first sacrifice, employed all her artifice to defeat their counsel, and to maintain her ascendant over Antony. For this purpose, with more care and assiduity than she mustered the forces of her allies, or collected the resources of her kingdom for the support of the war, she assembled from every quarter the means of dissipation and the instruments of pleasure.

Many Roman officers, who had hitherto embarked their fortunes with Antony, disgusted by the appearances of levity and dissipation which attended him on this occasion, withdrew from his cause, and threw themselves into the arms of his enemy. Plancus, in particular, with Titius, long dissatisfied with the influence and conduct of Cleopatra, deserted him. They brought with them into Italy particular accounts of Antony's levity, and of Cleopatra's insolent speeches, insinuating that she flattered herself with the hopes of becoming mistress of the Roman empire. They produced copies of Antony's will, already mentioned as having been sent to the records of the Vestals, and which, by its extravagance, procured credit to every other report which was raised to his prejudice, so much as to make it believed, that if he should prevail in the contest with Octavius, he meant to declare Cleopatra queen of the Romans, and to transfer the seat of the empire to Alexandria.

These reports, tending to render Antony an object of ridicule, or of scorn, were propagated with great effect among the people. They were even introduced in the senate, and employed as the pretence for a motion that was made to divest him of his present command in the east, and of that share of the sovereignty which he held in the capacity of triumvir, and to declare him incapable of holding the office of consul, to which he was destined for the ensuing year.

Plancus, in support of the motion that was made to this purpose, urging, together with the reports now mentioned, the manifold disorders which were imputed to Antony, and the many offences he had committed against the commonwealth, was answered with great courage and asperity, by persons who still ventured to espouse the cause of the absent triumvir. "While you were of his councils," said Coponius to Plancus on this occasion, "I doubt not but the conduct of Antony was sufficiently blameable."[10]

Octavius, however, being master at Rome, the motion was carried, and a decree was obtained, in consequence of it, to suspend Mark Antony in the exercise of all his powers. War at the same time was formally declared against the queen of Egypt, while Octavius, with his usual discretion, to avoid making enemies unnecessarily of those who must have been involved with Antony in any personal attainder, did not include him in this declaration. A proclamation, however, was published, "requiring all citizens to withdraw themselves from Antony, as being abandoned to the caprices of a stranger, and a woman, who, by a kind of fascination, led him in her train, and prevailed upon him to countenance, against his own country, a war which was to be conducted by the eunuchs Mardio and Pothinus, keepers of the palace of Alexandria; and by Ira and Charmion, the waiting women of Cleopatra, who hoped soon to reign in the capital of the Roman empire, as absolutely as they had for some time governed in the provinces of the East."[11]

In the sequel of these declarations, some taxes for the expense of the war were laid on the inhabitants of Italy; an uncommon stretch of power, which, on the approach of an enemy who was likely to divide the people, appeared to be impolitic and dangerous. All freed slaves, having two hundred sestertia or upwards, were required to pay an eighth of their effects, free citizens were required to pay a fourth of their yearly revenue; and these exactions being violently enforced, gave rise in many places to insurrection and bloodshed;[12] and the minds of men being greatly agitated, reports of presages and prodigies were circulated as usual, in times of great alarm, and on the eve of important events.

Antony, in the mean time, advanced with his fleet and army from Ephesus to Samos, and from thence to Athens, where, together with the queen of Egypt, he was received with a flattering pageantry, and with many complimentary addresses, in composing which, this people now exercised that ingenuity for which they were formerly celebrated in conducting matters of state and of war. Cleopatra was admitted to the freedom of the city of Athens. Antony, being already a citizen, led the procession, in which the republic came to con-

6 Dio. Cass. lib. l. c. 2. 7 Ibid. c. 3. 8 Ibid. c. 7.
9 Plut. in Antonio, near three millions sterling.

10 Vell. Pater. lib. ii. c. 83. 11 Plut. in Antonio.
12 Dio. Cass lib. l. c. 10

fer this honour on the queen; and made her a speech in name of his fellow-citizens, the Athenian people.

From thence Antony proceeded to the island of Corcyra, where all his forces assembled, and seemed to threaten Italy with an immediate invasion. He had undoubtedly got the start of his antagonist, might have surprised him, and divided the inhabitants of Italy, and other parts of the western empire. Of these, numbers were discontented on account of recent exactions, many were disposed to favour the absent party, or from animosity to a government, under which they had experienced oppression, were desirous of any change.

With all these advantages in his favour, Antony either never had the intention to invade Italy in the present season, or laid it aside, and determined to pass the winter in Greece. He sent his fleet into the gulph of Ambracia, and quartered his army in the Peloponnesus, or round th gulph of Corinth, where, besides the ordinary resources of the country, they had continual supplies of every necessary by sea, from Asia and Egypt.

U. C. 722.

Imper Cæs. Mar. Val. Messala Corsinus. Ex Kal. Mart. M. Mitius, ex Kal. Oct. Cn. Pompeius.

By the last arrangement, which had been concerted between Octavius and Antony, for the succession of consuls during eight years, of which this was the last, they themselves were now to have entered on the office; but Antony being set aside by a public act of the senate and people, Octavius assumed for his colleague, Messala, already mentioned as the particular friend of Marcus Brutus. This almost only remaining partizan of the republic had been among the proscribed, but was afterwards taken into favour, and reconciled to the successor of Cæsar.[1]

Octavius now holding the office of Roman consul, endeavoured to sink, under this designation of a legal magistrate, his pretensions as a military adventurer, and qualified the troops, which he employed against Antony, as the forces of the commonwealth, assembled to repel the attack of a foreign enemy. He drew them together on the coast of Apulia, and while he stationed the greater part of his fleet in two divisions at Brundusium and Tarentum, sent Agrippa with a squadron to ply off the harbours of Greece, and to interrupt the naval communications of the enemy.

By the vigilance and activity of Agrippa, many captures were made in the winter, and the conveyance of corn, arms, and military stores from Asia Syria, and Egypt, intended for the use of Antony's fleet and army,[2] was rendered difficult and extremely precarious. To supply their necessities, both his sea and land forces were obliged to plunder the country around them; and, in the want of horses and carriages, drove the inhabitants like beasts of burden, laden with corn and other provisions, to the sea coast. Antony, when he joined his fleet at Actium, being told that half his rowers had perished from scarcity and disease: "The oars," he said, "I hope are safe."[3]

In the mean time, Octavius brought his land forces to Brundusium and Tarentum; and either to show the strength of his party, or to secure the persons of those of whose fidelity he entertained any doubt, summoned all the Roman citizens of note to attend him on the coast. From thence, in order to profit by Antony's delay, and to fix the theatre of the war in Greece, he embarked with his army, and stood for the opposite coast of Epirus. He landed under the promontory of Acroceraunus, the same place at which Julius debarked in pursuit of the war with Pompey; and from this place, ordering the fleet to coast round the head lands, and the island of Corcyra, he marched with the army along shore towards the gulph of Ambracia.

This gulph opens into the channel that separates the islands of Corcyra, Leucada, and Cephalonia. It is narrow at its entrance;[4] but is wider within,[5] and stretches eastward[6] about twenty or thirty miles. At its opening, on the southern shore, stood Actium, and opposite to this place stood Toryné, afterwards called Nicapolis. Antony had taken possession of Actium, and having a proper harbour in the gut, commanded the whole navigation of the gulph.

Octavius advancing with his fleet and army from the northward, and having no opposition made to him by the enemy, took possession of Toryné, entrenched himself in a strong post on shore, and stationed his fleet behind him in a creek, which furnished a harbour sufficiently safe.[7]

Antony, already posted on the opposite side of the gulph, either did not think himself in condition to prevent the enemy from making this lodgment in his presence, or determined by some other motive, chose to act on the defensive; and thus the armies were stationed, Octavius in Epirus, and Antony in Acarnania, on the opposite sides of the entrance to the gulph of Ambracia.

The state of the forces on each side is variously reported. Plutarch says, that in entering on the war, Antony had five hundred galleys, of which there were many mounting eight and ten tire of oars; that the land army, which had been transported by his fleet, consisted of a hundred thousand infantry, and twelve thousand horse; that Octavius had two hundred and fifty galleys, eight thousand foot, and twelve thousand horse. Others place the superiority of numbers on the side of Octavius, but state them as more nearly equal.[8]

As the Egyptian fleet still commanded the passage of the gulph, Antony, after it was too late to disturb the enemy in making their lodgment, seized a post, with a considerable part of his army, on the side of Toryné, to restrain their excursions, and to cut off their forage. Octavius, on his part, detached Agrippa, with a powerful squadron, to make descents on the coasts, to ravage the towns that were in the possession of Antony, and to cut off the supplies that were brought him by sea.

According to these instructions, Agrippa took possession of Methone, on the coast of Messenia and of Patræ, near the mouth of the gulph of Corinth, entered that gulph, and made a descent near the city of Corinth, afterwards took posses-

1 Dio. Cass lib l. c. 10 2 Oros. lib. v. 9.
3 Ibid.

4 About half a mile, or five stadia.
5 One hundred stadia.
6 Stretches in land three hundred stadia, Polyb lib. iv. c. 63. 7 Plut. in Antonio. 8 Ibid

sion of the promontory of Leucada, which lay in the course of Antony's convoys,[9] and obliged him, after a check he had received in the neighbourhood of Toryné, by the defeat of the cavalry he employed on that side, to abandon his ground in Epirus, and to repass the straits to Actium.

In these operations passed the greater part of summer; but as nothing was decided, Domitius, who, in the preceding year, notwithstanding he was consul, had left his station in the city to join Antony, now disgusted with his conduct, went over to Octavius. A general distrust ensued in the party,[10] and Antony, being distressed for want of provisions, saw the necessity of making his retreat, or of risking a general action. His fleet having suffered greatly in winter from scarcity and from disease, he deliberated whether he should not abandon his ships, and rest his cause on the event of a battle on shore;[11] but Cleopatra, who governed all his councils, and who dreaded being deprived of a retreat by sea, urged him without delay to set sail for Alexandria. She proposed, that, to check the progress of the enemy, proper detachments should be left to keep possession of all the strong-holds in Asia and Greece; that these detachments should be supported from Egypt; and that Antony, in the mean time, should prepare the whole forces of that kingdom to contend for the empire of the world.

The partizans of Cleopatra, in the council of Antony, contending for this plan of retreat which she proposed, among other arguments against risking a battle, urged many fatal presages and signs of impending calamity, sufficient to strike a panic in the troops, and to render the flight they advised, in some measure necessary. It was determined, however, as a kind of middle course, that the fleet should put to sea; if permitted, withdraw from the enemy; but if attacked, give battle. As it was observed, that many of the ships were ill manned, and in disrepair, and some altogether unserviceable; these being selected and burnt, the remainder prepared for the sea.

When this resolution was taken, Antony called his officers together, put them in mind of the diligence with which he had made his preparations for the present war, and referred for proof to the armament itself, which was then in their view.—In a war, which was to turn on the event of naval operations, they had an undoubted superiority, he said, either in the number or loftiness and strength of their ships.—He contrasted his own reputation, the maturity of his age, his experience, and his success, with the opposite circumstances in the description of his enemy. He put his officers in mind, and wished them to remind the army, that they were about to contend for the empire of the world; that great as this object was, the loss of it, if they failed, was to be the least of their sufferings; that every indignity and insult was to be expected from an enemy,[12] who on former occasions had shown himself sufficiently averse to mercy. Having addressed himself in this manner to the officers who were to be left on shore, he ordered on board all those who attended him in the character of Roman citizens, or of whose inclination to the enemy he had any suspicion, and reinforced his fleet from the land army with as many archers and slingers as could ply in the ships.

Octavius, in the mean time, having intelligence of these deliberations and counsels, and seeing the bustle which the embarkation of so many men from the land, and the movements of ships to get in their stations, occasioned, he likewise prepared for action. In his address to the officers of his fleet, he still affected to consider Cleopatra as the principal party in the war. "Antony had condescended," he said, "to become her dependent and follower, and was now preparing, not to fight, but to accompany the queen of Egypt in her flight." In respect to the conduct of the action, he was inclined to let the enemy get under sail, and even to wait until they should have turned the promontory of Actium, thinking this would be the proper time for him to attack their rear, to pursue them in their retreat, and by these means to gain the advantage and reputation of a victory, without the hazard of a battle; but being dissuaded from this design by Agrippa, he took his resolution to meet them at the mouth of the straits, and if he prevailed, was in hopes he might put them out of condition to renew the war. For this purpose he reinforced his fleet with as many men from the land as could conveniently act on board.[13]

After both fleets were in readiness, they were detained in their harbours four days by a storm, and a high sea which set into the gulph. But on the fifth day the wind having abated, and the sea becoming smooth, Antony's fleet began to form in the straits. He himself, with Poplicola, embarked with the first division on the right, Cælius on the left, and an officer, whom Plutarch names Marcus Octavius, with M. Justeius in the centre.[14] His ships being heavier and loftier, but less active than those of Octavius, he hesitated for some time whether he should not remain in close order, and endeavour to bring on the action in the narrow entrance of the gulph, where his antagonists, for want of room, could not derive any great advantage from the superior agility of their vessels, or quickness of their motions.

While Antony deliberated on this matter, Octavius got under sail, turned the headland of Toryné, and formed in a line before the entry of the straits, about a mile from the enemy. The right division was commanded by M. Larius, the left by Aruntius, the whole by Agrippa.[15] Both armies, at the same time, were drawn out on the shore to behold the event; but the fleets, for some time, did not make any movement, and it continued uncertain whether Antony, being still in the road, might not return to his anchors; but about noon his ships began to clear the straits, and came forward where the sea-room was sufficient for their line. As in this movement the fleets came closer together, Agrippa began to extend his front, in order to turn the enemy's flank; but Poplicola, on the other side, to keep pace with him, stretching to the same side, the centre of both fleets was equally opened, and they engaged soon after, without any apparent advantage on either side.

The contest, for some time, remained unde-

9 Vell. Pater. lib. ii. c. 84.
10 Ibid.
11 Plut. in Antonio.
12 Dio. Cass. lib. l. c. 15—22.
13 Dio. Cass. lib. l. c. 23—30.
14 Plutarch. in Antonio.
15 Vell. Pater. lib. ii. c. 84.

cided. In the beginning of the action, the queen of Egypt's yacht had been near to the line, and she herself continued to look on the battle, till, overcome with anxiety, affright, and horror, she gave orders to remove her galley to a greater distance, and being once in motion fled with all the sail she could make; her vessel being distinguished by a gilded poop and purple sails, made her flight be conspicuous to the whole fleet,[1] and drew away from the line about sixty ships of the Egyptian squadron, who, under pretence of attending their mistress, withdrew from the action.

Antony, apprehending the consequence of this defection, whether in despair of his fortunes, or in some hopes to rally those who fled, put on board of a quick sailing vessel, and endeavoured to overtake them. Being observed from Cleopatra's galley, he was taken on board; but no longer capable of any vigorous or rational purpose, he became the companion of her flight, without any attempt to rally her fleet. Although he quitted the chance of a victory to follow the object of his passions, he could not endure to behold her, turned his eyes aside, threw himself upon the deck, and continued in the deepest anguish of shame and despair.

The flight of Antony, joined to that of Cleopatra, an event so little expected, was not for some time observed, and the fleet, notwithstanding the desertion of their leader, continued the action till four in the afternoon, when they were overpowered; and many of them being greatly damaged in their oars and rigging, were not in condition either to resist or to escape, and fell an easy prey to the enemy. Three hundred ships were taken or sunk, and about five thousand men were killed.[2] The strand was covered with wrecks and dead bodies. Octavius detached a squadron in pursuit of such of the enemy's ships as had got to sea from the engagement, and himself continued in the channel during the remainder of the day, and the following night, to gather the fruits of his victory.[3]

The land army of Antony, having from the heights on shore beheld the ruin of their fleet, retired to their camp as with an intention to maintain it to the last extremity. They flattered themselves, that their general, though forced to yield to his enemy at sea, would make for the nearest port, and again show himself at the head of his legions. These, they said, he never should have left to commit his fortunes to an uncertain element, and a treacherous ally. In these hopes they remained for seven days unshaken in their duty, and rejected all the offers which Octavius made to induce them to change their party. Being satisfied, however, at last, that their hopes were vain, they consulted their safety in different ways. Some laid down their arms; Canidius himself, who commanded them, withdrew in the night;[4] others, remaining together in small parties, took the route to Macedonia; but, being pursued by the enemy, were separately overtaken, and forced or persuaded to surrender. All the Roman citizens, who had taken refuge in the eastern provinces, all the foreign allies and princes, who made a part of the vanquished army, successively made their peace;[5] and the empire itself now seemed to be reduced under a single head.

Antony having continued his flight by the coasts of the Peloponnesus to the head of Tenarus, without appearing to recover his courage, made a halt at this place, rather from indecision and irresolution, than from any settled purpose respecting the conduct of his affairs. Here he was joined by some ships that remained in the action to the end of it; and being informed by them, that the fleet was entirely demolished, but that the army continued firm in their camp; he seemed to be revived by this last part of the account, and despatched an order to Canidius to make the best of his way into Macedonia, and from thence to continue his march into Asia. Such of his friends as came up with him at Tenarius, he treated with his usual liberality, divided his plate and jewels among them, and gave them orders, for the supplies they might want, on the keeper of his treasure at Corinth. In performing these acts of munificence, he seemed to recover his mind, and resumed some part of his usual manner, but returning at the same time to his former habits with Cleopatra,[6] he suffered himself again to be governed by her councils; and, in compliance with her desire, steered directly for Egypt, without making any attempt to rally his forces in Greece, or to join his army, which, in reality, by this time, had been separated, or obliged to make their peace.

The victor having entirely dispersed, or gained to his own party all the forces of his rival in Europe, sent such a part of his army into Asia as was thought necessary to finish the remains of the war, and permitted the veterans, whose turn it was to be disbanded, to return into Italy. He himself, in order that he might be at hand to observe the motions of Antony, and to renew his operations in the spring, proposed to pass the winter at Samos.[7] From thence, being master of a country in which his rival had once been favourably received, he exercised his power in punishing those who had taken part against him. Many towns, by his order, were laid under heavy contributions, and deprived of their municipal privileges. All the petty princes who held their territories by grant from Antony, except Archelaus[8] and Amyntas,[9] were dispossessed. Alexander,[10] the son of Jamblichus, was not only stript of his territories, but reserved in chains to make a part in the procession of the victor's triumph; and when that ceremony should be over, was doomed to die. The principality of Lycomedes[11] was given to a certain Mede, who had deserted from Antony, and who had brought with him a considerable body of the allies. The Cydonii[12] and Lampæi, on account of their particular services, were restored to their liberties.

Of the Roman citizens of rank, who had espoused the cause of Antony, some were pardoned, some laid under heavy fines, and others put to

1 Florus, lib. iv. c. 11.

2 Plut. in Antonio. Orosius says, 12,000 were killed in battle, 6000 were wounded, of whom 1000 died under cure, lib. vi.

3 Sueton. in Octavio.

4 Plut. in Antonio.

5 Dio. Cass. lib. li. c. 1.

6 Plut. in Antonio.

7 Dio. Cass. lib. li. c. 3, 4. Sueton. in Octavio, c. 17.

8 King of Cappadocia.

9 Of Galatia. Dio. Cass. lib. xlix. c. 32.

10 A prince of Arabian extraction.

11 On the frontier of Pontus.

12 The people of certain towns of Crete.

death.[13] Among those who were pardoned, was Sosius the late consul, who had absconded for some time after the battle of Actium, and remained in concealment, until, by the intercession of his friends, he made his peace. With him likewise is mentioned M. Scaurus, the uterine brother of Sextus Pompeius, who had been condemned to die, but spared at the intercession of his mother. Among those who were put to death is mentioned Curio, the son of that Curio, who, in the steps which led to the civil war, acted for some time in support of the senate, but afterwards so effectually served the ambition of Julius Cæsar.[14]

While Antony was still possessed of the kingdom of Egypt, or had any means of renewing the war, it was thought expedient that Octavius in person should reside in Asia. The administration in Italy was committed to Mæcenas and Agrippa; the first entrusted with the civil, the other with the military department; but acting under orders and instructions from Cæsar, which, though in form addressed to the senate, were previously submitted to these ministers; and, after having received such alterations and corrections as they thought proper, were likewise intrusted to their execution.

Agrippa, as has been mentioned, having borne his part in the victory at Actium, returned into Italy with a particular charge of the veterans who were now entitled to their dismission, and to the reward of their services. He was chosen for this trust, as having sufficient authority to repress the mutinous spirit which this order of men had ever discovered as often as they were encouraged by victory to state their pretensions and to overrate their merits. The task, however, was too arduous even for the daring courage and unblemished reputation of this officer. The troops had been told, after the late action, that, on account of the state of Cæsar's finances, the reward of their services must be deferred to the end of the war; such of them as were destined to act in Asia and Egypt, acquiesced in this delay, expecting to enrich themselves in the mean time with the spoils of those opulent countries.[15] But those who were sent back into Italy, expecting such settlements in that country as the veterans had formerly received, upon their arrival laid claim to immediate satisfaction, and complained that Cæsar, in employing his lieutenants to treat with them, meant to evade their just demands.

In consequence of earnest representations from Mæcenas and Agrippa, stating these discontents of the veterans as of the most dangerous tendency, Octavius, after he had determined to fix his residence at Samos for the winter, set sail for Italy in the most tempestuous season, and in his passage was twice exposed to great danger; once in doubling the headlands of the Peloponnesus, and again near to the rocks of Acroceraunus. Being arrived at Brundusium, he was met by many of the principal citizens of Rome, with the senate and magistrates, who, having committed the government of the city to the tribunes, were come forward to receive him, and to pay their court. He likewise found the discontented veterans still at the same place, and obstinate in their purpose of not suffering themselves to be disbanded, until they should have obtained their just gratification in money and allotments of land.

Octavius, having occasion for all the arts in which he was already so well versed, now affecting to hasten what he alleged had been only delayed to a more convenient time, proceeded to make way for these mutinous troops, by dislodging many possessors of land, on pretence that they had favoured the queen of Egypt in the late war; and, in order to provide the intended gratuities in money, he pretended to offer his own estate to sale, or proposed to pledge it as security for a loan. But no man having the courage to become either his creditor or the purchaser of his estate, he represented his having made the offer as a sufficient excuse to the army for the delay which he was still obliged to make in gratifying their just requests. But the riches of Egypt, he said, now forfeited by Cleopatra, would be an ample fund for the gratification of those who forebore their demands for the present, to have them more fully complied with hereafter.[16] Having, by these means, pacified the clamours of those who were most urgent; and having been, during his stay at Brundusium, vested a fourth time with the titles and ensigns of consul, he set sail again for the coast of Asia, with intention to give Antony and Cleopatra as little time as possible to recollect themselves, or to reinstate their affairs.

U. C. 723.

Imp. Cæs. 4to. M. Licinius Crassus, ex Kal. Jul. C. Antistius Vitus, ex Id. Sept. M. Tul. Cicero, ex Kal. Nov. L. Junius.

These unfortunate adventurers, whose arrival at the point of Tenarus has been mentioned, steered from thence for the coast of Africa, and parted from each other near to Paretonium, a sea-port of Lybia, which had been held by the kings of Egypt, as a barrier at some distance beyond the western frontier of their kingdom. In the neighbourhood of this place, Antony expected to be received by Pinarius Scarpus, whom he had placed at the head of his forces in that quarter.[17] But this officer, from whatever person he may have received his appointment, or however he may have been inclined, while the triumvirs divided the empire, was now, by the event of the battle of Actium, sufficiently determined in the choice of his party. He had declared for Octavius, and now ordered the messengers of Antony, and all the officers under his own command, who were disposed to enter into any correspondence with the vanquished party, to be put to death.

Upon this disappointment, Antony relapsed into his former melancholy, proposed to kill himself, and was prevented only by the persuasion of a few friends, who earnestly entreated him to try his fortunes once more, at the head of the forces of Egypt.[18]

Cleopatra, in order to outrun the news of her disaster, and to prevent the disorders that might attend the fall of her authority, made all possible haste into her own dominions. When her ships came in sight, she hoisted the ensigns of victory,

13 Dio. Cass. lib. li. c. 2. Ibid.
15 Ibid. c. 3, 4.

16 Dio. Cass. lib. li. c. 4.
17 Ibid. c. 5. Plut. in Antonio, p. 136. Both these writers seem to understand that Pinarius Scarpus had belonged to Antony, and deserted from him on this occasion.
18 Plut. in Antonio, p. 136, 4to. edit. Lond. ann 1724. Dio. Cass. lib. li. c. 5.

and entered the harbour of Alexandria with shouts of joy and triumph. Upon her landing, she gave an order to cut off, or to secure, some persons of whose affections she was doubtful, and then acknowledging the event of her late unfortunate expedition, took measures for the defence of her kingdom. Under pretence of collecting money for this purpose, she seized the effects of corporations and of private persons, and stript the temples of their ornaments and of their treasures. But, having still upon her mind all the impressions of her late defeat, she rather looked for a retreat, to which she might fly with the money she amassed, than for a station at which to withstand her enemy. Under these impressions, she formed a project to have her fleet dragged over land, from the Nile to the gulph of Arabia, and ordered ships to be built in the ports of that sea, trusting that her enemy could not, for some time, be in condition to molest her with any naval armament in that quarter.

After this project began, in part, to be executed, the Arabs, apprehending some danger to themselves, from the preparations which appeared to be making on their coasts, demolished the docks which the queen of Egypt had ordered to be fitted up, plundered her stores, and destroyed the ships which she had already built; so that she was reduced to the necessity of making her defence on the Nile, and of abiding the fate which threatened her country from this side.[1]

She had heard of Cæsar's having gone back into Italy; and from this circumstance, as well as from the difficulties of a winter navigation round the coasts of Greece, both she and Antony thought themselves secure for that season. In this, however, they were disappointed by the activity and resolution of their enemy, who, having lost no time unnecessarily, had, in order to avoid the difficulties of the winter navigation, ordered some galleys to be dragged over land at the isthmus of Corinth; and by this means, while he was yet believed to be beyond the sea of Ionia, was actually well advanced in his voyage to the Nile.[2] His plan was to invade the kingdom of Egypt on two sides at once; at Paretonium, on the side of Africa, by an army under the command of Cornelius Gallus; and at Pelusium, on the side of Syria, with an army which he himself was to command.[3]

Antony, upon his return to Alexandria, with the mortification of having been rejected by the Roman legions that were stationed on the frontier of the province of Africa, thinking it might strengthen his own party against that of Octavius, to point out an immediate offspring of the Julian family, and a succession of leaders to the party of Cæsar, declared Cæsarion, the reputed son of Julius Cæsar by Cleopatra, to be now of age, and qualified to enter upon the inheritance of his father. But while he exasperated Octavius by this species of personal insult, he appeared incapable of any rational plan of defence for himself or the kingdom he occupied. He even absented himself from the councils that were held on this subject, declined any share in the management of affairs, and withdrew from the palace.

While Antony continued in this humour, he was joined by Canidius, the late commander of his land forces at Actium. From this officer he had the melancholy account, that all his armies in Greece were dispersed; that Herod, the king of Judea, had declared against him, and all the princes he had lately placed upon different thrones in Asia had either followed this example, or been displaced; that he had not any possession, nor any certain friend beyond the limits of Egypt. Upon receiving this account, he seemed to recover from his melancholy, and acquired that species of ease which results from despair. He left his retreat, returned to the palace, and, with Cleopatra, gave himself up to dissipation, profusion, and continual riot. They formed parties of pleasure, consisting of such persons as professed their resolution to die rather than to fall into the hands of the enemy.[4] Antony had an officer retained to put a period to his life in the supposed extremity in which this choice was to be made, and Cleopatra had a collection of poisons for the same purpose.

In the midst of this seeming indifference to life, both the queen and her lover, however, submitted at times to make advances to Cæsar, and to sue for mercy. They despatched their messengers together; but as Cleopatra sent, on her own account, presents of a crown, a sceptre, and a throne of gold, and privately instructed her agent to sound the disposition of Cæsar with respect to herself, this crafty politician perceived that she wished to be considered apart from Antony, and encouraged her to hope for a separate treaty. While he made no reply to Antony, and in public insisted that Cleopatra herself should surrender at discretion, he, in private, encouraged the queen to hope for better terms, and even to imagine what he supposed her willing to believe, that she might still make some impression on his mind by the charms of her person.

As Octavius had an agent at the court of Egypt to insinuate these hopes, and to cultivate the disposition which the queen had shown to a separate treaty, Antony became jealous of the frequent conferences to which this agent was admitted, and ordered him to be whipped, and expelled from the court. Sensible, however, of the enormity of this outrage, he wrote to Octavius soon after to make an apology. "My misfortunes," he said, "have made me peevish, and this fellow had provoked me; but you may take your revenge on the person of my agent, who is with you." In the subsequent part of this letter he put Octavius in mind of their former intimacy, of their near relation, of their parties of pleasure, or rather debaucheries; and observed, that his frolics with Cleopatra did not deserve to be more seriously treated, than affairs of the same kind in which they had passed some idle hours together. He, at the same time, delivered up P. Turvilius, a Roman senator, who had been supposed accessary to the death of Julius Cæsar, and who had, for some time, been attached to himself; and he concluded his letter with some expressions of magnanimity, saying, that he was willing to die, provided he could obtain any favourable terms for the queen of Egypt.[5]

Octavius, however, continued inexorable; and urging his military operations on both frontiers

1 Dio. Cass. lib. li. c. 7. Zonaras, lib. x. c. 33.
2 Dio. Cass. lib. li. c. 5. 3 Orosius, lib. vi.
4 Plut. in Antonio. 5 Dio. Cass. lib. li. c. 9.

of the kingdom of Egypt, got possession of Pelusium and of Paretonium; of the first, it was said, in consequence of his intrigues with Cleopatra, and by her connivance; of the second, by the entire defection of the troops which Antony nad stationed for the defence of the place, and who now became an accession to the army of his rival.

Cleopatra, as if sensible of the suspicions she had incurred on the surrender of Pelusium, and desirous to recover the confidence of Antony, doubled her attention to his person, kept the anniversary of his birth-day with unusual splendour; and, to remove any suspicion of her having connived at the loss of Pelusium, delivered up the officer of the name of Seleucus, who had surrendered that place, that he might atone for his treachery by a suitable punishment.

Antony, observing the progress which his enemy made on the frontiers of the kingdom, and being weary of the project of ending his life in a riot, took a better resolution, and mustering what forces he could, both by sea and by land, was determined to try the fortune of a war, or to die, at least, sword in hand. When the enemy advanced to Alexandria, he attacked their cavalry, and put them to flight. Encouraged by his success in this encounter, he ordered all his forces to assemble on the first of August.[6] On this day he proposed to bring the contest to a decision at once, both by sea and by land:[7] but the Egyptian fleet being ordered to begin the action, struck their colours, and surrendered hemselves without a blow. The cavalry, at the same time, deserted to the enemy; and the infantry being routed, fled into the city.

Upon this dispersion of all his forces, Antony complained, that he was betrayed, and was heard to accuse the queen. This unhappy author of his misfortunes had taken refuge, during the action, with a few attendants, in the monument which, upon a plan of great magnificence, was then recently built for a royal sepulchre. Thither she had already transported all her jewels, money, and most valuable effects. The access of the place was contrived to be shut from within, in such a manner as not to be opened without great labour.[8] It was given out, that the queen had retired in order to kill herself at he tomb, in which she was to be buried; and soon after, the report was spread that she was actually dead.

Antony, being now arrived at the end of all his hopes, and of his efforts, made haste to follow the supposed example of the queen, and gave his sword, for this purpose, to Eros, a freed slave, who had promised to use it when required in the last action of friendship to his master; but Eros unable to fulfil his promise, instead of killing his master, plunged the sword into his own bosom. Antony then snatching the weapon, wounded himself; but not expiring immediately, he was told, as he lay bleeding, that Cleopatra was yet alive, and safe in the monument. Seeming to revive at these tidings, he gave directions that he should be carried to her presence. Upon his coming, she appeared on the battlements, but under pretence that she feared a surprise, refused to have the gates unbarred, and made it necessary to have him towed over the walls. Although she had wished to disengage herself from this unfortunate man, and had even submitted to betray him, now when she saw him laid at her feet expiring,[9] and covered with his blood, she beat her breast, and tore her hair in the agonies of real suffering, mixed with the affectation of pre tended passion.

Antony, having somewhat in his mind which he wished to express, called for wine, recovered strength enough to utter a few words, and expired:[10] thus ending his life in the fifty-third, or, according to others, in the fifty-sixth year of his age;[11] disposed even in the last scenes of it, to occupy the intervals of relaxation in riot and debauchery; and verifying, in all the steps of his manhood and age, the charge of extravagance and profligacy, which marked his youth, and his first appearances in public affairs. He was possessed of talents for the council and the field, which he never exerted for any valuable purpose, or rather never exerted at all, except when he was pressed by the most urgent necessity of his situation. Under this pressure, indeed, he sometimes repaired by his industry and vigour the breaches which were made by his dissipation or neglect. In consequence of his connexion with Julius Cæsar, and of the place he gained among the military factions, which endeavoured to engross or to divide his power, he was tempted to consider the Roman empire itself as the scene of his pleasures; and, in aiming at the sovereignty of the world, experienced those reverses which fully displayed the versatility and instability of his own character. But he fell, at last, deserted by every Roman citizen who had ever been attached to his interest; betrayed by that person to whose caprices chiefly he sacrificed his fortunes, and under the fatal experience, that the utmost efforts of resolution, incited by the sense of extreme necessity, will not always retrieve the errors of past dissipation and folly.

When Antony gave himself the wound of which he died, one of his attendants, extracting the dagger from his body, ran with it to Octavius, who seeing the weapon stained with blood, and being told what had passed, perhaps in imitation of Julius Cæsar, who is said to have wept for the death of Pompey, was observed to shed tears.[12] Suetonius reports, that he afterwards desired to see the body.[13]

Cleopatra, as soon as the scene in the monument was over, and she had recollected herself, sent an intimation of Antony's death to Cæsar, and then probably indulged her hopes, that the great obstacle to her peace being removed, she might obtain that consideration for her separate interests, which Octavius, by insinuations, or expressions of civility, had given her cause to expect.

After the late contest was in a great measure decided, the victor continued to encourage the queen of Egypt to hope for a separate treaty; and amused her with civilities, while he endeavoured to inform himself of her treasure, and to make sure of her as a captive to adorn his triumph, a circumstance esteemed of the highest importance at Rome; but he had avoided coming un-

6 Orosius, lib. vi. p. 268. 7 Dio. Cass. lib. li. c. 10.
8 Plut. in Antonio.
9 Dio. Cass. lib. li. c. 10. 10 Zonar. lib. x. c. 30.
11 Plut. in Antonio. 12 Ibid.
13 Sueton in Octav. c. 17.

der any engagements that should preclude him from the full use of his victory. Upon receiving her message, he sent Caius Procu'eius, a Roman knight, and Epaphroditus, an emancipated slave, to sooth her fears, to administer comfort, and if possible, without stipulating any conditions, to secure her person.

What Octavius chiefly apprehended from the unfortunate queen, was some violent attempt on her own life. His emissaries, therefore, having suffered her, at her own earnest request, to remain where she was until the funeral of Antony should be over, they made a strict search, in order to remove from her hands every weapon, or supposed instrument of death; and, under pretence of doing her honour, placed a guard on the monument. They prevailed upon her afterwards to remove to the palace, where she was attended with the usual state and dignity of a sovereign.[1] But being still kept at a distance from Cæsar, and in suspense with respect to his intentions, she expressed great anxiety, and seemed to meditate some desperate purpose. In order to divert her from any fatal resolution, which might deprive Cæsar's triumph of a principal ornament, she was told, that he consented to see her, and was to make her a visit in her own apartments. Upon this intimation, she ordered the chambers to be fitted up in the most elegant manner, and decorated, in particular, with the picture and bust of Julius Cæsar.—When the expected visit of Octavius was to be paid, she took care to have bundles of the late Cæsar's letters and memorials before her. She herself was dressed in mourning, which she knew was supposed, at all times, to become her, and which, on this occasion, might give an expression of tender melancholy that rendered her person and her state more affecting. When Octavius presented himself she rose from her couch; but as if overawed by his presence, with an air of modesty and dejection, fixed her eyes on the ground. In accosting him she called him Master. "To his father," she said, "she owed all her fortunes, and now willingly resigned them to the son. The memory of the great Julius should be a sufficient comfort in all her afflictions; she would even consider him as revived in the person of his son. But would to God," she said, bursting into tears, "that I had died before him, so should I have escaped the evils which his death, and the consequences of it have brought upon me!" Octavius bid her be of good courage; and assured her, that no hurt was intended her. But she, observing that he spoke these words with coldness, and turned his eyes away, threw herself upon the ground in agonies of despair. "I neither wish," she said, "nor can I continue to live. I should have died when Cæsar fell; and there is another now who calls upon me to follow him; suffer me to rest with him on whose account I die."[2]

This interview concluded with a request on the part of the queen, that she might be allowed to perform the obsequies of Antony, to which she proceeded with all the appearances of an affectionate widow in the deepest affliction; but, as there is no doubt that she had betrayed the person whom she now appeared so much to lament, it is probable that her tears, though pretended to be shed on account of the dead, were in reality, directed to move and to win his surviving rival. She still trusted to the effects of her beauty, and was, in her present situation, what she had been in the most serious councils of state, a mere coquette, who being naturally disposed to violent passions, could personate any character, or turn her real passions to account in serving any disguised purpose of vanity or ambition.

The scene which Cleopatra acted on the present occasion, in whatever degree she was possessed by real or affected despair, had no other effect on Octavius, than to make him redouble his intention to prevent any attempt which she might intend to make against her own life. Epaphroditus had orders to watch her with great diligence; a circumstance from which she had the sagacity to infer a fixed determination to carry her as a captive to Rome. She was soon confirmed in her suspicions; having intelligence that Octavius himself, being to march by land, had given orders that she, with her children, should be sent into Italy by sea. Equally anxious to avoid being led in triumph, as the victor was desirous to preserve her for this purpose, she instantly took measures to end her life. But in order to elude the vigilance of her keeper, she affected to be resigned to her fate, gave an inventory, and delivered up all her effects, reserving only a few jewels, which she professed an intention to deliver with her own hands, in presents, to Livia and Octavia. She even affected to dress in her usual gay and sumptuous manner; and pretending to have some business of consequence to communicate to Cæsar, she gave Epaphroditus a letter, and charged him to deliver it with his own hands. It contained expressions of exultation at having obtained her end, and having escaped from her enemies.

Octavius, on seeing this letter, instantly gave orders to prevent what he apprehended was her purpose; but the queen, at the arrival of the messenger, was already dead, and laid upon a couch of state. One of the women, who usually attended her, was likewise dead; the other was expiring; but while the messenger of Octavius was entering the chamber, observing that the crown had fallen from her mistress's head, she made an effort, with what strength she had left, to replace it. No mark of violence appeared on the body of the queen, except a small puncture in her arm; and she was therefore supposed to have died of a venomous bite, or of a scratch with a poisoned instrument. To render the last of these conjectures the more probable, it was said, that she always carried a pin in her hair the point of which was tainted with poison. She was now at the age of nine-and-thirty years, and of these had lived fourteen years with Antony.

Octavius, being disappointed of his design to lead the queen of Egypt as a captive in his triumph, had her effigy, with an aspick fixed upon the arm, fabricated to supply her place in the procession. He no longer kept any measures with her family or kingdom. Cæsarion, her son, supposed by Julius Cæsar, and of course a pretended heir to Cæsar's fortunes, had too high pretensions to be spared; endeavouring to make his escape into Ethiopia, he was taken in his flight, and killed. Antyllas, the son of Antony

1 Dio. Cass. lib. li. c 10. 2 Ibid. xli. c 2.

by Fulvia, being of an age to receive impressions which might render him dangerous, was likewise sacrificed to the safety of the conqueror. He had taken refuge at the shrine of Julius Cæsar, but was forced from thence, and slain. The other children, whether of Cleopatra or of Antony, were spared, and honourably treated. Those of the latter, by Octavia, being near relations of Cæsar, and afterwards intermarried with the reigning family, left a posterity who succeeded to the empire.[1]

Among the partizans of the vanquished party who were ordered for execution, only two or three Romans of note are mentioned: Canidius, who had commanded the land forces of Antony at Actium, and who still adhered to him in the wreck of his fortunes; Cassius Parmensis, a man of letters and a poet, who had been attached to Brutus and Cassius, but, having employed his wit against Octavius, was received by Antony, and lived with him in great intimacy; and Ovinius, who, having been a Roman senator, is said to have degraded himself by taking charge of the manufactures which were carried on in the palace of the queen of Egypt.

In limiting the severity of his executions to these examples, Octavius appeared greatly to restrain the cruelty which he had formerly exercised against his enemies; he, at the same time, gave proofs of his munificence, by releasing all those who were in custody at Alexandria, whether as prisoners of state, as captives, or hostages from foreign nations.[2]

1 Sueton. in Octav. c. 17. Dio. Cass. lib. li. c. 19. Plut. in Antonio.

2 Orosius, p. 269. Vell. Pater. lib. ii. c. 87

THE

HISTORY

OF

THE PROGRESS AND TERMINATION

OF THE

ROMAN REPUBLIC.

BOOK VI.

CHAPTER I.

The Merit or Demerit of Parties in the latter Period of the Roman Republic—Return of Octavius to Rome—His Triumphs and public Entertainments—Reform of the Army—Proposition to resign his Power—Consultation of Agrippa and Mæcenas—Preludes to the pretended Resignation of Octavius—His Speech in the Senate—His Consent to retain a part in the Government of the Empire—Distribution of the Provinces—Title of Augustus—The Establishment of Augustus.

ALTHOUGH, in compiling this history, it has been intended to avoid expressions of mere praise and blame, other than are contained in the detail of facts and specification of characters; and to state, in every instance, the transaction itself, rather than the judgment of the writer; yet it is hoped that where questions of merit or demerit are in any considerable degree problematical, and where readers are likely to take opposite sides, he too may be indulged in some general discussion.

U. C. 620.
U. C. 723.

We may suppose the Roman republic to have been hastening to its ruin from the sedition of Tiberius Gracchus, to the time on which we are now entered. A great revolution has been so long in dependence, and more blood has been shed in an age of boasted learning and politeness, than perhaps has been known to flow in any equal period of the most barbarous times.

In judging of those who were concerned in this transaction, we may form our opinions now upon speculative considerations, as they themselves joined their party from motives of interest, ambition, or public virtue. Although it be allowed that, in point of justice, we must give a preference to those who endeavoured to preserve the constitution of their country, and who acted merely in defence of themselves and their fellow-citizens; yet in this instance it will be alleged, that the event has had the effect of an experiment, to show that what they strove to perform was impracticable, and that notwithstanding the justice of their cause, the circumstances of the times were such as to have rendered their success not only desperate, but in a great measure inexpedient. They were born to a republic, it is true; but the people who were destined to govern in that republic could no longer be safely intrusted with government; and to contend for such a trust in behalf of men who were unworthy of it, was a dangerous error, for which the best intentions could not atone. Even the Roman senate itself could not supply all the exigencies of government over a dominion of such extent, and containing so many sources of corruption. Its own members were degenerated, and fallen from the virtue of their ancestors. They were trained up in a luxury at home, which was to be supplied by the most cruel rapacity abroad, in the provinces. Such an empire could be preserved only by the force and prompt executions of despotism. The change therefore from republic to monarchy, it may be alleged, was seasonable; and Cato, with Cicero, Brutus, and all the other partizans of the commonwealth, actuated by a mistaken, though commendable zeal for liberty, would have supported their fellow-citizens in their pretensions to government after they were unworthy of it; in this attempt they fell a necessary sacrifice to their own error; and in their ruin made way for an establishment better fitted to the condition of the age, and to the character of the people, than that for which they contended and bled.

In this manner of stating the subject, we lay the task of vindicating their own conduct on those who endeavoured to preserve, not upon those who destroyed, the republic. But in judging of the merits of men in so distant a scene, we must not proceed on conceptions drawn from the experience of subsequent ages, on our own predilection for monarchy in general, or even on our judgment of its expedience in that particular case; we must suppose ourselves in the situation of those who acted, and who, in the result of this contest, from the condition of equals, were to become master and servant, or lord and vassal. One party strove that they should be masters, the other that they themselves should not be slaves. The latter contended for the rights, which, together with their fellow-citizens, they had inherited, as Romans; they endeavoured to preserve the manners, as well as the institutions, of their country, against the destroyers of both. The other party, at first, under pretence of zeal for higher measures of popular government than those they enjoyed, endeavoured to corrupt the people whom they meant to enslave; and having, upon plausible pretences, got possession of the sword, they turned it against the established government of their country. Neither of those parties, probably, stated the speculative question which we may now be inclined to discuss, whether republic or monarchy was best accommodated to the Roman state in the height of its dominion, and in the full tide of luxury?

The wise, the courageous, and the just alone are entitled to power; the innocent alone are entitled to freedom. But they who are not conscious of having forfeited their right to either, are undoubtedly justifiable in persisting to maintain it. The virtuous who resign their freedom, at the same time resign their virtue, or at least yield up that condition which is required to preserve it. Citizens who were born to inherit this condition, and who had the courage to harbour and to cherish that elevation of mind which belongs to it, were entitled to maintain for themselves the post of honour to the last, and must for ever receive from those who respect integrity and magnanimity the tribute of esteem, even of tenderness, which is due to their memory.

If ever there was a body of men fit to govern the world, it was the Roman senate, composed of citizens who had passed through the higher offices of state, who had studied the affairs of their country in the execution of its councils, and in the command of its armies; and it will for ever be remembered, in behalf of those who wished to preserve its authority, that if their removal from the scene on which they acted was expedient or seasonable, it was so because that scene was become unworthy of their presence.

Some of the characters, indeed, that appeared in this cause, may require a separate treatment. In that of Cato, virtue was the result of a decisive and comprehensive reflection. To him rectitude of conduct was in itself, without regard to consequences, the supreme object of desire and pursuit. His penetration, as well as courage, in the early endeavours he made, and in the manly steadiness with which he persisted to oppose the designs of Cæsar and Pompey, while others wavered, and either did not perceive their intention, or tamely submitted to them, gave him a striking superiority over his contemporaries.[1] He is represented by Cicero, in some instances, as retaining his inflexibility, when some degree of compliance was more likely to preserve the republic. The same censure has been repeated by others; but Cato was present to the scene, had no by-views to mislead him, and there is not any reason to prefer the judgment of those who censure him to his own. Cicero temporised, made the experiment of what compliance on some occasions could effect, and even flattered himself that he had gained the affections of Cæsar and Pompey to the republic, by giving way to the arts which they employed to destroy it.

The fellow-sufferers of Cato in the same cause of the republic, were persons of a different character from himself. To him virtue was the end, to them it was the means which they employed for the attainment of their end, and they measured advantages by the success of their pursuits. Cato possessed independence in the courage and resolution of his own mind; they sought for it in the institutions of their country; they wished to preserve their own rights, and would yield them to no individual or set of men whatever. This character is indeed in a high degree meritorious; no more is required to form an excellent citizen, and no more was required but the prevalence or frequency of such a character at Rome to have preserved, and even to have reformed, that sickly and perishing constitution of government.

The natural antidote of vice is restraint and correction; but in great disorders, and where the system itself is corrupted, what is applied for a remedy is sometimes an evil, as well as the disease. They who peruse the history of Rome, under the continued effects of a revolution, which is now accomplished or fast approaching, will find no cause to congratulate the world, on its having escaped from the factions of Clodius and Milo, to incur the evils that arose under Caius and Nero.

The impossibility of preserving the republic, or its unfitness to remain at the head of so great an empire, is no doubt the most plausible excuse which is made for its subversion; but this apology neither Cæsar nor Pompey was entitled to make for himself. Cæsar affected a zeal for popular government, and Pompey strove to inflame all its evils, in order to render himself necessary to the aristocracy. Cæsar fomented political troubles, in order to weaken the hands of the senate, or in order to find a pretence to make war upon them; and at last, under the show of releasing the people from the tyranny of that body, drew that sword with which he accomplished the ruin of both.

The senate indeed had many difficulties to encounter; that of protecting the provinces from oppression, in which many of their own members were concerned; that of restraining the tumults and disorders of a licentious people, led by different factions, desirous of change, or im-

1 The impression of Cato's character remained so deep with posterity, as well as with the immediate witnesses of his conduct, that no authority on the part of those who wished to traduce him had any effect. It is remarkable, that even the authority of the Cæsars did not silence those who in other instances submitted to flatter them, nor prevent their joining in the praises of Cato. Virgil and Horace, though courtiers, could not be restrained on this subject. Vid. Æneid. lib. viii. ver. 670. Hor. lib. i. od. 12. He was revered, it has been said, rather as a good than as a great man; but mankind do not revere without an opinion of great ability, as well as benevolent intention. Vid Lord Bolingbroke's Patriot King.

patient of government; and that of conducting a pretended popular assembly, in whom the legislation and sovereignty of the empire was nominally vested. It is, however, difficult to judge now far so able a council, while they themselves remained in any degree uncorrupted, might not have found antidotes, or at least temporary expedients, to resist every other evil, if they had not been so ably attacked as they were by the first Cæsar and Pompey, who joined interests together, to break down the defences of a fortress, which they afterwards severally intended to occupy.

The ordinary train of affairs at Rome; the substitution of tumults for regular assemblies of the people; the practice of committing the provinces, with so many resources, and the command of such armies, with so little control, to the discretion of ambitious citizens; the dangerous powers which accompanied the higher offices of state, without any check upon those who were inclined to abuse those powers, the easy recourse which persons of dangerous pretensions, when rejected by the senate, had to popular riots, under the denomination of Comitia, or Assemblies of the People, made the destruction of the commonwealth in some measure necessary.

With such citizens as the Gracchi, as Apuleius, as Marius and Cinna, Clodius and Milo, it was difficult to preserve a republic; but with such citizens as Cæsar and Pompey, it was altogether impossible; or rather the republic may be considered as at an end from the time it was in their power to dispose of it.

The first class of these adventurers were misled by their passions, or fell into the vices of their situation. They endeavoured to rule by popular tumults or military force, and when they could not pervert the ordinary forms of the state to their purpose, employed violence to set them aside; but even in this, by their mutual opposition, they preserved a kind of balance, in which the freedom of the commonwealth seemed to remain.

Pompey and Cæsar promoted systematically all the evils to which their country was exposed. They had recourse to the populace for grants which the senate refused; they prolonged the term of provincial appointments, which were sufficiently dangerous, however short; they united together powers that were sufficiently dangerous when separate; united the command of armies in the provinces with the authority of office at Rome; and, instead of suspending the fate of the commonwealth by their mutual obstructions to each other, hastened its ruin by concerting together their measures against it; leaving the decision of their respective claims, till after they had rendered the republic a necessary prey to the one or the other.

Pompey for some time thought himself in actual possession of the monarchy; Cæsar, in the mean time, provided the most effectual means to ravish it from him. To state the difficulty of preserving the republic in such hands, as an excuse for their having destroyed it, were to offer the character of criminals as an excuse for their crimes. When the highwaymen are abroad, the traveller must be robbed; but this is not an excuse for the crime. Cæsar and Pompey are blamed, not because the republic had an end, but because they themselves were the evils by which it perished.

The necessity of submitting, at least for a time, to the government of single men, had been repeatedly experienced by the Romans, and was so in the highest degree at the times to which these observations refer; but this will not justify the pretensions of every profligate person who may affect to place himself in the station of sovereign. If upon this ground Cato and Brutus were to be blamed for resisting the power of Cæsar; the last, in his turn, must be blamed for resisting the power of Pompey and other citizens, in their respective ages, for rejecting the advances which were made by Marius, Cinna, Catiline, and other profligate adventurers, who attempted to place themselves at the head of the empire.

Of the two Cæsars, the first possessed the talent of influencing, of gaining, and employing men to his purpose, beyond any other person that is known in the history of the world; but it is surely not for the good of mankind that he should be admired in other respects. To admire even his clemency, is to mistake policy and cunning for humanity. The second Cæsar, in the part which he acted against the republic, is in many respects more excusable than the first. He entered the scene when the piece was much farther advanced, when his countrymen had submitted to monarchy, under the title of a perpetual dictatorship, and when he himself was considered as the heir of a person who had possessed this pre-eminence. He was therefore at least nearer to the condition of an hereditary prince, who may be allowed to consider sovereignty as his birthright, and who, however he may be disposed to promote the good of mankind, has a right to maintain his own station, and may be supposed to acquit himself sufficiently of his duty, by making a proper use of his power, without being under any obligation to resign it, or to admit of improper encroachments upon the estate to which he is born.

The first Cæsar strove against those who endeavoured to preserve their own rights and those of their country; the second, although he succeeded to the same quarrel, and actually paid no respect to the republic, more than was necessary to cover his design against it, yet appears, more than the first, in the light of a person who strove only with the rivals of his own ambition, and with his competitors for the succession of his uncle and adoptive father, who, having declared him the heir of his fortune, gave him a pretence to support the pre-eminence he himself had gained.

This apology, nevertheless, though more powerful in its application to the case of the second Cæsar than to that of the first, is very imperfect in its application to either. If Octavius had been educated under any impressions of hereditary right to the sovereignty of the Roman republic, the fate of the person from whom he derived his supposed right, and the subsequent, though temporary, re-establishment of the commonwealth, which he witnessed, and which he pretended to approve, were sufficient to have undeceived him, and to have taught him the part which he had to act as a Roman citizen, and the modesty with which he ought to have waited for the legal age and the constitutional election, in order to obtain those offices of state to which, in common with the other citizens of Rome, his condition no doubt highly entitled him.

Octavius, however, is not perhaps to be tried so much in the capacity of a Roman citizen born to the republic, as in that of leader of a party, born at a time when the competition for superiority was general, and when sovereignty or death were the alternatives to be chosen by persons of such rank and pretensions as his own. In this capacity he affected what his grand-uncle and adoptive father had taught him to aim at; the suppression of civil government, and the removal of all his own competitors for power.

As Pompey, with Cato and the principal supporters of the senate had sunk under the first Cæsar, so Brutus, Cassius, and the other restorers of the commonwealth, with the last of the family of Pompey, sunk under Octavius, Antony, and Lepidus; and the two last, in their turn, having sunk under Octavius, this successful adventurer now remains sole commander of all the armies of the republic, and sole master of all its provinces, from the banks of the Euphrates to the sea of Britain. And the contest for this mighty sovereignty being now at least decided, it remains that we observe what new form the world is to receive under the dominion of its master, or what mighty harvest is to be reaped by him who is in possession of the field, and who is now enabled to gather what so many heroes had sown or planted, and what so many pretenders to the same object would have ravished or torn from each other.

This able adventurer having, in other situations, conducted his affairs with so much discretion, as well as enterprise, continued in his present elevation to exercise the same profitable virtues. In the severities which he had formerly practised against those who opposed him, there was sufficient evidence of a cruel and sanguinary nature,[1] and it were monstrous to suppose that the murders which were perpetrated by his order, or with his consent, could be justified by the necessity of affairs in which his engaging at all was criminal. But as the horror of Sylla's cruelties, still remaining in the minds of the people, was a great bar to the success of any similar usurpation, and suggested to Julius Cæsar, in the beginning of his career, an opposite course of clemency and mercy; so the fate of this last adventurer, who, after having shown mercy to many of his opponents, fell at last by the hands of those he had spared, probably suggested to the triumvirate the necessity of securing themselves before they affected the reputation of mercy, and, as we shall see, suggested to this heir of Cæsar the caution not to affront, so directly as the other had done, that republican spirit, whose effects he had occasion to dread.

Octavius, though inferior to his uncle in the capacity of a soldier, being equally master of every necessary artifice, had recourse to the use of clemency when it suited the state of his affairs. His steps became gradually less bloody, from the first fatal proscription to the last victory which he obtained over Antony; and in this he reversed the order that was observed by the first Cæsar, beginning to affect moderation in a period of the war, corresponding to that in which the military executions of the other were observed to have become more decisive and bloody.

In the whole management of the contest with Antony, Octavius had conducted himself with a singular address. Stating himself as a Roman consul, merely, he discontinued the power of triumvir in his own person, in order to strip his antagonist likewise of that character. To avoid appearances which might divide any part of the Roman people against him, he overlooked Antony entirely in the pretended quarrel with the queen of Egypt, or he affected to consider him as a person under some fatal delusion, and in hazard of becoming a traitor to his own country, from his attachment to a stranger and an artful woman. The war was declared against the queen of Egypt alone, and, like any other foreign war, was undertaken by Octavius in the capacity of Roman consul, and with an observance of all the usual forms of the commonwealth.

Octavius was remarkable for employing disguises, which, though too thin to conceal the truth, furnished his own party, at least, with a pretence for supporting him, and considerably helped him forwards in the execution of all his designs. Affecting to be no more than consul, or ordinary magistrate, he exercised the power of a master, or military usurper, in the western provinces; and hastened, by the reduction of Egypt, and the suppression of his rivals who had taken refuge in that kingdom, to make himself equally sovereign in the east. In the absence of this consul the affairs of state in the capital were not permitted, as usual, to devolve on his nominal colleague, nor, in the absence of both consuls, to devolve on the officer that was next in rank; but were in the hands of Mæcenas, a person known for the minister or confidant of Octavius, without any other rank or title of office in the commonwealth. These circumstances were sufficient to discredit the professions which he continued to make of his zeal for the constitution of the republic; but when it is convenient for parties to be deceived, they shut their eyes upon every circumstance which tends to expose the deception.

It was not indeed necessary at present that the people should be imposed upon, in order to enable the head of the army to reign with an absolute sway in Italy and over all the western provinces. As the troops who were actually under arms looked forward to their general for future provisions and settlements, so the veterans then established in the country, looked up to him as the guardian of their property, and considered his power as the principal security of what they possessed. If it were necessary, in this case, to preserve the appearances of civil government, in order to conciliate the minds of the citizens, it was equally necessary to preserve the reality of absolute power, in order to gratify the army, and in order to continue to the veterans the principal security by which they held their lands. And this wary politician accommodated himself with uncommon discernment, to the feelings or prejudices of both.

The superior address of Octavius, in the contest with Antony, gave continual presages of victory on his side; and from the beginning of the war to its final decision at Actium, and to the last close of the scene in Egypt, partizans were continually passing from the losing to the

1 See the History of the Proscription, and his attendance at the sacrifices or executions done at Perusia. Sueton. in Octav. c. 15.

winning side. Upon the reduction of Egypt, the victor, though pretending to act in the capacity of Roman consul, did not, as in former times, refer to the senate the arrangements to be made in his conquest; nor did he wait the formality of a commission from Rome, authorising him to settle the provinces. He named a governor, and gave orders for the repair of all the public works, which, on account of their effect in distributing the inundations of the Nile, made, in that kingdom, a great and important object of state, and by their being neglected in the late troubles, had occasioned much distress.

The kingdom of Egypt was a principal granary for the supply of Italy, and it is probable that its consequence had been severely felt in the late interruption of its exports. Octavius therefore took measures to secure his possession of a country, by which he observed that the state of Italy and the capital of the empire might be greatly affected. He deprived the Egyptians of all the forms of their monarchy; and, in order to efface the memory of their national independence, and to discontinue pretensions which the inhabitants of Alexandria used to support by tumults and revolts, he abolished all their public assemblies and national councils. He forbade the resort of Egyptian nobles to Rome, and of Roman senators to Egypt. As there was reason to apprehend that there might still exist, under the ruins of this late opulent monarchy, or under the remains of Antony's party there, some sparks of fire which the ambition or intrigues of any considerable partizan might kindle into a flame, he chose for governor Cornelius Gallus, a person of equestrian rank and moderate pretensions, not likely to harbour ambitious designs; and made it a rule to have similar qualifications in future governors, and to perpetuate the other parts of an establishment which he now made, for the preservation of so important a territory, and the government of so factious a people.

While Octavius made these arrangements in Egypt, he secured a great treasure, of which a considerable part was found in the coffers of the late queen, and part arose from the contributions which he himself imposed on the city of Alexandria and other parts of the kingdom. And being, from these funds, prepared to acquit himself of the pecuniary engagements he had come under to the army, and enabled to make donations to the populace of Rome, whose favour was necessary for him in the farther prosecution of his designs, he set out on his return to Italy; but having stopped in the island of Samos, while the army in separate divisions was moving to the westward, he passed the winter at this place, deferring his arrival at Rome until the troops should be assembled, and every other circumstance prepared for the triumphal entries he meant to make into the capital.

During his stay in Samos, the neighbouring towns and provinces vied with each other in demonstrations of submission to his person, and of zeal for his cause. The inhabitants of Pergamus and Nicomedia made offer of divine honours to himself, and petitioned for leave to erect a temple for the purpose of performing these honours. Those of Ephesus and Nicæa, as being more modest or more delicate in their flattery, directed this compliment to his adoptive father, the late Cæsar, to whom, together with Roma, considered as joint deities, they proposed to erect a shrine and a temple.

In Italy, at the same time, similar or more important tributes of adulation and servility were paid to the victor. At Rome, all the honours with which the republic had been accustomed to reward the eminent service of her citizens, had been for some time lavished on those who were most successful in subverting her government. and these honours were now heaped on Octavius with a profusion proportioned to the ascendant he had gained by the suppression of all his competitors. The statues which had been erected to his rival Mark Antony were broken down, and the name of Marcus for ever forbid in that family: as if the extinction of this rival were an end of every war, notwithstanding that many hostile nations were yet in arms on the frontiers of the empire, the gates of Janus were ostentatiously shut, and Octavius declared to be the restorer of peace to the world. A triumphal arch was erected at Brundusium, on the spot where it was supposed he was to set his foot on shore. The anniversaries of his birth and of his victories were to be celebrated for ever as days of thanksgiving, and his name was to be inserted in the hymns or public prayers which were statedly sung, or offered up for the safety of the commonwealth.

U. C. 724.

Imper. Cæsar 5'o. Sext. Apuleius, ex Kal. Julii Polit. Valer. Messala.

On the first of January, while Octavius was still at Samos, he being admitted a fifth time into the office of consul, the senate and people took an oath of allegiance, or in words more nearly corresponding to the terms of their language, took an oath to observe his acts and decrees. They declared him tribune of the people for an unlimited time, and extended the powers of this office beyond the usual bounds of the city. They ordained, that from thenceforward the appeals usually made to the people should be made to Cæsar alone, and that in criminal judgments, what was called the vote of Minerva, an act of grace provided for the pardon of criminals when condemned only by a single vote of majority, should from thenceforward be ascribed to him, and consequently be termed, the Mercy, or the Vote of Cæsar.[1]

The precipitancy with which the Roman senate and people now rushed into servitude, had probably no mixture of that sullen design with which the partizans of the republic had prepared the first Cæsar for his fate. The retainers of the victorious party raised the cry of adulation, and they were followed, in expressions of servility, by persons who wished to recommend themselves in the most early advances, or who dreaded being marked out for resentment in case they appeared to be tardy in expressing their zeal. But what, under established monarchy, may be considered as the duty and the loyalty of subjects to their sovereign, and like filial affection, though sometimes partial and misplaced, is always a virtue, and salutary to mankind, in such rapid transitions, from the pretensions of citizens to the submission of slaves, is a mortifying example of the weakness and depravity to which human nature is exposed.

The apparent servility of all orders of men

1 Dio. Cass. lib. xxxi.

under the usurpation of Julius Cæsar, probably inspired the security which gave the conspirators such an advantage against him. The example, however, put Octavius, though less exposed, much more on his guard; and may serve to account for many of the precautions he took, and for many of the forms he observed, in the sequel of his government. He had occasion, indeed, to experience, in his own person, that his precautions were not altogether unnecessary. In the midst of the late demonstrations of joy for his victory, there were still a few who whetted their swords in secret against him, as the cause of their public degradation, and the author of their private wrongs. Lepidus, the son of the late degraded triumvir, and nephew of Marcus Brutus by his sister Junia, incited probably by this domestic example, and by so many motives of a private and public nature, had procured some accomplices, and was preparing to cut short the usurpation of Octavius on his return to Rome. But this design, no way justified by any considerations of prudence or public utility, was defeated by the vigilance of Mæcenas, and ended in the execution of the young Lepidus, and in the imprisonment of his mother Junia, who remained in confinement until she was admitted to bail, at the humble request of her husband, the late triumvir and associate in the empire with Octavius and Antony, and who, to the other marks of the humiliation which he now endured, joined that of being overlooked even by those who were supposed to have suffered by his tyranny.[2]

Octavius having, by his stay in the island of Samos, disconcerted the effect of this conspiracy, and given sufficient time for the transportation of his army, and the other apparatus of his triumph into Italy, set out for that country, and in his way visited the scene of his late victory at Actium. At this place, Apollo being the principal object of worship, he had, immediately after the action, selected from the captures a galley of each rate to be placed as an offering to the god; and at Toryné, on the opposite side of the straits, where his own army had been stationed before the engagement, he directed a city to be raised under the name of Nicopolis.[3]

The conqueror, upon his arrival at Rome, was received by Politus, who had succeeded to the office of consul at the resignation of Apuleius, and who, though now his colleague, dropped the pretension to equality, and performed the sacrifices of thanksgiving which had been appointed for his safe return. Octavius hitherto, either by the nature of the wars in which he had been engaged, or by the event of them, had not been entitled to a triumph; or being, by his temper and great caution, averse to ostentation, he had neglected to avail himself of this honour. But though he himself, in appearance, was no way governed by vanity, something was due to the public opinion, to the wishes of those who had shared in the glories of his victories, and to the impressions which even pageantry makes on the minds of those who are to be governed. He therefore determined to exhibit three separate triumphal processions. The first for his victory over the Panonians, the Japydes, and the Dalmatians; the second for his victory at Actium; and the third for the conquest of Egypt. In the first of these triumphs, Carinus, by whom the war of Illyricum had been chiefly conducted, was admitted to partake with the commander under whose auspices the subject of triumph had been gained. In the third was exhibited a scene, which, for riches and splendour, greatly surpassed any of the former, being enriched with the treasure he had amassed in Egypt, and with various trophies constructed from the spoils of that country. Among these were carried the effigy of the late queen, having, in allusion to the supposed manner of her death, the aspick represented on her arm. This pageant was followed by her surviving children, who were led as captives.

In these processions a circumstance was remarked, which indicated considerable innovation in the pretensions of the person by whom they were to be led. It had been usual for the officers of state to meet the triumphal march at the gates of Rome, and afterwards to advance before it into the city. In conformity with the first part of this custom, the consul and other magistrates met the procession at the gates; but suffering the conqueror to pass before them, fell behind, and followed in his train to the capitol. Here he deposited, in the temple of Jupiter, sixteen thousand pondo, or a hundred and sixty thousand ounces of gold, with fifty millions in Roman money, or above four hundred thousand pounds sterling;[4] and at the close of the ceremony distributed a thousand sestertii, or above eight pounds of our money a man to the troops; and this, to an army consisting of one hundred and twenty thousand men, amounted to a sum of near a million sterling. To the officers, besides his pecuniary bounty, he gave honorary rewards. To Agrippa, in particular, he gave a blue ensign in token of his naval victories; to the people he made a donation of four hundred sestertii, or about three pounds five shillings a man, and doubled the usual allowance of corn from the public granaries; discharged all that he owed, remitted all the debts that were due to himself, and refused all the presents which were offered to him from the different towns and districts of Italy.

These accumulations and distributions of foreign spoils at Rome, or the general expectations of prosperous times, produced great or very sensible effects in raising the price of houses, lands, and other articles of sale, whether in Italy or in the contiguous provinces; a circumstance which, joined to the new and strange appearance of the gates of the temple of Janus being shut, as a signal of universal peace, made these triumphs of Octavius appear an æra of felicity and hope to the empire.

They were followed by other magnificent ceremonies; the dedicating of a temple which had been erected to Minerva, and the opening of a great hall which had been inscribed with the name of Julius Cæsar. In that hall was placed a noted statue of victory which had been brought from Tarentum; and there too were hung up the trophies which had been collected in Egypt. The statue of Cleopatra, in gold, was placed in the temple of Venus, and at the same time the

2 Vell. Pater. lib. ii. c. 88. Liv. Epitome, lib. cxxxv.
3 Dio. Cass. lib. li. c. 1. Sueton. in Octav. c. 18.

4 Sueton. in Octav. c. xx.

shrine of Julius Cæsar, as well as those of Jupiter, Juno, and Minerva, were decorated with many ensigns or badges of victory.

On occasion of these solemnities, a variety of games were exhibited: that of Troy, in particular, was now instituted, being a procession formed by youth of high rank, mounted on horseback, and led by Marcellus and Tiberius, the nephew and the stepson of Octavius. Races were run in chariots and on horseback, by persons of high rank; and fights of gladiators were exhibited, in which, to the supposed disgrace of the times, it is remarked, that a Roman senator, of the name of Quintus Ventelius, was one of the combatants. Numerous parties of captives from the Daci and Suevi, in a form that might pass for real battles, were made to fight for their liberty, that was proposed as the prize of the victors. Many exhibitions were made of hunting and baiting of wild beasts, in which were presented a rhinoceros and hippopotamos or sea horse, animals, till then, unknown at Rome. In the time of these entertainments, which continued many days, Octavius either really was, or pretended to be taken ill, and left the honour of presiding at the shows to some private senators, who, together with many other members of their body, to increase the solemnity, feasted the people in their turns.[1]

Such had been the arts by which candidates for public favour, in the latter times of the republic, maintained in the capital the consideration they had gained by their services on the frontiers of the empire; and the continuance of these arts had now the more effect, that the people, who still had a claim to this species of courtship, were become insensible to any other privilege of Roman citizens, and were ready to barter a political consequence, which they were no longer fit to enjoy, for a succession of sports and entertainments that amused their leisure, or for a distribution of bread, which, without the usual and hard conditions of industry or labour, helped to give them subsistence.

It is observed, that in the preceding year, while the Egyptian war was yet in dependance, a concourse of Roman citizens, assuming the powers of the people in public assembly, bestowed on Statilius Taurus by a formal decree, in return for his munificence, in exhibiting matches of gladiators and the baiting of wild beasts, the privilege of naming annually one of the prætors. So irregular and absurd were become the proceedings of what were called the assemblies of the people; and the wary Octavius could not overlook the effect of these arts, in gaining their consent to the dominion he meant to establish. But while he indulged the people in their disposition to amusement and dissipation, he gave the necessary attention to his military arrangements, and took measures to secure the possession of that principal support, on which sovereignty, in such an empire, must be founded. He had experienced the danger which may arise from armies ill governed, and knew that a power may become insecure, by an abuse of the means by which it is gained. When to the troops, which he himself commanded in Sicily, were joined those o Lepidus and Sextus Pompeius, the engine, become too unwieldy for his management. and without any other principle of government, but fear, might baffle his skill to conduct it. He learned, upon that occasion, that the considerations of civil justice, and the respect which is paid to some form of political subordination, are necessary even to the discipline and order of a military establishment.

Upon this account, Octavius, immediately after his victories in Sicily, had proceeded with great address, to reduce and to purge the legions, by dismissing strangers and fugitive slaves, and by ordering the levies from thenceforward to be confined to citizens of Rome. The denomination of Roman citizen, indeed, was no longer appropriated to the descendants of the Alban or Sabin colony, nor even to the inhabitants of the municipal towns of Italy. It had been communicated to many cities and provinces beyond these limits, and it was likely now, with much greater propriety than ever, to be extended to the free, or well-born and respectable class of the inhabitants in all parts of the empire. By limiting, however, the levies of the army to this name of respect and of real privilege, Octavius restored, in some degree, the connection between the civil and military honours, taught the soldier to value himself on his condition as a citizen, and the citizen to consider as an honour the name of a soldier.

Upon this arrangement, the commander in chief of the army, as first magistrate of the commonwealth, had a double claim to obedience, and, joined to his military power, had an authority, derived from a principle of justice and of civil right, without which armies are no more than companies of banditti, whose force may be occasionally turned against the person who leads them, as well as against his enemies.

The legions assembled at Rome, on occasion of the late triumphal processions, were now to be distributed to what were intended as their ordinary stations in time of peace. Of these stations, the principal were on the Euphrates, on the Rhine, and on the Danube; but, before this distribution could be finally made, some troubles, which, notwithstanding the late signal of general peace, still subsisted in some parts of the empire, particularly on the Moselle and the Rhine, in the interior parts of Spain, and on the confines of Macedonia, required attention. To the first of these quarters, Nonius Gallus was sent to reduce the Treviri,[2] who, in concert with some German nations, made incursions into Gaul. Statilius Taurus was sent into Spain, against the Astures and Cantabri,[3] and Marcus Crassus, from Macedonia, had orders to repress the incursions of the Daci and Bastarni, Scythian nations, who had passed the Danube and the mountains of Hæmus, and who had taken possession of some districts in Thrace; but, upon the approach of Crassus, they repassed those mountains, and left the Romans again in possession of the lands, which they had formerly occupied in that quarter.[4]

The officers employed on these different services, were no longer, as formerly, supreme in their respective stations, and accountable only to the senate and people; they were understood to

1 Dio Cass. lib. li. c. 22, 23.

2 The Bishoprick of Treves.

3 The inhabitants of what is now called Asturia and Cantabria.

4 Dio. Cass. lib. lvii. c. 54—57. Tacit. An. lib. iv c. 5.

be lieutenants of a superior officer acting as general governor over all the provinces, and commander in chief of all the armies in the empire. This supreme command Octavius held under the well known name of *imperator*, which was usually given in the field to victorious generals, and which he, contrary to former practice, now retained even in the city; and, as we shall have occasion to observe, gradually appropriated to himself and his successors.

In the character which Octavius now assumed, he united, in support of his authority, the prerogatives of consul, censor, and tribune of the people; and thus, in divesting himself of the name of triumvir, he affected to re-establish the constitution of the republic, and to restore the ordinary magistrates and officers of state: but to a person, who valued safety no less than power, such an establishment was far from being sufficiently secure. The dignities of consul, censor, and tribune, being by the constitution of the republic separate and temporary, the unprecedented conjunction, and continuance of them in the same person, was a palpable imposition, which could be no longer safe than it was supported by force; and depending on the army merely, without any plea of right, presented an object of ambition to every adventurer, who could bring an army in support of his claim.

These considerations, probably, suggested to Octavius the necessity of endeavouring to strengthen his title. He had hitherto kept possession of the government under various pretences; but never declared any intention to realize, or to perpetuate the sovereignty in his own person. For some time, he had professed no more than a desire to avenge the death of his relation Julius Cæsar. Next, he pretended to remove some disorders which had crept into the commonwealth; and, last of all, to oppose the designs of Antony, who, at the breaking out of the quarrel between them, he suggested, was likely to sacrifice the rights of the Roman people to the caprices of a stranger and a woman.

These rivals, in their appeals to the judgment of the public, vied in their professions of zeal for the commonwealth, mutually challenged each other to resign their unconstitutional powers; and each retained his own power, under the single pretence that he was obliged to continue in arms, until he should have secured the republic against the designs of his antagonist.

This pretence being now removed, it was become necessary that Octavius should more fully explain himself, and declare upon what footing he was to hold the government. The chief partizans of the republic had fallen by their own hands, or by the swords of their enemies. All his rivals were cut off, and the whole military force of the empire centred in himself; but he had experienced, in the repeated mutinies of the army, the precarious state of his authority over men, who were directed by mere caprice or personal attachment, without any acknowledged title on the part of their leader.

An open usurpation of kingly power was still odious at Rome; it appeared as a direct attack, not only upon the forms of the Roman republic, but likewise as an attack upon the private right of every citizen who pretended to consideration and power proportioned to the rank of his family or his personal qualities; and though the people in general were disposed to submission yet the violence of a few, who might be willing to expose themselves as the champions of the commonwealth, was still to be dreaded. In this capacity, not only citizens having high pretensions in the civil line, but military officers likewise, might be dangerous to their leader; and choosing rather to claim preferments and honours as their right, than as the gift of a master, might publicly spurn his authority, or employ against him the hands of some secret assassin, whom in any successful attempt the law would protect, and the public voice would applaud.

Julius Cæsar, whose personal qualities were sufficient to have supported him in any pretensions, still found himself mistaken in relying on the attachment of his own officers, as much as on the submission of his fellow-citizens. He found persons of every condition, still animated with the spirit of republican government, combined for his destruction, and he fell a sacrifice to his excessive security, or rather to the vanity and ostentation with which he affected to hold his power. His successor on the present occasion, as he was by nature more cautious and had less ostentation, so he was taught, by this alarming example to disguise his ambition, or to proceed less directly to his object.

Octavius, therefore, having taken the most effectual measures to secure his power, still thought it necessary to affect a purpose of resigning it, and of restoring the republican government. It is reported, that he even held a serious consultation on this subject with his principal advisers and confidents, Agrippa and Mæcenas. This fact may be questioned; but in a character so entirely made up of artifice and design, it is not unreasonable to suppose that he wished to disguise his thoughts even to his most intimate counsellors, or to secure their approbation before he disclosed his real intentions.

Agrippa and Mæcenas are said to have been of different opinions respecting the propriety of their master's resignation; and the question accordingly, as it was supposed to be debated in this famous council, has furnished a curious theme to historians and rhetoricians. Agrippa encouraged Octavius to persist in his supposed intention to resign his power, and supported this opinion, by stating the advantages of republican government. "It is the tendency of the republic," he said, "to multiply examples of great men; it is the tendency of monarchy to diminish their numbers, and to sacrifice to one person, the pretensions and the elevation of many. Under the first species of government, the Roman state has attained to its present greatness; under the second, it may languish, and sink to the level of other nations." He put Octavius in mind of his duty to the senate, and to the Roman people, for whose rights, while he took arms against the murderers of his father, he had always professed the greatest respect:—bid him beware of the reproaches he must incur, if it should now appear, either that he had formerly employed the pretence of filial duty as a cloak to his ambition; or that, now finding the people at his mercy, he neglected their rights the moment it was in his power to violate them with impunity.—He mentioned the danger of attempting to reduce into servitude a people, who had been accustomed not only to freedom, but to dominion over other nations;—the difficulties that must arise in the government of so great an empire;—the thorns that are for ever fastened in the pillows of kings;—the dangers to which he must be exposed, from persons who should feel themselves injured by his seizing the government, or who should think themselves entitled to supplant him, and whose courage, in every attempt against his person, would be extolled as a noble effort of patriotism to restore the freedom of their country.

Mæcenas took the opposite side, and contended for the necessity of a new species of government, in circumstances so different from those in which the republic had been formed. "So great an empire," he said, "surrounded by so many enemies, required the authority and the secret counsels of a prince, aided, but not controlled, by the opinions of those who were qualified to serve him. The time, when the republic might rely on the virtue and moderation of the greater part of her citizens is now no more; men are governed by ambition or interest, and if one person decline the sovereignty, many pretenders will arise, who will again tear the republic asunder by their wars and contensions." He observed, that the fortune or destiny of Octavius had placed him at the head of the commonwealth; that he ought not to despise its gifts, or to throw the Roman people again into a state of confusion and anarchy, out of which he had been destined to save them. From these topics, he proceeded to consider the difficulties to be encountered in the administration of such a government, delivered maxims that contain the wisdom of monarchy, pointed at regulations calculated to preserve some species of civil constitution, yet depending on the will of the prince, and, according to the account which is given of his speech, suggested at this conference most parts of the plan which Octavius actually carried into execution.[1]

In the result of this consultation, it is said, that not only Octavius, but Agrippa likewise, embraced the opinion of Mæcenas; and that they, from thenceforward, considered the secure establishment of the monarchy as the common object of all their councils. They appear to have agreed, that Octavius should treat the senate as he had in this conference treated his friends; that he should propose to resign his power, affect to make his continuing to hold it the result of their own deliberations, and, by these means, obtain the sanction of a legal establishment.

To smooth the way to this end, some previous steps were yet to be taken. Much had already been done by Octavius to secure his power, to reconcile his new subjects, and, in case of any competition, to recommend himself to the public choice; but some caution was still to be employed in bringing forward a question, relating to the continuance of the present government, or the restoration of the republic. The senate, on whose readily embracing and acting the part that was expected from them the whole depended, was to be scrutinized and purged of all members, who were by the love of republican government, or by any other circumstances, likely to mar the design. A single voice in this assembly, given for receiving the demission, which Octavius was about to offer, might have greatly disconcerted his project, obliged him to throw aside his disguise, and might have made it necessary for him to continue holding by force what he wished to receive by consent, or even to have pressed upon him by the interests of all orders of men. In order to cultivate the dispositions with which he already endeavoured to inspire the senate and the people, he himself, in conjunction with Agrippa, entered on the office of consul for the sixth time, divided the fasces with him, as usual in the purest times of the republic, and in all the exertions of their authority, or in the discharge of their common duties, knowing how little he had to apprehend from the pretensions of his colleague, affected to rank with him on the most perfect footing of equality.

U. C. 725.
Imperator Cæsar VI. M. Agrippa.

The new consuls, in proceeding to their principal object, which was to reform the senate, and to fill it with such members as were likely to cooperate in the design they had formed, of obtaining for Octavius the sovereignty by a formal consent, made a review or census, as usual, of all the different orders of the commonwealth; and having, in consequence of the late troubles, much property as well as public honours in their power, they had an opportunity to enrich, as well as to promote those whom they wished to oblige; and accordingly made such a distribution of estates and dignities, as plainly showed, that obsequiousness to the will of Cæsar was the road to distinction and fortune.

At this census or review of the people, the Roman citizens were found to amount to four million one hundred and sixty-four thousand men fit to carry arms.[2] So much had their number, without any increase of population, augmented by the continual admission of the freemen of entire towns and provinces, upon the rolls of the people.

The senate had, during the devastations, and in the event of the civil wars, not only lost those who made its principal ornament, considered as a republican council, but had even undergone a great, if not an entire change of its members. It consisted now of persons occasionally intruded by the parties lately contending for superiority; many, in particular, named by Antony, and who, during the late struggles, endeavoured to support the cause of their patron. These, more especially, it was the object of Octavius to remove; but being desirous to court all orders of men, as well as to set aside his enemies, he affected a reluctance in expelling particular persons, and recommended to those, who were conscious of any disqualification, voluntarily to withdraw their names.

In consequence of this intimation, fifty senators retired, probably most of them conscious of a disaffection to the reigning power. One hundred and forty more were struck off the rolls. In discharging this invidious service, Octavius was guarded by ten chosen senators, who surrounded his person with concealed weapons, and is said himself to have been cased in armour under his robe. He, at the same time, endeavoured to pal-

1 Dio. Cass. lib. lii. c. 1—42.

2 The whole number of souls must have exceeded sixteen millions. Eusebii Chronicon. Cæsar Imperator VI. M. Agrippa, p. 163.

liate the severity of his censures in different ways, suffering those, who were excluded from the senate, still to retain the dress of that order, and to enjoy, at the theatre, and other public places, the usual precedence of the senatorian rank. Under pretence of rendering the order itself more independent and more respectable, he raised the money qualification of a senator from eight to twelve hundred thousand sesterces;[3] and, without any personal imputation, affected to exclude some senators for the want of this new qualification; others he contrived to gain by a very artful method of bribery, alleging, that the public should not be deprived of the services of worthy citizens merely by a deficiency in their fortune, he from his own coffers, made up the estates of several senators to the new qualification. A striking instance of the policy in which he excelled; at once the most effectual to obtain his purpose, and the most artful to palliate or to conceal his design.

By the forms which the present consuls, Octavius and Agrippa, affected to observe in the discharge of their public duties, the republic seemed so much to revive, that one Quintus Statilius was tempted to offer himself as candidate in free election for the office of tribune; but in this instance, Octavius thought himself obliged to resume the character of master. Although he employed the forms of the republic to reconcile the minds of men to his government, he knew how to distinguish what had a tendency to ravish that government out of his hands, or to embroil him in contests with the people: he therefore commanded this candidate for the office of tribune to withdraw his pretensions, and not to awaken, by his unseasonable canvas, the turbulent dispositions which had formerly so much afflicted the state.

In the arts which were practised on the citizens of Rome, shows, processions, and public entertainments always made a part, and they operated on this people, perhaps operate on all mankind, with such powerful effects, as not to be overlooked without the danger of mistaking the circumstances which lead to the most important events. Octavius, aware of this circumstance, on the present as well as on former occasions, having temples and other public works executed with great magnificence, celebrated the dedication, or the completion of them, with many pompous entertainments and shows; he furnished, at his own expense, the circus and theatres with continual entertainments, with the fights of gladiators, and the baiting or hunting of wild beasts. While he thus encouraged the people in their usual vices of idleness and dissipation, he avoided laying any new burdens, cancelled all arrears due to the treasury within the city, and increased fourfold the gratuitous distributions of corn. To these popular arts, he joined a species of amnesty of all past offences and differences; repealed all the acts, which, during the late violent times, the spirit of a party had dictated; and, to quiet the apprehensions of many, who were conscious of having taken part with his enemies, he gave out that all papers or records seized in Egypt, upon the final reduction of Antony's party, were destroyed; though in this Dion Cassius contradicts him, and alleges, that such papers were preserved and afterwards employed in evidence against persons whom he thought proper to oppress.[4]

At the close of this memorable consulate, Octavius laid down the fasces, and, agreeable to the forms of the republic, took the usual oath of declaration, that he had faithfully, and with his utmost ability, discharged the duties of his station. Being destined to the same office of consul for the following year, he resumed the ensigns of power; and thinking the senate and people, by the steps he had already taken, sufficiently prepared for the subject he meant to bring under consideration, he, on the Ides, or thirteenth of January, surprised them with a direct and full resignation of all the extraordinary powers which he held in the empire. This solemn act he accompanied with a speech, which, according to his usual practice, having committed it to writing, he read. Being sensible that his sincerity would be questioned, and that his having taken the most effectual measures to obtain and to secure the government was but an ill indication of his intention to resign it, he employed a great part of his harangue in removing suspicions, not merely by assurances of sincerity, but by arguments likewise drawn from general topics of probability and reason. To this purpose, he observed, that many persons, who were themselves incapable of such intentions, might doubt his sincerity, and that many, who could not behold a superior without envy, would be disposed to misrepresent his actions; but that the immediate execution of the purpose he had declared, would remove every doubt, would silence every attempt of calumny, entitle him to credit, and to their just esteem.

U. C. 726.

Imperator Cæsar VII. M. Agrippa III.

"That I have it in my power to retain the government," he said, "no one will question. Of my enemies, some have suffered the just effects of their own obstinacy, and others having experienced my clemency, are fully reconciled. My friends are confirmed in their attachment, by the mutual exchange of good offices between us, and by a participation in the management of affairs. I have no real danger to fear, and any alarm I might receive, would only hasten the proofs I am in condition to give of my power. I have many allies, and numerous forces, well attached to my person; money, magazines, and stores of every description; with what is of more consequence than all these put together, I am placed, by the choice of the senate and people of Rome, at the head of the republic.

"What I now do, I hope will explain my past actions, and silence those who impute my former conduct to ambition, or who suppose that I am not now sincere in the resignation which I profess to make. Having the sovereignty at present in my possession, I renounce it, and deliver into your hands, the army, the state, the provinces, not merely in the condition in which I received them, but in a condition much improved by my exertions.

"Let this action then evince the sincerity of the declarations I made, when, being engaged in the late unhappy contest, I professed that my intentions were to obtain justice against the murderers of my father, and some relief to the

3 From about 7000*l.* to 10,000*l.*

4 Lib. lii. c. 42, &c.

commonwealth from the evils with which it was afflicted.

"I wish, indeed, that this task had never been imposed upon me; that the republic had never stood in need of my services, and that the fatal divisions we have experienced, had never taken place. But since the fates had otherwise decreed, and since the republic, young as I was, required even my assistance, I declined no labour, I shunned no danger, I made efforts above my years and my strength. Neither toil nor danger, the entreaties of my friends, the threats of my enemies, the tumults of the seditious, nor the fury of those who opposed me, could turn me aside from the pursuit of your good. I forgot myself; I became altogether yours. The event, with respect to you, is known; for myself, the only reward I desire, is the sense of having delivered my country from the evils with which it was distressed, and of having restored you to the state of peace and tranquillity which you now enjoy. With these advantages, resume your political trust, and the forms of your constitution; take charge of your provinces, and the direction of your military forces; conduct every part according to the rules and precedents which were laid down by your ancestors.

"My conduct, in this resignation, will not appear unaccountable to those who have observed the moderation with which I have frequently declined the uncommon distinctions by which you offered to raise me above the level of my fellow-citizens; nor to those who know the real value of human possessions, will it appear a folly, that having such an empire in my power, I choose to resign it. If I am supposed to have any regard to justice, what more just than that I should restore to you what is your own? If I am supposed to be governed by prudence, what more prudent, than to withdraw from trouble, from general envy, and from the snares of my enemies? If I am supposed to aim at glory, the great object for which men have most willingly exposed themselves to hazards and toils, what more glorious than to dispose of empire to others, and to rest secure myself in the honours of a private station?

"Having the choice of many actions, which reflect honour on my father's memory, and may do so on my own, these actions I prefer to any other; that he, being offered the sovereignty of his country refused to accept of it; and that I myself, being in actual possession of that sovereignty, have resigned it. To these actions, the conquest of Gaul, of Mysia, of Egypt and Panonia, the victories obtained over Pharnaces, Juba, Phraates, the passage of the Rhine, and of the British sea, though far exceeding the achievements of former times, are yet of inferior account: even the merit of having conducted to so glorious an issue the unhappy contest in which we have been engaged, the having overcome as enemies all who withstood our reformations, the having protected as friends all who were pacific and well inclined to the commonwealth, the having by moderation and clemency stript civil war itself of many of its greatest evils, are not comparable to this; That being in a condition to reign, we have not been intoxicated with power: neither could he be seduced to accept of a crown which was offered to him, nor I to retain a dominion which is actually in my hands.

"I do not mention any past action from ostentation, or with a view to profit by the advantage it gives me, but merely to show, that I know the value of my present conduct, and have made it my choice, because I think it more glorious than any other conduct I could hold.

"I might, indeed, (not to drag any more the name of my father into this argument,) challenge any one to compare with myself in the part which I now act. Being at the head of great and well appointed armies attached to my person; being master of the seas within the pillars of Hercules; of all the towns and provinces of this mighty empire, without any foreign enemy, or domestic sedition to molest me; being cheerfully acknowledged and obeyed as sovereign in profound peace, I now willingly and of my own accord resign the whole, from a regard to my fellow-citizens, and from a respect for the laws of my country.

"What I have to apprehend, is not your insensibility to the merit of what I perform, but your doubt of its reality, and of the sincerity of my intention; but you give credit to illustrious examples recorded of former times. You admit that the Horatii and the Decii, that Mucius, Curtius, and Regulus exposed themselves to danger, even rushed upon certain destruction to establish for themselves a reputation after death. Why should not I, to enjoy, even during my lifetime, a fame far superior to theirs, perform the action which I now propose? Were the ancients alone possessed of magnanimity? or is the age become barren and unabled to bring forth such examples?

"Think not, however, that I mean to revive the late public distractions, or propose to commit the government to an unruly and factious multitude. No; broken with toil, and overwhelmed with labour as I am, I should prefer death to such a desertion of the public cause. To you, my fathers, who possess wisdom and virtue equal to the trust, I resign this government. Weary with solicitude and care, I retire from that envy which the best of men cannot escape, and prefer the glories of a private life to the dangers of empire. To your judgments and to that multiplicity of counsel which must in wisdom ever excel the reason and understanding of any single person, I now commit the republic. I therefore adjure you, in consideration of any service which I may have rendered to my country, either in a civil or military capacity, that you will suffer me to retire in quiet, and give me an opportunity to evince, that I know how to obey as well as how to command; and that, while in power, I imposed no condition upon others, with which, as a subject, I am not myself willing to comply. In this capacity, my conscience tells me, that unguarded and unattended I may rely for safety on your affection, and that I have nothing to fear, either in the way of violence or insult. But, if there should be a danger from any secret enemy, (for what person ever passed through scenes like those, in which I have acted, without creating some private enemies?) it is better to die, than to purchase security by enslaving my country. If the event should be fatal, posterity at least will do me the justice to own, that so far from seeking a kingdom at the expense of the blood of other men, I have freely resigned one at the hazard of my own. Who ever wrongs me, will have the immortal gods and you for their enemies; they will perish, as the murderers of my father have perished, leaving their names as monuments of divine justice and wrath. In this, every one has had his just retribution; my father is placed among the gods, and is vested with eternal glory; his murderers have undergone the punishment due to their crimes.

"All men are born to die; but he who dies, as well as lives with honour, in some measure disappoints his fate, and acquires a species of immortal life. I have lived, as I trust, with honour; the other and less arduous part of my task, I hope is likewise in my power. I now, therefore, restore to you the arms, the governments, the revenue, and all the legal powers of the commonwealth. Be not dismayed by the greatness of the object on the one hand, nor receive it too lightly on the other. My counsel, in what relates to matters of moment, shall be freely given.

"Let the law be the unalterable rule of your conduct. In the administration of government, a determinate order, though attended with some inconveniency, is preferable to fluctuation and frequent change, which, aiming at improvement, renders the condition of men precarious and uncertain.

"In private, therefore, as well as in public life, comply with the laws; not as persons who aim at impunity merely, but as persons who aim at the rewards which are due to merit.

"Commit the provinces, whether in peace or war, to men of wisdom and virtue; do not envy each other the emoluments that attend the public service: strive not for profit to yourselves, but for security and prosperity to the commonwealth; reward the faithful, punish the guilty; not only consider the public property as too sacred to be invaded, but consider even your private possessions as a debt which you owe to the state. Manage well what is your own; covet not what belongs to others; wrong not your allies or subjects; do not rashly provoke any power to hostility, nor meanly stand in fear of those who are disposed to be your enemies. Be always armed, but not against each other, nor against those who are inclined to peace. Supply your troops regularly with what is appointed for their pay and subsistence, that they may not be tempted to supply themselves by invading the property of their fellow-citizens; keep them under strict discipline, that they may respect their duty as guardians of the public peace, and not become, from a consciousness of their force, a school for violence and the commission of crimes.

"Such in general are the rules of your conduct, of which it is not necessary to make the particular applications: these are sufficiently evident. One thing only I will mention, before I conclude. If you conform yourselves to these rules, you will be happy, and you will owe thanks to me, for having placed the administration in your hands; but, if you depart from them, you will make me to repent of what I now do, and you will relapse into all the disorders from which I have so happily rescued the commonwealth."

Such is the purport of a speech, said to have been delivered by Octavius, in announcing his intention to resign the empire. The performance may not appear worthy of the person to whom it is ascribed, and, like other speeches recorded in ancient history, may have been framed by the historian.[1] The occasion, however, was remarkable, and this speech having been committed to writing, may have been preserved in the records of the senate. The historian may have copied it from thence; or, if disposed to fabricate a speech, could not in this case, without detection, substitute any fiction for what was real. The composition indeed may have suffered in the first translation,[2] as well as in this extract or paraphrase of it; but the matter, though not such as might have been expected from the conqueror of the Roman empire on a serious occasion, and in the actual exertion of al his abilities, yet is such as we may suppose Octavius to have employed in supporting an assumed character, and in proposing what he did not wish to obtain.

The references which, in ushering in this pretended resignation, are made to the disorders of the late republic; the arguments which are made use of to prove the sincerity of a purpose to resign the government of it, and the ostentation of great merit in making this sacrifice, are well enough suited to the part which the speaker was acting, and to the solicitude under which he spoke, not to make too deep an impression, nor to be taken at his word. The barefaced and palpable imposture in which he was engaged, did not admit of the dignity which might have been expected in so high a place; and, if the history of this pretended resignation were not confirmed by the united testimony of many writers, and still more by the lasting effects of it, in the forms and in the state of the empire, the want of dignity in other parts of this business, as well as in the tenor of this speech, might create a doubt of its veracity; but the same forms of resignation were again repeated, and great festivals[3] at certain periods were held on this account.

As soon as this speech was ended, notwithstanding the many evils which had been recently felt under the republic, it is probable, that if Octavius had appeared to be sincere in making it, his proposal to restore the commonwealth would have been received with joy. There were yet many who revered the ancient constitution, and lamented the loss of their own political consequence. Some, who would have been glad to renew the competition for power and dominion which had been recently decided, and many who would have rejoiced to find so much consequence at once bestowed on the order of senators to which they themselves had been unexpectedly raised; but as much care had been taken in the nomination of senators, to fill this assembly with unambitious men, who were likely to prefer peace to every other object, or with men of a servile cast, who would follow the cry when raised to confirm the emperor's power, it is probable. that proper persons were prepared to lead the way in the part which the senate was to take on this occasion.

The majority of the meeting indeed was surprised and perplexed. There could be no doubt, that Octavius wished to have his proposal rejected; but it would have been an ill manner of paying court, to appear to have penetrated his

1 Dio. Cass. 2 From the Latin to Greek.
3 The Decennalia.

design. It was necessary to affect implicit faith in the sincerity of his purpose, at the same time to withstand the execution of it in the most peremptory manner. This ground being pointed out by those who were in the concert, or by those who had discernment enough to perceive it, was instantly seized by the whole assembly.[1] They beseeched Octavius, as with one voice, not to abandon the commonwealth; observed, that services, still greater than those he had already performed, were yet due to the republic; that the fear of his intending to resign the government, had already filled the minds of the people with a cruel anxiety; that he alone could quiet their apprehensions, by not only remaining at the head of the empire, but by accepting the government in such a formal manner, as would give them assurance of his continuing to hold it.[2]

To this request, Octavius was inexorable; but he was prevailed upon not to lay the whole load of administration at once on the senate. He was willing to administer some part of the government for a limited time, and to retain the command of the army for ten years; to continue his inspection over some of the most refractory provinces, such as were yet unsettled, such as were wild and uncultivated, such as had many inaccessible retreats, under the favour of which the people still continued unsubdued, or still in condition to rebel. He agreed to take charge of such provinces on the frontier, as, being contiguous to warlike and hostile neighbours, were exposed to frequent invasion; but such as were already pacific, and accustomed to civil forms, such as were reconciled to the tribute which they paid, he insisted that the senate, as the more easy and profitable part of the government, should take under their own administration; and that they should be ready to relieve him of the whole, or any part of his burden, at the expiration of the period to which he limited his acceptance of the military command.

By this imaginary partition of the empire, the provinces which in Africa had formed the states of Carthage and Cyrene, with the kingdom of Numidia: in Europe, the more wealthy and pacific parts of Spain, the islands of Sardinia, Sicily, and Crete; with the different districts of Greece, Epirus, Macedonia, and Dalmatia; and beyond the Ægean sea, the rich province of Asia, with the kingdoms of Bithynia and Pontus, were committed to the jurisdiction of the senate.

The emperor still retained, under his own immediate charge, the more warlike districts in Spain, in Gaul and in Syria, with the kingdom of Egypt, and all the great military stations and resorts of the legions on the Euphrates, the Danube, and the Rhine.[3] Some time afterwards, under pretence of a war which arose in Dalmatia, he accepted of this province, in exchange for the island of Cyprus, and the district of Narbonne.

It was understood, that the emperor and the senate, in their quality of partners in the sovereignty, should have the nomination of governors in their respective provinces; that those named by the senate should be civil officers merely, with the title of proconsul, but without the power of the sword or any military rank, and they were not to remain in office longer than one year, that the officers to be named by the emperor were to have military rank, with the title of propraetor, and were to act in the capacity of his lieutenants accountable only to himself, and to hold their commissions during his pleasure.[4]

From the reformations which Octavius now made in the establishment of the provinces, it appeared that he himself clearly understood the circumstances by which those members of the empire had become too great for the head, and by which the dependencies of the republic had become the means of its ruin; that he looked back to the steps, by which the first Cæsar and himself had advanced to dominion, and wished to efface the track, in order that no one might follow it, or employ the same means to supplant himself, which Julius Cæsar had employed to subvert the republic.

The provinces of the Roman empire had been hitherto not so much the demesne of the commonwealth, as the property of private citizens, by whom they were conveyed from one to another by quick succession. As they were received in trust for the republic, without any particular assignment of a share in the profits[5] great part was diverted to private uses; or where great sums were to be accounted for to the state there was much extorted likewise to enrich individuals by peculation and oppression.

From their stations abroad, the officers of the republic returned with the spoils of the provinces to purchase importance at Rome. If they were frequently changed, the empty hand was often held out with fresh rapacity, and the full one brought back with quicker succession to corrupt the city: if continued too long, they acquired the force of great monarchs, got possession of armies and of revenue, and had sufficient resources of men and money to enable them to make war on the state. Marius and Sylla showed what could be done with armies levied from the opposite factions in the city of Rome; and Julius Cæsar showed what use could be made of the extensive territory, entrusted for a continued term of years to the government of the same person. The republic had often tottered under the effect of disorders which arose in the capital, but fell irrecoverably under the blows that were struck from the provinces.

It is evident, that the head of the empire, of whatever description, whether a commonwealth or the court of a monarch, could not be safe under this distribution of power and trust. Measures were accordingly now taken by Octavius to reform the establishment, and to reduce the provincial officers to their proper state of subordination and dependence. The duties they were to levy, and their own emoluments, were clearly ascertained. The greater provinces were divided, and separate officers appointed to each division.

1 Zonar. lib. x. c. 34. 2 Dio. Cass. lib. liii. c. 11.
3 Dio. Cass. lib. liii. c. 12. Strabo, lib. xvii. fine.

4 Dio. Cass. lib. liii. c. 13.
5 The provincial officers under the republic had no salary, nor public appointments. They were understood to subsist at the expense of the provinces; and in their journies were allowed to impress horses and carriages, and to demand every supply of provisions and forage for the numerous retinue or court that usually attend them. These powers being abused, it was proposed that the provincial officers should be supplied by contract; but the leaders of faction at Rome went forth to the provinces, with a power tha could not be restrained by any rules whatever.

Neither men nor money were to be levied without authority from the emperor and the senate, nor was any officer, to whom a successor was appointed, to remain in his command, or to absent himself from Rome above three months.[6] To secure the observance of these regulations, and to accelerate the communication from every part of the empire, an institution, resembling that of the modern posts, was for the first time introduced in the ancient world. Couriers were placed at convenient stages, with orders to forward from one to the other the public despatches. It was afterwards thought more effectual, for the purpose of intelligence, to transport the original messenger to Rome.

In this establishment, the senate and the emperor, in their respective civil and military characters, had their several departments, and their revenue apart; what was collected in the provinces of the senate, went to the Ærarium or public treasury; what was collected in the provinces of Cæsar, went to his own coffers. The latter professed being no more than a servant of the public, appointed for a limited time; but, in being head of the army, he secured the sovereignty, and meant to employ the senate only as an aid to retain the army within the bounds of their duty. In his proposal to divest himself of the government, there was sufficient reason to suspect his sincerity; but in this partial and supposed temporary resumption of government, the artifice was so obvious, as to become a species of insult upon the understandings of mankind. The Romans, nevertheless, on this memorable occasion had learned to be courtiers, could affect to want penetration and conceal their sentiments.

The senate, in return to the emperor's gracious acceptance of the government, proceeded to distinguish his person, and even the place of his residence, by many honorary decrees. They took into their serious consideration, by what title he should for the future be known. That of king had always been odious at Rome; that of dictator had been feared, ever since the sanguinary exercise of its powers by Sylla, and it had been formally abolished by law, soon after the demise of Julius Cæsar. The name of Romulus was proposed, and thought due to Octavius, as the second founder of Rome; but this name he himself rejected, not on account of the ridicule conveyed in it, but on account of the implication of kingly power. The title of Augustus was in the end accepted by him, rather as an expression of personal respect, than as a mark of any new or unprecedented dignity in the commonwealth.

While the senate bestowed on their emperor the title of Augustus, they ordered that the court of his palace should be for ever hung with laurel, the badge of victories that were ever fresh in the minds of the people, and with wreaths of oak, the usual distinction of those who had saved a fellow-citizen; in token that the Roman people were continually preserved by his acceptance of the sovereignty, and by the wisdom of his administration.

Octavius from henceforward came to be known by the name of Augustus. He had been some time the object of fear, and consequently of adulation to the people, and was now probably become the object of that fond admiration, with which the bulk of mankind regard those who are greatly elevated by fortune. Under the effect of this sentiment, or supported by the prevalence of it, citizens of high rank devoted themselves to Augustus, as they were told that the vassal devoted himself to his lord in some of the barbarous cantons of Spain and Gaul. They took an oath to interpose their persons in all his dangers, and if he must die, to perish with him. The dying, under pretence of bequeathing some legacy to Augustus, introduced his name in their wills, with a lavish encomium or flattering character Many appointed him sole heir, or, together with their children, the joint heir of all their fortunes. Some, on their deathbed, bequeathed particular sums to defray the expense of sacrifices to the gods for this signal blessing, *that Augustus was still living when they expired.*

CHAPTER II.

State of the Emperor—Condition of the Empire—Amount of the Revenue unknown—Military Establishments, &c.

IN what degree the court which began to be paid to Augustus, and which continued during his reign, proceeded from design and servility, or respect and affection, we must endeavour to collect from a farther view of his life, and must suspend our judgment until the scene of his trial is passed. At the late formal establishment of the monarchy in his person, he was in the thirty-fifth year of his age, and had still the aspect of youth. His complexion is said to have been fair, his eyes bright, and his features regular and elegant. He was well made in his person, and though below the middling stature, had so much the proportions of a tall man, as, except when compared with some person who overlooked him, to appear above the ordinary size. Two-and-twenty years of a life so little advanced, he had passed in the midst of civil wars, and in the contest for empire, which was begun by his adoptive father, and maintained by himself. During seventeen of those years he had himself been a leader of party, and veered in his professions and conduct with every turn of fortune; at one time courting the senate, by affecting the zeal of a citizen in behalf of the republic; at another time courting the veterans, by affecting concern for their interests, and a zeal to revenge their late general's death. He opposed himself to Antony, or joined with him as suited with the state of his affairs; made or broke concerts with the other leaders of faction, made and unmade treaties of marriage; even had intrigues of pleasure with women to forward

6 Dio. Cass. lib. liii. c. 13.

some political design;[1] and at an age when other young men have scarcely any object but pleasure, sacrificed every supposed private or public connexion, and every friend and every enemy to his ambition, or to the cool and deliberate consideration of his own conveniency.

By such means as these Octavius became sovereign of the Roman empire at the age of three-and-thirty years, the same age at which Alexander, with the greatest efforts of ability and courage, which were afterwards marred by equal instances of intemperance and folly, effected the conquest of the Persian monarchy. Much, no doubt, in the fortunes of men, is to be imputed to accident. To this they owe, at least, great part of the occasions on which they act; but the use of the occasion, and sometimes the preparation of it, is their own; and nothing besides the most consummate abilities can, through a great variety of scenes, retain the uniform appearance of a fortunate life. It is true, that Octavius, with the name of Cæsar, was become convenient or necessary to the military faction which he found already formed in the empire; that his youth, and other circumstances, prevented the alarm which might have led his enemies to take more effectual and earlier measures against him. But he did not fail to improve these advantages; affected, when necessary, to be the mere instrument of the army, or of the senate, for obtaining their respective purposes; preserved the same discretion in every state of his fortunes; and, with the same address with which he supplanted every rival in the contest for power, continuing to avoid every offensive appearance in the model of his government, he still retained the forms of the commonwealth; and, besides the title of Augustus, did not introduce any new appellation of dignity or of office.[2]

Every possible power under the republic had been implied in the titles of consul, censor, augur, pontiff, and tribune of the people. Some of them could, even under that form of government, have been united in the same person, as that of augur and pontiff, with the office either of consul or censor; and there was no law to forbid the accumulation of such dignities in the hands of the same person, probably because it was deemed sufficiently difficult to arrive at any of them apart. To constitute a despotic power, therefore, provided that these titles could be united in the same person, it was not necessary to introduce any new forms of office, nor even to assume the name of dictator. It was more effectual to unite the prerogatives of separate stations in the person of one man, or to bestow them on persons, who would be content to employ them at the pleasure of a master: and this method accordingly being suited to the wary policy and affected modesty of Octavius, could not escape him in the choice of his model.

In the character of consul, the new emperor presided in the senate, and was first executive magistrate in the city. In the character of tribune he could not only suspend all proceedings, whether of administration, of public council, or of justice; but likewise could punish with instant death any breach of the peace, or any attempt that was made on his own person. In the capacity of censor, which was now comprehended in the office of consul, he was the fountain of honour, could pry into every citizen's private life, and could promote or degrade, at pleasure, every person who had courted his favour, or incurred his dislike. In the capacity of augur and pontiff he could overrule the superstition of the times; and, last of all, in the capacity of imperator, or head of the army, he held, at his disposal, all the forces of the empire, both by sea and by land. The republic, at the same time, retained most of its forms. There were meetings of the senate, and assemblies of the people; there were laws enacted, and elections made; affairs proceeded as usual in the name of the consul, the censor, the augur, and tribune of the people. The only change which had happened, and that which the emperor endeavoured to disguise, was, that he himself acted in all these capacities, and dictated every resolution in the senate, and pointed out every candidate who was to succeed in the pretended elections.

In these appearances of republican government, however, which were preserved by Octavius, we are not to suppose, that there was any image of that mixed constitution, which subsists with so much advantage in some of the kingdoms of modern Europe. The Roman senate, under the emperors, was no more than a species of privy council, of which the members were named or displaced by the prince; and which, under some specious appearances of freedom in their speech, were actually the mere instruments of his will.

The comitia, or assemblies of the people, had still less of their original dignity or power. We have had occasion to observe, that even under the republic, when the number of citizens, fit to array in the field of Mars, amounted to no more than four hundred thousand men; it was impossible that any adequate number could be assembled for any purpose of legislation or election. In the present times, when the musters extended to four millions, and the Roman citizens were dispersed over the whole empire, the assembly of any proportionable number was still more impracticable. No precautions had ever been taken, even under the republic, to prevent the great irregularities to which the assemblies of the people were exposed, nor was it ever ascertained what numbers were necessary to constitute a legal assembly. In consequence of this defect, in the latter times of the republic, any tumultuary meeting, however thinly or partially assembled, took the sacred name of the Roman people, and gave officers to the state, or laws to the commonwealth. Every faction which, by violence or surprise, could seize the place of the assembly, so as to exclude their opponents, were masters of the elections, or sovereigns of the state.

After Julius Cæsar had taken possession of the city, he had no difficulty in commanding the elections, or the resolutions of the people; he even planned the succession that was to take place in his absence; and, being to set out for

1 Sueton. in Octav. c 69.

2 The title of *Princeps* had been usually given to the person whose name was first in the rolls of the senate, and Augustus assumed it in no other sense than this; that of Imperator had been given to every successful leader of an army, and in its application to Octavius, implied no pre-eminence above what other leaders had formerly enjoyed. These titles, indeed, by being from henceforward appropriated to the sovereign, acquired, by degrees, their significance in the original language; and in our translation of them into *Prince* and *Emperor*, are applied only to royal persons, and the sovereigns of extensive dominion.

Asia, he named the officers of state for five years. The triumvirs, in like circumstances, fixed the succession for different periods of an equal and greater length; and it was now understood, that the officers of state, though under the show of popular election, were actually filled up by the emperor.

The apparent respect which, under the present establishment, was paid to civil forms implied no abatement of the military power. On the contrary, instead of weakening, it served to support, as usual, the authority of that government, under which these forms were observed. By flattering the people with an idea that their political consequence was still entire, this semblance of the ancient republic reconciled them to the state of degradation into which they were fallen. It vested the emperor himself with a species of civil character, and with a political consideration which he could employ in support of his military power, and which, in some measure, secured him against the caprice of troops, who might think themselves entitled to subvert what they alone had established. It enabled him to treat their mutinies as acts of treason, and as crimes of state. He was no longer obliged to court their favour, or to affect condescension, in order to obtain their obedience. He accordingly, in consequence of the late votes of the senate, changed the style of his address to the legions, called them *Milites*, not *Commilitones; soldiers*, not *fellow-soldiers*, as formerly.

This was probably the whole amount of the political establishment now made by Octavius, and which he meant to employ as a stock on which to ingraft his military power. The senate and assemblies of the people were retained only in name, and were far from having the energy of collateral members in the government, such as could check or control the perpetual executive, which was now established in the empire: but we shall nevertheless be disappointed, if, upon a supposition of absolute power in the emperor, we expect, in his court, the splendour and magnificence of a royal estate.

Octavius still lived in the house of Hortensius, a Roman senator, which he occupied without making any addition to it, either in point of dimension or ornament. The equipage, retinue, or accommodation of the imperial family was not composed for show and magnificence, as in monarchies long established. Such an attempt in the eyes of a decayed republic might have had an improper effect, might have moved envy, and not procured respect.[3] The emperor indeed was attended with an armed guard; but this was intended for safety, and not for parade. He preserved, in his own person, the exterior appearances of a citizen, was accosted by the simple name of Cæsar, took his place in the senate, in the theatre, in the public assembly, in the bench of judges. At funerals he pronounced the oration that was delivered in honour of the dead; and even at the bar appeared in behalf of his clients.[4] The females of his house preserved the virtue of notable house-wives, and fabricated, with their own hands, the stuffs which he wore in his dress.

In respect to manners, and appearance of state, the emperor, with his family, was not raised above the condition of citizens; but he had full compensation in the extent and arbitrary effects of his power. While he retained the appearances of an equal, he took care to be master; and, with no higher pretensions than those of a citizen, was more than a king. While he suffered the senate and people to retain the ancient names and titles of sovereignty, he withheld from them the substance of any privilege whatever. He personated the simple senator and the citizen with all the terrors of military power in his hands, and preserved the force of a tyrant, because he could not assume the precedence and authority of a legal monarch.

If in this account of the sovereign's person and state our expectations of grandeur are not fulfilled, his dominions will surpass the highest and most enlarged conception we can form of their greatness. The Roman empire contained within itself, and in a very entire and populous condition, what had been the seat or territory of many famous republics and extensive empires, or what has since, in modern times, upon the revival of nations, furnished their possessions to no less considerable states and great monarchies. As it had swallowed up the states of Italy and Greece, Macedonia, the Lesser Asia, Syria, Egypt, Carthage, Numidia, Spain, and Gaul to the Rhine and the Danube; so there have sprung from its ruins many states now formed within the Alps, the kingdoms of Portugal, Spain, and France, with all the divisions of the Ottoman empire in Europe, Asia, and Africa. These are its fragments, or shreds of the vast territory of which it was composed.

This empire seemed to comprehend, within itself, all the most favourable parts of the earth; at least, those parts on which the human species, whether by the effects of climate, or the qualities of the race, have, in respect to ingenuity and courage, possessed a distinguished superiority. It extended to a variety of climates, and contained lands diversified in respect to situation and soil, distributing the productions of nature and art, so as to render its different divisions mutually useful and subservient to each other. The communication between these parts, though remote, was easy, and by a sea which, with the species of shipping then in use, and with the measure of skill which the mariner then possessed, could be easily navigated.

The Mediterranean being received into the bosom of this empire, gave to the whole a greater extent of coast, and to the inland parts an easier access to navigation, than could be obtained by any different distribution of its land and water. In consequence of this circumstance, the coasts of the Roman empire, without measuring minutely round the indentures of creeks and promontories, and even without including the outline of some considerable as well as many smaller islands, may be computed at thirteen thousand miles; an extent which, if stretched into a single line, would exceed half the circumference of the earth. Over this extensive coast, the empire was furnished with numerous seaports, and the frequent openings of gulphs and navigable rivers so that, notwithstanding the great extent of its

3 We may read in the journal of a voyage made by Horace, in company with Mæcenas, that much retinue, or equipage, did not accompany great power as they do in modern times. Vid. Sat. lib. i. sat. 5.

4 Dio Cass. lib. lv. c. 4.

territory, the distance of any inland place, the most remote from the sea, does not appear to exceed two hundred miles.

In forming this mighty dominion, the republic had united, under its territories, all the principal seats of industry then known in the western world, had come into possession of all the seaports the most famous for shipping, and for the residence of merchants, who had conducted the carrying trade of the world. Its subjects were possessed of all the profitable arts, and having all the means and instruments of trade, might be expected to reap all the fruits of commerce. But, in making these acquisitions, the capital of the empire had been a place of arms, and a mere nursery of statesmen and warriors, more occupied with the ideas of spoil and farther conquest, than with the attentions necessary to promote the industry or the prosperity of the nations subjected to its power. And it is probable that the Romans, in reducing so many separate nations to the condition of provinces, greatly impaired the sources of wealth, at the same time that they suppressed the pretensions to independence and national freedom.

It might be hoped, that the peace now given to the empire, and the protection which every province was to receive against the avarice and rapacity of subordinate oppressors, would revive the pursuit of lucrative arts, and encourage the Roman traders to settle where the natives were not in capacity to pursue the advantages of their situation. But even these circumstances, without the aid of a happier government than that which was now established, were not sufficient to repair the damage formerly sustained by the provinces in their reduction and subsequent oppression. So that although Carthage, with all its dependencies, Egypt, Syria, the Lesser Asia, and Greece, with all the trading establishments of Spain and Gaul, were united under one head, we are not to suppose, that the wealth of the empire ever equalled the sum of what might have been raised from the separate and independent states of which it was composed.

The commercial policy of Rome was limited, in a great measure, to the supply of Italy, and to the conveyance of what the provinces yielded to the treasury of the empire. Both these objects were entrusted to mercantile companies, who farmed the revenue, and who made commerce subservient to the business of their own remittances and exclusive trade.

It were, no doubt, matter of curiosity to know the whole amount of a revenue collected from so rich and so extensive a territory; but we are deprived of this satisfaction by the silence of historians, or by the loss of records in which this subject was stated. Vespasian was heard to say, That a sum, supposed equal to about three hundred and thirty millions sterling, was required annually to support the imperial establishment.[1] This emperor, however, being rapacious or severe in his exactions, might be supposed to exaggerate the necessities of the state; but as this sum is beyond the bounds of credibility, and must lead us to suspect a mistake in the numbers, it will not enable us to form any probable conjecture of the truth.

Under the republic, both the treasury of the state, and the fortunes of individuals, were supplied, in a great measure, by the spoils of vanquished enemies, brought to the capital with great ostentation by every victorious general. To this source of revenue we may join the presents that were made by foreign princes and states, together with the military contributions that were exacted from the provinces.

Julius Cæsar brought, at once, into the treasury, sixty-five thousand talents, or above twelve millions and a half sterling. As the lustre of a triumph depended very much on the sums that were carried in procession, and placed in the capitol, Roman officers were more faithful stewards of the plunder taken from their enemies, than they were probably of any other public trust.

It had been, for some time, the practice of the Romans to lay every burden on the conquered provinces, and to exempt themselves. This policy is dated from the conquest of Macedonia, the spoils of which kingdom being joined to their former acquisitions, put them in condition to effectuate this exemption. It was, however, but of short duration. The practice of taxing citizens was resumed in time of the civil wars, and the privilege, or rather the mere designation of Romans, being extended to the inhabitants of many parts of the empire, all the burdens that were borne by any subjects were, at the same time, brought home into Italy, and all the former distinctions gradually removed.

Under the establishment now made by Augustus, conquests were discontinued, or became less frequent; and the returns made to the treasury, from the spoil of enemies, failed in proportion; but the avidity of receiving presents, the worst form under which extortion can be exercised was still indulged, and, as in every other despotical government, became a considerable engine of oppression.[2]

The republic, for the most part, in the latter periods of her conquests, entered on the possession of territories without any capitulation, and considered not only the sovereignty, but the property likewise of the land and of its inhabitants, as devolving upon themselves. They, in some instances, seized on the persons as well as the effects of the vanquished, and set both to sale. They leased the lands at considerable quit-rents, or leaving them in the hands of the original proprietors, exacted, under the appellation of tithes, or fifths of corn, fruit, and cattle, a proportion of the produce. By diversifying the tax, the burden was made to fall upon different subjects, or was exacted from different persons, and by these means the whole amount was less easily computed, or less sensibly felt. The Romans, in continuing the taxes which they found already established in the countries they had conquered, or by imposing such new ones as suited their own character as conquerors, set examples of every species almost that is known in the history of mankind. They levied customs at sea-ports, excises on many articles of consumption, and a considerable capitation or poll-tax, in which they

1 Sueton. in Vespas. c. 16.

2 There being no rule by which to limit the extent of a present, the person who receives it, allowing the giver to proceed as far as his means, or his desire to pay court will carry him, still resents any imaginary defect, and employs terror and force to extort what he affects to receive as a gift.

made no distinction of rank or fortune. These modes of taxation, already known under the republic, and various in different provinces, now began to be regulated upon the maxims of a general policy, extending over the whole empire.

Some of the burdens laid by Octavius, as that which was imposed on the value of goods exposed to sale, were charged directly for the benefit of the army as a fund for the discharge of their pay, or an immediate supply for their subsistence or clothing; and by this sort of impropriation were unalterably fixed. The country, where any troops were quartered, was charged, for their use, with supplies of straw, forage, carriages, corn, bread, provisions, and even clothing.

From such particulars, we may form some conception of the mode and tendency of Roman taxation, although we have no certain accounts, or even probable conjecture, of the amount of the whole. Under the present or preceding state of the Roman government, there was no principle operating in behalf of the subject, besides the spontaneous humanity or justice of those who exercised the sovereignty; and as the provinces under the republic had been ill-protected against the rapacity of proconsuls and proprætors, they were now considered, together with the republic itself, as the property of a master; and the examples of taxation that were set by either, may instruct a sovereign how to profit by the wealth of his subjects, rather than admonish a free people how to constitute a revenue with the least inconvenience to themselves, or the least possible injury to the sources of wealth.

The situation of Italy, and the distribution of land and water in its neighbourhood, had made navigation familiar to the Romans in the earliest ages of the republic. A considerable part of their force, in many of their wars, consisted in shipping. The battle of Actium, which decided the fate of the empire, was fought at sea; and although the Romans, at this date, had subdued every nation within reach of their seas, and had no enemy to fear on that element; yet the transport of armies, the safety of their navigation, and the suppression of piracies, by which the supply of corn, and the conveyance of the public revenue from the provinces, were often interrupted, made a naval force, and a proper distribution of guard ships, necessary to the peace and government of the empire.

Three capital fleets were accordingly stationed by Augustus for the security of the coasts, one at Ravenna, near the bottom of the Hadriatic Gulph; one at Forum Julii, on the opposite side of the peninsula; and a third at Misenum, the principal promontory or head-land of Campania. Besides these, there were numbers of armed vessels destined to ply in all the gulphs and navigable rivers throughout the empire.

The ordinary military establishment consisted of about five-and-forty legions, besides cavalry and city and provincial troops. The whole, reckoning each legion, with its attendants and officers, at six thousand men, and making a reasonable allowance for cavalry, may have amounted to three hundred thousand. Of the manner in which this army was distributed, the following particulars only are mentioned: on the Rhine, there were stationed eight legions; on the Danube, two; on the frontiers of Syria, four; in Spain, three; in Africa, in Egypt, in Mysia, and Dalmatia, each two legions; in the city were nine, or, according to others, ten cohorts, in the capacity of guards, or prætorian bands, to attend the person of the emperor; and, together with these, three cohorts of a thousand men each, intended as a city watch, to be employed in preserving the peace, in extinguishing fires, and in suppressing any other occasional disorder.[3]

For the farther security of the empire, considerable territories on the frontier, which might have been easily occupied by the Roman arms, were suffered to remain in the possession of allies, dependant princes, or free cities and republican states, who, owing their safety to the support of the Roman power, formed a kind of barrier against its enemies, were vigilant to observe, and ready to oppose every attempt of invasion, and were prepared to co-operate with the Roman armies, and to support them with stores and provisions as oft as they had occasion to act in their neighbourhood. The republic had ever cultivated such alliances with powers that were contiguous to the place of their operations; and frequently, after having made the defence of their ally the pretence of a war, and after having availed themselves of his assistance, they, upon occasion of some breach or quarrel, joined the ally himself to the conquest which he had assisted them to make. This same policy which had been useful in acquiring the dominion of so great an empire, was still employed for its safety. In pursuance of this policy, the kings of Mauritania, of the Bosphorus, of the Lesser and Greater Armenia, of Cappadocia, Commagne, Galatia, and Pamphilia, with Paphlagonia, Colchis, and Judæa, together with the republican states of Rhodes, Cyrene, Pisidia, and Lycia. acted under the denomination of allies, as advanced parties on the frontiers of the empire, and encouraged by the prospect of a powerful support, were ready to withstand every enemy by whom their own peace, or that of the Romans, was likely to be disturbed.

3 Tacitus, lib. i.

CHAPTER III.

The Family and Court of Augustus—His pretended Resignation of the Empire renewed—The exercise of his Power becomes less disguised—Death of Agrippa.

IN the Roman empire, thus subjected to a monarch, though planted with races of men the most famed for activity and vigour, it has been observed, that the materials of history became less frequent and less interesting than they had been in the times of the republic, while confined to much narrower bounds. Under the dominion of a single person, all the interesting exertions of the national, the political, and the military spirit over great parts of the earth, were suppressed. Even in the capital of the world, so lately agitated with every difference of opinion or interfering of interests, the operations of government itself were become silent and secret. Matters of public concern, considered as the affairs of an individual, were adjusted to his conveniency, and directed by his passions, or by those of his family, relations, or domestics. The list of such persons accordingly, with their characters, dispositions, and fortunes, make a principal part in the subsequent history of this mighty empire.

Augustus still continued to employ Mæcenas and Agrippa as the chief instruments of his government. To their abilities and conduct, in their respective departments, he in a great measure owed the prosperous state of his affairs. He likewise persevered in his attachment to Livia, whose separation from her former husband has been already mentioned. Together with the mother, he received into his family her two sons, Tiberius and Drusus. Of these Tiberius, born in the year of the battle of Philippi, was now about twelve years old; Drusus, of whom she was pregnant at the time of her marriage with Octavius, and whom she brought forth about three months afterwards, was now about seven years old.

The emperor having no children by Livia, had offspring only a daughter, famous by the name of Julia, born to him by Scribonia, the relation of Sextus Pompeius, with whom he had contracted a marriage of political conveniency, and of short duration. Next to this daughter, in point of consanguinity, were his sister Octavia, the widow, first of Marcellus, and afterwards of Antony, with her children by both her husbands. Among these were, by her first husband, Marcella, married to Agrippa, and the young Marcellus,[1] who being married to the emperor's daughter Julia, was looked upon as the undoubted representative of the Octavian and Julian families, and heir to the fortunes of Cæsar.

Such then are the persons to whom many parts in the immediate sequel of this narration will principally refer; and such are the outset and first considerable lines of a very long reign, of which the materials will not furnish, nor the professed intention of this history require, a long or minute detail.

The establishment now made by Augustus has nearly completed the revolution of which it was proposed to give an account. The despotism, though exercised under the name of republic, and in the form of a temporary and legal institution, being in reality absolute, and without any qualification of mixed government, it could not be doubted that the same powers would be continued after the period for which they were now granted should expire, and that the empire, for the future, must for ever submit to the head of the army: but in what form of succession, or with what immediate effect on the character and condition of those who were subject to it, remains to be collected from the sequel of this and a few of the following reigns. Military government is almost a necessary result of the abuse of liberty, or, in certain extremities of this evil, appears to be the sole remedy that can be applied.[2] But, in order to know with how much care the evil itself ought to be avoided, we must attend likewise to the full effects of the cure.

It appears from the particulars which have been stated, relating to the first uses which Octavius made of his power, that he was not to be caught in the snare into which many others have fallen in consequence of great success. In his prosperity he still retained his vigilance, his caution, and his industry, and relied upon these alone for the preservation of what he had gained. Though now secure by the pretended forms of a legal establishment, he continued attentive to what was passing in every part of the empire, frequently withdrew from the seats of adulation and pleasure in the city of Rome to visit the provinces; and, without any view to conquest, or purpose of ostentation whatever, gave his presence where any affairs of moment were in dependence, merely to extend the effects of his government, and to realize the dominion he had planned.

The peace which immediately followed the victories obtained on the coast of Epirus and in Egypt, was the circumstance on which Augustus chiefly relied for the recommendation of his government, and he seems, from inclination as well as policy, to have early entertained a maxim favourable to peace with foreign nations, and which he afterwards openly inculcated, That the bounds of the empire should not be extended. He himself had made some acquisitions in Dalmatia and in Panonia. But his object in making war in those countries, had been, rather to exercise and prepare his army for the contest he expected with Antony, than for any purpose of extending his conquests; and he reduced Egypt to a province, merely to extirpate the last remains of his rival's party, and to prevent farther molestation from that rich and powerful king-

1 In relation to this young man, Virgil, in flattering Augustus, has composed so many beautiful lines in the sixth book of the Æneid.

———Si qua fata aspera rumpas,
Tu Marcellus eris, &c.

2 Non aliud discordantis patriæ remedium fuisse quam ut ab uno regeretur. Tacit. lib. i. c. 9.

dom. In his first plan of operations communicated to the senate, he expressed his disposition to acquiesce in the present extent of the empire; but it was necessary to secure the frontier from invasions, and to ascertain, though not to extend, its bounds. Soon after his new model of government was established, he took measures accordingly to repress the disorder which subsisted in some of the provinces, and to reduce to obedience some cantons on which the state had already a claim of sovereignty, though not fully acknowledged. He proceeded to punish others, who, at the breaking out of the civil wars, had taken advantage of the general distraction of the empire to resume their independency, or to make war on the Roman settlements. He had examples of both sorts to contend with in different parts; in Thrace, on the Rhine, and among the Alps, but chiefly in Spain.

Of all the provinces that became subject to Rome, those of Spain had been the most difficult acquisition; insomuch that, after all the wars so frequently renewed in that country, there were still some warlike cantons who continued to maintain their independence. Among these the Astures and Cantabri[3] being in actual rebellion, the emperor himself, at the head of a powerful army, still pretending a design to invade Britain, passed into Gaul, and there having fixed a rate of taxation for the province, turned into Spain. He obliged the rebels, upon his approach, to quit their usual habitations, and retire to the mountains. But finding that they were likely to protract the war, and to engage him in a succession of tedious and indecisive operations, he fixed his quarters at Tarraco,[4] and left the command of the army employed on this service to C. Antistius and Carisius. Soon after his arrival at Tarraco he entered on his eighth consulate. From that place he sent Terentius Varro to quell a rebellion of the Salassi and the other nations of the Alps, and sent M. Vincius to punish some German tribes, by whom the Roman traders frequenting their country, or settled among them, had been massacred. He himself, while his generals were employed in these services, remained two years at his quarters in Spain; and upon the elapse of his eighth consulate resumed that office for the ninth time.

U. C. 724.
Imper. Cæsar 8vo. T. Statilius Taurus. August 2do. Ætat. 36.

U. C. 728.
Imperator Cæsar 9no. M. Junius Silenus. August 3tio. Ætat. 37.

During the residence of Augustus in Spain, arrived the famous reference or appeal from the Parthians, submitting to his decision a contest for the throne of their kingdom.[5] The competitors were Phraates and Tiridates. The first having been in possession, was expelled by a powerful insurrection of the people in favour of his rival: but, after a little time, having assembled his forces and his allies, he attacked Tiridates, obliged him to fly in his turn, and to take refuge in the contiguous province of the Roman empire. This exile, having the son of his rival a prisoner, proceeded to Rome, and from thence to the quarters of the emperor in Spain. At the same time arrived an embassy from Phraates, then in actual possession of the throne, desiring that Tiridates should be delivered up to him, and that his son should be restored. Both parties offered honourable terms to the Romans, particularly the restoration of all the captives, and of all the trophies taken either from Crassus or from Antony, in their unfortunate invasions of that kingdom.

Augustus willingly accepted of these terms; but affecting to refer the Parthian dispute to the Roman senate, gave instructions that the son of Phraates should be restored to his father, but that Tiridates should not be delivered up to his enemy.[6]

By this transaction, though a pacific one, the disgrace incurred by the Roman legions in Parthia was supposed to be entirely effaced. And it being said that Augustus, on this occasion, had performed, by the authority of his name, what other Roman leaders had attempted in vain by force of arms, he had a variety of honours decreed to him by the senate. It passed, among other resolutions, that his name should be inscribed among those of the gods in the address of the public hymns; that one of the Roman tribes should be named the Julian tribe, in honour of him; that he should wear the triumphal crown at all public entertainments; that all Roman senators, who had been present at any of his victories, should attend his triumphs dressed in purple robes; that the anniversary of his return to Rome should be observed as a festival; that he should have the nomination of persons to be honoured with the priesthood, and should fill up the list to any numbers he thought proper. From this time forward, accordingly, the number was supposed to be unlimited.

Soon after the conclusion of this negotiation with the Parthians, the operations of the armies in Spain and Germany were brought to a successful period. Caius Antistius being attacked by the Cantabri, obtained a complete victory, and obliged that people again to take separate retreats in the woods and mountains, where numbers of them were reduced by famine, and others, being invested in their strong holds, and in danger of being taken, chose to perish by their own hands.

Carisius was equally successful against the Asturi; obliged them to abandon their habitations, or to submit at discretion.[7]

Terentius Varro, having invaded the Salassi or Piedmontese, on different quarters, made them agree to pay a cotribution, and, under pretence of levying it, sent an army in separate divisions into their country; and thus having them at his mercy, exercised a cruelty of which too many examples are to be found in every period of ancient history. He ordered, that all the children and youth of the nation, thus taken by surprise, should be put up for sale; the buyer being required to come under engagements, that none of this unhappy people, thus sold for slaves, should be restored to freedom, or allowed to return to their own country, till after an interval of twenty years.[8]

3 Nations inhabiting the mountainous coasts of the Bay of Biscay.
4 Tarragona.
5 Dio. Cass. lib. liii. c. 22 et 25. Orosius, lib. vi. c. 21. Velleius. Liv. Epitome, lib cxxxiv. Dio. Cass. lib. liii. c. 33.

6 Justin. lib. xlii. c. 5. Dio. Cass. lib. liii. c. 33. Velleius Pater. lib. ii. c. 91.
7 Dio. Cass. lib. liii. c. 25.
8 Ibid.

About the same time Augustus received from the army the title of Imperator, and from the senate the offer of a triumph, on account of the victories gained by his lieutenants. The last of these honours he declined; but took occasion to exhibit games in Spain, in name of his nephew Marcellus and of his step-son Tiberius, whom he wished to recommend to the army by this act of munificence. He likewise distributed lands, both in Spain and in the Cisalpine Gaul, to the soldiers who were discharged from the legions, and on this occasion built the Augusta Emeritorum[1] in Spain, and the Augusta Prætoria[2] on the descent of the Alps towards Italy. In conformity with his general plan of dividing the provinces, he separated Spain into three governments, the Bœtica, Lusitania, and Taraconensis. The first was included under the department of the senate, the other two had been reserved to himself.

Gaul was, at the same time, divided into four separate governments; the Narbonensis, Acquitania, Lugdunensis, and Celtica or Belgica. Upon this increase of the number of provinces, additional officers, particularly in the capacity of quæstors, became necessary. All who had, for ten years preceding the date of these arrangements, held the office of quæstor in the city, without succeeding to any foreign employment, were now ordered to cast lots for the vacant stations.

The general peace being again restored, by the successful operations of the army in different quarters of the empire, the gates of Janus once more were shut, and a column was erected on a summit of the Alps, bearing an inscription, with the names of forty-eight separate nations or cantons, who were now reduced to obedience under the auspices of Augustus.[3]

U. C. 729. The emperor being on his return to Rome, and having accepted of a tenth consulate, the ceremony of his admission into office was performed before his arrival on the first of January, with a renewal of the oaths formerly taken by the people, that they would observe his decrees.

Imper. Cæsar 10mo, C. Norbanus Flaccus. August. 4to, Ætat. 38.

The senate, at the same time, being informed that he intended to make a donation to the people, amounting to a hundred denarii for each person; but that, from respect to the laws which gave them a negative on such donations, he meant to defer the publication of his intention until he had their consent; they immediately passed a decree, giving him full exemption from every law or form of the commonwealth, and empowering him[4] to govern in all matters according to his own will. This decree, of which the effect was not so much to vest him with any new powers, as to remove the veil from that power of which he was already possessed, it is probable, from his caution in other matters, he would have gladly avoided. At his return, after so long an absence, he was received by all orders of men with every demonstration of joy. Having already been flattered in his own person with every mark of distinction and honour, he was now courted in the person of his favourite nephew Marcellus. This young man was admitted, by a formal decree, to a place in the senate among the members of prætorian rank, and was allowed to sue for the consulate ten years before the legal age. Livia too had a share in these flatteries, by a like privilege bestowed on her son Tiberius, though in order to retain some distinction between the favourite nephew and the step-son of the emperor, the decree in favour of Tiberius only bore that he might sue for the consulate five years before the legal age.

In the mean time Marcellus held the office of ædile, and Tiberius that of quæstor. The first, to signalize his magistracy, ordered that that part of the forum or space in which the courts of justice were held, which till then had been always uncovered and exposed to the open air, should be shaded with a covering or awning of cloth.[5]

During the absence of the emperor, the plans which had been formed for the better government of the city, for adorning it with public buildings, and for repairing the highways throughout Italy, were carried into execution by Agrippa. The repair of the highways had been assigned, in separate lots, to such of the senators as were supposed able to defray the expense of it; and, among these, the Flaminian Way had been assigned to Augustus himself. The town was divided into quarters or districts, under proper officers, annually chosen or taken by lot; and a watch was established, to prevent disorders, and to guard against fire.

The channel of the river, in a great measure choked up with heaps of rubbish from the ruins of houses, that formed considerable banks and islands in the midst of it, and, at every flood, forced great inundations into the streets, was now effectually cleared.[6] The Septa Julia, or place of assembly, called the Julian place, in honour of the emperor, was repaired, adorned, and dedicated. A temple was erected to Neptune, in memory of the late naval victories. The portico of the pantheon was finished about this time; within was placed, among the images of the gods, a statue of Julius Cæsar; in the vestibule, or portico, were placed those of Augustus and Agrippa.[7]

The emperor, upon his approach to the city, published, by virtue of the power lately conferred upon him by the senate, his intention to distribute to the citizens a hundred denarii a man. In this it appears that the Roman people had still retained the worst and most corrupting part of their republican privileges, that of receiving gratuities in money and corn, as well as that of being frequently amused with expensive shows. By the first they were supported in idleness, and by the other taught dissipation, and made to forget the state of political degradation into which they were fallen. At the games exhibited in the preceding year by the prætor Servilius, it is said, that three hundred bears, and an equal number of African wild beasts, were baited or hunted down.[8]

The restoration of peace being a principal point on which Augustus valued himself with the public, the gates of Janus, in a few of the first years of his reign, had been already three

1 Now Merida.
2 Now Aosta.
3 Plin. lib. xix. c. 1
4 Dio. Cass. lib. liii. c. 28.
5 Quantum mutatis moribus Catonis censorii qui sternendum quoque forum muricibus censuerat. Plin. Nat. Hist. lib. iii. c. 20.
6 Sueton. in August. c. 29, 30.
7 Dio Cass. lib. liii. c. 22 &c. &c.
8 Ibid. c. 27

times repeatedly shut.[9] But on a frontier so extensive, beset on the one hand by fierce nations, jealous of their liberties, and on the other, by armies, whose commanders were fond of opportunities to distinguish themselves, it was not possible long to avoid every species of war. Soon after the emperor had withdrawn from Spain, leaving the command in Lusitania tó L. Æmilius, the Cantabri and Astures, still impatient of the dominion to which they had lately, in appearance, made a perpetual submission, took a resolution again to shake off the Roman yoke. Proposing to give the first intimation of their design by a stroke of importance, they drew a considerable part of the Roman army into their country, under pretence of furnishing them with a supply of corn; and when they found them dispersed in small parties to receive the proposed distribution, they put the whole, or the greater part, to the sword. In revenge for this piece of treachery, Æmilius laid their country under military execution, and by a barbarous policy, to prevent future revolts, cut off the right hands of the prisoners whose lives he spared.[10]

At the same time Augustus himself, though somewhat contrary to the general system of his reign, entertained a project of extending the Roman settlements, or at least of making discoveries on the side of Arabia, and on the coasts of the Indian seas. He was tempted, probably, by the prospect of getting access to the rare and costly commodities, which the Arabians were known to receive from India,[11] and which they sold in the markets of Egypt and Asia at their own price. He expected to refund the expense of his armament from the great treasures of gold and silver which the Arabians were supposed to possess.

For this purpose Ælius Gallus, the proprætor of Egypt, was entrusted with the conduct of an expedition to the Gulph of Arabia. This officer spent a considerable time in fitting out a fleet of armed ships, which he afterwards found to be unnecessary, as the Arabians were mere traders, and had no ships of force. In passing the gulph with one hundred and thirty transports, he, by the unskilfulness of his mariners and pilots, sustained a great loss both in shipping and men, and in the delays which he afterwards incurred, or in attempting to penetrate the deserts of Arabia eastward, he lost a great part of his army, which perished by want of water, or by disease. And thus, after a fruitless attempt, in which he spent many months, returned to Alexandria with a small part of his army, without having gained any considerable advantage, or even obtained information of the sources of wealth which he was sent to explore.[12]

U. C. 730.

Imper. Cæsar 11mo. Tribunus plebis. Terentius Varro Murena mort. C. Calpurnius Piso.

While these transactions passed in the provinces and on the frontier of the empire, Augustus, then residing at Rome, entered on an eleventh consulate. His colleague, in the beginning of the year, was Terentius Varro Murena. But this consul died in office, and was succeeded for the remainder of the year by C. Calpurnius Piso.

August. 5to. ætat. 39.

Augustus himself, in this consulate was taken ill; and being supposed in danger, called his colleague, with a number of the principal senators, into his presence, to receive his last instructions relating to the empire. The title by which he affected to hold the government could not support him in pointing out a succession. He accordingly made no mention of any successor to himself, but delivered to the consul Piso, as being first officer of state, the memorials he had drawn up relating to the revenue and other public establishments. He gave to Agrippa his ring, which was the badge of his nobility, and which, according to the ideas of the Romans, had an emblematical reference to his power. He seemed to overlook his nephew Marcellus, though at this time the first in his favour, and probably destined to inherit his fortune. This circumstance, together with the general opinion of his dissimulation, made it be suspected that he had no real apprehensions of dying, and that he called his friends to this solemn audience, merely to show, on a supposed death-bed, his respect for the commonwealth. To elude the penetration of those who suspected his arts, and whom he still continued to dread, after his recovery, he desired that the will which he had made on this occasion should be publicly read; but the senate, already knowing the contents, and affecting to believe, without this evidence, the sincerity of his intentions to restore the republic, refused to comply. They appointed great rejoicings on account of his recovery, and amply distinguished and rewarded the physician, to whose skill it was supposed that they owed the preservation of so valuable a life.[13]

Although the circumstance of Augustus not having mentioned his nephew Marcellus, and the honour he had done to Agrippa, were probably not the effects of any serious design respecting the succession, they nevertheless became a subject of jealousy in the mind of the young man, and soon after occasioned the retirement of Agrippa from the court. This officer, under pretence of going into Syria, where he was appointed to command, set out from Rome, but stopped at Mitylene in the island of Lesbos, where he lived in retirement, without taking any part in public affairs.

During the stay of Agrippa at Mitylene, and in less than a year after his departure from Rome, happened the death of Marcellus; an event which Livia was, by some, alleged to have hastened, in order to make way for the advancement of her own sons; but the sickliness of the season and the mortality at Rome, during the two preceding years, might have accounted for the death of Marcellus, without any supposition of unnatural means;[14] and the event itself brought no immediate advantage to the sons of Livia. It was followed by the recall of Agrippa, and by a new arrangement, which removed the Claudii still farther from the place to which the mother was desirous to raise them in the consideration and favour of the emperor.

Augustus had now, for some years, without intermission, assumed and exercised the office of consul, but thinking its authority no longer necessary to support his power, he divested himself of the title, and gave a fresh proof of his modera-

9 Sueton. in August. c. 22. 10 Ibid. lib. liii. c. 29.

11 Strabo mentions, that in the port of Nus there were above 100 ships from India.

12 Dio. Cass. lib. liii. c. 29. Zonaras, lib. x. c. 33. Plin. lib. vi. c. 28. Str. lib. ii. p. 118. Ib. lib. xvi. p. 782.

13 Dio. Cass. lib. liii. c. 31. 14 Ibid. c 32, 33.

tion, by substituting in his place L. Sestius, one of the few who were still supposed to regret the fall of the republic. Sestius had been the friend of Marcus Brutus, adhered to the cause of the commonwealth in every period of the civil wars, and, though spared by the victors at Philippi, still ventured to retain the statue and picture of his friend.

The magnanimity of Augustus, in getting over these objections to the character of Sestius, was not neglected by the flatterers of his court; nor was his declining the consulate overlooked by the senate, in their zeal to devise new honours and additional concessions. The character of tribune, which had been annually conferred on the emperor for some years, was, on the present occasion, rendered perpetual in his person, and the privilege of proposing matters for the consideration of the senate, hitherto appropriated to the consuls in office, was now likewise extended to him. As a compensation for the dignity of consul, which he now declined, he was declared perpetual proconsul, both at Rome and in the provinces, and empowered to supersede every officer, even in his own government.[1] He was, at the same time, pressed to accept the title and power of dictator.

U. C. 731.
M. Claudius Marcellus Arseninus, L. Aruntius, August. 6to, ætat. 40.

The people, labouring under a a plague or epidemic distemper, which, in the usual mode of their superstition, they considered as a punishment inflicted by the gods for some public offence, and in particular for their having suffered the emperor to divest himself of the consulate, proposed that he should instantly assume this or a higher dignity. While the senate was assembled, multitudes crowded together in a riotous manner, and with threats required that a decree should pass to vest Augustus with the style and powers of dictator. They collected twenty-four fasces, the number usually carried before this officer, and repairing to the emperor's palace, called upon him to assume his power, and to rescue the people from their present calamities.

Augustus, who had sufficiently provided for all the objects of his ambition, without the alarming name of dictator, took this opportunity to establish his character for moderation. He intreated the people to desist from their purpose; and when still pressed, he appeared to be greatly agitated, tore his clothes,[2] and gave other signs of extreme distress. Being likewise pressed to accept of the office of perpetual censor, he, in the same manner, declined it, recommending, for the immediate discharge of its duties, P. Æmilius Lepidus and Munatius Plancus.

In acting this part, it is probable that Octavius guarded against the fate of Julius Cæsar; that he preferred security to the ostentation of power, and relied more on the caution with which he avoided offence, than he did on the vigilance of his informers and spies, or on the terror of his arms. He could not, however, at all times, avoid having recourse to these means of defence. During his present residence at Rome, he received information of a design formed on his life by Muræna and Fannius Cæpio, and brought them to trial. Velleius Paterculus, without any scruple, affirms the guilt of these supposed conspirators; but Dion Cassius insinuates, that the guilt of Muræna, at least, was rather indiscretion, and an unguarded freedom of speech, with which he was accustomed to censure the conduct of his superiors, than any formed design of so criminal a nature.

Muræna was the brother-in-law of Mæcenas, and himself appeared to be in favour with Augustus. Upon the surmise of an intention to seize him, together with Fannius, both absconded and fled. They were arraigned and tried in absence; but as the judges still enjoyed the privilege of voting by secret ballot, they availed themselves of it to acquit the accused.

The use of the secret ballot in criminal trials, when first introduced in the republic, as it diminished the power of the aristocracy, which was so necessary for the preservation of public order, no doubt had a tendency unfavourable to public justice. But now, when it might have been salutary, at least in all state trials, it was, under pretence of the false judgment given in the case of Muræna and Cæpio, so far abolished, that all persons who fled from trial, or who declined appearance, were, by an express statute, deprived of the benefit of it;[3] and this circumstance deserves to be mentioned as the first instance, perhaps, in which the judicial forms of the republic, formerly partial to the interests of the people, began to be changed in favour of despotism. This innovation was probably the more fatal in the sequel, that the emperor himself, under pretence of giving evidence, of urging prosecutions, or of appearing as an advocate for his clients, frequently attended the courts.[4] And it cannot be doubted, that as often as he appeared,[5] the part which he took, whether as a witness or as a pleader, must have had very great and improper influence in the cause.

In the beginning of this reign, are dated some regulations calculated for the peace and general order of the city. Among these, it is mentioned, that the number of prætors was reduced to ten; and that two of this number were appointed to inspect the public revenue;[6] that some feasts, which had been customary, were prohibited, and the expense of others restrained within moderate bounds; that the care of the public shows was entrusted to the prætors, with a competent allow-

1 Dio. Cass. lib. liii. c. 32. 2 Ibid. lib. liv. c. 1.

3 Dio. Cass. lib. liv. c. 3.
4 Ibid. Sueton. in August. c. 56.
5 Among the remarkable trials of this period is mentioned that of M. Primus, who having the command in Macedonia, was accused of having, without orders, made war on the Odrysians, a Thracian nation. He pleaded the orders of Augustus or of Marcellus; but the emperor himself, attending the trial, denied his having ever given such orders, and the defendant was condemned. He is said, at another time, to have appeared in behalf of his confidents Apulius and Mæcenas, who were arraigned of some undue influence in protecting a person under prosecution for adultery. After the prosecutor began to open the charge, Augustus himself came into court, and commanded him not to traduce his relations and friends; a stretch of power which, under legal government, ought to have given offence but in the present state of the Romans, only put the subject in mind how necessary it was for himself to court the imperial favour; and it was decreed accordingly, by the unanimous votes of all the senators, that in memory of this gracious interposition of the emperor, an additional statue should be erected to him.
6 Dio. Cass. lib. liii. c. 32.

ance from the treasury to defray the expense of them, but under an express prohibition to add, as they had been hitherto inclined to do, from ambitious motives, above an equal sum from their own private estates. The shows of gladiators were subjected to the control of the senate, and the number of pairs to be exhibited, on any particular occasion, restricted to sixty. The care of extinguishing and guarding against fire being in the department of the ædiles, a body of six hundred men, destined to this service, was put under the command of these magistrates. Persons of rank having given cause of complaint, by presenting themselves as dancers or performers on the public theatre, such examples were strictly prohibited.

As the emperor ever affected a desire to be entirely relieved of the government, he accompanied his most popular acts and regulations with a formal and ostentatious resignation of some particular parts of his power. The provinces of Narbonne and of Cyprus, which had been originally part of his trust, being in the first period of his reign restored to peace, he formally resigned them into the hands of the senate. But while he was occupied with these pacific or popular measures, the Astures and Cantabri, notwithstanding their former distresses, still passionately fond of their expiring liberties, having revolted yet a third time, were again reduced with great slaughter. Most of those who escaped from the swords of the Roman legions, perished by their own hands.[7] While this event, in appearance, terminated all the troubles which subsisted in the western part of the empire, an alarm was received from Egypt, of a formidable enemy appearing to intend the invasion of that kingdom. The Ethiopians, probably, encouraged by the low state to which, from the unfortunate expedition of Gallus against the Arabians, they supposed the Roman forces on the Nile to have been reduced, had, by the time that the alarm had been communicated to Rome, actually entered the province; and, before any assistance could be sent from other parts of the empire, were repulsed by Petronius, who succeeded to Gallus in the government of Egypt.

But before these events were known, the emperor had taken his resolution to attend to the defence of this kingdom in person, and was set out on his voyage. Having put into Sicily in his way, while he yet remained in this island, the usual election of consuls came on at Rome.[8]

U. C. 732.

Q. Emilius Lepidus M. Lollius Nepos. August 9no, Ætat. 41.

He himself was named, together with M. Lollius Nepos; but he declined accepting of the office, and affected to leave the Roman people, as of old, to a free choice. This novelty gave rise to a warm contest, in which Quintus Emilius Lepidus, and L. Silanus appeared as competitors, and were supported by numerous parties of their friends. The people began to recover the remembrance of their former power, and were encouraged or supported by the candidates in disorders or freedoms, from which they had for some time been restrained. Augustus himself was alarmed with these appearances of a reviving republic, summoned both the candidates to attend him in Sicily; and having reprimanded them for the disturbances they gave, forbade them to appear at Rome, until the depending elections were passed. The competition, nevertheless, was carried on with great warmth in their absence, and ended with much difficulty in favour of Lepidus.

This specimen of the supposed disorders to which the people were inclined, in the absence of an authority that was fit to restrain them, probably induced the emperor to hasten the recall of Agrippa, as a person on which he could devolve the care of the city. The breach which had been some time made in his family, by the death of Marcellus, remained unrepaired; and he seems to have hesitated in the choice of the person whom he was to place next to himself in power, and in succession to the government. His daughter Julia, the widow of Marcellus, had yet brought no addition to his offspring. She was now to be disposed of in a second marriage, and was likely to bestow on her husband the character of heir apparent to the fortunes of her father. It is said, that Mecænas advised the emperor to make choice of Agrippa. "This man," he said, "is already too high to remain where he is: he must be lifted up to a place yet higher, or be cast to the ground."[9]

Agrippa was accordingly, about this time, made to part with Marcella, the niece of Augustus, to whom he had been some time married, in order that he might become the husband of Julia, and by this title the first in the family of Cæsar.

The emperor, while in Sicily, having bestowed on the city of Syracuse, and on other towns of that island, the privilege of Roman colonies, and having made some other arrangements for the better government of the province, continued his voyage from thence into Greece. As he passed through Sparta and Athens, he treated the inhabitants of those once eminent cities with marks of favour or displeasure, according to the part they had taken in the late divisions of the empire.

The Spartans had, with proper hospitality, received Livia in her flight from Italy, and, in return, were now honoured with the presence of the emperor at one of the public meals, which they still affected to retain in memory of their ancient institutions. They likewise received a grant of the island of Cithera, which formerly had belonged to their territory.

The Athenians, on the contrary, it is said, were put in mind of their partiality to Antony and Cleopatra, and of the singular ostentation with which they admitted the queen of Egypt a citizen of Athens. In resentment of this behaviour, they were deprived of their sovereignty in Ægina and Eretria, and forbid to receive any presents in return for the freedom of their city, a distinction, which, it seems, was still earnestly courted, and from the sale of which they derived some revenue.

From these visits to Sparta and Athens, the emperor proceeded to Samos, where he remained for the winter.[10] Here he not only had a confirmation of the reports already mentioned, relating to the success of Petronius against the Ethiopians, but received an embassy from this people to sue for peace. They had addressed themselves to

7 Dio. Cass. lib. liv. c. 4. 8 Ibid. c. 5, 6.

9 Dio Cass. lib. liv. c. 6. 10 Ibid. c. 7

Petronius; and being referred to the emperor, desired that they might have guides to conduct them to him. "This emperor," they said, "or the place of his abode, we know not." Being conducted to Samos, on the route by which he was expected to arrive in Asia, they obtained a peace, without any of the submissions or unequal conditions by which the Romans were formerly accustomed to prepare the way, in every treaty, for the farther extension of their conquests.[1]

U. C. 733.

M. Apuleius, P. Silius Narva. August. 8vo, Ætat. 42.

In the spring, Augustus passed from Samos to Bithynia, in which, though one of the provinces that had been committed to the administration of the senate, he, by his own authority, made some reformations, and upon a complaint, that the people of Cyzicum had insulted with the rod, and put to death some Roman citizens, he stript them of several privileges which they had hitherto enjoyed. From thence, he continued his progress into Syria, and there likewise inflicted some severities on the citizens of Tyre and Sidon, as a punishment of their seditions and disrespect to his government.[2]

The Parthians had not yet restored the Roman captives, and the trophies of which they had got possession on the defeats of Crassus and Antony. This was the condition, on which the king had obtained the release of his son. Being now reminded of it, or alarmed by the approach of the Roman emperor to his frontier, he sent an embassy to perform this article. But of the Roman prisoners, many, soon after they were taken, perished by their own hands; others, being reconciled by degrees to their condition, and having settled, were unwilling to remove. They concealed themselves from the persons who were sent to assemble and conduct them to the frontier, and but a few were recovered. These, together with the restored standards and other trophies, were conducted with great pomp to the city of Rome.

Augustus had already received the congratulations of the senate and people, on the conclusion of his treaty with the Parthians, and knowing how much it was become a point of honour at Rome to repair the disgrace which Roman armies had incurred on the Euphrates and the Tigris, he indulged, on the conclusion of this transaction, a degree of vanity, which was unusual with him on other occasions. He ordered the rites of thanksgiving that were appropriated to the greatest victories; gave instructions to erect a triumphal arch; and, upon his return to Rome, entered the city in triumph.

The Romans, in conferring honours on those who performed any successful service, considered the advantage itself, more than the means by which it had been obtained, and indulged, with all the distinctions that military courage or personal ability could claim, every officer, under whose auspices they prospered, whether by artifice or valour.[3] On this principle, Augustus, without having performed any military operation whatever, took occasion to triumph over an enemy, before whom the armies of Antony and Crassus had perished.

The object of the emperor's journey to the east having been obtained by the restoration of peace to Egypt, he did not proceed in his progress beyond the province of Syria. From thence, in his letters to the senate, he declaimed every intention or wish to extend the bounds of the empire, and disposed of kingdoms on the frontier to the princes of Asia, who were considered as confederates or allies of the Romans Among these, he gave to Tarcondimotus a principality in Cilicia; to Archelaus, the Lesser Armenia; to Herod, over and above his own kingdom of Judea, the principality of Zenodorus, in its neighbourhood. He restored a prince, of the name of Mithridates, to the kingdom of Commagené, from which his father had been expelled; and, at the request of the people of Armenia, sent his step-son Tiberius Claudius Nero, now about twenty years of age, with a commission to remove Artabazus, then in possession of that kingdom, and to declare Tiridates, who was still at Rome, to be its sovereign. This revolution in Armenia however was, by the death of Artabazus, who fell by the hands of his own subjects, in part effected before the arrival of Tiberius.

While the emperor was thus employed in the provinces, the ordinary succession of magistrates took place at Rome, and he himself being named consul, together with Caius Sentius, again declined the title, without recommending a substitute. Great animosities arose among the candidates for this honour. Agrippa had been called away into Gaul, upon an alarm received on the German frontier, and from thence into Spain, to quell another revolt of the Astures and Cantabri. In his absence the consul Sentius and the senate, unable to repress the tumults, sent a deputation to the emperor, who was still in Asia, to know his pleasure respecting the election, and, in return, had a fresh proof of his magnanimity and candour in the recommendation of Lucretius, a known partizan of the republic, and one of those, who being among the proscribed, had escaped from the massacre.

U. C. 734.

C. Sentius Saturninus. Q. Lucretius Vespello. Ex Kal. Julii. M. Venucius Vipsanius Agrippa. August. 9no, Ætat. 43.

Augustus, during his stay in Syria, had accounts of the birth of a grandson Caius, the eldest of the sons of Agrippa, by his daughter Julia, and had a copy of the decree, by which the senate annexed the anniversary of this birth to the days of public rejoicing. On his way to Italy, he passed another winter in Samos, where he received the ambassadors of many nations, and among these, an embassy from India, attended with a numerous retinue, and charged with a variety of presents.[4] But what probably most entertained the curious in the western world, was the exhibition of an Indian sage or Brahmin, who having taken his resolution to die, was ambitious to make his exit in presence of the Roman court. Being indulged in this desire, and flattered with the attendance of a numerous crowd of spectators, he prepared a funeral pile, which he set on fire, and with much ostentation and gravity, threw himself into the midst of it.[5] His tomb was marked

1 Strabo, lib. vii. p 821.

2 Dio. Cass. lib. liv. c. 6.

3 Ibid. c. 8.

4 Among these are mentioned by Strabo a snake ten cubits long, though it appears from Suetonius, lib. xv. p. 719, that a snake of a much greater length was exhibited in the public spectacles at Rome, fifty cubits. Sueton. in August. c 43.

5 Dio. Cass. lib. liv c. 8. 10, 11. Vell. Pat. lib. ii. c. 39

with the following inscription. "Here lies Tarmarus or Tarmanochegas, an Indian of Bargosa, who, in the manner of his country, ended his days by a voluntary death."[6] In such actions, we may perceive the powerful attraction of glory, from whatever sort of performance it be supposed to arise.

When the emperor's intended return was announced at Rome, many honours were decreed to him, all of which he declined, except that of having an altar erected on the occasion to Jupiter Redux, and that of having the day of his arrival inserted, under the title Augustalia, among the festivals of the kalendar. On his approach to the city, the magistrates and the people prepared to go forth in procession to meet him; but either from an aversion to pageantry, which he ever shunned, except when necessary to serve some purpose, or from a desire of procuring fresh encomiums of moderation, he made his entry in the night to avoid this compliment. On the following day, he procured resolutions of the senate and people, promoting Tiberius, the eldest of the sons of Livia, to the rank of prætor, and bestowing on Drusus, the younger brother, the privilege of standing for any of the ancient honours of the commonwealth five years before the legal age. He himself, at the same time, accepted the office of censor, with a new title, that of inspector of manners,[7] for five years.

This new designation was annexed to the titles of Augustus, under pretence that such an authority was wanting to take cognizance of the disorders committed in the late canvass for the election of consuls; but, as the period was near approaching, at which he was to repeat the form of resigning the government, it is probable that he chose to be vested with the character of censor, in order to make the arrangements preparatory to this ceremony.

Near ten years had elapsed since the rolls of the senate had been made up, and in this interval many reasons may have occurred for removing some of the members, and for substituting others. The powers of censor, with which the emperor was now vested, enabled him, without any unprecedented stretch of authority, to effect his purpose; but, notwithstanding this circumstance, his usual caution led him to seek for palliatives, and to devise means to lessen or to divide the odium of so disagreeable a measure. He gave out, that the number of senators was become too great, and thus provided himself with an excuse for excluding many of them, without stating any personal objection. He at first proposed to take upon himself only the nomination of thirty members, and under a solemn oath, that he should name the most worthy. These thirty, under a like solemn oath, were directed each, to give in a list of five, which would have made up the number to one hundred and fifty. And these, if they had been agreeable to the emperor, would have probably made the first part of the roll. But as he was in many instances disappointed and displeased with the choice that was made, he selected only thirty of the whole, to whom he gave the same directions as before, each to name five; but being equally dissatisfied with this new nomination, he took the whole on himself; and alleging, that the officer who collected the names had made some mistakes, and that many, who were thus proposed to be members of the senate, had necessary avocations in the provinces, he undertook, by his own authority, to reform the list. This task, however, he performed under so much apprehension of danger to his person, that, as in the former instance of the same kind, he carried armour under his clothes, and had a guard of ten chosen senators, with concealed weapons, who had orders not to admit above one person at a time to approach him.[8] By his conduct in this matter, or by the severity of his censures, he was supposed to have made so many enemies, or he himself at least took such impressions of jealousy and distrust as kept him in alarm, and occasioned some trials and executions, by which he proposed to counteract or prevent the conspiracies which were forming against him.[9]

Upon observing how much the emperor was alarmed, it was moved in the senate, as an acknowledgment of the danger to which he was exposed, that the members should take arms, and in certain numbers by turns pass the night in the palace. "I am unfortunately addicted to snore," said Antistius Lubeo, who still possessed some remains of the republican spirit, "and am afraid, that I should be an unwelcome guest in the anti-chamber of the prince."[10]

U. C. 735.
P. Cornelius Lentulus Marcellinus. Cn. Cornelius Lentulus. Aug. 10mo, Ætat. 44.

The period for which Augustus had accepted the command of the armies, and taken charge of part of the provinces being about to expire, he repeated the form of his resignation, and was prevailed upon to resume his trust, though but for a term of five years longer. Agrippa being now the son-in-law of the emperor, and the first in his favour, as well as his nearest relation, was joined with him for the same term of five years, in the character of tribune of the people.

During the preceding part of the new establishment, Augustus had affected to limit the exercise of his power to the military department, or to the provinces committed to his charge. In the city, or in civil affairs, he acted in the name of the senate, or under the veil of some temporary office of magistracy. But in the period upon which he was now entering, he seemed to have thought himself safe in assuming a more direct authority. He accordingly received from the senate, an appointment of perpetual extraordinary consul, to be preceded in all public appearances by twelve lictors, and in the senate to have a chair of state placed between the ordinary consuls of the year. He likewise received unlimited authority to enact laws, to the observance of which, the senate offered to bind themselves by oath. In this, he took occasion to give a proof of his moderation, by preventing the oath to be administered; but he proceeded from henceforward in the exercise of his power, with fewer disguises than he had formerly employed.

Prerogatives, hitherto assumed under the name of some ordinary magistracy, were committed to officers, acting by the appointment of Cæsar, and by his sole authority. Among these, may be numbered the inspection of the public works; of

6 Strabo, lib. xv p. 720.

7 Præfectus Morum.

8 Dio. Cass. lib. liv. c. 13, 14, 15.

9 Sueton. in August. c 35.

10 Dio. Cass. lib. liv.

11 Ibid. c. 17.

the highways; the navigation of the river; the markets;[1] the public granaries; the preservation of the peace, or government of the city, which was now committed to a military præfect or governor. Other new institutions were made, to remedy evils of a recent date.

From the time of the civil wars, Italy had remained subject to many disorders. The inhabitants, alleging the dangers to which they had been exposed in their persons and properties, continued to form into bands, and taking arms, under pretence of defending themselves, employed those arms for lawless purposes; robbed, murdered, or by force confined to labour in their workhouses many innocent passengers, whether freemen or slaves, whom they thought proper to question or violate, under the appellation of disorderly persons. To remedy this evil, guards were posted at proper intervals, and a species of military patrole established throughout the country, with orders to protect travellers, to inspect the workhouses or receptacles of labouring slaves, and to suppress all associations, besides those of the ancient corporations.[2]

By the same authority Augustus revived some obsolete laws, and gave instructions to put them in force: such as the laws limiting expense, restraining adultery, lewdness, and bribery, together with the laws which had been provided to promote marriage, or to discourage celibacy. The limitation of expense may have had its propriety under a republic, where it is an object of state not to suffer the citizen by his manner of living, or by his affectation of magnificence, to ruin himself, or to aim at distinction above his equals; but the object of the sumptuary laws, now enforced, is not specially mentioned. It was probably the same with that of the laws revived by Julius Cæsar, and consequently the same with that of the laws long since obtained, under the republic, by the tribune Licinius, and chiefly respecting the consumption of provisions.

In limiting the excess of the table, Augustus was himself a striking example of sobriety, being extremely moderate and abstemious in the use of wine and of food;[3] and with respect to the other objects of his severity, although he himself was not equally free from imputation, he probably already experienced the necessity of certain restraints in his own family, and very properly thought it became him, in the capacity of magistrate, every where to watch over the purity of domestic manners. His zeal to recommend marriage, and to promote the settlement of families, probably suggested the same measures.[4]

The Romans, by means of the census, obtained a more regular account of the numbers of the people than any other nation, and they were exceedingly watchful of their population, even when they had least cause to apprehend a diminution of it. They made laws to encourage marriage, when the advantages enjoyed by any Roman citizen, as father of a family, were of themselves a sufficient encouragement. Augustus being to revive those laws, produced and read in the senate a speech at that time, still extant, which had been delivered by Metellus Numidicus on this subject, about a hundred years before the present date.

Even so far back, under the republic, the decline of domestic manners may have begun to be felt. Licentiousness and want of economy may have already broke into the establishment of Roman families; disorders happening in the state of matrimony, may have deterred the single from embracing it. But if the effect of such circumstances then began to appear, how much more may we suppose that the destructive civil wars, which followed; the removal of the ancient inhabitants of Italy, to make way for strangers and soldiers of fortune, must have operated to reduce the numbers of the people? These troubles ending in military government; the uncertainty of every man's condition depending on the will of a master; fear, melancholy, and dejection, felt amidst the ruins of a fallen republic, may have completed the accumulation of evils, and the effect may have suggested to Augustus the necessity of reviving the ancient laws of the republic for the encouragement of population; insomuch, that the extension and application of them became a principal object of his reign.

Suetonius, as usual in his manner, without regard to dates, brings into one view many particulars of the policy of Augustus relating to this subject. Among these, it is mentioned that he augmented the rewards of marriage, and the penalties on celibacy.[5] That he sometimes brought forward the children of his own family into the place of public assembly, and exhorted the people to profit by that example; but that his zeal in this matter was far from being acceptable to the people. That he was frequently accosted in the theatres and places of public resort, with general cries of aversion;—had representations from citizens of rank, that it was impossible to support the extravagance of women educated in high condition, and was obliged to correct many of the edicts he at first had published, and to abate much of their rigour;—that, in order to facilitate the settlement of families, he permitted free and noble citizens to marry emancipated slaves;[6]—that the law, nevertheless, was still eluded;—that pretended marriages were contracted with children or females under age, and the completion of course indefinitely deferred;[7] that to prevent such evasions or frauds, it was enacted that no marriage could be legally contracted with any female under ten years of age, nor the completion of any marriage be delayed above two years after the date of the supposed contract.[8]

As it was proposed to multiply marriages, so it appeared likewise of consequence to render the dissolution of those already formed more difficult, and to lay divorces and separations under proportional restraints.[9] Under this wretched policy it seemed to be forgotten, that where man

1 Dio. Cass. lib. liv. c. 17.
2 Sueton. in Octav. c. 32.
3 In his ordinary diet, when he wanted nourishment, he eat a little bread, with some dried fruit, without observing any stated time for his meals. He ordered his table indeed to be regularly served; but he himself joined the company irregularly, often after they were set, and frequently left them before they were done, and insisted that he should not be disturbed in this freedom by any ceremony of waiting for him, or by any troublesome attention whatever. Sueton. in Octav. c. 72, 73. 76, 77.
4 Sueton. in Octav. c. 69.

5 Dio. Cass. lib. liv. c. 16. 6 Ibid.
7 Sueton. in Octav. c. 34. 8 Dio. Cass. lib. liv. c. 16
9 Sueton. in Octav. c. 34.

kind are happy, nature has provided sufficient inducements to marriage. The sovereign, who charged himself with the care of the people, seemed to consider a state into which mankind are powerfully led, by the most irresistible calls of affection, passion and desire, as a kind of workhouse into which they must be driven by the goad and the whip, or a prison in which they must be detained under bars and fetters of iron. The people seemed to feel themselves become the property of a master, who required them to multiply, in order to increase the number of his subjects; and they resisted this part of his administration, more than any other circumstance of the state of degradation into which they were fallen.

U. C. 736. *C. Furnius, C. Julius Silanius, Aug. 11mo, Ætat.* 45.

Augustus, in this second period of his reign, while he extended the exercise of his power, still endeavoured to disguise it under some forms or regulations of the ancient constitution. For this purpose, he revived the laws against bribery, those against taking fees for the pleading of causes, and the laws that were made to enforce the attendance of senators. In these particulars, we cannot imagine that he so far mistook the situation into which he had brought the people, as to revive laws against bribery, after there ceased to be any free election; the laws against accepting of fees[10] for pleading of causes, after all the motives which formerly induced senators to lend their gratuitous protection, had ceased to exist;[11] the law imposing a fine upon members of the senate coming too late to their places, after the proceedings of the senate, were reduced to a mere form, by which the emperor enforced his own decrees.[12] In these instances, then, we must suppose that Augustus, in the usual strain of his policy, revived the laws of the republic, in order to make it be believed that the republic was still in existence. But notwithstanding his attention, by these and other methods, to conceal the extent of his usurpation, he could not escape the penetration of his subjects, nor even the animadversion of buffoons, to whom some degrees of freedom or of petulance are permitted, after they are withheld from every one else. Having banished a player of the name of Pylades, for a difference with another player of the name of Bathyllus, he afterwards, to please the people, recalled Pylades; and giving him some admonition to be upon his good behaviour for the future: "That is a jest," said the other, "for the more that the people are occupied with our quarrels, the better for you."[13]

The emperor having remained at Rome about two years after the commencement of the second period of his reign, continued, or began to carry on many works for the ornament, magnificence, or convenience of the city. To defray the expense of such works, he laid persons, who had obtained a triumph, or any military honour, under a contribution of some part of their spoils; and by these means, perhaps, made some officers pay for their vanity more than they had taken from the enemy. He was supposed to be lavish of military honours, which in reality began to lose their value, or to change their nature, being mere badges of court favour, not as formerly, the evidence or record of signal services rendered to the state, and supported by the testimony of victorious armies, and the voice of the people. It may be observed, as an evidence, how much the triumph was fallen in its value, that, for some advantage gained over the Garamantes,[14] an obscure nation on the frontier of the Roman province in Africa, it was bestowed on Balbus, a native of Gades in Spain, and but newly admitted a Roman citizen; while it was declined by Agrippa, to whom it was due for his eminent services, and who considered it as a piece of empty pageantry, which could add nothing to the consideration he already enjoyed.[15]

U. C. 736. *August. 11 mo, Ætat.* 45.

About this time Augustus received an accession to his family by the birth of another grandson, of the name of Lucius, the second son of Agrippa, by his daughter Julia; and by adopting both the brothers, conferred upon them the names of Caius and Lucius Cæsar, and, by the same act, published the destination of his fortunes.

In the midst of festivals, which were instituted on this occasion, the attention of the emperor was called anew to the provinces by alarms which were received at once in many parts of the empire.

U. C. 737. *L. Domitius Ahenobarbus, P. Cornelius Scipio. August. 12mo, Ætat.* 46.

Historians give us a list of particulars, exhibiting the troubles to which so extensive a territory was still exposed. The Commenii and Venones, nations inhabiting the valleys of the Alps, were in arms. The Panonii and Norisci had attacked Istria. The Danthæleti and Scordisci had invaded Macedonia. The Sauromatæ had passed the Danube. Some cantons, both of Dalmatia and Spain, had revolted. The Sicambri, Usupetes, and Tenchteri, German nations bordering on the Rhine, having seized on the Italian traders who frequented their country, in imitation of the Roman manner of punishing slaves, nailed them to the cross, and employing this insult as a declaration of war, passed the Rhine, and made a descent upon Gaul. They surprised and put to flight a party of horse which had been sent by Lollius to observe their motions. In pursuit of this advantage, they fell in with the main body, commanded by Lollius himself, equally unprepared to receive them, obliged him to retire with great loss, and with the disgrace of leaving the standard of one of the legions in the hands of his enemies.[16]

These revolts of the frontier provinces, or incursions of barbarous neighbours, may be considered as part of a war which lasted for ages, and terminated at last in the ruin of the empire. The defeat of Lollius was indeed the first signal calamity which had befallen the Roman arms under the auspices of the present emperor.[17] It was supposed to have greatly affected him, and to have caused the resolution which he took to pass the Alps, and to superintend, in person, the

10 Lex Cincia. The offender was subjected to a fine, equal to double the fee he had accepted.

11 Under the republic, the character of an able pleader led to the highest preferments and honours of the state.

12 Dio. Cass. lib liv. c. 18.

13 Ibid. c. 17.

14 Plin. lib. v. c. 6.

15 Dio. Cass. lib. liv. c. 11

16 Dio. Cass. lib. liv. c. 20. Vell. Pater. lib. 20. c. 97

17 Sueton. in Octav. c. 33.

measures that were necessary to repair this loss. His departure from Rome, however, at this time, is likewise ascribed to other motives. He had now, for about two years, been exposed in the city to the animadversion and censure which a people still petulant though not free, were ready, on so near a view, to bestow on his person and government; and it was part of his policy to withdraw, at proper intervals, from the observation of such a people, in order to preserve that respect and authority which too much familiarity is apt to impair. He accordingly took occasion from these alarms, on the west and northern frontier, to absent himself from the city; and despatched Agrippa at the same time, into Asia, where a contest which had arisen respecting the succession of the kingdom of the Bosphorus required his presence.

The emperor, leaving the administration of affairs at Rome in the hands of Statilius Taurus, set out for Gaul, accompanied by Mecænas and Tiberius, now in the rank of prætor, who made a part of his court. At his arrival in Gaul, the people were relieved of the alarm they had taken on the approach of the German invaders, who, not being prepared to make a continual war beyond their own boundaries, had repassed the Rhine. He proceeded, therefore, to receive the representations that were made to him relating to the administration of the province. Among these are mentioned complaints of extortion on the part of the governor. This officer, though now bearing a Roman name, that of Licinius, was himself a native of Gaul, and had been a slave in the family of Julius Cæsar. Having become by the bounty of his master, a freeman and a Roman citizen, he was afterward gradually raised, by Augustus himself, to the height of his present command, in which he committed enormous oppressions. Being convicted of the crimes which were laid to his charge, it is said, that the money of which he had robbed the province was seized, but not returned to the owners.[1]

U. C. 738. *M. Livius Drusus, L. Calpurnius Piso. August. 13mo, Ætat. 47.*

While the Germans fled from Gaul upon the report of the emperor's approach, the revolts of the Commenii and Venones, of the Panonii and Ligures Commati, were quelled at the same time by the different officers who had been employed against them. The Rheti and Vendelici, nations inhabiting the valley of Trent, having been long in the practice of plundering the Roman traders, of making incursions into Gaul, and even into Italy, were attacked first by Drusus, the younger of the sons of Livia, and being forced from their own country, moved in a hostile manner into the Roman province, where they were received by Tiberius, at the head of a considerable army; and being pressed at once by both the brothers, were obliged to make their submission, and to suffer the greater part of their men, able to carry arms, to be transplanted into other countries.[2]

The peace being thus established on the side of Germany, the emperor applied himself to restore some cities which had gone to ruin in different parts of the empire, and to plant new colonies in Gaul and in Spain. Whether these were settlements provided for the veterans and Emeriti, by dispossessing the ancient inhabitants, or new plantations made in waste and unappropriated lands, is uncertain. Suetonius informs us, that no less than twenty-eight different colonies were settled in Italy, towns built, and funds allotted to defray the expense of these newly established communities; and that persons, who had filled any office of magistracy in these colonies, were entitled to a vote in the elections at Rome.

Among the acts of Augustus, during his progress in Gaul, are mentioned the effects of his attention to the favourite object of encouraging population, with the premiums he gave, wherever he passed, to such persons as presented him with numerous families of children;[3] it is mentioned, that the city of Paphos being destroyed by an earthquake, he gave orders to have it rebuilt; and, as an earnest of his future patronage, gave the inhabitants leave to change the name to Augusta:[4] that he restored to the people of Cyzicum in Bithynia, the privileges of which he himself had lately deprived them: that his orders, to re-establish the king of Pontus in possession of the Bosphorus, which had been usurped by a pretended descendant of Mithridates, being successfully executed by Agrippa, he received the report of this service without having it communicated to the senate. And this is said to have been the first instance in which this form was omitted.

U. C. 739. *M. Licinius, Cn. Cornelius Lentulus. August. 14mo, Ætat. 48.*

A triumph having been offered to Agrippa, on this occasion, was again declined.[5]

Augustus had now passed above two years in Gaul, and obtained the end for which he went, whether of a temporary recess from Rome, or of making the necessary provision for the security of the province. Leaving Drusus, the younger of the sons of Livia, to command on the Rhine, and to continue the military services he had lately begun among the Alps, he himself set out on his return to Italy. But, willing to avoid the crowds which usually advanced to receive him on his approach to the city, he made his entry in the night. The senate, however, not to lose any opportunity of paying their court, ordered to be erected, in the usual place of their assembly, an altar, on which to offer a sacrifice of thanksgiving for his safe return; and to signalize the occasion by some circumstance of a gracious nature, resolved, that, from this date, whatever criminal within the city presented his prayer for forgiveness to the emperor in person, should obtain his pardon. Both these flattering decrees, presented to him on the day of his arrival, he rejected. On the following day, he received the salutations of the people on the Palatine Hill,[6] ordered the baths to be thrown open to them, and the usual attendance at such places to be given at his own expense. From

U. C. 740. *Tiberius Claudius Nero, Quincelius Varus. August. 15mo, Ætat. 49.*

1 Dio. Cass. lib. liv. c. 21.
2 Videre Rhæti bella sub Alpibus. Drusum, Gerentem, et Vendelici, &c. Horat. Carm. lib. iv. Od. 4. Dio. Cass. lib. liv. c. 22. Vell. Pater. lib. ii. c. 95.
3 Sueton. in Octav. c. 46.
4 Dio. Cass. lib. liv. c. 23.
5 Ibid.
6 The place of his own residence

this ceremony he proceeded to the capitol, and going up to the statue of Jupiter, stript the laurel from his fasces, and laid this badge of his victory at the feet of the pedestal. He then assembled the senate; but excusing himself from speaking, on account of a hoarseness, he delivered a paper to be read by his quæstor, containing a summary of his late operations in the provinces, and some new regulations, by which the army, for the future, were to be governed.[7]

Augustus had gradually, since his accession to the government of the empire, endeavoured to improve the discipline of the legions, and particularly to restore the dignity of the military character, by forbidding the admission of slaves. From this rule he never departed, except either upon extraordinary occasions, which required sudden augmentations of the army, or in recruiting particular bodies of men, such as the city-watch, appointed to guard against fire and other disorders. And he succeeded so far in restoring the discipline, which had been much relaxed in times of the civil war, that he had authority enough, on different occasions, to dismiss, without any provision or reward, all such as presumed to make any demands in a mutinous manner. He had entirely disbanded the tenth legion for mutiny. In urging the duties of the service, he generally decimated such bodies of men as gave way before an enemy, and punished with death the desertion of a post, whether in officers or private men. Less offences he punished with some species of ignominy or disgrace, as, by obliging the offender to stand a whole day unarmed before the general's tent, with some mark or badge of disgrace.[8]

By the regulations now presented to the senate for their approbation, the term of military service was fixed, if in the prætorian bands, at twelve years; if in the legions, at sixteen years. After this term, it was admitted that a soldier might claim his discharge.

It had been the practice in the course of the late civil wars to gratify the veterans, at their dismission, with grants of land; a practice which taught the armies to covet the possessions of their fellow-citizens, and to seek for pretences against them, which, in reality, rendered that species of property extremely insecure. But Augustus now thought himself possessed of a sufficient authority to reform this abuse, and to substitute, for these grants of land, a gratuity in money.[9] By publishing his regulation on this subject, he greatly quieted the fears and apprehensions under which the pacific inhabitants laboured in different parts of the empire.

The utmost efforts of the emperor were likewise required, on the present occasion, to preserve the mask under which he wished to conduct his government. The senate, though maintained in all its formalities, was observed to have no power, and began to be deserted. The civil offices were shunned as a burden, or as a conspicuous servitude. Many families of senators were gone to decay, and those who were called into supply their places, either had not, or denied that they had the legal qualification. The titles of magistracy continued for some time to be coveted, on account of the rank which they were supposed to bestow; but the frequency and prostitution of such honours now rendered them contemptible;[10] and, in some degree already an object of that ridicule which is so well expressed by the satirist in writings of a later date.[11]

To relieve senators, in part, of the burdens which they alone were hitherto appointed to bear, the emperor, while yet in Gaul, gave directions that the ten judges, who decided in all questions relating to public sales and confiscations, the three inspectors of the coin,[12] the officers who had charge of public executions,[13] and the wardens of the streets and highways,[14] should all, for the future, be taken from the equestrian order. It was now the practice to decline, not only servile or burdensome offices of this sort, but likewise what had been the highest stations under the republic; and it became necessary to force the acceptance of them under actual penalties. At first, all who had been quæstors, if still under forty years of age, were draughted by lot for the superior offices;[15] all likewise who had been quæstors, and who were possessed of the legal estate, if not above thirty years of age, were obliged to enrol in the senate.

From this forced enrolment or promotion, however, which may be considered as a general press for senators and officers of state, were excluded all such as had any bodily deformity or blemish, or who wanted the legal estate. In ascertaining the fortunes of senators the parties themselves were examined, and other evidence was brought to investigate the truth. Such as appeared to have made any diminution in their paternal inheritance were obliged to specify the losses they had sustained, and to give an account of their own manner of life.[16]

In the sequel of these measures, which were intended to preserve the appearance of a commonwealth, and to support the formalities of a civil institution, it is probable, although not mentioned by any of the historians, that Augustus accepted of a prolongation of his power for other five years;[17] and again assumed Agrippa with himself into the office of tribune for the same term. The ceremony of this resignation became, by degrees, a matter of form, and his resumption of the empire was made known by sports and entertainments, which rendered the occasion extremely agreeable to the people.

At this time a theatre, which had been begun by Marcellus, was finished and opened with great solemnity. A procession of noble youth was led by Caius the son of Agrippa, and adoptive son of the emperor. Six hundred African wild beasts were baited in the circus, and among them a tiger, it being the first time that this animal made its appearance at Rome.[18]

---

7 Dio. Cass. lib. liv. c. 25. 8 Sueton. in Octav. c. 23.
9 Dio. Cass. lib. liv. c. 25.

10 Dio. Cass. lib. liv. c. 30.
11 Perpetuo risu, pulmonem agitare solebat
Democritus quanquam non essent urbibus illis,
Prætextæ et Trabeæ, Fasces, Lectica, Tribunal.
Juven. Sat. x. v. 33
12 Triumviri Monitales. 13 Triumviri Capitales
14 Viginti Viri. 15 Dio. Cass. lib. liv. c. 26. 16 Ibid
17 His having accepted the empire for ten years, and at the expiration of this period, his having accepted of it for five years, are mentioned; and again, it is mentioned about his twentieth year, or five years after this date, that he accepted of it for ten years more.
18 Plin. lib. viii. c. 17.

In continuation of these entertainments, Julus, he son of Antony, being prætor, celebrated the birth-day of Augustus with the most expensive shows, and in his public character entertained the senate, together with the emperor himself, at a feast in the capitol.[1]

Tiberius, at the same time, in performance of a vow which he had made for the emperor's safe return from his last excursion to the provinces, gave splendid entertainments. Having introduced Caius Cæsar, the eldest of the emperor's adoptive sons, and placed him by himself in the prætor's chair at the theatre, he was received by the people with shouts of applause.

The emperor, however, gave signs of displeasure. "Such premature honours," he said, "could only serve to inspire the mind of a young man with presumption and pride."[2]

U. C. 740.

August. 15mo, Ætat. 49.

About this time died the famous triumvir M. Æmilius Lepidus, formerly the associate or the tool of Octavius and Antony, in the execution of their designs against the republic. While he was subservient to the interest of these competitors, he was allowed, in appearance, to hold a third part of the empire; but being unsupported by any real abilities or personal authority, he ceased to be of any consequence the moment he presumed to act for himself, and was too inconsiderable, even to be an object of resentment to those he had injured.

Augustus had suffered this fallen rival to remain, during his life, in the dignity of Pontiff, and, by keeping him in public view, deprived him of the consolation even of being forgotten.[3] The emperor, though himself desirous to hold this sacred character, and frequently pressed, by his flatterers, to supplant Lepidus, was too cautious to violate any supposed religious institution, and too politic to trifle with acknowledged rights, of which he meant, on occasion, to avail himself. But upon the death of Lepidus, he did not neglect to assume the only dignity which was wanting to complete the accumulation of prerogatives united in his own person.

U. C. 741.

M. Valerius Barbatus, P. Sulpicius Omilian in Mag. mort.

Agrippa had returned to Rome, about the same time, with the emperor; but soon had occasion again to depart from Italy, being sent to quell a rebellion that broke out in Panonia. Upon his arrival in this country, finding the natives already subdued by the fear of his approach, he accepted of their submission; and though still in the

C. Vagius abdicavit, C. Caninius.

August. 16mo, Ætat. 50.

depth of winter, set out on his return to Rome. After he had repassed the seas, on his way through Campania, he was taken dangerously ill. Augustus received the accounts of his danger, while he was exhibiting sports to the people in the name of his two sons, Caius and Lucius, and left the city immediately to attend his friend; but came too late, and after he expired.

This great man appears to have been worthy of the best times of the republic. He had magnanimity enough to have relied on his personal qualities alone for consideration and honour, and was fit to have been a citizen of Rome in its happiest age; but from the necessity of the times, and the principles of fidelity to the friend who trusted him, he became a principal support of the monarchy. His great abilities being employed to maintain the government and authority of the prince, and his credit with the prince employed in acts of justice and moderation to the people, he was neither an object of jealousy to the one, nor of envy to the other.

It was a singular instance of good fortune to have found such an officer, and a mark of understanding and steadiness, without jealousy, and without wavering, to have persevered in the choice. In this, and in some other instances, Augustus showed that his talent was not mere cunning, but a principle of able conduct, which is tried in nothing more than in the choice and employment of proper men. He raised Agrippa, though not a flatterer, from a low condition, to command his forces, to preside in his councils, and, last of all, by the marriage of his daughter, to the highest place in his own family.

At the funeral of his friend, the emperor took upon himself the office of principal mourner, accompanied the corpse from Campania to Rome; and having it brought into the forum, pronounced the funeral oration, having, while he spoke, a screen placed between himself and the dead body. In order to confirm and to increase the regard that was paid to the memory of the deceased, he not only ratified that part of the will, by which Agrippa bequeathed his gardens and his baths to the public, but in his name also made farther additions to the legacy.

Julia, at the death of her husband, was again pregnant, and bore a third son, who, from the family of his father, and the circumstances of his birth, was known by the name of Agrippa Posthumus.[4]

CHAPTER IV.

Marriage of Julia with Tiberius—Death of Drusus—Death of Mecœnas—Disgrace of Julia War in Panonia—Roman Legions cut off in Germany—Tiberius associated in the Empire—Death of Augustus.

U. C. 741.

THE death of Agrippa made way for Tiberius Claudius Nero, then about twenty-eight years of age, into a higher place than he yet held in the family and confidence of the emperor.

August. 16mo, Ætat. 50.

Octavius had received this young man in the arms of his mother Livia, had observed the progress of his childhood and youth, and had given him no distinguished place in his favour during the lives of Marcellus or Agrippa, to whom he had successively married his daughter; but being de-

1 Dio Cass. lib. liv. c. 25, 26. 2 Ibid. c. 27.
3 Ibid. c. 15. 4 Ibid. c. 28 29.

prived of both these supports, and his adopted children, Caius and Lucius being yet of tender age, he was led to receive Tiberius as a relation, the nearest to supply the place of those he had lost.

Livia, by whose arts the emperor now began to be governed, was, according to the report of historians, and, as we may infer from her own conduct, perfectly formed to the mind of her husband. In all matters, not only of business, whether private or public, but even in those affairs in which the sexes are least patient of each other's failings, she preserved or affected the most implicit submission to his will. She is said, not only to have connived at his infidelities, but as often as he was inclined to diversify his pleasures, even to have employed her sagacity and her knowledge of his choice in procuring him the means of indulging his fancy. Herself, the dupe of no passion which was likely to mislead her, she never lost an opportunity to advance her family, nor risked the miscarriage of her purpose, by hastening improperly the means of obtaining it. Favoured by the death of Agrippa, and the minority of the young Cæsars, she easily, without seeming to entertain any improper views for her son, procured his advancement. He was at first received by the emperor as a temporary aid in the government, and afterwards as a person fit to become the third husband of Julia; and by this connexion to occupy a rank in his family, which had been hitherto considered as the nearest to his own.

Tiberius, at the time that this resolution was taken in his favour, was already a husband and a father, having been married to Vipsania, the daughter of Agrippa, by whom he had a son named Drusus. He is said to have parted, with great reluctance, from Vipsania, then a second time pregnant, in order to make way for Julia, by whom he was to hold the second place in the empire.

Augustus had hitherto distinguished, by the marriage of his daughter, the person whom he meant to point out as his successor; but, his family being now become numerous, it does not appear that he had any thoughts of giving to this new son-in-law precedence of his adopted children, Caius and Lucius, who, bearing the name of Cæsar, already precluded any competition for rank in the empire.[5] This third marriage of Julia, he probably intended for a purpose, which it did not by any means serve, that of restraining the disorders to which this unhappy person was inclined.

Tiberius had begun his military services with some distinction in Gaul, and now coming into the place of Agrippa, was sent to repress a rebellion, which, upon the report of that officer's death, had again broke out in Panonia. Having succeeded in this service, he gave orders, that the youth of the vanquished nation should be sold into slavery, and that the buyer should come under an obligation to transport them far from their native country; a cruel action, but not to be imputed merely to the personal character of this young man, as it did not exceed what was frequent in the history of the Romans. Upon this occasion Tiberius had the honour of a triumph conferred by the senate; but by the emperor's directions, while he accepted of the triumphal robes, he declined to enter the city in procession.[6]

About the same time Drusus, the younger brother of Tiberius, then stationed on the Rhine, had repulsed a body of Germans, passed the river in pursuit of them, and laid waste the contiguous country of the Sicambri and Usipetes, which, lying between the Lippe and the Issel, is now the bishopric of Munster, or the province of Zutphen. Having embarked his army, he fell down the Issel to the marshy lands inhabited by the Frisii and Chauci, probably what are now the provinces of Friesland and Groningen, arrived without resistance at the sea, where the tides, to which his Italian mariners were unaccustomed, leaving them sometimes ashore, and almost out of sight of the sea, at other times threatening to overflow all the lands in their view, gave them at first considerable trouble; but having learned to accommodate themselves to this alternate flux and reflux of the waters, they took the benefit of the floods to re-ascend the river, and returned to their station on the frontiers of Gaul.[7]

Drusus, having thus explored the coasts of the northern ocean, set out for Italy; and, though already vested with the dignity of prætor, was made to accept of an inferior rank in the office of ædile; probably to set an example, encouraging others to comply with the forms of the republic which were still kept up; but which were at this time very much neglected by persons of rank.[8]

As the Roman armies had now, for some time, ceased to make offensive war, many of the barbarous nations took courage from this circumstance, and began to harass the provinces in their neighbourhood, passed the Rhine and the Danube in frequent incursions, and laid waste the frontiers of Gaul, Panonia, and Thrace; insomuch, that it appeared necessary, for the security of these provinces, to attack the enemy, and to furnish them sufficient occupation in the defence of their own country.

U. C. 721.
Q. Ælius Tubero, Paulus Trebius Max.
August. 17mo, Ætat. 51.

In the spring of the following year, Drusus accordingly having returned to his command on the frontiers of Gaul, passed the Rhine, overran the territory of the Chatti,[9] and penetrated to the Weser. In these operations, although the emperor's object, on this and every other service, was merely defensive, it appeared necessary, not only to occupy both banks of the Rhine, but likewise to have fortified stations on the Lippe, from which to observe the Germans in their future preparations to pass the river for the purpose of invading Gaul.

Drusus, for his services in this campaign, was saluted by the army, as had been customary in the times of the republic, with the title of Imperator; but this designation having been, for some time, appropriated to the sovereign as head of the armies of the empire, was now, by him, refused to Drusus. The title of proconsul, with the triumphal robes, were decreed to him instead of the other. On his return to Gaul, the Germans laid an ambuscade on the route by which

5 Dio. Cass. lib. liv. c. 31.

6 Dio. Cass. lib [illegible] c. 31.

7 Ibid. c. 32.

8 Ibid.

Supposed to be that of Hesse.

he was to pass, and threatened his army with imminent danger; but lost the advantage of the disposition they had made, by discovering their posture too soon, and by giving the Romans an opportunity to extricate themselves by a vigorous attack, in which they gained a decisive victory.

Upon the news of this event, which seemed to remove, for some time, the prospect of any farther trouble on the side of Germany, it was proposed, once more, to shut the gates of Janus.[1] But an irruption of the Daci, who passed the Danube on the ice, together with inroads made by the Thracians into Macedonia, and fresh insurrections in Dalmatia, still kept the empire in a state of war.

Lucius Piso, formerly governor of Pamphilia, was employed in repressing the attempts of the Thracians; and Tiberius, in reducing the Dalmatians. The last of these territories, which, in the general partition of the empire, had been committed to the senate, was now, on account of its frequent revolts, taken under the immediate inspection of the emperor.

While these operations took place, under the officers whom the emperor employed in the provinces, he himself remained at Rome; and the few circumstances which are mentioned, relating to affairs of state in the capital, are characteristic of the times, but not otherwise interesting or important.

The emperor himself, in his capacity of inspector of manners, took an account of the people, paying the highest regard to the distinctions of senator and knight, and to the honours which were constituted by titles of office, as those of prætor and consul. But these names of distinction, which he affected to preserve, having no real consideration or power annexed to them, only served to remind the people of dignities which no longer existed.

The senate itself, though filled with persons who bore the titles of prætorian and consular, and though, with affected respect, still preserved among the ruins of the commonwealth, being deprived of its ancient foundations, underwent a continual decay: and the honours to which citizens had formerly aspired, with so much ardour, were now neglected or shunned with disdain. The wealthy, fearing more the burdens to which they might be exposed, on the supposition of possessing great riches, than coveting the honours to which the qualification of senator entitled them, came to the musters with reluctance, and even concealed their effects.

To counteract this disposition, and to set an example of public duty, the emperor made a fair return of his own patrimonial estate, and, as far as was consistent with his sovereignty, endeavoured to raise the value of subordinate ranks, admitted members into the senate with lower qualifications than formerly; diminished the *quorum*, or number that was hitherto required to constitute a legal assembly: and, affecting great respect for the proceedings of the senate, ordered their journals to be regularly kept; and gave this matter in particular charge to the quæstors.

In other respects, the servility of the times seemed to outrun the exactions of the sovereign. Some of the courtiers, in their desire to flatter, and others, under the fear of being suspected of disaffection, began the practice of contributing sums of money to erect statues to the emperor: and he himself, in consequence of some dream, or directed by some species of superstition, made it a practice, on certain days, to ask, as in charity, from all who came in his way, some small pieces of money.[3] As he was in his temper sufficiently liberal, neither of these practices brought him under any imputation of rapacity. What was contributed to erect statues for himself he employed in multiplying those of the gods, particularly in erecting the allegorical images of Safety, Concord, and Peace. What he received as a charity was returned twofold.

The republican honours, though much faded on every other brow, still bore a considerable lustre among the emperor's titles, made a part of his state, and an engine of his power. Those of the priesthood, in particular, equally suited to every constitution of government, were easily brought in aid of his military power. For this reason the title of Flamen Dialis, or priest of Jupiter, was now added to the other dignities of the same kind which the emperor had recently assumed. It being deemed ominous, and presaging the greatest calamities, if a Flamen Dialis should die in office, this dignity formed an additional guard to the emperor's person. It had been vacant about seventy years from the demise of Merula, who being consul when Cinna forced his way into the city, and seeing no means of escape, in order to avert from his country the supposed evils which must have followed from his dying in the priesthood, divested himself, stripped the sacred crest or fillet from his hair, and being thus reduced to a private station, cut his own arteries, and sprinkled the altar of Jupiter with his blood.

This ceremony, it was supposed, had averted the evils to which the republic, to expiate the death of this sacred person, would have been otherwise exposed; and the priesthood had, from reverence to this illustrious martyr, been suffered to remain vacant till a person could be found that was worthy to succeed him; a condition which was now supposed to be fulfilled in the person of Augustus.

U. C. 743. *Julius Antonius Africanus, Q. Fabius Maximus. Aug. 18mo, Ætat. 52.*

About this date died Octavia, the widow of Marcellus and of Mark Antony. Her obsequies being performed with great pomp, the emperor himself pronounced the funeral oration, having a screen, as at the burial of Agrippa, to hide the body from his view.

Soon after this event, notwithstanding there was no recent alarm from the enemy on the Rhine, the emperor thought proper to change the place of his residence from Italy to the north of the Alps. Under pretence of observing the storms which still threatened the province of Gaul from the barbarous nations on its frontier, he took his station for the campaign at the confluence of the Soane and the Rhone, and from thence gave his instructions to the two brothers, Tiberius and Drusus, to whom the war was committed on the Save and the Rhine. Both having been successful in the services entrusted to them, joined the emperor at his quarters, and from thence ac-

1 Dio. Cass. lib. liv. c. 36.
2 Ibid. c. 34. Vell. Pater. lib. ii. c. 98.
3 Sueton. in Vit. August c. 91.

companied him to Rome, where they partook in the honours which were paid to him for the success of his arms.

U. C. 744.

Neri Claudius Drusus, Q. Fabius Maximus. Aug. 19mo, Ætat. 53.

In the following spring the two brothers resumed their commands, and the emperor returned to his former residence on the Rhone. Drusus passed the Rhine, overran the country of the Chatti, and penetrated to the Elbe, where he erected some trophies, and left some monuments of the progress he had made; but on the approach of winter, being obliged to retire, he was taken ill on the march and died.

Tiberius, who had been sent by the emperor on the first news of his brother's illness, came in time to see him expire. The funeral being to be performed in Italy, the corpse, during the march of the army to the Rhine, was carried by officers of the highest rank. From the Rhine it was conveyed on the shoulders of the principal inhabitants, who received it on the confines of their respective districts, and bore it to the next. Augustus himself, on the occasion, repaired to Rome; but being then in a military character, or in the actual exercise of a military commission, and not permitted, by the ancient forms of the republic, to enter the city, he spoke a funeral oration in the circus Flaminius, which was without the walls. Tiberius followed the corpse to the forum, and delivered another oration there. The obsequies were performed by persons of the equestrian and senatorian rank. The ashes were deposited in the tomb of Augustus.

The title of Germanicus having been conferred on Drusus, it remained in his family. He had issue two sons and a daughter; the eldest known by the name of Germanicus Cæsar, the younger by the name of Claudius, long neglected on account of his imbecility; and the daughter Livilla, hereafter to be mentioned as the wife of successive husbands.

Tiberius, soon after the funeral of his brother, entered the city in procession, to celebrate the success of his arms in Dalmatia. He gave a public feast to the people; and as in this entertainment only one of the sexes cou d partake, Livia and Julia were allowed to entertain the other.

The influence of Livia, and the elevation of her family, notwithstanding the hopes that were entertained of Caius and Lucius Cæsar, were now apparent, and procured her flattering decrees from the senate, that were offered in consolation for the loss of her son. Her statue was erected at the public expense, and she herself was vested with the privilege, reckoned so highly honourable at Rome, that of being the parent of three children.[4]

U. C. 745.

C. Marcius Censorinus, C. Asinius Gallus. Aug. 20mo, Ætat. 54.

In the beginning of the following year Augustus again entered the city in a kind of triumphal procession, carrying his laurel to the temple of Jupiter Ferretrius, instead of that of Jupiter Capitolinus. But he made no rejoicings, alleging, that he had suffered more by the death of Drusus than he had gained by the success of his arms. The consuls, however, took charge of the solemnities usual on such occasions, and among the public shows brought forth some captives, whom they obliged, for the entertainment of the people, to fight in the theatre.[5]

The period for which Augustus, at his last pretended resignation, had consented to accept of the government, being expired, he affected a purpose, as formerly, to resign the empire; and was again prevailed upon to resume it for ten years more. The decline of the civil establishment, of which he still wished to preserve the appearances, occupied his principal attention. The senate, as has been observed, underwent a continual degradation, and its assemblies were neglected. The members excused their neglect, by pretending, that the times of meeting being irregular, they had no proper intimation to attend; and that they were frequently engaged in trials and other public bnsiness when the senate was called.

To obviate such excuses for the future, the emperor appointed ordinary assemblies of the senate on particular days of each month, and ordered that those days should be kept clear of trials, or any other public business whatever, that might occupy the members. Having formerly reduced the number that was required to constitute a legal meeting, from four hundred to three hundred, he now directed, that in matters of less moment, even fewer might constitute such meetings, and that in fixing the quorum on any particular occasion, regard should be had to the importance of the business before them; that even without requiring the presence of any determinate number, the senate might form resolutions which, though not accompanied with the force of laws, should nevertheless be deemed of great authority. He, at the same time, ordered a list of the members to be published; increased the fine usually paid for absence, and, to facilitate the ordinary course of their proceedings, extended to the prætors the privilege of making motions, which had been confined to the consuls or to himself.

These several resolutions, before they passed into laws, were posted up in the senate-house, and every person was invited to offer his observations and corrections.[6]

About the same time are dated other regulations ascribed to Augustus, of which some related to the conduct of elections, and others to that of criminal trials. As to the first, although every office was filled by his own nomination, he affected to preserve the ancient forms; and in order to give some appearance of reality to the right of election, which he affected to leave with the people, he prescribed rules, which were to be observed in the manner of collecting the votes, and in restraining corruption. Among these it is mentioned, that he ordered, as soon as any candidate had declared himself, he should deposit a certain sum of money, to be forfeited in case he were detected in procuring any suffrage by corrupt means.

In respect to criminal trials, as the subject was more serious, the regulations now made by the emperor were of more effect. In this matter, he wished to set aside the forms of the republic, though by evasion, rather than by a formal repeal.

So long as the people were sovereigns of the commonwealth, it was part of the security which,

4 Dio. Cass. lib. xxxv. c. 1, 2

5 Dio. Cass. lib. lv. c. 5.

6 Ibid. c. 3, 4.

in their collective capacity, they provided for themselves, as individuals amenable to the laws, "that no slave could be tortured to give evidence against his master." As this law, in the present state of the government, might obstruct prosecutions that were instituted even for the emperor's safety, it was thought necessary to find some expedient by which to elude its force. For this purpose it was enacted, that such slaves as might be wanted in evidence against their masters should be conveyed by a formal process of sale to the emperor, and that, being in his possession, they might be put to the question, or cited as witnesses, even against their former masters.

This act is by Tacitus imputed to Tiberius, and in either emperor was considered as a dreadful innovation.[1] But the consideration of the emperor's safety was supposed to be a sufficient excuse for any deviation that was made from the forms of the republic.

In whatever degree the present emperor employed, in defence of his person, the severity of criminal prosecutions, and the fear of the executioner, he appears to have relied for his safety more on the disguises under which he concealed his usurpation, and on the moderation and the popularity of his manners. By the respect which he affected to pay to the senate and officers of state, he held up the forms of the republic as a kind of shield between himself and the zealots of the republican government. He endeavoured to gain the people by his affability, and frequently bore with familiarities from persons of the lowest condition. As an example of the temper with which he endured the saucy or petulant remains of military or republican freedom,[2] it is mentioned, that being called upon to act as counsel in behalf of a soldier who was to be tried for some crime, and having, under pretence of some other engagement, named a friend to undertake the cause: "This," said the soldier, "is not a proper return to me. In your danger I did not employ a substitute, but interposed myself." He received with seeming indifference the reports of spies and informers. To a person of this character, who accused Æmilius Ælianus of having frequently traduced him; "Prove me this," said he, "and I will show Ælianus, that I too in my turn can find faults in his character." Tiberius having once written him a warm letter, with a complaint of the same kind, he bid him beware of the heats of youth. "It is enough," he said, "that we can hinder people from doing us any harm;[3] we may allow them to say what they please." Yet in this he did not act from contempt of the public opinion; for in some instances he even condescended to answer accusations that were published against his private or public character.[4] His discretion and prudence prevented the occasions of much jealousy and resentment; and, in many parts of his reign, imitated the effects of generosity and elevation of mind, if they did not amount to the real possession of these characters.

Augustus having passed the winter at Rome, returned in the spring to his former station in Gaul, accompanied by Caius, the elder of his adopted sons, whom he now proposed to introduce to the military service; and by Tiberius, who, notwithstanding the rise of a new light in the person of the young Cæsar, who threatened to obscure his lustre, continued to receive fresh marks of the emperor's favour, and was considered as a principal support of his government. Being placed at the head of the army on the Rhine, he had charge of the war which had lately been committed to Drusus, his younger brother. But few particulars are mentioned of the campaign which followed in that quarter. He is accused, in one instance, of having violated the public faith, by having seized as prisoners, and sent in chains to different parts of the Roman provinces, the deputies of some German nations, who came in a public capacity to treat of peace: and of having laid waste the country in the neighbourhood of his province.

The Germans, however, were probably rather incensed than subdued by these measures. Their deputies, who had been made prisoners, that they might not be employed against their own nations as hostages, put themselves to death; and their countrymen retained the most vehement purpose of revenge. But whatever may have been the result, it is mentioned, that Augustus received from the army the title of imperator, and gave this title likewise to Tiberius; that he put him in nomination for consul on the following year, and, at their return to Rome, permitted him to make his entry into the city in triumph, while he himself declined the honour.

Soon after the emperor's arrival in Italy, he suffered a great loss by the death of Mecænas. This event made a breach in the civil department of his affairs, not less than that which the death of Agrippa had made in the military. The predilection of this minister for learning, and the intimacy in which he lived with persons of the best and most elegant accomplishments, who were recommended to him merely by their merit, has made his name proverbial among those of the patrons of letters. His inclination in this matter, if it did not form the taste of his master, happily concurred with it, and brought him acquainted with those elegant productions of genius which occupy the affections, as well as the fancy; and which, in a situation otherwise likely to instill pride, jealousy, and distrust of mankind, served at once as an antidote to these evils, and opened the way to better dispositions. Mecænas had served his prince with great fidelity, and, if not insensible to personal ambition, was at least satisfied with the elevation he had gained in the confidence of his prince. He retained the equestrian rank to which he was born, without endeavouring to accumulate the preferments or titles which were so much an object of ambition in the early part of this reign, and so easy an acquisition in the latter part of it.[5] It is observed, however, that he experienced, as is common, some vicissitude in his master's temper, and outlived the high measure of favour which he enjoyed, but without any interruption of his duty. As he lived, when most in favour, without any public envy, so he escaped every public insult when supposed in disgrace. While he presented the emperor with a continual model of elegance, ingenuity, and good temper, he took the liberty to check his passions, and served him no less by the sincerity of his speech, than by the ability of his conduct. An instance of the freedom he took

1 Tacit. Annal. 2 Dio. Cass. lib. lv. c. 4.
3 Sueton. in August. c. 56. 4 Ibid.

5 Tacit. Annal. lib iii. c. 30.

is mentioned on occasion of a trial in which Augustus himself, according to custom, sat in judgment on some criminals of state. Mecænas observing him agitated with passion, and likely to pronounce some precipitant or cruel sentence, and being hindered by the crowd from reaching his ear, handed a billet to him, which contained no more than two words, which may be translated into this homely expression, *hangman, begone!*[6] The admonition, however, had its effect, and the emperor adjourned the court.

The minister left his whole estate, as was the fashion of the age, to the emperor's disposal.[7]

By the successive diminutions of the list of confidants, on whom Augustus relied for the administration of his government, the influence of Livia, and the fortunes of her son Tiberius, received a continual advancement. The latter, after he had resumed the military habit, in his capacity of commander of the armies on the Rhine, being to enter on the office of consul, was received by the senate in the Curia Octavia, beyond the walls of the city. In his address to this assembly he spoke of the public works which he proposed to erect. Among these a temple of Concord, to be inscribed with his own name, joined with that of his brother; and of another temple, to be dedicated by himself, in conjunction with his mother Livia. He gave, in her name and in his own, upon this occasion, splendid entertainments to the senate, and to persons of distinction of both sexes. Having vowed an exhibition of public shows for the safe return of the emperor from his last campaign, he made all the necessary provision for the performance of his vow; but being obliged to set out for the army, he trusted the discharge of this duty with Piso, his colleague in the consulate, and with Caius, the eldest of the emperor's sons.

U. C. 746. *Tiberius Claudius Nero, Cn. Calpurnius, Aug. 21mo, Ætat. 55.*

This solemnity received a great addition from the sports and entertainments which were given at the same time by the emperor himself, to celebrate the memory of Agrippa, at the opening of the portico, of the hall, and of the pleasure-grounds which had been bequeathed by that officer to the Roman people.[8] Gladiators were exhibited at first in simple pairs, afterwards in numerous parties, that fought as in real battles. Such was the ferocity of the Romans in the choice of amusements, even after the character of the people ceased to be military, and when the public entertainments, formerly perhaps in part intended as nurseries for soldiers, had no longer any other object than that of ministering to their pleasure.

The Cæsars, Caius and Lucius, though yet too young for business of state, began to feel the spur of ambition, and were alarmed at the advancement of Livia's family. Even their own step-father, Tiberius, they were taught to consider as a rival in consideration and power. And it is said, that, in order to keep pace with him in his advancement to public honours, the youngest of the two brothers made application to be vested with the dignity of consul. The proposal was received by the people with applause, but discouraged by the emperor, who reflecting, as he pretended, on the presumption of his own youth, or on the necessity of the times which had brought himself forward into this station at an improper age, was pleased to say, "That he hoped never again to see a time when the office of consul must be intrusted to a person under twenty." To pacify the young man under this disappointment, he was advanced to the dignity of the priesthood, got admission into the senate, and had a place among the members of that body at the public theatre.

Soon after this date Tiberius, probably in consequence of the jealousy he had thus given to the emperor's adopted sons, underwent a great and sudden change in the state of his fortunes. Upon his return from the campaign on the Rhine, he was vested with the character of tribune of the people for five years; and, under pretence of a war likely to arise on the Euphrates, from the defection of the king of Armenia, who was disposed to join the Parthians, he was appointed to command the armies in Syria; but it soon after appeared, that this preferment and change of station were devised to conceal a species of exile or removal from the court. At his departure from Rome, he passed into Asia; but instead of continuing his route to his pretended destination in Syria, he withdrew to the island of Rhodes, where, under pretence of study, he lived some years in retirement.

U. C. 747. *D. Lelius Balbus, C. Antistius Vetus. Aug. 22do, Ætat. 56.*

The real cause of this retreat of Tiberius, whether the jealousies of the young Cæsars, the misconduct of Julia, or any other offence taken by the emperor himself, was never known; and we are deprived of any light which might have been thrown by Dion Cassius, on this, or the transactions of some of the succeeding years, by a manifest breach in the text of his history. This defect is very imperfectly supplied from Xiphilinus, Zonaras, or any other of the abbreviators or copiers of this historian.

U. C. 748. *Imperator Cæsar 12mo. P. Cornelius, Sylla. Aug. 23tio, Ætat. 57.*

U. C. 749. *C. Calvinius, Sabinus, L. Passienus Rufus. Aug 24to, Ætat. 58.*

In collecting from such authors, what is little more than the names of consuls, which serve to mark the progress of dates, we learn that in the first year after the retirement of Tiberius, the emperor himself having persisted, for seventeen years preceding this date, in rejecting the office of ordinary consul, now again accepted of it; that he intended, in this character, to solemnize the admission of his sons Caius and Lucius to the age of manhood;[9] that the ceremony was accordingly performed with respect to the eldest, who now assumed the ordinary dress of a man, was brought into the senate, and declared chief of the Roman youth;[10] but with respect to the youngest, that it was deferred till about three years afterwards, when the emperor again appeared in the character of consul.

U. C. 750. *L. Cornelius Lentulus, M. Valerius Messala. Aug. 25to, Ætat. 59.*

U. C. 751. *Imperator Cæsar 13tio, Ab. M. Plautus Silanus, Caninius Gallus. Aug. 26to. Ætat. 60.*

6 Surge, Carnifex.

7 The same year in which Mecænas died put a period likewise to the life of Horace. That of Virgil ended about ten years before. Dio. Cass. lib. lv. c. 7.

8 Dio. Cass. lib. lv. c. 8.

9 Sueton. in Octav. c. 26.

10 Zonaras, lib. x. c. 35

In one of the years of this period, or about the year of Rome seven hundred and fifty-one, is fixed by the vulgar computation the commencement of our era at the birth of Christ; an event not calculated to have an immediate influence on the transactions of state, or to make a part in the materials of political history, though destined to produce, in a few ages, a great change in the institutions, manners, and general character of nations.

At this date, from the imperfect records which remain, we have scarcely any materials of history, besides the occurrences of the court, and the city of Rome; the public entertainments that were given, the occasions on which they were exhibited, and the provision that was made in the capital for the subsistence and pleasure of an idle and profligate populace.

The emperor having again assumed the office of ordinary consul, that he might preside at the admission of his younger adopted son, Lucius Cæsar, to the age of manhood, continued to hold the office no longer than was necessary for this purpose. He exhibited magnificent shows as usual upon this occasion, and among others, one that is mentioned probably as a novelty, a shoal of six-and-thirty crocodiles of uncommon size, turned out to be hunted or fished in the bason of the circus Flaminius.[1] While the emperor gratified the people in their public diversions to a degree of debauch, he made some attempts to regulate the gratuitous distribution of corn, that other principal engine of abuse which the Roman citizens, though in other respects fallen from their sovereignty, still carefully retained among the relics of their democratical government.

The people of Rome, so long as they could overawe the senate by their assemblies or tumults, and so long as they had the disposal of preferments and honours, bartered their suffrages for sports and distributions of corn. For these too, they were now willing to sell their submission to the present establishment, and it was undoubtedly more safe to have deprived them of every other prerogative, than to restrain them in these. The numbers that were accustomed to receive corn at the public granaries, as we may judge from the number of two hundred thousand, to which it was now proposed to reduce them, had increased to an immoderate height; and as the circumstance of being subsisted gratuitously, encouraged idleness, so the very attendance required at these monthly distributions gave a considerable interruption to labour. The emperor endeavoured to apply some correction to both these evils, by reducing the number of pensioners, and by limiting the times of distribution to three particular terms in the year.[2] But in making this attempt he received so many complaints, that he was obliged to lay aside the design.

A populace thus supported in idleness must likewise be amused, and they received, in this particular, from their masters, whether acting from choice or policy, not only in the first period, but, in the subsequent ages of this monarchy, the most lavish indulgence. By Augustus in person, they were presented at different times with four capital exhibitions, consisting of all the entertainments in which they were known to delight, and with three-and-twenty great festivals, solemnized in honour of some other persons, as of his father Julius Cæsar, of his nephew Marcellus, of his friend Agrippa, and of his young relations now entering into manhood, and coming to the possession of public honours.

The sports themselves, though fierce and irrational in many instances, were splendid, magnificent, and sometimes interesting. The presence of the Roman people, in vast spaces or theatres fitted up to receive them, was always awful and sublime. The precedence of rank at these entertainments, was considered, even under the republic, as a principal object of state. The first benches were reserved for the senators; the next, at certain periods, had been allotted to the equestrian order; and the question, whether this order should be mixed with the people, or separated from them, made a subject at different times of much dispute and contention. The female sex too had their places, though at the fights of gladiators they were removed to a distance, being seated behind the other spectators; and from the athletic games were excluded altogether.[3]

The coarseness, nevertheless, of those public entertainments to which the Roman women were still admitted; the want of any interval, in their manners, between a rigorous severity, and the other extreme of an unbounded license, had, in many instances, the worst effect on their conduct. The emperor himself had a distressing example of this effect in his own family, by the flagrant debaucheries of his daughter Julia, who, having once quitted the reserve, and broke through the austerities of her father's house, had no longer any restraints of decency or established propriety to regulate her behaviour. It was reported, that, without any pretence of seduction, affection, or choice, she multiplied her paramours indefinitely, and even frequented the places of public debauch.

The emperor, though not supposed to be wanting in the tenderness of a parent, upon the detection of these disorders, proceeded against his daughter more with the rigour of an offended magistrate, than with the reluctant severity of a father. In the first transport of his passion, he hastened to lay his accusation before the senate, and obtained from this assembly an act of banishment against her, by which she was removed to a small island on the coast, reduced to low diet, and forbid to receive any visits; a species of imprisonment, which became common in the sequel of this and the subsequent reigns.

Scribonia, the mother of the unhappy exile, now arrived at a great age, and preserving in a state of separation from her husband, an unblemished reputation, gave way to the feelings of nature, and followed her child into this place of retreat or imprisonment. The father too, upon reflection, grievously lamented his rashness, in publishing, by a reference to the senate, the scandal of his own house, and bitterly regretted the severity by which he had empoisoned and rendered incurable the wounds of his own family. "If Agrippa or Mecænas had lived," he was heard to say, "I should have been restrained from this act of imprudence."[4]

In the sequel of this transaction, he indulged his resentment with less struggle against the supposed partners of his daughter's guilt; ordered Julius Antonius, with some other persons of

1 Dio. Cass lib. lv. c 10. 2 Ibid

3 Sueton. in Octav. c. 44. 4 Seneca de Ben. c. 32

high rank involved in the same charge, to be put to death. With respect to one of these criminals, who happened to be vested with the character of tribune, he affected a regard to the ancient laws of the republic, and was pleased to respite the execution of the sentence, until the time of his office as tribune should expire. Being told that Phœbe, the freed woman and confidant of Julia, when she heard of her mistress's fate, had put herself to death; "I had rather be the father of Phœbe," he said, "than of Julia."

Persons who were disposed to pay their court, ever ready to seize the opportunity, took occasion to flatter the emperor, even on occasion of this painful transaction. They hastened to show themselves in a situation like that of the prince, and to offer him the consolation of fellow-sufferers, in the distress he endured; made complaints in the senate of the license of their daughters and of their wives, and even raked up particulars of a very obsolete date. They too brought formal prosecutions, in order to obtain the interposition of law and public authority, to restrain the disorders of their children; but the emperor received this species of courtship with indifference, and refused to hear any accusation, of which the subject had preceded a fixed and very recent date.[5]

U. C. 752.
Cassus Cornelius Lentulus L. Calpurnius Piso.
Aug. 27*mo.*
Ætat. 61.

We are left at a loss for the sequel of this history, during the two years that immediately followed; but in a period, of which these were the principal transactions, we cannot be surprised that the chronicle is defective, nor indeed greatly regret the silence of a few years.

U. C 753.
C. Cæsar, Aug. Nepos, L. Emilius Paulus.
Aug. 28*vo.*
Ætat. 62.

The ordinary administration of Augustus, in pursuing the political, civil, and military forms, which he had established, no doubt was able and successful; but being once described, does not admit of repetition. The more interesting subjects of history, transactions that rouse the passions, and keep in suspense the expectations, the hopes, and the fears of men, were in this reign most carefully avoided. A powerful army was stationed on the Rhine, to keep the peace of that frontier. Even the court was lulled into perfect tranquillity by the want of any competition for the emperor's favour. This point being fully decided, by the place which was occupied by the Cæsars, Caius and Lucius; their supposed rival Tiberius, who had been sacrificed to their jealousy, still remained in his exile at Rhodes.

U. C. 754.
P. Vinucius Affinius Varus.
Aug. 22*do.*
Ætat. 63.

The defection of Armenia from the alliance of the Romans to that of the Parthians, the occasion upon which it had been pretended that Tiberius was destined to command in Asia, still subsisted; but the command of the armies in that part of the world, with the charge of recovering the kingdom of Armenia to its former state of dependance on Rome, was committed to Caius Cæsar, now first in the favour of the emperor, and highest in the expectations of the people.

It was thought proper, that both the brothers, about this time, should be sent to the command of armies; Caius to that of Syria, and Lucius to Spain; and these removals of the young Cæsars from court were supposed to be devised or procured by the empress Livia, because they made way, in a little time afterwards, for the recall of her son.[6]

But before any resolution taken at court in favour of Tiberius was publicly known, Caius Cæsar, in his way to the east, arrived in Greece, attended by a numerous train of officers. At Chios, he received a visit from Tiberius, professing the most submissive respect to the prince himself, and to the officers of his court; and from thence continued his route through the province of Asia, every where received as the son of the emperor.

The king of Parthia, upon the arrival of the young Cæsar in his neighbourhood, desired to have a conference with him, and they met on the Euphrates in a small island, each having an equal number of attendants. They afterwards mutually accepted of entertainments from each other in their respective quarters. Phraates agreed not to support the Armenians, in their defection from the alliance of the Romans, and Caius proceeded to take possession of their country, as a province of Rome. On his approach to Antagera, a place on the frontier of Armenia, the gates being shut against him, he presented himself under the walls, and while he summoned the governor to surrender, was struck by an arrow from the battlements. The wound he received, though in appearance not mortal, affected his health, and threw him into a state of dejection and languor, in which he desired to be recalled from his station, and expressed his disgust to affairs of state.

U. C. 755.
L. Ælius Lamia, M. Servilius Nepos.
Aug. 30*mo.*
Ætat. 64.

Caius being permitted to retire from his command by the emperor, who was mortified to find in him a pusillanimity so unworthy of the son of Agrippa, and of his own successor was carried to the coast in a litter, and there embarked for Italy; but having on his way put into a port of Lycia, he died at Lymira in that province.

Lucius, the other grandson of Augustus, by his daughter Julia, died some time before at Marseilles, in his way to Spain; and these deaths happening so opportunely for the family of Livia, laid this designing woman under suspicion of having been active in procuring them. The bodies of the deceased were borne through the provinces by officers of rank, and by the principal inhabitants, to be entered at Rome. Their shields and lances, richly adorned with gold, being gifts made to them by the equestrian order, when they were admitted to the age of manhood, were hung up as monuments in the hall of the senate.[7]

About this time, the third period of ten years, for which Augustus had accepted of the government, being expired, he went through the form of laying down, and re-assuming his power.

The people, at one of the entertainments which were given on this occasion, having applied to the emperor an applauded passage of

5 Dio. Cass. lib. lv. c . .

6 Vell. Pater. lib. ii. c. 103.

7 Zonaras, lib. x. c. 36. Vell. Pater. lib. ii. c. 102 103. Dio. Cass. lib. lv. c. 11, 12.

some poet, with the title of "lord or master," he gave signs of displeasure, and, on the following day, published a severe edict, forbidding the title of "master" being given to him by any person, or upon any occasion whatever.[1] "My name is Cæsar," he said, "and not master."

Augustus was now in the decline of life, had survived his principal confidants and friends, his nephew and grandchildren, on whom he had rested his hopes. He had been recently dishonoured in the conduct of his daughter, and had bound himself, by a formal act of the senate, to persist in the rigour of his treatment towards her. In these circumstances, it was thought that intercessions in favour of a child must be flattering to the father, and many applications were accordingly made in her behalf; but he remained inexorable, and being guided entirely by the influence of Livia, cast himself upon her family as a last resource. Under these circumstances, and from the approach of old age, he was observed to languish, and to lose much of his former vivacity.

Tiberius had been recalled to Rome soon after the departure, and before the death of the two Cæsars. Upon this last event, he was adopted by the emperor; but on condition, that he himself, though a father, having a son already mentioned of the name of Drusus, by his first wife Vipsania, should nevertheless adopt Germanicus Cæsar, the son of his brother, who being elder than his own son, was intended to have the advantage of seniority in all their future pretensions.

U. C. 756.
Sext. Ælius Catus, C. Sentius Saturnius. Aug. 31mo. Ætat. 65.

This successor to Agrippa and his family, being now the adopted son of Augustus, and heir apparent of his fortunes, had every where a numerous attendance of persons who wished to pay their court. Being appointed to his former station, at the head of the armies on the Rhine, his progress through the provinces to that frontier, was marked by the multitudes who flocked from all quarters to receive him. In his first campaign he penetrated to the Weser, and overran all the nations of that neighbourhood.[2]

The emperor, relying upon his newly adopted son for the conduct of the war on the Rhine, remained at Rome, where he was employed chiefly in reforming the senate, and in rebuilding the palace which had been lately consumed by fire. In the last of these works, he had offers of assistance from many of the senators, and from persons of his court, who brought him considerable sums in the way of voluntary contributions. Being unwilling, however, to let the burden thus fall entirely upon persons the most attached to himself, he laid a tax of twenty-five denarii on each corporation, and a capitation of one denarius on each private person; and having from this fund rebuilt the palace, which had hitherto been accounted a private property, he declared it for the future a public edifice, destined as a mansion for the supreme commander of the army, and head of the empire.[3]

Ten commissioners being appointed to inspect the rolls of the senate, and to restore its dignity, the first measure proposed for this purpose was to take away all appearance of constraint, and to leave every member at liberty to resign his seat; but the greater number, either fearing to be marked out as disaffected to the present government, or willing to partake in the bounty of Cæsar, who, in many instances, repaired the fortunes of senators that were gone to decay, still continued to hold their places, and affected zeal for the forms on which Augustus was pleased to rest his authority.

In this and other instances, it is instructive to observe with what care this sovereign of the empire endeavoured to flatter the vanity of Roman citizens, and to preserve the distinction of ranks, while in reality his policy was calculated to remove all distinctions, to render all ranks equally dependant on himself; or, if any distinction were suffered to remain, tended in the sequel, or under his successors, to render the most honourable conditions the least secure.

Augustus had returns made of all the most respectable families in Italy, and of those who had a property of above two hundred sestertia.[4] He laid great restraints on the manumission of slaves; a practice by which he alleged, that the privileges of Romans were rashly prostituted to the refuse of all nations, and to the meanest order of men. The Lex Ælia Sentia, which took its name from one of the consuls of this year, had, for its object, the reformation of this abuse. By this law was fixed the age at which a master should have the power of setting his slave at liberty, and the age of the slave at which he might be set free, together with the mutual rights and privileges of the patron or former master, and of the freed man, or emancipated slave.[5]

As the present government began to have proscription, as well as expediency on its side, every attempt on the emperor's life had the criminality of treason, and must have been condemned upon every consideration which established monarchy can suggest. Whoever made such an attempt might be considered as a dangerous and ill-advised assassin, who attacked the community itself in the person of its sovereign, and whose crime, in that particular instance, tended to involve the world anew in anarchy and bloodshed.

The privileges or pretensions of citizens, under the republic, were long since effaced. But a very few were left who had enjoyed, or even could remember the existence of them; yet private resentment, or the remains of republican zeal, and the supposed right of every person to repel usurpations, had produced some attempts of this sort during the present reign. Even in this advanced period of it, a conspiracy was detected, in which Cornelius Cinna, a grandson of Pompey, and descended of that Cinna, who, together with Caius Marius, was once at the head of the popular faction, formed a design to suppress the present usurpation of Cæsar, and to restore the republic, in which his ancestors had made so conspicuous a figure.

Augustus was greatly perplexed on the discovery of this plot; and having already, on like occasions, exhausted the means of severity, was now, it is said, persuaded by Livia to try the effects of clemency, and of a generous confidence. "This conduct," she observed, "would tend to disarm his enemies, and would interest

1 Orosius, lib. vi. fine. 2 Vell. Pater. lib. ii. c. 104.
3 Dio. Cass. lib. lv. c. 12, 13.

4 About 1600*l*. 5 Dio. Cass. lib. lv. c. 13.

numbers in his preservation by the ties of affection and gratitude."

The emperor, being accordingly prevailed on to take this course, ordered that the conspirator should be introduced to his presence, gave him to understand, that his guilt was discovered, and his accomplices known, remonstrated against an attempt so ungenerous and unprovoked, but relieved the young man of his fears, by assuring him of pardon, and of every other species of protection for the future. In these assurances he even went beyond what mere clemency required, affected to upbraid the author of a design on his own life with false modesty, in not demanding the honours to which he was justly entitled by his birth; and concluded with saying, That, as he trusted they were from henceforward to be friends, he should be glad to receive his applications in any matter by which he could contribute to his advancement or interest; and, in the mean time, named him for consul at the next succession to this dignity.

U. C. 757.

Cn. Cornelius Cinna Magnus. L. Valerius, Messalla Volusius. Aug 32do. Ætat. 66.

In this year are dated, among other measures, some regulations which were made by the emperor for the better government of the army; and, what was scarcely less important in the opinion of the times, for the conduct of entertainments in the public theatres. The military establishment consisted of six-and-twenty legions,[6] with nine or ten prætorian bands, composed of a thousand men each. Augustus, to restore the honours of the military character, had, from the beginning of his reign, made it a rule to exclude from his armies, as much as possible, all emancipated slaves. This exclusion, together with some reformations which diminished the profits formerly enjoyed by military men, rendered it extremely difficult, upon any sudden emergency, to complete the legions. Augustus found himself obliged to increase his bounty in order to recruit the army; but instead of giving more to those who enlisted, or increasing his levy-money, he chose to engage them by the hope of future advantages, to be reaped after certain periods of dutiful service. In the prætorian bands, he made a regulation, that, after sixteen years' service, the veteran should be entitled to his dismission, and a premium of twenty thousand sesterces.[7] In the legions, after twelve years' service, that he should be entitled to twelve thousand sesterces;[8] and, as a fund for these payments, it is probable that the tax of a twentieth on all legacies bequeathed to strangers, heirs of choice, or to distant relations, was imposed about this time. This tax did not extend to the inheritance of the ordinary heir at law, nor to legacies[9] made to the poor, or to persons in indigent circumstances.

With respect to the public entertainments, fresh regulations were made to keep places in the circus for senators and knights, apart from the commons, or lower class of the people.

It being observed, that the office of ædile, which formerly included the care of all public entertainments, was avoided; and that even the dignity of a vestal, which was wont to be so much desired by the most honourable families at Rome, ceased to be in request, it was decreed, that all the quæstors of any preceding year should cast lots for the office of ædile; and that the rules restricting the choice of vestals to persons of the most noble extraction, should now be considerably relaxed, or dispensed with; so that women, even descended from enfranchised slaves, might be admitted into this order: a very unlikely way to engage persons of superior rank to adopt it.

This year Agrippa Posthumus came of age, and assumed the dress of manhood; but, though adopted, as his elder brothers had been, into the family of the emperor, he appears not to have been thought worthy to replace them; and being obscured by the riper age and superior favour of Tiberius, he passed through this ceremony with fewer demonstrations of consideration or respect from the people than had been paid to his brothers.

The public was alarmed with earthquakes and inundations of rivers, which, however destructive, were considered more as the presages of future calamities than as present evils, and their significance in that point of view was confirmed by a famine, which immediately followed or accompanied these events. The inundation of the Tiber had overflowed the city for many days, so as to make it necessary to pass through the streets in boats. The markets could not be supplied; and this circumstance, joined to a real scarcity, which kept up the prices after the inundation subsided, occasioned a dearth which lasted for some years.

U. C. 758.

M. Æmilius Lepidus, L. Aruntius, ex Kal. Jul. Calicus Ca us Vibius. Aug. 33tio, Ætat. 67.

During this time of distress, it being thought impossible to find the usual supply of provisions, it was judged necessary to lessen the usual consumption; and for this purpose all gladiators,[10] all slaves kept for sale, and all foreigners, except physicians and public teachers, were ordered to be removed a hundred miles from the city.[11] Even the servants and attendants of the court were dismissed in great numbers, and a vacation was proclaimed in the courts of justice, in order that as many as could possibly be spared from the city should depart. The attendance of senators was dispensed with, and the law requiring the presence of certain numbers of that body to give validity to their acts was suspended. Commissioners were named to inspect the markets. All feasting, on the birth-day of the emperor, or on other days of rejoicing, was prohibited; and persons, wont to receive any part of their subsistence in corn from the public granaries, had double the usual quantity served out to them.

Notwithstanding these measures taken for the relief of the people, their discontents breaking forth in libels and seditious complaints, rewards were published for discovering the authors, and some being detected, were brought to trial, and punished.[12]

The emperor now willing, from the decline of his age, to be relieved of part of the ordinary

6 Dio. Cass. lib. lv. c. 23. Tacit. Annal. lib. iv. c. 5.
7 About 160*l*. 8 About 100*l*.
9 Dio. Cass. lib. lv. c. 24.
10 Dio. Cass. lib lv. c. 22. 11 Sueton. in Aug. c 42.
12 Dio. Cass. lib. lv. c. 26.

business of state, intrusted the receiving of foreign ambassadors to three persons whom he chose from the senate. At the same time he himself, with his ordinary council, continued to deliberate on all questions which arose relating to the internal government of the empire. He appears to have committed himself, without any prospect of change, to the influence of Livia and her family; and, to confirm him in this disposition, had frequent visits from Tiberius, who, though generally stationed on the frontier of the empire, carefully attended to the state of his interests at Rome, as they stood both with the emperor and with the people.

In the tide which was thus turned in favour of the Claudian family, the surviving Agrippa seemed to form an insurmountable bar; but this young man, being of a rude and brutal disposition, gave his antagonist every advantage in their supposed competition. Having, about this time, given some flagrant proof of this character in his behaviour to Livia, and even to the emperor himself, he was degraded from his place in the family of Cæsar, and sent, under a military guard, to the island of Planasia, near to Corsica, where he remained a prisoner during the remainder of this reign.[1]

From the disgrace of Agrippa Posthumus, it was no longer doubtful that Tiberius was destined to inherit the fortunes and power of Augustus. He alone was entrusted wherever great armies were to be assembled, and was employed in every service that was likely to end with lustre. Troubles on the frontier of Asia or Africa were entrusted to other hands; but the harder struggle with the Germans, Dalmatians, and other fierce nations of Europe, was committed to him. After having penetrated, in his last campaign, to the Weser and the Elbe,[2] he was called off to support his nephew and adopted son Germanicus, who, commanding the army on the side of Dalmatia, found himself too weak to execute the service on which he had been employed.

U. C. 759.

A. Licinius Nerva Ælianus. Q. Cæcilius Metellus Creticus. Aug. 34to, Ætat. 68.

The provinces east of the Hadriatic, and from thence probably to the Danube, had formed the plan of a general revolt. It was reported, at this time, that those nations could assemble eight hundred thousand men, and that they had two hundred thousand foot properly armed, with nine thousand horse. Being so powerful in point of numbers, they were enabled to divide their strength, and to carry on operations, at the same time, in different places. They destined one part of their force to invade Italy, by Tergeste and Nauportus; another to take possession of Macedonia; and a third to defend their own possessions at home. They had now joined to their own ferocity a considerable knowledge of the discipline and forms of the Roman legion, and conducted their present design with so much address as to escape observation until it was ripe for execution. They gave the first intimation of their hostile intentions by a general massacre of the Romans, who, as provincial officers or traders, were settled in the country, and cut off all the military posts which had been advanced to protect them. They entered Macedonia without opposition, and with fire and sword laid waste all the possessions and settlements of the Romans in that province.[3]

U. C. 760.

M. Furius Camillus, Sext. Nonius Geuntelianus. Aug. 35to. Ætat. 69.

Such was the beginning of a war with the barbarous nations of the northern and eastern frontier of the empire, which, during some ages, was, at intervals, interrupted and resumed, often put Italy itself upon the defensive, was always formidable, and at last fatal to the sovereignty of Rome.

The Romans, by the continual labours of seven centuries, had made their way from the Tiber to the Rhine and the Danube, through the territory of warlike hordes who opposed them, and over forests and rugged ways that were every where to be cleared at the expense of their labour and their blood: but the ways they had made to reach their enemies were now open, in their turns, for enemies to reach them. The ample resources which they had formed by their cultivation increased the temptation to invade them, and facilitated all the means of making war upon their country. By reducing the inhabitants of their provinces, in every part, to pacific subjects, they brought the defence of the empire to depend on a few professional soldiers who composed the legions.

U. C. 761.

Q. Sulpicius Camerinus, C Poppæus Sabinus, ex Kal Jul. M. Papius Mutil s, Q. Poppæus Secund s. Aug. 36to. Ætat. 70.

Under apprehension of these circumstances, Augustus was heard to say, on the present occasion, that if proper measures were not speedily taken for the defence of Italy, an enemy from the Danube and the Rhine might, in ten days, be seen from the battlements of Rome. New levies were accordingly made, and the order not to enlist emancipated slaves was suspended. The veterans, who had been discharged from the legions, were again ordered to repair to their colours; and citizens of every condition were required to furnish, in proportion to their estates or possessions, certain quotas of men for the service.

While the people, under so many symptoms of trepidation, were made sensible of their danger, Augustus seems to have thought it a proper opportunity to renew the part he had often acted in recommending population and marriage. He called together, in separate assemblies, first the married who had families of children, afterwards the barren and the unmarried; and finding the superiority of numbers on the side of the latter, expressed his concern in a public address to the people; enlarged on the consequences of population to the safety and prosperity of the commonwealth; revived the marriage-laws, and, by an act which took its name from Papius and Poppæus,[4] consuls of this year, gave additional rewards to the married, and laid new penalties on celibacy, with a considerable premium to the prosecutor by whom any person should be convicted of this offence.

Before these regulations should be enforced, a year was allowed to the unmarried to change their condition; and the rigour of former laws,[5]

---

1 Dio. Cass. lib. lv. c. 32.

2 Ibid. c. 27–30.

3 Velleius Paterculus, lib. ii. c. 110.

4 Lex Papia Poppæa.

5 Lex Voconia.

respecting the inheritance of women, which had hitherto been restricted to a hundred thousand sesterces,[6] was considerably abated. Females were allowed to inherit a larger sum; and, the better to testify the homage that was paid to female virtue, the vestals were admitted to partake in the privilege of Roman parents having three children.[7]

In the mean time, great efforts were made to keep the enemy at a distance, and to fix the seat of the war in their own country. Tiberius advanced for this purpose into Dalmatia, and the emperor himself set out for Ariminum, that he might be nearer the scene of operation to receive reports, to profit by intelligence, and to give his directions. He had, for some time, empowered the senate to continue their proceedings in his absence; as he ceased to attend the comitia or assemblies of the people, he made free with their privileges; and, under pretence of disorders occasioned by the elections, took upon himself the nomination of magistrates, or signified his choice to the tribes by a writ of recommendation. Public prayers were now offered for his preservation; and at his departure from the city, as if he were going on a service of great danger to his person, many vows were made, and sacrifices destined to be offered up in case of his safe return.[8]

Although the force of the empire was not yet fallen so low as to justify so much apprehension, the alarm nevertheless continued for three years.[9]

Tiberius upon his arrival in Dalmatia, found the barbarians, who had invaded that country, commanded by two leaders of the names of Bato and Pinetes. He formed his own army into three divisions, commanded by Germanicus, Sylvanus Lepidus, and himself. By this disposition he began his operations in three different quarters at once.

U. C. 762.

P. Cornelius Dolabella. C. Junius Silanus, ex. Kal. Jul. Ser. Cornelius. Aug. 37mo. Ætat. 71.

In the service which was committed to Sylvanus Lepidus, he met with little resistance. Where he himself commanded, the Romans were long detained in the blockade of a castle, which being built on a rock, was rendered inaccessible by the height of its situation, and by the depths of the glens and gulleys that were formed by the torrents with which it was surrounded. Bato had taken post in this place with a numerous body of his countrymen; and being provided with necessaries, endeavoured to tire out the enemy. But he himself, in the end, being weary of his inactive and hopeless situation, found means to escape, and left the remains of his countrymen, worn out with want and impatience, to surrender at discretion.

Where Germanicus commanded, the enemy had taken refuge in Anduba, a fortress similarly situated with the former; but which, after repeated attacks, was at last put into his hands by the dissension of the barbarians who defended it. These, having quarrelled, turned their swords mutually against each other. One of the parties set the quarters of their antagonists on fire, and both fell an easy prey to their enemies. Many of the women, to avoid captivity, threw themselves, with their children, into the flames.[10] Bato soon after surrendered himself; and being asked, what tempted him to make war upon the Romans? made answer, "You affect to treat every nation as your flocks and your property; but you intrust the care of them to ravenous wolves, not to shepherds and their dogs."[11]

At the close of the war, the title of imperator, with the triumphal ornaments, were decreed to Tiberius, and to his adopted son Germanicus;[12] but in the midst of the rejoicings which were made on this occasion, accounts of a different nature were received from the Rhine.

The Romans, wishing to command the passage of the river, had occupied, as has been observed, some country, and fortified some stations on the German side. By this disposition it was intended, in case the Germans should attempt a descent upon Gaul, that part of the Roman army should be so placed as to remain in their rear. And indeed while they kept possession of the navigation of the river, and of both its banks, they, in some measure, rendered every such attempt impracticable. In consequence of this disposition, the Germans had, for some time, discontinued the practice of making incursions into Gaul. They were become familiar with the Roman army that was stationed in their country, exchanged commodities with the Roman traders, and began to imitate their manners.

Such was the state of the nations situated between the Rhine and the Weser, when Quinctilius Varus, who had been left by Tiberius in the command of the German frontier, began to consider the natives of the country around him, as ripe for the ordinary impositions which the Romans laid on their subjects, and made some exactions for the supply of his army.

Some chiefs or leaders of the neighbourhood, particularly Segimerus, prince of the Chatti, and his son Armenius, had observed, with indignation, these encroachments of the Roman general, and the gradual decline of their country into a Roman province. Being at the head of a powerful canton, and much respected by all the nations of that quarter, they entered into a concert to cut off all the Romans that were posted on the German side of the Rhine; and to restore the independence of their people. They concealed their design by redoubling their attention to the Roman general; took their residence in his quarters, and applied to him for decision in all the disputes which arose among the natives; made him acquainted with the weaknesses and the strengths of their country, and served him as guides in conducting the marches, and in fixing the stations of his army.

While, by these artifices, Segimerus and Arminius lulled the Roman general into perfect security, they had their followers ready to assemble under arms, and brought all the chieftains of their neighbourhood under engagements to join them, as soon as their design should be ripe for execution. They proposed to draw the Roman general into a situation in which he could be attacked with advantage, while they themselves, without giving him any alarm, should have a pretence for advancing towards him with all their forces.

6 About 800*l*.
7 Dio. Cass. lib. lv. c. 1, 2. 10.
8 Ibid. c. 34.
9 Vell. Pater. lib. ii. c. 114
10 Dio. Cass. lib. lvi. c. 12. 14, 15.
11 Ibid. lib. lv. c. 56.
12 Ibid. lib. lvi. c. 17

To effect both these purposes, they procured an insurrection of some of the cantons over which Segimerus claimed a supremacy, and implored the assistance of the Roman army in suppressing the revolt. Varus, apprehending that the safety of the Romans, in all their possessions beyond the Rhine, depended on the support he should give to their allies, put his army in motion to quell this pretended rebellion, and advanced through difficult ways into the interior parts of the country. On this march he was attended by Segimerus and Arminius, and supplied with every requisite to promote the service, or to ensure its success. These chiefs had assembled their forces, and brought forth the inhabitants of the neighbouring country, under pretence of acting as irregulars to cover the march of the Roman legions. In performing this service, they pervaded the marshes and woods in his front, on his flanks, and his rear, and had actually surrounded him, when he came upon the ground on which they proposed to make their attack.

Here the forests and marshes were extensive and impassable, except by a single tract. The Romans were crowded together, and entangled with their baggage; and being in this condition attacked from every quarter at once, were unable to resist or to escape. Varus succeeded in gaining an opening which appeared at some distance in the woods; and there, with as many as could follow him, attempted to intrench himself; but the greater part of the army fell by the hands of the enemy. At night, seeing no hopes of a retreat, the general himself fell upon his own sword, and by his example induced many officers and soldiers to employ the same means of avoiding the cruelties or insults to which they were exposed.

A few having found means to retire under cover of the night, made their way to the Rhine. Here they were received by a party sent upon the first news of their disaster by Asprenas from Gaul, to favour their retreat.

It had been concerted by the Germans, that on the same day every Roman post in their country should be attacked. Lucius Ceditius, who commanded at Aliso, now supposed to be Elsemberg, being surrounded by superior numbers, forced his way through the enemy, and, under the greatest distresses, arrived on the Rhine. All the other posts were forced, and the troops who had occupied them taken or killed. Among the former, Caldus, an officer of rank, being a prisoner and in irons, upon some insult that was offered to him, struck himself on the head with his chains, and expired.

The Romans, on this occasion, lost three entire legions, or about eighteen thousand foot, and a considerable body of horse. Asprenas having remained on the German side of the Rhine only until he had collected the remains of the Roman army which had escaped from this calamity, withdrew into Gaul, and made dispositions to prevent any commotions in that province.

The first accounts of this disaster were received at Rome with the highest degree of consternation. The victorious enemy having cut off what was considered as the strength of the empire on the Rhine, were supposed to be following at the heels of the messenger who brought the news. Guards were posted in different quarters of the city to prevent disorders, and to quiet the fears of the people. A proclamation was issued to suspend the changes usually made in the provincial appointments, and requiring every officer to continue in his present command until express orders were given to the contrary. The sacred records were consulted, to find what religious processions or ceremonies had been performed on the invasion of the Cimbri, and on the breaking out of the Marsic war, and the same rites were now to be repeated. The emperor put on mourning, and for some months carried in his looks, and in the neglect of his person, every appearance of distress.[1] It was given out that, in the first transport of grief, he struck his head on the wall of his chamber. The Germans and Gauls that were at Rome, were secured and sent into the islands on the coasts of Italy. All citizens were ordered to arm, and many disappeared from the streets, to avoid being pressed to serve in the legions.

There remained a great army on the establishment of the empire; but this army being dispersed over an extensive frontier in Asia and Africa, it was not supposed that a sufficient force could be brought from thence in time to protect the capital against an enemy who was believed to be hastening to its gates. Very violent means were therefore employed to form an army in Italy, and men were forced under arms by the terror of military execution. The forces which were brought in this manner to the emperor's standard were placed under the command of Tiberius; and, as fast as they could be put into a regular form, began to move towards Gaul.

In these measures the Romans acted more from their own fears, than from a just apprehension of what was to be expected from the enemy. The most active and vigorous conquerors can seldom act up to the fears of those they have vanquished; and the Germans, on this occasion, content with having freed their own country from the presence of a Roman army, made no attempt to pursue their victory, and remained quiet in their own possessions.[2]

U. C. 763.
M. Æmilius Lepidus
F. Statilius Taurus,
ex Kal. Jul.
L. Cassius Longinus.
Aug. 38vo.
Ætat. 72.

In the following summer Tiberius and Germanicus, to recover the credit of the Roman arms, having passed the Rhine, laid waste the adjacent country, but not meeting with an enemy, returned without having given occasion to any signal event. They supposed that the natives were retired from the frontier, in order to tempt them to follow into the forests of that impervious country, and to engage them in difficult situations. But having done enough to enable the capital to recover from its panic, they brought back in autumn the Roman army into Gaul, and from thence themselves returned into Italy.

U. C. 763.
Aug. 38vo.
Ætat. 72.

In this year Drusus, the son of Tiberius, acted in the capacity of quæstor; sixteen prætors were employed. In the year following, the number of these magistrates was reduced to twelve. It being alleged that governors of provinces, to preclude the complaints which were often made against them upon their removal, extorted attestations and complimentary

1 Sueton. in Octav. c. 23.
2 Dio. Cass. lib. lvi. c. 23, 24.

addresses from the people they had oppressed, it was enacted, that no governor should receive any honorary gift or attestation from his province, during the continuance of his power, nor sooner than six months after his return to Rome.

The age of the emperor now led men to think of his successor; and predictions of his death were surmised abroad. This probably gave occasion to the edict which forbade soothsayers to utter predictions relating to the life of any person whatever. Among the circumstances that characterise the manners of the times, it is said, that Roman knights, or citizens of quality, had permission to exhibit themselves as gladiators.[3]

U. C. 764. *Germanicus Cæsar, C. Fonteius Capito, ex Kal. Jul. C. Vesellius Varro. Aug. 39no. Ætat. 73.*

Tiberius, at his return to Rome, after the noted services he had performed on the Save and the Rhine, had a triumphal entry. In ascending the capitol he dismounted from his carriage, and threw himself at the feet of the emperor, who stood in the way to receive him.[4] After the procession was over, shows were exhibited by Germanicus, in which two hundred lions were hunted down; and a portico which Livia had erected to the memory of Caius and Lucius Cæsar, being dedicated about this time, served to increase the solemnity.

Of the Claudain family, on whom the sovereign power seemed already to devolve, Germanicus, the grandson of Livia by Drusus, the younger of her sons, was most in favour with the people. He was recommended by an appearance of openness and candour in his manners, and by the facility with which he engaged, according to the custom of the ancient republic, in the defence of his clients, and in pleading their causes, whether before the emperor himself, or before the ordinary judges. Tiberius, on the contrary, seemed to be of a dark and suspicious temper, and was supposed to cover, under the appearances of moderation, which he studied to preserve in public and in presence of the emperor, a jealous and cruel disposition. But Livia, who, in the present period of her husband's life, had the entire government of him, preferred her son to her grandson, and employed all her influence to make the choice of a successor fall on Tiberius.

The emperor, in the mean time, pleased with the respite from trouble which these delegates of his power endeavoured to procure for him, reposed himself much on their care, and was pleased to be supplied with every change of amusement or pleasure for which it was known that he had any relish.[5] He was attended by agreeable women, musicians, comedians, and even declaimers on favourite topics in philosophy, who made a part of the scene at the close of his ordinary meals. At his entertainments he treated the guests with presents of dresses, trinkets, or money, and amused them with lotteries, in which they had chances that entitled them to prizes of different values, or with auctions of pictures, in which the back of the picture being turned to the company, they bid upon chance.[6]

3 Vell. Pater. lib. ii. c. 120. Dio. Cass. lib. lvi. c. 25.
4 Sueton. quoted by Piso.
5 Sueton. in August. c. 71. 6 Ibid. c. 74, 75.

Of these pastimes some were probably the amusements of the emperor's old age, and marked the decline of life. In his more vigorous years, we may suppose him to have been sufficiently occupied with the business of state, and with the attention which he gave in person to every question that arose in the government of so extensive an empire. Every transaction was still communicated to him, and despatched in his name; but from the symptoms which he gave of an inclination to retire from affairs, it is probable that his application was greatly abated. So long as he was accustomed to attend the senate in person, he generally received, on the days of their meeting, the compliments of the members at his own house or in the forum; from thence was conducted by them to the place of assembly, and, before they proceeded to business, commonly went round a circle of those who were present, and spoke somewhat obliging to each. This particular is mentioned, as a proof of his affability and condescension; but was in reality the highest circumstance of state which he ever assumed. As a private person, in the vigour of life, he suffered himself to be treated as an equal, and made one at the entertainments and parties of pleasure that were made by his friends; but in the decline of life, as he withdrew from the senate, so he desired to be excused from receiving the visits of the members, or even of his private friends; and, under pretence of being much occupied with the troubles which still subsisted on the frontiers of the empire, he declined going into company upon any occasion whatever.[7]

U. C. 765. *C. Silius, L. Munatius Plancus. Aug. 40mo. Ætat. 74.*

While the emperor thus, in a great measure, withdrew from the public view, the fourth period of ten years, for which he had accepted of the government, being about to expire, he again resumed his command with the usual forms, prolonged the tribunitian power in the person of Tiberius for other five years, and permitted his son Drusus from being quæstor, to be entered on the list of consuls without passing through the rank of prætor.

Augustus, in entering upon this new period of his government, in which he was no longer to attend the senate in person, received from this body, by a formal act, full powers, with the advice of his ordinary council, to determine all questions of state, and, with the concurrence of his adopted children, to enact laws of equal authority with those he had formerly passed in the senate. These powers he had already exercised; and we may suppose them to have been thus formally conferred upon him, chiefly that it might be made to appear how far the family of Livia, now included in the same act, were raised to an avowed participation of the imperial authority.

The first consultations of this new legislature were employed on the subject of the penal laws, which having remained without any considerable change from the times of the republic, were still, in respect to the forms of trial, better calculated to protect the subject than to gratify the passions of the sovereign. Banishment, by which, under the republic, criminals were at liberty to evade any sentence, and which, in reality, had

7 Dio. Cass. lib. lvi. c. 26.

nothing grievous besides the circumstance of their being obliged to travel from Rome, and to forego city preferments and honours, was, by a regulation now made, rendered more severe, and not suffered to remain, as the courtiers termed them, a mere elusion of justice. Under a sentence of banishment, by this regulation, the exile was no longer at liberty to choose the place of his retreat, nor suffered to retain his effects. He might reside in any island surrounded by fifty miles of sea, and in some islands which were mentioned, as Cos, Rhodes, Lesbos, and Sardinia, though less remote; but he was entirely debarred from the continent. He was allowed to retain of his estate, if it amounted to so much, five hundred thousand sesterces,[1] and might have a ship of a thousand amphoræ,[2] and two boats with twenty servants or slaves; but was not at liberty to pass from one island to another, nor to change the place of his abode.

So far the transition from the jealousy of the citizen against the severities of government, which is a part in the spirit of liberty, to the jealousy of the prince against the license of his subjects, which equally belongs to monarchy, was abundantly mild; but even this law, under the prospect of its immediate application, gave weight to the chains with which every citizen already felt himself loaded. The subjects of prosecution that were likely to draw the animadversion of a despotic court, were not injuries to society and offences to human nature, which the ingenuous ever wish to shun, as well as to restrain; but rather want of submission or respect, libels, petulant freedoms, and even merit itself, if such as to excite the jealousy of superiors. The new law, indeed, by the directions contained in it to take cognizance of libels and defamatory publications, under the denomination of treason, seemed to point chiefly at this species of guilt; but it was not the law itself, so much as the arbitrary application of it, that was likely to deprive every Roman of that degree of security or personal freedom to which he still had pretensions.[3]

U. C. 796.

Sext. Pompeius, Sext. Apulcius. Aug. 41mo. Ætat. 75.

In the same year mankind had still more reason to be alarmed; Tiberius was associated with Augustus in the government, and declared to have equal power with the emperor himself in all the provinces within his department.[4] On this occasion the new associate in the empire, to raise his consideration, and to amuse the people, exhibited no less than three separate triumphal processions; at the end of which, there being some disorders subsisting on the side of Dalmatia and Illyricum, which seemed to require his presence; and he being to set out for this province, Augustus was pleased to accompany him on the road to Beneventum They went to Astura by land; but as Augustus, when the wind was favourable, always preferred going by water, they embarked at this place, and steered for the coast of Campania. On their passage, Augustus was seized with a dysentery, but continued, as on a party of pleasure, to visit the different islands in the bay of Naples. At Capreæ he passed some days with uncommon gayety, and without appearing to suffer much from his distemper. At Naples he attended the public sports which were given upon his arrival. From thence he continued his route to Beneventum, where Tiberius, being to embark at Brundusium, took his leave, and the emperor set out on his return to Rome. But finding his strength decline on a sudden, he halted at Nola, a place in which his family had originally some possessions, and at which his father died. From the time of his arrival at this place he refused to listen to any business.[5] On the morning of the 18th of August, he asked if his illness had caused any tumults or insurrections, called for a mirror, and desired to be dressed. He said to those who attended him, "What think you now? Have I acted my part properly?" then repeated the form with which actors commonly end the representation of a play, desiring the audience, that if the piece was to their liking they should applaud.[6] "I found," he said, "a city of brick, and changed it into marble." In this he alluded to his policy in the state, as well as to his buildings at Rome.

Augustus died at three in the afternoon of the eighteenth of August, in the seventy-sixth year of his age. His body was transported from Nola to Bovillæ, carried by the magistrates of the several towns on the route. They moved in the night, and halted by day, to avoid the heat of the season. At Bovillæ it was received and carried forward to Rome, by a numerous company of the equestrian order.

The senate met to deliberate on the honours to be paid at the funeral; and the members vied with each other in the proposals they made to exalt the dead, and to express their own sorrow.[7] Some proposed, that the funeral procession should pass through a triumphal arch, preceded by the statue of Victory; and that the ceremony should conclude with a solemn dirge, or song of grief, to be performed by the children of all the principal families in Rome. Others moved, that on the day of his funeral the noble Romans should exchange the gold ring, which was the badge of their rank, for one of iron; that the ashes should be collected from the funeral pile by the highest order of priests.

At this funeral, in whatever form it was executed, two orations were pronounced; one by Tyberius, who had been recalled on the near approach of the emperor's death; the other by Drusus, the son of Tiberius, on whom the name and inheritance of Cæsar had now devolved.

1 About 4000*l*

2 The amphora, according to Arbuthnot, contained about seven gallons.

3 Dio. Cass. lib. lvi. c. 27, 28. Tacit. Ann. lib. i. c. 72.

4 Vell. Pater. lib. ii. c. 121.

5 Suet. in Aug. c. 100

6 Ibid.

7 Ibid

CHAPTER V.

The Will of Augustus—Review of his Reign—And of his Character—Tiberius returns to Nola—Issues without delay his orders throughout the Empire—In the Senate affects Reluctance to charge himself with the Government—Mutiny in Panonia—On the Rhine—Second Mutiny on the Arrival of Deputies from the Senate—Imposture of Clemens—Plot of Libo—Description of Tiberius—Death of Germanicus—And Trial of Piso.

AUGUSTUS had made his will about sixteen months before he died, bequeathing two thirds of his estate to Tiberius, the other third to Livia, with an injunction to take the names of Julia and Augusta. In succession to Livia and her son he substituted the younger Drusus, the son of Tiberius, for a third; and overlooking Claudius, one of the sons of the elder Drusus, and grandson of Livia, he bequeathed the remainder to the brother, Germanicus Cæsar, and his offspring, already consisting of three sons and as many daughters.[8] To this numerous list of heirs he substituted an ostentatious catalogue of principal citizens and senators But persisted so much in his severity to the unhappy Julia, as to forbid her a place in his monument. As a legacy to be distributed to the Roman people, he bequeathed four millions of sesterces, or about thirty-three thousand pounds sterling; as a fund for the tribes or wards of the city, to defray their respective corporation expenses, he bequeathed three millions five hundred thousand sesterces, or about twenty nine thousand one hundred and sixty-six pounds sterling; to the prætorian bands one thousand sesterces, or about eight pounds sterling a man; to the cohorts of the city five hundred, or about four pounds sterling a man; to the legions three hundred, or about two pounds ten shillings a man.[9] These sums he ordered to be paid immediately; leaving money in his coffers sufficient for this purpose. Other legacies, of which some did not exceed a hundred and sixty, or a hundred and seventy pounds sterling, he directed to be paid at different times, and alleged the scantiness of his estate, from which his heirs were not likely to draw above a hundred and fifty millions Roman money, or about one million three hundred thousand pounds sterling. The sums which he had received in legacies, amounting to about eleven millions sterling, he had expended in public works.

After his will was read, four separate memorials were produced. The first contained instructions for his funeral; the second, a list of the actions which he wished to have recorded on his tomb; the third, a state of the republic, including the military establishment, the distribution of the legions, the revenue, the public disbursements, the money actually lodged in the treasury, the arrears of taxes that were due, with a reference to the persons in whose hands the vouchers were to be found.

The fourth memorial contained political instructions or maxims, in which he dissuaded the people from the too frequent manumission of slaves, and from the too easy admission of foreigners to the dignity of Roman citizens; and recommended filling offices of state with persons of experience and reputation. The public service, he observed, never should be entrusted to a single officer, nor all the powers of the commonwealth be suffered to accumulate in the hands of any one person. Such exclusive trusts, he said, must lead to abuse, and end in a scarcity of persons fit to be employed. Such were the arguments of Catulus and Cato, when they pleaded against the exorbitant powers of Pompey and Cæsar; and the reasonings now ascribed to Augustus seems to be borrowed from theirs, and with too little regard to the difference of persons and times.

It is said, that in this memorial the emperor concluded with an injunction not to attempt any farther conquest or any farther extension of the empire.[3]

Such are the principal circumstances upon record, from which we are able to collect the character of this celebrated reign. The immediate effects of it, in many parts, appear to have been splendid and salutary. Among these we are to reckon the cessation of wars, and reformation of government in the Roman provinces. Under this establishment, instead of the consuls who, being annually elected by the people, as often renewed the passion of their country for war and conquest, there began a succession of emperors who were addicted to sloth and sensuality, more than to ambition; or if disposed to war, who in youth, or in some particular period of life, exhausted their passion for military fame, and became from thenceforward a powerful restraint on the ambition of their own officers. These they considered as rivals and objects of jealousy, or as dangerous instruments, ever ready to involve them in wars abroad, to disturb their government at home, or to divert their revenue from those pleasurable applications in which they wished to employ it.

Whatever was lost to citizens of rank or high pretension at Rome, by the establishment of the monarchy, was gained to the other subjects of the empire. The provinces, from being the temporary property of individuals, and stript to enrich a succession of masters, became the continued subjects of a sovereign, who as often as he understood his own interest, protected them against the oppression of his officers, and spared or nursed them as a continual source of revenue and of power to himself.

While these desirable effects naturally resulted from the new establishment, many circumstances of great lustre in the history of the age were ascribed to the sovereign. The seeds of ingenuity and of liberal arts, which had been sown, and which were already sprung up with so much

8 The three sons were Nero, Drusus, and Caius or Caligula; the three daughters Agrippina, Drusilla, and Livia or Livilla.

9 Dio Cass. lib. lvi. c. 32. Tacit. Annal. lib i. c. 8.

3 Dio. Cass. lib. lvi. c. 32. Tacit. Annal. lib. i. c. 8.

vigour under the republic, now began to be reaped in a plentiful harvest.

Literature, and all the more agreeable fruits of ingenuity, received under the first emperor a peculiar degree of attention and encouragement. Augustus was himself a proficient in letters, or, willing to be amused with the pursuits of the learned, read his own productions in the circle of his friends; and, what is more difficult for an author, heard without jealousy the compositions of others, by which his own were probably far excelled. He had saved from the wreck of his enemy's party, protected from the oppression of his own, and selected, as his favourites, the most ingenious men of the times.[1] By his munificence to these, his own name, as well as that of his minister, has become proverbial in the history of letters, and is deeply inscribed on monuments which can never perish, except by some calamity fatal to mankind.

The provinces greatly diversified in respect to situation, climate and soil, as well as in respect to the arts which they severally possessed, having the benefit of general peace, and the protection of a common sovereign, reaped the advantage of an easy communication and a flourishing trade. All the surplus wealth of the more cultivated parts of the earth being drawn to the capital, and being at the disposal of single men, was expended in works of magnificence, and if not of utility, at least of splendid caprice. From this fund, were erected those magnificent fabrics, of which the ruins, still mark the place on which stood the capital of the western world. The empire, at the same time, in all its parts, received those improvements which are the ordinary attendants of opulence and peace. The lands were cultivated; cities were built, adorned, or enlarged.

The rough and vigorous hands by which this great empire was formed, had carried the balance and the sword of state before they could manage the tools of the more ordinary and inferior arts, and had given empire to their country, before they had provided for themselves the ordinary means of accommodation or pleasure. A Roman citizen was not an artist, but he was a man fit to command every artist. He was possessed of courage, penetration, sagacity, and all the advantages which constitute the personal superiority of one man over another As a warrior and statesman, he was the reverse of those ingenious and feeble subjects, of whom each professes a particular part in the science or practice of human affairs, but of whom none is qualified to direct the whole.

In proportion, however, as this nation of masters forced into their service the industrious and the learned in different parts of the earth, the practitioners of every art, and the professors of every science flocked to the capital. Their productions, though spurned and rejected at first, were received by degrees, and in the reign of Augustus found the most ample rewards. By these means, the practice of every art was introduced at Rome, even Romans were taught to become artists and mechanics, and, by following a multiplicity of inferior pursuits and occupations, were taught to lower the haughty spirit of the conquerors of the world, to the level of the nations they had subdued.

In the times immediately preceding the civil wars, foreign letters, though fondly received by many of the first citizens of Rome, were still a novelty, and considered by the people as a foppish affectation. But the leaders in this fashion being the first officers and greatest men of the state, as Lucullus, Cicero, Cato, and Cæsar; such illustrious examples soon removed every prejudice, and engaged, in the pursuit of learning, every talent that could be diverted from the more violent pursuits of ambition or pleasure.

The civil wars for some time retarded the progress of letters; but when brought to an end, left the public in possession of the bias it had received. Octavius himself having, in his youth, received this bias, was probably, in his patronage of the learned, more led by inclination, and less by mere policy, than he was in other parts of the conduct with which he gained the favourable opinion of the world. He loved correctness and accuracy in all his compositions, and never delivered his mind on any serious matter, even in his own family, without memorials or written notes.

Although the effects of this reign, therefore, in many of the particulars we have mentioned, were the sequel of mere peace, and of the respite which the world began to enjoy from the disorders with which it had been lately afflicted, much likewise may be ascribed to the personal character of the prince. After the secure establishment of his power, his government began to be distinguished by appearances of moderation and justice, supported, in this part of his life, with a regular and ordinary tenor, which does not warrant any doubt of his sincerity, or any suspicion of any intention to impose upon the world, some purpose different from that which he professed to have in view.

In his character of legislator, he generally submitted his intended acts to public inspection, encouraged persons of every description to offer amendments, and sometimes adopted those which were offered to him.[2] In the exercise of the executive power, he took the assistance of a chosen council, with whom he deliberated on the ordinary measures of state. In accepting of the honours which were offered to him, he checked instances of extreme servility, and acquitted himself with great liberality or moderation in the use of the powers, which the flattery of dying persons frequently gave him over their families and estates. He became the guardian, rather than the co-heir, of the orphans, with whom he was joined in the father's will. Some he put in the immediate possession of the whole inheritance; others, while under age, he treated as his wards, and brought up with every advantage to the enjoyment of their fortunes, which they often received with considerable additions, made either by his care or by his bounty.

But what is of all other circumstances most peculiarly characteristic of this reign, was the judgment and address with which the emperor repressed the license of the military, to whom he owed his own elevation, the artful policy by

1 Horace was saved from the rout of the republican party at Philippi; and Virgil, from among the sufferers ejected from their property, to make way for the army of Cæsar.

2 Dio. Cass. lib. liii. c. 21.

which he affected to restore some fragments of the civil government that he himself had broken down, and the caution with which he retained the character and profession of a civil magistrate and of a citizen, while he governed as master. Joined to these, we may reckon the able choice which he made of officers fit to be trusted in the different departments of the public service; the constancy with which he persevered in employing them, and the liberality with which he made them feel that the prosperity of his fortunes was their own. While he gave these indications of a great mind and possessed these powerful supports of a prosperous life, he dispensed with much of the flattery that is paid to princes, and in conversation encouraged the manners of a free and equal society.[3]

How then are we to decide upon his character, marked by appearances of perfidy, cruelty, and even of cowardice in some parts of his life, distinguished by moderation, clemency, and steadiness in other parts of it? Are we to suppose what the emperor Julian insinuates,[4] that Octavius received in the later period of his life new lights, was become a new man; and that, by the lessons of Zeno, at an early period, this Cameleon might have fixed his colour, and been from the first, what he appeared to be in the last state of his fortunes, a real friend to mankind? The authority of Julian, no doubt, is highly respectable; but if a person in youth carry the marks of a bad disposition, and deliberately commit atrocious actions when his interest required them, we are still warranted to question the sincerity of his conversion, though, in a different state of his interest, even the whole tenor of his life should change.

Octavius does not appear to have had from nature, in any high degree, those dispositions to benevolence or malice which are the great distinguishing principles of virtue and vice. He seems to have been indifferent to mankind; but desirous of consideration and power, as objects of interest to himself. His ruling passion was a desire to reign. In his way to this end, he committed many crimes; but having once effected his purpose, he had no other criminal dispositions to gratify: or, after he was sovereign, standing in awe of a free spirit which he durst not insult, he, either from inclination or policy, and probably in part from both, preferred, as it is surprising that every one else does not prefer, the proper use of his power to the abuse of it.

Upon this principle, in a life so varied as that of Octavius, appearances of cruelty and of clemency, of caution and of enterprise, of violence and of moderation, may have equally found a place in the course of his actions. And in his person, we may read the same character of ambitious design, when he affected to join the senate in restoring the republic, or when he signed a warrant for the murder of those who were inclined to support that form of government; when he courted the protection of Cicero against Antony, or when he sacrificed the life of Cicero to the resentment of his enemy; when he made or broke off his treaties of marriage, and sought for aids to his ambition, even in the choice of his licentious amours; when he pardoned, and when he executed those who were detected in designs against his own life.

If we state ourselves therefore as judges on the solemn appeal which Augustus on his death-bed made to the sense of the world, it is probable, that as he was in some degree able to redeem, in the administration of his sovereignty, the enormities which he had committed in obtaining it, we shall bestow upon him neither the epithets of reproach and of infamy, which he appears to have deserved in the early period of his life, nor those terms of encomium and praise, which he seems to have merited in the longer and more elevated parts of his reign. Neither the friend nor the enemy of mankind, he was, by his personal and interested ambition, the cause of harm and of good; but upon the whole, if the history of the establishment made by him were to terminate with his own life; if the tranquillity of his reign be compared with the troubles of the preceding period; it will furnish, to those who contend for the preference of despotical government, an occasion of triumph.

Justice and peace are at all times the great objects of attention and care to mankind; but the degree in which they can be obtained, and the means which may be employed to obtain them, are different in different circumstances; different on the supposition of small or extensive states, of poor or of rich nations; and, in some circumstances, they may no doubt be better obtained by the wisdom and discretion of a single person, than by any system of public councils or popular assemblies, which the people to be governed are themselves fit to compose. When this is the case, it is fortunate that single men are found, who, without any criminal inclinations, are willing to undertake the government of nations. A succession of such characters, indeed, is more than human nature, by any known rule of substitution, whether by inheritance or by election, can continue to furnish. It is well, if, in a series of ages, where the government of the world is committed to the discretion of an individual, the good in any degree compensate the bad.

As Augustus had, to the last moment of his reign, affected to hold the sovereignty by a mere temporary appointment, he could not, in consistence with his own professions, either name a successor, or dispose of the empire as the inheritance of his family. At his death, therefore, some persons might hope to see the commonwealth restored; others might wish to see the late contest for dominion revived, and many questions might have arisen, that would have involved the empire in fresh trouble. These questions, however, with the projects or hopes that might be founded upon them, were in a great measure prevented, by the precaution which Livia had taken in having her son Tiberius, during the lifetime of the late emperor, associated with himself in the government.

When Augustus was seized with his last illness, Tiberius, in the capacity of his associate in the empire, as has been mentioned, set out for the armies in Dalmatia; but he received on his way, a message from his mother, intimating the last symptoms of approaching death in her husband. Upon this intimation, he returned to Nola, and arrived either before Augustus expired, or before his death was publicly known; and having given out, that, in a conference with

3 Dio. Cass. lib lvi. c. 43. 4 Vid. Cæsars of Julian.

hat experienced prince, he had received his last .nstructions for the government of the empire,[1] he took hold of the reins the moment the other was supposed to have dropped them, assumed his usual imperial guards, anu, by sending orders to all the provinces and military stations, took upon him to continue the same model of government, without any cessation or interval whatever.[2]

The new emperor, with the usual precaution to stifle competitors, ordered Agrippa, the surviving grandson of Augustus to be put to death, and took every other effectual measure to secure his own accession. At the same time, either in imitation of the cautious policy of the late emperor, or in pursuance of that hypocrisy and dissimulation to which he himself had been long accustomed, and to which he was naturally inclined, he affected, in his correspondence with the senate, to pay the utmost deference to their authority, and, in his letters, took care to employ all the modest expressions of a private citizen.

Being tribune of the people, he ventured only in this capacity, he said, to call upon the senate to give their orders respecting the funeral of Augustus. For his own part, he had taken his place by the corpse of the deceased, and in nothing else could take any public function upon him. The senate, he continued, would be pleased to order the guards that might be necessary to preserve the peace, and they would take every other precaution for the regular performance of this solemn duty.

When the funeral was over, and the senate was assembled for the opening of the will and memorials of the late emperor, Tiberius delivered himself in a voice, interrupted with sighs and tears; he observed, that a heavy burden, by the death of the only person who was able to bear it, had now devolved upon them all; that having himself been admitted to some share in the government, he had learned how arduous a task it was to be charged with the whole of it, and had learned to make a proper estimate of his own abilities;[3] but that in a state which could boast of so many illustrious men, they could not be limited in their choice, nor obliged to commit to one, what was sufficient to occupy the talents and abilities of many.

While he spoke to this purpose, and observed the aspect of his audience, frowning particularly upon those who gave any signs of assent, his known reputation for falsehood, the inconsistence of his actions with the professions which he now made, the murder of Agrippa, and the military guard which attended his person, effectually preserved the members who were present from becoming the dupes of a dissimulation, which it was equally dangerous to reject too abruptly, or to mistake for sincerity.

Most of the members, though sufficiently trained in the school of Augustus, to know the part they were to act on such occasions, had not yet performed this part upon such dangerous ground. They affected to believe that Tiberius was sincere, lamented that there should be any reluctance to accept of the government in the only person who was qualified to undertake it, and they beseeched him not to desert the republic in this extremity.

As the senators vied with each other in these feigned importunities, Tiberius seemed to be distressed, though not persuaded; and after he had remained some time undecided, in the end, as weary and silenced, though not convinced, he withdrew without making any reply, or without waiting for any formal resolution of the senate. In passing through the crowd, he was heard to say, "That a heavy load indeed had been laid on his shoulders, but that it could not be expected he was to bear it for ever; that old age at least must soon entitle him to respite." At the same time, those who were supposed to be most in his confidence, gave out, that his concern for the public, and the intreaties of the senate, had prevailed upon him to accept of the government; but the ridicule, which it was not permitted the senators to observe, was seized by the people. "Few men," it was said, "can perform all that they undertake; but this man, with a wonderful modesty, refuses to undertake even what he performs."[4]

While Tiberius, with so much palpable and even unnecessary craft, acted this farce in the senate, his title to the sovereignty underwent a more serious discussion in the provinces. The legions which were posted in different stations, though long confined under the authority of an able reign to the strictest duties and ordinary advantages of their profession, still retained the impression of their own importance, and of their power to dispose of the empire. They recolleted what some of them might have seen, and all of them had heard, of times in which they were courted by their leaders, retained with presents or gratuities, and rewarded at the expiration of their service with grants of land, and settlements in the richest and most cultivated districts of Italy. They had waited with impatience for an opportunity to give a new master to the world, and hoped, that, in performing this service, they might recover their consequence, and be entitled to rewards, such as military men had formerly received.

It cannot be doubted, that if there had been any officer at the head of the principal armies on the Rhine or the Danube, prepared to avail himself of this disposition in the army, the sword in the present, as in many other instances, must have decided who was to succeed in the throne of Cæsar; but Augustus having, in the choice of provincial and military commanders, guarded against any danger to his own government, had by the same means provided for the security of his successor's. The persons he employed, besides those of his own family, who depended entirely upon himself, were, for the most part, men of moderate ambition or mean pretensions; so that there was not now any person of rank prepared to take part in the revolts of the army.

Germanicus, the nephew and adopted son of Tiberius, might, by his popularity and by his pretensions, have become a formidable rival to his uncle, but was restrained by his moderation and the sense of his duty. A mutinous spirit nevertheless broke out first in Panonia, where three legions were commanded by Junius Blæsus; and

1 Sueton. in vit. Tiber. c. 21.
2 Tacit. Annal. lib. i. c. 3.
3 Varié disserebat de magnitudine imperii, sua modestia.—Tacit.

4 Sueton. in Tibe· c. 24. Dio. Cass. lib. lvii. c. 1.

afterwards on the Rhine, where a great division of the Roman armies, consisting of eight legions, were distributed in different stations, under the chief command of Germanicus himself.

The troops not having at any of their stations persons who were qualified to direct their discontents against the succession of Tiberius, clamoured only for an augmentation of pay, and an earlier discharge from the service, than, by the regulations of the former reign, they were allowed to expect. "Doomed," they said, "to drag out a life of hard service for thirty or forty years, and at the end, as their reward, to be banished to some barren mountain or sickly morass, which, under the name of a settlement or grant of land, they were required to cultivate or to drain, it was time that some regard should be paid to their merits, some relief provided for their sufferings." They contrasted their own condition, for ever stationed in the presence of ferocious enemies, and subsisting on ten asses a day, with that of the prætorian bands, having double their pay, and placed at ease amidst all the comforts and pleasures of the capital.

Excited by these considerations, the legions in Panonia refused to take the oath of allegiance to the new emperor, until their grievances should be redressed. They secured their colours, set at liberty all those who were confined for any military crime, and ceased to obey their officers, or to pay any regard to the ordinary duties and forms of the service.

Tiberius, though greatly alarmed, and sensible that this attack on his authority only needed a fit leader at the head of a few legions to reach him in the capital, and to supplant him in the empire, disguised his apprehensions, and proposing to soothe the discontents of the army, deputed to their quarters his own son Drusus, accompanied by Elius Sejanus, a young man already associated with his father Sejanus, in the command of the prætorian bands.

These young men, in the capacity of commissioners, attended by many persons of rank and consideration from the city, escorted by two cohorts of chosen men, together with the greater part of the prætorian cavalry and the German horse, which usually attended the person of the emperor, set out on their mission. They were furnished with a letter to be read at the head of the troops, but were empowered, without any specific instructions, to take such measures as the occasion might suggest. Having effected their march into Panonia, and approaching the station of the mutinous legions, they were received in the front of the camp by the whole body, but with an aspect rather of contumacy, than of respect or of duty.

The son of the emperor was conducted to the platform, from which it was usual for the troops to receive the commands, and to hear the addresses of their general. Having with some difficulty procured silence, he produced the letter which he had brought from his father, and which he had in charge to be communicated to the legions.

In this letter, Tiberius endeavoured to flatter and to soothe the discontents of the army; but to avoid committing himself too far, spoke of his intentions in general and ambiguous terms. "He might assure these brave legions," he said, "with whom he himself had so often acted, that they were the principal objects of his care; that as soon as he should recover his mind from his present grief, he would move the senate to take their just pretensions under consideration; that in the mean while he had sent his own son in order, without loss of time, to accommodate them in every thing that depended on himself; that many things must be referred to the senate, a wise and experienced council, who were not likely to withhold the proper indulgence from those who remained in the discharge of their duty, or to fail in the necessary rigour to those who ventured to depart from it."

After this letter was read, a centurion, who had undertaken to answer for the legions, made a demand in their name, that their pay should be sixteen asses a day instead of ten, and that they should be entitled to their discharge at the end of sixteen years, without being obliged, in the usual way, after they were supposed disqualified for the ordinary fatigues of the service, still to remain with their colours.

To these demands, Drusus declined giving any answer. "The matter should be reported to his father," he said, "and referred to the senate." Upon this reply, a general clamour arose. "Wherefore was he come, if not entrusted to relieve the army? He had no powers to relieve, but he had unlimited powers to distress, and to punish. So the father himself was accustomed to serve them, while he came to elude the prayers of the soldiers, by referring them to some one else, who was at a distance. Are we never," they said, "to see the face of the emperor? Is he to punish at discretion, but never to reward without consent of the senate? Our rewards, it seems, are to be carefully weighed and considered; but our fatigues and our punishments, are to be dealt without balance or measure."

In this disposition the assembly broke up, and the soldiers went roving about in disorderly parties, insulting their officers, and affecting to treat the authority of the emperor himself with contempt. Their presumption, however, was suddenly checked at night by an eclipse which took place in the moon, and which, in their superstitious way of interpreting natural appearances, formed an emblem of their own situation, and by its event was to prognosticate the sequel of their present attempts. Their despondence, during the progress of the eclipse, kept pace with the diminution of the moon's light; and, as at the time of the greatest obscuration, the sky itself was overcast with clouds, and every light suppressed in the total darkness of a stormy night, they received this event as a supernatural presage of their own fate, and in despair retired to their tents. They were soon afterwards persuaded to restore the colours which they had removed from their place; and in order to avert the evils with which they were threatened, to make seasonable offers of submission to the prince.

It was therefore thought proper, that Drusus should instantly avail himself of this favourable change, and, as much as possible, facilitate the return of the troops to their duty. For this purpose, he called them again to the place of audience, treated their mutiny as a transient fit of humour which was past, and gave them to understand, that although he was not to be awed by their threats, he was moved by their dutiful and submissive behaviour; that he should despatch an officer with their requests to the emperor, and should join his own intreaties to procure them immediate attention, and to obtain every favour that might be consistent with the order of the service.

After the departure of this messenger, the expectations of the legions were fixed entirely upon the return he should bring, and on the effect of the young Cæsar's interposition in their favours. In the mean time, the officers having resumed their command, and being obeyed in all the ordinary duties and forms of the camp, proposed to exert their authority in stifling the remains of a mutinous spirit, which had so far subsided. They accordingly gave orders to seize, and to punish the principal authors of the late disorders.

Under this exertion of power, the troops became as tame and submissive, as they had lately been refractory and ferocious. To signalize their zeal, some of the most guilty became the informers and instruments of justice against their own accomplices; and the humour from which this revolt proceeded, having sunk as it rose, without any rational plan, the mutiny appeared to be so entirely suppressed, and the discipline of the legions so effectually restored, that Drusus, with his company and the escort which attended them, departed for Italy, without waiting for the return of the officer he had despatched to the emperor.[1]

These disorders, however, were not peculiar to the troops in Panonia; they broke out with more violence, and a more dangerous tendency among those of the German frontier. On this side, eight legions were placed at two separate stations; one division under Cecina, on the borders of the low countries; the other under Caius Silius, on the Upper Rhine, both under the orders of Germanicus, who being adopted into the family of Cæsar, had been vested by Augustus with the command of these armies, and with the presidency of Gaul. This young man had married Agrippina, the daughter of Agrippa and of Julia Augusta, by whom he had a numerous issue, a circumstance generally attended with great popular favour among the Romans. He was now attended in his province by his wife Agrippina, with Caius, afterwards better known by the name of Caligula, the youngest of his three sons, now carried in the arms of the mother. He himself being extremely acceptable to the army, and to the people of the provinces, it was not doubted, that if the empire were to be disposed of, he would have had the wishes of mankind in his favour; and he became upon this account a principal object of jealousy to his adoptive father.

The troops that were stationed on the borders of the low countries under Cecina, comprehended the legions which had been hastily levied, and which, in order the sooner to replace the army that perished with Varus in the unfortunate expedition beyond the Rhine, had been formed without the usual selection. Being in a great measure composed of emancipated slaves, and other persons of mean condition. ney had not yet imbibed the sentiments of natk nal and military honour, which Augustus endeavoured to preserve in the legions. They considered themselves, at the death of that emperor, as discharged from their military oath. They rose against their officers, killed most of the centurions, and forced Cecina, with the tribunes, to withdraw from their rage.

The authors of this revolt, probably flattered themselves that Germanicus, although he did not at first openly countenance their mutiny, might however give way to their desires, and suffer himself to be elevated by their means to the throne of Cæsar. To preserve the appearances of order, until they should receive his commands, they appointed officers to act in place of those they had killed, performed most of the usual military duties, mounted the ordinary guards, and took the stated precautions, as in the presence of an enemy, for the safety and peace of their camp.

Germanicus, when the accounts of this alarming transaction were brought to him, was occupied in the affairs of the province, and in administering the oaths of allegiance on the accession of Tiberius. Sensible that his own high pretensions exposed him to be suspected of having encouraged these disorders, he repaired without delay to the camp, from which Cecina had been obliged to fly. Upon his approach, he was met by the legions; but instead of the respectful silence that was usual in receiving their commander in chief, was saluted with cries of discontent, and a mixture of expostulation and insult. He was followed by a multitude in the utmost confusion, to that part of the camp at which it was usual to harangue the army. That he might observe the different parts of his audience, or, in case any insult were offered, that he might distinguish the division from whence it came, he gave the signal for the whole to draw up in their legions and cohorts, and to display their colours.

So long as he spoke of the veneration due to the memory of Augustus, and of the glories acquired at the head of these very legions by the present emperor himself, he was heard with respect and attention; but when he touched on their want of duty, his voice could no longer be heard, and the whole presence was thrown into tumult. Some uncovered their scars, called for the rewards that were due to their services; others complained of the scantiness of their pay, of their toilsome marches, of their hard labour in forming entrenchments, and in rearing magazines of wood and of forage. "We have followed our colours," said some of the veterans, "above thirty years: Is death the only termination to be hoped for our labours?" They called for the legacy, which they heard was bequeathed to them by Augustus; they invited the prince to declare himself sovereign of the empire, and offered to support his pretensions with their swords.

On this proposal, Germanicus, as if seized with horror, came down from the platform on which he stood, and was hastening to retire, when numbers interposed to stop him. "My duty to the emperor," he said, "is more precious to me than my life;" and at these words, drawing his sword, he turned the point of it towards his own breast. Some of those who were near, laid hold of his arm; others called out, *let him strike;* and one, in particular, reaching his sword, said, *take this; it is sharper than your own.*

It is not to be questioned, that Germanicus might have led this army into Italy, and with a general consent placed himself at the head of the empire; but he seems to have apprehended the

1 Tacit. Annal. lib. i. c. 30.

rights of succession in the present emperor, with all the respect and fidelity that accompany the sentiments of loyalty and duty, under monarchies already established. Being desirous to withdraw from the tumult, and a way being made for him by the officers of his train, he retired to deliberate on the present alarming state of affairs.

The leaders of this mutiny were about to open a correspondence with the legions on the Upper Rhine. The enemy were in sight on the opposite banks of the river, and ready to take advantage of these distractions. Some of the officers present gave it as their opinion, that an army should be formed from the provincial cohorts to overawe the legions; but this was rejected by others, as likely to end in a civil war. Severity, it was observed by some, might exasperate; concession, it was said by others, might breed insolence; and the service was equally exposed to suffer, whether the troops were indulged in all their demands, or in none. It was suggested at last, that by a little artifice, without committing the authority of the emperor, the demands of the army might be satisfied. For this purpose, it was proposed that a letter should be feigned, as from Tiberius, so dated, that in writing it he could not be supposed to know of the disorder which now took place; that in this letter, he should be personated, as declaring, by a voluntary act of goodness, his intention to double the legacy bequeathed by Augustus; to fix the entire period of service at twenty years, and that of the ordinary duties at sixteen.[2]

A letter to this purpose being accordingly produced, the artifice was suspected, but the terms were agreed to, provided that the legacies were instantly paid; that those who had served twenty years should be discharged, and those who had served sixteen years, should be exempted as veterans from the ordinary duties of the camp. Many were accordingly discharged, and the more clamorous were paid up their share of the legacy, with such money as could be collected among the attendants of the prince. Others were persuaded to suffer a delay of payment, until they should come into quarters for the winter.

From this station, Germanicus repaired to that of the Upper Rhine, where with less trouble, and by means of the same gratuities, he prevailed on the legions of that division to withdraw into quarters. A mutiny of the troops on the Weser had broke out at the same time; but was suppressed by the courage and ability of the officer at their head.

It appears, that Tiberius, on hearing of these mutinies on the Rhine and the Weser, had recourse to the senate, and wished to avail himself of their authority in restoring the discipline of the army. He probably meant, in the name of this body, to inflict the necessary severities, while he reserved to himself the more popular office of granting indulgencies, or of making some gracious concessions.

A committee of the senate, of whom one Munatius Plancus is mentioned as the head, was accordingly sent to the quarters of the army, and arrived at the *Ara Ubiorum*,[3] where Germanicus, with two legions, after quieting the late mutiny, was retired for the winter. As soon as it was known, that deputies were arrived from the senate, to take cognizance of the state of the army, the soldiers apprehended that the late agreement was to be set aside; that the indulgencies granted to them were to be recalled, and that something ungracious was intended, which the emperor chose to execute in some other name than his own; for so the arts, by which the empire had been governed near fifty years, now began to be understood. In this persuasion, the soldiers, in a riotous manner, assembled round the quarters of their general; and as a signal, that they were not any longer to respect his authority, they tore the imperial standard from thence; and to deter civil officers, for the future, from interposing in their affairs, meant to have murdered Munatius Plancus, and the other deputies of the senate. These officers, however, took refuge at the colours of one of the legions, where, according to the practice of the Roman army, they had the protection of a sanctuary, and by this means escaped the fate that was intended for them.

Germanicus being still accompanied in his quarters by his wife Agrippina and her infant son, the youngest of his children, and apprehending that they could not be safe in this place of disorder, determined to remove them to some other station, where the troops, remaining in their duty, were likely to afford them protection. At their departure, the soldiers seeing the wife and the infant child of their favourite leader, followed by a numerous train of female attendants, fly from their camp, as from a place in which no respect was to be paid to sex, age, or rank, were struck with the effect of their own violence. Some crowded in the way of this melancholy train, and endeavoured to detain them; while others ran to the husband, and beseeched him to spare the legions so cruel a reproach, as was implied, in his supposing that the wife of Germanicus, the daughter of Agrippa, and the grand-daughter of Cæsar, with her infant child, were obliged to fly for safety from their quarters.

The prince, observing the disposition of the soldiers, seized the opportunity of regaining his authority; and making it a condition that they would return to their duty, complied with their request.

In the first moment of zeal to signalize their affection, multitudes, without knowing the cause of the change, passed with the impetuosity of popular tumults, by a rapid transition, from one extreme to the other, called out for justice on those who had been leaders in the late mutiny; and themselves became willing instruments in punishing such as were pointed out to them as authors of a guilt, in which the whole had been concerned. Germanicus and the principal officers withdrew from the scene, leaving a centurion on the platform to preside in this extraordinary course of justice. The prisoners that were brought to him, were hoisted up into view, and upon the verdict of the multitude, to spare or to punish them, were released, or thrown down from the platform, and suffered immediate death from the hands of their fellow-soldiers.

The same disorders had broken out, and still subsisted at Vetera,[4] the station of the fifth and

2 A Roman soldier, after he was exempted from the ordinary duties of the camp, was retained at his colours to encounter the enemy.

3 In the Bishopric of Cologne.

4 Nearly opposite the Cleves.

twenty-first legions; but Germanicus being now in condition to enforce his authority, advanced at the head of a powerful army, sent his instructions to Cecina, who was present with the mutinous troops, requiring that they should, of their own accord, bring the guilty to justice; and intimating, that if this were not done before his arrival, he was determined, without distinction of persons, to put the whole to the sword.

On this intimation, a considerable number of the soldiers entered into a concert for executing the vengeance required of them, and at a time appointed, began the slaughter of those who were most forward in the mutiny. As the camp was soon thrown into confusion, it became impossible to make any distinction of persons, and the massacre extended to all those who crowded in the way, and who were not apprised of the design. Germanicus, at his arrival, found the tents stained with blood, the passages strewed with heaps of the slain, and all the appearances of a camp surprised, and of an army put to the sword. Those who remained, affected for the present to pay respect to the authority of their leaders; but had shown themselves capable of the greatest extremes against their officers, as well as against their fellow-soldiers.

These were the principal difficulties which Tiberius encountered in effecting his succession; he had other alarms in the commencement of his reign, but of inferior moment. Such were the troubles occasioned by the imposture of Clemens, who had been a slave in the service of the posthumous Agrippa, and the conspiracy of Scribonius Libo, who, being encouraged by his affinity to the highest names in the republic, had formed some visionary design on the empire.

Clemens, upon the death of the late emperor, had gone to the place at which his master was detained in exile, meant to have conducted him to one of the armies in Gaul, where he made no doubt that the son of Agrippa, and the lineal descendant of Cæsar, would have found a favourable reception; but his design being prevented by the death of this unfortunate young man, he formed a project still more wild and romantic, founded in some resemblance which he himself bore to his deceased master, he took his name, and proposed to personate him. Pretending to have escaped from the cruelty of the usurper Tiberius, he frequently changed his place, and affected concealment; but suffered himself to be seen by those who were likely to be imposed upon, and to afford him protection or support. He was accordingly favoured by many persons of consequence, who were either deceived, or willing to countenance any attempt that was made to disturb the present succession. Among his supposed abettors, however, he had unfortunately one person employed by the emperor himself, to seduce and to circumvent him. By this emissary affecting to believe his story, and to aid him in asserting his pretensions to the throne, he was delivered over into the hands of his enemies, and was put to death by order of Tiberius, who, it is said, had the barbarous curiosity to visit him, and to examine his likeness to Agrippa before he was executed.

The emperor was soon after rather amused than alarmed, by the informations he received of the practices of Scribonius Libo, his other competitor for the throne of Cæsar. This young man, being by his mother, the grandson of Pompey, and by his father, the nephew of Scribonia, who was the first wife of Augustus, was consequently the cousin of Julia, and of her children. His affinity to the sovereigns of the world inspired him with thoughts and expectations above the condition of a subject, and laid him open to the arts of false and designing men, whom the fashion of the times encouraged with the prospect of impunity, and even of rewards.

Such men affecting zeal for the safety of the emperor, enticed the unwary to engage themselves in some supposed treasonable practice, in order to have the merit of informing against them. In this odious character, a senator of the name of Firmius Catus, practised upon the weakness of Libo, made him acquainted with professed magicians, astrologers, and interpreters of dreams, who flattered him with the hopes of empire; and after he was engaged in this idle or criminal correspondence, contrived, by means of one Flaccus Vesculanius, who frequented the court, to give secret information of the whole to the emperor.

Tiberius, employing all his artifice against this feeble antagonist, refused to see the informer, but directed him to continue his intrigue, and to report the progress of it by the same channel. While he concurred in laying this snare for the unhappy young man, he raised him to the dignity of prætor, treated him, at the feasts and entertainments of the palace, with uncommon marks of distinction, and took the malicious pleasure of observing how far these flatterers joined to the hopes of empire that were given him, contributed to swell his presumption.

In the mean time, and possibly before the design of the emperor, and of his informers, was ripe for execution, Fulcinius Trio, another noted informer, having intimation of the matter from one of the astrologers, who had been consulted by Libo, proposing to snatch the prey from his original accuser, and to have a preferable claim to the reward, carried his discovery directly before the senate; but the emperor being present when this information was delivered, did justice to the first informer, confirmed the charge, and with an odious accuracy, enumerated the piteous follies of which Libo had been guilty. The senators, pretending to be alarmed at such a treason, vied with each other in expressions of abhorrence, and many of them contended for the honour of conducting the prosecution which was to be formed against the criminal.

The slaves of the accused, agreeably to a late innovation in the law, were transferred in property to the emperor, that they might be put to the question, or that they might be received in evidence against their master.

Libo had the first intimation of what had passed, by a party of armed men, who, with orders to seize his person, broke into his house. Terrified by this appearance, he pleaded for mercy; or if this could not be obtained, implored that one of his own servants might be allowed to put an end to his life; and being disappointed in both these requests, he took poison or wounded himself, and was in the agonies of death, when according to Dion Cassius, he was, in order to secure the confiscation of his estate, carried before the senate to receive his sentence. By the decree which was given, the name and family of Libo were consigned to infamy, and the astrologers, his accomplices, were expelled from Italy, or put to death.

The emperor, when this sentence passed, affected regret for the unhappy young man, complained of his precipitancy in preventing the effects of mercy, and professed an intention to have spared his life.

From the time at which the mutinies on the Rhine and Danube were suppressed, and from the conclusion of this formal proceeding against Scribonius, as a traitor to the lawful sovereign of the empire, we may date the accession of Tiberius to the throne of Cæsar. He was now in the fifty-sixth year of his age; is described in his person as tall, robust, and healthy; erect in his walk; of a fair complexion, handsome countenance, large eye, but frowning; of few words, and slow of utterance; without any action or gesture while he spoke, besides a kind of involuntary motion with his fingers. His manner, notwithstanding his figure, was so ungracious, that Augustus, in recommending him to the public favour, thought proper to make an apology for this defect in his appearance, observing that his ungracious looks were mere accidents in the outward form of his person, not expressions of vice in his temper.[2] In his youth, he was addicted to debauchery; but as he advanced to manhood, being in awe of the emperor, he learned in many things to disguise his inclinations, and acquired a habit of reserve and hypocrisy.

Augustus on all accasions seemed to receive Tiberius with some degree of repugnance; so that when he came into company, the emperor, if engaged in any pleasurable conversation, changed the subject, and altered his countenance. Though in some degree reconciled to him, or obliged from necessity to employ him in the conduct of his affairs, and though observed sometimes to speak of him even in terms of affection and confidence, yet he gave more frequently, with respect to him, signs of aversion and distrust; and it is not unlikely that he fluctuated to the last in his opinion concerning him. Determined, however, by the influence and intrigues of Livia, or by the relation subsisting between them, he left him in possession of the empire, which he had long intended for persons more nearly related in blood, and more in his favour; but whatever were the motives of his choice, such was the belief of a deliberate and selfish design in all the actions of Augustus, that he was by many supposed to have chosen Tiberius, merely, that in the comparison of his own character with that of his successor, the preference might be given to himself.

Before the events which have been mentioned had put Tiberius in full possession of the government, and while he yet affected to decline it, the consuls, the senate, and all the principal citizens at Rome, had taken the oath of submission and allegiance. The whole army, and all the provinces soon after followed their example, and the world looked with anxious expectation for the full display of a character, hitherto for the most part wrapped up in reserve, and justly suspected of cruelty. Among the first discoveries that were made of his temper, it appeared that even his mother Livia had mistaken his disposition, or overrated her own ascendant over him. In procuring the empire to her son, she had joined to the zeal of a mother, a high degree of ambition, and a desire to emerge from a species of obscurity, in which she had lived in the reign of her husband. She flattered herself, that upon the accession of Tiberius, she was to possess a great part of the imperial power, or to exercise the whole in his name. Trusting to the deference, which he had hitherto affected for all her opinions, or to the gratitude which he owed to her for the high obligations she had conferred upon him, she instantly assumed all the consequence she expected to reap from his greatness, laid aside the caution and reserve which she had ever preserved in the reign of Augustus, advanced into public view, and, as if she had taken possession of the empire for herself, under pretence of bestowing it upon her son, took a principal part in all matters of state, and appeared on solemn occasions with her lictors, and all the other ensigns or formalities of a public station.[3]

The senate trusting to the mother's supposed knowledge of her son's inclinations, yielded to her in all the prerogatives she was pleased to assume, inserted her name with that of the emperor in all public acts, and, in the titles of Tiberius, styled him the son of Augustus as well as of Cæsar. They were not however suffered long to remain in this error. They were told by the emperor with an alarming coldness of manner, which left no doubt of his sincerity, "That the ambition of women should be kept within proper bounds, and that he should always endeavour to prescribe such bounds to his own."[4]

From the time in which this declaration was made by the emperor, it appears that Livia entirely dropt her pretensions to any part in the government, and became no less reserved in the reign of her son, than she had been in that of her husband.

As Augustus, in assuming the sovereignty, and in the whole of his reign was kept in awe by the republican spirit, which he supposed still to lurk with a dangerous violence in the minds of the people; so Tiberius, to the affectation of treading in the steps of his predecessors, joined a great measure of distrust in the dispositions of the people towards himself, and in their predilection for others, who might be supposed more worthy to reign. Among these, he looked upon Germanicus as the first or principal object of his jealousy. He had adopted this young man, merely in compliance with the late emperor's will, and considered him not only, as he was become by this act of adoption, a rival to his own son, but as he was, by the affection of the people, by the attachment of the army, and the high pretensions of his wife Agrippina, a most dangerous rival to himself. He could not forgive a person to whom the legions had made offers of the empire; and who, for having declined the offer, was deemed the more worthy of it. Although he endeavoured, under professions of the highest regard, to dissemble his feelings, and in making his report to the senate of the disorders which had lately taken place in the army, spoke of the conduct of his two sons, Germanicus and Drusus, with equal tenderness and applause; he

2 Suetou. in Tiber. c. 21. Tacit. Annal. lib. i.

3 Dio. Cass. lib. lvii. c. 12. Ibid. lib. lvi. fine.

4 Tacit. Annal. ib. i. c. 14.

had nevertheless suffered the retainers of his court to see through this disguise, encouraged them to charge Germanicus with want of capacity or courage on that occasion; and had taken his own resolution to remove him from a situation in which his popularity, the ambition of Agrippina, or the presumption of the troops under his command, might, in a moment, engage him in some dangerous design on the empire.

Upon these motives, therefore, it was proposed to remove Germanicus from the German station, and from the command of troops, by whom he was beloved, to the command of an army, inferior in point of character, and to which he was less known, or less an object of favour.

While this resolution was taken at home, Germanicus, after the suppression of the late mutinies, that he might not suffer the soldiers to brood over their grievances, gave them leisure to renew their complaints, or leave them to languish for want of employment, projected an expedition beyond the Rhine, and passed this river with twelve thousand men of the legions, twenty cohorts of the provinces, and eight alæ, or regiments of horse. By this sudden irruption, made before it was known that his troops were willing to obey him, he surprised a great body of barbarians assembled to take advantage of the disorder which they supposed to subsist in the Roman army, dispersed them with great slaughter, continued his march to the famous ground on which Varus had been cut off with his legions; and finding the field still covered with the unburied bones of the slain, gave directions to have them collected and interred. In this pious office the prince himself mixed with the private men, and put his hand to the work; a circumstance which, when reported at Rome, considerably increased the jealousy of the emperor. From thence he proposed to invade the territory of Arminius, and to punish that barbarian for his treachery to those unfortunate legions. In execution of this design, being provided with a thousand vessels, he embarked on the Ems, fell down this river to a considerable distance; and having landed on its eastern banks, and overrun the country from thence to the Weser, in his encounter with the natives obtained two considerable victories.

After these operations, Germanicus again returned to his ships in the Ems, and continued his navigation to the sea. Supposing that the mouth of the Rhine was contiguous to that of the Ems, he proposed, by a short voyage on the coast, to pass from the one to the other; and without exposing himself to be harassed in a march by land, to recover his former station on the frontier of Gaul. On this stormy coast, however, having met with difficulties with which neither his vessels nor his mariners were fit to contend, his fleet was dispersed; many of his ships were cast away on the continent, others wrecked on the contiguous islands, and some drove quite into Britain. He himself got on shore on the coast which is now called East Friezland, and saw with despair the apparent wreck of many vessels of his fleet, which seemed to be lost irrecoverably on the banks which were left by the sea at low water. From this disaster, however, he recovered the greater part of his forces. The vessels that were in company with his own, got afloat on the return of the flood, and the troops from on board of them were landed without any considerable loss. By this escape of his army, he was still in condition to make head against the natives of the country, who, intending to profit by the losses he had recently sustained, were assembled on the Weser; but being surprised by his sudden re-appearance, they fled before him, and separated to their different quarters.

Germanicus, upon his return from this expedition, and while he was meditating a renewa. of such operations on the following year, had intimation of the emperor's intention to remove him from his station on the Rhine. This intimation was accompanied with a message full of the most flattering commendation of his services. He was invited to Rome under pretence of celebrating a triumph, which had been decreed to him for his late victories; and for the purpose of assuming the consulate, to which he was destined on the approaching year as colleague to the emperor himself. As it was supposed, however, that, under an appearance of modesty, or unwilling to withdraw from a hazardous war in which the troops he commanded were still engaged, he might decline accepting of a mere honorary invitation, it was subjoined to these reasons of recall, that the remains of glory, if there were still any to be reaped in that quarter, ought to be reserved for his brother Drusus, there being no other enemy left from whom to collect his laurels.

An invitation to court, accompanied with the last of these considerations, though veiled under so many flattering pretences, was sufficiently understood to be a peremptory command, which Germanicus accordingly obeyed. On his arrival in Italy, only two cohorts or battalions were sent from Rome to receive him. But every circumstance tended to augment the jealousy of the emperor; the greater part of the prætorian bands, mingled with multitudes of the people of every sex, condition, and age, advanced of their own accord some miles from the city, and received him with uncommon acclamations of joy.[1] Having made his entry, as had been proposed, in triumph, he was, with the emperor himself, put in nomination for the consulate of the following year.

The popularity of which Germanicus now appeared to be possessed in the city, was no less mortifying to the emperor, than his power in the army was supposed to be dangerous. His presence, if it did not obscure the lustre of the emperor himself, seemed to place him in a continual state of competition with the other son of Tiberius; and the interests of these two princes, the one by adoption, the other by birth, the son of the emperor, though supposed to be on the best terms with each other, had divided the court.

Agrippina, the wife of Germanicus, inheriting the blood of Augustus, and ever carrying in her haughty looks the pretensions of the Cæsarian family, was become to Livia, whom she considered as a step-mother, no less an object of animosity, than she was to the emperor himself. Under these circumstances, the resolution to separate Germanicus from the German armies, and to place him in the command of the eastern provinces, a situation apparently honourable, but in which he should be surrounded with persons who might serve as a restraint, or as spies on his conduct, was now carried into execution. He was vested with a commission to restore the tran

1 Sueton. in Vita Caii.

quillity of Asia, that was disturbed by some disputes which had arisen on the succession to the kingdoms of Cappadocia and Armenia.

Germanicus, in the end of the third year of the present reign, set out upon this apparently honourable commission. Having a supreme authority in the several provinces through which he was to pass, from the sea of Ionia to the extremities of Egypt and of Syria, he visited, as chief in command, the cities of Greece, still revered as the principal seminaries of philosophy and literature; and upon his entry into Asia, proceeded to execute the commission on which he was sent. He reduced Cappadocia and Commagené to the form of Roman provinces, making some abatement of the taxes formerly paid to their own princes,[2] and settled Zeno, son to the king of Pontus, on the throne of Armenia. He afterwards ventured to continue his progress into Egypt, though contrary to an edict of the late emperor, which was still in force. On his return from thence he was taken ill, and died at Antioch in the thirty-fourth year of his age, with some suspicions of having been poisoned by Cn. Piso, the præfect of Syria, not without the connivance or the direction of Tiberius himself.[3]

It is not to be doubted, that the emperor looked upon Germanicus with great distrust, and might have sought for opportunities to sacrifice him to his own safety, or to that of his son Drusus; but it does not appear that he proceeded any farther on this occasion, than to remove him from a situation in which he furnished the court with continual occasions of mortification or jealousy, into one that was equally splendid in appearance, but tending to lessen his consequence in the empire; and that he meant only to place him in the command of armies over whom he had no personal influence, and who, if disposed to revolt, were less to be feared than the legions which were formed on the Rhine and the Danube.

In sending Germanicus into Asia, great attention indeed was paid to place in his way, as governor of Syria, the province which contained in itself the principal resources of the east, a person more likely to thwart and counteract him in every measure, than to become subservient to his ambition, or to promote his greatness. This intention was rendered extremely evident by the removal of Creticus Silanus, with whom Germanicus was about to contract an alliance by the intermarriage of two of their children, to make way for Piso, a man already unacceptable to Germanicus, and, in general, distinguished by a temper harsh and intractable, or likely to disagree with every superior.

It is likewise extremely probable, that Piso, as well as his wife Plancina, might have learned by their own penetration, that Germanicus and Agrippina had incurred the displeasure of Tiberius and Livia; and that they would not meet with any cordial support at the court of the emperor, in case of a disagreement with the officers who stood in their way in the provinces.

Some effects of an insolence, founded upon this supposition, appeared in the behaviour of Piso and Plancina, while Germanicus was yet on his way to Asia. Piso, having overtaken the prince, and passing him on the route, without the customary marks of respect or attention, from thenceforward seemed to set him at defiance. At their first interview in Syria, both were extremely guarded, and showed no signs of cordiality or confidence. Piso afterwards endeavoured to pre-occupy the affections of the army in opposition to Germanicus; and had the boldness to march in contempt of his orders, with a body of troops into Armenia. When the prince was taken ill, it was said, that Piso had spies to observe the progress of his disease, and seemed to await the event, as likely to place himself at the head of all the forces in Asia. Germanicus having recovered from his first fit of illness, had the conduct of Piso represented to him in such terms, that he ordered him into his presence, declared open enmity against him, and dismissed him the province. But, as he soon after relapsed, he accused Piso of having practised against his life, and charged all his friends, who were present at his death, to bring the author of it to a severe and just retribution.

Piso, hearing of the death of Germanicus, while he was yet on the coast of Asia, betrayed his animosity to the dead by public and indecent demonstrations of joy. He afterwards attempted, by force, to reinstate himself in the province of Syria, from which he had been ordered by Germanicus to depart; but was repulsed by Sentius, who had been chosen by the officers of the prince's train to keep the possession of the province till the pleasure of the emperor should be known.

Upon this event, Piso sent forward his own son to Rome, in order to prevent, as much as possible, the aspersions which were likely to be propagated against him in the city. He himself passed by Illyricum, to pay his court to Drusus, who was then in that province, and to implore his protection. Being received by this prince with coldness, though without prepossession, he from thence continued his voyage into Italy.

Agrippina, arriving soon after at Brundusium with the ashes of her deceased husband, was, by order of the emperor, received by a great military escort and the honours of war. She passed in a kind of funeral procession through multitudes that were collected from every part of the country to gaze upon her; and coming to Rome sufficiently impressed with the idea that her husband was poisoned, called for revenge upon the supposed authors of his death. Numbers contended for the honour of carrying her complaints before the tribunals of justice, and of being the accusers of her husband's murderers.

A prosecution soon after commenced against Piso; in which all that was known to be exceptionable in the preceding life and behaviour of the accused, was stated against him by Fulcidius Trio, the person already mentioned as having exercised the trade of informer in the case of Libo. The conduct of the accusation of poisoning, and the other crimes imputed to Piso in his late command, was committed to Vitellius and Veranus, persons peculiarly attached to Germanicus. The trial having begun before the emperor himself, was afterwards transferred to the senate. Two days were allowed to the accusers to enforce their charge, and three to the accused to make his defence. The prosecutors brought sufficient evidence of Piso's arrogance and extortion; of much undutiful behaviour to Germanicus himself in Asia: of disobeying his orders, of having made war beyond the limits of his pro-

2 Tac. An. lib. ii. c. 56. 3 Suet. in Vit. C. ii. c. 1.

vince, but no sufficient evidence of his having made any attempts by poison on the life of the prince. The charge indeed, as stated, or laid, was extremely incredible, that Piso should, at the table of Germanicus, and in the midst of servants, attendants, and friends, venture to mix poison in a dish from which numbers were to eat. To render this imputation still more improbable, it was observed, that the dead body had been exposed to public view in the market-place at Antioch, and that no external marks or indications of poison were found.

The principal evidence that was produced of any criminal practice against the prince's life consisted of a collection of human bones, some verses, pieces of lead marked with the name of Germanicus, and other supposed charms, which were found in his quarters, and which were considered as implements of sorcery, employed against the life of the person whose name was inscribed, and against whom they were supposed to take effect if the poison should fail.

The charge of murder, therefore, supported by such evidence, will appear to the modern reader entirely groundless, and must have been rejected even by the tribunal to which it was referred; but the accused, seeing that the torrent ran high against him, and probably to prevent the consequences of a formal sentence in the confiscation of his family estate, cut short the proceedings by a voluntary death; or, as was supposed by many, was secretly put to death by an order from the court, lest his public confession should appear to involve the emperor himself in the guilt.

On either supposition, the death of Piso being considered as an act of self-condemnation, or as a precaution in Tiberius to prevent a discovery, confirmed the people in their suspicion, that they were jointly concerned in the murder of the favourite prince.

CHAPTER VI.

Review of the first Period in the Reign of Tiberius—Applications of Penal Law—Disposition of Tiberius to a recluse Life—Place and Character of Sejanus—Death of Drusus, Son of the Emperor—Retirement of Tiberius to the Island of Capreæ—Jealousy of the Emperor against Agrippina and her Children—Death of Livia Augusta—Design formed against Sejanus—His Death—Prosecution of his supposed Accomplices—Artifices—Old Age—and Death of Tiberius.

THE death of Germanicus is considered by some historians as a remarkable epoch in the present reign.[1] Before this event, Tiberius, as if conscious that he held the empire by his good behaviour, was popular in his manners, and guarded in his administration; declined the extravagant honours which were offered to him; was easy of access; affected to live like a private citizen; returned visits, and accepted invitations to entertainments and feasts; visited the sick, attended funerals, and delivered orations in praise of the dead.[2] He treated the titular magistrates of Rome with the same ceremonious respect that used to be observed in times of the republic; rose, and stood, in the presence of the consul; took his place in the senate as a private member; was frequently seen in the courts of justice as an assessor, as an advocate, as an evidence, or as a spectator. To a person who saluted him with the title of *master*, "Insult me not," he said, "with that odious appellation. I am the master of my slaves, general of the army, and no more than prince, or first in the rolls of the senate and people." He took the title of Augustus only in his correspondence with foreign powers. In all his addresses, whether to particular members of the senate, or to this body at large, he was in the highest degree respectful and courteous. When engaged in debate, he endeavoured to qualify contradiction or difference of opinion with respect and regret. To a senator, named Haterius, on some such occasion, he said, "I hope you will forgive me, if, in my duty as a senator, I differ from you somewhat too freely." At a meeting of the senate, in referring some matter to their decision, he concluded with these words: "I have formerly said, and now say, that it becomes the person you have intrusted with so large a share of the public affairs, to consider himself as the servant of this assembly, as the servant of the people, and of every individual; nor do I repent me of this saying; for I have found you, and still find you, candid, indulgent, and kind masters."[3] He affected a continual deference to their judgment on every subject, whether of policy, revenue, or foreign correspondence; even seemed to wait for their orders in what concerned the command of the army, and pretended to be displeased, when officers, employed in the provinces, made their report directly to himself, without communicating the subject of their despatches first to the senate.

With these popular arts, which the senators indeed did not mistake for a real acknowledgment of their authority, he joined an administration in many things worthy of a wise and exemplary prince, indulged the people in the freedom of speech to which they had been accustomed, saying, that "in a free country, the mind and the tongue should be free." To those who brought him information of any slander spoken of himself, he affected indifference. "If you mind such accusations as these," he would say, "there will be no end of them." He gave a ready hearing and redress to all the complaints that were made to him from the provinces, and carefully limited the exactions of his officers within the bounds of established and ordinary fees.[4] To persons suffering by fire, earthquakes, or other public calamities, to the families of de-

1 Dio. Cass. lib. lvii. c 1

2 Ibid.

3 Sueton. in Tiber. c. 29.

4 Tacit. Annal. lib. iv. c. 6, 7

cayed senators, to the children of those who had bequeathed him their estates by will, he was munificent and liberal; took effectual measures to suppress the banditti, which, from the time of the civil wars, still infested the country; and endeavoured to diminish that constant source of corruption, the idleness which the people contracted in the too frequent repetition of shows and of public entertainments. He gave an abatement of some taxes which had been imposed by the late emperor, and in particular, mitigated the penalties which had been erroneously inflicted on celibacy.

Tiberius seemed to have perceived that the severities employed by his predecessor, to enforce marriage, served only to multiply the evils of the times, without administering any effectual remedy to that which was complained of. But what, in this enumeration of examples of his political conduct, would have done him most honour, had he continued to support it in the subsequent part of his reign, was the equanimity with which he rejected many frivolous accusations which were brought against the unwary by his own flatterers, or by the mercenary informers who began to swarm in his time.

In respect to criminal prosecutions, the change of government, which took place at Rome, had, without altering the legal forms, made a fatal change in the effect of the laws, and served to show, that the seeds of despotism may be laid in the freest establishments; and that when the characters of men are changed, the worst abuse may proceed from the best institutions.[5]

The securities of majesty, or the restraints provided against treasonable practices, were principal objects in the laws of the republic. The crimes[6] against which those restraints were provided, were, in reality, a trespass on the majesty of the commonwealth, including rebellion, breach of public trust, betraying the forces of the state to its enemies, or violating the person of the magistrate in the discharge of his office. These were justly reputed an invasion of the rights of the people, were public crimes, and might be prosecuted by any citizen, though not particularly interested in the issue of the trial.

In the time of the republic the prosecution of public crimes was considered as a duty; and the character of an informer, bringing to light what offended the commonwealth, though in some instances invidious, was not reckoned dishonourable.[7] In this character the most respectable and popular citizens sometimes braved the resentment of the most powerful offenders, or, when engaged in private enmities, sought their revenge, without incurring any dishonour as informers, by raising prosecutions on a public account.[8]

The mere permission, however, to become a public accuser, and the credit annexed to this character, were not, in all cases, sufficient to obtain prosecutions, or to prevail upon persons, not called upon by some material interest, to engage in so arduous and often so dangerous a task, as that of urging to justice offenders, who were powerfully supported by their fortunes, their rank, or the number of their adherents and friends. In the latter times of the republic, therefore, as the ardour of zeal for the commonwealth was supposed to wax cold, and motives of ambition and interest were required in aid of public virtue, it was enacted, that whoever convicted a person of any public crime incurring degradation or forfeiture, should be entitled to succeed to the dignity, whether of citizen, knight, or senator, from which the criminal was degraded. And lest even this consideration should not be sufficient to excite prosecutors, it was enacted, that a fourth part of the estate of the person convicted should be joined to the reward.

The office of an accuser, supported by a pure concern for the public safety, was commendable; but proceeding, in any degree, upon mercenary motives, even under the republic, when the cause to be supported was the majesty of the state itself, must have become, in a high degree, odious and contemptible; but under the present government, when the object of the law, as well as the motive for the application of it, were so much changed, the character of a prosecutor, though disguised under the ancient forms and titles, was, in the highest degree, vile and detestable.

Under the establishment of Augustus, the idea of majesty was transferred from the state itself to the emperor; and the principal object of the law being to guard his person, not only his safety and the authority of his government, but his most private concerns, made a part in the majesty which was to be preserved. Whatever implied disrespect, whatever alarmed his jealousy, or interfered with his caprice, even intrigues of debauch with women of his family, were constructed as treason. Under a continuation of this government, the evil was inflamed by the pretended zeal of spies and informers, who, partly to pay their court, and partly to merit the rewards which were promised from the confiscation of estates, endeavoured to keep on foot a continual inquisition, in which they brought to trial the most trivial indiscretions, as well as more real offences, against the person, authority, or dignity of the prince. The swarms of such persons who haunted the steps of the unwary, and filled the senate and the courts of justice with cruel or frivolous prosecutions; in which, by interesting the passions of the emperor, they endeavoured to make him a party, was one of the most grievous circumstances attending the late revolution of government.

Tiberius, notwithstanding this tendency of the establishment to which he succeeded, and his own temper, which was sufficiently prompt and sanguinary in preventing attempts on his person, or on his government, had the honour, during the first years of his reign, in some measure, to withstand this torrent, and to treat many frivolous accusations with a proper degree of contempt. A senator of the name of Falenius, being accused of having included, with other furniture in the sale of his house, a statue of Augustus;[9] another, of the name of Rubrius, being accused

5 Lex Majestatis.—Majestas est amplitudo et dignitas civitatis. Cicero de Orat. lib. ii. c. 39.

6 Public crimes.

7 Private crimes or offences could not be prosecuted by any person besides the party aggrieved or some person having an interest in the case.

8 Plutarch. in Lucullo, initio.

9 It is sufficiently known, that, in the heathen mythology, a place among the gods was sometimes conferred on mortal men; that an apotheosis was little more than canonization is in later times; and that this honour having been conferred on Augustus, his name and his statue were ranked among those of the gods.

of having taken a false oath by the name of Augustus; and Granius Marcellus being accused of having taken the head from a statue of that price, in order to substitute a head of Tiberius in place of it, a manner of paying his court rather ridiculous than criminal; in these and other instances of the same kind, Tiberius either took no part, or gave his instructions to the senate in very liberal and manly terms. On the subject of the prosecution that was raised against Falenius, "My father," he said, "was deified, that his divinity might be a safeguard and a protection, not a snare to the people. His image may, no doubt, be included, with those of the other gods, as part in the furniture of a house that is sold." With respect to the supposed perjury of Rubrius, he observed, that "if any one swear, and is perjured, the crime is the same, whoever be the god whose name is profaned. Augustus is no more to be regarded, in this matter, than Jupiter; and either of these gods, if offended, can avenge himself."[1] The third offence, or the shifting of heads from one statue to another,[2] being considered as a mockery of that adulation which was so easily transferred from one to another in the succession of princes, and as some degree of ridicule on the prince himself, was not so easily forgiven; though, for the present, overlooked, it was reserved as a subject of future resentment.

To whatever motive we ascribe a conduct so popular, and in many particulars so worthy of empire, it is observed, that its effects on the minds of the people were not such as might have been expected, and did not procure to the emperor the favourable opinion or credit to which he aspired. His manner, even when he affected humanity and condescension, was ungracious and alarming; and, notwithstanding any appearances to the contrary, his real character was supposed to be malicious and cruel. It is said, that in the midst of the hypocrisy and dissimulation by which he had endeavoured to disguise himself before his accession, he made some slips which betrayed the reality of this disposition; and that he had been surprised into acts of insolence and severity, in which, by mixing derision and sarcasm with cruelty, he had given the strongest proofs of a merciless nature. For the present it was observed, that his overacting the part of popularity, the ridiculous tyranny he exercised over the senate in requiring at once the affectation of freedom and the grossest servility; that the farce of affecting reluctance in accepting of a government which he had previously secured with the greatest care; the ridicule of dividing in the senate, or giving his vote with the minority, when a resolution was to be taken in favour of himself, served to join mockery and insult to the weight of his usurpation; that even his affectation of popularity, for the most part, increased the terrors of his government; that his presence in the courts of justice took away all freedom of judgment; and that the discretionary power which he assumed, of mitigating or reverting sentences, and of dispensing with laws, under pretence of correcting their general tendency by seasonable exceptions, only served to frustrate the pretensions to civil government, which, in imitation of Augustus, he still affected to preserve.

1 Deorum injuriæ Diis curæ. 2 Tacit. l. i. c 73

But in whatever sense the favourable appearances, which presented themselves in the beginning of this reign, were to be interpreted, they were no more than temporary, and, in the manners of this prince, gave way to the growing asperity of age, or to the presumption which took place in his mind, upon the removal of a person whom he considered as a dangerous rival, and who, in case of any public discontent, might have been made the instrument of overturning his government.

Soon after the death of Germanicus, the temper of Tiberius, which had probably gained strength from restraint, broke forth in many cruel and alarming effects. His vigilance, hitherto limited to one object, and his jealousy, directed against a single person, now found a multiplicity of subjects on which, with less disguise or reserve, to exert their force.

Among the particulars in which the emperor, in the first period of his reign, imposed the greatest violence on his own disposition, we may reckon the openness and accessibility which, with a temper naturally dark and reserved, he affected to maintain with the people; and one of the principal circumstances, probably, in which he proposed to indulge himself, on his being relieved from his fears of Germanicus, was in retiring from the public view, and in eluding the observation of persons whom he considered as spies on his actions. In the eighth year of his reign, and in the second year after the death of Germanicus, having associated his son Drusus with himself in the consulate, and leaving him in the administration of affairs in the city, he withdrew for some time into Campania, meditating, as Tacitus observes, a more entire and continued retreat. During the two first years after his accession he had confined himself to the walls of Rome, and remained in the city, as in the watch-tower, from whence he was to observe and prevent all designs that might be formed on his government. After those years were passed, he made some excursions to Antium,[3] and other towns or villages on the same coast, but never to any greater distance. In order, however, that the provincial officers might not think themselves altogether secure from his personal inspection, he frequently, even during this period, affected a purpose to visit the more distant parts of the empire; ordered his equipages, placed changes of horses and carriages, and permitted the usual sacrifices to be offered up for his safe return; but always, for some specious reason, delayed the execution of his pretended design. After having, in this manner, for some time amused the world, and, by the repetition of these and other artifices, furnished a key to the secret of his own conduct; his mysteries, for the most part, became extremely plain, and his true intentions easily perceived, merely because he never spoke truth.

But while the emperor thus endeavoured to debar the people from all access to his person, and to seclude himself from public view, he selected, as a proper instrument of his power, and, in appearance, as an object of his most implicit confidence, Ælius Sejanus, who has been already mentioned, as accompanying his son Drusus on his mission to the mutinous legions in Panonia. This person, supposed to have no dangerous pre-

3 About thirty miles from Rome.

tensions, or though false to others, supposed true to his master, he had placed at the head of his guards or prætorian bands, and distinguished him with a degree of affection and confidence hitherto without example in any former part of his life. This being the first of his intimate connexions, whatever may have been its motive, it did not admit of competition or participation, and rendered a person, who was dark and impenetrable to every one else, open and communicative to this favourite alone.

Sejanus is described by Tacitus as of a hardy and indefatigable constitution of body; of a bold spirit and an insatiable ambition, which he disguised under an affectation of modesty. He is described as a person possessed of great art in concealing his own vices, and of an insidious penetration in prying into those of others; versatile in his manners, and either careless and profuse, or vigilant and severe, as suited the occasion; insolent to those over whom he had any advantage, but fawning where he was the inferior, or had an interest to gain. In his youth he had attached himself to Caius Cæsar, the adopted son of Augustus; and afterwards succeeding his own father, in the station which he now occupied at the head of the prætorian bands, seemed to improve the access which this situation gave him to the person of the emperor, into an ascendant over his mind.

One of the first or most observable signs of the great elevation of Sejanus, was the proposed marriage of his daughter with the son of Claudius, the brother of Germanicus; a person, though at this time in a great measure neglected at court, yet nearly related to the emperor; and, in the sequel of events, himself destined to ascend the imperial throne.

Sejanus being thus pointed out as favourite, by a mark of honour which tended to gratify his vanity, he took measures, at the same time, the most efficacious, to establish his power. For this purpose he employed his credit in filling up with his own creatures, as fast as vacancies happened, the prætorian bands, the legions, and every civil as well as military department in the state; knowing that where government rests its authority on principles of reason and justice, the civilian, the senator, and the statesman are its principal instruments; but where it is founded entirely on force, its ministers are soldiers of fortune, and its powers rest chiefly with those military bodies who are in possession of the capital, or who surround the person of the prince. This adventurer, therefore, being already at the head of this powerful department, studied every method to concentrate its force, and to secure in his own person the direction of it. To this motive is imputed the change which he now made in the manner of disposing of the prætorian bands. These troops were hitherto quartered on the citizens, or distributed in the villages round the walls of the city, apprehending, it is alleged, that they might, in that way of life, imbibe the prejudices of the people, and become part of the families with whom they were mixed, he persuaded the emperor to detach them from that society; and, under the ordinary pretence of having the cohorts together, and more under the eye of their officers, erected a citadel and barracks for their reception; in this manner establishing in Rome itself, or contiguous to its walls, a fortress from which he could command the city, and employ the professional prejudices of those who occupied this garrison, most effectually against every person that was supposed disaffected to his person In this disposition, whatever may have been the object of it, there is no doubt that the prætorian bands became more detached from the people, and that the force and presumption of this formidable body became more tremendous to the other parts of the empire, and even to the emperor himself.

As Tiberius seemed to set no bounds to his confidence in the minister, and enabled him to employ all the powers of the empire in support of his own elevation, the jealousies or resentments of the favourite became equally fatal with those of his master, and being more numerous, involved the government of the emperor in perpetual animosities, prosecutions, and cruelties, which may have, for the present, gratified his severe and jealous temper, but which were in no way conducive to his interest.

Under the influence of this connexion, joined to his own disposition, Tiberius gave a ready ear to that numerous tribe of informers, who brought accusations against persons in any degree obnoxious or unacceptable to himself or to his favourite. In this predicament, the descendants of the ancient nobility, persons eminent by their birth, popular favour, or personal qualities, and considered as rivals in the apprehension of either, were the principal sufferers. The perpetual inquisition to which they were exposed, and which makes a principal article in the history of this and some of the succeeding reigns, must, by the frequent repetition of similar examples, become an object of disgust, as well as of indignation or pity. And it may perhaps have been true of this emperor, that even his character, though in itself sufficiently odious, may, for some time at least, have incurred additional detestation, from his having committed his administration into the hands of a servant, who multiplied the errors of his government, or gave them the directions of passions more numerous or less liberal than even those of the master.

As Sejanus was most vigilant and jealous in exacting observances, it became more dangerous to neglect the attention he required, than even that which was due to the prince. A courtship was accordingly paid to him by the retainers of the palace, by the senate, by the army, and by the people, more assiduous than even that which they paid to the emperor. In private, every species of flattery; in public, honorary decrees, were invented to gratify his vanity. The anniversary of his birth was joined to the festivals of the year. His name was inserted in the public prayers; and when any deputation was sent with addresses of respect to the emperor from the senate, from the equestrian order, or from any other public description of men, compliments were at the same time sent to his favourite. The effigies of both were carried together among the ensigns of the legions, and their statues were grouped together in the streets. Women of every rank thought themselves honoured by the addresses of this fortunate man, and became the tools of his ambition, or the prostitutes of his pleasure. By debauching the wife, he sometimes obtained intelligence what were the designs or ordinary pursuits of the husband; and by encouraging the zeal of spies and informers, who were now become the favourite retainers of the court, he was enabled to pry into the actions of every citizen, and to watch all the symptoms of disaffection to the emperor or to himself. Intoxicated with the extraordinary circumstances of his fortune, it is probable that he thought himself placed within reach of the empire, and measured his consequence with that of the persons who apparently stood before him in their pretensions to this elevation. The present emperor himself had succeeded to the government, not by his birth, but merely by having survived every person on whom his predecessor could rely for support, or through whom, by any line of inheritance, he could transmit his power. Pointed out by mere accident to the choice of Augustus, he had been first adopted into the family of Cæsar, and afterwards associated in the empire.

Sejanus computed that he himself was already possessed of more favour with the reigning emperor than Tiberius ever had enjoyed with the person to whom he succeeded; and that there was nothing in the farther progress of his fortune too arduous or difficult for him to undertake. The conduct of the young princes towards him had been provoking, and seemed to justify his resentment. They bore with impatience the intrusion of a rival into the emperor's favour. Drusus in particular was frequently heard to complain, that his father had chosen a favourite to supplant his own son, and had made a stranger little less than a colleague in the empire; that the steps which remained for Sejanus to make to this elevation were not so many, nor so difficult, as those he had already made. "And we must rely," he said, "on the *modesty* of this man for the bounds he may think proper to set to his farther pretensions."

This favourite had already formed an intrigue with Livia, or Livilla, the sister of Germanicus, married to Drusus. By this intelligence with the wife, he had notice of what passed in the conversations of the husband; and, in concert with this abandoned woman, determined to remove a person from whom he had so much to fear. They took into their confidence, for this purpose, Eudemus, a physician, who, under pretence of his profession, had a frequent and a secret access to Livilla; and, after some hesitation, and frequent change of their counsels, they found means, by the hands of one Ligdus, a eunuch, to administer poison to the prince, of which he died. The cause of his death, and the circumstances of this daring crime, were not known till about eight years afterwards.

In the mean time Sejanus, encouraged by the success of his first attempt, flattered himself that he might step into the place of the prince whom he had thus removed out of his way; and, in concert with Livilla, with whom he had already lived in habits of adultery, he waited for a decent interval to propose himself to the emperor as a husband for the widow of his son.

Tiberius, although he had, by his deceased son, a grandson of his own name; yet this young man being still under age, he thought proper, upon the breach which had recently been made in his family, to bring forward the two elder sons of Germanicus, Nero and Drusus, whom he presented to the senate, as the great-grand-children of Augustus, and the future supports of the commonwealth. "These," he said, addressing himself to the young men, "are your fathers. Such is the condition of your birth, that whatever concerns you, whether good or evil, must affect the empire." It is however singular, that this speech, made in behalf of the sons of Germanicus, appears to have awakened the jealousy of the person who made it. Observing that the audience were moved with these expressions, and supposing that the tenderness which was shown to the sons, was a remainder of that popular esteem which, in the father, had given him so much uneasiness, he appeared to be suddenly embarrassed; and, as if he had been reproached with intruding himself into a station which the world wished to have reserved for the parent of these young men, he proceeded to counteract his own apprehensions with his usual affectation of humility and moderation. "I beseech you," he said to the senate, "that I may be allowed, at a proper time, to resign the empire." And as he was always distrusted, and had the worst construction put on his words, these were supposed to be the expressions of mere embarrassment, and that he was in reality mortified with the demonstrations of joy which were given on this apparent restoration of the family of a favourite prince.

Sejanus, who bore with great impatience the admission of new rivals in the way of his ambition, improved these circumstances in the manner which he knew to be most effectual to awaken the emperor's jealousy, and to inflame the animosity already subsisting betwixt the empress Livia and Agrippina, the widow of Germanicus, and the mother of these young men. The effect of his artifices and insinuations operating on the distrustful mind of the emperor first appeared in the destruction of many persons who had been attached to Germanicus, and who still adhered to his family; and afterwards in the ruin of Agrippina herself, and in the death of the two elder of her sons.

The passions of jealousy and distrust, by which the mind of Tiberius was secretly devoured, but which he had endeavoured to conceal in the former part of his life, instead of abating in proportion as he became secure, only became less disguised and more violent in their effects against those who happened to be the objects of them. He listened without reserve to every spy or informer, and, under the pretence of treason, directed prosecutions against every person in any degree exposed to suspicion.

Under such prosecutions the accused, having no hopes to escape from a charge in which the passions of the sovereign were engaged against them, endeavoured, for the most part, to prevent by a voluntary death the confiscation of their estates. And this direful necessity, frequently repeated, being imputed to the merciless policy or suggestion of Sejanus, instead of drawing upon him public marks of indignation or hatred, greatly increased the court which was paid to him, and multiplied the professions of public regard.

The emperor, in the mean time, as he sought for security and peace of mind in a quarter in which they surely are not to be found, in the destruction of the most innocent objects of his suspicion, felt his odious passion of jealousy ripen into a general hatred of mankind, with a dislike, in particular, to those persons who had been the instruments of his distrust, and with an aversion to the very place at which he had multiplied its cruel effects. Conscious of what he endeavoured to conceal, and of what men were able to penetrate, he was jealous of every prying look, and detested every person whom he thought qualified to distinguish truth from appearances. At one time, he received the crowd of informers who haunted his court, as the most acceptable members of it; at other times, he abhorred them as persons who penetrated his character, and who, to their own advantage, and to the disgrace of his government, were practising upon his weakness. After having resided constantly in the city for many years, he began to multiply and to prolong his visits to some of his favourite retreats in the country, placed guards wherever he went, to keep the curious multitude at a distance, declined the attendance of those who wished to pay their court, and was accessible only to his favourite minister.

Sejanus, still appearing to rise in the confidence of his master on the ruin of every one else, ventured according to the agreement long since made with Livilla, to propose himself to the emperor as second husband to the widow of his son. It was the practice of Tiberius to require, even from persons who had daily access to him, that every proposal they made should be put in writing; and it was his practice likewise to give answers in the same form. Sejanus accordingly presented a memorial to the following purpose: "That he had been so long accustomed to look up to Augustus for protection, and to Tiberius for every effect of munificence and goodness, that his wishes and his prayers were carried to them more directly than even to the gods themselves; that the splendour of high fortune had no charms for him; that his delights were in the cares and toils of a soldier stationed for the defence of the emperor's person; that he had nevertheless already attained to the highest honours in the alliance of his family with that of Cæsar;[1] and from thence probably arose the farther hopes which he ventured to conceive. Augustus, when he deliberated on the marriage of his daughter, had condescended to think of a Roman knight. If a husband, therefore, should be thought of for Livilla, might he not presume to hope that the emperor would not overlook a person so profoundly attached to him, who coveted nothing, on this occasion, besides the honour of being chosen into this high connexion, and who had no ambition beyond the duties of his trust as a guard to the sacred person of his master. For himself he was willing to perish whenever the emperor should cease to protect him; but his family had many enemies, and needed to be raised into some such place of advantage, where they might be less exposed to the haughty and imperious insults of Agrippina and her offspring."[2]

In answer to this memorial, the emperor acknowledged the merits of his favourite; but did not give him any encouragement on the subject of his request. "Princes," he said, "were not, like private men, at liberty to follow their own inclinations, but must consult the opinion of the world; and observed, that, under this restraint, he must, for the present, suppress what he was most inclined to reply. That Livilla might determine for herself, whether, having been the wife of Drusus, she was to accept of a second husband; or if she had any doubts in the matter, she might consult her mother and her grandmother, fitter counsellors on that occasion than he could pretend to be; that the marriage which Sejanus proposed for himself would not allay the malice of Agrippina, but rather inflame it, and divide the family of Cæsar into parties; that it would be impossible for him, if he should form this alliance, to remain in his present condition: that Augustus, in deliberating on the choice of a husband for his own daughter, because he wished for a son-in-law whose pretensions were not likely to disturb the public peace, had turned his thoughts on some persons of equestrian rank; but that the example, nevertheless, was against Sejanus; for Augustus did not actually marry his daughter to a Roman knight, but first to Agrippa, and afterwards to himself." He concluded with insinuating that he had other views for his friend; owned that there was nothing too high for his merits; and his opinion in this matter, he said, he should in a proper time make known to the senate and to the people.[3]

Sejanus was alarmed by this intricate and ambiguous answer, and dreaded a change of his master's disposition. He had hitherto excluded every competitor from the emperor's favour; but a temper so prone to suspicion, he knew could be easily turned against him, and would receive encouragement from numbers, as soon as they should see the first signs of distrust. For these reasons, he is said at this time to have formed the design of persuading Tiberius to remove from the city. When at a distance, he trusted that, by means of the guards, who were the bearers of all expresses and messages, he might be master of the emperor's correspondence, and prevent the access of every suspicious person. With this view he exaggerated the troubles to which the sovereign was exposed at Rome; molested with trifles, and crowded, wherever he went, with multitudes of idle or importunate people; magnifying, at the same time, the pleasures of retirement, where free from the disgust and the avocation of inferior objects, he might bestow his attention on the conduct and result of affairs that were worthy of his notice.

Whatever effect we may suppose the representations of Sejanus to have had in persuading the emperor to retire from Rome, it is probable that, in forming this resolution, still more was owing to his own temper. Though deeply tinctured with pride, the inherent vice of his family,[4] Tiberius had not any share of that vanity which leads men to display their fortunes and persons in the view of the world. Content with the gratification of his appetites, and joining hypocrisy with the worst species of sensuality, he could submit to obscurity; and, although the resources of solitude were now diminished by the effects of age, yet a temper become more jealous of the world, and more averse to its notice, inclined him more to withdraw from the city, and to maintain from a distance that watch which he had hitherto kept over the actions, words, and even thoughts of its inhabitants. He accordingly, in the twelfth

1 The marriage of his son with the daughter of Claudius.

2 Tacit Annal. lib. iv. c. 39.

3 Tacit. Annal. lib. iv. c. 40.

4 Insita Claudiæ familiæ superbia.—TACIT.

year of his reign, under pretence of dedicating in Campania a temple to Jupiter and another to Augustus, withdrew from Rome, and after this time, during the remainder of his life, under various pretences, but with continual intimations of his intention to return, absented himself from the city. Having performed the ceremonies for which he had gone to Campania, he passed from thence to Capreæ, a small island under a headland, which was called the promontory of Minerva, making one side of the bay of Naples. It is probable that, after mature deliberation, he had fixed on this spot as a place of security and an agreeable retreat. It was covered by the high lands of Minerva from the northeast winds, and was open to breezes from the sea on the southwest. It was accessible only to very small vessels, and this only at a single place. The seas were open to his scouts, and no sail could approach without his knowledge and permission. In this secession it appears, that he divided the guards, having one part in the island for the defence of his person, and the other at Rome to enforce the mandates of his government.

Among the Romans who were admitted into this retreat are mentioned Sejanus, from whom the emperor was still inseparable, Curtius Atticus, a Roman knight, and Cocceius Nerva,[1] a senator of great dignity, who, possessing much knowledge in the laws and constitutions of the commonwealth, was still acceptable, or even necessary in the councils of a prince, who, except where his own passions were concerned, still wished to be reasonable and just. This person, however, from whatever cause, soon after ended his days on this island by a voluntary death.

Tiberius, in the latter part of his life, admitted likewise into his privacy at Capreæ, Caius, the third son of Germanicus, better known by the name of Caligula. The society, however, in which he delighted most, was made up chiefly of Greeks, professed men of letters, but more eminent as flatterers and ministers of pleasure. For such men he had no respect, but suffered them to amuse him with their speculations, or rather with a kind of literary buffoonery, in discussing ludicrous questions which he was pleased to propose; such as, who was the mother of Hecuba, and what species of music was sung by the Syrens?[2] These literary buffoons, however, no less than the objects of his political jealousy, experienced occasionally the effects of his capricious disgusts. One of them was banished to the island Cynaria for hinting a joke on the Doric accent, which the emperor had acquired at Rhodes in his pronunciation of Greek. Another, having found out that the emperor read books every morning, out of which he proposed his questions at night; and observing the book which the emperor had been reading, came so well prepared to answer every question, that his trick was suspected. He was banished from the emperor's company, and afterwards, by cruel usage, induced to lay violent hands on himself.

Were it established that ignominy could have no effect, nor the odious aspect of vice deter mankind from yielding to the vile considerations that lead to the practice of it, there would be no apology for molesting the world with many particulars, either of the past or subsequent part of this detestable reign. But it is likely that ingenuous minds may arrive at what is just, by desiring to shun what is odious and vile, no less than by admiring and aiming at what is noble and worthy. Certain follies and vices sometimes gain strength from the fashion and the example of persons in high station. But it is established by the feelings of mankind through every age, that malice, jealousy, and cruelty, can receive no lustre even from the purple and the throne of Cæsar, and Tiberius himself, considered as the monument of an infamy to be shunned, may be a teacher of humanity and of wisdom not inferior to Trajan or Aurelius.

This tyrant, though now withdrawn from the resentment of those he injured, did not suffer his vigilant jealousy to sleep over the rumours and reports of his informers and spies, but rather, with a more open and unguarded severity, watched over crimes which had no existence but in his own imagination, or in his remembrance of the countenance and aspect of the persons he disliked. In his present retreat, he seemed to multiply the objects of his hatred, in proportion as he himself was secure; and in order to compensate the distance to which he was removed, employed a proportional speed and decision to surprise, and to prevent those who were suspected of any designs against him. From Capreæ, his mandates, for the most part, were carried to the senate, and to the military officers at Rome, not as complaints against the supposed offender, or as instructions to the magistrate to make trial or inquiry into the guilt of the accused, but as warrants for their immediate execution.

Agrippina and her sons, with their adherents, and those of Germanicus, were principal objects of the present emperor's animosity and cruel dislike. This family being high in the favour of the people, he fancied that the young men might not be disposed to defer the completion of their hopes, until a natural event had bestowed a succession, which a daring attempt might accelerate. Nero and Drusus, the two elder sons of this family, having without any authority from the emperor been included by the senate in the forms of public prayer, their names were again expunged by his order, and with an admonition to the senate, not to inflame the ambition of youth with premature and exorbitant honours.

This forward attempt to place the sons of Germanicus on the steps of the throne, was supposed to proceed from the ambition of their mother Agrippina, who appearing to carry in her high looks and vehement temper the pretensions of the grand-daughter of Augustus, and the mother of future emperors, ever seemed to reproach Tiberius with having usurped, and with continuing to possess, what was due to herself and to her children. Sejanus did not neglect to cultivate the animosity of either party. He had informations conveyed to Agrippina, of a design that was hatching at Capreæ against her life, and excited her by these means to give the emperor provoking marks of her caution and distrust, which were easily interpreted as the symptoms of a guilty mind in herself, and hastened the preventions on his part, which he thought proper to employ against her.

As mutual provocations had passed between Agrippina and the emperor before his departure

1 Tacit. Annal. lib. iv. c. 58.
2 Sueton. in Tiber. c. 70

from Rome, and as she was become a principal object of his dislike, it is extremely probable that he had then resolved upon the ruin of her family, at least upon her own; and that he took his station at Capreæ for the more safe execution of an unpopular act, which might occasion some tumult in the city, or even a defection of the army. He proceeded, however, by degrees, in the execution of his purpose, and before his departure from Rome, had made a trial of his power against some of her relations and friends. Under this description, he had ordered the execution of Sosia Galla and Claudia Pulchra, two women of noble birth, who were related to her by blood, and much in her confidence.

Upon occasion of the last of these executions, Agrippina, who considered herself as aimed at in this cruel action, ventured, with a vehemence and impetuosity which made part of her character, to reproach the emperor with his tyranny, accosting him to this purpose, as he was engaged in his devotions at the shrine of Augustus; "It ill becomes a person," she said, "who affects to worship the parent, to practise the ruin of his offspring. The spirit of him you adore, is not transferred into the inanimate marble which you worship, but into his living posterity whom you oppress, and whom you cause to live in continual mourning, and in sorrow. Pulchra must perish now for the same reason that was formerly fatal to Sosia, for her being the unhappy relation and friend of those you are determined to ruin." Tiberius replied in a Greek quotation, implying *that she was hurt, because she was not allowed to reign;*[3] and in these words, contrary to his usual dissimulation, betrayed the rancour of his mind.[4]

After the retreat of Tiberius to Capreæ, Sejanus, to gratify the passions of his master, and to make way for his own ambition, continued his practices against the family of Germanicus. He had spies placed about them, and received frequent informations, in writing, of what passed in their company. He had an account of all the actions and words of Nero, the eldest of the two sons, from Julia Drusilla, the wife of this young man, who was engaged by her mother Livilla to betray her husband. He took measures to provoke both the brothers to angry and unguarded expressions, and had these effects of his own provocations carefully reported to the emperor. He had emissaries, who insinuating themselves into the favour and confidence of these young men, urged them to rash and desperate resolutions; such as that of calling upon the armies in Germany to support their rights, of taking refuge at the shrine of Augustus, and of appealing to the people. When these emissaries could not actually engage the persons against whom they were employed in the crimes they suggested, they had instructions to accuse them to the emperor of having deliberated on such dangerous projects.

While the sons of Agrippina were thus surrounded with snares, their most faithful retainers and friends were exposed to the same dangers, or actually fell, under the hands of the executioner. Among these, Titius Sabinus had been distinguished by his affection to Germanicus, and remained still attached to his family. He had been, upon this account, an object of the emperor's aversion, and likely to suffer under the first plausible pretence that could be found against him. Being selected, soon after the retreat of Tiberius, by the sagacity of those who wished to pay their court, as a proper object on whom to display their zeal, he was attacked at once by four persons of senatorian rank, Latinius Latiaris, Porcius Cato, Politius Rufus, and M. Oppius, all of them already promoted to the dignity of prætor, and now aspiring to that of consul. They agreed to pay their court, by some notable service, to the prince and his favourite. The first undertook, by insinuating himself into the confidence of Sabinus, to betray him into some criminal action or expression. The other three were to be placed within hearing of what should pass, in order to be cited as witnesses.

A snare so artfully laid could scarcely be avoided. The injured, wherever they think themselves safe, are apt to complain: and Sabinus, finding that his faithful attachment to the family of his late friend was warmly applauded by Latiaris, unwarily joined with the traitor in lamenting the iniquity of the times, and the cruelty of Sejanus and Tiberius. Conversations to this purpose being repeated at some supposed confidential interviews; but in the hearing of the other three, who were posted as witnesses, it soon appeared, that there was sufficient matter against Sabinus; and the information was conveyed to the emperor.

The informers, as a specimen both of their zeal and of their ability, gave a particular account of their conduct in bringing the treasonable thoughts of Sabinus to light. The information was applauded by the emperor, transmitted to the senate, and by them considered as a warrant for the immediate death of the accused. Being found by the officers, commissioned to seize him, paying his devotion at some public altar, he was dragged from thence to immediate execution. The particulars of the detection were published, in order to show with what zeal the emperor was served, and in order to restrain the disaffected, by a mutual distrust of each other, from entering into any such dangerous counsels.

The tragical death of Sabinus, a person generally loved and respected; his being dragged by the executioner through the streets at noonday in sight of the people, spread a general consternation in the city. All orders of men, under their first impressions, deserted the public places; but presently recollecting that their flight might be imputed to a participation of guilt, or at least to some degree of sympathy with the person who suffered, they immediately returned to the places of public resort, and affected their usual ease and tranquillity. But from thenceforward, for some time, it was observed, that a melancholy silence took place, even in the most secret conversations of relations and intimate companions, who, from this example, had learned to distrust each other.

Tiberius, upon receiving the report of Sabinus's execution, thanked the senate for the justice they had done on this enemy of the commonwealth, and mentioned a danger to which his person was still exposed from other enemies, more formidable than those they had already destroyed. In this ominous insinuation, he was supposed to point at Agrippina and her sons.

3 Ideo lædi, quia non regnaret.
4 Tacit. Annal. lib. iv. c. 52.

Asinius Gallus ventured to call for an explanation, by moving the senate to address the emperor, that he would be graciously pleased to make known the object of his apprehensions, and that he would accept of their services in the defence of his person.

Gallus had married Vipsania, from whom Tiberius was separated, when his marriage with Julia was determined. By this alliance, he became the relation of Agrippina;[1] and, what was still more dangerous, had presumed to succeed the emperor himself in a connexion, of which he still was envious and jealous. This circumstance rendered him, to the dark and vindictive mind of Tiberius, an object of deliberate malace. When his motion to address the emperor for an explanation of his fears was reported at court, it was considered as a saucy attempt to penetrate the secrets of government, as a contempt of authority, and a dangerous attack upon the majesty of the prince.

Tiberius would have seized this opportunity to execute his revenge against Gallus, if he had not been diverted from it by Sejanus himself, who wished rather to keep his mind intent on the destruction of Agrippina and her two eldest sons, who were equally objects of jealousy to the minister as to the emperor.

Such were the affairs which succeeded in the state, to the great political questions that formerly used to divide the senate and the people; and as the event of these affairs turned upon the caprice of individuals, they were very much affected by any alterations which happened at court. It being now the fourth year after the retreat of the emperor to Capreæ, a considerable change took place in the death of Livia Augusta, who, by her first marriage, was the mother of Tiberius, and by her second, the widow of Augustus, by whom she had no children. She appears to have been a woman of consummate address. According to Tacitus, a fond and partial mother, an obsequious wife, and uniting, in her own character, the abilities of her husband, with the duplicity of her son. Being asked, by what arts she had kept her place so long in the confidence of Augustus? "By the most scrupulous virtue," she said; "by implicit obedience; by not meddling in affairs of state; by overlooking his intrigues with other women."[2]

The authority of Livia had been a considerable restraint on the temper of her son; and being exerted to thwart him on some occasions, had contributed to the resolution he took of retiring from Rome. Both the mother and the son had their jealousies and their resentments; but as they seldom fixed on the same objects, such as were persecuted by the one, sometimes found a refuge with the other. They concurred in their aversion to Agrippina, but might have been divided in their inclinations towards her children. Livia, tainted with the rancour of a stepmother,[3] and incited by personal jealousies, ever saw in the person of Agrippina an air of superiority which seemed to reproach her as the wife of Nero, and but an intruder into the family of Cæsar. With respect to the widow of Germanicus, therefore, she was probably more implacable even than the emperor; but with respect to his children, these being descended of herself. it may be supposed that she could not possibly adopt the passions of Sejanus to their prejudice nor wish to remove them, in order to make way for the ambition of a stranger. The death of Livia was accordingly to those young men a fatal circumstance, and facilitated the execution of the designs, which the emperor or his favourite had formed against them. Soon after the funeral rites were performed, the storm which had been long impending over them accordingly broke out. A letter from the emperor was presented to the senate, accusing Agrippina, and Nero the eldest of her sons, not of any plot or conspiracy against the state, or of any breach of the public peace, but charging the young man with lewdness, and the mother with haughty looks, and a stubborn heart.

This letter was received in the senate with surprise. After some interval of consternation and silence, a motion was made to proceed in the matter to which it referred; but there being no specific charge, and no instructions to form a prosecution, it was observed, that the emperor might have given way to his displeasure in angry expressions, without intending any farther censure or judicial severities. Junius Rusticus, who had been appointed by Tiberius clerk or secretary of the senate, ventured to advise a delay, in order that the emperor might have time to reconsider the subject, and to make the senate acquainted with his real intentions.

In the mean time, the purport of this letter was rumoured abroad, and the senate was beset with multitudes of the people, who, carrying the effigies of Agrippina and her son, exclaimed that the letter in question must have been forged, that it was impossible the emperor could intend the destruction of his own family; and, after the senate broke up, there continued to be handed about in the streets invectives against Sejanus, alleged to be the speeches of members in that assembly.

When these particulars came to be known at Capreæ, they were represented by Sejanus as an insult upon the senate, and as a contempt of the emperor's authority. Libels, he said, were daringly published; the people were assembled in disorderly tumults, and nothing was wanting to complete the rebellion, but arms, and the personal presence of those leaders who were already followed in effigy.

Tiberius accordingly renewed his complaint to the senate, reprimanding them for not having proceeded on his former letter; but insinuated, that he did not aim at the life of Agrippina, nor at that of her son. In this, he seemed to require a sentence of exile or imprisonment; and the members, now as much decided as they had been lately perplexed and irresolute, were eager to distinguish their zeal. After four-and-forty elaborate speeches had been delivered, all tending to prove the necessity of immediate severities, it was resolved that Agrippina, with the eldest of her sons, should be banished; the first into the island of Pandateria, the place where her mother, the unhappy Julia, had been confined; and the other to Pontia, another island on the same coast.[4]

---

1 Vipsania was the daughter of Agrippa by a former marriage, and consequently the half sister of Agrippina.

2 Dio. Cass. lib. lviii. c. 2.

3 Novercalibus odiis.—Tacit.

4 Sueton. in Tiber. c. 33, 34.

The younger brothers were overlooked on the present occasion. Drusus, the second, being persuaded by Sejanus that the removal of his elder brother tended to his own advantage, by opening his way to the empire, took no part in the distresses of his family. He himself, however, was soon after put in confinement, and for some years kept a prisoner at Rome, in a secret recess of the emperor's palace.

Tiberius, in some instances, endeavoured to compensate the injustice which he practised against one set of persons, by acts of munificence to others, whom he selected as objects of his bounty, or who were of too little consequence to incur his jealousy. He seized an opportunity of this kind about the time that Agrippina and her son experienced his vengeance, by relieving numbers who had suffered by a fire which had recently consumed some part of the city, and others, who had suffered by the fall of a theatre erected at Fidenæ; a disaster, by which, according to Tacitus, about fifty thousand persons were killed or hurt. Continuing, however, with respect to those who incurred his aversion or his distrust, to exercise a cruelty which seemed to increase with age, or with the consciousness of his own demerit towards mankind, he proceeded against Asinius Gallus with singular marks of deliberate malice; took measures to prolong the sufferings of this favourite victim; wished to witness their effects, and to enforce the impression of them with peculiar circumstances of insult and mockery. For this purpose, he procured a deputation from the senate to be sent to Capreæ, and took care that Asinius Gallus should be one of the deputies. Upon their arrival, he received Gallus in a manner peculiarly gracious, admitted him as a party in all his entertainments, and as an ordinary guest at his table; but having in the mean time sent a complaint of treason against him to Rome, and directed that a warrant from the senate should be sent to seize his person, he continued his former behaviour, and detained him at Capreæ, under various pretences of kindness, until the warrant of the senate to seize him should arrive. He took care to be present when this warrant was executed, affected surprise, even pretended to be distressed, and, when the prisoner was removed, gave strict injunctions that no violence should be offered to him, nor any sentence passed against him, until he himself should return to Rome.

In this ambiguous injunction, Gallus was condemned to a lingering state of suspense, and of suffering without the knowledge of his crime, or of the person by whom he was accused; a species of refinement on cruelty which Tiberius had lately adopted, and, which he sometimes expressed. Having a petition presented to him, that one of his prisoners might be allowed to die: "I am not," he said, "sufficiently reconciled to him for that."

While Sejanus was considered as the author of most of these cruel acts, and was accordingly the general object of flattery as well as of terror, he was in reality the dupe of his master's cunning, and at this very time was already doomed to destruction.

Tiberius either moved by a mere change of caprice incident to unhappy men, or warned of some danger to his own person, from the height and from the views to which he had raised this favourite, had for some time secretly resolved on his ruin; but while he revolved this purpose in his own mind, and weighed the dangers to which he might be exposed in the execution of it, he redoubled the usual marks of his favour, and in all his despatches, in which he mentioned Sejanus to the senate, designed him, "My Sejanus, and the partner of my cares and my labours."

The public, as well as Sejanus himself, were imposed upon by these appearances. No honour was moved for the emperor, in which Sejanus was not included. Their statues still continued to be erected together, and were multiplied in every street; and when the emperor signified his pleasure that Sejanus should be named to the consulate, together with himself, the senate replied, by an act, vesting the prince and his favourite with this dignity for five years.

Hitherto, it is probable that Tiberius, well aware of the vigilance and penetration of his favourite, and of the numerous spies he had employed, had not confided his secret to any person whatever, and wished to remove him from his person, before he ventured to proceed any farther in his design. For this purpose he had chosen him for his own colleague in the consulate of the ensuing year; and, under pretence of delegating to him the whole functions of an office, which the emperor himself could not attend, he sent him to Rome.

For some time after the arrival of Sejanus in the city, the usual executions for treason were continued, and persons who had incurred the suspicion either of the prince or his minister, perished with their wives, and their children. Many of them, as usual, to prevent the effects of a formal sentence, laid violent hands on themselves, and some exhibited this horrid spectacle even at the bar of the senate.[5]

While Sejanus thus seemed to wield the imperial power, and to hold the lives of the people at his mercy, he was attended by multitudes, who pressed to his gate in such numbers, that the court of his palace could scarcely receive them. He slighted the attentions that were paid to him; but with unwearied jealousy remarked every appearance of neglect, and doomed to destruction persons who gave any signs of impatience, under the state of servility and debasement to which they were reduced.

In the mean time, Tiberius proceeded with great circumspection. He had accepted of the consulate merely to flatter his minister, and to increase his security, in being placed as the colleague of the emperor in that station. Being to destroy him, it was necessary that some one should be present, on whom the dignity of consul might devolve. For this reason, he divested himself of the office, and substituted in his own place C. Memmius Regulus, who on the first of May, was admitted as the colleague of Sejanus. From thenceforward, the conduct of the emperor threw the favourite himself and the public in general, into great perplexity. In some of his letters to the senate, he spoke of his health as declining, and of himself as a dying person. In his next, he announced his recovery, and a design of speedily visiting the metropolis. He commended Sejanus in one letter, he censured him in another

5 Dio. Cass. lib. lviii. c. 4.

sometimes favoured none but his partizans and adherents, at other times affected to prefer his rivals. It is possible that in these inconsistencies, he himself actually wavered between hatred and fear; and apprehending the great influence of Sejanus over the prætorian guards, hesitated in the execution of his purpose. It is likewise extremely agreeable to his character, to suppose that he meant, by holding forth some signs of displeasure, to urge the object of it to some act of indiscretion or insolence, which could be made the foundation of a plausible charge against him, and that he had spies on his conduct to lay hold of any pretence he should furnish for an impeachment; but that, fearing to drive him to some dangerous act of despair, he retracted in one message the provocation he had given in a former.

While Sejanus appeared, from some circumstances in the conduct of the emperor towards him, to be out of favour, he was suddenly raised to the dignity of pontiff, together with Caius Cæsar Caligula; and thinking this a favourable opportunity to recover his place about the person of his master, he desired leave to offer his thanks at Capreæ; but was told that he might spare himself the trouble, for that the emperor was soon to be at Rome.

To try the effect of a fresh mortification on the temper of this devoted favourite, Caius Cæsar Caligula was declared successor in the empire. The popularity of the family of Germanicus, made this declaration be received with universal joy; and being joined to other indications, that Sejanus no longer had the exclusive possession of the emperor's favour, greatly diminished the court that was paid to him.

From this time, it is probable that Tiberius took into his confidence Macro, an officer already of high rank in the prætorian bands, and whom he destined to succeed Sejanus in the command of that body. With Macro, he concerted the manner of removing this dangerous man, and formed a plan, which was to be intrusted to his execution. Sejanus was to be flattered with new hopes; he was to be surprised in the senate, while the guards were to be amused with, what was a new circumstance in this reign, the distribution of a donative from the emperor.

In proceeding to execute this design, in a manner which the emperor chose from his love of duplicity, or which, from his fear of the troops that were under the command of Sejanus, he thought himself obliged to contrive with so much circumspection, he intimated to the senate, and to Sejanus himself, that he speedily meant to vest him with the character of tribune, a dignity which rendered the person sacred, and which the Cæsars had in some measure appropriated to themselves. While this intimation was supposed to lull Sejanus in perfect security, Macro was despatched to Rome, and took care to arrive at an hour, when the senate had been, by order of the emperor, appointed to assemble. He met with Sejanus, just as he had posted his guard, and was entering at the door of the senate-house; and being asked, what commands he had from the emperor, and what letters for himself? answered, that he had brought his appointment to the tribunitian power, and was to lay it before the senate.

Sejanus took his place, with the usual attendance of persons who had accompanied him from his own house, and had the members of the senate still crowding around him as usual, when Macro presented the mandate of the emperor, and retired.

This paper was artfully drawn up, to gain time in the reading, and to keep all parties in suspense, while Macro should take his measures to secure the guards. In the preamble, the name of Sejanus was not at all mentioned; in the subsequent parts of the paper, he was sometimes extolled, and sometimes censured. Other affairs were intermixed with this, and the suspense which so long and so strange a performance occasioned in the minds of those who were present, amounted to some degree of stupefaction. But it concluded at last with a peremptory charge of treason against Sejanus; and the crowd of attendants instantly withdrew from the consul's chair on which he was seated. His colleague in office, Regulus, called upon him by name to stand up; but so much was he distracted, and so little accustomed to this tone of voice, that upon a second call, he started from his seat, and asked, if the words were addressed to him? Surprise had qualified him to take any vigorous resolution; and when he began to recollect himself, the precautions which had been taken by his enemies, rendered all his endeavours too late.

Macro, as soon as he had delivered the emperor's letter to be read in the senate, went to the guard which was posted at the doors, informed them that he brought a donative from the emperor, which they were then to share with their fellow-soldiers in the barracks; that for this purpose, they were immediately to be relieved by a party of the city watch. This being done, he led them to the citadel, or what was called the camp of the prætorian bands,[1] distributed the emperor's bounty, and at the same time taxed their commander with ingratitude to so kind a master; intimated his removal, produced his own commission to succeed in that important station, and by his authority, as well as by these precautions, prevented any disturbance among that formidable body of men.

Sejanus being deserted in the senate by those who had attended him into the house, and who a few moments before pressed to be first in his observation, was taken into custody of the party which had relieved his own guard, and was treated as a person accused of the highest crimes. On the first motion for a commitment, he was ordered to prison, and persons of every description began to give unfeigned or affected demonstrations of joy. From many who were present, the fear that was lately expressed in adulation and courtship, now burst forth in reproaches and insults. In others, who were more nearly connected with the prisoner, or more likely to be involved in his fate, the terror with which they were seized, was disguised under the affectation of joy. The populace as he passed through the streets, took their parts as usual in the storm which burst on this unfortunate man, and, that he might not have the consolation of passing unseen, tore away the lappet of his gown, with which he endeavoured to cover his face.

On the same day, the senate met again in a temple contiguous to the prison in which Se-

1 Castrum Prætorium.

janus was confined, and, without any specific charge or evidence of guilt, gave sentence of death against him, which was accordingly executed. The dead body, as usual in the case of treason, being made fast on a hook, was dragged through the streets, and cast into the river, where it was thrown up, or continued afloat during some days, under the continual insults of a multitude of people.

It is not easy to determine how far this minister was accountable for a tyranny, which occasioned so vehement and so general a resentment. His crimes were undoubtedly great, and the envy of his fortune was not to be assuaged by common sufferings. But as human nature is liable to error in the manner of punishing crimes, as well as in the commission of them, the rage which now animated the populace against Sejanus, mixed with a servile intention to pay their court to the emperor, led to an action as criminal and more odious than any of which he himself had been accused or suspected. The children of this unhappy man, a boy and a girl, though too young to partake in his guilt, or to furnish any subject of distrust or of jealousy to his enemies, were included in the same fate with the father; the girl with so much innocence, that she often asked the persons by whom she was seized, what she had done? assured them, with an infantine simplicity, that she never would do it again; begged that they would not carry her to prison; said that she never was obstinate, and that a few strokes of the rod were enough to correct her.

It is subjoined to this piteous detail, that, in compliance with a vile superstition, which the consideration of innocence could not restrain, she was ordered to be ravished previous to her execution, because it was ominous of misfortune to inflict the punishment of death on a virgin.[2] The bodies of these innocents, in the same manner with that of their father, were dragged through the streets, and cast into the river.

It is difficult to account, from any principles of human nature, for acts of such amazing depravity. Tyrants seldom exceed the bounds of resentment, jealousy, or fear; but the vile tools that are procured by servility to execute their purpose, in order to ingratiate themselves, often outrun, in their affectation of zeal, what tyranny or cowardice itself could not suggest or perpetrate.

Apicata, the widow of Sejanus, and the mother of these unhappy children, having first disclosed the conspiracy, by which Drusus, the son of Tiberius, had been poisoned, laid violent hands on herself, and, by the discovery she made, soon after brought on the ruin of the widow Livilla, with that of the other accomplices in that daring crime.

It was reported, that the anxiety of Tiberius, whether real or affected, was such, during the dependence of his design on Sejanus, that he instructed Macro, in case of any resistance from the guards, to bring forth Drusus, the son of Germanicus, then a prisoner in the palace, to assemble the citizens against them; that he had prepared shipping at Capreæ to waft himself, in case of necessity, to some of the military stations on the frontier; that he had formed a chain of posts from Rome to the nearest promontory of Campania, with orders to light fires, and to make other concerted signals, in case it should be necessary for him to consult his safety by flight. In his letter to the senate, in order to make a suitable impression of the danger to which he wished the public to believe he was exposed from the designs of Sejanus, he concluded, with expressing his wishes to be again at Rome; but desired that the consul, who remained at the head of the commonwealth, might come forth with the powers of the republic to conduct him in safety.[3] His design however having succeeded to his wishes, Drusus was still retained a prisoner in the palace, and the consul being arrived in Campania, with his lictors, to give the emperor a safe conduct to Rome, was every where considered as an object of ridicule.

After the execution of Sejanus, the city continued in a ferment during many days. The people having been disposed, for some time, to impute to the minister the system of tyranny which had been lately pursued, rejoiced in his fall, applauded the severities which were executed on the partners of his guilt, and willingly pointed out, as accomplices in his crimes, his relations and friends, and all who had ever moved for any of the extravagant honours that were lately bestowed upon himself; but, as in imputing the guilt of many cruel measures to Sejanus, they were too favourable to the emperor, so they probably over-rated the influence of the minister, who was in fact more the dupe, than the director, of his master's designs.

As it soon after appeared, that the cruel jealousies of this reign did not terminate with the death of the favourite, the people, as usual, ran to the opposite extreme, considered him as a mere instrument of his master's tyranny, as a person employed while his services were convenient, but in the end betrayed with a degree of perfidy, which rendered the cruelty of the tyrant, in that case, more odious than even when it was practised against the most innocent subjects.[4] So prone are mankind, in particular instances, to suspect the falsehood, or to exaggerate the wickedness of those, who, by general duplicity and malice, have incurred their detestation.

The death of Sejanus was so far from introducing any mitigation of the former tyranny, that it rather furnished a new set of pretences under which to exert its force. Intimacy with the fallen minister, or a supposed participation of his guilt, involved greater numbers, than had been formerly questioned on account of any other species of treason. Persons of every sex and of every condition, were cast indiscriminately into the same prisons; and the time of the senate was divided between the ordering of executions, and the appointment of honours, which were decreed to the prince for his vigilance in this matter. The title of father of his country was again offered to him; additional rejoicings were devised for the anniversary of his birth; a general thanksgiving was appointed to the gods; and a new statue was to be erected to liberty. All persons were forbidden to wear mourning for Sejanus; the anniversary of his death was to be kept as a festival, or celebrated with public entertainments and sports; and it was resolved in the senate, that the extravagant honours so profusely lavish-

2 Dio. Cass. lib. lviii. c. 11. Tacit. Annal. lib v. c. 5.

3 Dio. Cass. lib. lviii. c. 13.

4 Sueton. in Tiber. c. 55.

ed on that minister, should not be repeated in the case of any subject whatever.

These decrees, Tiberius, so far as they were intended to confer honours on himself, rejected with disdain, and even refused to see the deputies who were separately sent from the senate, from the equestrian order, and from the people, to congratulate him on this occasion. He despised the givers too much to be flattered wi. the gift, and was aware of their duplicity in pretending to offer him praise. Under this impression, at one of the last times he had attended the senate in person, he was observed to leave the assembly with scorn. "What a collection," he said, "of willing slaves."[1] There is, it seems, a degree of good nature as well as of weakness, in wishing to be flattered. This prince was equally exempted from both.

The senate, however, the more they were spurned, became the more sensible of their own degradation, and only endeavoured to vary the mode of their flattery. As Tiberius ever talked of his approaching return to Rome, and of his intended appearance in the senate, they passed a decree, that twenty of their own number, to be named by the emperor himself, should be armed with swords, and should have charge of his safety as often as he took his seat in their meetings. When this resolution was intimated to him, he returned thanks for their zeal, and with some derision desired to know, whether this senatorial guard should be young men or old men? whether they should continue for life, or be taken in rotation? and whether they should arm only at the door of the senate-house, or pass in arms through the streets?[2] and concluded with saying, that, if his life was worth preserving, he should think himself sufficiently safe, when attended by Macro and some tribunes of his guards, whom he would take the liberty to bring into the senate.

This reference to the guards had the effect of an admonition, and drew from the senate an attempt to pay their court likewise to this formidable body of men. Bounties in money and honorary distinctions were decreed to them; such as, that the prætorian soldier, at the expiration of the time for which he enlisted, should be allowed a place at the theatre on the bench of the equestrian order. In this, however, the compliment was not more successful than it had been in other instances. It was even resented by the emperor as an attempt to share the affection of the troops with himself. Junius Gallio, who had made the motion, was ordered into exile, and afterwards committed to prison in the city. And the senate, as a last effort to please this froward prince, seeing that the project to arm a part of their own number in his defence was not acceptable, resolved, that every member, in entering the house, should be searched for concealed weapons, as a precaution for the safety of a person who probably never meant to intrust himself in their hands.

In the midst of these servilities, the emperor met with some instances of a daring petulance, and with some even of a noble freedom, which he had the discretion to overlook, or to treat with affected respect. The defects of his person, he being bald, foul-faced, and bent with age, were exhibited by actors on the stage; and the monster, so represented, it was said, practised in secret the most detestable vices; alluding to the manner in which the emperor passed his time at Capreæ. But with respect to such buffooneries, he had the discernment to know, that a serious attempt to punish the authors, would only tend to confirm the application, and to increase its effects.

Among the numbers that were questioned as partners in the guilt of the late minister, and of whom many perished by their own hands, or by that of the executioner, Marcus Terentius, a Roman knight, had the courage to acknowledge his guilt, and pleaded his cause in a manner that suspended the proceedings of the senate against him.[3] "It were safer, perhaps, for me," he said, "to deny, than to confess, my connexion with Sejanus. But whatever may be the event, I must own that I attached myself to that minister; that I desired to be reckoned among his friends, and was proud of this title. In him I saw the first officer of the army, the first minister of the state, and the colleague of Cæsar; a powerful patron, and an irresistible enemy; one whose favour was preferment and honour, whose displeasure was ruin and disgrace. It was not for me to penetrate the councils of my prince, nor to decide on the reason of his conduct. It was my duty to honour whom he honoured; and in this, as well as in every thing else, to acquit myself as a faithful subject, by a perfect compliance with my sovereign's will. Please to recollect the period of this minister's favour, as well as of his disgrace. My conduct in both, and my defence, is the same with those of many others. We adhered to him, while the sovereign commanded us to do so; we left him the moment he was supposed to be the enemy of our prince." Upon this defence, the absurdity of punishing in others an error of which the emperor himself had set the example, suspended, for a moment, the rage of prosecution; and the prisoner, with consent of Tiberius, was acquitted.

An officer, named Lentulus Gentulicus, then at the head of the legions on the Upper Rhine, being some time afterwards accused as an accomplice with Sejanus, had the boldness to write, that his connexion with that minister was pointed out to him by the emperor himself; that the mistake was common to both, and that what was deemed innocent in one person, ought not to be imputed as a crime to another. "I have hitherto," he said, "been faithful in the discharge of my trust, and mean to continue so; but the first attempt to supersede me, I shall consider as a warning to defend myself. Matters, however, may remain in quiet; I am willing to acknowledge the emperor so long as I remain unmolested." Tiberius, now far advanced in years, governing by his reputation, and by the influence of forms established in the reign of his predecessor and his own, did not choose to risk his authority against a person, who, being at the head of an army, had the courage to hold such language; and affected, from this time forward, to treat Gentulicus with particular marks of favour and respect.[4]

Others were imprisoned, and carried to execution in troops and companies; and the emperor

1 Dio. Cass. lib. lviii. c. 13.
2 Tacit. Annal. lib. vi. c. 2.
3 Dio. Cass. lib. lviii. c. 18.
4 Tacit. Annal. lib. vi. c. 30

at last, as if tired with the pursuit of offenders in detail, or in separate divisions, ordered the jails to be cleared by a general execution of all persons confined as accomplices in the treason of Sejanus. In consequence of this order, numbers of dead bodies of every sex, age, and condition, were cast forth into the streets, and lying scattered about, or collected in heaps, until they began to corrupt, were thrown into the river.[5]

Mystery and concealment being the favourite arts of Tiberius, as often as he believed himself to be observed, he became jealous of every prying look, and detested such persons as seemed to be qualified to distinguish truth from appearances. At one time he received informers as the most acceptable members of his court; at other times, he appeared to detest them as persons who had detected his vices, and were hastening to make them known to the world. During the prosecution of his design against Sejanus, he encouraged his spies with additional rewards, and even with public honours. But after he had assuaged his passion in the blood of so many victims, he turned his disgust and aversion against the instruments of his cruelties, and ordered the city to be cleared of informers by a general slaughter.

In one of his letters to the senate, under the effects of disgust and aversion to measures which he had pursued for his own safety, but which he found to involve him in growing danger and guilt, he betrayed the distraction and anguish of his mind. "May I perish," he said, "under evils still worse than those I endure, if I know what to write, or what I should not write." These were probably the boils, ulcers, and sores, on the body of Tiberius, to which Julian alludes[6] in presenting him among his Cæsars.

In the memoirs which this emperor kept of the transactions of his reign, he stated the disgrace and execution of Sejanus, as a punishment inflicted on him for his cruelties to the family of Germanicus; and yet these cruelties, which were afterwards carried to much greater heights by the emperor himself, had been only begun under the influence of that minister.

Agrippina, with two of her sons, Nero and Drusus, had, during the administration of Sejanus, been taken into custody, or banished to some of the islands contiguous to the coast of Italy; but all of them perished after the death of Sejanus, either by the executioner, or by their own hands, urged to despair by the indignities they were made to suffer.

The mother perished in one or other of these ways in the island Pandateria, the place of her exile; and the eldest of her two sons was starved to death in one of the small islands called Pontiæ, to which he was confined.

The second son perished in the same manner, some time afterwards, in a prison to which he had been committed in the palace. A diary had been kept of all the expressions of impatience which, under this confinement, had dropt from him during some years; and the reproaches which were extorted from him, by his sufferings, were stated as the crimes for which he suffered.

A third son of Germanicus and Agrippina, Caius, better known by the name of Caligula, yet remained, to convince the Roman people, that the fond expectations which are formed of princes who die prematurely, are not always well founded. This young man, whether recommended to Tiberius by an early sympathy of their characters, or merely overlooked by him on account of his youth, not only escaped the persecutions in which his family was involved, but was at last embraced by the emperor as a support to his age; and making a part of his court at Capreæ, next to Macro, enjoyed the second place in his favour.

The emperor had a grandson by birth of the name of Tiberius; but Caius, who was his grandson by adoption, being elder, was pointed out by this circumstance of seniority, and by the favour which the people still bore to the family of Germanicus, as heir apparent to the empire.

Caius was encouraged by the grandfather, to whom falsehood appeared to be a necessary ingredient in every transaction, to expect the succession, while it was really intended for Tiberius. The first, though not qualified by address to extricate himself from any difficulties, acted, perhaps from mere insensibility or fear, the part which was fittest in his place, and which continued to render him sufferable at the court of Tiberius. He acquiesced in the fate of his mother and of his brothers, without uttering a single word of impatience or regret, regulated his own behaviour by the emperor's looks; and whether his countenance were gloomy or gay, formed his own upon the same model, carrying, under the aspect of extreme servility, while a subject, that detestable profligacy which rendered him afterwards so cruel a tyrant, and which gave occasion to the famous saying, "That his accession to the empire spoilt a good slave to make a detestable master."[7]

The accounts which are given of the latter part of the reign of Tiberius, have more the appearance of invective than of history. Even this hateful monster, it is said, was addicted to pleasure; but of so vile a kind, as to excite detestation and loathing, more than to increase the indignation which is felt at his cruelties and other crimes. His procurers had authority to employ seduction, money, and force; and, in their endeavours to supply his caprice, spared neither condition nor sex. It is difficult to conceive, that a world, enlightened by the reason and experience of so many ages; that citizens, acquainted with the character and the rights transmitted to them from their ancestors; that military men, yet rivalling the reputation of the ancient Romans, and having no interest in the horrid use that was made in the capital of the imperial and military power which they themselves bestowed and supported; should submit to be commanded for so many years by a superannuated monster, retired from the world, and supposed to practise every species of private abomination, as well as of public oppression.

In accounting for the patience of the Romans under this odious reign, we may observe, that, in the sense of a people who still retained the ferocity of their ancestors, though possessed of few of their good qualities, the cruelties which are mentioned had less effect than they have on our feelings. They were practised chiefly against

5 Tacit Annal. lib. vi. c. 19.
6 Vid. Cæsars of Julian.

7 Tacit. Annal. c. 20.

persons, who, being of the emperor's family, or raised by himself to be objects of general envy, were easily abandoned by the public to his will.

Senators of distinction at Rome, having no protection to expect from the populace, by whom they were hated, from the troops who were jealous of them, or from their own order, who were long since stript of every remnant of real power, were abandoned to the mercy of the tyrant. The followers of his own court at Capreæ, amongst whom the executioner made a principal personage, were still more in his power. They were commonly executed in presence of the emperor himself, who assisted in the refinements of cruelty which were practised against them. It was a favourite sport to throw those, whom he doomed to destruction, from a precipice into the sea, where they were received by a party from the galleys, who, with boat-hooks and oars, despatched such as were otherwise likely to escape.

After such an account of the character of this emperor, it is painful, in accounting for the success of his government, to acknowledge that he was a man of considerable ability; and that, while he indulged his passions in the capital, or at his own court, yet in the provinces, where the consequences of an error might have been fatal or dangerous to his power, he held the reins with a steady and a well-directed hand. Having possession of the empire by means of the army, he maintained his authority over this order of men by a well-placed application of discipline; not by any extraordinary indulgence, or bounty, which often corrupt, and render ungovernable, those whom they are intended to gain. On this subject, it is observed that he never made any general donation beside that of doubling the legacy which Augustus had bequeathed to the troops; and no particular one besides those which he made to the prætorian bands to secure their acquiescence in the fate of Sejanus; and to the legions of the east, as a reward for their not having paid, to this favourite, in the height of his power, the honours which were done to him by all the other armies of the empire.[1] He preserved his authority in the provinces by a jealous inspection of those who were entrusted with the administration of his affairs; and in this was, no doubt, greatly assisted by his indifference to personal friendships, which, in princes better disposed than himself, have often the effect of pernicious predilections and partialities. He checked all attempts at conspiracies, by the impression he gave of his vigilance, and by the mutual distrust with which he inspired his enemies, making their treachery to each other the road to preferments, honours, and wealth.

The ordinary rotation and succession to office and command, which Augustus, in continuation of the republican forms, had still maintained, Tiberius, by a very natural tendency of the monarchical spirit, in a great measure, or entirely, abolished. Such officers as were successful in keeping the peace of their provinces, he generally continued for many years, and sometimes for life. He avoided, as much as possible, the necessity of employing, at the head of armies, men of enterprise, forward ambition, or even superior capacity. He left the disorders, or troubles, that arose in any distant province, to the effect of time, rather than be obliged to employ, in repressing them, men who were likely to eclipse his own glory, or to awaken his jealousy. But as such men were likely ill to endure the state of obscurity in which they were kept, he soothed their discontents, sometimes, by flattering them with extraordinary honours. He named them for stations of high command; but still under various pretences detained them at Rome, where they were allowed to appear with the ensigns of their public character, but never to enter on the possession of its powers.

To these particulars we may join the advantages which Tiberius enjoyed by succeeding to Augustus, whose long and well-regulated government had left, throughout the empire, habits of submission and obedience, which could not be shaken by offences committed within the verge of the court, or in the capital, and against particular descriptions of men, in whom the empire at large took little concern.

The ordinary residence of this emperor, during eleven years in the later period of his reign, was in the island of Capreæ. This he had chosen as a place of security against any sudden attempts which might be made on his life. He nevertheless paid occasional visits to the continent of Italy, and made some stay at his villas situated in different parts of the country. In changing his abode, he kept the city of Rome in continual dread of his approach, sometimes presented himself in the neighbouring villages, and in the suburbs, but never entered the gates. At one time, he came by water to the gardens of the Naumachia, and, feeling himself incommoded by the concourse of people, placed guards to keep them at a distance, and soon after withdrew; at another time, in the last years of his reign, he advanced to the seventh mile-stone, and was in the sight of the battlements, but proceeded no farther. Being sensible of his decline and approaching dissolution, he undertook these journeys to keep the Romans in awe, and to check the hopes they were apt to entertain of an approaching deliverance from his tyranny. From the same motives, he prohibited the resort of the people to supposed oracles which he knew to be consulted with respect to the prospect of his own decease, and forbade all intercourse with astrologers and magicians, a class of men in whose skill he himself, though a contemner of the established superstition, had much faith.

On the approach of death, Tiberius, feeling his strength rapidly decline, strove to amuse the people with another voyage, in which he once more pretended an intention to visit Rome; and being attended by Caius, by Macro, and by his usual retinue of guards and parasites, he crossed the bay of Baiæ, to the head-land of Misenum, where he possessed a villa which had formerly belonged to Lucullus. At this place one of his physicians, under pretence of taking his leave for some days, pressed his hand, and took an opportunity to feel his pulse. From this stolen observation, it is said, that he ventured to inform Caius and Macro, that the emperor could not survive many days.

Tiberius being led by some appearances to penetrate their thoughts, or wishing to conceal the real state of his health, took his place, as usual, at table, affected to prolong the entertain

[1] In the armies of the west, the effigy of Sejanus was carried with the colours or ensigns of the legion.

ment, and addressed himself, at parting, with some particular words of attention to every guest: but after an effort of this sort, being retired to his apartment, he fainted away, and lay on his bed for dead. The report immediately ran from one end of the villa to the other. All the officers of the guards in attendance, and all the members and followers of the court, repaired to Caius with congratulations on his supposed accession to the empire. But while they were thus employed in paying their addresses to the successor, a servant arrived, and, in great consternation, announced that the emperor was revived, and called for assistance. The company, in a moment, was dispersed; and Caius, with extreme terror, saw the ruin which threatened him for his premature acceptance of the court that was paid to him. But Macro retained his presence of mind, and put a sudden stop to the feeble efforts of returning life in Tiberius, by gathering up the coverlet of his bed, so as to stop his breath until he was suffocated.

CHAPTER VII.

Succession of Caius to the Empire—The first Appearances of his Reign—Conclusion of the History—Observations on the Sequel—Accession of the Flavian Family—Vicissitudes of Character in the Emperors—Sources of Degradation in the Imperial Establishment—Its Preservatives—Its real and continual, though almost insensible, Decline.

TIBERIUS died in the seventy-eighth year of his age, and in the twenty-third year of his reign. By this event the imperial throne, for the first time since its establishment, became actually vacant. Men were left to form their conjectures of what was likely to happen, or, without any established rule of succession, to form their judgment of what was proper to be done on this emergency. Every question relating to the succession had been prevented at the demise of Augustus, by his having associated Tiberius in the government, a precaution by which the successor, instead of being left to rely on a controvertible title, was put in actual possession of the sovereignty. It is likely that Tiberius would have followed this example, if his grandson by birth, for whom he intended the empire, had been of a proper age to assume the government; but this young man was no more than seventeen years of age, while Caius, the grandson by adoption, was already five-and-twenty, had the better pretension, and was supported by the favour of the Roman people.

In these circumstances, the dying emperor thought it dangerous to declare for his grandson; but secretly drew up a will in his favour, of which he carefully lodged many copies, while he made the world believe, that he intended the succession for Caius. In this act of duplicity he had concealed his real intentions, even from Macro, the commander of the prætorian bands, on whom the execution of his purpose chiefly depended; and by these means rendered it entirely abortive.

Macro, having been for some time past in actual concert with Caius on the measures that were necessary to secure the succession; and both being equally surprised to find, at the demise of Tiberius, a formal conveyance of the sovereignty in a different channel, their first intention was to cancel this deed; but they soon found, that the testator had made so many copies of his will, and lodged them so securely, as to render their design impracticable. It was determined, therefore, as more advisable, to refer the matter to the senate, and to obtain an act, founded on a supposed right of seniority, preferring Caius to the throne of Cæsar.

By such an acknowledgment of right, the monarchy gained a new advantage, and perhaps one of the greatest of which it was then susceptible, that some rule of inheritance should be followed to prevent the ruinous contests which arise from an elective or disputed succession, and to give, if possible, together with a permanent right of the sovereign to his high estate, a corresponding right of every citizen to his rank, to his privilege, and to his property.

By this declaration in favour of Caius, it seemed to be admitted, that men were to look for a successor to the empire in the person who stood foremost, by birth or adoption, in the family of Cæsar; and the establishment of the monarchy appeared to be complete. The titles of emperor and prince,[2] or head of the army and of the senate, under which Augustus endeavoured to conceal the extent of his usurpation, came, in the course of his own and the succeeding reign, to signify what, among the designations of sovereignty and imperial power, they now actually import, and what, through a race of men, blessed with virtuous or moderate dispositions, might, as in other instances, have passed by hereditary succession to a very distant posterity; but in the persons who immediately succeeded to the government, the transmission of this inheritance was accompanied with much violence and frequent interruption.

Notwithstanding the acknowledgment now made in favour of hereditary right, the example of a formal resignation and resumption of the sovereignty, set by Augustus, and repeated by Tiberius, had entailed a kind of farce on the empire, to be acted, not only at the accession of successive masters, but in the same reign, at every period of ten years. At every such period the appointment of an emperor was supposed to be renewed: the occasion was attended with much solemnity, and the celebration of a great festival for the entertainment of the people.[3]

---

2 Imperator et Princeps. 3 The Decennalia

Caius, therefore, while he was far from admitting any doubt of his right to the sovereignty, nevertheless, mimicked the caution or artifice with which Augustus and Tiberius proceeded to assume the reins of government. He repeated the same professions of respect and of zeal for the commonwealth, the same expressions of personal modesty, the same unwillingness to undertake the government, the same reluctant compliance with the pressing requests of the senate and people, the same affectation of filial piety to his predecessor, and of indulgence or candour to those who had, in any way, obstructed his own advancement. It was become the fashion to affect destroying all papers and records, from which any one could fear to have matter of accusation brought against him; but it was become the practice to preserve them with great care.

While the new emperor passed from Misenum to Rome, he was attended on the highways by incredible numbers of people, who, animated by the affection which they bore to his father Germanicus, and by the hopes of exchanging a cruel and jealous tyrant for a youth of a noble and virtuous extraction, received him with acclamations of joy, calling him their propitious star, the child and the nursling of the Roman people, and bestowing upon him every other appellation of fondness and respect. It is scarcely to be doubted, as his mind was then elated with joy, for his deliverance from the insidious and cruel jealousy of his predecessor, and moved by the affection and cordiality with which his succession was acknowledged by all orders of men, that he must have felt a real, however temporary, gleam of good-will and affection of mankind. When officiously told of some offences which had been committed against his person or his pretensions, he said, "That he had done nothing to merit the hatred of any one, and should be deaf to the whispers of informers or spies." Affecting to follow the impulse of his own filial piety, and to be moved by the affectionate sympathy of the Roman people, he hastened to the island of Pandateria, where his mother Agrippina had suffered so long a confinement under the tyranny of Tiberius, raked up the ashes of her funeral pile, embraced her remains, and ordered them to be carried with great ostentation to Rome. Although decency required him to observe the forms, and to carry the aspect of mourning for his late adoptive father and predecessor, he complied with what he knew to be the wishes of the Roman people, affecting to reverse many orders that were established in the administration and policy of the preceding reign.

Here then, if not before, we may date the final and irretrievable extinction of the Roman republic, not only in the subversion of its own institutions, and in the actual substitution of different forms, but in the acknowledgment of a right which made the succession to imperial power hereditary, as well as the extent of it far beyond what was consistent with the prerogatives formerly enjoyed by the senate and people of Rome. At this termination, therefore, of the Roman republic, agreeably to the design of this history, the narration must cease or conclude, with a very general view of what befel the empire in the succession of masters, and in the result of its own greatness.

Notwithstanding the favourable appearances which presented themselves at the accession of Caius, he not having, either in his understanding or dispositions, the permanent foundation of any good character, his personal vices soon broke ou in one of the most brutal and sanguinary tyrannies of which there is any example in the history of mankind. Having no choice of amusement above that of the lowest people, he soon plunged, together with them, into every species of dissi pation and debauchery; remained whole days and nights in the theatres and in the circus, entertained with the fights of gladiators, the baiting of wild beasts, and all the other species of shows of which the Romans, once a warlike people, now a corrupted populace, were so immoderately fond.

Ambitious citizens under the republic, and even the late emperors, with their court, had occasionally given their attendance at such entertainments, more to please the humour of the populace than to gratify their own: but this em peror himself, in respect to the qualities of his mind, was to be ranked with the lowest of the vulgar. He considered the circus as the principal scene of his glory, and the number of shows he could procure as the measure of his greatness. That the scenes might not be interrupted, or the spectators be obliged to retire to their meals, he fed them in the theatre. He promoted persons to office of state, or marked them out for disgrace or ruin, according to the ardour or indifference which they seemed to have for these entertain ments. In the degree of extravagance to which he carried this matter, he incurred an immoderate expense; and, besides applying to this purpose the ordinary revenue of the empire, squandered, within the year, a saving of about two-and-twenty millions sterling, left in the treasury by his predecessor.

In the sequel of these vile misapplications of time, the satiety he experienced led him to indulge himself in the most scandalous and offensive debauch. A sense of the public hatred or contempt which he incurred, galled him with jealousy and disgust; and these passions soon ripened into a general enmity to mankind. Every species of brutal indulgence, qualified with the name of pleasure; deliberate murders, under the pretence of the execution of justice, ordered without any formalities of trial, perpetrated in his own presence, and attended with expressions of insult and scorn from himself, make up the sequel of a reign which began with some professions and propitious appearances of moderation and regard to the opinion of the world. But the degree to which human nature itself was disgraced and insulted, in these detestable abuses of power, hastened an attempt to relieve the empire from the dominion of this monster. He fell in about three years after he began to reign, in one of the passages of his own palace, by the hands of Chærea, an officer of his guard, who, without any intention to supplant or to succeed him in the empire, formed a conspiracy against his life.

The senate, for a few hours after this event, flattered themselves in the belief that the government had devolved on themselves; and Chærea, by whose hands the tyrant had fallen, fondly wished for the restoration of the republic; but the prætorian bands thought themselves entitled to dispose of the empire. Before their officers had taken any measures for this purpose, a few straggling soldiers pervading the courts and recesses of the palace, seized upon Claudius, the brother of Germanicus, and uncle of Caligula, who, as a changeling devoid of ordinary understanding, had been long neglected or overlooked in the palace. This being the person who seemed by his relation to the late emperors, to have the best claim to the name and succession of the Cæsarian or Claudian families, they raised him on their shoulders, yet trembling with fear, lest he should be involved in the fate of his kinsman Caligula, and hastening with their burden to the fortress or barrack, were received by their companions with shouts and acclamations, which announced to the senate and the people that a successor was given to the throne of Cæsar.

The inactivity of this new sovereign might have furnished the world with at least an innocent master, if his want of capacity could have been supplied without committing his power into hands equally disposed to abuse it with the worst of his predecessors. Fit only to be a pageant in the ceremonies of a court, or a tool to be employed by those who got possession of him, he came at last into the hands of the second Agrippina, the daughter of Germanicus, and sister of Caligula, who, though his niece, became his wife, and prevailed upon him to adopt the young Domitius Ahenobarbus, her son by a former husband; and by these means made way for his succession to the empire under the appellation of Nero.

This impetuous, severe, and profligate woman, equally ardent in the acquisition as in the abuse of power, mistook, for parental affection, the earnest passion with which she wished to govern in the name of her son. Having ability enough, however, where she was not misled by her passions, to distinguish the proper instruments of government, she endeavoured to procure for him in the tutory of Burhus, who was placed by her means at the head of the prætorian bands, and of Seneca, who was by her means likewise recalled from banishment to his place in the senate, the most able or specious direction which the times could afford.

Nero acting for some time what Burhus suggested, and speaking what Seneca dictated, appeared to be a prodigy of wisdom and ingenuity. But his own personal disposition, making its way in a little time through the mask of sayings and of actions which were not his own, gave sufficient evidence, that the circumstance of having been the mere puppet, though actuated by the most able and ingenious hands, does not bestow ingenuity or ability, and that a direction, however wise, received from others without discernment or knowledge of its value, cannot carry to the mind of those who submit to it the character of wisdom.

The name of Nero, after the person who bore it had, during a few years in the beginning of his reign, been supposed the model of royal and philosophic virtue,[1] has become proverbial for caprice, folly, brutality, insolence, and cruelty. To the contempt of his subjects he at last joined a contempt of that very dignity to which he himself was raised as sovereign of so great an empire. Having a talent for music, he became, or believed himself to be, a distinguished performer, exhibited his skill on the public theatres, and travelled through Greece in the character of an artist, to receive the applauses of a people supposed to excel in discernment and taste.

The contempt which Nero incurred in quitting the character of sovereign for that of musician, became more fatal to him than the general detestation which he had formerly excited. A revolt which took place at first in Gaul, was followed by a defection of all the armies of the empire, and reduced him to the necessity of quitting, together with his life, a situation of which he proved so unworthy. Next to the fears which assailed him on the prospect of death, he was most affected, it is said, with surprise, that the world could submit to lose the hand of so great a performer.

Such then, in the first period of this monarchy, was the progress of a sovereignty erected by the Cæsars with so much violence, bloodshed, and criminal address. According to our ideas of inheritance, the succession did not once take place in the family of the first founder, but was pieced out by continual adoptions from the Octavian, the Claudian, and, last of all, from the Domitian family.

The reign of Augustus has been generally applauded, and may be considered as a model for those, who wish to govern with the least possible opposition or obstruction to their power. It may serve likewise as a caution to those, who need to be told under what disguise the most detestable tyranny will sometimes approach mankind. The wary design which marked the character of Augustus, was followed by worse principles in the breasts of those who succeeded him; and the dominion he established, merely to subject the empire to his own power, without any disposition to abuse it, became, in the sequel, an instrument of the vilest tyranny, and brought upon the public stage of the world actors, whom their dispositions and characters must otherwise have condemned to obscurity, or exposed as a disgrace and a blemish to human nature.

The manners of the imperial court, and the conduct of succeeding emperors, will scarcely gain credit with those who estimate probabilities from the standard of modern times. But the Romans were capable of much greater extremes than we are acquainted with. They retained, through all the steps of the revolution which they had undergone, their ferocity entire, without possessing, along with it, any of those better qualities, which, under the republic, had directed their courage to noble, at least to great and national, purposes.

Augustus had established the military government with great caution, and even affected the appearances of a citizen, while he secured all the powers of a master. His successors retained in public the same familiarity of manners, without the same guard against its abuses, and affected to be popular in the city and in the camp, without the circumspection which preserved the first emperor from the contagion of mean and degrading examples. The state itself was just emerged from democracy, in which the pretensions to equality checked the ordinary uses which, under

---

1 The quinquennium Neronis, was a proverbial expression for what promised well, but turned out otherwise

monarchies, are made of fortune and superior condition. The distinctions of royalty, and with these the proprieties of behaviour, in high rank, were unknown. An attempt at elegant magnificence and courtly reserve, which, in established monarchies, makes a part of the royal state, and a considerable support of its dignity, were avoided in this fallen republic, as more likely to excite envy and hatred, than deference or respect.

The Roman emperors, perhaps, in point of expense, both public and private, exceeded every other sovereign of the world; but their public expenses consisted in the exhibition of shows and entertainments, in which they admitted the meanest of the people to partake with themselves. Their personal expenses consisted not so much in the ostentation of elegance or refined pleasure, as in a serious attempt to improve sensuality into a continual source of enjoyment; and their pleasures consisted, of consequence, in the excesses of a brutal and retired debauch. This debauch was supported by continual endeavours to excite satiated appetite, to prolong its gratifications, and to supply the defects of mere animal pleasure, with conceits of fancy and efforts of buffoonery or low humour.

The manners of imperial Rome are thus described in the remains of a satire,[1] as elegant in the style, as it is gross and disgusting in the matter, and which we may suppose to be just in the general representation, whatever we may think of its application to any of the princes whose names and succession have been mentioned.[2]

Although it would be absurd to imagine such a satire levelled at the corruptions of a modern court, whose principal weakness is vanity, and whose luxury consists in ostentation; we must not, therefore, reject every supposed application of it to the pollutions of a Roman barrack, or, what nearly resembled a barrack, the recesses of a Roman palace, where the human blood that was shed in sport, was sometimes mixed with the wine that was spilt in debauch.[3] The representations of Petronius may be applied, in some parts, to the court of Tiberius and Claudius, more properly than to that of Caligula or Nero, or may have been a general satire levelled at the corruptions of the times, without any such application. But with respect to one or other of those emperors, every part in the feast of Tremalchio may have been a genuine though disguised picture.

Even in the court of the sober Augustus, pleasure was but another name for debauch. Love was no more than the ebullition of temperament, without the allurements of elegance, or the seduction of affection or passion. In the license of the sexes, both of them alike resorted to the places of public debauch. Women of the highest rank affected the manners of prostitutes, and, to realize the evidence of their victories, collected the ordinary rewards of prostitution. Such was the debauch for which Julia, the daughter of Augustus, was infamous, and in which she exhibited, as has been observed, not the weakness of a mind misled by passion, or seduced by some partial affection, but the gross excess of an appetite unacquainted with decency and above restraint.

In this state of manners the first successors of Cæsar, not having the habits of a courtly decorum to preserve them from the contagion of mean and degrading vices, and not considering their own elevation as any other than a mere post of advantage, from which they could indulge every caprice with impunity, after a few attempts in the beginning of a reign to prejudice the world in their favour, plunged into every species of excess, that a vile disposition, set free from restraint, and exasperated by the sense of general aversion, could incur. Persons inclined to this course generally proceed in their vices, until they meet with some obstacle which necessity or fear presents to them, and where they meet with no such obstacle, they preserve no bounds.

A perfect freedom from all external restraint would be sufficiently dangerous for persons of the best dispositions; but to those who are cursed with the worst, such a freedom from restraint would be accompanied with certain ruin. It is indeed nowhere to be found; but the first successors of Cæsar flattered themselves that they had found it; and as they supported the first offences which they committed against the rules of propriety, by setting reason itself and the sense of mankind at defiance, they came to apprehend a species of pleasure in braving the detestation which they incurred by their infamies.[4] They pursued the first strokes of injustice and malice by a continual warfare of distrust, prevention, and revenge against those to whom they supposed that their persons or government were odious; and they persisted in this course until the extreme itself, being what nothing less than the possession of sovereign power could support, appeared characteristic of empire, and worthy of the descendants of Cæsar.

During this unhappy succession of Cæsars, the supreme power had been, for the most part, held or disposed of by the prætorian bands. These troops being posted in the capital, overawed the senate and people, and though not fit to contend with the legions who were still employed in actual service, they gave possession of the empire, at every vacancy, before the armies of the frontier had time to deliberate or to take part in the choice.

This pre-eminence, however, of the prætorian bands had been impatiently suffered by the legions of the Rhine and the Danube. They wished, at the death of Augustus, to have given a specimen of their consequence in naming a successor to the empire; but being then overruled by the dutiful spirit or moderation of Germanicus, they acquiesced in the government of Tiberius, and remained in quiet under all the successions which followed; until, being excited by the defection of Gaul, which happened under Nero, and impatient of the mockery of sovereignty exhibited in the infamies of that unhappy person, they entertained, almost in every quarter of the empire at once, the project of giving a better and more respectable sovereign to the world.

Within the compass of one year and a few months, after it was known that the province

1 That of Petronius.

2 Mr. Voltaire has with contempt rejected its supposed application to the manners of a court.

3 The Romans had combats of gladiators exhibited while they were at table.

4 Magnitudo infamiæ cujus apud prod gos novissima voluptas.

of Gaul had revolted from Nero, all the armies from the Rhine and the Danube, from Gaul, Syria, Spain, and Britain, were for their march towards Italy, for the important purpose of giving a sovereign to the empire. And it is remarkable, that this project did not originate with the leaders, or appear to be suggested by the ambition of generals, but arose from a spirit of commotion which pervaded the troops.

Every legionary soldier, excited by the desire of rapine, by the prospect of possessing the capital, and of rioting in the riches and pleasures of Italy, conceived the design of pushing forward his general to the head of the empire. They burst at once from their quarters, and, considering themselves as set free from every species of government, whether civil or military, set no bounds to their violence. Augmenting their fury by the consideration of the punishments they incurred, in case they should fail in their attempt, they passed through every city and province in their way, like a storm that wastes and destroys whatever is opposed to its course. Within the short period we have mentioned, a motley assemblage of provincial troops, dressed in the garb of their different countries, with different arms and different languages, mixed with the Roman legions, who, now for many years strangers to each other, met on the Po and the Tiber to dispose of the empire. And, in the sequel of their contest, whether as victors or vanquished, whether moved by insolence or despair, did equal execution on the pacific inhabitants.

These troubles, however, ended in the elevation of a great and respectable officer[5] to the throne of Cæsar, and in the substitution of the Flavian family to that of Claudius and of Julius. At the accession of Vespasian every army had tried its strength, and competitors from the court, the senate, and the camp had made trial of their fortune. The victors in this contest received a willing submission from the pacific inhabitants of the provinces, who were ready to congratulate themselves on the return of public tranquillity.

Fortunately the first emperors of the new family, Vespasian himself, and the eldest of his two sons,[6] come from the school of experience, had learned the value of reason, humanity, and justice in the government of mankind; and they accordingly exhibited a character which, in some of its parts, was still new on the throne of Cæsar: the character of wisdom, propriety, and humanity, assumed, for its own sake, and without any intention to circumvent the people, or to impose upon the world. But the fortunes of this second imperial family, like those of the first, soon devolved on a[7] person equally unfit to sustain them, and equally unfit to be suffered by the patience of an abject court or a submissive world.

As mankind are known to run, occasionally, from one extreme to another, the evils which had been experienced in the characters of some of the preceding emperors, perhaps helped to direct the armies of the empire, at times, to think of the opposite extreme; and they made a compensation, in some of their elections, for the mischiefs which they had brought upon the world in others.

Amidst the variety of examples that were set on the imperial throne, different emperors paid unequal degrees of respect to the civil forms which were handed down to them from the republic, and which were still retained at least in name. But the characters of sovereign in the empire, and head of the army, were necessarily united in the same person; and, in proportion as the army itself came to be corrupted, the imperial establishment suffered, not an occasional and temporary abuse, but a radical and irrecoverable decline of its character and force.

The prætorian bands were early debauched by their residence in the capital, the principal seat of licentiousness; they were inspired with presumption from the access which they had to practise on the vices of their sovereign, and they outran all the armies of the empire in profligacy insolence, and venality. They were, upon this account, broke or disbanded with indignation by Galba, the first provincial officer who was advanced to the purple; but this reformation only made way for others, who being placed in the same school of disorder and vice, soon equalled their predecessors in all the evils which they had brought on the capital, and on the empire.

The contagion of military arrogance gradually spread from the barrack or camp of the prætorian bands, to the legions of the frontier, and, together with the hopes of raising a favourite leader to the head of the empire, promised indulgence of crimes and exemption from every painful restraint. The practice of disposing of the empire was followed by that of selling it for pecuniary bounties, and formally capitulating with every new master for a relaxation of discipline and the impunity of crimes.

In proportion as the character of Roman citizen lost its consideration and its consequence, the name was easily communicated to all the subjects or natives of any province. But this promiscuous admission of every subject, under the same predicament of a Roman citizen, instead of raising the provincials to the dignity of Romans, sunk the latter to the level of provincial subjects; extinguished all the sentiments on which the legions of old were wont to value themselves, and, with their loss of self-estimation as Romans, probably diminished the interest they had in the preservation of the Roman name. They became by degrees, and at every succession, more mercenary and venal in the choice of their masters, more brutal in the exercise of their force against their fellow-subjects; and with a continual degradation from bad to worse, substituted for the order, courage, and discipline of Roman legions, mere ferocity, and a disposition to rapine and mutiny.

In composing such armies, the natives of the more rude and uncultivated provinces took the ascendant over those of the more civilized and pacific; and the empire itself sometimes received its master from its most barbarous extremities, and from the nurseries of brutality, ignorance, and violence.

From such a general tendency to corruption, it is not surprising that an empire, though once of such mighty power, should, in process of time, verge to its ruin; it is rather surprising, that a fabric, mouldering so fast within, should have so long withstood the storm with which it was naturally assailed from abroad. From the accession of Caligula to the admission of Alaric

5 Vespasian. 6 Titus. Domitian.

into Rome, was a period of no more than about four hundred years; but from the same epoch to the reduction of Constantinople by the Turks, was a period of one thousand four hundred and sixteen years. So long was it before the lights of civil, political, and military wisdom, erected by the Roman commonwealth, though struck out by the Goths and Vandals in the west, and continually sinking in the east, were entirely extinguished.

The fabric of the empire had many advantages to account for so long a duration, both in the nature of its materials and in the disposition of its parts. The provinces were conveniently situated for mutual intercourse and for mutual support; and there was an easy access from the seat of dominion, to the farthest bounds of the empire. The order established by Augustus, and confirmed by Tiberius, remained unaltered, even by many of their successors. The worst of the Cæsars suffered that order to subsist in the provinces, and never looked beyond the court and capital for the objects of their jealousy, and fit subjects of tyranny. Even in such hands the engine of empire continued to work, because the master neither pretended to understand, nor attempted to interpose in the operation of its distant parts. And the authority of government continued high in the extremities of this vast dominion, while it sunk or was abused in the centre.

Valour and discipline, the best preservatives of many other valuable qualities, being long in request, though sometimes impaired in the Roman legions, still formed examples of a noble and heroic virtue, which qualified some of those, who attained to the more high and respectable stations in the military profession, to fill with advantage the imperial throne.

The inhabitants of the empire in general were corrected of that ferocity, or reduced from that national spirit which renders subjects refractory. They were addicted to pacific arts, tractable, and easily retained within the bounds of their duty; and they acquiesced in any government, however negligent or incapable. Some of the emperors promoted this orderly and pacific disposition, by the confidence which they taught the subject to have in the security of his person and of his property, and by the encouragement which they gave to pursuits and applications which inspire the love of peace and tranquillity.[1]

It may appear strange, but it is true, that even under the government of mere soldiers of fortune, the principles of law, founded in the maxims of the republic, though in some things perverted to the purposes of despotic power, was made the object of a select profession, and was studied as a rule of peace and of property. The civil law was thus not only suffered to remain in force, but received, from the pleadings of advocates, the decisions of judges, and the edicts of princes, continual accessions of light and authority, which has rendered it the great basis of justice to all the modern nations of Europe.

Philosophy continued in repute from the times of the republic far down in the empire, and the doctrines of Epicurus, which had prevailed in the later times of the commonwealth, now gave way to those of Zeno and the Stoics. While men had rights to preserve, and hazardous duties to perform on the public scene, they had affected to believe, with Epicurus, that pleasure was the standard of good and of evil. But now, when the public occupations of state were withheld from them, and when personal safety was the highest object in their view, they returned to the idea, which seemed to have inspired the virtue of ancient times, that men were made happy by what they themselves were and performed, not by what they possessed. Under the discouragements of many a cruel and oppressive reign, men of education and of high descent accordingly had recourse to the philosophy of Zeno, as to a consolation and support: and although they were deprived of the opportunity to act upon their own ideas in any distinguished situation, they gave sufficient evidence of their sincerity, in the manly indifference with which they sometimes incurred the consequences of their independence and freedom of mind.

From these materials, the law was sometimes furnished with practitioners, the senate with its members, the army with commanders, and the empire itself with its head; and the throne of Cæsar, in the vicissitudes to which it was exposed, presented examples as honourable to human nature in some instances, as they were degrading and shameful in others. In these varieties, however, it is no disparagement to the good, to suppose that they were not able to compensate the bad, or to produce effects, to which the greatest abilities in a few individuals cannot extend.

The wisdom of Nerva gave rise to a succession, which, in the persons of Trajan and the Antonines, formed a counterpart to the race of Tiberius, Caligula, Claudius, and Nero; and it must be admitted, that if a people could be happy by any other virtue than their own, there was a period in the history of this empire, during which the happiness of mankind may have been supposed complete. This however is but a fond and mistaken apprehension. A people may receive protection from the justice and humanity of single men; but can receive independence, vigour, and peace of mind only from their own. Even the virtues of this happy succession could do no more than discontinue, for a while, the former abuses of power, administrate justice, restrain the guilty, and protect the innocent. Many of the evils under which human nature was labouring, still remained without a cure; and the empire, after having in the highest degree experienced the effects of wisdom and goodness, was assailed anew with all the abuses of the opposite extreme.[2]

1 Vespasian gave salaries of about 800*l.* a year to masters of rhetoric at Rome. Marcus Aurelius gave salaries to many teachers of philosophy at Athens. Hadrian established the school of liberal arts, called the Athenæum. Dio. Cass. lib. lxxi. c. 37. Sextus Aurelius Victor de Cæsaribus.

2 These extremes scarcely gain credit with the modern reader, as they are so much beyond what his own experience or observation can parallel. Nero seems to have been a Demon, and Aurelius a Divinity; and these prodigies, whether in the extreme of good or of evil, exhibited, amidst the ruins of the Roman republic, are no longer to be found. Individuals were then formed on their specific dispositions to wisdom or folly. In later times, they are more cast in a general mould, which gives a certain form independent of the materials. Religion, fashion, and manners prescribe more of the actions of men, or mark a deeper tract in which men are constrained to move.

For many ages, nevertheless, the frontier continued to be defended, and the internal peace of the empire to be tolerably secure. Commerce flourished, and the land was cultivated; but these were but poor compensations for the want of that vigour, elevation, and freedom, which perished with the Roman republic itself, or with the political character of the other nations which had been absorbed in this ruinous abyss.

The military and political virtues, which had been exerted in forming this empire, having finished their course, a general relaxation ensued, under which, the very forms that were necessary for its preservation were in process of time neglected. As the spirit which gave rise to those forms was gradually spent, human nature fell into a retrograde motion, which the virtues of individuals could not suspend; and men, in the application of their faculties even to the most ordinary purposes of life, suffered a slow and insensible, but almost continual decline.

In this great empire, the fortunes of nations over the more cultivated parts of the earth, being embarked on a single bottom, were exposed to one common and general wreck. Human nature languished for some time under a suspension of national exertions, and the monuments of former times were, at last, overwhelmed by one general irruption of barbarism, superstition, and ignorance. The effects of this irruption constitute a mighty chasm in the transition from ancient to modern history, and make it difficult to state the transactions and manners of the one, in a way to be read and understood by those whose habits and ideas are taken entirely from the other

The maxims of a christian and a gentleman, the remains of what men were taught by those maxims in the days of chivalry, pervade every rank, have some effect in places of the least restraint; and if they do not inspire decency of character, at least awe the profligate with the fear of contempt, from which even the most powerful are not secure. Insomuch, that if human nature wants the force to produce an Aurelius or a Trajan, it is not so much exposed to the infamies of a Domitian or a Nero.

INDEX.

N

O

P

Q

R

S

T

U

V

X

Y

THE END.

www.ingramcontent.com/pod-product-compliance
Lightning Source LLC
LaVergne TN
LVHW021321110826
845150LV00003B/640

* 9 7 8 1 4 2 5 5 5 6 8 2 2 *